BRITISH WRITERS

BRITISH WRITERS

GEORGE STADE

General Editor

SUPPLEMENT II

KINGSLEY AMIS

TO

J. R. R. TOLKIEN

CHARLES SCRIBNER'S SONS / NEW YORK

MAXWELL MACMILLAN CANADA/TORONTO
MAXWELL MACMILLAN INTERNATIONAL/NEW YORK OXFORD SINGAPORE SYDNEY

Charles Scribner's Sons   Maxwell Macmillan Canada, Inc.
Macmillan Publishing Company   1200 Eglinton Avenue East
866 Third Avenue   Suite 200
New York, New York 10022   Don Mills, Ontario M3C 3N1

Macmillan Publishing Company is part of the Maxwell Communication Group of Companies.

Library of Congress Cataloging-in-Publication Data

British writers. Supplement 2.

    Suppl. 2 George Stade, general editor.
    Includes indexes.
    Bibliography: p.
    Contents: Suppl. 1. Graham Greene to Tom Stoppard--
Suppl. 2. Kingsley Amis to J.R.R. Tolkien.
    1. English literature--20th century--History and
criticism.   2. English Literature--20th century--
Bio-bibliography.   3. Authors, English--20th century--
Biography. I. Scott-Kilvert, Ian. II. Stade, George.
III. British Council.
PR85.B688 Suppl.   820'.9   87-16648

ISBN 0-684-15798-5 (v. 1)   ISBN 0-684-16637-2 (v. 6)
ISBN 0-684-16407-8 (v. 2)   ISBN 0-684-16683-0 (v. 7)
ISBN 0-684-16408-6 (v. 3)   ISBN 0-684-17417-0 (v. 8)
ISBN 0-684-16635-6 (v. 4)   ISBN 0-684-18612-8 (Supp. I)
ISBN 0-684-16636-4 (v. 5)   ISBN 0-684-19214-4 (Supp. II)

Impression

1 3 5 7 9 11 13 15 17 19 V/C 20 18 16 14 12 10 8 6 4 2

PRINTED IN THE UNITED STATES OF AMERICA

The paper in this book meets the guidelines for permanence and durability of the Committee on Production Guidelines for Book Longevity of the Council on Library Resources.

Acknowledgment is gratefully made to those publishers and individuals who permitted the use of the following materials in copyright.

KINGSLEY AMIS Excerpts from "Against Romanticism," "An Ever-Fixed Mark," and "Two Impromptus" from *Collected Poems 1944–1979* by Kingsley Amis. Copyright 1956, 1967, and 1979 by Kingsley Amis. Reprinted by permission of Jonathan Clowes Ltd. on behalf of Kingsley Amis, and by permission of Hutchinson Century.

WILLIAM EMPSON Excerpts from "Aubade," "Autumn on Nan-Yueh," "Courage Means Running," "Missing Dates,"

"Poem about a Ball in the Nineteenth Century," "This Last Pain," "To an Old Lady," "Villanelle," and "The World's End," in *Collected Poems*, copyright 1949 and renewed 1977 by William Empson, reprinted by permission of Harcourt Brace Jovanovich, Inc, and Chatto & Windus, one of the publishers in The Random Century Group Ltd. Excerpt from "Let It Go" in *Collected Poems*, copyright 1949 and renewed 1977 by William Empson, reprinted by permission of Harcourt Brace Jovanovich, Inc., Lady Empson, and The Hogarth Press. Excerpt from "Song of

ACKNOWLEDGMENTS

the Amateur Psychologist" from *The Royal Beasts* by William Empson, reprinted by permission of Chatto & Windus, one of the publishers in the Random Century Group Ltd.

SEAMUS HEANY Excerpts from "At a Potato Digging," "Death of a Naturalist," "Digging," "Diviner," and "Water Fall" from *Death of a Naturalist* and from *Poems, 1965–1975;* excerpts from "Bogland," "The Forge," "Gone," "Rite of Spring," "Shoreline," and "Undine," from *Door Into the Dark* and *Poems, 1965–1975;* excerpts from "A New Song," and "The Tollund Man" from *Wintering Out* and *Poems, 1965–1975;* excerpts from "Exposure," "The Grauballe Man," "Hercules and Antaeus," "Punishment," and "Whatever You Say Say Nothing," from *North* and *Poems, 1965–1975;* copyright © 1980 by Seamus Heaney. Excerpts from "Casualty," "Elegy," and "Glanmore Sonnets" from *Fieldwork,* copyright © 1979 by Seamus Heaney. Excerpts from "Clearances," "From the Frontier of Writing," "Hailstones," "The Haw Lantern," "The Land of the Un-spoken," "The Mud Vision," and "Parable Island," from *The Haw Lantern,* copyright © 1987 by Seamus Heaney. Excerpts from "The Cleric," "The First Flight," "Sandstone Keepsake," and "Station Island," from *Station Island,* copyright © 1989 by Seamus Heaney. Reprinted by permission of Farrar Straus and Giroux, Inc., and Faber and Faber Ltd.

T. E. LAWRENCE Excerpts of letters of T. E. Lawrence re-printed with permission of J. M. Dent Ltd. and The Trustees of the Seven Pillars of Wisdom Trust. Excerpts from *The Home Letters of T. E. Lawrence and His Brothers,* copyright by The Trustees of the Seven Pillars of Wisdom Trust. Excerpt from *Letters to T. E. Law-rence* by A. W. Lawrence, reprinted by permission of The Estate of A. W. Lawrence and Jonathan Cape Ltd.

LE CARRÉ Excerpt of letter from John le Carré to George Leonard, reprinted by permission of John le Carré.

I. A. RICHARDS Excerpt from "The Daughter of Thought" in *Goodbye Earth and Other Poems,* copyright © 1985 by I. A. Richards, and renewed 1986 by D. Richards, and excerpts from "Hope"

in *The Screens and Other Poems,* copyright © 1960, 1959 by I. A. Richards, and renewed 1988 by Richard Luckett, reprinted by permission of Harcourt Brace Jovanovich, Inc. Excerpt from "The Proper Study" in *New and Selected Poems* by I. A. Richards, Carcanet Press, 1978.

STEVIE SMITH "Come, Death," "The Cousin," "From the Greek," "God the Eater," "Heber," "In My Dreams," "Lady 'Rogue' Singleton," "Me Again," "Not Waving But Drowning," "Pad, Pad," "The Songster," "The White Thought," "Why Do I . . . ," and excerpts from "The After Thought," "The Ambassa-dor," "Black March," "Childe Rolandine," "The Company," "Do Take Muriel Out," "The Donkey," "Dream of Nourish-ment," "Exeat," "Fairy Story," "Forgive Me, Forgive Me," "Freddy," "God and Man," "How Do You See," "Lightly Bound," "Lord Barrenstock," "Magna Est Veritas," "Mrs. Simp-kins," "The Orphan Reformed," "Papa Love Baby," "The River God," "Scorpion," "Silence and Tears," "So to Fatness Come," "Up and Down," "Unpopular, Lonely, and Loving," "The Wan-derer," and "Was He Married?" from *Collected Poems of Stevie Smith.* Copyright © 1972 by Stevie Smith. Reprinted by permission of New Directions Publishing Corporation, Agents for the Estate of Stevie Smith. Excerpt of 1957 letter to Hans Houserman reprinted by permission of New Directions Publishing Corpora-tion, Agents for the Estate of Stevie Smith.

STEPHEN SPENDER Excerpts from "Air Raid Across the Bay at Plymouth," "Auden's Funeral," "Elegy to Margaret," "The Express," "The Generous Days," "In 1929," "In Railway Halls," "My Parents," "Not Palaces," "One More Botched Beginning," "Perhaps," "The Public Son of a Public Man," "The Pylons," "Rejoice in the Abyss," "The Room above the Square," "Spiri-tual Exercises," "The Truly Great," "The War God," "What I Believe," "Ultima Ratio Regum," and "The Uncreating Chaos" from *Collected Poems 1928–1985* by Stephen Spender. Copyright 1934, 1940, 1942 and renewed 1961, 1962, 1968, 1970, and 1986 by Stephen Spender. Reprinted by permission of Random House, Inc. and Faber and Faber Ltd.

ACKNOWLEDGMENTS

Editorial Staff

SYLVIA K. MILLER, *MANAGING EDITOR*

VIDA PETRONIS, *Associate Project Editor*

MELISSA SOLOMON, *Assistant Editor*

MELISSA DOBSON, *Copyeditor*

BETH WILSON, *Copyeditor*

JONATHAN ARETAKIS, *Copyeditor, Proofreader*

GRETCHEN GORDON, *Copyeditor*

PATTERSON LAMB, *Copyeditor*

ANN LESLIE TUTTLE, *Copyeditor*

CAROL HOLMES, *Proofreader*

MELANIE BELKIN, *Indexer*

KAREN DAY, *PUBLISHER, REFERENCE BOOKS*

Contents

Introduction

The twenty-six articles in *British Writers, Supplement II* survey modern writers who for one reason or another are not represented in either Supplement I (1987) or in the initial seven volumes of *British Writers* (1979–1984).

All of the earlier volumes of *British Writers* were edited by Ian Scott-Kilvert, under the auspices of The British Council. The articles were drawn from the Council's Writers and Their Work pamphlet series—a series that is just one of many components in a worldwide program to improve the teaching of English language and literature. Supplement II represents a departure in that none of the subjects were ever part of The British Council's pamphlet series and in that the volume has been developed and published independently of the Council. In the process of preparing the list of subjects, librarians and teachers of first-year college students were consulted. Although all of the articles were commissioned by Scribners especially for this volume, every attempt has been made to remain faithful to the format of their predecessors.

Each article in *British Writers, Supplement II* ranges from ten to thirteen thousand words in length and is devoted to a single writer. And each article presents an account of the writer's works, life, and relations to his or her time, place, and literary surroundings. But from article to article the emphasis varies, as from writer to writer the relative importance of the life, the reading, and the situation varies. Whatever the relative emphasis, the works come first; other matters are taken up to the extent that they form or inform the works.

In style and scope, the articles are expressly written for that mythical but inspiring figure, the general reader, rather than for the specialist. They are written, that is, for high school, undergraduate, and graduate students, as well as for their teachers; for librarians and editors; for reviewers, scholars, and critics; for literary browsers; for anyone who wants to repair either an erosion or a gap in his or her reservoir of knowledge. The article that can at once inform the beginner and interest the specialist will have achieved its goal.

Of the figures to whom the articles in *British Writers, Supplement II* are devoted, Samuel Butler (1835–1902) is the oldest and Seamus Heaney (b. 1939) is the youngest. The work of these writers, then, is part of what we loosely call "modern" literature, which is sometimes subdivided by such terms as the *fin de siècle*, the Age of Transition, Modernism, and Postmodernism. Some of the writers, like Henry Green, are aggressively and self-consciously modern; others, like Kingsley Amis, are aggressively and self-consciously traditional—which is another way of being modern. But a proposed writer's age or relation to an era were not the only criteria that determined whether or not the author would be represented in *British Writers, Supplement II.*

Above all, the editor asked himself whether a writer under consideration was someone that American readers were likely to look up, and whether American readers were likely to look the writer up in twenty years; whether, that is, the writer's work was of enduring interest. Some of the writers included, like T. E. Lawrence, have already passed the test of time. Others, like Nadine Gordimer, are widely read now, and in the editor's opinion, will continue to be. And others, like Barbara Pym, have a smaller readership, which, still in the editor's opinion, will continue to grow. The editor, in determining which writers were to be included, also took into account a shift in reader interests and in critical theory that has not yet completely worked itself out. That shift, which is often thought of as a process of decanonization, includes a breakdown in the distinction between popular literature and the other kind, whatever we call it, and between criticism and literature. Thus three writers who worked mainly in the popular genres, Agatha Christie, John le Carré, and J. R. R. Tolkien, are included; and two critics (who also wrote poetry), I. A. Richards and William Empson, are included.

Some of the writers included are not "British" in one or another restricted sense of the term. Jean Rhys, for example, was born in the Windward Islands of the West Indies to a Welsh father and a Creole mother, and she lived for some years on the Continent. Brendan Behan was emphatically Irish, as is Seamus Heaney. Alan Paton and Olive Schreiner were South African, as is Nadine Gordimer. All of these writers, in varying degrees, had an adversarial relation to English culture. But Jean Rhys moved to England when she was sixteen, and in her main domicile in her subject matter, sensibility, styles, and readership was at least as British as Joseph Conrad. Ireland is one of the British Isles, no matter how understandably unpleasant that fact is to many Irish people; and Irish literature in the English language has long been considered part of British literature. The South African writers are "British" in a far looser sense, although it is true that they wrote in English, in what was until fairly recently a part of the British Empire, in styles, forms, and sensibility that are more British than Africaans or native African. But the main reason for including them, of course, is the editor's sense that American readers would want to look them up and could not do so elsewhere in articles like the ones included in this volume, that they were good writers, important writers, writers of enduring interest. As for the adversarial relation to English culture, it characterizes the work of a good many of the greatest English writers in the strictest sense. The inclusion of writers like Yeats, Joyce, O'Casey, Beckett, and Patrick White in earlier volumes of *British Writers* is a precedent for the inclusion of Irish and South African writers in this volume.

The articles in *British Writers, Supplement II* differ, then, according to their subjects and according to the different emphases placed on the writers' lives or political, social, or literary surroundings; they also differ according to the authors who wrote them. The articles were contributed by young scholars and old hands, by academicians and freelance critics, by poets, novelists, and playwrights; by experts in a genre or an era or a figure. They differ, therefore, in prose and intellectual style, in critical orientation, in attitudes toward their subjects, in relative proportions of exposition, interpretation, and evaluation. As a consequence, the experience of reading *Supplement II*, or any other volume of *British Writers*, is not the same as the experience of reading through an encyclopedia or a volume of literary history or a collection of critical essays by a single hand.

An encyclopedia characteristically strives for a uniform neutrality of style and attitude; it contains entries on small matters as well as large ones. In a literary history, works and writers tend to be pressed into their relative positions by the force of an overriding thesis. In a collection of essays there is at least the continuity of the author's personality and values. Neither *British Writers* as a whole, nor this supplement, however, is uniform in style or attitude; neither is shaped by a single thesis or set of values. But if you believe—as does the editor—that reality, in this case the imagined realities of a national literature, whether written from the center or from the periphery, does not lend itself to containment within a single mind or conceptual scheme, you will find a certain appropriateness to the variety of perspectives in the volumes of *British Writers*.

You will find, then, a variety among the writers equal to the variety of perspectives from which the authors of these articles address their subjects. But you will also find the family resemblances that make British writers British and that make modern British writers modern. Above all, you will find, I believe, that all these writers are well worth looking up.

GEORGE STADE

Chronological Table

CHRONOLOGICAL TABLE

1846 Repeal of the Corn Laws
The *Daily News* founded (edited by Dickens the first three weeks)
Standard-gauge railway introduced in Britain
The Brontës' pseudonymous *Poems by Currer, Ellis and Action Bell*
Lear's *Book of Nonsense*

1847 The Ten Hours Factory Act
James Simpson uses chloroform as an anesthetic
Anne Brontë's *Agnes Grey*
Charlotte Brontë's *Jane Eyre*
Emily Brontë's *Wuthering Heights*
Tennyson's *The Princess*

1848 The year of revolutions in France, Germany, Italy, Hungary, Poland
Marx and Engels issue *The Communist Manifesto*
The Chartist Petition
The Pre-Raphaelite Brotherhood founded
Zachary Taylor elected president
Anne Brontë's *The Tenant of Wildfell Hall*
Dickens' *Dombey and Son*
Elizabeth Gaskell's *Mary Barton*
Macaulay's *History of England* (1848–1861)
Mill's *Principles of Political Economy*
Thackeray's *Vanity Fair*

1849 Bedford College for women founded
Arnold's *The Strayed Reveller*
Charlotte Brontë's *Shirley*
Ruskin's *The Seven Lamps of Architecture*

1850 The Public Libraries Act
First submarine telegraph cable laid between Dover and Calais
Millard Fillmore succeeds to the presidency after the death of Taylor
Elizabeth Barrett Browning's *Sonnets from the Portuguese*
Carlyle's *Latter-Day Pamphlets*
Dickens' *Household Words* (1850–1859) and *David Copperfield*
Charles Kingsley's *Alton Locke*
The Pre-Raphaelites publish the *Germ*
Tennyson's *In Memoriam*
Thackeray's *The History of Pendennis*
Wordsworth's *The Prelude* is published posthumously

1851 The Great Exhibition opens at the Crystal Palace in Hyde Park
Louis Napoleon seizes power in France

 Gold strike in Victoria incites Australian gold rush
Elizabeth Gaskell's *Cranford* (1851–1853)
Meredith's *Poems*
Ruskin's *The Stones of Venice* (1851–1853)

1852 The Second Empire proclaimed with Napoleon III as emperor
David Livingstone begins to explore the Zambezi (1852–1856)
Franklin Pierce elected president
Arnold's *Empedocles on Etna*
Thackeray's *The History of Henry Esmond, Esq.*

1853 Crimean War (1853–1856)
Arnold's *Poems,* including "The Scholar Gypsy" and "Sohrab and Rustum"
Charlotte Brontë's *Villette*
Elizabeth Gaskell's *Ruth*

1854 Frederick D. Maurice's Working Men's College founded in London with more than 130 pupils
Battle of Balaklava
Dickens' *Hard Times*
Theodor Mommsen's *History of Rome* (1854–1856)
Tennyson's "The Charge of the Light Brigade"
Florence Nightingale in the Crimea (1854–1856)

1855–1920 Olive Schreiner

1855 David Livingstone discovers the Victoria Falls
Robert Browning's *Men and Women*
Elizabeth Gaskell's *North and South*
Tennyson's *Maud*
Thackeray's *The Newcomes*
Trollope's *The Warden*

1856 The Treaty of Paris ends the Crimean War
Henry Bessemer's steel process invented
James Buchanan elected president

1857 The Indian Mutiny begins; crushed in 1858
The Matrimonial Causes Act
Charlotte Brontë's *The Professor*
Elizabeth Barrett Browning's *Aurora Leigh*
Dickens' *Little Dorritt*
Elizabeth Gaskell's *The Life of Charlotte Brontë*
Thomas Hughes's *Tom Brown's School Days*
Trollope's *Barchester Towers*

CHRONOLOGICAL TABLE

1858   Carlyle's *History of Frederick the Great* (1858–1865)

George Eliot's *Scenes of Clerical Life*

Morris' *The Defence of Guinevere*

Trollope's *Dr. Thorne*

1859–1930   Arthur Conan Doyle

1859   Charles Darwin's *The Origin of Species*

Dickens' *A Tale of Two Cities*

George Eliot's *Adam Bede*

FitzGerald's *The Rubaiyat of Omar Khayyám*

Meredith's *The Ordeal of Richard Feverel*

Mill's *On Liberty*

Samuel Smiles's *Self-Help*

Tennyson's *Idylls of the King*

1860   Abraham Lincoln elected president

The *Cornhill* magazine founded with Thackeray as editor

William Wilkie Collins' *The Woman in White*

George Eliot's *The Mill on the Floss*

1861   American Civil War begins

Louis Pasteur presents the germ theory of disease

Arnold's *Lectures on Translating Homer*

Dickens' *Great Expectations*

George Eliot's *Silas Marner*

Meredith's *Evan Harrington*

Francis Turner Palgrave's *The Golden Treasury*

Trollope's *Framley Parsonage*

Peacock's *Gryll Grange*

Death of Prince Albert

1862   George Eliot's *Romola*

Meredith's *Modern Love*

Christina Rossetti's *Goblin Market*

Ruskin's *Unto This Last*

Trollope's *Orley Farm*

1863   Thomas Huxley's *Man's Place in Nature*

1864   The Geneva Red Cross Convention signed by twelve nations

Robert Browning's *Dramatis Personae*

John Henry Newman's *Apologia pro vita sua*

Tennyson's *Enoch Arden*

Trollope's *The Small House at Allington*

1865   Assassination of Lincoln; Andrew Johnson succeeds to the presidency

Arnold's *Essays in Criticism* (1st series)

Carroll's *Alice's Adventures in Wonderland*

Dickens' *Our Mutual Friend*

Meredith's *Rhoda Fleming*

A. C. Swinburne's *Atalanta in Calydon*

1866   First successful transatlantic telegraph cable laid

George Eliot's *Felix Holt, the Radical*

Elizabeth Gaskell's *Wives and Daughters*

Swinburne's *Poems and Ballads*

1867   The second Reform Bill

Arnold's *New Poems*

Bagehot's *The English Constitution*

Carlyle's *Shooting Niagara*

Marx's *Das Kapital* (vol. I)

Trollope's *The Last Chronicle of Barset*

1868   Gladstone becomes prime minister (1868–1874)

Johnson impeached by House of Representatives; acquitted by Senate

Ulysses S. Grant elected president

Robert Browning's *The Ring and the Book* (1868–1869)

Collins' *The Moonstone*

1869   The Suez Canal opened

Girton College, Cambridge, founded

Arnold's *Culture and Anarchy*

Mill's *The Subjection of Women*

Trollope's *Phineas Finn*

1870   The Elementary Education Act establishes schools under the aegis of local boards

Dickens' *Edwin Drood*

Disraeli's *Lothair*

Morris' *The Earthly Paradise*

Dante Gabriel Rossetti's *Poems*

1871   Trade unions legalized

Newnham College, Cambridge, founded for women students

Carroll's *Through the Looking Glass*

Darwin's *The Descent of Man*

Meredith's *The Adventures of Harry Richmond*

Swinburne's *Songs Before Sunrise*

1872–1956   Max Beerbohm

1872   Samuel Butler's *Erewhon*

George Eliot's *Middlemarch*

Grant reelected

Hardy's *Under the Greenwood Tree*

1873   Arnold's *Literature and Dogma*

Mill's *Autobiography*

Pater's *Studies in the History of the Renaissance*

Trollope's *The Eustace Diamonds*

1874   Disraeli becomes prime minister

Hardy's *Far from the Madding Crowd*

James Thomson's *The City of Dreadful Night*

CHRONOLOGICAL TABLE

1875   Britain buys Suez Canal shares
Trollope's *The Way We Live Now*

1876   F. H. Bradley's *Ethical Studies*
George Eliot's *Daniel Deronda*
Henry James's *Roderick Hudson*
Meredith's *Beauchamp's Career*
Morris' *Sigurd the Volsung*
Trollope's *The Prime Minister*

1877   Rutherford B. Hayes elected president after Electoral Commission awards him disputed votes
Henry James's *The American*

1878   Electric street lighting introduced in London
Hardy's *The Return of the Native*
Swinburne's *Poems and Ballads. Second Series*

1879   Somerville College and Lady Margaret Hall opened at Oxford for women
The London telephone exchange built
Gladstone's Midlothian campaign (1879–1880)
Browning's *Dramatic Idyls*
Meredith's *The Egoist*

1880–1932   Lytton Strachey

1880   Gladstone's second term as prime minister (1880–1885)
James A. Garfield elected president
Browning's *Dramatic Idyls Second Series*
Disraeli's *Endymion*
Hardy's *The Trumpet-Major*
James Thomson's *The City of Dreadful Night*

1881   Garfield assassinated; Chester A. Arthur succeeds to the presidency
Henry James's *The Portrait of a Lady* and *Washington Square*
D. G. Rossetti's *Ballads and Sonnets*

1882   Triple Alliance formed between German empire, Austrian empire, and Italy
Leslie Stephen begins to edit the *Dictionary of National Biography*
Married Women's Property Act passed in Britain
Britain occupies Egypt and the Sudan

1883   Uprising of the Mahdi: Britain evacuates the Sudan
Royal College of Music opens
T. H. Green's *Ethics*
Stevenson's *Treasure Island*

1884   The Mahdi captures Omdurman: General Gordon appointed to command the garrison of Khartoum

The *Oxford English Dictionary* begins publishing
The Fabian Society founded
Hiram Maxim's recoil-operated machine gun invented

1885   The Mahdi captures Khartoum: General Gordon killed
Marx's *Das Kapital* (vol. II)
Meredith's *Diana of the Crossways*
Pater's *Marius the Epicurean*

1886–1926   Ronald Firbank

1886   The Canadian Pacific Railway completed
Gold discovered in the Transvaal
Henry James's *The Bostonians* and *The Princess Casamassima*
Stevenson's *The Strange Case of Dr. Jekyll and Mr. Hyde*

1887   Queen Victoria's Golden Jubilee
Hardy's *The Woodlanders*

1888–1935   T. E. Lawrence

1888   Henry James's *The Aspern Papers*
Kipling's *Plain Tales from the Hills*

1889   Yeats's *The Wanderings of Oisin*
Death of Robert Browning

1890–1976   Agatha Christie

1890–1979   Jean Rhys

1890   Morris founds the Kelmscott Press
Henry James's *The Tragic Muse*
Morris' *News From Nowhere*

1891   Gissing's *New Grub Street*
Hardy's *Tess of the d'Urbervilles*
Wilde's *The Picture of Dorian Gray*

1892–1973   J. R. R. Tolkien

1892   Conan Doyle's *The Adventures of Sherlock Holmes*
Shaw's *Widower's Houses*
Wilde's *Lady Windermere's Fan*

1893–1979   I. A. Richards

1893   Wilde's *A Woman of No Importance* and *Salomé*

1894   Kipling's *The Jungle Book*
Moore's *Esther Waters*
Marx's *Das Kapital* (vol. III)
The Yellow Book begins to appear quarterly
Shaw's *Arms and the Man*

1895   Trial and imprisonment of Oscar Wilde
William Ramsay announces discovery of helium
The National Trust founded
Conrad's *Almayer's Folly*
Hardy's *Jude the Obscure*
Wells's *The Time Machine*

CHRONOLOGICAL TABLE

Wilde's *The Importance of Being Earnest*
Yeats's *Poems*

1896 Marconi sends first wireless telegraph signals to England

Failure of the Jameson Raid on the Transvaal

Housman's *A Shropshire Lad*

1897 Queen Victoria's Diamond Jubilee

Conrad's *The Nigger of the Narcissus*

Havelock Ellis' *Studies in the Psychology of Sex* begins publication

Henry James's *The Spoils of Poynton* and *What Maisie Knew*

Kipling's *Captains Courageous*

Shaw's *Candida*

Wells's *The Invisible Man*

1898 Kitchener defeats the Mahdist forces at Omdurman: the Sudan re-occupied

Hardy's *Wessex Poems*

Henry James's *The Turn of the Screw*

Shaw's *Caesar and Cleopatra*

Wells's *The War of the Worlds*

Wilde's *The Ballad of Reading Gaol*

1899–1973   Elizabeth Bowen

1899–1973   Noel Coward

1899 The Boer War begins

Elgar's *Enigma Variations*

Kipling's *Stalky and Co.*

1900 British Labour party founded

Boxer Rebellion in China

Reginald A. Fessenden transmits speech by wireless

First Zeppelin trial flight

Max Planck presents his first paper on the quantum theory

Conrad's *Lord Jim*

Edward Elgar's *The Dream of Gerontius*

Sigmund Freud's *The Interpretation of Dreams*

William Butler Yeats's *The Shadowy Waters*

1901–1910   Reign of King Edward VII

1901 William McKinley assassinated; Theodore Roosevelt succeeds to presidency and is elected to office later in the year

First transatlantic wireless telegraph signal transmitted

Chekhov's *Three Sisters*

Freud's *Psychopathology of Everyday Life*

Rudyard Kipling's *Kim*

Thomas Mann's *Buddenbrooks*

Shaw's *Captain Brassbound's Conversion*

August Strindberg's *The Dance of Death*

1902–1971   Stevie Smith

1902 J. M. Barrie's *The Admirable Crichton*

Arnold Bennett's *Anna of the Five Towns*

Cézanne's *Le Lac D'Annecy*

Conrad's *Heart of Darkness*

Henry James's *The Wings of the Dove*

William James's *The Varieties of Religious Experience*

Kipling's *Just So Stories*

Maugham's *Mrs. Cradock*

Times Literary Supplement begins publishing

1903–1988   Alan Paton

1903 At its London congress the Russian Social Democratic Party divides into Mensheviks, led by Plekhanov, and Bolsheviks, led by Lenin

The treaty of Panama places the Canal Zone in U.S. hands for a nominal rent

Motor cars regulated in Britain to a 20-mile-per-hour limit

The Wright brothers make a successful flight in the U.S.

Burlington magazine founded

Samuel Butler's *The Way of All Flesh* published posthumously

George Gissing's *The Private Papers of Henry Ryecroft*

Thomas Hardy's *The Dynasts*

Henry James's *The Ambassadors*

Shaw's *Man and Superman*

Synge's *Riders to the Sea* produced in Dublin

Yeats's *In the Seven Woods* and *On Baile's Strand*

1904 Russo-Japanese war (1904–1905)

Construction of the Panama Canal begins

The ultraviolet lamp invented

The engineering firm of Rolls Royce founded

Chekhov's *The Cherry Orchard*

Conrad's *Nostromo*

Henry James's *The Golden Bowl*

Kipling's *Traffics and Discoveries*

Georges Rouault's *Head of a Tragic Clown*

G. M. Trevelyan's *England Under the Stuarts*

Puccini's *Madame Butterfly*

First Shaw-Granville Barker season at the Royal Court Theatre

The Abbey Theatre founded in Dublin

1905–1973   Henry Green

CHRONOLOGICAL TABLE

1905   Russian sailors on the battleship *Potemkin* mutiny

After riots and a general strike the czar concedes demands by the Duma for legislative powers, a wider franchise, and civil liberties

Albert Einstein publishes his first theory of relativity

The Austin Motor Company founded

Bennett's *Tales of the Five Towns*

Claude Debussy's *La Mer*

E. M. Forster's *Where Angels Fear to Tread*

Richard Strauss's *Salome*

H. G. Wells's *Kipps*

Oscar Wilde's *De Profundis*

1906–1984   William Empson

1906   Liberals win a landslide victory in the British general election

The Trades Disputes Act legitimizes peaceful picketing in Britain

Captain Dreyfus rehabilitated in France

J. J. Thomson begins research on gamma rays

The U.S. Pure Food and Drug Act passed

Churchill's *Lord Randolph Churchill*

Galsworthy's *The Man of Property*

Kipling's *Puck of Pook's Hill*

Shaw's *The Doctor's Dilemma*

Yeats's *Poems 1899–1905*

1907   Exhibition of cubist paintings in Paris

Henry Adams' *The Education of Henry Adams*

Henri Bergson's *Creative Evolution*

Conrad's *The Secret Agent*

Forster's *The Longest Journey*

André Gide's *La Porte étroite*

Shaw's *John Bull's Other Island* and *Major Barbara*

Synge's *The Playboy of the Western World*

Trevelyan's *Garibaldi's Defence of the Roman Republic*

1908   Herbert Asquith becomes prime minister

David Lloyd George becomes chancellor of the exchequer

William Howard Taft elected president

The Young Turks seize power in Istanbul

Henry Ford's Model T car produced

Bennett's *The Old Wives' Tale*

Pierre Bonnard's *Nude Against the Light*

Georges Braque's *House at L'Estaque*

Chesterton's *The Man Who Was Thursday*

Jacob Epstein's *Figures* erected in London

Forster's *A Room with a View*

Anatole France's *L'Ile des Pingouins*

Henri Matisse's *Bonheur de Vivre*

Edward Elgar's *First Symphony*

Ford Madox Ford founds the *English Review*

1909–   Stephen Spender

1909   The Young Turks depose Sultan Abdul Hamid

The Anglo-Persian Oil Company formed

Louis Bleriot crosses the English Channel from France by monoplane

Admiral Robert Peary reaches the North Pole

Freud lectures at Clark University (Worcester, Mass.) on psychoanalysis

Serge Diaghilev's Ballets Russes opens in Paris

Galsworthy's *Strife*

Hardy's *Time's Laughingstocks*

Claude Monet's *Water Lilies*

Trevelyan's *Garibaldi and the Thousand*

Wells's *Tono-Bungay* first published (book form, 1909)

1910–1936   Reign of King George V

1910   The Liberals win the British general election

Marie Curie's *Treatise on Radiography*

Arthur Evans excavates Cnossus

Edouard Manet and the first post-impressionist exhibition in London

Filippo Marinetti publishes "Manifesto of the Futurist Painters"

Norman Angell's *The Great Illusion*

Bennett's *Clayhanger*

Forster's *Howards End*

Galsworthy's *Justice* and *The Silver Box*

Kipling's *Rewards and Fairies*

Rimsky-Korsakov's *Le Coq d'or*

Stravinsky's *The Fire-Bird*

Vaughan Williams' *A Sea Symphony*

Wells's *The History of Mr. Polly*

Wells's *The New Machiavelli* first published (in book form, 1911)

1911–1966   Flann O'Brien

1911   Lloyd George introduces National Health Insurance Bill

Suffragette riots in Whitehall

Roald Amundsen reaches the South Pole

Bennett's *The Card*

Chagall's *Self Portrait with Seven Fingers*

CHRONOLOGICAL TABLE

Prokofiev's *Classical Symphony*
Yeats's *The Wild Swans at Coole*

1918 Wilson puts forward Fourteen Points for World Peace
Central Powers and Russia sign the Treaty of Brest-Litovsk
Execution of Czar Nicholas II and his family
Kaiser Wilhelm II abdicates
The Armistice signed
Women granted the vote at age thirty in Britain
Rupert Brooke's *Collected Poems*
Gerard Manley Hopkins' *Poems*
Joyce's *Exiles*
Lewis's *Tarr*
Sassoon's *Counter-Attack*
Oswald Spengler's *The Decline of the West*
Lytton Strachey's *Eminent Victorians*
Béla Bartók's *Bluebeard's Castle*
Elgar's *Cello Concerto*
Charlie Chaplin's *Shoulder Arms*

1919 The Versailles Peace Treaty signed
J. W. Alcock and A. W. Brown make first transatlantic flight
Ross Smith flies from London to Australia
National Socialist party founded in Germany
Benito Mussolini founds the Fascist party in Italy
Sinn Fein Congress adopts declaration of independence in Dublin
Eamon De Valera elected president of Sinn Fein party
Communist Third International founded
Lady Astor elected first woman Member of Parliament
Prohibition in the U.S.
John Maynard Keynes's *The Economic Consequences of the Peace*
Eliot's *Poems*
Maugham's *The Moon and Sixpence*
Shaw's *Heartbreak House*
The Bauhaus school of design, building, and crafts founded by Walter Gropius
Amedeo Modigliani's *Self-Portrait*

1920 The League of Nations established
Warren G. Harding elected president
Senate votes against joining the League and rejects the Treaty of Versailles

The Nineteenth Amendment gives women the right to vote
White Russian forces of Denikin and Kolchak defeated by the Bolsheviks
Karel Čapek's *R.U.R.*
Galsworthy's *In Chancery* and *The Skin Game*
Sinclair Lewis' *Main Street*
Katherine Mansfield's *Bliss*
Matisse's *Odalisques* (1920–1925)
Ezra Pound's *Hugh Selwyn Mauberly*
Paul Valéry's *Le Cimetière Marin*
Yeats's *Michael Robartes and the Dancer*

1921 Britain signs peace with Ireland
First medium-wave radio broadcast in U.S.
The British Broadcasting Corporation founded
Braque's *Still Life with Guitar*
Chaplin's *The Kid*
Aldous Huxley's *Crome Yellow*
Paul Klee's *The Fish*
D. H. Lawrence's *Women in Love*
John McTaggart's *The Nature of Existence,* vol. I (vol. II, 1927)
Moore's *Héloïse and Abélard*
Eugene O'Neill's *The Emperor Jones*
Luigi Pirandello's *Six Characters in Search of an Author*
Shaw's *Back to Methuselah*
Strachey's *Queen Victoria*

1922–   **Kingsley Amis**
1922 Lloyd George's Coalition government succeeded by Bonar Law's Conservative government
Benito Mussolini marches on Rome and forms a government
William Cosgrave elected president of the Irish Free State
The BBC begins broadcasting in London
Lord Carnarvon and Howard Carter discover Tutankhamen's tomb
The PEN club founded in London
The *Criterion* founded with T. S. Eliot as editor
Eliot's *The Waste Land*
A. E. Housman's *Last Poems*
Joyce's *Ulysses*
D. H. Lawrence's *Aaron's Rod* and *England, My England*
Sinclair Lewis's *Babbitt*

CHRONOLOGICAL TABLE

O'Neill's *Anna Christie*
Pirandello's *Henry IV*
Edith Sitwell's *Façade*
Virginia Woolf's *Jacob's Room*
Yeats's *The Trembling of the Veil*

1923–   **Nadine Gordimer**
1923–1964   **Brendan Behan**

1923   The Union of Soviet Socialist Republics established

French and Belgian troops occupy the Ruhr in consequence of Germany's failure to pay reparations

Mustafa Kemal (Ataturk) proclaims Turkey a republic and is elected president

Warren G. Harding dies; Calvin Coolidge becomes president

Stanley Baldwin succeeds Bonar Law as prime minister

Adolf Hitler's attempted coup in Munich fails

Time magazine begins publishing

E. N. da C. Andrade's *The Structure of the Atom*

Bennett's *Riceyman Steps*

Churchill's *The World Crisis* (1923–1927)

J. E. Flecker's *Hassan* produced

Paul Klee's *Magic Theatre*

Lawrence's *Kangaroo*

Rainer Maria Rilke's *Duino Elegies* and *Sonnets to Orpheus*

Sibelius' *Sixth Symphony*

Picasso's *Seated Woman*

William Walton's *Façade*

1924   Ramsay Macdonald forms first Labour government, loses general election, and is succeeded by Stanley Baldwin

Calvin Coolidge elected president

Noel Coward's *The Vortex*

Forster's *A Passage to India*

Mann's *The Magic Mountain*

Shaw's *St. Joan*

Sibelius' *Seventh Symphony*

1925   Reza Khan becomes shah of Iran

First surrealist exhibition held in Paris

Alban Berg's *Wozzeck*

Chaplin's *The Gold Rush*

John Dos Passos' *Manhattan Transfer*

Theodore Dreiser's *An American Tragedy*

Sergei Eisenstein's *Battleship Potemkin*

F. Scott Fitzgerald's *The Great Gatsby*

André Gide's *Les Faux Monnayeurs*

Hardy's *Human Shows and Far Phantasies*

Huxley's *Those Barren Leaves*

Kafka's *The Trial*

O'Casey's *Juno and the Paycock*

Virginia Woolf's *Mrs. Dalloway* and *The Common Reader*

Brancusi's *Bird in Space*

Shostakovich's *First Symphony*

Sibelius' *Tapiola*

1926   Ford's *A Man Could Stand Up*

Gide's *Si le grain ne meurt*

Hemingway's *The Sun Also Rises*

Kafka's *The Castle*

D. H. Lawrence's *The Plumed Serpent*

T. E. Lawrence's *Seven Pillars of Wisdom* privately circulated

Maugham's *The Casuarina Tree*

O'Casey's *The Plough and the Stars*

Puccini's *Turandot*

1927   General Chiang Kai-shek becomes prime minister in China

Trotsky expelled by the Communist party as a deviationist; Stalin becomes leader of the party and dictator of the USSR

Charles Lindberg flies from New York to Paris

J. W. Dunne's *An Experiment with Time*

Freud's *Autobiography* translated into English

Albert Giacometti's *Observing Head*

Ernest Hemingway's *Men Without Women*

Fritz Lang's *Metropolis*

Wyndham Lewis' *Time and Western Man*

F. W. Murnau's *Sunrise*

Proust's *Le Temps retrouvé* posthumously published

Stravinsky's *Oedipus Rex*

Virginia Woolf's *To the Lighthouse*

1928   The Kellogg-Briand Pact, outlawing war and providing for peaceful settlement of disputes, signed in Paris by sixty-two nations, including the USSR

Herbert Hoover elected president

Women's suffrage granted at age twenty-one in Britain

Alexander Fleming discovers penicillin

Bertolt Brecht and Kurt Weill's *The Threepenny Opera*

Eisenstein's *October*
Huxley's *Point Counter Point*
Christopher Isherwood's *All the Conspirators*
D. H. Lawrence's *Lady Chatterley's Lover*
Wyndham Lewis' *The Childermass*
Matisse's *Seated Odalisque*
Munch's *Girl on a Sofa*
Shaw's *Intelligent Woman's Guide to Socialism*
Virginia Woolf's *Orlando*
Yeats's *The Tower*

1929 The Labour party wins British general election
Trotsky expelled from USSR
Museum of Modern Art opens in New York
Collapse of U.S. stock exchange begins world economic crisis
Robert Bridges's *The Testament of Beauty*
William Faulkner's *The Sound and the Fury*
Robert Graves's *Goodbye to All That*
Hemingway's *A Farewell to Arms*
Ernst Junger's *The Storm of Steel*
Hugo von Hoffmansthal's *Poems*
Henry Moore's *Reclining Figure*
J. B. Priestley's *The Good Companions*
Erich Maria Remarque's *All Quiet on the Western Front*
Shaw's *The Applecart*
R. C. Sheriff's *Journey's End*
Edith Sitwell's *Gold Coast Customs*
Thomas Wolfe's *Look Homeward, Angel*
Virginia Woolf's *A Room of One's Own*
Yeats's *The Winding Stair*
Second surrealist manifesto; Salvador Dali joins the surrealists
Epstein's *Night and Day*
Mondrian's *Composition with Yellow Blue*
Walton's *Viola Concerto*

1930– John Arden
1930 Allied occupation of the Rhineland ends
Mohandas Gandhi opens civil disobedience campaign in India
The *Daily Worker,* journal of the British Communist party, begins publishing
J. W. Reppe makes artificial fabrics from an acetylene base
Auden's *Poems*
Noël Coward's *Private Lives*
Eliot's *Ash Wednesday*
Wyndham Lewis's *The Apes of God*

Maugham's *Cakes and Ale*
Ezra Pound's *XXX Cantos*
Evelyn Waugh's *Vile Bodies*
Von Sternberg's *The Blue Angel* and Milestone's *All Quiet on the Western Front*

1931– John le Carré
1931 The failure of the Credit Anstalt in Austria starts a financial collapse in Central Europe
Britain abandons the gold standard; the pound falls by twenty-five percent
Mutiny in the Royal Navy at Invergordon over pay cuts
Ramsay Macdonald resigns, splits the Cabinet, and is expelled by the Labour party; in the general election the National Government wins by a majority of 500 seats
The statute of Westminster defines dominion status
Ninette de Valois founds the Vic-Wells Ballet (eventually the Royal Ballet)
Chaplin's *City Lights,* René Clair's *Le Million,* and Leontine Sagan's *Mädchen in Uniform*
Coward's *Cavalcade*
Dali's *The Persistence of Memory*
O'Neill's *Mourning Becomes Electra*
Anthony Powell's *Afternoon Men*
Antoine de Saint Exupéry's *Vol de nuit*
Walton's *Belshazzar's Feast*
Virginia Woolf's *The Waves*

1932 Franklin D. Roosevelt elected president
Paul von Hindenburg elected president of Germany; Franz von Papen elected chancellor
Sir Oswald Mosley founds British Union of Fascists
The BBC takes over development of television from J. L. Baird's company
Basic English of 850 words designed as a prospective international language
The Folger Library opens in Washington, D.C.
The Shakespeare Memorial Theatre opens in Stratford upon Avon
Faulkner's *Light in August*
Huxley's *Brave New World*
F. R. Leavis' *New Bearings in English Poetry*
Boris Pasternak's *Second Birth*
Ravel's *Concerto for Left Hand*

Rouault's *Christ Mocked by Soldiers*
Waugh's *Black Mischief*
Yeats's *Words for Music Perhaps*

1933 Roosevelt inaugurates the New Deal
Hitler becomes chancellor of Germany
The Reichstag set on fire
Hitler suspends civil liberties and freedom of the press; German trade unions suppressed
George Balanchine and Lincoln Kirstein found the School of American Ballet
André Malraux's *La Condition humaine*
Orwell's *Down and Out in Paris and London*
Gertrude Stein's *The Autobiography of Alice B. Toklas*

1934 The League Disarmament Conference ends in failure
USSR admitted to the League
Hitler becomes Führer
Civil war in Austria; Engelbert Dollfuss assassinated in attempted Nazi coup
Frédéric Joliot and Irene Joliot-Curie discover artificial (induced) radioactivity
Einstein's *My Philosophy*
Fitzgerald's *Tender Is the Night*
Graves's *I, Claudius* and *Claudius the God*
Toynbee's *A Study of History* begins publication (1934–1954)
Waugh's *A Handful of Dust*

1935 Grigori Zinoviev and other Soviet leaders convicted of treason
Stanley Baldwin becomes prime minister in National Government; National Government wins general election in Britain
Italy invades Abyssinia
Germany repudiates disarmament clauses of Treaty of Versailles
Germany reintroduces compulsory military service and outlaws the Jews
Robert Watson-Watt builds first practical radar equipment
Karl Jaspers' *Suffering and Existence*
Ivy Compton-Burnett's *A House and Its Head*
Eliot's *Murder in the Cathedral*
Barbara Hepworth's *Three Forms*
George Gershwin's *Porgy and Bess*
Greene's *England Made Me*
Isherwood's *Mr. Norris Changes Trains*

Malraux's *Le Temps du mépris*
Yeats's *Dramatis Personae*
Klee's *Child Consecrated to Suffering*
Benedict Nicholson's *White Relief*

1936 Edward VII accedes to the throne in January; abdicates in December

1936–1952 Reign of George VI

1936 German troops occupy the Rhineland
Ninety-nine percent of German electorate vote for Nazi candidates
The Popular Front wins general election in France; Léon Blum becomes prime minister
The Popular Front wins general election in Spain
Spanish Civil War begins
Italian troops occupy Addis Ababa; Abyssinia annexed by Italy
BBC begins television service from Alexandra Palace
Auden's *Look, Stranger!*
Auden and Isherwood's *The Ascent of F-6*
A. J. Ayer's *Language, Truth and Logic*
Chaplin's *Modern Times*
Greene's *A Gun for Sale*
Huxley's *Eyeless in Gaza*
Keynes's *General Theory of Employment*
F. R. Leavis' *Revaluation*
Mondrian's *Composition in Red and Blue*
Dylan Thomas' *Twenty-five Poems*
Wells's *The Shape of Things to Come* filmed

1937 Trial of Karl Radek and other Soviet leaders
Neville Chamberlain succeeds Stanley Baldwin as prime minister
China and Japan at war
Frank Whittle designs jet engine
Picasso's *Guernica*
Shostakovich's *Fifth Symphony*
Magritte's *La Reproduction interdite*
Hemingway's *To Have and Have Not*
Malraux's *L'Espoir*
Orwell's *The Road to Wigan Pier*
Priestley's *Time and the Conways*
Virginia Woolf's *The Years*

1938 Trial of Nikolai Bukharin and other Soviet political leaders
Austria occupied by German troops and declared part of the Reich
Hitler states his determination to annex Sudetenland from Czechoslovakia

Britain, France, Germany, and Italy sign the Munich agreement

German troops occupy Sudetenland

Edward Hulton founds *Picture Post*

Cyril Connolly's *Enemies of Promise*

Faulkner's *The Unvanquished*

Graham Greene's *Brighton Rock*

Hindemith's *Mathis der Maler*

Jean Renoir's *La Grande Illusion*

Jean-Paul Sartre's *La Nausée*

Yeats's *New Poems*

Anthony Asquith's *Pygmalion* and Walt Disney's *Snow White*

1939–   Seamus Heaney

1939   German troops occupy Bohemia and Moravia; Czechoslovakia incorporated into Third Reich

Madrid surrenders to General Franco; the Spanish Civil War ends

Italy invades Albania

Spain joins Germany, Italy, and Japan in anti-Comintern Pact

Britain and France pledge support to Poland, Romania, and Greece

USSR proposes defensive alliance with Britain; British military mission visits Moscow

USSR and Germany sign nonaggression treaty, secretly providing for partition of Poland between them

Germany invades Poland; Britain, France, and Germany at war

USSR invades Finland

New York World's Fair opens

Eliot's *The Family Reunion*

Isherwood's *Good-bye to Berlin*

Joyce's *Finnegan's Wake* (1922–1939)

MacNeice's *Autumn Journal*

Powell's *What's Become of Waring?*

1940   Churchill becomes prime minister

Italy declares war on France, Britain, and Greece

General De Gaulle founds Free French Movement

The Battle of Britain and the bombing of London

Roosevelt re-elected for third term

Betjeman's *Old Lights for New Chancels*

Chaplin's *The Great Dictator*

Disney's *Fantasia*

Greene's *The Power and the Glory*

Hemingway's *For Whom the Bell Tolls*

C. P. Snow's *Strangers and Brothers* (retitled *George Passant* in 1970, when entire sequence of ten novels, published 1940–1970, was entitled *Strangers and Brothers*)

1941   German forces occupy Yugoslavia, Greece, and Crete, and invade USSR

Lend-Lease agreement between U.S. and Britain

President Roosevelt and Winston Churchill sign the Atlantic Charter

Japanese forces attack Pearl Harbor; U.S. declares war on Japan, Germany, Italy; Britain on Japan

Auden's *New Year Letter*

James Burnham's *The Managerial Revolution*

F. Scott Fitzgerald's *The Last Tycoon*

Huxley's *Grey Eminence*

Shostakovich's Seventh Symphony

Tippett's *A Child of Our Time*

Orson Welles's *Citizen Kane*

Virginia Woolf's *Between the Acts*

1942   Japanese forces capture Singapore, Hong Kong, Bataan, Manila

German forces capture Tobruk

U.S. fleet defeats the Japanese in the Coral Sea, captures Guadalcanal

Battle of El Alamein

Allied forces land in French North Africa

Atom first split at University of Chicago

William Beveridge's *Social Insurance and Allied Services*

Albert Camus's *L'Étranger*

Joyce Cary's *To Be a Pilgrim*

Edith Sitwell's *Street Songs*

Waugh's *Put Out More Flags*

1943   German forces surrender at Stalingrad

German and Italian forces surrender in North Africa

Italy surrenders to Allies and declares war on Germany

Cairo conference between Roosevelt, Churchill, Chiang Kai-shek

Teheran conference between Roosevelt, Churchill, Stalin

Eliot's *Four Quartets*

Henry Moore's *Madonna and Child*

Sartre's *Les Mouches*

Vaughan-Williams' Fifth Symphony

CHRONOLOGICAL TABLE

1944   Allied forces land in Normandy and southern France
Allied forces enter Rome
Attempted assassination of Hitler fails
Liberation of Paris
U.S. forces land in Philippines
German offensive in the Ardennes halted
President Roosevelt reelected for fourth term
Education Act passed in Britain
Pay-As-You-Earn income tax introduced
Beveridge's *Full Employment in a Free Society*
Cary's *The Horse's Mouth*
Huxley's *Time Must Have a Stop*
Maugham's *The Razor's Edge*
Sartre's *Huis Clos*
Edith Sitwell's *Green Song and Other Poems*
Graham Sutherland's *Christ on the Cross*
Trevelyan's *English Social History*

1945   British and Indian forces open offensive in Burma
Yalta conference between Roosevelt, Churchill, Stalin
Mussolini executed by Italian partisans
President Roosevelt dies; succeeded by Harry S. Truman
Hitler commits suicide; German forces surrender
The Potsdam Peace Conference
The United Nations Charter ratified in San Francisco
The Labour Party wins British General Election
Atomic bombs dropped on Hiroshima and Nagasaki
Surrender of Japanese forces ends World War II
Trial of Nazi war criminals opens at Nuremberg
All-India Congress demands British withdrawal from India
De Gaulle elected president of French Provisional Government; resigns the next year
Civil war between Chiang Kai-shek and Mao-Tse-Tung begins in China
Betjeman's *New Bats in Old Belfries*
Britten's *Peter Grimes*
Orwell's *Animal Farm*
Russell's *History of Western Philosophy*

Sartre's *The Age of Reason*
Edith Sitwell's *The Song of the Cold*
Waugh's *Brideshead Revisited*

1946   Bills to nationalize railways, coal mines, and the Bank of England passed in Britain
Nuremberg Trials concluded
United Nations General Assembly meets in New York as its permanent headquarters
The Arab Council inaugurated in Britain
Frederick Ashton's *Symphonic Variations*
Britten's *The Rape of Lucretia*
David Lean's *Great Expectations*
O'Neill's *The Iceman Cometh*
Roberto Rosselini's *Paisà*
Dylan Thomas' *Deaths and Entrances*

1947   President Truman announces program of aid to Greece and Turkey and outlines the "Truman Doctrine"
Independence of India proclaimed; partition between India and Pakistan, and communal strife between Hindus and Moslems follows
General Marshall calls for a European recovery program
First supersonic air flight
Britain's first atomic pile at Harwell comes into operation
Edinburgh festival established
Discovery of the Dead Sea Scrolls in Palestine
Princess Elizabeth marries Philip Mountbatten, duke of Edinburgh
Auden's *Age of Anxiety*
Camus's *La Peste*
Chaplin's *Monsieur Verdoux*
Priestley's *An Inspector Calls*
Edith Sitwell's *The Shadow of Cain*
Waugh's *Scott-King's Modern Europe*

1948   Gandhi assassinated
Czech Communist Party seizes power
Pan-European movement (1948–1958) begins with the formation of the permanent Organization for European Economic Cooperation (OEEC)
Berlin airlift begins as USSR halts road and rail traffic to the city
British mandate in Palestine ends; Israeli provisional government formed

CHRONOLOGICAL TABLE

Yugoslavia expelled from Soviet bloc

Columbia Records introduces the long-playing record

Truman re-elected for second term

Greene's *The Heart of the Matter*

Huxley's *Ape and Essence*

Leavis' *The Great Tradition*

Pound's *Cantos*

Priestley's *The Linden Tree*

Waugh's *The Loved One*

1949   North Atlantic Treaty Organization established with headquarters in Brussels

Berlin blockade lifted

German Federal Republic recognized; capital established at Bonn

Konrad Adenauer becomes German chancellor

Simone de Beauvior's *The Second Sex*

Cary's *A Fearful Joy*

Arthur Miller's *Death of a Salesman*

Orwell's *Nineteen Eighty-four*

1950   Korean War breaks out

Nobel Prize for literature awarded to Bertrand Russell

R. H. S. Crossman's *The God That Failed*

T. S. Eliot's *The Cocktail Party*

Doris Lessing's *The Grass Is Singing*

Wyndham Lewis' *Rude Assignment*

George Orwell's *Shooting an Elephant*

Carol Reed's *The Third Man*

Dylan Thomas' *Twenty-six Poems*

1951   Guy Burgess and Donald Maclean defect from Britain to USSR

The Conservative party under Winston Churchill wins British general election

The Festival of Britain celebrates both the centenary of the Crystal Palace Exhibition and British postwar recovery

Electric power is produced by atomic energy at Arcon, Idaho

W. H. Auden's *Nones*

Samuel Beckett's *Molloy* and *Malone Dies*

Benjamin Britten's *Billy Budd*

Greene's *The End of the Affair*

Akira Kurosawa's *Rashomon*

Lewis' *Rotting Hill*

Anthony Powell's *A Question of Upbringing* (first volume of *A Dance to the Music of Time*, 1951–1975)

J. D. Salinger's *The Catcher in the Rye*

C. P. Snow's *The Masters*

Igor Stravinsky's *The Rake's Progress*

1952   Reign of Queen Elizabeth II begins

At Eniwetok Atoll the U.S. detonates the first hydrogen bomb

The European Coal and Steel Community comes into being

Radiocarbon dating introduced to archaeology

Michael Ventris deciphers Linear B script

Dwight D. Eisenhower elected U.S. president

Beckett's *Waiting for Godot*

Charles Chaplin's *Limelight*

Ernest Hemingway's *The Old Man and the Sea*

Arthur Koestler's *Arrow in the Blue*

F. R. Leavis' *The Common Pursuit*

Lessing's *Martha Quest* (first volume of *The Children of Violence*, 1952–1965)

Thomas' *Collected Poems*

Evelyn Waugh's *Men at Arms* (first volume of *Sword of Honour*, 1952–1961)

Angus Wilson's *Hemlock and After*

1953   Constitution for a European political community drafted

Georgy Malenkov succeeds Stalin

Julius and Ethel Rosenberg executed for passing U.S. secrets to the USSR

Cease-fire declared in Korea

Edmund Hillary and his Sherpa guide, Tenzing Norkay, scale Mt. Everest

Nobel Prize for literature awarded to Winston Churchill

General Mohammed Naguib proclaims Egypt a republic

Beckett's *Watt*

Joyce Cary's *Except the Lord*

Robert Graves's *Poems 1953*

1954   First atomic submarine, *Nautilus*, is launched by the U.S.

Dien Bien Phu captured by the Vietminh

Geneva Conference ends French dominion over Indochina

U.S. Supreme Court declares racial segregation in schools unconstitutional

Nasser becomes president of Egypt

Nobel Prize for literature awarded to Ernest Hemingway

Kingsley Amis' *Lucky Jim*

John Betjeman's *A Few Late Chrysanthemums*

William Golding's *Lord of the Flies*

CHRONOLOGICAL TABLE

Christopher Isherwood's *The World in the Evening*
Koestler's *The Invisible Writing*
Iris Murdoch's *Under the Net*
C. P. Snow's *The New Men*
Thomas' *Under Milk Wood* published posthumously

1955 Warsaw Pact signed
West Germany enters NATO as Allied occupation ends
The Conservative party under Anthony Eden wins British general election
Cary's *Not Honour More*
Greene's *The Quiet American*
Philip Larkin's *The Less Deceived*
F. R. Leavis' *D. H. Lawrence, Novelist*
Vladimir Nabokov's *Lolita*
Patrick White's *The Tree of Man*

1956 Nasser's nationalization of the Suez Canal leads to Israeli, British, and French armed intervention
Uprising in Hungary suppressed by Soviet troops
Krushchev denounces Stalin at Twentieth Communist Party Congress
Eisenhower reelected U.S. president
Anthony Burgess' *Time for a Tiger*
Golding's *Pincher Martin*
Murdoch's *Flight from the Enchanter*
John Osborne's *Look Back in Anger*
Snow's *Homecomings*
Edmund Wilson's *Anglo-Saxon Attitudes*

1957 The USSR launches the first artificial earth satellite, *Sputnik I*
Eden succeeded by Harold Macmillan
Suez Canal reopened
Eisenhower Doctrine formulated
Parliament receives the Wolfenden Report on Homosexuality and Prostitution
Nobel Prize for literature awarded to Albert Camus
Beckett's *Endgame* and *All That Fall*
Lawrence Durrell's *Justine* (first volume of *The Alexandria Quartet*, 1957–1960)
Ted Hughes's *The Hawk in the Rain*
Murdoch's *The Sandcastle*
V. S. Naipaul's *The Mystic Masseur*
Eugene O'Neill's *Long Day's Journey into Night*
Osborne's *The Entertainer*

Muriel Spark's *The Comforters*
White's *Voss*

1958 European Economic Community established
Krushchev succeeds Bulganin as Soviet premier
Charles de Gaulle becomes head of France's newly constituted Fifth Republic
The United Arab Republic formed by Egypt and Syria
The U.S. sends troops into Lebanon
First U.S. satellite, *Explorer 1*, launched
Alaska becomes forty-ninth state
Nobel Prize for literature awarded to Boris Pasternak
Beckett's *Krapp's Last Tape*
John Kenneth Galbraith's *The Affluent Society*
Greene's *Our Man in Havana*
Murdoch's *The Bell*
Pasternak's *Dr. Zhivago*
Snow's *The Conscience of the Rich*

1959 Fidel Castro assumes power in Cuba
St. Lawrence Seaway opens
The European Free Trade Association founded
Hawaii becomes the fiftieth state
The Conservative party under Harold Macmillan wins British general election
Brendan Behan's *The Hostage*
Golding's *Free Fall*
Graves's *Collected Poems*
Koestler's *The Sleepwalkers*
Harold Pinter's *The Birthday Party*
Snow's *The Two Cultures and the Scientific Revolution*
Spark's *Memento Mori*

1960 South Africa bans the African National Congress and Pan-African Congress
The Congo achieves independence
John F. Kennedy elected U.S. president
The U.S. bathyscaphe *Trieste* descends to 35,800 feet
Publication of the unexpurgated *Lady Chatterley's Lover* permitted by court
Auden's *Hommage to Clio*
Betjeman's *Summoned by Bells*
Pinter's *The Caretaker*
Snow's *The Affair*
David Storey's *This Sporting Life*

CHRONOLOGICAL TABLE

1961 South Africa leaves the British Common-
wealth
Sierra Leone and Tanganyika achieve in-
dependence
The Berlin Wall erected
The New English Bible published
Beckett's *How It Is*
Greene's *A Burnt-Out Case*
Koestler's *The Lotus and the Robot*
Murdoch's *A Severed Head*
Naipaul's *A House for Mr Biswas*
Osborne's *Luther*
Spark's *The Prime of Miss Jean Brodie*
White's *Riders in the Chariot*

1962 John Glenn becomes first U.S. astronaut
to orbit earth
The U.S. launches the spacecraft *Mariner*
to explore Venus
Algeria achieves independence
Cuban missile crisis ends in withdrawal
of Soviet missiles from Cuba
Adolf Eichmann executed in Israel for
Nazi war crimes
Second Vatican Council convened by
Pope John XXIII
Nobel Prize for literature awarded to John
Steinbeck
Edward Albee's *Who's Afraid of Virginia
Woolf?*
Beckett's *Happy Days*
Anthony Burgess' *A Clockwork Orange* and
The Wanting Seed
Aldous Huxley's *Island*
Isherwood's *Down There on a Visit*
Lessing's *The Golden Notebook*
Nabokov's *Pale Fire*
Aleksandr Solzhenitsyn's *One Day in the
Life of Ivan Denisovich*

1963 Britain, the U.S., and the USSR sign a
test-ban treaty
Britain refused entry to the European Ec-
onomic Community
The USSR puts into orbit the first woman
astronaut, Valentina Tereshkova
Paul VI becomes pope
President Kennedy assassinated and Lyn-
don Johnson assumes office
Nobel Prize for literature awarded to
George Seferis
Britten's *War Requiem*
John Fowles's *The Collector*

Murdoch's *The Unicorn*
Spark's *The Girls of Slender Means*
Storey's *Radcliffe*
John Updike's *The Centaur*

1964 Tonkin Gulf incident leads to retaliatory
strikes by U.S. aircraft against North
Vietnam
Greece and Turkey contend for control of
Cyprus
Britain grants licenses to drill for oil in the
North Sea
The Shakespeare Quatercentenary cele-
brated
Lyndon Johnson elected U.S. president
The Labour party under Harold Wilson
wins British general election
Nobel Prize for literature awarded to
Jean-Paul Sartre
Saul Bellow's *Herzog*
Burgess' *Nothing Like the Sun*
Golding's *The Spire*
Isherwood's *A Single Man*
Stanley Kubrick's *Dr. Strangelove*
Larkin's *The Whitsun Weddings*
Naipaul's *An Area of Darkness*
Peter Shaffer's *The Royal Hunt of the Sun*
Snow's *Corridors of Power*

1965 The first U.S. combat forces land in Viet-
nam
The U.S. spacecraft *Mariner* transmits
photographs of Mars
British Petroleum Company finds oil in
the North Sea
War breaks out between India and Paki-
stan
Rhodesia declares its independence
Ontario power failure blacks out the Ca-
nadian and U.S. east coasts
Nobel Prize for literature awarded to
Mikhail Sholokhov
Robert Lowell's *For the Union Dead*
Norman Mailer's *An American Dream*
Osborne's *Inadmissible Evidence*
Pinter's *The Homecoming*
Spark's *The Mandelbaum Gate*

1966 The Labour party under Harold Wilson
wins British general election
The Archbishop of Canterbury visits
Pope Paul VI
Florence, Italy, severely damaged by
floods

Paris exhibition celebrates Picasso's eighty-fifth birthday

Fowles's *The Magus*

Greene's *The Comedians*

Osborne's *A Patriot for Me*

Paul Scott's *The Jewel in the Crown* (first volume of *The Raj Quartet*, 1966–1975)

White's *The Solid Mandala*

1967 Thurgood Marshall becomes first black U.S. Supreme Court justice

Six-Day War pits Israel against Egypt and Syria

Biafra's secession from Nigeria leads to civil war

Francis Chichester completes solo circumnavigation of the globe

Dr. Christiaan Barnard performs first heart transplant operation, in South Africa

China explodes its first hydrogen bomb

Golding's *The Pyramid*

Hughes's *Wodwo*

Isherwood's *A Meeting by the River*

Naipaul's *The Mimic Men*

Tom Stoppard's *Rosencrantz and Guildenstern Are Dead*

Orson Welles's *Chimes at Midnight*

Angus Wilson's *No Laughing Matter*

1968 Violent student protests erupt in France and West Germany

Warsaw Pact troops occupy Czechoslovakia

Violence in Northern Ireland causes Britain to send in troops

Tet offensive by Communist forces launched against South Vietnam's cities

Theater censorship ended in Britain

Robert Kennedy and Martin Luther King, Jr., assassinated

Richard Nixon elected U.S. president

Booker Prize for fiction established

Durrell's *Tunc*

Graves's *Poems 1965–1968*

Osborne's *The Hotel in Amsterdam*

Snow's *The Sleep of Reason*

Solzhenitsyn's *The First Circle* and *Cancer Ward*

Spark's *The Public Image*

1969 Humans set foot on the moon for the first time when astronauts descend to its surface in a landing vehicle from the U.S. spacecraft *Apollo 11*

The Soviet unmanned spacecraft *Venus V* lands on Venus

Capital punishment abolished in Britain

Colonel Muammar Qaddafi seizes power in Libya

Solzhenitsyn expelled from the USSR

Nobel Prize for literature awarded to Samuel Beckett

Fowles's *The French Lieutenant's Woman*

Storey's *The Contractor*

1970 Civil war in Nigeria ends with Biafra's surrender

U.S. planes bomb Cambodia

The Conservative party under Edward Heath wins British general election

Nobel Prize for literature awarded to Aleksandr Solzhenitsyn

Durrell's *Nunquam*

Hughes's *Crow*

F. R. Leavis and Q. D. Leavis' *Dickens the Novelist*

Snow's *Last Things*

Spark's *The Driver's Seat*

1971 Communist China given Nationalist China's UN seat

Decimal currency introduced to Britain

Indira Gandhi becomes India's prime minister

Nobel Prize for literature awarded to Heinrich Böll

Bond's *The Pope's Wedding*

Naipaul's *In a Free State*

Pinter's *Old Times*

Spark's *Not to Disturb*

1972 The civil strife of "Bloody Sunday" causes Northern Ireland to come under the direct rule of Westminister

Nixon becomes the first U.S. president to visit Moscow and Beijing

The Watergate break-in precipitates scandal in U.S.

Eleven Israeli athletes killed by terrorists at Munich Olympics

Nixon reelected U.S. president

Bond's *Lear*

Snow's *The Malcontents*

Stoppard's *Jumpers*

1973 Britain, Ireland, and Denmark enter European Economic Community

CHRONOLOGICAL TABLE

Egypt and Syria attack Israel in the Yom Kippur War

Energy crisis in Britain reduces production to a three-day week

Nobel Prize for literature awarded to Patrick White

Bond's *The Sea*

Greene's *The Honorary Consul*

Lessing's *The Summer Before the Dark*

Murdoch's *The Black Prince*

Shaffer's *Equus*

White's *The Eye of the Storm*

1974 Miners strike in Britain

Greece's military junta overthrown

Emperor Haile Selassie of Ethiopia deposed

President Makarios of Cyprus replaced by military coup

Nixon resigns as U.S. president and is succeeded by Gerald Ford

Betjeman's *A Nip in the Air*

Bond's *Bingo*

Durrell's *Monsieur* (first volume of *The Avignon Quintet*, 1974–1985)

Larkin's *The High Windows*

Solzhenitsyn's *The Gulag Archipelago*

Spark's *The Abbess of Crewe*

1975 The U.S. *Apollo* and Soviet *Soyuz* spacecrafts rendezvous in space

The Helsinki Accords on human rights signed

U.S. forces leave Vietnam

King Juan Carlos succeeds Franco as Spain's head of state

Nobel Prize for literature awarded to Eugenio Montale

1976 New U.S. copyright law goes into effect

Israeli commandos free hostages from hijacked plane at Entebbe, Uganda

British and French SST Concordes make first regularly scheduled commercial flights

The U.S. celebrates its bicentennial

Jimmy Carter elected U.S. president

Byron and Shelley manuscripts discovered in Barclay's Bank, Pall Mall

Hughes's *Seasons' Songs*

Koestler's *The Thirteenth Tribe*

Scott's *Staying On*

Spark's *The Take-over*

White's *A Fringe of Leaves*

1977 Silver jubilee of Queen Elizabeth II celebrated

Egyptian president Anwar el-Sadat visits Israel

"Gang of Four" expelled from Chinese Communist party

First woman ordained in the U.S. Episcopal church

After twenty-nine years in power, Israel's Labour party is defeated by the Likud party

Fowles's *Daniel Martin*

Hughes's *Gaudete*

1978 Treaty between Israel and Egypt negotiated at Camp David

Pope John Paul I dies a month after his coronation and is succeeded by Karol Cardinal Wojtyła, who takes the name John Paul II

Former Italian premier Aldo Moro murdered by left-wing terrorists

Nobel Prize for literature awarded to Isaac Bashevis Singer

Greene's *The Human Factor*

Hughes's *Cave Birds*

Murdoch's *The Sea, The Sea*

1979 The U.S. and China establish diplomatic relations

Ayatollah Khomeini takes power in Iran and his supporters hold U.S. embassy staff hostage in Teheran

Rhodesia becomes Zimbabwe

Earl Mountbatten assassinated

The U.S. hands over Canal Zone to Panama

The USSR invades Afghanistan

The Conservative party under Margaret Thatcher wins British general election

Nobel Prize for literature awarded to Odysseus Elytis

Golding's *Darkness Visible*

Hughes's *Moortown*

Lessing's *Shikasta* (first volume of *Canopus in Argos, Archives*, 1979–)

Naipaul's *A Bend in the River*

Spark's *Territorial Rights*

White's *The Twyborn Affair*

1980 Iran-Iraq war begins

Strikes in Gdansk give rise to the Solidarity movement

CHRONOLOGICAL TABLE

Mt. St. Helen's erupts in Washington State

British steelworkers strike for the first time since 1926

More than fifty nations boycott Moscow Olympics

Ronald Reagan elected U.S. president

Burgess's *Earthly Powers*

Golding's *Rites of Passage*

Shaffer's *Amadeus*

Storey's *A Prodigal Child*

Angus Wilson's *Setting the World on Fire*

1981 Greece admitted to the European Economic Community

Iran hostage crisis ends with release of U.S. embassy staff

Twelve Labour MPs and nine peers found British Social Democratic party

Socialist party under François Mitterand wins French general election

Rupert Murdoch buys *The Times* of London

Turkish gunman wounds Pope John Paul II in assassination attempt

U.S. gunman wounds President Reagan in assassination attempt

President Sadat of Egypt assassinated

Nobel Prize for literature awarded to Elias Canetti

Spark's *Loitering with Intent*

1982 Britain drives Argentina's invasion force out of the Falkland Islands

U.S. space shuttle makes first successful trip

Yuri Andropov becomes general secretary of the Central Committee of the Soviet Communist party

Israel invades Lebanon

First artificial heart implanted at Salt Lake City hospital

Bellow's *The Dean's December*

Greene's *Monsignor Quixote*

1983 South Korean airliner with 269 aboard shot down after straying into Soviet airspace

U.S. forces invade Grenada following left-wing coup

Widespread protests erupt over placement of nuclear missiles in Europe

The £1 coin comes into circulation in Britain

Australia wins the America's Cup

Nobel Prize for literature awarded to William Golding

Hughes's *River*

Murdoch's *The Philosopher's Pupil*

1984 Konstantin Chernenko becomes general secretary of the Central Committee of the Soviet Communist party

Prime Minister Indira Gandhi of India assassinated by Sikh bodyguards

Toxic gas leak at Bhopal, India, plant kills 2,000

British miners go on strike

Irish Republican Army attempts to kill Prime Minister Thatcher with bomb detonated at a Brighton hotel

World Court holds against U.S. mining of Nicaraguan harbors

Golding's *The Paper Men*

Lessing's *The Diary of Jane Somers*

Spark's *The Only Problem*

1985 United States deploys cruise missiles in Europe

Mikhail Gorbachev becomes general secretary of the Soviet Communist party following death of Konstantin Chernenko

Riots break out in Handsworth district (Birmingham) and Brixton

Republic of Ireland gains consultative role in Northern Ireland

State of emergency is declared in South Africa

Nobel Prize for literature awarded to Claude Simon

A. N. Wilson's *Gentlemen in England*

Lessing's *The Good Terrorist*

Murdoch's *The Good Apprentice*

Fowles's *A Maggot*

1986 U.S. space shuttle *Challenger* explodes

United States attacks Libya

Atomic power plant at Chernobyl destroyed in accident

Corazon Aquino becomes president of the Philippines

Giotto spacecraft encounters Comet Halley

Nobel Prize for literature awarded to Wole Soyinka

Final volume of *Oxford English Dictionary* supplement published

CHRONOLOGICAL TABLE

Amis's *The Old Devils*
Ishiguro's *An Artist of the Floating World*
A. N. Wilson's *Love Unknown*
Powell's *The Fisher King*

1987 Gorbachev begins reform of Communist party of the Soviet Union
Stock market collapses
Iran-contra affair reveals that Reagan administration used money from arms sales to Iran to fund Nicaraguan rebels
Palestinian uprising begins in Israeli-occupied territories
Nobel Prize for literature awarded to Joseph Brodsky
Golding's *Close Quarters*
Burgess's *Little Wilson and Big God*
Drabble's *The Radiant Way*

1988 Soviet Union begins withdrawing troops from Afganistan
Iranian airliner shot down by U.S. Navy over Persian Gulf
War between Iran and Iraq ends
George Bush elected U.S. president
Pan American flight 103 destroyed over Lockerbie, Scotland
Nobel Prize for literature awarded to Naguib Mafouz
Greene's *The Captain and the Enemy*
Amis's *Difficulties with Girls*
Rushdie's *Satanic Verses*

1989 Ayatollah Khomeini pronounces death sentence on Salman Rushdie; Great Britain and Iran sever diplomatic relations
F. W. de Klerk becomes president of South Africa
Chinese government crushes student demonstration in Tiananmen Square

Communist regimes are weakened or abolished in Poland, Czechoslovakia, Hungary, East Germany, and Romania
Lithuania nullifies its inclusion in Soviet Union
Nobel Prize for literature awarded to José Cela
Second edition of *Oxford English Dictionary* published
Drabble's *A Natural Curiosity*
Murdoch's *The Message to the Planet*
Amis's *London Fields*
Ishiguro's *The Remains of the Day*

1990 Communist monopoly ends in Bulgaria
Riots break out against community charge in England
First women ordained priests in Church of England
De Klerk announces end of South African emergency measures and freeing of political prisoners, including Nelson Mandela
East and West Germany united
Iraq invades Kuwait
Margaret Thatcher resigns as prime minister and is succeeded by John Major
Nobel Peace Prize awarded to Mikhail Gorbachev
Nobel Prize for literature awarded to Octavio Paz
Amis's *The Folks that Live on the Hill*
Byatt's *Possession*
Pritchett's *Collected Stories*

1991 American-led coalition forces Iraqi withdrawal from Kuwait in Persian Gulf War
Rajiv Gandhi assassinated
Boris Yeltsin elected president of Russia

List of Contributors

BERNARD BENSTOCK. Professor of English, University of Miami. Editor of the *James Joyce Literary Supplement.* Author of two books on Sean O'Casey. Has written or edited fourteen books on James Joyce, most recently *Narrative Con/Texts in "Ulysses."* Author of a volume of essays, *Art in Crime Writing: Essays on Detective Fiction,* and co-editor of the *Dictionary of Literary Biography* series on *British Mystery Writers.* **Arthur Conan Doyle**

RALPH C. BOETTCHER. Professor of English, Duquesne University, Pittsburgh. Author of articles on Thomas Hardy, E. M. Forster, D. H. Lawrence, Robert Graves, and Joyce Cary as contributors to modern fiction, and on Peter Shaffer, Archibald MacLeish, and Neil Simon as modern dramatists. Publications include numerous book reviews. **Ronald Firbank**

BARBARA BROTHERS. Professor and Chairperson of English, Youngstown State University. Co-editor, *CEA Critic* and *CEA Forum,* official publications of the College English Association. Author of articles on Henry Green, Sylvia Townsend Warner, Barbara Pym, Elizabeth Bowen, William Butler Yeats, and Margaret Kennedy. Publications also include chapters in *Women's Writing in Exile, Rewriting the Good Fight: Critical Issues on the Literature of the Spanish Civil War, Old Maids and Excellent Women,* and *Twentieth Century Novelists.* Contributed to and co-edited (with Bege K. Bowers) *Reading and Writing Women's Lives: A Study of the Novel of Manners.* **Henry Green**

ROBERT CASILLO. Professor of English, University of Miami. Publications include *The Genealogy of Demons: Anti-Semitism, Fascism, and the Myths of Ezra Pound;* essays on Ezra Pound, John Ruskin, Adrian Stokes, Ernest Hemingway, Lewis Mumford, Alexander Solzhenitsyn, Stendhal, Madame de Stael, the films of Martin Scorsese, and American advertising. Author of two forthcoming books, on Italy and Italian-Americans in modernity, and on John Ruskin, Patrick Geddes, and Lewis Mumford. **Samuel Butler**

MASON COOLEY. Professor of English, College of Staten Island, City University of New York. Author of books on composition, and of essays on T. S. Eliot, Thomas Carlyle, George Eliot, Hippolyte Taine, Roland Barthes, and Barbara Pym. Publications include a book-length study, *The Comic Art of Barbara Pym.* **Barbara Pym**

JOSEPH DEVLIN. Poet and critic. Frances Steloff Fellow in Irish Literature, Columbia University. Author of the forthcoming *Comedy and Modern Irish Literature.* **Flann O'Brien**

SUZANNE FOX. Poet, critic, and freelance writer. Administrator of the National Poetry Series and Adjunct Professor, New York Institute of Technology. Has contributed poems and articles to a variety of periodicals and has written widely in the fields of business and finance. **Stevie Smith**

DAVID GALEF. Assistant Professor of English, University of Mississippi. Has published fiction and essays in a wide variety of periodicals, including *Punch, Confrontation, Shenandoah, American Literature, Twentieth Century Literature, Verbatim,* and many others. Specializes in twentieth-century literature, with an emphasis on Modernism. **Brendan Behan**

JUDITH KEGAN GARDINER. Professor of English and Women's Studies, University of Illinois at Chicago. An editor of *Feminist Studies.* Has published extensively on twentieth-century writing by women, Renaissance and English literature, and feminist theory. Publications include *Craftsmanship in Context: The Development of Ben Jonson's Poetry* and *Rhys, Stead, Lessing, and the Politics of Empathy.* **Jean Rhys**

DAVID GRAVER. Assistant Professor of English and Comparative Literature, Columbia University. Has published articles on twentieth-century American, British, European, and South African drama and theater in *New Theatre Quarterly, Theatre Journal, The Drama Review,* and *Maske und Kothurn.* Publications include critical studies in progress on early twentieth-century avant-garde drama and contemporary British historical drama. **John Arden**

SIOBHÁN KILFEATHER. Assistant Professor of English and Comparative Literature, Columbia University. Forthcoming publications include a study of women's writing in eighteenth-century Ireland and an edition of critical essays on Samuel Richardson. **Elizabeth Bowen**

JEFFREY KINDLEY. Playwright. Taught at Columbia College (1970–1976). **Noel Coward**

KARL KROEBER. Mellon Professor in the Humanities, Columbia University. Has published extensively on English and Continental romantic poetry, nineteenth-century fiction, the graphic arts, and oral literatures of American Indians. His books include *Romantic Narrative Poetry, Styles in Fictional Structure, Romantic Landscape Vision: Constable and Wordsworth, British Romantic Art,* and *Romantic Fantasy and Science Fiction.* **J. R. R. Tolkien**

DAVID ADAMS LEEMING. Associate Professor of English and Comparative Literature, the University of Connecticut. Has published numerous books and articles on mythology, Henry James, and James Baldwin. A particular interest is Stephen Spender, with whom he has conducted several interviews since 1970. **Stephen Spender**

GEORGE J. LEONARD. Novelist, author, Associate Professor of Interdisciplinary Humanities, San Francisco State University. Has been a lecturer at Beijing Advanced Teacher's College. Publications include *Beyond Control, The Ice Cathedral* (novels), "Claude Simon" in Scribners' *European Writers,* and

articles and reviews on aesthetics. Extensive screenwork. **John le Carré**

RANDY MALAMUD. Assistant Professor of English, Georgia State University. Has published articles on T. S. Eliot, Virginia Woolf, and Truman Capote. His book, *The Language of Modernism,* explores patterns of linguistic and stylistic experimentation in modern literature. **Alan Paton**

ANNE McCLINTOCK. Assistant Professor of English, Columbia University. Teaches cultural and feminist studies. Author of *Maids, Maps, and Minds: Gender and Unmaking of Empire.* Currently writing *Power to Come: Women and the Sex Industry.* Author of numerous articles on South African culture and politics, feminist theory, and the politics of sexuality. Her articles have appeared in *Social Text, Critical Inquiry, South Atlantic Quarterly,* and the *Village Voice.* **Olive Schreiner**

ROB NIXON. Assistant Professor of English, Columbia University. Contributor to the *Village Voice.* Has published widely on culture and politics in Africa, Britain, and the Caribbean. Author of *London Calling: V. S. Naipaul, Travel Writer and Postcolonial Mandarin.* **Nadine Gordimer**

JOHN RICHETTI. Leonard Sugarman Professor of English and Chairman of the English Department, University of Pennsylvania. Co-editor of Cambridge University Press Studies in Eighteenth-Century Literature and Thought. Author of books and essays on the early English novel and philosophical prose in the eighteenth century. Books include *Popular Fiction Before Richardson: Narrative Patterns 1700–1739, Defoe's Narratives: Situations and Structures,* and *Philosophical Writing: Locke, Berkeley, Hume.* **Kingsley Amis**

MICHAEL ROSENTHAL. Professor of English and Comparative Literature, Columbia University. Author of *Virginia Woolf* and *The Character Factory: Baden Powell's Boy Scouts and the Imperatives of Empire.* Author of numerous book reviews and essays on literature, which have appeared in the *New York Times Book Review,* the *Partisan Review, Raritan,* and *South Atlantic Quarterly.* **Lytton Strachey**

JOHN PAUL RUSSO. Professor of English, University of Miami. Visiting Professor, University of

Rome (1987), University of Genoa (1990). Has written extensively on poetics, eighteenth-century literature, history of criticism, and history of culture. Publications include *Alexander Pope: Tradition and Identity* and *I. A. Richards: His Life and Work.* **I. A. Richards**

GREGORY A. SCHIRMER. Associate Professor of English, University of Mississippi. Has written extensively on Irish literature and modern British literature. Publications include *The Poetry of Austin Clarke* and *William Trevor: A Study of His Fiction.* Also editor of the forthcoming *Austin Clarke: Essays and Reviews.* **Seamus Heaney**

ROBERT VISCUSI. Professor of English and Executive Officer, Wolfe Institute for the Humanities, Brooklyn College, City University of New York. Has published *Max Beerbohm, or the Dandy Dante: Rereading with Mirrors* and edited *Victorian Learning.* Has also published widely on nineteenth- and twentieth-century British literature, Anglo-Italian literary relations and Italian writing in America. **Max Beerbohm**

STANLEY WEINTRAUB. Evan Pugh Professor of Arts and Humanities, The Pennsylvania State University. Editor of *Comparative Literature Studies* and former editor of *SHAW: The Annual Bernard Shaw Studies.* Author or editor of fifty books on Victorian and twentieth-century life and literature, including biographies of T. E. Lawrence, Aubrey Beardsley, Bernard Shaw, James McNeill Whistler, the Rossettis, and Queen Victoria. Publications include (with R. Weintraub) *Lawrence of Arabia: The Literary Impulse* and *A Stillness Heard Round the World: The End of the Great War.* **T. E. Lawrence**

ROBIN W. WINKS. Randolph W. Townsend Jr. Professor of History, Yale University. Specializes in comparative British, British Imperial, and American History, and also teaches on mystery, crime, and espionage fiction. Has taught in universities in Sydney, Malaysia, and Beirut, among others. Eastman Professor at Oxford University (1992–1993). He has written or edited eighteen books, among them *The Historian as Detective, Detective Fiction, Modus Operandi, Colloquium on Crime,* and *Cloak & Gown.* **Agatha Christie**

MICHAEL WOOD. Professor of English, University of Exeter, England. Has also taught at Columbia University and St. John's College, Cambridge. Author of books on Stendahl, García Márquez, and American film, and of many articles on literature and cinema. **William Empson**

BRITISH WRITERS

KINGSLEY AMIS

(1922–   )

John Richetti

EARLY LIFE

Kingsley Amis was born on 16 April 1922 and grew up in south London, in suburban Norbury. He attended local primary schools until he won a scholarship in 1934 to the City of London School, a "public" school for what the English call "day boys" (that is, a private school for commuting students) near Blackfriars Bridge. The scholarship marked for Amis a distinct and crucial step up in social class and in career possibilities beyond those of his family. His parents, William and Rosa Lucas Amis, were from Nonconformist (Baptist), lower-middle-class backgrounds; his father was a senior clerk in the export department of Colman's Mustard Company. An only child, Amis by his own account in "A Memoir of My Father" (1967, collected in the 1970 volume *What Became of Jane Austen?*) had an uneventful childhood as a normally rebellious adolescent who found intense pleasure and escape from the boredom of family life in various forms of popular culture such as science fiction, films, and pop music that took him out of what he evokes as the fairly dreary narrowness of lower-middle-class suburban existence. He admits, nevertheless, that his parents did teach him to be honest, responsible, thrifty, and industrious, and family finances were probably stretched to give a difficult but obviously brilliant son the best education possible.

At the City of London School, his frame of reference and his distance from his social origins widened considerably, as he made friends and began to take an interest in jazz and classical music, architecture, and modern poetry. When England entered into war with Germany in the summer of 1939, the school was evacuated to the country. In another brief memoir, "City Ways" (1958, also collected in *What Became of Jane Austen?*), Amis tells of how he joined the chapel choir and recalls that he found "singing in four-part harmony" to be "the apex, still unrivalled in my experience, of non-sensual pleasures." This deep pleasure in music, especially jazz of the premodern sort, has clearly continued for Amis and plays an important role in many of his novels.

In "City Ways," Amis describes how life at public school brought him new insight into social diversity and possibility: "My fellows, I saw dimly, were drawn from a wide variety of social strata: accents varied from those that discomforted me to those that made me feel superior." After his initial terror as he entered this strange new world, Amis remembers making his mark among the boys as an excellent mimic of the masters, and he has fond memories of his school days. "Life at a large day-school in a large city embodies a freedom which I should guess to be unique, a freedom based on heterogeneity. Where there is no orthodoxy there can be no conformity and no intolerance."

In the rigidly hierarchical world of prewar England, at least as Amis remembered it in the late 1950's, such a school seemed to him the perfect alternative society. As he describes in retrospect, the critical view of the adult world he had as an adolescent was ideal preparation for the novelist:

The boy in his early teens . . . sees the world with the delighted, faintly hostile astonishment of the tourist, who is entertained to the limits of endurance by its quaint tribal customs, its grotesque ritual dances, its capering, scowling, gesticulating witch-doctors. And if he later becomes a novelist he must strive to recapture, not indeed the undifferentiating vision of childhood, but the adolescent's coldly wondering stare.

("City Ways")

Although he failed to win a scholarship at St. Catherine's College, Cambridge, Amis did receive a university grant from St. John's College, Oxford, where he studied English literature during the academic year 1941–1942 and formed close and enduring friendships with Philip Larkin, John Wain, and Elizabeth Jennings, each of whom became well-known writers with whom his work was later linked. His university career was interrupted when he was called to service in the British Army during World War II. Although never actually in combat, he served from 1942 to 1945 as a lieutenant in the Royal Signal Corps in Normandy, Belgium, and Germany. Amis later drew on those experiences in a series of short stories about military life published in a volume called *My Enemy's Enemy* (1962). Back at Oxford after the war, he completed a "first-class" degree in English in 1947. The next year he married Hilary Ann Bardwell, with whom he had two sons, Martin and Philip, and a daughter, Sally. In the meantime, he did research toward a B. Litt. degree at Oxford—his thesis, on Victorian poetry and the reading public, was never completed—and in 1949 Amis became a lecturer in English at the University College of Swansea, one of the four colleges that make up the University of Wales, a post he held until 1961. Amis' success as a novelist began with his publication of *Lucky Jim* in 1954. He continued to teach, however, and spent the academic year 1958–1959 as a visiting fellow in creative writing at Princeton University. There he delivered a series of lectures on science fiction, later published as *New Maps of Hell* (1960). In 1961 he was named a fellow and director of studies in English at Peterhouse College, Cambridge.

That appointment soon proved unhappy. Amis found Cambridge dull and intellectually provincial, his colleagues shallow, self-satisfied, obsessed with academic politics, and even hostile to him as both a newcomer and an outsider. F. R. Leavis, then the most eminent member of the English faculty, reportedly said that Peterhouse could not be taken seriously after its having given a fellowship to a "pornographer." Looking back at his Cambridge experience the next year, Amis concluded that what really made academic life impossible for him "was paradoxically what made me most reluctant to leave: teaching" ("No More Parades," in *What Became of Jane Austen?*) which he says he enjoyed but found all-consuming. In 1963

Amis resigned his fellowship to devote all his energies to writing.

A MAN OF LETTERS

ASIDE from his second marriage to the novelist Elizabeth Jane Howard in 1965, and their divorce in 1980, the rest of Amis' life, except for a semester as a visiting professor at Vanderbilt University in Nashville, is a story of ceaseless activity as a versatile man of letters—perhaps the most productive, well-known, and at times politically controversial literary figure on the English scene in the second half of the twentieth century. In the early 1990's, Amis was still working as a journalist, social commentator, and prolific reviewer of books, jazz, and wine, as a poet and, especially, as a novelist who has turned out a wide variety of books in different genres, both popular and serious, from social comedy to science fiction to murder mysteries.

Amis began his writing life as a poet influenced by W. H. Auden and then briefly by Dylan Thomas. He has continued to write verse, but has shifted from the paradoxical prophetic mode he copied from Auden and the emotional-rhetorical style of Thomas to a much quieter, realistic, and reticent manner he shares with his friend Philip Larkin. He published his first volume, *Bright November,* just after he left Oxford in 1947, and a second volume, *A Frame of Mind,* in 1953. In 1956 his collected poems, *A Case of Samples (Poems 1946–1956)* appeared, and that same year Amis also published some of his poems in a collection called *New Lines,* which he edited with the conservative diplomat and poet Robert Conquest. His association with that anthology marked him as a member of a group of English poets who came to be called "The Movement." Including figures like Larkin, Donald Davie, Thom Gunn, and D. J. Enright, these poets rejected what Amis in one of his essays at the time called the "New Romanticism," which was exemplified during the 1940's in the poetry of Dylan Thomas and Edith Sitwell. In place of what they saw as a poetry full of obscurity and rhetorical bombast that was in fact empty of real meaning, the Movement figures proposed clarity and irony, an avoidance of emotional self-indulgence, and an attention to form and to particular experiences. One of Amis' most anthologized poems, "Against Romanticism" (1957), puts the case explicitly for rejecting poetry that tries "to discard real time and place, / Raging to build a better time and place." Instead, Amis urges "visions that we need":

Let mine be pallid, so that it cannot
  Force a single glance, form a single word;
An afternoon long-drawn and silent, with
  Buildings free from all grime of history,

    . . .

Let there be a path leading out of sight,
And at its other end a temperate zone:
  Woods devoid of beasts, roads that please the
    foot.

Amis' poems are an important part of his work, and his values as a poet will be familiar to any reader of his novels. His poems are frequently glum and even grim, but like Larkin's and John Betjeman's, they often cultivate a sardonic glee in the face of mortality. Like his novels, they often render with sympathy but with ironic and playful distance the compensatory fantasies and sad compromises of middle-class life. "An Ever-Fixed Mark" is typical. The title is from a Shakespeare sonnet, in which love is an "ever-fixed mark that looks on tempests and is never shaken." Amis' poem looks back to adolescent homosexual affairs at school and remembers two boys, Buck, who "used to perform / Prodigious feats in the dorm," and Ralph, who was in love.

He did the whole thing in style—
Letters three times a week,
Sonnet-sequences, Sunday walks;
Then, during one of their talks,
The youngster caressed his cheek,
And that made it all worth while.

But now, as the last stanza observes, Ralph's friend is a homosexual prostitute, while Buck's playmates, "family men," merely "eye a Boy Scout now and then." The moral: "Sex is a momentary itch, / Love never lets you go."

The special comic mordancy of that poem and many others carries over into Amis' fiction. But as a novelist Amis has always had a difficult time getting away from the expectations created by the distinctive success and the racy subject of his first novel, *Lucky Jim,* by far the most popular of his

books. It went through ten impressions in 1954, was made into a film in 1958, and has continued to be read ever since. Even though his *The Old Devils* (1986) was awarded the prestigious Booker Prize as the best novel of that year, Amis has over the years been dismissed by many critics as a limited writer, a novelist with one subject, social comedy of a sometimes bitterly realistic sort that has lost its interest as times have changed and new social problems come to the fore. Despite some truth in that charge, Amis' work at its best is not only wonderfully funny (and technically interesting as it exemplifies comic and satiric writing) but also deeply serious, expressing his ambition to align himself with the English comic and moral tradition of fiction stretching back to the eighteenth-century novelists such as Henry Fielding and Samuel Richardson.

In his novels as well as in his literary and political journalism, Amis values clarity and a skeptical common sense; his overseeing narrative technique is uncomplicated and straightforward, and the reader always knows just what is happening, although perhaps not always why. A notorious opponent of those tendencies in literature that have come to be called "modernism" and are associated with novelists like Virginia Woolf and James Joyce, Amis has been consistently assertive in his rejection of narrative experimentation and the cosmopolitan attitudes about art that go along with it. But he is not simply a philistine. As various sympathetic critics have noted, his attention to language as the fundamental subject of fiction marks him, almost in spite of himself, as a post-Joycean novelist whose work differs in this regard from the older tradition of social realism practiced by Arnold Bennett and H. G. Wells (continued by English novelists from the 1950's such as C. P. Snow), for whom language is simply a means for rendering a reality outside of words.

In Amis' comic novels, "style" is essential in that he renders his characters' special personalities as self-expressive manipulations of language that collide with and subvert or challenge standard discourse. Most of his novels feature a recurring linguistic exuberance whereby Amis pays close attention to the specific ways reality is manifest in speech and in language rather than in external action and scene. In the typical Amis comic novel, style is more important than plot or character development. Especially in his later work, Amis presents the surface of a character, his or her voice, and its interaction with other ways of speaking. He wittily ventriloquizes these linguistic surfaces and lets the reader add the implicit psychological depths. Through his characters, Amis examines the relationships between language and consciousness; or, if that sounds too solemn a description for his comic fiction, we can say that it subjects the language of contemporary culture to a deflating ironic scrutiny. To that extent, Amis deserves to be called an inheritor of an important aspect of the tradition of the modern novel that he seems to reject.

At the same time, he is also a satirist of postwar England and a novelist of manners with a number of immediate predecessors who have clearly influenced his work. Although Amis' novels are realistic and concerned with social and moral issues, they resemble P. G. Wodehouse's in their quirky linguistic energy and sometimes zany inventiveness. In his comic rendering of the interactions of personality in a shifting social scene, Amis has affinities with his friend from the previous generation of novelists, Anthony Powell, whose multivolume series *A Dance to the Music of Time* chronicles the breakup of upper-class society after World War I. In his later novels, as a sometimes gloomily reactionary satirist disgusted by contemporary life, Amis can also be compared to Evelyn Waugh, whose satirical novels such as *Vile Bodies* (1930) and *A Handful of Dust* (1934) ridicule the moral emptiness of British upper-class life in the 1920's.

Amis began to write *Lucky Jim* in 1951, after his wife received a legacy of two thousand pounds that enabled them to buy a house in Swansea with a small study where he could work. When the book was published in 1954, it was an overnight sensation that led reviewers to associate Amis with a group of writers described by the journalistic tag "angry young men." By the end of the 1950's, *Lucky Jim* could plausibly be linked to a number of other recent works that seemed to readers to define a distinctly new and urgent response to the profound social changes taking place in postwar England: John Wain's *Hurry on Down* (1953), Iris Murdoch's *Under the Net* (1954), John Osborne's play *Look Back in Anger* (1956), John Braine's *Room at the Top* (1957), and Alan Sillitoe's *Saturday Night and Sunday Morning* (1958).

What these works have in common is that they highlight the discontents and confusions of a transformed postwar England. From them, critics and journalists extracted a composite picture of a compelling antihero for the postwar era in Britain, one with a new consciousness of himself and of society. Epitomized for many at the time by Amis' Jim Dixon and especially by Osborne's Jimmy Porter from *Look Back in Anger,* this hero repudiates and ridicules the old class loyalties and distinctions but also questions in strong, often bitter terms the new society that seems to be emerging in England. Irreverent, mockingly resentful of old class privileges, impatient with tradition, scornful of any sort of cultural or moral pretension, cynical about politics and politicians, rude and boisterous toward anything he sees as the least bit phony—even sacred cows like art and literature—this new hero can be vulgar and ruthlessly self-seeking, but he has an energy and vigor that make him attractive and, most of all, alive. In this pure state, of course, he is an archetype and as such does not exist. Anger of this sort is not really what drives the heroes of Amis' early novels, but they do share some of the new hero's characteristics.

Amis himself, like some of his heroes, shared only a few of these qualities with the popular conception of the angry young man. But he and the others grouped with him did represent something new in English literary life, something unique to the postwar years. For many intellectuals, World War II had profoundly altered European culture and civilization. Reactionary writers like Evelyn Waugh and the more popular novelist Angela Thirkell described with horror the dawning of a new age of mass society where the old privileges of birth and inherited wealth, and the graceful and cultivated existence of the few that such wealth made possible, were to be swept away.

Like the writers with whom he was identified at the time, Amis obviously did not belong to the privileged classes who until then had dominated English life and letters. His career as a lower-middle-class scholarship boy turned academic and professional man of letters is paradigmatic for the new postwar era, and his later turn away from the Labour party toward a more conservative and traditionalist stance can be seen as part of a subsequent trend as well. As postwar society expanded and needed more technocrats and managers, political reformers said that the ranks of the ruling minority needed to be opened up to the bright sons of the lower-middle and working classes. The Labour party's overwhelming victory at the polls in 1945 had initiated the construction of the new welfare state, and this new order involved, among other things, the liberalization and extension of higher education, which was no longer to be a class privilege but rather, in theory, to be open to anyone with ability. Unfortunately, the postwar period brought unexpected austerity and a protracted continuation of wartime deprivation and rationing, as the British economy struggled to recover from the devastation of the war. The Labour government's introduction of sweeping reforms such as a national health service and other social welfare programs, as well as the nationalization of key industries like steel and coal mining, was accompanied by Britain's economic decline and subordination on the world stage to the United States. By 1951, the economy still lagged behind the energetically rebuilding defeated nations, Germany and Japan. Disillusion with the Labour party's program led to a Conservative victory that year. Many younger writers in the early 1950's, like Amis early products of the new promised order, were responding to these fading hopes and disappointments, expressing their own outrage at the slow pace of real social change and the persistence of entrenched privilege that the Labour government's restructuring of British society had failed to eliminate.

LUCKY JIM

ALTHOUGH such social issues are not at all explicit in *Lucky Jim,* they are the essential background and the ultimate target of the book's comic energy. Amis in those days, he has confessed, was an enthusiastic supporter of the Labour party, and he has Jim wonder out loud why the rich should not pay more: "If one man's got ten buns and another's got two, and a bun has got to be given up by one of them, then surely you take it from the man with ten buns" (ch. 4). But Amis' hero is no altruist, and the novel concerns his attempt to perpetrate his own sort of fraud in a world he denounces privately as dishonest. He is a recently appointed probationary lecturer in medieval history at a provincial university who is desperately trying to hang on to his job by convincing everyone in authority that he is a responsible person and dedicated teacher and scholar. In fact, as quickly becomes apparent, Dixon hates everything about academic life—his subject, lecturing, his colleagues, and especially the pretentiously arty and deviously absentminded head of his department, Professor Welch. He also hates Welch's family, especially Welch's son, a painter, and Dixon's rival in love, the odious Bertrand.

Jim's secret loathing for his circumstances provides the novel's point of view and swings it from comedy to occasional violence and potential nightmare, which quickly turn back again to comedy as we realize that Jim is not only the victim of the world he loathes but also of his own engaging fecklessness. Jim's wildly inventive expressions of his resentment of the academic establishment provide a hilarious distorting perspective on personalities and events that makes the novel much more than social observation. For Jim's fury is as much at his own hopeless inability to act honestly and speak forthrightly as it is at the pretentiousness and incompetence he sees surrounding him. As Jim in the opening pages talks to the evasive Welch,

he pretended to himself that he'd pick up his professor round the waist, squeeze the furry grey-blue waistcoat against him to expel the breath, run heavily with him up the steps, along the corridor to the staff cloakroom, and plunge the too small feet in their capless shoes into a lavatory basin, pulling the plug once, twice and again, stuffing the mouth with toilet paper.

(ch. 1)

The comedy for the moment is the disparity between these violently exact fantasies and the truth of Jim's obsequiousness, as he promises to attend one of Welch's arty weekends featuring diversions like madrigal singing and dramatic readings that he hates. He would rather be in the pub. At the same time, Jim is subject to his own form of comic self-loathing, real rather than imagined and funny entirely at his own expense—as when he wakes up at the Welches' with a hangover:

He lay sprawled, too wicked to move, spewed up like a broken spider-crab on the tarry shingle of the morning. The light did him harm, but not as much as looking at things did; he resolved, having done it once, never to move his eyeballs again. A dusty thudding in his head made the scene before him beat like a pulse. His mouth had been used as a latrine by some small creature of the night, and then as its mausoleum. During the night, too, he'd somehow been on a cross-country run and then been expertly beat up by secret police. He felt bad.

(ch. 6)

Amis is vague about Jim's social class and background, but the novel is about Jim's resentment not just of his immediate academic overseers but of those who are at ease in the larger world of privilege and pleasure that Jim longs to be a part of. Trapped in a destructive and passionless relationship with his manipulative, hysterical, unattractive, and badly dressed female colleague, Margaret, Jim watches as the hated Bertrand Welch arrives with an attractive girl:

The sight of her seemed an irresistible attack on his own habits, standards, and ambitions: something designed to put him in his place for good. The notion that women like this were never on view except as the property of men like Bertrand was so familiar to him that it had long ceased to appear an injustice.

(ch. 4)

Faced with his own imagined (and real) deprivations and second-rate existence, Jim's imagination improvises compensatory violent fantasies, and he makes wonderful secret faces at those he hates, such as his "sex life in ancient Rome face" or his "Chinese mandarin face." But he also at times acts as a satiric mirror and corrector of the external world he loathes. That is, he passes occasionally from his fantasies of comic revenge for his own dreary life to impassioned satiric denunciation of incompetence and selfishness. For example, as he contemplates Welch's evasive silence to his question about his reappointment, he makes the shift from wishing "to tie Welch up in his chair and beat him about the head and shoulders with a bottle until he disclosed why, without being French himself, he'd given his sons French names" (ch. 8) to wanting simply to say "quite quietly and very slowly and distinctly, to give Welch a good chance of catching his general drift: Look here, you old cockchafer, what makes you think you can run a history department, even at a place like this, eh, you old cockchafer?" (ch. 8).

In moments like this, Jim aspires to tell the truth as he sees it about a phony world, and eventually he does just that, in the novel's hilarious drunken climax, with a lecture he delivers on "Merrie England" to a crowd that includes the officers of his university. As he speaks he finds that he is mimicking the speech first of Welch and then of the principal of the college, and then as he grows more and more flushed and confused with the liquor he's drunk

he began to infuse his tones with a sarcastic, wounding bitterness. Nobody outside a madhouse, he tried to imply, could take seriously a single phrase of this conjectural, nugatory, deluded, tedious rubbish. Within quite a short time he was contriving to sound like an unusually fanatical Nazi trooper in charge of a book-burning reading out to the crowd excerpts from a pamphlet written by a pacifist, Jewish, literate Communist.

(ch. 22)

Drunk and fed up, Jim explodes with the anarchic verbal inventiveness that has been merely private till now; he tells the truth as he has understood it all along about his academic specialty: "Had people," he wonders earlier in the book as he contemplates reading his students' essays on their examinations, "ever been as nasty, as self-indulgent, as dull, as miserable, as cocksure, as bad at art, as dismally ludicrous, or as wrong as they'd been in the Middle Age?" (ch. 8).

Lucky Jim is more than a sustained satire of academic life or a novel of social realism. Like Amis' subsequent novels, it actively resists the generalizations critics want to apply to it. Its subject is an intensely imagined individual and his difficulties in rejecting a world he wants to be a part of. In this ambivalence, it doubtless reflects Amis' own feelings. It is one of the funniest of recent English novels because its hero is part of the joke, better than the people he satirizes mainly in his honesty and in his luck. And also, it should be emphasized, Jim is superior to those around him in his verbal facility, his capacity (like Amis the schoolboy) for mimicry of the masters that undercuts the fake discourse of everyday life with an exhilarating self-assertiveness. It can perhaps be said that Jim is rewarded with a happy ending for that combination of stand-up comic talent and ultimate honesty: he loses his job after the disastrous lecture, but he is offered a better one in London as the private secretary of the rich uncle, Julius Gore-Urquhart, of his new girlfriend, Christine, stolen from the odious Bertrand. And off he goes to London to his new job and beautiful sweetheart. Lucky Jim indeed!

KINGSLEY AMIS

THAT UNCERTAIN FEELING

Lucky Jim received the Somerset Maugham Award in 1955, and Amis published his second novel, *That Uncertain Feeling,* the same year. Ironically enough, around Christmas of that year Maugham wrote an essay for the London *Sunday Times* (25 December 1955) about the new heroes exemplified by Jim Dixon, in which he denounced them as a "white collar proletariat" who "do not go to the university to acquire culture, but to get a job." They have, Maugham complains, no manners. "Charity, kindliness, generosity are qualities which they hold in contempt. They are scum." Maugham had clearly not read *That Uncertain Feeling,* which is in some ways a fairly serious sequel to *Lucky Jim* and a radical revision of the angry-young-man stereotype. For all his linguistic energy and the satiric negation of order it encourages, Amis has "always been a moralist," as he remarked in an interview with Peter Firchow in 1974 (in *The Writer's Place: Interviews on the Literary Situation in Contemporary Britain,* 1974, p. 37). That aspect of his work becomes evident in *That Uncertain Feeling.* Its feckless hero discovers that his integrity is, after all, more important to him than pleasure, profit, or social advancement.

John Lewis is a threadbare young Welshman, struggling to support a wife and two children on the meager salary of an assistant librarian in a Welsh city, Aberdarcy. Lewis does fit the stereotype of the new hero in some ways, and his view of society coincides with the cynical disaffection Maugham complained of. Sitting in a pub, Lewis picks a spot where he can see his bus coming but remarks that one disadvantage of his seat is that it affords

visual and aural contact with the pub's other patrons . . . an occasional grocer or butcher in his Yacht Club blazer and lavender trousers, a publican or two in subfusc accompanied by an ignorant doctor or two in sportive checks, the odd golfing-jacketed cinema-manager, cafe-owner or fish-shop proprietor.

(ch. 11)

If these people, he reflects, represent "the new privileged classes in 'our society,' you could console yourself with the thought that there was a lot to be said for them compared with the old privileged classes. At least this crowd had enough bad taste to drink brandy before 'dinner.'" Vulgar and crudely self-seeking, such people for Amis' hero are at least honest in their pursuit of gratification, and his contempt for their ignorance and their bad taste in clothes is tempered by his admiration for the straightforward vigor they possess and he himself lacks.

The plot turns on a brief affair Lewis has with the wife of a rich industrialist who runs the town council and the library committee. When she arranges for her husband to have Lewis promoted to sub-librarian, he decides to break off their affair and turns down the job. In the last chapter of the novel, we find him back in his home village employed in the office of the coal mine where his father works. This flight from adultery and the corruption of modern life in the city to honest work and domesticity in the country has struck some critics as sentimental and inconsistent. Amis' moral stance is balanced unevenly against his skeptical analysis of human nature and life in Britain after the war. Moreover, Lewis' pastoral choice looks odd next to the satirical analysis of himself and others that Amis conducts through his hero.

Lewis is his own narrator in *That Uncertain Feeling,* and Amis gives him (like Jim Dixon) a comic, nearly manic self-awareness that approaches the external world as a challenge for farcical role playing. "When nothing's going on or likely to start going on, which is a lot of the time, I start practising certain poses and tones and phrases, for no very clear reason" (ch. 1). Lewis' perspective on his fellow creatures is like his own view of his external self, and it exemplifies a satiric distance in Amis' work that is both comic and at times quite chilling in its lack of compassion for his characters. Satire, traditionally, assumes a harshly judgmental and necessarily partial or even distorting perspective. Like caricature, satire exaggerates in order to tell a brutal sort of truth. Amis' heroes, by and large, specialize in this cruel rendering, much of it produced in this novel by the hero's social and sexual resentments. Since such resentment is hardly an adequate motive for satire as normally understood, Amis thus makes his hero to some extent the target of his own implicit judgment, an example of a traditional satiric strategy critics have labeled "the satirist satirized." Needless to say, such distancing on the author's part—of what he has after all invented—may simply be a way of disavowing what he himself really feels. The social resentment and, especially, the misogyny that Amis plants in his hero in *That Uncertain Feeling* continues to find expression in most of his later work.

When Lewis meets the upper-class Elizabeth Gruffydd-Williams, with whom he will have an affair, he notices with irritation her upper-class English voice and manner and then her appearance: "she was attractive in a square-shouldered, taut-bloused way, with skin the colour of the top of the milk and hair the colour of tar" (ch. 1). At one point, Elizabeth declares to him passionately, "I desire you utterly. . . . I want all your desire" (ch. 9). Looking back on this later, Lewis thinks that "its embarrassing quality was confined to its stylistics. There was nothing at all wrong with its paraphrasable content" (ch. 9). This uncomplicated desire on her part makes up, he confesses, for "the fairly numerous things about her that repelled me." Even during their one consummated sexual encounter later in the novel, Lewis will preserve an aspect of this jaggedly externalized view of her, and the emphasis in the descriptions of her and others will be on grotesquely isolated, or at least strongly marked or highlighted, observations that do not always fit together into whole human beings. Amis' narrative technique typically involves a single perspective on people and events, with extensive reported dialogue of a sometimes cryptic sort predominating over thorough descriptions of scenes or settings. The result is a partial and fragmented view of externalized others, who appear as bits and pieces of the narrator's detached observation of them and their speech, often rendered so as to imitate the disconnected quality of actual speaking. Amis' narrator-hero thus blurs the line between a comic view of human action and its mechanical dismissal—for example, in this description of his first embrace of Mrs. Gruffydd-Williams:

She got up and put her arms round my neck. Wriggling a little, she leaned against me and tried kissing me, as a motorist on a cold morning might abandon the starter button and get going with the handle. I fired on the first swing and very soon we were swaying about, as if a gaucho had got us round the ankles with his lasso or bolas.

(ch. 9)

That is comic writing of a high order, but it depends on an exclusion of sympathy for human emotions that can be repellent when one reads a lot of Amis all at once.

I LIKE IT HERE

ONE of the conditions of the Maugham prize was that the recipient go abroad for a year, so Amis and his family went to Portugal. Since that country was ruled by the dictator Antonio Salazar, whose regime had for years been denounced as repressive by liberal political observers, Amis made a deliberately provocative choice by going there. His third novel, *I Like It Here* (1958), is based on that time in Portugal, and the book is clearly his most directly autobiographical work. Garnet Bowen represents a sort of negative self-portrait of Amis:

Until a couple of years ago Bowen had been supposed to be a novelist who was keeping himself and his family going on the proceeds of journalism, wireless talks and a bit of lecturing. In the last six months or so he had started being supposed to be a dramatist who was keeping himself and his family going by the same means. He had never really supposed himself to be much more than a journalist, wireless talker and occasional lecturer.

(ch. 1)

Now Amis was never just that, although he had certainly performed all those functions. In a sense, *I Like It Here* begins his deliberate cultivation of a public pose as a mere entertainer, a writer who refuses to take himself "seriously" in the conventional sense and who outrages other writers and intellectuals by his boorish enthusiasm for beer and sex, his aggressive xenophobia, his philistine contempt for anything cultivated or artistic, and his aggressively conservative political views. So when Bowen's wife suggests that they go to Italy, Garnet replies, "All those rotten old churches and museums and art galleries" (ch. 1). This philistinism is meant to be amusing and unconventional, part of the satirizing of mindless, automatic enthusiasm for the fake romance attached by some English writers more or less since Lord Byron to going "abroad," that is, as Bowen explains, to "the Romance-speaking family of nations, with a few Greeks and southern Slavs thrown in."

In the end, this only mildly amusing satire of the romance of travel is quite misleading. As the novel develops, Bowen gradually comes to a deeper understanding of himself and his role as a writer, and he winds up validating to some extent the premise of novels that take their heroes to exotic places to discover the truth about themselves. The great irony Amis arranges is that Bowen begins to find that travel and new circumstances do just what they are supposed to, if not quite as neatly. Riding as the terrified passenger on a motorcycle through the streets of Lisbon, Bowen both accepts and then dismisses these insights:

If he lived he would ever afterward work harder, write more of his own stuff, do more with the kids, live in the United Kingdom. In his belly there was a plucking, a knocking, a shifting like the tide coming stealthily in among rock and weed. First adding "eat and drink less" to his ever-afterward list, he reflected that abroad was held to deepen your knowledge of your compatriots as well as all the other things it was held to do, and felt there might be something in this. In addition, abroad reputedly gave you fresh insight into—wait for it— yourself. So, for that matter, would a sharp go of locomotor ataxia or a visit from the dough-faced Christian physicist who had lived above him in Swansea. And anyway, he already had as much insight into himself as he cared to have.

(ch. 11)

Part of Bowen's purpose in going to Portugal is to engage in what amounts to espionage for a publishing firm with which he hopes to land a job. The firm has received a novel called *One Word More* from someone living in Portugal and claiming to be Wulfstan Strether, a distinguished writer who has not been heard from since 1946 and has been assumed to be dead. Bowen's assignment is to see if this Strether is the real thing. After spending some time with this man, whom he calls Buckmaster, Bowen decides for various reasons that he is indeed Strether. A key incident in this sequence is a visit the two of them pay to Henry Fielding's grave in Lisbon. Here are Bowen's thoughts:

Perhaps it was worth dying in your forties if two hundred years later you were the only noncontemporary novelist who could be read with unaffected and whole-hearted interest, the only one who never had to be apologised for or excused on the grounds of changing taste. And how enviable to live in the world of his novels, where duty was plain, evil arose out of malevolence and a starving wayfarer could be invited indoors without hesitation and without fear. Did that make it a simplified world? Perhaps, but that hardly mattered beside the existence of a moral seriousness that could be made apparent without the aid of evangelical puffing and blowing.

(ch. 15)

Buckmaster/Strether, on the other hand, intones that Fielding was "the darling of the comic muse,"

and in his—for Bowen (and Amis)—flatulent eloquence and self-importance disparages comedy like Fielding's as inferior to "the authentic voice of tragedy. That alone can speak to us of the loneliness and dignity of man." That is to say, for Buckmaster/Strether, Fielding is not his equal. Such a performance convinces Bowen that this is his man, since an imposter would not have dared "to put himself on show as the kind of prancing phoney who'd say he was better than Fielding."

As the critic and fellow novelist David Lodge has argued in his *Language of Fiction* (1966), *I Like It Here* belongs to a special genre, the kind of novel that is turned not so much upon the external world as "inward upon literary art and upon the literary artist himself" (p. 261). Such novels, Lodge observes, are autobiographical and full of literary jokes and parodies. The most important joke in Amis' novel is implicit in Strether, the name of Henry James's hero in *The Ambassadors* (1903), who is sent to Paris to redeem a young friend from a life of European decadence and winds up being seduced by it himself. Amis reverses the situation, as Bowen finds life abroad something that makes you when you get home "realise how much you like it here" (ch. 16).

Amis' third novel is, then, a crucial exploration of his identity as a writer. Through Bowen, Amis dramatizes his literary values, not expounding them in a didactic way but embodying them in a character who affirms them through experience and subjects them by his own moral limitations and selfish weaknesses to the skeptical examination of the reader. For all his boorishness and gleeful anti-intellectualism, Bowen has high and clearly articulated standards of artistic truth. After quoting a passage from Buckmaster/Strether's novel, he thinks how much he would like to put the author in the stocks "and stand in front of him with a peck, or better a bushel, of ripe tomatoes and throw one at him for each time he failed to justify any phrase . . . on grounds of clarity, common sense, emotional decency and general morality" (ch. 9). Bowen is Lucky Jim with a writer's mission, out to purge literature of the phony and affected self-indulgence of mere aestheticism and to revive the comic and moral tradition exemplified in Fielding.

But Amis also includes Bowen's sense of the limitations of these values and that insular tradition. As he is shown around the harbor of a Portuguese fishing village, he hears the story of a man they see on one of the ships: the man's father, a Finn, was the victim of a mutiny by the crew of his fishing ship. The crew was taken back to Finland to stand trial, and the ship remained in the harbor. When he came to claim the ship, the captain's son found he could not sell it in Portugal—it is unsuitable for sardine fishing—and could not afford to sail it back to Finland. So he has remained in the village, living on his ship and working in a fish shop. "A powerful, useless thrill" runs through Bowen as he hears this, "a marvellous story for someone, but not, unfortunately, for him" (ch. 12). What is required, he first jokes and then ruefully admits, is "a rather worse or much older writer. Well, just say a writer, instead of a man who was supposed to be a writer. That would get it." A worse or much older writer, thinks Bowen, because this sort of situation, exotic and romantic like something out of Joseph Conrad, is now unacceptable, part of a vanished modern tradition of high and tragic art. As David Lodge points out, Amis is implicitly commenting in this sequence on the "difficulty of being committed" to aesthetic and moral principles that "seem more reliable but drabber than the principles on which most great 'modern' art was based" (p. 267).

TAKE A GIRL LIKE YOU *AND* ONE FAT ENGLISHMAN

I Like It Here, it seems safe to say, is much more than a rehearsal of Amis' self-satisfied English provincialism, which is certainly a factor in all his fiction but is increasingly accompanied as he matures by the self-conscious complications of novelistic imagination. As Amis remarked in a 1973 essay, "Real and Made-Up People" (*Times Literary Supplement,* 27 July 1973), the novelist projects himself into "an entity that is part himself and yet not himself," and he can thereby "see more clearly, and judge more harshly, his own weaknesses and follies." That exercise will help both him and his readers to acquire more tolerance for the same weakness in others. Amis' next two novels demonstrate the difficulties of that program, since they attempt to present opposite kinds of characters: complicated innocence in *Take a Girl like You* (1960) and monstrous selfishness in *One Fat Englishman* (1963).

Innocence in *Take a Girl like You* is embodied in Jenny Bunn, a young and stunningly attractive schoolteacher from the north of England who comes to work in a town near London. Amis' difficult objective is to do equal justice to opposite views of sexual relationships. Jenny is reluctant to join in the "liberated" sexual life offered by the hero, Patrick Standish. Jenny is, nonetheless, deeply attracted to Patrick, an experienced and sophisticated thirty-year-old bachelor who teaches classics at the local grammar school. Amis projects himself into both these characters, giving their points of view more or less equal space in the novel. The effect of this balance, as critics have pointed out, is something like that of Samuel Richardson's *Clarissa* (1747–1748), in which the heroine and her seducer, Robert Lovelace, express opposing personalities in sexual combat that ends in rape and death for the heroine. Amis' novel, of course, is ironic rather than tragic and melodramatic like *Clarissa,* although it ends in something like rape. He clearly sympathizes with Patrick's point of view, giving him the satirical sharpness of his earlier heroes and some of Amis' own sophisticated taste for jazz. But it is Jenny who has the more convincing point of view and may be said to win the reader's sympathy. She does this because she is able to expose the liberated sex Patrick offers as a convenient cover for his own selfish pleasures, for a male domination and power he takes for granted. She thus performs the kind of analysis of the conventional that consistently wins Amis' moral admiration:

She could see the point of sex being *frank, free and open,* as Patrick had unwisely put it to her once and as she had put it back to him again a couple of dozen times since. What was meant by the expression in practice was a frank, free and open (and immediate and often repeated) scuttle into bed with some man; to tell them all to drop dead, however frankly, freely and openly, did not count as that.

(ch. 15)

Next to that sort of tough analysis of sexual relationships, Patrick's own wishes seem callow and self-indulgent as he looks forward to sleeping with Jenny and evokes rather powerfully the actualities he wants to avoid:

Even here and any time now that simple and final encounter might take place—to believe it for a moment, before the image was blurred and fouled by the inevitable debris of obligation and deceit and money and boredom and jobs and egotism and disappointment and habit and parents and inconvenience and homes and custom and fatigue: the whole gigantic moral and social flux which would wash away in the first few minutes any conceivable actualisation of that image.

(ch. 11)

Take a Girl like You is an ambitious novel, so much so that it never resolves this clash of moralities and wills, and it was in this sense the most difficult writing Amis had up to then attempted. He had, in fact, begun it in Portugal in 1955, but put it aside when he realized that he lacked the experience to write such an ambitious book. It marks a shift in his fiction, obviously, away from novels focused on quirky individuals like Jim Dixon and Garnet Bowen and toward novels that attempt to understand diverse characters more fully within a complex of social codes and circumstances. For that reason, *One Fat Englishman* is probably his most puzzling and unsatisfactory work, since it seems to interrupt that development. A caricature of satiric malevolence, Roger Micheldene weighs sixteen stone (245 pounds) and is someone without a single redeeming quality, the most disagreeable character Amis ever imagined. For that reason alone, he has an unreality that makes him amusing but a step back in novelistic complexity from the world of *Take a Girl like You.* "Of the seven deadly sins, Roger considered himself qualified in gluttony, sloth, and lust but distinguished in anger" (ch. 1). Roger's anger is directed at everything he finds in America, and much of the material in the book is clearly based on Amis' year at Princeton.

An editor at an English publishing house, Roger has come to America partly on business but mostly in pursuit of his mistress, twenty-nine-year-old Helene Bang, wife of Dr. Ernest Bang, a philologist from the University of Copenhagen who is a visiting fellow at Budweiser College in Pennsylvania. Unlike Amis' earlier "angry" heroes, Roger is an upper-class Englishman, a snob, and a Catholic. Amis makes no attempt to explain Roger's ugly and relentless pursuit of gratification or his hatred of everything around him, and he seems to be defying the reader to find any moral point or psychological coherence to his narrative. To be sure, Roger is frustrated in most of his designs. He loses his mis-

tress to a young Jewish novelist he despises, and his companion on the ship back to England is an insufferable American Anglophile whom Roger hates. Perhaps the best approach to *One Fat Englishman* is to consider it an experiment—an exercise in imagining a monster—and a challenge to readers, perhaps the very readers who share some of Micheldene's views (like Amis himself) but will be appalled by his ruthless cynicism and brutality.

Some critics have suggested that the novel is Amis' attempt to purge himself of the worst aspects of his own alter ego, and that Roger is an exaggerated version of the public persona Amis had by this time acquired. One of the most important moments in the emergence of that public identity as a reactionary was the essay, "Lone Voices," published in 1960 (and later collected in *What Became of Jane Austen?*), in which Amis warned that the expansion of Britain's university system would be a disaster. "MORE," he wrote in what became his most notorious phrase, "WILL MEAN WORSE." Admitting more students will lower standards, in fact wreck them beyond repair, Amis maintained. Amis was still a university lecturer then, and he claimed to speak from experience about the decline of higher education. Traditional more than reactionary in its emphasis, his essay is a moderate defense of an older idea of a university as a center of learning rather than a training ground for technocrats. Amis attacks what he sees as the mindless sloganeering of progressive politicians who want to destroy that institution.

His larger target, here and everywhere else in his writing, is trendy, self-satisfied, pseudogeneralization that passes for knowledge. As his novels repeatedly dramatize, Amis passionately rejects system and abstraction and promotes the individual and the concrete. His notorious political conservatism can be seen as an expression of this empirical skepticism, for what Amis really hates about leftist politics is its abstract notions of economic man and impersonal historical forces. As he said in a 1968 talk at the London Conservative Party Political Centre (published in pamphlet form that same year), "Lucky Jim's Politics," growing older meant that he had "lost the need to be political which means, in this country, the need to be Left. I am driven into grudging toleration of the Conservative Party because it is the party of nonpolitics, of resistance to politics."

KINGSLEY AMIS

IN this same talk, Amis looked back genially on the "free publicity" that he received from being identified for the public as one of the angry young men, but he also meditated on "how nice it would be if one's novels were read as novels instead of sociological tracts." His scorn is directed at those who would "rather read a book as a puree of trends and attitudes than as a work of art having its own unique, unparaphrasable qualities." For Amis the first concern of the writer is to render "what he takes to be permanent in human nature." These traditional attitudes toward art may look surprising, at first, coming from a novelist whose works do in fact engage his actual contemporary world and who makes a great point about avoiding the so-called eternal verities and tragic truths of the sort espoused by Buckmaster/Strether in *I Like It Here.* His problem in the novels since *One Fat Englishman* appeared in 1963 has been to reconcile his strongly held beliefs about art with an imagination engaged (and often enraged) by what he sees as the shabby disorder of contemporary culture. Amis has alternated in the last twenty-five years between novels that return to the social satire and black humor of his early work and to other kinds of "experimental" novels, a few of them merely entertainments but several of them original variations on traditional fictional forms. Some of these require little comment, since Amis has written them, clearly, to show that he can as a professional writer produce whatever the market seems to want. For example, in 1968 he published a James Bond adventure, *Colonel Sun,* under the pseudonym Robert Markham. Years later, in *The Crime of the Century* (1987), he tried his hand at a six-part serialized murder mystery that ran originally in London's *Sunday Times.*

Amis' most successful venture into crime writing, however, is *The Riverside Villas Murder* (1973), which is of interest not so much for its contribution to the genre of the murder mystery but rather for its careful evocation of the suburban world in which Amis grew up in the 1930's. The central character is a fourteen-year-old boy, Peter Furneaux, exactly Amis' age in 1936 when the story takes place, and like Amis he goes to a public school in the city, Blackfriars Grammar School. Peter helps solve the story's murder, which turns out to have been committed by Mrs. Trevelyan, one of his neighbors. She has killed her former lover, and she has also seduced Peter and introduced him to sex. Cunningly, Amis turns the murder-mystery plot into a novel of growing up, as Peter discovers the adult world of sex and betrayal in these intertwined histories.

The difficult passage from childhood to adult consciousness is a perennial theme in fiction, of course, that in England stretches back to the beginning of the novel with Daniel Defoe, Richardson, and Fielding and continues on to Charles Dickens and George Eliot in the nineteenth century. However, it is revealing that Amis has chosen to explore this theme exclusively within the confines of fictional genres where it does not normally appear. His other treatment of growing up is his one full-length work of science fiction, *The Alteration* (1976), which was awarded the John W. Campbell prize for work in that genre. This approach to what is necessarily the most personal material a novelist can deal with may be Amis' way of keeping his distance and turning emotion into the controlled art he admires.

The Alteration turns on a clever hypothesis: suppose Henry VIII's elder brother, Arthur, had not died, and England had remained a Roman Catholic country. From there, Amis imagines an alternative present, a 1976 in which all of Europe (but not America) is repressively ruled as a sort of fascist theocracy, a modern Christendom still at war with Islam and presided over by a pope who happens to be an Englishman. The boy hero this time is, again like Amis, a choir boy, ten-year-old Hubert Anvil, who is the finest boy soprano in the world. The alteration of the title refers to the Church's plan to castrate Hubert and thereby preserve his voice to sing God's praises. Precocious and sharply intelligent, Hubert is still too young to understand exactly what the loss of sexuality will mean, but he senses that he will be a diminished and incomplete person after the operation. Eventually he runs away, finding refuge with the ambassador from America ("New England"). Perhaps with a glance at some of Kipling's adventure stories about boys, Amis leads us through an exciting chase, but it all ends sadly when Hubert, with his departure to freedom in New England seemingly imminent, is forced to stay and undergo castration to save his life; one of his testicles has turned over and its blood supply is choked off. (The diagnosis is bilateral torsion, a real if rare occurrence.)

The Alteration is a thoughtful book, rich in political, moral, and theological implications, a far cry from the lurid sensationalism of much of the pulp science fiction the young Amis devoured in Norbury. Although there are a number of in-jokes (Pope John XXIV is from the north of England and sounds suspiciously like Harold Wilson, the Labour party prime minister at the time of the novel's publication), Amis here and elsewhere can be a deeply serious novelist of ideas. At his best, however, he manages to combine that seriousness with a satirical wit that is his signature and strength. Such a combination is achieved in *The Green Man* (1969), a ghost story, possibly the best of Amis' experiments with fictional genres, and perhaps his best work since *Lucky Jim.*

The Green Man is the name of the country hotel owned and run by the narrator, Maurice Allington. Amis begins with a joke, a description of a real hotel taken from the British *Good Food Guide,* along with a short list of satisfied guests (actual people, including some of Amis' friends) who have recommended it. Allington himself is a sort of inside joke: a fifty-three-year-old alcoholic and womanizer, a cultivated hotelier, a graduate of Peterhouse College, Cambridge, with a taste for poetry, a fear of death, and a range of wittily misanthropic attitudes that echo Amis' own public pronouncements. This resemblance between Amis and his narrators, in both his early and later fiction, is always something of a joke and a trap for the reader, one that some of his critics often fall into. In this case, the familiarity of Allington's Amis-like attitudes is part of the casually exact realism that sets up the novel's taut and frightening supernatural encounters.

As the *Good Food Guide* entry informs us, the Green Man is known for its ghost: Dr. Thomas Underhill in the late seventeenth century was accused of murdering his wife and a local farmer, both of whom were brutally torn to pieces. After experiencing various eerie manifestations and conducting his own research into them, Allington is visited by Underhill's ghost and learns how he trafficked with evil spirits to serve his lusts and had his murderous bidding done by a creature, the Green Man of the title, a sort of native English wood demon made of twigs and leaves. Eventually, after learning all these secrets of the spirit world, Allington manages to destroy Underhill and his Green Man, who almost kills Allington's thirteen-year-old daughter, Amy. Amis' narrative control in these scenes is remarkable; his writing is taut, economical, and totally gripping in rendering the creature as it bears down on Amy:

I faced about. The thing was coming up fast now, its legs driving powerfully and arms crooked, still accelerating. If it were left to itself, Amy would never reach the village. I stood in its path and marked out a place in the left groin that seemed made only of twigs and creepers, so perhaps vulnerable to a fist. I saw its face now for the first time, an almost flat surface of smooth dusty bark like the trunk of a Scotch pine, with irregular eye-sockets in which a fungoid luminescence glimmered, and a wide grinning mouth that showed more than a dozen teeth made of jagged stumps of rotting wood: I had seen a version of that face before. Then the green man was upon me, its dissimilar arms held out before it, and that cry as of wind through foliage issuing from its mouth, exultant as much as menacing.

(ch. 4)

In the meantime, we have been kept amused by Allington coping with problems in the hotel, seducing his friend's wife, arranging an orgy with her and his wife, and neglecting Amy, who watches television all day. *The Green Man* has two sets of events, the comic-satirical rendering in Amis' best manner of the world of the randy, wittily nasty owner of a hotel-restaurant near Cambridge and the serious investigation of the nature of evil in the universe; these strikingly divergent worlds are brilliantly linked by Allington's personality. He resembles to some extent, and is therefore tempted by, the sinister Underhill, who sees that Allington exploits others for his pleasure, that his dissatisfaction with these fleshly pleasures points to a deep intellectual and spiritual emptiness. Underhill offers him not only knowledge and power but peace of mind. It is precisely Allington's identity as the wearily sophisticated Amis alter ego that puts him at the center of this encounter and makes him sensitive to the presence of evil. Allington's sins are a sign of his moral intelligence; his dissatisfaction and self-disgust point to a capacity for selfless heroism that he lives up to fully. Like other recent Amis heroes, he discovers that the universe is a game in which good and evil are randomly intertwined.

Allington learns this firsthand when he is visited by God, who appears not as a pillar of fire or a voice from the whirlwind but as a well-dressed young man who discusses with him, over a glass of scotch, the nature of the universe. Amis' touch is just right, as he avoids metaphysical melodrama through this ironic domestication of the deity, who is like the sort of chap Amis might meet at his club. The created universe is a game, God explains, and now that he has set it in motion evil is simply a part of it. In one of the best scenes Amis has ever written, God urges Allington to stop Underhill. When he asks how and whether he will succeed, the young man

> sighed, swallowed audibly, and smoothed his fair hair. "No. I don't know. I only wish I did. People think I have foreknowledge, which is a useful thing for them to think in a way, but the whole idea's nonsense logically unless you rule out free will, and I can't do that."
>
> (ch. 4)

Allington resists, and when God threatens punishment, he replies bitterly that he's not worried about that, since he knows "how hard you can be on people who couldn't possibly have done anything to offend you." The young man replies, in a couple of pages of dialogue that summarize Amis' views on the problem of evil:

> "I know, children and such. But do stop talking like a sort of anti-parson, old man. It's nothing to do with offending or punishing or any of that father-figure stuff; it's purely and simply the run of the play. No malice in the world. . . .
>
> "It's not that I want to be cruel, not that so much as finding that's what I seem to be turning out to be. Not an easy situation, you know. I just realized that I was there, or here, or wherever you please, and on my own, and with these powers. I must say I wonder how you'd have managed." He sounded slightly cross. "You can't imagine what it's like to be faced with a set of choices that are irrevocable and also unique."
>
> (ch. 4)

Amis has been described as an "anti-theist." When the Russian poet Yevgeny Yevtushenko (on a visit to Cambridge in 1962) asked him, in English, "You atheist?" Amis reports that he answered, "Well yes, but it's more that I hate him." Amis' indignation extends, in other words, from human satirical targets to the entity that seems to have engineered human suffering.

This resonant, grandly grim theme is the subject of another of the "experimental" novels, *The Anti-Death League* (1962), less successful perhaps than *The*

Green Man but interesting as yet another variation on a standard fictional formula, in this case the spy thriller. *The Anti-Death League* has a plot too complicated to summarize adequately, but it is uniquely somber and serious among Amis' novels. It has no comedy at all. Using a sparse and austere third-person narration, Amis lets the characters' dialogue do most of the expository work, which adds to the mystery surrounding the events. What the reader only gradually pieces together is that the main characters are a group of officers on a military base somewhere in the English countryside engaged in a mission ("Operation Apollo") to test a top-secret weapon to be used against an enemy ultimately identified as the Chinese. The air of mystery and unreality Amis thus creates evokes the paranoia of the Cold War. In the end, the characters turn out to be pawns of an elaborate hoax designed to trick the Chinese into thinking that Britain will employ huge numbers of tactical atomic rifles if the Chinese carry through with their plan to invade India.

But the book's theme is metaphysical as well as political, since the malevolent inscrutability of the system is matched by that of the moral universe the characters see themselves living in. One of them, the alcoholic homosexual Max Hunter, is the founder and sole member of the anti-death league ("incorporating Human Beings Anonymous"), the anonymous announcement of which is his grimly subversive joke to protest the random, gratuitous evil that seems to operate in the world. When that principle manifests itself in the breast cancer of his mistress, Catherine Casement, another young officer, James Churchill, lapses into catatonic despair. His friend, the chaplain Major Ayscue, attempts to rouse him by a strange confession, a powerful exposition of Amis' anti-theism:

> To believe at all deeply in the Christian God, in any sort of benevolent deity, is a disgrace to human decency and intelligence. Of course it is. We can take that as read. I was so convinced of it when I was your age that I saw the Church as the embodiment of the most effectively vicious lie ever told. I declared a personal war on it. That was why I joined—so as to be able to work against it more destructively from within. I used to have a lot of fun in those days with things like devising an order of service that would please God much more than merely grovelling and begging for mercy or praising him for his

cruelty in the past and looking forward to seeing some more of the same in the future. Selected members of the congregation getting their arms chopped off and/or their eyes put out as a warm-up. Then a canticle about his loving-kindness. Then some whips and scorpions treatment on children under sixteen, followed by a spot of disembowelling and perhaps a beheading or two at the discretion of the officiating priest, with the choir singing an anthem about the beauty of holiness.

(p. 308)

Those readers who know Amis only from novels like *Lucky Jim* or as a curmudgeonly journalist would probably be surprised at the intensity of that speech. Amis really means it, even though his usual mode of describing an unjust universe is rather more sardonic, as in these lines from a poem, "Two Impromptus," with which he closed his *Collected Poems: 1944–1979* (1979):

> Only the actions of the just
> Smell sweet and blossom in their dust,
> Which does the just about as much
> Good as a smart kick in the crotch.

CHRONICLES OF MODERN LIFE

THE rest of Amis' novels since 1963 explore the world invoked by these lines, charting different sorts of everyday injustice and the normal unpleasantness of life as they have appeared to him since then. Amis has watched developments in British culture since the 1960's with increasing dismay, and in a series of novels beginning with *I Want It Now* (1968) right up through his 1990 novel, *The Folks That Live on the Hill,* he has continued his career as a satirist of special and sometimes controversial nastiness. The "swinging sixties" were an especially distasteful period for him, their "liberated" (the quotation marks would be his) sexual mores and dominant left-wing political trends coinciding with his own turn to conservatism, perhaps provoking it further to the right. With the publication of *Jake's Thing* (1978) and *Stanley and the Women* (1984), Amis has also been accused of making what some critics see as his lurking misogyny offensively explicit, and he has become the target of intense criticism from feminists.

What stands out, even in these more or less real-istic novels, is the undiminished energy and variety of Amis' writing, his exploration over the years of different aspects of the contemporary scene, and his modulation from a social satirist to a wry observer of the complicated emotions surrounding old age and mortality. Indeed, even when he is most fiercely satirical, Amis is still a novelist whose characters are more than simple targets, and his novels have surprises and moral twists in store for the perceptive reader.

For example, *I Want It Now* and *Girl, 20* (1971) are Amis' satirical rendering of the 1960's, and both of them are now somewhat dated. But each of these books winds up complicating what looks like a simple moral situation. The earlier book is the weaker of the two, since its initially repellent hero, the rising media personality Ronnie Appleyard, simply finds love and domesticity at the end. He begins as Amis' most blatantly offensive character since *One Fat Englishman,* rather worse in fact than Roger Micheldene, since he is a professionally "liberal" television interviewer whose sole concern is his own enrichment. As always, Amis has a grudging admiration for uncomplicated individual rapacity, for people like Ronnie who are honestly selfish, at least to themselves. Ronnie has not, Amis explains, the least interest in power as such: "Fame and money, with a giant's helping of sex thrown in, were all he was after" (ch. 1).

The novel is about Ronnie's pursuit of the neurotic and promiscuous but sexually unfulfilled heiress, Simona Quick. This chase, from London to the Greek islands to Nashville, Tennessee, allows Amis to etch in acid a portrait gallery of the decadent rich and to lead his hero through his accumulating disgust with this sort of person to sexual tenderness and love for Simona. There are incidental satirical pleasures along the way, but the book's ending seems half-hearted and disappointingly simple. *Girl, 20* is much more interesting, although it, too, continues Amis' assault on 1960's culture.

Sir Roy Vandervane, a fifty-three-year-old, moderately famous second-rate composer and conductor, has embarked on his latest affair, with seventeen-year-old Sylvia, who is unhappy that they can never go out in public together. Sir Roy asks his friend and the narrator of the story, the newspaper music critic Douglas Yandell, to act as her escort by accompanying them and Roy's daughter on a visit to a jazz club. Yandell's reluctant cooperation matches his disapproving recording of Roy's pursuit of youthful vigor not only with his mistress but with other aspects, musical and political, of the swinging scene.

Yandell's narrative includes some very funny set pieces, such as a visit to a wrestling match and Sir Roy's performance (with a rock group) of his composition "Elevations 9," a chamber violin concerto with parts for sitar, bass guitar, and bongos. But Yandell's sour and disgusted view of Sir Roy and his own joylessly controlled emotional life point to unresolvable issues. Yandell, that is, has no coherent moral base for his disgust with Sir Roy's selfish yearnings. When he asks the appalling Sylvia, "What makes you such a howling bitch?" the target of his satire answers in a blast of unpunctuated rage for which Yandell has no response:

I expect it's the same thing as makes you a top-heavy red-haired four-eyes who's never had anything to come up to being tossed off by the Captain of Boats and impotent and likes bloody symphonies and fugues and the first variation comes before the statement of the theme and give me a decent glass of British beer and dash it all Carruthers I don't know what young people are coming to these days and a scrounger and an old woman and a failure and a hanger-on and a prig and terrified and a shower and a brisk rub-down every morning and you can't throw yourself away on a little trollop like that Roy you must think of your wife Roy old boy old boy and I'll come along but I don't say I approve and bloody dead. Please delete the items in the above that do not apply. If any.

(ch. 3)

Truly appalling as she is, Sylvia in this speech at least has a satiric energy superior to Yandell's sour disapproval and lack of will. He himself is drawn to Roy's daughter, Penny, but when he finds that she is available, his musing on the prospect of an affair with her is repulsive: "attractive but irrelevant, like the free offer of a new and prodigious set of hi-fi equipment" (ch. 9). In the end, Sir Roy runs off with Sylvia, and Yandell is horrified to discover that Penny has become a heroin addict. She rejects his offer to look after her: "Thank you for asking me, but you wouldn't stick at it, would you?" (ch. 10). She is right, and Amis' narrator implicitly dramatizes in his weakness and lack of moral commitment the failure of satire based simply on aesthetic disgust.

That complexity is less of a factor in the enormously controversial *Jake's Thing,* which looks like a late-middle-aged sequel to *Lucky Jim.* Jake Richardson is a classical historian who teaches at Oxford but spends most of his time in London. Unlike Jim, he has been enough of a historian (he has written four books) to secure for himself a comfortable academic existence, and he has also had an active sexual life, including three wives. At nearly sixty, however, Jake finds that his sexual drive has evaporated, and he has embarked on a course of medical and psychological treatment to restore his urge.

Sex and group therapy (with an American "facilitator") are obvious targets for Amis' satire, as is the intellectual vapidity of the academic scene. Unmistakably, this is Amis' own view of the world. But Jake himself, as an essentially tormented character struggling toward self-understanding, may be another matter. Giving great offense to many readers, who tended not unreasonably to assume that this represents the author's own standpoint, Amis has Jake discover after a long and successful libidinal career that he does not like women. The revelation comes after his potency returns with a one-night stand with an old flame. As he nurses a hangover the next day, he confesses to his homosexual colleague that he despises women "intellectually," that he is "a male chauvinist pig" (ch. 22). For Jake to bring himself to admit these truths in this sort of banal language is the ultimate humiliation.

Read backwards, as it were, from that self-discovery, *Jake's Thing* is not a simple satire. The book's comic moments consistently humiliate Jake; for example, in one sex-therapy session he is in the pit of an operating theater, surrounded by doctors and students and technicians:

He found himself sitting on an ugly and expensive-looking straight-backed chair without his trousers and underpants. Otherwise he was neatly, almost formally dressed on the clean-linen-for-scaffold principle: dark-grey suit jacket, cream shirt, well-knotted regimental tie, grey socks and much-polished black shoes.

(ch. 8)

Jake, in other words, is assaulted and indeed mastered by the things he hates. When he arrives at his college, Comyns, it is being picketed by women carrying placards that read "Piss Off Comyns

Pigs." As Jake tries to rush through the line, he is assaulted by shouts that include "Richardson! Bloody Richardson! Wanker! Wanker Richardson!" The scene is comic enough for a reader but nightmarish for Jake himself:

Instead of the blows he had foreseen, kisses descended, breasts were rubbed against him and his crotch was grabbed at. There was a great deal of warmth and flesh and deep breathing . . . he could see no more than an inch or two: My Body Is Mine But I Share, he read at close quarters, holding his glasses on with his left hand and his case with his right. He felt frightened, not of any physical harm or even of greater embarrassment, but of losing control in some unimagined way.

(ch. 10)

For most readers—it seems likely—Jake Richardson as victim of his own past, as tragic or at least pathetic loser in human relationships, will be a hard case to swallow. There is, perhaps, too much of Amis the provocative satirist in the third-person narration that ends with Jake learning that his problem is physiological and can be cured. Amis has him refuse the medicine, and his paraphrase of Jake's misogynistic analysis of women's shortcomings, including "their preemption of the major share of feeling" (ch. 28) is a wittily malicious last word that is clearly heartfelt. Amis' self-indulgence in his own prejudices mars the end of the novel, but he makes up for it in *Stanley and the Women* by using a first-person narrator to confront and to complicate similar issues.

Stanley Duke is a far cry from the usual witty and satirical Amis narrator; he is a confused, eventually overwhelmed man who discovers that his nineteen-year-old son from his first marriage, Steve, is severely and later violently schizophrenic. Jake fights back against his tormentors, but Stanley can only wonder who's telling him the truth—Dr. Nash, the male psychiatrist who says simply that Steve is suffering from paranoid delusions and recommends chemotherapy, or Trish Collings, the woman psychiatrist who calls it something other than madness, "a problem in living, something involving not just him but also the people close to him" (ch. 2). In her jumpy evasiveness, Dr. Collings reminds Stanley of his first wife, Nowell. Indeed, in the therapy session Dr. Collings arranges, she and Nowell seem to become one female enemy, blaming everything on Stanley. His rendition of this moment projects subtly the kind of percep-

tion without understanding that makes him such an interesting narrator in the context of Amis' career.

Collings got up and Nowell went across and I could have sworn they were going to kiss, but without going that far they made it clear enough that they got on famously together. Then they both turned and looked at me. I knew that look, I would have known it even if I had never seen it before—it was the look of two women getting together to sort a man out. And on my way here I had said to myself well anyway, it would be fun to see those two wills battling against each other. My trouble was that I kept mixing women up with men.

(ch. 2)

Stanley himself is no misogynist, but plenty of hatred for women manifests itself in *Stanley and the Women*. The other men Stanley encounters, including his former wife's current husband, contribute to the book's evocation of unconditional warfare between the two halves of the human species. Amis may well be dramatizing his own baffled hostility toward women, but in doing so he does novelistic justice to the complexities of social and psychological issues by implicating Stanley's feelings about women with his confused emotional reaction to his son's madness. A reader is not meant to sort these things out neatly, although taken out of context there is much in the book to alarm and disgust feminists, or indeed anyone interested in communication between the sexes. Consider the concluding episode for a troubling last instance. Stanley suspects that his wife, Susan, has deliberately slashed her arm with a knife and blamed it on Steve so that he will be sent back to the hospital; she confronts Stanley with the suspicion and leaves him, after a barrage of abuse—"you lower-class turd. I don't know how I've put up with you so long" (ch. 3). Stanley searches for the truth, and he seems to have found it when his friend Cliff, a doctor, calls her slashed arm a textbook case of a self-inflicted wound. Sitting in a pub, Cliff and Stanley drunkenly rehearse the book's misogynist refrain. The novel ends with the two men at Cliff's house later that evening, where Susan calls: "Can you ever forgive me?" she says.

Cliff's evidence may or may not be conclusive; the boozy exchange in the pub between him and Stanley on men and women continues the book's rehearsal of a destabilized world of sexual relationships, which Amis renders in all of its confusion and even violence. To some extent, *Stanley and the Women* is a narrative experiment using deliberately inflammatory material, from a novelist who thrives on keeping his readers guessing.

Both misogyny and radical self-disgust are complementary obsessions of a male satiric tradition that reaches back in Western culture to ancient Greece, through the Christian fathers of the church, and—closer to home—to native English satirists important to Amis, such as Pope and Swift. In repeating these obsessions, Amis is certainly not playing literary games. The hatred of women by men, or in Jake's case the projection of self-hatred onto them, is set in the context provided by life in twentieth-century England as Amis engages it in his novels.

To some extent, Amis redeems himself from charges of obsessive hatred of women by returning in *Difficulties with Girls* (1988) to Jenny Bunn and Patrick Standish from *Take a Girl like You.* Married now and living in London, where Patrick works in publishing, the Standishes are still locked in manipulative competition, with Patrick womanizing and Jenny wondering how to cure him. Once again, she has the last and best word by seeing through his plot to even the moral balance by tempting her into a retaliatory affair with a friend of his. "I don't think," she says, "I can go on loving you indefinitely, not like this. Of course, we might get on better that way. Then you could be a shit to your heart's content" (ch. 16). Matters are resolved when Jenny becomes pregnant, but her meditation on the future, the last words of the novel, shows that she has no illusions, that she understands men like Patrick in ways that may well make them fear women like her: "Jenny was happy. She was going to have him all to herself for at least three years, probably more like five, and a part of him for ever, and now she could put it all out of her mind" (ch. 19).

Amis' misogyny may be a real enough part of his personality, but for the purposes of reading his fiction it could possibly be a false issue, better understood as part of his wider, complicated vision of modern life and mortality in general. Misanthropy and the self-loathing that goes with it are implicit in his earliest work, but so is a high hilarity and manic inventiveness that give even a somber book like *Stanley and the Women* flashes of black humor. *Ending Up* (1974) is an odd book in this regard. It treats the last three months of the lives of five

septuagenarians who live together to make their modest means go further. Each of them dies grotesquely in the last chapter on the same day in a connected series of accidents. The key figure in this menage is Bernard, a former soldier. Told that he has three months to live, he spends much of this very short narrative playing malevolent practical jokes on the others. Amis makes it all grotesque rather than funny, and the book seems deliberately too short and cryptic to generate much sympathy for the characters. It illustrates the degree to which black humor like Amis' can fail if it lacks sympathy and verbal wit. Bernard's tricks generally fall short of their aim, and it is the neat arrival of death all around that takes care of him and his housemates. So, too, Amis the novelist cannot reconstruct these five lives and extract meaning and coherence from them, or perhaps he decides that the task is impossible. Such retrospection, his bleak little novel seems to say, is pointless, futile.

But Amis in more recent years seems invigorated, returning in 1988 to the irrepressible Jenny Bunn in *Difficulties with Girls* and in effect resolving some of his troubling themes of advancing decrepitude, guilty remorse for a life ill spent, and terminal self-loathing in the prizewinning *The Old Devils* (1986). The devils of the title are a bit younger and much more affluent than the oldsters in *Ending Up,* but the novel is about looking back to a past that began about thirty-five years ago. Alun Weaver, a media personality who has made a career out of his Welshness, a sort of Dylan Thomas without poetic talent, returns to Wales with his wife, Rhiannon. With Malcolm, Peter, Charlie, and Garth, his old chums, they renew old friendships and bring excitement and reexamination of their shared past to a circle that has become dull and settled. Alun renews other relationships, including his affair with Sophie, Charlie's wife, and he leads his old friends on a pub crawl to old haunts. With his flaunted and still vigorous sexuality, his unabashed self-assertiveness, his energy for pleasure and drink, and especially his verbal wit, Alun Weaver marks the return of the dominating energy of the protagonists of Amis' early novels, but now the aging hero exists in a context of mellow retrospection and failed or not-quite-fulfilled lives, his own as much as the others.

Alun's homecoming is a brilliant but inevitably doomed burst of self-assertion, for the old devils are too old to sustain it for long. Gulping the last of many whiskeys, Alun coughs, sprawls across a sofa, and dies. As Charlie watches, Alun seems to be performing "an unusually thorough imitation of a man collapsing with rage or revulsion" (part 8). But this last fling had been wonderful while it lasted. For instance, Amis describes a morning when Alun goes out early to get the newspapers:

On his return he stood facing the bay in pale sunlight, took some deep breaths and thought to himself, if a waft of industrial pollution had ever been perceptible here there was no question of any now. When other thoughts, to do with time and age and all that, started to occur to him, he rather consciously went indoors to breakfast, a scheduled fatty's flare-up presenting two boiled eggs turned out on to fried bread and fried potatoes as well as bacon and tomatoes. While he ate it he worked animatedly at the *Times* crossword. "You *fiend*," he said, writing in a solution. "Oh, you . . . you *swine*."

(part 7)

That is a wonderful if self-deluded moment for Alun, and the reader's necessary ambivalence toward him here and throughout the narrative creates the special ironic maturity of *The Old Devils*. Like so many of Amis' other heroes, Alun has a complicated relationship to his creator. One can see in Alun's wit and guiltless pursuit of pleasure Amis' amused projection of aspects of himself and also, perhaps, a kind of self-loathing. Alun can be considered an expression of Amis' own indefatigable wit and resourcefulness as a writer but also as an emblem, in his doomed gaiety and predatory selfishness, of Amis' sense of his own moral failings and of a looming mortality he now shares with his older characters.

Kingsley Amis was knighted in 1990, and by that time his reputation as a conservative elder statesman of English letters seemed to have solidified, partly perhaps because of the spectacular arrival on the literary scene of his son, Martin, whose violently nihilistic satiric novels make his father's work look mildly traditional by contrast. Amis' novels like *The Old Devils* in 1986 and *The Folks That Live on the Hill* in 1990 mark a mellowing of the younger satirist. Without giving up his verbal and stylistic energy, Amis seems to have acquired a deepened compassion for his characters, to have replaced scorn and contempt with tolerant amusement and a good amount of fellow feeling. To be

sure, Amis' work remains full of comic outrage at modern life, but it also features an implicitly unsparing self-examination and a darkening engagement with mortality and failure.

SELECTED BIBLIOGRAPHY

I. COLLECTED WORKS. *A Case of Samples (Poems 1946–1956)* (London, 1956); *Collected Poems: 1944–1979* (London, 1979); *Collected Short Stories* (London, 1980).

II. SEPARATE WORKS. *Bright November* (London, 1947), poems; *A Frame of Mind* (Reading, 1953), poems; *Lucky Jim* (London, 1954), novel; *That Uncertain Feeling* (London, 1955), novel; *I Like It Here* (London, 1958), novel; *New Maps of Hell: A Survey of Science Fiction* (London, 1960), criticism; *Take a Girl like You* (London, 1960), novel; *The Anti-Death League* (London, 1962), novel; *My Enemy's Enemy* (London, 1962), short stories; *One Fat Englishman* (London, 1963), novel; *The Egyptologists* (London, 1965), novel, with R. Conquest; *The Evans Country* (Oxford and London, 1967), poems; *Colonel Sun* (London, 1968), novel, pub. under the pseudonym Robert Markham; *I Want It Now* (London, 1968), novel; *The Green Man* (London, 1969), novel.

What Became of Jane Austen? and Other Questions (London, 1970), essays; *Girl, 20* (London, 1971), novel; *Selected Short Stories of G. K. Chesterton* (London, 1972), edited by Amis; *Ending Up* (London, 1974), novel; *The Riverside Villas Murder* (London, 1973), novel; *Rudyard Kipling and His World* (London, 1975), biographical essay; *The Alteration* (London, 1976), novel; *Jake's Thing* (London, 1978), novel; *The New Oxford Book of Light Verse* (London, 1978), introduction and compilation by Amis; *Russian Hide and Seek* (London, 1980), novel; *Stanley and the Women* (London, 1984), novel; *The Old Devils* (London, 1986), novel; *The Crime of the Century* (London, 1987), novel; *Difficulties with Girls* (London, 1988), novel; *The Folks That Live on the Hill* (London, 1990), novel.

III. BIOGRAPHICAL AND CRITICAL STUDIES. K. Allsop, *The Angry Decade* (London, 1958); C. Shapiro, ed., *Contemporary British Novelists* (Carbondale, Ill., 1963); D. Lodge, *The Language of Fiction* (New York, 1966); R. Rabinovitz, *The Reaction Against Experiment in the English Novel, 1950–1960* (New York, 1967); B. Bergonzi, *The Situation of the Novel* (Pittsburgh, 1970); D. Salwak, *Kingsley Amis: A Reference Guide* (Boston, 1978); P. Gardner, *Kingsley Amis* (Boston, 1981); N. McEwan, *The Survival of the Novel: British Fiction in the Later Twentieth Century* (London, 1981); P. Swinden, *The English Novel of History and Society 1940–1980* (London, 1984); R. Stevenson, *The British Novel Since the Thirties* (London, 1986); R. Bradford, *Kingsley Amis* (London, 1989).

JOHN ARDEN
(1930–   )

David Graver

OF ALL THE angry young playwrights to write critical, uncompromisingly vivid dramas about Britain's social ills and class-ridden malaise for the Royal Court Theatre in the late 1950's and early 1960's, John Arden was the most accomplished craftsman of dialogue and plot. In addition, he has proven over the years to be the most ardent and principled experimenter in the form and function of theater. His abiding discontent with the traditional place of theater in Britain's high culture took him beyond the limited innovative parameters of the Royal Court, even when colleagues such as John Osborne and Harold Pinter were uncritically coming to terms with the conservative luxuries of West End success. Arden's own success came from his forging plays, in collaboration with Margaretta D'Arcy, for politically committed amateur groups and for other nontraditional settings. This direction led to financial straits and critical neglect for Arden, but also allowed him to create some of the most original and powerful plays written in Britain in the twentieth century.

Arden's and D'Arcy's commitment to addressing intertwined notions of anti-imperialism (particularly the question of Britain in Northern Ireland), socialism, and feminism and their boycott of large commercial theaters have made it difficult for them to gain financial backing for many plays, but the projects they have completed display a theatrical richness and conceptual sophistication equal to all and eclipsing most other contemporary British drama. Many critics would not agree with this estimation, but such a response perhaps shows the limitations in conventional criteria of good drama rather than any flaws in the major works of Arden and D'Arcy.

Although Arden's own work has enjoyed more widespread approval than his work in collaboration with D'Arcy, his debt to D'Arcy's suggestions and support has been considerable from the very beginning of his career. The two met in 1955, two years before Arden's first commercial productions, and he credits her with introducing him to the work of Bertolt Brecht, Samuel Beckett, August Strindberg, Ernst Toller, and Brendan Behan as well as guiding him into the London theater scene. Without D'Arcy, Arden might likely have never become the playwright he is. The couple married in 1957, the year Arden's first full-length play, *The Waters of Babylon,* premiered at the Royal Court. Since then they have raised four sons and written more than thirteen plays together, ranging in length from short one-acts to a twenty-six-hour, six-part marathon. But in the beginning Arden wrote most of his plays alone.

EARLY WORK

BORN 26 October 1930, Arden was the only child in a large extended family dominated by his aunts, great-aunts, and grandmothers. Among the innovative young playwrights of the late 1950's, he was an anomaly. Most of his colleagues came from working-class backgrounds, while Arden was thoroughly middle-class. His father was the manager of a glass factory in the West Yorkshire town of Barnsley, and his paternal grandfather owned a wine business that had been handed down through several generations. The Arden family were proud of a bourgeois pedigree that boasted two centuries of mayors and other local dignitaries as well as vague connections with the family of Shakespeare's mother. Arden's mother, née Layland, hailed from the Lancashire town of Otley, where her father's job as an insurance salesman and the family's connections with the Methodist church and the Labour Party placed them somewhat lower in the bourgeois pecking order than the Ardens.

Whereas most of Arden's fellow dramatists had little formal education, Arden was trained in architecture at Cambridge and Edinburgh. Many of his colleagues had professional theatrical training; in contrast, Arden's familiarity with the theater derived exclusively from his participation in high-school productions, from attending provincial shows, and from avid theatergoing while stationed in Edinburgh during his military service in 1948 and 1949 as a lance-corporal in the British Intelligence Corps. Most significantly, while playwrights such as Osborne, Arnold Wesker, and Pinter used prose dialogue exclusively to delineate often searingly tense dramatic situations from which the characters are incapable of escaping, Arden rigged out his dialogue with a spectacular array of regional dialects, invented archaisms, blank verse, and rhymed ballads, and he sent his characters careening through plots of intrigue that rival nineteenth-century melodrama and Jacobean tragedy in complexity.

Arden's first major play, *The Waters of Babylon* (produced without decor at the Royal Court on 20 October 1957), provides a good example of his general style. Set in London in 1956, the play draws together characters speaking English in accents hailing from Poland, the West Indies, Ireland, Yorkshire, the Conservative wing of Parliament, and cockney slums. Their verbal styles range from the poetic to the grotesque. Here are two members of the protagonist's prostitution ring discussing prospective employees they have spotted at train stations:

BATHSHEBA: Two today from Trinidad and there was one from Jamaica. I brought them along for to see Mr. Krank. Will he keep them, maybe? No, I don't know. Not what I'd call real proud-jetting young women, not what I'd call flying fish or torpedoes. No sir, just kind of sad and quiet gentle sea-weed laid out dark on a hard cold beach. You've been along to meet a train too?

CASSIDY: The Irish Mail, no less. And there they stepped down from it, six beautiful doxies, Sea-weed?—No sea-weed but all roaring gorse, wild whitehorn, a chiming tempest of girls, turned that dirty Euston into a true windswept altitude, a crystal mountain-top for love. Or for Mr. Krank's finances, which is more to the bloody purpose.

(act 2, scene 1)

Note the giddy distance from this to the broken bombast of the parliamentarian holding forth in Hyde Park:

LOAP: We feel, and, I say, the Prime Minister feels, that, to this circumstance, that is to say, the forthcoming visit of the Russian Leaders—as a necessary if indeed a not entirely inappropriate manifestation, or, yes, a trend towards possible peace, ah, mutual co-operation, co-habitation . . . co-, to coin a phrase, co-existence with the mighty Soviet Union.

(act 2, scene 2)

So much of the characters' lives is packed into the words they speak that Arden has little use for a realistic scenic decor. In general, he never looks for the setting of the drama to confine, direct, or in any way set the terms for the actions undertaken by the characters. In this respect, Arden's plays make use of the classic vocabulary of drama established by Aristotle and Georg Wilhelm Friedrich Hegel rather than the modern vocabulary ushered in with naturalism in the late nineteenth century. In other words, Arden's characters create the action of the play through the free exercise of their individual wills and the conflicts among characters that arise from the decisions each has made. Arden never allows forces beyond the control of the characters' volitions to exert a primary influence on the course of the action. Forces such as the unconscious, the past, disease, or the physical milieu, which figure prominently in the drama of Strindberg, Henrik Ibsen, and Maksim Gorky, are of only marginal interest in Arden's plays. Arden does not, however, give his characters the kind of timeless, absolute willpower that the philosopher Hegel would have preferred and that prompted Hegel to suggest that only princes are appropriate for the grand dramatic actions of tragedy. Arden's characters usually have very limited personal powers, and they make decisions based on their social class, their personal history of experiences, and sundry other constraints and influences. The difference between Arden's characters and those in the realistic plays of high modernism (of Gerhart Hauptmann, Ibsen, Strindberg, Anton Chekhov, and others) is that no matter how many social, physical, and biographical factors impede the choices of action available to Arden's characters, those characters are always left with significant choices to make, choices that shape the dramatic action in which they are involved. In realistic, high-modern plays, the characters are usually incapable of significantly influencing the course of events by their volitional decisions.

Since Arden constructs his dramas around the free decisions of his characters and the words they utter to one another, he has little use for the detailed sets that a playwright like Hauptmann or Ibsen would use to confine and direct the dramatic action. Instead of participating in the representational action of the play, Arden's sets facilitate the theatrical display of that action. Props are simple and functional, designed to emphasize the actions of the characters rather than to prevent them from acting. In *Waters of Babylon,* for instance, Arden describes the stage arrangements thus:

The sort of scenery I had in mind was the eighteenth or early nineteenth century sort, which involved the use of sliding flats or drop curtains which open and close while the actors are still on the stage—a method still in use in provincial pantomimes.

(author's note)

The twentieth-century technical advances in the illusionary powers of the stage are of no interest to Arden. He prefers instead a matter-of-fact acceptance of obviously artificial dramatic conventions as long as these conventions swiftly, efficiently, and forcefully convey the story to the audience. Arden's methods of "presenting the pretence" of drama owe much to his study of Bertolt Brecht but are also enlivened by his interest in the humor, sensuality, and spectacle of popular entertainments such as pantomime. When his characters speak directly to the audience, for instance, they do not simply reveal their values and motivations in a gesture of Brechtian alienation but often engage the audience with a sardonic wit that owes as much to the traditions of the medieval Vice and the stand-up comedian as it does to Brecht. We can see this in the way Krank introduces himself to the audience in *The Waters of Babylon:*

Breakfast, what sort of breakfast, this coffee is not very fresh, is it? After the nature of an archaeological deposit, more water more coffee into the pot every morning, but at the bottom it has been there six weeks, seven, it's like drinking bitumen. Why don't I wash my cups and plates more often than only once a week? 'Cause I am a man of filthy habits in my house, is why.

(act 1, scene 1)

Another feature *The Waters of Babylon* shares with most of Arden's early plays is its emphasis on the machinations of astonishingly roguish and sleazy characters whom Arden allows to defend themselves so articulately that they are almost endearing. The protagonist Sigismanfred Krankiewicz (alias Krank), a Polish expatriate, claims to be a concentration-camp refugee but, in fact, was a concentration-camp guard and now makes his money as a pimp, slumlord, and confidence man while pretending to work as an architectural assistant. He is surrounded by other slumlords and pimps, by prostitutes, petty thieves, corrupt politicians, and political fanatics; miraculously, he comes off as the play's most sympathetic character, both for his manipulative skills and his relative personal honesty.

The major reason the audience can admire Krank is because he so tenaciously holds his own at the center of an elaborate maze of intrigues. The audience need not be overly concerned with his questionable character when there is so much to wonder at in the plot that wraps itself around him. As the play begins, Krank is already leading a triple life: a pimp by night, an architect by day, and a speculator in overcrowded tenements over breakfast and on weekends. He engages Charles Butterthwaite, an old, discredited, derelict Labour politician from the North, to help him manipulate the local district councillors and keep the health commission off his back just as a fanatical Polish nationalist, Paul, pressures him into providing a room in his tenement for the construction of a bomb to be thrown at Khruschev, then first secretary of the Communist party of the Soviet Union, on his visit to London. Butterthwaite hatches a plan for creating a municipal lottery that will endear Krank to the chief power in the district, the councillor Joseph Caligula (originally from Barbados), and allow him to siphon off funds for his own use. Krank hopes to use the money swindled from the lottery to pay off Paul and avoid being involved in his terrorism; but just as this plan begins to develop it is complicated by the suspicious meddling of Henry Ginger, a fanatical English nationalist, and Alexander Loap, a conservative member of Parliament.

Loap's interventions are given further twists because his mistress once worked for Krank and is the long-lost sister of Krank's current underling, Conor Cassidy. Cassidy has friends in the Irish Republican Army and quickly sets his own designs on the bomb Paul begins building in one of Krank's back rooms. Caligula's inconvenient honesty and his romantic entanglement with Krank's West Indian prostitute Bathsheba, as well as Krank's own erotic intrigues with his employer, the architect Barbara Baulkfast, provide further complications. After many misunderstandings, inopportune confrontations, and muddled intrigues, Krank's elaborate machinations disintegrate in a chaotic display of botched swindle and revenge that leaves Butterthwaite under arrest, Paul on the run, and Krank mortally wounded by a shot aimed at Ginger. With his dying breath Krank ties up the other loose ends of the plot. By way of a eulogy and conclusion, Butterthwaite leads a ballad in the form of a four-part round that describes hiding in a cellar.

LIVE LIKE PIGS

The following year, 1958, Arden's next stage play, *Live Like Pigs,* was given a full production at the Royal Court, and he gave up his job in an architect's office to become a full-time playwright. The title of this play is taken from George Bernard Shaw's 1892 drama *Widowers' Houses:* "those dirty, drunken, disreputable people who live like pigs." Arden again indulges his fascination with scurrilous and unbalanced characters as he charts the consequences of forcing a group of vagabonds into a municipal housing project "in a north-country industrial town." In the play's seventeen scenes, all located in or in front of their new flat, the nomadic Sawneys progressively make a shambles of their lives, their living quarters, and the comfortable existence of their dull neighbors, the Jacksons. Arden says,

When I wrote this play I intended it to be not so much a social document as a study of differing ways of life brought sharply into conflict and both losing their own particular virtues under the stress of intolerance and misunderstanding.

(introductory note)

In this play Arden makes one of his closest approaches to realism, in that the physical milieu seems partly responsible for the course of the action. When the wild life of the Sawneys is crammed into the small space of the housing proj-ect, it reaches a critical mass and explodes. It is important to realize, however, that this housing project, despite its dreary lack of variety, is by no means oppressive in itself. In Gorky's *The Lower Depths* (1902), the dirty, cramped tenement clearly does exert its malevolent influence over the characters, but in *Live Like Pigs,* the housing project plays more the part of an innocent bystander abused by its unfortunate proximity to human forces with which it is incapable of reckoning.

To focus this drama on "differing ways of life," Arden avoids the elaborate intrigues and strong central character he exploited in *The Waters of Babylon* in favor of charting multifarious interactions among a broad array of vivid characters. The Sawney group is composed of Sailor, a seventy-year-old tyrant with white hair hanging below his shoulders and a drooping moustache, "the most barbarous yet least savage of the group"; Rachel, Sailor's lover and a part-time prostitute, a forty-year-old "tall handsome termagant"; Col, Rachel's son, a loutish youth of eighteen with "swift and violent mannerisms"; Rosie, Sailor's daughter, in her early twenties, sullen and weary but with "a basic sense of satire and true depth of passion"; Sally, Rosie's daughter, "a wicked little ten-year-old"; and Rosie's other child, an infant. The Sawneys initially overwhelm but are eventually attacked by their next-door neighbors, the Jacksons, "an undistinguished but not contemptible family" who are "in the process of being promoted from the working-class proper into the lower-middle." Their teenage daughter, Doreen, is both attracted and frightened by Col's aggressive manners, while Mr. Jackson gets more excitement than he bargained for from Rachel. Another group descends upon the Sawneys' flat to cause them as much grief as they cause the Jacksons. This group is led by Blackmouth, the father of Rosie's children, an escaped convict, "twenty-eight years old, lean, and sexy . . . both insolent and obsequious" with "clear indications of underlying mental unbalance." He brings with him his latest love, the seventeen-year-old, feverish Daffodil, who "has an old, old face like that of a malicious fairy," and Daffodil's mother, the Old Croaker, "a batty old hag, alternately skittish and comatose." A small group of well-meaning but ineffectual social-welfare officials complete the cast.

For the Sawney and Blackmouth groups, Arden has invented his own lyrical version of street slang and given each character a distinct version of it. Compare, for instance, these passages:

ROSIE: There's no one can touch that old Sailor once he's got his strength in. My mam, when she wor living, he'd be out on a job . . . then into the boozer till closing—likely fight a pair o' men into canal dock, knock a copper over after—then home like a traction engine and revel her three times down to Rio without he'd even take off his boots.

(scene 2)

SAILOR: They call me a killer. . . . They gave me that name. Times I sail the sea they gave it. So take you one look at 'em: forcsle, deck, or captain's bridge—"Watch out for that boy, he's a killer."

(scene 4)

CROAKER (she sings [to Mrs. Jackson]):
Come all you little black cats.
He chases the dirty rat
The rat is sharper than the cat
And fetches the blood right out of his back . . .
I'd sooner love a biting rat, I would, than any day with our Rachel; ee-ay-yai—

COL (to Croaker): What you gabbing over the fence, you old haystack? How's our chirping Daffodil today?

CROAKER (in a sort of trance): Eh? Who is it? Col?

COL: You know me as well as your own toe nails, you do.

(scene 9)

Although this play is loosely based on a true incident, in his introductory note Arden declares it a "poetic" rather than "journalistic" look at the clashes among lower-class cultures. He has invented the life-style of the Sawneys rather than observed it. He is more interested in the dynamics of a difficult social situation and the theatrical staging of that situation than he is in drawing lessons about social problems. As in *The Waters of Babylon,* Arden's chief purpose in *Live Like Pigs* is to hold the audience's attention with bold innovations in theatrical form. He creates a world never seen before on the English stage and presents this world to his audience in a manner never practiced by his contemporaries. For Arden, following Brecht, the contact between audience and stage is as important as the world represented on the stage. In *The Waters of Babylon,* he has Krank address the audience directly

in conspiratorial and illusion-breaking speeches similar to Shakespeare's Richard III or the Chorus in *Henry V;* in *Live Like Pigs* he has various characters sing verses from a ballad directly to the audience before each scene.

At this point in his career, Arden's interest in social problems and theatrical innovations was more sensual than ideological. He stood quietly with his fellow playwrights Osborne, Wesker, and Ann Jellicoe against nuclear armament, British imperialism, and social injustice, but his plays stood on their own as spectacular scenes of dramatic conflict. His political convictions might lead him to certain themes, but his artistic sensibilities always carefully detached his finished plays from any particular political line. He was so successful at making *Live Like Pigs* apolitical that most critics were completely baffled by it. It was even harder to understand than *The Waters of Babylon* because it did not have a central character to admire and no one was quite sure what was meant by the central conflict of the piece, which culminates in a siege by the Jacksons and their law-abiding neighbors against the Sawney household. Critics on the left castigated Arden for his unfair ridicule of the welfare state; critics on the right attacked what they saw as his romantic admiration of the criminal Sawneys. Very few people realized at the time that Arden was attempting to display problems that had no immediate solutions. Over the years, however, critics and audiences have come to appreciate the humor, sensuality, and intellectual rigor upon which *Live Like Pigs* draws for its raison d'être.

SERJEANT MUSGRAVE'S DANCE

IN 1959, Arden wrote another then-unappreciated play, which is now viewed as a masterpiece. *Serjeant Musgrave's Dance* has received more performances than any of his other plays, and has been canonized in drama anthologies on both sides of the Atlantic. It is set sometime between 1860 and 1880 in a northern coal-mining town—Arden had in mind his hometown, Barnsley, about fifty or sixty years before he was born. Sergeant "Black Jack" Musgrave and three privates appear during a bitter cold snap in the dead of winter looking for volunteers during a tense strike at the mines. They take up lodgings and begin recruiting at the widow Mrs.

Hitchcock's pub. The mayor and parson suggest that they press the strike leaders into uniform; the colliers drink sullenly and promise nothing; the sinister bargee who brought the soldiers taunts and tries to manipulate and betray everyone. Meeting secretly in a graveyard, the soldiers reveal that they are deserters come to town to wreak an unspecified vengeance for crimes committed overseas in the service of the British Empire. Their individual reasons for embarking on this mission are troublingly diverse: Hurst is an anarchist, Attercliffe is a pacifist, Sparky does it for the memory of a dead friend and his respect for Musgrave, and Musgrave himself is wrapped in a dark religious zeal hardened by his icy military discipline. The next day they plan to train a Gatling gun on the crowd attending their recruitment rally, display the skeleton of a local soldier who died overseas, and "make a whole town, a whole nation, understand the cruelty and greed of armies, what it means, and how to punish it" (act 1, scene 3).

The soldiers' plans begin to go awry during the night. Attercliffe accidentally kills Sparky, who is trying to run off with the barmaid Annie, and some colliers attempt to steal the Gatling gun for their own cause. Sparky's body is hidden and the colliers are brought into an uneasy alliance, but the mayor has called for dragoons from a neighboring town to protect him from the miners, so Musgrave and his men have control of the rally for only a short time. Musgrave hangs the uniformed skeleton from an elaborate market clock and does his dance—five innocent foreigners died for the death of this soldier, so twenty-five innocent Englishmen must pay the price for them. Hurst is anxious to start the massacre by killing the mayor and parson, but when Annie reveals the death of Sparky, the colliers withdraw their support, and Attercliffe steps in front of the Gatling gun. Just then the dragoons arrive, kill Hurst, and arrest Musgrave and Attercliffe. In the last scene, Mrs. Hitchcock visits them as they await the gallows. She says the miners were too worried about feeding themselves and their families to worry about the injustices of the Empire. Musgrave is silent and in despair, but Attercliffe wonders if their principles might not eventually encourage others to act: "They're going to hang us up a length higher nor most appletrees grow, Serjeant. D'you reckon we can start an orchard?" (act 3, scene 2).

Among the most notable features of this play is its innovative and complex employment of themes and forms. First, the play is a protest against imperialism. Although set in a vaguely nineteenth-century past, the play makes, in Arden's words, "quite deliberate" reference to an incident in Cyprus the previous year, in which a British soldier's wife was shot and soldiers killed five people in reprisal. Arden chose to set his play in the nineteenth century because this was a period "of naked rather than apologetic imperialism" (*Arden on File,* p. 20). Despite its urgent political theme, however, the play is contemplative rather than didactic. In finely wrought confrontations it weighs the importance of domestic labor issues against imperial foreign policy and compares three distinct responses to the atrocities of empire: anarchic terrorism, calculated violent protest, and pacifism. Pacifism, represented by Attercliffe, Mrs. Hitchcock, and Annie, is given prominence but is by no means unconditionally endorsed. The complex difficulties of the social and political situation represented in the play make impossible a clear, specific response to the problem. The orchard that Attercliffe and Arden call for at the end does not represent more martyred religious fanatics and pacifists but more people willing to see the urgency of political problems and to look for solutions.

Besides the inherent difficulties of the political issues that Arden presents, the possibility of finding solutions to these problems is also obscured by the unruly complexity of the central characters. Most of the minor characters, such as the mayor, the parson, and the constable, are sketched out in what Arden calls "silhouette." In an interview with Frank Cox (quoted in Malcolm Page, *Arden on File*), Arden explains: "I've purely emphasized in the mayor those aspects of the man's character that deal with his attitude to the coal industry and his attitude to the military" (p. 20). For the four soldiers and two women, however, Arden has constructed much more elaborate characters. So, while the social problems facing the soldiers are given a sharp, pressing abstraction, the soldiers cannot respond to these problems without first confronting the fears, prejudices, desires, and obsessions in their own minds and struggling with the difficulties involved in understanding themselves and making themselves understood by others. Personal anxieties and idiosyncrasies constantly interfere with Musgrave's carefully laid plan for the moral redress of social evils. In the end, the stubborn humanness of the characters triumphs over Musgrave's cold religious dogma. First, Sparky agrees to throw over the plot in order to run off with Annie, then Annie confronts the soldiers with the murder of their colleague, and finally Attercliffe cannot bear to see any more death. Unfortunately, this triumph is also a defeat, because the town stays in the hands of the avaricious mayor and the Empire continues to be protected by dragoons willing to follow orders. All of the all-too-human soldiers die.

Just as the play's political issues stand apart, in their abstraction, from the psychological realism of its central characters, so also do the ritualistic structures and motifs that shape and decorate the drama. The play makes reference to medieval skits concerning the battle of Winter and Spring. Musgrave plays the king of winter: the temperature drops suddenly when he arrives. When the dragoons arrive to reestablish order, the temperature rises. The townspeople engage in a dance that celebrates, perhaps, the old order, the dragoons, or the warm weather, and the play ends with Attercliffe singing a song about green apples and germinating seeds. The allegorical significance of this ritualistic structure, however, is fraught with irony bordering on sarcasm. The dragoons have come to break the strike as well as to arrest Musgrave, and the townsfolk dance more from intimidation or general confusion than from any heartfelt relief over the turn of events. The return of order in this community does not promise to be as salubrious as the return of spring. Moreover, at the end of the play Attercliffe attempts, with some hesitation, to appropriate the imagery of spring for the anti-imperialist cause. He suggests that he and Musgrave might well become martyrs for their political ideals, divine scapegoats whose deaths assure the fertility of the community and whose spirits may be resurrected in the revolutionary deeds of future rebels.

Aside from the struggle for allegorical vindication in the references to the battle between winter and spring, a number of other aestheticized ritual motifs appear throughout the drama. Musgrave's song and dance is the best example of this. Malcolm Page in his critical study of Arden's plays suggests that Musgrave's dance

recalls King David in his dance before the Ark (I Chron. 15:28, 29). . . . Both are warriors executing a long-forgotten ritual before a holy relic (the skeleton); both are symbols of authority; both have a new order in mind.

(p. 46)

The women in the pub also occasionally utter cryptic fragments of ritualistic chants. Annie, for example, intones: "a little bit of wind and a little bit of water. . . . But it drowned three score of sailors, and King of Norway's daughter" (act 2, scene 1). The bright-red soldiers' uniforms and mayor's gown moving against the somber black and white of snow and night, the graveyard, portentous card games, the totemlike market cross/clock, and the skeleton Musgrave hangs from it as a macabre anti-imperialist fetish all contribute to the atmosphere of sinister, fragmented rituals. The prolonged exposition of the play, "using two acts for what is normally done in one" as Arden admits (*Arden on File*, p. 21), results in the drama's opening backward into time as it simultaneously moves forward, creating a static present in which events are suspended as if in the conventions of an unknown liturgy. Through this murky, ritualized world the bargee prances like a demon in a medieval mystery play, disrupting the solemnity with his irreverent and cynical asides while ultimately serving the ceremonious spectacle.

Against these richly symbolistic ritual motifs, Arden expertly balances a strong melodramatic strain. In *John Arden*, Page quotes Alan Brien:

The characters' reactions [in *Musgrave*] have always to be several sizes too large for their actions. The mention of a man's name in a pub resounds like a cannonade. The drop of a trunk on a quayside starts off tremors of an earthquake. The hoisting of a skeleton to a flagpole is expected to change the world.

(p. 51)

Many of the characters and situations seem directly drawn from melodrama: the grotesque bargee named Bludgeon, the forbidden tryst in a stable, the barmaid forsaken by a soldier and half-mad from the loss of her child, the scheming politicians, the whispered plot with its growing complications, the frequent singing of ballads, and the show-stopping dances. Even the arrival of the dragoons resolves the plot with an ironically appropriate melodramatic gesture.

Critics attending the early performances of *Serjeant Musgrave's Dance* could not decide whether to judge the play as a political argument, a realistic character conflict, a symbolistic ritual drama, or a melodramatic spectacle. Ultimately, the play's unique ability to be all of these at once won it justifiable honor and popularity. Arden acknowledges that it has a number of faults, particularly a certain murkiness in the exposition and the lack of "enough hard thinking in the last third of the play" (*Arden on File*, p. 22). Nevertheless, it may be the first twentieth-century play in English to approach Shakespeare's command and synthesis of dramatic elements from popular and high culture and to wed this sophisticated theatrical vocabulary with the Brechtian demands for alienation and political engagement. Indeed, Arden forwards Brecht's theories significantly by showing that the emotional distancing from the action involved in Brecht's "alienation effect" need not imply flat characters or obvious plots. Where Brecht strips the drama to its bare essentials so that spectators stand back in shock, Arden packs the stage so tightly with unruly dramatic and theatrical elements that the spectators can find no room there for their emotional empathy—they instead stand back in puzzled admiration.

THE WORKHOUSE DONKEY

In 1963, Arden came back to the style and themes of his first play with even more assurance and wit in *The Workhouse Donkey.* Although it is not entirely consistent with *The Waters of Babylon,* this play examines the political machinations of Arden's earlier character, Butterthwaite, when he was still "the Napoleon of the North," and it explains his fall from grace. Besides the finely crafted qualities it shares with *Babylon, The Workhouse Donkey* is most notable for its introduction of strong female characters who direct the course of the plot and for Arden's flippant claim in the introduction that he would have liked to have made the play thirteen hours long. Arden's female characters have always spoken convincingly for themselves, but in this play the problems and possibilities of feminine agency, that is, the opportunities for and constraints on the actions of women in a male-dominated society, begin to occupy more of his attention. This concern became central in most of his subsequent work. Likewise, his interest in long plays culminated twelve years later in the twenty-six-hour cycle appropriately titled *The Non-Stop Connolly Show.*

In *The Workhouse Donkey* we also see Arden's proclivity to develop an array of distinct dramas all from one specific milieu or group of characters. His keen sense of the possibilities inherent in personalities and situations is not exhausted by a single dramatic action, and his ingenuity produces an endless supply of plots and intrigues. From memories of his hometown of Barnsley and his work as an architect Arden developed *The Waters of Babylon, Live Like Pigs, Serjeant Musgrave's Dance, The Workhouse Donkey,* and the television plays *Soldier, Soldier* (written in 1957) and *Wet Fish* (written in 1960). From the history of England and Scotland under the Tudor and Stuart monarchies he composed *Armstrong's Last Goodnight* (1964), the radio plays *Pearl* (1978) and *Garland for a Hoar Head* (1982), and the novel *Books of Bale* (1988). A nineteenth-century Irish experiment in communal farming prompted D'Arcy and Arden to write both *Vandaleur's Folly* (1981) and *The Manchester Enthusiasts* (1984). The Christmas Nativity provided material for *The Business of Good Government* (1960) and for the radio broadcast "Keep Those People Moving!" (1972). The legends of Camelot generated a trilogy of plays titled *The Island of the Mighty* (1972), the life of James Connolly prompted a six-part, twenty-six-hour production (1975), and the history of the Christian church under Emperor Constantine inspired a nine-part radio series titled *Whose Is the Kingdom?* (1988).

EXPERIMENTS AND HISTORICAL PLAYS

Until 1965, Arden's drama fell into two broad categories: (1) formal and thematic innovations in conventional theater and (2) experiments that alter the material and media of theater. Besides his work at the Royal Court Theatre in London, he actively sought other forms of dramatic representation. Indeed, his first success as a playwright was an award for his 1956 radio drama *The Life of Man,* a modern reworking of the tale concerning Dionysus captured by pirates. He also wrote two television plays: *Soldier, Soldier,* which developed a few dramatic situations reincarnated two years later in *Serjeant Musgrave's Dance,* and *Wet Fish,* set in an architect's office and featuring Krank from *Waters of Babylon* and Sir Harold Sweetman from *The Workhouse Donkey.* After *Wet Fish,* Arden permanently abandoned television plays because the organization of the industry did not allow him the authorial control he desired. Moving further from the beaten track of most professional playwrights, he wrote the one-act *When Is a Door Not a Door?* (1958) on commission from a drama school to "provide eleven parts of roughly equal size." Two years later his collaborations with Margaretta D'Arcy began when she provided suggestions and assistance in the writing of *The Business of Good Government,* a one-act Christmas play designed for an amateur performance in a church near the Arden and D'Arcy home, and *The Happy Haven* (1962), a full-length conventional stage play about the director of a retirement home plotting to experiment upon his wards with an elixir of youth. The parts of the elderly in *Happy Haven* were to be played commedia del l'arte style by young actors in masks.

In the summer of 1963 Arden invited anyone interested to his home in Kirkbymoorside, a small country town in Yorkshire, for a month-long "festival of anarchy." Fifty performers of various ilk showed up, including poets, clowns, and a potter. Shows were held nightly for as many as eighty people in the Arden and D'Arcy living room. Skits were improvised by local residents; films were shown and made. Arden was uneasy about the chaotic course of events and never repeated such an unstructured experiment, but it provides vivid testimony to his interest, along with D'Arcy, in creating cultural events on a grand scale for a specific community. In 1964, Arden and D'Arcy proved that plays for local amateurs could work equally well for highly trained, innovative professionals. They wrote *Ars Longa, Vita Brevis* for a group of Girl Guides. Later, the play, dealing with a militaristic art teacher shot in the line of duty by his own principal, was performed by Peter Brook during his celebrated "Theatre of Cruelty" season in London.

In contrast to the diverse experimentation in amateur and anarchistic performance at this time, Arden's conventional stage plays in 1963 and afterward focused intensely on historical drama. The exuberant playfulness of *Waters of Babylon* and even *Live Like Pigs* seems to have been directed into the amateur pieces, leaving the cold, serious world of *Musgrave* to be shaped more precisely into the confrontation of irreconcilable social interests at particular historical moments. This work begins with *Ironhand* (1963), an adaptation of Johann Goethe's *Götz von Berlichingen;* it continues with *Armstrong's Last Goodnight* (1964), about a barbaric Scottish robber baron and the poet/ambassador forced into betraying him; and it ends with *Left-Handed Liberty* (1965), commissioned for the 750th anniversary of the Magna Carta and focusing on King John's po-

litical machinations. Despite their historical subjects, these plays share more in common with the "un-historical parable" *Musgrave* than they do with Shakespeare's history plays or the contemporary ones by Osborne or Bolt.

Arden's historical dramas are not about memorably decisive events or characters of enduring power and influence. His Magna Carta play, for instance, begins after the document is signed and concerns an unexpectedly affable and conniving King John who maneuvers to reassert his authority until his plans are suddenly cut short by his accidental death. In general, Arden's plays dramatize the problematic confrontations of distinct social groups and the dynamics of decision-making involved in the attempts to resolve their differences. The plays are not so much about history as about decision and compromise. They deal with the difficulties of making history rather than with the shape history takes. History never becomes solidified in these plays: dilemmas endure; victories are tentative and vulnerable to undermining or renegotiation. Events take on a vaguely allegorical quality, so that an encounter in the border country of Scotland in 1530 leads to "an exercise in diplomacy" similar to ones carried out in the Congo on the eve of colonial liberation. Arden's attention is not on the movement of history but on the individual's ability to move within history.

Besides this important shift in the intellectual concerns of his plays, Arden's history plays also testify to the continuing power of his dramatic craft and innovation. *Armstrong's Last Goodnight,* for instance, is written entirely in an archaic Scottish dialect that Arden has carefully designed to lend a distant, otherworldly aura to the play without making it incomprehensible. *Left-Handed Liberty* exploits dramatic conventions drawn from medieval morality plays and from Shakespeare's *Richard III* to make King John and the papal legate Pandulph both characters in the play and commentators on it, sometimes drawing the audience into their thirteenth-century world, at other times stepping into the twentieth-century to look back at the events of their lives.

SHIFTING AESTHETIC PRIORITIES

The high point of Arden's critical acclaim and commercial success came in 1965 and 1966. In 1965

Armstrong's Last Goodnight was produced by London's National Theatre, while *Left-Handed Liberty* played at the prestigious Mermaid Theatre. The following year, *Serjeant Musgrave's Dance* had a successful run in New York, and Arden and D'Arcy began dividing their time between life in London and in the remote reaches of County Galway, Ireland. This period also marked a major shift in Arden's dramatic endeavors: he ceased writing for the commercial theater and devoted most of his time to collaborative work with D'Arcy for amateur, juvenile, or leftist theater groups. He also became more active in nonviolent socialist politics, serving as chairman and contributing writer for the weekly *Peace News.*

Despite his general satisfaction with the craft of his earlier works, Arden was very dissatisfied with the effects of their performance, as he explains in the preface to *Plays: One:*

I was troubled by a general lack of warmth, a withdrawn coldness, a too-precisely-defined correctitude of artistic technique which seemed to tell the audience: "thus far and no further—we are the professionals."

(p. 5)

He turned to collaborations with D'Arcy because he thought she had a better understanding of the social constraints imposed upon artistic practice by cultural institutions and of the possibilities for subverting those constraints by performing theater outside the traditional institutionalized organizations. He describes their work together in *To Present the Pretence:*

I found a *story* which appealed to me, for whatever reason, and began to write it. . . . She will think of a *subject* that requires to be dramatised: and will relate it to the conditions of the time and the potential audience to be sought for it. Only then will the idea of a story . . . become uppermost in her mind.

(p. 12)

D'Arcy's talents for identifying potential audiences and relating politically charged subjects to the conditions of the time led the pair far from the terrain of drama with pretensions to high art and left most of the critics, who were finally learning to love the older Arden style, bewildered or indignant.

The transition from an aloof, amoral professionalism to an engaging, politically involved solidarity was not easily made. Although the variety of theatrical forms with which Arden and D'Arcy experimented is very impressive, the quality of the language and the ingenuity of the action did not equal that of Arden's earlier work for quite some time. The plays by the pair did not compare favorably with Arden's best early work until *The Island of the Mighty* in 1974, and they did not manage to raise the art of political propaganda to heights that challenged their less politically vociferous work until the astonishing *Non-Stop Connolly Show* in 1975. Other plays they wrote between 1965 and 1975 are noteworthy primarily as milestones on the way to these two major works.

The Royal Pardon (1966) is a children's play set in a "legendary" past and concerns a soldier back from war who joins a traveling theater troupe. The soldier and all those involved in the troupe are pursued by a zealously repressive constable until their performance of a King Arthur play wins them a prize and a pardon. The work is designed to be at its best in an informal setting where audience and acting spaces overlap. The fast-paced plot, witty stage business, humorously doggerel flights of verse, and political and cultural commentary make this play appealing not just to children but to anyone who is willing to relax and enjoy it. It was designed, Arden and D'Arcy explain in a prefatory note, to "question a whole list of the guff that surrounds a tired British theatre, especially the myth that to be serious you have to be pompous and intense" (p. 1). The performances of *The Royal Pardon,* in which Arden acted and which he and D'Arcy directed, provided an example of vital, immediate theater that they then strove to emulate in their drama for adults. This play also marks their first thematic treatment of the theater's place in the cultural and political life of a society. This issue occupies them again in *The Island of the Mighty* and is taken up by Arden alone in his radio play *Pearl* and in both his novels.

In 1967, while teaching at New York University, Arden and D'Arcy directed an eleven-hour event they called "Vietnam carnival," which involved a series of scenes written in collaboration with the cast and interspersed with performances by other groups and individuals. The purpose of this project was threefold: to make good on Arden's call, in the introduction to *The Workhouse Donkey,* for a loosely organized, informally presented, day-long theatrical happening; to harness and focus the kind of chaotic communal artistic energy unleashed in their earlier "festival of anarchy"; and to protest U.S. aggression in Vietnam.

Returning to London in 1968, Arden and D'Arcy wrote, directed, and acted in two plays for experimental theater collectives, *Harold Muggins Is a Martyr* and *The Hero Rises Up*. The first returned to the milieu of Krank's London but in a more slapstick, comic-book fashion with obvious political references. The second treated Admiral Nelson's conquests at sea and in bed in the style of nineteenth-century melodrama. The plays are boisterous, irreverent, and impeccably countercultural, but they lack the sustained craft and wit of earlier and later endeavors. In these productions Arden and D'Arcy directed less attention to the literary qualities of the dramatic text in order to devote more attention to the cultural politics of the theatrical event as a whole. Besides writing and directing the plays, they demanded control of publicity and production management.

In the same year, a one-act play written by Arden in 1963 also reached the stage: *The True History of Squire Jonathan and His Unfortunate Treasure*. Squire Jonathan lives in a tower with his chest of treasure, where he waits for the woman of his dreams to arrive; meanwhile, he listens to the black charcoal-burners from the nearby forest, who taunt him when they pass. When his desired great blonde woman arrives he slowly convinces her to trade her clothes for his jewels but finds himself impotent at the crucial moment because he suspects she is in league with the Black Men. She scorns his fears and exits nude through a window into the arms of the Black Men. The play is notable for its surreal, fairytale quality, its unpretentious brevity, and the threefold layering of its significance. In the preface to the published play Arden claims it was prompted by an unsatisfactory love affair of his youth, in which "a large blonde beautiful Scot" explained she would not marry him because he was a poet. Harold Hobson, in *Arden on File*, suggests two other interpretations: "It may be a parable of the ineffectualness of capitalism (since the lady eventually escapes); or a demonstration that it is possible to combine striptease with considerable elaboration of language" (p. 44). It is, most likely, all three: autobiography, parable, and a countercultural striptease.

Arden concluded four years of collaborative alternative theater experimentation with a more ob-

viously autobiographical work, the 1970 radio play *The Bagman; or, The Impromptu of Muswell Hill*. This play, collected in *Two Autobiographical Plays* (1971), is set in a fantastic, vaguely medieval, dreamlike world similar to that in *Squire Jonathan* but with a more elaborate and precise allegorical import. The narrator's dreamlike search for an evening paper leads him into a hostile town of fat people; the countryside surrounding the town is infested with starving folk prone to cannibalism. The only thing protecting him from the suspicion and violence of the townspeople is his bag of puppets, who act out whatever scenes his audience desires once he calls the puppets to life with a magical chant. For the town's common citizens, the puppets enact scenes of war and revolution between rich and poor; for the town's nobility, they enact scenes of orgiastic dissipation; but for the revolutionaries from the countryside, they refuse to act:

> Men of war do not require
> To see themselves in a truthful mirror
> All that they need to spur them to action
> Is their own most bloody reflection
> In the eyeballs of their foe.
> We are neat and well-considered little people—
> If you bring us into battle
> You bring us into grief and woe . . .
>
> (p. 86)

When the narrator returns to his comfortable neighborhood on Muswell Hill, he notices fat and thin men in the crowds milling home from work and is disturbed by this evidence of class oppression but feels incapable of remedying the situation. The thin men need food, but the bag of a poet never carries such nourishment. Political action is needed, but the narrator remains purely a poet: "All I can do is look at what I see" (p. 88).

POLITICAL DRAMA

IN 1970, Arden and D'Arcy traveled through India, where Arden's political commitments took a significant turn. The appalling degree of poverty and oppression there convinced him that nonviolent protest was often not a sufficient means for attaining social justice. More important for his work alone and with D'Arcy, the long traditions of theatrical art among India's impoverished peoples, and the contradictory social forces sustaining that art, suggested more forceful methods of making political theater. On their return from India, Arden and D'Arcy settled in County Galway, Ireland, and worked up a number of occasional agitprop theatrical productions in 1971. In Arden's preface to *The Bagman,* published the same year, he distances himself sharply from the state of mind he held while writing the play in 1969 and declares that "the attitude of the central character at the end of the story is reprehensible, cowardly, and not to be imitated" (*Two Autobiographical Plays,* p. 17).

From then on Arden was not content simply to "look at what he sees." He stopped writing plays with ambiguous social messages or an aloof celebration of dramatic spectacle and began writing, primarily in collaboration with D'Arcy, plays that called for concrete social action. This decisive turn in the intent of their work began to cause the playwrights problems in 1972. They became involved in a bitter dispute with the management of the Royal Shakespeare Company because they claimed the RSC production of their *Island of the Mighty* altered the play to celebrate imperialism rather than criticize it. Another of their new plays, *The Ballygombeen Bequest* (1972), which accused British businesses of oppressing the rural poor in Ireland, involved them in a lengthy libel suit, which ended in the play's being revised to eliminate the naming of names and retitled *The Little Gray Home in the West.* Mainstream critics began to condemn their work as propaganda, and mainstream theaters refused to commission or produce their new work because of both the more-volatile political themes it treated and the involvement in production demanded by the playwrights.

Arden and D'Arcy were demanding no more involvement in production than that granted playwrights such as Beckett, but the political motivations of their proposed innovations made much of the mainstream theater industry extremely uncomfortable. The ostracism Arden and D'Arcy suffered since 1972 had two unfortunate effects. First, it denied them the financial security necessary for producing a large body of high-quality stage plays, and second, it withheld recognition from the major achievements they had made in advancing the complexity and power of politically engaged drama.

THE ISLAND OF THE MIGHTY

THE last more or less conventional stage play written by Arden and D'Arcy is *The Island of the Mighty.* Its formal innovations, borrowing from both agitprop and historical costume drama, as well as its thematic breadth and complexity, make this one of their most significant plays. It treats legends surrounding King Arthur in a three-part structure that rivals in scope the trilogies of Aeschylus. The playwrights immediately distance the story from its most familiar romance renditions by using the names found in early Welsh sources rather than those in Malory—Guinevere becomes Gwenhwyvar and Mordred becomes Medraut, for example. Furthermore, the legends are reshaped as history and draw upon modern theories of cultural anthropology and feminist or Marxist historiography to give the story a precise setting in the volatile movement of European populations during the fifth century. Finally, the immediate theatricality of the story is heightened as attention is drawn to the pretense of the performance. Masks, music, and song are featured frequently. A small platform stage, upon which all the dramatic scenes are enacted, is erected upon the theater stage. Various Chief Poets take turns standing beside the platform to narrate events or sing commentary. Scenes of vigorous action spill off the platform and spread across the stage. Characters step forward to break the spell of representation and talk directly to the audience.

The Island of the Mighty begins on the eve of the Anglo-Saxon invasion of Britain. Arthur is the general of a Roman-style mounted army and is responsible to the lords of various small kingdoms for the protection of Britain from Strathclyde to Cornwall. He is seventy years old and walks with a limp. The trilogy ends—after Arthur's death and his army's dissolution—by following a few Celtic refugees into the wilds of Galloway and the woods of Wales. Part 1, narrated by Merlin and the Pictish Poet, establishes the dramatic situation by describing the life-styles, material interests, and religious beliefs of the Britains as witnessed in the wanderings of two young, displaced noblemen, Balin and Balan. Part 2, narrated by Merlin and Aneurin, moves quickly—from the landing of the Anglo-Saxon army, through Arthur's political maneuvering and marriage to Gwenhwyvar, to his fatal battle with Medraut at Camlann. Part 3, narrated by Aneurin, charts the breakup of Arthur's army, Merlin's madness, and the retreat of common Celtic folk before the Anglo-Saxon invasion. Arden and D'Arcy have identified three central themes for the trilogy as a whole: (1) the collapse of Arthur's imperial rule, (2) the position of the poet in society, and (3) the oppression of common people. Each of the three parts treats these themes in a unique way.

Part 1 follows Balin and Balan across Britain after their family holding and all their kin are destroyed by an English raiding party. Balan vows to live free and alone and wanders toward Galloway; Balin looks to join an army that will take revenge on the English, but his impulsive proclivity to violence makes him unwelcome in every group he joins, until he too finds himself in Galloway. There the two brothers unwittingly kill each other in an archaic fertility rite organized by the Picts. Over the course of the play the two brothers wander in and out of two distinct stories: the quarrel between the Wildcat Picts of Galloway and the Prince of Strathclyde and the attempted seizure of power by King Pellam. These conflicts span the ideological spectrum of fifth-century Britain. On one extreme are the pagan, matriarchal Picts, with roots deep in Celtic and pre-Celtic indigenous customs and beliefs. On the other is King Pellam, a fanatically Christian descendent of Roman aristocracy armed with the spear that killed Christ and bent on establishing God's kingdom in Britain. Garlon, an impoverished robber and cutthroat who lives by his cynical wits and holds all theological doctrine in contempt, completes the survey of religious beliefs.

The Chief Poets in this play correspond to the distinct societies portrayed in various ways. The Pictish Poet is nameless and functions as an officiating priest. His songs are incantatory and magical, relying for their effect primarily upon hypnotic rhythm and repetition. The sixty-five-year-old Taliesin is a conservative servant of the Christianized Celtic elite. He officiates at ceremonies but acts primarily as an ambassador and advisor. The forty-five-year-old Merlin carries the office of chief poet even further from religion and song than Taliesin. His songs celebrating Arthur's twelve victories, songs that were written long ago, function more like political advertising than sincere praise, and during the play he devotes most of his energy to espionage and court intrigue. One other poet makes a veiled appearance. He is not physically present or acknowledged by name but his songs are in the throats of the poor and oppressed throughout England, as Garlon attests when he sings one of them:

> John Baptist out of the desert walked
> And all he wore was a cloth of hair
> And all he could cry was "Beware beware—
> The naked man has come to steal your coat!"
> Who fetched the King's soldiers to run him in?
> Lord Jesus who was both Priest and King,
> Who forgave the rich men all their sins
> So long as they said that they loved him
> And would whip their people till they loved him
> too—
> Lord Jesus, a great revenge is coming upon you!
>
> (part 1, scene 4)

Besides setting the scene for the events to follow, part 1 prefigures the plot of the trilogy in two of its episodes. Both display the breakdown of religious customs, the disintegration of communities, and a tragic inability to understand and come to grips with the historical situation. In the first episode, King Pellam's dream of a divinely sanctioned monarchy is shattered when Arthur's men overrun his camp and Balin dares to run him through with the lance that pierced Jesus' side. In the second episode, the Pict's custom of keeping a lame king, who guarantees fertility and prosperity by dying in ritual combat each year to make way for a new king, ends when Balin and Balan kill each other in the ritual. As well as Pellam's foolish faith in religious relics, we see the tragic effects of ignorance in Balin's failure to join forces with Garlon when they both face the same threats and in Balin's and Balan's failure to recognize each other under the cat masks they wear into battle.

The motifs of ritual dogma and social disintegration repeated in short vignettes throughout part 1 are stretched into an elaborate intrigue plot of national dimensions in part 2. The Pict ritual of a lame God/King reappears as part of a secret pre-Celtic legend of liberation tenaciously passed down the generations by Britain's poor, oppressed, and marginalized peoples. As the plot proceeds, the neat sense of historical development, by which Merlin and Arthur live and rule, disintegrates before an atavistic fantasy of freedom created a thousand years earlier when the Celtic "men of the long sword" overthrew the original matriarchal culture

33

ruled by Branwen and her brother/husband, Bran. It turns out that Arthur's position of authority in Britain (as well as his lame leg) resulted as much from an incestuous liaison with his sister, a hereditary Daughter of Branwen, as it did from his patrilineal connection with imperial Rome. Hidden family relationships, ruses and stratagems, and startling coincidences—as elaborate as those in any nineteenth-century novel or melodrama—accumulate over the course of the play, ending in the death of Arthur, the collapse of British military power, and Merlin's madness. Where Merlin's supple diplomacy and vigorous espionage clearly had the advantage of both the Pictish Poet's rituals and Taliesin's conservative political interests in part 1, in part 2 Merlin's understanding of the developing situation proves disastrously inferior to that of Aneurin, poet of the oppressed, whose song is heard anonymously in part 1, and to that of Morgan, the unacknowledged wise woman from whom Merlin first learned the trade of poetry. Unfortunately, because Aneurin and Morgan have no political power, their knowledge of the desperate hopes circulating in the society of women and common folk is useless in preventing catastrophe.

Part 3 functions as a prolonged denouement for the play, but it does not do this by unraveling the plot of part 2. Part 2 departs from the conventions of well-constructed intrigue by forsaking the satisfactions of climax, denouement, and closure. Instead, the tangled knot of British imperial ambition, popular insurrection, and general self-destruction is swept away by the English invasion and Aneurin's rise to the position of narrating poet. Aneurin is more concerned with the plight of common people, one of whom he becomes, than with the vacillations of martial power and court politics. Hence, part 3 unravels the consequences of social disorder for the general population rather than for the rulers who were swept away. The elite figures of the first two parts remain of interest only insofar as they now move among the people they once ruled.

Considerable attention is devoted to Merlin, whose madness testifies to the ethical vacuity of the ideals he once served. He placed his talents and his soul at the service of Arthur's imperialism, so when Arthur's power ends, he no longer has a justification for his life. First he turns against his own profession, wounding Taliesin with a spear for at-tempting to prevent the Battle of Camlann; then he turns against humanity and wanders west and north, away from the English invaders. Besides embodying the hopeless dissolution of Arthur's realm, Merlin also figures forth a more humble, honest, and immediate approach to existence. In a lucid period he acknowledges his intellectual debt to Morgan and spends the last moments of his life singing the praises of a cowman's wife. This rapprochement to the salt of the earth distinguishes Merlin from Taliesin, who never forsakes his elitist values even when the class he served has been completely obliterated. Taliesin, whose wound festers and grows, absorbing his entire personality in its pain and damnation, becomes a demon that haunts Merlin. Merlin, on the other hand, has harrowed hell and found the path to an earthly paradise where his talent for song can serve human life rather than political domination. Unfortunately, once on this path he is exceedingly vulnerable: the Cowman kills him because he cannot imagine that Merlin only wants to sing to his wife.

As a whole, *The Island of the Mighty* is more than just a chronicle of Britain. It is an analysis of the political and ideological dynamics of imperialism and oppression. Part 1 delineates the imperial order and the rebellious impulses it holds in check on its periphery; part 2 delineates the contradictory interests and animosities that crack the imperial order from within; and part 3 explores the wasteland left after the empire's demise, where a new order begins to inscribe itself. Indeed, as part 3 ends we see Bedwyr, Arthur's old standard-bearer turned priest, inventing legends of Camelot in order to bury forever the pagan Branwen and establish a new, Christianized, patriarchal myth for the scattered remnants of the nation. Aneurin's final song about Lazarus suggests that Bedwyr's efforts will be in vain: it says that the oppressed of the world eventually come back. Aneurin's song, then, is in some respects optimistic; it is also terrifying, however, for he suggests that the oppressed never rise from the dead in a healthy state. As with the resurrection of Bran and Branwen, the revolution they usher in will be stamped with the irrational cruelty and enforced ignorance in which they have been too long entombed.

> We are going to come back
> And we are going to take hold

So hideous and bloody greedy
We take hold of the whole world!
(part 3, scene 13)

Aneurin leaves the audience with a song similar to Musgrave's wild chanting dance:

Up he goes and no one knows
How to bring him downwards
Dead man's feet
Over the street
Riding the roofs
And crying down your chimneys
Up he goes and no one knows
Who it was that rose him
But white and red
He waves his head
He sits on your back
And you'll never never lose him. . . .
(*Musgrave*, act 3, scene 1)

If the image is the same, however, the handling of it has changed considerably. Musgrave is caught up in the dance of the unquiet dead. He embodies the dance and succumbs to it. Aneurin stands to one side of the stage, like all the narrating poets in *The Island of the Mighty*, and describes the threatened resurrection. His life has given him an intimate knowledge of the tomb from which the corpse will rise and the course its shambling feet will take, but he has also acquired the wisdom (or timidity) to stand aside and observe.

Serjeant Musgrave's Dance is built from the same raw outrage that propels the eponymous event. Consequently, its structure breaks up with the event. As the plot reaches its climax it is already unraveling uncontrollably. The greater bulk of *The Island of the Mighty* gives the play more stability and allows it to contain the wild rebellion of the earlier play, just as Aneurin contains the rage that overwhelms Musgrave. In 1959, Arden had been interested in the theatrical power of righteous indignation driven to desperation. In 1972, Arden and D'Arcy were interested in theatrically dissecting the social and cultural conditions that produce material desperation and the ensuing wild dreams of revolt. The world of emotional collisions that filled Arden's stage in 1959 has been shrunk to fit the small players' platform in *The Island of the Mighty*. The power of the theatrical flourish is still there but now we can see around it. Arden and D'Arcy step away from their characters in order to give the audience a broader perspective, both of the world the characters inhabit and the theatrical ploys involved in delineating that world.

Indeed, where Arden takes his skills for granted in the early plays, here Arden and D'Arcy make the artist's skills a central theme. They repudiate the image of the disinterested poet used in *The Bagman* in favor of a portrayal that demonstrates the ways in which aesthetic form is tied to the poet's personal economic and political interests as well as to the broader functions that poetry serves in society. With a deftly politicized, yet naturalistic approach to character, the playwrights demonstrate how personal inclinations and social circumstances combine to create a poet's moral and political allegiances. Aneurin champions the oppressed not because it is right but because his patron's lack of interest in the arts leaves him open to the influences of a more responsive audience, namely women and peddlers. On the other hand, despite Merlin's education in feminist culture at the feet of Morgan, he becomes a poet of the patriarchy because opportunities and ambition lead him in that direction. Thus, art is seen to be shaped by the same influences as the rest of society. It enjoys no more moral freedom than any other sector of society and significantly less power than some. Aneurin's marginality gives him a certain clarity of vision that Merlin tragically lacks, but this marginality also makes him less historically significant than Merlin.

THE NON-STOP CONNOLLY SHOW

AFTER *The Island of the Mighty*, Arden and D'Arcy turned their attention away from the politics of art to examine other forms of political action. With D'Arcy credited as the first author, they produced three plays about Ireland between 1972 and 1978: *The Ballygombeen Bequest* (1972) (revised in 1978 as *The Little Gray Home in the West*), *The Non-Stop Connolly Show* (1975), and *Vandaleur's Folly* (1978).

Arden considers *The Non-Stop Connolly Show* the most significant and satisfactory work of his career. This play treats the entire life of James Connolly, labor activist and Irish revolutionary, in a six-part cycle that requires twenty-six hours to perform. In the vast scope of this play, D'Arcy and Arden were able to bring together and refine most of their many theatrical and political interests. To be performed, the play demands the kind of carnivalesque community support and involvement that the playwrights became familiar with through their "festival of anarchy," "Vietnam carnival," and observation of Indian folk epics. In placing the work on stage, D'Arcy and Arden draw again from Indian performance techniques, as well as from Brecht, agitprop, and mime, to combine masks, costumes, movement, song, and dance in a thrillingly immediate and cost-effective spectacle. The play itself is structured upon what the authors call an "intertwining of serpentine motifs" (*Arden on File*, p. 55) drawn from the elaborate plots of melodrama, the brash exaggerations of political cartoons, the uncanny incarnations of allegory, and the cornucopia of socialist and labor controversies in which Connolly was embroiled.

D'Arcy and Arden feel that James Connolly deserves the lavish attention this play bestows upon him because he was "the first working-class leader to enter the world conflict in the cause of socialism" (*Non-Stop Connolly Show*, pt. 6, p. 109). He was born to Irish parents in the industrial slums of Scotland in 1868. After gaining a reputation as a speaker and organizer for the Scottish labor movement, he went on to found the Irish Socialist Republican Party in Dublin, to work with the Industrial Workers of the World in the United States, and to head the Belfast chapter of the Irish Transport Workers' Union during a long, bitter lockout and general strike. He was executed by the British military for the lead he took in the Dublin Easter Rising of 1916. Aside from his importance as a historical figure who deserves more attention than he has received, Connolly probably appealed to D'Arcy and Arden because dramatizing his life allowed them to draw together their interests in social history, the imperial ambitions of capitalism, and contemporary Irish politics. In *To Present the Pretence*, Arden points out that Connolly's life also presented them with some major obstacles that they summarized in this little jingle:

> My name it is James Connolly
> I neither smoke nor drink:
> Come to the theatre for twenty-six hours
> And watch me sit and think . . .
>
> (p. 96)

Aside from the final, fateful insurrection and siege at the Dublin post office, Connolly's life does not resolve easily into striking theatrical tableaux. His time was consumed primarily in maneuvering through lengthy committee meetings, writing position papers, petitioning for financial and political support, and balancing in his mind and among his friends the ideals he sought against the opportunities that each situation offered. The difficulties involved in representing such a life in traditional dramatic terms was increased by D'Arcy's and Arden's determination to represent Connolly as a hero without flaws.

D'Arcy's and Arden's idealization of Connolly is not so much a case of socialist hagiography as a desire to present the clearest possible picture of both the socialist agenda for civil and economic justice and the world conflict that socialism must wage with capitalism to realize its agenda. The idealization of Connolly is not intended to turn him into an idol of socialism but, rather, to make him a reliable witness to the controversies of socialist action in the real world. When he attends important socialist congresses in the United States or Europe his personality does not obscure issues addressed there. Those critics who accuse this play of being shallow propaganda are themselves guilty of a very shallow notion of political controversy, a notion that takes capitalism's propaganda seriously. They betray a prejudice against socialism that does not allow them to see the meticulous objectivity with which D'Arcy and Arden represent the often-contrary workings of various socialist groups. This play is, of course, propagandistic in the sense that the authors have reached a "partisan" conclusion about the problems they present, but they want the audience to judge these conclusions for themselves. The playwrights attempt to bring the audience to their side through the depth and complexity of their argument rather than by the shallow swiftness of political clichés one normally associates with propaganda. The clarity of Connolly's personality aids in elucidating the contending socialist strategies involved in the question of workers' rights.

As committed playwrights as well as committed socialists, D'Arcy and Arden are not satisfied simply with clear ideas. They want these ideas to work on the stage. To make the socialist controversies of Connolly's life theatrically concrete, they dramatize the connections between world events and

Connolly's writing and organizing. The Boer War in South Africa, American imperial designs on Latin America, civil unrest in Ireland, socialism and political instability in Europe, and the machinations, local and international, of various capitalist concerns tumble across the stage in vivid cartoon renditions to instigate and complicate Connolly's organizing and educating efforts. His editorials and speeches move on the same stage as government proclamations, troop movements, and riots and engage these events in dramatic, if often frustratingly ineffectual, debate.

To make Connolly's thoughts comparable with the actions of national governments and international corporations, D'Arcy and Arden turn away from naturalistic dramatic representation to a Brechtian "elucidatory exposition," which schematically demonstrates the connections between events rather than attempting to portray these connections realistically. Cartoon caricature, blank or rhymed verse, song, decorative placards, and expository narrative help enliven and organize the demonstrative scenes.

The various manifestations of capitalism throughout the play are embodied in the ubiquitous figure of Grabitall, taken from an American socialist cartoon circa 1914, and his chorus of Three Employers. By turns Grabitall plays an English lord with vast Irish holdings, J. P. Morgan (during the U.S. section), and the Dublin newspaper magnate Murphy. During the first four parts Grabitall also acts as narrator and nay-sayer to all Connolly's ambitions. The play's central agon is between Connolly and Grabitall, but they rarely meet face-to-face. Between them move Grabitall's hired minions and numerous historical figures of all political stripes, who are as likely to sing about their part in the action as actually enact it. Riotous confrontations occur frequently, but when the issues become too complicated for dramatic vignettes, they flourish in the cantering rhythm and rhyme of expository declarations:

GRABITALL: I have fallen victim to an inexplicable crisis in international trade.
I don't pretend to understand it, but my stockbroker, who is highly paid
Informs me that my shares in steel and coal and shipping have begun to drop.
I must sell one of my gilded carriages and get rid of half my stable—

A coachman and some grooms must be given, as they say, the chop:
What a pity, he was a cheerful coachman and exceedingly able.
Until this loss to my prestige has been recouped I cannot rest content.
My Irish tenants, I suppose, must pay some small increase of rent.

(part 1, scene 13)

While the rhythms and rhymes are sometimes flippantly doggerel, the astonishing command of idiom common to most of Arden's work is as strong as ever in this collaboration. The artificiality of the meter never prevents the playwrights from rendering the speech of each character particular to a specific social milieu and personal temperament. The accents range from Bill Haywood's western twang to ruling-class London lisps to Scots and Irish brogues to the unearthly poetic cries of the War Demon.

In the sixth part, as the world goes to war and Connolly marches toward his death, the theatricalized pressure of circumstance moves beyond the demonstrative conflicts of Brechtian drama to an icy world of allegory and ritual. The effect is first to rob Connolly of his power to act rationally and sweep him toward his death, but then to allow him to speak from beyond the grave and glory in the progress the working class has made, since his defeat, along the road that he blazed.

The obvious allegorical and ritual elements of part 6, such as the War Demon and the prologue from Irish legend, reverberate subtly throughout the entire play. The length of the play alone does much to de-emphasize its dramatic aspect and heighten its ritual force. In dramatizing the life and times of Connolly through a cycle of six individual plays, D'Arcy and Arden have in many ways actually refused to be dramatic by either Brechtian or Aristotelian standards. While the theatricalization of social relationships dear to Brecht and the recognitions and reversals in the plot dear to Aristotle figure repeatedly throughout the play as a whole, the notion of condensing social history into a handful of confrontations or moments of decision that can be played in one evening is forsaken by D'Arcy and Arden, despite its endorsement by Aristotle and Brecht. D'Arcy and Arden draw instead upon Indian folk-play cycles, in which basic situations unroll in almost endless permutations and in which decisions must be made over and over again in a ritual combat of endurance, rather than in the short sprints of catastrophe or commitment found in Western traditions.

The play as a whole is not so much a story as the beginning of a story—the story of proletarian emancipation. Each part is a kind of false start. The repetitive clashes between workers and capitalists each add a bit to the discourse and eventually harden into the demon-infested allegory of part 6, which ends Connolly's life, gives it meaning, and sets the terms for the ensuing revolutionary story played out in the real world.

Even within the play, however, Connolly has some measure of success. The first four parts are all narrated by Grabitall, who makes an early promise "to confound all my enemies before they are even born" (part 1, scene 1). During these parts, Connolly is so enmeshed in working-class infighting and the struggle to feed his family that he rarely catches a glimpse of his real enemy, Grabitall. In part 5, however, an impartial narrator takes over and the Great Lockout and ensuing general strike finally bring Connolly face-to-face with the bosses. In part 6, numerous characters provide their own narration, but they must vie with the War Demon for control of the plot. In the end, Connolly is overcome not by his own flaws but by the oppressive momentum of circumstance. He is one of many who fall, but his defeat is not as important as the example of determination he has set throughout his life.

The play ends with an image of resurrection similar to that in *Musgrave* and *The Island of the Mighty* but with a change of emphasis. Instead of calling forth moldy corpses to haunt the world, Connolly dwells on bringing comfort to those entombed alive:

We were the first to show the dark deep hole within
Could be thrown open to the living sun.
. . . We were the first. We shall not be the last.
This is not history. It has not passed.

(part 6, scene 10)

The long and elaborately articulated form of *The Non-Stop Connolly Show* allows for the representation of social action in a detail and variety seldom achieved on the Western stage, but it also allows for representation to become a meaningful social action in itself in a number of ways not typical of Western drama. In creating such a massive masterpiece of political drama, D'Arcy and Arden both exploit and denigrate the notion of the masterpiece. The scope of the play is designed to elevate the figure of James Connolly and champion his historical and political significance but also to deny the commercial marketability of his historical significance: this play will never fit the criteria of conventional entertainment set by the institutions of bourgeois culture—it will never play Broadway. In refusing to fit the cultural space provided for drama by the funding and organizing mechanisms of government and big business, the play demands that an alternative cultural space be created for it.

Aside from making their uncompromising demand for an alternative, workers', socialist cultural space, however, the play and the playwrights are extremely adaptable and accommodating. Here again this play makes an extraordinary advance over their earlier efforts at countercultural theater. Within an alternative cultural space D'Arcy and Arden allow standard questions of aesthetic autonomy to give way to questions of what is most valuable for a particular place, occasion, and audience. The play has been presented in its continuous entirety as a kind of ritual celebration of the Irish (and international) socialist movement; it has been cut up for an informal lunchtime readers' theater; and it has been reduced to pertinent skits and scenes for union meetings, picket lines, and street theater. With this play D'Arcy and Arden have realized their dreams of making a strong theatrical statement that serves a political cause completely, without forsaking any of its own intrinsic strengths.

PEARL

UNFORTUNATELY, drama that serves the cause of socialism is not the same as drama that brings in a steady income. D'Arcy's and Arden's political Irish plays were, to a significant degree, precariously underwritten by the continuing revenue of *Serjeant Musgrave's Dance*, but as Arden proved resolute in refusing to return to his old dramatic style, the opportunities for staging his work, let alone the works written with the uncompromisingly militant D'Arcy, virtually dried up. This situation led Arden to two significant shifts in his artistic career: first to radio plays, and then to novels.

Beginning in 1978, Arden was regularly commissioned by the BBC to write radio plays, initially with the proviso that D'Arcy not contribute and that the plays not treat contemporary Irish themes. After writing five plays on his own, he at last won approval to write again with D'Arcy. They produced *The Manchester Enthusiasts* in 1984 and completed their monumental *Whose Is the Kingdom?* in 1988.

Of Arden's independent radio plays, *Pearl*—broadcast in 1978—is the most substantial. Set on the verge of the British Civil War (1640), it treats social history, the politics of theater, and autobiographical themes. The play concerns a half-Irish actress (D'Arcy is half Irish) and a Yorkshire playwright who conspire to write a new kind of play, one that will appeal to the republican aspirations of the Puritans and display the revolutionary power of theater. Their intentions are, however, sabotaged in production by the stage manager Captain Catso, who is in league with the reactionary Royalists. While the autobiographical references are obvious here, they can probably be found in most of Arden's work. In *Arden on File*, he provocatively stated, "I myself constantly write secret plays within my ostensible ones . . . in order to relieve myself of certain personal preoccupations" (p. 85).

The unmistakable references to Arden's and D'Arcy's quarrel with the Royal Shakespeare Company over its production of *The Island of the Mighty* add a layer of meaning to *Pearl* but do not get in the way of its fine analysis of culture, theater, politics, and social history. The social, political, and aesthetic arguments made in the play, as well as its engrossing story, are formed with elements drawn from a number of Arden's and D'Arcy's earlier works. The actress, Pearl, and playwright, Backhouse, have the unmitigated charm and moral rectitude found in Connolly and in the central couple of *The Royal Pardon*. Their naive political enthusiasm and amorous sensuousity, however, also give them a more traditional dramatic appeal. The precise dramatization of class conflict and ideological tensions peculiar to a particular historical moment, which is found in *The Island of the Mighty* and *The Non-Stop Connolly Show*, is repeated here, but the relationship between social forces and dramatic representation has been given a new shape.

In *The Island of the Mighty*, the forces of historical change lie in the hands of the invading English, who are only rarely present on the stage. The play traces the behavior of characters who are basically powerless before the juggernaut of social change. In *The Non-Stop Connolly Show*, social forces are personified in exemplary or allegorical characters. Rather than reacting to undramatically collective threats in the wings, these characters play out social conflicts on the stage. In *Pearl*, the social forces are represented on the (radio) stage by particular characters rather than generalized exemplary or allegorical ones. The plans of Pearl and Backhouse are foiled by the vividly individual Countess Belladonna and her mercenary minion Captain Catso, rather than by cartoon abstractions along the lines of Grabitall. Gideon Grip represents the revolutionary idealism of the imminent Puritan revolt, and Catso embodies the cynical opportunism that will eventually subdue the revolution. Arden successfully draws upon his talent for creating dramatic plots driven by individual characters in order to represent the social forces at work in a particular historical moment.

In *Pearl*, Arden also expands upon his earlier work (both his own and his collaborations with D'Arcy) by giving prominence to female characters. He and D'Arcy complained of the underrepresentation of women in drama in their introduction to *Vandaleur's Folly*, but the solution they offered there (given the underrepresentation of women in history) was to demand that all the male parts be played by women. In *Pearl*, Arden begins to dramatize the unwritten role of women in history. Women are certainly prominent in *The Island of the Mighty* but here, for the first time, they are central. The narrator and protagonist is Pearl, her antagonist is Belladonna, and of the eleven most important characters in the play, five are female.

The pessimistic estimation of social justice common to most of Arden's plays seems particularly dark in *Pearl* because of the chilling way in which it has been embodied in characters of remarkable cynicism and vindictiveness. The emotional attachment to Pearl and Backhouse and their project, which Arden encourages, adds to the listener's distress when the forces of evil destroy them. The sensibility of this play is closer to the dark mood of Jacobean tragedy than to the more optimistic intricacies of Victorian melodrama. Whereas the defeats of Musgrave, Merlin, and Connolly are all mitigated by lessons learned and hopes for the future, in *Pearl* the dream of a socially progressive theater is utterly crushed by superior wealth and brutality:

> . . . and from that day to this the word of the Common People of England, most powerful in the strength of the Lord, had little or nothing to do with the word of their poets or the high genius of their actors.
>
> (scene 18)

This unusually definitive defeat of progressive forces does not indicate a change in Arden's sensibility so much as a change in his subject matter. When concerned with social oppression, he and D'Arcy always acknowledge the tenacious demands of the defeated; when concerned with the social function of theater, Arden's own experience encourages him to be more critical and pessimistic. Unlike oppressed peoples, the theater does not threaten to resurrect its demands for social justice spontaneously.

WHOSE IS THE KINGDOM?

From the beginning, Arden made a virtue of the necessity of working in radio. He was quick to realize that this medium freed him from some of the problems he faced in writing for the theater: productions were less costly to mount, he could count on a larger and broader audience, and his words reached his listeners free of the dubious manipulations of unsympathetic directors. In 1988, Arden and D'Arcy combined their talents once more to produce a major masterpiece specifically for the radio medium. Their nine-hour *Whose Is the Kingdom?* was designed to air in one-hour segments. Here their interest in theater as a community cultural event finally found a well-supported, widely received realization: the play was broadcast by the British Broadcasting Corporation in weekly installments; a discussion of historical and religious issues by a panel of experts followed each segment, and a packet of written material was available for listeners upon request.

Whose Is the Kingdom? charts Christianity's transition from an underground to an official religion during the reign of the emperor Constantine. Events transpiring between 305 and 337 A.D. are enacted within a narrative frame voiced by Kybele, an Epicurean philosopher and refugee in Ireland brought to trial by the Chief Druid of Armagh. (D'Arcy was imprisoned in Armagh Gaol for her Irish-republican sympathies in 1978.) The scenes portrayed range from Ireland to the border of Persia, from battlefields to bedrooms, from secret councils to public debates.

Arden's and D'Arcy's long interest in the political implications of Christianity combine here with their interest in the nature of imperial rule. While convincingly evoking the life of fourth-century Rome, with its elaborate political and religious controversies, the playwrights also present the political machinations and police actions of the English empire, given a critical distance by their classical garb. Secret agents lurk outside Christian academies and libraries; police provoke and then attack rioters; class divisions lead to policy debates among dissident groups; the issue of women's rights is separated by the male politicians from the issue of religious freedom. "Apparent unity brings disunity, fear, repression. . . . Repression brings paranoia, paranoia brings tyranny: both Church and State begin to fall apart," explain the playwrights in the table of contents of the published script (p. v).

As the play begins, Christianity holds together a broad array of people from slaves to patricians. Over the course of Constantine's reign the religion is forged into an instrument of empire and the common people embraced by it are either crushed or slip away into quiet nonconformity. The play is an object lesson in power politics and in the inability of power politics to suppress opposition definitively. In the end nothing is settled: "A patching up in the midst of chaos leaves all the loose ends that have continued ever since" (p. v).

Arden's and D'Arcy's interest in the role of women in history, first evidenced in *Island of the Mighty* and made central to *Pearl*, is maintained here. Emperor Constantine's control of the world is shown to depend significantly upon the political acumen of his barmaid mother, Helen, and is threatened by the criticisms of his wife, Fausta, who has a profound emotional hold on him despite her virtually powerless political position. The primary narrative voice belongs to the female philosopher Kybele, and women preachers, slaves, and pagan priestesses match the men in dramatic importance and historical impact throughout the play. While women are as central to *Whose Is the Kingdom?* as they are to *Pearl,* their influence upon the course of history is even more varied and pervasive in this play than in the earlier one.

THE NOVELS

DURING the six years that Arden and D'Arcy worked upon *Whose Is the Kingdom?,* pecuniary pressures prompted Arden to stretch his talents to the writing of novels. His first, *Silence Among the Weapons* (1982), was nominated for the prestigious Booker Prize, and his second, *Books of Bale,* appeared the same year as *Whose Is the Kingdom?* Both novels continue his interest in the history of empires and the historical importance of theater.

Silence Among the Weapons takes its title from an aphorism attributed to Gaius Marius: "Once the weapons are out, the laws fall silent." The novel is set between 91 B.C. and 81 B.C. in Asia and Italy. The events are narrated by Ivory, a lame, Greek-speaking theatrical agent, whose career is disrupted by the imperial intrigues, civil rebellion, and state-sponsored terrorism that attend the consolidation of the Roman Empire. Besides evoking the life of common people in the first century B.C. "who live at the lower end of society and only see bits of the power figures round corners" (*Arden on File,* p. 74), Arden is keen to suggest similarities between Rome's influence over the Mediterranean and the United States' influence over Latin America. In cultivating the novel's relevance for modern political and cultural issues, however, Arden never neglects the purely sensual pleasures of an intriguing story involving exotic characters in a vividly delineated world.

Books of Bale is set in Tudor England and concerns the life and work of John Bale (1495–1563)—author of England's first historical drama—as well as the activities and opinions of his largely fictional wife and granddaughter, professional minstrels and women of daringly independent thought and action. Arden displays his narrative skills more spectacularly here than in his first novel. Events in the life of John Bale alternate with those in the life of his granddaughter and are delineated by various narrators in various styles ranging from characterless omniscience to impassioned epistolaries to stream of consciousness. The variety and vitality that Arden has always brought to the creation of dramatic characters are instilled also in this novel's narrative voices.

Themes from *Pearl, Silence Among the Weapons,* and the D'Arcy/Arden Irish plays are worked together in *Books of Bale.* The political implications of theater and religion, the intrigues and terror of imperialism, the English subjugation of Ireland, and the situation of women in a male-dominated society are all brought to life within the novel's minutely detailed representation of sixteenth-century life. That the issues occupying the novel's characters have also occupied Arden in his troublesome career as a playwright and that Arden drew upon the atmosphere of modern Indian theater to create many of the details of sixteenth-century English theater welds the novel's Tudor England to the contemporary age. The autobiographical elements in the work are given a humorous emphasis by the proliferation of Johns: in addition to the author and the eponymous protagonist, major references are made to King John (the subject of historical plays by Arden and Bale), John the Baptist, and St. John the Divine.

Clearly, Arden's shift from playwright to novelist did little to mitigate his interest in theater. Indeed, the novels give him the narrative omniscience needed to explore all aspects of the theater: the audience, the box office, the management, and the historical moment, as well as the boards of the stage and the action of the characters. The success of his novels means that "the broken chains of theatre" no longer hurt his wrists but, as he boasts in his introduction to *Awkward Corners,* these chains "haven't fallen completely off . . . gathered in the fist, they still make a useful flail" (p. 6).

Few living writers can match the linguistic breadth and literary invention present in Arden's major works, both alone and with D'Arcy; even fewer can match the achievements he and D'Arcy have made in so many distinct forms of literary endeavor. From *The Waters of Babylon* to children's plays to *The Non-Stop Connolly Show* to *Whose Is the Kingdom?* to *Books of Bale,* Arden (usually with D'Arcy) has enriched and widened the form and concept of drama. Very seldom has he been content to repeat the model of his past successes. The failures and weak points in his oeuvre, which can generally be attributed to his grappling with novel issues that are difficult to master, are justified by the major accomplishments to which his trials ultimately lead. Arden is universally praised for his early work. In time that praise surely will extend to his late novels and to the rich political theater and radio drama that he has written with D'Arcy.

SELECTED BIBLIOGRAPHY

I. BIBLIOGRAPHY. M. Page, *Arden On File* (London, 1985).

II. COLLECTED WORKS. *Three Plays* (Harmondsworth, 1964, repr. New York, 1966), collects *The Waters of Babylon, Live Like Pigs,* and *The Happy Haven* (written with M. D'Arcy); *Soldier, Soldier, and Other Plays* (London, 1967), also includes *Wet Fish, When Is a Door Not a Door?,* and *Friday's Hiding* (written with M. D'Arcy); *Two Autobiographical Plays* (London, 1971), contains *The True History of Squire Jonathan and His Unfortunate Treasure* and *The Bagman; or, The Impromptu of Muswell Hill; Plays: One* (London, 1977), collects *Serjeant Musgrave's Dance, The Workhouse Donkey,* and *Armstrong's Last Goodnight; To Present the Pretence: Essays on the Theatre and Its Public* (London, 1977); *Awkward Corners* (London, 1988), essays by Arden and M. D'Arcy.

III. SEPARATE WORKS. *Serjeant Musgrave's Dance* (London, 1960), play; *Live Like Pigs,* in T. Maschler, ed., *New English Dramatists 3* (Harmondsworth, 1961), play; *The Happy Haven,* in T. Maschler, ed., *New English Dramatists 4* (Harmondsworth, 1962), play, with M. D'Arcy; *The Business of Good Government* (London, 1963), play, with M. D'Arcy; *The Workhouse Donkey,* in *Plays and Players* (August–September 1963), play; *Ars Longa, Vita Brevis,* in *Encore* (March–April 1964), pp. 13–20, play, with M. D'Arcy; *Armstrong's Last Goodnight* (London, 1965), play; *Ironhand* (London, 1965), play; *Left-Handed Liberty* (London, 1965), play; *The Royal Pardon* (London, 1967), play, with M.

D'Arcy; *The True History of Squire Jonathan and His Unfortunate Treasure,* in *Plays and Players* (August 1968), play; *The Hero Rises Up* (London, 1969), play, with M. D'Arcy; *The Ballygombeen Bequest,* in *Scripts* (September 1972), play, with M. D'Arcy; *The Island of the Mighty* (London, 1974), play, with M. D'Arcy; *The Non-Stop Connolly Show,* 5 vols. (London, 1977–1978), play, with M. D'Arcy; *Pearl* (London, 1979), radio play; *Vandaleur's Folly* (London, 1981), play, with M. D'Arcy; *The Little Gray Home in the West* (London, 1982), play, with M. D'Arcy; *Silence Among the Weapons* (London, 1982), novel; *The Old Man Sleeps Alone,* in *Best Radio Plays of 1982* (London, 1983), radio play; *The Manchester Enthusiasts* (London, 1984), radio play, with M. D'Arcy; *Books of Bale* (London, 1988), novel; *Whose Is the Kingdom?* (London, 1988), radio play, with M. D'Arcy.

VI. CRITICAL STUDIES. V. Manchester, "Let's Do Some More Undressing: The 'War Carnival' at New York University," in *Educational Theatre Journal* (December 1967); J. R. Taylor, "Presented at Court: John Arden," in his *Anger and After* (London, 1969); S. Trussler, *John Arden* (New York, 1973); A. Hunt, *Arden: A Study of His Plays* (London, 1974); P. Marsh, "Easter at Liberty Hall," *Theatre Quarterly,* no. 20 (1975–1976); M. Anderson, in his *Anger and Detachment* (London, 1976), includes commentary on Arden's work; C. Clinton, "John Arden: The Promise Unfulfilled," in *Modern Drama,* 21 (March 1978); C. Itzin, *Stages in the Revolution* (London, 1980), includes commentary on the political nature of Arden's work; R. O'Hanlon, "The Theatrical Values of John Arden," *Theatre Research International,* 5, no. 3 (Autumn 1980); J. Hilton, "The Court and Its Favours," in C. W. E. Bigsby, ed., *Contemporary English Drama* (London, 1981); H. I. Schvey, "From Paradox to Propaganda: The Plays of John Arden," in Hedwig Bock and Albert Wertheim, eds., *Essays on Contemporary British Drama* (Munich, 1981); J. Elsom, in his *Post-War British Theatre Criticism* (London, 1981), includes commentary on *Armstrong's Last Goodnight;* F. Gray, *John Arden* (London, 1982); M. Page, *John Arden* (Boston, 1984); M. Cohen, "A Defence of D'Arcy and Arden's *Non-Stop Connolly Show,*" in *Theatre Research International,* 15, no. 1 (1990).

MAX BEERBOHM

(1872–1956)

Robert Viscusi

MAX BEERBOHM was born in 1872, the year that the Albert Memorial went up in Kensington Gardens. That pile honored Queen Victoria's late consort by summoning in crowds the shades of the most notable figures in the history of Western culture: Dante, Beethoven, Virgil, Homer, and a cast of hundreds of others to pay homage to the shade of the departed prince. The stolid riot of appropriation that plays across the bas-reliefs of this extravaganza represents the high-water mark of British imperial self-confidence. Max Beerbohm is most easily remembered as a part of the long movement to undermine that Olympian arrogance.

Beerbohm entered public life as a brilliant player in the great homosexual crisis of the 1890's, having achieved his first fame as an English "decadent" in the spring of 1894, just a year before Oscar Wilde endured the spectacular scandal that sent him to Reading Gaol. A few years later Max was thriving as a dramatic critic in Edwardian London, thus taking part in the most energetic theatrical revival in England since the closing of the playhouses in 1642. After twelve years in this role, Max surprised his friends and his public by resigning his post and then retiring from life in London. He left the city and the nation in May 1910, when he married the American actress Florence Kahn and they moved to Rapallo on the Italian Riviera. This small event was in its way as much a part of the Edwardian sunset as the actual death of the English monarch a few weeks later—or as that mysterious moment in December 1910 when, according to Virginia Woolf, human character changed. Max and Florence lived in Rapallo for the rest of their lives, except for sojourns in England during the two world wars. Florence died in 1951, but Max survived, appropriately enough, until the final fall of night upon the British Empire. He died, after marrying Elisabeth Jungmann, an old family friend who had cared for him, in 1956, the year that Egypt nationalized the Suez canal. The long slide from the world of great empire to the world of little England produced an endless train of absurdities and contradictions. And Max, who was a humorist of genius, made his career by making the most of them.

"Except in union with some form of high seriousness," Max once asserted, "humour does not exist for me" (*More Theatres,* 1969, p. 269). Is this a Victorian sentiment? Not entirely. Rather, it is a fruitful complication. It is worth remarking that from Victorian high seriousness to Beerbohm's humor-in-union-with-high-seriousness is neither an easy nor an obvious pass, because although humor can readily dismantle an imposing attitude, what Beerbohm's sentence suggests is that the attitude can survive with, or even through, the humor. This unlikely coexistence summarizes the artistic policy of the most puzzling, and one of the most durable, of the writers whose names are associated with the imperial late afternoon of the British 1890's: Henry Maximilian—after 1939, Sir Max—Beerbohm. "Max," the signature of his thousands of caricatures and the name by which he was mostly known throughout his career, has always been a treasure of initiates, a writer's writer, a caricaturist's caricaturist, and the author of the definitive Oxford novel, *Zuleika Dobson, or An Oxford Love Story* (1911). He is also now emerging as the greatest British humorist of his generation and even the twentieth century.

To consider Beerbohm is to consider contradictions—not merely the sobriety of farce concealed inside the farce of sobriety, but a great number of paradoxes in his career and reputation. For example, his one novel was rejected by his own publisher, but it has never been out of print since it first appeared in 1911. Max himself, never quite a star and always insistent upon the "smallness" of his gifts and ambitions, has nonetheless been the subject of a dozen books, among them a substantial biography, two copious bibliographies, and a good number of more or less learned commentaries. The implausibilities of the case are numerous, but the resolution has its own harmony: Max was the voice of the contradictions of his moment.

EARLY LIFE AND INFLUENCES

BEERBOHM was equipped to look at things from two sides. Born on 24 August 1872 in Kensington, a borough of London, last child of a prosperous corn merchant who had migrated to London in 1850 from Memel, in German-speaking Lithuania, Max Beerbohm grew up in a world that remained slightly foreign to its surroundings. Julius Beerbohm and his first wife, Constantia Draper, had four children: Ernest (b. 1851), Herbert (1852), Julius (1854), and Constance (1854). All the male children of this marriage were sent to the father's school, Schnepfenthal College, in Thuringia, Germany. None of them thrived there. When his first wife died, Julius took her younger sister Eliza Draper to Switzerland in order to marry her—thus evading the Deceased Wife's Sister's Bill (familiar to students of the sober hilarity in Matthew Arnold's *Friendship's Garland* [1871] and *Culture and Anarchy* [1869]). Eliza Beerbohm gave birth to Agnes (1865), Dora (1868), and Henry Maximilian (1872). The children of the first marriage thus were nearly adults when young Max entered the world, and he tended to look at them, particularly Julius, Jr., and Herbert, as "gods." Julius was an adventurous sort who traveled to South America in the company of a rich woman and wrote a book about Patagonia. Herbert decided to become an actor, a decision that did not please his bourgeois father until he began to make a resounding success of it. Calling himself Herbert Beerbohm Tree (*Beerbohm* means "berry tree"), Herbert, though innocent of formal training, brought to acting an energetic enthusiasm and a hectic whimsy that carried him to the heights of actor-managership while he was still in his middle thirties and Max was in the fourth form at Charterhouse, a boarding school in Surrey.

Max was raised in a more conventional British manner than his older half brothers. The results were in fact in his case more mixed. The stringencies of their German schooling had inspired definitive acts of rebellion in his half brothers: Julius

became a playboy whose career was marked by disastrous speculations and huge debt; Ernest disappeared into South Africa. Max was given the less remarkable education provided at the local preparatory school in Kensington, where he learned a little drawing and a good deal of Latin, making ready for his entry into Charterhouse, where he would miss the comforts, privacies, and freedoms of home but would contrive to avoid trouble and to leave for Oxford University at the end not altogether undistinguished. His distinctions were not strictly scholastic, however. They consisted in his drawing caricatures to illustrate the comic poem "An Epic of Hades," a spoof of the masters written by his house monitor, and in his publication (private) during his last year there of a brief Latin satire "Carmen Becceriense, Cum Prolegomenis et Commentario Critico, Edidit H. M. B."—a parody of the school edition of Horace published by one of the Charterhouse masters, T. E. Page, reprinted in *Max in Verse* (1963). The subject of the poem is itself school-satirical, being an elaborate rhetorical joke about the quality of the music made by the Charterhouse piano teacher Arthur Becker. "Carmen Becceriense" is as notable for its latinity as for its wit and thus is a production as clearly inside the values promoted by the school as it is, for the bite of its sarcasms, planted firmly on the outside.

The capacity that young Max demonstrated for projecting simultaneously the world on both sides of the wall was not then, as it has never been, a gift that was widely distributed. It gave to Beerbohm's point of view a sense of ease, a sense of being at home in the institutions of power—the universities, clubs, journals, theaters, courthouses—of his time, at the same time that it enabled him to see these same edifices, as it were, as they looked to the people straining to peer into the windows over the palings on the sidewalk. The result of this doubled and self-opposing perspective was a unique satiric vision, at once comfortable and unsettling, that was to be the leading characteristic of Max Beerbohm's whole performance as a public artist.

PUBLIC ARTIST AND DANDY

THE term "public artist" is meant to comprehend the various aspects of a career sharply marked, according to a famous Augustan paradox, by the diversity in its sameness. Beerbohm, from the time that he entered Oxford in 1890, figured on the public stage in a wide variety of roles: he was known as a caricaturist even while still in his first year at Oxford; by the time that he left (without taking his degree) four years later, he had made a name as an essayist, achieving this with a debut in the first issue of the quintessential 1890's journal, *The Yellow Book,* as the author of a brilliant essay in paradox and gay stylistics that bore the quintessential 1890's title, "A Defense of Cosmetics" (renamed "The Pervasion of Rouge" in the *Works of Max Beerbohm,* 1896). Caricaturist and essayist, he soon added further arrows to his quiver by publishing an extremely successful novella (*The Happy Hypocrite: A Fairy Tale for Tired Men,* 1897, afterwards adapted into a play, a radio play, and even, in the fullness of time, an Italian opera) and a series of parodies of established authors titled "A Christmas Garland Woven by Max Beerbohm" (published in the Christmas supplement of the *Saturday Review* in 1896 and followed ten years later by another collection in the *Saturday Review* with the same title, and eventually by a book, *A Christmas Garland,* in 1912), and by assuming in 1898 the chair of dramatic critic of the *Saturday Review,* a position vacated by George Bernard Shaw, who introduced his successor with the tag line forever afterwards associated with Beerbohm's career. "The younger generation is knocking at the door," Shaw wrote, "and as I open it there steps spritely in the incomparable Max."

A remarkable sobriquet for a man not yet twenty-seven years of age. Who was this incomparable Max? He was the public artist who brought together all the roles of caricaturist, parodist, essayist, story writer, and critic, under the more generic and dramatic rubric of "dandy." As a public artist, Max enclosed all his other roles in the generous folds of his well-tailored coats.

The twentieth century still has the occasional dandy in arts and letters: Tom Wolfe in his ice-cream suit, Elton John in his thousand hats, Andy Warhol in his white hair and leather jackets. But these are individual artists whose dandyism is part of an individual politics. Dandyism, however, was still a flourishing tradition, almost a movement, during the latter part of the nineteenth century, when Max was growing up. It was, in art and literature, a frequent phenomenon for an artist to devise himself a public character and to live inside of

it like a Japanese actor, ceremonially masked and costumed. The archetypal dandy, Beau Brummell, practiced no other arts but those of impeccable clothes, high-stakes gambling, and superior attitudes. His inheritors, however, carried the approach into such wider arenas of dominance as poetry (Charles Baudelaire), painting (Comte D'Orsay), fiction (Sir Henry Bulwer-Lytton), politics (Benjamin Disraeli), and drama (Oscar Wilde). A style of male display, a ritual of dominance, dandyism deployed old habits of cosmopolitan patriarchy, concentrating them in a new vocabulary that eschewed the excessively florid, the powdered wigs and gold lace of an earlier generation, and developed instead a subtle interplay of whites and grays and buffs and blacks, a modern palette that is with us still in Wall Street and the Strand. Its subtlety allowed dandyism to become the language of social mobility, suitable to an age of rapid urbanization and of spectacular arrivistes. In the chronicles of dandyism as in the birth order of his family of origin, Max came at what consciously saw itself as the end of a long line.

The end was signaled by the arrival on the public stage of Oscar Wilde, who had graduated from Oxford notoriously into Piccadilly wearing a velvet suit and carrying a lily in his hand. Wilde's originality as a dandy was to bring on the sunset. He made his pose the self-conscious ironic fulcrum of a career that exploited every contradiction in his personal, cultural, and historical situations. "I was a man," he wrote in an undated letter believed by scholar Rupert Hart-Davis to have been penned in 1897,

who stood in symbolic relations to the art and culture of my age. I had realized this for myself at the very dawn of my manhood and, had forced my age to realize it afterwards. Few men hold such a position in their own lifetime and have it so acknowledged. It is usually discerned, if discerned at all, by the historian, or the critic, long after both the man and his age have passed away. With me it was different. I felt it myself, and made others feel it.[1]

Wilde consciously played this symbolic role, which he saw as one of definition, even of consummation: "I treated Art as the supreme reality, and life as a

---

[1]In Rupert Hart-Davis, ed., *The Letters of Oscar Wilde* (London, 1975), p. 466. All subsequent references are to *Letters.*

mere mode of fiction: I awoke the imagination of my century so that it created myth and legend around me. I summed up all systems in a phrase, and all existence in an epigram" (*Letters*, p. 466). He accomplished these heroic goals by devising in many spheres a highly concentrated art that embraced extreme contradictions like wide parentheses including everything else within their embrace. Thus in his personal life, he played the paterfamilias and the pederastic adventurer; as an artist, he explored the possibilities of a glittering public mask that was paralleled by a sordid private reality; and as a historical actor, he made himself the martyr of the very hypocrisy that had given shape to his public masquerade and his public art, allowing himself to display in the dock of the Old Bailey the precise doubleness of vision that had made him what he was and that would, upon his conviction for sodomy, unmake him altogether as a felon in Reading Gaol.

Max's career as a writer grew inside the resonant force field of contradictions set up by Wilde's career. Already a dandy at school, already successful as an undergraduate in the social and literary arts of self-dramatization, very much the inheritor of his family's theatrical bent, Max arrived on the public stage well able to make capital of precisely the complex hypocrisies upon which Wilde had constructed his flamboyant success. Max came to a premature fullness of power in 1895, the year of Wilde's downfall, writing an essay titled "Be It Cosiness" in *The Pageant* (1895) in which he pronounced himself "outmoded," a "classic," and announcing his retirement from the field.

This was an ingenious response to the general hue and cry that followed Wilde's disgrace. And Max turned the gesture into a running gag in the titles of his subsequent collections of essays, *More* (1899), *Yet Again* (1909), and *And Even Now* (1920). The compliment to Wilde, in Max's mind, needed to be permanent. Indeed, while Oscar Wilde was still in prison, Max published his fable, *The Happy Hypocrite: A Fairy Tale for Tired Men*, the subtitle of which refers doubly to Wilde and the content of which amounts to a spiritual justification of the dandy martyrdom that Wilde had assumed. Max, throughout his varied production—which includes, among his books, a collection of parodies, a novel, collections of dramatic criticism, and eleven bound volumes of caricatures—always ex-

ploited the position of dandy that Wilde had brought to a definitive, heroic pitch, the character of the genteel outsider, the spy of truth in the palace of lies.

A crucial aspect of Wilde's originality lay in his combining a personal capacity for contradiction with dandyism's gift for representing itself in the newspapers. Wilde, to a greater extent even than Byron, lived and died in the public prints, thus making it clear the degree to which dandyism's monochrome display reflected the technology by which this movement in art and culture had communicated itself to the general public. And this is the aspect of his art that taught the most to Beerbohm.

Wilde was in literature what Herbert Beerbohm Tree, his coeval, was in the theater: a brilliant publicist, a man who had learned to adapt the lessons of high culture to the profit centers of Piccadilly and the Strand, where the crowds had always fancied a gentleman, provided he had a sense of humor and a cocky cut to his collar. Tree and Wilde sometimes collaborated—Max's big brother had the distinction of creating the role of Lord Illingworth in Wilde's *A Woman of No Importance* (1894). The keen eye of Max the sixth-form parodist had already learned a great deal from these triumphant wits and their colleagues, who frequented Herbert's greenroom during his great success in the production of W. P. Outram Tristam's play *The Red Lamp* in 1887. Even as the masters at Charterhouse were taking the boy through the ritual syllabus of the young lord at school, such mentors as Wilde and Tree were teaching him how to make the lordly popular.

For a writer and artist this meant that he did not aim directly at the library but rather at the newspapers. Dandyism had understood this road for a long time—indeed, from the days of the Regency. "How very delightful Grego's drawings are!" wrote young Max Beerbohm, in his essay "Dandies and Dandies," collected in *The Works of Max Beerbohm* (1896), praising the caricaturist of Brummell and his contemporaries for guiding him "as Virgil, Dante" into the netherworld of by-now-long-dead dandies (p. 3). Translated, this praise meant that dandyism was a movement that had survived itself not in the poetry anthologies but in the bound volumes of the comic weeklies.

Comic journalism, dandyism, theater: these are

not three divisions of a career but three levels of interpretation—to which, at the end, will be added a fourth. As levels, each presupposes the last and leads to the next, and all are, finally, interdependent.

COMIC JOURNALISM

Max Beerbohm as a writer was formed by the reading of dozens of illustrated funny papers—the happy genre of popular journalism that reached its apex in the often ferocious and always copiously allusive, or class-solid, columns and caricatures of that most successful periodical in the history of English literature, *Punch.* Parody, cartoon, outrageous assertion, farcical violence: these are the hallmarks of this style of journalism. These are the delights most frequently shared by admirers of Beerbohm's work.

As an essayist, Beerbohm was an exaggerator. "I shall write no more," he announces at the close of *The Works of Max Beerbohm,* his first book, published when he had reached the age of twenty-three (p. 178). The self-mockery in that gesture is the other side of the weakness for comic extremes that allows him to discuss the ruling family as "our royal pets." His prose fairly bubbles with this gestural extravagance of diction, delectable samples of which its initiates frequently cite to one another, almost in the manner of the tired old comedians who know the items in the joke book so well that they can make each other laugh simply by citing the catalogue numbers. One of the most frequently quoted of Max's lines, from *And Even Now,* comes at the end of the passage about to be cited. It is worth considering carefully for what it suggests about the possibilities inherent in the exaggerations of comic journalism, possibilities that Beerbohm exploits with admirable thoroughness in this classic exordium to his essay entitled "Laughter":

M. Bergson, in his well-known essay on this theme, says . . . , well, he says many things; but none of these, though I have just read them, do I clearly remember, nor am I sure that in the act of reading I understood any of them. That is the worst of these fashionable philosophers—or rather, the worst of me. Somehow I never manage to read them till they are just going out of fash-

ion, and even then I don't seem able to cope with them. About twelve years ago, when everyone suddenly talked to me about Pragmatism and William James, I found myself moved by a dull but irresistible impulse to try Schopenhauer, of whom, years before that, I had heard that he was the easiest reading in the world, and the most exciting and amusing. I wrestled with Schopenhauer for a day or so, in vain. Time passed; M. Bergson appeared "and for his hour was lord of the ascendent"; I tardily tackled William James. I bore in mind, as I approached him, the testimonials that had been lavished on him by all my friends. Alas, I was insensible to his thrillingness. His gaiety did not make me gay. His crystal clarity confused me dreadfully. I could make nothing of William James. And now, in the fullness of time, I have been floored by M. Bergson.

It distresses me, this failure to keep pace with the leaders of thought as they pass into oblivion.

(pp. 303–304)

Readers who do not at least smile at the punch line will have a rough time with Max Beerbohm, because not only is that sentence meant to raise a bit of the laughter under examination in his essay, but it also represents the acme of what, stretching a little Beerbohm's own paradox of humorous high seriousness, we may call the academics of high journalism. That is, the *filosofia buffa* is only the beginning of the joke. Deeper into it, we meet the pleasant self-mockery of a reader who sarcastically cannot cope but who also probably *really* cannot make very much of his "dull but irresistible urge to try Schopenhauer." Invited to identify with this little confession, we are then offered the pleasures of a shared sneer at the supposed pleasures of speculative prose. "Thrillingness" is a definitive coinage in this arena. It calls our attention, it *means* to call our attention, to the prose we are at that moment reading instead of academic philosophy. What prose is this? This prose is journalism, tuned to its highest pitch. Not only who, what, where, and how, but, supremely, *when.* When and when and when. "Twelve years ago . . . years before that . . . a day or so . . . time passed . . . his hour . . . tardily . . . the fullness of time . . . as they pass into oblivion." This is prose that deploys a journalist's freedom to converse with the gods, while it never forgets journalism's license to speak in and from the street. "And now," he says with his poker face, "in the fullness of time, I have been floored by M. Bergson." "Floored," for readers who appreciate the distance between the levels of diction, is just about breathtaking. In the convolutions of narrative, with time schemes running in two directions continuously from the first M. Bergson to the last, we are never lost, but we are more than a little exhilarated to land so definitively upon the repetition of the name. The elegance of the exercise as form is Beerbohm's answer to the uncited gaieties that failed to make him gay. Comic journalism at this level is as gay, in the old sense of deliriously delightful, as an overture of Mozart.

And like an overture of Mozart, it implies a setting that a later age needs consciously to call to mind. The silks and dominoes of eighteenth-century Prague have a permanent place around the orchestra of *Le Nozze di Figaro.* Likewise, one ought never to reconsider the opening of "Laughter" without calling to mind the senior common room at Merton College, whose dons gave the finest finish imaginable to Max's sense of what a literary institution could do in the way of devastating irony. Max wrote, one should remember, for a generation of readers who knew the lyrics to the patter songs in *H. M. S. Pinafore* and *The Mikado,* no less well than they did the verses of *The Lady of Shalott* or *In Memoriam* or *Men and Women* or *Casa Guidi Windows* or, especially, the notorious final paragraph of Walter Pater's essay on Leonardo da Vinci, which Oscar Wilde and his friends used to chant as a marching song on their way to and from pretending to dig ditches for socialism and William Morris out on the Cowley Road. Max wrote for a generation accustomed to a still-open commerce between the civilized world and the varieties of journalistic reflection.

Max's readers, that is, were accustomed to a high level of conversation in their weekly papers—not just the comic papers had brio in those days. The political and cultural reviews like the *Westminster Gazette,* the *Quarterly Review,* and the *Saturday Review* spoke to a readership of people who generally combined a degree of travel, languages, schooling, and savoir vivre with that freedom from dishwashing, lawn mowing, child tending, and cutlet selecting that makes a reader's day so much more ample and self-collected than most of us nowadays can begin to imagine. Telephones existed but still carried an air of expense and high technology that kept them from totally dominating daily life as they later did. The protections of class that era permitted still al-

lowed these readers to enjoy the freedom of play that we find in their periodicals. Max was totally a child of this class, totally its student and its drawing-room entertainer. He confidently expected to have readers whose attention could respond to his use of "floored." Thus it is that in his essays, most of them published in weekly and monthly reviews long before they were collected in individual volumes, we find him playing an arabesque of variations against the whole panoply of modes frequent in luxury journalism.

He showed himself master, for example, of the correspondence columns, in copious, very funny exchanges with such heroes and heroines of the best-seller lists as Arthur Conan Doyle and Marie Corelli. As a parody interviewer and revealer of the secrets of the great, he displayed a cunning so devastating that Oscar Wilde, one of his earliest victims, complimented him on having a style "like a silver dagger." As a dramatic critic, he bows only to Bernard Shaw. As a book reviewer, he could be by turns learnedly charming and dryly withering— in short, consummate. His collections of essays are filled with sublime versions of the sorts of thing one even now encounters in the better newspapers: expressions of the flaneur's nostalgia as he strolls past the building site where they are dismantling a fine old auditorium in favor of some faceless block of luxury flats, detailed accounts of mornings spent in the courtroom listening to the brilliant improvisations of pimps and confidence men, reflections upon the meaning of the institutions of daily life— ranging from such fetishes of the bourgeois household as the bindings of books and the stoking of fires to such weightier matters as what it means to speak French or why it is a problem having servants. All of this amounted to a wide and varied conversation, carried on for the benefit of a readership whose drawing-room manners Max understood down to the tiniest niceties. But Max's journalism also had greater heights and depths than one might suppose. These we glimpse only as he opens for Henri-Louis Bergson, Arthur Schopenhauer, and William James the passage into oblivion. We have a wider, calmer view of these spacious liberties if we consider Max's journalism in those genres that allowed him the greatest liberties. These were parody and caricature.

As a parodist in English, Max has very few equals—Geoffrey Chaucer and James Joyce are the names that come to mind. Max's parodies present to us an entire generation of writers—Henry James, Rudyard Kipling, A. C. Benson, H. G. Wells, G. K. Chesterton, Thomas Hardy, Frank Harris, John Galsworthy, G. S. Street, Joseph Conrad, Edmund Gosse, Hilaire Belloc, George Bernard Shaw, Maurice Hewlett, George Moore, George Meredith—each dispatched in a few pages, with an economical thoroughness that suggests the literary portraiture of Dante Alighieri. The student of *A Christmas Garland* comes away with an understanding of the words and works of an astonishing variety of writers. The parodies are not only funny, they are deadly accurate—x-rays of permanent flaws. Here is H*nry J*m*s, as Max calls him, describing a brother and a sister deciding whether to look into their Christmas stockings:

The gaze she fixed upon her extravagant kinsman was of a kind to make him wonder how he contrived to remain, as he beautifully did, rigid. His prop was possibly the reflection that flashed on him that, if *she* abounded in attenuations, well, hang it all, so did *he!* It was simply a difference of plane. Readjust the "values," as painters say, and there you were! He was to feel that he was only too crudely "there" when, leaning further forward, he laid a chubby forefinger on the stocking, causing that receptacle to rock ponderously to and fro. This effect was more expected than the tears which started to Eva's eyes and the intensity with which "Don't you," she exclaimed "see?"

"The mote in the middle distance?" he asked. "Did you ever, my dear, know me to see anything else? I tell you it blocks out everything. It's a cathedral, it's a herd of elephants. It's the whole habitable globe. Oh, it's, believe me, of an obsessiveness!"

(pp. 7–8)

Such work explores with considerable resonance the possibilities of self-reflexive fiction. Beerbohm employs the genre of burlesque parody, as the brilliant writers of *Punch* had taught him to do, in order to exaggerate James's mannerisms and even to turn them back upon James himself—"Oh, it's, believe me, of an obsessiveness!"—and, as he commits this wonderfully framed self-interrupting self-interruption of a self-reflecting self-reflection, he manages to convey the sense that his own eyes are absolutely wide open, displaying with a bland self-assurance this concentration of tightly wound ingenuities that he knows to be entirely his own. The

calm intricacy of this work, which does not need either to exaggerate its own importance or to spread itself across great expanses of paper, owes as much to the concentrated aristocratic excellences of Latin poetry, which Max also had learned to parody, as it does to the more careless freedoms one is likely to find on display in even the more luxurious weekly reviews.

A central question for the student of Beerbohm's work is precisely this combination of excellences: What enables him thus to transform the genres of occasional farce into occasions, which this James parody exemplifies perfectly, of an excellence so thorough as to suggest permanence, canonicity, classic status?

DANDYISM

THE answer is dandyism. It is Max's dandyism that makes him a classic. This answer is, appropriately, a paradox. According to its great philosopher, Baudelaire, dandyism is the art of the evanescent. The dandy walks down the street like a set of mirrors on legs, reflecting the changing fashions of kaleidoscopic modernity, not so much unconcerned with permanence as he is unmoored from the very possibility of its consideration. Nonetheless, it is Max's concentration upon dandyism, both as a theory and a practice, that gives him his power to transmute the trivial into things of high and lasting value.

The process is the by-now familiar contradiction of modernism, of which dandyism was an early avant-garde, that time and motion are the most stable of essences. This concentration upon the elusive has furnished us with most of the monuments of modern art, from futurism to abstract expressionism, while attempts to make history stop in its tracks have generally been relegated to the attic of discarded academies. Dandyism, with its painters of modern life and its twinship with the gods of haberdashery and haute couture, was born on a newspaper stand and knew that its one chance of endurance was to fix its attention obsessively upon what was passing, trivial, and, because of those very qualities, to become painfully eloquent of its historical specificity.

As suggested earlier, Max did not invent this

understanding of dandyism. Instead he inherited it—*learned* it, we can say, if we mean by *learning* the total appropriation of an entire life's understanding—from Oscar Wilde. Wilde's life and martyrdom, from the younger dandy's point of view, exemplified in every possible way the range of meanings open to the art of dandyism, its capacity to achieve permanence by subsuming within its own body the contradictions of its society.

Wilde's martyrdom is not accidental to dandyism. Dandyism is an art that has much to do with the bodies of its adepts. It is vital to underscore this point. Before its other aspects—before its value as visual art, its innovations in costume, its comic-strip simplicity, a simplicity transferable into newspapers—dandyism is first of all a physical discipline. It is of the body. The dandy puts clothes on his body. He can take hours, if necessary, over his cravat, as Brummell often did, and as Max liked to remind his readers. The dandy is the dancer of drawing rooms. His simple vocabulary of costume, like the transparent textures of classical music, exacts perfection in performance. What is the point of this praxis? It teaches the dandy the moral consequence of social gesture. He learns to read ties, lapels, top hats. But not only clothes. Also the men who wear them. Hands, necks, hair, legs, noses: all of these enter the language of social conversation.

Wilde, understanding this, was able to make sublime observations, noting that a widow's "hair has gone quite gold from grief," or writing Lady Bracknell's reappraisal of young Cecily in *The Importance of Being Earnest* (1904), after learning that the girl's fortune is a hundred and thirty thousand pounds:

There are distinct social possibilities in your profile. The two weak points in our age are its want of principle and its want of profile. The chin a little higher, dear. Style largely depends on the way the chin is worn. They are worn very high, just at present.

(p. 307)

Max, long before meeting Wilde, had already learned how deeply style depends upon the way the chin is worn. The question of family dandyism will be entertained a little more fully later on. At the moment, it is only necessary to point out that Max, whose father and three grown-up half brothers were all dandies, came by this mandarin prac-

tice about as naturally as it is possible to do. And he learned early how to draw.

Of course it is in his drawings that the fullness of his understanding of dandyism shows itself. Max's caricatures display a quality that has perhaps no precise parallel in the work of any other visual artist. This might be explained by a series of partial parallels. Max is a cartoonist, like a portrait artist of the Renaissance. But unlike the Renaissance portrait artist, he is a cartoonist whose characters are also known to us from a great deal of other portraiture. Max's subjects are people exceedingly well-known to his audience, people who read the illustrated papers, people who have seen photographs. In fact, Max's are not so much portraits as they are commentaries on self-display. Max, then, is a caricaturist, like Honoré Daumier. But unlike Daumier, he is also a superb writer whose caricatures speak articulately, often with a devastating parodic accuracy in the captions. When Max draws Arnold Bennett, the caption also *speaks* Arnold Bennett. Max is a writer-artist, like William Blake. But unlike William Blake's, the characters in Max's art are all actors upon the stage of contemporary history, so the understanding of his work does not require that one enter the private universe of a person given to hallucinations—or even, as Blake's apologists would have it, a Swedenborgian engraver addicted to moral allegory. In short, Max Beerbohm's caricatures present an articulate vision of the historical world around him.

In doing so, they fulfill, and indeed bring to a close, the ambitions of nineteenth-century dandyism. When Beau Brummell administered to the Prince Regent lessons in the shooting of cuffs and the angling of the chin, he was asserting for the first time in the halls of royal British politics the overwhelming power of semiotics—what the present age has sometimes called stylistics. The implication of Brummell's masquerade is that the monarch himself can never rise above the category to which he belongs: the king is a subset of the kingly. Later dandies enforced this logical hierarchism with a velvet glove. Disraeli played Queen Victoria as if she were a harpsichord. Oscar Wilde invented a legend of sexual allure for the rather blowsy actress Lillie Langtry, and the fruit of his labor was the pleasure of watching the copious Prince of Wales make the lady his mistress. Stéphane Mallarmé, in some ways the severest of all literary dandies, invented a poetic in which style was so exiguous as to exclude, often, the possibility of any other kind of sense. Max's caricatures fit into this tradition—indeed they consummate its highest ambitions—by re-creating the historical world of his time entirely in terms of its style.

In Max's caricatures, Chesterton's flowering bellies reveal his medieval soul, liberally "beef and beery." The pianist Ignacy Paderewski's hair is also his cacophonic aesthetic of flying fingers and frequently dropped notes. Oscar Wilde's chin angles so determinedly towards the ceiling as to transform him into the lily he is carrying and the vegetable god he is going to die into. The cockeyed red-nosed gluttony of the Prince of Wales is often carefully related to the hardened hand grenade of his leathery self-indulgent mother, the Empress of the Indies. Bernard Shaw appears not only as the hero of his own unhealthy skin and unattractive beard but as the bagman who patches his clothes with rags of Friedrich Nietzsche and Schopenhauer. The socialist Webbs are nightmare apparatchiks whom our century has taught us to fear rather than laugh at. There is the occasional foray into the past, as well—not usually very well done: Beerbohm's Shakespeares and Napoleons are more often part of his jokes about Frank Harris and Thomas Hardy than they are in any sense portrayals of themselves. Sympathy can, however, bring him a little further sometimes: Beerbohm manages to portray Dr. Johnson's bulk, unlike Chesterton's, as both firm and gelatinous, more suggestive of self-protection than of self-indulgence. But the main focus of attention is on things that Max has actually seen, the world of arts and letters and public affairs of his own youth, thoroughly transformed by his mastery of dandy stylistics.

This transformation rises to the level of a fully articulated historical vision in many instances. The series of cartoons "Mr Gladstone Goes to Heaven" (in *Max's Nineties,* 1958) is an altogether indelible representation of the moral economy of parliamentary posturing during the late Victorian age. Nothing is lacking. Mr. Gladstone's florid and self-accompanied aria of moral hysteria, his grotesque scholarship, his malodorous puritanism, his ill-concealed self-indulgence—all this and more is tilted on its axis by one glimpse of the disillusioned urbanity of the dandy prime minister Disraeli. In his book of caricatures *Cartoons: "The Second Childhood of John Bull"* (1911), Max even entered that universe of allegorical demiurges created and ruthlessly

overexploited by nineteenth-century newspaper artists, a land of no subtleties where the men wear jackets and pants tailored of bunting. In this instance, the ferocity of Max's disapproval of the Boer War (1899–1902) made the cartoons successful, although the precedent was not good for him, and in later years, whenever he allowed himself to use the personifications of patriotism—the United States's Uncle Sam or the French Republic's Marianne—the chances were good that his imagination was flagging.

Max's masterpiece in this art is his tribute to another great writer-artist, in some ways his closest precursor in this exclusive arena, Dante Gabriel Rossetti. *Rossetti and His Circle* (1922) is a full exploration of the world of Rossetti, from his childhood in the exiled outer darkness of the risorgimento, when his father Gabriel Rossetti and Giuseppe Mazzini argued politics and invented modern Italy a hundred times, to the Pre-Raphaelite brotherhood, with whom Dante Gabriel and William Michael Rossetti, along with Holman Hunt and Edward Burne-Jones, reinvented medieval Italy a hundred times, to the later days of Swinburnians and aesthetes, whom Max himself, preoccupied by that disappeared generation and living in Italy during the second half of his life, reinvented a hundred times for himself as memories. It is the most unusual work of literary and artistic history imaginable. In it, writers and artists as varied as Thomas Carlyle and John Stuart Mill, William Morris and Jane Morris, Theodore Watts-Dunton and Christina Rossetti, make their appearance, each of them making (as Max wrote once in a stage direction for " 'Savonarola' Brown") "remarks highly characteristic of themselves" and each of them indelibly portrayed through the unmistakable language of style that is spoken by a person's clothes and body no less distinctly than by his or her inscriptions on a page.

Or in conversation. Dandies specialized in conversation. Beau Brummell, indeed, did not write at all. Others did write, but all believed what Wilde taught, that the man who can dominate a London dinner table can rule the world. Wilde himself was a superb conversationalist, more than once memorialized by Max Beerbohm as the best talker he ever heard. Those who heard Max were, however, themselves given to similar encomiums. Max's mastery of this art was quite full enough to allow for a rich appreciation of the capacities of those masters he had the good fortune to know. Parody had taught him, or perhaps it equally reflected, a loving attention to the speech of others. One certainly sees the effects of this in the inspired dialogues—it seems scarcely adequate to call them captions—that accompany Max's caricatures. But it shows itself, inevitably, at its best when Max is engaged in the purest form of dandy art—self-portrayal. Late in his career, Max now and then wrote essays to perform on the BBC. In these, one occasionally catches a bit of what he must have been capable of, after a pint of Falernian or two, under the lemon trees on the terrace of the house in Rapallo, Italy, where he lived from 1910 until his death on 20 May 1956. People came to see him, he said, on their way from Somerset Maugham's at Cap Ferrat, in southern France, to Bernard Berenson's in Settignano, outside Florence. He rarely disappointed these visitors, we are told. This is what he sounded like from there, speaking to the radio microphone on the subject of London, in "London Revisited," collected in *Mainly on the Air* (1946):

One of the greatest of Englishmen said that the man who is tired of London is tired of life.

   Well, Dr. Johnson had a way of being right. But he had a way of being wrong too—otherwise we shouldn't love him so much. And I think that a man who is tired of London may merely be tired of life *in London.*

(p. 3)

Nothing much, that opener. A set of variations on a famous cliché—comparable, let us say, with Mozart's variations on "Twinkle twinkle little star." The plan is to take the simple statement and transform it with other simplicities. First he compliments Johnson, then he introduces his statement, then he compliments Johnson again, then he takes it back. Then he praises Johnson's fault as a virtue. Then he introduces the first person singular. Then he rewrites the proverb adding the three words "merely," "in," and "London." What do these variations amount to? The gestures of a monologue that is in fact a dialogue. The dandy changes sides from sentence to sentence. This draws in the audience, because dandy conversation is, like all dandy self-portrayal, in fact a form of social portraiture. The dandy is a mirror. In conversation or in monologue, he mirrors the interlocutor.

The interlocutor is not always the listener. In the passage cited above, the interlocutor is also Dr. Johnson. And in the radio talk that followed, the voice of Dr. Johnson was in fact, as the psychiatrists elegantly put it, introjected. In disagreeing with an opinion of Dr. Johnson's, Beerbohm is appropriating the voice of that notorious Jeremiah, in order to make a prophetic utterance of very considerable force:

London never had any formal or obvious beauty, such as you find in Paris; or any great, overwhelming grandeur, such as Rome has. But the districts for which I loved her, and several other districts too, had a queer beauty of their own, and were intensely characteristic—inalienably Londonish. To an intelligent foreigner, visiting London for the first time, what would you hasten to show? Except some remnants here and there, and some devious little nooks, there is nothing that would excite or impress him. The general effect of the buildings that have sprung up everywhere in recent years is not such an effect as the intelligent foreigner may not have seen in divers other places—Chicago, for example, or Berlin, or Pittsburg. London has been cosmopolitanised, democratised, commercialised, mechanised, standardised, vulgarised, so extensively that one's pride in showing it to a foreigner is changed to a wholesome humility. One feels rather as Virgil may have felt in showing Hell to Dante.

   It is a bright salubrious Hell, certainly. But still—to *my* mind—Hell.

(pp. 7–8)

His mind. Beerbohm saw dandyism as the mental representation of the greatness of the nineteenth century that created it. Not only did this lend point to his condemnation of the "-ised" London of the 1930's. But it also explained, as it were, just before sundown, the manner in which his age had learned to communicate across the divisions of class.

   Dandies appealed, let us say, equally above and below. Above, they were admired for their mastery of style, for their capacity to teach its nuances to the young aristocrats that must master it in order to enter the fullness of their roles. Below, these dandies were beloved for their arrogance, their willingness to snub princes and dukes. They had a mediating function that offered them a very wide range of social reference. It also offered them, as here, the possibility of speaking with more than one voice at a time. In "London Revisited" Max would speak with the voice of Dr. Johnson, and in other talks he would echo the old music-hall performers whose manner he knew unreasonably well for a man of his caste. The memories had a melody the old man could still render.

As a youth, in his debut, he had been master of the polyphonic sentence whose turns can still astonish:

For behold! The Victorian era comes to its end and the day of sancta simplicitas is quite ended. The old signs are here and the portents to warn the seer of life that we are ripe for a new epoch of artifice. Are not men rattling the dice-box and ladies dipping their fingers in the rouge-pot? At Rome, in the keenest time of her degringolade, when there was gambling even in the holy temples, great ladies (does not Lucian tell us?) did not scruple to squander all they had upon unguents from Arabia.
(*Works,* pp. 85–86)

We may take it as Max's debt to journalism that this debut did not lead to a Joycean, or at least a Lylyan, prose later on in life. The Bible, Martin Tupper, Carlyle, Robert Browning, Lucian—all are visible through the texture of a handful of lines. "Degringolade," when the *Oxford English Dictionary* records a first use of it in the *Saturday Review* in 1883, is still a French word with an acute accent on the *e.* No more. Now it is in the chorus of French words sounding in the background of the dandy cantilena. Now it is, and indeed the entire performance is, the interior music of a scattered self—not an interior monologue, as practiced by Browning before and by Joyce afterwards, but an explosion into the sentences of a polyglot receptivity, all held together by the sense that the speaker is a coherent character, a "mask."

Wilde said to a woman whom Beerbohm frequented, "When you are alone with him . . . , does he take off his face and reveal his mask?" (Ada Leverson, "Reminiscences," in Violet Wyndham, *The Sphinx and Her Circle,* 1964). And Max has this to say about the theory of it: "Gracious goodness! why do not we have masks upon the stage? Drama is the presentment of the soul in action. The mirror of the soul is the voice" ("The Defense of Cosmetics"). Thus it is that he conceptualized the relationship between the outer dandy and the inner: the outer coherence, the mask, allows the complexities we hear in this many-tongued diction, these sentences echoing with incomplete gestures of counterpoint and allusions not quite made articulate. The art is exactly adapted to the needs of cosmopolitan London in its apogee, gives precisely the sense of the starched order of things still intact, while strange languages were already being spoken at the windows and old certainties announced themselves in sentences that only a few years before had not yet seemed so brittle.

MAX AND THE THEATER

MAX saw the dandy's mask as continuous with the actor's. He scarcely had any choice in this matter. For the overwhelming presence in his life from young boyhood to full manhood was that of his half brother/half cousin Herbert Beerbohm Tree, son of his father and his mother's elder sister, and king of the London theater. "King" is not too strong a word. Herbert defied his elderly father's disapproval. Without training, without proper initiation, he managed somehow to rise not merely to actor-managership, but to *triumphant* actor-managership, a category of dominance only imaginable today in Hollywood. That is, he was director, producer, star, and proprietor of the building, a vast theater called Her Majesty's that he built himself in the Haymarket. Monster of a million dreams, master of a vast matinee public, licensed to play Antony, Caesar, Lear, Hal, Falstaff, Henry Higgins, Svengali, Hamlet, Romeo, whatever took his fancy, he was also captain of the couch, with at least one second family of children, established separately from his official leading lady and two daughters, and separate, too, from the long parade of costarring beauties that shared the pleasures of the dome apartment he had built above the ceiling of the theater.

Max was candid about what it was like growing up in this person's nimbus. On the first page of "From a Brother's Standpoint" (in *Herbert Beerbohm Tree,* 1920), a memorial essay written following Tree's sudden death in 1917, Max says,

Herbert was for many reasons an enviable man, but I think that what most of us envied him was that incessant zest of his. Nothing ever seemed to derange for one moment that large, wholesome appetite for life and art. Difficulties that would have crushed any man of no more than ordinary power to cope with them were for Herbert a mere pleasant incentive—or rather, as he was the last man to need any incentive, a mere pleasant challenge to be lightly accepted and quickly dealt with on the way to something else.

(p. 187)

A man of action as well as of imagination, Herbert was generous even to a fault—all in all, an eminence altogether too lofty for the young sibling to contemplate equaling. But rivalry is inevitable in such a situation. It is easy to conceive of Beerbohm's career as a writer as a project to construct for his own use an alternative theater. Unable to compete with Herbert on his chosen ground, Max invented an imaginative kingdom and made it his own.

Not that he ran away. Indeed, he kept close to Herbert, perhaps too close for the comfort of either. In many ways it was necessary. When Max was only twenty-three and down from Oxford, without any regular employment, Tree appointed him private secretary and brought him along on a theatrical tour of the United States. Max did not like the United States. It was not casual, his reference forty years later to Chicago and Pittsburgh as types of Hell. Nonetheless, Chicago was kind to him.

As an undergraduate Max had made many friends among Oscar Wilde's circle of young intimates—particularly Reggie Turner, Max's closest friend, who was later to be Wilde's most faithful supporter, long after others had deserted him as a pariah, staying with Wilde in Paris until the moment of his death. Max was fascinated by the homosexual world of Oxford, although some of his letters and some of his biographers insist that this fascination was purely mental. Whatever the case, it was certainly lucky for Max that Herbert had brought him to Chicago just as Wilde decided to accuse the Marquess of Queensberry of libel. The morning after Wilde's disgrace was in the newspapers, Max wrote Reggie Turner to announce that an ingenue in Herbert's troupe, Kilseen Conover, had accepted his offer of marriage. The marriage never took place, but Max returned to England safely engaged to an attractive young woman during the height of the furor over Wilde's homosexuality, a time when less fortunate young bachelors found themselves scurrying to join cricketing clubs and to take up boxing.

Not all Max's connections to Herbert had this same urgency, but necessity was what always drove them. The most important of these, no doubt, was Max's acceptance of Shaw's offer to appoint him his successor as dramatic critic of the *Saturday Review*. This was a signal honor: Shaw was already quite distinguished in London. It was an important post: the *Saturday Review* was an influential, though not stodgy, periodical. Max was being assured access to the best readership in London. Would he have had all this at age twenty-seven without his connection with Herbert? No—not that he had not made his own name, but his own name was so much easier to make for the recognition that preceded it. His own knowledge of the world was so much wider for his having spent so much time in Herbert's greenroom during his formative years, years when Herbert was already enjoying that universal patronage that London gave, and still sometimes gives, to its leading actors. And certainly, Max's acquaintance with Wilde and many other theater people, from Ellen Terry to Harley Granville-Barker to Bernard Shaw, grew directly from the family business. That the theater was the family business no doubt inspired Max's reluctance to accept the offer at the *Saturday Review*. He did not want to do it, but he needed the money. "I am not fond of the theatre," he writes in his opening essay, under the fetching title "Why I Ought Not to Have Become a Dramatic Critic" (28 May 1898), later collected in *Around Theatres* (1924). He gives many reasons he should be disqualified. But he concludes: "The Editor of this paper has come to me as Romeo came to the apothecary, and what he wants I give him for the apothecary's reason" (vol. 1, p. 6).

Shaw is a more forceful critic, because his eye is single and his prose benefits in power from that concentration. Max's dramatic criticism can sometimes echo the same cave of voices we have already encountered. That is to say, he provides the divagations of a seeing, hearing intelligence rather than gives voice to a purpose. But, as a dramatic critic, Max Beerbohm is, nonetheless, much more a concentrated person than he ever shows himself elsewhere. Again, necessity rules. He is his big brother's little brother. There is no escaping it:

I can imagine that a man who had never been in a theatre might, were he suddenly sent forth as a dramatic critic, be able to write really charming and surprising and instructive things about the stage. But my readers must not look for any freshness or cerebration from me. I could find my way blindfold about every theatre in the metropolis, and could recite backwards most of the successful plays that have been produced in the last ten years. . . . Out of my very cradle I stepped upon the fringe of the theatrical world, and my familiarity with the theatre has been a matter of circumstance rather than of choice.

(vol. 1, p. 3)

That is to say, like it or not, he was technically equipped to do a very workmanlike job as a dramatic critic, and this was exactly what he did. The only regular employment he ever held, Max Beerbohm's tenure at the *Saturday Review* ran from June 1898 through May 1910, corresponding with the last part of Queen Victoria's reign and just about all of King Edward's. Beerbohm wrote over six hundred review essays: an estimable chronicle, at the minimum, and often very much more than that.

But as the passages cited will have already made very clear, the person in question is very different from the usual Max. He cannot play so freely here as elsewhere. He is too old in the theater; having been born into it, he knows too much to let himself float so freely among his voices as elsewhere. The contrast between the academic and the journalist that makes the best of his caricatures and gives his finest essays their air of being spoken simultaneously from two sides of a wall, this doubleness rarely makes an appearance in Max's dramatic criticism. And when it does, it does so with an air of deliberate fun. Sometimes it is funny, anyway, as when, on 12 May 1900, he reviewed *Quo Vadis?* together with *You Never Can Tell,* which he refers to as *Nil Praedicandum (Around Theatres,* vol. 1, pp. 134–140). This is worth a smile, at least. But much more frequent is the voice we have already heard: very competent, determinedly self-deprecating, and under everything, always a little angry, always a little impatient. The theater really *is* too much like work for him, as is weekly journalism, as is the need to keep before his eyes the spectacle of his brother Herbert, who was never so good an actor as he was a successful one, and always much richer than Max, who liked nice things and once even tried to marry one of Tree's leading ladies, Constance Collier, whom he could not, it turned out, either afford or adequately keep happy by night. Collier returned to Tree's affections, an event he celebrated by casting her as Cleopatra.

All of this being so, it would still be a very fool-

ish reader who skipped the dramatic criticism of Max Beerbohm. He is always excellent company. It would be easy to multiply examples of how very amusing he can be. Here is one. Sarah Bernhardt took it into her head to play Hamlet. Max's account, "Hamlet, Princess of Denmark" (17 June 1899), is instructive. "From first to last," he points out, "no one smiled" (vol. 1, p. 61). One smile would have brought the house down. As to Bernhardt,

the best that can be said of her performance is that she acted (as she always does) with that dignity of demeanour which is the result of perfect self-possession. Her perfect self-possession was one of the most delicious elements in the evening's comedy, but one could not help being genuinely impressed by her dignity. One felt that Hamlet, as portrayed by her, was, albeit neither melancholy nor a dreamer, at least a person of consequence and unmistakably "thoro'bred." Yes! the only compliment one can conscientiously pay her is that her Hamlet was, from first to last, *très grand dame.*

(vol. 1, pp. 65–66)

As far as serious consideration of theater goes, he is not much interested in theory, but he has plenty to say about the most notable theatrical phenomenon of his day, George Bernard Shaw, whom he admires but can never take quite seriously. In general he is remarkably judicious with the better playwrights of his time, quite open to Henrik Ibsen if not to Maurice Maeterlinck, and as one would expect, extremely worth reading whenever Oscar Wilde is in question.

But there is no escaping the reflection that he understood almost too much about Edwardian theater. The best thing to come out of this understanding is not, in the end, to be found in Beerbohm's dramatic criticism at all, but in the collection of tales that he published a decade after giving up dramatic criticism forever and retiring to live splendidly in Italy: *Seven Men* (1919), later expanded to *Seven Men and Two Others* (1950). These tales are exercises in the genre of "imaginary portraits" practiced by Walter Pater, but developed here by Max Beerbohm into something altogether his own. In these tales the dandy and the dramatic critic work remarkably well together. The dandy is there because one of the seven men of the title is Beerbohm himself, appearing as a character—or mask, we can say—who plays interlocutor to the leading figures in each of the tales. *Seven Men* is a varied work. Each of the six tales in the expanded version is quite different in kind from the others, and the four best of them—"Enoch Soames," "A. V. Laider," "Hilary Maltby and Stephen Braxton," and " 'Savonarola' Brown"—call to mind the short fiction of Italo Calvino and Jorge Luis Borges.

These stories benefit from Max's long consideration of the dramatic art. " 'Savonarola' Brown" actually includes a play, a blank-verse tragedy about Savonarola that puts on every historical pageant from the crowd scene in *Julius Caesar* to the very popular Edwardian verse tragedies of Stephen Phillips, who wrote such now-forgotten wowsers as *Paolo and Francesca* and *The Odyssey* in a workmanlike jogtrot blank verse that Max found an irresistible, and unresisting, target. The humor may not bite as it once did, but if blank versification ever comes back into vogue, there will be people to write these lines again:

> Savonarola will not tempted be
> By face of woman e'en tho' 't be, tho' 'tis,
> Surpassing fair. All hope abandon therefore.
> I charge thee: Vade retro, Satanas!
>
> (p. 188)

The pleasure, nonetheless, is not the college humor it appears to be. In fact, what the whole grotesque play amounts to is a nightmare recollection of the kitsch his work required him to consider seriously for many years.

Other stories show him even more plainly reflected in the destinies of his imaginary portraits. "Hilary Maltby and Stephen Braxton" is a psychological drama built around the sexual terror of 1895, the year of Wilde's catastrophe, and around Beerbohm's own powerful fantasies of greatness, fantasies that it is reasonable to see as part of his lifelong response to the overpowering presence in his life of his brother Herbert. The most engaging of these portraits and the most ingeniously structured is that of "Enoch Soames," the unknown poet who sells his soul to the devil in return for the privilege of visiting the Reading Room of the British Museum a century later in order to read his vindication in the pages of literary history. The only trace of himself he finds, however, is an inaccurate reference to the very story Beerbohm is writing.

That Max understood how his ambitions might encounter themselves in nightmare or in farce is certainly the effect of his dramatic encounter with Herbert, the dramatic antagonist of all his own ambitions, in the dark of the theater, night after night. This relationship is what put him in the way of a journalistic career and what, in fine, put his dandyism into that dramatic relationship with its audience that gives Beerbohm's art the culturally mediating quality we have been following in the present account. Journalism, dandyism, theater: three frames for interpreting a single act. There is a fourth, less a matter of genre than these three, but no less important than any. We might call this the history of the literary institution, but in the present instance it makes most sense to call it Oxford.

ZULEIKA DOBSON

Max Beerbohm once boasted that it was Oxford that had made him insufferable. This was true. Max responded very deeply to the poetry of Oxford. Some of his most effective essays are variations on its themes. His literary imagination wove itself a texture of Oxford writers: Rossetti and Arnold and Pater and Wilde, chief among them. His masterpiece turned out to be the "Oxford novel" still regarded as definitive for that subgenre of British fiction. *Zuleika Dobson, or An Oxford Love Story* is, indeed, definitive, not only in its category, but also in the interpretation of the entire oeuvre of its author.

It does not seem so at first glance. It has a definitely insubstantial appearance. It is not thick, and it is not difficult to read. The reputation of inscrutability, so essential a measure of greatness in twentieth-century literature, has never hung about *Zuleika Dobson.* Not that it is without drawbacks: the writing is beautiful, marked by a self-conscious exquisiteness that some readers cannot forgive; the plot is absurd and even grotesque. Zuleika Dobson is a woman that young men cannot resist loving. But she can only love a man who spurns her. Imagining that the undergraduate Duke of Dorset, a consummate dandy and snob, has snubbed her, she falls in love with him. But she is mistaken. He loves her. Consequently she rejects him. He resolves to commit suicide for the love of her, which he promises to do just as soon as the Eights Races are over. He makes good his promise, and all the other undergraduates follow him to their graves. While some people find this amusing, there are some whom it horrifies, perhaps understandably, and there are some others, more numerous, whom it puzzles. "What is the point or pattern of *Zuleika Dobson?*" Edmund Wilson asks in *Classics and Commercials* (p. 411).

Beerbohm has chosen a plot of visible unlikeliness in order to call the reader's attention to the nature of the work. It is a novel that, upon even slight examination, glitters with that combination of evident patterning and elaborate irony that moves the reader into an immediate position of collaboration, suspicion, cleverness. Here, the opening of *Zuleika Dobson:*

That old bell, presage of a train, had just sounded through Oxford station; and the undergraduates who were waiting there, gay figures in tweed or flannel, moved to the margin of the platform and gazed idly up the line. Young and careless, in the glow of the afternoon sunshine, they struck a sharp note of incongruity with the worn boards they stood on, with the fading signals and grey eternal walls of that antique station, which, familiar to them and insignificant, does yet whisper to the tourist the last enchantments of the Middle Age.

(p. 1)

Part of the peculiarity of this novel is that its structure requires especially careful attention to this paragraph, because, while it does not have the appearance of one, it is an epic invocation. *Zuleika Dobson* has twenty-four chapters, and is in fact constructed as a comic epic in prose, a genre first perfected in English by Henry Fielding, the author of *Joseph Andrews* (1742) and *Tom Jones* (1749); *Zuleika Dobson* is structured around the Alexandrian Homeric pattern of twenty-four books, having that number of chapters and preserving many of the features of Homeric arrangement. These features include an intricate use of chiasmus in the disposition of episodes and a thoroughgoing circularity of motif. How does the genre apply to the reading of the opening?

It will be clear that we must attend to the familiar voice of the dandy journalist, who invites us to collaborate in his arch ironies: "That old bell" and the "grey eternal walls" and "that antique station"

cannot be old, eternal, or antique. A railroad in Oxford is irreducibly *new.* And we are emphatically in Oxford, whose touchstone, venerability, is thus emphasized. Also emphasized for the reader is a certain superiority to the tourist who reads the railroad station for its medieval architecture. It will be clear, too, that the bell signifies the beginning of an action and the portent—"presage," Beerbohm writes, with a certain technical insistence—of strange doings, divine doings, it turns out, with gods and muses and ghostly writers flitting about, and the hand of fate on everyone. Another clarity—or is it?—is given in the phrase that occupies the privileged position at the end of the paragraph: "the last enchantments of the Middle Age."

The reference is to Matthew Arnold's famous apotheosis of Oxford in his "Preface" (collected in *Lectures and Essays in Criticism,* 1962):

Beautiful city! so venerable, so lovely, so unravaged by the fierce intellectual life of our century, so serene! . . . And yet, steeped in sentiment as she lies, spreading her gardens to the moonlight, and whispering from her towers the last enchantments of the Middle Age, who will deny that Oxford, by her ineffable charm, keeps ever calling us nearer to the true goal of all of us, to the ideal, to perfection, to beauty, in a word, which is only truth seen from another side. . . . Adorable dreamer, whose heart has been so romantic! who has given thyself so prodigally, given thyself to sides and to heroes not mine, only never to the Philistines! home of lost causes, and forsaken beliefs, and unpopular names, and impossible loyalties!

(p. 290)

This is the necessary gloss for reading the depths of the novel, and this is the answer to Edmund Wilson's question. *Zuleika Dobson* uses Oxford as the battleground where Beauty and the Philistines meet. Characteristically, for an imagination that knew how to speak on both sides of the wall, Beerbohm's novel confuses the two sides of the struggle, but it nonetheless presents them plainly enough.

On the one side, representing all that Oxford stands for is the warden of Judas College, Dr. Dobson, "an ebon pillar of tradition": staid, disconnected, concerned only with the eternal security of his college. On the other, representing everything he wards against, is his granddaughter, Zuleika, a music-hall magician, an international star, a famous beauty dueled over by princes, and the very queen of philistia, whose tag line, frequently repeated, is "I don't know much about music, really, but I know what I like." Zuleika arrives in Oxford on the railroad, that sign of compromised antiquity we met in the first paragraph. As she steps out of the train "in a toque a-twinkle with fine diamonds," the sides are drawn. The struggle will be decided over the bodies and souls of the youth of Oxford.

These are Dr. Dobson's wards, it appears. But they are, immediately, his granddaughter's captives. Zuleika, a figure of newspaper legend, inspires love in all young men. But her tragedy is that she cannot give her own heart to anyone except a man that refuses her. The dilemma is neat enough. The youth of Oxford, to a man, fall for her and are accordingly rejected. But one among them, the young, the impossibly rich and accomplished and dazzling dandy Duke of Dorset, has so steep a tilt to his chin that he *seems* immune to Zuleika. A false impression, this lasts long enough to allow her to declare love for him and then, upon learning of his true feelings, to spurn him dramatically. Drama, indeed, in the sense of well-made plays and stock-company warhorses, is everywhere present, every scene having its striking attitudes and eloquent gestures of supplication, of remorse, of anger, giving the whole enterprise a sort of Gilbert-and-Sullivan robustness of cheerful familiarity—even when, in the end, all of the undergraduates, once the outcome of the Eights Races is decided, kill themselves for love of Zuleika, heartless trashy queen of music-hall prestidigitation that she is. Dr. Dobson, though troubled by this denouement, afterwards reflects that he is the guardian of Judas *College,* rather than of its undergraduates, and that the College emerges no worse off than any of the other colleges—all equally depopulated.

Strange humors, but the meditation is one, in the end, meant to rise above the philistine glories— Zuleika is presented entirely in terms of her newspaper clippings—that it contemplates. Was there a tragedy? Max wonders. "What then? Not Oxford was menaced. Come what might, not a stone of Oxford's walls would be loosened" (p. 191). This remarkable equanimity is the opening of a consummate meditation, inserted by Max exactly at the center of his concentric structure, just at the end of its twelfth chapter, in which he develops his

sense of the deepest meaning of Arnold's prose poem. In this passage, the fantasy is that the author is bodiless and omniscient as he contemplates the university and its threatened undergraduates:

There lay Oxford far beneath me, like a map in grey and black and silver. All that I had known only as great single things I saw now outspread in apposition, and tiny; tiny symbols, as it were, of themselves, greatly symbolising their oneness. There they lay, these multitudinous and disparate quadrangles, all their rivalries merged in the making of a great catholic pattern.

(p. 191)

It is a meditation equally medieval, for its great catholic pattern and its *discordia concors,* and modern, for its deep understanding of what a symbolic landscape might actually consist of, how it might be that a landscape is also its own map, how a dandy's colors, "grey and black and silver," might reveal a continuity of commitment even where there was a tragedy of contradiction. This is a powerful vision. It enables Max to see the rituals of everyday Oxford as deeply suggestive of their own place in much larger schemes, so that the Duke's relations with the landlady's daughter display a wide range of overtones in English social history, so that the dandy's relations with the female demiurge make thoroughly clear the very limitations in his own stance.

For *Zuleika Dobson*'s point, at the end, is to describe the end of dandyism itself. Max, who had memorized Wilde and Shaw from backstage and who in 1910 had married the actress Florence Kahn, who specialized in Ibsen, recognized that the sort of man of whom he was the last example, had excluded his own feminine as far and as long as was going to be possible. All his life he felt closest, of all his siblings, to his sister Dora—Sister Dora, as she was known, an Anglican nun in adult life, and always to Max the Beatrice of a childhood idyll in Pre-Raphaelite Kensington, the muse of a medieval sweetness that somehow Oxford, even as it solicited such delights, failed to accommodate. The figure of Zuleika rises like the vindication of all that was suppressed in the forced homophilia of the public schools and the romance quadrangles. It represents the assumption into the larger motherhood of Oxford even the rejected daughters of its dons, even the self-divisions of its undergraduates.

Illi almae matri: Zuleika Dobson is dedicated to the tutelary goddess of Oxford. The dedication makes plain that Max's Oxford is not merely itself, but, as he suggests, the symbol of itself, a larger type of what might suffer and struggle among its lost causes and impossible loyalties. Thus, *Zuleika Dobson* announces no less than the end of a way of life, eyes open to all its contradictions, and open too to the always greater possibilities of another and a wider existence.

SELECTED BIBLIOGRAPHY

I. BIBLIOGRAPHIES. A. E. Gallatin and L. M. Oliver, *A Bibliography of the Works of Max Beerbohm* (London and Cambridge, Mass., 1952); J. G. Riewald, *Sir Max Beerbohm, Man and Writer: A Critical Analysis with a Brief Life and Bibliography* (The Hague, 1953); R. Hart-Davis, *A Catalogue of the Caricatures of Max Beerbohm* (London, 1972). Mark Lasner's forthcoming bibliography for the Soho Bibliographies will be the most complete to date.

II. COLLECTED WORKS. *The Collected Edition of the Works of Max Beerbohm,* 10 vols. (London, 1922–1928); *Max's Nineties* (London, 1958), caricatures; *Max in Verse: Rhymes and Parodies,* S. N. Behrman, intro., J. G. Riewald, ed. (London, 1963), poetry; *More Theatres: 1898–1903,* Hart-Davis, ed. (London, 1969), dramatic criticism; *Last Theatres, 1904–1910,* R. Hart-Davis, ed. (London, 1970), dramatic criticism; *A Peep Into the Past and Other Prose Pieces,* R. Hart-Davis, ed. (London, 1972).

III. SEPARATE WORKS. *Caricatures of Twenty-Five Gentlemen* (London, 1896), caricatures; *The Works of Max Beerbohm* (London, 1896), essays; *The Happy Hypocrite: A Fairy Tale for Tired Men* (London, 1897), novella; *More* (London, 1899), essays; *The Poets' Corner* (London, 1904), caricatures; *A Book of Caricatures* (London, 1907), caricatures; *Yet Again* (London, 1909), essays; *Cartoons: "The Second Childhood of John Bull"* (London, 1911), caricatures; *Zuleika Dobson, or An Oxford Love Story* (London, 1911), repub. with the author's illustrations as *The Illustrated Zuleika Dobson,* N. J. Hall, ed. (New Haven, 1985), novel; *A Christmas Garland* (London, 1912), parodies; *Fifty Caricatures* (London, 1913), caricatures; *Seven Men* (London, 1919), stories.

And Even Now (London, 1920), essays; *Herbert Beerbohm Tree, Some Memories of Him and of His Art* (London, 1920), collection of essays, with others; *A Survey* (London, 1921), caricatures; *Rossetti and His Circle* (London, 1922), new ed., *Rossetti and His Circle,* N. J. Hall, ed. (New Haven, 1987), caricatures; *Things New and Old* (London, 1923), caricatures; *Around Theatres,* 2 vols. (London, 1924), dramatic criticism; *Observations* (London, 1925), caricatures; *The Dreadful Dragon of Hay Hill* (London, 1928), fiction; *A Variety of Things* (London, 1928), miscellany; *Heroes and Heroines of Bitter Sweet* (London, 1931), caricatures; *Lytton Strachey* (Cambridge, 1943), lecture; *Mainly on the Air* (London, 1946), essays and broadcasts.

IV. LETTERS. *Max Beerbohm's Letters to Reggie Turner,* R. Hart-Davis, ed. (London, 1964); *Max and Will: Max Beerbohm and William Rothenstein, Their Friendship and Letters, 1893–1945,* K. Beckson and M. M. Lago, eds. (Cambridge, Mass., 1974); *Letters of Max Beerbohm, 1892–1956,* R. Hart-Davis, ed. (London, 1988).

V. BIOGRAPHICAL AND CRITICAL STUDIES. H. Jackson, *The Eighteen Nineties* (London, 1913); B. Lynch, *Max Beerbohm in Perspective* (London, 1921); E. Wilson, *Classics and Commercials: A Literary Chronicle of the Forties* (New York, 1950); J. G. Riewald, *Sir Max Beerbohm: Man and Writer: A Critical Analysis with a Brief Life and a Bibliography* (The Hague, 1953); S. N. Behrman, *Portrait of Max* (New York, 1960); E. Moers, *The Dandy: Brummell to Beerbohm* (New York, 1960); D. Cecil, *Max: A Biography* (London, 1964); J. Felstiner, *The Lies of Art: Max Beerbohm's Parody and Caricature* (New York, 1972); B. McElderry, *Max Beerbohm* (New York, 1972); J. G. Riewald, ed., *Beerbohm's Literary Caricatures, from Homer to Huxley* (Hamden, Conn., 1974); K. L. Mix, *Max and the Americans* (Brattleboro, Vt., 1974); J. G. Riewald, ed., *The Surprise of Excellence: Modern Essays on Max Beerbohm* (Hamden, Conn., 1974); G. Franci, *Il sistema del dandy: Wilde, Beardsley, Beerbohm* (Bologna, 1977); L. Danson, *Max Beerbohm and The Mirror of the Past* (Princeton, 1982); P. Santaniello, *Max Beerbohm, l'uomo e l'artista* (Napoli, 1983); I. Grushow, *The Imaginary Reminiscences of Sir Max Beerbohm* (Athens, Ohio, 1984); R. Viscusi, *Max Beerbohm, or the Dandy Dante: Rereading with Mirrors* (Baltimore, 1986); L. Danson, *Max Beerbohm and the Act of Writing* (New York, 1989).

BRENDAN BEHAN

(1923–1964)

David Galef

BRENDAN BEHAN belongs to a time-honored Irish tradition, a lineage of artists as public figures, of writers who wasted their powers through drink and conversation and died before they had outdistanced middle age. Comparisons with Oscar Wilde and Dylan Thomas are inevitable, if unfair. At his best, Behan possessed a gift of expression both epigrammatic and raucous. Much of it he got on the page; the rest he dispensed freely to audiences ranging from prison mates to drinking mates. His subjects ranged widely from religion to sex, politics to philosophy, but always with an Irish slant, a consciousness of a nation plagued by its own history. As with Joyce, his background was his art, and both were linked to Dublin.

Brendan Francis Behan was born 9 February 1923. His family lived on 14 Russell Street, in the seedy North Side of Dublin, where Joyce set his Nighttown scene, as Behan liked to point out. His father, Stephen Behan, was a housepainter, and his mother, Kathleen, had her hands full trying to raise seven children, two from a previous marriage. In later years, Behan painted a picture of working-class squalor to suit his roughneck image, but in fact he grew up in a cultured household. Brendan's father could read both French and Latin, and would read aloud everything from Charles Dickens to Guy de Maupassant, changing his voice for each character to please the children. As Brendan's half brother Rory recalls, "he read the preface of *John Bull's Other Island* to us so often that Brendan knew it by heart by the time he was twelve" (O'Connor, pp. 14–15). His mother, for her part, possessed an inexhaustible store of Irish folklore and ballads, which she would sing on any occasion, a habit Brendan adopted. Music and drama ran in the family: his maternal uncle Peadar Kearney, besides being manager of the Abbey Theatre, had written the Irish national anthem, "The Soldier's Song."

The family was not well off, however, and Bren-

dan's formal education stopped when he was fourteen. His two formative influences were Roman Catholicism and Irish nationalism, the first instilled by the Christian Brothers School and by his mother, the second learned from both parents and from the streets. Stephen Behan, a Free-Stater, had served time for his patriotism, and in fact Brendan's first view of his father was blocked by the bars of a jail cell. Brendan joined the I.R.A. youth group Fianna Éireann ("Irish Warriors") when he was eight years old and moved on to an I.R.A. brigade six years later. By his early teens, he had begun to produce stories for the Fianna magazine and journalistic articles for the Republican journals. He and his father were to diverge later over the issue of guerrilla warfare, Brendan insisting on its necessity. For him, the I.R.A. became a faith in itself. In 1939, at the age of sixteen, Brendan was arrested in Liverpool with a suitcase full of explosives that he had intended to use to promote the Republican cause. He was tried, convicted, and sent to Borstal, the English system of reform schools, for three years.

Behan's Borstal experience, though recounted with humor and passion in his autobiographical *Borstal Boy* (1958), marked him for life. At Walton Prison, where he was held pending his trial, he was denied his Catholic faith by a prison chaplain who excommunicated him for not renouncing the I.R.A. It was a world of lags and screws—the slang terms for prisoners and guards—where infractions of the regulations often meant beatings and solitary confinement. Later, he was kept at Feltham Prison for a month, awaiting his sentence, and finally he was shipped off to the Borstal at Hollesley Bay, where he spent the bulk of his sentence. If a bildungsroman is a story in which a protagonist must come to terms with the world, then *Borstal Boy* fits the category, although the world of confinement presents a strange microcosm.

BRENDAN BEHAN

BORSTAL BOY

THOUGH published in 1958, *Borstal Boy* began seventeen years earlier as the sketch "I Become a Borstal Boy," an account of Behan's trial in Liverpool in 1940, and was published in the magazine *The Bell* in 1942. A longer version was later published in the Paris magazine *Points* (Winter 1951–1952), under the title "Bridewell Revisited." The final manuscript, though it may at times appear loose and sprawling, has a three-part structure. Its sections describe first Behan's stay at Walton, then his wait at Feltham, and finally his years at the Hollesley Bay Borstal. Surprisingly, the tone throughout is plucky and humorous, from the opening depiction of Behan's arrest:

Friday, in the evening, the landlady shouted up the stairs:
  "Oh God, oh Jesus, oh Sacred Heart. Boy, there's two gentlemen to see you."
  I knew by the screeches of her that these gentlemen were not calling to enquire after my health, or to know if I'd had a good trip. I grabbed my suitcase, containing Pot. Chlor, Sulph Ac, gelignite, detonators, electrical and ignition, and the rest of my Sinn Fein conjuror's outfit, and carried it to the window. Then the gentlemen arrived.
  A young one, with a blonde, Herrenvolk head and a B.B.C. accent shouted, "I say, greb him, the bestud."
(p. 3)[1]

Behan is a master at both verbal and situational irony, evident here in the religious invocation *cum* arrest warrant to the facade of a gentlemanly visit. And where there is no apparent irony, he will either find one or insert it. While Behan is waiting to be taken down to the station, the fatherly sergeant in command claims that even the most committed of the I.R.A. types can't name the six counties they are supposed to be fighting for, and Behan manages to list five before the sergeant concludes his point in triumph. But as Behan mentions, "I left out County Tyrone, for he was a nice old fellow" (p. 5). Later, as a way of ingratiating himself with a man named Donohoe, Behan mentions that Donohoe was his mother's name and adds as an aside, "It was not her name, but civility costs nothing" (p. 30).

[1]References to *Borstal Boy* cite page numbers from the first American edition.

This willingness to accommodate others is undoubtedly what helps Behan get by. At the Dale Street lockup, his Irish accent marks him as an I.R.A. type, disliked among the English prisoners, but he links up with another boy named Charlie. Charlie becomes his mate—or his China, in the rhyming prison slang that makes "mate" into "China plate" or just "China." Charlie calls him Paddy, the generic name for an Irishman, and offers snout (tobacco) and chocolate, two commodities in scarce supply in prison. Later, Behan procures another China named Ginger, and the three support each other. Certain details, such as soaping a China's back, or a screw's sarcastic reference to the cells as "married quarters because that is where sex takes place," indicate the homoerotic nature of these relationships, but no overt sexuality is depicted. Behan, whose bisexuality remained a half secret to his death, undoubtedly felt it wouldn't square with the hard-drinking image he projected.

In any event, the deprivations of prison life seem to have an enlivening effect on the prisoners. The soulless regimen makes religious services a real pleasure. The restricted diet makes even bully beef a gustatory delight. The enforced isolation makes human contact—of any kind—particularly poignant. As Behan writes after a near confrontation with a fellow countryman, "Fighting is better than loneliness" (p. 10). And the strictly enforced rules, from the thumb-scarring business of sewing mailbags to the proper way of cleaning a chamber pot, are all described with a fidelity to detail that is both grim and amusing. The ritual of morning inspection, for example, emphasizes what Behan sees as the anal-retentive quality of the British—literally: "When all was ready for inspection you could have the morning bowel movement. Not before. Business before pleasure" (p. 47). The olfactory impression Behan gives of a British jail, "the smell of shit and soap," is exact and pungent (p. 60).

Despite the repressive nature of incarceration, a great deal of spirit is reflected in the language of *Borstal Boy.* The description of Christmas dinner at Walton is Dickensian in its splendor, and it is no coincidence that Dickens was one of Behan's favorite childhood authors. At the same time, no Bob Cratchit would exclaim, "Oh dear dilapidated Jesus," or describe a fellow inmate as "a proper white-livered whore's melt" (pp. 33, 77). The genesis of most of these phrases is, of course, the narrator himself, who tells stories, pitches the "old

BRENDAN BEHAN

blarney" (p. 222), and sings an endless procession of ballads. In a sense, the hero of the novel—Behan insisted the work was a novel, not an autobiography—is language itself.

Whether the book is novel or autobiography, the protagonist shares Behan's views on life and its hardships. No matter what the screws mete out, he can see the funny side of it. As he comments, "I have a sense of humour that would nearly cause me to burst out laughing at a funeral" (p. 132), and this is the key to the comic rhythm of *Borstal Boy:* not the English black humor of Waugh, but the kind of humor at an Irish wake, an attempt to cheer up the survivors. Behan's descriptions are often capped with bits of this philosophy: "It's a queer world, God knows, but the best we have to be going on with," and "When all fruit fails, welcome haws" (pp. 69, 281). These same sentiments (and wording) are later echoed in *Confessions of an Irish Rebel* (1965). Prison, and perhaps life outside as well, is best met with a cheerful fatalism.

After the indoor world behind bars, the Borstal at Hollesley Bay comes as a surprise. Under the relatively benign auspices of a new governor, C. A. Joyce, it was a progressive institution with an emphasis on outdoor activities and open communication. In fact, it was run along the lines of a British public school, and Behan seems to have flourished there. Though some critics have complained that the last third of the book is inferior to the first segments, it may simply be that deprivation makes for more interesting reading than satisfaction. Here, where Behan is allowed to work in the fields and eventually take up his old job as housepainter, he begins to assume a real ease of manner. More important, he is surrounded by other boys who have endured predicaments similar to his own, and friendship crosses the divide of patriotism. The focus on himself seems less self-congratulatory and more open than in the earlier sections. In Walton, he defines himself in geographical opposition to others: "No, be Jesus, I was from Russell Street, North Circular Road, Dublin" (p. 77). After several months at Hollesley Bay, he is able to joke with another boy named Ken, who claims he likes the Irish: " 'They're very popular with themselves,' said I" (p. 228). By the time Behan is set free, he seems genuinely reformed. But there has been so little contact with the outer world that his future comportment remains an open question. At the end, as the immigration inspector greets Behan in

Gaelic, he adds, "It must be wonderful to be free." "It must," replies Brendan, boarding the train to Dublin and home (p. 365).

RETURN TO PRISON AND EARLY WORK

FOR Behan, returning to Dublin meant a merge with his old identity. Though the I.R.A. was then in disarray, he was still eager to prove himself. At the 5 April 1942 commemoration of the Easter 1916 uprising, he got his chance. Though Behan later exaggerated his part, the incident began with the police attempting to disarm an I.R.A. man. In the confusion, Behan grabbed a pistol from an acquaintance of his and shot at a detective. He then escaped with another I.R.A. friend named Flaherty, with the police in pursuit. The two of them hid out for several days in homes sympathetic to the I.R.A. Finally, two I.R.A. men convinced Behan to give up his gun, and the next day Behan walked unarmed into the hands of the police. In *Confessions of an Irish Rebel,* he claims to have been arrested in bed before he had a chance to use his gun, but as his biographer Ulick O'Connor notes in *Brendan:* "It is more than probable that Brendan was at his old trick of polishing up the facts to make a good story" (p. 67).

As O'Connor further points out, Behan was lucky: though the judge sentenced him to fourteen years, other men had been sentenced to death for similar crimes. And so, in 1942, Behan returned to jail, this time to Dublin's Mountjoy Prison. There, until his release in the general amnesty of 1946, he spent much of his time reading and scribbling away, observing and recording. It was in Mountjoy that he began his serious apprenticeship as a writer. Sean O'Briain, a fellow prisoner at the time, describes Behan's method of composition in those days, "lying down on his bed with a blanket over him": "As he finished a page he would peel it off—fling it in the air and let it land where it might—on the floor or anywhere at all, and seldom if ever did he collect the papers of any story together again" (in Mikhail, ed., 1982, p. 17). It is no surprise that most early manuscripts have been lost. This haphazard method of production was characteristic, and even in later years, Behan seemed to care little about a piece after it was written.

His first full-length play, "The Landlady," was

63

probably written around 1943, a year and a half into his stay at Mountjoy. The main character was based on his grandmother, Christine English, who leased several houses on Russell Street, including the one the Behans lived in. The other dramatis personae were also derived from Behan's personal acquaintance, even if they tended to speak like Sean O'Casey's characters. The play was slated for a prison production, but was canceled when many of the prisoners protested it as blasphemous. Later, Behan rewrote the play in Gaelic and sent it to the Abbey Theatre. It was rejected (one act remains in the Abbey archives), but he kept on trying.

In 1947, a one-act play, "Gretna Green," was put on at an I.R.A. fund-raiser. As with most of Behan's dramas, the play has little action: three men talk about the imminent execution of two I.R.A. men in jail. It was put on at the Queen's Theatre at a modest loss, and the playscript is no longer extant. Two points about the production are worth noting, however. First, Behan was to play one of the parts himself, but backed out at the last minute. "I'm a writer," he told the company, "not an actor" (in Mikhail, ed., p. 22). Second, in what was to become a habit, he appeared at the performance quite drunk. Both incidents are significant in revealing an essential feature of the emerging artist's character: he was insecure and unable to face life sober, despite the boisterous show he put on for everyone.

In prison, however, away from unsteadying influences, he was both studious and industrious. He read continually, with the eclectic interests of an autodidact. He began intermittent work on his reform-school recollections, which culminated finally in *Borstal Boy*. It was also in Mountjoy that he learned fluent Gaelic, a language that was to prove as important to him as French to Beckett. Other prisoners recall his reciting long passages from Brian Merriman's bawdy Gaelic verse epic, *The Midnight Court*, written in 1796. He translated Merriman's work and began writing poetry of his own, mostly in Gaelic. Between 1945 and 1950, his poems began appearing in Gaelic magazines. In 1950, he achieved a signal honor: a collection of the best Irish verse written between 1939 and 1949, entitled *Nuabhéarsaíocht*, was published with Breandán Ó Beacháin represented by two poems. At twenty-seven, he was the youngest poet in the anthology.

Behan's career as a poet was short-lived; he stopped writing poetry as soon as he began making money from his prose writings. Much of his verse remains untranslated and uncollected, with the exception of a few poems in *Brendan Behan's Island* (1962), including one addressed to Wilde and the other to James Joyce. In both the poet is a little too conscious of his own rising notoriety. Still, in his best efforts, Behan achieves the rueful air of a Thomas Hardy transplanted to a different climate, as in "Loneliness":

> In the silence of prison
> The train's cold whistle.
>
> The whisper of laughing lovers
> To the lonely.
> (trans. in O'Connor, p. 120)

Though he would later distinguish himself from what he claimed were real poets, like Dylan Thomas, Behan had two talents that make his writing sing: an eye for image and an ear for rhythm.

After his release from prison in 1946, he knocked about Dublin for a bit. He was beginning to acquire a name for himself, partly from his writing and partly from his growing reputation as a pub raconteur. There really is no adequate label for Behan's manner of holding forth. Anthony Cronin—Irish poet, lawyer, broadcaster—characterized it as *"cabaret intime"* (quoted in Mikhail, ed.; p. 29), which is as good a description as any for the jokes, ballads, quips, stories, and impersonations Behan would offer in the course of an evening. The group that hung around him was composed of a hazy merging of Trinity College students and aspiring writers, including the young J. P. Donleavy, Patrick Kavanagh, and eventually Cronin. McDaid's was the usual hangout, followed by a visit to the Catacombs, a private club run by a man who used the bottle-deposit money to pay his rent.

At the time, Behan was supporting himself with his old job of housepainting. In his off-hours, he worked on what he called his prison novel, *Borstal Boy*, and published small articles sporadically. But his I.R.A. past—or his lust for notoriety—soon got him in trouble again, when he got involved in an attempt to free a fellow I.R.A. member, Dick Timmins, from Wakefield Jail. Behan's account of the incident in *Confessions of an Irish Rebel*, like his version of the 1942 shooting, is to the greater glory of the author. It involves a "borrowed" lorry from the

BRENDAN BEHAN

Royal Army Service Corps, a little subterfuge, and a lot of drinking. In fact, Behan had nothing to do with the escape and met Timmins only once, shortly before other individuals smuggled Timmins out of England. Behan, however, in England under a false passport, was nabbed by detectives in Manchester. Since, through the 1939 Prevention of Violence Act, he was barred from returning to England under penalty of imprisonment, the combination of charges got him four months in Strangeways Prison in Manchester.

When he got out in July of 1947, he returned to his former haunts in Dublin. The nights of drinking and tale-telling began all over again, tempered by bouts of work. Behan's pugnacity when drunk was unpredictable, but it was usually tolerated as part of his "character." Not everyone was so tolerant, however. After a drunk-and-disorderly charge got him a month in jail, Behan decided it was time to give Dublin, and himself, a rest. In the tradition of Joyce and Samuel Beckett, he journeyed to Paris. Paris in the late 1940's was dominated by Jean-Paul Sartre and Albert Camus, perceptible influences in Behan's first major play, *The Quare Fellow* (1956).[2] Behan did not take to Jean Genet, despite Genet's prison background; Behan claims, in *Confessions of an Irish Rebel,* that the Frenchman "rose the hair on my head" (p. 144).[3] But Behan at this stage knew what he wanted to do. Living on handouts and in others' flats, he nonetheless kept up a steady regimen of writing that produced solid results.

HOLD YOUR HOUR AND HAVE ANOTHER

BY 1950, he was able to support himself solely from his writing. Largely through journalism, he was able to earn sums that distinguished him from the average writer manqué in Paris. At the same time, the ability to make a living from his typewriter meant freedom from a regular job. Behan often claimed (borrowing from Dylan Thomas), "A job is death without the dignity." In 1954 the *Irish Press* commissioned him to write a regular series of columns, eventually collected in *Hold Your Hour and*

Have Another (1963). The columns suited Behan's literary temperament perfectly: They were anecdotal, capturing the Dublin character and the language of its citizens. They were also brief, a definite advantage for a writer whose longer plots tended to go astray. Five hundred words was the right length for Behan to present a scene, relate a story, or just comment on life, for which he was paid the respectable sum of five pounds.

As the series evolved, Behan invented—or coopted—a group of characters: Mr. Crippen, who killed more of his own than the enemy during the Irish Civil War by serving bad liquor; Maria Concepta, once principal soprano in a foundry; Mr. Kinsella, who killed "bores" alongside Lord Roberts in Africa; Mrs. Brennan, always "in suspenders" (that is, in suspense) over one thing or another; and a curious character whose name is pronounced locally as Brending Behing. As with Behan's pub talk, the subjects range all over, from a group of Irish musicians called the Suffering Ducks to a painter who sat on the throne of England while redoing the royal apartments. Many of the stories are drawn out over a pint or two, Mrs. Brennan chiming in with her sincere accolade, "That was massive," at the end (p. 130).[4]

Occasionally the columns degenerate into strung-together jokes. "Overheard in a Bookshop" uses the premise of a former cookshop worker stuck in a bookshop because of a labor department mistake. A man who asks for a copy of the New Testament is told it's not out yet—"We have the old one of course, but I suppose you've read that" (p. 14). The gags are mostly ancient, including the old "Joyce is useless" (Joyce's *Ulysses*) line, but the rhythm of Dublin-speak comes across flawlessly. In the end, the woman clerk catches the overhearer Behan actually reading a book in the shop and accuses him of robbery. Behan clearly has his talent of mimicry down to a tee, including the malapropisms he would later use in *Richard's Cork Leg* (1973).

The best columns in the collection are the vignettes, which describe some of the more memorable minor characters in Dublin or anywhere in literature. In "The Hot Malt Man and the Bores," for instance, a Bottle of Stout man is drinking in a pub on the second floor, marking the time with the exactitude of a schedule. Just as a double-decker

[2]Dates of plays given in the text refer to dates of first production. See this essay's bibliography for publication data.
[3]References to *Confessions of an Irish Rebel* cite page numbers from the first American edition.

[4]References to *Hold Your Hour and Have Another* cite page numbers from the first American edition.

65

bus stops in front of the pub, the Bottle of Stout man drops below window level "like a trained guerilla fighter" (p. 64). The second tier of passengers can see directly into the pub, and vice versa. No one takes advantage of this phenomenon, except "a hatchet-faced oul' strap who swept the features of each of us with a searching sharpness and then, not altogether satisfied with what she'd seen, nodded grimly and almost threateningly as the bus bore her off" (p. 65). When Kinsella describes her as "a right hatchet," the Bottle of Stout man takes offense: she happens to be his wife, the woman he loves. This confuses Kinsella, who can't understand how the man could know this without having seen the woman himself. The response is utterly logical: " 'I recognized her from your description,' said the Bottle of Stout man, with the quiet dignity of a trained mind" (p. 65). The kicker is equally inspired. When the Hot Malt man asks why the other does not go to another pub, one where his wife cannot check up on him, the Bottle of Stout man confesses to sentimentality: " 'This is how we met. She looked in at me off the top of a tram. I'll never forget it' " (p. 66).

The elements of this miniature tale are talk, drink, and the contradictions of love, the sources for so much of Behan's art. Here, the technique is lighthearted, something like P. G. Wodehouse's Mr. Mulliner mixed with a dash of George Bernard Shaw. The columns are also a showcase for Behan's cheerful fatalism, the determination to go on in spite of misfortune, imprisonment, and the general absurdity of life. Or, as Mrs. Brennan remarks after hearing about a man who had his thumb amputated, but mercifully not his head: "When all is said and done, a body does have two tums" (p. 128).

SHORT STORIES

MUCH of Behan's free-lance work during the years 1950–1954 is either forgettable or forgotten, but two short stories written around this period are worth more than a cursory mention. In 1950 the magazine *Envoy* published a piece entitled "A Woman of No Standing" (collected in *Brendan Behan's Island*), about a man's mistress who sticks by him in his decrepitude, tending him in the Pigeon House sanatorium until his death. The story opens with a discussion between Ria and Máire, the man's estranged wife and daughter, overheard by the narrator. The two women are chiefly concerned about the disgrace of it all. After the man's death that night, the priest gives orders that the mistress is not to be allowed to attend the funeral. As for Ria and Máire, they are "charmed that he'd no mortal sin on his soul to detain him in torment for any longer than a few short years of harmonious torture in Purgatory" (p. 58). Behan is up to the Joycean trick of letting his characters hang themselves through their own words and deeds. In fact, the story resembles a cast-off piece from *Dubliners*.

The narrator attends the funeral, expecting the mistress to appear in rich mourning attire, or pull up in a fancy car "owned by a new and tolerant admirer," but she does not come (p. 58). Finally, at the grave, Máire suddenly points out a figure in the background. The narrator looks, but sees only "a poor middle-aged woman, bent in haggard prayer, dressed in the cast-off hat and coat of some flahool old one she'd be doing a day's work for" (p. 59). When the narrator says he expected something more in the line of a fur coat, " 'Fur coat, how are you,' said Ria scornfully, 'and she out scrubbing halls for me dear departed this last four years—since he took bad.' " The moment of this epiphany extends to a final scene in a pub, where the woman passes by, "her head down and a pale hunted look in her eyes" (p. 59).

The theme of twisted lives in Dublin, of guilt and recrimination akin to Stephen Dedalus' "agenbite of inwit," is further pursued in "The Confirmation Suit," which appeared in the *Standard* in 1953 and was also later collected in *Brendan Behan's Island*. Structurally, the story is more complex than "A Woman of No Standing"; its plot is derived from an incident in his brother Rory's childhood, narrated as if it had happened to Brendan himself. Reference is made to his favorite grandmother, his prying Aunt Jack, and an elderly tenant named Miss McCann, who works at her sewing machine to produce shrouds for the dead. The side plot of Aunt Jack's prying into the grandmother's life establishes the theme of well-meaning but unwanted assistance. When it comes time for Brendan to get his confirmation suit, Miss McCann kindly offers to make it if the family will provide the material. But the suit ends up looking like a Lord Fauntleroy costume, with lapels like "little wee things," buttons "the size of saucers," and Brendan ashamed to be seen in it (p. 150).

He hits upon the simple stratagem of wearing a

heavy overcoat to hide the suit in church, though the heat is so great that he all but faints. After that, he briefly puts on the suit every week to show Miss McCann. His mother calls this hypocrisy and threatens to tell the old woman about his deceit, but he never thinks she will go through with it. Only after he visits Miss McCann and sees her weeping over her sewing machine does he realize his ploy has been discovered. Miss McCann dies the next winter, and in atonement Brendan attends the funeral with his topcoat off, despite the rain: "People said I would get my end, but I went on till we reached the graveside, and I stood in my Confirmation suit drenched to the skin. I thought this was the least I could do" (p. 153). In Behan's sharp view of himself and Catholicism, the spiritual debt is paid only at the grave.

THE SCARPERER

BEHAN'S growing literary reputation helped him get more newspaper work, though he was clearly preparing himself for something greater. His last major journalistic effort was actually a novel, serialized in thirty installments for the *Irish Times* in 1953. Behan approached the editor with the idea, hoping to get cash up front, but his habits of drinking up advance money were too well known. Still, Behan was capable of discipline when he chose. He went away to the Aran Islands, where he could work in quiet, and in a few days produced enough material to guarantee an advance of ninety pounds. The serial ran under the title *The Scarperer,* after a slang term for a prison escapee, and was finally published in book form posthumously in 1964. The serial appeared under the pseudonym Emmet Street, as Behan explained, to keep the Dublin literati from associating it with that Irish lout who wrote pornography in France, Brendan Behan.

The plot of *The Scarperer* loosely revolves around a prison escape and its consequences, but it contains several twists along the way. The opening scene takes place in a pub called The Shaky Man's, where a man named Eddie Collins gets Tralee Trembles arrested for drunk and disorderly conduct, after first supplying him with the alcohol. Collins' plan, secretly discussed with his boss the scarperer, is to free an Englishman nicknamed Limey from Mountjoy Prison. Tralee is duly incarcerated, then chloroformed and put in Limey's cell

to fool the guards when Limey escapes. Once out, however, Limey is kept by the scarperer for a far grander scheme: to act as a stand-in corpse for the French criminal Pierre le Fou, who would like the police to think him dead. In the end, the criminals are caught through the accidental providence of an Irishwoman in Paris and another case of mistaken identity.

The story contains more than enough machinations to satisfy a Dickens addict, and the ingenious structure holds together well. Behan must certainly have been aware of the heavy hand luck has in the work, but the theme seems somehow in keeping with his generally cheerful fatalism. Signs of chance riddle the novel, from the opening mention of an Irish sweepstake to a lecture advertised in Paris for "WHAT MAKES THINGS HAPPEN." Though critical opinion is divided as to whether the novel adds up to much, it does indicate that Behan could handle the niceties of traditional plot and sequence, which were often weak in his later plays. Of course, the real joy in the book is Behan's knack for getting down the Irish vernacular and the characters who speak it. Pig's Eye, "a hard chaw that ganged around the quarter" (p. 70), and a patriotic prostitute named the Goofy One who sings ballads from the paddy wagon are just two Dubliners who give the novel its texture.

Given Behan's background, there is also a fair degree of inside knowledge, including the details of a Continental smuggling operation that Behan was briefly involved in. The description of Mountjoy Prison is exact, down to the prisoners' term for the hang house: "We used to call it the dance-hall" (p. 25). In fact, the prison scenes constitute both the grimmest and liveliest section in the novel, a peculiar combination of effects that became Behan's trademark. By this time, he was a seasoned writer, looking around for an apt vehicle for his talents. With his flair for the dramatic, the stage seemed a natural extension of his own personality.

RADIO PLAYS

RADIO Éireann had already commissioned two playlets from him in 1952: *Moving Out* and *A Garden Party,* both collected in *The Complete Plays.* In scope, these radio plays resemble anecdotes more than fully developed drama, but they do display Behan's knack for quiddities of character, and they are also as close to family sketches as Behan ever ventured. *Moving Out* depicts the Hannigan family's move from the slums of Dublin to a new development in Ardee Road. The incident is drawn from the Behans' own shift from Russell Street to Crumlin. Because the husband, Jim, wants to stay put—insisting "I'm not going out to the Bog of Allen for a bath" (p. 322)—the family decamps without telling him, and poor Jim must find his way to the new development in the dark. When Jim finally locates the place, he finds that his old neighbors have moved along with him.

A Garden Party portrays the Hannigan family once they have settled in at their new address, but, as with *Moving Out,* the plot also rests on a joke. When Chris, the wife, wants Jim to dig up the garden for planting, Jim naturally protests against the extra work. (There may be an additional joke here: the Irish nationalist who will not plant on his own soil.) His neighbor Gibbons is being similarly nagged. But when Gibbons reads in the newspaper of a local robbery, he thinks up an ingenious dodge. Disguising himself over the telephone as an informant, he convinces the police that the swag is buried in the yard outside his house. When the police come to search the area, he gets all the dirt in his garden turned up, along with Jim's.

The most enjoyable figures in both plays are the secondary characters, the Dublin eccentrics that Behan could mimic flawlessly. One speech in particular, Mrs. Carmody's complaint in *Moving Out,* has the ring of a minor classic:

Says I, says I, it's a while now since we had a pig's cheek and himself was always partial to a bit, especially the ear, but there's pig's cheeks and pig's cheeks in it. The one old Daly handed me was the most ugly looking object you ever put an eye to. It was after being shoved up again the side of a barrel by all the other cheeks and was all twisted. A class of cock-eyed, ma'am, if you follow my meaning. "God bless us and save us," says I in my own mind, "if I put that up to him with the bit of cabbage, and that twisty look in his eye, when he goes to put a knife in it, he'll throw me out." So I says to old Daly, says I, "God bless us and save us, Mr Daly," says I, "but that's a very peculiar looking pig's cheek." And says he, "What do you want for two shillings," says he. "Mee-hawl, Mac Lillimore?" The impudent ould dog. Says he, "Hold on a minute, and I'll see if I can get you one that died with a smile."

(p. 325)

If nothing else, the radio plays showed once again Behan's main strength, to dazzle with language. But the limitations of theme and plot kept Behan a local name, a fact he had to work against. By 1954, he had completed work on a full-scale drama that would bring him international fame.

THE QUARE FELLOW

The Quare Fellow had its genesis as early as 1946, with an early draft of the first act completed near the end of Behan's incarceration. The main events of the play—the anticipated hanging of a murderer and the prisoners' response—are loosely based on the lives of two prisoners at Mountjoy, one of whom was eventually saved from the rope after being judged insane. Originally written in Gaelic as a one-act radio play, the play was entitled "Casadh Súgáin Eile" (The Twisting of Another Rope, after Douglas Hyde's *The Twisting of the Rope* [1901], the first Gaelic drama on the Irish stage). When Radio Éireann turned it down, Behan expanded it, reworked it, and sent the finished English version to the Abbey Theatre in early 1954. The directors liked the play but found it too long and asked Behan to shorten it. Behan's response this time was to take the play elsewhere. After another rejection from Dublin's Gate Theatre, it was recommended to Alan Simpson of the Pike Theatre, who took it at once.

Not that the play did not need some judicious pruning and alteration: Carolyn Swift, Simpson's partner at the Pike, had to cut some passages, transfer others, and ask Behan to rewrite certain parts. Simpson suggested the play be retitled *The Quare Fellow,* after the term used by the prisoners for the condemned man. Thus began Behan's collaboration with his directors, a process that would continue under Joan Littlewood and her Theatre Workshop. Literary gifts are rarely all-encompassing, and Behan's great strength lay in his depiction of character and the sheer power of his words, not in plot or organization. Even after suitable alteration, the play's action was oddly anticlimactic, yet somehow the suppressed mood is entirely apt. It supports an existentialist closeness to death while leaving room for the human drama that occupies center stage. The power of the play also derives from its focus on authority and its effects, not just on those ruled by it, but on the rulers, as well.

From the opening scene, the play is concerned with both the repressed and the irrepressible. Despite the prison sign reading "SILENCE," the play starts with a song, and a rather bawdy one, at that: "And that old triangle / Went jingle jangle, / Along the banks of the Royal Canal" refers not only to the metal triangle rung by the prison guard, but also to the sexual urgings of the prisoners. One prisoner's comment about "two for a haircut and a shave" refers to the two men condemned to die (*Complete Plays,* p. 40). These double references continue throughout the play; they are a way of enlivening the dull facts of prison and turning even the horror of death into a semblance of comedy. The prevailing philosophy is best expressed by Dunlavin, an old lag who has somehow kept his sense of self-worth in prison. When one of the condemned men learns that his sentence has been commuted to "life," Dunlavin replies, "And a bloody sight better than death any day of the week" (p. 51). There is an affirmation, a brio, in Behan's spokesmen that raises them above fatalist gloom.

Yet the world of lags and screws is not by any stretch of the imagination a cheery place. The scope of the prisoners is circumscribed, their desires reduced to the creature comforts of food, alcohol, and tobacco, all three in insufficient amounts. Still, as in Behan's later *Borstal Boy,* if deprivation has dulled the body, it has sharpened the senses and the imagination. When Dunlavin talks with the neighboring prisoner, they mention the consolation given by the Bible—whose thin pages make an excellent rolling paper to smoke the coir mattress stuffing in their cells. Necessity forces invention: perhaps for this reason, the oppressed in the play seem livelier than their oppressors.

If the play has a hero, it is Warder Regan, a clear-sighted individual who sees the moral horror in state executions. He occupies a middle ground between the lags and the screws, knowing the depravity of the prisoners yet never losing sight of their essential humanity. What Holy Healey, the hypocritical Department of Justice head terms "a sad duty," Regan calls "neck-breaking and throttling" (p. 67). The open secret within the prison is that hanging often fails to kill the victim, who must squirm at the end of the rope until he chokes. The hangman himself makes a point of getting so drunk before an execution that he has to be helped out of

the pub by his teetotal assistant Jenkinson. Later, in a bitter speech to the chief warder, Regan claims they might as well make a show of the job and give the public its money's worth rather than cloaking it all in secrecy. For this frankness, he may well lose his job.

Because the prison is a stunted but real reflection of the outer world, the same prejudices tend to hold. Even in jail, religion divides the prisoners, though, as Prisoner A comments, "I never saw religion do anything but back up the screws" (p. 99). Later, Jenkinson's hymn to the quare fellow (who never appears onstage) is undercut by the hangman's calculating the length of rope for the drop. The class system also operates in jail, with a high-toned English murderer having his sentence commuted to life imprisonment, while a bogman who butchered his brother becomes the quare fellow. As for the cause of Irish nationalism, Behan is surprisingly harsh for an ex-I.R.A. man: "The Free State didn't change anything more than the badge on the warders' caps" (p. 59).

At times, the irony is crippling. The condemned man whose sentence has just been commuted to life tries to commit suicide in his cell. The prisoners seem to grieve over the quare fellow's hanging but afterwards fight over his letters, which can be sold to the newspapers. The headstone for the quare fellow is marked only with a number, and an incorrect one at that, since 7's are easier to chisel than 9's. Even Regan, when asked by Healy why he stays in the service, remarks, "It's a soft job, sir, between hangings" (p. 71). Still, the bleakness achieves a certain poetry of its own. In a particularly Beckettian sequence, several prisoners describe what to expect in the Bog, where lifers serve out their sentences:

YOUNG PRISONER 1: Not with you going to the Bog to start life in a couple of days, where you won't see a woman.
YOUNG PRISONER 2: A child.
YOUNG PRISONER 1: A dog.
YOUNG PRISONER 2: A fire.

(p. 58)

Behan diverges from Beckett in the significance of these signs of life. For Beckett, they are poignant but ultimately pointless. For Behan, more practical and materialist, they represent what makes life worth living. At the end of the play, a prisoner once again takes up the tune of the old triangle, and the play ends in song.

The Quare Fellow had its opening night in Dublin at the Pike Theatre on 19 November 1954 to almost entirely favorable reviews. Behan suddenly found himself compared with Sean O'Casey and J. M. Synge; his Dublin reputation was made. The play ran for six months, but because of the large cast of actors to pay and the small seating capacity of the Pike, the production actually lost money each week. Then, in January 1956, Behan was approached by Joan Littlewood of the Theatre Royal about the possibility of a London production. Though Behan had earlier sold the London rights to Simpson, he now sold them again to Littlewood, a maneuver he was to repeat with sections of *Borstal Boy.* Still, if Behan thought he was selling the same play, Littlewood had her own ideas. Undoubtedly, Littlewood made both *The Quare Fellow* and *The Hostage* (1958) financial successes, but her alterations of the plays—popularizations, some critics have charged—exceeded the legitimate bounds of directorial control.

The modus operandi of Littlewood's avant-garde Theatre Workshop was to establish total communication between the actors and the audience, often subordinating major elements of the play to this task. At the first rehearsals of *The Quare Fellow,* for instance, she told her actors simply to mill around up on the gray roof of the theater, in order to instill in them a sense of a prisonlike atmosphere. Improvisation was encouraged. Littlewood also streamlined some of the looser characterization in the play, reassigning certain speeches and fusing two of the warders' roles into one.

The tremendous success of the Theatre Royal production, which was eventually transferred to the Comedy Theatre in the West End by the Abbey Company, can be attributed to several factors, not the least of which was the social climate at the time. British theater had been fairly tepid during the previous decade, and the stage was set for the advent of the "angry young men." John Osborne's recent *Look Back in Anger* (1956) had demonstrated how ready the public was, not for moral outrage, but for outrage at conventional morality. Behan's focus on prison life also fed the public's aroused interest in a formerly ignored segment of the population. The critic Kenneth Tynan, responsible for launching many playwrights' careers, was particularly taken with the play's language: "It is Ireland's

sacred duty to send over every few years a playwright who will save the English theatre from inarticulate dumbness" (quoted in O'Connor, p. 183).

That Behan was practically a born rebel did not hurt either. He was, as he well knew, made to play the part. Shortly after *The Quare Fellow* opened in London, Behan gave his famous drunken interview with Malcolm Muggeridge on the BBC program *Panorama.* That anyone, even an upstart Irish playwright, would appear inebriated in such a situation, caused exactly the sensational uproar that might have been expected. From then on, Behan was a notorious character to the press, his most minor activities recorded as news. Echoing Wilde in "Let's Go to Town," one of his *Irish Press* columns (collected in *Hold Your Hour and Have Another*), he wrote: "Good or bad, it's better to be criticized than ignored" (p. 18).

BORSTAL BOY

IN early 1955, Behan had married the Irish painter Beatrice ffrench Salkeld, and it was her steadying influence that now helped him cope with his newfound publicity. Behan's problem was with excess: too much success went to his head, and too much money was apt to be spent all on drink. After one prolonged bender landed him in the hospital, he discovered that he was a borderline diabetic, a condition to which he ascribed his great thirst and sudden irascibility. It also meant that unrestrained drinking could result in a coma. But during this period Behan had his writing to occupy him. In the summer of 1957, the British publisher Hutchinson had given him a substantial advance for the manuscript of *Borstal Boy,* and now, despite periodic binges, he was able to keep himself to a fairly regular work schedule as he moved toward the completion of the book.

He was also busying himself with more dramatic work. In the spring of 1957, the BBC Home Service broadcast *The Big House,* a farcical allegory of the current state of Ireland. (This work was eventually adapted for the stage and first performed on a bill with *Moving Out* and *A Garden Party* at the Pike Theatre in Dublin on 6 May 1958. This version is collected in *The Complete Plays.*) The plot loosely revolves around the ancestral house Tonesollock, which mutters like a Graeco-Gaelic chorus. The house is a stand-in for Ireland, deserted by the owners Ananias and Boadicea Baldcock when the Republican cause and its explosions get too close for comfort. Ensconced in a London suburb, the Baldcocks represent Ireland's much-hated absentee landlords. Meanwhile, a Dublin swindler named Chuckles Genockey begins to sell off parts of the house, beginning with the lead from the roof. His partner is Angel, an Englishman. Respectively, the two represent down-and-out Ireland and rapacious English commercialism. Along the way are various other voices of Ireland, including Green Eyes, a scrap dealer and double symbol for Ireland and envy; Dionysius O'Looney, the butler who sells out the Baldcocks; and Granny Grunt and Granny Growl, two patriots who would not say no to a drink.

Behan, of course, is playing Shaw's game of showing what both the British and the Irish have done to Ireland. If the British have looted Ireland, many Irish have been willing accomplices. If Ireland is war torn, it is partly from internecine strife over politics, class, and religion. Significantly, O'Looney talks of a Protestant minister who sleeps in the house on occasion. Baldcock's given name, Ananias, may also refer to the man in Acts 5 of the New Testament who sells his property but withholds the church's due share. Unfortunately, the comic elements in the play soon get out of hand, and much of the structure dissolves in cheap laughter. The gutted house gets the final comment, echoing its lines in the beginning, still claiming its many possessions and its long endurance, but now comparing its sheeps and bullocks to its citizens. Clearly, Behan the playwright had distanced himself somewhat from Behan the I.R.A. man. As he notes later in *Confessions of an Irish Rebel,* "The first duty of a writer is to let his fatherland down" (p. 87). This is not in the least to say that Behan did not care for Ireland, simply that he did not care for what was being done to it on all sides. His last major play, *An Giall,* later translated as *The Hostage,* takes a far more searching look at those sides, as well as at the victims in the middle.

AN GIALL *AND* THE HOSTAGE

In the spring of 1957, Gael Linn, a society for the promulgation of Irish language and culture, asked Behan to write a play in Gaelic. Though he was working on *Borstal Boy* at the time, he accepted the commission and then spent the next year taking sporadic swipes at the playscript. He eventually claimed to have batted out the play in twelve days, but this refers more to the final revisions produced frantically as the performance date drew near. As with *The Quare Fellow,* the play took as its main incident a bit of history close to home, in this case a British Tommy captured by the I.R.A. during a 1955 raid in County Down. Though the soldier was eventually released unharmed, as the story runs in *Brendan Behan's Island,* "The incident moved me and remained in my mind because I thought it was tragic for young fellows from England to be stuck in Northern Ireland" (p. 14). Conflating the event with another incident, a fatal ambush of Tommies during the War of Independence, Behan had the materials for a tragedy on the futility of war.

The plot of *An Giall* contains a love story within a war tale, forming a vexed tragicomedy that pits ideals against personal relations. The entire action of the play takes place in the bedroom of an old tenement house in Dublin. Patrick, an old patriot who has lost a leg to the cause, presides over the house and bickers with his wife, Kate. The house itself, nicknamed The Hole, is now half I.R.A. barracks and half whorehouse, a sign of general decay. Though Patrick tends to reminisce about the old glory days at the drop of a line, he realizes that "the Irish Volunteers and the War of Independence are as dead as—as dead as the Charleston" (Wall trans., p. 30). The owner of the house, Monsúr, with the zeal of an Englishman turned pro-Irish, remains a super-patriot. After the I.R.A. capture a British soldier in retaliation for the planned execution of an I.R.A. boy in the dock, it is Monsúr's idea to hide the hostage in the house.

As befits the theme of a cause gone sour, talk overrides action in the first act. Patrick's annoyance, aired frequently, is that of an old veteran viewing the new recruits, and little pleases him. He sees corruption in the ranks: when Monsúr talks of a patriot held in Mountjoy Prison, Patrick knows it is for petty thievery and not for the cause. On the other hand, when an I.R.A. man comes in wearing a Fainne and a Pioneer pin (symbols attesting to Irish-speaking ability and temperance), Patrick dresses him down for what he sees as naive purity. Even Kate is suspect: when he asks where Kate was during the 1916 uprising and she replies that she was not born then, he cries, "Excuses! . . . They've enough gab out of them, more than enough boasting, forty years after the real fighting" (p. 32). But Patrick does a fair amount of boasting himself, his war stories changing to suit convenience.

The real issue, how the struggle defeats both sides, gradually emerges through the women characters. After Patrick describes incessantly how he lost his leg in the war, Kate replies with an old but pointed joke: "If that is the sort you call a Civil War, I wouldn't like to see an uncivil war" (p. 33). Teresa, the girl who works in the house and who will eventually care for the hostage, has an equally clear-eyed view of the turmoil. After Monsúr claims how lucky the young man in jail is, awaiting the gallows for the cause, Teresa has a simple rejoinder: "Monsúr is stupid" (p. 47). The abstract cause matters far less than the individuals who support it. As the first act closes, the I.R.A. men bring in the British hostage, precisely the flesh and blood ignored on both sides.

The growing romance between Teresa and the hostage, named Leslie, occupies the second act. Appropriately, both are the same age, eighteen; symbolically, both are orphans born during wartime, victims of history. Leslie is far cruder about this than Teresa, upsetting her by joking, "We're nothing but a pair of bastards" (p. 59). On the other hand, Teresa knows all about Ireland's misery with Britain, whereas Leslie asks, with no intentional irony, "Why, were some people doing something to Ireland?" (p. 56). As the two become more involved with each other, they kiss, and Leslie asks for a photograph of her. She gives him one, along with a medal of the Virgin Mary, though he is Protestant. The tact and delicacy with which Behan handles the growing relationship is perhaps his most impressive feat in the play: no undue sentiment, only a series of quiet lines that shows the pair's cultural divide as well as their mutual attraction. The tension derives from Leslie's situation: held as a hostage against the execution of the I.R.A. boy in jail, he is used as barter. When the radio announces that the death penalty will go ahead as planned, Teresa throws her arms around Leslie just as Patrick enters the room, and the act closes on that note.

The final act represents a series of denials. Patrick assures Leslie that the hostage threat is only a bluff, that he will be set free regardless, but Leslie will not be comforted. He alternates between mak-

ing plans with Teresa and thinking about his last request. The end comes abruptly and accidentally when gunfire signals that the house is being stormed by the police. The I.R.A. men rush into the room to hide Leslie, tying and gagging him and shoving him inside an old clothespress. By the time the detectives leave, though, it is too late: Leslie has suffocated to death. As the assembled men rationalize that it was all in a good cause, Teresa simply repeats the unassailable truth, that Leslie is dead and that they are responsible. All that is left is to mourn, and the drums and pipes played for the I.R.A. boy at the start of the play now sound for Leslie.

An Giall opened on Joyce's Bloomsday, 16 June, of 1958, in Damer Hall, Dublin. It enjoyed generally favorable reviews, and after a few months Littlewood offered to produce it in Stratford if Behan would work up an English translation. He worked on it during a stay in Sweden, at which time he also re-read the final proofs of *Borstal Boy.* He was more successful with the second job than the first. When he arrived back in England, he had made little progress on the translation, retitled *The Hostage,* though the opening was slated for October. The final product, though unquestionably a dramatic and financial success, was certainly an unfaithful translation of the original. Much has been written about the process that changed *An Giall* into *The Hostage.* The most accurate explanation is that it was a collaborative effort, written under great pressure by the playwright and his director and performed by a cast that freely interpreted the resulting script.

Certain changes in the playscript are more tangible than others. There are, for example, five more characters in *The Hostage* (really seven added and two deleted or merged), and the play itself is somewhat longer. As most critics note, the extra characters add little to the plot or theme but are there mostly for comic relief: Rio Rita, the homosexual sailor, and Princess Grace, his black boyfriend; Mr. Mulleady, a down-at-the-heels civil servant in pursuit of the "sociable worker" Miss Gilchrist; a prostitute or two, and a Russian sailor who appears as a client of the establishment.

Despite some grim jokes, *An Giall* is almost frighteningly calm, despite an anticipatory dread of death akin to that in *The Quare Fellow.* *The Hostage,* on the other hand, deals with death by covering it over in laughter, sex, and drunkenness. Where *An Giall* opens with funeral music, *The Hostage* has a wild Irish jig in progress, and the occupants of the establishment drink stout instead of tea. Patrick's wife, Kate, has been changed to his consort, Meg, with more idealistic views, and Monsúr is now Monsewer, whose glorification of the cause is now based on the delusion that he is still of commander rank. In the process, the antinationalistic lines have lost much of their force, their satiric edge blunted in the general send-up of everything from Irish ballads to the royal family. It is Brendan Behan as a lesser Bertolt Brecht.

Amid the sifting of old jokes, there are still some pointed lines in *The Hostage:* when the I.R.A. officer claims he would never betray the cause, Pat observes sourly, "You've never been in prison for the cause" (*Complete Plays,* p. 178). The worst part, as Pat notes, is "the other Irish patriots in along with you" (p. 179). Somewhat later is a reference to the author Brendan Behan, whom Leslie regards as too anti-British and the officer claims is too anti-Irish. But in general the condemnations are far more broadside: Meg and Pat agree that pound notes make the best religion and politics in the world, and Mulleady sings, "There is no one, no one, loves you like yourself" (p. 183). With the narcissistic undercurrent throughout the play, the romance between Leslie and Teresa is more a lustful adventure, including a bed scene in the second act. At the end of the play, Leslie still dies, but this time he is shot in the general confusion of police and I.R.A. men running about. Of course, in the music-hall tradition nothing is for keeps, and after the body is covered Leslie gets up to sing: "Oh death, where is thy sting-a-ling-a-ling! / Or grave thy victory" (p. 237). Death and warring factionalism have been beaten back by general merriment and song.

The Hostage premiered on 14 October 1958, at the Theatre Royal in Stratford and was an immediate success with the British critics. In 1959, it was selected to be the United Kingdom entry for the Théâtre des Nations Festival in Paris and was eventually named best play of the French season in 1962. In the ensuing years, it acquired an international reputation, despite some critics who balked at the play's wholesale endorsement of "anything goes." Behan was not immune to the force of this criticism, once reviling Littlewood and her adaptation during the first run of the play. Still, if *The Hostage* is a bastardization, Behan could accept the

charge, even embrace it. As he wrote in *Brendan Behan's Island:*

I've always thought T. S. Eliot wasn't far wrong when he said that the main problem of the dramatist today was to keep his audience amused; and that while they were laughing their heads off, you could be up to any bloody thing behind their backs; and it was what you were doing behind their bloody backs that made your play great.

(p. 17)

Behan, at least, had had his fling with greatness. The rest of his career was more the aftermath.

RICHARD'S CORK LEG

WITH *The Hostage* still in its first month, *Borstal Boy* was finally published. Critics on both sides of the Atlantic gave it warm praise, and the public embraced the image of a brawling Irishman made good, an image Behan always felt he had to live up to. When *The Quare Fellow* was performed in New York's Circle in the Square Theater (November 1958), the reaction was more muted than it had been in England, but by this time Behan the public figure was beginning to bulk larger than Behan the writer. When *Borstal Boy* was banned in Ireland, it merely added to the aura of the rebel artist.

For Behan, sustained success meant more public appearances and more drinking. Having found that his drunken performances were good for publicity, he began making a habit of them. In addition, his literary reputation extended so far that he found it difficult to write, especially when there was so little necessity to do so. He no longer had to produce polished work when interviews and engagements were offered daily. At base, Behan was an artist who wrote for money, and when talking was able to produce the same results—a money-paying audience—he switched over to that mode.

Behan's great success as a raconteur was the rationale for the method of his remaining works, the words spoken into a dictaphone and later edited. His first attempt at this method of composition resulted in one act of a play in Gaelic, "La Bréagh San Réilg" (A Fine Day in the Graveyard), but soon Behan began translating it in the hopes of an English production. In the process, the play acquired a new title, *Richard's Cork Leg*. The name derives from a rueful reflection by Joyce on his rejected play *Exiles:* that the play would have had a better chance if he had given the main character Richard a cork leg. If nothing else, Behan's play does show the effect of this tongue-in-cheek advice: *Richard's Cork Leg* includes everything from bawds to a black named Bonny Prince Charlie, with a lot of literal graveyard humor, since the first act takes place in a cemetery. Behan took some time over the first partial draft, and in fact visited Forest Lawn cemetery for further material when he was in California in 1961.

Unfortunately, Littlewood was disappointed in the piece, and when an indignant Behan took the Irish version to Gael Linn, they also turned it down. It is not too hard to see why: the play seems more a pretext for a motley collection of jokes than a unified dramatic statement. Granted that some critics had made precisely this accusation against *The Hostage,* the earlier play had at least a structure from which to depart, whereas the new work had little coherence to begin with.

The plot loosely follows two bawds, Maria Concepta and Rose of Lima, plying their business in the graveyard after being chased away from their usual haunts. There, they meet the main character Cronin, an unemployed Dubliner who hangs around with the Hero Hogan, an I.R.A. type who fought in the Spanish Civil War on the Republican side. Hogan is interested in breaking up a meeting of Blueshirts, or Irish fascists who fought for Franco; Cronin is interested in airing his own views. Eventually, a young woman named Deirdre Mallarkey comes along to scatter the ashes of her uncle, and Cronin attempts to seduce her. Somewhere along the way, Bonny Prince Charlie, a black man who claims to be American but who eventually reveals himself to be British, makes several comic entrances and exits. He also demonstrates his plan to bring the cemetery up to date with mechanically animated corpses and recorded hymns. Behan's growing preoccupation with death is thus rendered comically in a vision that presages Evelyn Waugh's *The Loved One* (1948). (The play's reference to "Blessed Evelyn Waugh," on the other hand, is there simply because Behan found that it always got a laugh.) Eventually, the scene shifts to the home of Deirdre's mother, Mrs. Mallarkey, where

Hogan shoots at a Blueshirt and Cronin gets shot by a policeman in the confusion. As in the end of *The Hostage,* all the characters end up singing, including the recently deceased Cronin.

If the play has a theme, it follows Cronin's views, which are remarkably similar to Behan's own. Disillusioned over politics and religion, he detests the Communists but appreciates their value as an irritant: "All the big-bellied bastards that I hate, hate the Reds" (*Complete Plays,* p. 252). The long list of organizations that follows shows clearly that Cronin has come to suspect causes of all kinds. On the other hand, he still pities the individual, claiming, "I stand by the damned anywhere" (p. 276). This staunch support of outsiders is not new in Behan, but the emphasis on intellectuals and creative types is. Cronin is currently unemployed, Behan's metaphor for the state of the artist, and he is trying to come to terms with a job that few regard as a profession. In a particularly bitter passage, with more than a hint of autobiography, Behan has Cronin declaim:

The English and Americans dislike only *some* Irish—the same Irish that the Irish themselves detest, Irish writers—the ones that *think.* . . . They give me beer, because I can say things that I remember from my thoughts—not everything, because, by Jesus, they'd crucify you, and you have to remember that when you're drunk, but some things, enough to flatter them.

(p. 280)

But such passages are few and vitiated by the surrounding sideshow, precisely the sort of crowd-pleasing elements Cronin rails against. In the end, the play lacks sufficient thrust and direction.

Richard's Cork Leg was never completed, though in March 1972 Alan Simpson put on a posthumous production by piecing together Behan's drafts and writing some additional material himself. The play premiered at the Peacock Theatre in Dublin, moved to the Opera House in Cork, and also had a run at the Royal Court Theatre in London. The play was Behan's last sustained writing, apart from his dictation books and some thirty pages of a novel entitled "the catacombs." The novel was to be about the same bohemian Dublin crowd of J. P. Donleavy's *The Ginger Man* (1955), but Behan never got any further than about thirty pages, which remain unpublished.

BRENDAN BEHAN

DICTATED BOOKS

IF regular writing had turned into a dead end, Behan could still crank out the books he was under contract to produce. The first of these, *Brendan Behan's Island*, was commissioned by Hutchinson and was to be a book about Ireland, with illustrations by Paul Hogarth. It was completed with the assistance of a publishing executive at Hutchinson, Rae Jeffs, who acted as both amanuensis and caretaker for Behan during the last stormy years of his life.

Brendan Behan's Island was published in 1962, and while Behan's rambles about Ireland make for amusing enough reading, the book is a patchwork job. Here are Behan's anecdotes of Dublin and its inhabitants, his love of the Blasket Islands and his hatred of the Anglo-Irish, and some vintage witticisms. Interspersed throughout the book are reprinted earlier pieces: "A Woman of No Standing," "The Confirmation Suit," "The Big House," and various poems. The pacing and tone are meant to mimic Behan holding forth in a pub, but the performance is hard to sustain, and the speaker, perhaps having drained a few, seems a bit drained himself. Every so often, Behan's inimitable inflection asserts itself—as in "The English, God love them, expect every language to be like their own" (p. 71)—but mostly what the reader gets are echoes.

As Behan's drinking episodes grew worse, he occasionally ended up in the hospital. Undoubtedly, he knew that he was drinking himself to death but found it almost impossible to stop. Despite his status as a public figure, he always had doubts about himself, and alcohol buoyed his self-confidence. For a nine-month period of the year 1960–1961, he managed to avoid drink almost altogether—he arrived for a visit to New York with a milk bottle in his hand—but back in Ireland his resolve broke down. In an attempt to alter his life by changing his surroundings, he eventually fled back to New York. There, at the Chelsea Hotel, he managed to dictate another book, *Confessions of an Irish Rebel*. In a sense, *Confessions of an Irish Rebel* is a sequel to *Borstal Boy*, since it begins where the earlier book ends, with Behan's leaving prison in 1946. In this volume are Behan's accounts of the police shooting in 1942, his mission to free Dick Timmons from jail, and other exploits. Most of the tales are livelier than a strict accuracy would permit, and most are punctuated with by-then repetitious pronouncements on life. The book ends with an account of his marriage to Beatrice, a touching tribute to the woman who showed extraordinary patience with him.

His last book, *Brendan Behan's New York* (1964), was dictated back in Dublin during his last months and published shortly after his death. The idea for the book was sound enough, a celebration of all that appealed to Behan in New York: the bustling crowds, the jazzy atmosphere, the characters in the bars, and the sheer inexhaustibility of the place. By this time, however, the quick patter that had enthralled audiences had degenerated into a rambling monologue, with one digression after another. The book contains a lot of celebrity counting and spliced-together anecdotes, all carried by a self-important air that is meant to sound breezy. Perhaps the most telling sentence occurs near the end, where he comments, "I will have forgotten this book long before you have paid your money for it, I can assure you" (p. 115). It indicates that Behan himself had grown tired of what he was doing.

His final days were spent in and out of Dublin bars, numbing his hurt pride and fear of death with alcohol, keeping up an interminable conversation in order to prevent being cut off. Near the end, his supporters dwindled to a small cadre of his old I.R.A. friends, who treated him as a comrade rather than a failed celebrity. Behan, realizing how far he had fallen from his early days pledged to the cause, requested a full military funeral. After a final series of alcoholic seizures, he ended up in Dublin's Meath Hospital, where he died on 20 March 1964. Two days later, an eight-man I.R.A. Guard of Honor saw the coffin to its resting place in Glasnevin cemetery, as the crowds watched along the streets. It was, as Behan might have quipped, the return of a native son to the old sod.

In the years since Behan's death, his reputation has suffered the slow declivity of time. Literary work on Behan falls roughly into two camps: the critical analyses of his writing and the personal reminiscences, with the second group bulking far larger than the first. Though his works continue to be read and performed, the vital presence of Behan himself is missing. Borstal boy, renegade Catholic, I.R.A. man, pub raconteur, local genius, and general roustabout, Behan once wrote, "If I am anything at all, it is a man of letters" (*Confessions of an Irish Rebel,* p. 209). The Irish writer Flann O'Brien, however, came nearer the truth in a tribute written just after Behan's death, excerpted in Ulick O'Connor's *Brendan:* "He is in fact much more a player than a playwright, or, to use a Dublin saying, 'He was as good as a play' " (p. 318). At times he was far better.

SELECTED BIBLIOGRAPHY

I. Bibliography. Peter René Gerdes, ed., *The Major Works of Brendan Behan,* European University Papers Series 24, vol. 10 (Frankfurt, 1973), provides detailed analyses of the major works, also refers to every traceable piece of Behan's writing, including uncollected material and juvenilia.

II. Collected Works. *The Complete Plays,* A. Simpson, ed. (New York, 1978), an omnibus volume, providing the definitive versions of all the plays that survive, including Behan's radio plays and Simpson's completion of *Richard's Cork Leg; Poems and Stories* (Dublin, 1978).

III. Separate Works. *The Quare Fellow* (London, 1956; New York, 1957), play; *The Hostage* (London, 1958; New York, 1959), play; *Borstal Boy* (London, 1958; New York, 1959), autobiographical novel; *Brendan Behan's Island: An Irish Sketch-book,* with drawings by P. Hogarth (London, 1962; New York, 1962), anecdotes, stories and other works, includes *The Big House; Hold Your Hour and Have Another* (London, 1963; Boston, 1964), articles; *Brendan Behan's New York,* with drawings by P. Hogarth (New York, 1964), anecdotes and stories; *The Scarperer* (New York, 1964), novel; *Confessions of an Irish Rebel* (London, 1965; New York, 1965), memoirs; *Richard's Cork Leg,* A. Simpson, ed. (London, 1973; New York, 1974); *Poems and a Play in Irish* (in Gaelic), P. N. Dhorchaí, ed. (Dublin, 1981), includes the play *An Giall; An Giall / The Hostage,* R. Wall, ed. and trans. (Washington, D. C., 1987), plays.

IV. Letters and Interviews. S. McCann, ed., *The World of Brendan Behan* (New York, 1966); E. H. Mikhail, ed. *Brendan Behan: Interviews and Recollections,* 2 vols., continuously paginated (Totawa, New Jersey, 1982); E. H. Mikhail. "The Letters of Brendan Behan," in Heinz Kosok, ed., *Studies in Anglo-Irish Literature* (Bonn, 1982).

V. Biographical and Critical Studies. A. Simpson, *Beckett and Behan and a Theatre in Dublin* (London, 1962); M. Muggeridge, "Brendan Behan at Lime Grove," in *New Statesman* (27 March 1964); R. Jeffs, *Brendan Behan: Man and Showman* (London, 1966); D. Behan, *My Brother Brendan* (New York, 1966); T. E. Boyle, *Brendan Behan* (New York, 1969); A. Burgess, "The Writer as Drunk," in his *Urgent Copy: Literary Studies* (New York, 1969); U. O'Connor, *Brendan* (Englewood Cliffs, N.J., 1970); R. J. Porter, *Brendan Behan* (New York, 1973); B. Behan, *My Life With Brendan,* with D. Hickey and G. Smith (London, 1973); R. Wall, *"An Giall* and *The Hostage* Compared," in *Modern Drama,* 28 (1975); C. Kearney, *The Writings of Brendan Behan* (New York, 1977); E. H. Mikhail, ed., *The Art of Brendan Behan* (New York, 1979); P. Arthurs, *With Brendan Behan* (New York, 1981); P. C. Hogan, "Class Heroism in *The Quare Fellow,"* in *Études Irlandaises,* (December 1983); P. Bordinat, "Tragedy through Comedy in Plays by Brendan Behan and Brian Friel," in *West Virginia University Philological Papers,* 29 (1983); R. Brown, *"Borstal Boy:* Structure and Meaning," in *Colby Library Quarterly,* 21 (December 1985); B. Cardullo, *"The Hostage Reconsidered,"* in *Éire-Ireland: A Journal of Irish Studies,* 20 (Summer 1985); W. Witoszek, "The Funeral Comedy of Brendan Behan," in *Études Irlandaises,* 11 (December 1986); W. Huber, "Autobiography and Stereotypy: Some Remarks on Brendan Behan's *Borstal Boy,"* in W. Zach and H. Kosok, eds., *National Images and Stereotypes,* vol. 3 of *Literary Interrelations: Ireland, England and the World* (Reutlingen, Germany, 1987); Desmond Maxwell, "Brendan Behan's Theatre," in M. Sekine, ed., *Irish Writers and the Theatre* (Gerrards Cross, England, 1986; Totawa, N.J., 1987).

ELIZABETH BOWEN
(1899–1973)

Siobhán Kilfeather

ELIZABETH BOWEN, in her long and productive career as a writer, was devoted to a meticulous examination of how a literature of manners might respond to the catastrophic violence and radical social change of the twentieth century. The novel of manners has always, of course, been concerned with ideals and behavior under stress; in eighteenth- and nineteenth-century fiction, manners function as a structure for examining the desires, hostilities, and fears that are indirectly expressed in human relations. A literature of manners deals with the texture of social relations and with the types of subjectivity created through the habits and customs of indirect expression. The primary site of such an examination is the home. How do people desire and fear one another? How do people live together as families and as friends?

The novel of manners provides a particularly suitable forum in which to examine interpretations of female experience. Jane Austen described her subject as "three or four families in a country village"; many readers, however, have discerned the various pressures social change, changes in the structure of the family, the slave trade, and foreign wars bring to bear upon the lives of her characters in indirect ways. Bowen writes about the ways in which quotidian domestic life in Ireland and Britain is shattered by war, by the breakup of the British empire, by changes in popular understandings of sexuality, and, above all, by changes in the modern understanding of time. She examines the ways in which conventions of indirection in speech and manners, by Austen and Henry James in their use of conventions represented in the free indirect discourse, are transformed by direct violence. These themes converge in Bowen's best-known work, *The Heat of the Day* (1949), a novel about World War II, and in the stories collected under the title *The Demon Lover* (1945, published the next year in the United States as *Ivy Gripped the Steps*). An obsession with the past and with the violence of change characterizes her most successful writing: *The Last September* (1929), "The Disinherited" (1934), *The House in Paris* (1935), *The Death of the Heart* (1938), "Ivy Gripped the Steps" (1941), "Sunday Afternoon" (1941), "Mysterious Kôr," (1944), *The Heat of the Day, A World of Love* (1955), and *The Little Girls* (1964).

Bowen was born into a class and a community that were at once marks of privilege and conditions for stress. Her parents were upper-middle-class Irish Protestants who traced their families' settlement in Ireland to the seventeenth century. Bowen described herself and her community as Anglo-Irish; her community had a history of supporting British government in Ireland and identifying with British interests abroad. She grew up in a period when a national independence movement was developing in Ireland.

LIFE

ELIZABETH Dorothea Cole Bowen was the only child of Florence Colley Bowen, whose family came from Clontarf, near Dublin, and of Henry Bowen, a barrister who practiced in Dublin and owned an estate with an eighteenth-century country house at Bowen's Court, County Cork. The Colleys were a stable, respectable, sociable, well-connected family. The Bowens were inclined to be nervous and high-strung. Elizabeth was born on 7 June 1899, at 15 Herbert Place, Dublin, her parents' town house. Her early childhood was divided between Dublin in the winter and Bowen's Court in the summer. *Seven Winters* (1942) is a memoir of this childhood. Bowen describes the security of the seasonal movement between town and country and her family's security in its class, community, and privileges. She does not recall any sense that she was a member of a minority community, but she does recollect that Roman Catholics were considered "different," and that this difference could not be discussed: "As to the difference between the two religions, I was too discreet to ask questions—if I wanted to know. This appeared to share a delicate, awkward aura with those two other differences—of sex, of class" (*Seven Winters,* p. 50).[1] In Bowen's fiction there is always a concern with how much anyone can know or should want to know about the differences of sex, class, race, and religion. The discretion that governed her early life in Ireland is refigured in her concern with the problematic status of knowledge for her characters. Both *The Death of the Heart* and *The Heat of the Day* focus on the dangers of knowing too much. *The Death of the Heart* begins when Anna reads Portia's diary and the fiction of family feeling in Windsor Terrace begins publicly to unravel. *The Heat of the Day* is a spy thriller, and, like the best of the genre, it depicts surveillance as a governing structure in "private" sexual and social relations as well as in the operations of the state. In *The Last September* Bowen looks at the precariousness of the structures that supported Bowen's Court and Herbert Place.

When Elizabeth Bowen was six years old her father had a nervous breakdown. During this period he was obsessively attentive to his daughter and Florence Bowen was advised to separate from her husband as much for Elizabeth's sake as for her own. She took Elizabeth to England, where they moved among a succession of villas on the Kent coast and were more or less looked after by relatives. Henry Bowen made a gradual recovery but was never well enough to have his wife and child back for longer than a visit. In 1912 Florence was diagnosed as having cancer and that year she died in Hythe. Elizabeth described her response to the traumas of her childhood as a "campaign of not noticing" (*Bowen's Court,* 1942, p. 308). Elizabeth's stammer was perhaps one legacy of her father's illness; as Victoria Glendinning notes in her biography of Bowen, one word over which she always faltered was "mother."

After her mother's death Bowen was educated at a Kent boarding school, Downe House, and spent

most of her summers in Ireland. She wrote of her schooldays in "The Mulberry Tree" (1934, in *Collected Impressions,* 1950):

The war having well outlasted my schooldays, I cannot imagine a girl's school without a war. The moral stress was appalling. We grew up under the intolerable obligation of being fought for, and could not fall short in character without recollecting that men were dying for us.

(p. 188)

Bowen experienced more "appalling moral stress" during the Irish War of Independence. Initially her response was to feel that her identification with England during World War I had exhausted her reservoir of imaginative sympathy for Ireland. In numerous direct and indirect ways, however, she returned to thinking about the War of Independence and the Irish Civil War throughout her career. Her family's most direct involvement with the Irish wars was her cousin Captain John Bowen-Colthurst's scandalous "execution" of a well-known writer and pacifist, Francis Sheehy Skeffington, during the week of the Easter Rising in 1916. The Bowens do not appear to have had strongly articulated, overt political sympathies, but they found themselves interpellated as pro-British during the War of Independence. In 1921 several Protestant-owned "big houses" in the vicinity of Bowen's Court were burned down, and Elizabeth's father wrote to her advising her to prepare herself for the destruction of their home. The worst did not happen, but Bowen was so strongly haunted by the image of the house on fire that she used it as the conclusion to her first Irish novel, *The Last September.* Writing of her childhood, she describes fire as "the thing of which I was most frightened" (*Collected Impressions*).

Bowen more than once suggests that her upbringing in Ireland contributed to her treatment of sex as possessive of "a delicate, awkward aura" (*Seven Winters*). In her 1946 introduction to Sheridan Le Fanu's *Uncle Silas* (1864, in *Collected Impressions*) she discusses a convention characteristic of much Irish Protestant writing, the displacement of Irish themes into English contexts:

Uncle Silas has always struck me as being an Irish story transposed to an English setting. The hermetic solitude and the autocracy of the great country house, the de-

---

[1]Page numbers refer to original American editions, when one was published, and otherwise to English editions.

monic power of the family myth, fatalism, feudalism, and the "ascendancy" outlook are accepted facts of life for the race of hybrids from which Le Fanu sprang. For the psychological background of *Uncle Silas* it was necessary for him to invent nothing. Rather, he was at once exploiting in art and exploring for its own more terrible implications what would have been the norm of his own heredity. . . .

Uncle Silas is, as a novel, Irish in two other ways: it is sexless, and it shows a sublimated infantilism.

(p. 4)

Bowen identifies as Irish themes family myth, feudalism, fatalism, sexlessness, and infantilism. Her own writings are profoundly concerned with these issues and her recognition of Le Fanu's transposition of these concerns to an English setting is an important key to Bowen's fiction. The sexlessness and infantilism of Irish fiction are most thoroughly explored in *The Last September* and *A World of Love,* novels that emphasize the intergenerational romance and the obsession with the past that are both the chief resource in Irish writing and the locus of its paralysis.

Henry Bowen remarried in 1918. His wife was the sister of Stephen Gwynn, the first writer Elizabeth met. After leaving school Elizabeth divided her time between her father's house in Ireland and her aunt's home in Harpenden. She went for two terms to art school in London, and afterward took a course in journalism. In 1921 she became engaged to a British Army officer, but after the couple visited some of Elizabeth's family in Italy the engagement was broken off. This incident seems to have been the basis for the terminated romance in *The Last September.* At art school she had begun to write stories; her first collection, *Encounters,* was published in 1923. That same year Bowen married Alan Cameron, a war veteran whose health had been damaged by gas poisoning, and who worked as a civil servant in Northampton. In 1925 the Camerons moved to Old Headington, Oxford, and in 1935, when Alan joined the BBC, they moved to 2 Clarence Terrace, Regent's Park, London. Elizabeth's father had died in 1930, and she had inherited Bowen's Court. For the following thirty years she spent a good part of every year in County Cork.

Bowen uses the obsessions and frustrations of her own sexual and romantic history as material for her fiction. Although her marriage to Cameron was in many ways happy and sustaining, Bowen had three important extramarital love affairs on which

she drew for material for her fiction. In the mid 1930's she was involved with Humphry House, a lecturer in English at Oxford. At the time of their meeting House was engaged, but the affair continued after his marriage and through his wife's pregnancy. Inevitably, such a relationship brought intense pressure to bear on Bowen and the Houses. (It is unclear how much Cameron knew about Bowen's affairs.) In her fiction Bowen repeatedly returns to the circulation of desire, hostility, and guilt among trios. In 1935 House and his family went to India for a couple of years. When he returned to England his relationship with Bowen settled into a steady friendship. In 1936 Bowen became infatuated with Goronwy Rees, an editor at the *Spectator.* The promised affair was frustrated during a holiday at Bowen's Court when Rees fell in love with Bowen's friend Rosamond Lehmann. Rees recognized himself in the character of Eddie, the charming but slightly hysterical young lothario in *The Death of the Heart.* Eddie carelessly, and so all the more cruelly, betrays all his friends in order to soothe his ego: "I have to get off with people . . . because I cannot get on with them, and that makes me so mad" (p. 257). Rees was so upset at this portrait that he threatened legal action, but he was dissuaded by various friends, including E. M. Forster, from pursuing his grievance.

Bowen's most important friendship, apart from that with Cameron, was with Charles Ritchie, a Canadian diplomat based in London for most of World War II. They met at the christening of Bowen's goddaughter, Perdita Buchan, in 1941, and were soon involved in an intimate friendship that lasted the rest of Bowen's life. After the war Ritchie became a career diplomat, representing his country first in Paris and then in New York. He married his cousin, but he and Bowen continued to meet and correspond frequently, and Ritchie was with her in her last illness. Bowen told him that he was the model for Robert Kelway in *The Heat of the Day,* the novel she dedicated to him.

During the war Bowen worked as an ARP warden in London and an intelligence gatherer for the British government in Ireland. After the war Cameron's deteriorating health obliged him to retire from the BBC. He continued to work part time as an educational advisor to EMI, and to help Bowen manage her career, which was becoming increasingly complex with negotiations over rights and translations, British Council lecture tours, interviews, and literary journalism. Although Bowen worked constantly at writing and was always very successful, the maintenance of Bowen's Court was a massive drain on the couple's income. They moved permanently to Ireland in 1951 for the last year of Alan's life. In the 1950's and 1960's Bowen spent part of almost every year in the United States, lecturing and teaching creative writing at, among other places, Princeton, Berkeley, Stanford, Vassar, Bryn Mawr, Amherst, Reed, and the University of Washington, Seattle. She liked the United States. Teaching there helped her to make a living and allowed her to see more of Ritchie. She also spent time as writer-in-residence at the American Academy in Rome. Since the war she had felt herself less at home in England. She was politically conservative and a snob. In a letter to William Plomer dated 24 September 1945 she writes: "I can't stick all these little middle-class Labour wets with their Old London School of Economics ties and their women. Scratch any of those cuties and you find the governess" (in *The Mulberry Tree*, 1986, p. 207). There was more to her alienation from England, however, than a dissatisfaction with social change. As she described it in *A Time in Rome* (1960), "Anywhere, at any time, with anyone, one may be seized by the suspicion of being alien—ease is therefore to be found in a place which nominally *is* foreign: this shifts the weight" (p. 27). The suspicion of being alien in Ireland was one to which her background and upbringing had accustomed her. In her later life, as she came to write more about her Irish identity and the history of England's relation to Ireland, her own history of loyalty to England provoked an unease.

Bowen did, however, return to England. In 1960 she recognized that she could no longer afford the upkeep of Bowen's Court. She offered it to the only possible male Bowen heir, her father's nephew, Charles Bowen, who was farming in Africa; when he declared himself unable to take on the house, she sold it. She had hoped that it would become the family home of the new owners, but within a year they demolished it. Bowen first returned to Old Headington, where she had lived with Cameron in the early years of her marriage, and then to Hythe where her mother had died. Elizabeth Bowen died at Hythe on 22 February 1973 and was buried in Ireland, near the site of Bowen's Court.

Almost from the very beginning of her career Bowen's writing was well-received by other writers, by critics, and by readers in general in Ireland,

Britain, and the United States. She received a number of honors in the last twenty years of her life: she was made a Companion of the British Empire in 1948 and received honorary doctorates from Trinity College, Dublin, in 1949, and from Oxford in 1956, as well as various fellowships at American universities. She is the subject of critical biographies by Glendinning (1977) and Patricia Craig (1986) and a number of critical and academic studies, notably *Elizabeth Bowen: An Estimation* by Hermione Lee (1981). Although critics praise her descriptions of "life with the lid on"—a phrase she used when writing about Jane Austen in *English Novelists* (p. 25)—and the toughness with which "her people faced the secrets from which society no longer protected them"—to quote V. S. Pritchett—Bowen's reputation has never been as high as that of the major modernists. It is my intention, in what follows, to describe Bowen's major fiction and to suggest some ways of reading those aspects of her work that remain elusive or difficult.

EARLY STORIES: LOVE AND MOURNING

BOWEN wrote to Graham Greene about her writing (letter quoted in *Why Do I Write? An Exchange of Views Between Elizabeth Bowen, Graham Greene, and V. S. Pritchett*):

I am sure that in nine out of ten cases the original wish to write is the wish to make oneself felt. It's a sign, I suppose, of life's decreasing livableness *as* life that people should feel it possible to make themselves felt in so few other ways. The non-essential writer never gets past that wish. But actually, as I suppose anybody who *has* written for twenty or twenty-five years knows, that initial wish to make oneself felt evaporates after the second or at latest the third book: after that point writers divide off into those who, honestly planning to make money, have reason to think themselves, now, on to something good, and those who, now, find themselves ridden by an impersonal obsession on the subject of writing for its own sake.

(p. 55)

One of the most frequent situations in Elizabeth Bowen's fiction is that of a girl who wishes to make herself felt but who does not yet know how—or indeed if—she might do so. The influence of Henry James has been often noted and sometimes lamented, even by Bowen herself, who worried about her convoluted syntax (she was nervous about developing "stylistic ticks") and recognized that her writing sometimes seemed self-parodic. Many of Bowen's evasions and elaborations are the result of her using the girl to tell the reader things that the girl does not know or recognize. James, particularly the James of *What Maisie Knew* (1897), is not the only influence here. Two nineteenth-century Irish novels were particularly important for Bowen: Le Fanu's *Uncle Silas* and *The Real Charlotte* (1894) by Edith Somerville and Martin Ross. In both these stories a young girl is preyed upon by an apparently benevolent older relation who is secretly working to destroy her. The intergenerational hostility and the heroine's vulnerability to forces from the past that seek to mold her—forces that she does not fully comprehend—are themes taken up in much of Bowen's fiction. The young women in her fiction are embedded in a process of elaborate self-narration that complicates and obfuscates their relation to society. They are described in language so dense and convoluted that to the reader they seem to be detached from bodies and from social intercourse. This apparent detachment gives Bowen's heroines a ghostly quality.

Life's decreasing livableness as life is partly a consequence of new social formations that make apparent the privileged subject (the young girl) in her relation to the world. Bowen's fiction seems to hearken back to a society in which choices were not apparently determined by money or the fear of violence. Although she was often under financial pressure herself, Bowen did not follow her friend Virginia Woolf's feminism by making women's need for financial independence a subject of her writing. Money matters for Bowen's characters, but she resists letting them acknowledge how important it is to them. Bowen is not interested in representing people who recognize their desires as socially constructed. Her response to materialist interpretations of identity is to create characters who inhabit their lives in strikingly immaterial ways—characters who live like ghosts in their world. In *Why Do I Write?* Bowen described to V. S. Pritchett her own sense of being "unrelatable" to society:

Perhaps one emotional reason why one may write is the need to work off, out of the system, the sense of being solitary and farouche. Solitary and farouche people don't have relationships: they are quite unrelatable. If you and I were capable of being altogether house-trained and made jolly, we should be nicer people but not writers. If

I feel irked and uneasy when asked about the nature of my (as a writer) relation to society, this is because I am being asked about the nature of something that does not, as far as *I* know, exist. My writing, I am prepared to think, may be a substitute for something I have been born without—a so-called normal relation to society. My books *are* my relation to society.

(p. 23)

It is helpful when thinking about Bowen to remember that she felt "irked and uneasy" about this relation to society, and to ask what her writing suggests about her fears and anxieties. Her early experiences of family breakdown and of civil strife may well have troubled her sense of relation to other people. She never felt happy with systems of thought that ask for people's lives to be justified on the grounds of their usefulness. Bowen does, however, situate her characters in a context, and that context is history. They have historically constructed, rather than socially constructed, identities.

In *A World of Love,* a novel almost self-parodically characteristic of Bowen's themes and style, the narrative opens with a description of Jane walking in anachronistic clothing, like a ghost in the Irish landscape: "Wearing a trailing Edwardian muslin dress, she stepped out slowly towards the obelisk, shading her eyes" (p. 5). Jane falls in love with the long-dead writer of some love letters perhaps addressed to her mother or cousin. One evening at a dinner party at a neighbor's home, her attention wanders from the loose, disembodied dialogue and she thinks she sees his ghost. Jane does not know the events or passions of the past, but she is constructed by them. She is the quintessential Bowen character in that she hopes to understand the value of her life through understanding what she loves, and in these novels love is a product of history.

The best stories in Bowen's first two collections, *Encounters* and *Ann Lee's* (1926), are those concerned with children trying to define themselves in their relation to an adult world not centered on them. Bowen later wrote of these stories: "I was beating myself against human unknowableness; in fact, I made that my subject" (preface to *Early Stories,* 1951, p. xviii). Both Rosalind in "Coming Home" and Roger in "The Visitor" face the crisis of imagining the deaths of their mothers. These children learn to distinguish themselves from their mothers by the painful realization of the differences between themselves and their parents. The problems of the unknowableness of either the self or the other are foregrounded; the children act and react in response to their fears and suspicions. In "Coming Home" Rosalind eventually discovers that nothing has happened to her missing mother and has to come to terms with the fact that she does not fully occupy her mother's attention. By facing the idea of their parents' mortality these children begin to prepare for their own dissolution. In her later novels *The House in Paris, The Death of the Heart, The Little Girls,* and *Eva Trout* (1968) Bowen would return to her concern in these first stories with the presence of death in childhood. Bowen's children come to grieve almost as soon as they come to consciousness.

THE HOTEL

In her early stories Bowen seems to be translating and processing her own experience of family breakdown and of loss. In her first novel she uses her brief engagement to John Anderson and its collapse after her holiday with her aunt Edie in Italy, but this material is much more effectively transformed in fiction than any writing about her parents would be for some years. *The Hotel* (1927) is a novel about women in love with women and the ways in which the arrival of men into a female community does and does not affect that love. Sydney Warren accompanies her sickly cousin Tessa on a holiday to the Italian Riviera. She meets Mrs. Kerr, a fascinating and manipulative older woman with whom she becomes infatuated. Mrs. Kerr seems fond of Sydney but, especially after her son Ronald arrives, she cannot give Sydney the attention the younger woman craves. James Milton, a clergyman, arrives at the hotel and begins to court Sydney. They are briefly engaged, but Mrs. Kerr's conversation causes each to doubt the other and they break the engagement.

Jane Rule's inclusion of Bowen in her study, *Lesbian Images* (1976), is mainly justified by a reading of *The Hotel,* although erotic relations between women provide implicit tensions in a number of her plots, particularly in "Mysterious Kôr," *The House in Paris,* and *The Little Girls.* (Bowen often had intense friendships, sometimes erotically charged, with other women. In *A World of Light* [1976] the American novelist, May Sarton, describes how she was in love with Bowen in the mid-1930's.) *The Hotel* opens

with a quarrel between Miss Pym and Miss Fitzgerald, the acknowledged lovers of the novel, and ends with their reconciliation. The hotel on the Italian Riviera is dominated by women. When James Milton arrives he unwittingly outrages the hotel by taking a bath in a bathroom reserved for two elderly ladies. Milton emerges from the sanctuary of female underwear and toiletries scarlet and erect, oblivious to the violation caused by his masculine presence. In naming her clergyman Milton, Bowen sets up a comic tension between the different representations of female experience in male and female literary traditions. Her Milton is an expert on culture and civilization, particularly on the Renaissance, and from his first walk with Sydney their conversation is laden with heavy allusions to literary and artistic tradition. He sees Sydney as a Beatrice Cenci figure. At the same time Milton is made painfully aware that to the women in the hotel he appears to be a Mr. Collins looking for his Charlotte Lucas. Sydney herself, with her ambiguous desires marked in her androgynous name, resists the feminization he would impose on her.

The characters are perhaps too much placed through their initial descriptions. A representative passage is the first description of Sydney's cousin Tessa, a sympathetically treated hypochondriac:

Several complaints had, it is true, been suggested to her by her doctors before leaving England and she had come abroad with a perfectly open mind as to the possibility of most of them. Not one, however, had proved itself entirely satisfactory. She wanted something that would settle down with her, simple and unexigent like an old family servant, so that they might get to know each other and understand each other's little ways. She was distressed by any suggestion of impermanence; she was a homely woman. One had to have Something in one's life. She lay on a velvet sofa in her bedroom with the head pulled round away from the window and wished that she were a religious woman and that it were time for lunch and that Sydney would soon come in.

(p. 26)

These passages of characterization are very successful and typical of the skill with which Bowen presents the dozen hotel residents in the novel. The single sentence that links Tessa's yearning for faith with her desire for lunch and for Sydney's company is almost Augustan in its poise and discrimination. Bowen, in addition to her admiration of Austen, was particularly fond of the earlier eighteenth-century novelists and satirists.

The dramatic interaction between the characters is not so well executed. At one point Bowen rather self-consciously has Sydney say,

I have often thought it would be interesting if the front of any house, but of an hotel especially, could be swung open on a hinge like the front of a doll's house. Imagine the hundreds of rooms with their walls lit up and the real-looking staircases and all the people surprised doing appropriate things in appropriate attitudes as though they had been put there to represent something and had never moved in their lives.

(p. 115)

The characters in *The Hotel* compare their world, with its sense of female community and the importance of marriage, to the world of Austen's *Pride and Prejudice* (1813). However, Bowen is not as at home as Austen in making comic action represent something emotionally significant. Indeed, her failure to be quite at home in a comedy of manners is made explicit by the novel's foreign setting.

Mrs. Kerr, the older woman with whom Sydney is infatuated, declares, "You know, women's lives *are* sensational" (p. 18). Bowen sends up these self-centered lives at the same time as she gives maximum credit to how these women feel. The events of the novel are small, private incidents, but they are felt as momentous by the characters. Female experience is privileged as both more intense than male experience and as comically self-regarding.

The novel is at its most powerful and yet most unsure when it investigates female eroticism. Although Bowen's women are like Austen's in that they inhabit a world in which marriage is the normative custom into which ambition and eroticism are channeled, they differ from Austen's characters in that they are able to articulate lesbian love as a possible alternative. Sydney does not describe her attraction to Mrs. Kerr as lesbian, but she does recognize that it is a romantic attraction, and that recognition governs her self-perception within the relationship. The best scene in the novel, dramatically and emotionally, is the one in the patisserie where Mrs. Kerr dismisses Sydney's affection:

"I begin now to guess you've expected much more of me and that I've been taking and taking without so much as a glance ahead or a single suspicion of what you would want to have back. I'm afraid we've gone wrong through your not quite understanding. You see, I'm so fond of you, but—"

"But?"

"Well, simply but! I mean, there is nothing else there. It has always seemed to me simple to like people and right to be liked, but I never can feel that much more is involved—is it? I have a horror, I think, of not being, and of my friends not being, quite perfectly balanced. I think moderation in everything—but perhaps I am cold . . . Will you take my purse now—if you won't eat any more?—and go in and pay for the cakes?"

To Sydney the cumulative effect of this succession of touches (especially the last: herself brandishing with commercial insistence a long bill that her bewildered debtor felt unable to meet) was one of vulgarity. The attribution to herself of an irritable sex-consciousness vis-à-vis to Ronald did not hurt but sharply offended. Mrs. Kerr, however, sitting there with her half-smile, her evident deprecation of the interlude, her invincible air of fastidiousness, had maintained her own plane whereon "vulgarity" would be meaningless. Sydney could only suppose that cruelty, as supremely disinterested as art, had like art its own purity which could transcend anything and consecrate the nearest material to its uses.

(pp. 196–197)

The cruelty and complacency of Mrs. Kerr's withdrawal are well-portrayed in the evasions and self-congratulation of her syntax. Sydney's role in the scene is less effective. She is made to reflect on Mrs. Kerr as Bowen would have the reader reflect. These moments of lucid criticism endow Sydney with precisely the kind of self-consciousness she so painfully lacks in the rest of the novel.

THE LAST SEPTEMBER *AND* BOWEN'S COURT

THE characteristic problem of first novels—a blurring of the distinction between protagonist and narrative—is resolved by Bowen in her second novel, *The Last September,* published in 1929, two years after *The Hotel,* a novel that revisits many of the concerns of *The Hotel.* Lois Farquar, like Sydney Warren, is a young woman of intense feelings and vague ambitions who becomes engaged for want of anything else on which to fix her attention. Once again an older woman intervenes to end the engagement. As in *The Hotel,* people play tennis, entertain visitors, and make up picnics, but this leisure is placed in a context very different from that of the Riviera. It is 1920, and Lois lives with her uncle and aunt, Sir Richard and Lady Naylor, at Danielstown, County Cork, a "big house" modeled on Bowen's Court. At first it seems as if the inhabitants of Danielstown and the neighboring landed estates can ignore the Troubles, even though much of their social life is involved with the locally garrisoned British army officers and their families, whose business in Ireland is the repression of the independence movement. The leisure, courtesy, and "manners" of Danielstown provoke questions similar to those raised about ancestral houses by W. B. Yeats in "Meditations in Time of Civil War" (1923):

> O what if levelled lawns and gravelled ways
> Where slippered Contemplation finds his ease
> And Childhood a delight for every sense,
> But take our greatness with our violence?

In *The Last September,* as later in the history of her family home, *Bowen's Court,* Bowen examines the possibility that violence is the very foundation and condition of civilization. The delights of a privileged childhood at Danielstown or Bowen's Court are produced by means of the domination of the land and of other populations. Like Yeats, Bowen investigates what it would mean to think of her own writing as a product of a civilization that is also an agent of domination. During World War II Bowen would return to these concerns as she considered the preservation of a specifically British culture (represented for her by a certain kind of writing) that has as its foundation the structure of empire.

The Naylors of Danielstown feel guilty and uneasy about the harassment of local people, including their own tenants, consequently they turn a blind eye to the "rebels" around them. They entertain British army officers and their families, identify themselves with the union, and are complicit with British action to quell the "rebellion." The British in Ireland are represented as vulgar and insensitive. "Vulgarity" is a term of moral discrimination for Bowen, as it was for Sydney Warren. The "Anglo-Irish" are, by and large, courteous and well-meaning, and yet they accept the systems of violence and misrepresentation that maintain their homes and privileges. How do good people come to do the wrong thing day by day? What fault of manners permits the erosion of morality? These seem to be the questions posed by *The Last September.*

The relationship between past and present in the novel articulates these questions. The very title expresses one of the ways in which temporality plays on the imagination—the last September at Danielstown, however much it marks the end of a style of living, can never be the "last" September. As Yeats remarks in so many of his poems, every anniversary of an event recalls that event with particular force. The epigraph to the novel is from Marcel Proust's *The Past Recaptured* (1927): "Ils ont les chagrins qu'ont les vierges et les paresseux" ("Virgins and idlers have their troubles"). Although *The Last September* is set only eight years previous to its publication date, it is self-consciously historical: "In those days, girls wore crisp white skirts and transparent blouses clotted with white flowers" (p. 3). It is the first of Bowen's novels to mark its interest in the functions of temporality in narrative with a tripartite structure: an arrival, a visit, and a departure. Bowen repeats this tripartite structure in *Friends and Relations* (1931), *The House in Paris, The Death of the Heart, A World of Love,* and *The Little Girls.*

Lois Farquar's life is governed by the past in two important ways. She is living in an estate built from the spoils of conquest, a place now threatened by a violence that is the latest stage in a historical struggle. Lois is represented as largely ignorant of this history, although her romance with Gerald allegorizes her family's idealization of Britain and dependence on British force. Lois's life is also significantly related to the past, in her own and in others' imaginations, through the figure of her dead mother, Laura, who haunts the novel like a ghost. Hugo Montmorency, the visitor whose arrival opens the narrative, had been in love with Laura, and he and his wife search for her in Lois.

This is the novel in which Bowen is most obviously concerned to distinguish her projects from those of the Irish renaissance writers, Yeats in particular. In much of his early poetry Yeats constructed female figures and female voices as emblematic of the nation. In the collections of poems contemporaneous with *The Last September, The Tower* (1928) and *The Winding Stair and Other Poems* (1933), Yeats reexamines configurations of gender in the light of his own developing scepticism about the essentially Roman Catholic ordering of sexuality in the Irish Free State. In poems about domesticity, education, national politics, and sexuality (as in "A Prayer for My Daughter" or the "Crazy Jane" poems) women remain emblematic figures rather than historical agents, although they sometimes represent a critique of Catholic nationalist ideology. In "The Seven Sages," a poem from *The Wind-*

ing Stair that traces an alternative genealogy of Protestant nationalist thought in Ireland through the figures of Jonathan Swift, George Berkeley, Oliver Goldsmith, Henry Grattan, and Edmund Burke, one eighteenth-century woman, Esther Johnson (Swift's friend "Stella"), briefly appears, only to be dismissed from historical significance. In *The Last September* Bowen tries to develop different ways of situating women within a Protestant tradition and different ways of understanding the production of female sexualities in Ireland. Laura Farquar, Lois's dead mother, is emblematic of female mystery and desirability. Like Francesco Petrarch's Laura, she is represented as an icon rather than as a specific character. Her strange, sudden marriage to Farquar represents the dangers and seductions of the north. For southern Protestants in Bowen's fiction there is a powerful tension between kinship and alienation in their imagination of the north. (Three years later Bowen titled one of her English novels *To the North,* and in that novel the north is clearly marked as deathly.) The older people at Danielstown try to retrace Laura's character in her daughter, but Lois resists their interpretation. She is the niece rather than the daughter of the house; she is placed at a tangent to ideas of tradition and inheritance.

In Lois's engagement to Gerald Lesworth, the young army officer, Lois flirts with the possibility of a symbolic act of union with Britain. Lady Naylor intervenes to show the young people that in the eyes of the family Lesworth is worthless. In a scene of social comedy very much in the manner of Oscar Wilde, the Anglo-Irish Lady Naylor interviews the English Gerald in a sitting room decorated with British regimental photographs and union jack cushions, and conveys to him the inadequacy of English society, given Anglo-Irish expectations.

"Such a day," she sighed briskly. "We have lunched with the Boatleys. What a delightful colonel he must be. *She,* you know, is Irish; a Vere Scott. We must seem ridiculous to you, over here, the way we are all related."

"Topping, I think," said Gerald.

"Oh, I don't know! Now you lucky people seem to have no relations at all; that must feel so independent."

"I have dozens."

"Indeed? All in Surrey?"

"Scattered about."

"That sounds to me, of course," remarked Lady Naylor, pulling her gloves off brightly, "exceedingly restless. But you all *came* from Surrey, didn't you?"

"More or less," said Gerald, who was not sure. The Boatleys had not been sure where he came from, either; her day so far had been unsatisfactory.

(p. 262)

Bowen indulges herself here in a chauvinistic reversal of stereotypes, a revenge on an English literature and society in which the Irish are so often dismissed as "nobodies." There is also some irony in Lady Naylor's comfortable self-satisfaction as a member of a society in which everybody is related to everybody else, when that society is shown to be torn apart by internecine warfare. The very vocabulary of "independence" and "troubles" describes domestic and family problems more aptly than that of "civil war." The novel's famous penultimate line, which records the destruction of Danielstown, depends on the particular conflation of love and hatred in every Irish community: "The door stood open hospitably upon a furnace." This final, direct confrontation with the fire is in stark contrast to the strategies of evasion that characterize the behavior of Lois and the Naylors in their relation to the world around them. Throughout the novel Lois is seen to turn away from confrontations. She meets a man hurrying through the garden one evening and suspects that he is a "volunteer" (in the Irish Republican Army). There may be IRA guns hidden on the plantation. On another occasion she almost encounters a gunman. When she is out driving and comes across the Black and Tans, a violent, undisciplined supplement to the regular British army presence in Ireland, she turns aside to avoid them.

What Lois craves in the relationship with Gerald is immediate, physical passion. Things fall apart when he agrees to be reinscribed socially by Lady Naylor's judgment. In the lovers' final meeting Lois wants Gerald to possess her with something of the force that his presence as a soldier in Ireland represents. When he remains trapped inside his own fiction of chivalry—he has promised Lady Naylor not to "kiss" Lois—she cries out to him: " 'Gerald you'll kill me, just standing there' " (p. 281). This standoff between the two mimics the structure of relations between the English and Irish that dominates the book: the combination of English physical power and moral indifference is destroying Ireland. In fact, it is Gerald who is killed, shot by the IRA shortly after his parting from Lois. Ironically, the Naylors are able then to accept him as an individual rather than as a member of a race and class, while his own family in England are obliged to transform him into an emblematic figure in order to make his death significant. Lady Naylor, who sent him off unhappy to his death, prides herself on writing a letter of condolence to his mother. Yeats's "terrible beauty" is echoed and challenged when Lady Naylor describes her exchange with Gerald's mother to Mrs. Trent:

[I]t was a shock, too, for Lois. You see they had really played tennis so often and were beginning to be quite friends. She did not take it as hard as I feared, girls of her generation seem less sensitive, really. . . . I don't know, perhaps that is all for the best. But it was terrible, wasn't it? I still think: how terrible—But he did have a happy life. I wrote that to his mother; I said, it must always be some consolation to think how happy his life had been. He quite beamed, really; he was the life and soul of everything. And she wrote back—I did not think tactfully, but of course she would be distressed—that it was *her* first consolation to think he died in so noble a cause.

(p. 301)

That last sentence is rich with the complexities Bowen encountered when writing about Ireland. The Wildeian comedy of Lady Naylor's selfishness—"of course she would be distressed"—plays against the real lack of apprehension in Mrs. Lesworth's assumption that to an Irish Protestant the British presence in Ireland would be "so noble a cause." The naming of that difference as "untactful" is crucial to Bowen's writing about the fusion of personal and political concerns in Ireland. Lady Naylor is self-condemned in the stupidity of her mistaken employment of manners as a social structure for disguising violence, but manners—here invoked as "tact"—are important in dealing with violence. Bowen persistently discriminates between manners in the service of honesty and manners that are opposed to honesty. Manners in the service of honesty are idealized, but Bowen does not underestimate the ways in which that ideal comes under stress in a world of physical violence.

Some of Bowen's self-understanding as a writer comes from a perception of herself as a historically constructed agent whose sensibility was forged in the context of political violence. At the same time, she represents women as only tangentially the producers of violence. Her account of her Irish male contemporaries in her introduction, "The Short Story," to *The Faber Book of Modern Stories* (London, 1937) makes clear how much she credits

experience in a writer's development of a literary style:

The Irish Sea makes a bigger break in sentiment than the Atlantic, and Irish and American writers of the short story have—for all their differences in temper—strong common qualities. Extroverted coldness in art, objectivity, may be the fruit of a life that is, or has been lately, physically exciting or uncertain, life that is quick, rough or lived at high nervous tension, in which either sexual or political passion makes society unsafe. Precipitate feeling makes for hard form in art. The younger Irish writers have almost all carried arms; American civilisation keeps the Americans, nervously, armed men: fact there overtops fancy. There is a state of living in which events assault the imagination, stunning it: such a state of living enforces its own, a now no longer unique, literature.

(p. 11)

Sexual passion is here regarded as likely as political passion to destabilize society. For all her affinities with the Bloomsbury group and middle-class English literary life, Bowen seems to have characterized her own writing as exhibiting "extroverted coldness." *The Last September* stands with her other great wartime novel, *The Heat of the Day,* as the fictions in which events most assault the imagination. At the end of *The Last September* Lois has left Danielstown and Ireland, not for art school, as had once been proposed, but for Tours, where she is to work on her foreign languages. With the burning of Danielstown representing an apparent closure of the past, Bowen turned her fictional attention away from Ireland, to that "place which nominally *is* foreign." Almost everything she produced in the 1930's was about England and France.

ENGLAND AND FRANCE: FRIENDS AND RELATIONS, *"THE DISINHERITED,"* TO THE NORTH, *AND* THE HOUSE IN PARIS

IN so far as Bowen revisits questions raised in *The Last September* in her next novel, she returns to the issue of community as discussed by Gerald Lesworth and Lady Naylor, an issue announced in the novel's title, *Friends and Relations.* This slightly affected social comedy deals with the skeletons in the closet of an upper-class English family, and particularly with those scandals central to family life: illegitimacy, adultery, and incest. Irish women writers (in English) have traditionally shown a fascination for legitimacy. In allegorizing the union between England and Ireland as a sexual union, Bowen's female predecessors, most notably Maria Edgeworth and Sydney Owenson, called the legitimacy of that union into question. *Friends and Relations* begins with a marriage that is clearly announced as the union not so much of two individuals as of two families: "The morning of the Tilney-Studdart wedding rain fell steadily from before daylight, veiling trees and garden and darkening the canvas of the marquee that should have caught the earliest sun in happy augury" (p. 13). This inauspicious opening to the family connection introduces a narrative in which Edward Tilney and Laurel Studdart have to come to terms with the revelation that the groom's mother, Lady Elfrida, had had an affair with a big-game hunter, and that Edward is developing desire for Laurel's sister Janet, who later marries the game hunter's nephew. Lady Naylor boasted to Gerald that everyone in Ireland was related; in *Friends and Relations* the vision of an incestuous, claustrophobic society (now in Cheltenham and London) is taken to parodic extreme. Insofar as the novel is about Edward Tilney's anxiety that he may be the product of an illegitimate union, the subject matter is not completely removed from Bowen's desire to understand her position as an Irish Protestant writer. The novel ponders the difference between kinship and affinity, another Yeatsian problematic. The novel is at its best in its attempt to think through nominally perverse desires and the eroticism of forbidden unions. On the whole it rejects the enforcement of normative sexualities, although family structures are left intact at the conclusion. The novel's major fault is that it employs crude stereotypes to critique stereotypes and does not always succeed in creating a gap between its own method and what it is criticizing. This is particularly evident in the representation of an awakening lesbian sexuality in one of the minor characters, Theodora Thirdman, a large, frustrated, bullying adolescent. Bowen's uneasy self-projection in this character is marked by the curiously crude name—if "thirdman" points to a third gender, one might also note that Theodora is an anagram of Bowen's middle name, Dorothea.

Friends and Relations is the only novel in which Bowen regards the past with some optimism, depicting our relation to the past as more comic than tragic. In spite of the rigid ways in which families reproduce themselves, for individuals things do change and people become more tolerant. Where there is violence it is kept parodic and distant. The big-game hunter participates in imperial violence, but he does not bring that violence home with him. It remains in the background. Glendinning describes *Friends and Relations* as "the Elizabeth Bowen novel that even Elizabeth Bowen enthusiasts tend to forget about" (p. 98). It is best appreciated as a light counterpoint to the concerns of her major fiction.

It is tempting to read Bowen's interest in sexual perversity as resistance on her part to the normative sexual practices of the inter-war years. It is perhaps more accurate to describe her interest in sexuality as part of a wider concern in British society with the ways in which the very idea of normative sexualities was falling apart in the 1920's and 1930's. Changes in the work force, new pressures on families after the large loss of men in the war, the depression, increased secularization of the laws around sexual morality (particularly around divorce), were producing new versions of "respectable" sexualities. In particular, wider access to divorce opened up divisions between an authorized Christian discourse on sexuality and the increasingly acceptable, more permissive secular discourse. Within both discourses, respectability was an issue, particularly with regard to social class. The concern in *Friends and Relations* with sexual scandal quickly becomes an examination of conventions of class. The novel's failures of tone are largely a problem of genre, since its particular form of social comedy is too intertwined with the language of the class it attempts to criticize to attain a critical distance.

Bowen returned to examine the social construction of sexuality a couple of years later in "The Disinherited," the best story from her 1934 collection, *The Cat Jumps*. (Bowen chose to include "The Disinherited" in her edition of *The Faber Book of Modern Stories* in 1937.) Two young women—one single and the other married, one from the village manor and the other from the new housing estate—go out one evening to a wild, promiscuous party held in a decaying, almost gothic, mansion. Davina, the poor niece of a gentrified family, has sex with her aunt's chauffeur, Prothero. She recognizes this social miscegenation as a form of self-hatred, although she never discovers that the subtext to their union is Prothero's murder, in a fit of passionate jealousy, of a previous sexual partner. In the context of Bowen's other work the story is wildly melodramatic, but that very melodrama is more representative of the violence and stress of social change in England than the muted comedy of *Friends and Relations.*

To the North (1932) is the first Bowen novel to record her growing love of London. It is another story about two women. Cecilia Summers, recently widowed, comes to live in St. John's Wood with her sister-in-law, Emmeline. The initial movement north is Cecilia's return from Italy to London. On the journey she meets Markie Linkwater, one of the sharp, callous, predatory, sexually attractive young men who characterize Bowen's fiction in the 1930's. Markie seduces Emmeline, while Cecilia composes herself to make a second marriage to Julian, safe but passionless. This is one of Bowen's most Jamesian novels, a crisis of distance and misunderstanding. It deals with the failures of language in everyday life, but also attempts to demonstrate what language may achieve in rendering complex moral states in fiction. The silences between people in this novel are more important than any words they speak. Bowen is by no means as skilled as James in using syntax to relay convoluted and evasive states of mind and gaps in communication. When characters enter rooms they bring far too much with them—and find too much already there:

Were she dead, she could not have come from further away. But from this distance, her silver dress sweeping the stairs, all the more Emmeline seemed to arrive at a party, one of those parties from which one is always absent, which heroes and one's friends' friends attend in some kind of heaven; the eternal Party to which Cinderella drove up, upon whose light the doors close. "Here you are, . . ." Julian said, holding out a hand—that, though smiling his way, Emmeline did not see—as her shadow came down the white wall.

To the extent that the novel is concerned with the relation between public and private identities, and in particular with the function of secrets in human relations, the syntax does some work in foregrounding Emmeline's and Julian's distance from themselves and the role of fantasy in that distance. By and large, however, the language of the narrative is too affected to be engaging—it seems merely perverse rather than interestingly perverse.

It is not surprising to find that—as happens in so many popular films of the 1930's—Bowen's treatment of illicit sexual passion ends up with the melodramatic destruction of the lovers. As Bowen becomes more interested in the problem of "life's decreasing liveableness as life," she becomes even more interested in the violence of death, and in the presence of death in life. In the passage quoted above, the most typical Bowen sentence is the first: "Were she dead, she could not have come from further away." James Joyce, particularly the Joyce of "The Dead" (1914), is as strong an influence as Henry James on *To the North.* Like Joyce, Bowen is fascinated by the ways in which being in love is similar to being in mourning. The apprehension of another person's absolute difference—an apprehension that is a consequence of the kind of attention paid by a person who loves—is uncannily like a confrontation with death. The feeling that the present is haunted by the past and that the dead occupy the same space as the living is a characteristic Irish literary response to the anxieties of colonization and dispossession and in particular to the massive depopulation caused by the famine in the mid nineteenth century. At the end of Joyce's story "The Dead," there is a movement from inside to outside, from individual identity constructed in social spaces out into a landscape where the living and the dead seem to be made equivalent. Bowen strives for a similar effect at the end of *To the North.* Emmeline and Markie leave Cecilia and Julian after a party in St. John's Wood. Emmeline has offered to drive Markie to King's Cross, but instead she takes the northern road. The idea of the north has something of the resonance of the west in Joyce's story. At the moment when Markie realizes that she intends to kill them he has something like a Joycean epiphany:

"Look *out*—" he began: and stopped at her glittering look that while so intently fixing him showed in its absence of object a fixed vacancy. She looked into his eyes without consciousness as though in at the windows of an empty house. His throat tightened, the roof of his mouth went dry: she was not here, he was alone. Little more than his memory ruled her still animate body, so peacefully empty as not even to be haunted.

(p. 305)

Bowen differs from Joyce in casting her emphasis on the relationship between the two. They confront one another's vacancy. It is in *To the North* that Bowen pushes her interest in the unlivableness of life in the twentieth century into a fascination with ghosts and haunting that informs her writing for the rest of her career.

The House in Paris makes explicit the vision of the relationship between past and present implied in Bowen's earlier work. The first and third parts are both named "The Present," while the middle section is called "The Past." Part one is very much influenced by James, in his use of children as magnets, as conduits, and as censors of information about adult sexuality, particularly in his novel *What Maisie Knew.* In *The House in Paris,* two children, Henrietta and Leopold, meet for a day in the house in Paris belonging to Mme. Fisher and her daughter, Naomi. They are both passing through. Henrietta is being sent, like a parcel, to her grandmother. Leopold is waiting for his mother, who does not come. Bowen writes, "There is no end to the violations committed by children on children, quietly talking alone" (p. 20). The children begin to create for one another an articulated sense of identity. Henrietta "was anxious to be someone, and, no one having ever voiced a prejudice in her hearing without impressing her, had come to associate prejudice with identity. You could not be someone without disliking things. . . ." (p. 13). She ruthlessly interrogates Leopold about the missing mother for whom he is waiting:

The displeased cool manner in which Henrietta had peered behind the roses, and her glance at the clock, made Leopold value her: she showed he was nothing to her. All he had said, having left her cold, was still his. Where he came from, kindness thickened the air and sentiment fattened on the mystery of his birth. Years before sex had power to touch his feelings it had forced itself into view as an awkward tangle of his motives. There was no one he could ask frankly, "Just how odd *is* all this?" The disengaged Henrietta had been his first looking-glass.

(p. 23)

At the end of the first part of "The Present," when Leopold's mother does not come, Bowen makes her transition to "The Past" by suggesting how inadequate any explanation between two people, particularly between mother and child, would necessarily be. Instead she invokes the value of an imaginary relation: "So the mother who did not come to meet Leopold that afternoon remained his

creature, able to speak the truth" (p. 65). The middle section of the novel—"The Past"—which explains the mysteries of Leopold's birth and background, is staged as the narrative of what might have been said "on the plane of potential, not merely likely behavior" (p. 66), where people would be willing and able to communicate and language would be transparent. Under the umbrella of that conceit, of course, "The Past," as narrated to the reader, is by no means transparent and uncomplicated: "This is, in effect, what [Karen] would have had to say" (p. 67).

Surprisingly, "The Past" begins by returning the reader to the world of *The Last September.* It is ten years earlier and Karen Michaelis, Leopold's mother, is traveling by boat to Ireland. Much of "The Past" is concerned with this state of being between places and events. Karen is engaged to Ray Forrestier, an old family friend, but not yet married. She goes to Ireland to compose her thoughts, but the realization that her aunt Violet is dying confounds her expectations, as does Ireland itself.

It was hard for Aunt Violet's family to see why the Bents could not have chosen to settle—for instance—in Devonshire. Perhaps Uncle Bill clung to the edges of his own soil; and it was like Aunt Violet to set, so unconsciously, a premium on her company by living across the sea. Florence had seemed less distant; the Michaelis connection all knew Florence well. "Abroad" was inside their compass. But the idea of Aunt Violet in Ireland made them uncomfortable; it seemed insecure and pointless, as though she had chosen to settle on a raft.

(p. 75)

At first this excursion to Ireland seems oddly beside the point in such a tightly constructed novel. But it is in Ireland that Karen learns what it might be both to yearn for security and to crave for the margins of her society, to court risk. Karen has finished art school, had her time of adventure in Paris, and is waiting to be married. While she is in Ireland, her fiancé, Ray, is literally at sea, on his way to a diplomatic post in the East—his letters arrive on ship's notepaper. Karen's family have given her nothing to fight against:

Had the Michaelises been bigoted, snobbish, touchy, over-rich, over-devout, militant in feeling or given to blood sports—in fact, absurd in any way—Karen's new friends might have found them easier to stomach. But they offered nothing to satire; they were even, in an easy endearing way, funny about themselves.

(p. 69)

In Ireland Karen begins to learn how powerfully the past constructs people's imaginations. Her aunt's husband lives in a room dominated by the picture of his ancestral home, destroyed in the Troubles. It is this memory, rather than the soil, that keeps him in Cork. Even more significantly, in watching her aunt die, Karen becomes possessed with the desire to do something radical with and to herself, to make herself felt in the world. Back in London she meets up with her friend Naomi Fisher and Naomi's fiancé, Max Ebhart, a French Jewish banker, people she has known from her stay in Paris, in the very house where the novel begins and ends. Gradually the narrative reveals the sexual tension between Karen and Max, who seem almost pressed together by Naomi. Like the biblical Naomi, Karen's friend is the very emblem of generosity, fidelity, and domestic comfort, and the narrative examines how ruthless and oppressive those qualities may be. Karen and Max meet together twice, on the margins of their two countries, once in Boulogne and once in Hythe. In Boulogne they talk about history, and the narrative glosses their conversation with an interpretation of the place of memory in personal relationships:

They had been nowhere together, their childhoods had been different, of what people they had in common they dreaded to speak. Their worlds were so much unlike that no experience had the same value for both of them. They could remember nothing that they could speak of, and memory is to love what the saucer is to the cup. . . . But to walk into history is to be free at once, to be at large among people. . . . History is unpainful, memory does not cloud it; you join the emphatic lives of the long dead. May we give the future something to talk about.

(pp. 155–156)

This novel is Bowen's tour de force of formal elegance. The significance of place, for example, is explored not only in the house in Paris, but through a series of other houses, each of which becomes a place to think about death: the house in Ireland where Karen takes time out from her sexual passions and is confronted with her aunt's imminent death; the Michaelises' London house, which is most vividly described at the moment when Aunt Violet's death is announced; the house of Naomi's dead aunt in London; the hotel in Hythe where Leopold is conceived.

In her "Notes on Writing a Novel" (1945) Bowen begins by writing about plot: "Plot might seem to be a matter of choice. It is not. The particular plot is something the novelist is driven to. It is what is left after the whittling-away of alternatives" (in *Collected Impressions,* p. 249). Later she adds, "Plot must further the novel towards its object. What object? The non-poetic statement of a poetic truth" (p. 250). The particularly focused and accomplished plot of *The House in Paris*—the drama of a child searching for his identity by searching for his parents, who in their turn had searched for their identities in the sexual act that produced him—has occasioned the most interesting critical commentaries on Bowen. A. S. Byatt's introduction to the Penguin edition of the novel is an excellent account of the elegant and precise ways in which Bowen's concerns with sex, time, and identity are woven together in the narrative. Victoria Glendinning describes the novel as being concerned with "the politics of passion" (p. 116), and quotes one of its most powerful statements about Karen: "Nobody speaks the truth when there's something they must have." In the politics of passion women seem to be the more powerful players, because they are more experienced. Max, Leopold, and Ray seem oddly victimized. Max is driven to his suicide by his vulnerability to Mme. Fisher's willingness to say whatever is necessary, even to sacrifice her daughter, in order to get what she wants. At its conclusion the novel is profoundly pessimistic about how much reality anyone can bear.

SECRETS AND IDENTITY: THE DEATH OF THE HEART

The Death of the Heart further examines the destructiveness of a passion for knowledge about other people. The novel begins when Anna Quayne reads the diary of her sixteen-year-old sister-in-law Portia and finds out that Portia does not like her. Anna does not love Portia, but regards that as being beside the point. The incident of the diary becomes the occasion for a sustained interrogation of what it means to write, and what writing has to do with memory, experience, and audience.

The plundering of the diary also instigates an inquiry into what it means to have secrets, and how much a fiction of secrecy is bound up with the construction of subjectivity. Late in the novel Portia discusses her diary with Anna's friend, St. Quentin, who is a writer. He argues passionately against keeping a diary, which he claims is quite distinct from a novel:

I should never write what had happened down. One's nature is to forget, and one ought to go by that. Memory is quite unbearable enough, but even so it leaves out quite a lot. . . . But a diary (if one did keep it up to date) would come much too near the mark. One ought to secrete for some time before one begins to look back at anything. Look how reconciled to everything reminiscences are. . . . Also, suppose somebody read it?

(p. 67)

The yoking of secretion and secrecy in St. Quentin's vision of memory and writing is crucial to the ways in which writing itself is a metaphor for the articulation of subjectivity in the novel.

Anna first objects to Portia's diary because of its implication that Portia presumes to judge the world around her. In the 1930's many of Bowen's friends and contemporaries were engaged in explicitly political writing. In *Why Do I Write?* Bowen repudiated the idea that writers of fiction should have a political influence. She uses *The Death of the Heart* to argue that all writing is about the exercise of judgment, and that making judgments is the activity that constitutes individual identities. At the end of chapter one, when Anna has related Portia's history to St. Quentin, he asks, "But why was she called Portia?" The question is unanswered within the text, but one reason that suggests itself is that Portia, like Shakespeare's heroine of the same name, is like a Daniel come to judgment. Insofar as the novel is about being sixteen and losing one's innocence, then coming to judgment is figured as the necessary and sufficient compensation for such a loss.

Portia begins to lose her innocence when she hands over her diary to Eddie, Anna's protégé and antagonist, with whom Portia falls in love. She fails to recognize that Eddie may use the secrets of the household as weapons against Anna. Portia also makes the mistake of believing that because she offers Eddie access to her most secret thoughts and feelings that she will engender in him an obligation to her. She is horrified when he betrays her in the most careless and crass fashion, holding hands with her rival, Daphne, when they are all at the cinema together. Portia is like a nicer and more grown-up version of Henrietta in *The House in Paris.* She expresses herself through prejudices. She does not always know how far those prejudices are predetermined by the family histories to which she is vulnerable but of which she has little knowledge. Her closest friendship, for example, is with Matchett, a servant. She knows that Portia's elderly father had an affair with a young widow and that Portia is the product of that affair. The distinctively modern configuration of this old story is that Quayne's wife insisted that he divorce her and marry the widow. The wife's noblesse on this occasion is patently vicious: she turns Portia's family into exiles by so ruthlessly doing the apparently right thing. Matchett's fondness for Portia partly represents the reaching out of one lonely person to another, but it also, in opposing that sentence of exile, represents a critique of this respectable family.

WORLD WAR II: LOOK AT ALL THOSE ROSES, THE DEMON LOVER, *AND* THE HEAT OF THE DAY

DURING World War II Elizabeth Bowen worked as an ARP warden in London and was there during the Blitz. She also did war work for the British Ministry of Information by gathering intelligence in the Republic of Ireland, which was neutral. The war altered some of her attitudes to the usefulness of a writing that is politically engaged and she was willing to write propaganda, particularly where it would bring the British and Irish closer together. The majority of Bowen's writing during the war, however, expresses a complex and often critical attitude to the interplays between violence, civilization, and freedom in English life. Having made a commitment to England for the duration of the war, in 1942 she published an autobiography of her childhood, *Seven Winters,* and the history of her family home, *Bowen's Court,* in both of which she affirms her ties to Ireland. *Bowen's Court* is a meditation on the relationship between violence and culture in which Bowen declares, "We have everything to fear from the dispossessed." Indeed, some of her propagandizing in the 1940's was directed at explaining Irish neutrality to England, as well as trying to persuade the Irish to join the war effort. In *English Novelists* she describes the place of a nationally "great" literary tradition in forging a sense of English identity. Writing about English history, however, she is careful to present it as a political construct that falls apart when it is read back through the eyes of the dispossessed. She writes in "Doubtful Subject" (1939, in *Collected Impressions*), a review of two recent histories of Ireland:

Peace-lovers seek the past because it is safely over—and nothing in Ireland is ever over. England's past is at present one of her chief assets; it must have only one adjective—"glorious." And England's past in Ireland has not been glorious: its residue is a sort of embarrassment. When the Englishman looks at Ireland, something happens which is quite unbearable—the bottom drops out of his sense of right and wrong. That *méfiance* holds good in a generation: few Englishmen who served in His Majesty's Army in Ireland in those years that just preceded the Treaty care to be reminded of that country again.

So, ignorance of Irish history, in the English and most of the Anglo-Irish, has not been seen as a blot on culture—till now.

(p. 173)

It is at this point in her life, when she is most aggressively active for England, that Bowen begins to distance herself from normative Anglo-Irish political attitudes, belatedly referring, in a 1936 review of three books about Dublin, to the "scandalous and infinitely regrettable Union" (*Collected Impressions*, p. 176).

Bowen published two collections of short stories during the war, *Look at All Those Roses* (1941) and *The Demon Lover*. These war stories are justly celebrated for their evocations of the fear in London, as the city comes to terms with danger. They dwell on the changes wrought on people's expectations over time. They are particularly concerned with characters who, like Bowen, were young during World War I, and find in World War II both repetition and new horrors. They examine how World War II makes newly present the memory of the dead from the first war. The literature that Bowen turned to in the war was the literature of her childhood, particularly stories of empire by Joseph Conrad, Saki, Rudyard Kipling, Erskine Childers, and Rider Haggard. In a 28 February 1947 broadcast on Rider Haggard she explains what the author meant to her in childhood:

I saw Kôr before I saw London; I was a provincial child. Inevitably, the Thames embankment was a disappointment, being far, far less wide than Horace Holly had led me to expect. I was inclined to see London as Kôr with the roofs still on. The idea that life in any capital city must be ephemeral, and with a doom ahead, remained with me—a curious obsession for an Edwardian child. At the same time I found something reassuring and comforting in the idea that, whatever happened, buildings survived people. Long, even, before I had read *She*, I would run across any amount of fields to look at any ruin, even the ruin of a cottage. Yes, it seems funny now. . . . *She*, the book, glutted my imagination with images and pictures of which I could not, it seemed, have enough.

(*The Mulberry Tree*, p. 249)

Growing up in Ireland, where so many of the ruins, from forts and monasteries to castles and famine cottages, are traces of colonization and exploitation, Bowen's interest in ruins is necessarily a political interest. Bowen's need to believe that cultural artifacts are more enduring than people was radically shaken in the Blitz. She wrote to Virginia Woolf on 5 January 1941, after the bombing of the Woolfs' home in Mecklenburgh Square: "All my life I have said, 'Whatever happens there will always be tables and chairs'—and what a mistake" (in *The Mulberry Tree*, pp. 216–217). The war stories look hard at what happens to individuals when the material world begins to crumble around them.

The only serious mistake in these stories is a mistake about class. In *The Death of the Heart* one of the most successful strokes is Matchett's attachment to the Quayne's furniture and her choice to serve their possessions (which are her possessions) rather than the family. However, in one of Bowen's most popular stories at the time of the war, "Oh, Madam . . ." (in *Look at All Those Roses*), this same idea does not work as well, despite the notable popularity of the dramatized version. This dramatic monologue is the speech of a maid to a silent interlocutor, her mistress, after the bombing of the house. The maid is more attached to the house and possessions than the mistress is, and clearly this is intended to be a touching account of working-class spirit and fidelity. As Angus Wilson points out in his introduction to *The Collected Stories of Elizabeth Bowen*, Bowen's ear for dialect is not good here. Perhaps "Oh, Madam . . ." is irritating and provoking rather than touching because Bowen's apprehension of violence is too powerful for her to joke about it successfully. On the other hand, Bowen may simply have fallen victim to the vanity and self-centeredness of a privileged life and really have fantasized that the maid's language of fidelity is appropriate and worthwhile.

In contrast, Bowen shows a sharp ear for the complacencies and self-deceit of members of her own class in "Careless Talk" (in *The Demon Lover*), a story about the ways in which some people who cannot buy fresh eggs can always survive on potted shrimp and grouse. Joanna, whose house has been destroyed in the Blitz, comes up to London from the country where she is raising chickens and caring for evacuees. She meets some old friends in a smart restaurant. The men are full of self-importance about secret war work. The women are enjoying the glamor of a little inconvenience. Everyone is noisily self-obsessed, but that does not seem inappropriate in a context where those selves are being violently attacked.

"Mysterious Kôr" (in *The Demon Lover* and *Ivy Gripped the Steps*) is the best of the war stories. Pepita and Arthur wander about London on a bright moonlit night during the blackout. They dread their return to the tiny flat Pepita shares with Callie. They want to sleep together, but Pepita is expected to sleep with Callie, and Arthur on the divan. They play a game, a retreat into Pepita's fantasy that London is Kôr, a lost city in central Africa, from H. R. Haggard's *She* (1887). Arthur does not know quite what to make of the game. Really he wants to get on to sex. "What next?" he keeps asking. "I thought girls thought about people," he remarks. "What, these days?" she said. "Think about people? How can anyone think about people if they've got any heart? I don't know how other girls manage: I always think about Kôr." To think about Kôr is to think about the power of symbols to empty themselves of specific significance. Pepita does not think specifically of Africa and empire, of Ayesha, the goddess who governs Haggard's Kôr, and female sexuality, of white supremacy and the war, even of herself and Arthur, but of a pure empty place. The story ends with her sleeping in bed, Callie's cold body seeking her warmth, Arthur fretting in the next room, and Pepita herself escaped into a dream of Kôr.

Given Bowen's own work as an intelligence gatherer in Ireland during the war, *The Heat of the Day* may be read as a particularly self-reflexive study of the nature of loyalty and betrayal. Stella Rodney is in love with Robert Kelway, a soldier wounded at Dunkirk. She is harassed by a man named Harrison who claims that Kelway is a Nazi spy. Harrison is a British spy, and therefore self-congratulatory about his motives. He blackmails Stella, telling her that he will spare Robert if Stella will have sex with him. She is merciless in her recognition of what he is asking: " 'I'm to form a disagreeable association in order that a man be left free to go on selling his country' " (p. 36). This unlikely situation is the occasion of Bowen's most explicitly feminist writing. The dilemma facing Stella is that she instinctively does value personal loyalties over abstract or more removed concepts like patriotism or freedom. Like everyone in wartime London, she recognizes her own ties to those more distant ideals. She is a widow with a son in the army. Stella's dilemma is that her loyalty is called upon at the very moment when she realizes that she does not know her beloved. But as Robert becomes increasingly obscure to her understanding, Harrison becomes clearer. Stella begins to recognize that the erotic surveillance Harrison has conducted over her affair with Robert is contiguous with his other practices as an agent of the state, and that sexuality is always under the surveillance of the state. Given the state's attempt to control female sexuality, Stella comes to a position vis-à-vis the war effort that is very close to that articulated by Virginia Woolf in *Three Guineas* (1938): she finds herself asking if a woman should have a country. At this point in the novel she is obliged to travel to neutral Ireland to safeguard her son's inheritance there, and thus confronts the possibility of an analogy between feminism and postcolonialism in their dissent from patriotic configurations. Had Robert Kelway been a Communist rather than a Nazi, as many of Bowen's friends would have liked, his "betrayal" of his country might have been rationalized and Stella's anguish eased. As it is, she ends up supporting Robert not so much out of loyalty to someone increasingly strange, but as a gesture of resistance against the management of women in nationalist ideologies.

1950's AND 1960's: A WORLD OF LOVE, A TIME IN ROME, THE LITTLE GIRLS, *AND* EVA TROUT

In the 1950's and 1960's, even as her reputation grew, Bowen felt herself to be increasingly out of touch with contemporary sensibilities and styles of writing. *A World of Love* is more a synthesis of earlier themes than a new development. It is a ghost story set in Ireland, narrated around the experience of a young girl and concerned with the construction of identity through desire and in time. The heroine, perhaps like Bowen herself, wants to live in an earlier generation. The novel is clever about postwar nostalgia and the ways in which it manifests itself through style. Jane irritates her family by rooting around in attics and wearing old clothes. It is the first novel of Bowen's widowhood; its interest in grief and haunting and its plangent tones may be read as the work of mourning:

Life works to dispossess the dead, to dislodge and oust them. Their places fill themselves up; later people come in; all the room is wanted. Feeling alters its course, is drawn elsewhere, or seeks renewal from other sources. When of love there is not enough to go round, inevitably it is the dead who must go without: we tell ourselves that they do not depend on us, or that they have not our requirements. Their continuous dying while we live, their repeated deaths as each of us dies who knew them, are not in nature to be withstood.

(p. 65)

Bowen wrote about ghost stories in general that "obsessions stay in the air which knew them, as a corpse stays nailed down under a floor" (*Afterthoughts,* p. 207). This is a very precise understanding of what it means to be haunted. The corpse stays nailed down, it is hidden but in place, a smell in the air. A ghost story set in Ireland becomes a fresh opportunity for Bowen to reflect upon the ways in which Ireland's apparently interminable troubles are informed by the presence of the dead.

In the decade of the "angry young men" and new postwar subjects and style, *A World of Love* takes the risk of sentimentality indicated by its title and the epigraph from Thomas Traherne's *Centuries of Meditations* (a seventeenth-century manuscript first published in 1927): "There is in us a world of Love to somewhat, though we know not what in the world that should be. . . . Do you not feel yourself drawn by the expectation and desire of some Great Thing?" The novel offers a world of suffering and loss and asks what expectations of love might grow out of such a world. Perhaps this, rather than *The Last September,* should be read as Elizabeth Bowen's

attempt to articulate what all the losses of her childhood meant to her.

It is not surprising to read the first phrase of Bowen's only "travel book," *A Time in Rome* (1960), and discover that "too much time in too little space" is announced as her concern. Bowen had a fellowship at the American Academy in Rome and found the city "the ideal environment for a born stranger." Bowen finds in the revealed palimpsest of the city a correlative for the hinged door of *The Hotel,* the skeleton furnace of Danielstown, and the blitzed buildings of London that preoccupied her earlier writings.

Bowen's last two novels, *The Little Girls* and *Eva Trout,* have not generally been as popular as her earlier works. The attempt in *Eva Trout* to produce a 1960's atmosphere is distinctly odd, as her 1930's melodrama is no longer in touch with popular genres. *Eva Trout* is the story of an heiress whose search for a child ends in her death at the hands of that child. After a career of writing powerfully about children's passions for their parents, Bowen seems curiously disengaged from the description of what it might feel to be a parent.

The Little Girls is a more significant achievement, although it contributes little new to Bowen's concerns. It returns to the structure of *The House in Paris*—present, past, present—and to a triangular relationship. Three elderly women, who have not seen each other since they were eleven years old, come together for a reunion. The middle section describes incidents from their girlhood at a seaside school. They pledge their friendship by burying a chest: "Each girl was to place in the coffer, before its burial, one undeclared object, of which the nature was to remain known to herself only" (p. 137). The point of this gesture toward futurity is that none of them shall ever know the contents. A return to the narrative present brings the three women together, each now much less easy with the contemplation of her own mortality. The novel concludes with the recovery of the chest and the revelation (surprising to the women) of what each had buried. *The Little Girls* is formally accomplished. The foundation of the vanities of age is interestingly revealed by an excavation of childhood. The seaside town is unsentimentally reconstructed. In the end, however, the plot does not resonate with the significances of Bowen's earlier fiction.

ELIZABETH BOWEN

CONCLUSION

The blurb to almost every Bowen novel in print carries a quotation from Glendinning's 1977 critical biography: "She is a major writer. . . . She is what happened after Bloomsbury, . . . the link that connects Virginia Woolf with Iris Murdoch and Muriel Spark" (p. xv). The claims being made here—not only that Bowen is a "major" writer, but also that she may be situated in two traditions, one of British women writers and the other of postmodern realists—needs to be re-examined. The formation of literary value implied in the term "major writer" no longer seems as helpful as when Glendinning published her biography. One might also question the usefulness of placing Bowen in a British female tradition that situates her between an influential English feminist like Woolf and two Anglo-Celts of very different political persuasions. Bowen's importance for feminist history and criticism is not her minimal engagement with issues of women's political and social oppression but her interrogations of the relationship between gender and national identity and her understanding of the role of the state in producing various sexualities and identifications of sexual conduct. Heterosexuality, homosexuality, incest, adultery, illegitimacy, and celibacy are all represented in Bowen's novels as socially constructed. She is an important Irish writer in that she offers a substantial critique of both Yeats and Joyce, the dominant figures in anglophone Irish literature of this century, and suggests alternative ways in which Irish writers might address questions of identity, history, and time.

Bowen is not an innovator in plot or style. What she contributes to fiction in English is an extraordinary attention to tradition. Language, conventions, and manners that have been taken for granted she places under stress. She addresses mainstream, middle-class English life as someone sufficiently alienated by race and gender to cast a cold eye upon it. During her life she sustained her fair share of losses, both of people and place. She uses the effects of sudden and violent change upon the individual imagination to describe an individual's self-representation at the moment when death seems imminent. Her fiction is likely to be of most interest to readers who feel that at least one kind of useful action and self-reflection is accomplished in the work of mourning. In *The Heat of the Day,* Stella's son Roderick claims that "art is the only thing that can go on mattering once it has stopped hurting" (p. 337). It may be the work of contemporary cultural studies to take apart that claim, but there can be no doubt that it is one to which Elizabeth Bowen was deeply committed.

SELECTED BIBLIOGRAPHY

I. BIBLIOGRAPHY. J. M. Sellery, *Elizabeth Bowen: A Descriptive Bibliography* (Texas, 1977).

II. COLLECTIONS. *The Early Stories* (New York, 1951), contains *Encounters* and *Ann Lee's; Pictures and Conversations,* ed. by S. C. Brown (London, 1975; New York, 1975); *The Collected Stories of Elizabeth Bowen* (London, 1980; New York, 1981); *The Mulberry Tree: Writings of Elizabeth Bowen,* ed. by Hermione Lee (London, 1986; San Diego; 1987).

III. SEPARATE WORKS. *Encounters* (London, 1923; New York, 1923); *Ann Lee's and Other Stories* (London, 1926; New York, 1926); *The Hotel* (London, 1927; New York, 1928); *The Last September* (London, 1929; New York, 1952); *Joining Charles and Other Stories* (London, 1929; New York, 1929); *Friends and Relations* (London, 1931; New York, 1931); *To the North* (London, 1932; New York, 1933); *The Cat Jumps and Other Stories* (London, 1934); *The House in Paris* (London, 1935; New York, 1936); as editor, *The Faber Book of Modern Stories* (London, 1937); *The Death of the Heart* (London, 1938; New York, 1939); *Look at All Those Roses* (London, 1941; New York, 1941); *Seven Winters: Memories of a Dublin Childhood* (Dublin, 1942, limited edition; London, 1943); *Bowen's Court* (London, 1942; New York, 1942); *English Novelists* (London, 1942); *The Demon Lover and Other Stories* (London, 1945), published as *Ivy Gripped the Steps and Other Stories* (New York, 1946); with Graham Greene and V. S. Pritchett, *Why Do I Write? An Exchange of Views Between Elizabeth Bowen, Graham Greene, and V. S. Pritchett* (London, 1948; Folcroft, Pa., 1969); *The Heat of the Day* (London, 1949; New York, 1949); *Collected Impressions* (London, 1950; New York, 1950); *The Shelbourne: A Centre in Dublin Life for More Than a Century* (London, 1951), published as *The Shelbourne Hotel* (New York, 1951); *A World of Love* (London, 1955; New York, 1955); *A Time in Rome* (London, 1960; New York, 1960); *Afterthought: Pieces About Writing* (London, 1962); *Seven Winters: Memories of a Dublin Childhood and Afterthoughts: Pieces on Writing* (New York, 1962); *The Little Girls* (London, 1964; New York, 1964); *The Good Tiger* (New York, 1965; London, 1970); *A Day in the Dark and Other Stories* (London, 1965); *Eva Trout or Changing Scenes* (New York, 1968; London, 1969).

IV. CRITICAL STUDIES. J. Brooke, *Elizabeth Bowen* (London, 1952); S. Tweedsmuir, *A Winter Bouquet* (London, 1954);

R. Macaulay, *Letters to a Friend 1952–1958,* ed. by C. B. Smith (London, 1962); R. Lehmann, *The Swan in the Evening* (London, 1967); C. Ritchie, *The Siren Years: Undiplomatic Diaries 1937–1945* (London, 1974); E. J. Kenney, *Elizabeth Bowen* (Lewisburg, Pa., 1975); J. Rule, *Lesbian Images* (London, 1976); M. Sarton, *A World of Light: Portraits and Celebrations* (New York, 1976); V. Glendinning, *Elizabeth Bowen: Portrait of a Writer* (London, 1977; New York, 1978).

H. Lee, *Elizabeth Bowen: An Estimation* (London, 1981); M. McGowan, "The Enclosed Garden in Elizabeth Bowen's *A World of Love,*" in *Eire-Ireland,* 16 (Spring 1981); B. B. Watson, "Variations on an Enigma: Elizabeth Bowen's War Novel," in *Southern Humanities Review,* 15 (Spring 1981); D. W. Meredith, "Authorial Detachment in Elizabeth Bowen's 'Ann Lee's,'" in *Massachusetts Studies in English,* 8 (1982); A. Quinn, "Elizabeth Bowen's Irish Stories," in *Studies in Anglo-Irish Literature,* ed. by H. Kosok (Bonn, 1982); H. S. Chessman, "Women and Language in the Fiction of Elizabeth Bowen," in *Twentieth-Century Literature,* 29 (Spring 1983); J. E. Dunleavy, "Mary Lavin, Elizabeth Bowen, and a New Generation: The Irish Short Story at Midcentury," in *The Irish Short Story: A Critical History,* ed. by J. F. Kilroy (Boston, 1984); B. Hooper, "Elizabeth Bowen's 'The Happy Autumn Fields': A Dream or Not?" in *Studies in Short Fiction,* 21 (Spring 1984); D. M. Laigle, "Images of the Big House in Elizabeth Bowen," in *Cahiers du Centre d'Etudes Irlandaises,* 9 (1984); J. Medoff, "'There is no elsewhere': Elizabeth Bowen's Perceptions of War," in *Modern Fiction Studies,* 30 (Spring 1984).

D. Gauthier, "L'Image du réel dans les romans d'Elizabeth Bowen," in *Études Anglaises,* 91 (1985); J. Halperin, "Elizabeth Bowen and Henry James," in *The Henry James Review,* 7 (Fall 1985); B. O'Toole, "Three Writers of the Big House: Elizabeth Bowen, Molly Keane and Jennifer Johnson," in *Across a Roaring Hill: The Protestant Imagination in Modern Ireland,* ed. by E. Longley and G. Dawe (Belfast, 1985); A. C. Partridge, "Language and Identity in the Shorter Fiction of Elizabeth Bowen," in *Irish Writers and Society at Large,* ed. by M. Sekine (Totowa, N.J., 1985); M. Scanlan, "Rumors of War: Elizabeth Bowen's *Last September* and J. G. Farrell's *Troubles,*" in *Eire-Ireland,* 20 (Summer 1985); P. Craig, *Elizabeth Bowen* (London, 1986); R. B. Kershner, "Bowen's Oneiric House in Paris," in *Texas Studies in Literature and Language,* 28 (Winter 1986); A. Ashworth, "'But why was she called Portia?': Judgement and Feeling in Bowen's *The Death of the Heart,*" in *Critique,* 28 (Spring 1987); J. Bates, "Undertones of Horror in Elizabeth Bowen's *Look at All Those Roses* and *The Cat Jumps,*" in *Journal of the Short Story in English,* 8 (Spring 1987); H. Bloom, ed., *Elizabeth Bowen* (New York, 1987); J. Coates, "The Rewards and Problems of Rootedness in Elizabeth Bowen's *The Heat of the Day,*" in *Renascence,* 39 (Summer 1987); M. Jarrett, "Ambiguous Ghosts: The Short Stories of Elizabeth Bowen," in *Journal of the Short Story in English,* 8 (Spring 1987); T. O. Johnson, "Light and Entertainment in Elizabeth Bowen's Irish Novels," in *Ariel,* 18 (April 1987); J. Coates, "The Recovery of the Past in *A World of Love,*" in *Renascence,* 40 (Summer 1988).

SAMUEL BUTLER

(1835–1902)

Robert Casillo

SAMUEL BUTLER WAS born on 4 December 1835 at Langar Rectory, near Bingham, Nottinghamshire. He was the son of the Reverend Thomas Butler and Fanny Worsley and the grandson of Dr. Samuel Butler, who was headmaster of the famous Shrewsbury School and became bishop of Lichfield. By Butler's own account his childhood was one of the unhappiest a writer ever suffered. Raised in a loveless clerical family that his father ruled with an iron hand, he kneeled before he could crawl and began learning Latin at the age of four.

Regularly punctuated by religious exercises and his father's sermonizing, domestic life at Langar resembled a perpetual Sunday school. The young Butler often suffered corporeal punishment for spiritual and intellectual infractions. In his memoir, "Father and Son," written between 1883 and 1898, Butler said that his father was "sure to be against me," and was "my most implacable enemy from childhood onward" (*Butleriana,* 1932, pp. 25–26). This unhappy upbringing, which Butler fictionally portrays in *The Way of All Flesh* (1903), was the decisive period of his life. The absence of parental love first starved and then crippled his affections, so that thenceforward he remained emotionally timid. Throughout his life Butler repeated his hostility to his father by constantly venting his grievances on the world. His attacks on intellectual authorities and his view of himself as a Victorian Ishmael are evidence of this. However, his early miseries were somewhat alleviated by his love of George Frideric Handel's music, which often figures in Butler's writings, and of Italy, which he visited twice before the age of twenty and later adopted as his second country.

At Cambridge University, which Butler attended from 1854 to 1858, he wrote humorous sketches dimly foreshadowing his mature attitudes. Appearing in 1858 in the *Eagle,* a school publication, "On English Composition and Other Matters" rejects literary ornamentation in favor of plain and honest expression: the writer should know and say what he really thinks and feels. Yet Butler was preparing for ordination in accordance with his father's wishes, and his environment gave him little cause to doubt this goal. He later noted that Cambridge was uncharacteristically free of religious controversy during his undergraduate days, and that the Christian miracles were generally accepted. Nonetheless, Butler's latent antireligiosity surfaced in his undergraduate spoof of the overenthusiastic evangelical Simeonites. His dislike of zealotry remained with him and was reinforced by the Cambridge ethos of intellectual moderation.

While preparing for ordination as an amateur lay assistant among the London poor, Butler was shocked to discover no discernible moral differences between the baptized and unbaptized students in his Bible class. With his faith in dogma thus weakened, he refused to take religious orders and quarreled bitterly with his father over his career choice. Canon Butler rejected on moral grounds his son's proposal to become an artist; Butler announced his intention to live without his father's financial support. "I have duties to myself to perform," said Butler, "even more binding on me than those to my parents" (*The Family Letters,* p. 76) Finally Canon Butler gave him £4400 to establish a sheep farm in the vicinity of the new colony of Canterbury in New Zealand. On his first night at sea he neglected for the first time to say his prayers, while during the voyage he read Edward Gibbon, that satirist of Christianity. He arrived at Canterbury early in 1860.

Butler's four and a half uncharacteristically happy years in New Zealand greatly widened his experience. Just as New Zealand inspired the unforgettable mountain landscapes of *Erewhon* (1872), so its frontier environment may have contributed to that work's curious perspectivism and awareness of the conflict between "primitivism" and "progress," the organic and the mechanical. Butler's sheep farming may also have catalyzed his later speculations on evolution. However, the earliest literary result of Butler's New Zealand adventure was the prosaic *A First Year in Canterbury Settlement* (1863), which his father compiled and edited from Butler's letters home and saw through publication. Butler's parents were unaware that their son's religious inquiries had led him deeper into skepticism. Not willing to accept the doctrine of the Trinity, Butler imagined himself a unitarian. In 1862 his studies of the Gospel accounts of the Resurrection, which he had begun while preparing for ordination, forced him to conclude that Christ did not die on the cross. He declared in the same year, writing to a Cambridge friend, that "for the present, I renounce Christianity altogether" (in H. F. Jones' *Memoir,* p. 98).

Yet the greatest challenge to Butler's religious beliefs came from Charles Darwin's *On the Origin of Species by Means of Natural Selection* (1859), which he read in 1860 with enormous enthusiasm. Butler later told Jack B. Yeats, whom he met at Heatherley's art school in London, that *The Origin of Species* destroyed his belief in a personal god. It also inspired him to write a dialogue that the *Press,* a Canterbury newspaper, published in 1862. This short piece provides Darwin's defender with an explanation of natural selection so lucid that Darwin himself thought it worth reprinting. But though the dialogue was seen as a defense of Darwin, it actually dramatized the opposition between science and religion. Not only does Darwin's opponent complain of the heartless logicality of natural selection, but Darwin's defender believes in religion and aims honestly to define its difference from science. Butler typically gave both sides of an issue; here he is skeptical of both religion and Darwinism.

A similar skepticism of natural selection underlies two later essays Butler wrote for the *Press.* Published in 1863 under the pseudonym Cellarius and entitled "Darwin Among the Machines," the first essay argues for the immediate destruction of all machinery, for machines, being logically the next stage of evolution, will ultimately develop in organization and efficiency to the point where they dominate humanity. Butler did not fully realize the anti-Darwinian implications of the essay, which suggests that natural selection is inherently mindless and mechanical. Nor did Butler initially grasp the implicit anti-Darwinism of the second essay, "Lucubratio Ebria," published anonymously in 1865. This essay counters the thesis of the earlier one in arguing that machines, being artificial extensions of limbs, always remain under human control, and that those persons with the greatest amount of mechanical power—that is, the rich—are the most developed organisms. In short, humanity exerts a degree of free will over merely mechanical forces. Even more interesting, the essay proposes that limbs are machines that organisms have created for themselves. This idea, as Butler understood only later, challenges Darwin's explanation of evolution as the result of the natural selection of fortuitous rather than purposive organic variations. Still, Butler seems to have meant "Lucubratio Ebria" as something of a joke, as its very title dismisses it as the product of an inebriate mind.

Butler sold his sheep farm at a profit sufficient to enable him to return to England and to live independently of his parents. In New Zealand he had met Charles Paine Pauli, a handsome, well-dressed, and charming young man whom Butler idolized as the very opposite of himself. Some critics see Butler's self-sacrificing adoration of Pauli as his attempt to become an ideal father to an ideal son. Others view their relationship as latently or even secretly homosexual, arguing that its easy detectability and special unacceptability in an underpopulated and extremely conservative colonial setting necessitated Butler's and Pauli's departure for England. Yet their friendship cooled soon after their arrival in London in 1864. Even so, Pauli persuaded Butler to give him a substantial yearly allowance, which Butler provided even during his own extreme financial difficulties. In 1897, the year of Pauli's death, Butler discovered that Pauli had a substantial independent income and had been bilking two other persons. He was the great love of Butler's life and a model for Towneley in *The Way of All Flesh.*

EREWHON *AND* THE FAIR HAVEN

UPON arriving in London, Butler set up bachelor's quarters at 15 Clifford's Inn and began pursuing a career as a painter at Heatherley's art school. A man of strong habits, he would remain at Clifford's Inn until his death on 18 June 1902. Although painting claimed most of his attention into the early 1870's, in 1865 he published several short pieces that anticipate his later writings. "Lucubratio Ebria" was written in England in that year, as was "The Mechanical Creation," published in the *Reasoner* and amounting to a reiteration of "Darwin Among the Machines." Butler's "Precaution in Free Thought," also published in the *Reasoner,* typifies his peculiar combination of intellectual independence and conservatism in arguing that, to quote Lee E. Holt's summary of Butler's position (in his *Samuel Butler,* p. 34) while each generation has the right to develop its own ideas, reformers ought to take care "not to push for a growth which the roots will not support." As in his later evolutionary writings, Butler fears the destructiveness and unfamiliarity of abrupt change and favors gradual, even tentative progress; hence caution is seen as a necessary means of preserving social unity and continuity.

Butler's most important literary effort of 1865 was a pamphlet entitled *The Evidence for the Resurrection of Jesus Christ as Given by the Four Evangelists, Critically Examined,* which Butler's companion Henry Festing Jones described as Butler's apology for not becoming a clergyman. A development from his skeptical inquiries into the Gospels, the pamphlet argues in close detail that textual inconsistencies undermine the credibility of Christ's Resurrection; the lack of corroboration between the Gospels makes it impossible to affirm that Christ died on the cross. Butler was disappointed that the pamphlet went unnoticed, yet he would return to its arguments in *The Fair Haven* (1873), *Erewhon Revisited* (1901), and *The Way of All Flesh.*

At Heatheriey's art school in 1870 Butler met Miss Eliza Mary Ann Savage—a major event in his personal life. Despite her drab existence as a governess and manager of a lady's club, Miss Savage had mental and verbal brilliance, a quick, acerbic wit, and an ironic view of life from the perspective of a social outsider. Gradually their friendship deepened into psychological and intellectual intimacy. They often exchanged letters and notes, and Butler welcomed her shrewd criticisms of his manuscripts, among them *Erewhon* and *The Way of All Flesh.* Miss Savage wanted to marry Butler, but he preferred to remain emotionally detached; he was not attracted to her, as she lacked physical beauty. After her death in 1885 he wrote three sonnets in which he expresses repulsion at her face and figure

and remorse over having rejected her. Nonetheless, Miss Savage greatly influenced Butler's writing, for she appreciated his originality and encouraged him during a period of critical and commercial failure.

Even as he pursued his career in painting, Butler continued to speculate on evolution, ethics, religion, and a host of other subjects. In 1870, on a trip to Venice, he so impressed a Russian woman with the novelty of his thought that she told him: "Et maintenant, monsieur, vous allez créer" (and now, monsieur, you must create). Within two years Butler had published *Erewhon,* his first major work and his only commercial success, however modest. As *Erewhon* constituted Butler's sole claim to a literary reputation throughout his life, he described himself as *homo unius libri,* a man of one book. Although his family knew that he had written it, he published it anonymously for fear of offending them, as *Erewhon* is a biting satire on modern life and thought; because of its audaciously irreverent treatment of religious and scientific themes it has prompted some misleading comparisons with Jonathan Swift. But soon enough Butler's authorship was revealed. As Butler revealed only later in *Erewhon Revisited,* the narrator of *Erewhon* is John Higgs, an English everyman who, while working on a sheep farm in an unidentified country resembling New Zealand, is led by commercial ambition to cross a mountain fastness into the undiscovered land of Erewhon (an anagram of nowhere). Arrested by the Erewhonians, Higgs spends his time observing and commenting upon their civilization until, accompanied by his Erewhonian beloved and future wife, he escapes in a balloon. *Erewhon* abundantly exemplifies Butler's penchant for turning values upside down, for exploiting the comedy of incongruity. Sometimes Higgs speaks for Butler; sometimes he is absurd. At points Victorian values are vindicated; at others Erewhonian superiority is implied; at others Victorian foolishness or wisdom is mirrored by the Erewhonians.

The germ of *Erewhon* lies in the two Darwinian essays Butler wrote for the *Press;* they are the basis for the three chapters entitled "The Book of the Machines." Centuries before Higgs's arrival, an Erewhonian philosopher had argued—as Butler did in "Darwin Among the Machines"—that machines are evolving automatically, by natural selection, and that their ever-increasing efficiency and organization will ultimately enable them to enslave humanity: hence they must be abolished immediately. The Erewhonian philosopher's chief opponent countered with arguments echoing "Lucubratio Ebria," contending that machines are extensions of human limbs, that they only increase humanity's mastery over nature, and that the most developed human beings command the most mechanical power. He further held that limbs are tools that organisms have created for themselves. The antimechanists won the debate, and the Erewhonians lapsed into a medieval technological capability. Some critics have suggested that "The Book of the Machines" seeks to reduce Darwin's theory of natural selection to absurdity by showing that it implies the triumph of mechanism. Others claim that it predicts the dehumanizing mechanization of modern life. However, Butler told Darwin in a letter of 11 May 1872 that these chapters had not a "particle of serious meaning" and implied no disrespect toward Darwin's theory (letter included in Jones's *Memoir,* vol. 1, p. 156). Nor is it likely that Butler was prophesying technological determinism, for as a voluntarist he probably believed that machines would remain under human control. Even so, "The Book of the Machines," like the essays it stems from, anticipates Butler's attack on the theory of natural selection as a falsely mechanical interpretation of nature, one that denies to organisms the freedom to shape their existence from within.

Darwin exerts a crucial influence as well upon Butler's portrayal of Erewhonian morality, which is naturalistic, deterministic, and utilitarian. Higgs discovers that the Erewhonians view disease as immoral and criminally punishable. This attitude is reinforced by the practice of requiring infants to assent, by proxy, to "birth formulae," absolving their parents of responsibility for their physical and moral failings, and also by the Erewhonian philosophy of the unborn, which depicts embryos as pestering their parents for postnatal existence. At the same time, the Erewhonians legally punish any misfortune or disgrace—for instance, ugliness or commercial failure—as a social offense. Crime is defined, conversely, as impaired mental or physical health: criminals are placed in the hands of "straighteners," who somewhat resemble psychiatrists. Not surprisingly, these beliefs often tempt the sick to cover their illness through criminal means. But though Erewhonian morality may seem a meaningless spoof, Hans-Peter Breuer points out in "The Source of Morality in Butler's *Erewhon*"

(1973) that Butler almost certainly recommends it as consistent with Darwin's view that nature punishes the diseased and unfortunate while granting success to the biologically favored. Butler's approval of Erewhonian morality is not invalidated by his later criticism of the theory of natural selection in its neglect of organic purposiveness, since he never denies the importance of luck in evolution, or that natural selection acts, as Breuer says, upon what it finds. Erewhonian morality appeals to Butler's social conservatism, since it reflects the fact that societies reward the lucky and condemn the unlucky.

Some critics claim that when Higgs is being Victorian, the Erewhonians are sensible, and vice versa. Others hold that Butler's lack of a unified or systematic point of view makes for an inconsistent and multidirectional satire. And for others, Butler's repeated inversion of moral values indicates topsy-turvyism for its own sake, to the point that *Erewhon* becomes farcical and even meaningless. Actually, *Erewhon* sometimes endorses Victorian attitudes Butler espouses elsewhere in his writings. And while the satire lacks a unifying thematic focus, it presents a consistent attitude toward reality, as evidenced by its typically Butlerian plea for balance and equilibrium, common sense and compromise.

One sees this in Butler's satire on the Erewhonian Colleges of Unreason, which are modeled on Oxford and Cambridge. Specializing in an ancient, useless, and purely speculative language known as "hypothetics," whose prestige lies in its venerable antiquity, the professors of these schools inculcate vagueness and fence-sitting. Apart from his conviction that classical education is impractical, Butler here expresses his hostility to extremism as manifested in priggish academic jargon and double-talk. On the other hand, insofar as the Colleges of Unreason do not encourage students to think for themselves, or to surpass their neighbors, they anticipate Butler's view in his *Note-Books* (1912) that genius, though necessary for social progress, is often dangerously novel and extreme. The Professors of Unreason agree with another principle expressed in the *Note-Books,* that while extremes, taken alone, are logical, they inevitably meet; a strictly logical proposition must lead to contradiction. Contrariwise, the mean is illogical, yet preferable to the sheer absurdity of the extreme. Thus endowed with a sense of balance, the professors

SAMUEL BUTLER

advocate not pure unreason but its necessity as a counterpoint to reason.

A similar desire for balance underlies Butler's satire on the Erewhonian Musical Banks. Housed in beautiful, venerable, yet unvisited buildings reminiscent of English churches, the Musical Banks dispense a currency that is supposedly the basis of all commercial transactions, but that is actually of no practical value, being merely ornamental. All business is conducted by means of a separate monetary system. The banks are called "musical" because all transactions are conducted to the sound of hideous music. Here then is a satire on conventional religion, which can be seen as going ignored in daily life. Yet despite the fact that this satire coincides with the period of Butler's intensest religious skepticism, it does not necessarily seek to discredit all religion. Rather, Higgs's observation that some bank coins are ugly, while others are beautiful and good, implies that religion has some value. Higgs further observes that the Musical Banks testify to the presence of a "kingdom that is not of this world," and of which we know only that "it exists and is powerful," being founded on the "unseen power . . . to which [we give] the name of God" (p. 119).[1] Butler's demand for equilibrium requires that, just as practical currency is balanced by impractical, so the seen world must be balanced by the unseen—a point Butler underscores in a paragraph added to the 1901 edition, in which he admits a preference for religious faith as opposed to scientific hubris: "The Erewhonian Musical Banks, and perhaps the religious systems of all countries, . . . attempt to uphold the unfathomable and unconscious instinctive wisdom of millions of past generations, against the comparatively shallow, consciously reasoning, and ephemeral conclusions drawn from that of the last thirty or forty" (p. 119).

Although the Erewhonians profess to believe in supernatural deities, they unofficially worship the quotidian goddess Ydgrun. The name is an anagram of Mrs. Grundy, and Ydgrun, like her English counterpart, represents conformism, the tacit acceptance of the standards and judgments of one's neighbors. Refusing to insist on points of dogma and other extremes, the Ydgrunites are morally flexible and even lax when occasion demands.

Thus their behavior, though slightly balanced on the side of virtue, is not excessively virtuous. At the same time, the Ydgrunites recognize the importance of good luck and conventionally estimate success in terms of beauty and material advantage. Since Ydgrun typifies the antiextremism and utilitarian pragmatism Butler celebrates throughout his career, he no doubt wants us to admire the high Ydgrunites as paragons of social and biological success. The Ydgrunite is, as Higgs recognizes, the equivalent of the Victorian gentleman or "swell," whom Butler apotheosizes in his later works; and his admiration for them reveals his longing for qualities he himself did not possess. Besides having wealth and good looks, they dress well and exhibit a "nice," casual amiability that, should they disapprove of anything, keeps them from speaking out. And because they see both sides of an issue, they escape self-righteousness and logical rigidity—in short, they lack the priggishness to which Butler traced much of his misery at others' hands.

The Erewhonian prigs include the professors of hypothetics, the antagonist of machines, and the philosopher introduced in the 1901 edition. Claiming divine revelation, the philosopher asserted that, as animals are "our fellow-creatures," we have no right to eat slaughtered meat, only that of animals dead from natural causes. Butler's sympathy is with those Ydgrunites who kill animals in secret and pretend that they had committed suicide—a deception justified by common sense. He also no doubt agrees with the Erewhonian philosopher who reduced his predecessor's argument to absurdity by ironically proposing that, if animals are our brethren, so too are plants, and should not be eaten. To take this idea seriously would mean mass starvation. However, the worst prig in *Erewhon* is probably Higgs, who sometimes justly criticizes Erewhonian beliefs, but whose religious dogmatism blinds him to inconsistencies in his own. Even worse, Higgs combines priggishness with hypocrisy, for although upon entering Erewhon he intends to convert its inhabitants to Christianity, at the work's conclusion he intends to sell them into slavery. This is Butler's comment on the Victorian compromise between high-toned religious sentiments and ruthless commercialism.

Published in 1873, Butler's *The Fair Haven* is the first in a long line of commercially unsuccessful books. This is a fictional work, not a novel as such but a satire, in which Butler obliquely expresses his

[1] Page citations throughout the essay refer to the Shrewsbury edition of Butler's works, unless otherwise noted.

101

religious skepticism. What is the epistemological status of miracles, especially the Resurrection? Does not the credibility of Christianity hinge upon Christ's rising from the dead? *The Fair Haven* thus grows out of Butler's 1865 pamphlet, *The Evidence for the Resurrection of Jesus Christ.* But unlike the pamphlet, *The Fair Haven* is an ironic fiction whose irony was lost on many readers. This misapprehension resulted partly from the fact that Butler ascribed the work to two fictional authors, whose statements one is invited to accept unsuspectingly; the main reason, however, is that Butler's irony is extremely subtle and all-pervasive.

The introductory section of *The Fair Haven* consists of William Bickersteth Owen's memoir of his brother, John Pickard Owen, whose faith was shaken, as was Butler's, first by the realization that good conduct bears no necessary relation to the fact of baptism and then by his discovery of inconsistencies in the Gospel accounts of the Resurrection. Pickard Owen thus fell into extreme skepticism, running desperately from sect to sect, doctrine to doctrine. This fictional memoir enables Butler to state indirectly his own attitudes and opinions. Bickersteth Owen observes that children's ideas of God are "modelled upon the character of their father" and that "all children love their fathers and mothers, if these last will only let them." Moreover, "so soul-satisfying is family affection to a child, that he who has once enjoyed it cannot bear to be deprived of the hope that he is possessed in Heaven of a parent who is like his earthly father— of a friend and counsellor who will never, never fail him" (pp. 8–9).

Here Butler expresses his resentment of his father's unloving treatment of him as well as of Canon Butler's punitive version of Christianity. Butler also reveals his longing, which persisted throughout his life, for an emotionally nourishing conception of the divine. Perhaps the most remarkable irony of the memoir is that Pickard Owen attains such a conception during his skeptical phase. Criticizing Christianity for its emphasis on self-denial and its lack of the ideals of "generosity and nobility of conduct" (p. 40), he contrasts the "peevish" Christian view of life with the joyful and balanced values typified by classical paganism, the Italian Renaissance, and Shakespeare's plays. Although Bickersteth Owen offers such statements as examples of his brother's spiritual confusion, they support the same values that Butler later

celebrates in *Life and Habit* (1878) and in the *Note-Books.*

The no less ironic main text, entitled "The Fair Haven," is Pickard Owen's account of his long journey from skepticism to the "fair haven" of orthodoxy. Describing himself as a "broad Churchman" (p. 20), the forty-year-old Pickard Owen contends that he has reconciled religion with reason. His claims are hardly strengthened by the fact that, shortly after completing his work, he dies insane. Pickard Owen's aim is to vindicate Christianity, but only after permitting the rationalizing textual critics of the New Testament to have their say. But though he wants to summon them only to refute them, he unwittingly disproves his own position. First he considers the argument of the German scholar David Strauss, who theorized that Christ died on the cross and that reports of his reappearance resulted from hallucinations. Rejecting the likelihood of collective hallucination, Pickard Owen insists that the Apostles, being weak in faith and shaken by the Crucifixion, would have accepted only solid evidence of Jesus' immortality. Turning next to Dean Henry Alford's analysis of Gospel accounts of the Resurrection, he accuses Alford of intellectual cowardice for attesting that the Gospels can be harmonized even if it is not yet possible to do so. Yet Pickard Owen's credibility collapses through his own inability to reconcile the Gospels' inconsistencies. Indeed he admits that we have "no evidence of Christ's having died," and that a "jury of educated Englishmen" would not accept the evidence of his death (ch. 8). These rashly candid admissions apparently undermine Christianity's supernatural foundations, if not Christianity itself. Yet rather than yield to logic, Pickard Owen "explains" that the Almighty intended the Gospels' portrayal of Christ to be inaccurate, and that they are true *because* of their inconsistencies. Their confusion is God's way of revealing the "Christ-ideal," which gains by its vagueness, since it allows each person to fill in the picture of Christ with whatever he or she requires. Pickard Owen dies a classic example of blind faith and sanctimoniousness.

In view of the evidence Pickard Owen marshals against belief in the Resurrection, *The Fair Haven* must be seen as a satire on the irrationality of orthodox Christianity. Nonetheless, it was widely interpreted as a vindication of Christian dogma. Darwin, to whom Butler sent a copy, not only admired the work's dramatic power but added that he would not have suspected the author of being unorthodox. Christian readers were taken in by Butler's irony and their unwillingness to face the facts. It would be a mistake, however, to suppose that in so ironic a work as *The Fair Haven* the irony points in only one direction, or that Butler, in attacking Christian dogma, sought to undermine all religion. At its most subtle, the work implies that Pickard Owen's spiritual crisis results from a lack of balance, which leads him to apply mere reason to ultimate questions that are beyond the power of reason to answer. And insofar as the main issue of faith is left unresolved, *The Fair Haven* can be seen as an attack not only upon dogma but upon reason itself, its pretensions to the attainment of final truth.

It is therefore possible to find, as Basil Willey suggests in *Darwin and Butler: Two Versions of Evolution* (1960), a residuum of the possibility of faith even in Pickard Owen's sanctimonious contention that faith in God does not finally depend on such "facts" as the Resurrection:

After all, it is not belief in the facts which constitutes the essence of Christianity but rather the being so impregnated with love at the contemplation of Christ that imitation becomes almost instinctive; this it is which draws the hearts of men to God the Father, far more than any intellectual belief that God sent our Lord into the world, ordaining that he should be crucified and rise from the dead. Christianity is addressed rather to the infinite spirit of man than to his finite intelligence.

(ch. 9)

This passage anticipates Butler's attempt to reinterpret Christianity in accordance with the theory of evolutionary instinct developed in his scientific writings.

AN ATTACK ON DARWINISM

By the early 1870's Butler's life had begun to take on its distinctive pattern. Although some of his paintings were exhibited at the Royal Academy, he was neither critically nor commercially successful as a painter, and by 1877 he had transferred his professional ambitions to a literary career. His best painting is probably *Family Prayers* (1864), a satiric

reminiscence of Langar, in which the stiff, almost primitive rendering of the figures underscores their lifelessness. He did not altogether abandon his artistic interests, as he continued to paint on the side and in 1886 applied unsuccessfully for the Slade Professorship of Art at Oxford. Butler's decisive turn to literature was encouraged by the success of *Erewhon,* for which he was briefly lionized. But thereafter he had little commercial success as a writer, and indeed, with the exception of *Erewhon Revisited,* he published his books at his own expense.

For a number of years Butler was a member of the Whig literary circle surrounding Crabb Robinson, a living relic of the Romantic period, and also of the Century Club, a fraternity of minor literati. But being a maverick and by no means a good mixer, he left the club around 1880, citing his conservative opposition to its liberal views. By this point he had settled into the largely solitary domestic existence for which the ladies at Heatherley's had dubbed him "The Incarnate Bachelor" (reported in Jones's *Memoir,* vol. 1, p. 140). Oddly reminiscent of his childhood at Langar, the influence of which he seems never to have escaped, Butler's life was remarkably routinized and rather dull, consisting of meals at assigned intervals; visits to the British Museum, where he did his writing; occasional evening entertainments with his small coterie of friends; and a solid eight hours of sleep. On Wednesdays he visited Mlle. Dumas, a prostitute, until her death in 1892; every year he had his Italian vacation, which he considered essential to his intellectual refreshment. Just as ideas provide the chief interest in most of Butler's writings, so his mental life and more specifically his books came to dominate his being. "My books," he said, "are to me the most important thing in life. They are in fact 'me' much more than anything else" (reported in C. G. Stillman, 1932, p. 88).

From 1876 onward Butler's social isolation was alleviated by his friendship with Henry Festing Jones, a part-time lawyer sixteen years his junior. Unlike Pauli, Jones was devoted, if not slavish, in his admiration for Butler and shared his interest in music, painting, science, Italy, and other subjects. He visited Butler regularly and often accompanied him to the theater, on long walks, and on his yearly vacations to the Continent; indeed, they even shared Mlle. Dumas. Butler valued Jones's critical judgment of his works and even described him, much overgenerously, as their coauthor. During the 1880's Butler and Jones learned musical counterpoint and collaborated on a number of mainly Handelian-style compositions. To no small extent their friendship was a mutual admiration society that sometimes descended into foolishness: while Jones acceded to Butler's judgments of most things, Butler seriously praised a fugue by Jones as the best composition since Handel. In any case they remained close friends until Butler's death, and in 1919 Jones published a two-volume celebratory memoir of Butler that greatly added to his reputation.

Worse than the poor sales and critical neglect of his works, the darkest cloud over Butler in the 1870's was that of financial failure. The high estimation or perhaps overestimation of material wealth in his works reflects his recognition of the commanding influence of money in his own life. In the early 1870's Butler made bad investments, most seriously in a Canadian tanning company, and in 1874 he went to Montreal in a desperate attempt to rescue his money. As *Life and Habit* shows, he perceived his Canadian experience as a personal crisis, a time of struggle between his past and future selves. On the one hand, he wanted to preserve the continuity of his life and personality in the face of economic catastrophe; on the other, he wanted to respond to adversity by striking out on a new intellectual path, namely his writing career and in particular his scientific works. Over the next decade he had no choice but to call upon his father's assistance. Meanwhile he doggedly pursued his scientific writings despite growing financial pressure and intense critical opposition. Relief came at last in 1886, with the death of his father, whose legacy resolved Butler's money problems henceforeward.

In a letter dated 8 March 1873 Miss Savage told Butler that the dramatic power of *The Fair Haven* showed that he was capable of writing a "beautiful novel" (letter included in Jones's *Memoir,* vol. 1, p. 173). That year Butler began an autobiographical novel that, following its posthumous publication under the title *The Way of All Flesh,* came to be recognized as his finest achievement. Insofar as the work is a dramatization and exemplification of Butler's maturing ideas, it needs to be seen in relation to his scientific writings as well as to his *Note-Books,* large portions of which he wrote contemporaneously with the novel.

Butler's scientific works, which he held highest in his own estimation (see C. E. M. Joad, 1924, p. 19), are the key to nearly his entire corpus. *Life and Habit* is the most important one. Its starting point is the argument, deriving from "Lucubratio Ebria," that limbs are tools organisms have created for themselves. But if organisms create limbs for their own convenience, how is it, asks Butler, that they learned how to make them? How does an egg, without conscious understanding, become an adult organism? Butler contends that a growing organism unconsciously remembers and instinctively repeats the accumulated practices—that is, the unconscious, instinctive habits—of its ancestors. Unconscious memory is therefore identical to heredity, and each organism is identical to its parents. Butler adds that memories of ancestral habits are latent in a developing organism, and that when it finds itself in situations similar to those its ancestors encountered, long-forgotten trains of association are activated, thus enabling it to adapt instinctively to its surroundings. On the other hand, each organism finds itself in at least slightly novel circumstances and thus has its own peculiar needs. In attempting to adapt to new conditions, an organism can, by its own efforts, acquire new habits and traits slightly different from those of its ancestors. These become part of its memory, are added to the ancestral store, and are passed on to its offspring. Butler insists, however, that successful adaptation is most likely to occur when an organism finds itself in only somewhat unfamiliar situations, for too abrupt a change or too great a "cross" in its experience is likely to defeat it. In short, Butler believes that organisms inherit characteristics acquired by their forefathers and that, therefore, organisms partly design themselves. The constant repetition of similar conditions underlies the stable, hereditary factor in evolution, while the variational factor is the more important, since it leads to the modification of species.

Another key argument in *Life and Habit* is that consciousness is always evidence of an organism's doubt and unfamiliarity in experience, the failure of activity to become habitual and therefore instinctive. However, a conscious organism's knowledge grows more perfect until, through repetition and familiarity, activity based on that knowledge becomes habitual and thus less conscious. It follows that only those things we do unconsciously are completely known and experienced. This holds true for both the developing embryo, which acts completely by instinct, and for the trained pianist, who plays a complex score without thinking about it. The pianist illustrates Butler's notion that consciousness is a "vanishing tendency" (*Note-Books*, p. 49) as well as his paradox that perfect knowledge is perfect ignorance, that is, unconsciousness. Thus, according to Butler, the best thief is the kleptomaniac.

Butler's high estimation of instinct has major ethical implications. He argues that evolutionary success or "perfection" is the special privilege of those persons who unconsciously achieve their own happiness, in the sense of mental and physical pleasure. For Butler, such instinctive hedonism is the very sign of "grace" (p. 8)—not in the Christian sense of otherworldly benefaction, but in the worldly, Latin sense of pleasure, favor, or thanks. As the highest examples of grace, he offers the Hellenic ideal of effortless physical health and beauty as manifest in Greek and Italian art—the Venus de Milo, the Discobolus, and Donatello's St. George (p. 32). In his own time its exemplars are those who have "good health, good looks, good temper, common sense and energy," and who maintain all these things "without introspection" (p. 27). He refers to the un-self-reflective, hence bibliophobic children of the "best class" (p. 29), the Victorian "swells" he celebrates in numerous works for their instinctive grace. By contrast, Butler identifies the very antithesis of grace as "law" in the sense of merely conscious, introspective, and hence insufficiently mastered action, and exemplifies it in all "ugly, rude, and disagreeable people" (p. 27). What Butler sees as the dominance of law over grace in postclassical Western civilization he attributes to the influence of the antihedonic legalist St. Paul, who "stole the word" grace in conceiving it as only a spiritual virtue (p. 33), and therefore "drove it into the wilderness."

Throughout his career Butler would strenuously defend the Hellenic over the Hebraic ideal. *Life and Habit* should thus be read concurrently with his 1875 poem "A Psalm of Montreal" (collected in the *Note-Books*, pp. 392–393), which records his disgust at discovering, in a Canadian museum, that the guardians of public morality had consigned copies of the Antinous and the Discobolus, two "swells" of the ancient world, to a room filled with "skins, plants, snakes, [and] insects" (see Jones's *Memoir*, vol. 1, p. 218). This is not to suggest that Butler numbered himself among the graceful, for in *Life and Habit* he describes himself as "damned" (p. 35). Nor should his concept of grace be understood as encompassing only a materialistic hedonism, as it yields a justification for faith in the spiritual world. As Butler points out, grace is also an attribute of those who, unlike introspective religious rationalists, believe unconsciously in God and hence repeat the proven unconscious wisdom of their ancestors. And insofar as the church, whatever its shortcomings, still "uphold[s] a grace of some sort" (p. 34), its teachings are perhaps ultimately reconcilable with evolutionary science.

The implications for Butler of *Life and Habit* cannot be ignored. It was begun during a personal crisis, when Butler faced the uncertainties of a literary career as well as the possibility of financial collapse. One recalls his point that organisms generally achieve successful adaptation when confronting only *moderately* unfamiliar circumstances, which permit them to adjust more readily to newly acquired habits. In a spirit of resolution rather than panic Butler dramatizes this conflict between his past and future selves in his recollection of the bells of Montreal, where he had vainly sought to retrieve his investments:

It is one against legion when a creature tries to differ from his own past selves. He must yield or die if he wants to differ widely, so as to lack natural instincts, such as hunger or thirst, or not to gratify them. It is more righteous in a man that he should "eat strange food," and that his cheek should "so much as lank not," than that he should starve if the strange food be at his command. His past selves are living in unruly hordes within him at this moment and overmastering him. "Do this, this, this, which we too have done, and found our profit in it," cry the souls of his forefathers within him. Faint are the far ones, coming and going as the sound of bells wafted on to a high mountain; loud and clear are the near ones, urgent as an alarm of fire. "Withold," cry some. "Go on boldly," cry others. "Me, me, me, revert hitherward, my descendant," shouts one as it were from some high vantage-ground over the heads of the clamorous multitude. "Nay, but me, me, me," echoes another; and our former selves fight within us and wrangle for our possession.

(p. 43)

Just before completing *Life and Habit* Butler learned of Darwin's criticism of the French naturalist Jean-Baptiste Lamarck for what Darwin described as Lamarck's discredited theory of the inheritance of acquired characteristics. Butler read Lamarck and realized not only that his own thinking was closer to Lamarck's than to Darwin's, but that he much preferred the theories of the former. According to Lamarck, organisms develop new uses for organs as a result of changing needs occasioned by the environment. As disuse enfeebles an organ, use develops it; and as the acquired characteristic is transmitted to offspring, in time a new species emerges. Butler agreed with these points, although Lamarck never attributed the inheritance of acquired characteristics to unconscious memory as the basis of heredity. After reading Lamarck, Butler added several chapters to *Life and Habit,* stating on what he saw as Lamarckian grounds his objections to Darwin's theory of natural selection. The key conceptual difference he cites is the role of teleology, or purpose, in evolution. Whereas for Darwin changes in species result primarily from nonpurposive external agencies, for Butler they result from purposive, self-designing efforts by organisms. To be sure, Lamarck seems to have viewed organic changes not as resulting from purpose or design but as occurring automatically. Yet in *Luck, or Cunning* (1887) Butler claims that Lamarck's denial of design is only "skin deep" (p. 7).

The response to *Life and Habit* was largely hostile, and not merely because of its anti-Darwinian argument. Critics objected to Butler's pose as the "man in the street" (reported in Stillman, p. 132) who appeals to supposedly sense notions such as the evident purposiveness of organisms. They did not consider Butler's style appropriate for scientific writing, complaining of his love of paradox, his literalizing of analogies—for instance the identity of heredity and memory—and his satiric irony, for which he had already won a reputation. Indeed, the *Athenaeum,* a publication that published Butler, suspected a hoax.

Butler extended his critique of Darwinism in *Evolution, Old and New* (1879). The famed naturalist Alfred Russel Wallace described it as an interesting, important, and even necessary supplement to Darwin's theory; nevertheless, it was mainly attacked or ignored. The work argues that Darwin was not, as many believed, the first theorist of evolution, but that the neglected Georges-Louis Buffon, Erasmus Darwin (Charles Darwin's grandfather), and Lamarck had preceded him with more insightful theories of their own; moreover, that Darwin had deliberately ignored or belittled his predecessors. Here we see Butler in his increasingly characteristic role as intellectual maverick and vindicator of for-

gotten genius. His major intention, however, is to show that Darwin's theory of natural selection explains little, and certainly not the origin of species. To explain that, Butler contends, it is necessary to combine the ideas of Darwin's predecessors with Butler's own teleological theory of evolution as primarily the result of the inheritance of acquired characteristics through unconscious memory.

Butler shows that Buffon, Erasmus Darwin, and Lamarck all recognize organic descent with modification yet explain it with varying emphases. For Buffon, modification results from two causes, the primary being changed conditions, the secondary being the organism's changing needs under such conditions. Although Buffon does not speak explicitly of the inheritance of acquired characteristics, Butler contends that he assumed the validity of that idea. Like Butler, Erasmus Darwin viewed children as "elongations" of their parents, thus recognizing the unity of parents and offspring, but explained this as the result of imitation rather than memory. He further anticipated Butler (and Lamarck) in seeing organic variation as the direct consequence of living needs. As for Lamarck, like Butler he sees changed conditions as the indirect cause of variation; the direct cause is the organism's varying needs arising from those changed conditions.

In the broadest sense the importance of these naturalists for Butler is that they rejected either explicitly or implicitly the traditional idea that organic purposes are governed by an *external* teleology. In other words, they reject the view that nature's design and its designer are unchanging, that nature works toward final causes or ends predetermined by a single, nonnatural intelligence, namely God. By contrast, Buffon, Erasmus Darwin, and Lamarck argued for an *immanent* teleology, whereby nature's design emerges slowly and unpredictably, as the result of small adaptive changes initiated by organisms themselves. Butler, too, rejects final causes along with the idea that nature's plan is predetermined by some external intelligence that is "not an organism." Instead, nature's plan constantly evolves as organisms bequeath to their offspring new traits acquired through their own tentative, yet purposive, efforts:

No plant or animal, then, . . . would be able to conceive more than a very slight improvement on its organization at a given time, so clearly as to make the efforts towards it that would result in growth of the required modification; nor would these efforts be made with any far-sighted perception of what next and next and after, but only of what next.

(p. 42)

What is the crux of Butler's opposition to Darwin? Darwin's chief aim was to show how those variations that provide an advantage in the struggle for survival are "selected" by the environment and how the accumulation of such selected variations finally results in new species. Although Darwin, much to Butler's annoyance, spoke of organic variations as fortuitous, he did not believe that the success of his theory required him to explain causes. It is now agreed that Darwin demonstrated how natural selection works, and that variations result from genetic and biochemical causes. As for Butler, it must again be emphasized that he never denies the reality of natural selection or that luck plays an enormous role in evolution. He insists, however, that Darwin failed to explain the origin of species because he did not explain the origin of variations—precisely what Butler mistakenly attributes to the voluntary use and disuse of organs and to the hereditary transmission of acquired characteristics through unconscious memory. For Butler it is these factors, not natural selection, that constitute the primary cause of evolution. Butler complained that Darwin's tendency to speak of natural selection as a means falsely suggested that external factors caused variations. He also took mischievous pleasure throughout his scientific works in showing that in successive editions of *The Origin of Species* Darwin had weakened his original theory by giving greater emphasis to use and disuse.

Yet Butler's quarrel with Darwin goes deeper. Insofar as the theory of natural selection emphasizes fortuitous variations and environmental factors, it horrifies Butler as the apotheosis of a mechanical universe ruled by chance and devoid of intelligence and will. Darwin, he charges in the introduction to *Luck, or Cunning,* had "pitchforked" the mind "out of the universe." For Butler the ultimate superiority of his own theory is in recognizing the intelligent purposiveness, the "cunning" of organisms. In *Evolution, Old and New* he accepts the view of the distinguished biologist St. George Mivart that the universe is "sustained and directed by an infinite cause" (quoted in B. Willey, 1960, p. 82), which is the mind. Butler believes as well that evolution is a "moral struggle" (p. 39): organisms seek to improve the value of their existence by "faith" in their own efforts and in the unconscious memory deriving from their ancestors (see *Life and Habit,* p. 56). Undoubtedly this conception of faith is rooted in Butler's belief in his personal struggle against his family's opposition to his own desires for self-realization. It is not surprising that *Evolution, Old and New* concludes with speculations on the possibility of reconciling evolutionary science with religious belief.

Unfortunately, Butler's opposition to Darwin at least partly degenerated into a personal grudge. His next work, *Unconscious Memory* (1880), devotes tedious pages to the *"Kosmos* affair," the most unattractive episode of Butler's literary career. In 1879 Darwin published a prefatory essay to *Erasmus Darwin,* the substance of which, explained Darwin, consisted of an English translation of an article by Ernest Krause originally published in the German journal *Kosmos.* Butler read Darwin's book and found statements attacking recent attempts to revive Erasmus Darwin's ideas, which Butler suspected as referring to *Evolution, Old and New.* His suspicions were confirmed, so he thought, when he found that Krause's article, which was in fact written before his own book, contained no such statements. Butler concluded that Krause, with Darwin's approval and perhaps at his instigation, had expanded the original article in order to attack *Evolution, Old and New;* moreover, that Darwin had tried to conceal his deception. Although Darwin's failure to mention the discrepancy between the two works seems to have been an oversight, Butler implied publicly that Darwin was trying to sabotage him as he had supposedly sabotaged Buffon, his grandfather, and Lamarck. Darwin tried to make amends, then retreated into embarrassed silence. While Butler was justified in asking for an explanation, his accusations testify not only to his intensifying and somewhat paranoid antagonism toward authority figures, but also to his growing frustration at the neglect of his own ideas. Writing of his struggle against "vested interests" (*Evolution, Old and New,* p. 173). Butler described himself as a "literary Ishmael" who had the "entire scientific community against [him]" (*Luck, or Cunning* p. 14), and whose scientific writings "were still-born, or nearly so, as they fell one after the other from the press" (*Butleriana,* p. 64).

Butler had more important aims in *Unconscious Memory.* It includes a translation of the German biologist Carl Ewald Hering's lengthy "On Memory as a Universal Function of Organized Matter," in which Hering had preceded Butler in arguing that unconscious memory underlies heredity and that personal identity therefore extends through the generations. Hering speculates that memory results from the molecular vibration of the nerve fibers in response to internal and external stimuli, heredity thus being explicable as the transmission of vibration patterns. Although Butler argues for the plausibility of the vibration theory, elsewhere he seems more skeptical; but he was glad to find a distinguished scientific ally. *Unconscious Memory* also contains a translation from Edward von Hartmann's *Philosophy of the Unconscious* (1869), which attributes many vital phenomena to unconscious forces. Butler points out, however, that von Hartmann hypostatizes or "deifies" the unconscious as an impersonal entity independent of the will and personality of organisms; he offers, in short, another version of external teleology. By contrast, Butler identifies the unconscious with inherited instincts traceable to the conscious, voluntary effort of organisms to adapt to their environment. Yet the major intellectual development in *Unconscious Memory* is Butler's turn to monism. In his previous scientific writings he had argued for vitalism, that is, for the existence of a living principle irreducible to mechanical or chemical causes. Here he asserts that there is no absolute distinction between the organic and the inorganic, the purposive and the nonpurposive: all matter is already imbued in some degree with life. As Butler wrote to H. M. Paget on 20 May 1880: "I have finally made up my mind that . . . every molecule of matter is full of will and consciousness, and that the motion of the stars in space is voluntary and of design in their parts" (letter included in Jones's *Memoir*, vol. 1, p. 333).

Butler wrote two more scientific works of interest: *Luck, or Cunning* and "The Deadlock in Darwinism," consisting of three essays originally published in the *Universal Review* in 1890. ("The Deadlock of Darwinism" is included in the second volume of *Collected Essays* in the Shrewsbury edition.) Polemical in tone, and marred by mean-spirited denigrations of Darwin's genius, *Luck, or Cunning* acknowledges the importance of luck in evolution yet argues that organisms, including plants, are capable of intelligent, voluntary adaptation, and that this testifies to a universal mind. Discussing his book in a letter to Mrs. Alfred Tylor, Butler observes that "no name can be so fittingly applied" to such an intelligence as "God" (reported in Jones's memoir, vol. 2, p. 41). He admits the unorthodoxy of his position but insists upon his religiosity, which is directed against the "present mindless, mechanical, materialistic view of Nature" (quoted in Wiley, p. 305). By now Butler had come to find the religious emphasis on unconscious faith and invisible power more appealing than dogmatic scientific rationalism. He insists, though, that no fundamental antagonism ought to exist between religion and science, as they properly confirm and supplement each other. Just as God is the "ineffable contradiction in terms whose presence none can enter, or ever escape" (*Luck, or Cunning,* p. 115), so religious faith is inseparable from the true theory of evolution. Another polemic, "The Deadlock in Darwinism" takes on the neo-Darwinians Alfred Russel Wallace and August Weismann, who defined natural selection as the sole cause of evolution. Butler saw special urgency in opposing Weismann's germ cell theory, which holds that, since germ cells are alone the carriers of the hereditary component, and since they are unaffected by changes in somatic cells, there can be no transmission of acquired characteristics. As Butler admits, Weismann's theory filled him with an "instinctive loathing" of the idea that "habit, effort, and intelligence" count for "nothing" in evolution (p. 40). But though Butler pointed out equivocations in Weismann's theory, it is in the main line of modern biological thought, while Lamarckianism has few proponents.

THE NOTE-BOOKS

BUTLER's *Note-Books* is, with *Erewhon* and *The Way of All Flesh,* the third pillar of his reputation and crucial to understanding his life and thought. Beginning in 1874, Butler kept extensive notebooks, which he revised, edited, and indexed at intervals, and which he edited in 1891 for the last time. Henry Festing Jones published an incomplete single-volume edition of the notebooks in 1912; they now run to three volumes. When in the *Note-Books* Butler quotes Buffon's observation that "le style c'est l'homme" (style is the man, p. 104), he does so in support of his own belief that literature is valuable only in how it reveals the author. Like Butler's other works, the notebooks reflect his personality in their resistance to ornament and self-conscious eloquence, their unaffected plainness, directness, and logical clarity. Less typically, the notebooks convey something of Butler's warmer side, as in his vignettes of London life and sketches of his manservant, Alfred. Mainly, though, the notebooks are the product of a life devoted to rigorous if unsystematic thinking. Aphoristic, anecdotal, and essayistic by turns, they typify Butler's love of paradox and chiasmus, satire and irony. They offer surprising if sometimes strained analogies, unsettling shifts of perspective, subversive yet invigorating mockery of conventional ideas and institutions, and at points an intellectual cruelty that P. N. Furbank saw as moral anarchism. To support this argument, he quoted the notebooks:

There will be no comfortable and safe development of our social arrangements—I mean we shall not get infanticide, and the permission of suicide, and cheap and easy divorce—till Jesus Christ's ghost has been laid; and the best way to lay it is to be a moderate churchman.

(in Furbank, p. 31)

More than validating Butler's description of himself as the *"enfant terrible* of literature and science" (p. 182), the notebooks are the testament of a Victorian outsider who, with a forced show of joyousness, compared himself to the Hebrew priest Melchizedek: "He was a really happy man. He was without father, without mother, and without descent. He was an incarnate bachelor. He was a born orphan" (p. 25).

At the center of the *Note-Books* is Butler's vision of a monistic universe in which all things forever change and pass into each other in constant conflict and contradiction. Nothing has a clear beginning or end, limit or boundary: not life or death, self or not-self, organic or inorganic nature, memory or intelligence. And as opposites always interpenetrate, so nothing exists absolutely, but always in relation to something else. Hence there can be no absolute principles, no metaphysical foundations. Ideas are "baseless" and "rotten at the roots" (p. 314), and "everything must be studied from the point of view of itself . . . and . . . its relations" (p. 301). So too, in a world of flux all words and concepts are necessarily makeshift, provisional, a matter of convenience. "There is no such source of error," writes Butler, "as the pursuit of absolute truth" (p. 302), while definitions are merely the

"enclosing [of] a wilderness of idea within a wall of words" (p. 222). Logic, dogma, and all other forms of intellectual absolutism vainly attempt to fix reality within a conceptual system, to find stability amid endless flux. Moreover, logical absolutes are inherently extreme, and extremes prove untenable in a world in which opposites converge. As Butler says, "Truth should never be allowed to become extreme; otherwise it will be apt to meet and to run into the extreme of falsehood" (p. 302). Indeed, "an eternal contradiction in terms meets us at the end of every enquiry" (p. 306).

Butler thus arrives at an antirationalist position. Since dogma and logic lead to contradiction, they must be balanced by faith or intuition, which spring from the unconscious and which are therefore more trustworthy than merely reflective reason. Butler even prefers common sense to intellectual absolutes. Yet what must be emphasized is that his antirationalism leads Butler, in the *Note-Books* as elsewhere, to a tentative acceptance of religion. Despite its dogmatism, religion surpasses positivistic science in its appeal to faith and in its recognition of the paradoxes of life, the mysterious penetration of the seen and the unseen. Butler had learned in his quarrel with Darwin and his supporters that scientists are more dogmatic than clergymen.

In the *Note-Books* Butler aims toward balance, compromise, a via media of the mind. One sees this especially in Butler's apothegms: "Though Wisdom cannot be gotten for gold, still less can it be gotten without it" (p. 171), or "Absolute virtue is as sure to kill a man as absolute vice is" (p. 20), and "It is the function of vice is to keep virtue within reasonable bounds" (p. 21). Again, Christianity is "at once very moral and very immoral. . . . There is no knowledge of good without a knowledge of evil also" (pp. 17–18). Sometimes, though, the balancing act becomes mechanical, self-parodic: "You may have all growth or nothing growth, just as you may have all mechanism or nothing mechanism, all chance or nothing chance, but you must not mix them. Having settled this, you must proceed at once to mix them" (p. 301). Nonetheless the ideal of balance in the notebooks underlies Butler's continued support of the Hellenic over the Hebraic principle. He celebrates Hellenism for its appreciation of the unconscious as the source of physical grace and spontaneity, its rejection of dogma and logical extremism as inimical to hedonistic instinct, its harmony of body and mind. Contrariwise, Butler identifies the Hebraic principle with St. Paul, who, notwithstanding his rejection of the Jewish law in favor of Christian grace, Butler insists upon viewing as legalistic and intolerant. According to Butler, St. Paul was wrong not only to despise money (which Butler loves), but also, to define grace as a solely spiritual endowment, to devalue the beauty and freedom of the physical body. For Butler, St. Paul remains the arch-prig, the man of rules.

In his *Note-Books,* as elsewhere, Butler deplores priggishness as the vice of professionalism. He regards the typical professional as a myopic grotesque whose self-conscious overcomplication of the rules, methods, and language of his own discipline renders him incapable of honesty or spontaneity. Rather the professional's delight is to inflict his system upon other people. Denouncing professors as typical prigs, Butler protests the enforcement of classical education and insists that students should learn only that which instinctively attracts them. He also despises artistic professionalism, finding only insincerity in John Cardinal Newman and Robert Louis Stevenson, two highly self-conscious literary artists. Composers of marked technical difficulty such as Bach and Beethoven suffer from too much "gnosis," too much knowledge; Butler prefers Handel's comparatively simple style as revealing "agape," sincere emotion. (For Butler's musical views, see *Note-Books,* pp. 89–132.) Likewise he finds agape in the early Italian artists, whose works are free of affectation, and who learned by unsystematic apprenticeship rather than by slavish adherence to the academic rules and formulae ushered in by the high Renaissance. Indeed, Butler contends that he would have succeeded as a painter had academicism not suffocated his creative instinct.

Butler's rejection of intellectual absolutism in his *Note-Books* leads him to a theory of truth reminiscent of the American pragmatists. Like Butler, the pragmatists rejected apriority, metaphysical absolutes, and closed systems in favor of an emphasis on action, development, and the extension of human power; for them the value of ideas is in achieving useful results. So, too, the pragmatists tended to measure success in conventional terms, as the increase of conveniences and comforts. "In the complex of human affairs," writes Butler, "we should aim not at a supposed absolute standard but at the greatest coming-together-ness or convenience of all our ideas and practices; that is to say, at their most harmonious working with one another" (*Note-Books,* 1917 ed., p. 310). To determine the practically convenient, Butler appeals to common sense or the opinion of the great majority of sensible and successful people. Thus for Butler the best knowledge is worldly knowledge: children should be taught in school how to make money, while students of art should learn how to market their pictures.

In the *Note-Books* Butler again identifies evolutionary success as equivalent to successful adaptation. At the same time, like many other nineteenth-century writers, he evaluates society according to a naturalistic, evolutionary model, and thus pragmatically valorizes adaptation as the mark of social success. Who, then, does Butler consider the best-adapted socially? Like most people, he dislikes social rebels and reformers, since their discontent proves them to be ill-favored, ill-adapted, and excessively self-conscious. And since nature, and by analogy society, evolves by small changes, social revolutionaries are guilty of extremism, *trop de zèle* (too much zeal). Similarly, from the evolutionary point of view, most geniuses, because they are too deviant, too great a "cross," are likely to be abused or neglected—or to achieve success only posthumously. For Butler, then, the Victorian gentleman or "swell" demonstrates nature's paramount success at the present stage of evolution. His adaptive advantages are evident in his enjoyment of health, wealth, good looks, abundant and handsome children, kindness, social esteem, casual wordliness, complaisance, freedom from priggishness—in short, that unconsciousness Butler proclaims as the sign of grace. For Butler, "good breeding" in terms of fine manners and procreative advantage is the "summum bonum" (p. 27).

Not accidentally, the ideas of grace and summum bonum belong to a religious lexicon. Butler is serious when he says that the greatest social successes are divinely favored; this contention results from his reinterpretation of Christianity in accordance with Lamarckianism and hedonism. He had come to see God as working in nature, as an unconscious or instinctive force, and God's laws as consistent with the laws of humanity's well-being in the evolutionary process. And since our well-being demands comfort and pleasure, God not only sanctions our instinctive hedonism but wants us to adapt to our environment as best we can. Hence Butler insists that the most successful people *do* serve God and Mammon: "To love God is to have good health, good looks, good sense, experience, a kindly nature and a fair balance of cash in hand. 'We know that all things work together for good to them that love God.' To be loved by God is the same as to love Him. We love Him because He first loved us" (p. 26). Yet Butler's defense of hedonism carries an indispensable corollary. Insofar as we normally "have our likings found for us" (p. 208), grace is attainable only if we first find out what our instinctive desires and pleasures really are. Butler had learned this lesson painfully, and so too does Ernest Pontifex in *The Way of All Flesh.*

The authorial stance of the *Note-Books* is fundamentally paradoxical. Butler's claim to speak for common sense is in many ways a pose, as his ideas are often crankily eccentric. This rhapsodist of the swell had neither good looks nor charm nor wife nor children. His books were ignored or attacked, his friends were few, and only after 1886 did he achieve security, not riches. The sometimes jaundiced tone of the *Note-Books* is that of the failed outsider. To assuage these disappointments Butler says that he writes only for himself or, like Stendhal, in expectation of a more appreciative posthumous audience; while there is no immortality in ultimate terms, we may gain a measure of it through posthumous fame. Reiterated in Dr. Gurgoyle's essay in *Erewhon Revisited,* this is also the theme of Butler's sonnet "Not on Sad Stygian Shore," one of his few good poems, in which immortality is to live on the "lips of living men" (in *Note-Books,* p. 427).

THE WAY OF ALL FLESH

THE book for which Butler is now best known is *The Way of All Flesh.* It combines several forms, among them the discursive essay, the conversion narrative, and the bildungsroman, or novel of education; but it is above all an autobiographical novel in which Ernest Pontifex struggles for intellectual and economic independence from his family. Butler began writing it in 1873 and worked on it intermittently until he completed it in draft form in 1884; then he laid it aside for good. Throughout its composition he was encouraged by Miss Savage's

appreciative and wittily insightful commentary. Yet Butler revised only the first part of the novel, and some have suggested that he lost interest in it after the death of Miss Savage in 1885, which deprived him of his ideal audience. In any case *The Way of All Flesh* was published posthumously in 1903 and was gradually acknowledged as a great novel, a time bomb, to quote V. S. Pritchett, "to blow up the Victorian family" (quoted in Jeffers, 1981, p. 4).

The development of Ernest Pontifex must be seen in relation to Butler's ideas, many of which the novel discusses and exemplifies. These include his ideas of unconscious memory as the heredity link between generations, the identity of parents and offspring, and the capacity of the individual organism to acquire its own specific traits through voluntary and cunning adaptation to new circumstances. Above all, Ernest Pontifex embodies Butler's idea that the most vital powers within each person derive from the instinctive, unconscious self, which contains the accumulated wisdom of past generations. Butler sees the unconscious as an intelligent force that can, if not impeded by overwhelming obstacles, direct the organism on a successful course.

In keeping with Butler's evolutionary theories, *The Way of All Flesh* focuses first on Ernest Pontifex's ancestors. An example of both grace and evolutionary success, his great-grandfather John Pontifex rises in the world, shows an instinctive, hence unself-conscious, talent for painting, music, and carpentry, and, being natural and spontaneous, shuns dogmatism. Next comes the unlikeable and ungraceful George Pontifex, Ernest's grandfather, whom Butler modeled on his impression of his own grandfather, Dr. Samuel Butler. Later, in writing his grandfather's biography, Butler found that he liked him and wanted to change the novel's portrait, though he never did so. Conventional minded and priggish, George Pontifex browbeats his children and responds pretentiously to art and nature. Nonetheless, he is an evolutionary success in Butlerian terms, for his strong will and worldliness combined with his essential hedonism enable him to improve his family's social standing. By contrast, George's son Theobald calls to mind Butler's theory in *Life and Habit* that too great an evolutionary success causes instinctive energy to ebb temporarily in the next generation. Bullied by his father into the ministry, drawn by inertia into a dull marriage, the rigidly puritanical Theobald is the sheer antithesis of grace as unconscious perfection, the very exemplar of Butler's view of the clergyman as a "kind of human Sunday." Reducing religion to a mechanical routine, Theobald stands for repression over instinct, the letter over the spirit. This arch-prig is the terror of Ernest, his son.

Ernest grows up in an atmosphere of joyless piety enforced by parental discipline. Theobald and his wife, Christina, do all they can to crush Ernest's will and spontaneity; and they do it in the name of Christ. He is taught to kneel before he can crawl, lisps the Lord's prayer before he speaks, and gets a beating for mispronouncing "come" as "tum." As Ernest grows up, Theobald's sermons fill him with a guilty sense of duty, and he continues to suffer corporeal punishment for trivial offenses. His native interests in art, music, and carpentry—his great-grandfather's endowment—receive no encouragement. Ernest's mother extorts confidences from him through a show of affection, then earns his lasting distrust by betraying him to his father. At the aptly named Roughborough public school Ernest is expected to play sports and learn the classics, which he hates, while at Cambridge he is expected to prepare for ordination. And all the while Theobald's tight purse strings insure his son's dependence.

Although Butler said that Theobald and Christina were modeled on his parents, it is not exactly clear how closely these literary characters correspond to their originals. Notwithstanding the claim of Henry Festing Jones that Theobald and Christina *are* Butler's father and mother (see Jones's *Memoir,* vol. 1, pp. 19–20), Butler probably blackened the picture somewhat. R. S. Garnett's *Samuel Butler and His Family Relations* (1926) shows that Canon Butler was in many ways a model clergyman, and that Jones's memoir ignores the canon's more patient and reasonable letters to his son. Also, that the canon published *A First Year in Canterbury Settlement* suggests that he was less of a stumbling block than his son believed. Nonetheless, in evaluating Butler's view of his parents it is interesting to recall Sigmund Freud's point that fundamentally the neurotic does not lie.

Fortunately Ernest has two friends who embody Butlerian wisdom. A brilliant unmarried woman, Ernest's aunt Alethea treats him as a surrogate son, encourages his natural bent for music and carpentry, and secretly bequeathes to him a legacy that he

is to receive at age twenty-eight; for she foresees that her nephew needs first to learn the importance of money. No less valuable to Ernest is Overton, a friend of the Pontifex family and the novel's narrator. As his name suggests, Overton is Ernest's mentor and helper in the struggle to find his true self; indeed, he refers to Ernest as "my godson." Overton's presence insures that the reader evaluates events from a Butlerian point of view, as his many reiterations of Butler's ideas on evolution and ethics reveal him as the author's mouthpiece.

Near the midpoint of the novel Overton remarks that Ernest had been taught to believe in his own depravity, and had lived by other's ideas, not according to his unconscious impulses. And had Ernest been capable in his childhood of attending to his unconscious, this is what he would have heard:

You are surrounded on every side by lies which would deceive even the elect, if the elect were not generally so uncommonly wide awake; the self of which you are conscious, your reasoning and reflecting self, will believe these lies and bid you act in accordance with them. This conscious self of yours, Ernest, is a prig begotten of prigs and trained in priggishness. . . . Obey *me,* your true self, and things will go tolerably well with you.

(p. 131)

Although Ernest embraces his true self only at the novel's crisis, before this awakening his unconscious rebels in small ways. Staring at a painting of Elijah in the family dining room, he wants to give this undernourished prophet healthy, abundant food—this wish being a projection of his own thwarted desire for healthy satisfactions. At public school he shirks his studies, spends his allowance freely, and smokes in secret. At Cambridge he writes an essay expressing his genuine dislike of the Greek dramatists as well as satiric pieces on the unsightly Simeonites, priggish evangelicals who instinctively repel him. He is spontaneously attracted to the Cambridge swells, rich, handsome, amiable gentlemen favored with unconscious grace. Yet his upbringing leads him against his true nature to embrace the Simeonites' zealous puritanism. He is ordained and goes to work in the London slums, where the stage is set for a crisis.

Ernest enacts Butler's disturbing discovery that there is no predictable difference in moral conduct between the baptized and the unbaptized. He is shaken too by his encounter, in chapter 59, with the plain-speaking Mr. Shaw, who has the common man's distrust of priggishness, and who alerts Ernest to the dishonesty of Richard Whateley's *Historic Doubts,* a smugly sophistic satire against critics of the Christian miracles. Shaw also points out damaging inconsistencies in the Gospel accounts of the Resurrection, none of which Ernest had noticed. Impressed by Shaw's candor, Ernest, like Butler and Pickard Owen, examines Dean Alford's argument that we should accept these inconsistencies on trust; and like them he finds this position untenable. Ironically, his disbelief in the Resurrection aids in his rebirth.

However, the most dramatic and illuminating moment of Ernest's crisis occurs in Chapter 57, which depicts his chance encounter with Towneley, an acquaintance from his Cambridge days. The very incarnation of the swell, Towneley combines the gentleman's "nice" consideration for others with a pragmatic and hedonistic morality; indeed, when Ernest meets him he is about to visit a lower-class prostitute. And when Ernest asks Towneley if he likes the poor, he answers instinctively with an emphatic "No, no, no." At this moment Ernest realizes that he, too, dislikes the poor, that "no one was nicer for being poor," that class barriers are insuperable, and that he would most like to resemble Towneley (p. 254). In this ironic conversion Ernest accepts grace not in the Pauline but in the Butlerian sense. Yet still being naive, he is bilked of his money by an unscrupulous, priggish clergyman, and when he decides to visit a prostitute, he mistakenly propositions a respectable woman, for which he is arrested and receives a six-month prison sentence.

Ernest's disgrace is a fortunate fall, whereby he loses his life in order to save it. The essence of his conversion lies in a vitalistic redefinition of faith and grace in terms of an intuitive acceptance of the healthy prompting of organic instinct, that is, his true, unconscious self. Ernest needs the shock of imprisonment and a complete disruption of his life to force him to adapt to new conditions. The organism, writes Butler in *Luck, or Cunning,* can "profit even by mischance so long as the disaster is not an overwhelming one." Ernest's disgrace separates him at once by choice and necessity from his family, thus winning him the freedom of the orphan Melchizedek, to whom Butler compares himself in his *Note-Books.* In fact, his "one chance lay in separating himself completely" from his parents (p.

303). Once released from prison, he is free to struggle in a new social environment, to exercise his will, and to draw upon his unconscious instincts. Resolving to "fall" (p. 291), he lives among the lower classes, owns and runs a shop, marries and has children. Consistent with Butler's evolutionary theories, Ernest's attempts at adaptation are tentative, and he makes mistakes. But then, having disemburdened himself of wife and children, and supported by his aunt's legacy, Ernest becomes a respected moral philosopher of the Butlerian stamp. His goal is to save others from the lies and errors he himself has suffered and thus to assist in the social and biological progress of humanity.

Like Butler, Ernest believes that no true metaphysic is possible, that belief has no ultimate basis. He rejects all dogmatism and extremism in favor of an intellectual and spiritual equilibrium resulting from the balance of opposites. As Christianity and the denial of Christianity inevitably meet as extremes, so one must be inconsistent consistently, mingling virtue with vice and truth with error. Meanwhile, the absence of a credible metaphysic only renders more urgent the necessity of faith. Ernest bases his faith not on supernatural revelation but on unconscious instinct, which accepts the "evidence of things not actually seen" (ch. 65), and which is essentially a belief in the validity of one's existence. Overton does not miss the irony in Ernest's nearly returning to the orthodox Christian idea that "the just shall live by faith" (ch. 65). Now, however, Ernest identifies Christ with his own intelligent instincts. For him, the true Christian attitude is the "pursuit of his truest and most lasting happiness" (ch. 68), namely pleasure, while "pleasure," in the sense of "tangible material prosperity," is the "safest test of virtue" (ch. 19). Sharing Butler's view that the most worthy persons are those who best adapt to the social and physical environment, Ernest sees the "swell" as the most perfect saint. Yet Ernest admires more than he resembles this type, for he owes his success to his recovery of the spontaneous instinct of his great-grandfather, John Pontifex. Being a bridge between generations, Ernest lives up to the name Pontifex, which means "bridge maker."

A major novel and Butler's finest achievement, *The Way of All Flesh* abounds in powerful scenes. Few readers will forget Theobald's beating of Ernest, from which Overton catches Theobald emerging "red-handed"; or Christina's playing cards with her sisters for Theobald's hand in marriage; or Theobald's and Christina's carriage drive home after their wedding, when the glum Theobald realizes his entrapment; or the scene in which he first asserts his domestic tyranny. *The Way of All Flesh* is also innovative in its intensive use of the interior monologue, which intimately renders the mental life of the characters. Yet perhaps the novel's greatest strength lies in its constant, full-bodied invention. For instance, rather than summarizing the characters' letters, Butler gives them in full, and each conveys the personality of the writer through nuances of tone and phrasing. Thus Theobald's blandly unctuous manner only partly masks his "will-shaking game" (p. 157), a threatening, coercive intent. Most of the novel's weaknesses are concentrated in that part of the narrative dealing with Ernest's life after prison. Whereas Butler found inspiration in Ernest's struggle with his family, the last third of the novel is often underdramatized or obvious, as when Ernest returns home to flaunt his economic independence: there is too much emotional identification here between author and hero. A clumsy coincidence reminiscent of the conventional Victorian novel allows Ernest to extricate himself from his marriage through his accidental discovery that his wife is already married. Although Towneley is represented as an evolutionary ideal, Ernest's abandonment of him suggests that this " 'swell' who sins gracefully" (p. 302), as Claude T. Bissell calls him in "A Study of *The Way of All Flesh*" (1940), is less than perfect. But a more serious difficulty was noted by U. C. Knoepflmacher in "Ishmael or Anti-Hero? The Division of Self" (1961). Ernest is supposed to be a rebellious vitalist recovering the unconscious of John Pontifex. Actually he resembles Overton, a sterile bachelor and exemplar of conscious thought; far from being a Thomas Carlyle or a D. H. Lawrence, Ernest espouses an unadventurous meliorism that resembles Butler's.

LATER WORKS

APART from his *Note-Books,* Butler spent the rest of his career on minor projects. Yet *Alps and Sanctuaries* (1882) and *Ex Voto* (1888) remain interesting for their unexpected warmth and their original contribution to the Anglo-American genre of Italian travel writing. These works capture Butler's more relaxed holiday mood among a people who he believed to have retained much of the pagan ideal of unconscious grace and freedom from dogmatic and moralistic extremism. So often a maverick, Butler nonetheless adheres to the prevailing Pre-Raphaelite view expounded by John Ruskin, the influential art critic, that Italian art reached its zenith from about 1300 to about 1500. The early Italian painters demonstrated "agape" in their lack of aesthetic pretensions, their sincere religiosity, and their literalistic, antiformalistic love of natural detail. But by the middle of the sixteenth century academicism had transformed most Italian artists into self-conscious prigs obsessed with classical models and idealist formulae. Michelangelo and Leonardo had only "gnosis," pretending to arcane mysteries and refusing to "kiss the soil" (p. 6). Yet having accepted the Ruskinesque aesthetic, Butler was compelled to vindicate its neglected exemplars. On his frequent visits to the obscure villages and shrines of the Italian Alps he discovered the works of the sculptor Giovanni Tabachetti and the painter-sculptor Gaudenzio Ferrari, two little-known sixteenth-century artists whose champion he became. For Butler, they had preserved the vitality of the earlier Italian tradition. Writing in *Alps and Sanctuaries* of Ferrari's Crucifixion Chapel at Varallo-Sesia, Butler doubted whether there is a "more remarkable work of art in North Italy" (p. 155). And in *Ex Voto*, whose subject is the Sacro-Monte at Varallo-Sesia, Butler describes Tabachetti's *Journey to Calvary* as the "most astonishing work that has ever been achieved in sculpture" (p. 62). But though Ferrari is now widely recognized as a major artist, Tabachetti remains virtually unknown.

Throughout his later career Butler's musical interests remained strong and inspired three little-known works in the earlier classical style that he wrote with Henry Festing Jones. Published in 1885, *Gavottes, Minuets, Fugues, and Other Short Pieces for the Piano* was followed by *Narcissus: A Cantata in the Handelian Form* (1888) and by *Ulysses*, which Jones completed after Butler's death and published in 1904. *Narcissus* was performed in 1892; *Ulysses* in 1905. Yet the greater significance of *Ulysses* is that in composing it Butler was inspired to reread the Homeric original, which led him to his prose translations of *The Iliad* (1898) and *The Odyssey* (1900), and to his study, *The Authoress of the "Odyssey"* (1897). In Butler's view, the most esteemed contemporary prose translations of Homer, those of Andrew Lang, were a mishmash of self-conscious archaism, pseudopoeticisms, and false sublimity, and hence the verbal equivalent of "Wardour Street" (pp. 6–7), where phony antiques were sold. Although Butler admits that "Wardour Street" has its uses, since Coleridge's "Ancient Mariner" is a more effective title than "Old Sailor," he also says in the Note-Books that "great licence must be allowed to the translator in getting rid of all those poetical common forms which are foreign to the genius of prose. If the work is to be translated into prose, let it be into such prose as we write and speak among ourselves" (p. 197). As for The Odyssey, Butler says in The Authoress, "a tale so absolutely without any taint of affectation . . . will speed best being unaffectedly told." Butler's Homeric translations had two chief purposes, one of which is typically paradoxical. For though he undertook this labor out of genuine love, he also viewed classical education as a "great humbug" (quoted in Joad, p. 133), and wanted to spare his audience the effort of reading the original works. At the same time, the narrative rapidity and direct, if often commonplace, diction of Butler's translations is intended to make Homer come alive for modern readers. He boasted that whereas Lang seeks to "preserve a corpse" (Note-Books, p. 197), his own translations aim to "originate a new life and one that is instinct . . . with the spirit though not the form of the original" (p. 197). In a furious review, the Academy called Butler's Odyssey "wholly superfluous" and complained that in eschewing archaisms he had betrayed the tone of the work (in Holt, Samuel Butler, p. 133). But the Athenaeum admired Butler's directness and naturalness, while W. H. Salter praised Butler for "dispelling the dreadful shades of 'classicalism'" (quoted in Stillman, p. 272). Gilbert Highet, writing in The Classical Tradition (1970), is probably right that Butler's simplifying method misses Homer's poetry, yet as a translator Butler anticipates Ezra Pound's attempt to render ancient poets in a vital contemporary idiom.

Butler's Authoress of The Odyssey reflects his assumption—fashionable in his own day but now unpopular—that "art is interesting only in so far as it reveals an artist" (p. 6). He rejects the view of Friedrich Wolf and other German scholars that the Homeric epics are composite pieces that later editors stitched together; as always, Butler insists on individual design. But if on this point many would

have agreed with him, the main thesis of The Authoress invited controversy, for Butler argued that, whereas the militaristic Iliad was written by a man for men, The Odyssey was written by a woman for women. His argument relies heavily on textual evidence allegedly proving feminine authorship. Just as feminine interests such as homes and gardens predominate in The Odyssey, so the poem vindicates the honor of women. The female characters are noble, while the males are foolish and need the women to assist them, and in contrast with later epics, women hold a prominent place in the underworld. Again, Butler's alleged authoress is ignorant of matters a male author supposedly would have been familiar with, such as sports and animal husbandry. After visiting Sicily, Butler concluded that The Odyssey was written by an aristocratic Sicilian woman who lived in ancient Trapani between 1100 and 1050 B.C., and who appears in the poem as Nausicaa, the charming daughter of Alcinous, king of the Phaeakians. Both Scheria, the home of Nausicaa, and Ithaca are modeled on Trapani and its environs; Odysseus' far-flung voyage is mainly a circumnavigation of Sicily and its adjacent islands. Since Butler's authoress apparently repeated local details in describing distant settings, he finds her consistent with his own values of aesthetic realism, or rather literalism. "No artist," writes Butler in The Authoress, "can reach an ideal higher than his own best actual environment. Trying to materially improve upon that which he or she is truly familiar invariably ends in failure" (p. 218). Yet more than an embodiment of literal-mindedness, Butler's authoress is another misunderstood, forgotten genius needing his vindication.

The chief importance of The Authoress lies in its attempt to make Greek literature come alive to modern readers. Like the great German archeologist Heinrich Schleimann, who excavated Troy and Mycenae, Butler believed in the historical reality of Homer and anticipated James Joyce's and Pound's attempt to render the modern epic as vivid and concrete as its Greek predecessor did. Nonetheless, apart from its extreme literal-mindedness, The Authoress has serious shortcomings. Unwittingly sexist, Butler finds in the author's apparent "love of a small lie" (p. 124), evidence of a feminine hand. The poem's emphasis on feminine honor is quite consistent with a patriarchal culture such as ancient Greece and hence too with masculine authorship. Nor is Butler persuasive in his contention that a Greek colony existed in Trapani in 1050 B.C. *The Authoress* found supporters in the literary critic John F. Harris and the classical scholar B. Farrington, George Bernard Shaw and Robert Graves considered it irrefutable, but it has not won scholarly acceptance. Perhaps it is best understood as the imagined love affair of a confirmed, aging bachelor with a beautiful young woman rendered safely inaccessible by a distance of three thousand years.

Butler's other extended excursion into literary criticism in his later years was *Shakespeare's Sonnets Reconsidered,* which he began in 1895 and published in 1899. Butler rejects the view, contemporaneously advanced by Sir Sidney Lee, that the sonnets were an exercise in conventional Renaissance love poetry. Rather, he once again seeks to determine the literal facts or story which, in his view, must stand behind a great work of literature. In doing so Butler challenges critical orthodoxy in two key ways. First, he insists that critics must face the unwelcome truth that the theme of the sonnets is not friendship but Shakespeare's homosexual love for WH, whom Butler identifies as William Harvey. While the identity of WH remains debatable, later criticism has in fact acknowledged the homosexual theme in these poems. Second, Butler holds that the sonnets are not the product of Shakespeare's later years, as was generally believed, but of his youth; moreover, that Shakespeare's homosexuality, for which he was "bitterly penitent," is forgivable as a youthful indiscretion, whereas it would be damnable as the act of an older man. Butler is quite possibly reading into the sonnets his own youthful relationship with Pauli, whom he loved desperately, and who rejected him in a manner reminiscent of WH's rejection of Shakespeare. In any case, Butler learned the sonnets by heart and in some instances rearranged them in accordance with what he saw as their underlying narrative. He claims unconvincingly that Sonnet 107 refers to the defeat of the Spanish Armada, so that the sonnets can be dated between 1585 and 1588. No less implausibly, Butler finds evidence in Sonnet 32 that WH and his friends laid a trap for Shakespeare in order to expose his homosexuality. Thus when Shakespeare says, in Sonnet 35, that he "travel[ed] forth without my cloak," he means that he allowed himself to be entrapped and disgracefully roughed up. In Sonnet 37 the phrase "made lame by Fortune's dearest spite" literally means, according to

Butler, that Shakespeare was injured by WH's practical joke, so seriously, in fact, that he was incapacitated for a year. These readings testify to Butler's extreme literal-mindedness, his inability to accept metaphor as metaphor; and it is understandable that his study of Shakespeare is now regarded as a mere curiosity.

Although inferior to *Erewhon* as a work of the imagination, *Erewhon Revisited* is pervaded by an unexpected warmth and tenderness along with the conciliatory spirit Butler achieved in his last decade. The satirical elements in this work are farcical and peripheral: the emotional center of the novel lies predominantly in John Higgs's quest for his lost Erewhonian son. Butler bids an imaginative farewell to the New Zealand landscapes where he spent the happiest days of his youth. And in dramatizing Higgs's search for his son, Butler expresses his unsatisfied wish for paternity and for a father-son relationship founded on trust, fidelity, and sacrifice.

After two decades in England, the dying Higgs returns to Erewhon in quest of his son, George, whose mother is Yram, now the wife of a prominent Erewhonian. Wearing a disguise, Higgs enters Erewhon, meets George, and finds him to be intelligent, amiable, handsome. Yet their friendship is complicated by Higgs's discovery that his escape from Erewhon had been interpreted as a miraculous event and had given rise to a new religion whose deity is Higgs himself, glorified as the Sunchild. Its doctrinal core consists of half-understood, half-remembered sayings of Higgs. Founded on popular enthusiasm, its institutional support comes from vested interests, including the priggish, power-hungry professors Hanky and Panky. Even worse, George views his father, whom he knows to be the Sunchild, as an impostor, and he tells Higgs that, should his father ever return, he would accept him only if he revealed his identity, even at the risk of execution. Higgs declares his identity at a major religious convocation, proving his willingness to sacrifice himself for love of his son. At this point Higgs is almost killed at the urging of Professor Panky, who defends Sunchildism for selfish reasons. George, however, averts tragedy through a series of pragmatic deceptions. He earns Higgs's admiration when he takes his father under his protection and passes him off as a harmless madman. He also disarms Hanky and Panky by exposing their illegalities, for which they are punished, though moderately. Thanks to George's improvisations, all difficulties are smoothed over in an atmosphere of tolerant, good-natured laughter. At the novel's conclusion Higgs and George have each other's absolute trust, and their moving farewell reveals Butler's profound personal investment in an idealized father-son relationship.

Although Sunchildism remains alive after Higgs's departure, its teachings are intellectually flimsy and its alleged miraculous origins incredible, and indeed it is challenged by skepticism and materialism. What then will become of it? This question of belief stems from Butler's inquiry into the Christian miracles in his 1865 pamphlet on the Gospels, *The Fair Haven,* and *The Way of All Flesh.* Despite some subtle equivocations, these works seem to reject Christian miracles on empirical grounds and thus to discredit Christianity itself. For similar reasons the preservation of Sunchildism seems unjustified. Nonetheless, *The Fair Haven* argues, not necessarily ironically, that the core of Christianity depends not on the "fact" of the Resurrection but on the ethical and spiritual values embodied in the "Christ-ideal." Butler's essay of 1879, "A Clergyman's Doubts," allows room for belief in the Resurrection by extending the principle of antiextremism to skepticism itself. And again, from the late 1870's onward Butler is powerfully attracted to religion as faith in the unseen. In his preface to *Erewhon Revisited* he observes that he had always belonged to the more advanced wing of the English Broad Church Movement, adding that the later parts of the novel express his position. What Higgs says calls to mind the Christ-ideal in *The Fair Haven:*

Then I must tell you. Our religion sets before us an ideal which we all cordially accept, but it also tells us of marvels . . . which we most of us reject. Our best teachers insist on the ideal, and keep the marvels in the background. If they could say outright that our age has outgrown them, they would say so, but this they may not do. . . .

Make me [Higgs, as the Sunchild] a peg on which to hang all your own best ethical and spiritual conceptions. If you will do this, and wriggle out of that wretched relic, with that not less wretched picture [votive objects celebrating the "miracles" of Sunchildism]—if you will make me out to be much better and abler than I was, or ever shall be, Sunchildism may serve your turn for many a long year to come.

(pp. 219–220)

For all its failings, religion is preferable to the hubris of positivistic scientists, who in substituting hard facts for faith in the unseen impose a harsher dogma of their own. " 'Better,' we think," says Higgs, " 'a corrupt church than none at all!' Moreover, those who in my country would step into the church's shoes are as corrupt as the church, and more exacting. They are also more dangerous" (p. 221).

ICONOCLAST OR THE ULTIMATE VICTORIAN?

WITHIN a decade of Butler's death in 1902 his fame had grown enormously. Although *The Way of All Flesh* initially had little impact, it soon won many admirers. Butler's growing reputation was signaled by the "Erewhon dinners," which Henry Festing Jones organized and which continued from 1908 until World War I; honored by George Bernard Shaw, Gilbert Cannan, Augustine Birrell, and others, Butler had inspired a prestigious cult. In 1912 the *Note-Books* were published to wide acclaim. Butler was the beneficiary of a new mood of intense anti-Victorianism that lasted roughly into the 1930's.

To many it seemed that no writer of his time had done as much as Butler to debunk Victorianism. He had exposed not only its domestic tyranny and hypocrisy but its tiresome earnestness, its false pieties and life-denying conventions, its love of great reputations and dogmatizing prophets, its trumpeting of big causes and ideologies. He stood for an anti-Victorian style of life that, founded on biological criteria of human conduct, and in the interests of balance and compromise, gave free play to irony, antirationalism, and an instinctive hedonism. Butler's admirers also claimed that many of his ideas had anticipated and even inspired Friedrich Nietzsche, Henri-Louis Bergson, Sigmund Freud, William James, and Alfred North Whitehead. In England Butler's attack on domestic tyranny influenced H. G. Wells (*The New Machiavelli,* 1911), Lytton Strachey (*Eminent Victorians,* 1918), and E. M. Forster; his pervasive influence on the Bloomsbury group has often been noted. Of all writers, Shaw is probably most like Butler and most deeply indebted to him. "The late Samuel Butler," wrote Shaw in his preface to *Major Barbara* (1905), was "in his own department, the greatest writer of the latter half of the nineteenth century." Shaw's anti-professionalism, love of paradox, inversion of apothegms, domestic satire, and savage irreverence toward the middle class often call Butler to mind. But Shaw also took Butler's scientific writings seriously, praising them in his prefaces to *Major Barbara* and again in *Back to Methuselah* (1921), in which Shaw embraces vitalism and Lamarck over what he, too, sees as the mechanical, soulless theory of natural selection.

Since the 1930's, however, interest in Butler has declined somewhat with the waning of anti-Victorianism. Certainly the familial problems of Ernest Pontifex seem remote to contemporary readers. On the other hand, Butler lost some of his appeal with the gradual discovery that he was not quite the iconoclastic modern he had appeared to be. The *Note-Books* and Jones's memoir revealed that Butler's values and conduct were in many ways conventionally bourgeois, as we have already seen. Malcolm Muggeridge in *The Earnest Atheist* (1936) fiercely derided Butler as the "Ultimate Victorian." Muggeridge saw him not as a vitalist but as a bookishly abstract middle-class bachelor whose works stand self-condemned as the expression of a sterile program of life. Although Muggeridge's judgments were vitiated by his complete lack of sympathy for Butler and a false equation of the man and his works, he correctly saw that Butler's writings often carry the flavor of his cramped existence—its solitary detachment, dull routine, overestimation of money and social success, excessive calculation and cerebration, emotional timidity to the point of passionlessness. It did not help that in an increasingly ideological age Butler either ignored politics or espoused an insensitive conservatism. Edmund Wilson, in his "The Satire of Samuel Butler" (1938), complained of his lack of interest in the condition of the working classes; Clara Stillman of his contempt for women's rights. Indeed, for all his expectations of social evolution, Butler welcomed class differences and even described the upper and lower classes as distinct species. These attitudes reflect his self-centeredness, his class position (as a rentier), and his evolutionary theories, which he extended to society, and which led him to overvalue adaptation and gradual change over more daring kinds of innovation.

A fair assessment of Butler needs to weigh the boldness and originality of many of his ideas against the no less frequent inadequacy of the values, feelings, and interests expressed in his works. Butler, among a number of late-nineteenth-century writers, had a significant and on the whole salutary influence on the culture in helping to legitimate unconscious instinct as an inescapable and in some ways vitalizing element in mental life. Yet Shaw rightly complained that Butler mistakenly valorized the unconscious—that is, unself-conscious, instinctive activity—over conscious thought. According to Shaw, Butler should have realized that not *all* our actions ought to be unconscious, but only those that interfere with or distract the reason. Indeed, Butler's insistence that the most important forms of human activity are instinctive raises the paradox, if not contradiction, that this defender of the will against mechanism nonetheless conceived of the individual as ruled far less by conscious volition than by impersonal forces. There remains in any case something valuable in Butler's hedonism, his belief that we must find our true feelings and desires and pursue our self-interest (within legal limits). Like Stendhal's, these values are admirably individualistic and libertarian, yet Butler is a tepid example of Stendhal's ideal. For all his talk of pleasure, Butler's stunted emotional life, combined with his narcissism, limited the range of his responses in his life and works. Stendhal glorifies risk and the unexpected as indispensable to pleasure, whose measure is intensity, and the height of which is love. Butler's spiritual timidity landed him in a routinized, blandly comfortable existence, with few nonintellectual challenges and little risk: yearly vacations to Italy, regular visits to his prostitute. Butler's greatest pleasures were neither emotional nor sensual but cerebral, and his works suffer for lack of the very balance he celebrates. A self-confessed egoist, Stendhal could still escape himself; Butler's narcissism made it difficult for him to enjoy things with which he could not spontaneously identify and thus appropriate as his own. Hence the shocking range of his instinctive and unshakable antipathies: Aeschylus, Virgil, Raphael, Dante, Michelangelo, Charles Dickens, George Eliot, Alfred Lord Tennyson, Dante Gabriel Rossetti, Richard Wagner, Carlyle, Johann von Goethe, and many more. Butler was only slightly exaggerating when he said in the *Note-Books* "I hate all poetry."

Butler's chief appeal remains that of a satirist who employed paradox and irony to devastate dogmas, conventions, received ideas, intellectual pretensions, and orthodoxy. There is as well an admirable sense of fairness—arising no doubt from his own feelings of personal injustice—in his defense of abused or neglected figures. Yet his satire does not run that deep, being limited mainly to the priggish and dogmatic: for the rest he accepts and even welcomes the human average in all its lax conformism. It is wrong, then, to compare Butler with Swift, as he lacks Swift's bitterness and indignation toward human depravity. Moreover, Butler's works are weakened by that naughtily irresponsible desire to shock to which he alludes in describing himself as the enfant terrible of art and literature. He seems at times to pursue paradox for its own sake or as a merely mechanical means of achieving intellectual novelty. His controversialism is not altogether innocent, for he often adopts his adversarial stance out of perverse combativeness, or else to place himself in the secretly cherished role of Ishmael or outcast. This impulse, which partially motivated his ultimately unpleasant debate with Darwin, had its origin—as did much of Butler's writing—in his hatred of his father as an authority figure. The later Butler is compelled to demolish intellectual reputations in order to set up his personal discoveries. His eagerness to defend the forgotten Lamarck and Tabachetti, with whom he identified, smacks of paranoia. Although Butler claimed to write only for himself and to believe that posterity would come to honor him, his urge to belittle reigning reputations suggests a frustrated desire not so much for intellectual acceptance as for intellectual domination. And this is what Butler achieved, but only within his small coterie of friends, among whom his opinions went unchallenged, and who thus allowed him to indulge in the priggishness he elsewhere abhorred.

Yet in judging Butler one must avoid the error P. N. Furbank exposes in Muggeridge's diatribe, that of supposing that Butler's works are invalidated by his resentments, narrow intellectual interests, and stunted emotional range. Amounting to ad hominem sabotage, Muggeridge's portrayal misses Butler's verbal originality, his power of stimulating fresh perspectives, his daring insights, his gift for detecting humbug, his frequently high spirits and occasional tenderness. These and other virtues insure a place for Butler's works as minor classics. It furthermore seems uncharitable—in the one Pauline sense of grace that Butler accepted—to

focus on his shortcomings rather than to admire him for having won his creative and personal freedom against circumstances that would probably have defeated most others. Butler's struggle for self-determination, which is the underlying theme of his scientific writings, found major expression in *The Way of All Flesh.* The most revealing statement of the measure by which to judge his life and works is in the *Note-Books:* "I had to steal my own birthright. I stole it and was bitterly punished. But I saved my soul alive" (p. 181).

SELECTED BIBLIOGRAPHY

I. BIBLIOGRAPHY. H. F. Jones, *Samuel Butler, Author of "Erewhon" (1835–1902): A Memoir* (London, 1919), contains a short but useful bibliography; H. F. Jones and A. T. Bartholomew, *The Samuel Butler Collection at Saint John's College, Cambridge* (Cambridge, 1921); A. J. A. Hoppé, *A Bibliography of the Writings of Samuel Butler and of the Writings About Him* (London, 1925); C. A. Wilson, *Catalogue of the Collection of Samuel Butler (of "Erewhon") in the Chapin Library, Williams College* (Portland, Maine, 1945); S. B. Harkness, *The Career of Samuel Butler (1835–1902): A Bibliography* (New York, 1955), an indispensable bibliography containing a chronological listing of books, articles, letters, paintings, sketches, musical compositions, and editions, as well as a list of reviews and criticism in books, newspapers, and periodicals; H.-P. Breuer and R. Parsell, *Samuel Butler: An Annotated Bibliography of Writings About Him* (New York, 1990).

II. COLLECTED WORKS. *Selections from Previous Works, Remarks on Mr. G. J. Romanes' "Mental Evolution in Animals" and "A Psalm of Montreal"* (London, 1884); *Essays on Life, Art, and Science* (London, 1904; New York, 1983); *The Humour of Homer and Other Essays* (London, 1913; New York, 1967); *The Collected Works of Samuel Butler,* ed. by H. F. Jones and A. T. Bartholomew, 20 vols. (London, 1923–1926; New York, 1923–1926), also known as the Shrewsbury Edition, it is the standard scholarly text of Butler's writings and contains useful introductory materials and indices; *Butleriana,* ed. by A. T. Bartholemew (London, 1932; Folcroft, Pa., 1976); *The Essential Samuel Butler,* ed. by G. D. H. Cole (London, 1950).

III. SEPARATE WORKS. *A First Year in Canterbury Settlement* (London, 1863; New York, 1915); *The Evidence for the Resurrection of Jesus Christ, as Given by the Four Evangelists, Critically Examined* (1865), an anonymous pamphlet of which three copies are in the British Museum and three at St. John's College, Cambridge University; *Erewhon; or, Over the Range* (London, 1872; New York, 1907), published with *Erewhon*

Revisited (New York, 1927), with an introduction by Lewis Mumford; *The Fair Haven: A Work in Defence of the Miraculous Element in Our Lord's Ministry upon Earth, both as against Rationalistic Impugners and Certain Orthodox Defenders, by the Late J. P. Owen, Edited by W. B. Owen, with a Memoir of the Author* (London, 1873; New York, 1914); *Life and Habit: An Essay After a Completer View of Evolution* (London, 1878; New York, 1910); *Evolution, Old and New: or the Theories of Buffon, Dr. Erasmus Darwin, and Lamarck, as Compared with That of Mr. Charles Darwin* (London, 1879; Salem, Mass., 1914); "God the Known and God the Unknown," eight articles published in the *Examiner* (24 May–26 July 1879), published in book form (London, 1909; New Haven, 1917). *Unconscious Memory: A Comparison between the Theory of Dr. Ewald Hering, Professor of Physiology at Prague, and the Philosophy of the Unconscious of Dr. Edward von Hartmann; with Translations from these Authors* (London, 1880; New York, 1910); *Alps and Sanctuaries of Piedmont and the Canton Ticino* (London, 1882; New York, 1913); *Gavottes, Minuets, Fugues, and Other Short Pieces for the Piano,* with H. F. Jones (London, 1885); *Luck, or Cunning as the Main Means of Organic Modification? An Attempt to Throw Additional Light upon the Late Mr. Charles Darwin's Theory of Natural Selection* (London, 1887); *Ex Voto: An Account of the Sacro Monte or New Jerusalem at Varallo-Sesia, with Some Notice of Tabachetti's Remaining Work at the Sanctuary of Crea* (London, 1888; London and New York, 1890); *Narcissus: A Cantata in the Handelian Form,* with H. F. Jones (London, 1888); *Erewhon* (London, 1901), substantially expanded text.

The Life and Letters of Dr. Samuel Butler, Headmaster of Shrewsbury School 1798–1836, and Afterwards Bishop of Lichfield (2 vols., London, 1896; 1 vol., New York, 1924); *The Authoress of the "Odyssey," Where and When She Wrote, Who She Was, the Use She Made of the "Iliad," and How the Poem Grew Under Her Hands* (London, 1897; New York, 1922); *Shakespeare's Sonnets Reconsidered* (London, 1899; New York, 1927); *Erewhon Revisited Twenty Years Later, both by the Original Discoverer of the Country and by His Son* (London, 1901; New York, 1910), published with *Erewhon* (New York, 1927); *The Way of All Flesh* (London, 1903; New York, 1910), ed. by Daniel F. Howard (Boston, 1964), the most reliable text, derived directly from Butler's manuscript; *Ulysses: A Dramatic Oratorio in Vocal Score, with accompaniment for the pianoforte,* with H. F. Jones (London, 1904). *The Note-Books of Samuel Butler: Selections,* ed. by H. F. Jones (London, 1912; New York, 1917); the complete and authoritative text is *The Note-Books of Samuel Butler,* ed. by H. Breuer, 3 vols. (Lanham, Mass., 1984).

IV. TRANSLATIONS. *The Iliad of Homer, Rendered into English Prose* (London, 1898; New York, 1921); *The Odyssey, Rendered into English Prose* (London, 1900; New York, 1920).

V. LETTERS. *Samuel Butler and E. M. A. Savage, Letters 1871–1885,* ed. by G. Keynes and B. Hill (London, 1935); *The Correspondence of Samuel Butler and his Sister May,* ed. by D. F. Howard (Berkeley, Calif., 1962); *The Family Letters of Samuel Butler (1841–1886),* ed. by A. Silver (Stanford, Calif., 1962).

VI. CRITICAL STUDIES. W. Bateson, *Darwin and Modern Science* (Cambridge, England, 1910), examines Butler's *Life and Habit* theory from the viewpoint of a scientist; A. D. Darbishire, *An Introduction to Biology and Other Papers* (London, 1917), reveals the influence of Butler on Darbishire's scientific thought; H. F. Jones, *Samuel Butler, Author of "Erewhon" (1835–1902): A Memoir,* 2 vols. (London, 1919), contains a wealth of indispensable information concerning the life and works; C. E. M. Joad, *Samuel Butler, 1835–1902* (London, 1924; Boston, 1925); R. S. Garnett, *Samuel Butler and His Family Relations* (London and Toronto, 1926), defends Butler's parents against his accusations; S. Farrington, *Samuel Butler and the Odyssey* (London, 1929), defends Butler's Homeric theories; H. K. Lunn, *After Puritanism (1850–1900)* (London, 1929), contains an early attack on Butler; C. G. Stillman, *Samuel Butler, A Mid-Victorian Modern* (New York, 1932; London, 1932); M. Muggeridge, *The Earnest Atheist: A Study of Samuel Butler* (London, 1936); E. Wilson, "The Satire of Samuel Butler," in *The Triple Thinkers: Ten Essays on Literature* (New York, 1938).

C. T. Bissell, "A Study of *The Way of All Flesh,*" in *Nineteenth Century Studies,* ed. by H. Davis, et. al. (Ithaca, N.Y., 1940), examines Butler's novel in relation to his scientific theories; L. E. Holt, "Samuel Butler and His Victorian Critics," in *Journal of English Literary History,* 8 (June 1941); P. N. Furbank, *Samuel Butler (1835–1902)* (Cambridge, 1948); L. E. Holt, "Samuel Butler's Rise to Fame," in *Publications of the Modern Language Association,* 57 (September 1942); G. D. H. Cole, *Samuel Butler* (Denver, 1948); P. Henderson, *Samuel Butler: The Incarnate Bachelor* (London, 1953; Bloomington, Ind., 1954); J. Barzun, *Darwin, Marx, Wagner* (Garden City, N.Y., 1958); J. Jones, *The Cradle of Erewhon: Samuel Butler in New Zealand* (Austin, Tex., 1959); D. F. Howard, "The Critical Significance of Autobiography in *The Way of All Flesh,*" in *Victorian Newsletter,* 17 (Spring 1960); P. B. Maling, *Samuel Butler in Mesopotamia* (Wellington, New Zealand, 1960); B. Willey, *Darwin and Butler: Two Versions of Evolution* (London, 1960; New York, 1960); U. C. Knoepflmacher, "Ishmael or Anti-Hero? The Division of Self: *The Way of All Flesh,*" in *English Fiction in Transition,* 4, no. 4 (1961); G. G. Simpson, "Lamarck, Darwin and Butler: Three Approaches to Evolution," in *The American Scholar,* 30 (1961); P. Greenacre, *The Quest for the Father: A Study of the Darwin-Butler Controversy* (New York, 1963); L. E. Holt, *Samuel Butler* (New York, 1964; rev. ed., 1989); V. S. Pritchett, "A Victorian Son," in *The Living Novel and Later Appreciations* (New York, 1964); R. E. Schoenberg, "The Literal-Mindedness of Samuel Butler," in *Studies in English Literature,* 4 (Autumn 1964).

G. Highet, *The Classical Tradition* (New York, 1970); A. G. Brassington, *Samuel Butler in Canterbury: The Predestined Choice* (Christchurch, New Zealand, 1972), sheds new light on Butler's friendship with Charles Paine Pauli; H. Breuer, "The Source of Morality in Butler's *Erewhon*," in *Victorian Studies,* 16 (March 1973); H. Breuer, "Samuel Butler's 'The Book of the Machines' and the Argument from Design," in *Modern Philology,* 72, no. 4 (1975); H. Breuer, "Samuel Butler's *Note-Books:* The Outlook of a Victorian Black Sheep," in *English Literature in Transition,* 22, no. 1 (1979); J. L. Wisenthal, "Samuel Butler's Epistle to the Victorians: *The Way of All Flesh* and Unlovely Paul," in *Mosaic,* 13, no. 1 (1979); R. Gounelas, "Samuel Butler's Cambridge Background and *Erewhon,*" in *English Literature in Transition, 1880–1920,* 24 (1981); T. L. Jeffers, *Samuel Butler Revalued* (University Park, Pa., 1981), brilliantly assesses Butler's values; A. Fleishman, *Figures of Autobiography: The Languages of Self-Writing in Victorian and Modern England* (Berkeley, 1983), demonstrates Butler's originality as an autobiographical novelist; R. Norrman, *Samuel Butler and the Meaning of the Chiasmus* (New York, 1986), analyzes the obsessively chiastic structure of Butler's thought.

AGATHA CHRISTIE

(1890–1976)

Robin W. Winks

AGATHA CHRISTIE IS probably the fifth best-selling author of all time, exceeded only by the Bible, which was surely the work of many hands, and by Shakespeare, Barbara Cartland, and perhaps Erle Stanley Gardner, or Josef Stalin. By 1980, Christie's books had sold over four hundred million copies, half of these in the United States alone, and her works had been translated into well over fifty languages. Through her writing she became a Dame Commander of the British Empire and was hailed as the "Queen of Crime." She also became the target of much envy and critical abuse, especially for commentators who thought mystery and detective fiction vulgar, a form of pandering to low tastes and slow intellects, or simply frivolous. Christie wrote sixty-six crime novels, fifteen plays, two autobiographical works, two volumes of poems, 157 short stories that fill eighteen volumes, and six novels under the name of Mary Westmacott. On the occasion of her eightieth birthday she published *Passenger to Frankfurt* (1970), certainly one of the worst books of her long career, and yet it sold in its first edition more copies than anything she had ever written.

Some critics are prepared to take Agatha Christie seriously solely on the basis of her popularity, arguing that she deserves close attention as an indication of popular taste and as a point of entry into popular culture. This condescending view fails to take into consideration that readers attentive to so-called serious novelists remained, and remain, faithful to her books, and that Christie was, at her best, a writer of clear and engaging prose, a gentle (and at times sly) social critic, and a master of that element so essential to storytelling—plot. Some readers find in her, and especially in her early work, more than a hint of racism, and certainly of snobbery; some think her an antifeminist, conservative and lacking in compassion, especially toward the working class. Yet other readers regard her as an early feminist who cleverly poked fun at male shibboleths and was ever mindful of the frailties of human nature. That there is wide disagreement about the nature and importance of her work is an indication both of her vitality and of the precarious position mystery and detective fiction occupies in the literary world.

Agatha Christie was born Agatha Mary Clarissa Miller on 15 September 1890, in Torquay, an attractive resort town on the Devon coast. Though much larger than her fictional English village of St. Mary Mead, Torquay was, at least until well after World War II, as much of a legendary English country town as one might find. Landed gentry occupied ancestral estates nearby, where rural farmers tugged at their proverbial forelocks, and retired colonels with exotic knowledge of the far-flung corners of the British Empire let their Darjeeling tea steep under padded cozies while rereading Trollope in front of a roaring fire. She drew upon the reality, and even more the memories and myths, of her childhood for many of her settings and characters. The house in which she was born and lived as a child, Ashfield, appears in modest disguise in several of her novels, its many chimneys and sprawling rooms, its croquet court and greenhouse becoming backdrops to murder.

Christie's father, Frederick Miller, was a charming American who was well-placed in New York society. Her mother, Clarissa "Clara" Boehmer, was born in Belfast, lost her father when she was nine years old, and was brought up by an aunt and uncle. She married her cousin Frederick in 1878, and they had three children, of whom Agatha was the last and much the youngest, there being a gap of ten years between herself and the next child. Thus Agatha, whose mother was thirty-six and father forty-four at the time of her birth, lived something of the life of an only child. Her father died when she was eleven, and thereafter she was extraordinarily close to and dependent on her mother.

Although Christie received no formal education, she read widely and learned writing and mathematics from her father and fluent demotic French from her governesses and dressmaker. She traveled with her mother to Egypt, spending three months in Cairo in 1910. Although by 1909 she had hopes of making a career as an opera singer, at eighteen, recovering from influenza and housebound, she wrote her first short story, "The House of Beauty." It would be nearly eight years before she would publish it. She submitted her work to a successful writer of mystery stories, Eden Phillpotts, who encouraged her to persist, and in 1920 she published her first book, in America, *The Mysterious Affair at Styles.*

Agatha Miller had, in the meantime, married a dashing young aviator and war hero, Archibald Christie. They had one child, Rosalind, in 1919. Four more novels followed and then, in 1926, the already popular mystery novelist published *The Murder of Roger Ackroyd* and was, quite suddenly, famous.

It is impossible, in assessing Christie's sudden fame, to separate her ingenious novel from the bizarre circumstances that followed its publication. *The Murder of Roger Ackroyd* was published in Britain by Collins and in the United States by Dodd, Mead (which would remain her publishers thereafter until her death) and would, in time, sell over a million copies. The book remains a superb litmus test to determine a reader's propensity for mystery fiction, and to this day it can still generate controversy, although only those who have not fully grasped a central tenet of the genre—that one must suspect everyone, and in doing so, must take note of every fact and give those facts, at least initially, equal weight and concern—could agree with the critics who, in 1926, accused Christie of cheating. For after creating an attractive, intelligent, and very likeable country doctor who is the narrator of the story, she reveals that he is also the murderer. The attentive reader will have noted one, two, perhaps three clues, certainly not more, but will have dismissed them because of the author's skillful use of sleight of hand, character, and language. While one newspaper declared *Roger Ackroyd* to be "the best thriller ever," another thought it "tasteless and unfortunate," and years later the influential American critic Edmund Wilson would rhetorically ask "Who Cares Who Killed Roger Ackroyd?" in a scathing attack on the entire body of mystery fiction (Wilson, *Classics and Commercials: A Literary Chronicle of the Forties,* New York, 1960). Dorothy L. Sayers, who had published a stunning first mystery only three years before, defended Christie, declaring that she had held to the canons of fair play.

One result of the furor over *Roger Ackroyd* was the compilation by Monsignor Ronald Knox some three years later of a set of "Ten Commandments of Detection," a decalogue that was endorsed by the Detection Club, of which he was a founding member. One of these commandments, that the criminal "must not be anyone whose thoughts the reader has been allowed to follow," was believed to be directed at Christie, and although some of the strictures are expressed humorously, the commandments were meant to define an emerging tradition of fair play between author and reader.

It would seem that Christie, having already violated the first commandment, deliberately set out to break the remaining nine during her long writing career. One, that the detective may not prove to have committed the crime, she publicly broke only near the end, in a book written during the London blitz but intended for posthumous publication, *Curtain* (1975). But although she became president of the Detection Club herself in 1958, she could not have taken the rather fussy, if also funny, Knox commandments seriously if she expected her work to remain original.

Seven months after the publication of *The Murder of Roger Ackroyd,* Christie disappeared, and became the object of a nationwide search. Archie Christie was suspected of having murdered her; some thought her disappearance was a publicity stunt to boost *Roger Ackroyd*'s sales or to thumb her nose at her critics. She was the subject of banner headlines day after day until, after ten days, she was discovered registered under the last name of her husband's mistress at a hotel in the spa town of Harrogate. The press immediately demanded a full explanation from her, but she never provided one, and to this day biographers debate whether her disappearance was occasioned by her growing unhappiness over her husband's unfaithfulness and her subsequent amnesia—the majority view then and now—or whether she was exacting a form of vengeance on her husband and his new love. She and Archie Christie were divorced shortly afterward.

Christie's fame grew thereafter, as did her command of the genre. Most critics agree that her best work began in 1926 and continued through the early 1950's. Interested in archaeology, she visited a dig at Ur, near Baghdad, where she met a young scholar, Max Mallowan, with whom a friendship developed that, in September 1930, led to marriage. Max Mallowan was fourteen years younger than Christie, but mature, calm, and respectful of her work and career. This would be a most happy marriage, marked by frequent trips to the Near East, on the Orient Express or by Nile River steamer, all grist for Agatha's mill. Following her husband's knighthood in 1967, Christie became Lady Mallowan. Book followed book, and the public came to expect another Christie for Christmas.

Always shy, Christie immersed herself in her work and her marriage, enjoying Greenway, her Devon estate, where she gardened, walked, and read. Her books and short stories were turned into plays; plays and stories were turned into motion pictures. *The Mousetrap,* a play written in 1947, opened at London's Ambassadors Theatre in November 1952 and became the longest running play in history, the curtain not falling until 1989. When the play opened, Christie gave the rights to her grandson, then ten years old; over the years he became a millionaire from this single literary property. Another highly successful effort, *Witness for the Prosecution,* followed in 1953.

Toward the end of her career, Christie began writing less original works. Her plots became strained, more nearly fitting thrillers than mysteries. Although not up to her earlier standards, some good books were produced, though so too were some markedly unsatisfactory efforts. One novel, *Endless Night* (1967), demonstrated her facility for ingenious plotting and seemingly effortless prose, and she kept up her tradition of violating the established rules of the genre in *The Pale Horse* (1961), but there were distinct failures; despite soaring sales, *Hallowe'en Party,* published in 1969, and *Passenger to Frankfurt,* which came out the following year, were proof of sharp decline. She had not written such nonsense since *The Mystery of the Blue Train* (1928), which she dismissed as her worst book. (She was no better judge of her own work than most writers are, for she said that *Crooked House,* published in 1949, was her favorite, in a judgment few critics would support; though on another occasion she named *Ordeal by Innocence,* 1958, a much better

book.) There were two fine late books, *Curtain*—which bore the apposite subtitle, *Hercule Poirot's Last Case,* after her series detective, the little Belgian, Hercule Poirot—published in 1975 though written many years before, and *Sleeping Murder,* also written in the 1940's and deliberately held back to appear after her death, subtitled *Miss Marple's Final Case* (1979).

Christie died on 12 January 1976. By then nearly everyone who could read had cared who killed Roger Ackroyd.

THE MYSTERY OF MYSTERIES

WHY do people read mystery and detective fiction? Why is Agatha Christie so vastly popular, so representative of the attractions of the genre? Why, indeed, do people care who killed Roger Ackroyd?

Many ingenious theories have been offered in an attempt to explain why mysteries and detective fiction retain such a hold on the public imagination. Since such fiction is most commonly associated with the West, these theories often presuppose some connection between industrialization, capitalism, and Western philosophies of rationalism. Since mystery fiction is much less common in the Soviet Union, and was scorned in Nazi Germany, the theories also assume that freedom and democracy are essential to its growth. However, detective fiction sells in translation in vast quantities in societies that produce relatively little of it—Spain and Italy, for example, which, though once dictatorships, are now democracies—so it is clear that there is a difference between those conditions that foster authorship and those that encourage widespread readership. Some commentators detect a difference between cultures that are essentially Roman Catholic in their religious convictions and those that are either nominally Protestant or statistically secular. None of these observations tracks well, however, since detective fiction thrives in secular lands even though it has not, at least until quite recently, in an officially atheistic society such as Russia.

One may say that mystery fiction is popular because it entertains, provides escape from everyday realities, and is, quite simply, fun. Many scholars would find so simple an explanation insufficient, for each culture defines entertainment, as each society defines crime, somewhat differently. Nonetheless, there is much to commend this straightforward explanation. People like to be puzzled and, up to a point, fooled—although not too much, and perhaps not over issues that matter most to them.

Agatha Christie and Dorothy Sayers both realized to an exquisite degree just where the line ought to be drawn. Most readers of mystery fiction do enjoy being fooled, and are, generally speaking, literate enough to appreciate the verbal sleight of hand essential to the genre and the variable meanings assigned to a phrase. It is in this sense that the best mystery fiction may be said to be cerebral, even when the central action—of an American private-eye novel by Raymond Chandler, for example—is violent. Sayers in particular recognized that readers wish the detective to be just a bit ahead of them in the reasoning (or at times purely revelatory) process, but not too far ahead; alert readers will usually pick up on the clues a page or two after Lord Peter Wimsey, Sayers' series figure, has done so. That this happens time and again cannot be by accident, and one must conclude that she, and Christie, both understood the value of giving the detective only a little more rope than they gave their readers. Only inattentive readers, or readers with little regard for how language is used, will be caught in the end utterly by surprise, and those who *are* usually denounce the book as unfair and the genre as unrealistic and silly.

Christie's popularity was built during the golden age of detective fiction. Through the 1920's Britain was attempting to recover from a war that had decimated its younger generation. Escapism was the mode, in music, sexual mores, alcohol use, and literature. Mystery fiction looked in both directions: By focusing on a crime, almost always a murder, it spoke to the loosened morality of a period that followed upon years of legalized killing. Yet, by holding to a series of rules, or by acknowledging the existence of rules precisely by mocking them, mystery fiction also appealed to those who longed for the orderly and rational life that, they believed, had preceded World War I. However mysterious events might seem to be, however much facts might not be made to cohere, in the end the detective, whether amateur, as was Lord Peter, or professional, as was Hercule Poirot, would demonstrate a rational connection between all that had happened. To this extent, then, mystery fiction was conservative in its leanings, encouraging readers to believe that even though their prewar, orderly world had been demolished, there was an ultimate order in human events if only one were astute enough to detect it.

The interwar period, from 1919 to 1939, was the heyday of Freudian analysis, and mystery fiction presented its share of psychological conflicts. Seemingly placid figures were revealed to be hiding smoldering hatreds; highly conventional sexual lives were discovered to be perverse by the canons of the time; motivations that seemed simple were found to rest on the most complex of human instincts and emotions. The scientific rationalism of Edgar Allan Poe and Sir Arthur Conan Doyle was believed to be insufficient to account for human motivation. Indeed, detective and mystery fiction was based in good measure on the search for *the* motive, the key that would explain an entire pattern of cause and effect, which psychology referred to collectively when it spoke of motivation.

Mystery fiction appears to have been the favorite reading of the English, and in time, of the American middle class (though as science fiction developed, it also would hold a preferred place in the American imagination). The world envisioned by mystery fiction was artificial yet recognizable, not so much a parody as it was a nostalgic view of real places. Thus Christie's fictional St. Mary Mead, in which the spinster lady Miss Marple conducted her investigations, was at once endearing and a little sinister, a place not beyond, yet certainly approaching, a twilight zone. The artificiality of the final product, the degree to which mystery fiction became formulaic in the hands of many highly successful writers of the time, such as Margery Allingham and Ngaio Marsh, was an attraction, for it offered dependability, even predictability, to readers fed up with the instability of their world.

Members of the Detection Club were concerned that mystery fiction not be confused with "cheap thrillers" in which nothing mattered except pell-mell action. (Edgar Wallace, a highly successful writer of the time, frequently—and rightly—was accused of writing just such books.) Thus when Ronald Knox declared as his fifth commandment that "no Chinaman must figure in the story," he did not mean to be taken literally. Here "Chinaman" was a surrogate for the sinister Orientals and evil geniuses that distinguished the cheap thriller, the kind of one-dimensional figure whose culture was seen as precluding any solidarity with the Western understanding of motivation. Hidden behind the commandment, therefore, was the very real if often covert racism of most thrillers and much mystery fiction of the time. Christie was not immune to the conventions of the 1930's, and in her earlier books there are passing anti-Semitic remarks that are all the more obvious today for being so perfunctory.

The scientific, logical method of deduction (which was, in truth, more often induction) that Doyle's Sherlock Holmes had made so popular in the late Victorian and Edwardian periods remained popular in a transmuted form. While the war had taught people that life was not rational, it also left them hungering for a system of fair play, for a genre based on conventions and rules. Several historians of mystery fiction have noted that it is much like Restoration drama: bloody, tense, and cathartic, bound by a set of clearly bounded imperatives. P. D. James (the pseudonym for Phyllis White, the hugely successful mystery writer of the 1980's) is seen as the logical inheritor of Christie's mantle, the writer who has most successfully extended the genre while remaining within its traditions. It is not coincidental that one of James's earliest books, *Cover Her Face* (1962), takes its title from Restoration drama, or that her much-criticized 1982 novel, *The Skull Beneath the Skin* is, I believe, to be understood only as a self-conscious and highly crafted parody of at least a dozen of Christie's works.

The conventions of mystery fiction as developed during the golden age were, then, both satisfying and open to challenge. Christie was particularly skilled at using the conventions while treading close to their edge. These conventions included the centrality of "the body in the case," for murder most foul was deemed essential to a genuine mystery novel. (When Dorothy Sayers provided no murder in *Gaudy Night* in 1936, she was criticized for it.) Character was to play an important role; the agent of the final resolution could not prove to be acting out of character, although the reader could be judged to have misread that character. Search for motive, often conducted through a series of police interrogations—the questioning of the suspects and witnesses—provided a sense of motion even where there was none. The various suspects' alibis, by which they showed that they could not have committed the crime, and the final proof that one alibi was false, often turned on the most careful deductions of time and place, of railroad time-

tables and clocks that proved to be five minutes fast, of apparently locked rooms that somehow could be penetrated, of apparently reliable witnesses who confess they have lied. Motive and alibi are the the most traditional building blocks of all mystery fiction.

Of course, there must also be detection, and for detection there must be clues, and with the clues there must be red herrings. The clue—literally the "clew," or ball of thread which, as one unravels it, leads the way out of a labyrinth—must be laid down with care so that it may be taken up again as one backtracks along the trail, reexamining the evidence in the new light that each subsequent clue gives rise to, while the red herring—named from the practice of trailing a red herring across a bloodhound's path to confuse it—must be indistinguishable until the end from the true clue. At that end the criminal should prove to be the "least likely person," and since at any given stage of the plot, the least likely person would be identifiable, the clues must shift the focus from one person to another. Often, using the technique of the "double bluff," a person suspected at an early stage and then cleared would become the focus of investigation again.

These conventions meant that mystery fiction was, above all, pure plot, and this in turn dictated a certain rhythm to the proceedings, one that rose to a climax followed by a denouement in which the detective explains all to an assembled cast of suspects. To aid the plot, the author often would provide a map by which the reader could visualize the layout of the estate, the country house, or the town in which the murder was committed. That such maps or diagrams were useful suggests that crime fiction was particularly visual in its nature, and this characteristic, combined with reliance on plot, meant that mystery stories were readily adaptable to film. The 1930's were a time of great growth in the film industry, which snapped up popular mystery writers to prepare scripts or to outline possible plots. There was easy movement between the two art forms.

The visual significance of many of the clues in mystery fiction also meant that place, locale, landscape were of great importance. In real life a crime takes place within a discrete setting that may well have contributed to the nature of the crime: the darkened street, the lonely moor, the crowded hall. The better mystery writers took their readers on a vicarious journey, demonstrating the significance of place in relation to clues. Middle-class readers who might never hope to see inside a country gentleman's private library or to take tea on a cruise ship, much less ride on the Orient Express or enjoy a holiday on a remote island off the Cornwall coast, could see and experience such places from the comfort of their armchairs. Travel literature always has been popular with those who can afford only a little bit of the real thing, and mystery fiction drew upon the same impulse that brought entertainment to the armchair traveler.

Another convention of the time, stemming in particular from the work of Conan Doyle, was the detective's "sidekick." Christie used this convention well, her Captain Arthur Hastings playing Dr. Watson to Hercule Poirot. A trusted friend and confidant, sometimes the person who tells the story and through whom the reader comprehends the action, the sidekick is best when intelligent but somewhat less so than the hero. The device provides the detective with a reason to think out loud, to engage in passages of explication and explanation, bringing the reader into his confidence while ostensibly thinking through for his companion the meaning of a particular chain of events or the significance of a certain clue. Ideally the sidekick is slightly behind the readers, who compensate for trailing a page or two behind Wimsey or Poirot by being a page or two ahead of the sidekick in their understanding of the clues.

Hastings was a particularly happy invention, for Poirot, as a Belgian and something of a fop, would be seen as a foreigner with a certain number of foibles. If Christie were to comment on English society, she had two choices, the foreign view belonging to Poirot or the domestic view belonging to Hastings, and she could count on her readers to understand the latter and to sympathize with his conventionality, thus making Poirot appear all the more unusual. Although Poirot declares that Hastings suffers from an absence of order and method, he both likes and respects him; in this way Hastings becomes the reader, since a successful mystery novelist must have respect and affection for his or her audience. In fact Hastings appears in only eight Christie novels but his function is so important, when he is not present she often creates a similar figure.

Given these conventions, it is understandable that *The Murder of Roger Ackroyd,* and to a lesser ex-

tent *Murder on the Orient Express* (1934), which was published in the United States as *Murder in the Calais Coach,* should create a sensation for the way in which Christie interpreted fair play. Seldom have the books of popular writers given rise to the kind of controversy *Roger Ackroyd* did. Christie achieved her notoriety while remaining within the canons of acceptable language, needing neither censorship nor scandal to promote her work after her divorce from Archibald Christie.

In short, the popularity of mystery fiction, and of Agatha Christie in particular, may best be attributed to the public desire for sheer story, for grown-up tales that can, for busy adults, replace the brothers Grimm and Hans Christian Andersen at bedtime. Christie observes: "With method and logic one can accomplish anything" (*Poirot Investigates,* 1924); "Very few of us are what we seem" (*Partners in Crime,* 1929); "Speech . . . is an invention of man's to keep him from thinking" (*The ABC Murders,* 1936); "The worst is so often true" (*They Do It with Mirrors,* 1952). Such observations come close to paranoia; they are also at the heart of storytelling.

Finally, another quality of mystery fiction is that the storytelling has some modest practical applicability. Poirot says that "method, order, and the little grey cells" will lead to the truth; he notices details that do not fit a pattern, he remarks of a fact that "It is completely unimportant. That is why it is so interesting" (*Roger Ackroyd*); he takes notice of people who are behaving out of character. In this manner he alerts the reader to the role of inquiry and observation in everyday life, sharpening the senses, while praising both intuition and reason. The methods of inquiry, much like those of the historian, grant to the seemingly illogical a sense of logic, teach something about cause and effect, and alert one to the significance of the discordant note in an entire composition.

These explanations for the perennial popularity of mystery fiction omit three broad theories that have won followings of their own. The first, which may be loosely labeled the Marxist theory, sees detective fiction as a subtle attack upon, or unsubtle defense of, the status quo. The second, the psychological theory, holds that fans of crime fiction are motivated by the trauma of having witnessed their parents engaged in sexual intercourse, "primal scenes" of mystery and horror. The third, which may be called the environmental theory, although it also draws upon psychology and focuses on childhood, asks why people enjoy being frightened and suggests that mystery fiction helps put terror at a distance, on the printed page, into the experience of unreal figures, so that it may be internalized and thereby held at bay. This theory suggests that only children are attracted to mystery fiction because they often had to think through life's mysteries, especially those of which they would not speak openly by themselves, cerebrally rather than emotionally. Some biographers have found significance in the fact that Christie herself was brought up virtually an only child. The "only child" theory argues that solitude results in a compulsion toward order, which leads a person toward the kind of fiction that both restores order and gives the reader, through association with the triumphant detective, a sense of omnipotence.

All of these theories may be true, or partially true, contributory to an understanding of the perennial popularity of mystery fiction. They can be applied to Agatha Christie. They may be more applicable to Western societies than to non-Western. None detracts from the established fact that people read such fiction in great quantities because they enjoy it.

Agatha Christie's writing falls into five groups: those novels and stories which feature Hercule Poirot; those which bring Miss Marple to the fore; those which feature Tommy and Tuppence, that is Prudence and Thomas Beresford; the novels she wrote under the pseudonym Mary Westmacott; and her plays. Let us take each group in turn.

POIROT, MARPLE, ET AL.

CHRISTIE's first book, *The Mysterious Affair at Styles,* was written in 1916, while she was working in a wartime medical dispensary in Torquay. The book was turned down by four publishers before The Bodley Head published it in 1920. An instant success, the book raised the general level of mystery fiction, introduced Hercule Poirot, a retired Belgian detective, and demonstrated the author's knowledge of the use of poisons. Many of the elements that would come to distinguish her work were present. The story is told by Captain Hastings, recently home from the wartime front. It concerns the murder of an autocratic grande dame who, after being a widow for many years, has married a man twenty years younger than herself, a man thought to be a fortune-hunting bounder. When she dies, her new husband is the obvious suspect, especially when strychnine poisoning is found to be the cause of death. Suspicion falls in turn on a small, closed band of friends and relations.

In Styles, which is actually Styles Court, a somewhat stately home near the village of Styles St. Mary in Essex, Christie is able to display the social nuances of English society in the midst of war. She, and other mystery writers, will do so with such care that their work will be seen as an extension of the comedy of manners, of which Jane Austen was perhaps the finest practitioner, and in later years it would be fashionable to see certain mystery writers as descendants of Austen. Christie did not trace her inspiration to so grand a source, however, stating in her *Autobiography* (1977) years later that she wrote largely in response to her sister's challenge to attempt the kind of story they both enjoyed reading and from her desire to break into print. She knew poisons from her work in the dispensary, and she knew Torquay, where a body of refugee Belgians were residing. From such simple associations she began to weave her story.

Had Christie realized how popular Hercule Poirot would become, no doubt she would have made him younger in her first book. Already retired and walking with a limp in *Styles,* he would live on until *Curtain* in 1975, aged at least 85—and more likely 120. A private inquiry agent, he was, at Styles, "hardly more than five feet four inches" tall, although he made up for his diminutive stature by carrying himself with dignity and demonstrating unrivaled meticulosity: "His head was exactly the shape of an egg, and he always perched it a little on one side. His moustache was very stiff and military." In subsequent books he would lose his limp and intensify his already obsessive demand for order, squaring up pads on his blotter and books on his shelves with fanatical precision. According to the conventions of the time, Poirot could be forgiven his arrogant air of omniscience, his vanity, and his pomposity, because he was a foreigner.

Even in this first novel Christie displayed a nononsense attitude toward crime. She neither theorized about it nor, except on occasion in the mouth of a vicar who was usually made to sound just a wee bit foolish, did she moralize. Poirot declared that he had "a bourgeois attitude to murder. I disapprove of it." Thus the reader could get on with solving the crime with few moral qualms, moving at a steady gait through the clues, using common sense to follow not too far behind the great detective. Yet well ahead of Hastings, who is even more obtuse in *Styles* than in later adventures.

Including collections of short stories, Poirot would appear in forty-four books. Christie tired of Hastings, who appeared in her first three books and only intermittently thereafter. He appears to good effect in *The ABC Murders,* one of the most ably plotted of all the Poirot books. Here a homicidal maniac appears to be moving through the alphabet, having killed an Ascher in Andover, a Barnard in Bexhill-on-Sea, a Clarke in Churston, each of these places being a town on the same railroad line. The murders are preceded by a warning letter to Poirot challenging him to solve, or to forestall, each crime. At Doncaster an apparent mistake is made, for the murderer makes an attempt on the life of a man named Earlsfield. Poirot realizes there is a distinct method in this madness, and using the *ABC Rail Guide* he solves the puzzle. This is the quintessential golden age mystery; every element of the puzzle novel demonstrates the author's great skill and imagination. Numerous detective novels since have been derived more or less directly from Christie's plot; indeed by 1936 she was taking their proliferation as a compliment.

After *The Murder of Roger Ackroyd,* Poirot was an established figure, though not until 1934, in *Murder on the Orient Express,* would he again achieve so distinct a triumph. In the 1920's Christie had written ten books that were mysteries certainly but thrillers as well, although the thriller element in her plotting would gradually decline. With *The Murder at the Vicarage* (1930) one sees the thriller element subordinated—though never quite eradicated, as it was in *Endless Night* and *Passenger to Frankfurt.* A certain hesitation and mild experimentation followed *Murder at the Vicarage* until, with the *Orient Express,* her true direction became abundantly apparent.

Frequently said to be one of Christie's most outrageous novels, *Murder on the Orient Express* was written while Christie was on a dig in the Middle East. Traveling there on the Taurus Express, one of the constituents of the fabled Orient Express, the series of trains that had captured the traveling public's imagination since 1883, Christie was stranded in her coach due to a washed-out roadbed and heavy snowfall. She had ample time to study the precise layout of the train's sleeping compartments, the swing of its doors, the nature of her fellow travelers, and the intricacies of the dinner service. Her always fertile imagination turned the unfortunate journey into the basis for a remarkable mystery.

One convention of golden age mystery fiction was the locked room puzzle; another was the notion of a murderer at large among an ever-diminishing group of people who appear unable to escape their fate, since they are snowed in at a mountain cabin, trapped together on an isolated island, or cut off in a country estate because of a raging flood. Christie took these conventions and placed her murderer, and apparently her victim, an unpleasant American in this case, within the very tight confines of the Istanbul–Calais train, which has been forced to stop somewhere in Yugoslavia because of a heavy snowfall. Most of the action, in fact, takes place within only two coaches, where a mixture of national stereotypes are amusingly brought together: the romantic Russian, the sturdy German, the talkative American, the suave Hungarian, the winsome English woman, the blimpish British colonel, the phlegmatic Swede, and so forth. The indomitable Hercule Poirot is also aboard. The plot, triggered by a kidnapping markedly similar to the Lindbergh case of 1932, raises questions about the nature of guilt, the desirability of capital punishment, and the relativity of justice. In the end all of the major figures prove to be guilty, which both broke a commandment and posed questions about how society defines crime and punishes criminals.

Perhaps no book of Christie's so clearly revealed the difference between American and British mystery fiction. Her solution to the mystery was incredible in the truest sense of the word: quite improbable, yet logically viable, as the solution to a puzzle must be. Dashiell Hammett had been taking the American mystery in the opposite direction, toward an abundance of overt violence—his first book, *Red Harvest,* published in 1929, involved twenty-four murders—and cynicism. Hammett's successor, Raymond Chandler, would denounce *Murder in the Calais Coach* (the American title for the *Orient Express*), for he disliked its fairy-tale undertones, its dubious real-life legitimacy, the solution that worked rather as a crossword puzzle works, and the aridity, as it saw it, of the conventions by which he felt British detective fiction was bound.

From 1930 on, American and British mystery writing diverged steadily, one holding to and improving on the puzzle story, the other exploring the type of mystery that would later be referred to as the "quest story," in which the dogged search for an answer replaces strict reliance on "the little grey cells."

In 1935 Christie published two Poirot novels, the second of which, *Death in the Clouds* (published in the United States as *Death in the Air*) honed the puzzle story to its sharpest. An airborne Orient Express, the *Prometheus,* flying from Paris to London with eleven passengers in a rear compartment, is the scene of an unusual murder that takes place in full view of everyone, with no one having witnessed it. By this time Christie was so well established that she could indulge in numerous private jokes and much self-parody. It is thought that the murdered woman, at first believed to be asleep and then found to be dead, her throat marked by a tiny puncture mark, has been killed by "arrow poison" from South America (one crime-fiction commandment prohibits rare South American poisons), or by a lethal wasp (it is unclear how one would have entered the plane). Although there would be better books to come, there were none more typical of Christie's style.

By now Christie was writing with much conscious humor. In *Cards on the Table* (1936) she explored the psychology of four bridge players to determine the most likely suspect in a murder. An undercurrent of gentle mockery concerning card players, locked-room mysteries, and the function of the dummy in bridge distracts the reader from the tight construction. A famous crime novelist, Mrs. Adriadne Oliver, is an obvious self-portrait, and Christie does not spare her sharp tongue when discussing the essential futility, and the great fun, of a game she clearly means to equate with mystery fiction.

Many critics regard Christie's *Ten Little Niggers,* published in 1939, as her masterpiece. In a sense it is a mirror image of *Murder on the Orient Express.* Ten people are invited to an isolated island for a party. Each has been responsible for someone's death, whether by intent or through negligence. The island is owned by the person seeking to avenge the deaths. One by one the guests are murdered, each dying in a sequence determined by the appropriate verse of a nursery rhyme called "Ten Little Niggers," the words of which hang in every bedroom on the estate. (When the book was published in the United States, it was titled *And Then There Were None,* from the closing line to the rhyme, the English title being deemed offensive. In later years the title would be changed to *Ten Little Indians,* which would be confusing, due to the different version of the rhyme employed. Thus did social awareness invade the unreal world of Christie's fiction.) The novel is markedly tense, as close to a gothic thriller and modern suspense novel as the author would come. Widely praised and much discussed, the book would become a highly successful motion picture and is, under one of its titles, Christie's best-known work today. It is, as reviewers of the time remarked, her most nearly perfect mystery, quite superior to anything else appearing in the genre at the time.

But *Ten Little Niggers* was not a Poirot volume, and although she would return to his little gray cells often in the future, she clearly wished to break out of the mold into which the little Belgian was threatening to trap her. In *Murder at the Vicarage* she had introduced a second series figure, Miss Jane Marple, to whom she had returned in short stories from time to time but not, for twelve years, in a novel. In 1942 she committed herself to Marple, in a tour de force that was at once a commentary on the clichés of the genre, including her own *Roger Ackroyd,* and a humorous yet chilling mystery of great ingenuity, *The Body in the Library.* She later correctly judged the opening chapter to be the best she had ever written.

The body of an unknown young woman is discovered in the library of Gossington Hall, the country home of Colonel Bantry and his wife, Dolly. Identified as Ruby Keene, a teenage dance hostess "or something" at a hotel in a nearby resort town, the body proves particularly troublesome. Dolly Bantry's friend, Jane Marple, who is elderly—although Christie would not make the same mistake twice; the reader is given fewer hints as to her exact age than were given about Poirot's at Styles—and nosy, solves the mystery through persistence, a penchant for gossip, and the ability to eavesdrop with skill.

In creating Jane Marple, Christie was saying something about the stereotype of the small-town gossip. Marple is an unusual detective—an old, seemingly harmless woman, whom no one suspects. In fact, she can eavesdrop because no one even *sees* her. Marple is rather relentless: at the end of *The Body in the Library* she declares herself "quite pleased" to contemplate the murderer being hanged. One would not wish to live with a guilty secret in St. Mary Mead with a Miss Marple peering out through her lace curtains. In this way Christie comments on the essential narrowness of small-town life.

As mysteries, the Marple books are fully as good as the Poirot novels. They demonstrate the great power that lies in the hands of those with a taste for solitude and a belief that evil may be found anywhere under the sun, even in a small and unsophisticated village. The third Miss Marple tale, *The Moving Finger* (1942), which followed immediately upon *The Body in the Library,* was in design much like the card game of which she had written only four years before. Clues are laid out, then withdrawn, then used again in a complex dance that is both highly stylized and wondrously misleading. *4.50 from Paddington* (1957; published in the United States as *What Mrs. McGillicuddy Saw!,* a much more apposite title), despite farfetched moments, astutely explores how one can misread what one has seen. The busybody old lady, Miss Jane Marple, is revealed as a tough-minded exponent of capital punishment who concludes that there are some crimes for which death is the only appropriate end.

Tommy and Tuppence Beresford are much less successful characters than Poirot and Marple, certainly in retrospect; the books in which they are featured have not aged well. Introduced in *The Secret Adversary* in 1922, they would appear four more times in Christie novels, over fifty-two years: *Partners in Crime, N or M?* (1941), *By the Pricking of My Thumbs* (1968), and *Postern of Fate* (1973), the last published when the author was eighty-two and arguably her worst novel. Tommy and Tuppence seem, quite simply, self-indulgent and silly. Poirot was self-indulgent and full of nervous quirks and affectations but never silly—he was redeemed always by the rigor of his mind. Jane Marple was never self-indulgent, and the icicle in her eye kept her from ever being silly, although at times she appeared, or chose to appear, dithery. But the conventions of the golden age favored the kind of society couple Thomas Beresford and Prudence Cowley (later Mrs. Beresford) wished to be. This was a time when nicknames, often generated in grade school, followed adults to their graves:

Muffy and Fluffy, Boopsie and Bobbsie, Tommy and Tuppence were all unfalteringly endearing young people who drank their martinis and drove fast cars and danced the night away. If they happened to be creatures of an Agatha Christie, they also solved crimes, using a good bit of intuition and much romantic blather—in Tommy and Tuppence's case, speech directly out of P. G. Wodehouse and the drawing-room comedy—and a modicum of logic. Here, in a direct shoot-out, an American would win hands down, for Dashiell Hammett's Nick and Nora Charles, first introduced in *The Thin Man* in 1934, would carry away the dancing-and-drinking honors with ease and have grit left over for dealing with underworld toughs. Tommy and Tuppence are intolerable. Fortunately for Christie's reputation they are also nearly forgotten.

Christie tried her hand at creating other figures, but none took hold in a series or engaged her affections enough to lead her to return to them. There was Parker Pyne, in a collection of short stories, *Parker Pyne Investigates* (1934). There was Harley Quin, an unhappy pun, who was introduced in *The Mysterious Mr. Quin* (1930) and not revived. There was Inspector Battle, first made known in *The Secret of Chimneys* (1925), who returned on four occasions, once to work with Poirot (in *Cards on the Table*), and he nearly entered the pantheon, for the last Inspector Battle, *Towards Zero* (1944), is a fine example of the double bluff and, rather than beginning with the murder deemed essential to mystery fiction, works toward the murder in a careful construction of cause and effect rather than, as in most mystery fiction, a reconstruction.

Christie was quite prepared to abandon the notion of a central detective entirely. *Ten Little Niggers* is the best example, and perhaps the only truly satisfying one. Without a detective against which character might be read, or through whom development might be seen, she often fared poorly: three of her least satisfactory books, *Endless Night, Passenger to Frankfurt,* and the somewhat earlier *They Came to Baghdad* (1951) seem directionless for want of a director. *Death Comes as the End* (1944) pleased some readers, though more for its curiosity value than its plot. Set in Thebes, in ancient Egypt, and based on letters discovered in a tomb in the early 1920's, the novel is a labored and transparent effort to give everyday domestic details the kind of weight they might bear in St. Mary Mead. The device does not work and even the Christie magic cannot save this historical stew.

Although Christie was too multifaceted a writer to depend wholly on series figures, she well understood their value. Once the reading public was addicted to Poirot and Jane Marple, they could be counted on to buy each new book as it appeared. New readers, first stumbling on one of these figures in a later novel, would be likely to seek out the earlier ones, helping to make certain that dozens of Christie works would be in print at one time. Today one may visit virtually any airport in the Western world and find a shop with at least a dozen Christies set out in a row. So addicted did they become, countless intelligent readers would report being nearly to the end of a Christie mystery before discovering that they had already read the book. Some commentators take this to mean that the books induce a certain mindlessness, for one cannot imagine approaching the end of Herman Melville's *Moby Dick* unaware of having read it before. Certainly it is true that the speed at which a Christie novel moves, and the sleight of hand woven through it, necessitates the reader's attention to detail and a subsequent inattentiveness to the basic structure of the story. In this sense Christie's mystery books are trees, not forests.

THE WESTMACOTT NOVELS

But Christie wished to produce romantic novels as well, and to do so she chose a pen name: Mary Westmacott. These noncrime novels are not taken seriously today, eclipsed as they are by Christie's mysteries, and inferior to the romantic novels of Daphne Du Maurier and Barbara Cartland. They are seldom read anymore. They are not without merit, however, and they are more autobiographical than any of Christie's other work, with the obvious exception of her explicitly autobiographical accounts.

The first Westmacott, *Giants' Bread*, appeared in 1930. Christie had had aspirations of becoming an opera singer, and here her subject is music. The book was reviewed quite favorably given that no one knew the author's true identity. The principal figure, Vernon Deyre, is a composer who has moved into experimental forms. The plot is complicated and hardly convincing, but life in pre- and postwar London is effectively evoked. In one sequence Vernon, who has been shipwrecked, must decide which of two women to pull onto a raft, an ex-lover or his wife. The scene is implausible, melodramatic, and in retrospect implicative of Christie's attitude toward her first husband, but she was able to carry it off precisely because readers did not know who Westmacott was.

Christie returned to the Westmacott pen name four years later, in *Unfinished Portrait* (1934), still apparently determined to see whether she could achieve success through so-called "straight" novels and still obsessed with the need to write covert autobiography. This novel, perhaps because it is the most consciously autobiographical—indeed, Christie scholars have noted how closely it corresponds to early portions of her *Autobiography*, published posthumously in 1977—is the best of those written under the Westmacott pseudonym. It succeeds not by virtue of its plot or style—on both grounds it fails—but because of the anguish it reveals, an anguish that would, by 1977, be reported in tranquillity. This was the fifth Christie published in 1934; such intense productivity attests to Christie's obsessiveness in fleshing out her own "portrait."

Most critics prefer another Westmacott novel, *Absent in the Spring,* which appeared ten years later, in 1944. Certainly it is the most mature Westmacott, a clear-eyed portrait of a middle-class woman who is the victim of self-deception. Christie tells us that she wrote the novel, all fifty thousand words of it, in three days, composing the first chapter "in a white heat," then the last chapter, and then the material that inexorably carries the one to the other. It was, she wrote, "the one book that . . . satisfied me completely" (*Autobiography,* p. 484). Some readers believed that it was about a person, or type of person, Christie hated. Clearly it exorcised something within her. Still, one must not make too much of the autobiographical element, for *Absent in the Spring* was also a variant on her mysteries, a demonstration that things are not as they seem, even to oneself.

PLAYS

In addition to short stories and two books of poetry, as well as her two works of autobiography,

Agatha Christie wrote plays, fifteen in all. Most were adaptations of her novels, notably *Ten Little Niggers* (1943), her first venture into adaptation, and *Towards Zero* (1956). By far her two greatest successes on the stage were fleshed out from short stories, however. These were *The Mousetrap* (1952), adapted from "Three Blind Mice," which first appeared in a collection of that title in 1950, and *Witness for the Prosecution* (1953), from the short story published in a collection with that title (1948).

Despite the record-breaking commercial success of *The Mousetrap,* no case can be made for Christie as a major dramatist. Her novels and short stories generally were adapted for the stage by someone else, and the plays are simply stripped-down versions of her novels and stories, by which the plots stand revealed as contrived and thin. Still, she had a shrewd head for drama, and a knack for keeping action flowing across the stage almost unceasingly, surprise following surprise to keep the audience gasping. Undemanding and clever, these plays were ideal for the typical matinee audience, up from the country and eager to be entertained. They do make clear how tight, how lean her basic constructions were when unadorned, how wickedly clever and how cleverly simple. They also attest to her professionalism, for all writers who must live from their writing learn how to cut the same loaf of bread in more ways than one. The short story "Three Blind Mice," which became the record-setting play, began as a radio drama. Thus it lived nearly as many lives as those blind mice, as radio skit, short story, lead piece in a published book, play, and object of intense imitation.

Interestingly, *The Mousetrap* has not become a motion picture, although *Witness for the Prosecution* was turned into a very successful film in 1957; a new ending, however, added by Christie, seriously lessens the story's impact. Christie usually disliked the motion picture versions of her work. *Ten Little Niggers* was made into a film on three occasions, each time drawing upon the play rather than the book. *Murder on the Orient Express,* released shortly before her death, became the most commercially successful British film ever made, and it was happily, if clumsily, faithful to the original book, although Albert Finney's portrayal of Poirot was a far cry from what Christie had envisioned. Still, Christie is said to have enjoyed it, and the adaptation was more nearly a mystery than any other

motion picture derived from her work in the last thirty years.

THE FINAL DUO: CURTAIN *AND* SLEEPING MURDER

CHRISTIE would have one last laugh on those who had sought to keep her beholden to an arbitrary set of commandments. In the 1940's, as we have seen, she had written two novels, one featuring Hercule Poirot, the other Jane Marple, and had laid them down like good wines to mature. It was her intention to have her publisher bring both out posthumously. She changed her mind with the first, *Curtain;* Sir William Collins persuaded her to let the book appear in 1975. The publisher needed another best-seller; perhaps Christie herself realized she needed a strong book after the critical failures of her last five novels, beginning with *Hallowe'en Party* in 1969, and of her last play, *Fiddlers Three* (1972). *Curtain* broke another commandment—that the detective may not be the murderer—but to do so it saddened many readers, and while the ending was almost universally proclaimed to be a total surprise, one senses that the critics were being kind, for in fact the ending emerges from the gloom toward the reader with an unwanted logic few who had followed her career could escape.

But as planned, Miss Marple's last case, *Sleeping Murder,* appeared posthumously in 1976, nine months after its creator died. Although critics also praised this book, one feels they were being entirely too gracious, gratifying the public's desire that the mistress of crime close her career with a strong performance. Indeed, while much better than anything she published in the late 1960's or in the 1970's, there are weaknesses in the narrative that suggest Christie may have tinkered with it during the period of her decline. Nonetheless, *Sleeping Murder* effectively employs a favorite Christie plot, the attempt in the present to retrace the roots of a crime that has occurred in the past (in this case, eighteen years before), an exercise in excavating the sedimentary layers of the human psyche. One reviewer declared that Christie had "saved the best for last" (as cited in Osborne, p. 291), and while the judgment was not sound, the sentiment was welcome. By holding back two of her better manuscripts, she was able to salvage the old respect that had been given the originality of her mind.

CONCLUSION

THE case, however, can be made that Christie was less original than she was credited as being. Miss Marple was not the first spinster detective, for in *Unnatural Death* (1927) Dorothy Sayers introduced an inquiry agency headed by a Miss Climpson and run entirely by women. Rather, Christie was the first writer of mysteries to make an elderly and obviously genteel woman the solver of crimes over an entire series of books. The basic idea for *The Murder of Roger Ackroyd* was given to her by Lord Mountbatten in a rather sketchy letter. Several of her stories were suggested by news articles, personal experiences, or settings. The basic idea in a short story might show up again in a novel, and certainly there are strong hints of Poe, Doyle, and Phillpotts in her early work. If the Lindbergh case, in some measure, inspired *Murder on the Orient Express,* a series of British crimes in which black magic was believed to have played a role lay behind *The Pale Horse.* Although Christie used trains ingeniously in four major novels, Graham Greene had already taken the reading public on the *Stamboul Train* in 1932. She first put forward the central plot of *Cards on the Table* a year earlier in *The ABC Murders,* and she frequently foreshadowed her own books. Nursery rhymes, Knox's decalogue, and the clichés of her own and other books all become points of departure for her plots. If, in the 1930's, Mrs. Belloc Lowndes, most noted for a classic novel based on the crimes of Jack the Ripper, *The Lodger* (1913), wrote stories about Hercules Popeau, one of them entitled "A Labour of Hercules," it bothered Agatha Christie not at all when she called one of her collections of Hercule Poirot stories, published a decade later, *The Labours of Hercules.*

Christie was original because of the way in which she developed plot, unraveled motive, and put utterly fresh twists on timeworn devices. Even books of less substance than her undoubted classics revealed her quite remarkable ability to build motive, to misdirect the reader, and to weave complex plots that turned and turned again. *Mrs. McGinty's Dead* (1952; in the United States, *Blood Will Tell*), concerns the death of a washerwoman, struck on the head for a few pounds, and unfolds as a portrait of lower-middle-class life after World War II. *The Clocks* (1963), *Endless Night,* both masterpieces of plotting, or *The Moving Finger* and *The Hollow* (1946) belie the conventional judgment that Agatha Christie was not a stylist. Her prodigious productivity, her (as critic Robert Barnard remarked) "effortless drive," and her mastery over the art of persuasion and obfuscation combined to produce a body of work of quite remarkable originality.

In *The Clocks* Hercule Poirot apparently speaks for Christie when he engages in an unaccustomed series of judgments about mystery writers. Doyle, he says, is the great teacher, who gives pleasure through his language. *The Leavenworth Case* (the work of Anna Katharine Green, published in 1878), sometimes said to be the first modern mystery story, he admires for its period atmosphere. *The Mystery of the Yellow Room* (1908), the work of Gaston Leroux, he praises for its logic, and *The Adventures of Arsene Lupin* (1909), by Maurice Leblanc, for its vitality. American writers, he remarks, are "a little too obsessed with drink," reporting the exact amounts of rye and bourbon consumed on every page. In *Elephants Can Remember* (1972) Christie had shown how the elderly (the elephants of the title) do not forget, and she had not forgotten the way in which Raymond Chandler had dismissed her kind of book. In vitality, logic, atmosphere, and social scene, above all in the simplicity and trickery and pleasure of language, Agatha Christie was, as Poirot said of Doyle, a master teacher.

SELECTED BIBLIOGRAPHY

I. BIBLIOGRAPHY. N. B. Wynne, *An Agatha Christie Chronology* (New York, 1976), contains several useful checklists; R. H. Fitzgibbon, *The Agatha Christie Companion* (Bowling Green, Ohio, 1980), a full bibliography of all Christie publications in Great Britain and the United States, with useful entries on the short stories, plays, and film adaptations, and a fine index to characters; T. W. Johnson and J. Johnson, eds., *Crime Fiction Criticism: An Annotated Bibliography* (New York, 1981), annotates 47 critical books and articles on Christie through 1980, all in English; W. Albert, *Detective and Mystery Fiction: An Inter-*

national *Bibliography of Secondary Sources* (Madison, Indiana, 1985), annotates 109 titles, including significant studies not in English; D. Riley and P. McAllister, eds., *The New Bedside, Bathtub & Armchair Companion to Agatha Christie,* 2d ed. (New York, 1986), presents one- and two-page commentaries on each novel in the order they were published.

II. SEPARATE WORKS. [Works listed are novels unless indicated otherwise.] *The Mysterious Affair at Styles* (London, 1920; New York, 1920); *The Secret Adversary* (London, 1922; New York, 1922); *Murder on the Links* (London, 1923; New York, 1923); *The Man in the Brown Suit* (London, 1924; New York, 1924); *Poirot Investigates* (London, 1924; New York, 1925), short stories; *The Road of Dreams* (London, 1924), poetry; *The Secret of Chimneys* (London, 1925; New York, 1925); *The Murder of Roger Ackroyd* (London, 1926; New York 1926); *The Big Four* (London, 1927; New York, 1927); *The Mystery of the Blue Train* (London, 1928; New York, 1928); *Partners in Crime* (London, 1929; New York, 1929), short stories; *The Seven Dials Mystery* (London, 1929; New York, 1929).

Black Coffee (London, 1930 [production]), play; *Giants' Bread* (as Mary Westmacott, London, 1930; New York 1930); *The Murder at the Vicarage* (London, 1930; New York 1930); *The Mysterious Mr. Quin* (London, 1930; New York, 1930), short stories; *The Sittaford Mystery* (London, 1931), published as *Murder at Hazelmoor* (New York, 1931); *Peril at End House* (London, 1932; New York, 1932); *The Thirteen Problems* (London, 1932), published as *The Tuesday Club Murders* (New York, 1933), short stories; *The Hound of Death* (London, 1933), short stories; *Lord Edgware Dies* (London, 1933), published as *Thirteen at Dinner* (New York, 1933); *The Listerdale Mystery* (London, 1934), short stories; *Murder in Three Acts* (New York, 1934), published as *Three Act Tragedy* (London, 1935); *Murder on the Orient Express* (London, 1934), published as *Murder in the Calais Coach* (New York, 1934); *Parker Pyne Investigates* (London, 1934), published as *Mr. Parker Pyne, Detective* (New York, 1934), short stories; *Unfinished Portrait* (as Mary Westmacott, London, 1934; New York, 1934); *Why Didn't They Ask Evans?* (London, 1934), published as *The Boomerang Clue* (New York, 1935); *Death in the Clouds* (London, 1935), published as *Death in the Air* (New York, 1935); *The ABC Murders* (London, 1936; New York, 1936); *Cards on the Table* (London, 1936; New York, 1936); *Murder in Mesopotamia* (London, 1936; New York, 1936); *Death on the Nile* (London, 1937; New York, 1938); *Dumb Witness* (London, 1937), published as *Poirot Loses a Client* (New York, 1937); *Murder in the Mews* (London, 1937), published as *Dead Man's Mirror* (New York, 1937), short stories; *Appointment with Death* (London, 1938; New York, 1938); *Hercule Poirot's Christmas* (London, 1938), published as *Murder for Christmas* (New York, 1939); *Murder Is Easy* (London, 1939), published as *Easy to Kill* (New York, 1939); *The Regatta Mystery* (New York, 1939), short stories; *Ten Little Niggers* (London, 1939), published as *And Then There Were None* (New York, 1940).

One, Two, Buckle My Shoe (London, 1940), published as *The Patriotic Murders* (New York, 1941); *Sad Cypress* (London, 1940; New York, 1940); *Evil Under the Sun* (London, 1941; New York, 1941); *N or M?* (London, 1941; New York, 1941); *The Body in the Library* (London, 1942; New York, 1942); *The Moving Finger* (New York, 1942; London, 1943); *Five Little Pigs* (London, 1943), published as *Murder in Retrospect* (New York, 1943); *Absent in the Spring* (as Mary Westmacott, London, 1944; New York, 1944); *Death Comes as the End* (New York, 1944; London, 1945); *Towards Zero* (London, 1944; New York, 1944); *Sparkling Cyanide* (London, 1945), published as *Remembered Death* (New York, 1945); *Come, Tell Me How You Live* (as Agatha Christie Mallowan, London, 1946; New York, 1946), memoir; *The Hollow* (London, 1946), published as *Murder After Hours* (New York, 1946); *The Labours of Hercules* (London, 1947; New York, 1947), short stories; *The Rose and the Yew Tree* (as Mary Westmacott, London, 1948; New York, 1948); *Taken at the Flood* (London, 1948), published as *There Is a Tide* (New York, 1948); *Witness for the Prosecution* (New York, 1948), short stories; *Crooked House* (London, 1949; New York, 1949).

A Murder Is Announced (London, 1950; New York, 1950); *Three Blind Mice* (New York, 1950), short stories; *The Under Dog* (New York, 1951), short stories; *They Came to Baghdad* (London, 1951; New York, 1951); *Mrs. McGinty's Dead* (London, 1952); *A Daughter's a Daughter* (as Mary Westmacott, London, 1952; New York, 1963); *They Do It with Mirrors* (London, 1952), published as *Murder with Mirrors* (New York, 1952); *After the Funeral* (London, 1953), published as *Funerals Are Fatal* (New York, 1953); *A Pocket Full of Rye* (London, 1953; New York, 1954); *Destination Unknown* (London, 1954), published as *So Many Steps to Death* (New York, 1955); *Spider's Web* (London, 1954 [production]), play; *Hickory Dickory Dock* (London, 1955), published as *Hickory Dickory Death* (New York, 1955); *The Burden* (as Mary Westmacott, London, 1956; New York, 1963); *Dead Man's Folly* (London, 1956; New York, 1956); *4.50 from Paddington* (London, 1957), published as *What Mrs. McGillicuddy Saw!* (New York, 1957); *Ordeal by Innocence* (London, 1958; New York, 1959); *The Unexpected Guest* (London, 1958 [production]), play; *Verdict* (London, 1958 [production]), play; *Cat Among the Pigeons* (London, 1959; New York, 1960).

The Adventure of the Christmas Pudding (London, 1960), short stories; *Double Sin* (New York, 1961), short stories; *The Pale Horse* (London, 1961; New York, 1962); *The Mirror Crack'd from Side to Side* (London, 1962), published as *The Mirror Crack'd* (New York, 1963); *Rule of Three* (London, 1962 [production]), three one-act plays; *The Clocks* (London, 1963; New York, 1964); *A Caribbean Mystery* (London, 1964; New York, 1965); *At Bertram's Hotel* (London, 1965; New York, 1966); *Star Over Bethlehem* (as Agatha

Christie Mallowan, London, 1965; New York, 1965), stories for children; *Third Girl* (London, 1966; New York, 1967); *Endless Night* (London, 1967; New York, 1968); *By the Pricking of My Thumbs* (London, 1968; New York, 1968); *Hallowe'en Party* (London, 1969; New York, 1969); *Passenger to Frankfurt* (London, 1970; New York, 1970); *The Golden Ball* (New York, 1971), short stories; *Nemesis* (London, 1971; New York, 1971); *Elephants Can Remember* (London, 1972; New York, 1972); *Fiddlers Three* (Guilford, England, 1972 [production]), play; *Akhnaton* (London, 1973), unproduced play; *Poems* (London, 1973; New York, 1973); poetry; *Postern of Fate* (London, 1973; New York, 1973); *Poirot's Early Cases* (London, 1974), published as *Hercule Poirot's Early Cases* (New York, 1974), short stories; *Curtain* (London, 1975; New York, 1975); *Sleeping Murder* (London, 1976; New York, 1976); *An Autobiography* (London, 1977; New York, 1977), autobiography; *Miss Marple's Final Cases and Two Other Stories* (London, 1979), short stories.

III. CRITICAL STUDIES. G. C. Ramsey, *Agatha Christie: Mistress of Mystery* (New York, 1967), one of the earliest examinations of Christie's work; J. Feinman, *The Mysterious World of Agatha Christie* (New York, 1975); B. Legars and J. Thibaudeau, "Agatha Christie," in *La nouvelle critique,* XCVI (November 1976); H. R. F. Keating, ed., *Agatha Christie: First Lady of Crime* (London, 1977; New York, 1977), consists of fourteen essays, some of them substantial; A. Krause and M. Peters, "Why Women Kill," in *Journal of Communication,* 25, no. 2 (1977); G. Robyns, *The Mystery of Agatha Christie* (New York, 1978), recommended for its coverage of Christie's private life; R. Barnard, *A Talent to Deceive: An Appreciation of Agatha Christie* (London, 1980; New York, 1980); R. Toye, *The Agatha Christie Who's Who* (New York, 1980), helps to sort out Christie's many characters; F. Rivière, *Agatha Christie: Duchesse de la mort* (Paris, 1981), the best study not in English; C. Osborne, *The Life and Crimes of Agatha Christie* (London, 1982), provides the fullest publishing history; J. Morgan, *Agatha Christie* (London, 1984; New York, 1985), the best biography of Christie; M. S. Wagoner, *Agatha Christie* (Boston, 1986), attempts the most complete assessment by studying the nonmystery writings.

NOEL COWARD

(1899–1973)

Jeffrey Kindley

THE NAME NOEL COWARD has meant many things since Coward first succeeded in thrusting it upon the public in 1924 by writing and starring in a determinedly sensational look at contemporary neuroses called *The Vortex.* From the beginning his name meant wit and charm and confident, commercial theatricality. But the name had other connotations as well.

In the 1920's Coward's name also suggested immorality. Talent too, of course, but tainted by decadence—an "unhealthy" talent. It meant drugs and jazz and sex and bright young things bent on self-destruction. To those in the know it meant homosexuality.

By the 1930's Coward's name meant something a good deal less suspect to the multitude and, happily for Coward, even more marketable. It meant sophistication. It meant elegantly costumed men and women with long cigarette holders trading quips in the moonlight. And it meant romantic nostalgia, gift wrapped in elaborate confectionary period musicals.

In the 1940's it meant heart-on-the-sleeve, stiff-upper-lip patriotism. It meant "London Pride" and the war effort and celebrations of British indomitability. To his countrymen and women Noel Coward meant "Our Noel," guardian of the home fires and upholder of the Queen.

In the 1950's, as patriotism unabashed lost ground to patriot bashers and the drawing room was superseded by the kitchen sink, Noel Coward came to mean passé. The name was a synonym for the outmoded theatrical establishment, the dead and despicable *derrière-garde.* It meant elitist retrograde sentimental sludge.

In the 1960's the name Noel Coward was suddenly and surprisingly regilded. It meant style. It meant "the Master": the by-now bald eminence who had written thirty-one full-length and seventeen one-act plays, seven musicals and five revues

(he directed twenty-nine of these productions and starred in nineteen) as well as the music and lyrics of hundreds of songs, many of which he introduced on stage as singer and dancer.

Throughout all these years, from 1924 on, one thing was indisputably clear, clear to his opponents and adherents alike: the name Noel Coward meant star.

When he died in 1973, three years after attaining a much-publicized knighthood, it was universally acknowledged that a phenomenon unique in the history of the theater was gone. No playwright before him had been such a complete man of the theater. Not Shakespeare. Not Molière.

There is a difference, however, between being acclaimed as a theatrical phenomenon and being acclaimed as a playwright. Coward was certainly a celebrated figure during his lifetime, but his work was often overshadowed by his personality—as evidenced by playwright John Osborne's ambiguous tribute: "Mr. Coward . . . is his own invention and contribution to this century. Anyone who cannot see that should keep well away from the theatre" (Morley, *A Talent to Amuse,* p. 298).

What about his plays? Were they nothing but airy charm, insubstantial pageants faded like Prospero's—or were they perhaps as distinguished as their author? Had the world, blinded by his panache and popularity, failed to detect a major playwright in the boulevardier and box-office magician? Well, yes and no. "Major" he was and will likely remain to those who regard the comedy of manners a praiseworthy genre. The author of *Hay Fever* (1925) and *Private Lives* (1930) has earned himself a permanent place in the history of English dramatic comedy alongside William Wycherley, William Congreve, Oliver Goldsmith, Richard Sheridan, and Oscar Wilde. "Minor" he will always be to those who condescend to the genre, who consider it primarily an opportunity for belated social research. "Microscopic" will no doubt be the verdict of those who survey his literary output solely for something of enduring philosophical value.

He was of the theater, theatrical, and many of the plays and musicals he wrote were as thin and ephemeral as their playbills. Look beyond his five or six enduring works and one surveys a desert of dated vehicles, enlivened every so often by an oasis of charm—a scene or a song or the memory of a star performance. One has to see him for what he was, a man of the theater, and try to understand why his best plays are so durably enchanting. Bubbles that do not burst all but defy analysis, but every once in a while an artist produces them, and they shimmer through the centuries, floating far above contention.

BEGINNINGS

To know Noel Coward at thirteen was to know Noel Coward for all time. Micheál MacLiammóir, a fellow child actor who played with him in *Peter Pan*, speaks of "his intense loyalty, even then, to the theatre; it gave Noel everything in the world he dreamed of or wanted." "He was always quite certain of everything," says MacLiammóir, who describes him as "decidedly puckish, witty, dry, clipped and immensely competent" (Morley, *A Talent*, p. 25). Coward was a boy who loved the stage, learned its discipline extremely early, and lived by its rules all his life.

He was born on 16 December 1899—which means, quite conveniently, that his achievements in the twentieth century correspond in date to his age. Despite the impression he gave in later life of having been raised in the lap of luxury, he was in fact born to a family with very little money who lived in a small, inelegant suburb of London and struggled to retain some vestige of gentility. He was firmly ensconced on the stage as a professional actor at age eleven (partly in the hope of augmenting the family income), directed his first play at twelve, met his eventual costar Gertrude Lawrence at thirteen, and wrote his first plays and songs at fourteen. The rest of his career is in some sense a willed fifty-year-long prolongation of his preadolescence. Or, as critic Kenneth Tynan put it in 1953 in "A Tribute to Mr. Coward", "Forty years ago he

was Slightly in *Peter Pan,* and you might say that he has been wholly in *Peter Pan* ever since."

Growing up in the theater, Coward learned several things. He learned, obviously enough, to play a part—which meant, in his terms, not only to impersonate a character but to exert a certain fascination that would get him noticed. He also learned that the best part to play was the star's; that the audience told you what was good and what was not; that plays closed in no time if they did not please the audience; and that there were certain kinds of plays the audience traditionally enjoyed more than others. In lieu of a more formal education (Coward's was intermittent at best and ended for good at age thirteen) these theatrical precepts sustained him quite nicely for the next fifty years. Other playwrights began with the intention of expressing themselves artistically or conveying a message. Coward began with the intention of holding an audience: What would be effective? What would work?

His mentor at age eleven was actor/author Charles Hawtrey, the first of a new breed of nondeclamatory actors who prized naturalness on stage and seemed, by dint of a stage technique at least as sophisticated as any of his predecessors', not to be acting at all. This early exponent of the apparently unperformed performance had a profound effect on Coward, who would develop his own distinctive "sine qua nonchalance" as actor and author.

The two writers who contributed most to the development of his style were both boyhood favorites: E. Nesbit and Saki (H. H. Munro). Nesbit's books for children—*The Enchanted Castle* (1907), *The Magic World* (1912), and many others—fascinated Coward all his life with their offhand unapologetic bohemianism, their implicit conviction that children know all there is to know but are obliged to keep still about it by stuffy adults. It was an attitude that informed his best comedies: the sense of enlightened childlike "us" against stuffy adult "them." "Of all the writers I have ever read," Coward said in 1956, "[E. Nesbit] has given me over the years the most complete satisfaction and, incidentally, a great deal of inspiration" (Lesley, *The Life of Noel Coward,* p. 371).

And Saki? More than Wilde, more than anyone, this master of the maliciously witty short story was the writer who influenced the creation of Coward's unique brand of badinage. Cole Lesley, in *Remem-*

bered *Laughter: The Life of Noel Coward* (1976), quotes an exchange from a story by Saki—"There was apple-blossom everywhere." "Only on the apple trees, surely."—as "dialogue exactly to Noel's taste" (pp. 29–30). The quick, astringent reply, subverting sentimentality but not entirely canceling it out, is indeed the quintessence of Coward.

The Noel Coward style crystallized while he was still in his teens. But polishing it up and putting it over—impressing his persona upon the public—took time and work. Before he was twenty-five he had written two novels, an opera, innumerable songs and sketches for revues, and thirteen plays. Most of these projects fell by the wayside. The ones that did not were written with a sharp eye on the market, and to list them is to make a synopsis of the era's most marketable commodities.

One was a light comedy manufactured to its producer's specifications about a supposedly rich uncle and his heirs (*"I'll Leave It To You,"* 1920); one was a smudged carbon copy of George Bernard Shaw's 1897 *You Never Can Tell* in which the younger generation cleverly comes to the rescue of its errant elders (*The Young Idea,* 1922); one was the steamy romantic story of a repressed English wife who surrenders to the lust of an Italian troubadour and learns about life (*Sirocco,* 1927); one was a Ruritanian melodrama in which "Fate played marionettes" with a hapless queen and her true love, caught in the midst of a revolution (*The Queen Was in the Parlour,* 1927); one was a sex comedy about two married women anticipating a visit from a past lover while their husbands are off playing golf (*Fallen Angels,* 1925).

And one was *Hay Fever* and another was *The Vortex.* In 1924 a producer told Coward he liked both of these last plays and couldn't decide which to put on. What did Coward think? Coward unhesitatingly urged him to produce *The Vortex* because it, unlike *Hay Fever,* contained "a whacking good part" (introduction to *Play Parade,* vol. 1, p. x)—a *star* part—tailor-made for its author to play.

He was about to become a sensation.

THE VORTEX

THE stage directions at the beginning of the published edition of *The Vortex* reveal a great deal about the play: "THE SCENE *is the drawing-room of Mrs. Lancas-*

ter's flat in London. The colours and decoration are on the verge of being original. . . . Persons shown are Helen Saville and Pauncefort Quentin. . . . Helen is a smartly dressed woman of about thirty. 'Pawnie' is an elderly maiden gentleman" (*Play Parade,* Vol. 1, p. 427).[1]

The drawing room setting is no surprise. We are in Arthur Wing Pinero territory, only a step away from Somerset Maugham's recently successful *Our Betters* (1917) and *The Circle* (1921). But "on the verge of being original"? What a wealth of social history, what a wealth of *attitude,* is implicit in that phrase. And how immediately the playwright's own arch argot becomes inseparable from his characters'. The designation "persons shown" is a nod to nineteenth-century dramatic tradition in its archaic formality—an indication that Coward is striving to be a part of British theatrical tradition even as he's about to set off a few depth charges. That Helen is smartly dressed tells us little except that the author is conscious of fashion. But that Pawnie "is an elderly maiden gentleman" speaks volumes.

Less than thirty years before Coward wrote *The Vortex,* Oscar Wilde was sentenced to two years with hard labor for "committing acts of gross indecency with other male persons." His conviction had many consequences, one of which was to make homosexual artists not just circumspect about revealing their sexual preferences but wholly clandestine. "The love that dare not speak its name" dared least to speak it on the stage, where the Lord Chamberlain was empowered to forbid the production of any morally objectionable play. "Maiden gentleman" may seem a quaint euphemism to us now, but in 1924 it signaled the discreet reemergence on stage of the homosexual voice—a voice never absent, of course, but once again tempting recognition. Pawnie's function in the play is largely to be the catty half of an opening expository dialogue, remarking that this or that is "too marvelous" or "too divine" or "too tiresome for words!" and delivering such Wilde-and-water epigrams as: "He's divinely selfish; all amusing people are" (p. 429). But there's no mistaking that his very presence on stage, resurrecting the spirit of Wilde, is provocative.

[1]Citations for plays in volume 1 of *Play Parade* refer to original American edition. All other references to plays, unless otherwise noted, are to original English editions of the *Play Parade* series, volumes 2–6.

And what is *The Vortex* about? It's about twenty-four-year-old Nicky Lancaster and his aging beauty of a mother who has a lover his own age. The plot was suggested by an incident at a party: the glamorous mother of a friend of Coward's was flirting with a youthful admirer when someone exclaimed within the son's hearing, "Will you look at that old hag over there? She's old enough to be his mother." Coward's sympathetic embarrassment was the germ of *The Vortex*. The play provided him with a star part (no surprise there, although he had to fight a bit to ensure that he played it), a star part that was the highly polished first draft of the Noel Coward persona.

Nicky Lancaster is an "extremely well dressed" young man, "tall and pale, with thin, nervous hands" (p. 441), who "will be perfectly happy as long as he goes on attracting people; he loves being attractive" (p. 429): "He *doesn't do* anything except play the piano—he can't play any games, he's always trying to be funny" (p. 480). He is not the sort that a girl would be expected to fall in love with; he is "that sort of chap . . . you know—up in the air—effeminate" (p. 454) and profoundly attached to his mother. "The beautiful Flo Lancaster!" Nicky rhapsodizes with post-Proustian fervor, "I can remember her when I was quite small, coming up to say good night to me, looking too perfectly radiant for words" (p. 474).

Returning home after a year in Paris, Nicky looks "a debauched wreck of [his] former self" (p. 467) but proclaims himself "gay and witty and handsome" (p. 468) nonetheless. He carries "a divine little box" (p. 459) full of cocaine in his pocket, plays jazz with symptomatic frequency, and lapses into hysteria at the drop of a hat. Nicky's drug habit has progressed, as he coyly and not too inaccurately puts it, "a little beyond aspirin" (p. 488).

What was so shocking about Nicky Lancaster? The theater critics and the audience were in total agreement on this: he was a drug addict—the first drug addict of his class ever to appear on the British stage. Furthermore, what would have been far too shocking to admit was that Nicky Lancaster gave every indication of being gay. Of course almost every individual who sat in the audience of *The Vortex* must have understood, on some level, that Nicky was one of the "pretty boys, witty boys, too, too, too / Lazy to fight stagnation" whom Coward would recognize at an ironic remove five years later in *Bitter Sweet:* the brotherhood of the notorious green carnation. But no one said so, at least not in print.

Perhaps this was because there were only so many shocks the public could absorb at one time, and *The Vortex* introduced drug addiction and sexual promiscuity (albeit in tiny doses) to a theatrical drawing room that had not too long ago been rocked by the admission of genteel adultery. But underneath the much-publicized decadence (cocktails! drugs! gigolos!) there was lurking a fact of life that the public would rather not have acknowledged: homosexuality. Was it deep conviction that prompted Coward to be so daring? Certainly not, or else there wouldn't have been so many veils, so much calculated coyness. More likely it was a sense of stageworthy raciness that allowed him to gauge (accurately enough) what the public would tolerate and what it might find titillating if presented as up-to-the-minute realism.

Intimations of homosexuality aside, Coward's own investment in the self-consciously "degenerate" milieu of *The Vortex* was minimal. He detested drugs and never used them. He looked askance at liaisons between older women and younger men but obviously did not feel too strongly about the issue. "I have had a few causes," he told the *New York Times* disingenuously in 1970. "[In *The Vortex*] I disapproved of elderly ladies having young lovers." He neglected to mention that he had celebrated a certain Mrs. Wentworth-Brewster in song for carrying on far more flamboyantly than the beautiful Flo Lancaster.

He was no reformer, any more than he was the sin-driven sybarite that the press immediately made him out to be (a role he adored and gleefully played to the hilt, so long as it helped at the box office). What he had done was to take a sensational situation—the implicitly incestuous triangle of son, mother, and youthful lover—and combine it with the then-fashionable vice of drug addiction to produce a potent theatrical cocktail that made him, suddenly, the voice of his generation, a new force in British theater, and a star with "a whacking good part."

The worldly wise Helen Saville, Florence's best friend, expresses Coward's own point of view within the play. She disapproves of drugs, cautions

Florence against taking a youthful lover, feels that "it's silly not to grow old when the time comes" (p. 441) and believes that "if you don't face things in this world, they only hit you much harder in the end" (p. 483). Helen's homilies were acknowledged by the public about as much as they were by Nicky and his mother; they may have been the moral ground-bass of the play, but it was the far more fascinating riffs of rampant immorality that caught the audience's ear.

Social comment in *The Vortex* was sub-sub-Shavian and vaguely portentous—a matter of malaise attested to rather than diagnosed—but it obviously struck a plangent note of mid 1920's desperation:

NICKY: It's funny how mother's generation always longed to be old when they were young, and we strain every nerve to keep young.

BUNTY: That's because we see what's coming so much more clearly.

NICKY: Wouldn't it be terrible to know *exactly*—I feel frightened sometimes.

BUNTY: Why?

NICKY: We're all so hectic and nervy. . . .

BUNTY: It doesn't matter—it probably only means we shan't live so long. . . .

NICKY [*suddenly*]: Shut up—shut up.

(pp. 452–453)

Insofar as it was a widely accepted fever chart for the disease of postwar world-weariness, *The Vortex* retains a place in social history, but there is little claim to be made for it now as drama. It blew the dust off the drawing room all right, but it did not destroy, or even greatly rearrange, its furniture. The play concludes with a scene so spuriously effective that only a boy bred in the theater could have imagined it: mother and son, admitting their sins, pledge to renounce them and be whole again. She strokes his hair as the tears roll down her cheeks. The curtain falls.

Perhaps the deus ex machina of psychoanalysis rescued this pair, perhaps not. Whatever their fate in our imaginations, they had a spectacularly successful stage life during the London and New York productions of the play. *The Vortex* made Noel Coward an international celebrity and guaranteed that the public would be on the alert for his next efforts—which is to say *The Vortex* served its purpose handsomely.

HAY FEVER

COWARD had another and immensely better play in his back pocket when *The Vortex* swept him into celebrity, but he was unaware of it. He had written *Hay Fever* "in about three days" and "was rather unimpressed with it." "This was an odd sensation for me," Coward blithely admitted in the first of his two autobiographies, "as in those days I was almost always enchanted with everything I wrote" (*Present Indicative,* p. 179).

It was a masterpiece of the most unpretentious sort, patronized initially by its author as well as the critics. James Agate of the *Sunday Times,* prissily admitted that although "there is neither health nor cleanness about any of Mr. Coward's characters . . . many moral plays are not enlivened with such delicate imbecility" (8 June 1925). Only gradually did the play assume a place as one of the most remarkable comedies of the twentieth century.

The great thing about *Hay Fever* is that it sets a lower value on sincerity than any play ever before written; sincerity itself is its butt. It celebrates the put-on: emotional manipulation for the sheer fun of it. Ben Jonson and Molière may have touched on this territory, but their characters always *wanted* something, so they never inhabited the realm of pure play. Love and money, the carrots for comic characters from Aristophanes on, do not entice Coward's in the least. Coward's main characters, the Bliss family, do not scheme to acquire or accomplish anything; they merely amuse themselves at the expense of others—playing at life with a shared secret code of theatrically expressed false emotions. Even Jack and Algernon in Oscar Wilde's *The Importance of Being Earnest* (1895) are Bunbury-bound, in pursuit of pleasures elsewhere, and hence more goal-oriented than the Blisses.

A hateful bunch of perennial preadolescents they may be—undeniably rude and selfish and oh-so-immature—but who cares? The audience certainly does not. Conventional morality does not apply during this three-act weekend. The Blisses' country house in Cookham is a child's dream Eden, exempt from all ordinary rules. The poet W. H. Auden in *The Dyer's Hand* (1962) defined a few of such an Eden's axioms:

The self is satisfied whatever it demands; the ego is approved of whatever it chooses.

Whatever people do, whether alone or in company, is some kind of play. The only motive for an action is the pleasure it gives the actor, and no deed has a goal or an effect beyond itself.

The Serpent, acquaintance with whom results in immediate expulsion [is] any serious need or desire.

(p. 41)

The creation of this kind of Edenic, amoral atmosphere—this playground for uninhibited self-projection—may not seem like such an accomplishment, but it is rarely achieved in art, and when achieved it eventually finds lasting admirers. Why should we value a release from everything we regard as serious? Perhaps because it returns us, temporarily, to a state of mind in which the dread realities of the adult world are robbed of threat by our ability to manipulate them imaginatively—a state all children know well—a state of Bliss, if you will.

Combine Saki's world of wryly observed country-house parties with E. Nesbit's children's world of bohemian independence, add in Coward's observations of the actress Laurette Taylor's and playwright Hartley Manners' New York household ("a highly-strung family, deeply theatrical and prone to elaborate word games which always ended in hysteria," says Sheridan Morley on page 64 of his 1969 biography of Coward), mix well with the playful camp theatrics of Coward's child-actor peers, and you have the ingredients for *Hay Fever*, if not the genius that made the play a thing of lasting value.

A summary of the plot reveals how little except comic invention keeps the play aloft. Simon, Sorel, and their parents, actress Judith and novelist David Bliss, have each invited a guest to their country house for the weekend without informing anyone else. Romantic dalliance is what they have, somewhat vaguely, in mind; alleviating boredom is closer to their true motive. As boredom is what the guests in their various ways almost instantly engender—the family cannot even draw them into their usual histrionic charades—the Blisses are forced to fall back on their resources and create a scene or two (or three or four) to keep things lively. Misalliances spring up everywhere before any of the supporting cast of guests knows what is happening. Tentative kisses are taken as signs of love undying, hands and hearts are said to be sworn instantaneously, and

recriminations rain, all too theatrically, on everyone. The next day the abused and appalled guests sneak off en masse as Judith, Simon, and Sorel get caught up in a new game of the imagination: rewriting David's latest novel.

Hay Fever, oddly enough, is really *The Vortex* through the looking glass. Mother, intent on staying young and beautiful, tries to attract a lover half her age. Father is too focused on his own concerns to care. Son and daughter are charming, talented misfits who blame their mother for their slapdash upbringing and wonder how anyone could possibly expect them not to be abnormal.

On the comic side of the looking glass, however, everything that was cause for breast-beating in the overheated atmosphere of *The Vortex* is cause for tongue-clucking and finger-wagging here:

SOREL: But, Mother darling, don't you see it's awfully undignified for you to go flaunting about with young men?

JUDITH: I don't flaunt about—I never have. I've been morally an extremely nice woman all my life—more or less—and if dabbling gives me pleasure, I don't see why I *shouldn't* dabble.

SOREL: But it *oughtn't* to give you pleasure any *more.*

JUDITH: You know, Sorel, you grow more damnably feminine every day. I wish I'd brought you up differently.

(vol. 1, pp. 508–509)

Henry Wadsworth's Longfellow's "Life is real! Life is earnest!" (from "A Psalm of Life," 1838) is not stitched on any sampler in the Bliss household; their implicit motto is more likely to be Wilde's: "A little sincerity is a dangerous thing, and a great deal of it is absolutely fatal" (from *The Critic As Artist,* Part 2).

In *The Vortex,* at the end of act 2, Florence Lancaster comes downstairs to find her young admirer in the arms of her son's fiancée. "You utter cad!" she cries, every bit as enraged as Phaedra, and orders him out of the house, hysterically screaming: "Love! You don't know what it means. You've lied to me—all these months. It's contemptible—humiliating. Get out of my sight!" (p. 482). And then she runs after him, pathetically begging him to come back.

In act 2 of *Hay Fever* Judith Bliss plays this same time-honored discovery scene twice over, but she plays it with a decided difference. Her responses are no less stagey, but her awareness of her own staginess gives her great satisfaction and inspires her to turn mock-desperation into a minor art form. First she finds her young admirer in the arms of her daughter, Sorel, who momentarily misjudges her mother's state of shock, worrying that the serpent of serious desire has been let loose in the garden:

JUDITH: What a fool I've been! What a blind fool!
SOREL: Mother, are you *really* upset?

Judith quickly shifts into martyred *Marschallin* mode (emulating the heroine of Richard Strauss's *Der Rosenkavalier*), playing the cliché-ridden role of the injured but eternally noble older woman to the hilt:

JUDITH: There's nothing to be sorry for, really; it's my fault for having been so—so ridiculous.
SOREL: Mother!
JUDITH [*sadly*]: Yes, ridiculous. . . . I'm getting old, old, and the sooner I face it the better.
SOREL [*hopelessly*]: But, darling . . .
JUDITH [*splendidly*]: Youth will be served. . . . You've answered the only call that really counts—the call of Love, and Romance, and Spring.
(pp. 546–547)

Another splendid theatrical recovery is required of Judith when she comes downstairs to find her husband, David, kissing Myra Arundel, her son Simon's weekend guest who "goes about using Sex as a sort of shrimping-net" (p. 510). Judith responds by proclaiming grandly that "life has dealt me another blow, but I don't mind" (p. 555) and envisioning herself (in a speech that would have held any audience she ever played absolutely enthralled) wandering mournfully abroad, a desolate woman, forlorn amid Italian cypresses.

We have not gone to the other side of the looking glass, really; we have merely gone to the other side of the proscenium. *Hay Fever*'s antic mirror-melodrama is life from a player's point of view: life as a thing less real than theater, therefore in need of some artful heightening to put it over. Coward stumbled upon a new kind of high comedy without realizing that this breezy, briskly written celebration of a houseful of "posing, self-centred egotists . . . artificial to the point of lunacy"—as Myra calls them (p. 559)—would endure as an exhilarating,

blessedly careless and completely unmoral glimpse of Eden.

Very often plays can be plundered for their authors' intentions and evaluated accordingly, but *Hay Fever* cannot. Coward thought it a dubious trifle, but it captured and continues to evoke a spirit he possessed and did not think to prize: the spirit of play.

EASY VIRTUE, "SEMI-MONDE," AND BITTER SWEET

THE success of *The Vortex* led to productions, also successful, of a musical revue entitled *On with the Dance* (1925), the sex comedy *Fallen Angels* (enlivened by Coward's characteristically brisk banter but basically an extended revue sketch) and *Hay Fever*.

He followed these up with *Easy Virtue*, a crowd-pleasing drama written as a star vehicle for actress Jane Cowl, which went back to Pinero for its theme: a glamorous woman with a past (she has run away from a "perfect brute" of a husband, who has divorced her) suffers the slings and arrows of her young husband's outrageously priggish upper-middle-class family until she musters the courage to denounce their "stereotyped views of virtue and charity" (vol. 2, act 2). She makes a daring third-act appearance at a family party in a low-cut dress emblazoned with jewels—and then deserts her backsliding bore of a spouse (who refuses to condone her insistence on reading Proust instead of joining him at tennis) and heads back to the moral high ground of Paris. English country life—an easy target—is dished and ditched in three very familiar acts. Worldly wisdom detonates hypocrisy. The audience (no doubt wishing to dissociate itself from the bourgeois values that have been blown to smithereens) applauds through countless curtain calls.

The trouble with *Easy Virtue* is not so much its facile triumph of bohemianism over straw-man stodginess as its retooled Victorian form. Coward always had a conservative respect for theatrical formulae, and throughout his career this sense of "what the audience wants because they've wanted it before" inhibited him, except when he was feeling exceptionally frisky and full of himself, from daring to be entirely Noel Coward. The free spirit who wrote *Hay Fever* and *Private Lives* for the fun of it (and undervalued them precisely because they *were* such fun) wrote dozens of other plays because he thought they were the kind of entertainment the public would appreciate. His boyhood apprenticeship in the theater taught him to trust the audience even more than himself.

Trusting the audience became a painful responsibility in 1926 and 1927. Coward was very much like Larita, the heroine of *Easy Virtue,* who admits: "I've got an unworthy passion for popularity—it hurts my vanity not to be an unqualified success" (p. 541). His string of initial hits, which established him as the theatrical man of the moment in both London and New York, was followed by six productions of diminishing glitter. *The Queen Was in the Parlour,* his overwritten Ruritanian melodrama, limped along in London—as did a far more accomplished eighteenth-century whimsy called *The Marquise* (1927), written for and illuminated by the actress Marie Tempest. *"This Was a Man"* (1926), which was banned from production in England because its hero broke into laughter when he heard that his wife had seduced his best friend, closed quickly in New York (its opening night audience had almost entirely decamped before act 3); *The Rat Trap* (1926), a play written when he was eighteen about a couple of young writers caught in a painful marriage, was briefly performed in Hampstead to very bad reviews; *Home Chat* (1927), an insipid comedy about supposed marital infidelity without a flicker of Coward's by-now-famous wit, was booed at its opening ("We expected better!" shouted someone in the audience; "So did I!" retorted Coward from the stage), and the opening night of *Sirocco* (1927) was a memorable fiasco at which members of the audience not only booed but actually spat at its author as he came out of the stage door.

Reading these plays now is every bit as enervating as attending them must have been (with the exception of *The Marquise,* which advocates and achieves "Lightness of Touch" but is written in a somewhat stilted quasi-historical idiom that dampens the fun). Some were unwisely resurrected early efforts, some merely injudicious attempts at rushing unready products to what seemed to be a welcoming market.

In 1926 Coward wrote a play called "Semi-Monde" which was, as he describes it, "as jagged with sophistication as all get out" (Lesley, *The Life,* p. 124). It depicted liaisons, both heterosexual and homosexual, in the lobby and bar of the Ritz Hotel in Paris over a three-year period. Those who criticize Coward for disguising his own homosexuality by writing exclusively about heterosexual relationships should read "Semi-Monde" to discover what the Lord Chamberlain succeeded in suppressing: an amorous life in every way equivalent to the heterosexual (except, of necessity, more furtive) and in no way more dramatically revealing. "Semi-Monde" was not produced during Coward's lifetime, nor was it ever published; it was considered too scandalous when it was written, and he himself was apparently ambivalent (perhaps from fears about its quality as much as its content) about having it produced. Three years later Vicki Baum's novel *Grand Hotel* (1929) dealt famously with the same milieu and made "Semi-Monde" a permanent back number. Reconsidering the play in 1957, Coward remarked that "to call it good clean fun would perhaps be going too far, but at least it wasn't about the Death Wish, and compared with Existentialism it becomes *Rebecca of Sunnybrook Farm"* (Lesley, *The Life,* p. 124).

Coward pulled himself out of his slump by writing a splendid musical revue in 1928, *This Year of Grace!,* and an even more splendid musical (or "operette," as he called it), *Bitter Sweet,* in 1929. *Bitter Sweet* is somewhat outside the category of dramatic literature in that it depends upon the potency of its music, which contrasts the frenetic, discordant jazz of the late 1920's with lush romantic melodies evocative of Vienna in the 1880's, as much as it depends upon its script. It tells a story no less familiar than that of *Easy Virtue* or even *Sirocco:* the story of a woman who dares to defy convention and risk all for love. And yet this version of the tritest of tales works far better than his earlier efforts because it establishes two worlds of opposing values: a present in which romance is derided as a delusive ideal, and a past in which it was believed to be genuine.

This sentimental dialectic, however specious it may seem, expresses a real conflict of Coward's. Although he became famous as an apostle of the new cynicism and played the part tongue-in-cheek for all it was worth, he was at heart an old-fashioned romantic with a decidedly moralistic bent. "The public image of himself in top-hat and tails, the immortal spirit of the charming twenties, was merely one of his admirable inventions," wrote novelist Rebecca West after his death. "It was a disguise worn by an odd and selective kind of Puritan" (in Gray, *Noel Coward,* p. 149). The lyrics of his most celebrated revue songs are cautionary, warning flappers that they are "living in a world of lies" where "false things soon decay." His harshest view of the era's "hectic desperation" was contained in "Twentieth Century Blues," the song that concluded the play *Cavalcade* in 1931:

Why, if there's a God in the sky, why shouldn't he grin?
High above this dreary Twentieth Century din,
In this strange illusion,
Chaos and confusion,
People seem to lose their way.
What is there to strive for,
Love or keep alive for? Say—
Hey, hey, call it a day.

(vol. 1, p. 179)

Bitter Sweet revealed what Coward put in his personal balance against chaos and confusion: a belief in love and duty that was not too far removed from Matthew Arnold's. "Your conception of life [is] grotesque" (vol. 1, p. 273), says the play's moral spokeswoman, Lady Shayne, to the bright young things jigging about to jazz. What seems extraordinary, in retrospect, is how serenely Coward managed to straddle the fence of public opinion; he was at once the advocate of old-fashioned values and—by virtue of his cold-eyed depiction of the contemporary scene—the voice of the determinedly decadent younger generation.

PRIVATE LIVES

DURING four days in 1929 Noel Coward wrote *Private Lives* in a Shanghai hotel as a vehicle for himself and Gertrude Lawrence. The idea had occurred to him a month or so earlier in Tokyo but, as he writes in *Present Indicative* (1937), he "had learned the wisdom of not welcoming a new idea too ardently" (p. 320)—presumably by writing *"This Was a Man"* and *Home Chat* at white heat and finding himself knee-deep in ashes. He delayed writing the play until he was recovering from influenza and had nothing else to do.

Coward's swiftness of composition, which he was the first to publicize, always set critics' teeth on

edge. He knew it would, of course, but self-confidence was his calling card, and he no doubt reckoned that his insouciance earned him as many points with the public as disaffected critics cost him. *Hay Fever* took three days to complete, *Private Lives* four. Drama critic James Agate complained in the *Sunday Times* that Coward's plays were rumored to have been written before breakfast and demanded to know "what kind of work he intends to do after breakfast, when he is clothed and in his right mind" (Morley, *A Talent,* p. 97).

Of course it is ludicrous to imagine that a longer gestation period would have improved *Private Lives.* It was written fast and played fast. He and costar Gertrude Lawrence both knew "if we let it sag for a moment that it would die on us" (*Present Indicative,* p. 338). It exhilarated its audiences from the word go. Quickness—the impulsive seizing of the moment—was its subject.

T. E. Lawrence, who met Coward while the play was in rehearsal, sized him up very neatly in an August 1930 letter to a friend: "He is not deep but remarkable. A hasty kind of genius. I wonder what his origin is? His prose is quick, balanced, alive: like Congreve's probably, in his day. He dignifies slang when he admits it" (Lesley, *The Life,* p. 133). This off-the-cuff estimate, with its implicit understanding that haste was no hindrance to Coward's talent but actually essential to it, is blessedly devoid of the Victorian assumption that genius is the apotheosis of effort, and it does more than countless reviews to suggest what is unique and valuable about his writing. "Your work is like swordplay; as quick as light," wrote Lawrence of Arabia to Noel Coward after he had seen *Private Lives.* "I could not always tell when you were acting and when talking to one another" (Lesley, *The Life,* p. 136).

Swiftness and verisimilitude were the hallmarks of Coward's best work. Kenneth Tynan, in *The Sound of Two Hands Clapping,* said that Coward "took the fat off English comic dialogue; he was the Turkish bath in which it slimmed" (p. 60)—which meant that he sacrificed the self-conscious epigrams of Wilde and the preternaturally articulate loquacity of Shaw in favor of something more like conversation as we know it, gaining in rapid byplay what he lost in quotability, as in this passage from *Private Lives:*

ELYOT: I was wondering what was going on inside your mind, what your plans are really?

SIBYL: Plans? Oh, Elli!

ELYOT: Apart from loving me and all that, you must have plans.

SIBYL: I haven't the faintest idea what you're talking about.

ELYOT: Perhaps it's subconscious then, age-old instincts working away deep down, mincing up little bits of experience for future use, watching me carefully like a little sharp-eyed, blonde kitten.

SIBYL: How can you be so horrid.

ELYOT: I said Kitten, not Cat.

SIBYL: Kittens grow into cats.

ELYOT: Let that be a warning to you.

(vol. 1, pp. 187–188)

This kind of breathless naturalistic point-counterpoint exchange was something new on stage, never heard before. Even the classic repartee of Beatrice and Benedick in *Much Ado About Nothing* or Millamant and Mirabell in William Congreve's *The Way of the World* seems labored—less likely ever to have been uttered by actual human beings—when contrasted with Coward's quick and casual thrusts and parries.

Private Lives, to Coward, was "a shrewd and witty comedy, well-constructed on the whole, but psychologically unstable; however, its entertainment value seemed obvious enough, and its acting opportunities for Gertie and me admirable" (*Present Indicative,* p. 322). It was in fact a revolutionary play that redefined what comedy could be. *The Importance of Being Earnest* had turned sincerity upside down, inverting Victorian values; *Hay Fever* had denied the importance of sincerity altogether, substituting a world of theatrical free play. *Private Lives* went a step beyond *Hay Fever.* It envisioned a world in which the concept of sincerity is a false ideal because it implies that we know what we want, moment to moment; what we *really* want is to reinvent ourselves forever, as we did when we were children at play.

At the beginning of act 1 Elyot Chase and Amanda Prynne think they know what they want: to settle down with their sedative and unthreatening new spouses and experience the much-celebrated marital peace which passeth all understanding, forgetting their tempestuous former marriage. Elyot's new wife, Sibyl, presents a prospect of love that's "steady and sweet . . . tremendously cosy; and unflurried by scenes and jealousies" (p. 186). Amanda's new husband, Victor, is an exemplary-seeming chap whose true identity is soon discerned by his wife: he's really a

"fat old gentleman in a club armchair" (p. 204) disguised as a marriageable man in his thirties.

Coward felt a bit bad that Victor and Sibyl were "little better than ninepins, lightly wooden, and only there at all to be repeatedly knocked down and stood up again" (introduction to *Play Parade,* vol. 1, p. xiii)—but he need not have worried; their conventionality is far easier to accept than the conventionality of the high-minded straw figures who correspond to them in *Easy Virtue* and *Sirocco.* Sibyl and Victor are deftly and convincingly sketched, and they serve their purpose in the play without seeming to be the "extra puppets" Coward feared they were.

What Elyot and Amanda want, really, is the old bond they shared—a bond more imaginative than sexual—that gave them license to look on the world as a place of self-deluded serious people and celebrate their point of view as free-spirited outsiders. Their marriage was a collusion of preadolescent kindred spirits (much like the intense friendship of Coward and Gertrude Lawrence); it fell apart after a series of childish rows in which they struck each other and Amanda broke gramophone records over Elyot's head.

What the audience knows full well is that these two sophisticated children are soul mates, alike in their inability to adapt to the adult world because they are permanent creatures of impulse, immune to reality:

ELYOT: Things that ought to matter dreadfully, don't matter at all when one's happy, do they?

AMANDA: What is so horrible is that one can't stay happy.

(p. 231)

Well yes, one can—in the theater, anyway. *Private Lives* blessedly abolishes all restrictions and realities for Elyot and Amanda, allowing these "figures of fun" free rein. "That sacred and beautiful thing, Love" is "a very poor joke" (p. 231). As for death, "Death's very laughable, such a cunning little mystery. All done with mirrors" (p. 232). Despite its prosaic marriage/remarriage underpinnings, it's an oddly poetic play, both in execution and in outlook. It depends upon skillfully sustained vivacity of cadence for its effects, and it says what carpe diem lyrics have always said: "Come and kiss me, darling, before your body rots, and worms pop in and out of your eye sockets" (p. 232). Pity the poor philosophers and futile moralists who would spoil the fun of these "very small, quite idiotic school-children" who want nothing more than to "savour the delight of the moment" (p. 232).

The basic joke that enlivens *Private Lives* is that its soigné, worldly-wise principals are in fact only schoolchildren, prone to bickering and bashing each other, set adrift in a world of incomprehensible beings called adults. The subsidiary joke, revealed at the end of act 3 when Sibyl and Victor begin carrying on and calling each other names, is that *all* adults are equally childish, however skillfully they manage to disguise it. These are Saki jokes, E. Nesbit ironies, and we're not too far removed from Sir James Barrie, either. Many of the play's first critics felt that it succeeded in spite of its childishness, whereas of course it succeeds because of it. What keeps it gloriously alive—quick for all time—is its testament to human immaturity.

POST-MORTEM *AND* CAVALCADE

SHERIDAN Morley, in his biography of Coward, detected a "curiously patronizing attitude" in forty years of Coward's critical notices, remarking that the words "flippant" and "trivial" recurred "with alarming frequency," whereas few other contemporary writers of comedy treated their themes "with more weight or underlying seriousness" (Morley, *A Talent,* pp. 96–97).

This is an extraordinarily wrongheaded and disingenuous defense. Flippancy—disrespectful levity—was Coward's forte, the essence of his comic genius. Seriousness, where present in his work, is scarcely an asset; it drags down a few of the comedies and overloads most of the sentimental melodramas. Moralistic critics may have found it insufferable, as playwright Sean O'Casey did in 1937, that this "infant phenomenon" (p. 87) should make triumphs out of trivialities without shaking "even a baby-rattle of life in the face of one watching audience" (p. 98). And yet that is what he did, and that is what future generations will continue to applaud him for.

It was Coward himself who nonchalantly flung down the gauntlet that his critics picked up and refused to relinquish for forty years. Playing the part of Elyot Chase in *Private Lives* he denounced "all the futile moralists who try to make life unbearable." "Laugh at them," Elyot says to Amanda.

"Be flippant. . . . Flippancy brings out the acid in their damned sweetness and light" (p. 232).

Elyot Chase was the 1930 edition of the Noel Coward persona, and Coward played the role of sophisticated, mocking, conscienceless cavalier in the press as well as onstage, just as he had done with the previous role he had both written and played: the brilliant but debauched Nicky Lancaster in *The Vortex.* It was shrewd self-advertising. It made him a very visible, world-renowned star. It also threatened to make him the prisoner of his own arch archetype, and he knew it. He wanted to prove his versatility by attempting something deeper.

Three decades later, in his introduction to volume 5 of the *Play Parade* series, he admitted that "in my deep Christian subconscious there was the gnawing suspicion that I was nothing but a jester, a foolish, capering lightweight with neither depths nor real human understanding" (p. xxxi). To dispel this suspicion and silence the critics' unrelenting cries of flippancy and triviality, he wrote two new plays in 1930 and 1931, both historical dramas about English life in the early decades of the twentieth century: *Post-Mortem* and *Cavalcade.* The first was never produced on stage because he was persuaded by friend and drama critic Alexander Woollcott that it belonged in a desk drawer. The second was one of the great successes of his career, resulting in what he accurately recorded in his autobiography as "mounting paeans of praise—not a discordant note" (*Present Indicative,* p. 352).

Reading the two plays sixty years later one sees that, just as Woollcott predicted, *Cavalcade* was destined for success, *Post-Mortem* for failure. Their juxtaposition is fascinating and reveals a great deal about Coward's facility for juggling ideologies in the interest of theatrical effectiveness: *Post-Mortem* is a savage indictment of a society that *Cavalcade* sentimentally celebrates. The wonder is that one man should have written both plays in the course of a year.

Post-Mortem begins in 1917 at a World War I company headquarters on the front line. John Cavan, the idealistic son of a publisher whose newspaper fatuously portrays the patriotic glories of war, is shot by an enemy sniper. As he dies he still holds onto his belief that "poor old England" will learn from the experience of war and be better off.

In six visionary scenes presumed to occur as he lies dying on a stretcher, John reappears in 1930 as a ghost to talk to his mother, his fiancée, a fellow officer who had been his intellectual sparring partner, his father, and a group of his former comrades. He is progressively stripped of his illusions about the world he was fighting to save. His mother has been devastated by his death. Boredom and unenlightened self-interest have degraded his fiancée and friends-in-arms. His father's rampant hypocrisy has blighted the life of a truth-telling fellow officer, Perry Lomas, who has written a book about the war as it really was. Perry shoots himself in the head after denouncing the "ignorant carnage" that in no way mitigated the "poverty, unemployment, pain, greed, cruelty, passion, and crime" (vol. 1, p. 395) of British society. The play concludes with John Cavan acknowledging as he dies that the war was indeed "a poor joke" (p. 423).

This is not *Private Lives,* obviously. Sincerity is paralyzingly reinvoked in *Post-Mortem;* high-flying hypocrites and moral will-o'-the-wisps end up as intensely despised flies in amber. By far the best scene is the satirical, expressionistic mad tea party (a total stylistic departure for Coward, anticipating W. H. Auden and Christopher Isherwood's 1935 *The Dog Beneath the Skin*), in which Sir James Cavan and his entourage of yellow journalists, buyable bishops, and paid public scolds reduce his son's war experience to tabloid trivialities, prompting John to cry out that "War is no evil compared with this sort of living":

SIR JAMES: England is proud of you, my son.
JOHN: England doesn't know me, or any like me. England now can only recognize false glory. Real England died in defeat without pretending it was Victory.

(p. 413)

Post-Mortem gave every appearance of being a heartfelt play, but the heart that felt it was (like Judith Bliss's in *Hay Fever*) pledged first and foremost to the theater. Coward himself had had a medical discharge from the army in 1918 after brief, noncombative service. What inflamed his imagination to write *Post-Mortem* was an acting appearance in R. C. Sherriff's antiwar play *Journey's End* (1929); he stayed in character, in a sense, until he had written something comparably profound. "I wrote *Post-Mortem* with the utmost sincerity," he claims in *Present Indicative;* "In fact, I tore my emotions to shreds over it" (pp. 334–335). And then, having proved his seriousness to his own satisfaction, he began work on *Cavalcade,* a flag-waving

pageant that sentimentally refuted the cynical truths of *Post-Mortem* point by point.

Cavalcade was inspired by a different kind of reading matter entirely: an old issue of the *Illustrated London News* that showed a full-page picture of a troopship leaving for the Boer War. Coward had been wanting, ever since *Private Lives* opened, to write something for the theater on a far grander scale: a historical spectacle. After rejecting the Roman Empire and the French Revolution as subjects, he prudently settled on the first thirty years of English history in the twentieth century (from the Boer War to the bored-with-war jazz babies). He invented a patriotic English family to follow and skillfully depicted their tribulations in a changing world, emulating Oscar Hammerstein's successful 1927 adaptation of Edna Ferber's *Show Boat* (1926) with composer Jerome Kern. In three acts and twenty-two scenes, a cast and crew of over four hundred people recreated the triumphs and sorrows of the era. Jane Marryot, the noble matriarch of the family, toasts her husband Robert in the play's penultimate scene:

Let's drink to our sons who made part of the pattern and to our hearts that died with them. Let's drink to the spirit of gallantry and courage that made a strange Heaven out of unbelievable Hell, and let's drink to the hope that one day this country of ours, which we love so much, will find dignity and greatness and peace again.

(vol. 1, p. 178)

"That was deeply sincere and as true as I could make it," wrote Coward in *Present Indicative* (p. 353).

In *Post-Mortem* he had ruthlessly impaled a similarly sanctimonious mother, Lady Stagg-Mortimer, who proclaimed that "every woman of England should be proud and glad to give and give and give, even the flesh of her flesh and the blood of her blood," by sarcastically adding "and the tripe of her tripe" (vol. 1, p. 559). He had taken pains to show that even the unbelievable hell of war was preferable to the hypothetical "dignity and greatness and peace" of the society that spawned it because "war makes you leap, and leap again into bloody chaos, but there are redeeming moments of vision which might, in smug content, be obscured for ever" (vol. 1, p. 627).

While *Post-Mortem* was buried in his desk drawer, *Cavalcade* made him the toast of the nation. Which play represents what he truly believed? Why, both—and neither. "Coward was a performer who wrote: not a writer who happened to perform" (pp. 1–2), commented critic John Lahr. A performer's mind is more adaptable than a writer's; it is accustomed to seeing the truth from whatever point of view it is assigned. Coward saw that the "truth" of *Cavalcade*—that patriotic side of himself that he had sentimentally revealed—was immensely popular with the public, and he continued to exploit it in World War II by writing *This Happy Breed* (1943) and *Peace in Our Time* (1947), two other chauvinistic plays that earned him favor.

The moral indignation of *Post-Mortem* was a note he chose never again to strike. "Ethical motive," wrote T. S. Eliot magisterially in his essay "A Dialogue on Dramatic Poetry", "is not apparent in Mr. Coward" (*Selected Essays of T. S. Eliot,* New York, 1960, p. 32). Written to reveal his depths, *Post-Mortem* hardly achieved its goal—but it did reveal what an extraordinary chameleon its thoroughly theatrical author could be.

DESIGN FOR LIVING, POINT VALAINE, TONIGHT AT 8:30, *AND* PRESENT LAUGHTER

THROUGHOUT the 1930's Coward created one star vehicle after another, each tailor-made to display the celebrated-actor glamor of very vivid stage personalities. "Idealistically speaking," he said, "of course the play is the thing. . . . But overidealism in the theatre is as perilous as it is in any other profession that depends on the vagaries of public taste for its livelihood." The star system was simply "a form of insurance" for the audience-minded author.

He wrote *Design for Living* in 1932 to fulfill a promise he had made to Lynn Fontanne and Alfred Lunt eleven years earlier when they were all impoverished actors in New York, a promise "that when all three of us had become stars of sufficient magnitude to be able to count upon an individual following irrespective of each other, then, poised serenely upon that enviable plane of achievement, we would meet and act triumphantly together." While on vacation in Chile after the successful launching of *Cavalcade* he was abruptly called to account by a telegram from the now celebrated Lunts that said: OUR CONTRACT WITH THEATRE GUILD UP IN JUNE WHAT ABOUT IT?

The play—written this time in ten days, working mornings only—was based on their real-life situation as three success-hungry artists whose dreams came true, but altered reality by imagining that both men were sexually involved with the female member of the trio. "The homosexual daydream of sexual abundance" (p. 82) is what John Lahr calls this plot, as if heterosexual daydreams were not every bit as omnivorous; box-office spice is more like it. Just as Coward's relationship with Gertrude Lawrence informed the creation of *Private Lives* (they constantly bickered but were always glad to be reunited in a new show because nobody understood them quite so well as they understood each other), so did his relationship with Lunt and Fontanne inform *Design for Living* (they were envious of each other's successes but felt themselves to be kindred spirits inhabiting a rarefied artistic realm all their own).

The trouble was that *Design for Living* was not, like *Private Lives,* a free-spirited fantasy; it was tainted by self-justification. Earnestness had crept in from the start. In telling the story of three artistic people (Lunt played a painter, Coward a playwright, Fontanne an interior decorator) Coward felt obligated to address a few of their world's larger and more platitudinous issues. Thus we have:

GILDA: You can't blame me for hating success, when it changes all the—the things I love best.
OTTO: Things would have changed, anyhow. It isn't only success that does it—it's time and experience and new circumstances.

(vol. 1, pp. 52–53)

"My mind functions best when I am dealing with people," Coward astutely remarked when in his sixties, "and it is at its worst when there is some abstraction to worry about" (Marchant, p. 176). To make matters worse, the trio's enlightened unconventionality is more often pompously asserted than witnessed. "We are different," declares Otto. "Our lives are diametrically opposed to ordinary social conventions; and it's no use grabbing at those conventions to hold us up when we find we're in deep water. We've jilted and eliminated them, and we've got to find our own solutions for our own peculiar moral problems" (p. 58). Bohemianism, in this play, begins to sound like a painful duty.

"When *Design for Living* sounds serious," said Brooks Atkinson in the 25 January 1933 *New York Times,* "you wish impatiently that Mr. Coward would cut the cackle and come to the main business, which is his brand of satire and comedy." He finally does, in a glorious farcical put-on by Coward's and Lunt's characters in act 3 that harks back to the inspired lunacy of the Blisses in *Hay Fever*. But we get only a glimpse of Eden in this essentially sober world of anguished escapades. When Gilda (Fontanne's character) cries out near the end of the play, "I'm not serious! That's what's so dreadful. I feel I ought to be, but I'm not" (p. 106), her admission feels very much like Coward's own cri de coeur. The adult world is too much with these characters; getting and spending. "Let's play the game for what it's worth," they cry, "secretaries and fur coats and de-luxe suites on transatlantic liners at minimum rates!" (p. 76). They bore us silly. Only when they contemplate rice pudding—"How glorious" (p. 48)—or sex—"I want to make love to you very badly indeed, please!" (p. 59)—do they sound the authentic Coward note of childlike enthusiasm.

The verbal weave is much looser in *Design for Living* than it had been in *Private Lives*. The brisk exchanges that characterize Coward's best work are far less frequent here; characters take longer to say what they mean. Coward's dialogue at its sharpest is stichomythia, line countering line. One can almost glance at a page of Coward playscript and assess its dramatic energy: lengthy speeches mean turgid sincerity; swift interchanges, flippant fun.

The play ends when its three main characters determine to live in a permanent ménage à trois, casting Gilda's husband of convenience (suitably named Ernest) out of their lives forever. *"They break down utterly and roar with laughter"* (p. 111), say the stage directions. Anarchy commences all too late in *Design for Living*; the stage is set for comedy just as the curtain falls.

Coward wrote two musicals in the 1930's in addition to the 1932 revue *Words and Music: Conversation Piece* and *Operette* were successively paler carbons of *Bitter Sweet*'s nostalgic romanticism, set, respectively, in picturesque Regency Brighton and picturesque Edwardian London, showcasing the talents of actress/singers Yvonne Printemps and Peggy Wood. Pastel nostalgia and pastiche romance were seductive sirens promising paid-in-advance matinees, but they did not exactly spur him on to greater creative achievements.

Nor did *Point Valaine*, the 1934 play he wrote for the Lunts. This was a wholly uncharacteristic Som-

erset Maughamish melodrama set in the British West Indies, and it revealed fewer of Coward's talents than any play he'd written since *Home Chat*. "Snap out of your deep romantic despair and be a man, my son," one character counsels another. "Cry later on, when you're alone. We can all cry when we are alone" (vol. 6, p. 103). "Strong moonlight" betrays the principals into passionate entanglements. Something of the sort (Coward later called it "the innocent desire to create two whopping good parts for the Lunts" [Marchant, p. 262]) no doubt betrayed Coward into committing this passionately stupid play.

Point Valaine left him overdrawn at the bank and concerned that he might be overdrawn with his audience. Determined to summon up the old box-office magic that was at its most potent in *Private Lives*, Coward set to work on not one but nine new plays for which he would be reunited with Gertrude Lawrence. The result was *Tonight at 8:30*, a minirepertory of nine (briefly ten) one-act plays performed three at a time in varying combinations. This 1936 theatrical novelty, which once again brought him and his costar great acclaim for their performances, did less to demonstrate his versatility than it did to reconfirm the narrowness of his range, but it most certainly had its moments.

Three of the plays are essentially serious in tone, if not necessarily in content: *The Astonished Heart*, *Shadow Play*, and *Still Life*. *The Astonished Heart*, whose theme according to Coward was "the decay of a psychiatrist's mind through a personal sexual obsession" (introduction to *Tonight at 8:30*), is merely a trendy rhetorical retread of the age-old other-woman story that deals with psychiatry less percipiently than *The Vortex* dealt with drug addiction. *Shadow Play* is the hallucinatory fantasy, induced by a sleeping pill, of a woman who expects to be divorced by her husband; her marital history flits past in brief, sometimes musical, interludes. Melodrama is kept at a distance by the lightness of these elliptical encounters. "Small talk—a lot of small talk with quite different thoughts going on behind it" (vol. 4, p. 179) is what she and her husband share—and what Coward at his best always trafficked in. Kenneth Tynan shrewdly notes that playwright Harold Pinter's "spare, allusive dialogue owes a great deal to Coward's sense of verbal tact" (*The Sound*, p. 59). Although the play concludes unconvincingly, it evokes a mood of evanescent understanding akin to Elyot and Amanda's in

Private Lives and seems in fact like a glimpse of their troubled future. *Still Life* is a rarity in Coward's work: a naturalistic short story for the stage, almost entirely unaffected. It's about two people, both married, who meet periodically in a railway station and fall in love, then separate forever, driven apart by duty. It was made into the film *Brief Encounter* in 1945. Of all Coward's "serious" plays *Still Life* has the best claim to profundity because it asks for it least; it simply records what happens when two convincing characters get caught up in a passion that threatens to capsize their quite ordinary lives and then leaves us to draw our own conclusions.

Tonight at 8:30's comedies are a mixed bag. *We Were Dancing* is an unsparkling account of a love affair begun in moonlight enchantment and aborted at dawn when the heroine's husband strikes up a friendship with her lover. *Fumed Oak* and *Family Album* are mildly amusing situation comedies, subgenus suburban and Victorian, in which fiscal facts reduce family feeling, somewhat mean-spiritedly, to shreds. The three best comedies are *Hands Across the Sea,* a manic piece about a beleaguered hostess trying to entertain unrecognized guests from abroad; *"Red Peppers,"* the backstage bickering and onstage routines of a music-hall duo; and *Ways and Means,* in which an impoverished couple accustomed to the high life resort to desperate measures. These three are distinguished by their blessedly swift and scatty dialogue. Each also describes a child's-eye view of the world: the characters cope with social responsibilities that are all but incomprehensible, assert themselves in insult matches, and trust to grownups or blind luck to come to their rescue. The three plays may not be vintage Coward, but they are the next best thing: the vin ordinaire of his impertinent imagination.

The last star vehicle of the 1930's, *Present Laughter* (not published until 1943), Coward described, in his introduction to volume 4 of the *Play Parade* series, as "a very light comedy . . . written with the sensible object of providing me with a bravura part. It was an enormous success. I received excellent notices and, to my bewilderment and considerable dismay, the play also was reasonably acclaimed" (p. xv). Once again he underestimated his achievement. *Present Laughter* is not quite in a class with *Hay Fever* or *Private Lives* because, paradoxically, it is a better-made play; the careful craftsmanship of farce, beautifully realized in *Pres-*

ent Laughter, is less liberating to Coward's imagination than the practically plotless high jinks of the earlier plays, in which whimsicality counted for more than construction. But *Present Laughter* was nonetheless a spectacular fireworks display of sustained wit, and the leading role of Garry Essendine was the definitive Noel Coward persona—a part that he would continue to play offstage for the rest of his life.

Garry Essendine is an actor, first and foremost. He is an immensely popular middle-aged matinee idol, master of his own adoring entourage, acerbic moral pundit, and apparent cynosure of the Western world. He's "just a simple boy, stinking with idealism" (vol. 4, p. 371), who never gets tired of everybody's adoration and obeisance. Garry is a sly self-caricature, Coward's own egoism blown up to Judith Bliss proportions:

GARRY: I'm always acting—watching myself go by— that's what's so horrible—I see myself all the time eating, drinking, loving, suffering—sometimes I think I'm going mad—

(p. 328)

Histrionic to the core, he is also capable of the occasional tart sincerity, and he genuinely loves his tight little band of intimates. Garry differs from Coward's previous stage personae in being intensely opinionated, principally about the theater:

GARRY: If you wish to be a playwright you just leave the theatre of to-morrow to take care of itself. Go and get yourself a job as a butler in a repertory company if they'll have you. Learn from the ground up how plays are constructed and what is actable and what isn't. Then sit down and write at least twenty plays one after the other, and if you can manage to get the twenty-first produced for a Sunday night performance you'll be damned lucky!

(p. 353)

"Of course Garry Essendine is me," Coward declared in an interview with the *Daily Mail* (16 February 1972). He has the same opinions, the same crisp wit, the same delight in role-playing, the same mother-hennishness, the same elegant dressing gowns—but he's also a great comic character because his vastly overinflated ego that makes him foolish is observed at an ironic remove. The essence of Essendine is the essence of Coward: the wise child. Remember how Micheál MacLiammóir described Coward at age thirteen: "decidedly puckish, witty, dry, clipped and immensely competent." In *Present Laughter* that child comes into his own as a dramatic character and tells everyone else on his particular playground how to behave. Nobody listens, of course, but that is what is so endearing about his megalomaniac alter ego: for all his fulminations, he is never quite as much in command as he thinks he is. The play ends with Garry stealing away from his incorrigible companions, just as Elyot and Amanda stole away from their squabbling mates. Tiptoeing away from conflict was always the characteristic Coward denouement, implying the eternal existence of pastures—and playgrounds—new.

THIS HAPPY BREED, BLITHE SPIRIT, AND "DAD'S RENAISSANCE"

COWARD'S attentions understandably shifted away from the world of light comedy as war with Germany threatened the civilization he had previously taken for granted. As soon as he completed *Present Laughter* in 1939 he began work on *This Happy Breed,* the patriotic chronicle of a middle-class family from 1918 to 1938. This was *Cavalcade* redux, without the pageantry: a domestic melodrama that asserted, as its patriarchal hero says to his infant grandson at the play's conclusion, that the English are "a race that's been bossy for years and the reason it's held on as long as it has is that nine times out of ten it's behaved decently and treated people right" (vol. 4, p. 554). *This Happy Breed*'s celebration of the status quo was well received, when it was first staged in 1943, by a war-torn public eager for affirmation. Coward's screenplay for the film *In Which We Serve,* a celebration of the British navy that he produced and codirected with David Lean in 1942, further established him as a patriot, as did his tours to entertain the troops and the songs he wrote in wartime, both sentimental and satiric. All these efforts, together with *Peace in Our Time,* a 1947 play that imagined Britain under German occupation, were potent but ephemeral. To evaluate the plays now as dramaturgy is to do them a disservice; they remain relics of a time in which their nationalistic fervor was greatly appreciated.

The one great comic success Coward enjoyed in the 1940's was *Blithe Spirit,* an "improbable farce" written in 1941. It ran far longer than any of his other plays (1,997 performances) and has constantly been revived all over the world throughout the past half century. In a sense *Blithe Spirit* was Coward's best contribution to the war effort. Air raid warnings punctuated its performances and death was much on the minds of its bomb-threatened audience, but inside the vulnerable shell of St. James's Theatre death was temporarily treated as a joke and real fears were assuaged by restorative laughter. Regarded in its historical context, *Blithe Spirit* is a reminder that comedy, however frivolous, can sometimes assume a social purpose merely by being a much-needed anodyne.

The play itself was something new for Coward: it depended upon its plot far more than its wit to achieve distinction. Synopses of his greatest comedies, even including the deftly made *Present Laughter,* cannot begin to suggest what makes them so appealing, but a synopsis of *Blithe Spirit* reveals many—perhaps most—of its attractions. Charles Condomine, a novelist who is planning to write a book about a fake spiritualist, invites a local psychic, Madame Arcati, to conduct a séance in his home. The séance evokes the ghost of his first wife, Elvira, whom only he can see and hear. Elvira (a free spirit even when she was alive) is dead set on making trouble between Charles and his new wife, Ruth. Trying to arrange Charles's death and reclaim him for herself, she inadvertently kills Ruth instead. Charles is then dogged by two ghostly wives until Madame Arcati manages to dematerialize them and he escapes female domination forever.

It sounds like fun, and for the most part it is. The inspired comic device of an unperceived participant in stage activity (Elvira) leads to one farcical misunderstanding after another. But if one listens to the language of the play, one finds very little of Coward's accustomed flair. The dialogue is strangely flat, provoking laughs all too often by mimicking the form of former witticisms, as when Elvira criticizes Ruth for trying to get her husband to go to bed: "The way that woman harps on bed is nothing short of erotic" (vol. 5, p. 558). Charles and his two wives lack zest, perhaps because there are so few moments in which they seem actually to be enjoying themselves. Their complaints about each other (that Charles is pompous, weak-willed and irascible, Ruth stolid and ungiving, Elvira manipulative and morally unstable) are all depressingly earnest adult complaints and all quite true. Sexual passion and passionate wit are things of the past in *Blithe Spirit*. Even Elvira, embodiment of the first fine careless rapture, finds more pleasure in thwarting Ruth than she does in being alone with Charles.

The child in the piece—and the one fully realized comic character—is the medium, Madame Arcati, whom critic Frances Gray aptly described as showing "the soul of an intelligent twelve-year-old shining through a middle-aged body" (p. 173). This cliché-spouting Girl Guide in bohemian attire is set up before her entrance as either a fool or a charlatan, but she soon proves herself to be neither. She steals the show from the sour, sophisticated Condomines with her passionate attachments to an eclectic array of phenomena: birdsong, bicycling, moss beetles, dry martinis, minor royalty, and ectoplasmic manifestations. Her innocent enthusiasm is a fresh breeze that blows through the play and a reminder that Coward's imagination was always best engaged when his protagonists embodied a spirit of preadolescent abandon.

After *Blithe Spirit* came a lengthy series of theatrical disappointments, both for Coward and for his audience. Some of the postwar comedies and musicals were either sentimental bouquets to bygone times, such as *Sigh No More,* a 1945 revue; *Pacific 1860,* a nostalgic 1946 musical romance, set in the fictional colony of Samolo, which Coward described as having "less a run than a convulsive stagger" in his introduction to volume 5 of *Play Parade* (p. xix); *Quadrille,* a 1952 romantic Victorian comedy written for the Lunts; and *After the Ball,* a 1954 musical play based on Oscar Wilde's 1892 *Lady Windermere's Fan.* Others were satirical glances at modern society from an increasingly reactionary point of view, such as *Ace of Clubs,* a 1950 musical about Soho gangsters, which Coward dubbed an "attempt to break away from a tradition I had established for myself" in his introduction to volume 6 of *Play Parade* (p. xii), but the play left Coward stranded, too far from his native milieu; *Relative Values,* a 1951 comedy that disparaged the idea of social equality by inventing a maid with a long-lost sister, now a movie star, who is romantically involved with her employer's son; *South Sea Bubble,* a comedy, written in 1949 but first produced in 1956, once again about life in imaginary Samolo, where happy natives are proud to be citizens of the British

Queen; and *Nude with Violin,* a 1956 comedy that cynically dismissed modern art. Some of these plays closed quickly, others ran for a season, bolstered by the box-office attractiveness of their stars; none, except the ersatz *Ace of Clubs* and *After the Ball,* was more than a five-finger exercise in the Noel Coward manner.

While Coward had been biding his time, producing new variations on essentially prewar themes, a whole new world of theater had sprung up, and he hated it. This was the English new wave of proletarian playwrights, spearheaded by John Osborne in the revolutionary *Look Back in Anger* in 1956, who forced the British public to acknowledge its disenfranchised working-class citizens. "Coward knew how to be popular," writes John Lahr, "but he was no longer pertinent. The English New Wave was pertinent but would never quite learn how to be popular" (p. 140). Their conflicting values came to a boil after *Look After Lulu!,* Coward's maladroit 1959 adaptation of Georges Feydeau's farce, *Occupe-toi d'Amélie,* was presented at the Royal Court Theatre, cradle of the "angry young men." The production, which starred Vivien Leigh and transferred to the West End, was criticized as a commercial sellout of the theater's ideals. In the *Sunday Times* (22 January 1961) Coward commented that "theatrically, one of the more depressing aspects of the present transitional phase through which the civilized world is passing is the monotonous emphasis on the lot of the Common Man; for the Common Man, unless written and portrayed with genius, is not, dramatically, nearly so interesting as he is claimed to be." "The bridge of a sinking ship," Kenneth Tynan retorted, "is scarcely the ideal place from which to deliver a lecture on the technique of keeping afloat" (*Right and Left,* London, 1967, p. 87).

Coward's ship continued to sink in the early 1960's. *Waiting in the Wings* (1960), a heartfelt melodrama about retired actresses in a charity home, and *Sail Away* (1961), a musical comedy about a group of Americans on a cruise, made no more than a ripple as they were plummeted to oblivion by the critics.

And then came the extraordinary turn of events, beginning in 1963, which Coward called "Dad's Renaissance." What kicked it off was a modest but highly acclaimed production of *Private Lives,* which had not been revived in London for nearly twenty years. "Can it be," a critic (quoted in Morley, *A*

Talent, p. 303) asked, "that we have underrated Coward all these years, and that *Private Lives* so far from being a badly dated relic is in fact the funniest play to have adorned the English theatre in this century?" The answer was yes, and it seems likely to remain yes for all time.

One successful revival followed another in 1964: a musical version of *Blithe Spirit* in New York, television productions of *Present Laughter, Blithe Spirit, The Vortex,* and *Design for Living,* and a triumphant *Hay Fever* (directed by "The Master" himself, the first living playwright to be so honored) at London's National Theatre. What had been derided as mannerism was now celebrated as style; what had seemed ephemeral was still miraculously alive and undated. The best of Coward's frivolities—which critic Cyril Connolly, writing for the *New Statesman* in 1937, had dismissed as "written in the most topical and perishable way imaginable, the cream in them turns sour overnight"—were every bit as fresh as when they had first been played.

LATE WORKS

ENCOURAGED by all this acclaim, in 1965 and 1966 Coward wrote and starred in one last vehicle, *Suite in Three Keys* ("a sort of acting orgy swan-song" is how he saw it [*Diaries,* p. 512]), which consisted of three short plays set in the same luxurious hotel in Switzerland. *Shadows of the Evening* is a melodrama about a man facing death philosophically; deploring preachiness, he nonetheless preaches quite earnestly a Montaignean doctrine of stoic skepticism: "I make no claim to omniscience. I only know that I *don't* know and that faced with this insoluble mystery all the priests, philosophers, scientists and witch doctors in the world are as ignorant as I am. . . . I intend to utilize the days that are left by fortifying my mind against fear" (p. 488).[2] What might be touchingly true in a diary is numbingly false, unfortunately, as dramatic assertion, because the character has no claim on our attention except as spokesman for the author's personal beliefs. *Come into the Garden Maud* is a heavy-handed reworking of *Fumed Oak,* depicting rich vulgar Americans instead of working-class South Londoners, a

situation comedy about a henpecked husband who flies the coop.

The most adroit and substantial play in the trio was *A Song at Twilight,* in which Coward seemed at first glance to be venturing a late revision of his by now almost adamantine persona. Sir Hugo Latymer, the leading character, is "an elderly writer of considerable eminence" (p. 357) who sounds very much like Garry Essendine of *Present Laughter* twenty-five years later, grown decrepit and disagreeable under "the constant strain of having to live up to the self-created image he has implanted in the public mind" (p. 375). That image omits something he would rather not have his public (or his sexless secretarial wife, Hilde) know about: his homosexuality. Along comes Carlotta Gray, an actress with whom he once had a celebrated affair. She asks permission to quote his love letters in her memoirs; he arrogantly denies it. On her way out the door she offers to return the letters, adding casually that she will keep his correspondence with Perry Sheldon, "the only true love of your life" (p. 402). The curtain descends on act 1 as she makes her melodramatic exit.

Act 2 begins with Sir Hugo, unnerved, summoning Carlotta back and attempting to buy the compromising letters to Perry. What offends her is not his homosexuality but his dishonesty and callousness in keeping up heterosexual appearances. "You waved me like a flag to prove a fallacy" (p. 424), she claims, and "you wrote [Perry] off like a bad debt" (p. 420), acknowledging him in his memoirs only as an "adequate secretary":

CARLOTTA: It was your dishonesty and lack of moral courage in those far-off days that set you on the wrong road for the rest of your life.
HUGO: It is hardly for you to decide whether the course of my life has been wrong or right.
CARLOTTA: You might have been a great writer instead of merely a successful one, and you might also have been a far happier man.

(pp. 423–424)

A Song at Twilight was taken by many as a soul-searching *apologia pro vita sua,* but it was not really; it was a biographical fantasia, concocted by combining an incident from belletrist Max Beerbohm's life (a comic encounter with an old flame in later years) with a trenchant character study of novelist Somerset Maugham, whose indiscretions made

[2]Citations for the plays in *Suite in Three Keys* refer to *Plays: Five.*

good gossip in the 1960's, and adding in a tried-and-true blackmail plot. "Coward had neither impulse nor cause to accuse himself of Hugo's nastiness, and the circumstances of his private life in no way resembled those of Hugo," writes critic Robert F. Kiernan (1986), noting that the character is "a type of homosexual that Coward disliked, and he scorns Hugo for marrying, for denying his inclination in private, and for slighting a man who was once his lover" (p. 136).

Why then had Coward raised the issue of a writer's concealed homosexuality, if not to remove a mask and portray himself truthfully on stage? For the same reason that he had flirted with the subject forty-two years earlier in *The Vortex:* because it provided a frisson of notoriety that piqued the public interest. *A Song at Twilight* was less an apologia than a lifelong self-dramatist's last gasp. The sexual freedom of the 1960's gave him the opportunity to be the first English dramatist to address a provocative taboo. Frances Gray observed that Coward wrote the final draft while the Sexual Offences Act, legalizing homosexuality, was passing through the House of Lords (p. 108). Audiences who had long since surmised Coward's sexual preferences were nonetheless titillated by his dropping of the seventh veil. But he did not drop it, really; he performed a discreet striptease in which Carlotta spoke what he felt while his character demurred:

HUGO: According to the law in England, homosexuality is still a penal offence.

CARLOTTA: In the light of modern psychiatry and in the opinion of all sensible and unprejudiced people that law has become archaic and nonsensical.

HUGO: Nevertheless it exists.

CARLOTTA: It won't exist much longer.

HUGO: Maybe so, but even when the actual law ceases to exist there will still be a stigma attached to "the love that dare not speak its name" in the minds of millions of people for generations to come. It takes more than a few outspoken books and plays and speeches in Parliament to uproot moral prejudice from the Anglo-Saxon mind.

CARLOTTA: Do you seriously believe that now, today, in the middle of the Twentieth century, the sales of your books would diminish if the reading public discovered that you were sexually abnormal?

HUGO: My private inclinations are not the concern of my reading public. I have no urge to martyr my reputation for the sake of self-indulgent exhibitionism.

(pp. 417–418)

Kiernan aptly remarks that *A Song at Twilight* is "a curious theatrical contrivance: Coward playing an unattractive homosexual while speaking out for the legalization of homosexual acts through the voice of a heterosexual woman" (p. 137). The play, if approached as autobiography, is a mirage—but so was everything else that Coward wrote. It flirts with reality and retreats into illusion when Hugo, Carlotta, and wife Hilde sentimentally settle their differences—which is to say that it is irrevocably caught, like its author, between candor and the box office.

CONCLUSION

"IF I had to write my own epitaph," Coward once said, "it would be: 'He was much loved because he made people laugh and cry'" (*Harper's Bazaar,* August 1960). "I have no great or beautiful thoughts," he said of himself. "More than anything else I hate this pretentious, highbrow approach to things dramatic. The primary and dominant function of the theatre is to amuse people, not to reform or edify them."

Amuse them he did and amuse them he will. As to his importance in the development of Western theater, Coward pondered the subject himself in 1958 in the introduction to volume 5 of the *Play Parade* series:

Deeply embedded in most people's minds is the conviction that a work of art can only merit the adjective "Important" if it deals with a serious matter in a serious manner. Since the grey dawn of the Christian era this superstition has persisted, presumably because laughter, frivolity, joy and humour are concomitants of pleasure and for those who accept the dubious assumption that the brief years we live on this earth are merely a preparation for a nobler life to come, pleasure is obviously suspect. . . . Personally I have never been able to share this wary attitude to enjoyment. I prefer comedy to tragedy and laughter to tears. . . .

It must not be imagined, however, that in my early years I was not beset by doubts. . . . I searched my mind, for long years I searched, to find a theme solemn enough on which to base a really important play. It was only a little while ago, when I was cheerfully emerging from my forties into my fifties, that, to quote Madame Arcati, "It came upon me in a blinding flash" that I had already written several important plays—*Hay Fever, Private Lives, Design for Living, Present Laughter* and *Blithe Spirit.* These plays were important because they had given a vast number of people a great deal of pleasure.

(pp. xxx–xxxii)

The name Noel Coward is destined to endure, not just as a synonym for star or style or wit or sophistication; in its most comprehensive significance it will always mean one thing: pure pleasure.

SELECTED BIBLIOGRAPHY

I. COLLECTED WORKS. *Collected Sketches and Lyrics* (London, 1931; New York, 1932); *Play Parade,* vol. 1 (New York, 1933; London, 1934), contains *Design for Living, Cavalcade, Private Lives, Bitter Sweet, Post-Mortem, The Vortex,* and *Hay Fever; Play Parade,* vol. 2 (London, 1939), contains *This Year of Grace, Words and Music, Operette, Conversation Piece, Fallen Angels,* and *Easy Virtue; Play Parade,* vol. 3 (London, 1950), contains *The Queen Was in the Parlour, "I'll Leave It to You," The Young Idea, Sirocco, The Rat Trap, "This Was a Man," Home Chat,* and *The Marquise; The Noel Coward Song Book* (London, 1953; New York, 1984); *Play Parade,* vol. 4 (London, 1954), contains *Tonight at 8:30* (includes *We Were Dancing, The Astonished Heart, "Red Peppers", Hands Across the Sea, Fumed Oak, Shadow Play, Ways and Means, Still Life, Family Album*), *Present Laughter,* and *This Happy Breed; Play Parade,* vol. 5 (London, 1958), contains *Pacific 1860, Peace in Our Time, Relative Values, Quadrille,* and *Blithe Spirit; Play Parade,* vol. 6 (London, 1962), contains *Point Valaine, South Sea Bubble, Ace of Clubs, Nude with Violin,* and *Waiting in the Wings.*

Plays: One (London and New York, 1979), contains *Hay Fever, The Vortex, Fallen Angels,* and *Easy Virtue; Plays: Two* (London and New York, 1979), contains *Private Lives, Bitter Sweet, The Marquise,* and *Post-Mortem; Plays: Three* (London and New York, 1979), contains *Design for Living, Cavalcade, Conversation Piece,* and *Tonight at 8:30* I [*Hands Across the Sea, Still Life, Fumed Oak*]; *Plays: Four* (London and New York, 1979), contains *Blithe Spirit, Present Laughter, This Happy Breed,* and *Tonight at 8:30* II [*Ways and Means, The Astonished Heart, "Red Peppers"*]; *The Collected Stories of Noel Coward* (New York, 1983); *Plays: Five* (London and New York, 1983), contains *Relative Values, Look After Lulu!, Waiting in the Wings,* and *Suite in Three Keys* [*A Song at Twilight, Shadows of the Evening, Come into the Garden Maud*]. *The Collected Verse of Noel Coward* (London, 1984; New York, 1985).

II. SEPARATE WORKS. *Present Indicative* (London and New York, 1937), autobiography; *Future Indefinite* (London and New York, 1954), autobiography; *Pomp and Circumstance* (London and New York, 1960), novel.

III. JOURNALS. *The Noel Coward Diaries,* ed. by G. Payn and S. Morley (London, 1982; Boston, 1982); *Autobiography* (London, 1986).

IV. REFERENCE WORKS. R. Mander and J. Mitchenson, eds., *Theatrical Companion to Coward* (London and New York, 1957); J. Russell, ed., *File on Coward* (London, 1987; New York, 1988).

V. CRITICAL STUDIES. A. Bennett, preface to *The Plays of Noel Coward* (New York, 1928); S. Maugham, preface to *Bitter Sweet and Other Plays* by Noel Coward (New York, 1929); S. O'Casey, "Coward Codology," in *The Green Crow* (New York, 1956); T. Rattigan, "Noel Coward: An Appreciation of His Work in the Theatre," in *Theatrical Companion to Coward* (London and New York, 1957); E. Albee, "Notes for Noel About Coward," introduction to *Three Plays by Noel Coward* (New York, 1965); M. Levin, *Noel Coward* (New York, 1968; rev. ed., 1989); S. Morley, *A Talent to Amuse: A Biography of Noel Coward* (London and New York, 1969; rev. ed. with new epilogue, Boston, 1985); C. Castle, *Noel* (London, 1972); W. Marchant, *The Pleasure of His Company: Noel Coward Remembered* (Indianapolis and New York, 1975); K. Tynan, "A Tribute to Mr. Coward," in *A View of the English Stage, 1944–1963* (London, 1975); K. Tynan, "In Memory of Mr. Coward," in *The Sound of Two Hands Clapping* (London, 1975); C. Lesley, *The Life of Noel Coward* (London, 1976), published as *Remembered Laughter: The Life of Noel Coward* (New York, 1976); C. Lesley, G. Payn, S. Morley, eds., *Noel Coward and His Friends* (London and New York, 1979); J. Lahr, *Coward the Playwright* (London, 1982; New York, 1983); R. F. Kiernan, *Noel Coward* (New York, 1986); F. Gray, *Noel Coward* (New York, 1987).

ARTHUR CONAN DOYLE
(1859–1930)

Bernard Benstock

As THE CREATOR of Sherlock Holmes, Sir Arthur Conan Doyle has guaranteed himself an immortality second only to that of his fictional detective, although he persevered throughout his life as a writer to achieve fame for his literary labors in various other genres and often tried to rid himself of the Holmes who established his fame and provided him with a considerable fortune. To imagine the history of detective fiction without Conan Doyle's seminal contribution is as difficult as attempting to conjecture the extent of Doyle's fame had he not written the Holmes stories. Yet Conan Doyle also wrote adventure novels, historical novels, mysteries, business novels, romantic novels, various types of short fiction and war reportage, as well as plays, poems, memoirs, travel literature, and assorted nonfiction—enough of a life's work for any writer. A prolific author in these various genres, whose life was also crammed with activities not directly related to literature, Conan Doyle survives for posterity almost exclusively for the sixty Holmes narratives (four novels and fifty-six short stories), which stand apart on a pedestal of their own.

It would be perverse to attempt to imagine Doyle's fame had he never embarked on detective fiction and never written the Holmes narratives. His historical adventure stories, which he particularly valued, *The White Company* (1891) and *Sir Nigel* (1906)[1] might have left him with a following among younger readers in the twentieth century, but could hardly have survived past his lifetime. His later science fiction, however, might have exploited the contemporary interest in that genre; yet books like *The Lost World* (1912), which concentrate on ancient beasts and exotic terrain, would soon prove to be out of fashion with modern science fiction, which is based on space exploration and

focuses on the future rather than on the past. Doyle's views of the medieval world and Revolutionary France in the historical romances now seem obsolete and stilted, especially when compared with the Victorian England of his day portrayed in the Sherlock Holmes works. The confirmed patriot and the chivalric gentleman in Conan Doyle dominates *Micah Clark* (1889) and *Uncle Bernac* (1897); but these aspects of himself are diffused and complicated when Holmes and Watson are at the center of the fiction.

Incredibly well known in his own lifetime and since, Conan Doyle has been the subject of numerous biographies, and himself contributed his autobiographic writings, especially his *Memories and Adventures* (1924), all of which add together the facts of his life with the ancillary legends. The story of the desperate young physician who whiled away his time, when patients were not forthcoming, by writing his first Sherlock Holmes novel, *A Study in Scarlet* (1888), professes to portray the would-be author's first venture into writing; yet Doyle had published a mystery story while in medical school, and had thereafter published several other stories and written a novel about the world of business that was not accepted for publication until after the first Holmes work, "The Mystery of Sasassa Valley," was in print. That he sold the copyright for *A Study in Scarlet* for a mere twenty-five pounds sterling before publication is supposed to indicate what little impact that first Holmes novel was expected to have on the literary world, and perhaps the little significance that Doyle himself attached to the work; yet only a few years later he was demanding and getting twice that for a short story, and still later a thousand pounds for twelve stories—apparently much to his own surprise.

The young writer had little to follow in 1886 in terms of a literary tradition in the detective genre. Émile Gaboriau and Edgar Allan Poe were the only

[1]Dates in parentheses after full-length works indicate the year of publication in book form, usually the year after serialization.

primary precursors, although gothic novels, works of "scientific" fantasy and horror, novels involving criminal activities, and adventure tales provided materials for a new hybrid form. The Gaboriau novels and Poe stories were valuable sources for Doyle, and, although Holmes in *A Study in Scarlet* sneers at their detectives, Inspector Lecoq and Auguste Dupin, Doyle himself was far more respectful of Gaboriau and Poe as authors, and on occasion his debt to them was barely this side of plagarism. The choice between the novel and the compact story was constantly open to him, primarily determined by what he perceived the market would bear. Doyle soon realized the economic advantages of quickly disseminated short fiction in periodicals. The continuance of a serial detective in regular magazine appearances determined his major emphasis on the short story, but the temptation to weave a romantic, historical adventure tale into a Holmes story also proved irresistible.

To the Holmesian devotee the canon of sixty narratives stands as inviolate, with no pejorative attached to the insistence that the formulaic structure remains intact throughout; yet to many a literary critic an unevenness exists in the work and some stories are decidedly superior to others, although these critics often disagree about which ones. Doyle was at times under pressure to produce Holmes stories on demand and under contract, and both the onerousness of the task and the desire to get on with other literary work put Sherlock Holmes's life in jeopardy, his creator frequently willing to sign the death warrant with a stroke of the pen. After several attempts to bring the series to a close were foiled when his demands for increased payment were met, Doyle made what he thought was his irrevocable decision in 1893, barely six years after introducing Holmes to the reading public: his hero was to meet his death heroically, carrying the notorious Professor Moriarty, that "Napoleon of crime," to his death over the Reichenbach Falls in Switzerland, which the Doyle family had visited on holiday. "The Final Problem," then, spelled the end of the detective and the series; but public outcry and insistent publishers resulted in "The Adventure of the Empty House" (1903),[2] and the return of Sherlock Holmes—it turns out that Holmes himself had

falsely advertised his own death for his own safety. Holmes's existence thereafter was safe as long as Conan Doyle was alive, and considering the hordes of imitations, pastiches, and spin-offs that followed, remains safe to the present day.

The degree to which the Holmes mystique has taken hold—so tenaciously as to eclipse Arthur Conan Doyle from the primacy usually afforded the successful author—can be seen in the establishment of Sherlock Holmes as a cult figure. Very early in the process a spate of parodies appeared in several languages, almost as quickly as the stories were being translated. These numerous variants, like "Shamrock Jones," attest obliquely to the unique achievement, and directly to the enormous popularity, of the world's first "unofficial consulting detective," as Holmes called himself in *The Sign of Four* (1890). Although these pastiches continue to the present day, far more indicative of the unusual nature of the Holmes mystique are the various societies around the world, satellites of the originating group called The Baker Street Irregulars, named after the band of street urchins employed several times by Holmes as his fleet-footed gatherers of information.

The group of intellectuals and bon vivants who formed the society dedicated themselves assiduously to following the exploits of their hero, taking as gospel every word in the printed texts and assuming Sherlock Holmes to be a real person, rather than a fictional creation, thus eliminating Arthur Conan Doyle from consideration. A "biography" of Holmes's life was constantly in progress, the events of every narrative feeding information into a composite portrait of his life and activities, and the "gaps" in chronology ingeniously filled in. In one important way Doyle himself encouraged the hypothesis of Holmes's existence, while dispensing with the existence of Conan Doyle: almost all the Holmes stories were folded into narratives that were the writing up of Sherlock's cases by his friend and cohort, Dr John H. Watson, himself almost as capable of legendary amplification as Holmes. Fifty-six of the narratives were attributed by Doyle to Watson, and it was not until late in the series that Holmes himself was allowed to narrate two of his adventures; two more appeared in the form of third-person narration. (These last two the Sherlockians allow to be attributed to the insignificant Doyle.) The cultic celebrants of the Holmesian mystery schedule festivities for Queen

---

[2] Dates in parentheses after stories indicate year of first publication.

ARTHUR CONAN DOYLE

Victoria's birthday, May 21, but ignore that of Conan Doyle, the next day.

What once consisted of virtuoso performances of mock scholarship and social pleasantry has mushroomed into a worldwide "industry," assuming excessive proportions when devotees appear unaware of the basic frivolity underlying the bald assertions made behind the mask. Refining Conan Doyle out of existence in this irreverent manner, however, complements the author's attempts to refine Holmes out of existence. Yet the life of Arthur Conan Doyle has been written several times, constantly reaffirming his unquestioned existence, although no one would attempt to tell Doyle's story without telling that of Holmes as well.

LIFE

DOYLE was born on 22 May 1859 in Edinburgh, Scotland, the eldest son of the ten children of Charles and Mary Foley Doyle. His family was not without artistic interests; although not an artist by profession, Doyle's father was responsible for some of the early illustrations for the Holmes stories. The family was Roman Catholic and Doyle was educated by the Jesuits, but as an adolescent he found himself veering away from Catholicism, without converting to any other creed. At school he excelled in various sports, skills he later gave Sherlock Holmes, just as he eventually revealed a painter among Holmes's maternal ancestors. At the age of seventeen he entered medical school at the University of Edinburgh, where he earned his degrees and qualified as a physician, a profession that he attached to Watson. At the university he took classes with Dr Joseph Bell, whose skills in diagnosis extended beyond the medical into various aspects of character study and detecting clues regarding a subject's profession and habits, characteristics that make Bell the single most significant source for the kinds of unusual talents displayed by Sherlock Holmes.

In childhood and adolescence an avid reader of the popular fiction of the day, especially adventure stories, historical romances, and gothic novels, Doyle himself turned to writing within the popular literary tradition while he was preparing for the medical profession. He also utilized aspects of his own experiences in the early fiction, especially an unpleasant incident in his initial partnership with another surgeon; and although his literary works are generally classified as anchored in popular cultural conventions, much of what he observed throughout his life filtered into his literary works. The practice of medicine, off to a tenuous start first as a ship's surgeon and later, once he had his M.D., as a physician with more time on his hands than patients in his office, gave way to the literary vocation that lasted throughout his life.

Although Doyle was forty years old and a husband and father when the Boer War broke out, he attempted to enlist as a soldier but was dispatched instead as a surgeon. Thus Dr Watson's experiences in the Afghan War, which immediately precede his meeting with Sherlock Holmes, replicate Doyle's own. For Doyle, who by this time preferred being called Conan Doyle, the Boer War extended his literary range into the writing of contemporary history instead of his usual historically based fictions: *The Great Boer War* (1900) was for a while regarded as an authoritative text on the subject. But the British venture in South Africa had met with a great deal of suspicion and antagonism throughout Europe, and few nations were at all receptive to what was almost universally viewed as an offensively imperialistic adventure. Conan Doyle then undertook the composition of a pamphlet justifying the British military venture and exonerating the British soldier from charges of brutality: *The War in South Africa: Its Cause and Conduct* (1902) resulted in Doyle's being knighted. The inscription on his tombstone reads "Knight," then "Patriot, Physician, & Man of Letters," with no mention of Sherlock Holmes, although between the writing of his two works on the Boer War he resurrected the dead Holmes and included him in his single most famous work of literature, *The Hound of the Baskervilles* (1902).

In 1906 Louise Hawkins, whom Doyle had married in 1885, died; a year later he married Jean Leckie and settled in a new house in Sussex that remained his residence until he died on 7 July 1930. At the time of his second marriage the Holmes tales numbered three novels and three dozen stories, almost two-thirds of the final output. By this time Doyle had found another way to carry the Holmes mystique beyond the confines of literary fiction: he undertook to reopen two criminal cases on which the courts had already rendered verdicts, and managed to have one of the convictions reversed with a success that Holmes would have admired. At the same time he was concentrating his literary efforts on a new genre, science fiction, re-creating a world of dinosaurs discovered on the South American continent and featuring a new serial character, Sir George Edward Challenger, whom Doyle even took to impersonating on occasion.

As was true for millions of others, Conan Doyle's life was altered by World War I, most seriously in a conversion to spiritualism that strengthened a tendency which had been present since his first youthful doubts about Catholicism. The deaths of several members of his immediate family, in the year 1918–1919, including a son and a brother, affected him dramatically. The emphasis on spiritual contact with the dead dominated his remaining years, as he wrote and lectured on the subject and spent much of his personal wealth in propagating the new faith. During the first years of the war, however, when optimism for a quick victory prevailed, Conan Doyle devoted himself to writing the kind of war propaganda that had earned him a knighthood after the Boer War, and indulged in predictions and blueprints for new war matériel, including a prophetic plan for a tunnel connecting Britain to the European mainland.

In 1914 Conan Doyle wrote the final Holmes novel: *The Valley of Fear,* published in 1915, proved to be very much in line with the first Holmes novel of almost three decades earlier—in tone, mood, structure, and design. As the world was changing drastically for Doyle himself, time stood still for Holmes: care was taken to preserve the atmosphere that had fixed the successful formula for the fiction. Nonetheless, the 1917 story, "His Last Bow," brings Holmes out of retirement to serve his nation in World War I.

Of the three facets of Sir Arthur Conan Doyle's personality—the hardheaded man of science, the romantic adventurer, and the proselytizing spiritualist—only those of the scientist and the romancer are apparent in the Sherlock Holmes narratives, and are often at odds with each other. In many ways the tension between rationalist and sentimentalist, personified respectively in Holmes and Watson, achieves a functional balance that makes the fictions so successful, maintaining an equilibrium in which disbelief can be suspended. The best of the short tales often depend on the validity of Holmes's analytical methods of deduction and the storytelling skills that Watson insists on employing to embellish the bare facts of each particular case—

despite Holmes's frequent protests. As a repeated bone of contention between them, the Watsonian method of narration is all the more effective because it is constantly being displayed in proportion to the Holmesian method of detection. The seamless weave between the operative methods is not possible in the four longer narratives, however, where the divided ways of storytelling demarcate separate genres coexisting within each narrative.

BALANCE OF MODES AND GENRES

In fashioning his first detective novel, Conan Doyle may well have had one eye on Poe and Gaboriau, but the other was clearly on Sir Walter Scott and Thomas Mayne Reid. *A Study in Scarlet* establishes the narrational voice of the storyteller in what purports to be "a reprint from the reminiscences of John H. Watson, M.D.," whose initial obligation is to introduce Holmes and locate him within the focus of his abilities and eccentricities as a potential detective. But once that has been achieved in the first two chapters, the lurid murder investigation takes command of the stage, and the active ingredients of the hunt augment the ratiocinative process of Holmes's thinking: in essence, a Holmes who seems intent on being an armchair investigator is propelled into action instead, and the five remaining chapters of part 1 speedily result in the apprehension of the murderer. All that remains is for Holmes's neat summary of how he arrived at his deductions—but that is suspended until the final two chapters of part 2, when the interrupted "reminiscences" are concluded. In the interim, the portion subtitled "The Country of the Saints" begins a new tale, a story in third-person narration, that will eventually dovetail with Watson's suspended narrative. The new story is an adventure romance presented as retrospective exposition, in a style unrelated to that of the previous section and familiar to readers of adventure fiction.

Being wrenched from the gaslit, foggy streets of London to the Great Alkali Plain of Mormon Utah can be an unnerving experience for the reader of classic detective fiction, but the rules of the genre were not yet fixed and Doyle depended on an allied genre of adventure stories to give magnitude to his novel. The same necessities were operative soon after, when he embarked on the writing of *The Sign of Four;* but in this latter work the forced separation of the two aspects of the plot—the immediacy of detection and chase and the filling in of the exposition—are not nearly as disruptive, with only the last two chapters given over to the tale told by the villain—within the framework, this time, of Watson's "reminiscences." The love story at the center of the first plot does not have equal relevance in the second book, which does, however, conclude with the love story of John Watson and the client who brought the case to Holmes.

Although *The Hound of the Baskervilles* is not dependent on this bipartite structure and stands as Conan Doyle's most integrated long narrative, the fourth novel, *The Valley of Fear,* returns to the original formula, even closer to the balanced separation of the two plots in *A Study in Scarlet* than the more digested use of the background tale at the end of *The Sign of Four.* Again the two parts are separately titled—"The Tragedy of Birlstone" and "The Scowrers"—and again the story returns in the second part to an American locale; but instead of a lapse into "objective" narration, part 2 is presented as a first-person narration by the surviving participant in the action of the two parts. In this particular structuring a very brief epilogue is given to Watson for the purpose of revealing the eventual fate of that survivor. The two extrapolated tales, that of the murderous and fanatical Mormons and that of the villainous secret society (here called the Scowrers), are expected to stand on their own in complement to the detection yarn, and are as much a part of Conan Doyle's literary predilections as such historical adventures as *The White Company* and *Micah Clarke,* his most admired works in that genre.

The much-admired *Hound of the Baskervilles* probably owes its reputation to its relentless atmosphere of horror rather than to its sustained method of literary presentation. Although the typical Holmes story may seem to be permanently associated with the mysterious fogbound streets of London, many of them actually take place in rural areas as desolate and dangerous as the Grimpen Moors of Baskerville. "It is my belief, Watson," Sherlock Holmes states in "The Adventure of the Copper Beeches" (1892), "that the lowest and vilest alleys in London do not present a more dreadful record of sin than does the smiling and beautiful countryside" (*Complete Sherlock Holmes,* 1960, p. 323).[3] As *The Hound of the Baskervilles* moves through its successive stages—

from the Holmesian accumulation of clues to the gathering of the involved participants, and on to the dual tracks of a murderer at work on further mischief and a detective at work on solving one crime and preventing another—an integrated narrative unfolds. Yet the unswerving allegiance to a single narrational method may have more to do with the relative absence of Sherlock Holmes from the story, rendering it more of an action novel than a detective novel, than with a perfect fusion of the detection and action genres.

Conan Doyle began writing the novel without intending it as another Holmes tale, but at a later stage of composition revised the original scheme and made *The Hound* into a vehicle for his famous detective. Sending Watson into the field of action allowed for a narrative technique in which his reports and diary entries transmit the central parts of the events, and Holmes, who has now gained a reputation as a master of disguise, served as one more mysterious element, as well as an active detective at the scene. Whereas the usual superimposition of a corroborative adventure yarn upon a novel of detection may have allowed the two interacting genres to show their separate characteristics, the superimposition, instead, of the analytical detective on a tale of horror produced a full-length novel with the tight single weave for which the short stories earned their reputation. And despite the force of the continual terror in *The Hound,* all the possibilities of the supernatural that give it its power are finally dispelled by the hardheaded analyses of the scientific investigator, so that the ghost story is eventually drained of its "spiritual" elements.

Conan Doyle's dedication to spiritualism became the overwhelming factor of his later life, and in the 1920's, when Holmes stories were mere afterthoughts, replaced almost all other endeavors and concerns, exhibiting itself in numerous séances, lectures, world tours, and books and articles. An unusual facet of his preoccupation involved the eminent conjurer Harry Houdini, whose international fame equaled that of the creator of Sherlock Holmes. Sir Arthur and Houdini maintained an uneasy friendship and a determined debate until the magician's untimely death in 1926, a debate that Conan Doyle continued beyond the grave.

In "The Riddle of Houdini," the first item in Conan Doyle's *The Edge of the Unknown* (published in 1930), he presents a complex case for and against Houdini: the magician had been as dedicated a de-

---

[3]All further page references in the text are to the 1960 edition of *The Complete Sherlock Holmes.*

bunker of spiritualism as Conan Doyle had been its defender, the two sharing a zealous campaign to unmask false mediums but differing when it came to a belief in "true" mediums. "The Riddle of Houdini," however, contends that the magician was not primarily a conjurer but himself a true medium, either unaware of his spiritualist powers or too much aware that as a practicing magician he amassed enormous wealth, whereas as a proclaimed spiritualist he would engender only mistrust and hostility.

Conan Doyle manages to use against Houdini those incredible feats the magician accomplished before the eyes of hundreds and thousands of onlookers, insisting that such feats could not possibly have been merely a matter of agility and dexterity but must have derived from preternatural powers, despite Houdini's vociferous denials of such powers. He also reveals the handful of instances when Houdini came close to admitting more than he usually dared, even producing his own photographs of spiritual emanations and acknowledging the existence of a medium he considered authentic.

Conan Doyle's posthumous re-creation of Houdini parallels his earlier creation of Sherlock Holmes, a character with whom he strongly identified but from whom in various ways (primarily through the parallel creation of Dr Watson) he distanced himself. It is significant in this later context to recall the circumstances of *The Hound of the Baskervilles,* where the basic problem could have proven to be either "preternatural" or scientifically explainable, and where Holmes's insistence on natural causation proved to be accurate: "The more *outré* and grotesque an incident is," Holmes insisted, "the more carefully it deserves to be examined, and the very point which appears to complicate a case is, when duly considered and scientifically examined, the one which is most likely to elucidate it" (p. 764). "The Riddle of Houdini" also calls for the open and thorough examination of the evidence, but in the final analysis Conan Doyle's spiritualist Houdini is expected to triumph over the rationalist and skeptical detective.

THE HOLMES–WATSON PARTNERSHIP

PERHAPS even more intrinsic to Conan Doyle's determination of the detective genre than either the operative puzzle or the exciting hunt is the vital relationship between the detective and his companion, that devoted but far less astute partner in the investigations. Although it has certainly served as a model for many such companionate relationships in detective fiction, it has deeper psychological roots than others, dating from the earliest days of the friendship, in which Watson is a wounded army medical officer living on a meager pension and Holmes is an eccentric loner just starting work in his first professional job. Their economic straits, resulting in their sharing the quarters at 221B Baker Street that will become Holmes's famous consulting rooms, reflect Doyle's own financial difficulties as a young medical man supporting his mother and siblings when his alcoholic father was hospitalized.

The depressed mood at the beginning of *A Study in Scarlet* is determined by Watson's shoulder wound, his physical and mental exhaustion, and his poverty. Holmes, on the other hand, displays an eccentric and reclusive character, and assumes his chosen profession as a "consultant" with little inclination for active investigation outside the confines of his consulting room. The events of the case and the bonding of the two men effect important changes in both of them by the end of the novel, as Holmes is quick to perceive about his own situation. "I must thank you for it all," he says to Watson after his initial burst of activity. "I might not have gone but for you, and so have missed the finest study I ever came across" (p. 36).

Critics have either puzzled over or scoffed at the discrepancy regarding Watson's Afghan War wound, which in the second novel is in the leg rather than the shoulder. Rather than authorial carelessness, the change might be attributed to the demands of the particular text, in which Watson proves to be "game for a six-mile trudge," brushing aside Holmes's solicitousness ("Your leg will stand it?"). The near invalid and the near recluse emerge from *A Study in Scarlet* as active and alert partners in crime-solving, having propped each other up and dispelled each other's neuroses—to a certain extent.

Yet *The Sign of Four* opens with similar aspects of dependency: Holmes is revealed as a confirmed addict of morphine and cocaine, much to Dr Watson's disapproval; when Holmes offers to share his drugs with his friend, Watson responds "brusquely": "My constitution has not got over the Afghan campaign yet. I cannot afford to throw any extra strain upon it" (p. 89). Holmes without a criminal case to investigate is at loose ends and cynical, asking "Was ever such a dreary, dismal, unprofitable world?" (p. 93). Watson is despondent and fatalistic, "an army surgeon with a weak leg and a weaker bank account. . . . If my future were black, it was better surely to face it like a man" (p. 97). The renewed activity resulting from the new case proves restorative to both, Watson in particular rescued by his having fallen in love with and become engaged to their client, Mary Morstan. But for Holmes, "there still remains the cocaine-bottle" at the end of the adventure, and only the succeeding cases manage to separate him from the addiction; in "The Adventure of the Missing Three-Quarter," Watson takes full credit for it: "For years I had gradually weaned him from that drug mania which had threatened once to check his remarkable career" (p. 622).

The somewhat symbiotic relationship between Holmes and Watson has attracted a great deal of critical attention, and even some suspicion from psychoanalytic critics, fixed as it is within the confines of male bonding—despite the various marriages that temporarily detach Watson from 221B Baker Street. (The first Mrs Watson died, and he later remarried, but given the complex chronology of the stories, it is never certain whether he remarried more than once, so that Sherlockians have had a field day in their reconstruction of Watson biography, some even allowing him as many as five wives.) Rare moments of sentimental indulgence are offset by analytical dissection by Dr Watson, but generally the cases unfold systematically with the assumption that Watson will follow wherever Holmes leads, handing over his medical practice on occasion to a fellow practitioner for the duration. One rare moment of soul-baring occurs late in the canon, in "The Adventure of the Three Garridebs" (1924), when Watson receives a flesh wound, much to Holmes's concern. Watson suddenly realizes "the depth of loyalty and love which lay behind that cold mask," and acknowledges, "All my years of humble but single-minded service culminated in that moment of revelation" (p. 1053). But soon after, in "The Adventure of the Creeping Man" (1923), he is clinically self-analytical, noting, "If I irritated him by a certain methodical slowness in my mentality, that irritation served only to make his own flame-like intuitions and impressions flash up the more vividly and swiftly. Such was my

humble rôle in our alliance" (p. 1071). Not unlike Don Quixote and Sancho Panza, they play their chivalric roles in serving (and saving) their country.

Although the Holmes stories appear to be relatively formulaic, there are significant distinctions among them, primarily between the more loosely constructed and almost contemplative ones, such as "Silver Blaze," and the quicker-paced and often grim ones, such as "The Adventure of the Speckled Band" (1892). The latter is one of the most perfect of its kind, a classic Holmes narrative equally divided between the London setting (221B Baker Street) and the country manor house (in Surrey). The familiar gambit is the unexpected arrival of the distraught client, heavily veiled and dressed in black, in this case awakening the household very early to tell her story of inexplicable horror. The exposition involves the death of her twin sister under mysterious circumstances, and the tyranny of a villainous stepfather, a medical man from one of the oldest families in the county, whose fortune had been so eroded by dissolute ancestors that he is now dependent on his dead wife's legacy, much of which he would lose by the marriage of either of her daughters. He is a man of violent temper, once jailed in India for the killing of a servant and now a terror in his village, soon proven when he breaks in upon Holmes and Watson, once his stepdaughter has left, and demonstrates his furious strength by bending the steel poker—which Holmes calmly bends back once the doctor has stormed out. As one of Conan Doyle's most heinous villains, the doctor is also one of the few miscreants who makes the mistake of openly insulting Sherlock Holmes, sharpening the detective's resolution to bring him to heel.

More important, this introductory exposition contains many of the familiar elements that give a Holmes narrative its distinctive coloring: Watson's dredging up of an old case now that the principals are dead; Holmes's indifference to being paid for his services, especially with so sympathetic a client; and Watson's extolling Holmes for his "rapid deductions, as swift as intuition, and yet always founded on a logical basis." Once the client is on the premises, emotions are heightened by her display of pity and terror, her face having prematurely aged; the story she tells evokes a stormy night in a decrepit manor house where no servants will stay for long. Her sister's death is a locked-room mystery, with no discernible cause of death but accompanied by a whistle in the night and the loud clang of metal and marked by her strange last words. The desolate setting is augmented by a band of Gypsies camping on the grounds (the essential red herring also present in "Silver Blaze") and such wild animals as a cheetah and baboon roaming free. Despite the urgency and horror, Holmes indulges in a display of his powers of observation to impress the terrified woman: that she had traveled to London by train and dogcart (return ticket in her glove, mud on her left sleeve).

The Surrey half of "The Adventure of the Speckled Band" involves the surreptitious inspection of the room where the sister died, followed by a calm interlude during which Holmes and Watson discuss the clues, quickly followed by a night vigil in the dark room and the actions that result in the backfiring of the villain's scheme to rid himself of his remaining stepdaughter. All that remains then, once the intended victim is saved and her tormenter is dead, is Holmes's elaboration of the entire plot, which is presented to Watson during the return trip to London. This "active" segment of the narrative also contains the requisite elements: Watson urged to bring his revolver and even cautioned that he may not wish to participate in the vigil because of the danger involved; the process of Holmes at work, examining the floor and walls with his magnifying lens, observing such strange factors as a dummy bell rope, a ventilator in the wrong wall, a bed clamped to the floor, an iron safe in the doctor's room, along with a saucer of milk and a looped dog lash; the trek across the grounds in the dark, with a chill wind and a signal light, enhanced by the sudden appearance of the hideous baboon. To which should be added the snake as instrument of death, thus involving an untraceable poison that obviously would confound the coroner. There is also that usual combination of chilling and moralistic pronouncements: "a most dark and sinister business," "a strange contrast between the sweet promise of spring and this sinister quest," "when a clever man turns his brains to crime," and the need to prevent a "subtle and horrible crime." As a final touch Holmesian modesty is introduced when he admits that his first suppositions were wrong and that the Gypsies were not the "speckled band" he had at first assumed.

Few writers, certainly among those who wrote detective fiction, have ever been as painstaking as Conan Doyle in both establishing the narratologi-

cal ground rules and maintaining a continuous discussion about them within the fictions themselves. What Conan Doyle could take for granted, however, was the grounding of the Holmes stories in an acceptable concept of reality, despite the efforts made to create an atmospheric ambience that would lend a gothic aspect to Holmes's surroundings. Fog and rain and murky London at night, as well as dark country lanes and moors and isolated manor houses, play their part in his work, but they are just as often quickly passed over for accuracy of detail and specifics of location. Illumination by gaslight and candles, communication by post or courier or telegraph, transportation by hansom cab and the London Underground and the British railway system: these are some reliable markers of the last decades of the nineteenth century; although the influences of contemporary, politics sometimes make themselves felt, time nevertheless seems to stand still in these tales, partially because many are culled from the past achievements of the detective, from scrapbooks and memorabilia. The time is specified by the absence of modern technology: although an occasional telephone or electric light or automobile intrudes in some of the later stories, even something as "essential" to the genre as fingerprinting is generally ignored; there are relatively few instances in which modern method is mentioned, and only one in which "the well-marked print of a thumb" is of any consequence—in "The Adventure of the Norwood Builder."

NARRATIVE METHOD: HOLMES VS. WATSON

BEYOND the obvious accomplishment of capturing the public imagination at an opportune moment, the Sherlock Holmes stories are successful as chronicles of important aspects of late Victorian culture and as narratives that depend on a balance of modes. The bonding of Holmes and Watson satisfies the masculine ethos of adventure literature, but the aspect of that bonding which is primarily a tension between the two satisfies a far more aesthetic requisite: few writers of crime fiction other than Conan Doyle have managed to establish a persistent hostility between the fictional detective and the fictional chronicler of the fiction. What Watson favors is a sensationalist presentation of the crimes and the hunt for the villain, in opposition to Holmes's insistence on a coldly scientific statement of the events. What is achieved is a narrative close to Watson's intentions but one that describes and glorifies Holmes's methods, fictional romance cloaked in the aura of ratiocination. From the second narrative on, once the protagonists are in place, the active tension is introduced and perpetuated as an ongoing argument between them, in one out of every six of the chronicled adventures.

Yet it is Holmes himself who immediately sees the possibilities of his activities as publishable stories, and for all of his insistence on the unromantic and clinical approach, he contains the "touch of the artist" within his own personality. That he immediately visualizes the events of his operative investigation as already recordable in printed form is evidenced by his imaginative titling of the case. "A study in scarlet, eh? Why shouldn't we use a little art jargon" (p. 36), he declares with enthusiasm, violating his later insistence on no such frills embroidering his analytical deductions. (It is not until "The Greek Interpreter," 1893, the twenty-third work, that we are informed Holmes's grandmother's brother was a French painter named Vernet; "art in the blood is liable to take the strangest forms," the analytical Holmes comments [p. 435].)

This early venture into artistic titling is no aberration, but indicative of the dual role Holmes himself plays in the fabrication of the tale, aware of its artistic value. In *The Sign of Four* he calls attention to the fact that the perpetrator of the cabal had already captured its mysterious essence by naming it "the sign of the four," Holmes adding, "as he somewhat dramatically calls it" (p. 120). But he admits that footprints in creosote and the deployment of a bloodhound "prevented the case from becoming the pretty little intellectual problem which at one time it promised to be" (p. 119). In a later story the "artistic touch" is rather inadvertent, but all the more compelling because of the inadvertence. Holmes telegraphs to Watson, suggesting which of his cases to chronicle next: "Why not tell them of the Cornish horror" (p. 955). The London press, that bastion of sensationalism, had termed the case "the Cornish Horror," and although Watson accepts Holmes's suggestion, he gives it the more discreet title, "The Adventure of the Devil's Foot" (1910), focusing on the *root* of the problem rather than the hysterical reaction to it, but nonetheless obtaining both advantages.

The ways in which Holmes can be employed to undercut one aspect of the narrative technique for the benefit of the other is seen as soon as *A Study in Scarlet* is in print, allowing him the function of literary critic as well as of detective. "Detection is, or ought to be, an exact science and should be treated in the same cold and unemotional manner. You have attempted to tinge it with romanticism," he accuses Watson in *The Sign of Four*, "which produces much the same effect as if you worked a love-story or an elopement into the fifth proposition of Euclid" (p. 90). Holmes then pronounces his dictum: "The only point in the case which deserved mention was the curious analytical reasoning from effects to causes, by which I succeeded in unravelling it" (p. 90). That *The Sign of Four* is so much a replica of *A Study in Scarlet* attests to Watson's refusal to change his manner of presentation despite Holmes's criticism. But Watson himself had acted as critic in an earlier instance, targeting a text by Holmes without knowing the identity of the author, calling it "a remarkable mixture of shrewdness and of absurdity," a mixture that provides the basic formula for all the Sherlock Holmes stories.

The Conan Doyle stories were always the target of complaints from literal-minded critics who objected to discrepancies, and inconsistencies, and violations of verisimilitude, criticism that left the author unfazed. Letters to newspapers frequently reported these infelicities during Conan Doyle's lifetime; one of his most famous stories, "Silver Blaze" (1892), in particular came under scrupulous attack. Although an active sportsmen interested in various sporting activities, Conan Doyle was not particularly knowledgeable about horse racing, yet he managed to evoke the world of the racecourse very effectively in "Silver Blaze"—but not without serious mistakes regarding the care and running of racehorses. When these mistakes were pointed out to him, he shrugged them off with indifference: it was the aura of the track that he had captured, and his story conveyed that aura with excitement and immediacy. Accounting for the discrepancies as if they were intentional became the sport of the professional Sherlockians (as they became known in the United States) and Holmesians (as they are known in the United Kingdom).

Holmes's complaints about Watson's literary style appear throughout the canon, from *The Sign of Four* to "The Problem of Thor Bridge" (1922), one of the last half-dozen stories. There are both a dogged persistence and elements of inconsistency in the substance of these complaints: a tendency to "embellish so many of my own little adventures"; a "meretricious" effect of "retaining in your own hands some of the factors in the problem which are never imparted to the reader"; "your fatal habit of looking at everything from the point of view of a story instead of as a scientific exercise." Having insisted from the beginning on "analytical reasoning from effects to causes," Holmes reverses himself in "The Adventure of the Copper Beeches," contending, "You have erred, perhaps . . . in attempting to put colour and life into each of your statements instead of confining yourself to the task of placing upon record that severe reasoning from cause to effect which is really the only notable feature about the thing" (p. 317). Conan Doyle may have been as careless about the distinction between inductive and deductive reasoning as he was about maiming racehorses, but he kept up the controversy between Holmes and Watson for dramatic effect and internal justifications for his narrative methods.

Rather than subvert the ends of literary creation, Holmes's dicta regarding these methods call attention to the art in the artifice, the constant duality of shrewdness and absurdity, a fiction that claims its origins in reality and yet profits from its artificial embellishments. When Holmes sums up his impressions of the events in "The Adventure of Wisteria Lodge" (1908, first published as "The Singular Experience of Mr. J. Scott Eccles"), he labels the case a "chaotic" one: "It will not be possible for you to present it in that compact form which is dear to your heart," he tells Watson (p. 887). When the story does see the light of day, it is subdivided into two sections; although it is one of the longest of the short stories—though not as long as "The Naval Treaty" (1893)—its compactness seems intrinsically sufficient. It comes as a surprise, however, that Holmes should consider Watson's recasting as "compact," despite all the "embellishments" that he presumably denigrates.

On occasion Holmes is willing to offer praise, although on such occasions he does so rather backhandedly, as when he lauds Watson for giving "prominence not so much to the many *causes célèbres* and sensational trials . . . but rather to those incidents which have been trivial in themselves, but which have given room for those faculties of deduction and of logical synthesis which I have made

my special province" ("The Adventure of the Copper Beeches," 1892, p. 316). Conan Doyle derives major effects from both the Holmesian brain in action and the eccentric and self-consciously sensational personality of Sherlock Holmes.

Late in the process Conan Doyle further justifies his preference for the Watsonian method when he allows Holmes temporarily to become his own chronicler. The challenge had been posed much earlier when Watson, in "The Adventure of the Abbey Grange" (1904), said to Holmes, "with some bitterness," "Why do you not write them yourself?" (p. 636). In "The Adventure of the Blanched Soldier" (1926), Holmes takes up the challenge, but with unusual humility: "I am compelled to admit that, having taken my pen in my hand, I do begin to realize that the matter must be presented in such a way as may interest the reader" (p. 1000). In this instance he seems to be quite purposeful in the writing of the tale, unlike the situation in "The Adventure of the Lion's Mane" (1926), where the events overtake him in his retirement, although in both cases Watson is absent so that not only has Holmes lost his chronicler, but he has no opportunity to characterize Watson as Watson had so consistently been characterizing him.

That the writing style remains consistent with Watson's in the Holmesian narrations, and in the two third-person narrations—"His Last Bow" and "The Adventure of the Mazarin Stone" (1921)—as well, attests to the fixity with which Conan Doyle determined that the style and structure of his detective fiction were determined not by the persona of the narrator but by the inner dynamics of the narrative. What Holmes grudgingly learns in "The Adventure of the Blanched Soldier" is that a narrative conceals as it reveals, that embellishments are aspects of sleight of hand: "Alas, that I should have to show my hand so when I tell my own story! It was by concealing such links in the chain that Watson was enabled to produce his meretricious finales" (pp. 1007–1008). When the same limitations prevail in "The Adventure of the Lion's Mane," Holmes is not as sanguine in facing the necessity of writing his own story without the varnish of embellishment:

Thus I must act as my own chronicler. Ah! had he been with me, how much he might have made of so wonderful a happening and of my eventual triumph against every difficulty! As it is, however, I must needs tell my tale in my own plain way, showing by my words each step upon the difficult road which lay before me as I searched for the mystery of the Lion's Mane.

(p. 1083)

Despite Conan Doyle's own praise for this effort of his old age, "The Adventure of the Lion's Mane" does not display Holmes at his best: he depends for his solution on a piece of information stored in his brain that he is unable to retrieve at will—the delay in retrieval results in an attack on a second victim, although not a fatal one. As much as Holmes as chronicler lauds his "eventual triumph," Holmes as detective proves to be a has-been in retirement, and Conan Doyle reveals his waning talent in old age. The Watsonian skills in romanticizing and sensationalism and embellishment might have made Holmes appear more triumphant than Holmes himself is able to, since what Watson was chronicling was the Holmesian personality rather than the cases that could have been presented with cold, unemotional facts. Holmes allows himself to acknowledge Watson's contribution to his professional reputation when he admits in "Silver Blaze," "I made a blunder, my dear Watson—which is, I am afraid, a more common occurrence than anyone would think who knew me through your memoirs" (p. 336). The scientist in Conan Doyle constantly seeks to validate the creative process that is exemplified in Dr Watson.

Conan Doyle's skillful deployment of Watson allows him a control of the means of narration that makes the character of Sherlock Holmes the major focus of the stories, so that in having Holmes fail to appreciate his dedicated chronicler he sharpens the focus all the more. In a moment of rare humility Holmes even admits that "your old friend here has given an exaggerated view of my scientific methods" ("The Adventure of the Sussex Vampire," 1924, p. 1039), flying in the face of his more frequent assertions that Watson's sensationalism detracts from a view of those methods. Watson himself then confesses to being torn between cases that are interesting in themselves, despite Holmes's less spectacular efforts in solving them, and those which are examples of his genius but intrinsically less interesting—a dilemma that he characterizes as a choice between Scylla and Charybdis—offering as examples "The 'Gloria Scott' " (1893) and *A Study in Scarlet,* assuming that the reader knows which is which. In effect, Conan Doyle has condi-

tioned his readership to finding both positive advantages—interesting cases and examples of genius—in each of the tales, and the critical dispute that occurs between Holmes and Watson remains strictly a show trial between the participants.

Conan Doyle has arranged for a constant tension to be operative within the canon between crime puzzles and feats of detection, proportionately balanced at the highest points of achievement but interesting in their dissension when the stress falls on one aspect rather than the other. Watson officiates at the balancing act, a narrative device to keep both potentials realizable. Nonetheless, the pivotal factor is invariably Sherlock Holmes, who had achieved so enormous a degree of personal popularity with readers that Conan Doyle was compelled to steer a course which took him well away from his passion for a good adventure story and to find ways occasionally to reconcile the two genres. Watson's ambivalence reflects that of the author, as seen in his statement in "The Adventure of the Illustrious Client" (1924): "Then he [Holmes] told the story, which I would repeat in this way. His hard, dry statement needs some little editing to soften it into the terms of real life" (p. 991). The Holmesian ego accounts for the insistence on the dry statement, but allows Watson's softening to take precedence once the hero has made his statement.

At the center of the Holmesian ego is that odd mixture of shrewdness and absurdity which reveals itself in Holmes's statements. Despite his control as chronicling voice, Watson has to accept the intrusion of dialogue, a major component in the narrative method that assists in softening the hard, dry facts. Watson's persistence in shaping that narrative is offset by Holmes's tendencies to explicate, elucidate, pontificate throughout. "I never can resist a touch of the dramatic," he confesses in "The Naval Treaty"—the dramatic for Holmes is often a euphemism for the practical joke, these touches providing heightened resolutions for such tales as "The Naval Treaty," "Silver Blaze," "The Adventure of the Norwood Builder" (1903), and "The Adventure of the Mazarin Stone." In these instances Holmes is providing Watson with sensational endings for the tales, belying his insistence on only "analytical reasoning." "I have an impish habit of practical joking," he admits; "Also that I can never resist a dramatic situation" ("The Adventure of the Mazarin Stone," 1921, p. 1022). At a heightened moment in "The Adventure of the Bruce-Partington Plans" (1908), after having fulfilled his function as an unemotional thinking machine and having solved the problem by analytical reasoning, his ecstasy turns him to literary immortality, as he alerts Watson: "Get foolscap and pen, and begin your narrative on how we saved the State" (p. 925).

Compared with Holmes's enthusiasms, Watson's narratives are models of restraint, ironically, because the chronicler is unable to keep clear of the performer as reigning star. It was Holmes, after all, who in "The Red-Headed League" quoted Flaubert: "L'homme c'est rién—l'ouevre c'est tout." Neither Watson nor Holmes is ever consistent on whether the focus should be on the detective or on the puzzle, the facts or the fancy, the rational or the dramatic, the inductive or the deductive. As Conan Doyle was constantly aware, the sixty Holmes narratives have their own organic and counterintentional reasons for being, as the nature of "antagonism" in the genre becomes apparent as an operative force.

Although Holmes and Watson are permitted individually to manipulate the dramatic situation and are manipulated by the inner dynamics of the mode of narration, these contradictions are neither resolved nor detrimental, but are artistically *contained* by the narrative. From Holmes's perspective Watson's chronicles are "little fairy tales," but he refers to them in his way with nostalgic fondness. There are moments at the end of a case, as in *The Hound of the Baskervilles,* for example, when he senses that the experience itself, in which he was fully in command at the time, is over, and the recapturing of that experience in literary prose (where Watson is fully in command) is about to begin. He lingers over the events at that conclusive moment, desirous of retaining his powers into the next stage, projecting his own blueprint for the writing: "I shall soon be in a position of being able to put into a single connected narrative one of the most singular and sensational crimes of modern times" (p. 753). Holmes has one more role to play before passing on the completed material to the chronicler: that of oral storyteller, first-person narration with himself in the dual roles of narrator and protagonist, unstinting in his presentation of the "sensational."

Yet when an unusual amount of time intervenes between the solving of the crime and the telling of the tale, Holmes proves to be a rather bumbling storyteller. "I cannot guarantee that I carry all the facts in my mind" (p. 761), he concedes, a failing that covers for the absence of certain facts which would have resulted in perfect closure, the wrapping up of all loose ends and answers to all remaining questions. The literal, scientific mind abdicates its function, as it does again with comic effect in "The Adventure of the Norwood Builder": Unable to get the perpetrator of the crime to explain what animals he used for the blood left behind as a false clue, Holmes jovially instructs Watson to make an arbitrary choice for his chronicle. "If ever you write an account, Watson, you can make rabbits serve your turn," he suggests, usurping the chronicler's prerogative in making the arbitrary choice (p. 510).

Conan Doyle is in effect exercising his authorial prerogative to educate his readers in the complexities of the narrative problems in the Sherlock Holmes stories as the continuing dialogue between the involved practitioners interweaves with the events. A primary target against which to set the literary method is that of the newspaper, so that journalistic narrative can serve as a contrast to Conan Doyle's art. Throughout the Holmes stories Conan Doyle displays a pixyish humor, but in *A Study in Scarlet* he also shows himself to be a master of literary pastiche, as he runs his plot material through three London daily papers, all of them managing to get things wrong on two levels: they have not yet accumulated the relevant facts and they lack the mode of narration necessary for evocative retelling. In evaluating the case in "The Adventure of the Engineer's Thumb" (1892) in retrospect, Watson comments:

The story has, I believe, been told more than once in the newspapers, but, like all such narratives, its effect is much less striking when set forth *en bloc* in a single half-column of print than when the facts slowly evolve before your own eyes, and the mystery clears gradually away as each new discovery furnishes a step which leads on to the complete truth.

(p. 274)

The literary artifact, therefore, is credited with letting "the facts slowly evolve," replicating actual experience, in contradistinction to the artlessness of newspaper reportage. Midway through "The Adventure of the Six Napoleons" (1904), Holmes has occasion to chuckle over a newspaper account that he condemns as "highly sensational and flowery."

The merits of the Holmes stories are also demonstrated by their author in contrast with another "literary" form, that brand of commercial fiction that lacks the artistic flair of Conan Doyle's offerings. Dr. Watson makes the value judgment in "The Boscombe Valley Mystery" (1891) when he tries to read a "yellow-backed novel" while Holmes is on the trail of a murderer: "The puny plot was so thin . . . compared to the deep mystery through which we were groping, and I found my attention wander so continually from the fiction to the fact, that I at last flung it across the room and gave myself up entirely to a consideration of the events of the day" (p. 209). The convention being entertained here is that the particular fiction of the day—the Holmes crime narrative—has the imprimatur of reality and that all other fiction, by comparison, is devoid of real facts.

Having dispensed with these two easy foils, the newspaper and the yellow-backed novel, the Sherlock Holmes story establishes its sovereignty, in which the chronicling Watson has his vested interest. In his scrupulous reportage of Sherlock Holmes's adventures, he jealously guards his territory, expressing his irritation when an internal narrator, Jonathan Small in *The Sign of Four,* holds forth at length in what amounts to his confession, Watson critical of the "somewhat flippant and careless way in which he narrated it" (p. 150). He is eager to reassert his narrative function, so that even dialogue is not immune from the chronicler's artistic pruning; and although the reader might assume that recorded speech is always presented exactly as intended by the speaker, the chronicler's blue pencil has been known to intervene on occasion: in "The Adventure of the Missing Three-Quarter" (1904) Watson quite casually refers to "many repetitions and obscurities which I may omit from his [Overton's] narrative" (p. 623).

The most overt example of these Watsonian rewritings occurs in *The Valley of Fear,* where John Douglas has written out in his own words the past events in Vermissa Valley and handed them over to Dr Watson: "Tell it your own way," he allows, "but these are the facts." Watson then takes over the narrational responsibility, prefacing *his* story of the Scowrers by saying, "I may lay before you a singular and terrible narrative—so singular and so terrible that you may find it hard to believe that even as I tell it, even so did it occur" (p. 815). The narrational tone and attitudes throughout that long portion of the novel mark it as vintage Watson, a replication of sorts of "The Country of the Saints," the long second part of *A Study in Scarlet,* with the typically Watsonian perspective perpetuating Conan Doyle's strong predilection for the adventure tale.

The Watson–Holmes tug-of-war over literary procedures works itself out to favor Watson for logic, but nonetheless affords Holmes a measure of operative idiosyncrasy. In *The Hound of the Baskervilles,* where Conan Doyle employs a succession of narrative modes to convey a long tale, Watson is obliged to report by mail to Holmes, acknowledging the irrevelancies within his reports—in other words, the "fiction" that makes the "facts" operate as a digestible narrative: "All this, however, is foreign to the mission on which you sent me," he notes early on, "and will probably be very uninteresting to your severely practical mind. I can still remember your complete indifference as to whether the sun moved round the earth or the earth round the sun" (p. 713). (To the reader, who does know the difference and is not as indifferent, Watson makes his logical appeal on behalf of his method.) Holmes, on the other hand, is not indifferent to a good resolution: "A fitting windup to an extremely interesting case," he comments in *The Sign of Four* (p. 157), not on his own participation in the windup, but on the closing remarks of Jonathan Small—although Watson still gets to add his own fitting windup.

Holmes's diverse role can be viewed, for example, in "A Case of Identity" (1891), when he and Watson are discussing the strangeness of human behavior and the contents of police reports, Holmes insisting that "a certain selection and discretion must be used in producing a realistic effect" (p. 191), positioning himself in Watson's camp at this instance more than in his own. At a moment of rare humility early in the case of "The Man with the Twisted Lip" (1891), he says, "I'll state the case clearly and concisely to you, Watson, and maybe you can see a spark where all is dark to me" (p. 233). Holmes can be credited with being disingenuous, but nonetheless he has exchanged roles, allowing that imaginative sparks must come into play in contact with dry facts; and it is of course his own imagination that solves the case and provides the material for a good story.

What Conan Doyle is constantly emphasizing is the "unique" quality of his detective fiction, how it rises to the heights of great storytelling through its uncompromising position within operative reality, yet superior to other means of narrative. When Sir Henry Baskerville begins to become aware of a mystery affecting him, he says to Holmes, "I seem to have walked right into the thick of a dime novel" (p. 688), an accurate observation that must be immediately belied for the sake of the narrative. The double bind insists on the difference between fiction and reality, as well as the difference between the fictitiousness of the dime novel (or yellow-backed novel) and the reality of the Holmesian fiction. In *The Valley of Fear* Holmes establishes the tricks of his trade—the tricks, that is, of Conan Doyle's trade:

> Watson insists that I am the dramatist in real life. . . . Some touch of the artist wells up within me, and calls insistently for a well staged performance. Surely our profession . . . would be a drab and sordid one if we did not sometimes set the scene so as to glorify our results. The blunt accusation, the brutal tap upon the shoulder—what can one make of such a *dénouement?* But the quick inference, the subtle trap, the clever forecast of coming events, the triumphant vindication of bold theories—are these not the pride and the justification of our life's work? At the present moment you thrill with the glamour of the situation and the anticipation of the hunt. Where would be that thrill if I had been as definite as a timetable?
>
> (p. 809)

Timetables are a basic bit of persiflage of Holmes's modus operandi, necessary for the trappings of reality but inoperative for the functioning of the narrative, and Holmes is quick to comment, "If criminals would always schedule their movements like railway trains, it would certainly be more convenient for all of us" (p. 809)—but these observations are interrupted by events and activities, the narrative superseding the commentary, and as quickly subsuming it.

The flow of those events and activities as narrative at times can be problematic, as Conan Doyle became aware early in the gestational stages of the Holmes canon, and he allows the frequent interruptions by Sherlock Holmes, accusative and self-castigating, to alert his readers to the active and complex process of narration. At the resolution of "The Problem of Thor Bridge," Holmes despairs of his deductive prowess: "I fear, Watson . . . that you will not improve any reputation which I may have acquired by adding the case of the Thor Bridge to your annals. I have been sluggish in mind and wanting in that mixture of imagination and reality which is the basis of my art" (pp. 1069–1070). Holmes's reputation with the readers of the canon, however, is for infallibility tempered by a hint of fallibility, the basis itself for the operative mixture. We have come full circle: this mixture of imagination and reality that Holmes professes at the end of the cycle returns us to Watson's inadvertent accusation at the beginning, that he finds a "remarkable mixture of shrewdness and of absurdity" in Holmes's article, "The Book of Life" (in *A Study in Scarlet*). When Holmes interrupts a Watson description in "The Adventure of the Retired Colourman" (1926) with the caustic remark, "Cut out the poetry, Watson," he underlines one of the elements that Conan Doyle never wanted deleted from a Sherlock Holmes narrative, its intrinsic poetry. Conan Doyle's methods of presentation gravitate between a scientific Scylla and a poetic Charybdis, much as Holmes's methods of deduction negotiate similar channels, despite his determined insistence on the cerebral.

THE POLITICS OF CRIME

THE England over which Holmes and Watson preside as guardians remains essentially late Victorian and early Edwardian, where crime was hardly unknown but certainly not a major social problem. For the effectiveness of the Holmes stories, Conan Doyle had to "create" a serious criminality to challenge Sherlock Holmes's ingenuity, yet at the same time reassure his reading public that these fictions did not reflect real danger in their lives. To this effect he varied his method between two extremes: on one hand, Holmes broods over the lack of crime and resorts to drugs to offset his boredom, and on the other hand, he exults over a "foeman worthy of our steel" (as in *The Hound of the Baskervilles,* where he uses this phrase twice). Initially, Conan Doyle created Professor Moriarty to be the instrument of Holmes's demise, the "Napoleon of crime" perishing with Holmes and leaving the world free of serious crime and no longer needing Holmes's ministrations. In "The Final Problem" Holmes reveals to Watson the existence of a vast criminal empire that he has succeeded in destroying, so that Moriarty's death would now end all threats to society. Just as Holmes had regretted the absence of any serious crime at the beginning of *A Study in Scarlet,* so in "The Adventure of the Norwood Builder," the second story in *The Return of Sherlock Holmes,* he expresses the sentiment that "London has become a singularly uninteresting city since the death of the late lamented Professor Moriarty" (p. 496).

Endowing the Holmes stories with the requisite atmosphere, however, meant stress on London as a "cesspool" (*A Study in Scarlet*) and a "dark jungle" ("The Adventure of the Empty House"), although in "The Five Orange Pips" (1891) the reigning sentiment is that "we are in a civilized land here," where the criminal violence of other nations (the United States in this case) cannot reach—and yet of course it does. Several of the early stories are not criminal cases at all, but puzzles for Sherlock Holmes to solve where crime is suspected but finally shown not to be evident. In "The Adventure of the Blue Carbuncle" (1892) Watson acknowledges that "of the last six cases which I have added to my notes, three have been entirely free of any legal crime" (p. 245), and although this particular case involves a serious larceny, Holmes allows the thief to depart unapprehended and unpunished, assuring Watson that he has learned his lesson and will henceforth be a law-abiding citizen. As for the major crime of murder, considered essential in the twentieth century for all crime novels, there are certainly numerous murder cases for Sherlock Holmes, but they are in the minority in the short stories (although present in all four of the novels). In one instance, in "The Adventure of Charles Augustus Milverton" (1904), Holmes allows the murderer to escape and condones the murdering of the blackmailer.

Like many other crime writers who followed in his footsteps, Conan Doyle displays a particular antipathy for blackmail, and both in the Milverton case and in the earlier "A Scandal in Bohemia" (1891) he allows Holmes and Watson to break into a private residence with the intention of stealing the blackmail evidence. It is not unusual for a staunch supporter of the status quo and upholder of the mores of upper-middle-class society to view the blackmailer as a major threat, especially when a stringent moral code that did not necessarily re-flect the life-style of some members of the dominant social group was in effect. Yet Conan Doyle is also careful to assure that the blackmail victims in his cases are relatively blameless, even if they are the prey of blackmailers, real or potential. Sherlock Holmes is frequently allowed to make moral decisions that transcend the legal guilt of those he apprehends, and in some cases—with Watson providing the approval of the solid middle class—he acts as judge and jury. Where the murder victim is revealed as particularly heinous, as in "The Adventure of the Abbey Grange," the detective and his companion decide that it was justifiable homicide and allow the killer to go free—and even invite him back in a year's time to marry the widow.

With at least sixty criminals for Holmes to apprehend (although some stories have no crimes at all, others have more than one involved criminal), it would be impossible to avoid unmasking native residents of England as the culprits. Nonetheless, Conan Doyle provides a host of "foreigners" as the perpetrators of crime in England, implicitly supporting certain xenophobic tendencies prevalent in his Britain. Particularly virulent are the American Mormons in *A Study in Scarlet* (the author apparently accepting the existing mistrust in his country of that "unorthodox" religious group) and the Irish–American gangsters in *The Valley of Fear* (the author in this case taking the side of those who considered the "Molly Maguires" of the Pennsylvania mines to be criminals rather than radical activists). The most exotic killer, however, is the diminutive Andaman Islander in *The Sign of Four,* a tale replete with Hindus and Muslims and Sikhs and Pathans, although the operative villain is a low-class Englishman.

Conan Doyle's tendency to balance various perspectives evenhandedly allows that villain to sound convincing in voicing his strong anticolonial sentiment when he repeats the tempting offer made by the Indians who conscripted him: "We only ask you to do that which your countrymen came to this land for. We ask you to be rich" (p. 147). Even more powerful are the arguments of the Scowrers (Conan Doyle's version of the Molly Maguires) regarding "a war of two classes with all in, so that each struck as best it could" (p. 841), and condemning the police as "paid tools of the capitalists, hired by them to club or shoot your poorer fellow citizen" (p. 831). But these sentiments are immediately suspect because the first is a pretense by the Pinkerton detective who infiltrated the Scowrers and the second is a cynical rationalization by the criminal leader of the organization.

The England that these stories describe is a tolerant and peace-loving country into which various foreigners infiltrate; some of them come for criminal purposes and others bring with them less civilized modes of behavior. American gangsterism is, of course, an accepted concept; Holmes claims that "Americans are readier with pistols than our folks are," but this statement is in "The Problem of Thor Bridge" (p. 1062), written when Prohibition was in full swing in America. Despite Conan Doyle's special fondness for Americans and his announced vision of a reunited United States–United Kingdom, American gangsters make their appearance in his England in such tales as "The Adventure of the Dancing Men" (1903) and "The Adventure of the Three Garridebs." In *The Valley of Fear,* however, when the Pinkerton detective is tracked down and eventually killed, Moriarty's criminal empire gets the credit as the extended arm of the Scowrers.

For more politically obvious reasons, Germans—or at least people with German accents and German names—are frequently the criminals in the Holmes cases, more so in the tales written during the years immediately prior to World War I; but the list of suspicious aliens is a long one and includes Greeks, Italians, Russians, Austrians, Bohemians, Czechs, Slavs, Hungarians, Malayans, and Sumatrans. The colonies provide Australians, New Zealanders, and Canadians, but this is also a two-way road, since certain characters are "sent" to the colonies when they prove to be undesirables rather than indictable criminals. The New World provides a large number of people who display antisocial behavior—Brazilians, Costa Ricans, Creoles, Central Americans, West Indians, and Peruvians—although they are not necessarily criminals as much as people from countries where the possibilities of criminal behavior are particurarly discernible. For obvious reasons Conan Doyle steers clear of either the Scots or the Irish; when it becomes a matter of a violently Celtic personality, the culprit is described as "of Welsh blood, fiery and passionate." And Gypsies of course are routinely suspect, as in "Silver Blaze," but too obvious to be seriously implicated.

A mild element of chauvinism appears on occasion in the tales, taking the form of a warning at the resolution of *A Study in Scarlet:* "A lesson to all foreigners that they will do wisely to settle their feuds at home, and not to carry them on to British soil" (p. 86). The warning notwithstanding, Italian immigrants wield their knives in the streets of London—as in "The Adventure of the Six Napoleons"—and Italian secret societies attempt to assassinate their defectors in respectable London neighborhoods—as in "The Adventure of the Red Circle" (1911). In the former the criminal activities are placed on the doorstep of a Neapolitan "connected with the Mafia," which Holmes describes as "a secret political society"; in the latter the organization is fictionalized as "a Neapolitan society, the Red Circle, which was allied to the old Carbonari."

From *A Study in Scarlet* the stress is often on such foreign entities "invading" peaceful England, although long before he realizes that the Mormons are at the heart of the mystery, Holmes dismisses the idea that the case involves "Socialism and secret societies." Nonetheless, the popular press keeps referring to the "Vehmgericht" and the "Carbonari," and when Holmes learns of the Mormon connection, he asserts, "Not the Inquisition of Seville, nor the German Vehmgericht, nor the secret societies of Italy, were ever able to put a more formidable machinery in motion than that which cast a cloud over the state of Utah" (p. 62). To augment these exotic menaces, there is also the Ku Klux Klan, which in "The Five Orange Pips" reaches to England to claim its victims.

While continually reaffirming the basic security of British society and the moral basis on which the nation's strength resides, the Holmes stories also call attention to a need for vigilance against external threats to the system, some aspects of which are already present on the immediate periphery. In "The Adventure of the Six Napoleons" the reader is taken on a tour of the complex layers of London life: "In rapid succession we passed through the fringe of fashionable London, hotel London, theatrical London, literary London, commercial London, and, finally, maritime London, till we came to a riverside city of a hundred thousand souls, where the tenement houses swelter and reek with the outcasts of Europe" (p. 588). There is a conflation throughout the tales between criminal societies and underground political organizations that becomes more political in the later ones, where the emphasis may well be merely comic and far-fetched, as voiced by an Englishman in "The Adventure of the Six Napoleons": "A Nihilist plot!—that's what I make it. No one but an anarchist would go about breaking statues. Red republicans—that's what I call 'em" (p. 588). Or it may be in deadly earnest: "We are reformers—revolutionists—Nihilists, you understand" (p. 619), even if the political positions are somewhat confused in a jumble of labels and scare words. The latter instance is from "The Adventure of the Golden Pince-Nez" (1904), a tale that uncovers Russian terrorists in a quiet English village in the year 1894.

The threat posed by imperial Germany results in the handful of espionage stories, Holmes being more frequently credited with serving his country than there are actual cases to document his career as a counteragent, although the four spy stories may be seen as providing the genesis of that particular subgenre. The existence of master spies offers the necessary "foemen" worthy of Holmes's steel in "The Adventure of the Second Stain" (1904) and "The Adventure of the Bruce-Partington Plans," where the names of these known operatives are given as "Oberstein," "La Rothière," and "Eduardo Lucas" in the first, and "Adolph Meyer," "Louis La Rothière," and "Hugo Oberstein" in the second (Lucas having been killed in the first).

By 1914 the German threat had of course become a reality, and three years later Conan Doyle wrote his ultimate spy story, set in the opening moments of the war: "His Last Bow," subtitled "An Epilogue of Sherlock Holmes." Disguised as an Irish American in the pay of the German embassy, Holmes has come out of retirement to serve his country, and manages to foil a nefarious plot against the nation, in a situation that allows a platform for political propaganda. One of the German diplomats denigrates the British as "docile, simple folk," although the other cautions against judging them superficially: "It is that surface simplicity of theirs which makes a trap for the stranger. One's first impression is that they are entirely soft. Then one comes suddenly upon something very hard, and you know that you have reached the limit and must adapt yourself to the fact" (p. 971). In his anti-British guise Holmes pretends to gloat over British inertia and unpreparedness, and the power of the Irish insurrection ("a devil's brew of Irish civil war") to undermine the war effort. Conan Doyle

threw himself wholeheartedly into that war effort: managing to do his own local recruiting after his age prevented him from being enlisted, obtaining an honorary commission and having his own uniform specially tailored, sending ideas for weapons and tunnels to be used in the War to the government, and maintaining a voluminous correspondence with British generals, as well as visiting the battlefields and publishing his propaganda writings, of which "His Last Bow" seems to be little more than an afterthought.

Throughout his life Conan Doyle held strong political views, and even stood for Parliament on two occasions, losing both times despite his public renown. These views could hardly be expected to surface in his detective fiction, a genre usually dismissed as escapist and consequently irrelevant to the political realities of the time; yet more than just an obvious national pride, a fervent patriotism in time of war, and a defense of national values and the status quo, filter through the Sherlock Holmes narratives. One might dismiss the two references in these narratives to the Boer War, about which Conan Doyle wrote extensively and passionately, as merely the indicators of a date in time (which is all they are); but one cannot overlook the allusion in "The Adventure of the Second Stain" to a letter "from a certain foreign potentate who has been ruffled by some recent Colonial developments of this country" (p. 653), a misguided attitude that could at the time of the story prove an embarrassment if publicly exposed—putting to rest the condemnation of Britain's role in the South African war.

Conan Doyle frequently tried to assess the international political schemes in which Europe was enmeshed in the years preceding 1914, so that in his first spy story, "The Naval Treaty," he refers to a "secret treaty between England and Italy" that must not leak out—"The French or the Russian embassy would pay an immense sum to learn the contents of these papers" (p. 450)—and in "The Adventure of the Second Stain" we are told, "The whole of Europe is an armed camp. There is a double league which makes a fair balance of military power. Great Britain holds the scales" (p. 653).

On the home scene Conan Doyle campaigned diligently for changing the divorce laws under which women were inhumanely disadvantaged, a campaign that is unmistakably asserted in "The

Adventure of the Abbey Grange" and "The Adventure of the Devil's Foot"; Conan Doyle's equally virulent opposition to women's suffrage, however, does not surface at all in the Holmes stories. It was conceivable that a bad marital situation could lead to violence, as in "The Adventure of the Abbey Grange" and "The Adventure of the Devil's Foot," but since Conan Doyle could not imagine a criminal occurrence evolving from women casting their ballots, the issue never arises in Holmes's narratives.

CONCLUSION

THE enduring popularity of Conan Doyle's series of Sherlock Holmes fictions depends primarily on the creation of a self-contained world that defines its own dynamics and adheres to its own rules but remains centered in an acceptably realistic frame. Each narrative fulfills its own logic within that construct and amplifies the whole, so that the various discrepancies that are of such interest to the Sherlockians and Holmesians as subject matter for their versions of "higher criticism" fail to disturb the existing framework. Watson's wound is alternately in the shoulder and in the leg, his wife once calls him James instead of John, both Professor Moriarty and his brother are named James, Holmes attended Oxford *and* Cambridge, Inspector Lestrade is "ferret-like" in *A Study in Scarlet* but has "bulldog features" in "The Second Stain," *The Sign of Four* takes place simultaneously in July and September, but these discrepancies hardly disturb the seamless weave of the Holmesian ambience.

Composed of moody atmospheric touches, concentrated enigmas, and sustained action, with occasional gothic moments and even elements of the grotesque, as well as "pawkish" humor, philosophic asides, and moralistic observations, the canon has an intrinsic validity that time has only mellowed in a reexperiencing of the historic context. As an insignificant character observes in *The Sign of Four*, "It is a romance! . . . An injured lady, half a million in treasure, a black cannibal, and a wooden-legged ruffian. They take the place of the conventional dragon or wicked earl" (p. 129). Sherlock Holmes would find it necessary to object, but as an author Dr Watson would recognize the basics there of the literary formula.

SELECTED BIBLIOGRAPHY

I. BIBLIOGRAPHIES. H. Locke, *A Bibliographical Catalogue of the Writings of Sir Arthur Conan Doyle, M. D., LL. D., 1879–1928* (Tunbridge Wells, U.K., 1928); R. B. De Waal, *The World Bibliography of Sherlock Holmes and Dr. Watson: A Classified and Annotated List of Materials Relating to Their Lives and Adventures* (New York, 1974); B. R. Reece, *A Bibliography of First Appearances of the Writings of A. Conan Doyle* (Greenville, S.C., 1975); R. L. Green and J. M. Gibson, *A Bibliography of A. Conan Doyle* (Oxford and New York, 1983); D. A. Redmond, *Sherlock Holmes Among the Pirates: Copyright and Conan Doyle in America, 1890–1930* (New York, 1990).

II. COLLECTED WORKS. *The Professor Challenger Stories* (London, 1952); *The Complete Sherlock Holmes,* 2 vols. (Garden City, N.Y., 1953, 1960), continuously paginated; *Strange Studies from Life: Containing Three Hitherto Uncollected Tales* (New York, 1963); *The Annotated Sherlock Holmes,* 2 vols., William S. Baring-Gould, ed. (New York, 1967); *Tales of Terror & Mystery* (Garden City, N.J., 1977); *The Best Supernatural Tales of Arthur Conan Doyle,* E. F. Bleiler, ed. (New York, 1979); *Further Adventures of Sherlock Holmes* (New York, 1981); *The Unknown Conan Doyle: Essays on Photography,* J. M. Gibson and R. L. Green, eds. (London, 1982); *The Unknown Conan Doyle: Uncollected Stories,* J. M. Gibson and R. L. Green, eds. (London, 1982); *The Illustrated Sherlock Holmes* (New York, 1984); *Adventures of the Speckled Band and Other Stories of Sherlock Holmes* (New York, 1985); *Sherlock Holmes: The Complete Novels and Stories,* 2 vols. (New York, 1986); *Thirty-three by Conan Doyle* (New York, 1986); *Strange Studies from Life & Other Narratives: The Complete True Crime Writings of Sir Arthur Conan Doyle* (Bloomington, Ind., 1988); *Tales for a Winter's Night* Chicago, 1988).

III. SEPARATE WORKS. *A Study in Scarlet* (London and New York, 1888); *Micah Clarke* (London, 1889); *Mysteries and Adventures* (London, 1889); *The Mystery of Cloomber* (London, 1889); *The Captain of the "Pole-Star" and Other Tales* (London, 1890); *The Firm of Girdlestone* (London, 1890); *The Sign of Four* (London, 1890); *The Doings of Raffles Haw* (New York, 1891); *The White Company,* 3 vols. (London, 1891); *The Adventures of Sherlock Holmes* (London, 1892), the first collection of Sherlock Holmes stories; *The Great Shadow* (Bristol, 1892); *The Great Shadow and Beyond the City* (Bristol, 1893); *The Refugees,* 3 vols. (London, 1893); *An Actor's Duel and the Winning Shot* (London, 1894); *The Memoirs of Sherlock Holmes* (London, 1894), the second collection of Sherlock Holmes stories; *The Parasite* (London, 1894); *Round the Red Lamp: Being Facts and Fancies of Medical Life* (London, 1894); *The Stark Munro Letters* (London, 1895); *The Exploits of Brigadier Gerard* (London, 1896); *Rodney Stone* (London, 1896); *Uncle Bernac: A Memory of the Empire* (London, 1897); *The Tragedy of the "Korosko"* (London, 1898); *Songs of Action* (London, 1898), poems; *A Duet, with an Occasional Chorus* (London, 1899).

The Great Boer War (London, 1900); *The Green Flag and*

Other Stories of War and Sport (London, 1900); *Hilda Wade: A Woman with Tenacity of Purpose* (London, 1900), written with G. Allan; *The Immortal Memory* (Edinburgh, 1901); *The Hound of the Baskervilles* (London, 1902); *The War in South Africa: Its Cause and Conduct* (London, 1902); *The Adventures of Gerard* (London, 1903); *The Fiscal Question: Treated in a Series of Three Speeches* (Hawick, U.K., 1905); *The Return of Sherlock Holmes* (London, 1905), the third collection of Sherlock Holmes stories; *An Incursion into Diplomacy* (London, 1906); *Sir Nigel* (London, 1906); *The Croxley Master: A Great Tale of the Prize Ring* (New York, 1907); *The Story of Mr. George Edalji* (London, 1907); *Through the Magic Door* (London, 1907); *Round the Fire: Stories* (London, 1908); *The Crime of the Congo* (London, 1909); *Divorce Law Reform: An Essay* (London, 1909).

The Last Galley: Impressions and Tales (London, 1911); *Sir Arthur Conan Doyle: Why He Is Now in Favour of Home Rule* (London, 1911); *Songs of the Road* (London, 1911); *The Case of Oscar Slater* (London, 1912); *The Lost World* (London, 1912); *The Speckled Band: An Adventure of Sherlock Holmes* (New York and London, 1912); *The Poison Belt* (London, 1913); *The German War* (London, 1914); *Great Britain and the Next War* (Boston, 1914); *To Arms!* (London, 1914); *The Valley of Fear* (London, 1915); *A Visit to Three Fronts* (London, 1916); *The British Campaign in France and Flanders*, 6 vols. (London, 1916–1919); *His Last Bow: Some Reminiscences of Sherlock Holmes* (London, 1917), the fourth collection of Sherlock Holmes stories; *Danger! and Other Stories* (London, 1918); *The New Revelation* (London, 1918); *The Vital Message* (London, 1919); *Spiritualism and Rationalism* (London, 1920); *The Wanderings of a Spiritualist* (London, 1921); *The Case for Spirit Photography* (London, 1922); *The Coming of the Fairies* (London, 1922); *The Poems of Arthur Conan Doyle: Collected Edition* (London, 1922); *Our American Adventure* (London, 1923); *Three of Them: A Reminiscence* (London, 1923); *Memories and Adventures* (London and Boston, 1924); *Our Second American Adventure* (London, 1924); *Psychic Experiences* (London, 1925); *The History of Spiritualism*, 2 vols. (London, 1926); *The Land of Mist* (London, 1926); *The Case-Book of Sherlock Holmes* (London, 1927), the fifth collection of Sherlock Holmes stories; *Pheneas Speaks* (London, 1927); *The Maracot Deep and Other Stories* (London, 1929); *Our African Winter* (London, 1929); *The Edge of the Unknown* (London, 1930); *The Field Bazaar* (London, 1934).

IV. THEATRICAL WORKS. *Jane Annie; or, The Good Conduct Prize: A New and Original English Comic Opera* (London, 1893), written with J. M. Barrie; *A Duet (A Duologue)* (London, 1903); *Waterloo* (London and New York, 1907). *The Crown Diamond* (London, 1921).

V. LETTERS. *Letters to the Press*, J. M. Gibson and R. L. Green, comps. (London, 1986); *The Secret Conan Doyle Correspondence*, L. Harper, ed. (Provo, Utah, 1986).

VI. BIOGRAPHICAL STUDIES. J. Lamond, *Arthur Conan Doyle: A Memoir* (London, 1931); H. Pearson, *Conan Doyle: His Life and Art* (London, 1943); A. C. Doyle, *The True Conan Doyle* (London, 1945); J. D. Carr, *The Life of Sir Arthur Conan Doyle* (London and New York, 1949); M. Hardwick and M. Hardwick, *The Man Who Was Sherlock Holmes* (London and New York, 1964); P. Nordon, *Sir Arthur Conan Doyle: L'Homme et l'oeuvre* (Paris, 1964), trans. by F. Partridge as *Conan Doyle: A Biography* (London, 1966); I. Brown, *Conan Doyle, a Biography of the Creator of Sherlock Holmes* (London, 1972); C. Higham, *The Adventures of Conan Doyle: The Life of the Creator of Sherlock Holmes* (New York and London, 1976); R. Pearsall, *Conan Doyle: A Biographical Solution* (London and New York, 1977); J. Symons, *Conan Doyle: Portrait of an Artist* (London, 1979); O. D. Edwards, *The Quest for Sherlock Holmes: A Biographical Study of Arthur Conan Doyle* (Edinburgh, 1983); J. L. Lellenberg, ed., *The Quest for Sir Arthur Conan Doyle: Thirteen Biographers in Search of a Life* (Carbondale, Ill., 1987).

VII. CRITICAL STUDIES. H. W. Bell, *Sherlock Holmes and Dr. Watson: The Chronology of Their Adventures* (London, 1932); T. S. Blakeney, *Sherlock Holmes: Fact or Fiction?* (London, 1932); V. Starrett, *The Private Life of Sherlock Holmes* (New York, 1933; rev. and enl. ed., Chicago, 1960), and, as ed., *221B: Studies in Sherlock Holmes* (New York, 1940); H. W. Bell, ed., *Baker Street Studies* (London, 1934); E. W. Smith, ed., *Profile by Gaslight: An Irregular Reader About the Private Life of Sherlock Holmes* (New York, 1944); D. Sayers, *Unpopular Opinions* (London, 1946); G. Warrack, *Sherlock Holmes and Music* (London, 1947); G. Brend, *My Dear Holmes: A Study in Sherlock* (London, 1951); E. W. McDiarmid and T. C. Blegen, eds., *Sherlock Holmes: Master Detective* (La Crosse, Wis., 1952); S. C. Roberts, *Holmes and Watson: A Miscellany* (London, 1953); E. W. Smith, ed., *The Incunabular Sherlock Holmes* (New York, 1957); M. Harrison, *In the Footsteps of Sherlock Holmes* (London, 1958).

W. S. Baring-Gould, *Sherlock Holmes of Baker Street: A Life of the World's First Consulting Detective* (New York and London, 1962); M. Hardwick and M. Hardwick, *The Sherlock Holmes Companion* (London, 1962); W. Klinefelter, *Sherlock Holmes in Portrait and Profile* (Syracuse, N.Y., 1963); M. Harrison, *The London of Sherlock Holmes* (Newton Abbot, U.K., 1972); P. Haining, ed., *The Sherlock Holmes Scrapbook* (New York, 1974); S. Rosenberg, *Naked Is the Best Disguise: The Death and Resurrection of Sherlock Holmes* (Indianapolis, 1974); M. Pointer, *The Public Life of Sherlock Holmes* (Newton Abbot, U.K., and New York, 1975); M. Harrison, ed., *Beyond Baker Street: A Sherlockian Anthology* (New York, 1976); J. Tracy, ed., *The Encyclopaedia Sherlockiana* (Garden City, N.Y., 1977); B. L. Crawford, Jr., and J. B. Connors, eds., *Cultivating Sherlock Holmes* (La Crosse, Wis., 1978); T. H. Hall, *Sherlock Holmes and His Creator* (New York, 1978); C. Steinbrunner and N. Michaels, *The Films of Sherlock Holmes* (Secaucus, N.J., 1978); H. R. F. Keating, *Sherlock Holmes: The Man and His World* (New York, 1979).

S. R. Bullard and M. Collins, *Who's Who in Sherlock Holmes* (New York, 1980); J. Tracy, ed., *Sherlock Holmes: The*

Published Apocrypha (Boston, 1980); E. M. Liebow, *Dr. Joe Bell: Model for Sherlock Holmes* (Bowling Green, Ohio, 1982); D. A. Redmond, *Sherlock Holmes: A Study in Sources* (Kingston and Montreal, 1982); U. Eco and T. A. Sebeok, eds., *The Sign of Three: Dupin, Holmes, Peirce* (Bloomington, Ind., 1983); R. Butters, *First Person Singular: A Review of the Life and Work of Mr. Sherlock Holmes, the World's First Consulting Detective* (New York, 1984); M. Harrison, *A Study in Surmise: The Making of Sherlock Holmes* (Bloomington, Ind., 1984); J. McNabb, *The Curious Incident of the Hound on Dartmoor: A Reconsideration of the Origins of the Hound of the Baskervilles* (Toronto, 1984); A. E. Rodin and J. D. Key, *The Medical Casebook of Dr. Arthur Conan Doyle: From Practitioner to Sherlock Holmes and Beyond* (Malabar, Fla., 1984); P. A. Shreffler, ed., *The Baker Street Reader: Cornerstone Writings About Sherlock Holmes* (Westport, Conn., 1984); D. R. Cox, *Arthur Conan Doyle* (New York, 1985); W. D. Goodrich, *The Sherlock Holmes Reference Guide* (Bloomington, Ind., 1985); G. E. Sundin, *Sherlock's London Today: A Walking Tour of the London of Sherlock Holmes* (Des Plaines, Ill., 1985); R. A. Brown, *Sherlock Holmes and the Mysterious Friend of Oscar Wilde* (New York, 1988).

WILLIAM EMPSON

(1906–1984)

Michael Wood

WILLIAM EMPSON IS one of the twentieth century's greatest critics, and a poet whose work will always find a place in the anthologies. His reputation has at various times glittered, faded a little, and now seems to be glowing again. In comparison with the moral and social directness of the writing of F. R. Leavis and Lionel Trilling, Empson's criticism has seemed eccentric; compared with the theoretical work of Roland Barthes or Paul de Man, it has seemed a little too full of blunt common sense. On inspection, it appears that Empson questions the traditions that create the very idea of the eccentric, and that his common sense invites, although it does not spell out, theoretical considerations of the most far-reaching kind. Empson's early poems, strongly influenced by the work of John Donne and other metaphysical poets, seek to place the intense personal emotions of lovers and isolated thinkers in the context of the vast scientific and social discoveries of the modern age—among the galaxies, so to speak, but also among alien gods and the dark new territories of the psyche. Later poems engage issues of courage and responsibility in an always slightly distanced political context.

LIFE

EMPSON was born at Yorkefleet Hall, Yorkshire, on 27 September 1906. The youngest of the five children of Arthur Reginald and Laura Micklethwaite Empson, he was educated at Winchester College and Magdalene College, Cambridge. The first part of his first-class Cambridge degree was in mathematics; the second, in English. He was about to take up a fellowship for further study when he was discovered to have been more than entertaining a young woman in his rooms, and in June 1929 was sent back to Yorkshire in disgrace—those were stern days in sexual matters. Empson took the matter seriously but not gloomily, and wrote a witty poem about the hypocrisy and gossip of Cambridge, "that strange cackling little town" ("Warning to Undergraduates," from *The Royal Beasts*). He seemed set for a literary rather than a scholarly career anyway. He had written movie, theater, and book reviews as an undergraduate—Empson reviewed Fritz Lang's 1926 masterpiece, *Metropolis,* for example—had had a short play performed in the student theater, and was gathering poems for a first collection, which he offered to a publisher at the same time as *Seven Types of Ambiguity,* which appeared in 1930.

Empson had to wait for five years to see his first volume of verse, although quite a few poems had already been published in magazines and he was acquiring a reputation, having been reviewed by F. R. Leavis ("a tough intellectual content," Leavis found, and "an intense preoccupation with technique"). By 1935 Empson had taught English at two universities in Japan (following the traditional practice of English scholars teaching English literature in the East), and had also, in that same year, published his second critical book, *Some Versions of Pastoral.* From Japan, after a time back in London (1934–1937), he went to China, where he accompanied the universities on the Long March and wrote one of his happiest and most memorable poems, "Autumn on Nan-Yueh." When World War II broke out in 1939, Empson returned to London, where he worked with George Orwell in broadcasting and later became a Chinese editor for the BBC. Meanwhile, Empson published a second volume of verse, *The Gathering Storm* (1940), a title Winston Churchill seems to have borrowed; and versions of his *Collected Poems* appeared in 1949 and 1955. In 1941 Empson married Hester Henrietta Crouse; they had two sons. After a postwar stint at Peking University, interspersed with visits to Kenyon College in Ohio, in 1953 he assumed the chair of English literature at the University of Sheffield, where he remained until his retirement in 1971. He died in London on 15 April 1984.

Empson wrote few poems after 1940 and, as far as is known, none after 1952, apart from a faint ceremonial flutter for the queen's visit to Sheffield in 1954. His poetic silence has been the cause of much speculation. Empson said he gave up writing verse because his work was "too tight," but the remark itself requires interpretation and we may think other thoughts. Had Empson perhaps become happy enough not to need to write poetry? He always insisted that poetry was therapy, a matter of getting thoughts and feelings into acceptable verbal order, of persuading fright or doubt, for example, into memorable lyrical form. The poem "Success" (1940)[1] gracefully thanks a companion for taking "torment and the fear" away ("Lose is Find with great marsh lights like you"), and suggests that "verse likes despair." But the poem also ruefully reflects on how "all losses haunt us," so that even torment and fear might be missed when they were gone. There is plenty of wit and energy left here, and despair cannot be the only thing verse likes. More convincingly we might argue that Empson felt that writing poetry had become too dangerous for him, still conceivable as art but the reverse of therapy, a sort of desperate springboard for insanity. "Let It Go" (1949), one of the very last of Empson's poems, suggests that while "blankness" is strange, "talk" is likely to be worse. I quote the whole poem, since its very brevity and terseness mime its worry about both words and their absence:

It is this deep blankness is the real thing strange.
  The more things happen to you the more you can't
    Tell or remember even what they were.

The contradictions cover such a range.
  The talk would talk and go so far aslant.
    You don't want madhouse and the whole thing there.

Seven Types of Ambiguity was reprinted many times (1947, 1953, 1955, 1961, and later), and continued to exert an enormous influence on the New Criticism. The book seemed to give support to an anti-intentionalist stance and encourage over-subtlety, an interpretation which Empson sometimes regretted. *The Structure of Complex Words* (1951), which Empson had begun in China, extends the exploration of language initiated in *Seven Types,* and *Milton's God* (1961) is an embattled exploration of Milton's struggles with his theology. We may like to remember that Empson's first recorded poem, written when he was thirteen, concerns a little girl called Anne who refuses to have angels guarding her bed and throws pillows at them to scare them off.

Empson wrote reviews and essays in the 1960's and 1970's; edited Coleridge; and gathered some old and new work in *Using Biography* (1984) and what was to become *Essays on Shakespeare* (1986). A second posthumous collection, the voluminous *Argufying* (1987), revealed just how much uncollected material there had been. *The Royal Beasts* (1986) brought together some unpublished and uncollected poems, a play, a fable, and a ballet, all of them quite old—the play, for instance, was the undergraduate production mentioned earlier. The story seemed to be over, effectively to have been over since the Milton book, when Empson posthumously surprised everyone with a startling new work: *Faustus and the Censor,* a manuscript patiently recovered and edited by John Henry Jones, and published in 1987, three years after Empson's death.

POEMS

MANY of the pieces gathered in *Poems,* Empson's 1935 volume, had been written and published earlier, and it makes sense to look at these before turning to the criticism, since Empson was practicing ambiguity before he elaborated a theory of it. He hoped the word "air," for instance, in his first printed work, "Poem About a Ball in the Nineteenth Century" (1927), would suggest not only "tune" but also "atmosphere" and "grand manner"—the latter as in "to give oneself airs." The three meanings in this case do not so much clash as hover around each other, casting faint semantic shadows, leaving the reader in a mild, not unpleasant uncertainty.

The poem is a verbal exercise in the manner of Gertrude Stein, a trail of associations in words, but

---

[1]The date in parentheses after the title of a poem indicates the year of its initial publication, except where indicated.

it does not exactly, as Empson later apologetically remarked in the "Notes" to *Collected Poems*, "disregard meaning." It generates meaning through echoes and similarities and modulations of sound rather than through logic or a conceptual program, and conjures up a rather poignant sense of a slight but vanished world. If read aloud (or if heard as read by Empson on the recording he made in 1959), it acquires an odd incantatory power, and is all the more mysterious for its "air" of nonsense:

feather feather, dancing and to declare for turning
    turning
a feather as it were for dancing, turning for dancing,
    dancing
being begun turning together, together to be become,
    barely a
feather being, beware, being a peacock only on the
    stair,
staring at, only a peacock to be coming, fairly
    becoming for
a peacock, be fair together being around in air,
    peacock to
be becoming lastly, peacock around to be become
    together,
peacock a very peacock to be there.
    . . .
Will he be there, can he be there, be there?

Being a feathered peacock.

Only a feathered peacock on the stair.

This poem, with its intimations of Wallace Stevens as well as of Gertrude Stein, is important for what it suggests about Empson's view of language. He was a strenuous opponent of the then fashionable doctrine of "pure poetry," and always insisted that good poems were more than sound and sensibility, that they contained arguments and propositions, could be discussed, even quarreled with. Picking up the accusation that critics are dogs who bark at poetry, he thought there might be two sorts of dogs,

those who merely relieve themselves against the flower of beauty, and those, less continent, who afterwards scratch it up. I myself, I must confess, aspire to the second of these classes; unexplained beauty arouses an irritation in me, a sense that this would be a good place to scratch; the reasons that make a line of verse likely to give pleasure, I believe, are like the reasons for anything else; one can reason about them; and while it may be true that the roots of beauty ought not to be violated, it seems

to me very arrogant of the appreciative critic to think that he could do this, if he chose, by a little scratching.
(*Seven Types*, p. 9)

Empson's own poems, apart from the one just quoted, are crowded with intellect and allusion, sometimes almost muscle-bound with meaning. But the *possibility* of multiple, floating implications is important to both kinds of poetry—indeed, we may want to see the associative kind as the key to the other. If we could not play with words in the manner of "Poem About a Ball . . . ," we could not play with concepts and images in the manner of John Donne. The scratching dog, we notice, does not claim his scratching will necessarily explain beauty, only that an explanation would be worth having and that the scratching will not do any harm.

Another early poem, "Song of the Amateur Psychologist" (1926, published only posthumously, in *The Royal Beasts*), introduces us to a persistent fear in Empson's work, and to an image that makes the findings of Freud seem both domestic and threatening. The mind is presented as a cellar that continues infinitely down into the dark:

> Let us descend now
> but carefully, they are high steps
> and steep, for walking.
> After a dozen of them
> there is an even darkness
> that has waited so long
> it is not a light thing to disturb,
>   . . .
> Might there not be—might there not—
> the unchained
> the insane perspective
> the no end
> and your cry recoiling— . . .

We may hear an echo of T. S. Eliot's cadences here, and Empson later said he was not sure how much of his poetic mind Eliot had invented (*Argufying*, p. 361); but we also hear the eerie alternations of sound *and* meaning in "unchained" and "insane," and note the seemingly frivolous double meaning of "light." There is room for wit and playfulness even in these underground zones; the mind is unwilling to concentrate exclusively on its gloom.

Even more than the new psychology, the new physics and the new anthropology attracted and perturbed Empson's generation in England. Einstein's work on relativity and Sir James Frazer's comparative compilations of ritual practices and mythology, coming in the wake of Darwin's radical revision of human biology, suggested that science, religion, and culture all needed rethinking. This was one of the great affinities between the early twentieth century and the early seventeenth. "The New Philosophy calls all in doubt," Donne had said, alluding to the beginnings of modern science, and much that had for some time been certain now seemed to be in doubt again. These developments were exciting but also unnerving, and many writers took refuge in extreme religious or political solutions, burying their doubts in strenuous belief. Empson was as troubled as anyone else, but felt that doubt was a virtue as well as a difficulty, and that in the end courage and intelligence were all we had—that revealed religion, illuminating if studied across the world, East as well as West, was a regression if simply embraced. Empson's responses to his trouble, in his poems and in his criticism, often seem breezy, even flippant; but the trouble is powerfully felt, and the breeziness is a symptom—how else is a writer to stay cheerful, if doubt is all he has? This unaided intellectual and moral courage is what Roger Sale, in his "The Achievement of William Empson" (1973)—the best essay yet written on Empson—calls heroism. Empson thought we needed to live intelligently, Sale says, not because he or we are intelligent, but because he sensed "the horrors that would rise up if one did not." Thinking of fascism and much that has followed, of the hatred of intelligence that has consumed so much of our century, we might want to say quite starkly that Empson was right, the horrors *have* risen up.

In the poems, these concerns often appear as wit and allusion rather than as central subject matter. The curvature of space, for example, in "The World's End" (originally titled "Relativity," 1928) makes romantic escape a disappointed dream. "Fly with me then," a lover says, "to all's and the world's end"; but where would such a flight take them?

> Space is like earth, rounded, a padded cell;
> . . .
> The shadow clings. The world's end is here.
> This place's curvature precludes its end.

"Precludes," Empson suggested in his later note to the poem, could mean "stops from happening" and also "already shut." The same poem tells us that "Satan's voice rattled the whole of Hell," because Milton makes Hell hollow and echoing, thereby seeming to anticipate modern physics. The line is a good instance both of Empson's close reading and of his light touch with a quick, compact allusion. Other poems evoke entomology, Lucretius, bicycles, space travel, cooling planets, the stars formed in a lake by the foam of toothpaste, cave paintings, proverbs, Christianity, botany, mechanical engineering, and much else. "Homage to the British Museum" (1932) offers a strong example of Empson's amused but frightened intelligence. "There is a Supreme God in the ethnological section," we are told. "His smooth wood creeps with all the creeds of the world." "Creeps," because the creeds cling like lice, and because we may find many of these creeds creepy. But Empson invites us to attend to them all: "let us absorb the cultures of nations / And dissolve into our judgement all their codes." We need, he says, to "give ourselves the benefit of the doubt," a remarkable renewing of a tired phrase: doubt would be a real benefit if we could take it seriously. We are to "offer our pinch of dust all to this God, / And grant his reign over the entire building." The God is the Polynesian Tangaroa, and the pinch of dust is what Christians offered to the Roman gods. It sounds like the skeptical pinch of salt, but it may help us to more than mere survival.

One of the most memorable and often quoted of these poems is "To an Old Lady" (1928), an austere and yet moving salutation to the poet's mother. Empson remarked in the sleeve-notes to the recorded version of the work that his mother did not recognize herself in the poem, and thought it was about *her* mother, but that this displacement perhaps helped to show that the poem had a reach beyond the merely personal. It opens grandly, but with an odd dryness, quoting *King Lear* in such a contextless way that the statement seems authoritative but unreachable:

> Ripeness is all; her in her cooling planet
> Revere; do not presume to think her wasted.
> Project her no projectile, plan nor man it;
> Gods cool in turn, by the sun long outlasted.
>
> Our earth alone given no name of god
> Gives, too, no hold for such a leap to aid her;
> Landing, you break some palace and seem odd;
> Bees sting their need, the keeper's queen invader.

No, to your telescope; spy out the land;
Watch while her ritual is still to see,
Still stand her temples emptying in the sand
Whose waves o'erthrew their crumbled tracery;

Still stand uncalled-on her soul's appanage;
Much social detail whose successor fades,
Wit used to run a house and to play Bridge,
And tragic fervour, to dismiss her maids.

Years her precession do not throw from gear.
She reads a compass certain of her pole;
Confident, finds no confines on her sphere,
Whose failing crops are her sole control.

Stars how much further from me fill my night,
Strange that she too should be inaccessible,
Who shares my sun. He curtains her from sight,
And but in darkness is she visible.

The poem accepts age and change and, by implication, death; accepts distance; respects dignity. The confidence of this lady is much admired; we are not to condescend to her. And yet she does belong to another world, another planet; or, rather, we do, since although the earth seems to be hers and ours, we are elsewhere with our telescope, would need to land on the earth to reach her. It is "strange," and perhaps painful, that she should be so remote, and that we should be able to see her only in darkness. What is distant and only intermittently seen, I think, is not finally a person but a style, an order, a version of certainty. It is yesterday's certainty; and the sobriety of the poem, the stateliness even, in the wit involving missiles, bees, and broken palaces, seems carefully designed to exclude all nostalgia. But then where are we? "Ripeness is all" seems a sardonic prescription if the ripeness belongs only to the past or always comes too late. It means "Leave her alone," but also "Don't count on it." The implication, perhaps, is that we should study the darkness carefully but not exclusively. There is also the world of light, and the sun long outlasts the gods.

The form of this poem is in many ways characteristic of Empson: four-line stanzas, five beats to the line, regular (if ingenious) rhymes on a simple *abab* scheme. There are rather ornate syntactical inversions ("Still stand her temples," "Years her precession do not throw," "Stars how much further from me fill"), and the occasional flavor of Alexander Pope's courtly concision, as exemplified, say, in "The Rape of the Lock." But the diction includes "projectile," "telescope," and "gear" as well as "appanage," "tracery," and "o'erthrew." Old and new worlds meet here in fragile suspension—playing "bridge," perhaps—and if we take this poem as placed at the opposite pole from "Poem About a Ball . . . ," we have a measure of Empson's range and consistency. Free verse or strict verse, the impulse is always to get language to enact both its own and our history, to write out *where we are.* The ball is over, leaving only (perhaps) a feather on a stair; the old lady is going, becoming a memory. We are on our own, and need all our wits about us.

The poem "Villanelle" (1928) alerts us particularly to Empson's interest in the fragile life or discreet death of old forms, as does his commentary on the sestina in *Seven Types of Ambiguity.* A villanelle is a poem of three-line stanzas (and a concluding four-line stanza) in which the two outer lines of the first stanza serve alternately as refrains for the other stanzas—until the last, when the two refrains come together to close the poem. The poem thus plays throughout with the *aba* rhyme, and the effect is that of an intellectual and musical development, with the theme phrases subtly changing their meanings as they return in new contexts. For example:

It is the pain, it is the pain, endures.
Your chemic beauty burned my muscles through.
Poise of my hands reminded me of yours.

What later purge from this deep toxin cures?
What kindness now could the old salve renew?
It is the pain, it is the pain, endures.

The infection slept (custom or change inures)
And when pain's secondary phase was due
Poise of my hands reminded me of yours.

. . .

You are still kind whom the same shape immures.
Kind and beyond adieu. We miss our cue.
It is the pain, it is the pain, endures.
Poise of my hands reminded me of yours.

"Immures" seems fussy, a stretching out for rhyme, and the image of the poise of the hands seems obscure, "poise" perhaps not being strong or visual enough. But the recurrence of the word (and the idea) of pain is haunting, and the poem as a whole eloquently embodies a sense of loss, a sickness that will not go away. Empson wrote three other villanelles, but later in his career: "Reflection from Anita Loos" (1940), where the refrain lines are "No man is sure he does not need to climb" and (the thought from Anita Loos) "A girl can't go on laughing all the time"; a political piece ("The ages change, and they impose their rules" / "We must endure, and stand between two fools") dating from 1937–1940 and published in *The Royal Beasts;* and "Missing Dates" (1937), collected in *The Gathering Storm,* one of the bleakest and yet most successful of Empson's poems, in which the daunting topic of waste, which also figures largely in Empson's critical works, is addressed and, if not mastered, at least fully faced, framed in a feat of lucid style. This is the complete poem:

> Slowly the poison the whole blood stream fills.
> It is not the effort nor the failure tires.
> The waste remains, the waste remains and kills.
>
> It is not your system or clear sight that mills
> Down small to the consequence a life requires;
> Slowly the poison the whole blood stream fills.
>
> They bled an old dog dry yet the exchange rills
> Of young dog blood gave but a month's desires;
> The waste remains, the waste remains and kills.
>
> It is the Chinese tombs and the slag hills
> Usurp the soil, and not the soil retires.
> Slowly the poison the whole blood stream fills.
>
> Not to have fire is to be a skin that shrills.
> The complete fire is death. From partial fires
> The waste remains, the waste remains and kills.
>
> It is the poems you have lost, the ills
> From missing dates, at which the heart expires.
> Slowly the poison the whole blood stream fills.
> The waste remains, the waste remains and kills.

It is perhaps worth commenting on the old-fashioned, elliptical turn of syntax that Empson favors: "It is not the effort nor the failure tires"; "It is the Chinese tombs and the slag hills / Usurp the soil"; "not the soil retires." Empson uses this turn everywhere: the effect is one of speed and strangeness, the mind somehow both in a hurry and belonging to an older world where people spoke like this. Both elements of the effect are important, of course. Empson has no time to waste; he is a modern man. But he also needs to signal continuities where possible. Not all the dates are missed.

The ending of "This Last Pain" (1932) is perhaps better known than anything else Empson wrote.

The last line has become a sort of proverb, part of the English vocabulary:

> Imagine, then, by miracle, with me,
> (Ambiguous gifts, as what gods give must be)
> What could not possibly be there,
> And learn a style from a despair.

Empson came to dislike the poem for what he felt was a certain dandyism—Oscar Wilde would not have disowned the argument—and for giving what might be construed as support for a return to religious faith. In *Some Versions of Pastoral* he evokes the White Queen in *Alice,* who "believes the impossible for half an hour before breakfast, to keep in practice," and represents, in Empson's view, a satirical comment on Cardinal Newman. But the movement of the poem is really more complicated than this, more ambiguous in the extended sense we shall shortly consider, and the ironies are nicely balanced. It is the context, the buildup that matters; the logical and historical point at which style is going to be our only hope. The very idea of such a hope is questioned, I think, even as it is (quite seriously) proposed.

The "last pain" of the title is that the damned in hell know what they are missing in heaven. This knowledge, Empson suggests, *is* hell and heaven, all there is, for believers or unbelievers. Happiness is what we watch for, not what we have. We need the wisdom of fools, but not blind folly or fantasy. We need to know that our very hopes are real *because* they are invented, products of our need:

> All those large dreams by which men long live well
> Are magic-lanterned on the smoke of hell;
> This then is real, I have implied,
> A painted, small, transparent slide.

This "reality" is what we are to keep creating, the feat of imagination and style for which the poem calls at its end. But Empson's tone and imagery also warn of the dangerous appearance of ease offered by this genuinely difficult thought. The slides of reality are easily procurable, he wryly says:

> These the inventive can hand-paint at leisure,
> Or most emporia would stock our measure;
> And feasting in their dappled shade
> We should forget how they were made.

The dappled shade (and indeed the rhyme of "shade" and "made") recalls Andrew Marvell's "The Garden," with its intricate ironies about escape from the noise of the world. We need Marvell's intelligence as much as we need his fantasy. Empson here is insisting, perhaps more firmly than he himself noticed, that it is no good stocking up on home made or mass-produced slides. We need to remember how they are made, to imagine what could not possibly be there, but also to imagine ourselves imagining, like a Brechtian actress showing that she is showing. On this condition we might actually learn from despair, and style would be an achievement, not a disguise.

SEVEN TYPES OF AMBIGUITY *AND* SOME VERSIONS OF PASTORAL

EMPSON wrote the bulk of *Seven Types of Ambiguity,* a landmark in the practice of literary interpretation, while he was still a student at Cambridge. The story goes that he asked his tutor at Magdalene College, I. A. Richards, for a little more time in which to develop an undergraduate essay, and finally showed up with a draft of the book. Richards, who was interested in language, psychology, and the theory of literature, had published *Principles of Literary Criticism* (1924) and was about to publish *Practical Criticism* (1929). The latter book was based on testing the reading of Cambridge undergraduates (and a few graduate and nonacademic members of the audiences at Richards' lectures) when they did not know the name of the author of a particular piece. Richards concluded that what we call reading is usually a matter of implementing assumptions and prejudices, and that we must start again, *learn* to read, attend to the words on the page: "There cannot be much doubt that when we know we are reading Milton or Shelley, a great deal of our approval and admiration is being accorded not to the poetry but to an idol" (1939 ed., pp. 315–316).

Later in the career of this idea, the "words on the page" were to become a rather lazy slogan, inviting students to ignore history, biography, and anything else they might know. At this stage, though, the idea was fresh, indeed revolutionary. To encounter Shakespeare without knowing he was Shakespeare altered almost everything, opened up entirely new possibilities of pleasure or disappointment or lucidity. "The critical reading of poetry is an arduous discipline," Richards said; "few exercises reveal to us more clearly the limitations under which, from moment to moment, we suffer" (1939 ed., pp. 350–351). But then—and here we see how Richards could have had an even stronger influence on Empson than Eliot did—Richards concluded: "The lesson of all criticism is that we have nothing to rely upon in making our choices but ourselves. The lesson of good poetry seems to be that, when we have understood it, in the degree in which we can order ourselves, we need nothing more" (1939 ed., p. 351).

Seven Types of Ambiguity was Empson's attempt to order himself critically, but also to acknowledge the various forces that must challenge and escape any order we are likely to find. Empson owed much to Richards, but he took greater intellectual risks than his mentor, had a more flexible and inventive mind, and left a richer and more open legacy. The young Empson's imagination was also caught by *A Survey of Modernist Poetry* (1927), by Laura Riding and Robert Graves, whom Empson called the "inventors" of the method he was using. His "verbal analysis" was the immediate ancestor of what was to become "close reading." Graves and Riding invite us to think, for example, of an "intensified inbreeding of words," and suggest that "making poetry easy for the reader should mean showing clearly that it is difficult" (p. 75). Like Empson, they are interested in multiple meanings, although they are more nervous about plurality than he is, anxious to collapse the meanings back into one before the show is over: "If we must choose any one meaning, then we owe it to Shakespeare to choose at least one he intended and one embracing as many meanings as possible, that is, the most difficult meaning. It is always the most difficult meaning that is most final" (p. 74). Empson would say we quite often do not have to choose one meaning, and would prefer the word "ambiguous" to the word "difficult." "Difficult" suggests a problematic relation between writer and reader; "ambiguous" hints at minds—the writer's and the reader's—doing their complicated daily work.

Empson, in Roger Sale's fine formulation, "sees ambiguity not as a verbal trick but as a secret of the heart" (p. 35). Of the heart and of the mind Empson says:

> People, often, cannot have done both of two things, but they must have been in some way prepared to have done either; whichever they did, they will have still lingering in their minds the way they would have preserved their self-respect if they had acted differently; they are only to be understood by bearing both possibilities in mind.
>
> (*Seven Types,* p. 44)

Ambiguity is not so much a hesitation as a sense of how complex the world is, even when decisions have been made, even when the decisions feel right. We could say it is a hesitation after the fact or, as Empson calls it, "an indecision and a structure." It is characteristic of Empson that he should worry not about the correctness of what we do but about our threatened self-respect, and about the story we are going to tell ourselves. Other relevant (although not synonymous) words here are honor, honesty, integrity, and conscience. All of them appeal to felt values; all of them imply an ongoing, more or less convincing mental narrative, a relation of the self to the self. Ambiguity arises when one story clashes with or compounds or diverts another.

Empson repeatedly writes of "puzzlement" as the trigger for a piece of analysis. For instance, "I felt sure that the example was beautiful and that I had, broadly speaking, reacted to it correctly. But I did not at all know what had happened in this 'reaction'" (p. x).[2] The poem makes the reader think, and the reader's thought constructs the poem: "The process of getting to understand a poet is precisely that of constructing his poems in one's own mind" (p. 62). Unlike many later theorists, Empson assumes that the reader's poem and the poet's poem are not too different, and quite deliberately, if erratically, takes both sides, so that sometimes an ambiguity is an intention or a dilemma, and sometimes it is a perceived array of implications. I think it fair to say that *Seven Types of Ambiguity* offers a (disorderly) theory of reading that does not require a doctrine of intention, and relies primarily upon possibilities of meaning that are available in the general fund of a language, in what the Swiss linguist Ferdinand de Saussure

would have called *langue,* the accumulated history of a word or a structure. Empson is interested in the way particular writers and readers reach into this fund, put it to use. However, it must also be said that Empson talks often (and belligerently) about intention, particularly in his later work, and would think it recklessly unhistorical of us to push his own early doctrine (or certain aspects of that doctrine) too far—too far, that is, from what an author might conceivably have meant.

Empson later said that his term "ambiguity" had been "more or less superseded by the idea of a double meaning which is intended to be fitted into a definite structure (*The Structure of Complex Words,* p. 103), whereas his critics have always thought he merely meant to talk about multiple meaning. Empson invited this response by being rather vague about his types ("In a sense the sixth class is included within the fourth") and by indulging in dizzying afterthoughts about whether he had placed his examples where they needed to be ("the last example of my fourth chapter belongs by rights to the fifth or to the sixth") (*Seven Types,* p. 190)—Empson can sound like Chico Marx haggling with Groucho over a contract in *A Night at the Opera.* Empson also made an almost comically humble claim for his conceptual apparatus:

> I think my seven types form an immediately useful set of distinctions, but to a more serious analysis they would probably appear trivial and hardly to be distinguished from one another. I call them useful, not merely as a means of stringing examples, but because, in complicated matters, any distinction between cases, however irrelevant, may serve to heighten one's consciousness of the cases themselves.
>
> (pp. 253–254)

Empson's types can indeed appear trivial, or at least awkwardly assembled, but we should not be deceived. There are deep matters in this book, and their name, precisely, is ambiguity.

Empson says he has arranged his types "in order of increasing distance from simple statement and logical exposition" (p. 7), but what he has actually done is to explore cases of contradiction, intermingling logical and psychological criteria as he goes, thoroughly exploiting what he calls "the ambiguity of 'ambiguity'" (p. 6). Thus Ambiguity One is a mild possibility of double or multiple meaning; Ambiguity Two occurs when different meanings

---

[2]References to *Seven Types of Ambiguity* cite page numbers from the 1953 revised edition.

are finally resolved into one. Ambiguity Three is the opposite, dealing with "apparently unconnected meanings" (p. v). A little pressure on that "apparently" could no doubt push Type Three back into Type Two. Ambiguities Four and Five are based on assumptions about the author's mind (complicated, getting clearer in Four; confused but discovering an idea through writing in Five). Ambiguity Six looks very much like a stepped-up version of Three: "What is said is contradictory or irrelevant and the reader is forced to invent interpretations" (p. vi). Ambiguity Seven returns to psychology, signaling "full contradiction, marking a division in the author's mind" (p. vi). At this stage "two systems of judgement are forced into open conflict before the reader" (p. 226), we see what is ordinarily not seen, and we again encounter the obscure cellar of the psyche, the place below our customary consciousness where many of the decisions that affect us are taken: "Such a process, one might imagine, could pierce to regions that underlie the whole structure of our thought; could tap the energies of the very depths of the mind" (p. 226).

Ambiguity, in other words, would not merely be written, a particular poetic effect; it would be a feature of the way *we are written,* an aspect of the human program. But perhaps the program works best if we do not tinker with it or ask too many questions about it. Empson devotes much of his brilliant last chapter to worrying about this question, and to piling up impressive arguments against himself. "The object of life, after all," he says in this vein, "is not to understand things, but to maintain one's defences and equilibrium and live as well as one can; it is not only maiden aunts who are placed like this" (p. 247). Again: "It does not even satisfy the understanding to stop living in order to understand" (p. 245). Empson's answer to his argumentative and more cautious twin is that not everyone needs to descend into the cellar or care about contradictions—indeed, the task is not recommended for those whose defenses are shaky. But for those who can face the descent, who can analyze their reactions (to poems or anything else) without losing touch with their initial reaction, and without being shocked by what they find, the exercise must, Empson hopes, produce the sort of moral and mental agility so much needed in the modern world. It would give us "a certain power of dealing with anything that may turn out to be true; and

people have come to feel that that may be absolutely anything" (p. 247). He cannot conceal his sympathy, Empson says, "with those who want to understand as many things as possible, and to hang those consequences which cannot be foreseen" (p. 248). However, it would be irresponsible not to recognize that this gamble *is* a gamble.

The writing of *Seven Types of Ambiguity* is fast, forceful, slangy, seemingly casual. Empson enjoys words like "trick" and "machinery," phrases like "wandering about in your mind" and "lying about his mind"—as if the mind were an attic or storeroom as well as a cellar, as if our relation to the mind were like our relation to a mischievous friend or a recalcitrant car. There is much charm and energy in this style, but also a certain amount of delusion, since complicated matters cannot always be canvassed by such speed and bluster. Empson's later vocabulary dips further and further into apparent negligence, offhand assaults on what he takes to be an excessive scholarly decorum. Keats, for instance, "skids round the corner from self-pity to an imaginative view of the world"; Satan is "a rippingly grand aristocrat"; God is "a jovial though pompous old buffer." But the delusion is a generous one, and in any case scarcely affects the overall stance. Empson mentions Wittgenstein in a poem but does not speak of him otherwise, yet his position here has real affinities with that of the philosopher. "What *we* do," Wittgenstein said in *Philosophical Investigations* "is to bring words back from their metaphysical to their everyday use" (New York, 1967, p. 48). Empson also thinks the everyday use of words may take us further than we ordinarily assume, and should help to diminish our intellectual arrogance. "Philosophy," Wittgenstein memorably remarked, "is a battle against the bewitchment of our intelligence by means of language" (p. 47). Empson's brand of literary criticism is precisely that—except that being bewitched by language is also part of the struggle, so that to be entirely cured would be to have lost rather than won the battle. The bewitchment is to be understood, reasoned about—but not banished.

At other times Empson's writing, although fast, does not seem casual, since it is fueled by the extraordinary power of the insight it expresses. Empson thought his method was "the main point of the book"; we may feel that his critical performance, what the method shows, is even more the point. Looking, for example, at Macbeth's familiar line,

"Time, and the hour, runs through the roughest day," Empson notes the odd singular verb, which seems to make time and the hour one thing but does not stop us from thinking of them as different, perhaps even opposite. But then he goes on to point out the almost invisible double meaning of "runs through":

Time and the hour force the day to its foregone conclusion, as one runs a man through with a dagger, or *time and the hour* are, throughout the day, after all, always quietly running on. The remark does not seem as ambiguous as it is because it is a shelving of indecision rather than an expression of it.

(pp. 201–202)

This was the sort of thing that drove some of Empson's early readers mad. In a footnote Empson himself says the analysis "seems too elaborate." I think we might now claim that we probably do not (and need not) imagine Shakespeare plotting such subtleties, setting them up for the connoisseurs, but that the idiom "run through," however casually used, must bear its violent meaning when used in a play about murder. It takes an Empson to notice it, perhaps; but once noticed, it becomes a constituent feature of the work, an enrichment of interpretative possibility. We could hardly send it back to oblivion even if we wanted to. It hangs in the mind, like one of Perry Mason's comments, stricken from the court record but lingering invisibly to persuade the jury.

Here is an even more "elaborate" example. Empson is commenting on a line from Thomas Nashe, "Brightness falls from the air":

Evidently there are a variety of things the line may be about. The sun and moon pass under the earth after their period of shining, and there are stars falling at odd times; Icarus and the prey of hawks, having soared upwards towards heaven, *fall* exhausted or dead; the glittering turning things the sixteenth century put on the top of a building may have *fallen* too often. In another sense, hawks, lightning, and meteorites *fall* flashing from heaven upon their prey. Taking *brightness* as abstract, not as meaning something bright, it is as a benefit that light *falls*, diffusely reflected, from the sky. In so far as the sky is brighter than the earth (especially at twilight), brightness is natural to it; in so far as the earth may be bright when the clouds are dark, *brightness falls* from the sky to the earth when there is a threat of thunder.

(p. 26).

Empson paraphrases the possible broad meanings as " 'All is unsafe, even the heavens are not sure of their brightness,' or 'the qualities in man that deserve respect are not natural to him but brief gifts from God; they fall like manna, and melt as soon' " (p. 26). He thinks there may be a sense of threat in the line, too, particularly since the poem evokes a time of plague: "There is a taint of darkness in the very *air.*" Most of us are probably too dizzy to go any further, but Empson feels he must mention the "rather cynical theory" that Nashe may have meant "hair" rather than "air," Elizabethan pronunciation being rather uncertain in these regions. "Oddly enough," he continues, the possibility, "though less imaginative . . . carries much the same suggestion as the other version"; but then Empson cannot help wondering whether Nashe was *using* the uncertain pronunciation of his time to promote ambiguity: "It is conceivable that Nashe meant both words to take effect in some way."

It is not conceivable to me, and no doubt to many others; but it is important to understand what Empson is doing here, and by extension what this whole book is about. Empson is not so much interpreting a line as laying out the ingredients of several interpretations, all the interpretations he can think of. Or, to put that another way, he is inspecting interpretation itself, watching it at work, offering an anatomy of reading. *Seven Types of Ambiguity* is a book of possibilities, an indication of the reach of the inquisitive and thoughtful mind. What we do with these possibilities is another matter, but we cannot even consider that until we know they are there.

There is a word that covers many of these complications, and is perhaps even more comprehensive than "ambiguity." The word is "irony," which we need to understand not only as a stance or a structure but also as the multifarious reflection of a frame of mind, a complex cultural achievement. In this sense it is the subject both of *Seven Types of Ambiguity* and of Empson's next critical work, *Some Versions of Pastoral.* "Human life," Empson says, "is so much a matter of juggling with contradictory impulses (Christian–worldly, sociable–independent, and such-like) that one is accustomed to thinking people are probably sensible if they follow first one, then the other, of two such courses" (*Seven Types,* p. 197). I am not sure how accustomed "one" is to making this assumption about "people." I am sure one was even less accustomed to it

188

in the years 1930–1935 than one is now, and Empson acknowledges that such behavior may merely seem foolish. But that makes his claim all the more striking.

Irony in this sense is a global name for what Empson calls the "shifts and blurred aggregates of thought by which men come to a practical decision" (*Seven Types,* p. 68). It is close to Henry James's sense of irony as a projection of "the always possible other case," and to Eliot's notion of wit as involving "probably, a recognition, implicit in the expression of every experience, of other kinds of experience which are possible."

Of other kinds of experience, but also the one at hand, the different experiences hold in some kind of precarious, troubled, or even comic balance: We can think of Hamlet worrying about the afterlife, or of Harold Lloyd clinging to the hands of a clock. "An irony," Empson says, "has no point unless it is true, in some degree, in both senses": we do not merely mean something other than what we say, we mean what we say as well:

The fundamental impulse of irony is to score off both the arguments that have been puzzling you, both sets of sympathies in your mind, both sorts of fool who will hear you. . . . The essential is for the author to repeat the audience in himself, and he may safely seem to do nothing more. No doubt he has covertly, if it is a good irony, to reconcile the opposites into a larger unity, or suggest a balanced position by setting out two extreme views, or accept a lie . . . to find energy to accept a truth, or something like that.

(*Some Versions,* pp. 60–61)

Empson notes, for instance, that "all politeness has an element of irony"; and the mode he calls comic primness, most fully displayed for him in *The Beggar's Opera,* relies on emphatically *not* saying what we expect to hear ("A man cannot be expected to hang his acquaintance for nothing"—as if prompt and proper payment for informing on one's friends would make everything all right) or saying the right thing, as Tony Nuttall very well puts it, in the wrong tone of voice (Swift wrote, "Yesterday I saw a woman flayed and you will scarcely believe how it altered her person for the worse").[3] The character (a person in a play, or the assumed persona of a

[3]A. S. Nuttall, "Solvents and Fixatives: Critical Theory in Transition," in *The Modern Language Review* (April 1987).

writer) seems strangely not to share the perspective and priorities of author and reader, to treat what we see as horror as the normal run of the world. The result is that we either miss the horror (the irony) or find it dramatically highlighted by the deadpan delivery.

Some Versions of Pastoral is a slightly deceptive title, and the title of the American edition, *English Pastoral Poetry* (1938), is even more so, not because the book does not consider pastoral but because Empson finds pastoral where no one else would dream of looking. He thinks the chief "trick" of conventional pastoral is "putting the complex into the simple," as when a group of sophisticated Elizabethan courtiers play (in poetry or in life) at being swains and shepherds. A good instance is the court in exile in *As You Like It,* leading a simplified existence that cannot forget the complications it claims to have left behind. *Don Quixote* is a travesty of a chivalric novel in which the times are seen to be wrong for chivalry; but it almost becomes a travesty of a pastoral novel when Quixote encounters both real and mock shepherds. Empson identifies pastoral wherever this "trick" is found, even if the scene does not look at all pastoral at first sight: in modern proletarian literature, in the realm of dramatic double plot, in commentaries on Milton, in *The Beggar's Opera,* in *Alice in Wonderland.* In all these cases an interesting mock simplicity hints at a real complexity. "It is the very queerness of the trick," Empson says, "that makes it so often useful in building models of the human mind" (p. 94). It is worth noting that Empson says "queerness" and not "frequency" or "range." Like Dostoevsky, who speaks out "queer and clear" in Empson's poem "Success," he finds deep, general, *ordinary* truths in what seems strange behavior. "Probably," he says rather casually, "the cases I take are the surprising rather than the normal ones" (p. 23). But the surprising cases make us rethink the norm.

Empson's investigation results in a series of remarkable readings and insights, and a work that many regard as his finest critical achievement. The essay on double plot, for example, looks at Faustus, Falstaff, and Donne's sonnets, and ends with a fine, glancing remark about *Wuthering Heights,* a whole critical study compacted into a sentence that Empson seems merely to have dropped, like litter: "And *Wuthering Heights* is a good case of double plot in the novel, both for covert deification and telling the same story twice with the two possible endings"

(p. 84). The essay on *Alice in Wonderland* convincingly puts Freud among the Victorian pigeons, disarmingly suggesting that "to make the dream-story from which *Wonderland* was elaborated seem Freudian one has only to tell it" (pp. 258–259). *Some Versions of Pastoral* is certainly the most fluent of Empson's books and contains the largest doses of the grand, throwaway wisdom that is his characteristic signature: "The belief that a man's ideas are wholly the produce of his economic setting is of course as fatuous as the belief that they are wholly independent of it" (p. 19). But the book is perhaps not as brilliant locally as much of *Seven Types of Ambiguity,* and lacks that first work's troubling intimacy with deep and raging contradictions, the sense of fear beneath all the boisterous ingenuity.

If there was a tilt toward psychology in *Seven Types of Ambiguity,* there is in *Some Versions of Pastoral* a leaning toward social studies. It is true that Empson says the book "is not a solid piece of sociology," but we may be surprised to find him thinking of it as piece of sociology at all. He reminds us that "literature is a social process"; and here, as in the earlier book, he speaks repeatedly of "forces," by which he seems to mean political or social pressures. "Pastoral" itself is a social idea, a means of negotiating, among other things, matters of class and visions of alternative social orders; and it is in this context that the question of waste arises.

"The waste remains," we remember from "Missing Dates," "the waste remains and kills." Since pastoral simplifies the world but knows it is simplifying, the ideas that are "naturally at home with most versions of pastoral" are those we associate with limitation, even when much wit and courage have gone into the scenario or the phrase. This is one of the ways in which we learn a style from a despair; but the style does not deny the despair. Empson comments on Gray's "Elegy," for instance, which mourns the waste of human talent but suggests the waste is natural. The case is "pathetic, but the reader is put into a mood in which one would not try to alter it." As Empson says, we do not have to be communists to find this stance complacent, too contented with the stratified social order of its time. "And yet," he continues with remarkable lucidity, "what is said is one of the permanent truths": "It is only in degree that any improvement of society could prevent wastage of human powers;

the waste even in a fortunate life, the isolation even of a life rich in intimacy, cannot but be felt deeply, and is the central feeling in tragedy" (p. 5). Tragedy embodies this feeling, but pastoral displaces it, helping us to know what it is we need to say and not to say. We may find ourselves thinking, for example, in Empson's resounding words, "that life is essentially inadequate to the human spirit," and must think this in our bleaker moments; but then Empson reminds us "that a good life must avoid saying so," not because we cannot face the truth but because we do not have to wallow in it, and because there are other truths, too, moments or zones where life and the human spirit get along better. The dark feeling is genuine; but it is a feeling, not a divine revelation. Pastoral permits us to acknowledge these truths without drowning in them.

MORE POEMS

EMPSON was modest about his verse—a good deal more modest than he was about his ideas, particularly in later life—and consistently thought of himself as a minor poet. This is probably right, as long as we remember that most poets are minor poets, and that complicated historical and cultural factors always enter into such adjudications. William Butler Yeats is a major poet now but once was thought to be dubious, though famous. Is T. S. Eliot still a major poet? Is W. H. Auden a major poet despite his conviction that he was minor? Empson said of one of his own later poems, collected in *The Gathering Storm,* "The Teasers" (1940), that he thought it was "nearly very good, above my level altogether," but that it did not quite earn the moral it was claiming to offer: "Make no escape / build up your love, / Leave what you die for and be safe to die." Empson lacks Auden's range and ease but often manages a compacted, reflective elegance that is altogether stricter than anything Auden offers. Empson understands himself and us better than most poets do. If we are uncomfortable with his verse, it is because it puts us on the spot and because the verse itself, although it knows how to be terse and intelligent, does not always know how to breathe, where to turn for escape.

Escape is the great theme of Empson's later

poems, usually figured by the many-faceted image of flight. "Courage Means Running" (1936) is a brilliant meditation on the adage that discretion is the better part of valor. This unlikely, self-serving proposition cannot be true, the poem suggests, but it is not always as disreputable as it looks, since it has the merit of recognizing fear. It is "Usual for a man / Of Bunyan's courage to respect fear," Empson says; "No purpose, view, / Or song but's weak if without the ballast of fear." This is not to give in to fear but to know it, and to recognize its presence behind other moves we make.

> To escape emotion (a common hope) and attain
> Cold truth is essentially to get
>
> Out by a rival emotion fear. We gain
> Truth, to put it sanely, by gift of pleasure
> And courage, but, since pleasure knits with pain,
>
> Both presume fear. To take fear as the measure
> May be a measure of self-respect.

"Get out" means both "get away" and "solve," in the mathematical sense: a neat suggestion that the intellect has all kinds of escape routes, ways of leaving town while pretending to stay at home. Pleasure/pain, courage/fear: these are opposites, not ambiguities; but they are also relatives, members of a family. The family needs to know it is one, and to find ways of getting along. Here, as in other respects, Empson is trying to keep disparate ideas and emotions, as he says of the plot elements of his fable, "The Royal Beasts," "within reach" of each other, trying to take a divided world as "one place."

Empson's deepest and funniest, most self-mocking meditation on the subject of fear is "Aubade" (1937), with its villanellelike refrains, full of paradox and casual understatement: "It seemed the best thing to be up and go" or "The heart of standing is you cannot fly." An aubade is a traditional medieval form in which a lover regrets the dawn, which returns his mistress to her duties and (usually) to her husband. "It seemed the best thing" mimes an English diffidence; this is how lovers say good-bye when they are trying not to look at their feelings. "The heart of standing": courage perhaps is merely circumstantial, you face the music because you have nowhere to go. The poem also plays on the word "rising," which means both getting up

in the morning, leaving your lover's bed and going home, and political revolt, an uprising against a government:

> But as to risings, I can tell you why.
> It is on contradictions that they grow.
> It seemed the best thing to be up and go.

Lovers and nations, in the sort of conjunction Empson learned from Donne, are caught in contradictions, need to move and sometimes cannot move. "Lying" is another crucial word: Are we staying in bed or avoiding the truth, or both? The poem is set in the Far East, and opens with an earthquake: Where are you to fly from one of those? The lovers are "two aliens," a Western man and an Eastern woman; the earthquake is quite a small one; and she has to get back to her child or her husband (someone, in any case, who will "bawl" when he wakes). Is it really the best thing to be up and go? No, the best thing would be to stay, but you can do that only if the option of flight is not available. This is not a romantic view of human courage, but it exactly describes the way many commitments, emotional and political, are made and missed. We need to note the subtle shift from "you" to "we" in Empson's refrain when it appears for the last time: "The heart of standing is we cannot fly." The "you" seemed impersonal, a generalization rather than an attack, applicable to everyone but only in the broadest sense; but "we" are who "we" individually are. Can we really say we would not fly if we could?

"Autumn on Nan-Yueh" (1940), Empson's longest and most lighthearted poem, again examines the notion of flight, in an ever-widening context. Nan-Yueh, Empson tells us in a note, "is a sacred mountain about seventy miles southwest of Changsha"; he was there with the Chinese universities for a term in 1937. "If flight's as general as this," the poem begins, "And every movement starts a wing." Angels, eagles, the whole aviary of Romantic birds: the very idea of paradise, considered in this light, seems airborne. Empson has taken a plane to where he is (and also a train and buses; even metaphors have to remember exceptions and particulars), and he is, he says, in flight as well: "I flew, I fled." Empson thinks of the holy mountain and of the universities in exile, wittily adapting a phrase from Yeats ("The soul remembering") to describe what teachers have to do when they have no library on which to rely. The mind has its own flying horses, lifting Empson, for instance, to a quotation from Virginia Woolf. He next thinks of witches on their broomsticks; of whether drinking helps us escape or brings us closer to our fear; wonders whether being against escapism (as so much writing in the 1930's rather sententiously was) is not itself a cozy escape: "It struck me trying not to fly / Let them escape a bit too far."

Empson then launches into a good-humored attack on what he calls "the revolutionary romp," on the grounds that politicized writers tend to stumble into the very conventions they have denied:

> You find a cluster of them cloys.
> But all conventions have their pomp
> And all styles can come down to noise.

"*Can* come down": the precision is important. Dreams, Empson now argues, skillfully playing Freud off against Yeats, are not escapes from reality but are themselves the dark realities we may need, quite properly, to escape. And what about the actual fliers fighting the Chinese war? The material reality reminds Empson that he needs to distinguish between politics and being (too eagerly) politicized:

> Politics are what verse should
>   Not fly from, or it all goes wrong.
> I feel the force of that all right,
>   And had I speeches they were song.

The last line glances at Yeats's phrase "True song though speech," and might almost be taken as expressing Empson's ideal in poetry: song without speech would be mindless music; speech without song, mere doggerel or prose. But has Empson speeches at this moment? What could he tell the world, or his countrymen at home? The world and England, he feels, can get along without his advice.

And in any case, his advice, once he tries to formulate it, crumbles into bewilderment:

> What are these things I do not face,
>   The reasons for entire despair . . . ?

This is compressed and rather difficult writing. Empson is saying, I think, that he does *not* despair

entirely, as some others do, but that may be because he is not facing all there is to face. He cannot name "the large thing" that seems to be causing all the trouble—the time, remember, is 1937—but he does not think it is nationalism or race, and is wittily skeptical about economists, who currently "have the floor, . . . have the flair." He reflects on Marx and Stalin, and defends "the tedious triumphs of the mind" against those who require quick action (although he understands their impatience); he wonders what he is doing in China, and decides he may be performing a useful task, not "good for nowt" (a Yorkshire phrase), and that it is not "shameful" to want to be where things are happening. The poem ends with these fine lines:

> I said I wouldn't fly again
>   For quite a bit. I did not know.
> Even in breathing tempest-tossed,
>   Scattering to winnow and to sow,
> With convolutions for a brain,
>   Man moves, and we have got to go.
> Claiming no heavy personal cost
>   I feel the poem would be slow
> Furtively finished on the plain.
>   We have had the autumn here. But oh
> That lovely balcony is lost
>   Just as the mountains take the snow.
> The soldiers will come here and train.
>   The streams will chatter as they flow.

"Man moves": this is a version of the old saw about man proposing and God disposing. For Empson man proposes, no one disposes, and we should all say how we feel about the propositions. It is a question of generosity and imagination rather than of political or other alignment. The "convolutions" of the brain seem to be a sort of joke on us, but our brains are what we have. The long way round may appear endless, but it is not all tedious. Empson said of this poem in his "Notes" to *Collected Poems*, "I hope the gaiety of the thing comes through; I felt I was in very good company." It does; he must have been. The adventure of flight does not conquer fear; it includes it.

THE STRUCTURE OF COMPLEX WORDS

CLEANTH BROOKS, reviewing *The Structure of Complex Words* in 1952, said Empson was "the incorrigible amateur, the man with a knack." But he is trying very hard to be professional in this work, or at least to tidy up the mess the professionals have left. The problem, hindsight suggests, is that the professional linguists Empson studied were rather rigid members of the old school, and that the ordinary language philosophers who could have helped him were just getting started. (J. L. Austin was lecturing at Oxford on what he called "sense and sensibilia" in the late 1940's, and Wittgenstein's *Philosophical Investigations* appeared in 1953.) The effect is of an enormously intelligent and gifted writer who has partly gotten lost through looking for too much clarity, and has partly invented ordinary language philosophy on his own. The early chapters of the book are cluttered with symbols for the notation of meaning and mood (A for sense, (A) for sense at the back of the mind, + and − for warmer and colder intimations, £ for mood, ? for covert reference, and so on). We have to fight our way through thickets of such shorthand, and then need to restore the examples to longhand in order to understand what is going on.

Empson's chief topic is what he calls equations among the senses of words. He proposes four types of equations: 1. Where the context calls for a meaning which is not the chief or usual meaning of the word, so the chief meaning is there but not in the foreground; 2. Where the chief meaning *and* a series of implications are invoked; 3. A reversal of 1, so that the chief meaning is in the foreground *as* meaning, but not immediately applicable to the object (the usual mode of metaphor); and 4. Where the different meanings are offered as the same meanings, as in many forms of paradox. This is rather complicated, even in my simplified summary, and Empson himself concedes that "a classification . . . can cover a field without telling us anything important about it" (p. 54). The interesting thing here, though, is not the act of classifying but the brilliant suggestion of an equation *within a word*. This radically alters our sense of how language works (or it affords a new way of grasping the sense we have of its workings), and it changes the notion of what a dictionary is. What the dictionary lists as separate meanings would all have to be active all the time, although in different degrees at different moments. The "equation" is more metaphorical, and less technical, than Empson thinks it is. It is what holds the meanings together, keeps them in play—like a rally in tennis, which may be

long or short, slow or fast, balanced or unequal, cover quite different areas of the court, but still operates within the rules of the game.

The trouble with Richards' view of meaning, Empson says—*The Structure of Complex Words* is dedicated to Richards, who is described as "the source of all ideas in this book, even the minor ones arrived at by disagreeing with him"—is that it takes the sense of a word as "something single," and therefore must explain everything else that seems to be "in" the word as an aspect of feeling. Empson agrees that there are feelings in words but also says that "much of what appears to us as a 'feeling' . . . will in fact be quite an elaborate structure of related meanings." "Language is essentially a social product," Empson writes, "and much concerned with social relations, but we tend to hide this in our forms of speech" (pp. 56–57). Words like "surely" and "certainly" are "simple in meaning and indeed in emotion but socially complicated" (p. 18), modest agents in really intricate maneuvers. Our jokes and tag words, all the small change of language we take for granted, "carry doctrines more really complex than the whole structure of [our] official view of the world" (p. 174). "Doctrines" is too definite a word, and the claim is too strong; but it is an important claim nevertheless.

What Empson calls the "shrubbery of smaller ideas," everything popular and "unofficial" in a culture's way of going about its ordinary life, here finds precisely the social and intellectual significance that most theories of art and life deny to it. "This may be an important matter for a society, because its accepted official beliefs may be things that would be fatal unless in some degree at bay" (p. 158). The Elizabethan worldview, in other words, was seriously held by the Elizabethans; and so was a whole group of irreverent, skeptical counterviews, the sort any culture needs to stay sane and human. Falstaff is the disreputable but also the necessary other face (and flesh) of Henry V's kingdom, and in his piece on this character in *Essays on Shakespeare*, Empson makes short work of much high moralizing on this subject: Falstaff is "a very rich joke," and if we feel Shakespeare has deliberately degraded him in order to make a point, Empson wonders just "what we expect our own old age to be like."

Empson's engagement, as the title of his book suggests, is now with particular words rather than with images or idioms or pieces of grammar. And

WILLIAM EMPSON

with words rather than what writers make of them. He is interested not in individual uses of language but in its social and emotional hinterland, all the things words may mean, or might have meant. Empson's equations are not wrought ambiguities but pools of implication, so that language itself, and not some literary magic, seems to carry the meaning. This distinction is rather dubious in practice, since Empson is using so many literary examples, but it does have a real theoretical interest. We might not be able to tell in any given case whether Pope or Shakespeare was personally bending the meaning of a word or illuminating the trail of its history, taking a word over or pointing to a contemporary shift in its sense, but that would not be a reason for thinking the activities are not different.

It is in this spirit that Empson studies "wit" in Pope's *Essay on Criticism,* "all" in *Paradise Lost,* "dog" in *Timon of Athens,* "honest" in *Othello,* "sense" in *The Prelude,* and so on. The heart of the book is the chapter "Fool in *Lear,*" first published in 1949, and connected in mood and interest with Empson's other writings on Shakespeare at this time (on *Hamlet* and on Falstaff, both 1953, and both collected in *Essays on Shakespeare*) and with his masterly essay on *Tom Jones* (1958, collected in *Using Biography*).

Empson leads up to his *Lear* essay by a study of Erasmus' *Praise of Folly.* "Folly" in the Renaissance had a range of meanings running from simplemindedness to sanctity, marked by the various senses of "dupe," "clown," "lunatic," "jester," "knave," and the rest. Shakespeare shares Erasmus' feeling that simplemindedness may at times *be* sanctity (what could be more foolish, Erasmus suggests, than getting yourself crucified to save a sinful species?), but more often associates folly with clowning or ridicule, and in very painful situations. Macbeth asks, "Why should I play the Roman fool, and die / On my own sword?" Is the question whether he should play the fool, or is the stress, as Empson would like to think, on *"Roman* fool": "so as to make him imply that he has got to play some kind of clown's part anyway" (*Structure,* p. 120). Either way the role of the clown is prominent, as it is in a bitter line from *Twelfth Night:* "Infirmity, that decays the wise, doth ever make the better fool." Suffering, contrary to traditional consolations, ruins wisdom but improves folly. Empson calls this a "black little piece of fun" but brilliantly sees in it the larger suggestion that "tragic experi-

ence may lie behind wit and . . . that simplicity is learned through adversity" (p. 122).

In *King Lear* a desolate simplicity is learned through adversity but also through madness, that is, "not merely through suffering, but through having been a clown" (p. 146). The old king, Empson suggests, "has made a fool of himself on the most cosmic and appalling scale possible; he has got on the wrong side of the next world as well as on the wrong side of this one" (p. 155). The famous "Ripeness is all"—we remember the opening of Empson's poem "To an Old Lady"—suggests not maturity but an emptying out, a region of the mind where wisdom and folly are both bleached away. In this reading, Shakespeare looks toward Beckett. We learn that "there is no worst" because the worst is a name, and there may be unnameable horrors to come. Hopkins is desperately thinking through this argument in his sonnet that begins "No worst, there is none." We have already looked at Empson's own poem "Let It Go," published in the same year as the *Lear* essay and picturing its speaker as a clown like Lear, edging toward craziness in words, opting in the end for sanity and silence: "You don't want madhouse and the whole thing there."

Empson found in the world of *Tom Jones* an answer to the madhouse, a place where "talk" was still possible. He admired Fielding's lucidity and decency, the spaciousness of his irony; the essay is offered as a "defence" of an underread and undervalued novel. Empson argues that Fielding presents a "doctrine" in *Tom Jones,* "a highminded though perhaps abstruse one": that it is possible, in spite of the more plausible-seeming claims of Thomas Hobbes and other skeptics, to experience the feelings of other people virtually as if they were our own, so that kindness or sympathy would not be exceptional or noble but instinctive, a source of simple pleasure. Fielding surely thinks this experience is possible rather than frequent, but the possibility is enough for his argument. What Fielding calls love, as distinct from appetite or desire—also good, natural things—is thus the deployment of an aspect of human nature: selfish and selfless at the same time.

Empson is drawn to the generosity of such a view, and his later work is full of the search for heroes, Marvell and Joyce particularly being conscripted as good men even more than good writers.

Much of this moral detective work (gathered in *Using Biography*) is very erratic, and has a bluntness and crudity of aim that the younger Empson would have scorned. The Fielding essay, however, is both fervent and subtle. Empson twice stresses Fielding's "Proust-like" delicacy, and he manages something of the same effect himself. Fielding's irony is Empson's ambiguity released from its restrictions, a means of sanely seeing round difficult questions "like a judge." This may slightly idealize judges. Empson also describes Fielding as expressing "imaginative sympathy for two codes [of honor] at once." "The society which Fielding describes is one in which many different codes of honour, indeed almost different tribes, exist concurrently" (*Using Biography*, p. 141).

This is like the divided modern world that Empson wants to take as "one place," not homogenized but harmonized by the imagination and understanding of difference. The situation in *Tom Jones* allows him to state his general literary creed, which is no less difficult to practice because it can be so simply stated: "Modern critics . . . have become oddly resistant to admitting that there is more than one code of morals in the world, whereas the central purpose of reading imaginative literature is to accustom yourself to this basic fact" (*Using Biography*, p. 142). Once again, Empson sounds up-to-date, a modern critic himself, a firm pluralist, and yet also full of a quite old-fashioned confidence about what "the central purpose of reading" (and of many other things) is. The madhouse is closer than this cheery tone suggests, because if "modern critics" are not blinkered or dogmatic about morals, they are likely to deny or relativize all morals. When Empson realizes where he is, he begins to bluster, rather as creatures in cartoons start to fall when they realize the stairway is missing. A late lecture by Empson entitled "Rhythm and Imagery in British Poetry" (1961) confesses the problem. He sees that much of this material—codes of honor, functions of the imagination, desire, religion, relation to the means of production and to human biology, and a great deal more—must work in the dark, rely on a sort of cultural unconscious, and that the "main function" of a critic "must be to mediate between the unconsciousness of the artist and the unconsciousness of the public." "When I was young," Empson continues, "I did not mind this, but I find now I have become one of the old

buffers who were always made fretful by it. I think modern art has gone too far" (collected in *Argufying*, p. 147). Too far in several directions, probably; but not all old buffers know they are old buffers, and some buffers have never been young.

GOD ON TRIAL

EMPSON is fond of legal metaphors, and one of the most notorious (and attractive) pronouncements in *Milton's God* puts God himself in the dock. The context has Empson saying again, only more fully, what he says in the Fielding essay:

The fundamental purpose of putting elaborate detail into a story is to enable us to use our judgement about the characters; often both their situation and their moral convictions, or their scales of value, are very unlike our own, but we use the detail to imagine how they feel when they act as they do, so that we "know what to make of them." Understanding that other people are different is one of the bases of civilization.

(p. 94)

Empson quotes J. S. Diekhoff as saying that God is on trial (what Diekhoff seems to suggest is that Satan seeks to arraign God, but that the attempt misfires because the accused becomes the ideal witness to his own innocence), and concludes impressively, "and the reason is that all the characters are on trial in any civilized narrative." No exemptions, no special pleading. The thought is appealing and Empson writes very persuasively about Satan's mistrial, by God and Christian theology; he writes less persuasively about God's misconduct, although it is shocking to be reminded that one of the traditional delights promised to the blessed in heaven was the sight of their fellows in hell being tortured. Culturally licensed sadism seems to be the only name for this and, as Empson says, it brings us uncomfortably close to the spirit of the concentration camp.

There is plenty of indignation in this book, but Empson seems to want to blame God for the whole modern madhouse, and his excited rhetoric often carries him away. It is true that Milton says he set out to "justify the ways of God to man," and that "justify" implies a serious possibility of argument.

It is not true that this justification necessarily implies that God is on trial, and still less that Milton is regularly "struggling to make his God appear less wicked" (p. 11), or anxious "to justify God for creating a world so full of sin and misery" (p. 95). Empson is breaking his own rule, having convicted and sentenced God before the trial has half started. When he writes that "you ought not to obey a God if your conscience tells you that his orders are wrong" (p. 160), there seems to be a genuine muddle, a failure of the secular imagination to understand the world of belief. Of course Empson is right about worldly orders, and even the orders of a church. He also is right if he means that an atheist ought not to obey the orders of a God in whom he or she no longer believes. But God and the conscience *cannot* give different orders for a believer: the question is logical, not moral or political. Conscience is one of the forms that God's presence takes. It could be at odds with everything except itself. Your conscience could hardly tell you that its orders are wrong.

Faustus and the Censor in one way continues *Milton's God,* although its tone is quite different. It offers a triumphant alternative where the earlier book could afford only a spirited defense. Milton, according to Empson, did what he could for his "appalling God," but Marlowe did even better, refusing God's orders and inventing a Faustus who is not damned, a Mephistopheles who is not a devil. Mephistopheles is a middle spirit, one of the sort who stole children and were full of mischief but lived in a theological limbo. Such spirits have no soul, and Mephistopheles wants Faustus'. Faustus will not need it, since he does not believe in heaven and hell, and will be happy to die like a beast once his time is up. This is an elegant solution, circumventing much medieval horror, and this is what happens in the end, Empson says. What awaits Faustus, he realizes, is neither heaven nor hell but sheer oblivion, just what the tricky but finally faithful Mephistopheles had promised. He cries "Ah Mephistopheles," and "dies in the arms of his deceitful friend with immense relief, also gratitude, surprise, love, forgiveness, and exhaustion. It is the happiest death in all drama" (p. 122). This, Empson argues, is the spectacular and subtle play Marlowe wrote. Then he fell foul of the censor, and he or someone else rewrote the whole thing, introduced Lucifer, turned the middle spirits into dark demons, Christianized Faustus' fault, and made sure he was damned at the end.

Empson clearly believes he is reconstructing history, and equally clearly he cannot be doing that. The best we can say is that his version of events is not historically impossible. At times the argument seems so contorted that we cannot say even that. There is talk of hell in Empson's conception of the play, for example, even before the censor gets to work; and Empson explains much of this as deviousness on Mephistopheles' part. He is not really a devil, but he pretends to be one in order to soften Faustus. We can reject this argument at once on grounds Empson himself would have to accept: because it trivializes some of the best lines in the play. "Why, this is hell, nor am I out of it," Mephistopheles says in answer to Faustus' question about exactly where hell is. Hell is not a place, it is a state of the soul, and Faustus ought to know better than to ask. Hell may well remain, as Empson thinks, an awful human invention, one of our most grisly cultural achievements; it would still have a dignity and a power that a mere Mephistophelian trick would lack, and hellish states of soul have certainly outlasted the theology that named them.

However, Faustus does speak, even in the version of the play we have, of "eternal death" where we might expect him to speak of eternal torture, and he does call Lucifer "Chief Lord and Regent of perpetual night," which sounds oddly peaceful. Empson's reading makes sense of the Faustus who says he does not believe in hell, and catches the flickering grandeur of many of his claims about magic. Empson has found two heroes here, Faustus and Marlowe; and the writing is full of energy and generosity, has none of the bullying and bad faith that mar *Milton's God.* We may want to think of this extraordinary critical creation as a form of historical novel, since we might wish Marlowe had written this different play even if we do not quite believe he did. It is true, too, that whatever Empson himself regards himself as doing, his idea of evidence is critical rather than historical: "The best evidence for this theory of the play is that it gives point and thrust to so many of the details" (p. 123). "All this part is so brilliant when restored that I feel I cannot have gone wrong" (p. 129). Empson can go wrong, and perhaps he has; but the book has great power as a form of fable, an extended metaphor for what happens when we read, for those mixed acts of attention, distraction, and insight that constitute interpretation. Even Empson's misreadings, if that is what they are, never do less than illuminate the process of reading, and there are gleams here of the excitement of *Seven Types of Ambiguity,* the sense of newly discovered riches poured out in sheer prodigality.

LEGACY

In *Some Versions of Pastoral* Empson defines "richness" as "readiness for argument not pursued" (p. 139). The definition, although casually offered, takes us a long way toward understanding Empson's work and its continuing importance. In many views of the world, old and new, arguments not pursued, like chances not grasped, are simply lost, abolished by the pressure of what we call the real. For Empson (as for T. S. Eliot or Robert Frost, also specialists in roads and passages not taken), they are a form of wealth. That wealth is individual, since "readiness" might be more active and useful to us than "ripeness," and cultural, since we understand each other by imagining possible behavior as well as by observing what we actually do.

To this proposition we can add the further claim, adumbrated in *Seven Types of Ambiguity* and developed in *The Structure of Complex Words,* that words themselves possess such richness that their *other* uses always lurk in them, since language stores both pursued and unpursued arguments. Language *is* history, an archive of possibilities—particularly of unspoken or half-spoken possibilities, everything that lurks in jokes, proverbs, ironies, and popular idioms, the secret as well as the open agenda of a culture.

Empson's work thus connects close reading to the history that close reading has often seemed to deny; and also, although he would have hated the thought, it prepares the ground for what came to be called deconstruction, with its suspicion of cultural conspiracy in the metaphors we use. Empson has long been regarded as a major force behind much of the American New Criticism from the 1930's to the 1950's, an unruly but unavoidable example. He is currently being rediscovered as a "theorist," that is, as one who brought philosophi-

cal and other concerns to bear on the business of literary criticism. It is true that his philosophy is technically rather loose, but it is intensely applied, the action of an admirably restless intelligence. Paul de Man, pursuing an argument of his own in relation to Empson, writes of "poetic consciousness as . . . essentially divided, sorrowful, and tragic"; of a fundamental ambiguity that "prevails between the world of the spirit and the world of sentient substance." This is to turn Empson into a Hegelian in spite of himself, and it is a measure of the reach of Empson's implied theory that the move should even seem possible. But Empson's sense of the split between spirit and substance reflects familiar human disappointment rather than an eternal ontological gulf, and the divided consciousness produces energy as well as sorrow. Empson's cheerful tone, in his poems and in his criticism, is often bravado, a form of English bluff. What it hides, however, is not melancholy but panic, not the morgue but the madhouse. Empson shows us our fear but also shows us, in the underexplored spaces of language and imagination, the rich resources we have for facing it.

SELECTED BIBLIOGRAPHY

I. BIBLIOGRAPHY. F. Day, *Sir William Empson: An Annotated Bibliography* (New York, 1984).

II. SEPARATE WORKS. *Seven Types of Ambiguity* (London, 1930; rev. ed. New York, 1955); *Poems* (London, 1935); *Some Versions of Pastoral* (London, 1935); *The Gathering Storm* (London, 1940); *Collected Poems* (New York, 1949; enl. ed., London, 1955); *The Structure of Complex Words* (London, 1951); *Milton's God* (London, 1961; rev. ed., 1965); *Using Biography* (London, 1984); *Essays on Shakespeare,* D. Pirie, ed. (London, 1986); *The Royal Beasts and Other Works,* J. Haffenden, ed. (London, 1986); *Argufying: Essays on Literature and Culture,* J. Haffenden, ed. (London, 1987); *Faustus and the Censor: The English Faust-book and Marlowe's Doctor Faustus,* J. H. Jones, ed. (Oxford and New York, 1987).

III. RECORDING. *William Empson Reading Selected Poems* (London, 1959).

IV. BIOGRAPHICAL AND CRITICAL STUDIES. F. R. Leavis, "Cambridge Poetry," in *Cambridge Review* (1 March 1929); J. C. Ransom, *The New Criticism* (Norfolk, Conn., 1941); C. Brooks, "Hits and Misses," in *Kenyon Review,* 14 (Autumn 1952), a review of *Structure of Complex Words;* S. E. Hyman, "William Empson and Categorical Criticism," in his *The Armed Vision: A Study in the Methods of Modern Literary Criticism* (New York, 1955); H. Kenner, "Alice in Empsonland," in his *Gnomon: Essays on Contemporary Literature* (New York, 1958); J. H. Willis, Jr., *William Empson* (New York, 1969); P. de Man, "The Dead-End of Formalist Criticism," in his *Blindness and Insight* (New York, 1971; rev. ed., Minneapolis, 1983); R. Sale, "The Achievement of William Empson," in his *Modern Heroism* (Berkeley and Los Angeles, 1973); R. Gill, ed., *William Empson: The Man and His Work* (London and Boston, 1974), a collection of important essays on Empson and his work, includes a substantial bibliography; P. Gard-

ner and A. Gardner, *The God Approached: A Commentary on the Poems of William Empson* (London and Totowa, N.J., 1978); C. Norris, *William Empson and the Philosophy of Literary Criticism* (London, 1978); C. Norris, "Reason, Rhetoric, Theory: Empson and de Man," in *Raritan,* 5 (Summer 1985); T. Eagleton, "The Critic as Clown," in his *Against the Grain* (London, 1986); F. Kermode, "On a Chinese Mountain," in *London Review of Books* (20 November 1986); R. Wellek, "William Empson," in *A History of Modern Criticism: 1750–1950,* vol. 5 (New Haven, 1986); J. Culler, "Empson's Complex Words," in his *Framing the Sign* (Oxford, 1988).

RONALD FIRBANK

(1886–1926)

Ralph C. Boettcher

THE DISTINGUISHED critics Mark Longaker and Edwin C. Bolles in *Contemporary English Literature* (1953) dismiss the novels of Ronald Firbank as "trivial impertinences" (p. 342). And Cyril Connolly, in his essay "The Novel-Addict's Cupboard," in *The Condemned Playground* (1946) writes that "it is quite useless to write about Firbank—nobody who doesn't like him is going to like him, and he can be extremely aggravating and silly—but," he immediately adds, "he was a true innovator, and his air of ephemerality is treacherous in the extreme." This assessment follows Connolly's judgment of "the poetry of Horace and Tibullus, the plays of Congreve, the paintings of Watteau and Degas, the music of Mozart, and the prose of Flaubert"—and the fiction of Firbank—as attempting "to portray the beauty of the moment, the gaiety and sadness, the fugitive distress of hedonism." Further, he catalogs Ernest Hemingway, Evelyn Waugh, Anthony Powell, and F. Scott Fitzgerald as "among the Firbank derivatives" (p. 115).

"Ephemeral" may be insufficient in describing the fiction of Firbank to the reader most comfortable with a narrative whose logic is predicated upon causal relations. In his or her initial encounter with Firbank the reader may, in fact, lose the thread of the narrative altogether as it weaves its way through a sequence of scenes displayed largely by long passages of dialogue that may seem—or indeed may be—threadbare.

Among the features of Firbank's fiction that may further disenchant the reader are the characters. Few are memorable, some dull, most remarkable only for their eccentricities. There is the queen in *The Artificial Princess* (1934) who, wearing her crown, loves to drive or sit by the roadside to fix flat tires; or the "tangerine figure" of an ancient in *Valmouth: A Romantic Novel* (1919), who says, "The last time I went to the play . . . was with Charles the Second and Louise de Querouaille, to see Betterton play Shylock in *The Merchant of Venice*" (p. 440).[1] In the sometimes mad world Firbank has created, identification with most of the characters may be virtually impossible. And except for the sentimental *Odette d'Antrevernes* (1905), Firbank's novels, unlike those by Charles Dickens, the Brontës, John Galsworthy, or even Virginia Woolf, may be judged deficient in sentiment.

These alleged defects notwithstanding, his novels, relatively unfamiliar and consigned to minor status, have called forth lavish praise from distinguished critics. Among them are E. M. Forster, who praises Firbank in an essay in *Abinger Harvest* (1936) to be discussed at the end of this essay; and Sir Osbert Sitwell who, in a touching memoir of Firbank in *Noble Essences* (1950), judges his books "deliciously unlike any others in the world. . . ." (p. 100).

Connolly's catalog of derivatives—he should also have included Firbank's friend Aldous Huxley, whose fiction, notably *Crome Yellow* (1921), suggests indebtedness to Firbank—is substantiated by Evelyn Waugh in his succinctly perceptive essay on Firbank in *Life and Letters* (1929) and reprinted in *The Essays, Articles, and Reviews of Evelyn Waugh* (1983). Recognizing in Firbank, among other defects, a degree of silliness, an apparently inherent "ineradicable fatuity," Waugh hastens to add that "these defects, and perhaps some others, may be granted to his detractors, but when everything has been said which can intelligently be brought against him there remains a figure of essential artistic integrity and importance" (p. 56). In essence Waugh says that by abjuring the cause-effect components of the raw materials of the narrative, Firbank has created a new art form.

---

[1]References to Firbank's novels are from *The Complete Ronald Firbank* except for *A Study in Temperament*, "Lady Appledore's Mésalliance," and *The New Rhythm*, which are from *The New Rhythm and Other Pieces*.

The critic and novelist Carl Van Vechten was the first to recognize Firbank's genius in America; he was responsible in 1924 for the publication and subsequent financial success of *Prancing Nigger*. (This was Van Vechten's title; it was published a year later in England under the title Firbank preferred, *Sorrow in Sunlight*).

The American critic Edmund Wilson, however, is probably Firbank's most trenchant critic. Both Carl Van Vechten and Ronald Firbank are praised by him in his essay "Late Violets from the Nineties" (1923). In his essay "Firbank and Beckford" (1926) Wilson draws close parallels between Firbank and the also relatively unknown William Beckford, but Wilson's major contribution to the criticism of Firbank is the essay "A Revival of Ronald Firbank," published in 1949 and reprinted in *Classics and Commercials* (1950). Subsequent studies by other critics have enlarged the portrait of Firbank, but none have excelled the incisiveness of Wilson's commentary, of which the following is representative:

One may have thought, when one first looked at his books in the twenties, that they were foamy improvisations which could be skimmed up in rapid reading. Yet when one tried to run through them, one found oneself pricked by something that queerly impressed; one was aware of artistic seriousness, even if one did not linger to find out what the writer was up to. When one returns to them today, one realizes that Ronald Firbank was one of the writers of his time who took most trouble over their work and who were most singlemindedly devoted to literature. The memoirs of him testify to this. His books are not foolish trifles, scribbled down to get through the boredoms of a languid and luxurious life. They are extremely intellectual, and composed with the closest attention: dense textures of indirection that always disguise the point. They have to be read with care, and they can be read again and again, because Firbank has loaded every rift with ore.

(p. 491)

Finally, there is a poetic tribute to Firbank by W. H. Auden in his "Letter to Lord Byron," originally published in *Letters from Iceland* (1937) and reprinted in *Collected Longer Poems* (1969):

There's every mode of singing robe in stock,
  From Shakespeare's gorgeous fur coat, Spenser's muff
Or Dryden's lounge suit to my cotton frock,

And Wordsworth's Harris tweed with leathern cuff.
Firbank, I think, wore just a just-enough. . . .

(p. 58)

A HAUT MONDE LIFE

ARTHUR Annesley Ronald Firbank was born in London on 17 January 1886. He was the second son of Thomas Firbank and Jane Garrett, the daughter of an Irish clergyman. His paternal grandfather, Joseph Firbank, was in the coal pits as a miner at the age of seven; with hard work, knowledge acquired in night classes, business acumen, and good luck, he amassed a large fortune as a railroad contractor. A compassionate man respected by all his peers, he was temperamentally different from his son and grandson, but Ronald may have inherited his grandfather's business perspicacity. It was this man's fortune, in any case, that provided for Firbank the means to live a life of ease, with the leisure to indulge in the arts, to travel—and to write.

His parents were gifted people of refined sensibility. His father evidently inherited some of Joseph Firbank's energy and verve. Knighted in 1902, he was a member of Parliament and held executive posts in several industries. He was also active in many clubs and was well known both as a sportsman and a collector of art objects. Firbank's mother, a beautiful, charming, and gracious woman, was probably the chief determinant in the formation of Firbank's personality. Directing his genius toward the arts when he was a child, she continued to be a major influence on his affairs all his life. He returned her affection in kind. She was, in fact, the only love of his life, and like Baudelaire, whom he admired, his relation with his mother throughout his life would be of interest to the Freudians. Ronald's delicate health as a child—differing diagnoses of which include asthma and throat infection—intensified her lavishly affectionate nature, and probably abetted, albeit reluctantly, by her husband, she spoiled him.

His formal education began in 1900, when he was fourteen. In the fall of that year he entered Uppingham, a public school; when he returned home for Christmas vacation however, "his mother kept him there" (Benkovitz, *Ronald Firbank*, p. 24). No information is available about his experience at

Uppingham, but as Ifan Kyrle Fletcher notes in *Ronald Firbank: A Memoir*, "a small tragedy is concealed behind the bare entry in the School Registry 'Arthur Annesley Ronald Firbank: Entered September, 1900. Left April, 1901'" (p. 20).[2] Little imagination is required to conjecture the trauma of this initial confrontation with an army of rough-and-tumble boys of his own age—the clashes on the playing field, the lack of privacy in the dormitory, and especially because of his artistic temperament, the inevitable "ragging." To those horrors must be added the routine and especially the discipline of classroom instruction. His education was resumed, surely not a moment too soon, by private tutors.

In the fall of 1902, he was sent to France to learn French and to prepare for a career, possibly in diplomacy. This was the beginning of long sojourns in France for the next four years, notably in Tours and later in Paris. His aspiration for a career in the diplomatic service, however serious he may have been about it, was abortive; and less significant than his study of the language was his discovery of French literature, especially the poetry of Charles Baudelaire, Paul Verlaine, Stéphane Mallarmé, and Henri De Régnier, and the novels of Gustave Flaubert and Théophile Gautier. He also came to admire the symbolic dramas of the Belgian poet and dramatist Maurice Maeterlinck.

The year 1905 is significant because it is the beginning of his career as a writer and his emergence—already begun in Paris—as a man about town. He published that year at his own expense (as he would all except one of his works) a slim paper-covered volume containing the short story *Odette d'Antrevernes* and the short sketch *A Study in Temperament*. In Madrid from late February until late July, he became part of its fashionable society. He entertained, as Ifan Kyrle Fletcher says, "with exquisite grace" (p. 24), in his lavishly appointed apartment, his rooms always gleaming with the light of candles, the air always filled with the aroma of incense as he conversed wittily in French.

He continued this haut monde style of living when he entered Cambridge in 1906, after a brief period in London where he was tutored for admission. His critics ponder his choice of rooms in Trinity Hall, for at the time it was occupied primarily by sportsmen, the rowers and the hunters who were seldom distracted by the challenges of the academy. The hearty Trinity Hall men viewed with quizzical interest his furniture draped in red silk and the modern paintings on his walls, these in an aura of burning incense mingling with the fragrance of fresh flowers, usually out of season. Scattered on tables was a collection of Gothic, Greek, and Egyptian statuettes; always prominent was a heavily framed photograph of his mother in court dress. Intimidated, perhaps, by his flamboyance, or awed by the knowledge that he had already published a book—or perhaps because they were guests at his parties for which he became well known—they ragged him only once, and it was a minor confrontation. He spent most of his time at Cambridge entertaining his friends, traveling to London and Paris, carrying back to Cambridge reports of evenings in the theater or exhibitions at museums. He took no examinations, and left after five terms.

His father's death in 1910 caused momentary panic because the value of his estate was discovered to be considerably smaller than Firbank and his mother had thought, but it was sufficient, at all events, for both to live quite comfortably. When living with his mother in London after his father's death, he was frequently seen at the theater, ballet, and galleries. He traveled extensively—to Egypt in 1911 and then on the Continent, until the outbreak of the war.

Declared unfit for military service, he took refuge from the horrors of war in 1914 by fleeing to Oxford, where he became a virtual recluse. His outrage at the cataclysmic events in Europe ironically galvanized his creative urge, and he began to write seriously, producing in rapid succession *Vainglory* in 1915, *Inclinations* in 1916, *Caprice* in 1917, and in 1919, *Valmouth*.

Impressed with *Vainglory*, Sir Osbert Sitwell made it a point to call on Firbank when he visited Oxford. Sitwell writes that

Ronald Firbank had, during two whole years, spoken to no one there except his charwoman and a guard on the train to London. . . . He felt himself totally out of place in a khaki-clad, war-mad world, where neither music nor gaiety existed, and in which one could no longer travel

---

[2]Differing from Fletcher, Benkovitz states that Firbank entered Uppingham in May 1900, (p. 22), and that his name "was still on Uppingham's list for 1901 because the statutory term's notice had not been given" (p. 24).

except about the business of death. . . . [The war] had deprived him of all outside interests, until finally ennui forced him to write the book about which he had talked for so many years. These volumes were, therefore, far more truly than any others in the English language the product of conflict. He was in the best, the least boring, sense a "war writer."

(*Noble Essences*, p. 82)

His departure from Oxford in 1919 initiated the last and most productive phase of his life. Although none of his works met with enthusiastic critical response, he began to receive some serious attention. (Fletcher recalls this incident in his *Memoir:* The reviewer for *The Scotsman* found *Inclinations* "pleasant, vivacious, and stimulating." "Stimulating to what?" Firbank archly wondered [p. 57].) He had the support of, among others, Sir Osbert and Dame Edith Sitwell, Wyndham Lewis, and Aldous Huxley. The publication of *Valmouth* enhanced his growing reputation. His play, *The Princess Zoubaroff,* published in 1920, was a disappointment for him, for he was never to see it produced. With air travel now available, his wanderlust revivified. He visited North Africa and the West Indies, and of course he continued his peregrinations on the Continent. The novelette *Santal* was published in 1921, and the novel *The Flower Beneath the Foot* in 1923.

The grief he experienced at the death of his mother in 1924 may have been assuaged somewhat by the relative success that same year in America of *Prancing Nigger,* a novel inspired by his experience in the West Indies.

Having completed the novel *Concerning the Eccentricities of Cardinal Pirelli* in Rome in 1925, he traveled to Egypt where he began *The New Rhythum and Other Pieces.* This work is unfinished, for returning to Rome, he died there of pneumonia on 21 May 1926 after about a year of deteriorating health. He was buried in the Protestant cemetery, but later his remains were transferred to the Catholic cemetery at Verano.

AESTHETE AND INNOVATOR

FIRBANK had become a legendary figure long before he died. Many who knew him refused to believe the news of his death, convinced that he was sequestered somewhere, screaming with laughter at his own obituaries. The search for an adjective that describes him in the various manifestations of his personality would have to include, among others, "bizarre," "neurotic," and "hypersensitive." Nevertheless, he was also a devoted son and, within the limitations of his circle at least, generous and kind. "It is difficult to say anything definite about anyone as vague as Ronald Firbank," writes his friend V. B. Holland in "Ronald Firbank," an essay reprinted in Fletcher's *Memoir.* "There seems to be nothing to grasp hold of, merely a fleeting impression here and there, of his gestures, of his half-said phrases, of his laughter, and of his tangled hair" (p. 101). He was enigmatic—seldom if indeed ever willing to reveal himself.

Above all he was an aesthete, born ironically too late to be in the company of the so-called decadents in France and England and the exponents of the Aesthetic movement in England in the 1890's— Joris Karl Huysmans, Paul Verlaine, Aubrey Beardsley, and Oscar Wilde, among others. Yet in many ways his life and his art are an amalgamation of their lives and art continued into the twentieth century. His novels display the instruction he received from Huysmans' *A Rebours* (Against the Grain [1884]) and in many ways, Firbank was as sensuous as the hero of that novel, Des Esseintes. Like Verlaine, he was a convert to Roman Catholicism and homosexual; and some of his prose has the grace and delicacy of Verlaine's poetry. Aubrey Beardsley's satiric drawings and especially his *Under the Hill* (1896) opened further vistas for Firbank's art. Although he was not epigrammatic as was the legendary Wilde, he did share his wit somewhat, and in some ways he was another Dorian Gray.

Unlike the rotund Wilde, Firbank was tall and slender and had, as Jocelyn Brooke states in her encapsulation of the existing commentary on his delicate physique, "the equivocal air of a female impersonator" (p. 34); his willowy, undulating walk always attracted attention. His cheeks appeared lightly rouged; the long nails of his well-kept hands were stained with carmine. In public he usually wore dark, well-cut suits invariably complemented by a bowler, gloves, and a cane. He habitually waved his hands over his head when he spoke—he had a high-pitched voice—and his confreres recall his "perpetual" giggle that frequently erupted into hoarse hysterical laughter. Like Wilde's Dorian Gray he was terrified by the prospect of losing his handsome features in growing old; consonant with his belief that only art endured, he frequently sat for portraits by artists such as Augustus John, Wyndham Lewis, and Alvaro Guevera. To preserve his figure, he dieted strenuously. Sir Osbert Sitwell tells of their having dinner with a friend who had ordered for them a sumptuous meal; Firbank ate nothing but one green pea. He seemed to subsist on champagne.

Sometimes in his commitment to the cult of the beautiful he could be rude. Fletcher recalls that once when about to be presented to an American staying in London, Firbank turned away, muttering, "He is much too ugly!" (p. 47). His passion for the theater did not prevent him from squirming agitatedly in his seat at times, his head nearly touching the floor, his feet extended into the air, or from rummaging under his seat in the middle of an act.

Fletcher believed that "elements of grace, wisdom, wit, reserve, nervousness, masochism, and perversion mixed in strange but attractive proportions" (p. 46) in his personality. He was especially shy with women. He did not make friends easily, and did not easily retain them. As for the loneliness consequent upon the absence of the joy of friendship, Brooke writes that he once announced, "I can buy companionship" (p. 36). But this flippancy disguised a need for friendship that more often than not was unfulfilled. Sir Osbert Sitwell recalled "a pathetic instance of this unhappy outlook" one day at the Café Royal in London, which was bohemian in atmosphere and patronage and one of Firbank's favorite haunts: "Firbank entered and walked up to one of his friends . . . and asked [him] to give him luncheon. The young man replied that he could not do so, for he had no money; upon which Firbank took a pound note out of his pocket, pressed it into the hand of his friend and, sinking at the same time into the seat opposite, exclaimed, 'How wonderful to be a guest!' " (*Noble Essences,* p. 96).

He was not without friends, numbering among them, in addition to the Sitwells, Rupert Brooke, Aldous Huxley, and Carl Van Vechten. One would expect, furthermore, by the way he is described by even his most sympathetic confreres, that his appearance and behavior would have made him easy prey for thieves—or worse—in his travels; yet his wanderings all over Europe, to Cairo, Constantinople, and the West Indies are reported without unpleasant incident.

He loved the social whirl but not without pain. Yet the pace of his socializing must have been unsettling, his elegance inadequate, his adoration of the beautiful unfulfilling, because with his aestheticism he had a penchant for satire, and satire arises if not out of indignation at the presence of evil, then out of amusement at human folly. In either case, the satirist is, to varying degrees of one variety or another, a moralist. Fletcher notes that a friend who met Firbank in Paris in 1910 recalls that he was "profoundly moved by the mystic element of religion" (p. 31). This was not long after he had left Cambridge, where he had become a convert to Catholicism.

After developing a friendship with and evidently coming under the influence of Monsignor A. S. Barnes, the Roman Catholic chaplain at Cambridge, Firbank was received into the Roman Catholic church in 1907. His interest in medievalism and his attraction to the Roman Catholic liturgy—like many of the aesthetes of the 1890's who became Roman Catholics—may have been initially motivational in his conversion, his latent mysticism notwithstanding.

For how long and how seriously he remained a Catholic, in any case, is questionable. On leaving Cambridge, he considered applying for a position in the Vatican, reasoning that a retreat, as Fletcher states, would be in order "As much for my looks as for the welfare of my soul" (p. 35). Neither retreat nor position materialized, and later he was to say to his friend Lord Berners, as Berners notes in his essay "Ronald Firbank," in Fletcher's *Memoir,* "The Church of Rome wouldn't have me and so I laugh at her" (p. 149). His frustrated ambition may have provided the motive for his fantastic hagiographies and his satirical portraits of the Roman Catholic clergy in his fiction. There is some irony, in any case, in the removal of his remains from the Protestant to the Catholic cemetery in Rome, because he was only nominally, surely, a Catholic at his death.

His search for a higher reality, a transcendental plane, took on other forms as well. His first trip to Egypt in 1911 was the genesis of what developed into a profound reverence for the Egyptian pantheon. Fascinated by the sphinx, he became convinced that by some infused knowledge—the ultimate mystical experience—he would solve its awesome mystery. In addition to the Egyptian statuettes always prominently displayed in his rooms, he had a sizable collection of Egyptian amulets. His enthusiasm for Egyptology asserted itself occasionally in his novels. In *Vainglory,* Mrs. Henedge suggests, "from behind, the Goddess Hathor as a sacred cow" (p. 132), and Mrs. Shamefoot takes delight in "a magnificent image of the god Ptah" (p. 118).

Moreover, whatever the element of his attraction to Islam may have been, *Santal* soars beyond approbation of the Muslim pursuit of sanctity. And Mrs. Yajñavalkya, central in *Valmouth,* murmurs, "I miss a mosque . . . and de consolation ob de church; but when I turn to Allah, I suppose de Holy Mihrab near to me and den . . . all is well" (p. 439).

Like many of his contemporaries, his explorations into the transcendental included the occult, and for a short time he investigated magic ritual. Finding Aleister Crowley worthy of serious study, he probably read Crowley's *The Equinox* and *The Scented Garden of Abdullah*. He evidently was familiar with the works of Alias Lévi, and in *Caprice* Mrs. Sixsmith announces that she is "fond of thoughtful, theosophical reading" (p. 355); her favorite authors are Madame Blavatsky and Mrs. Annie Besant. Firbank, furthermore, was superstitious; habitually consulting fortune-tellers, he always took their prognostications seriously, often to his dismay, if not to his despair.

If romanticism manifests essentially the exploratory, the transcendental, and the bourgeois, as William York Tindall states in *Forces in Modern British Literature* (1953), these transcendental pursuits make Firbank a Romantic, his romanticism refined, of course, by the ambience of the 1890s. Equally significant in his Romantic persuasions is his position as a member of the upper middle class, for the middle class generally provided the substance of his novels and is the focus of his satire. It is likely that his disposition as a satirist and an aesthete developed simultaneously, and that his sensitivity and sensibility as an artist alerted him to the elements of artificiality, shallowness, and malice that he perceived in his own echelon of society. His hatred of vulgarity was matched by his contempt for pomposity and pretentiousness. Sometimes he is the amused observer—his range includes his own work and his reputation as a novelist—and occasionally the scornful moralist; in either case he is always incisive in his assessment of human folly.

Firbank scholars identify, in addition to his affinity for fin de siècle literature, other influences in his work. Edmund Wilson was the first to indicate a relationship between the *Humour* comedies (*Every Man in His Humour,* 1598; *Every Man Out of His Humour,* 1599) of Ben Jonson and the novels of Firbank: the subordination of plot to character, the structure and orchestration of characters, the presence of both broad and subtle humor, the social satire. Firbank's *The Princess Zoubaroff* is nearly always offered by critics as a companion piece to William Congreve's *The Way of the World* (1700) in the literature of the comedy of manners; but Congreve's attributes—his wit, his fragile curve of action, his blithesome buoyancy—are more evident in Firbank's novels. Edward Martin Potoker in his monograph on Ronald Firbank indicates structural similarities between Firbank's novels and Laurence Sterne's *Tristram Shandy* (originally published in nine volumes, from 1760 to 1767) to suggest that Firbank was more than sufficiently familiar with the novel to use successfully some of Sterne's techniques. Among these are the displacement of the logical continuity of action by free association of ideas. Like *Tristram Shandy,* nearly all of Firbank's novels proceed by indirection rather than causal relations, the focus being the author's consciousness. Potoker also sees Firbank's humor, his "brand of whimsicality" (p. 39), as comparable to Sterne's.

A general pattern in Firbank's novels is a sequence of scenes or set pieces developed largely if not entirely through dialogue. Narration and description are, as a rule, minimal. "Plot" is not applicable except perhaps to *Caprice* and *Prancing Nigger;* a thread of action provides a loose cohesiveness for the scenes. Chronology and continuity are at times tenuous or even nonexistent, and the unwary reader must sometimes exercise ingenuity in making the necessary connections. A parallel in modern poetry is the use of ellipses by Gerard Manley Hopkins and free association by T. S. Eliot. In this structural idiosyncrasy, Firbank becomes like Joyce, Woolf, and others unique in contributing to the continuity of modern fiction.

As Firbank's forte in dialogue, a similar observation may be made about his contribution to the dialogue novel that began with George Eliot. In spite of his contempt for realism, he kept a careful record of overheard conversation, faux pas, and other trivia on strips of paper that he translated into his fiction. His dialogue, usually brilliant, is also occasionally banal. *Inclinations,* for example, is filled with passages such as these:

"Is that you, Mabel?" she asked.
"How's the poor head?"
"I've been drowsing."
"I'm glad you could manage that."
"Isn't the band *awful?*"

"Boom, boom, boom. . . ."
"Did you have a nice time?"

(p. 255)

A characteristic device is his use of ellipses to create a conversational vacuum that the reader is invited to fill. In this snippet from *The Flower Beneath the Foot,* for example, a young man registers horror, disbelief, and chagrin (let us say) on hearing that fleas have been found at the Ritz Hotel: ". . . . .! . . . .? . . .!!" (p. 509). In chapter 8 of the same novel, a third of the page is filled with rows of dots (compare the blank pages of *Tristram Shandy*) to disclose the awful interiority of Countess Yvorra's prayer. He frequently uses stichomythia. A unique motif is passages of fragments of overheard conversations—"confusion of voices"—to suggest the chatter in a crowded room.

His characters for the most part are flat in the sense that E. M. Forster suggests in *Aspects of the Novel* (1927): their conduct is generally predictable, and they do not change significantly. Women are dominant in his gallery of characters, drawn mostly from his own social stratum and usually presented in lavish dress. Dialogue is the chief means of characterization, but he uses description as well. Here, for example, is the Mistress of the Robes in *The Artificial Princess:*

Flushed to the colour of a Malmaison, she was looking conspicuous in silver tissue and diamonds, her long train spread, shimmering, over the steps behind, with the exquisite restraint of a waterfall in a poem. Above, from the fortifications of a lofty tiara, an Ostrich feather fluttered in her hair, as from a Citadel. . . . Clearly she was a Rubens, with her ample figure, florid colouring, and faintly pencilled moustache, a Rubens on the verge of becoming a Jordaens from a too ardent admiration of French cooking, and a preference for sleep.

(p. 55)

The names of characters are occasionally onomatopoeic: the pedantic Professor Inglepin and the willowy Winsome Brookes in *Vainglory,* the vacuous Hon. Mrs. Edward Facile-Manners in *The New Rhythum* are examples. In addition, characters' names are generally whimsical: In *Vainglory,* for example, Lady Anne Pantry sits "in the china-cupboard, a room fitted with long glass shelves, on which her fabled Dresden figures, monkey musicians, and sphinx marquises, made perfect blots of colour against the gold woodwork of the walls" (p. 120). In *Caprice,* Sally Sinquier purloins pieces of the family silver. Firbank also delights in cataloging extravagantly named characters in a social setting. Those attending Sally Sinquier's triumphant debut in the theater, for example, include "Dismalia Duchess of Meath-and-Mann, Lady Di Flattery, Lord and Lady Newblood." Some twenty more names follow, concluding with "Marquesa Pitti-Riffa and Sir Siegfried Seitz" (p. 380).

Firbank's arbitrary use of italics and capitalization of common nouns, the capricious indirection of his narration and description, and his frequent use of pronouns with remote antecedents compound the reader's confusion. More peculiar, perhaps, for so careful a writer, is the abundance of dangling introductory clauses and phrases; this, for example, from *Prancing Nigger:* "Joying frankly in excess, the fiery noontide hour had a special charm for him" (p. 621). On the other hand, his inversion of syntax, especially in his use of the adverb, recalls the syntactical distortions of Gerard Manley Hopkins, who sought to enhance the value of words. Firbank also uses inversion to humorous effect: in *The New Rythum,* for example, Mrs. Van Cotton is described as "waving comprehensively her fan" (p. 88), and in *Valmouth* Mrs. Thoroughfare detects "Lieutenant Whorwood grooming assiduously his romantical curls" (p. 465). Alliteration is a favorite rhetorical device. In *Vainglory* Mrs. Shamefoot's luggage is described thus: "A number of sagacious smaller cases clambered about it now into frantic streets, and sunny open piazzas, like a small town clustering about the walls of some lawless temple" (p. 115). To these features of Firbank's work must be added sly innuendoes in his dialogue, the colorful eccentricities of his characters, his control of crowds in social gatherings, and the subtlety of his satire, all of which contribute to his place among the innovators of contemporary English fiction.

EARLY WORK

His first work, the volume containing *Odette d'Antrevernes* and *A Study in Temperament,* offered by Arthur Annesley Ronald Firbank, was ignored by critics and, generally speaking, readers alike. Firbank, in spite of this general indifference, was sufficiently pleased with *Odette d'Antrevernes* to republish it, slightly revised, in 1915 under the title *Odette: A Fairy Tale for Weary People.* Like his only play, *The Princess Zoubaroff,* *Odette* discloses the influ-

205

ence of Maurice Maeterlinck in its exotic romanticism, its action bathed in moonlight to provide a dreamlike setting suitable to mystical experience.

Odette, a young orphan living in an old chateau in the Loire Valley, is entranced by the story of the child Bernadette's vision of the Blessed Virgin Mary. "She, too," Odette thinks, "would seek the Holy Virgin . . . would speak with the Holy Mary, the Mother of the Lord Seigneur Christ" (p. 20). After a week of steadfast prayers, Odette steals out into the rose garden late at night; instead of the anticipated vision, she discovers a woman emitting long, sad cries, lying "amongst the pale-yewed daisies . . . a woman with painted cheeks and flaming hair; a terrible expression . . . in her eyes" (p. 23). Filled with compassion, Odette takes from her neck a silver cross given her by her mother, and places it around the woman's neck. Promising to find work—honest work—the woman bids Odette goodbye. Returning thoughtfully to her chateau, Odette feels older. "For suddenly, she realized that Life was no. a dream; she realized for the first time that Life was cruel, that Life was sad, that beyond the beautiful garden in which she dwelt, many millions of people were struggling to live, and sometimes in the struggle of life one failed . . ." (p. 25).

Firbank's critics dismiss this early work as worthless juvenilia, but the fact that Firbank was nineteen years old when he published it is relevant in its critical evaluation. It has only a tenuous relationship with the mature works, of course. He would never again, for example, write with such unabashed sentimentality. Some of the action is embarrassingly maudlin: seeing the sobbing woman as the "Holy Mother . . . in pain," for example, Odette stoops down and timidly kisses her feet (p. 22). Later "an immense unaccountable pity" for "this shattered wreck of a human soul" siezes her, and once again Odette bends down to kiss "the woman on her burning lips" (p. 23). The dialogue between prostitute and innocent displays the worst features of melodrama—and yet the story is not without charm. Some descriptive passages compare favorably with the later Firbank: "Far away, at the end of the long avenue of fragrant limes, wound the Loire, all amongst the flowery meadows and emerald vineyards, like a wonderful looking-glass reflecting all the sky; and across the river, like an ogre's castle in a fairy tale, frowned the château of Luynes, with its round grey turrets and its long, thin windows . . ." (p. 17). And the final paragraph makes overtures to symbolism:

"And Odette turned as she walked and looked behind her, to where, by the roadside, and dying beneath the golden sun, the red roses that she had gathered for the Holy Mother, shone in the morning light like drops of crimson blood" (p. 25).

The short sketch *A Study in Temperament* anticipates, in its characterizations, its aesthetic dimensions, its satire, and its subtle humor, the fiction that was to follow. Lady Agnes Charters is compensated for her hatred of receiving guests on Friday afternoons by the sense of relief she always feels when the event is over. For her reception this afternoon, in a "becoming and a shady corner in her boudoir" (p. 21), she wants to be discovered reading; she randomly chooses a small volume bound in gray ("A touch of grey will improve my dress," she thinks), a felicitous choice: "It is so delightful to be seen reading Maeterlinck! So decadent!" (p. 22).

She finds life very dull. She seldom sees her husband, "but then there is something so very early Victorian in seeing one's husband, except, of course, sometimes at meals" (p. 21). In a private conversation during the afternoon, her lover tells her, ". . . you want an object in life. Art alone isn't enough. Grub Street is so very grimy, and good works are out of date. But aren't there other objects? Isn't there *another* object?" (p. 24). He offers himself as that object, imploring her to leave her husband that they might take flight together abroad.

The sketch ends as she tells her maid to prepare for a possible journey. The ambiguity of the conclusion becomes somewhat opaque as she contemplates dyeing her hair red. "I am very beautiful," she thinks, "but I think it would be an improvement to dye my hair red—very gradually, of course—I should so hate anyone to notice—" (p. 29). Her final utterance suggests, in its subtlety, that the flight will become a reality: "Yes, I shall certainly dye my hair red."

The satiric tone, suggestive of Oscar Wilde, extends to Firbank's portrayal of the guests. One, unable to marry the famous musician Paderewski, found consolation in marrying a man who reminded her of *Lohengrin,* her favorite opera ("The idyll lasted only a fortnight" [p. 26]). Another, an American poetess, Miss Hester Q. Tail, has a penchant for spouting epigrams. Expecting her to deliver a dazzling bon mot on idols, her partners in conversation receive her triumphant, "The ideal idol . . . is made in Japan!" (p. 25).

Yet Miss Hester Q. Tail, limited as she may be, offers some insight (shocking to Lady Agnes) into the nature of the society of which they are all a part:

... modern life is only remarkable for its want of profile, and lack of manners. To be smart is to be artificial. To be artificial is to be smart. There is not a man or woman in London society that dares to be him or herself. We are surrounded by invisible laws and conventions, we all sin, and cover our sins in chiffon and diamonds. The chiffon is quite transparent, everyone can see through it, still chiffon is a veil, and then the diamonds! We are all vulgar at heart, and if the diamonds glitter, what does it matter where they come from or how they are bought? To be artificial, and to be a little more improbable and impossible than one's neighbor, is to be a perfect success!

(p. 26)

Never again in his fiction would Firbank be so explicit in his indictment of upper-middle-class society, to which he himself belonged.

A kind of companion piece to *A Study in Temperament* is "Lady Appledore's Mésalliance (An Artificial Pastoral)" (collected in *The New Rhythm*), probably written before 1908. Offered by A. A. R. Firbank, it has autobiographical undertones in its characterization of Wildred, a young aristocrat whose fortune is concentrated mostly in the coal industry; awaiting the settlement of a claim that will secure for him a comfortable income, he takes work as a gardener on the estate of Lady Appledore. A young widow, beautiful and cultivated—she reads *The Rubáiyát of Omar Khayyám*—she finds Wildred attractive, for in addition to being handsome, he is fluent in French and reads the poetry of Verlaine in the moonlight. It is accidentally revealed to Lady Appledore, who has fallen in love with Wildred, that he is not a commoner at all but has noble antecedents; this legitimizes her love, and the two marry. A gossip at the end of the story, unaware of Wildred's true identity, describes his marriage to Lady Appledore as a "mésalliance," which indeed it may have been, since the marriage is referred to in the past tense.

The failure of the marriage may explain, in part, the story's subtitle. The central characters, all of them of the old aristocracy, would be comfortable in the artificial elegance of a painting by Thomas Gainsborough. The pastoral setting glows under sunlight and moonlight, lush with hyacinths, foxgloves, hair ferns, and fruit trees; every page adds to the catalog of flowers and is permeated by their fragrance. Exotic birds sing amid the yellow tassels of the laburnum flower, and peacocks float down from cedar trees to spread their tails in the sun.

The setting also provides a frame for satire. A housemaid, a rustic who could have sprung from the pages of Thomas Hardy, thinks it must be unpleasant to be a cow. The butler agrees: "I am no friend to cows ... they are such licentious animals. Things as has no tables of kindred and affinity are not to be respected" (p. 56). But music is to be respected, and the butler, discovering Wildred's rich, warm voice, invites him to sing for the servants one evening. They play the banjo, the concertina, "and when her ladyship is out driving, and all the doors are closed, Squire, the pantry boy, plays us selections on the bassoon" (p. 56). Conspicuous in this narration is an old gardener who sits up all night with a sick orchid.

Lady Appledore does not escape the satirist's thrust. She loves "remote books." She delights in treatises on industry. A "short essay on the Manufacture of Strawberry-punnets" fills her "to enthusiasm. 'It soothed me, it lulled me like nothing else,' she told a royal lady, who was complaining of feeling nervous at night. 'It is delicious to know something about the Moors ... they *must* have been dears'" (p. 55).

In *A Study in Temperament* and "Lady Appledore's Mésalliance," Firbank moved well beyond the juvenile *Odette d'Antrevernes;* fragile and imperfect as it may be, "Lady Appledore's Mésalliance" demonstrates remarkable maturity. All three works are substantial landmarks in Firbank's apprenticeship.

Miriam J. Benkovitz's *A Bibliography of Ronald Firbank* (1982) suggests two possible dates for the completion of the novelette *The Artificial Princess*—1906 and 1910. Firbank appears to have laid the manuscript aside, forgotten about it, and then to have rediscovered it, to his delight, in 1925, among some belonging to his deceased mother. Published posthumously in 1934, it is not among his best work. By the time he wrote the novel, in any case, his style had solidified; *The Artificial Princess* provides the direction for all of his subsequent work.

Firbank scholars read it as a parody of Oscar Wilde's *Salomé* (1894). The framework, a fantasy, is characteristically inconsequential. The setting is a mythical East European monarchy; the action, focusing on the celebration of the princess's birthday, by incident, allusion, and reference, vaguely parallels the Salome legend. The princess's mother, like Herodias, has married her brother-in-law.

Having a predilection for dancing, the princess vents her frustration by whirling through a "riotous valse" (p. 39) and dances before her mirror "in just a bracelet and a rope of pearls" (p. 53). In the celebration of her birthday, she has obtained the king's word "that she might ask, during dessert, for anything she pleased" (p. 53).

She dispatches a lady in waiting, the Baroness Rudlieb, to invite a saint, John Pellegrin, to her birthday festivities. On her mission the baroness is diverted by a "young man her husband had often sworn to kill" (p. 49); the invitation, which passes through many hands, is not delivered. The saint, however, does appear, a gardenia in his lapel, his dusky gold hair seeming "decidedly waved" (p. 67). He enjoys himself immensely at the party. The princess, staggered by the thought that he may have a "common nature," says to him, "You are a dear, excellent creature . . . and you think of us far too well. If you could see us in the searching light of morning you would condemn us in fiery words. . . . I daresay if you look about you will find bribery and corruption in our very midst" (p. 72).

Bribery and corruption, however, are not manifest in this collection of characters, in this comic fantasia where the royal family dines in restaurants and the king patronizes casinos. He has a glass eye and it is "difficult to say which was which. 'He has only one eye, and I never know which is looking at me'" (p. 59), the queen complains. She has "a passion for motoring," driving "for hours and hours with her crown on . . . [to] the delight of all those foreigners, and especially Americans" (p. 30). She insists "on mending her punctures herself, and it was no uncommon sight to see her sitting with her crown on in the dust." Her reasons for doing so are complex; but probably "wishing to edify her subjects was the real cause. She had been called a great many things, but nobody ever said she was proud; this was her pride . . ." (p. 45). The Baroness Rudlieb is "a thin weary person" (p. 28), whose elusive charm probably

lay simply in her untidiness; she had made it a study. Untidiness with her, had become a fine art. A loose strand of hair . . . the helpless angle of a hat; and, to add emphasis, there were always quantities of tiny paste buttons in absurd places on her frocks that cried aloud to be fastened, giving her an air of irresponsibility which the very young Courtiers seemed to find quite fascinating.

(p. 29)

The princess is artificial—as James Douglas Merritt has indicated—because she has acquired her title by the second marriage of her mother, and because of her fervent desire, as she tells Baroness Rudlieb, to be "a new Salomé" (p. 32). She is androgynous: "Like a Virgin in a missal her figure lacked consequence—sex. 'My tall-tall schoolboy'" (p. 28), her mother calls her. Not at all plain, however, the princess looks "like some radiant marionette" (p. 28). Musing on the state of things in general, she thinks,

Why are present-day sins so conventional—so anaemic? A mild, spectacled priest could trample them out with a large pair of boots. I prefer a Prophet who will insult me! It is then a pleasure to retaliate. I have always suspected mine to be a Salomesque temperament. Naturally, it would be treason to speak with candour of the king, but he would make a superb Herod.

(p.36).

An amplification and more careful development of this theme would give the novel greater density. Whatever Firbank intended in his use of the Salome legend, its main function appears to be merely cohesive, and that cohesiveness is tenuous at best.

Vainglory, his first full-length novel, is a portrait of late-Edwardian upper-middle-class society. The title evokes, among other things, the cry from chapter 12 of Ecclesiastes: *Vanitas vanitatum, omnis vanitas!* Not always satiric, however, it is nevertheless a glowing revelation of the pursuit of specious glory by an overripe society.

Mrs. Shamefoot's obsession with commemorating herself in the stained glass window of a cathedral—her desire "to be caught in a brutality of stone"—provides the framework of the novel. She epitomizes the women in her circle: "overshadowed by a clever husband, and by an exceedingly brilliant mother-in-law, all that was expected of her was to hold long branches of mimosa and eucalyptus leaves as though in a dream at meetings, and to be picturesque, and restful and mute." Sufficiently self-assured and self-centered, however, "she had developed into one of those decorative, self-entranced persons so valued by hostesses at dinner as an ideal full stop" (p. 81). Unsuccessful, however, in her initial attempts to have a stained-glass monument erected in her honor, she is finally able to realize her dream by making a sizeable contribution toward a cathedral severely damaged by lightning.

Within this fragile frame is a panorama of brilliant set pieces, concatenated by characters and developed by satire. A party is given, for example, to provide the world in general and London society in particular with a fragment of a line by Sappho recently discovered by a university professor. Following "an anguishing obbligato," the professor declaims to the assembled guests "impressively the imperishable line." The response, if somewhat skeptical, is generally approbatory. Lady Listless, "looking quite perplexed," nevertheless finds the lines "delicious! Very charming indeed!" The forthright Mrs. Thumbler, however, queries, "Will anyone tell me what it means in plain English?" "In plain English," the professor tells her, "it means: 'Could not . . . for the fury of her feet!' " When the professor interprets the lines as descriptive of the poet's apparent flight, Mrs. Thumbler seems "inclined to faint." " 'Could not,' " she murmurs "helplessly, as though clinging to an alpenstock, and not quite sure of her guide." A priest "suspiciously" inquires "But no doubt there is a *sous-entendu?*" "Indeed, no!" the professor answers. "It is probable, indeed, that Sappho did not even mean to be caustic. Here is an adventurous line, separated (alas!) from its full context. Decorative, useless, as you will; a water-color on silk!" "I don't know why," Lady Georgia confesses, "it thrills me, but it does!" (p. 92).

Firbank satirizes himself in the character of Claud Harvester, who "was usually considered charming. . . . In style—he was often called obscure, although, in reality, he was as charming as the top of an apple-tree above a wall. As a novelist he was almost successful. His books were watched for . . . but without impatience" (p. 82). As other characters observe,

"He has such a strange, peculiar style. His work calls to mind a frieze with figures of varying heights trotting all the same way. If one should by chance turn about it's usually merely to stare or to sneer or to make a grimace. Only occasionally his figures care to beckon. And they seldom really touch."

"He's too cold. Too classic, I suppose."

"Classic! In the *Encyclopædia Britannica,* his style is described as *odd spelling, brilliant and vicious.*"

(p. 199)

His dialogue, generally brittle, always revealing, is complemented by the classical precision of the description of his characters. Mira Thumbler, for example, is "a medieval-looking little thing, with peculiar pale ways, like a creature escaped through the border of violets and wild strawberries on a tapestry panel" (pp. 88-89). Her colleague Miss Compostella is someone whom no one would have taken "to be an actress; she was so private-looking. . . . Excessively pale, without any regularity at all of feature, her face was animated chiefly by her long red lips. . . . But somehow one felt that all Miss Compostella's soul was in her nose. It was her one delicate feature: it aspired" (p. 82). Lady Listless has "the look of a person who had discovered something she ought not to know" (p. 90). Winsome Brookes, the musician, sometimes suggests in "the over-elaboration of his dress . . . a St. Sebastian with too many arrows" (p. 84). Monsignor Parr has "heavy opaque eyes. Something between a butterfly and a misanthrope, he was temperamental, when not otherwise . . . employed" (p. 81). The ellipsis in this last is Firbank's, a void meant to titillate the reader's imagination.

In drawing on his descriptive powers, Firbank at times achieves a lyricism in the best tradition of English prose. A character reflects, for example, on English towers, which

so seldom mellowed rightly. They were too rain-washed, weather-beaten, wind-kissed, rugged; they turned tragic and outlived themselves; they became such hags of things; they grew dowdy and wore snapdragons; objects for picnics; rendezvous of lovers, haunts of vice . . . ; they were made a convenience of by owls; they were scarred by names; choked by refuse, and in the end they got ghoulish and took to too much ivy, and came toppling down.

(p. 175)

The novel is developed largely by dialogue in which there are pauses "just long enough for an angel to pass, flying slowly" (p. 117). However, it has sufficient descriptive and narrative passages to demonstrate a skillful blend of methods of exposition. *Vainglory* is an appropriate title—ironic, however, in its suggestion of a surprising humility, if characteristic levity, in Firbank's satiric assessment of the novels of Claud Harvester, an obvious self-portrait.

After the abundant wealth of *Vainglory,* the relative poverty of *Inclinations,* published a year later, is remarkable. In this novel Geraldine O'Brookomore, a biographer, plans a journey to Greece to gather material for a new book. Not quite sure why—although her lesbian tendencies surface later—she invites Mabel Collins, a young woman sensitive in temperament but limited in intelligence, to accompany her. Mabel emerges as the central character of the novel; her desire to escape the ugly house in Bovon, Yorkshire, where she lives, her frustrated attempt to lead a better life, gives the book its title (of course, the inclinations of Geraldine O'Brookomore also come into play). Aboard ship, Mabel meets Count Pastorelli of Orvieto; they elope. The novel ends when Mabel—a countess now—returns to Bovon with her baby to await the arrival of the count "to take her back with him to Italy, where he has prepared for her benefit a violet and rose salotto. . . ." (p. 313). One has the uncomfortable feeling that he will not appear.

The reader will immediately recognize parallels to Forster's *Where Angels Fear to Tread* (1905), but they are slim and Forster's is much the better novel. *Inclinations* is almost entirely dialogue, much of it stichomythia, most of it pedestrian; only infrequently is the dialogue interrupted by brief passages of narration and description. Here is an example, at the conclusion of chapter 3, of the "confusion of voices," snatches of overheard conversation that Firbank would refine in later novels:

> "Babes-in-the-Wood."
> "We think of crossing over to witness the autumn in Versailles."
> ". . . goes to auctions."
> "The slim, crouching figure of the Magdalen is me."
> "Those break-neck brilliant purples."
> "Pish!"
> "A scarlet song."
> " 'Order what you please from Tanguay,' he said—'a tiara, what you please.' "
> "—You'd think they'd been set by Bœhmer!"
> "O-o-o-h!"
> "You have the catalogue."
> "Mrs. Elstree took it with her."
>
> (pp. 233–234)

Neither Mabel Collins nor Geraldine O'Brookomore excites interest, and only among the tourists in Athens are there flashes of wit. In the orchestration of characters, men are insignificant. Count Pastorelli never appears; he is seen only through Mabel's eyes and devices like Miss O'Brookomore's reaction to him: "Take my word for it," she says, "he's not so pastoral as he sounds" (p. 237). When Mabel remarks that she thinks he has asked her to marry him, Miss O'Brookomore responds,

> "He's proposed?"
> "Of course it's purely verbal . . ."
> "What did he say?"
> "First he asked to speak to me . . . and then he said, 'Little miss,' he said, 'when Love springs under your nose! . . .' That was his expression."
> "A pretty one. But it has nothing to do with marriage. Oh, Mabel! . . ."

Looking grim, she instructs Mabel, "You've yet to learn, I find, what frivolous things men are. . . ." (pp. 260–261).

Her anxiety intensifies. Chapter 20, given here in its entirety, expresses her deepest fears:

> Mabel! Mabel! Mabel! Mabel!
> Mabel! Mabel! Mabel! Mabel!
>
> (p. 284)

And Chapter 21 is a letter Mabel addresses to Geraldine (the heading and postscript are incidental):

> Dear Gerald,—I was married this morning and we leave to-morrow early for Corfu don't worry about me dear I'm alright O darling I'm the happiest girl in Greece I wore my little amber tricorne satin cap dear and Oio gave me the violets I shall get my trousseau bit by bit I suppose as we go along I had wanted rather badly to be married in the Kapnikaraea but it was a Registry after all good-bye now Gerald and take care of yourself dear do in haste yrs always affectionately
>
> Mabina Pastorelli
> (p. 285)

In part 2 Mabel, "the countess" now, has returned to Bovon with her infant daughter. Short, tighter in structure, part 2 has greater density than part 1. Firbank, aware of weaknesses, however, revised chapter 4 (why only chapter 4?) of part 2 in 1925. The changes, reflecting his growth in style, provide an ironic contrast to the rest of the novel.

The 1916 version of chapter 4 features a montage of banal conversation at a dinner Mrs. Collins has arranged for her daughter's homecoming. It ends with a recitation of an innocuous bit of doggerel that concludes:

"Charming!"
"How very, very, very, very vulgar!" the Countess frowned.
"Was it the devil, my dear?"
Mrs. Collins rose.
"Gentlemen," she murmured, "*à tout à l'heure!*"
"Let's all go into the garden, Mabsey."
"There's no moon."
"There are stars."
Miss Dawkins peered out.
"It's dark like Gethsemane," she said.

(p. 302)

Here the chapter ends.

The revision—which sees the above dialogue excised—replaces much of the colorless conversation of the original with characterization. Into the gathering, for example, sails "a mite of a woman enveloped fancifully in a fairy-hued cashmere shawl. . . ." She is held "by local opinion, to be eccentric for preferring to live all alone, which may possibly have had its dangers for a person of her condition and sex; nevertheless, on occasion, to convince an intrusive stranger, she had a male in the house, she would discharge a cartridge out of window, and knot her hair across her chin in front in a thick cascade to imitate *a beard*" (p. 303). Another guest, whose wife is "a woman for whom undergraduates had shot themselves" asks "with a leer" for "la petite Comtesse" (p. 304); and the rector bestows "a frigid smile on the infant papist" (p. 308), her baby having been baptized at St. Peter's in Rome (and during the ceremony smacking "His Holiness"). These changes dramatically indicate that part 1 could have profited by revision—and condensation—as well. "Silly" is an appropriate adjective some critics use in evaluating this generally tedious work.

CAPRICE *AND* VALMOUTH

The theme of innocents abroad in *Inclinations* continues—with some inversion—in *Caprice,* published a year later. Sarah Sinquier (usually referred to in the book as Sally) is the daughter of an Anglican canon in a cathedral town of considerable wealth; finely wrought, she is sensitive, artistic, and intelligent, a romanticist of the most refined proportions. Strident in her ambition to become an actress, she is representative of the typical adolescent, who must escape the offensive confines of her environment to achieve self-fulfillment.

Gathering together her jewelry, pearls that were a gift from her godmother ("It should bring grist; perhaps close on a thousand pounds" [p. 326]), and some of the family's silver, consoling herself with the thought that her parents "shall have *sofas* in their box on the night of my debut. . . ." (p. 327), she flees to London. There she raises sufficient cash in pawning her booty to finance a production of *Romeo and Juliet* in which, as a star, she is a critical success. The morning after opening night, she wanders onto the empty stage; executing "a few athletic figures to shake off sleep" (p. 381), she trips over a mousetrap and falls into a well beneath the stage to her death.

This—and *Prancing Nigger*—are the only Firbank novels that can be said to have a legitimate "plot." The emphasis, nevertheless, continues to be on characters in scenes. On Sally's first day in London, for example, she receives the shocking news that Mrs. Bromley, the woman who was to act as her agent, to offer "experience and advice" in introducing Sally to the London theater, has died the night before. After dazedly wandering around London, nearly "fainting from inanition," she looks for "some nice tea-shop, some cool creamery," and discovers the Café Royal—a graphic fictionalization of one of Firbank's favorite bohemian haunts in London.

Miss Sinquier fluttered in.
By the door, the tables all proved to be taken.
Such a noise!
Everyone seemed to be chattering, smoking, lunching, casting dice, or playing dominoes.
She advanced slowly through a veil of opal mist, feeling her way from side to side with her parasol.
It was like penetrating deeper and deeper into a bath.
She put out her hand in a swimming, groping gesture, twirling as she did so, accidentally, an old gentleman's moustache.
Thank heaven! There, by that pillar, was a vacant place.
She sank down on to the edge of a crowded couch, as in a dream.

The tall mirrors that graced the walls told her she was tired.

"Bring me some China tea," she murmured to a passing waiter, "and a bun with currants in it."

(p. 333–334)

Bursting into tears in that bohemian milieu, she is comforted by Mrs. Sixsmith who, via typically Firbankian innuendo, almost immediately becomes suspect. She quickly passes judgment on Mrs. Bromley, to her a total stranger: "I expect this Mrs. Bromley was nothing but an old procuress. . . . A stage procuress" (p. 336). Learning that Sally had no artistic connections in town, she presents some of her theatrical confreres including "blackening her nose with a cigarette . . . the most resigned of women—Miss Whipsina Peters, a daughter of the famous flagellist—and a coryphée herself" (p. 336).

Mrs. Sixsmith offers her services to dispose of Sally's pearls through "an old banker-friend of mine—Sir Oliver Dawtry" (p. 337). He also arouses the reader's suspicion. He was once in close touch with the stage, and recalls that an actress who played "the wife" in *Macbeth* "was positively roguish" (p. 342).

Mrs. Sixsmith is one of Firbank's most graphically drawn women—flamboyant, avaricious, scheming. One is not likely to forget her "fingers super-manicured, covered in oxydised metal rings" (p. 349). Meeting Sally in a restaurant the evening she begins to take charge of Sally's affairs, Mrs. Sixsmith looks "staid as a porcelain goddess in a garment of trailing white with a minute griffin-eared dog peeping out its sheeny paws and head wakefully from beneath her train" (p. 339). (She will later tell Sally that she cannot return to the Café Royal because she owes "money there . . . To all the waiters" [p. 352].) Typical of Firbank's married women, she is estranged from her husband. "Careless of an intriguing world about her" (p. 338), Sally continues her production of *Romeo and Juliet* under Mrs. Sixsmith's proffered guidance.

The conversation Mrs. Sixsmith has with Sally's father after her funeral is revealing. Sally's father asks her if Sally had any debts.

"Indeed she had . . . she owed me money. Much money. But I won't refer to that . . . Sally owed me one thousand pounds."

"She owed you a thousand pounds?"

"She was infinitely involved."

"Upon what could she spend so much?"

"Her clothes," Mrs. Sixsmith replied with a nervous twitter, "for one thing, were exquisite. All from the atelier of the divine Katinka King . . . The white mantilla for the balcony scene alone cost her close on three hundred pounds."

"And where, may I ask, is it now?"

"It disappeared," Mrs. Sixsmith answered, a quick red shooting over her face, "in the general confusion. I hear," she murmured with a little laugh, "they even filched the till!"

(p. 383).

That this is a fabric of lies is suggested by her thoughts as she wonders at dusk on the cathedral green. Contemplating the wealth of the "fine palatial houses" of the cathedral town, she becomes aware of "new visions and possibilities." She recalls the day when Sally "had spoken of a massive tureen" in her father's house *"too heavy even to hold."* Sally's father had asked her for anecdotes of Sally's "broken brilliance" and Mrs. Sixsmith will accommodate him, "indulging him with 'Salliana'" (pp. 385–386). As the novel closes, she knows that with her experience and opportunity and time he will be useful to her—another figure to be manipulated in the stealthy machinations of her avarice.

An ironic—and poetic—contrast to Mrs. Sixsmith's evil is a description of the ringing of churchbells. Following is the first paragraph of the story:

The clangour of bells grew insistent. In uncontrollable hilarity pealed S. Mary, contrasting clearly with the subdued carillon of S. Mark. From all sides, seldom in unison, resounded bells. S. Elizabeth and S. Sebastian, in Flower Street, seemed in loud dispute, while S. Ann on the 'on the Hill,' all hollow, cracked, consumptive, fretful, did nothing but complain. Near by S. Nicaise, half paralysed and impotent, feebly shook. Then, triumphant, in a hurricane of sound, S. Irene hushed them all.

(p. 319)

And as the story ends, the ringing of churchbells accompanies Mrs. Sixsmith's final racing thoughts:

From all sides, seldom in unison, pealed forth bells. In fine religious gaiety struck S. Mary, contrasting clearly with the bumble-dumble of S. Mark, S. Elizabeth and S. Sebastian in Flower Street seemed in high dispute, while across the sunset water S. Ann-on-the-Hill did nothing but complain. Near by S. Nicaise, half-paralysed and impotent, scarcely shook. Then triumphant, in a hurricane of sound, S. Irene hushed the lot.

(p. 386).

In addition to its rich irony, the novel is remarkable for other features as well. Its panorama of life in the London theater early in the twentieth century is particularly notable. It is crowded with theatrical characters like Mrs. Mary, an eminent actress who, when she auditions her, decides that Sally is "Comedy" by the way she enunciates "Abyssinia" and "Joan" (p. 346). Her actor husband, Mr. Mary, is knighted by mistake, a motif Evelyn Waugh would sucessfully exploit in *Scoop* (1938). This novel is comparable to *Prancing Nigger* because the narrative, free of Firbank's characteristic omissions, is tightly constructed. The ambiguity that surrounds Sally's death is irrelevant. The disclosure of the full nature and extent of Mrs. Sixsmith's evil in the final chapter is also uncharacteristic of Firbank's fiction. But it is another feature sufficiently powerful to make this novel unique among his works.

Valmouth, the last of the novels he wrote at Oxford, is an elaborate series of scenes set in an imaginary health resort on the west coast of England. Nearly all of the inhabitants are centenarians or older. "Nowadays," Mrs. Hurstpierpoint comments, "around Valmouth centenarians will be soon as common as peas!" And when her companion, Mrs. Thoroughfare, sniffs "the air . . . there's no air to compare to it" (p. 390), the effect of the warm sirocco winds on the exotic inhabitants of the imaginary island of Nepenthe in Norman Douglas' *South Wind* (1917) immediately springs to mind. The air of Valmouth, promoting longevity, evidently also stimulates what W. H. Auden in his poem "Petition" labels "the intolerable neural itch"—"normal" or otherwise. After *Concerning the Eccentricities of Cardinal Pirelli,* this is the most sexual of Firbank's novels. For some critics, *Valmouth* is his masterpiece.

The arc of the action is, as usual, virtually flat. Dick Thoroughfare, a naval officer, son of Mrs. Thoroughfare and heir to her large fortune, spurns Thetis Tooke, the chaste dairy maid—who would be comfortable in any pastoral fiction of the nineteenth century—for the alluring Niri-Esther, whom one character describes as a "little madcap negress" (p. 467) but who is allegedly a "Tahaitian" princess. The novel ends as their wedding is about to take place in the basilica of Valmouth. No one can find the groom, however, and Niri-Esther runs "out of the house . . . into the garden, where, with her bride's bouquet of malmaisons and vanessa-violets," she "waywardly" pursues a butterfly (p. 477).

Her flight into the garden may be more felicitous than her march down the aisle, for in a drawing room of the basilica, Mrs. Thoroughfare discovers her son's "middy-chum Jack Whorwood who was not much over fifteen" (p. 398), the youngest member of Dick Thoroughfare's crew. She says, "My boy is very fond of you," to which he responds, "And I'm very attached to him" (p. 465). Some time before, Dick Thoroughfare had said, "That little lad . . . upon a cruise, is, to me, what Patroclus was to Achilles, and even more" (p. 398).

Similar proclivities abound. Mrs. Eulalia Hurstpierpoint nurtures a passion for Niri-Esther. Lady Parvula de Panzoust's "aphrodisiac emotions nicely titillated" is "in her element" (p. 454) contemplating a rendezvous with the young rustic David Tooke. "I know I should despise myself," she thinks, "but I don't. . . . Such perfect cant, though, with four 'honeymoons' in the hotel, to be forced oneself to take to the fields" (p. 453). But David will content her caprice only in marriage. "Marriage!!!!!!" is her breathless response. "I fear he must be cold, or else he's decadent" (p. 456). Figuring that half a loaf is better than none, she seeks relief with the captain of a ketch or, one can assume, any convenient man. Such behavior leads us to expect bizarre inclinations among the inhabitants of Valmouth. Consequently, when we read that "a coastguard was surprised to see two women wrestling on the beach below, their outlines dim against the western sky" (p. 461), we are surprised to discover a few pages later that what we took to be an instance of lust was really a work of mercy. A nun, describing the incident, tells that she had saved a young woman from drowning. The woman was Thetis Tooke, suicidal because of her rejection by Dick Thoroughfare. But for the nun "the sea would have absorbed her. . . . However, she is now comfortably installed in the Convent of Arimathaea, and already shows, it seems, signs of a budding vocation! So peradventure she will become a Bride of the Church" (p. 470). Even this apparently fortunate resolution must be read in the context of satire, because the nun relating the event is a wild-eyed neurotic; indeed, all the ecclesiastics in the novel are tinged—to a greater or lesser degree—with absurdity.

Most prominent in the canvas of exoticism is Mrs. Yajñavalkya, perhaps the most colorful Firbank character. A black woman, the aunt of Niri-Esther, she is a chiropodist, masseuse, and procuress; she is a dominant figure in Valmouth society. Never described physically she is disclosed chiefly through conversation.

A revealing scene is her visit to Lady Parvula to treat an inflamed toe. She observes, "I have known what love is, I! . . . Dair are often days ven I can neither eat, nor drink, nor sleep, ven my fingers hab no strength at all (massage den is quite impossible)—I am able only to groan and groan and groan—ah, my darling" (p. 416). Commenting on Niri-Esther's "vainglorious" clothes, Mrs. Yaj—as she is frequently called in the novel—remembers that until she "was past eighteen, I nebber had more in de course ob a year dan a bit ob cotton loincloth. You may wear it how you please, my poor mother would say, but dat is all you'll get! And so, dear me, I generally used to put it on my head" (p. 418).

Later, while visiting Mrs. Tooke, who cannot find her Bible, Mrs. Yaj says,

"You should read de Talmud for a change."

"It sounds a poor exchange."

"Do you really believe now, Mrs. Tooke my dear, in de Apostolic Succession? Can you look me in de eyes and say you do?"

"I ha'n't paid any heed lately to those chaps, Mrs. Yaj; I'm going on to Habakkuk."

"Was he not de companion ob de Prodigal son?"

"Maybe he was, my dear. He seems to have known a good many people."

"Dat is not de name now ob a man, Mrs. Tooke, to observe a single wife, nor even a single sex. . . . No! Oh no; a man wif a name like dat would have his needs!"

(p. 434)

Mrs. Yaj, always prominent in the affairs of Valmouth, is last seen in the basilica for the wedding of her niece and Captain Thoroughfare.

The setting changes chapter by chapter; each is developed virtually independently. Chapter 8 presents a formal gathering of the centenarians of Valmouth "escorted by twittering troops of expectant heirs and toad-eating relatives, foregathered together, like so many warlocks and witches . . ." (pp. 439–440). The epicenter of the novel, it gathers together all the major characters, who take part in a kaleidoscopic exchange involving gossip, rumors, and arrangements for liaisons. The gathering ends with Thetis Tooke's impassioned cry at the sight of her beloved. The chapter utilizes all of Firbank's techniques, including the presentation of a long catalog of exotic names. The affair provides an ideal opportunity for Firbank to impose on the narrative bits of overheard conversation:

"Heroin."

"Adorable simplicity."

"What could anyone find to admire in such a shelving profile?"

"We reckon a duck here of two or three and twenty not so old. And a spring chicken *anything to fourteen.*"

"My husband had no amorous energy whatsoever; which just suited me, of course."

"I suppose when there's no more room for another crow's-foot, one attains a sort of peace?"

(p. 448)

This "jargon of voices" (p. 448) continues longer than necessary to make its point, and perhaps the novel itself is much too long. Its full title, *Valmouth: A Romantic Novel,* is appropriate as satire because none of its characters experience, nor is any capable of experiencing, authentic romantic love. If "romantic" is read in the sense of the exploratory dimension of romanticism, the title is also appropriate as satire because its disclosure of human nature is for the most part unflattering. The grotesque overtones of the novel, in any case, resist the buoyancy of satire; sometimes incidental features, such as the novel's fictitious hagiographies, are, at best, tasteless. The following is an example:

One day St. Automona di Meris, seeing a young novice yawning, suddenly spat into her mouth, and *that* without malice or thought of mischief. Some ninety hours afterwards the said young novice brought into the world the Blessed St. Elizabeth Bathilde, who, by dint of skipping, changed her sex at the age of forty and became a man.

(p. 426)

Yet the novel displays virtuosity, and for many admirers of Firbank's fiction, it is his most satisfying performance.

SANTAL *AND* THE PRINCESS ZOUBAROFF

BETWEEN *Valmouth* and *The Flower Beneath the Foot,* Firbank published a novelette, *Santal,* and his only play, *The Princess Zoubaroff*. Critics generally describe both as failures, but *Santal* is a charming variation on the theme of innocents abroad.

Santal is set somewhere in the Near East—Tunis, let us say, since as Benkovitz suggests in her bibliography, Firbank went there to gather material for a story that would be a version of "Odette in an Arab setting—a child seeking Allah" (p. 35).

The central character, Cherif, is an orphan. His father died "while carving a sunflower upon a door of a mosque" (p. 479); his mother died soon after. Cherif has "a tiny head, like the proudest of camels, and forlorn, profound eyes . . ." (p. 479). Demoralized by living with his temperamental and taciturn aunt, "her silence being occasioned by her husband, refusing to better his calling, for it was her misfortune to be married to a man whose profession it was to hawk live chickens by the legs about the streets" (p. 482), Cherif flees to fulfill his desire to become a marabout. Packing his "Koran, a lead amulet, the Antar, six pomegranates, and a few loose sticks of Santal to burn at passing shrines" (p. 494), he sets out to find another hermit, another marabout, who as spiritual director will accompany him to Mecca. The tale ends as Cherif, on his way to Mecca, reads in the Koran,

The Lord hath not forsaken thee, neither hath he been displeased. And surely the Future shall be better for thee than the Past, And in the end shall thy Lord be bounteous to thee and thou be satisfied.

A "great resignation" filling his heart, "his face turned toward the kindling East," he prays, "Lord Allah! Show compassion to thy child Cherif" (p. 498).

No mockery, this; Firbank's reverence for Islam is in marked contrast to his contempt for Rome. The portrait of Cherif is touching; furthermore, this short work displays Firbank's narrative and descriptive powers at their best. In the pulsating city Cherif falls asleep "lulled by the distant drum and tambourine of a snake-charmer" (p. 489), and one can almost smell the air, "aromatic with [the] resinous sweet scent" (p. 490) of santal. Cherif likes to

linger in the courtyard of the Mosque, by the vine-shaded fountain that murmured sonorously in its midst. Green ferns, of a freshness indescribable fringed its brink. . . . But the wonder of the Mosque was a golden dove that lived all alone in the minarette. Occasionally

the Guardian would leave ajar the door of the tower, when Cherif rarely failed to ascend. It was good to peer out of the city rooftops toward the distant desert, especially in the early morning when the sun would break through the white dews of dawn, or to lie and watch the slow floating clouds that would evoke strange thoughts of Mecca. Sometimes, at noon, a brilliant blue mirage would form upon the horizon, offering an illusion of the sea.

(pp. 480–481)

Interlaced with such lush passages are flashes of conversation that remind us of the other side of Firbank:

"Safia, the lately repudiated wife of Abou Zazâa, takes a Hammam every day!"

"She is growing so exotic."

"They say she's in love with a peacock's feather."

"Give me a black moustache," Amoucha sighed, "and two passionate legs!"

"Unless," Nejma murmured, going into little shivers of laughter, "unless it be a beard."

(p. 486)

But the emphasis on the innocence of Cherif and his pursuit of self-fulfillment—the oldest story in the world—is what makes *Santal* a success.

The Princess Zoubaroff is a loosely structured play of fifty scenes divided into three acts. The scenes are short—scene 12 of act 1, for example, consists of four brief speeches; the final scene consists of two. The arbitrary divisions between scenes are indicated by entrances and exits. Intrinsic to the structural defects of *The Princess Zoubaroff* are insipid action, asthenic characters, and pallid dialogue. The setting is Florence, Italy, in the summer and fall. In the first scene two young men, Adrian and a honeymooning Eric, are planning to leave their wives. They disappear from the action of the play after scene 5 of act 1 only to return, in the final scenes, after having spent the summer together. They return *"looking wonderfully recouped and rejuvenated—as though their extensive holiday had done them good. Which has benefited from his freedom most—which looks the handsomer—it is not easy to determine"* (p. 759). Adrian's wife, in the meantime, has had a son. A discussion of his ignorance of the boy's name ends the play:

ADRIAN   [*with the pram moving towards the house, followed by Eric and Lord Orkish*]: By the by, I don't even know my child's name!

ERIC: He gives me the impression rather of *an Hermione* . . .

ADRIAN: Hermione? Nonsense, Eric. He has an air of Claud. Or Gervase even.

ERIC: Gervase?

ADRIAN [*to baby*]: Hello, Gervase!

LORD ORKISH [*prosaically*]: His name's Charles.

ADRIAN [*disappointed*]: Charles!

LORD ORKISH: Charles Augustus Frederic Humphrey Percy Sydney.

ADRIAN: I intend to call my son *Gervase*.

ERIC: Why not Gerry?

ADRIAN: No; Gervase.

ERIC: Gerry!

[*Exeunt, Gerrying and Gervasing one another to the house*]

(p. 765)

In their absence the Princess Zoubaroff, a character who vies for centrality, has founded a religious community that has enlisted, among others, the men's wives. She is "a very pale, vaguely 'sinister looking' woman of about thirty-five" (p. 705). The community she founds, sans habit, discipline, rule, or religion, promotes tête-à-têtes and pink teas, and like all the disintegrated marriages of its novices, promises soon to disintegrate as well.

The conventual activity of the princess, a fertile source for ridicule by an author who would "laugh at" or "mock" the church, is without the bite of satire. Worthy of note is the wives' lack of indignation at their husbands' desertion. Adrian and Eric's escapades and their evidently permanent relationship (Eric says in the final scene of the play ". . . if Enid [his wife] puts in an appearance again, I shall take the first express to Rome" [p. 763]) is disclosed with approbation. In that sense, the play was ahead of its time.

The flaccid dialogue is relieved only occasionally by flashes of wit: from scene 4, act 1:

PRINCESS: I am always disappointed with mountains. There are no mountains in the world as high as I would wish.

ADRIAN: No?

PRINCESS: They irritate me invariably. I should like to shake Switzerland.

(p. 706)

And later in scene 15:

NADINE [*introducing*]: My husband.

BLANCHE [*genially*]: I think we slept together once?

ADRIAN: I don't remember.

BLANCHE: At the opera. During *Bérénice!*

ADRIAN: Why, of course.

(pp. 722–723)

One searches in vain for other passages to redeem the tedium of the play. As stated earlier, critics have compared it to Congreve's *The Way of the World*, but the comparison is strained; the play belongs only tangentially to the genre of the comedy of manners. Given Firbank's love for the theater, one can only speculate on the reasons for the play's dismal theatricality.

THE FLOWER BENEATH THE FOOT

The Flower Beneath the Foot, which initiates the last phase of his career, might be described as another "romantic novel"; both structurally and thematically it is patterned on the earlier novels. The setting is another imaginary kingdom, Pisuerga, a vague amalgam of northern Africa, Italy, France, and England. The action focuses on the love of Mademoiselle Laura Lita Carmen Etoile de Nazianzi, a lady in waiting at the royal court, for Prince Yousef, the heir to the throne. Laura's love is unrequited, however, and the king and queen, in any case, consider the relationship a mésalliance; they offer in Laura's place the princess Elsie, the daughter of King Geo and Queen Glory of England. The novel ends as the heartbroken Laura, having retired to the Convent of the Flaming Hood, watches from her cell window the wedding procession of Prince Yousef and Princess Elsie. Laura, of course, is the flower beneath the foot.

In no other novel, perhaps, is the range of Firbank's satire so varied and so broad. A parody, for example, of gossip columns found in the typical tabloid is the "hebdomadal *causerie* in the *Jaw-Waw's Journal* on matters appertaining to society, signed by that ever popular diarist 'Eva Schnerb' " (p. 517). She writes of one of the women at a ball wearing "an 'aesthetic' gown of flame-hued Kanitra silk edged with Armousky fur (to possess a dear woolly Armousk as a pet is considered *chic* this season), while over her brain—an intellectual caprice, I wonder?—I saw a tinsel bow . . ." (p. 543). Firbank satirizes chic as the epitome of fashion in Madame Wetme, the wife of a café owner: "Madame Wetme's religion, her cruel God, was the *Chic:* the God Chic" (p. 518). His range includes science. Archaeologists in an expedition "among the ruins of Chedorlahomor, a *faubourg* of Sodom" (p. 501) report finding "a superb tear-bottle . . . severely adorned with a matron's head." There is "no doubt whatever" that it is "an authentic portrait of Lot's disobedient, though unfortunate, wife. Ample and statuesque (as the salten image she was afterwards to become), the shawl-draped, masklike features are by no means beautiful. It is a face you may often see today . . . a sodden, gin-soaked face that helps to vindicate, if not, perhaps, excuse, the conduct of Lot . . ." (p. 581). The convoluted plot of a novel being written by a lady novelist is a burlesque of nineteenth-century fiction. ". . . I've such a darling description of a cornfield," she says. "I make you *feel* England!" (p. 559). In the same vein, Firbank once again satirizes himself:

"The *Passing of Rose* I read the other day," Mrs. Montgomery said, "and *so* enjoyed it."

"Isn't that one of Ronald Firbank's books?"

"No, dear, I don't think it is. But I never remember an author's name and I don't think it matters!"

"I suppose I'm getting squeamish! But this Ronald Firbank I can't take to at all. *Valmouth!* Was there ever a novel more coarse? I assure you I hadn't gone very far when I had to put it down."

"Its *out*," Mrs. Bedley suavely said, "as well," she added, "as the rest of them."

(p. 532)

Even in his depiction of Laura's grief in her seclusion in the convent, he cannot resist satirizing—gently, to be sure—religious life. There is the nun's general rush for the refectory after Mass. "Preceded by Sister Clothilde and followed, helter-skelter, by an exuberant bevy of nuns, even Mother Martinez, who, being shortsighted, would go feeling the ground with her cane, was propelled to the measure of a hop-and-skip" (p. 588).

The pompousness and pretentiousness of the entire echelon of the English diplomatic service is satirized. Lady Somebody Something, the wife of the English ambassador, is focal in a number of episodes. In a conversation with Lady Something, a countess praises Shakespeare: "How gorgeous! How glowing! I once knew a speech from 'Julia Sees Her . . .' perhaps his greatest *oeuvre* of all. . . ." To which Lady Something replies, "Friends, Comrades, Countrymen . . . I used to know it myself!" (p. 505). The visiting Queen of Thleeanouhee of the

Land of Dates develops a passion for Lady Something:

"Let us go away by and by, my dear gazelle," she exclaimed with a primitive smile, "and remove our corsets and talk."

"Unhappily Pisuerga is not the East, ma'am," Lady Something replied.

"Never mind, my dear; we will introduce this innovation. . . ."

(p. 542)

Lady Something's role is characteristic of another of Firbank's unique contributions to fiction: a ridiculous incident becomes a leitmotiv woven into the action, with each succeeding reference enlarging upon its absurdity. The sequence begins in chapter 2. At a state dinner, the Queen of the Land of Dates casually remarks that they do not use china in her country.

"I could not be more astonished," the King declared, "if you told me there were fleas at the Ritz," a part of which assertion Lady Something, who was blandly listening, imperfectly chanced to hear.

"Who would credit it!" she breathed, turning to an attaché, a young man all white and penseroso, at her elbow.

"Credit what?"

"Did you not hear what the dear King said?"

"No."

"It's almost *too* appalling. . . . Fleas," she murmured, "have been found at the Ritz."

(pp. 508–509)

In chapter 5 she comes to offer help to the Hon. "Eddy" Monteith, who is ill:

"Had I known, Lady Something, I was going to be ill, I would have gone to the Ritz!" the Hon. 'Eddy' gasped.

"And you'd have been bitten all over!" Lady Something replied.

"Bitten all over?"

"The other evening we were dining at the Palace, and I heard the dear King say—but I oughtn't to talk and excite you—"

(p. 538)

In chapter 6, in a conversation between a countess and the queen, the countess demurely murmurs,

"Guess who is at the Ritz, ma'am, this week!"

"Who is at the Ritz this week, I can't," the Queen replied.

"Nobody!"

"Why, how so?"

"The Ambassadress of England, it seems, has alarmed the world away. I gather they mean to prosecute!"

(pp. 545–546)

In chapter 10 the "pending legislation, involving . . . the crown," and the "injudicious chatter" of Lady Something "(who even now, notwithstanding her writ, would say to every other visitor that came to the villa: 'Have you heard about the Ritz? The other night we were dining at the Palace, and I heard the King,' *etc.*)" is wearing the ambassador out (p. 557). Later, in a conversation with Sir Something, Lady Something says,

". . . A clairvoyant once told me I'd 'the bump of Litigation'—a *cause célèbre* unmistakably defined; so it's as well, on the whole, to have it over."

"And quite probably; had your statement been correct—"

The Ambassadress gently glowed.

"I'm told it's simple swarming!" she impenitently said.

(p. 561)

Successful in its humor, the sequence judiciously ends with this scene.

Evelyn Waugh's debt to Firbank is evident in his use, in a more serious vein, of this device in *Decline and Fall* (1928). Mr. Prendergast, as starter of a race in a boys' school, shoots one of the runners in the foot. The boy languishes throughout the action of the novel, having to have his foot, then later his leg, amputated, and eventually he dies at the end of the novel.

In Firbank's satiric portrait of his society, he adds a touch of fin de siècle humor in the character of the Hon. "Eddy" Monteith, who is diverted from entering the Jesuit Order by joining the Chedorlahomor archaeological expedition. He luxuriates in the sensuous: "Lying amid the dissolving bath crystals" while his manservant bathes him, he falls "into a sort of coma, sweet as a religious trance," and later it is "delicious" for him "to relax his powder-blanched limbs upon a comfy couch." When his manservant tells him he is looking "a little pale . . . about the gills," the Hon. Eddy winces. "I forbid you ever to employ the word gill, Mario," he exclaims, "It is inharmonious, and in English it jars; whatever it may do in Italian" (pp. 536–537).

Paradoxically, this blend of aestheticism, par-ody, burlesque, and satire, does no damage to the poignancy of the conclusion. In a number of ways, this may be the most mature work of Firbank's; it is in the judgment of most of his critics, in any case, the most "Firbankian" of his novels.

Prancing Nigger, the American title for *Sorrow in Sunlight,* is both misleading and—to Firbank, at least—repugnant, but Carl Van Vechten was probably right in his insistence that the former would be more attractive in the market. *Prancing Nigger* is misleading because it is a term of endearment Mrs. Mouth uses in speaking to her husband—an interesting but relatively minor character who is by no means a "prancer."

This was the only novel Firbank did not subsidize; it even made some money for him. Published in America in 1924, its modest success there gave rise to the possibility of a musical adaptation, a project that did not materialize. The novel was published in England that same year under its original title.

A word needs to be said here about the frequent use of the term "nigger" in Firbank's fiction. We must accept the unpleasant reality that the term, odious as it is, was common at the time Firbank was writing. That does not excuse its use, of course, but more to the point is that Firbank had a special interest in and affinity for blacks that became clearly evident after the war years. The warmth of his regard, in any case, pervades *Prancing Nigger.* In it no distinction is made between black and white society; it would be false to say that we tend to forget that the Mouths are black, but their color, like that of the white people, does not matter. There is certainly no irony in Mrs. Mouth's being the heroine of this novel.

Mr. and Mrs. Ahmadou Mouth live with their three children, Edna, Miami, and their younger brother, Charlie, in the little fishing village of Mediavilla on an island broadly suggestive of Haiti. The village is virtually paradisiacal:

The few thatched cabins that comprised the village of Mediavilla lay not half a mile from the shore. Situated between the savannah and the sea, on the southern side of the island known as Tacarigua . . . its inhabitants were obliged, from lack of communication with the larger island centres, to rely to a considerable extent for a livelihood among themselves. Local Market days, held, alternatively, at Valley Village or Broken Hill . . . were the chief source of rural trade, when such merchandise as fish, coral, beads, bananas and loincloths would exchange hands amid much animation, social gossip, and pleasant fun.

(p. 600)

Mrs. Mouth, indifferent to the innocent rusticity of Mediavilla, decides that the family must move to Cuna-Cuna, the island's glamorous capital city. "We leave Mediavilla for de education ob my daughters,' she would say; or, perhaps: 'We go to Cuna-Cuna for de finishing ob *mes filles!' "* (p. 594). Mr. Mouth, happily indolent and satisfied with the status quo, has no enthusiasm for the migration. A God-fearing man, furthermore, he cries, "How often hab I bid you nebba to mention dat modern Sodom in de hearing ob my presence!" (p. 595). Miami wants to remain in Mediavilla because she would be leaving behind her beloved, a young fisherman named Bamboo.

Their reluctance notwithstanding, off the family goes to merge quickly into Cuna-Cuna's society—and almost immediately to experience the evil of urbanity. They rent a villa from the wealthy and influential Madame Ruiz whose son, Vittorio, a musical virtuoso, immediately makes Edna his mistress. Young Charlie, who walks to Cuna-Cuna on foot for the purpose of collecting butterflies, is approached in a bar by "a girl with gold cheeks like the flesh of peaches" who addresses him, "softly from behind: 'Listen, lion!' " (p. 625). And later, as he strolls in the evening air of the city, "incipient Cyprians, led by vigilant, blanched-faced queens, youths of a certain life, known as bwam-wam bwam-wams, gaunt pariah dogs with questing eyes, all equally were on the prowl" (p. 625). Charlie is last seen "fast going to pieces, having joined the Promenade of a notorious Bar with its bright particular galaxy of boys" (p. 636).

Bamboo, still in Mediavilla, having gone in a boat out to sea when an earthquake strikes the island, is devoured by sharks when the boat overturns. In her grief, Miami recalls Mediavilla as a "gust of the hot trade wind" brings into the city "an odour of decay. . . . The trade winds! How pleasantly they used to blow in the village of Mediavilla. The blue trade wind, the gold trade wind caressing the bending canes. . . . City life, what had it done for any of them, after all?" She contemplates Edna as a harlot—"(since she had left them there was no other word)" (p. 635)—and the corruption of young Charlie.

Mrs. Mouth also discovers imperfections in the paradise she thought Cuna-Cuna would be, but like her husband, despite his being scandalized by its blatant sinfulness, she is remarkably adaptable. The novel ends when Edna and Vittorio watch from their balcony the grieving Miami in a penitential procession. "And smiling down on [Edna's] uplifted face, he asked himself whimsically how long he would love her. She had not the brains, poor child, of course, to keep a man forever. Heighho. Life indeed was often hard. . . . [the ellipsis is Firbank's]" (p. 642).

Vittorio is the focus of Firbank's satire of the white society the Mouths encounter in Cuna-Cuna. "At the age of five he had assaulted his Nurse, and, steadily onward, his passions had grown" (p. 612). He is an ironic reminder of Thomas Hardy's Alec D'Urberville. Edna becomes part of his "venetorial habits" (p. 612) at their first meeting at the Ruiz villa. At his invitation to sit down beside him on a grassy bank, she finds "De groung's as soft as a cushom. . . ." "You'll find it," he says, "even softer, if you'll try it nearer me." Calling her "Exquisite kid," "Bad baby," and "Dark, bright baby," he soon has her in his arms (pp. 622–623).

The satire radiates further to include Cuna-Cunians at large. During the earthquake that horrifies "a half-crazed crowd," young Charlie, dazed by the experience, finds himself in the vicinity of three older women.

Clustered back to back near by upon the grass, three stolid matrons, matrons of hoary England, evidently not without previous earthquake experience, were ignoring resolutely the repeated shocks.

"I always follow the Fashions, dear, at a distance!" one was saying: "this little gingham gown I'm wearing I had made for me after a design I found in a newspaper at my hotel."

"It must have been a pretty old one, dear—I mean the paper, of course."

"New things are only those you know that have been forgotten."

"Mary . . . there's a sharp pin, sweet, at the back of your . . . *Oh!*"

A marvelous innuendo follows: "Venturing upon his legs, Charlie turned away" (p. 626).

The characters of the Mouths are disclosed, of course, largely by dialogue. Mrs. Mouth is at once resolute and resilient, superstitious and realistic, earthy but aspiring to and finding comfort beyond the mundane planes of existence. Her reading of her cards evokes fear that her "lil jewel Edna . . . will wilt away" (p. 596) in the dark jungle of Mediavilla, and other disclosures by the cards disconcert her as well. "Lordey, Lord; what is it den you want?" asks her husband. " 'I want a villa with a water-closet'—Flinging wiles to the winds, it was a cry from the heart" (p. 596). (Water closets—privies—become a kind of leitmotiv in the novel.) Later in Cuna-Cuna, the cards reveal "somet'in' dat look like a death. . . . An' from de lie ob de cards . . . it seem as ef de corpse were ob de masculine species" (p. 607). After the death of Bamboo, she tries to comfort Miami. "Dat death was on de cards, my deah an' dair is no mistakin' de fac'; an' as de shark is a rapid feeder it all ober sooner dan wid de crocodile, which is some consolation for dose dat remain to mourn" (p. 636). When Mr. Mouth relates Miami's grief to "de disgrace ob Edna," Mrs. Mouth replies, "She is her own woman, me deah sah, an' *I* cannot prevent it!" (p. 636). When Mr. Mouth emphatically dismisses Mrs. Mouth's belief that Edna and Vittorio will very likely marry later, she reminds him, "Prancing Nigger, you seem to forget dat your elder daughter was a babe ob four w'en I put on me nuptial arrange blastams to go to de Church" (p. 637). At the reception she and the Duchess of Wellclose dispute the use of a chair, but neither "creatures [are] easily abashed." Insisting that the chair is taken, the Duchess, in an attempt to intimidate Mrs. Mouth, gives "her a look that would have made many a Peeress in London quail." Mrs. Mouth is unmoved. "From de complexion dat female hab, she look as doh she bin boiling bananas!" she comments "comfortably, loud enough for the duchess to hear" (p. 632). She insists on providing her children with the best that life has to offer. She tells Mr. Mouth, "Prancing Nigger, I hope your Son an' Daughters will yet take dair Degrees, an' if not from de University, den from Horne. From heah." "She had taken the girls to the gallery at the Opera one night to hear 'Louise,' but they had come out, by tacit agreement, in the middle of it; the plainness of Louise's blouse, and the lack of tunes . . . the suffocation of the gallery . . . Once bit twice shy, they had not gone back again [Firbank's ellipses]" (p. 617). She obviously tempers her enthusiasm for the aesthetic with sagacity. She also muses—as one

would expect in Firbank's world, mad or realistic—on the dull side, the drawbacks of married life, the difficulty, "at times, to endure such second-rate company as that of a querulous husband" (p. 636). And the Firbankian complement to that flaw in married love is the tragic grief of Miami and the grief of Edna to come.

This is the most realistic of Firbank's fiction—and the most pleasant. Scenes mesh easily in the development of his narrative; the dialogue is unsurpassed by any other of his works. The changes wrought on insularity and innocence by a new environment may come from his reading of Henry James; of course, the theme of the corruption of innocence by an evil environment reaches back into antiquity. His satire, applied with a feather touch to glowing figures in a spectacular setting, gives the final gloss to this colorful portrait of West Indian life.

POSTHUMOUS WORKS

BEFORE his death, Firbank paid Grant Richards to publish his final novel, *Concerning the Eccentricities of Cardinal Pirelli*; nevertheless, the book was published posthumously in 1926. Critics usually place this among Firbank's best works, but the glowing surface of its prose and dialogue is clouded by its inane framework.

Structured in the manner of Firbank's earlier works, the novel recalls the sensuality associated with the decadent movement of the 1890's, the *maladie de fin de siècle*. The baroque Spanish setting tends to place its action in the Renaissance, but its final effect is contemporary. It is a series of set pieces that begin with Don Alvaro Narciso Fernando Pirelli, Cardinal-Archbishop of Clemenza, baptizing a week-old police-dog, and end with his sudden death, he "nude and elementary now as Adam himself" (p. 697), during a wildly lascivious nocturnal pursuit of a choirboy in his basilica.

Critical in assessing the character of the cardinal are his ruminations in the cloister of the "slowly decaying monastery of the Desierto" where he has retreated from a probable censure by the Vatican:

The forsaken splendour of the vast closed cloisters seemed almost to augur the waning of a cult. Likewise the decline of Apollo, Diana, Isis, with the gradual downfall of their temples, had been heralded, in past times, by the dispersal of their priests. It looked as though Mother Church, like Venus or Diana, was making way in due turn for the beliefs that should follow: "and we shall begin again with intolerance, martyrdom and converts."

(p. 679)

This "Prince of the Church," if not already an apostate must, except for one instance, be construed as a pagan—and he is blatantly hypocritical, sexually perverted, and at times, fatuously imbecilic. He is also androgynous. One of his delights is in joining the crowded city at night:

Disguised as a caballero from the provinces or as a matron (disliking to forgo altogether the militant bravoura of a skirt), it became possible to combine philosophy, equally, with pleasure. . . .

Although a mortification, it was imperative to bear in mind the consequences of cutting too dashing a figure. Beware display. Vanity once had proved all but fatal: "I remember it was the night I wore ringlets and was called 'my queen.' "

And with a fleeting smile, Don Alvaro Pirelli recalled the persistent officer who had had the effrontery to attempt to molest him: "Stalked me the whole length of the Avenue Isadora!" It had been a lesson. "Better to be on the drab side," he reflected.

(pp. 650–651)

Sexuality is the dominant motif of the novel and the focus of its satire; references to sex in its various manifestations appear on virtually every page. A duquesa, for example, views critically a "portrait of a Lesbian, with dying, fabulous eyes," and then gives a "swift discerning glance at an evasive 'nude,' showing the posterior poudrederizé of a Saint" (p. 674). A boy offering a "good and pleasant night" to the Cardinal adds, "And if you should want me, sir . . . [Firbank's ellipsis] the youthful acolyte possessed the power to convey the unuttered" (pp. 682–683). A poetess is "besieged by admirers, to 'give them something . . . Anything of her own.' Wedded, and proclaiming . . . her lawful love, it was whispered she had written a paean to her husbands . . . [Firbank's ellipsis] beginning Thou glorious wonder! which was altogether too conjugal and intimate for recitation in society" (p. 664). For the secretary of the cathedral chapter, " 'Business'

indeed had seldom been livelier, and chapels for Masses of special intention were being booked in advance as eagerly as opera boxes for a première, or seaside-villas in the season" (p. 684). And he fulfills a woman's request that a mass be celebrated for her lover's safety. Another woman for the Feast of the Circumcision "invariably caused to be laid before the high-altar of the cathedral a peculiarly shaped loaf to the confusion of all who saw it" (p. 678).

Chapter 6, the best in the novel (but insufficiently redemptive), embodies Firbank's sophisticated use of stream of consciousness. It focuses on Madame Phoebe Poco, who is "the venerable Superintendent-of-the-palace" (p. 665), that is, Pirelli's housekeeper, and an informant on his affairs for the Vatican. Repairing a chasuble, she muses on the difficulty of her position: "It's not the door-listening," she decides, "so much as . . . when he goes a-wenching." Her thoughts stray to "the pontifical supremacy of Tertius II, for already she was the Pope's Poco, his devoted Pheobe, his own true girl: 'I'm true blue, dear. True blue' " (p. 665). Hearing a church bell, "which, tradition said, had fused into its metal one of the thirty pieces of silver received by the Iscariot for the betrayal of Christ" evokes her reflection that "they seem to have asked small fees in those days" (p. 666). "Fees" induces the thought of her resolution to use her pay as a Vatican spy for masses for the repose of her and her husband's soul. And so the stream meanders. Later, "freshening a little" the chasuble that had been stained with the police dog's urine when Pirelli was baptizing it, she labels the incident "a disgraceful business altogether" (p. 667). A variety of other stimulants—hearing the bells ring, replacing the chasuble, seeing the vestry cat perched on the ledge of a confessional, remembering that it is a Sunday evening of corrida ("Oh, mandolines of the South, warm throats, and winged songs, winging . . .")—alters the stream. It ends when she enters the garden to see Pirelli "plunged in prayer" (p. 669). A comparison of Firbank's use of this technique with that of James Joyce, Ford Madox Ford, and Virginia Woolf would be relevant; suffice it to say that Firbank's contribution is unique.

The cardinal's ostensible piety coalesces with the final vision of him after his death at the end of the novel: "Now that the ache of life, with its fevers, passions, doubts, its routine, vulgarity, and boredom, was over, his serene, unclouded face was a marvelment to behold. Very great distinction and sweetness was visible there, together with such nobility, and love, all magnified and commingled" (pp. 697–698). This passage conflicts dramatically with the cardinal's passionate pursuit of the elusive choirboy through the darkened basilica; its bid for sympathy is positively ludicrous. As another significant contribution to the "mad world" of Ronald Firbank in which duchesses ride buses and queens fix flat tires, *Concerning the Eccentricities of Cardinal Pirelli* might be admissible if it were not fundamentally in bad taste, seldom, if ever, funny, and generally oppressive in its satire.

Having finished this novel, he began work on what he called the "New York" novel shortly before his death. The financial success of *Prancing Nigger* in America was probably the impetus for his desire to write a novel with a New York setting. He wrote to his publisher in America from Cairo in the winter of 1925, as Alan Harris records in the introduction to *The New Rhythum and Other Pieces,* "Since I was never there . . . you may be sure it'll be the New Jerusalem before I have done with it. However, I hope to come out next year and develop it all" (pp. 13–14). Beginning the novel in anticipation of his visit—which he never made—he acquired a dictionary of American slang and colloquialisms. The unfinished novel has been collected in *The New Rhythum.*

The satire in this fragment is probably the most heavy-handed in the Firbank canon. The pursuit of high society for the wealthy New Yorkers in the novel is a "highly strenuous" (p. 87) vocation. Mrs. Harry Rosemerchant (née Catherine Corabilt) attends a reception given by Bertie Waldorf *"to watch me have a tooth drawn"* (p. 74). Bertie delights in giving teas "to hammer Jewellery," "to talk Scandal," "to gather Gardenias" (p. 95). Mrs. Rosemerchant attends a tea to pick strawberries, the ballroom of Bertie's Upper Park Avenue apartment having been made into a strawberry patch. Bertie's apartment also has a chamber, as one of the guests surreptitiously discovers, "wholly devoid of chairs, the floor strewn with countless cushions in whose midst was a harp with jade stops and rose-red strings. 'The scene of more than one orgy, I shouldn't wonder,' she reflected" (p. 100).

Mrs. Rosemerchant befriends the "Winner of the All American Beauty Prize, and perhaps one of the loveliest women in existence—Miss Dreadfu-line Hancock of Bloody Brook, Mass." (p. 72). Mrs. Rosemerchant renames Dreadfuline, a former laundress, "Heliodora"—and she becomes an intimate companion. They dance ecstatically on the warm green grass of Mrs. Rosemerchant's garden, "bobbing and dipping, gliding and running, clasping and parting, swaying and turning together" (p. 84). Driving home from a ball, they hold hands. Mrs. Rosemerchant finds her husband's jealousy of her "adorable friend" (p. 104) exasperating.

Other hints of sexual irregularity include the suggestion, from a woman "of almost fearsome beauty, recalling Medusa" (p. 79) to the women planning a charity ball, that whips be offered as a cotillion favor. A wealthy and "pious" widow indulges in flagellation as part of her religious fervor; for one of her devotees the "thorny twigs of her birching bouquet were softened by a few premature chrysanthemums" (p. 107).

The arrival from Europe of a "Greek marble of the Golden Age, none other than Praxiteles' long lost 'Hercules with a fearsome bottom' from the god's great temple at Eleusis" (p. 85) causes universal excitement. A beflagged marquee is erected on the wharf to entertain honored guests for the debarkation, and it is received with the playing of *The Star-Spangled Banner* and proselytizing by the Salvation Army. "A brief causerie upon the art of Praxiteles, as contrasted with modern American tendencies and ideals" (p. 93) precedes the unveiling. To everyone's surprise, the statue looks like Nick Tickel, the boxer: "It was Nick; Nick to the very life; without his breeches. 'Gosh, if it ain't our Boy!' " (p. 93).

Firbank's attempt to reproduce American speech—"reckon" is a common verb along with expressions such as "I guess," "Gosh," and "Gee"—is not successful, and for the most part, his New Yorkers sound British. A visit to New York, furthermore, in addition to accustoming him to American speech, should have corrected the errors he makes in describing the city. Yet there are touches such as this: "Detecting in a far-off corner the magnificent abdomen of the Reverend Cedric Potts, Mrs. Rosemerchant made towards him. Looking like iceless butter in August, he was descanting with the graces of a screen-favourite, to Iris Iquiavi, the poetess, whose polished verse perhaps accounted for her face half massaged away" (p. 80). Who could quarrel with prose such as this?

CONCLUSION

IN a charming essay on Ronald Firbank in *Abinger Harvest*, E. M. Forster compares the work of Firbank to a butterfly:

To break a butterfly, or even a beetle, upon a wheel is a delicate task. Lovers of nature disapprove, moreover the victim is apt to reappear each time the wheel revolves, still alive, and with a reproachful expression upon its squashed face to address its tormenter in some such words as the following: "Critic! What do you? Neither my pleasure nor your knowledge has been increased. I was flying or crawling, and that is all that there was to be learnt about me. Impossible to anatomize me and find what breeds my heart. Dissect the higher animals if you like, such as the frog, the cow, or the goose—no doubt they are all full of helpful secrets. By all means write articles on George Eliot. Review from every point of view Lord Morely of Borely's autobiography. Estimate Addison. But leave me in peace. I only exist in my surroundings, and become meaningless as soon as you stretch me on this rack.

(p. 113)

That may be, after all, the best way to read and judge Firbank; that is, within the perimeter of the world he has created as a fantast—a world in which exoticism is without restraint, wit displaces ratiocination, and aesthetics is of the highest value. *Ars gratia artis* is the only absolute. "Play," Forster concludes, "is [butterflies'] business. If for an instant they swerve from it they are swept into the nets of allegory. They may or may not possess will-power, may or may not desire to hover over a certain hedge, but the will is a trifle in the realm of the lower air which they inhabit and invite us to share" (p. 118).

Yet Firbank was a romanticist, and that means he was an explorer—however limited—if not of reality, at least of experience. His explorations expose, among a multitude of other things, the relations between the sexes as generally unsatisfactory, grief as common as fatuity in human affairs. Androgyny, homosexuality, and flagellation are presented as expressions of human behavior generally (if not always) within the frame of satire, a position that posits, at least, intellection and volition as fundamental components of the human personality. "When he attempts satire," however, Forster writes, "or wistfulness (as in *Santal*), he fails at once, he was incapable of totting up life" (p. 116).

Perhaps, or perhaps more pointedly, the force of Firbank's satire is substantially diminished by the absence of a view toward correction that authentic satire calls for. These observations on Firbank's satire notwithstanding, most critics extol it as a particularly brilliant facet of his art.

As an artist writing for the sake of art he was radiant, and the analogy of the butterfly is apt. No violation is done to this assessment in the further observation that in one sense, most of Firbank's fiction is as enigmatic as Firbank himself was. The indirection of manner in his fiction hazards misreading, and no two readings may be the same; but further readings, as Edmund Wilson suggests, may bring forth additional riches. In his art, furthermore, he was not always successful—sometimes, in fact, he was exasperating, sometimes a thumping bore, sometimes even offensive. Yet however his novels are read, interpreted, or judged, the reader will discover that butterfly imagery is frequent, sometimes developing into symbol, therein. Butterflies may indeed solve the problems proffered by the critic. In *Prancing Nigger*, young Charlie Mouth whom Forster interprets as "the glorified symbol of the writer himself" (p. 117), marches happily at dawn into Cuna-Cuna with his butterfly net and encounters a customs official.

"Have you nothing, young man, to declare?"
". . . Butterflies!"
"Exempt of duty. Pass."

(p. 614)

SELECTED BIBLIOGRAPHY

I. BIBLIOGRAPHY. M. J. Benkovitz, *A Bibliography of Ronald Firbank*, 2d ed. (Oxford, England, 1982).

II. COLLECTED WORKS. *The Works of Ronald Firbank*, 6 vols. (London, 1929), 5 vols. (New York, 1929); *Five Novels by Ronald Firbank* (Norfolk, Conn., 1949) includes *Valmouth, The Flower Beneath the Foot, Prancing Nigger, Concerning the Eccentricities of Cardinal Pirelli* and *The Artificial Princess; Three Novels by Ronald Firbank* (Norfolk, Conn., 1951) includes *Vainglory, Inclinations,* and *Caprice; The Complete Ronald Firbank* (London, 1961; Norfolk, Conn., 1962).

III. SEPARATE WORKS. *Odette d'Antrevernes and A Study in Temperament* (London, 1905); *Odette: A Fairy Tale for Weary People* (London, 1915); *Vainglory* (London, 1915; New York, 1925); *Inclinations* (London, 1916); *Caprice* (London,

1917); *Valmouth: A Romantic Novel* (London, 1919); *The Princess Zoubaroff: A Comedy* (London, 1920; New York, 1956); *Santal* (London, 1921; New York, 1955); *The Flower Beneath the Foot: Being a Record of the Early Life of St. Laura de Nazianzi and the Times in Which She Lived* (London, 1923; New York, 1924); *Prancing Nigger* (New York, 1924), published as *Sorrow in Sunlight* (London, 1924); *Concerning the Eccentricities of Cardinal Pirelli* (London, 1926); *The Artificial Princess* (London, 1934); *The New Rhythum and Other Pieces* (London, 1962; New York, 1963).

IV. BIOGRAPHICAL AND CRITICAL STUDIES. I. K. Fletcher, *Ronald Firbank: A Memoir* (London, 1930); E. M. Forster, "Ronald Firbank," in his *Abinger Harvest* (London, 1936; New York, 1955); C. Connolly, "The Novel-Addicts Cupboard," in his *The Condemned Playground* (New York, 1946); O. Sitwell, "Ronald Firbank," in his *Noble Essences* (Boston, 1950); E. Wilson, "A Revival of Ronald Firbank," in *Classics and Commercials* (New York, 1950); J. Brooke, *Ronald Firbank* (London, 1951); E. Wilson, "Firbank and Beckford" and "Late Violets from the Nineties" in his *The Shores of Light* (New York, 1952); M. Longaker and E. C. Bolles, *Contemporary English Literature* (New York, 1953); W. Y. Tindall, *Forces in Modern British Literature 1885–1956* (New York, 1956); H. Jackson, *The Eighteen Nineties* (New York, 1966); M. J. Benkovitz, *Ronald Firbank* (New York, 1969); J. A. Kiechler, *The Butterfly's Freckled Wings* (Bern, Switzerland, 1969); J. D. Merritt, *Ronald Firbank* (New York, 1969); E. M. Potocker, *Ronald Firbank* (New York, 1969); B. Brophy, *Prancing Novelist* (New York, 1973); E. Waugh, "Ronald Firbank," in *The Essays, Articles, and Reviews of Evelyn Waugh,* edited by D. Gallagher (Boston, 1983).

NADINE GORDIMER

(1923–   )

Rob Nixon

OVER THE PAST forty years, Nadine Gordimer has emerged as the most resourceful writer to have distilled fiction from the experience of apartheid. Her international literary eminence is complemented by her role within South Africa as an activist in the culture of resistance, and an articulate opponent of censorship, detention without trial, and Bantu education, and as an assiduous organizer of writers across the racial divide. Augmenting Gordimer's importance is the parallel between the beginnings of her career and the rise to power of the Afrikaner-dominated National Party, which has ruled South Africa uninterrupted since 1948. Her nine novels, more than two hundred short stories, and numerous essays of political and literary commentary thus offer a uniquely imaginative record of the high era of apartheid. This record gains depth from Gordimer's acute sensitivity to the history of her times. Among contemporary writers in English she displays an unequaled ability to integrate the shifting political moods of her society into the very form and texture of her fiction.

Gordimer has forged her considerable oeuvre out of circumstances that combined privilege and embattlement. This situation required of her an uncommon imaginative resilience. At home she has endured challenges from right and left flanks: the state banned several of her novels (most notoriously *Burger's Daughter* [1979]), while during the heyday of black consciousness in the 1970's, many black authors dismissed all white writing as a luxurious irrelevance. In the United States, Gordimer has had occasion to fend off the reverse criticism: that her engagement with politics and her socialist convictions have restricted her literary vision.

In accruing her reputation, Gordimer has never skirted controversy; she has steered an awkward course between those readers who crave more commitment and those who cry for less, with the censors, breathing heavily, seldom far behind. These pressures, for the most part, have helped her to hone her fiction and have led her to reflect profoundly on questions of artistic answerability. A localized but never provincial writer, Gordimer has garnered strength from an international cast of authors who have felt compelled, in the midst of social turbulence or when confronted by pronounced injustice, to pursue artistic freedom by exercising social responsibility: Bertolt Brecht, Albert Camus, Ernesto Cardenale, Milan Kundera, Czeslaw Milosz, and Ivan Turgenev, among others. It was Upton Sinclair's *The Jungle* (1906) that first stirred Gordimer to think about politics; the critics to whom she has been most attentive include Walter Benjamin, Ernest Fischer, Antonio Gramsci, and György Lukács, all of whom are associated with Marxist philosophies.

At first glance, Gordimer's attitude toward commitment may appear divided against itself. She insists that only *Burger's Daughter,* from among her novels, embodies an expressly political intent. Yet by the same token, she observes, as Stephen Clingman records in *The Novels of Nadine Gordimer,* that "politics is character in South Africa" (p. 10)—a determining pressure rather than an arbitrary backdrop. The best clue to her resolution of these positions occurs in her dense, suggestive piece, "The Essential Gesture," collected in the eponymous 1988 volume of critical writing. There Gordimer argues that a writer in her position can best fulfill her responsibility, not by contracting into orthodoxy, but through delving into the uncertainties of imaginative risk. The integrity of that risk taking is a version of answerability, though always a lesser one than the extraliterary pursuit of social justice. Gordimer's South African experience taught her to be equally skeptical of a sense of creative obligation on the one hand and, on the other, of a view of writers as pure, individual sensibilities flying free of ideology.

In that 1984 essay and in an autobiographical fragment written some twenty years earlier, Gordimer makes a limpid distinction between her own literary genesis and that of many black South African writers: "The problems of my country did not set me writing; on the contrary, it was learning to write that sent me falling, falling through the surface of 'the South African way of life'" (*Essential Gesture,* p. 26). By contrast, those directly oppressed by apartheid often achieve a cleaner synthesis of creativity and social responsibility, because "it is out of being 'more than a writer' that many black men and women in South Africa *begin* to write" (*Essential Gesture,* p. 290). Gordimer's literary ambitions, then, predated any alertness to politics; indeed, the initial impetus to write was provided more by her mother's perversity than by the singular deviancies of apartheid.

Gordimer was born on 20 November 1923 in Springs, a gold-mining town of stifling provinciality that lies to the east of Johannesburg. Her Jewish parents diverged widely in background and demeanor. At thirteen, her father fled a Lithuanian village where czarist anti-Semitism barred him from attending high school. In Springs he learned watch making and opened a jeweler's shop. Gordimer portrays him as a man of arrested emotional development who, despite childhood immersion in poverty, educational deprivation, and bigotry, disappointed her deeply with his recalcitrant racism toward black South Africans. The more profound influence was Gordimer's English-born mother, a woman whose ample creativity had been denied adequate professional outlets. Gordimer speaks of her as the dominant member of the household and a sincere do-gooder who founded a day-care center in a nearby black township.

When she learned that Nadine had an enlarged thyroid (a common, unproblematic ailment) she barred her from all outdoor activity and withdrew her, aged eleven, permanently from school. Thereafter, Gordimer suffered an education of erratic tutoring and never gained a high school diploma. Not until she was thirty did she ferret out the motives behind her mother's exaggerated reaction: miserably married, she had been in love with the family

doctor and had used her daugher's "illness" to maximize contact with him and pursue a never-consummated relationship. Thus she had guaranteed Nadine a damaged, friendless childhood, in which the company of books became an attractive alternative to the company of small-town adults. In this way, a mother's selfishness inadvertently prodded a daughter toward a literary vocation.

EARLY WORK

HER MOTHER'S insistence that she be tutored within the confines of home meant that Gordimer lacked the qualifications for admission to a university. Commuting from Springs, she audited courses for one year at the University of Witwatersrand, an institution in whose intellectual life she would later feature prominently. Despite her limited formal education, however, Gordimer had been publishing stories since the age of fifteen. But it was not until 1949, the year of both her first marriage and her permanent move to Johannesburg, that she broke through in literary terms. In that benchmark year she had a story appear in *The New Yorker* for the first time—the beginning of a long association with the magazine and the first hint of her international standing. 1949 saw, too, her inaugural book in print, a collection entitled *Face to Face: Short Stories.* That volume, *The Soft Voice of the Serpent and Other Stories* (1952), and her first novel, *The Lying Days* (1953), retain interest principally as measures of the distance, political and aesthetic, that Gordimer traversed. Helen Shaw of *The Lying Days* faces the classic colonial dilemma pondered by writers as diverse as Olive Schreiner, V. S. Naipaul, Patrick White, and Katherine Mansfield. How is she to read (and by analogy, how is Gordimer to render) her inadequately imagined society? Those around Helen point overseas to "home," while nothing in her imported European reading can ratify the reality of her immediate life. Apartheid exacerbates Helen's intimations of artificiality: she awakes to horror upon witnessing the police shoot a black protestor, but she remains estranged from the possibility of taking action. Her gender, too, conspires to keep her a spectator in a world in which agency is the prerogative of swaggering men. *The Lying Days* discloses Gordimer's intuitive sense of the turbulence South Africa underwent in the thirties and forties as a result of rapid industrialization and the National Party's ascent to power. But as yet Gordimer lacked the historical knowledge to secure her intuitions, and the novel, like Helen, seems somewhat adrift in a sea of vague revolt, unanchored by imaginative or ideological conviction.

In South African memory, Sophiatown is both a place and a time. During the 1950's—dubbed by writer Lewis Nkosi "the fabulous decade"—a ghetto in Johannesburg became the hub of a cultural renaissance led by black journalists, writers, jazz players, and intellectuals. *A World of Strangers* (1958) is Gordimer's Sophiatown novel, an engaged yet skeptical testament to an era whose heady bohemianism would be devastated by the government's bulldozing of Sophiatown and terminated, in 1960, by the Sharpeville massacre. As evidenced by *A World of Strangers,* Sophiatown became, for a thin stratum of middle-class blacks and whites, a center for conscientious multiracialism, often in an atmosphere of strained bonhomie. Flouting taboos, notably through interracial drinking and sex, became both a style of life and a surrogate politics.

A World of Strangers stages a preliminary, ambiguous assessment of the prospects of liberal good will (with a gloss of hedonism) as a reforming influence on apartheid. The novel's perspective is that of Toby Hood, an English visitor who becomes charmed by Sophiatown's penumbral verve, a welcome counter to the cheerlessness of white Johannesburg. The bookish Toby alludes several times to E. M. Forster's cross-cultural novels; indeed, *A World of Strangers* is shadowed by Forster's exploration of the limits of individual decency before the violence of colonial domination. Toby's cool detachment and his liberty to play the outsider are undermined by the death of his closest black friend when the police raid a speakeasy. The killing exposes the false parity of a relationship conducted under circumstances of skewed racial power; the fantasy of occupying, through friendship, a magic circle outside apartheid, degenerates into culpable sentimentality.

Gordimer advances this theme further in *Occasion for Loving* (1963). Here, the shimmering promise of transcendent intimacy arises not from male friendship but from (in South African argot) "sex across the color bar." Recalling her own bravado during the fifties, Gordimer remarks in an interview in *Paris Review*, "I felt that all I needed, in my own behavior, was to ignore and defy the color bar. In other words my own attitude toward blacks seemed to be sufficient action" (p. 93). In Gordimer's callow confidence in attitude serving as a proxy for activism, one discerns an extension of her mother's assiduous charity toward blacks. Indeed, in exposing the hazards of liberal paternalism, *Occasion for Loving* simultaneously works through the manipulative mother-daughter relationship of Gordimer's upbringing. The emergence of a love triangle among the English visitor, Ann Davis, her white South African husband, Boaz, and a black artist, Gideon Shibalo, is observed through the novel's principal figure, Jessie Stilwell. Jessie's mother deceived her into believing she had a "bad heart" as a way of denying her self-reliance and easing her mother's loneliness. Gordimer thereby probes the analogies between the crippling dependencies induced by the family and those engendered by apartheid.

Occasion for Loving enters a long tradition of Southern African literature centered on the traumas of miscegenation, a tradition stretching from William Plomer's *Turbott Wolfe* (1925) and Sarah Gertrude Millin's *God's Step-Children* (1924) to Doris Lessing's *The Grass Is Singing* (1950), Alan Paton's *Too Late the Phalarope* (1953), Richard Rive's *Emergency* (1964), Nkosi's *Mating Birds* (1983), and Athol Fugard, John Kani, and Winston Ntshona's collaborative play, *Statements After an Arrest Under the Immorality Act* (1972). But Gordimer's novel cuts across the prevailing tendency in this literature to celebrate the fidelity of love or desire in the face of dehumanizing laws. For in the final instance, Ann recoils from her black lover and flees the country, husband in tow, whereupon the lovelorn, abandoned Gideon slumps into bitterness and alcoholism. Gordimer's third novel thus adds a twist of tragedy to the closing scene of *A World of Strangers* in which Toby, departing for England, promises to revisit South Africa. At this his jazz musician friend chides: "Who knows with you people, Toby, man? Maybe you won't come back at all. Something will keep you away. Something will prevent you . . ." (p. 266). In both novels, Gordimer—by this stage steeped in Jean Paul Sartre and Camus—gives great play to the *mauvaise foi* of return-ticket intimacy. Middle-class whites dabbling in multiracialism, she suggests, often make impossible emotional demands of blacks, who remain fenced in by absent alternatives.

In terms of a long view of Gordimer, *Occasion for Loving* initiates her questioning of the routine dichotomy between personal integrity and the warped laws of the public domain:

There was no recess of being, no emotion so private that white privilege did not single you out there; it was a silver spoon clamped between your jaws and you might choke on it for all the chance there was of dislodging it. So long as the law remained unchanged, nothing could bring integrity to personal relationships.

(p. 279)

Ineluctably, the law becomes not only an imposition on human relations but, in refracted form, a psychological emanation that affects even those who oppose it.

THE MIDDLE YEARS

FROM the outset, Gordimer's prose manifested descriptive skills almost unexampled among contemporary writers. Yet, as the author herself concedes, in the early novels, her narrative command would sometimes slacken to episodic effect. Given the controlled brilliance of her short story writing and her narrative difficulties over longer stretches, it is not surprising that her most immaculate work of fiction, *The Late Bourgeois World* (1966), should assume the compressed form of a novella. *Burger's Daughter* is ultimately a more ambitious and momentous work, but nothing in Gordimer's oeuvre surpasses the sustained prose power and self-assurance of *The Late Bourgeois World*.

The book emerged out of the political gloom. By the time *Occasion for Loving* appeared in 1963, the energy and hope associated with the defiance campaigns of the fifties had already begun to attenuate. A further three years of bannings, censorship, new racist laws, infiltrations, assassinations, mass trials, and hangings guaranteed that resistance would reach its nadir.

The novella's compelling title is drawn from Ernst Fischer's *The Necessity of Art* (1963), a Marxist critique of the alienated aestheticism that Fischer sees as symptomatic of the decay of community into fragmented individualism. Arguing for the original utility of art, Fischer urges that society recover its vision by unearthing the possibilities in art for collective transformation. This idea is of direct significance to the tone and debates of Gordimer's novella as, out of the futureless despair of the mid-sixties, she aspires to conceive of fitting aesthetic and political forms of responsibility. In so doing, she avoids sanctimonious distinctions between the bourgeoisie and revolutionaries. The novella's most prominent activist, Max Van Den Sandt, blurs such categories as he conducts a life-long revolt against his elitist family under the banner of political radicalism. A saboteur in a splinter sect, he gets detained, betrays his comrades to the state, and takes his own life. It is important that *The Late Bourgeois World* not be misconstrued as opposing revolutionary practice; rather, it assails weak individuals like Max whose self-absorbed flirtation with revolution is reactive, romantic humbug that incriminates him as part of the detritus of the age.

The novella launches itself from two complementary epigraphs: Franz Kafka's "There are possibilities for me, certainly; but under what stone do they lie?" and Maxim Gorky's epigrammatic "The madness of the brave is the wisdom of life." These apply directly to Max's estranged wife, Liz, the novella's narrator. How, in a draconian climate in which liberal decencies are straws in the wind, is she to move beyond quietism and despair? In keeping with Gordimer's developing socialist convictions and with the titular allusion to Fischer, the tentative answer, instead of emerging from the realm of private morality, assumes the form of economic redress. A black revolutionary, Luke Fokase, implores Liz to find a bank account through which his organization can channel overseas funds undetected. Liz dismisses his request, then recalls that she possesses power of attorney over the account of her senile, ailing grandmother, who lives off the dividends of mining shares passed down through the family. Given that the apartheid laws are rooted in the exploitative economy of mining, Liz's decision to abuse her authority over the account (at least in terms of bourgeois morality) can be read as a way of commandeering the spoils of apartheid to bring about the system's demise. In a sense, Liz dislodges *Occasion for Loving*'s choking silver spoon and puts it to good use.

During the late sixties and early seventies, Gordimer began to deliberate with fresh intensity her position on the African continent. This preoccupation surfaces in closely observed travel essays on

Ghana, Botswana, the Ivory Coast, and Madagascar; in *Livingstone's Companions* (1971), a lively collection of stories exploring post- and neo-colonial conditions north of the border; and in the critical work, *The Black Interpreters: Notes on African Writing* (1973).

In the year prior to publication of *Livingstone's Companions,* Gordimer brought out *A Guest of Honour,* an epic novel and her only one set in its entirety beyond the confines of South Africa. For her purposes, she devised a Central African country, drawn largely from the example of Zambia, in the throes of excited postindependence debate and political maneuvering. Gordimer's venturesome break with her long-established setting is both typical of her resourcefulness—liberating her imaginatively from the staleness of late-sixties South Africa—and, paradoxically, less of a break than it might at first appear. By the time Gordimer embarked on *A Guest of Honour,* the state's imposition of apartheid had suffocated all significant revolt. But an explosive tension developed between the mood, in South Africa, of directionless despair, and the heady expectations in Africa at large, as one country after another gained its independence. In both *A Guest of Honour* and *The Conservationist* (1974), Gordimer works the unstable territory between apartheid's internal supremacy and its intensifying regional isolation.

A Guest of Honour opens with Colonel Evelyn James Bray, a retired colonial official, invited back to an unnamed Central African country for the birth of its independence. Bray's African reputation is high; while purportedly serving the British crown, he had the prescience to advance the anticolonial cause of the People's Independence Party, led by Adamson Mweta and Edward Shinza. Such insubordination prompted his expulsion. Now Bray returns to a different nation; the opposition has fractured into rivalry over power, and he is forced to take sides between his two friends and his political allies. Although Bray is the ruling Mweta's guest, he finds himself increasingly drawn to the arguments of the African socialist Shinza, who aligns himself with the interests of the poor rural populace and the workers in the heavily centralized mines and fishing industries.

Extending her fascination, begun in *The Late Bourgeois World,* with the economic underpinnings of politics, Gordimer plays off Mweta's policies, which subordinate the national interest to the whims of the international mining magnates, against Shinza's conviction that the president has been reduced to "the black watchman standing guard outside the white man's enterprise" (p. 488). When Mweta ships in mercenaries to smash internal dissent, Bray determines to travel to Europe to raise arms for Shinza. This traumatic decision, by a presidential guest with a distaste for violence, bears comparison with Liz's choice, at the close of *The Late Bourgeois World,* between the conventions of her inherited morality and the pressure to act. Bray's wracking decision is prefigured in the two epigraphs to the novel. His options lie stretched between opposing conceptions of bravery, between the lonely, principled doubt of Turgenev's "An honourable man will end by not knowing where to live" and Ernesto "Che" Guevara's insistence that action requires simple beliefs: "Many will call me an adventurer—and that I am, only of a different sort—one of those who risks his skin to prove his platitudes."

While fleeing the country, Bray is trapped in an ambush and is murdered by the very forces he sought to aid, as Shinza's men mistake him for a German mercenary. The irony is immense but not supreme. Just as Gordimer exploded Max's naive idealism so as to explore tougher forms of radicalism, she has Bray killed, not as a form of comeuppance for romantic meddling, but to demonstrate that in the muddy waters of politics principled action should not anticipate personal reward. Bray's lover insists that Bray would have comprehended his death. The force of Gordimer's critique is directed not against Bray, but against the old colonials who would view him as "a martyr to savages" (p. 503) and against *Time*- and *Newsweek*-style travesties of the events.

Gordimer typically refuses to simplify her characters' lives by segregating their exploration of ideological dilemmas from their anguished and often contradictory immersion in sexual and familial politics. On this score, *A Guest of Honour* is no exception. The novel's dialogue contains some discussion of Wilhelm Reich's ideas about the authoritarian personality and, as Judie Newman determines in her study of Gordimer, there is broader evidence that Gordimer was intrigued by Reich's efforts to reconcile Karl Marx and Sigmund Freud. A crucial subtext of the novel traces the new nation's ominous failure, despite the rituals of independence, to break with a vision of the leader as "father of the state" (p. 15). Gordimer's wariness of the crossover between familial and authoritarian models of government has proved prescient: "strong man" rule has repeatedly dogged neocolonial African states. Her foresight is revealed, too, in the novel's adhering to the principles of African socialism while exposing the immense obstacles blocking their application, and marking not the triumph of those beliefs but their convoluted deferral.

A Guest of Honour ranks with Chinua Achebe's *A Man of the People* (1966), Ngugi wa Thiong'o's *Petals of Blood* (1977), and Paule Marshall's *The Chosen Place, The Timeless People* (1969), as one of the great fictional renditions of the all-too-common demise of *uhuru* (freedom) into neocolonialism. Gordimer's book stands, too, as a formidable novel of ideas; while never formulaic, it integrates strong currents of contemporary radical thought. Gordimer has spoken of her immersion, at the time, not just in Reich, but also in the political philosophies of Frantz Fanon, Julius Nyerere, Kwame Nkrumah, and Amilcar Cabral, all alluded to over the course of the novel. Her alertness to such thinking deepens her exploration of the often contradictory structures of dependency and revolt, a subject she would pursue further in *Burger's Daughter.*

Between these two huge works lies the experimental, relatively slight achievement of *The Conservationist.* Like much of Gordimer's previous fiction, the novel explores questions of white belonging. But the titular character, Mehring, emerges as the antithesis of Bray, no self-acknowledged guest of honor, but someone whose ownership of a farm and surface command of its black tenants obscure his deeply alienated relation to the earth and its denizens.

Gordimer's title is charged with irony. Mehring fancies himself a tender of nature, someone who nurtures God's earth in order that future generations may enjoy the fruits of the past. As such, he stands for all self-appointed guardians of that ominous anachronism, "the South African way of life," which romanticizes the farm and outdoor living in an ambience of white supremacy. The irony is redoubled when it becomes apparent that Mehring is simply a prominent industrialist, a weekend farmer with a squanderous, absentee relationship to the land. He represents not the old style rural Afrikaner, imprisoned by his laager mentality, but the new, worldly wise corporate white who rose to prominence during the economic boom of the late sixties. Thus Mehring sentimentalizes playing the farmer between business trips to Japan. Gordimer exposes, in the process, the extent to which the conservation of the "age-old," white way of life, entails—to borrow Terrence Ranger and Eric Hobsbawm's phrase—the elaborate, self-deceiving "invention of tradition."

In the annals of colonialism, the expropriation of the land has been reiteratively characterized through sexual registers—virgin territory, penetration, rape. Gordimer positions *The Conservationist* in a subversive relationship to this tendency, for, in the fullest sense of the phrase, it is a book about land lust. Under circumstances in which apartheid has reserved 87 percent of the country for white ownership, Mehring's flirtation with farming is really a species of proprietary onanism. Despite his preoccupation with conservation, Mehring's life is wholly unregenerative: divorced and politically estranged from his son (who is, moreover, indifferent to the farm), he spends much of his waking life in fantasy monologues with a long-lost girlfriend. He inhabits an issueless world that forebodes white disinheritance. The novel closes with Mehring about to copulate with a woman hitchhiker when an ominous, never-to-be-identified male figure approaches. Mehring's panicked thoughts give precise expression to his mental bracketing of property and sex, while pointing equally to his inevitable abandonment:

He's going to leave her to them . . . he's going to make a dash for it, a leap, sell the place to the first offer. . . . He's going to run, run and leave them to rape her and rob her. She'll be all right. They survive everything. Coloured or poor-white, whichever she is, their brothers or fathers take their virginity good and early. They can have it, the whole four hundred acres.

(p. 250)

Were *The Conservationist* solely a novel about Mehring, it would be limited to a critique of a barren ethos. But, as we have seen from *A Guest of Honour,* in this phase of her work Gordimer was reaching for affirmative values. These she had located, in that earlier novel, in African socialism. To offset Mehring's life-threatening values with a spirit of renewal, Gordimer had to turn to another black tradition, in a manner that illuminates a representational crisis endemic to white South African literature. Novelist J. M. Coetzee remarks, in his essay collection, *White Writing: On the Culture of Letters in South Africa,* upon "the uneasy set of options" (p. 5) that have dogged white literary representation of blacks from the eighteenth century onward. Most often, the texts of European visitors and white settlers have effaced blacks from the landscape or fused them with it. Ever since, one might extrapolate, white writers have had to choose between the sins of omission and the sins of presumption. But of all white South African writers, Gordimer has ventured most convincingly into black characterization—notably in *A World of Strangers, Occasion for Loving, The Late Bourgeois World, A Guest of Honour,* and *Burger's Daughter.* Yet in all these works, she draws on her extensive exposure to township culture and her friendships with the urban bohemians and political leaders, with whom she shares significant values. When her writing shifts, as in *The Conservationist* and later, *July's People* (1981), to a rural locale, her predicament becomes more complex, for she draws on a shallow reservoir of common experience. In class terms, the Bantustan peasantry and farmhands are remote from her, while characterization is further complicated by her linguistic estrangement from them, as very little English is spoken in the countryside. It is understandable, therefore, that the depiction of blacks in *The Conservationist* should take a symbolic turn. Indeed, the novel's most powerful black presence is a biologically silent but mythologically articulate corpse.

Early in the narrative, the body of a murdered man disturbs the Africans on Mehring's farm; the corpse is given a cursory, indifferent burial, without the proper observances. That body remains a force throughout and, by the close, has been unearthed by a portentous storm in a gesture that intimates the return both of the white psyche's repressed and apartheid's oppressed. Gordimer reinforces this vision of cyclical revival through a contrapuntal design, alternating between the throttled narcissism of Mehring's mind (a state accentuated by her deployment of stream of consciousness) and citations from Zulu mythology. These, as Judie Newman has shown, Gordimer garnered from Henry Callaway's *The Religious System of the Amazulu.* From this ingenious opposition flows a series of reversals. The conservationist is bereft of a tradition to conserve, while his tenants dwell in a present animated by precolonial rituals, a present that opens out onto the future. Likewise, the de-

generate Mehring is evacuated of life, while the mysterious black cadaver, swept up in rituals of regeneration, comes to incarnate the living body politic.

Notwithstanding its subtlety of craft and the fact that it earned Gordimer Britain's prestigious Booker Prize, *The Conservationist* seems too detached to rank among the author's finest writing. On the one hand, Mehring, of all her leading protagonists, lies furthest from her sympathies; on the other, the narrative's affirmative impulse is borne by mythological ciphers. I say ciphers, because the anthropological extraction of the myth from oral tradition followed by its subsequent translation into novelistic form depletes its energy. Thus, overall, Gordimer's intelligence of design often seems eerily uninhabited. The limitations of *The Conservationist* are best dramatized by the remarkable books that succeeded it: *Selected Stories* (1975) and *Burger's Daughter* (1979), Gordimer's seventh novel and indubitably her most commanding work.

SHORT STORIES

ONE might never guess, from the criticism on Gordimer, that her energies have been split equally between short stories and novels. The former are not even touched upon in the two finest studies of her fiction—by Judie Newman and Stephen Clingman—and are, in general, left critically remaindered as if they were five-finger exercises. Yet, as *Selected Stories* amply demonstrates, in the briefer form Gordimer does more than limber up for the real performance, often achieving effects unattainable in the novels. Had she never gone on to produce three further collections of short stories, her 1975 selection, drawn from five volumes and spanning the first thirty years of her career, would have been sufficient to mark her as one of the most versatile exponents of the genre since Chekhov.

Technical and political factors have given an edge to her aptitude for the form. I have suggested that Gordimer's acute powers of observation are not always matched by a corresponding level of narrative control. Over the shorter stretch her pacing is invariably infallible, as she writes with a secure sense of the destiny of her material. Indeed, many of the most intense portions of her novels read like self-contained short stories: one thinks, for instance, of the much anthologized excerpt from *Burger's Daughter,* where Rosa witnesses an old black man brutalizing a donkey and recognizes that she has no conception of how to live or intervene in her own country.

In her introduction to *Selected Stories,* Gordimer remarks on the androgynous ambition behind her writing, her deeply felt need to move freely between female and male points of view. Few contemporary novelists hazard the range of governing perspectives found in her novels—from the male Oxbridge journalist in *A World of Strangers* to the daughter of a South African communist in *Burger's Daughter;* from the reprehensible farmer-cum-industrialist in *The Conservationist* to the idealized, globe-trotting single mother who weds an African head of state in *A Sport of Nature.* All the same, it is in Gordimer's two-hundred-odd short stories that she truly gets to chance new vantage points. One can surely read her restless quest for diverse perspectives as a form of defiance, a way of transgressing the bounds of her segregated society, charting people and places who are not meant to be on her experiential or imaginative maps. To get an inkling of the social range across which she remains affecting, one need only read in succession "The Last Kiss" (1960), "Which New Era Would That Be?" (1956), "Something for the Time Being," (1960), and "A City of the Dead, A City of the Living" (1982). The finest of her individual collections, *Not For Publication* (1965), offers a compact sample of her daring, versatile powers of empathy. "A Chip of Glass Ruby" probes the tension between an Indian woman who throws herself into the Defiance Campaigns and her admiring but politically cautious husband. "Some Monday for Sure" is narrated by a black refugee who escapes South Africa by walking halfway across the continent after becoming involved in a sabotage operation. A lonely white garage clerk tells her story in "Good Climate, Friendly Inhabitants." When an itinerant mercenary exploits her badly, the woman becomes wholly reliant on the "bossboy" as her confidant, but is unable to recognize that dependence. Gordimer thereby stages a brilliant inquiry into the character of "ordinary" lower-middle-class racism.

Gordimer's proficiency for the shorter form has helped her press further than any other South African writer toward overcoming the deprivation that comes of legislated isolation. Yet, just as her childhood passion for writing preceded any alertness to politics, so too, her first awareness of alienation stemmed not from apartheid but from her sense of being a bookish, housebound freak of a girl in a boorish mining town. This early sense of her own deviance and her ostracism has given a rich resonance to her writing on the subject, when, with maturity, she came to delve into the alienating effects of racial segregation.

Gordimer has remarked how, as an adolescent, she achieved communion through the body, not the mind, which remained sealed in reverie and intellectual solitude. Shared sexual attraction became her "Rapunzel's hair," whereby she could periodically enter the lives around her. Unlike many authors best known for their political obsessions—V. S. Naipaul being a notable example—Gordimer has never been awkward or skittish around sexual themes. She can be profoundly insightful into what she has called "the blankness of concealed distress" (*Selected Stories,* p. 65) that shrouds sexual desire in a repressive society. "A Bit of Young Life" (1956) and "A Company of Laughing Faces" (1965) both evoke, from youthful perspectives, the heavy shame and ineluctably private bewilderment that weigh on any woman who risks sexual spontaneity. In the later short stories, like those gathered in *A Soldier's Embrace* (1980), Gordimer's earlier fixation with her society's punishment of callow errancy gives way to some excellent writing on the frayed, weary sexuality of late middle age. "Time Did," narrated by a woman whose husband has just confessed his infidelities, is the finest of these.

As *Occasion for Loving* reveals at length, to trespass sexually "across the color bar" is to enter a zone of concentrated trauma, where the personal and the political meet head-on. Several of the short stories continue to approach miscegenation as symbolic revolt—the orgasm as guerrilla sortie—or vicious power play. If interracial sex sometimes lapses into theatrical illegality, Gordimer intimates that it can also be *the* place where interracial trust is won, whereas the best-intentioned of friendships often buckle beneath the strains of the segregated public domain. Thus Gordimer's early experience of the body as Rapunzel's hair, as a way out of solipsism, is revived in scenes of interracial intimacy, principally between black men and white women.

As the critic Dorothy Driver has observed, Gordimer "seldom focuses exclusively on a black consciousness engaged with itself rather than with a white world." Given the lineaments of Gordimer's experience, this tendency is scarcely surprising; indeed, to write otherwise might well be judged presumptuous. However, it is significant that her fascination with those border zones of interracial contact seldom extends beyond encounters between black men and white women. Her black women invariably seem less fully imagined than her men and are usually left with walk-on parts. Even the exception to this rule, Aila in *My Son's Story,* remains somewhat abstractly sketched and lacks the intimacy of Gideon Shibelo (*Occasion for Loving*), Luke Fokase (*The Late Bourgeois World*), and Sonny (*My Son's Story*). Gordimer's inability to generate resonant black female characters stems in part from the composition of the interracial circles in which she moved: black women were poorly represented among the bohemians, intellectuals, political leaders, and other professional classes. Moreover, Gordimer's insistence on sexual chemistry as a crucial catalyst for interracial communication, meant that, in autobiographical terms, she accrued the confidence to portray black men to a degree that she never achieved with black women.

Yet the most powerful of all the obsessive concerns in the shorter fiction is Gordimer's indictment of white society's inability to think beyond racial paranoia. This failure of imagination has produced a travesty of community, a community most intimate through its shared fears. The newly independent Africa of *Livingstone's Companions* (1971) issues successive challenges to that community of dread, most forcefully in "The African Magician," a tale narrated by a colonial on a river trip down the Congo. When a local conjurer appears on board and hypnotizes his assistants, the whites seek to expose his charlatanism by challenging him to test his powers on one of their number. Instantly, he binds a young white woman in a spell, producing in her a beatific abandonment of will:

She had never made such a gesture to her husband, or any man. She had never stood like that before her father—none of us has. How can I explain? One of the disciples might have come before Christ like that. There was the peace of absolute trust in it. It stirred a needle of fear in me—more than that, for a moment I was horribly afraid; and how can I explain that, either? For it was beautiful, and I have lived in Africa all my life and I know them, *us,* the white people. To see it was beautiful would make us dangerous.

(p. 258)

When prejudices become so settled, the threat of trust breaking out—the threat of human recognition—becomes much more disturbing than danger itself. Indeed, from "Is There Nowhere Else Where We Can Meet?" (1953) to "Something Out There" (1984) and "Once Upon a Time" (1989), Gordimer suggests that the true peril emanates from within a community that is self-besieged. "Once Upon a Time" conveys this conviction brilliantly. A fairy tale of suburban life set in the era of President P. W. Botha's "total onslaught," it points up the paradox of security, how an obsession with protecting a style of life eventually becomes a surrogate life-style, displacing or eroding the very comforts it was intended to secure. The most vocal inhabitants of the story's Johannesburg suburb are the burglar alarms, communing so incessantly in their "electronic harpies' discourse" that no one pays any heed, so thieves and housebreakers can proceed unhindered. The man and his wife encircle their property in a coil of serrated blades—"pure concentration camp style, no frills, evident efficacy." But the only intruder whom they maim is their son: playacting the valiant prince who revives Sleeping Beauty, he gets sliced to bits in a thicket of metal thorns.

Gordimer's stories reveal a special talent for charting those subliminal realms where racial and sexual fears make their rendezvous. "The Life of the Imagination" (1972), which draws on her mother's fantasy romance with a small town general practitioner, is the most acute of these tales. An artistic woman, diminished by the maternal rounds of a stunted marriage, is suddenly revived through an affair with her child's doctor. Her preoccupation with the rituals of concealment culminates in a scene in which her lover tiptoes past the children's room to reach her marital bed. Yet on departing, the doctor leaves the door ajar; the night wind blows in, bearing other, deeper fears. In her condition of guilty abandonment, the romance that had offered escape from the tedium of provincial life fades, leaving the woman vulnerable to the clichéd dread of black intrusion. Her sexual anxieties become racialized and her racial terror sexualized:

> She was empty, unable to summon anything but this stale fantasy, shared with the whole town, the whole white population. She lay there possessed by it, and she thought, she violently longed—they will come straight into the room and stick a knife in me. No time to cry out. Quick. Deep. Over.
>
> (*Selected Stories,* p. 368)

BURGER'S DAUGHTER *AND CENSORSHIP*

IF racial and sexual fears have always pulsed strongly through Gordimer's fiction, she gained an unusually public sense of their connection in battling the Calvinist censors who banned *Burger's Daughter.* Her most famous and most radical work, this is a book of towering intellectual ambition wherein Gordimer simultaneously engages the insights of Freud and Marx, returning, with enhanced sophistication, to that site of tension where familial revolt crosses social insurrection.

Within her oeuvre, *Burger's Daughter* is also unprecedented in its historical scope. The action ranges from the fifties, when both the African National Conference (ANC) and the South African Communist party were prominent, through the bleak, heavily repressive sixties, the ascent of black consciousness in the seventies, to the 1976 Soweto Uprising and beyond, ultimately foreshadowing the revival, in the eighties, of nonracialism as political philosophy and anti-apartheid strategy. Gordimer conceived of *Burger's Daughter* as, in part, a way of paying homage to the generation of white activists whom she knew and admired in the fifties and early sixties. As such, the titular Burger, a person of great human warmth—idealistic yet altruistic—offsets *The Late Bourgeois World*'s Max Van Den Sandt, a rash, narcissistic radical who falls catastrophically in love with the image of himself manning the revolutionary vanguard.

For her portrait of Lionel Burger, Gordimer drew heavily on the example of the South African communist Bram Fischer, who shares with writer Breyten Breytenbach and clergyman Beyers Naude the distinction of being the most famous of Afrikaner renegades. In 1966, the year that saw the publication of *The Late Bourgeois World,* Gordimer had published an essay entitled, "Why Did Bram Fischer Choose to Go to Jail?" sketching his defection from a racist upbringing, his leadership in the legal defense of Nelson Mandela and the other Rivonia defendants, his disappearance underground, and his capture, destined for the jail where he was to die.

Thirteen years elapsed before Gordimer gave fictional body to selected aspects of this outline. Yet, as the title intimates, *Burger's Daughter* commemorates Fischer/Burger without centering on his example. There are several reasons that explain why, by the late seventies, Gordimer had become more exercised by the predicament of his fictional daughter. Political icons (like Fischer, or Nelson Mandela, or Steve Biko, or Mahatma Gandhi) are resistant to novelistic transformation; saintliness is an inert, psychologically shallow condition and narrative art cannot flourish by expressing static reverence for cultural heroes. (One is reminded of *Paradise Lost* and the notorious tedium of Milton's God.) Through Rosa, who barely knows her father, Gordimer produces an admiring but external portrait; indeed, Rosa's distance from Burger becomes part of her case, as a daughter, against him, and sets the stage for the child's revolt. Thus Gordimer's novel economically probes the psychology underlying the perennial forms of familial conflict and explores the wracking choice, distinctively acute under apartheid, between personal and public responsibility. The Burgers, after all, resemble a political institution: the father "knew that his schoolgirl daughter could be counted on in this family totally united in and dedicated to the struggle" (p. 12).

Gordimer's respect for people who can be "counted on" does not, however, blind her to what gets discounted. The family's focus on the mother's detention exacerbates the repressed privacy of fourteen-year-old Rosa's "monthly crisis of destruction, the purging, tearing, draining of my own structure" (p. 16). When a society is erupting into conflict, the eruption of the body into puberty goes unnoticed; political bloodletting renders menstrual bleeding invisible. Like Chris Menges' 1988 film, *A World Apart* (which bears the influence of *Burger's*

Daughter), Gordimer's novel charts a difficult course in exploring the ways public answerability may inevitably foster private neglects. This is made most explicit through Rosa's simulated engagement to the young Communist prisoner Noel De Witt, as a way of guaranteeing him visits from the outside world. Yet no one observes Rosa's private pain when she, the proxy fiancée, falls in love with Noel; her love affair is a political construction accidentally "contaminated" by private romantic feelings. Rosa's official engagement is to the struggle—a more honorable version of "married to the mob." Without detracting from Burger's political fortitude, Gordimer exposes as always inadequate the attempt to yoke inner desires wholly to public causes. As such, the novel articulates Gordimer's fixation with what she has called "the psychology of history" and maps the crosscurrents, permeating all corners of society, between political and sexual repression.

Burger's Daughter stands as Gordimer's response to a painful challenge to her political relevance and imaginative authority in South Africa. The ascent of black consciousness in the seventies and the decline of ANC-style nonracialism caused many antiapartheid whites, of both liberal and radical persuasion, to feel remaindered by history. "Black Man you are on you own," Biko cautioned, and his words resonated through the structures of political and cultural organizations that refused white participation. This challenge was so urgent that it required, in answer, something tougher than a nostalgic return in memory to the nonracialism of the fifties. The altered conditions for activism and for writing ensured that Fischer could offer a symbolic starting point but no longer a practical inspiration.

South Africa's recent history is routinely referred to as pre- or post-1976. The dividing event, the uprising led by Soweto schoolchildren, occurs only toward the end of *Burger's Daughter,* but the novel takes its bearings from that momentous action, which, to a significant extent, was infused by black consciousness. In a stroke of intuitive brilliance, Gordimer seized upon the common appellation for 1976—"the revolt of the children"—and recognized its layered possibilities for a novel that explores generational conflict in psychological and political terms.

Gordimer's response to this explosive historical moment entailed, above all, that she reconceive the formal possibilities of the novel. As Stephen Clingman has observed, the design of *Burger's Daughter* is profoundly dialectical. In the first phase, Rosa's identity is fused to her father's revolutionary legacy; in the book's second, antithetical movement, Rosa withdraws from the family and its stifling political expectations, ventures overseas, and affirms an autonomous identity. While in Europe, Rosa grows intimate with Fischer's sexually liberated first wife, Katya, who helps demystify the father and sanction Rosa's romantic and sexual defection from familial responsibility. Finally, after a devastating exchange with Zwelinzima, the adopted "half-brother" of her childhood but now a black consciousness exile in London, Rosa reassesses her position and returns to South Africa to forge her own form of political commitment, which ultimately delivers her, like Lionel, into jail. The novel's closing synthesis reconnects Rosa with the family's ideological heritage, but Gordimer is emphatic that, given Rosa's personal maturation and the intervention of black consciousness, her activism does not simply recapitulate her father's politics. The needs, the possibilities have changed.

The novel thus poses the paradox of the antiauthoritarian father who, from the daughter's perspective, remains a representative of authority. The second, European movement of the narrative, stages the child's counterrevolution. The psychological necessity for this is familiar, but, in a South African context, there are sound political reasons, too. Rosa's rejection of her legacy is cathartic because it replaces the static organizing principle of inheritance—with all its baggage of birthrights, "natural" allegiances, and "natural" successions—on which white supremacy is founded, with an active principle of individual choice. In Rosa's words: "I was struggling with a monstrous resentment against the claim . . . of blood, shared genes, the semen from which I had issued and the body in which I had grown" (p. 62). Once this revolt has succeeded, it remains, in the final episodes, for that individual to recover her sense of social purpose.

Burger's Daughter positions itself at exactly that intersection where the personal and the political cross. Thus Rosa's remark concerning her father—"I wanted to know how to defect from him" (p. 284)—resonates in both realms, while a reference to the public "trial of her parents" (p. 89) takes on Freudian undertones. Nowhere is this crossover more explicit than in Gordimer's sustained effort to ring the changes on the concept of freedom. (In contemporary literature, *Burger's Daughter* shares this obsession with V. S. Naipaul's *In a Free State,* although the two books arise from quite different political affiliations.) For Lionel Burger, freedom is an awaited collective condition, not a present or individual possibility. At the other extreme stands Rosa's vaguely liberal lover, Conrad, for whom freedom exists within "the closed circuit of the self" (p. 86). In France, the apogee of Rosa's familial revolt occurs when she languishes in a condition of anonymity liberated from responsibility: "Bernard Chabalier's mistress isn't Lionel Burger's daughter; she's certainly not accountable to the Future . . ." (p. 304). Yet, having been seduced by the notion of freedom as a life of maximum individual choice unburdened by commitment, she discovers that such a conception of personal liberty is not absolute but ideological. The chief catalyst for this altered attitude is Zwelinzima Vulindlela, the man she once knew as her adopted black brother. On a parallel track to Rosa, Zwelinzima has had to free himself from the long shadow of white paternalism, symbolized by the mock-respectful name given to him in childhood—Baasie, "little boss." In his irate, sardonic attack on white meddling in the liberation struggle, Zwelinzima reintroduces into the novel a notion of freedom as entangled in obligation. Resenting the manner in which his dead father has vanished from public memory while Lionel Burger is lionized, Zwelinzima declares: "Whatever you whites touch, it's a take-over. . . . Even when we get free they'll want us to remember to thank Lionel Burger" (p. 321). It is after her hostile exchange with Zwelinzima that Rosa decides to return to South Africa and pursue a vision of freedom that entails commitment. The novel's closing conception of freedom is of a bond between an individual and an unavoidable course of action—a form of deeply felt necessity, the opposite of whimsy. As such, the novel reaffirms, by analogy, Gordimer's own formulation of the writer's freedom, which I alluded to at the outset of this essay. For Gordimer, as for Rosa, the challenge is to tack a course between unthinking, stifling orthodoxy and the false freedom of atomistic autonomy.

The analogy between the predicaments of Gordimer and her protagonist can be pressed further by returning to that visceral scene in which Zwelinzima confronts Rosa:

Everyone in the world must be told what a great hero he [Burger] was and how much he suffered for the blacks. Everyone must cry over him and show his life on television and write in the papers. Listen, there are dozens of our fathers sick and dying like dogs, kicked out of the locations when they can't work any more. Getting old and dying in prison. Killed in prison. It's nothing. I know plenty blacks like Burger. It's nothing, it's us, we must be used to it, it's not going to show on English television.—
—He would have been the first to say—what you're saying. He didn't think there was anything special about a white being a political prisoner.—

(p. 320)

Although Rosa defends her father and proceeds to find her niche of relevance, Zwelinzima's accusation remains so powerful that it can be read as anticipating the very terms of *Burger's Daughter*'s rejection. Faced with the charge of white irrelevance, a less audacious writer than Gordimer might have slumped into silence; instead, she staged, out of a preemptive rather than a defensive impulse, precisely the kind of reception that her novel could anticipate from black consciousness quarters.

Burger's Daughter exposed, with unprecedented clarity, the crucible of pressures from which Gordimer's writing has emerged. If, in the Zwelinzima scene, the novel confronts the possibility of its own dismissal, the book's last words prophesy a very different kind of rejection. A French friend is reading a letter from the now jailed Rosa:

There was a reference to a watermark of light that came into the cell at sundown every evening, reflected from some west-facing surface outside; something Lionel Burger once mentioned. But the line had been deleted by the prison censor. Madame Bagnelli was never able to make it out.

(p. 361)

Three weeks after publication, crates bearing copies of *Burger's Daughter* to South Africa were embargoed and the novel was banned. Some months later, the Publications Control Board lifted the banning order, but only after a huge international furor. Earlier novels by Gordimer had suffered similarly: *A World of Strangers*, which the authorities deemed to "undermine the traditional race policy of the Republic," was unobtainable in South Africa for twelve years, *The Late Bourgeois World* for ten. But no previous action by the South African censors had set off anything like the outcry provoked by their treatment of *Burger's Daughter*.

One fascinating spin-off of the affair was Gordimer's *What Happened to Burger's Daughter: or How South African Censorship Works* (1980). It is mandatory reading for anyone who would understand the strained conditions under which literature has been produced in South Africa, at least between 1963 and 1980. Gordimer's documentation of the case summons an array of contradictory opinions. One committee member advised that "banning this novel will make it sought out surreptitiously in this country. Censorship can be counterproductive, making this novel a threat when it might, in fact, not be a threat." Another, who urged the banning, found the novel biased but brilliantly researched—"a fact which makes its one-sidedness even more dangerous." An influential judge railed: "Don't buy it—it is not worth buying. Very badly written. . . . This is also why we eventually passed it. We knew our people wouldn't read it anyway. You know us *boere* find it a bit irritating when someone practices politics so badly."

For a more precise sense of what Gordimer was up against one can turn to her earlier essay, "Censored, Banned, Gagged," which cites the notorious Publications and Entertainments Act of 1963:

A publication is deemed "undesirable" if it, or any part of it, is

indecent or obscene or is offensive or harmful to public morals; is blasphemous or offensive to the religious convictions or feelings of any section of the inhabitants of the Republic; brings any section of the inhabitants into ridicule or contempt; is harmful to the relations between any sections of the inhabitants; is prejudicial to the safety of the State, the general welfare, or the peace and good order.

The definition of what may be considered indecent, obscene, offensive, or harmful to public morals includes the portrayal of

murder, suicide, death, horror, cruelty, fighting, brawling, ill-treatment, lawlessness, gangsterism, robbery, crime, the technique of crimes and criminals, tippling, drunkenness, trafficking in or addiction to drugs, smuggling, sexual intercourse, prostitution, promiscuity, white-slaving, licentiousness, lust, passionate love scenes, sexual assault, rape, sodomy, masochism, sadism, sexual bestiality, abortion, change of sex, night life, physical poses, nudity, scant or inadequate dress, divorce, marital infidelity, adultery, illegitimacy, human or social deviation or degeneracy, or any other similar or related phenomenon.

(*The Essential Gesture*, p. 61)

The detection of any of the above provided sufficient grounds for a work to be quashed.

Gordimer has gathered renown not only from her fiction but from her standing as one of the century's most resolute adversaries of censorship. She has penned dozens of essays and delivered scores of addresses on the issue as it affects South African authors and writers worldwide. With typically broad vision she used the attention that the banning of *Burger's Daughter* provoked to campaign for the creative liberty of those South African writers, predominantly black, who do not share her international visibility. Her stand finds its most outstanding articulation in the 1980 essay, "Censors and Unconfessed History," republished in *The Essential Gesture*.

THE LATER WORK

COMPARED to the iron-fisted repression and almost unchallenged state dominance of the 1960's, the 1970's proved to be a decade of resurgent resistance in South Africa. Black South Africans drew heart from the mid-decade fall of Portuguese colonialism in neighboring Mozambique and Angola while the black consciousness movement, trade unions, and student organizations spearheaded repeated challenges to apartheid rule. As a consequence of the momentous 1976 uprising, South Africans had become, by the end of the decade, obsessed with imminent time. Black South Africans, gauging history to be on their side, sensed (in Aime Cesaire's phrase) "the rendezvous of victory." Many white South Africans also conceded, for the first time, the probable collapse of white rule and began to hear the death knell of what they fondly called "the South African way of life."

One has only to scan the literature, black and white alike, to gauge how the nation's writers sought to command the future through metaphors of dawn, birth, revolutionary redemption, apocalypse, and historical closure. *The Late Bourgeois World,* an early instance of this tendency, was succeeded by Alex La Guma's *In the Fog of the Season's End,* Coetzee's *Dusklands* and *Waiting for the Barbarians,* Pieter-Dirk Uys's *Paradise is Closing Down,* Karel Schoeman's *Promised Land,* Mongane Wally Serote's *To Every Birth Its Blood,* and Gordimer's own "Some Monday for Sure." *July's People* (1981) falls squarely within this tendency. Like many of the above works, Gordimer's novel gives body to a postapartheid future that seemed at the time inexorable yet vague, imminent yet slow in coming forth. Nothing conveys this historical mood more precisely than the epigraph to *July's People,* drawn from Antonio Gramsci's *Prison Notebooks:* "The old is dying and the new cannot be born; in this interregnum there arises a great diversity of morbid symptoms."

As Stephen Clingman has recognized, *July's People* is less preoccupied with detailed envisaging of what is to come than with "seeing the present through the eyes of the future" (p. 202). In other words, the novel enacts the desire to escape the unendurable, sickly suspense of the present by consigning it to the detritus of the historical past. Gordimer stages this desire by chronicling the twinned fates of two families, one white, one black, in the wake of a guerrilla takeover of Johannesburg. Neither party is overtly political but the novel discloses the extent to which, at the deepest level, their relationship has been contoured by economic forces. The man whom Bam and Maureen Smales know only as July has been their faithful manservant for many years. Under the migrant labor system, he divides his life between the townships and a remote Bantustan where his family resides, but which he manages to visit only once every two years. July belongs to an older generation, remote from the spirit of youthful insurrection that swept the nation in the seventies, and still defers to authority, whether that of his white employers or his rural chief. July is not an intimation of the future; he is stationed very much in the interregnum.

Bam and Maureen belong to that class of suburban professionals who dislike apartheid but steer clear of politics. They believe in civilized reform, see themselves as enlightened, and join contact groups to meet blacks; Bam, an architect,

presents conference papers with titles like "Needs and Means in African Rural Architecture." Yet they do not know July's name (Mwawate), are ignorant of his family and of the conditions of his split life, and lack even rudimentary familiarity with his language. The relationship is founded on a species of self-deluding liberalism that generates opacity.

When Johannesburg erupts into violence, Bam and Maureen, their children, and July bundle into the family's light truck and make the three-day journey to the Bantustan where they take shelter in July's hut. That voyage is the first of the novel's series of elaborate reversals: it becomes a retributive reenactment of forced removal, the government policy that drives all unwanted blacks—"superflous appendages" in official parlance—into Bantustan dumping grounds. And so the Smaleses are initiated into black experience by being deprived of their freedom of movement. Hemmed in, uncertain when or if the waiting will end, they receive a mandatory education in the sensation of statelessness. Through such layered reversals, Gordimer stages an inquiry into the psychology and economics of dependency, one that probes the Janus-faced character of power in master-servant relations and is inevitably shadowed by Hegel. July has been reliant on the Smaleses not just for his job but, more important, for keeping his "pass" in order. But in the Bantustan, his paternalistic employers are transformed into his wards. July assumes quiet control over the simple insignia of power, notably the car keys. But it is left to Daniel, July's son and the implicit agent of the future, to abscond with the "master's" gun on his way to join the guerrillas.

Over the course of the novel, the Bantustan emerges as the underbelly of suburbia. Previously, Bam and Maureen had enjoyed excursions into the wilderness; now their relationship to it becomes profoundly untouristic. The middle class category of leisure dissolves and scenery turns to unsubmissive bush as they are schooled in the rough arts of necessity. Likewise, they learn the contingency of desire on the privacy of the master bedroom. Yet Gordimer is emphatic that the white man and woman experience what Maureen calls the "explosion of roles" (p. 117) differently. In the past, Bam's control of technology and his role as provider braced his social authority; robbed of these, he suffers complete mortification. Maureen, on the other hand, turns increasingly to July for her needs and discovers, in the process, that their former "working relationship" was a charade incapable of leaving even a residue of rapport.

The revealed sterility of the Smaleses' lives recalls Mehring's condition in *The Conservationist.* Symptomatically, both novels are left open-ended, with Mehring vulnerable to the approach of a man of uncertain purpose, while Maureen Smales abandons her family and rushes headlong toward an unmarked helicopter containing "saviours or murderers" (p. 158). Maureen's fate, however, seems the less foreclosed of the two: although nakedly unprepared for a postapartheid future, her flight may turn out to be suicidal or liberatory.

These, Gordimer's two most rural novels, also share limitations. In each, rather than inhabiting the same plane as white characters, black figures are invested with symbolic portent. Somewhat like the Africans in *Heart of Darkness,* if less absolutely, July exists primarily as a foil for an inquiry into the character of white civilization once the fabric of civic life has been rent. In the final instance, *July's People* seems an intelligent experiment, yet somewhat inert, and the tension between Maureen and July never rises to the compelling level that animates, for instance, the showdown between Ross and Zwelinzima.

The eighties saw Gordimer commit herself to writing past the uncertainties of the contemporary deadlock. As in *July's People,* this impulse also informs stories like "A Soldier's Embrace" and "At the Rendezvous of Victory," both set in the aftermath of a popular guerrilla triumph, and the closing pages of *A Sport of Nature* (1987), which usher in the postapartheid era. Much of this work, however, seems bloodless. Moreover, even though no fiction of Gordimer's is without strong writing, when advancing the future her prose often becomes symptomatically labored, as in this passage from *July's People:*

It began prosaically weirdly. The strikes of 1960 had dragged on, one inspired or brought about by solidarity with another until the walkout and the shut-down were lived with as contiguous and continuous phenomena rather than industrial chaos. While the government continued to compose concessions to the black trade unions exquisitely worded to conceal exactly concomitant restrictions, the black workers concerned went hungry, angry, and workless. . . .

(pp. 6–7)

A Sport of Nature, too, moves into the future, if only in the final chapter. However, the entire novel can be read as an attempt to reconceive South Africa and the nuclear family. Its historical sweep, international setting, and return to themes of political and familial reconstruction mark the novel as a sequel to *Burger's Daughter.* The book's epigraph, taken from the Oxford English Dictionary, defines a sport of nature as "a plant, animal, etc., which exhibits abnormal variation or a departure from the parent stock or type . . . a spontaneous mutation; a new variety produced in this way." Hillela, the novel's strong-minded, adventurous heroine, incarnates this concept. From childhood on, she refines her gift for errant brilliance, taking shape as a healthy deviant from the norms of a society perverted by racial bigotry and from the norms of that other aberration, the nuclear family.

The progeny of her mother's adultery, Hillela is sent down from Rhodesia for consorting with a "coloured" youth; she then departs her adopted home in Johannesburg after being caught in a sexual liaison with her cousin, Sasha. Hillela's flouting of conventions culminates in her marriage to an ANC guerrilla. After his assassination, she travels the world as a political refugee and a single mother carrying an interracial child—the icon of a postapartheid South Africa. She subsequently marries an exiled African leader who regains his seat of power, establishes a successful state, and rises to the head of the Organization of African Unity. In the final scene, the now illustrious couple return to Cape Town for the installation of South Africa's first black-led government.

Gordimer once remarked that "whites of former South Africa will have to redefine themselves in a new collective life within new structures" (*Essential Gesture,* p. 264). If "former South Africa" conveys the author's impatience to get beyond the dragging interregnum, Hillela is the fictional embodiment of that sentiment. The ultimate iconoclast and breacher of taboos, Hillela's greatest delight is in not having reproduced herself—as a South African and as a woman. She emerges as a politically engaged pied piper, a fairy-tale activist leading the way to unimagined freedoms.

Sasha's reflection on the utopian impulse perhaps comes closest to capturing the convictions that motivate the novel:

Utopia is unattainable; without aiming for it—taking a chance!—you can never hope even to fall far short of it. . . . Without utopia—the idea of utopia—there's a failure of the imagination—and that's a failure to know how to go on living. It will take another kind of being to stay on, here. A new white person. Not us. The chance is a wild chance—like falling in love.

(p. 187)

A Sport of Nature reveals Gordimer's romance with the idea of such a being, but unfortunately, a rift develops between conception and execution. After the strongly imagined first hundred pages, the prose becomes diffuse and rarefied. The political panoramas are too general, while Hillela, for all her sensuality, remains only partially realized. An instinctively phantasmagoric writer might have pulled this project off, but Gordimer's talent is grounded in the intimate observations of realistic prose and can seem cumbersome in flight. Nor are matters helped by her choice of a distant, disengaged perspective replete with remarks such as, "When she who people say was once Hillela thinks of that time—and no-one who knew her then knows whether she ever does—that is all she retains of it" (p. 17). Unlike Rosa, Hillela is never known from the inside and is too slightly conceived to support this burden of vagueness. Moreover, while Gordimer's choice of an erratic, inconsistent perspective dramatizes the immense labor of founding a new kind of individual, that same perspective revives and exacerbates her old difficulties with narrative cohesion, resulting in writing that, for all its bursts of brilliance, is ultimately scattered.

After the disappointment of *A Sport of Nature,* Gordimer reaffirmed her formidable talent with *My Son's Story,* her most impassioned novel yet and her most compelling since *Burger's Daughter.* The book's brilliance stems largely from Gordimer's recognition of deceit as *the* subject for someone as fascinated by stirrings in the loin as she is by the stirrings of history. Sexual deceits are clandestine, they flee the light, head underground. In South Africa, they share this condition with outlawed political activity which finds people tunneling out double lives, mixing the exhileration of illicit solidarity with the relentless dread of exposure. On the fulcrum of the lie—which may tilt lives toward selfish narcissism or selfless idealism—Gordimer balances her profound inquiry into the character of sexual, emotional, and political commitments; what it means, in short, to be counted on.

In the resistance movement, the protagonist, Sonny, counts. A mixed race (so-called "coloured") schoolteacher, he at first hovers on the political fringe, drawing his principal pleasures from Gramsci, Shakespeare, and Kafka, from the passion of his teaching, and from family life. But after losing his job for heading a student march and getting detained for two years, he throws himself zealously into the mass movement for democracy, where he gathers renown as a rousing orator and a savvy underground strategist.

Sonny adjusts himself to a permanent double life stretched between his family, who are indifferent to politics, and the cause of liberation. An upright man, Sonny nonetheless lives a devious life, for under the surveillance of a police state, an unbending commitment to honesty would be reckless, even, dare one say, unprincipled. Thus Sonny shows loyalty to his comrades by safeguarding their confidences, and loyalty to his family by withholding information that would endanger them under torture or arrest.

And then, in those vast fields of protective silence, sexual deceit begins to mushroom. The habitual, unexplained absences continue as before, but get devoted as often to clandestine love-making as to clandestine politics. That split, however, misleads: Sonny increasingly treats his liaisons with Hannah, a white activist who campaigns for detainees' rights, as a natural extension of his life of risk. Hannah is everything his demure, homebody wife is not: now finally "the cause was the lover, the lover the cause" (223). Gordimer displays impeccable instincts for the aphrodisiac aura that clings to political courage.

Sonny and Hannah pursue razor-edge lives that require them to cheat constantly on the state. From there it is but a simple step to becoming bonded through the confidential thrill of more selfish deceits:

They were so successful that now and then somebody would introduce them: I don't think you've met . . . this is . . .

Sonny and Hannah: presented each to the other, as strangers, by a third person.

(p. 70)

And so a talent for privacy gives way to the first unnecessary lie, then to dishonesty as ever-present substance abuse.

Yet in truth this intimate duo comes closer to a ménage à trois: Big Brother is always party to their liaisons. As a "known" subversive, Sonny will be watched by the wide, sleepless eye of the state until either he or apartheid is entombed. A further decisive observer scans Sonny's infidelities: Will, his fifteen-year-old son who, skipping school, stumbles on his father's deceit in a cinema foyer. The truant son faces the truant father and his blond lover who from then on becomes a ghostly, unnamed presence at the center of their family life.

When Gordimer adopts a wholly external perspective—as in *July's People* and *A Sport of Nature*—that distance lapses all too often into detached indifference. Wisely, in *My Son's Story* she revives the tactic that proved so persuasive in *Burger's Daughter,* switching between an outside view of an esteemed revolutionary and the inner swirlings of his angry, skeptical adolescent offspring. Will, wrenched out of innocence, struggles to cope with his unsolicited complicity in the deception of his mother. To add to the trauma, he intuits the affair as his father's last-ditch effort to assert his superior virility: "He's not moving aside, off women's bodies, for me" (94). What could be more Oedipal than an aging father, who clings to the name Sonny, staging his infidelities before a son named Will?

Gordimer's novel is soaked in the political tensions of the day. Police firing on mourners grouped around a grave; machinations within the union; guileful communications between prisoners and the world outside; brittle, old-school socialists who refuse, even in the wake of changes in Eastern Europe, to update their forms of radicalism. A lesser writer might have contented herself with these broad public themes around brutality and resistance, but Gordimer insists on giving equal attention to the segregations, surveillance, faction fighting, buried malice, courage, opportunism, and diplomatic lies which mark that other, oh-so-civil war waged between the walls of home.

A decade back in Gordimer's fiction, Burger's daughter revolted against her family's assumption that she too would be nothing more than politically correct. She invoked her father's enemies to aid her flight into exile. Will's adolescent uprising finds an even more violent expression. In defiance, his parents had bought a house in a conservative, working class Afrikaans suburb; they were the only "coloureds" on the block. One night, during their absence at a political gathering, neo-Nazis scorch the family home. Will, looking on at the charred relics of the site of his humiliation, his father's infidelities, his sister's attempted suicide, persistent police irruptions, and the arrest of both parents, exhorts the flames to complete the purgation: Let it burn.

Gordimer has portrayed herself as an androgynous writer and often chooses male perspectives in order to fathom women as men view them. This tactic comes off brilliantly in *My Son's Story:* by entrusting her narrative to Sonny and Will, she is able to stage the full force with which, in "seeing" Aila, they render her invisible:

[People] mistook her gentleness for disdain; perhaps he mistook it, too, in another way, taking the gentleness for what it appeared to be instead of the strength of will it softly gloved.

(p. 7)

In running between women, Sonny loses his instincts for Aila's ways, and errs in treating her as known. Will, but not his father, intuits that Aila has long possessed a silent knowledge of her husband's betrayals. Under cover of silence and neglect, she can plot another life. So when Sonny awakens to her knowledge, the time for confessions and scenes has passed, for she has moved far, far off, beyond retrieval. Her behavior disarms him utterly:

Sonny forgave himself; but this was futile. Aila had never reproached him, so there was nothing for her to forgive. . . . Even the harm he had done her was no claim on her; he saw that.

(p. 258)

In a quite unpredictable turnaround, Aila proceeds to surpass Sonny not just in familial respect but also in political prestige.

Remarkably, Gordimer manages this elaborate inversion without belittling Sonny's political integrity or caricaturing Hannah. The novel never underestimates that unspeakable pain which strikes when fiery desire for one person and the rich trust of another confront each other as totally incompatible states of grace. Gordimer writes as if she knows, and sympathizes with both.

With *My Son's Story* Gordimer has found—as she did in *Burger's Daughter*—a plot and a prose equal to the weight of her ideas. Importantly, her success coincides with her abandonment of futuristic writing; the world to come jars with her earthy, nineteenth-century realist sensibility. She is also wise to return to the urban roots of her experience—rural Africans will never appear as more than symbolic figments in her writing, whereas she has befriended and socialized with mixed race, middle-class intellectuals like Sonny for thirty or forty years.

Among the many surprises sprung by this book, nothing surpasses Gordimer's outrageous choice of perspective. Surely no precedent exists for a passionately feminist novel, composed by a white woman, in which the leading character is a black man and the most intimate voice that of his teenaged son. And this, moreover, from a writer inhabiting the world's most segregated society. But, from childhood onward, Gordimer has been possessed by a transgressive spirit. Read from one angle, *My Son's Story* illicitly appropriates so-called "coloured" experience; from another, it expresses a utopian defiance, Gordimer's determination to exceed the bounds of her partition-ridden society, charting lives that are meant to be barred from her experiential and imaginative maps. Does this novel, then, document her racial arrogance or her refusal to perpetuate an apartheid of the mind?

In 1956 Gordimer published a story entitled "Which New Era Would Be?" A brash young Jennifer flounces into the ghetto from the suburbs, brimming with concern for the plight of the oppressed. When she has breezed back out again, Jake Alexander, a burly "coloured," muses scathingly:

These women felt as you did. They were sure of it. . . . There was no escaping their understanding. They even insisted on feeling the resentment you must feel at their identifying themselves with your feelings.

(*Selected Stories,* p. 83)

Thirty-four years later, a version of that outrage recurs when Will first sights Hannah Plowman and dismisses her as "a blonde women with the naked face and apologetic, presumptuous familiarity, in her smile, of people who come to help" (p. 14). "Presumptuous familiarity": in a phrase, Will, no less than Jake, hurls an accusation at his author. In *Burger's Daughter,* in her finest stories, and most recently, in *My Son's Story,* Gordimer quite consciously gives her skeptics just enough rope to hang her on. Some might read that as a sign of her honesty. After a novel that inquires so mercilessly into the subtle maneuverings between probity and deceit, one would prefer to call it something else, something more extraordinary—a mark of her irrepressible daring.

CONCLUSION

As *A Sport of Nature* testifies, Gordimer has come, over time, increasingly to situate herself as an African writer. If her great fictional preoccupations are the human consequences of apartheid and the possibility of their transcendence, she has nevertheless honed a complementary talent for evoking her physical environs. Her political concerns would remain abstract were they not embedded in minutely observed African landscapes: "Pelicans on the water turn the lake into a child's bathtub filled with plastic toys. The flamingoes will not stir until late afternoon, when the colour under their wings as they rise seems to leak into the water like blood from a cut finger" ("Pula," in *Essential Gesture,* p. 207). So, too, with this impression of the ostentatious night scream of the tree hyrax: "Among the barks, grunts and cries there was one Greek and immortal in its desperate passion, gathering up echoes from all the private wailing walls of the human soul" ("The Congo River," in *Essential Gesture,* p. 168).

Yet, to Gordimer, such evocations of nature must seem comparatively painless alongside the dilemmas that wrack all South African authors who seek to imagine their fractured nation whole. She is only one of a succession of writers, black and white, to reflect on this torment when she observes: "In a society as deeply and calculatedly compartmentalised as South Africa . . . the writer's potential has unscalable limitations" ("The Novel and the Nation," p. 52). The outstanding integrity of her work derives in no small part from her commitment to respect and flex those limits simultaneously, acknowledging bounds to her authority while refusing to view them as an excuse for imaginative timidity.

Although the men she knows as "the mad scientists" of apartheid have entertained dreams of absolute separation, Gordimer has always managed to get beyond merely reactive, Manichean writing that would remain an inverted symptom of apartheid. Her fiction is not peopled with murderous whites or saccharine blacks; she prefers to station herself in the troubled zone of attempted reconciliation, where she scours pretensions for signs of resilient hope. Scanning four decades of work, one is struck by how often Gordimer's most distinguished writing occurs at those awkward junctures where black and white strive, in a manner half-genuine, half-skeptical, to confirm contact. Her insights can be ruthless. One recalls, for instance, Steven Sithole's remark in *A World of Strangers,* that a jazz-opera, imagined collaboratively by a Sophiatown musician and a suburban counterpart, is "more of a white man's idea of what a black man would write, and a black man's idea of what a white man would expect him to write, than the fusion of a black man's and a white man's world of imagination" (p. 201). Likewise, in this scenario from *Burger's Daughter,* Rosa pinpoints the cross-purposes of black and white women staging a tea-group for the furtherance of mutual understanding:

I skirted Flora's assembly and sat down at the back. . . . Everyone—I began to see them properly—bunched together in the middle and back seats, the black women out of old habit of finding themselves allotted secondary status and the white ones out of anxiety not to assume first place. . . . Dressed in their best, one after another, black women in wigs and two-piece dresses pleaded, were complaining, opportuning for the creches, orphans, blind, crippled or aged of their "place." They asked for "old" cots, "old" school primers, "old" toys and furniture, "old" braille typewriters, "old" building material. They had come through the front door but the logic was still of the back door. They didn't believe they'd get anything but what was cast-off; they didn't, any of them, believe there was anything else to be had from white women, it was all they were good for.

(pp. 202–203)

Without the alchemy of hope, such knowing exposés, however brilliant, could easily calcify into cynicism. But Gordimer is not content to rest in the knowledge that she opposes apartheid, for, as she puts it, that would be to "remain negatively within the white order" (*Essential Gesture,* p. 278). She has advanced well beyond routine negativity: unlike much white South African writing from Alan Paton to Christopher Hope, her prose does not clank with the self-imposed manacles of racial guilt, an aesthetically repetitive and politically obstructive emotion.

In 1991, Gordimer became the first South African and the first woman in twenty-five years to receive the Nobel Prize for literature. The timing could not have been more apt: she is the only South African writer publishing regularly whose literary career spans the entire history of official apartheid. Her first book, *Face to Face*, appeared in 1949, just months after the National Party seized power, and by the time she received the Nobel tribute, apartheid was spinning to its demise.

While writers commonly grow less rebellious with age and fame, Gordimer has kept her faculty of revolt very much alive. Over four violent, tumultuous decades, she has emerged as the poet laureate of apartheid's morbid symptoms. She has emerged, too, as a great rarity, a contemporary writer whose vision is informed by a restless idealism. Whether lacerating white presumptions or reaching after alternatives to South Africa's blighted present, Gordimer's writing expresses her determination not just to document her society, but to hasten its transformation.

SELECTED BIBLIOGRAPHY

I. BIBLIOGRAPHIES. R. Green, "Nadine Gordimer: A Bibliography of Works and Criticism," in *Bulletin of Bibliography,* 42 (March 1985); S. Clingman, *The Novels of Nadine Gordimer: History from the Inside* (London, 1986).

II. SEPARATE WORKS. *Face to Face: Short Stories* (Johannesburg, 1949).

The Soft Voice of the Serpent and Other Stories (New York, 1952; London, 1953); *The Lying Days* (London and New York, 1953), novel; *Six Feet of the Country* (London and New York, 1956), short stories; *A World of Strangers* (London and New York, 1958), novel.

Friday's Footprint and Other Stories (London and New York, 1960), short stories; *Occasion for Loving* (London and New York, 1963), novel; *Not for Publication and Other Stories* (London and New York 1965); *The Late Bourgeois World* (London and New York, 1966), novel.

A Guest of Honour (London and New York, 1970), novel; *Livingstone's Companions* (London and New York, 1971), short stories; *On the Mines* (Cape Town, 1973), with photographs by D. Goldblatt and C. Struik; *The Black Interpreters: Notes on African Writing* (Johannesburg, 1973), literary criticism; *The Conservationist* (London, 1974; New York, 1975), novel; *Selected Stories* (London, 1975; New York, 1976); *Some Monday for Sure* (London, 1976), short stories; *Burger's Daughter* (London, 1979; New York, 1980), novel.

A Soldier's Embrace (London and New York, 1980), short stories; *Town and Country Lovers* (Los Angeles, 1980), short stories; *What Happened to Burger's Daughter: or, How South African Censorship Works* (Johannesburg, 1980), an essay on censorship; *July's People* (London and New York, 1981), novel; *Something Out There* (London and New York, 1984), short stories; *Lifetimes Under Apartheid* (London and New York, 1986), with photographs by D. Goldblatt; *A Sport of Nature* (London and New York, 1987), novel; *The Essential Gesture: Writing, Politics and Places* (London and New York, 1988), literary and political essays and travel writing; *My Son's Story* (London and New York, 1990), novel.

III. SELECTED ARTICLES AND REVIEWS. (*Note:* Items marked with an asterisk have been collected in *The Essential Gesture.*) "Writing Belongs to Us All," in *The Forum* (September 1954); *"Where Do Whites Fit In," in *Twentieth Century* (April 1959); *"Chief Luthuli," in *Atlantic Monthly* (April 1959). *"The Congo River," in *Holiday* (May 1961); *"A Bolter and the Invincible Summer," in *London Magazine* (May 1963); *"Great Problems in the Street," in *I Will Still Be Moved,* edited by M. Friedman (London, 1963); *"Censored, Banned, Gagged," in *Encounter* (June 1963); "A Writer in South Africa," in *London Magazine* (May 1965); *"Why Did Bram Fischer Choose Jail?" in *New York Times Magazine* (14 August 1966); *"One Man Living Through It," in *The Classic,* 2, no. 1 (1966); "How Not To Know the African," in *Contrast* (March 1967).

*"Merci Dieu, It Changes," published as "The Life of Accra, the Flowers of Abidjan: A West African Diary," in *Atlantic* (November 1971); *"Pula!" in *London Magazine* (February/March 1973); *"Speak Out: The Necessity for Protest," (Durban, 1971); *"A Writer's Freedom," in *New Classic,* no. 2 (1975); "Catalogue of the Ridiculous," in *The London Times* (2 July 1975); *"Letter from Johannesburg, 1976," published as "Letter from South Africa" in *New York Review of Books* (9 December 1976); "What Being a South African Means to Me," in *South African Outlook,* 107 (June 1977); "From Apartheid to Afrocentrism," in *South African Outlook* (December 1977); *"A Vision of Two Blood-Red Suns," published as "Transkei: A Vision of Two Blood-Red Suns," in *Geo* (April 1978); "A Brilliant Bigot," in *Times Literary Supplement* (15 September 1978); "No Place Like Home," in *Geo* (August 1979).

*"Censors and Unconfessed History," published as "New Forms of Strategy–No Change of Heart," in *Critical Arts* (June 1980); "The Prison-house of Colonialism," in *Times Literary Supplement* (15 August 1980); *"The Unkillable Word," published as "Censorship and the Word,"

in *The Bloody Horse* (September-October 1980); *"Relevance and Commitment," published as "Apprentice of Freedom," in *New Society* (December 1981); *"Madagascar"; *"Living in the Interregnum," in *New York Review of Books* (20 January 1983); *"The Essential Gesture," in *The Tanner Lectures on Human Values,* S. M. McMurrin, ed. (Salt Lake City, 1985); "Letter from Johannesburg," in *New York Times Magazine* (8 September 1985).

IV. INTERVIEWS. B. Bachs, Interview with Nadine Gordimer, in *The Road from Sharpeville* (London, 1961); C. Stott, "I Must Stay and Fight," in *Star* (Johannesburg; 13 June 1969); S. Gray and P. du Plessis, "Nadine Gordimer Interviewed," in *New Nation* (September 1972); "A Writer Is Always Writing the Same Story," in *Rand Daily Mail* (Johannesburg; 27 July 1972); M. Ratcliffe, "A South African Radical Exulting in Life's Chaotic Variety," in *The Times* (29 November 1974); C. Dalglish, "The Writers Who Are Hardest Hit," in *Rand Daily Mail* (Johannesburg; 3 May 1978); N. W. Ellis, "In Black and White," in *Harpers and Queen* (November 1978); D. Loercher, "South African Political Novelist Nadine Gordimer: 'I Know I Have Not Been Brave Enough,'" in *Christian Science Monitor* (21 January 1980); P. Schwartz, "Gordimer Still Clings to a Sense of Wonder," in *Rand Daily Mail* (Johannesburg; 24 July 1981); P. Schwartz, "Interview—Nadine Gordimer," in *New South African Writing* (24 July 1981); J. Jurwitt, "The Art of Fiction LXXVII," in *Paris Review,* no. 88 (Summer 1983); R. Boyers, C. Blaise, T. Diggory, and J. Elgrably, "A Conversation with Nadine Gordimer," in *Salmagundi* (Winter 1984).

V. CRITICAL STUDIES. L. Abrahams, "Nadine Gordimer: The Transparent Ego," in *English Studies in Africa* (September 1960).

C. Hope, "Out of the Picture: The Novels of Nadine Gordimer," in *London Magazine,* 15, no. 1 (1975); K. Ogungbesan, "Nadine Gordimer's *The Late Bourgeois World:* Love in Prison," in *Ariel,* 9, no. 1 (1978); K. Parker, *The South African Novel in English* (London, 1978); M. Wade, *Nadine Gordimer* (London, 1978); R. Green, "Nadine Gordimer's *A World of Strangers:* Strains in South African Liberalism," in *English Studies in Africa* (March 1979); K. Ogungbesan, "Nadine Gordimer's *A Guest of Honour:* Politics, Fiction, and the Liberal Expatriate," in *Southern Review* (Adelaide, Australia), 12 (1979).

I. Wettenhall, "Liberalism and Radicalism in South Africa Since 1948: Nadine Gordimer's Fiction," in *New Literature Review,* 8 (1980); M. Heinemann, *'Burger's Daughter:* The Synthesis of Revelation," in *The Uses of Fiction,* edited by O. Jefferson and C. Martin (London, 1982); R. Holland, "The Critical Writing of Nadine Gordimer," in *Communiqué,* 7, no. 2 (1982); P. Rich, "Tradition and Revolt in South African Fiction: The Novels of André Brink, Nadine Gordimer and J. M. Coetzee," in *Journal of Southern African Studies,* 9, vol. 1 (1982); D. Driver, "Nadine Gordimer: The Politicisation of Women," in *English in*

Africa (October 1983); C. Heywood, *Nadine Gordimer* (Windsor, Berks., England, 1983); A. JanMohamed, *Manichean Aesthetics. The Politics of Literature in Colonial Africa* (Amherst, Mass., 1983); N. Bailey, "Living Without the Future: Nadine Gordimer's *July's People,"* in *World Literature Written in English* (Autumn 1984); R. Boyers, ed., "Nadine Gordimer: Politics and the Order of Art," in *Salmagundi* (Winter 1984); L. White and T. Couzens, eds., *Literature and Society in South Africa* (London, 1984); J. Cooke, *The Novels of Nadine Gordimer: Private Lives/Public Landscapes* (Baton Rouge and London, 1985); B. Greenstein, "Miranda's Story: Nadine Gordimer and the Literature of Empire," in *Novel* (Spring 1985); M. Trump, "The Short Fiction of Nadine Gordimer," in *Research in African Literatures* (Fall 1986); J. Newman, *Nadine Gordimer* (London and New York, 1988).

HENRY GREEN
(1905–1973)

Barbara Brothers

In 1950, at the height of his literary career, Henry Green traveled to the United States to publicize the Viking edition of his book *Loving*. But he did not register at the hotel as either Henry Green (his nom de plume) or Henry Vincent Yorke (his true name). H. V. Yonge was the name he created for this occasion. He remarked to Harvey Breit, who came to interview him, that Henry Green was not the name he signed to pay his bills. Nor did he think it suitable to register as Yorke, since he was not in New York in the role of managing director of H. Pontifex & Sons, the family firm, which he had joined when he left Oxford in 1927 without taking a degree.

Green never used his pseudonym to hide his identity. He was evasive but not secretive about himself and the crafting of the novels he worked on each day during his lunch hour, the time his son Sebastian remembers his father reserved for writing. He published an essay titled "The English Novel of the Future" (1950), but in it he said less about how he and others *would* write than about what his practice had been. He discussed his writing with various interviewers and published several essays in *The Listener*, based on talks he had given for the BBC, about how to read his novels. Yet the comments he made illuminate only how and why he wrote as he did. In an interview with Harvey Breit reprinted in *The Writer Observed*, Green would explain the stories he told in his novels no further than to say they were about love and the "everyday mishaps of ordinary life" (p. 105). His description of his novels is accurate. The books are not about war, social justice, or private morality, subjects chosen by many of the politically conscious writers of the 1930's. Nor are they about art, the artist, or quests for self-knowledge, subjects frequently identified with modernist writers. Rather, they portray people in the situations Green

has called *Blindness, Living, Party Going, Caught, Loving, Back, Concluding, Nothing,* and *Doting*.

A comical playing with names, identities, and the ironies of situation and interpretation characterizes Green's presentation of himself. Indirection—he once said he approached life "crab-wise"—also typifies the manner in which Green narrates the stories in his nine novels and autobiography published between 1926 and 1952.

LIFE

Green decided that there was a need to take "stock," to record his life, before the war that was about to begin in 1939 made an end of it. *Pack My Bag: A Self Portrait* (1940), however, is a strange record, one without labels and with the pseudonymous name Green on the title page. As is true of the novels, the narrator has a story to tell but no moral nor conclusions to draw. It is a record of impressions rather than a connected narrative of names, dates, and places, or of spiritual and intellectual milestones. The facts the reader learns about Green's life are the year of his birth (1905), but not the month or the day (29 October); the name of his family home, Forthampton Court (the estate was on the Severn River near Tewkesbury Abbey in Gloucestershire), but not the name of the public school he attended (Eton); the name of the family gardener (Poole), but not the names of Green's parents or ancestors.

Green claims that he decided not to use names because, on the one hand, he did not want to offend anyone, and on the other, he felt the reader may be disturbed if his or her experience of a place was different from the writer's. However, rather than seriously attempting to provide anonymity to people or to scenes, Green refuses to name names, dates, and places in order to remind his readers how much personal baggage names carry, and therefore how limited they are in communicating what something has meant to one. Readers of Green do not have to be particularly artful or tenacious sleuths to unearth the name of his father, Vincent Yorke, or that of his mother, Maud Evelyn Wyndham (of the Petworth House Wyndhams); that of the woman who became his wife, Adelaide Mary Biddulph (married 27 July 1929); or that of the friend, Anthony Powell, with whom he roomed at Oxford. Green was friends with a number of well-known writers of his time: he served as best man for Evelyn Waugh at his second marriage and was written about by Eudora Welty, whom he met at one of the numerous gatherings of literary friends he frequented before and during the war. He liked to listen—and not just to those in the pub he frequented near his home—and he liked to talk. He was, according to his friends, an entertaining storyteller. He became a recluse only after retiring in 1959. He died in London on 15 December 1973.

Pack My Bag teases the reader in other ways. The organization is loosely chronological—boyhood, boarding school days, public school years, student days at Oxford, and, finally, employment in the foundry in Birmingham. But the narrative is episodic. One thing does not lead to another, either causally or sequentially. We are presented with a collection of souvenirs, but we are not told the relationships between the vignettes Green selects to represent his life. The memories he records seem, at times, to be merely pictures randomly drawn from a box of family snapshots: "There was the butler with his outfit of gold teeth and one black one whistling through his pantry window" (p. 10);[1] and there was "one of the maids, that poor thing whose breath smelled, come in one morning to tell us the *Titanic* had gone down, it may be that much later they had told me I should have remembered at the age I was then and that their saying this had suggested I did remember" (p.8).

Green's anecdotal, oblique presentation of character, event, and place re-creates his life in the manner of an Impressionist painter: The lines and colors of the objective world blur as they are re-

called by the idiosyncratic and erratic eye of memory. To reproduce the image as it is fixed in the imagination, Green takes liberties with normal syntactic expectations. He strings together clauses and phrases, compresses through elision, and juxtaposes without parallelism in order to trace the alogical movements of the mind. Thus he makes the butler's teeth the focus of the picture he provides. They, not the butler, appear to be whistling through the pantry window. In the passage about the maids, the bad breath of the one and the act of remembering assume more importance than the sinking of the *Titanic*.

Whether or not readers find Green's factual omissions and his syntactic jugglings a satisfactory style for an autobiography is another matter. That style, however, reveals more of Green than would any narration that carefully supplied the facts and dates of experience and treated life as if it were a journey with a beginning, middle, and end of which we could make verifiable sense. His narrative mannerisms call attention to just how individual perceptions are and how "retouched" and "over-painted," to use his words, are memories; but overpainting, in the senses of "painted over" and "too much paint," will tell us what little we can know of him, just as, if we were to tell our own stories, our changes and emphases would tell us what little others might learn of us, and what little we might learn of ourselves. All representations of reality are stylizations, thick with one's "spittle," as Green comments in his autobiography.

Green reveals who he is in re-creating the eccentricities of the particulars of his life—the maid's bad breath, a packet of Wrigley's gum, a blue Persian kitten, fishing in the Severn, or his mother saying "chairs boys." These are small things. They are what Green remembers. Green, like the philosopher F. H. Bradley, whose last words Green said provided him with his title, does not feel we can learn much more about ourselves.

Green's seeming reluctance to be photographed was a pose (the first two photographs of him in American magazines show him with his hand covering his face in *Time* [10 October 1949] and from the rear in *Vogue* [1 October 1949]). He granted interviews, looked straight at the camera, and heard well enough what suited his purposes. As with his camera shyness, his celebrated difficulty in hearing (he never wore a hearing aid, and at least

---

[1] All page references are from first American editions unless otherwise noted.

one person who talked to him six months before he died was unaware that he was slightly deaf) appears to have been an artful guise. At times, he used that guise to convey a sense of himself and of his amusement at the ways in which things are never quite what they seem to be. At other times, he used it to deflect intellectual conversation about life, which he claimed neither to enjoy nor to find meaningful.

Green, much like a dramatist, weaves stories by arranging scenes in which people talk or, particularly in his autobiography, remember. He does not present an exposition of his ideas about life in his autobiography and interviews; in his novels, no narrators comment upon the characters and their actions. What we know is limited to what we see and hear.

When Terry Southern queried Green on the possible connection between the "mysteries" of Green's person and those suffused throughout his works, Green replied, "What's that? I'm a trifle hard of hearing." Later, Green deliberately mistook Southern's description of his works as "subtle". "I don't follow. *Suttee,* as I understand it, is the suicide—now forbidden—of a Hindu wife on her husband's flaming bier. I don't want my wife to do that when my time comes" (p. 65). Green's artfully constructed dodge links "subtle," abstract and safe, with "suttee," concrete and threatening. The association reminds Green's interviewer and audience of the mishaps of life—the "menaces" that lurk behind seemingly innocent facades. At the same time, the incongruity of the association makes it humorous. Green will not explain himself. He is indirect, not obscure.

Readers of Green's fiction need to pay attention to how he presents what he presents. For Green, style is as important as subject: Only through the manner of expression can the feelings produced by what is perceived be depicted. The sensation of a thing, not its name, is its reality. The specificity of labeling and detail, the technique of realistic art, is wrong, in Green's view. It leads a reader or a viewer to forget that what is real is the sensation or feelings produced by activities, things, and others. Thus Green, unlike Ernest Hemingway or later so-called minimalist writers, does not eschew figurative language and poetic descriptive passages in setting a scene or depicting characters' responses to their surroundings or other characters.

EARLY NOVELS

IN *Blindness* (1926), the youthful would-be writer records in his diary: " 'If you take a photograph of a man digging, in my opinion he is sure to look as if he were not digging' (Van Gogh)" (p. 30).[2] The statement might well appear in *Pack My Bag,* though the novel was begun while Green was a student at Eton and published when he was twenty-one and at Oxford. What is interesting is not the parallel that can be drawn between Green's activities and friends at Eton and those recounted and revealed by John Haye in approximately the first thirty pages of the novel but, rather, the similarity between the consciousness of the autobiographer and that of the fictional hero Green creates for his *Kunstlerroman,* his novel about growing up to become a writer. Unlike James Joyce's *A Portrait of the Artist as a Young Man,* correspondences between the author's life and that of the novel's protagonist John can be found after the introductory section only in the setting, a country estate. *Blindness* is not a fictionalized autobiography, but we do learn much about Green as writer. More self-reflective than Green's other characters, John ponders what we can learn from stories that others tell, and he thinks about the meaning of images and symbols. The novel is a remarkable accomplishment, exploring, as the title suggests, the relationship between "I" and "eye."

Blindness relates the melodramatic story of a seventeen-year-old boy, John Haye, who is blinded when a window of the train on which he is returning home for vacation is shattered by a stone tossed at the passing train. Green saves the novel from the bathos inherent in youthful fears of tragic victimization by the self-mocking tone of John, who finds his life boring and sometimes forgets that anything has happened to him; by the matter-of-fact acceptance of his situation by those around him; and by the parodying of John's misfortune with that of his sweetheart, Joan, whose mother is dead and who lives in poverty with her father, a drunken ex-minister. Green labeled the three parts "Caterpillar," "Chrysalis," and "Butterfly," as if to underscore that this is a novel of development; but

[2]Page references for *Blindness* are from the British edition published by Hogarth in 1977. Page references from this British edition correspond with those of the first American edition.

the ambiguities of his story and of its ending make questionable in what ways, if any, John has come to a greater understanding of himself and the meaning of life.

One of the beauties of *Blindness* is the way in which Green captures certain characteristics of the young, such as the dreams of self-importance, the desire for love, and the fears that life may be over before one has had a chance to live. Those dreams are presented both seriously and comically. John creates for himself a pastoral love affair with Joan as his maiden; he renames her June for his day-dream. The idyll ends as they sit on a hillside for the last time before he leaves for London. In his own eyes, he is the hero of a medieval romance. Joan, however, sees herself as the lovely heroine of a cheap romance she has read. She feels she is being deserted by her lover, though John has offered to take her with him. By telling John how "stupid" the girl in the novel was for committing suicide, Joan implies that she is maturer and wiser than the heroine (p. 198). To John, Joan's reading tastes reveal once again how "lamentably stupid" she is (p. 192), and he must finally recognize that June is Joan. The exaggerated stories John and Joan create for themselves are even more fantastic and grotesque than the ones they are supposedly living, a situation emphasizing that, though youthful feelings of anxiety are real, they are more traumatic in the imagination than in actuality.

John's diary entries, which form the first part of the novel, introduce us to his interest in the arts, including his involvement with the school art society; his wide-ranging reading from the Russians to Carlyle and Ruskin; and his distaste for the materialistic, scientific, and athletic mentality of so many of the other boys and masters at school. Not an admirer of photographic art, as his entry on Van Gogh demonstrates, John ponders the connection between perspective and perception in his musings upon his circumstances and the people with whom he lives at his country home, Barwood. Blindness is both the subject of his thoughts and the circumstance that creates the opportunity for his reflections.

Sitting on the lawn and momentarily pitying himself for his inability to see, John asks himself, "What sense of beauty had others?" (p. 86). He becomes aware that those around him do not lack an appreciation for what is beautiful; they just have differing perceptions. For Herbert, Salonica is

beautiful because of a flower that he remembers growing on the hills; Egbert delights in the memory of a covey of partridges. John's stepmother spends hours in the rose garden—flowers represent beauty for her—and Harry, who has charge of the horses, always notes the condition of fences and fox coverts. Personal experience, John notes, sets apart what one individual attends to and sees from what another attends to and sees.

The subjectiveness of perception is emphasized through John's thoughts about his mother, who died in childbirth. Nanny has emphasized to John how beautiful his mother was, but in her reveries the first Mrs. Haye is a hussy, always flirting with her husband's men friends. Nanny, the stereotype of the prudish spinster, seems to have rewritten the past because of her own sexual fears and frustrations, telling John only what she thinks is proper. On the other hand, John idealizes the mother he has never known. In typical Green fashion, the narrator alerts the reader not to trust John's judgments: "and now that [John] was blind he had come to treasure little personal things of her own, a prayer-book of hers, though that, of course, was mistaken" (p. 156). We never do learn if either John or Nanny has come close to grasping something of the real Mrs. Haye's character.

When John hears a blackbird "screaming" in flight, he reflects that it might have appeared only as a "smudge" if he had seen it. However, he goes on to make clear that what he perceives through his new "spiritual" sight is no more accurate and true than what he might have seen with his eyes—it is just different.

The ironic parodying of story, character, and symbolic meaning through repetition with a difference forces the reader of *Blindness* to confront multiple possibilities of interpretation. Only those carefully trained by modernist expectations of meaning to be found by examining clusters of symbols or images could feel confident that John has developed self-knowledge and spiritual insight. Is John's "rising through the mist, blown on a gust of love, lifting up, straining at a white light that he would bathe in" (p. 252-253) an epileptic fit or a vision (John had earlier remarked that they were much the same thing)? The physical climax of his sexual fantasies? A spiritual rebirth?

John's reflections and the narrator's reminders emphasize that characters are at times mistaken in their interpretations and at other times have so embroidered them as to make it impossible to decide whose interpretation is correct. As Green would write in "The English Novel of the Future," a reader cannot be any more sure of having the right reading of a novel than of knowing the answers to life's mysteries. A writer should stimulate readers to recognize how limited their knowledge is of themselves and life, and how different people are because of their individual personalities and experiences. Since people see things differently, "there can be no precise meaning in a work of art." Writers must emphasize this by making novels as "diffuse and variously interpretable as life itself."

Reading *Blindness* reminds us that what remained constant throughout Green's life and writing was his way of seeing the world and presenting himself to the world. He created a "web of insinuations," whether he was posing for the camera or the interviewer, whether he was writing fiction or autobiography, whether he was writing as a teenager seeking to become a novelist or as a published, mature author. John thinks, "Art was what created in the looker-on, and he would have to try and create in others [*sic*]" (p. 159); Green states in "The English Novel of the Future" that art requires "a work of conscious imagination on the part of the viewer" (p. 21).

Green's mannered passages of exposition, his playing with sentence structure, his departures from "good English," his startling, sensuous, and incongruous images, even his humor, are all part of a distinct and varied style that Green states is to serve the purposes of gaining the reader's attention, of conveying the sensibility of the author, and of giving the sense of the subject. He notes that he has always represented "very closely what I see . . . and what I hear . . . but I say it is 'non-representational' because it is not necessarily what others see and hear" (Southern, p. 66). His practice and his statements led some writers—C. P. Snow, for example—to attack him and call him a narcissistic aesthete more concerned with style than with human issues. Other writers, as Southern comments, have praised him as a "writer's-writer's writer" (p. 62). John Updike wrote in the introduction to the reissue of three of Green's novels (1978): "For Green . . . is so good a writer . . . that I can launch myself upon this piece of homage and introduction only by . . . [imitating] that voice so full of other voices . . . tremulous with a precision that kept the softness of groping, of sensation, of liv-

ing" (p. 7). Updike seems to have read the Green I read.

When Green left Oxford to work at the family's engineering foundry, he felt that he had become, for the first time in his life, one of those who—unlike the rich, the intellectuals, and the artists of his circle—experienced life rather than sat around talking about it. Perhaps, as he remarks in *Pack My Bag,* the men and women he met and observed in Birmingham had a vitality missing in those from his own class because they had to survive by the work of their hands and had little except conversation or stories for diversion. They were interested in people and not in intellectual talk about people.

Living (1929) conveys Green's admiration for those with whom he worked. For some critics, such as Walter Allen, Green succeeded so well that the book could be called the first proletarian English novel. For others, the recurrent images of circles and spirals, appearances of and references to pigeons and other birds, and omissions of articles, which made his sentences seem strange, constituted evidence that Green was more poet than novelist, more a player with words and symbols than an observer of life and people. Another factor contributing to Green's being grouped with the modernists—geniuses, according to some but elite formalists in the eyes of many British writers and critics of the 1930's and after—was the seeming geometric patterning of his novels, a phenomenon of which Georgio Melchiori makes much in his study of Green and other twentieth-century writers.

As in *Blindness,* Green divides his narrative into scenic snapshots, but here the scenes are much shorter. They are also more easily discernible in *Living* because the sets of characters change and Green inserts spaces between the scenes. What links them is not chronology—this happens and then this takes place. Rather, the scenes are linked by what they have in common: dinnertime at the Dupret (factory owner) home and at the Craigan (factory worker) household; rivalry and bad feelings among the men in the management offices and among the laborers in the factory; lovers yearning for each other but unable to communicate their feelings to each other at the cinema and at a country house party. The rapid changing of scenes creates the sense of motion in the novel and, rather than plot, shapes the flow of the narrative. Green eschews plot because he believes that if life has one, we do not understand it. He does not play with how to tell a story in order to impress us with his artistry but to convey his sense of what life is like. He does not ignore social problems because he is intensely absorbed with structure and symbols. He ignores social problems and experiments with ways of writing and of expressing his perceptions because human problems—people falling in and out of love, working and growing old—are what engage his attention and what he would like to engage ours.

Living is about being young and trying to become an adult by acquiring the responsibilities of a home, a family, and a job. At the center of one cast of characters is Lily Gates, who lives with her father and Craigan, an aging molder from the factory. Lily is not allowed to take a job as a packer at Waley's; until she marries, she is expected to keep house for Craigan and her father. Though she loves Craigan, who is not a blood relation, and thinks of and addresses him as "grandad," she desires children and a home of her own. At the center of the other cast is Richard Dupret, son of the factory owner, who has come from London to begin his work in the family business by helping to run the foundry in Bridesley, Birmingham. Like Lily, he is not tied to his father by bonds of affection. His mother is family to him, but he, too, wants someone with whom he can create his own home.

Living is a love story or, rather, two love stories, both triangular: Jim loves Lily, Lily loves Bert, and Bert is too frightened to love anyone; Richard loves Hannah, Hannah loves Tom, and Tom loves his independence and adventure. Lily becomes disenchanted with Jim, who is always taciturn and undemonstrative: He is unable to laugh or touch, as she sees other men do with other women in the cinema. So she turns to the dapper, more outgoing Bert, but Bert is not the strong and daring man she pictures him to be. Nor is Hannah ever going to behave with the abandon of the romantic heroine in whose image Richard re-creates her in his reveries. Bert and Hannah are not the individuals Lily and Richard imagine them to be. Lily and Richard must wait for someone else who will fulfill their desires to love and be loved.

Moving back and forth between the two groups of characters, whose lives come into direct contact with each other only in a few scenes in the factory, Green contrasts the blunderings and dreams of the young, Lily and Richard, with the power and desire of their elders to maintain their position of authority in the workplace and in the home. The novel is as much about the young shedding the bonds of parental control as about the young finding someone to love. It is about the relationship between parents and children. Craigan's desire for Lily to marry Jim Dale, his helper at the foundry who rooms with them, is selfish. If she were to marry Bert, he would lose her. Until he lies ill and dying in his bed at the conclusion of the novel, Craigan exerts the power of love to keep Lily by his side.

Richard Dupret's home life is sterile. He and his mother sit at the dinner table alone, his father in bed recuperating after he slipped on dog "mess" and fell. She fusses for a footman to bring her a handkerchief, and they talk of social engagements while his father fails to respond to the prostitute hired by Mrs. Dupret to revitalize him. Clearly, Green mocks the artificiality of the lives of the rich, and Richard Dupret's nose-picking is an apt metaphor for the attitude of Green toward the activities—or, perhaps more accurately, the lack thereof—of the upper class. Yet Richard's desire to get on with his life and take some real responsibility for the running of the foundry and his frustrations in love are just as sympathetically portrayed as are Lily's desire for a husband and baby and her frustrations in "better[ing] herself" (p. 218).

In the contest between the young and the old played out at work as well as in the home, Green favors the young, not because they are more virtuous but because it is their turn to have a go at things. Nor is this a novel about the class struggle, the miserable and wretched poor about to be transformed into militants who will overthrow their cruel and heartless victimizers. Green does not idealize the poor for their lack of material comforts any more than he chastises the old for trying to hang on to what life they have left. He simply cares enough about the workers to present them as human beings and not as idealized members of the proletarian class in the manner of a writer such as George Orwell: Aaron Connolly is a tightwad who deliberately and spitefully drops a wrench from a crane, narrowly missing other workers below; Tupe is a "babble baby" (p. 23);[3] Joe Gates drinks too much and would rather talk than work. Those in management have similar human failings—

---

[3]Page references for *Living* are from the British edition published in 1929.

Bridges exaggerates, Tarver is paranoid, and those in the front office occasionally ignore the safety of the workers. Neither group is able to control the outward circumstances of their lives; all men and women, both the young and the old, know joy and sorrow.

The opening scene of the third chapter focuses on the joy and wonder of love and family that is expressed in Mr. and Mrs. Eames's delight in each other and their two children: "Why do we bring kids into the world, they leave you so soon as they're grown, eh?" (p. 24). "Because" is the only answer Mrs. Eames can think of. For her, bearing a child is like the wonder of migrating birds: It provokes feelings of the grandeur of life. Green's analogy reminds the reader that his novel is about *Living.*

Ten years after Green published his novel about the workers living in an industrial town in the North, he depicted in *Party Going* (1939) the life of the London Mayfair set, the lost and brittle young people who had figured so prominently in the social satires by British writers of the 1920's and 1930's. The novel opens with the sentence "Fog was so dense, bird that had been disturbed went flat into a balustrade and slowly fell, dead, at her feet" (p. 7).[4] For those who read the novel as a vehicle for social commentary on the vacuous and doomed upper class, the fog is emblematic of the spiritual desolation of the young who escaped death in World War I.

Repeated references to decay and death in the descriptive passages of the novel serve to reinforce a reading of the novel as a 1930's prose version of T. S. Eliot's *The Waste Land.* Julia, making her way to the station to join Max, crosses a footbridge with "stagnant water beneath" (p. 19); she observes upon arriving at the station that "it was like an enormous doctor's waiting room and that it would be like that when they were all dead and waiting at the gates" (p. 59). The station's waiting room is also described as a "huge vault of glass," and luggage is "in piles like an exaggerated grave yard, with the owners of it and their porters like mourners with the undertakers' men" (p. 15, 40). Two nannies who observe Miss Fellowes, elderly aunt of one of the party goers, pick up the dead pigeon, act "like the chorus in Greek plays" (p. 72). On his

way to the station, Alex, another of Max's party, likens "what he saw to being dead and thought of himself as a ghost driving through streets of the living" (p. 37). Those waiting near the tracks for trains to take them home are compared in a long, extended metaphor to "ruins"—they were "places that is where life has been . . . what used to be in them lost rather than hidden" (p. 201).

The rich, waiting to depart for a holiday of sun and romance in the south of France in the relative comfort of their railway station hotel rooms, as well as their servants and the less well-to-do commuters—without a place to sit, bathe, eat, or drink—seem about to perish. The juxtaposing of the rich and the workers, and the picture of Nero fiddling while Rome burns hanging upon the wall of one of the rooms occupied by Max and his friends, provide further structural and symbolic evidence that the novel is to be read as a critique of the wealthy.

The poetic license Green exercises in the phrasing of the opening sentence, which makes prominent "bird," "fog," and "dead," and the repeated references to the triad tease the reader to find a meaning hidden behind the words and images. What does the bird portend? Of what is the fog emblematic? What is the real journey that awaits those gathered in the terminus? Menaces abound. But does Green mean for us to interpret the bird's fate and the fog as a statement of the condition of England and its upper classes or as symbols predicting their doom? Everyone's doom? Does the ominous meaning associated with the bird, a dead pigeon, suggest only the characters' psychological states induced by fog and waiting? Just how assuredly can a reader argue for the rightness of a reading based upon a divination of the bird when Green repeatedly calls attention to mistakes his characters are making in interpretation, mistakes that arise from a character's personal desires and previous experiences?

Numerous birds and references to birds flit through the novel; not all of the birds are ones that fly. Miss Fellowes gives the dead pigeon to a character named Robin Adams (an examination of an earlier typescript in the British Museum reveals the name changed from Robert to Robin); Julia sees sea gulls but recalls them as doves and thus mistakenly believes them to portend a favorable conclusion to her pursuit of Max. Thomson, Julia's servant, is told to go "pick up some bird, alive or dead . . . and

---

[4]Page references for *Party Going* are from the British edition published in 1939.

HENRY GREEN

get yourself your cup o' tea if you feel like it" (p. 159). Thomson's friends use "bird" as a slang term for a young woman. Max sees Amabel, one of the other rich young women who flock about him, as a bird, her hands "like white doves" (p. 226) and Julia is upset because Angela had called Embassy Richard "Embassy Dick like any bird" (p. 164).

Our difficulties and that of the characters in knowing what is happening to Miss Fellowes should warn us that Green, unlike his modernist predecessors, is playing with the partialness and partiality of the act of interpretation, and denying that coincidences will necessarily provide the clue to the mysteries of the self, others, or existence. In "Henry Green: Time and the Absurd," I discuss Green's parodying of modernist conventions, distinguishing, for example, his practice from that of Joyce, Woolf, and other, earlier, twentieth-century writers. Is Miss Fellowes, who picks up and washes the dead bird and then wraps it in brown paper and carries it with her, dying? Some of the characters in the novel assume that is to be her fate as she lies ill in one of the hotel rooms. The mysterious detective—we cannot be sure he is the house detective—thinks she is. The hotel doctor's diagnosis, however, is that she is drunk. The description of her lying in bed, feeling the room move as if she were on a ship at sea, and finally vomiting, and our remembering that she has had a whiskey or two in the station bar, seem to lend more credence to the doctor's diagnosis than to the detective's more severe perception.

If people, as the narrator or stage director remarks about the quite different motives for Max's guests going on a party, "are continually doing similar things but never for similar reasons" (p. 114), how can we be sure that any interpretation does more than reflect our own assumptions and desires? Even our responses to such a seemingly objective label as *hospital* are quite different, as Green commented in an essay for *The Listener,* and depend upon our experiences. In addition, Green drops frequent reminders in the novel that memories are unreliable. Julia, for example, is so on edge with Max—she is hoping to marry him after their trip together—that she cannot remember statements she made to him a few moments earlier.

Green does not cast himself as seer or prophet. He does not pretend to read the birds. He likes to observe people observing birds, talking to each other, flirting, and even gossiping about someone

so silly as Embassy Richard and something so superficial as his attempts always to be on the guest list of embassy parties—or at least to pretend that he is. The wealthy may indeed have nothing more worthwhile to think about than the next party. But Green's tone is one of amusement and delight, especially in his depiction of the jockeying of men and women for the attention of members of the opposite sex. For instance, in Green's description of the picture of Nero, the emperor is fiddling to "eight fat women reclined on mattresses in front" (p. 92). For Green, the mysteries of sexual attraction and people's preoccupation with sex enliven all our lives, regardless of class. It is not one thing for one group and another thing for another group. In Green's novels, whether a person is going home or going out, he or she is looking for someone's hand to hold and lips to kiss.

NOVELS OF THE 1940's

WORLD War II formed the backdrop for Green's next three novels. The situation of war acted as a catalyst to Green's creative energies. He wrote *Caught* (1943), *Loving* (1945), several short pieces for *Penguin New Writing* and *Folios of New Writing*, and *Back* (1946) while continuing to work in London for the family business and volunteering for the Auxiliary Fire Service. *Caught* draws on his experience as a fire fighter but, as Green reminds his readers in a prefatory note, it is not the particulars of how one fights a fire but the "effect of that time" that he sought to capture. The feeling of being an alien, a stranger in a strange land, is the subject of *Caught* as well as of the remarkably rich and varied novels Green published about the war years.

Caught tells the stories of Richard Roe, a gentleman like Green who leaves his London office to attend training classes, and Bert Pye, a professional fireman. Separated by class and age, unable to communicate with one another because of those differences, the two men are nervous and distracted in each other's company. Further complicating their ability to communicate with one another is their shared knowledge that Pye's sister had abducted Roe's son. But their apprehensiveness is only a heightened version of that experienced by the other men in the London Fire Brigade. The threat of imminent death and the anxiety the men suffer

254

regarding their abilities to meet the tests that are ahead make them distrust and fear one another, and they experience "twelve months' bickering" (p. 183).[5] Only when the "phony war" that lasted from September 1939 to the summer of 1940 ends, and the conflagration of the Battle of Britain is finally upon them, do they momentarily weld themselves into a group.

An outsider, Roe attempts to curry favor by buying drinks, participating in late-night cockroach races, and telling his boss, Pye, where to find the two women who had picked Roe up one night when he was off duty. The other men remind Roe of his status by pushing dirt under his bed, calling him a "pansy," and nicknaming him "Savory Row," a street where the "well-breeched" buy their clothes (p. 88). The whole associative process that produces Richard's nickname is set off by Pye's calling him savoury Roe (he smells!) when Pye mistakenly believes Roe turned him in to Pye's supervisor, Trant, whose knowledge of Pye's absence from duty resulted from another chance association. Personal paranoia feeds the situational paranoia created by waiting for the bombs to fall; fears about surviving destruction from the heavens trigger uncertainties about the meaning of even the most trivial actions of others.

Pye's unpreparedness for his leadership role as substation officer and his fear that his senior officers will hold him responsible for his sister's actions intensify his uneasiness, and the insistence by the authorities that he pay for the upkeep of his sister in the asylum in which they have placed her increases his bitterness with a government of which he has long been critical. Nor is Pye helped by having officers over him who are experienced leaders; like himself, they are inept and untrained for their responsibilities. Trant, for example, is more interested in saving his own skin than in helping his men to do their best.

Caught is a psychological study that mocks the journey into the interior of the self as a vehicle for self-discovery. Memory and the stream of consciousness that so many modernist writers presented as revealing the essential self concealed beneath the meaningless surfaces of outward appearances are unreliable. The journey into the self, with only the coincidences of free associations to

guide one, ends on a desert island. Lost in the past, the individual is cut off and abandoned like the fire fighter in *Caught,* who holds a hose and waits for the water that will never come.

In the novel, Green goes so far in his critique of Freudian and Proustian ideas as to make the pursuit of and belief in their systems dangerous as well as faulty. Pye's anticipation of action at the fire station leads him to recall another war. His experience in France in World War I is linked in his mind with the earth of the trenches, and the earth of the trenches becomes the earth in the moonlit lane where he made love for the first time. He cannot recall the face of the girl and begins to think of his sister, whom he remembers creeping home that same evening, possibly after having "whored" as he has. He wonders why she never married. Those associations are dangerously cemented together when his sister's doctor tells him a fatuous Freudian story of a family trauma that is supposed to unlock the doors of Pye's preconscious mind. The doctor has asserted that in Pye's sister's family history lies the answer to her problem. Could the girl with whom Pye had sex in the lane and his sister, who was creeping home, be one and the same? His effort to resolve his dilemma and know the truth is futile and leads him to insanity and suicide.

Through Pye's fate, Green makes questionable the claims of Freudian psychology and parodies the reliability of memories involuntarily recalled. One thing does indeed lead to another, but randomly so. As Green remarked of Freudian ideas in *Pack My Bag,* "We are warned that what happened in those [childhood] days . . . lies in wait, in ambush for when one has grown up. So they say, but it never does" (pp. 14–15). It does not, that is, unless some overzealous psychoanalyst leads us to plot our lives according to his scenario. Green is as vehement in his condemnation of Freudian hubris, naively and mistakenly based upon the belief that life can be explained through psychological law, as was D. H. Lawrence in *Psychoanalysis and the Unconscious.* Green, however, makes his stories act as commentator. Unlike Lawrence, he shunned ascending the pulpit to deliver directly his comments upon writing, life, and people.

Roe is also depicted as entrapped by his past. His first wife is dead, and he sentimentalizes their life together. He jealously guards her memory, refusing even to discuss her or acknowledge her death to the

[5]Page numbers for *Caught* are from the British edition published in 1943.

members of his unit. The more threatened and isolated he feels, the more he romanticizes the life he and his wife shared. His nostalgically inaccurate daydreams and memories supply him with the stability and comfort that he cannot get from those at the fire station or even from his wife's sister Dy, who cares for his son, Christopher, in the country.

Unlike Pye, however, Roe succeeds in coming to terms with his past. He knows that he has colored his memories and that, as he tells Dy, "[o]ne changes everything after by going over it" (p. 179). Richard sharply dismisses Dy's attempt to assure him that the individual's subjective impressions are reality, and he also will not allow her to assume that his need to speak of his experiences in the Blitz is the result of nearly being blown up. It is as if Green wants to remind us through Roe's remarks that art is not to relieve some psychic pressure from the unconscious; it is to share one's experience with another. By sharing in fighting the fires, the regulars and the volunteers have overcome their differences and have been enabled to live in the present. By Roe's speaking to Dy about what that time was like for him, he comes to live in the present with her and Christopher.

Green's next novel, *Loving,* also about paranoia and the war, is set in Ireland. Green calls attention to the absence of curtains in the butler's room of Kinalty Castle in the opening of the novel—"For this was in Eire where there is no blackout" (p. 3). The war is going on offstage, as it were, but the actions, gestures, and conversations of those at the castle who are onstage remind the reader that the effect of the war was felt by noncombatants as well as by those fighting men and fires in places such as London, Shanghai, Madrid, and Dresden, cities where so many bombs were dropping in the 1930's and 1940's. Throughout the novel, the servants worry that they may be raped by Hitler's soldiers, massacred by the IRA, or seized and thrown into military service if they return to England. Although their fears are real, their anxieties about the war mask, substitute for, and heighten their personal insecurities and anxieties about sex, growing old, and dying.

So much for the dark side of the fairy tale Green relates. As his title suggests, this novel is not a tragedy; his tale that begins "once upon a day" has a happy ending—"Over in England they were married and lived happily ever after." Rivalries, thievery, secrets, characters who share the same name—all are ingredients in the fairy tale Green creates; they provide no end of possibilities for the kinds of incongruent misreadings and misapprehensions that tickle Green's fancy and ours. In their efforts to keep their jobs and enjoy some sex and love, the characters tell tales—some are falsehoods, some are merely imaginary, and some are confidences—and interpret all that they hear and see in light of their personal anxieties and fears of having their (mostly minor) betrayals discovered. It hardly seems a crime that Edie, one of the two underhousemaids, swipes some peacock eggs to give herself a facial or that the waterglass the cook frets about having lost is most likely the gin she drinks and not a liquid for pickling eggs. But great anxieties and confusions arise from the characters' efforts to conceal their minor misdeeds and secret indulgences.

Green plays with the discrepancies between appearance and reality, and not just in the tales that his characters tell and their contradictory interpretations of those tales. One cannot tell a person by his or her cover. Edie and Kate talk like young servant girls—dropping their *h*'s, clipping their words, and using slang from the cinema—but Edie, in particular, looks like a princess, a young woman as portrayed in the paintings of Degas or Renoir: "In that light from the window overgrown with ivy her detached skin shone like the flower of white lilac under leaves" (p. 22) or "For what with the peacocks bowing at her purple skirts, the white doves nodding on her shoulders round her brilliant cheeks . . . it made a picture" (p. 248). For all its poetic descriptive passages, the novel is very funny and, as its opening suggests, does not place great stock in the artist's ability to reveal large truths through the formal patterns and symbols with which he or she plays; the artist can tell us imaginary stories of once upon a time but cannot reveal the real or the absolute behind or beyond appearance.

The alteration of the fairy tale opening—"once upon a time" becomes "once upon a day"—emphasizes the transient nature of life. What is happening on that day is death, the death of Eldon, the butler, whose job his understudy, the head footman, Charley Raunce, expects to assume, but not without Raunce having to assert with both the owners and the other servants his right to head the household behind the green baize doors. To prepare himself for his job, Raunce studies Eldon's notebooks, which contain information about how Eldon has doctored the accounts. Also recorded in the notebooks is a mysterious note about Captain Davenport "[digging] after the old kings in his bog" (p. 30). Eldon evidently supplemented his income by a little blackmail, for the phrase refers to Dermot Davenport's affair with Violet Tennant, whose husband is in the service. Violet's adultery, which she naively hopes to hide from her mother-in-law and the servants, is juxtaposed with the courting of Raunce and Edie. Will their wooing lead to love and marriage? How honest are each person's intentions and tales of love? While the opening emphasizes impermanence, the story is not about death but about loving. Death is merely the backdrop for the novel's action, as it is for life.

Kinalty Castle is a "folly in Eire that had still to be burned down" (p. 220). The Tennants of the castle have little to recommend them, though it is only Mrs. Tennant of whom we see much, since her son is home just for a brief leave. She claims to be helping in the war effort—"have to keep up morale," she says—by maintaining her Irish estate. She is described as having "blue-washed silver hair," and puts her head out the window like a "parrot embarrassed at finding itself not tied to a perch" (p. 203). She sits in "an antique Gothic imitation of a hammock slung between four black marble columns and cunningly fashioned out of gold wire" (p. 219). Around Mrs. Tennant and her daughter-in-law are "milking stools, pails, clogs, the cow-byre furniture—all in gilded wood" (p. 220), a description recalling the Petite Trianon at Versailles, thereby making the room an imitation of an imitation and a reflector of the artifice and sham that characterize the owners and the servants as well. (To construct an interpretation of the novel as a social satire, readers have to ignore that the novel is focused on the servants.) On the castle grounds is a dovecote built like the Leaning Tower of Pisa and Skullpier Gallery, a complete copy of a Greek temple that can be seen from the Gothic windows of the castle.

The dovecote serves as a frequent gathering spot for the characters of the novel. Nanny Swift takes her charges there to tell them a fairy tale. She remains, however, "shuteyed and deaf" (p. 57) to the birds that, the others note, are "quarrelling, murdering, and making love again" (p. 60). The birds' activities contradict a reading of the doves as eternal symbols of peace and love. No romanticist nor believer in the priestly powers of the artist, Green restores birds, water, peacock eggs, and rings into real things in a real world. But Nanny does not want to look at real birds. She prefers the storybook land she has created and closes her eyes to intrusions upon her world of childish innocence. When Violet, the mother of the children for whom Nanny is now caring and to whom she had been governess, is caught naked in bed with her "fronts bobbin" and her neighbor–lover beside her, Nanny insists that all Violet needs is a laxative to cure her upset nerves. Her Violet could not have been guilty of so serious an affront. The contrast between what Nanny would like to see and hear and what is actually going on is one of the many incongruencies upon which Green plays in the novel.

The prince and princess of this romantic tale are Raunce, the forty-year-old, dyspeptic butler, and Edie, a young housemaid who is innately practical about securing a husband and safe financial future for herself. Green plays with the meanings for the word "tale," using it three times in the last four pages of the novel to describe Charley's changing explanation to Edie of why she should now leave the castle. The fairy tale that Green evokes as the frame of the story of Edie and Raunce is like the tales Raunce tells, one kind of ordering of human experience. Love is an imaginative way of seeing another. In Charley's vision of Edie dressed in purple and attended like royalty by the peacocks and doves, he finds strength. The worlds of make-believe and reality unite as they grow in concern for each other, and they leave the known, secure future at Kinalty Castle for the uncertainties of a war job in England. Like the princess in a fairy story, a girl may find her prince; but he is likely to be somewhat dishonest and not too healthy, and the never-never land to which he carries her away will be one in which there is loving but also death. But that is life.

Some readers of *Loving,* noting Raunce's dyspepsia attack at the end of the novel and the linking of Raunce's illness with the death of Eldon through the narrator's remarks—"Yet he used exactly that tone Mr. Eldon had employed at the last when calling his Ellen" (p. 248)—interpret the novel as a tragedy and label Green's narrator unreliable. Green's narrator *is* unreliable, but not in the sense that literary critics use the word. More accurately, Green severely limits the omniscience of his narrators. They do little more than set the stage, describe the outward appearance of the characters, record the dialogue, or, on rare occasions, remind the readers that they lack the knowledge of which character has the right interpretation. Green's narrators are no more privileged than are other individuals in understanding human behavior or motives.

Green found the dark reading of some of the reviewers and critics amusing. In "The English Novel of the Future" Green considered this amusement to be evidence of how little people believe of what they are told: "It is not to be supposed that any reader believes any more of what he is told in narrative than he ordinarily believes, in life, of what someone is telling him. In life we most of us have the most extraordinary reservations about what we hear" (p. 23). Green goes on to say that he did not envision Raunce dying of dyspepsia. He intended to indicate merely that Raunce was lovesick. Green enjoyed having confirmation of his skepticism about what readers believe of what they are told.

In *Back,* the last of Green's novels to use World War II as a backdrop, Mrs. Frazier, Charley Summers' landlady, attempts to warn him not to pay too much attention to correspondences: "Once you start on coincidences why there's no end to those things" (p. 37). She then tells him a story which illustrates that life is full of strange and sometimes significant likenesses. Charley's problem seems as weighty a philosophical problem as Hamlet's: When is a likeness significant and when is it not? Charley, like a character created by Samuel Beckett or Eugène Ionesco, finds himself a protagonist in a metaphysical farce. But Charley and the minor characters in *Back* who, to some extent, share Charley's plight, are memorable and distinguishable, making the novel so much more than an absurdist dramatization of the incongruities, incomprehensibilities, and illogic of twentieth-century life. In spite of not exploring the recesses of the mind and the family history of the principal character, *Back* is a psychological study of an ex-soldier's attempt to rejoin society. It is also a critique of contemporary society and a parody of parables, symbols, and other devices by which we attempt to make sense of our world. Like *Loving,* the novel ends in an affirmation of love, though some reviewers and critics were reluctant to accept the happy ending that Green supplied for the novel.

Back opens in a cemetery where Charley, a for-

mer prisoner of war with a peg leg, has come to seek the grave of his former sweetheart, Rose. Rose, his one link with the past, died during the war: "[Charley] thought how Rose would have laughed to see him in his usual state of not knowing, lost as he always was, and had been when the sniper got him in the sights" (p. 6). Disoriented, he finds himself entangled in roses, trapped by his memories of Rose, which are like the trap in which he "had lost his leg in France for not noticing the gun beneath a rose" (p. 3). Not merely roses or reds like Rose's hair remind Charley of his lost love; even the conversational use of the verb "rose" seems to him to conceal a reference to her. Charley finds himself bombarded by roses. So immersed is he in his memories of Rose, linked as they are to his experience in the war, that he mistakes her half sister, Nancy Whitmore, for Rose, deciding that the young woman's claim to be Nancy is but another concealment and betrayal (he believes Rose has become a prostitute to support herself). As in the prisoner-of-war camp, he finds the "roses grown between the minutes and the hours, and so entwined that the hands were stuck" (p. 7).

By making Charley's quest to reunite himself with his past and become a part of the society to which he has returned a quest to find Rose, his lady love, Green evokes literary associations between his tale and Guillaume de Lorris's *Roman de la rose.* Certainly Charley was Rose's humble servant, and she wielded a great deal of power over him, as the letters that he had kept reveal. But those letters also reveal the incongruity of reading the tale as a modern romance of the rose. Charley does not fit the role of heroic knight, though his surroundings appear as strange to him as if he had awakened to find himself cast as a medieval courtly lover. Rose is a leech and a very mundane married woman, taunting Charley in the letters with her availability at a time when he cannot be there, putting him off to a future date because she is pregnant, reminding him of the mules he forgot to buy her, and asking him to visit her parents for her. Whatever the relationship was between Charley and Rose—and Green makes it questionable whether Charley took Rose to bed in more than his imagination—it ennobled neither of them.

Green creates other equally improbable parallels for Charley's search for redemption and meaning. At the end of the opening graveyard scene, Charley is described as bowing his head and thinking he has "denied [Rose] by forgetting, denied one whom, he knew for sure, he was to deny again, then once more yet, yes thrice" (p. 12). He thinks he has denied her a second time when he tells an acquaintance at lunch that he had had a child by her, and then a third time when he comments that Rose was nothing more than "a tale" (p. 176). If Charley and Rose were not lovers, then the last denial is an affirmation of their real relationship and no denial at all. The second denial is no denial, for he has not forgotten her or claimed that they did not have a relationship. It can be one only in the dictionary sense of contradiction if they were not lovers. Did they or did they not have a relationship? And what does Charley really believe? Green's overly obvious biblical allusion does not help the reader to make sense of the story: Charley may be Rose's disciple but he is no Apostle Peter, stumbling as he does in expressing himself if he says anything at all, and Rose may have died young, but no one would take her for a Christ figure. Green only teases the reader with the promise of meaning revealed through allusion. He parodies allusion as he parodies the modernist use of symbols to create depth and reveal truth, for we cannot use the allusion to verify our interpretations of character or story.

The misinterpretations of words, phenomena, actions, and gestures by Charley and the other characters propel them into a series of comic collisions that become the plot of the novel. Nancy mistakes James Phillips, Rose's husband, for a "Ministry snooper" (p. 100), and Charley mistakes her remark of shock—"So it's come"—for her recognition of the fact that she has been exposed for leading the life of a prostitute under an assumed identity, rather than, as she believes, that she has been discovered to be living alone and not reporting it. We know that personal problems trigger the identifications but frequently not what is the truth of the matter.

The game of sign and identification is further complicated by deliberate lies. As she sits with him in the room she has rented to him, Mrs. Frazier tells Charley that he should "enjoy this scuttleful while you may . . . for there's not another in the cellar"; however, the narrator informs us: "She said this with an easy mind, who had a ton and a half stowed safe in the other cellar" (p. 35). Mr. Grant, Rose's father, tells Charley that he particularly asked him not to tell Nancy that he was the one who sent Charley to her apartment. He also insinuates that Charley should apologize for having come to see Mrs. Grant. But Charley knows that Mr. Grant never made any such request of him at the time he gave Charley Nancy's address, and that it was Grant who insisted he come to see Mrs. Grant.

The lies the characters tell reveal their concerns and, therefore, something of themselves. (Green has always maintained that we can learn more about people through their lies than we can through their half-truths, which are as accurate as Green believes persons can be.) The lies, nevertheless, confuse Charley as he seeks to understand what is going on around him. His confusion is heightened by the inconsistencies of his experiences. He is told by his boss that a letter canceling a contract is a "try-on," but then is told that he should not consider all instances of this kind a "try-on" (p. 124). The contradictions with which Charley must live are not different from those with which the other characters must deal; however, his experiences in the war have made him less able to cope.

Mrs. Grant's return to the past to escape the reality of Rose's death—at least that is one possible explanation of her behavior—mirrors Charley's actions. Her loss of "connections" is another example of the mental switchboard's failure to handle incoming and outgoing calls, and it could be serious. Mr. Grant remarks, "Well, once you begin to lose the picture of this or the other in your mind's eye, it's hard to determine where things'll stop. . . . I knew a man once, in the ordinary run of business, who started to misremember in that fashion. Wasn't long before he'd lost all his connections" (p. 14). Sometimes Mrs. Grant calls Charley "John," but when her husband is not in the room, she reveals that she knows Charley is not her brother, who was killed in the last war. Reenter Mr. Grant, and she begins to talk about the terrible Zeppelin raids that have been occurring, acting as if she believes she is living during World War I. Charley cannot be sure whether Mrs. Grant does or does not recognize him as she peeps through her fingers. The reader is even less sure about her illness when we find her becoming fit and hardy after the death of her husband. Was her illness a way to pay him back for the adulterous affair that produced Nancy? Was it a way to keep him home where he belonged?

Green treats the institutions of society, government, and business as comic figures, as fixated and mechanical as Charley in his quest for Rose. Life in postwar England has become a pea soup of initials and jargony gobbledygook letters:

When last autumn at the instance of the Ministry, Section S.E.C.O., we accepted your esteemed order no. 1526/2/5812 for 60 (sixty) size N.V. Rotary Extraction Pumps and 60 (sixty) size O.U. Centrifugal Feed Pumps, we pointed out both to your goodselves and to Mr. Turner of S.E.C.O. that we could only undertake this contract on the clear understanding that you would be in a position to urge through sufficient quantities of the pump body castings, which are to be in the secret acid-resisting metal to your special requirements.

(p. 121)

While hiding behind cryptic initials, the government runs every aspect of the individual's life—rationing food and clothing, telling citizens where to live and work, deciding which companies will produce what, and waging a war that seems to have no purpose other than the disruption of the lives of its citizens and the maiming of those unfortunate enough to serve it in battle. Government has become a bureaucracy, omnipotent as well as anonymous, and has substituted the abstract for the personal. Personal relationships and profound experiences have been reduced to the language of clichés, bed hopping, back slapping, and bragging about sex that passes for male companionship. When James meets Charley in the cemetery, he reduces Charley's loss of a leg to "Yes, well there you are" (p. 9).

Charley mistakes the artificial for the real when he attaches himself to Rose. As he comes to know Nancy, he learns that she is not the person he knew named Rose (thorn and now-dead snare of the world he has inhabited), but a woman in full bloom, worthy of being called a rose. Green suggests this vision-version of Nancy through the rich imagery of fecundity in the concluding scene in the novel and through Nancy's nursing of Mr. Grant after his stroke and her remaining to care for Mrs. Grant after he has died. Charley has resolved his own problem of mistaken identity, and unlike the story within a story that Green inserts into *Back*—the tale of the Countess d'Egmont, who pines away with love for a young man who is the double for her dead lover—Charley's Nancy is very much alive and committed to Charley.

The inserted story, *Souvenirs de la Marquise De Créquy: 1710 à 1800,* provides an oblique commentary on the story. Omitting the moralizing passages of the story as well the parts about French society, Green faithfully translates the narrative, though he adds a line at the end: "She seemed, as she in her turn lay dying before my eyes, to fuse the memory of these two men into one, into one true lover" (p. 120). Green compounds the ironies of his story within a story: The memoir was a fabrication written by Maurice Cousin, there being no Marquise de Créquy. Charley, in spite of the parallels between the countess's and his own mistaken quest, finds the story "ridiculous" and fails to see why James Phillips gave him the story to read. Thus the story does nothing more than furnish some interesting coincidences, none of which, including the added line, provide the answers to either the characters' or the readers' quest for meaning. We did not need the added line to note that Charley calls Nancy "Rose" when in bed with her for the first time on a "trial trip" (p. 246). We would have to ignore the narrative of the novel to use that last line of the story to support turning the bed Charley is sharing with Nancy into his deathbed.

In *Concluding* (1948), Green once again focuses his comic eye on the aesthetic ordering of the novel. Green's division of the novel into three units suggests the traditional idea that stories have a beginning, a middle, and a conclusion—an exposition, a complication, and a resolution—but the complications go unresolved, and the final scene is no more conclusive than the ending of today's episode of a television soap opera. Will the lovers Sebastian and Elizabeth marry, the traditional resolution of the comic plot, or will Edge and Rock keep their establishments from being disturbed, the old society thus predominating? Will Rock foil Edge and keep his cottage, or will he spend his last days in the state institution for scientists? Does Mary return, or has she run off with a lover? Does Adams merely watch, or has he had to drown Mary to keep his evening exploits with the girls quiet? Will the estate itself become nothing more than a pig farm?

Concluding allows such questions to dangle—not to have us tune in to tomorrow's episode but to shock us into the realization that only the writers of soap operas and detective fiction know the answers to what happened and why. The story thus fails to become the melodrama it threatened to become; and the incidents of suspense, which have become the object of comic laughter, are thrust into the background, important only because they obliquely reveal character. As is true of Green's other novels, characters act in the belief that life is supposed to have a meaning, but their failure to discern that meaning brings feelings of persecution and fear. Green forces his readers to accept what his characters must accept—narratives and life, as he notes in "The English Novel of the Future," are "variously interpretable" (p. 22).

The setting for the novel, a futuristic society run by the state, has led a number of critics to identify the purpose of the novel as satire. But *Concluding*, for all its criticism of bureaucracy, is a spoof of the anti-utopian novel rather than a dystopia. Green reduces the state to the level of character, ridiculous for its mechanical rigidity but hardly the all-powerful monster of Orwell's *1984* or Huxley's *Brave New World*. In fact, the state is less menacing in *Concluding* than in *Back,* where its destructiveness is depicted in the physical terms of loss of a human limb. It may be that the power of the state has increased until all are "frozen in the high summer of the State" (p. 76),[6] the staff not free to leave the institute and Edge and Baker not free to get rid of the staff; but the characters' lack of action stems more directly from their being frozen by their own fixations. The Kafkaesque atmosphere results from the treachery of the world, which, like the individuals themselves, will not surrender its essence. Not only does the state, like the genre or structure of a novel, seek to impose its system, but the individuals attempt to define each other by their own needs. The result is a confusing overlay of patterns like the entrance hall of the school, which is replete with a black-and-white tiled floor—covered first by parquet blocks and then spread with Chinese Kidderminster rugs—and ornate paneled walls, the lower paneling made up of white and black lozenges and the upper of multitudes of carved cupids. Standing in the room are British dragons.

The state, ten years previous to the day of the action of the story, took the estate from its "life tenant" (p. 17) and turned it into an institute to train girls as future state servants. If readers recall Mrs. Tennant from *Loving,* they may be of the opinion that this is not such a bad idea. At worst, one

aristocrat and attendant hierarchy have merely replaced another. Edge, the new Mrs. Tennant, whose official title is principal, a position she shares with Miss Baker, wants to establish Tradition, with a capital *T,* for her girls. Thus, in spite of the fact that one of her girls is missing (and she was a particular favorite of Edge's), the Founder's Day dance must be held, and the hall must be decorated in the swags of rhododendron and azaleas that have become a part of the ritual. It is obvious that Edge is as little concerned with the individual well-being of her girls as Mrs. Tennant was with the welfare of her servants. Looking out over the dance floor, Edge thinks, in response to Rock's prodding, "Why cannot the sad man realise I will not be bothered tonight with individuals" (p. 213). Like Mrs. Tennant, her concern is for possessions: "her third Terrace," "the crescent of her House," and "her Lake" (p. 15). Rock even refers to Edge as a parrot, recalling the narrator's image of Mrs. Tennant.

In the novel, the state does nothing more threatening than send a letter directing that henceforth pigs will be raised on the estate of Petra. A comically offensive directive, the missive may lead to the state's undoing by directing the attention of those at the school back to sex and the natural functions of life. There are no purges, no secret police, no great attempts to wipe out the past. Rock is even likely to be honored for work done fifty years earlier during the old regime.

Rock, whom some critics take to be the protagonist of the novel and a stand-in for Green, is admirable in his concern for his granddaughter Elizabeth, for his efforts on behalf of his animals, and even for his advanced age, which would make it seem that he deserves to be left in the peace he desires in the place that he loves. But Rock is also guilty of victimizing others. He, too, generalizes and makes objects of other persons. Not only does he see Edge and Baker as one, both "Babylonian harlots" (p. 34), he also suggests to the principals that Adams, whom some see as his friend, may be responsible for the disappearance of the students Mary and Merode.

Most poignant and least forgivable is his blindness (or perhaps deafness would be the better term, since Green identifies Rock with this affliction) to what his beloved granddaughter's needs really are. Birt is her future, as Elizabeth tells her grandfather, but Rock would end her relationship with the man

---

[6]Page references for *Concluding* are from the British edition published in 1948.

if he could. Both Rock and Edge are blocking characters, the representatives of the old society, which Northrop Frye, in his description of the comic *mythos* in *Anatomy of Criticism,* states must be overcome by the young man and woman who are in love. The old order must fall so that a new society can crystallize. In the novel, this necessity is dramatized by Rock's fear that Birt's presence is part of the principals' plot "to break a poor old fellow down by simply driving his sad girl out of her wits" (p. 11). Rock has sublimated his fear of losing Elizabeth to his expressed fear of losing his cottage, and he accuses Birt of plotting with the principals and using Elizabeth to gain the cottage. Edge, however, does not approve of Birt and Elizabeth's relationship. She fears that the "display of animalism" (p. 216) that she witnesses in Elizabeth and Birt's dancing will lead her girls astray and disrupt her spinsterish establishment. She is obviously upset not only by the example that their relationship sets for her girls but also by the fact that their "disgraceful behaviour" (p. 218) exposes the emptiness of her own life.

The "justice" to which Edge and Rock continually refer, however, is not justice but justification, a justification of their own desires. Birt recognizes this as he cries to Elizabeth: "Justice. . . . Old men have no idea at their age. They're too old" (p. 118). Both Elizabeth and Birt realize that the ostensible battle over the cottage is actually one for the security and comfort that love provides and a chance to have a life of one's own. The reader is reminded of the generational struggle depicted in *Living,* which Green once referred to as his version of *Fathers and Sons.* Though Rock smugly reflects that he has Elizabeth's dancing shoes in his dispatch case, the narrator reminds us that Rock has forgotten that she will now be forced "to take the young man outside" (p. 254). The comic resolution does not fall within the covers of the book—Green said of his practice as a writer that he strove to create a novel that would go on living after the reader had read the last page. Rock may be "well satisfied with his day" (p. 254), but the sensuousness of the descriptive passages, the young schoolgirls' success in escaping into the woods, and Birt and Elizabeth's beautiful and frequent assignations do not bode well for elders. The new day looms ominously for Edge and Baker as well as for Rock. But surely that is how we would expect things to turn out.

Rock does not come off well as the personifica-tion of the strong individualist pitted against the state, a reading of his character upon which those critics who interpret the novel as a dystopia depend. Rock uses the state to threaten others, both the principals and the woodsman Adams. And we have every reason to believe that he would use his influential friends to keep Adams, as well as Edge and Baker, in place if he needed to do so.

But it is not just the old who are "malevolently hostile" (p. 153), as Baker describes Rock and as he would certainly describe her. The novel makes it seem that all persons have reason to fear others, even those whom they love and who love them. Paranoia abounds as it does in *Caught, Loving,* and *Back.* An atmosphere of intrigue, of scheming and fear, pervades the relationships among the girls. Jealous of Mary for the favor she has won because of her good work, Moira, who would rather play, tries to make her out as a crybaby to the cook. The cook, however, misunderstands her remark and concludes that Mary has gone home because of a death in the family, one more rumor, one more twist to the story of Mary's disappearance, the details of which are garbled like those which emerge in a game of gossip played by the girls. Elizabeth feels that the young girls are a threat to her future and refers to them as "fiends" (p. 171). Rock also thinks of them as fiends who deliberately taunt and tantalize him with their ripe, young bodies. He is too old to participate safely in the sexual merry-go-round of kissing, petting, and changing partners, and he will be defeated by the young who are in the prime of their sexuality.

While parodying what he sees as the artificial world of symbols that the Romantics made of the natural world, Green redirects our attention to nature and man as a part of the natural world. As in his other novels, birds circle and dart on the horizon. But in *Concluding,* the most repeated image is the sea: Elizabeth and Birt make love on the "sea bed" of the forest; the sunlight is "like a depth of warm water"; and Birt, "bent to the tide, like seaweed in the ocean," leans over the girl (p. 55, 56). Earlier in the novel, Green had described the students as having arisen from their "heavy tide of dreams . . . each in a flow of her eighteen summers" (p. 22). The girls—indeed, all of the characters—seem to be adrift on the sea of life.

In his critical study of Green's writing, John Russell asserts that the message of *Concluding* is that through technology and the state, man has undone himself and the natural world of which he is a part. But Green is not a writer of problem novels—a few asides is all that he allows himself—any more than he is a romanticist in his view of the natural world or his conception of the role of the artist. For him, both darkness and light are part of the natural order, an omnipresent fact the characters in his novel attempt to escape. Comically, they try to impose a pattern upon life in order to satisfy their desire for permanence and intelligibility, but life will not be contained. The most that we can learn is that, as in the natural order, day will give way to night and youth to old age. By implication, the "high summer of the State" (p. 76) will give way to fall and the decay of winter as have other systems, feudal and religious. With the coming of spring, the old will relinquish the reins of power to the young, who will establish a new family and a new order. *Concluding,* thus, does not really conclude.

LATE NOVELS

GREEN's last two novels, *Nothing* (1950) and *Doting* (1952), seem to form a coda to his work. Superficial comedies of manners, they are distinct from his earlier work, though misunderstandings and mistakes multiply as in his earlier novels. Those misunderstandings and misapprehensions, however, seem neither as witty and funny nor as meaningful and poignant as those that give off sparks in the novels already discussed. Rather than obliquely pointing to larger social and metaphysical issues, the last two novels turn inward, mirroring nothing more than the sexual partnering and repartnering of the characters, which in the end may, indeed, seem to be nothing. In spite of the playfulness of the words and metaphors, the spirit of these novels seems frequently to be as dull and lifeless as the neither rich nor poor and neither young nor old people whom Green depicts carrying on and going on, "much the same" (p. 252),[7] as he remarks at the end of *Doting,* as the day before. Sameness is not likely to challenge the imagination of the reader, not while reading and not after the book has been closed. Perhaps the problem is simply that there are no characters who provoke the reader's sympathy or interest.

Nothing is a romantic comedy that inverts the conventions of the genre. Instead of a handsome young man seeking a young girl's hand in marriage, a middle-aged widow contrives to get a forty-five-year-old widower (who may be the father of her eldest son) to propose marriage. Jane Weatherby's efforts to catch John Pomfret are threatened, however, not just by his interest in another woman, but by the courtship and engagement of their children. Members of the younger generation are cast in the role of blocking agents. Another twist of the traditional plot of the comedy of manners is introduced when rumors that Philip Weatherby may actually be the son of John and Jane—they had an affair—reach Mary Pomfret and Philip. But the revelation of real parentage, a stock comic device that makes possible an otherwise impossible marriage in eighteenth-century drawing room comedies, is never made; it is instead the stock device parodied here, as Green has parodied so many other conventions of the novel.

Also reversed are our expectations of who should be making love and who should be talking in bed. Philip and Mary's affair lacks passion. Their parents' past love life and the possibility that their relationship might be semi-incestuous interests them more than making love. They sound out their parents and their old friends, only to have their questions given equivocal answers. The engagement ends when Mary announces that she is going to visit an old friend of her father's in Italy and so will have no leave time left for their marriage. Philip appears indignant at first, but his indignation is never personal. Instead, it is directed at Mary's apparent lack of seriousness over her job: "But I'm bound to tell you throwing up your job on a whim as you are must affect me" (p. 237).[8] Not much affected at all, Philip believes life is a serious intellectual project. He is so unfeeling that his mother even worries that he might be a "pansy." After Mary, who is clearly no Shakespearian Beatrice, leaves the pub, he blanches momentarily, then looks around to see if anyone has noticed: "No one appeared to be watching however. After which he finished both light ales and then left with much composure" (p. 238). Gender roles as well as

---

[7]Page references for *Doting* are from the British edition published in 1952.

[8]Page references for *Nothing* are from the British edition published in 1950.

generational roles are inverted in this contemporary comedy of much ado about mating that pairs the former bed partners of John and Jane.

Green has not made his cast of characters or their trivial existence come to life as he did for the shallow Mayfair set in *Party Going*. Though the question of whether Philip is Jane Weatherby's son by John Pomfret, against whom her husband had started proceedings before Philip's birth, seems an important one, it is never really answered. The reader is not sure whether John and Jane can answer it or whether, given the delicacy of the situation, they decide merely to make use of the present gossip and comments for their own ends—getting back together again and separating their children.

In *Doting*, the ingenuities of the form—the repeated scenes, for example, of the opening and ending—and maneuvering of the characters mirror each other in a funhouse atmosphere. On stage in the opening party is an almost naked dancer wooing two mechanical snakes from a wicker basket. A subject of conversation is the poet Campbell Anthony, Annabel's friend who is collecting love poems to be included in an anthology he calls *Doting*. He supports himself by working at the Ministry of Propaganda. Ignored by the Middletons, a juggler tosses twelve balls with his "lazy-seeming hands" with such skill that each ball "could be thought to follow grooves on violet air" (p. 7). He climaxes his act by balancing on his chin a billiard ball on which is balanced a pint beer mug that in turn supports another ball upon its handle. The precariousness and preciseness of the juggler's feat along with its artificialities suggest Green's art as he arranges words to imitate the dialogue of persons caught in the trivia of living.

The Middletons and Annabel Paynton—two years older than Philip—the "favoured daughter of a now disliked old friend . . . invariably asked to make even numbers . . . on the boy's first night of his holidays" (p. 1), make up the gaudy and silly party with which the novel opens. Mr. Middleton, though somewhat embarrassed when caught by his son, entertains himself by peering down Annabel's dress as she leans over to watch the floor show below. He considers the play they have just seen "squalid" (p. 1) but, in typical fashion for one of Green's characters, fails to see any relationship between his actions and those of the fictive characters in the play (compare Charley Summers' ignoring any likeness between his mistake and that of Madame d'Egmont).

In the concluding scene, the restaurant to which the Middletons take their friends for a party is called Rome. On one side, separated by a glass window, is an arena for wrestling. Instead of the groans of the wrestlers, the customers are treated to the sounds of band music, which is also for dancing. If they still feel bored they can watch a floor show, get drunk, or eat, or do all three simultaneously.

Each artistic performance serves as a parody of the novel—Campbell Anthony's volumes mocking the subject and title; the dancer's swaying and twisting mirroring the characters' shifting sexual involvements that form the plot of the novel; and the juggler's act reflecting the novel's circular structure. Green views his fictive world and literary methods through comic lenses. He said of *Doting* in an interview with Nigel Dennis: It is "the story of a middle-aged, married businessman who loves his wife but dotes on a young girl. His efforts to have his cake (his wife) and eat it (his girl), and the horrific plots and counterplots which this provokes within and without the family circle" are what makes the novel go round (p. 87).

Green's plots are always slight, never "horrific," and remind us of how little we can know about life and ourselves as we bumble through. He was, however, always more than a player with words and symbols, more than a poet painting sensuous images and scenes, though the vibrancy of his descriptions and the comedy of his characters' misconnections provide reason enough to read and reread his novels. As he told Terry Southern, life is "basically absurd." But his novels are not about nothing. They are about people falling in and out of love and trying to communicate with one another. Somewhat miraculously, his characters sometimes succeed. Green wished to re-create life and people in his fiction. That he succeeded, his readers agree, however much they may disagree in their interpretations of his novels.

SELECTED BIBLIOGRAPHY

I. BIBLIOGRAPHY. R. Heinzkill, "Henry Green: A Checklist," in *Twentieth Century Literature,* 29 (Winter 1983), a special issue on Green.

II. ARTICLES, ESSAYS, REVIEWS, AND TRANSLATIONS. "A Private School in 1914," in *Folios of New Writing,* 1 (Spring 1940); "A Rescue," in *Penguin New Writing,* 4 (March

1941); "Mr. Jonas," in *Folios of New Writing,* 3 (Spring 1941); "Apologia," in *Folios of New Writing,* 4 (Autumn 1941), essay on C. M. Doughty's *Travels in Arabia Deserta;* "The Lull," in *New Writing and Daylight* (Summer 1943); Madame de Créquy, "The Waters of Nanterre," in *Horizon,* 10, no. 60 (1944), a translation; "The English Novel of the Future," in *Contact,* no. 1 (August 1950); "Autobiographical Sketch," in *New York Herald Tribune Book Review* (8 October 1950); "A Novelist to His Readers: Communication Without Speech," in *The Listener,* 44 (9 November 1950); "Edward Garnett," in *The New Statesman and Nation,* n. s. 40 (30 December 1950); "A Novelist to His Readers—II," in *The Listener,* 45 (15 March 1951); "A Fire, a Flood, and the Price of Meat," in *The Listener,* 46 (23 August 1951); "The Spoken Word as Written," in *Spectator* (4 September 1953), review of *The Oxford Book of English Talk;* Review of Virginia Woolf's *A Writer's Diary,* in *London Magazine,* 1, no. 1 (February 1954); "An Unfinished Novel," in *London Magazine,* 6 (April 1959); "Firefighting," in *Texas Quarterly,* 3 (Winter 1960); "Before the Great Fire," in *London Magazine,* 7 (December 1960); "For Jenny with Affection from Henry Green," in *Spectator* (4 October 1963).

III. COLLECTED WORKS. *Loving, Living, Party Going* (Harmondsworth, U.K., and New York, 1978), introduction by J. Updike; *Nothing, Doting, Blindness* (New York, 1980).

IV. SEPARATE WORKS. *Blindness* (London and New York, 1926); *Living* (London and New York, 1929); *Party Going* (London, 1939; New York, 1951); *Pack My Bag: A Self Portrait* (London, 1940); *Caught* (London, 1943; New York, 1950); *Loving* (London, 1945; New York, 1949); *Back* (London, 1946; New York, 1950); *Concluding* (London, 1948; New York, 1950); *Nothing* (London and New York, 1950); *Doting* (London and New York, 1952).

V. LETTERS. G. Jefferson, "Green and Garnett," in *The London Magazine,* 18, no. 2 (June 1978), unpublished correspondence.

VI. INTERVIEWS AND BIOGRAPHICAL SKETCHES. H. Breit, "Henry Green," in *The New York Times Book Review* (19 February 1950), repr. in H. Breit, *The Writer Observed* (Cleveland, 1956); N. Dennis, "The Double Life of Henry Green," in *Life* (4 August 1952); T. Southern, "The Art of Fiction XXII," in *Paris Review,* 5 (Summer 1958); A. Ross, "Green, with Envy: Critical Reflections and an Interview," in *London Magazine,* 6 (April 1959); B. Johnson, "A Note on Henry Green in Retirement," in *Michigan Alumnus Quarterly Review,* 46 (August 1960); J. Russell, "There It Is," in *Kenyon Review,* 26 (Summer 1964); S. Blow, "Silent Green," in *Manchester Guardian* (8 August 1973); V. S. Pritchett, "Henry Yorke, Henry Green," in *London Magazine,* 14 (June–July 1974), memorial address; D. Lambourne, " 'No Thundering Horses!'; The Novels of Henry Green," in *Shenandoah,* 26, no. 4 (1975); J. Lees-Milne, "Henry Yorke and Henry Green," in *Twentieth Century Literature,* 29 (Winter 1983), special issue that also contains reminiscences by D. Lygon, reprint of Pritchett

memorial address, and K. Odom's interview with J. Lehmann about Green.

VII. CRITICAL STUDIES. W. Allen, "An Artist of the Thirties," in *Folios of New Writing,* 3 (Spring 1941); P. Toynbee, "The Novels of Henry Green," in *Partisan Review,* 16 (May 1949); P. Quennell, "Four English Novelists," in *Vogue* (1 October 1949); M. Schorer, "Introduction to Henry Green's World," in *The New York Times Book Review* (9 October 1949).

C. P. Snow, "Books and Writers," in *Spectator* (22 September 1950); R. Phelps, "The Vision of Henry Green," in *Hudson Review,* 5 (Winter 1953); G. Melchiori, *The Tightrope Walkers: Studies of Mannerism in Modern English Literature* (London, 1956), "The Abstract Art of Henry Green"; A. Quinton, "A French View of *Loving,*" in *The London Magazine,* 6 (April 1959), special issue on Green; E. Stokes, *The Novels of Henry Green* (London, 1959).

M. Cosman, "The Elusive Henry Green," in *Commonweal* (9 September 1960); J. Russell, *Henry Green: Nine Novels and an Unpacked Bag* (New Brunswick, N.J., 1960); E. Labor, "Henry Green's Web of Loving," in *Critique,* 4 (Fall–Winter 1960–1961); B. Davidson, "The World of *Loving,*" in *Wisconsin Studies in Contemporary Literature,* 2 (Winter 1961); A. K. Weatherhead, *A Reading of Henry Green* (Seattle, Wash., 1961); E. Welty, "Henry Green: A Novelist of the Imagination," in *Texas Quarterly,* 4 (Autumn 1961); T. Churchill, *"Loving:* A Comic Novel," in *Critique,* 4, no. 2 (1961); J. Hall, *The Tragic Comedians: Seven Modern British Novelists* (Bloomington, Ind., 1963); S. Shapiro, "Henry Green's *Back:* The Presence of the Past," in *Critique,* 7 (Spring 1964); B. Johnson, "Henry Green's Comic Symbolism," in *Ball State University Forum,* 6 (Autumn 1965); D. Taylor, "Catalytic Rhetoric: Henry Green's Theory of the Modern Novel," in *Criticism,* 7 (Winter 1965); M. Turner, "The Imagery of Wallace Stevens and Henry Green," in *Wisconsin Studies in Contemporary Literature,* 8 (1967); R. Ryf, *Henry Green* (New York, 1967), Columbia Essays on Modern Writers, no. 29.

C. Hart, "The Structure and Technique of *Party Going,*" in *Yearbook of English Studies,* 1 (1971); N. Page, *Speech in the English Novel* (London, 1973); B. Bassoff, *Toward Loving: The Poetics of the Novel and the Practice of Henry Green* (Columbia, S.C., 1975); J. Unterecker, "Fiction at the Edge of Poetry," in A. Friedman, ed., *Forms of Modern British Fiction* (Austin, Tex., 1975); B. Brothers, "Henry Green: Time and the Absurd," in *Boundary 2,* 5 (1977); K. Knodt, "The Night Journeys in Henry Green's *Living* and *Party Going,*" in *Ball State University Forum,* 19 (1978); K. Odom, *Henry Green* (Boston, 1978); F. Kermode, *The Genesis of Secrecy* (Cambridge, Mass., 1979), contains a discussion of *Party Going;* C. J. Allen, "Inference and the Nature of Mind in Henry Green's *Concluding,* in *Revue des langues vivantes,* no. 1 (1979); J. Updike, "Green Green," in *The New Yorker* (1 January 1979).

R. Mengham, *The Idiom of the Time: The Writings of Henry Green* (Cambridge and New York, 1982); A. Stead, "The

Name's Familiar: An Aspect of the Fiction of Henry Green," in D. Jefferson and G. Martin, eds., *The Uses of Fiction: Essays on the Modern Novel in Honour of Arnold Kettle* (U.K., 1982); B. Brothers, *"Blindness:* The Eye of Henry Green," in *Twentieth Century Literature,* 29 (Winter 1983), special issue, edited by A. K. Weatherhead, that includes critical essays on Green's short stories and novels as well as on teaching Green; S. Carlson, "Readers Reading Green Reading Readers: Discovering Henry Green Through Reader Response," in *Language and Style,* 17 (Spring 1984); P. Swinden, *The English Novel of History and Society, 1940–80* (New York, 1984); A. Gibson, "Henry Green as Experimental Novelist," in *Studies in the Novel,* 16 (Summer 1984); M. North, *Henry Green and the Writing of His Generation* (Charlottesville, Va., 1984); O. Holmesland, *A Critical Introduction to Henry Green's Novels: The Living Vision* (Houndmills, U.K., 1986); V. Cunningham, *British Writers of the Thirties* (Oxford, 1988); M. E. Gorra, *The English Novel at Mid-Century: From the Leaning Tower* (Houndmills, U.K., 1990).

SEAMUS HEANEY

(1939–   )

Gregory A. Schirmer

SEAMUS HEANEY WAS born the year W. B. Yeats died—a notable coincidence, given that Heaney was eventually to be regarded, both inside and outside Ireland, as the most important Irish poet writing after Yeats. Also in that year, 1939, W. H. Auden (in an elegy on Yeats) made the peculiarly modern observation that "poetry makes nothing happen," a statement that few poets in Auden's wake—and certainly not Heaney—have been able to dismiss without at least some second thoughts. Indeed, for Heaney, an Ulsterman, the question of the value of the poetic enterprise has been particularly pressing; he has watched his literary career develop alongside a steady escalation of sectarian violence in his native Northern Ireland, and while it is one thing to make claims for the validity of art, to justify giving your life to writing poems, in a time of relatively low political voltage, it is quite another to do so when men, women, and children are being killed almost daily in your backyard.

As Yeats had done before him, Heaney has consistently made those claims, and much of his poetry—arguably the best of it—embodies with conviction and candor the poet's struggle to come to terms with urgent political and social realities without compromising the integrity of his art, and without abandoning his faith in art's ability to get at human truths lying beneath the surface of everyday events. In an essay in which he describes T. S. Eliot writing poems in the middle of the bombing of London during World War II, Heaney clearly elucidates that belief in the efficacy of art, a belief that inspires and informs almost all his poetry:

Here is the great paradox of poetry and of the imaginative arts in general. Faced with the brutality of the historical onslaught, they are practically useless. Yet they verify our singularity, they strike and stake out the ore of self which lies at the base of every individuated life.

In one sense the efficacy of poetry is nil—no lyric has ever stopped a tank. In another sense, it is unlimited. It is like the writing in the sand in the face of which accusers and the accused are left speechless and renewed.

(*The Government of the Tongue*, p. 107)

This view of the relationship between art and the world requires, among other things, aesthetic distance. Heaney's ability to stand back from the violent conflict between Catholic and Protestant, nationalist and unionist, probably owes more than a little to the circumstances of his life, especially his early years. He was born on 13 April 1939, the oldest of nine children of a Catholic couple, Margaret and Patrick Heaney, living on a farm called Mossbawn, in County Derry, about thirty miles northwest of Belfast. By Heaney's account, the community was a cheerfully mixed one, with Catholics and Protestants living "in proximity to and in harmony with one another." Even the local geography encouraged what Heaney referred to as his capacity for "a kind of double awareness of division": To the west of Mossbawn lay a walled and wooded demesne and a community with the British name of Castledawson; to the east lay bogland, a mysterious, treacherous, powerfully alluring tract of swamp that ran up to the west bank of the river Bann and a village with the distinctly Irish name of Toome. It is no accident that much of Heaney's poetry is rooted in this landscape. For Heaney it represents more than the locale of his childhood memories; it embodies in a highly concrete form many of the political, religious, and cultural divisions that have come to preoccupy his art.

From St. Columb's College in Londonderry, a boarding school to which he won a scholarship in 1951, Heaney went to Queen's University in Belfast, where he was an undergraduate from 1957 to 1961 and where his interest in poetry first began to flower. At Queen's, Heaney read widely in both English and Irish literature and published (under the pen name *Incertus*) some poems in the university's literary magazine. The year after he graduated, while doing postgraduate work at St. Joseph's College of Education in Belfast, Heaney came to know the English writer Philip Hobsbaum, who had recently come to Queen's to teach and organized a group of young poets, including Derek Mahon and Michael Longley, of which Heaney soon became an active part. In August 1965 he married Marie Devlin, a schoolteacher from County Tyrone. During the next few years, while teaching at a secondary school in Belfast and later as lecturer at St. Joseph's, Heaney began placing poems in journals, and in 1966 Faber and Faber brought out his first full-length book of poems, *Death of a Naturalist,* to considerable acclaim. Heaney spent most of the next six years teaching at Queen's and writing. His two sons, Michael and Christopher, were born in 1966 and 1968, respectively. Another book, *Door into the Dark,* appeared in 1969, and a third, *Wintering Out,* in 1972, both of which greatly enhanced Heaney's steadily rising reputation.

In the academic year 1970–1971, Heaney was a guest lecturer at the University of California, Berkeley, a move that proved to be the first step toward a more or less permanent exile from his native Ulster. The decision to go to Berkeley came less than a year after the civil rights movement on behalf of Ulster Catholics had erupted into violence. In California Heaney found an equally charged political atmosphere and, more important, he became convinced there by what he saw among anti–Vietnam War activists that poetry need not be alienated from politics. As he said later in an interview:

I could see a close connection between the political and cultural assertions being made at that time by the minority in the north of Ireland and the protests and consciousness-raising that were going on in the Bay Area. And the poets were a part of this and also, pre-eminently, part of the protest against the Vietnam war. So that was probably the most important influence I came under in Berkeley, that awareness that poetry was a force, almost a mode of power, certainly a mode of resistance.

("An Interview with Seamus Heaney," *Ploughshares,* p. 20)

A year after his return from California, Heaney and his wife moved with their two sons from Belfast to a house in a rural area of County Wicklow, south of Dublin, known as Glanmore. It was a momentous move in several ways. First, Heaney was giving up the security of his teaching post at Queen's and committing his life fully to writing poetry. Second, he was quite consciously making himself into an exile. The move was seen by some of his fellow Ulstermen as a betrayal, but in Heaney's view it was a necessary break, giving him the distance he needed to write and to think about his writing. The four years in Glanmore were, Heaney later wrote, "an important growth time when I was asking myself questions about the proper function of poets and poetry and learning a new commitment to the art." That new commitment led to two important books, each of which, in different ways, confronted the crisis that Heaney had left behind in Belfast—*North,* published in 1975, and *Field Work,* published in 1979.

In 1976, Heaney and his family, which now included a daughter, Catherine Ann, born at Glanmore three years earlier, moved to Dublin, where he had been teaching since 1975 at Caryfort College, a teacher-training institution. Heaney also, in these years, began strengthening the connection with the United States begun during his year at Berkeley, giving frequent readings in America. In 1981 he resigned his post at Caryfort, and a year later accepted a one-semester-a-year position at Harvard University. In 1984, Heaney was appointed Boylston Professor of Rhetoric and Oratory at Harvard, and he began dividing his time between Dublin and Cambridge. In 1984 he published *Sweeney Astray,* a translation of a Middle Irish romance, and *Station Island,* his sixth collection of poems. Another collection, *The Haw Lantern,* appeared in 1987. In 1989 Heaney was elected Professor of Poetry at Oxford University.

In the 1980's Heaney published two collections of critical essays—*Preoccupations: Selected Prose, 1968–1978* (1980) and *The Government of the Tongue: The 1986 T. S. Eliot Memorial Lectures and Other Critical Writings* (1988)—in which he defines the essentially Romantic poetics that underlies his art. For Heaney, the composition of a poem is a matter of "listening," of "a wise passiveness, a surrender to the energies that spring within the center of the mind" (*Preoccupations,* p. 63). It cannot, therefore, be willed, and cannot be dictated to by specific events, political or otherwise. "The fact is," Heaney writes, "that poetry is its own reality, and no matter how much a poet may concede to the narrative pressures of social, moral, political and historical reality, the ultimate fidelity must be to the demands and promise of the artistic event" (*Government,* p. 101). And so the poet must find ways of engaging the world around him in his work without sacrificing that "ultimate fidelity." In "Feeling into Words," a lecture given in 1974, five years after the outbreak of violence in Ulster, Heaney said that political pressures had forced him to realize that his art could not turn its back on what was happening in the streets of Belfast and Londonderry; but what he needed, he said, was not polemical arguments but "images and symbols adequate to our predicament":

> I felt it imperative to discover a field of force in which, without abandoning fidelity to the processes and experience of poetry . . . it would be possible to encompass the perspectives of humane reason and at the same time to grant the religious intensity of the violence its deplorable authenticity and complexity.
>
> (*Preoccupations,* pp. 56–57)

That "authenticity and complexity" is the poet's domain; his aim must be, Heaney says, to reach down and back into his country's history, psychology, and mythology to uncover all the forces "implicit in the terms Irish Catholic and Ulster Protestant."

DEATH OF A NATURALIST

HEANEY's first book, published three years before the Ulster violence began in earnest, carries few traces of those forces. The poems in *Death of a Naturalist* describe Heaney's experiences growing up in Mossbawn, and do so, for the most part, neutrally. Standing behind many of them is the twentieth-century Irish poet Patrick Kavanagh, to whom Heaney has acknowledged a large debt. Kavanagh's commitment to writing about his own postage stamp of ground, a piece of land in rural County Monaghan not far in distance or character from the County Derry of Heaney's childhood,

made it possible, Heaney said, for him to focus with confidence on the experiences and landscapes of his upbringing. Heaney once said that Kavanagh, more than any other Irish poet, including Yeats, gave all writers coming after him "permission to dwell without cultural anxiety among the usual landmarks of your life." Heaney's evocations of those landmarks differ from Kavanagh's, however, in their Keatsian sensuousness, their richness of sound and image. Here, for example, is a description, taken from the title poem of *Death of a Naturalist,* of a flax dam:

> All year the flax-dam festered in the heart
> Of the townland; green and heavy headed
> Flax had rotted there, weighted down by huge sods.
> Daily it sweltered in the punishing sun.
> Bubbles gargled delicately, bluebottles
> Wove a strong gauze of sound around the smell.

The rich, fecund atmosphere of the dam is felt here partly in the irregular, heavily stressed lines, and in a medley of internal sound patterns, alliterative and assonantal ("flax-dam festered," "heavy headed," "rotted" and "weighted," "strong gauze," and "sound around," among others).

There is something of the musical irregularities of Gerard Manley Hopkins lurking in such passages—and Heaney had read and admired Hopkins at Queen's University: ". . . when I first put pen to paper at university, what flowed out was what flowed in, the bumpy alliterating music, the reporting sounds and ricocheting consonants typical of Hopkins's verse"—but the English poet most important to Heaney's early work is Wordsworth. For one thing, as the title of the volume suggests, *Death of a Naturalist* is very much concerned with the destruction of youthful illusion, and can in fact be read as a rural Irish version of Wordsworth's notion of the necessary fall from innocence into experience. But Wordsworth and the Romantics are also crucial to Heaney's poetry because of their theories of poetry. In "The Diviner," Heaney takes a phenomenon of the rural life he knew as a child and transforms it into a metaphor for a Romantic concept of poetic inspiration:

> Cut from the green hedge a forked hazel stick
> That he held tight by the arms of the V:
> Circling the terrain, hunting the pluck
> Of water, nervous, but professionally

Unfussed. The pluck came sharp as a sting.
The rod jerked down with precise convulsions,
Spring water suddenly broadcasting
Through a green aerial its secret stations.

The bystanders would ask to have a try.
He handed them the rod without a word.
It lay dead in their grasp till nonchalantly
He gripped expectant wrists. The hazel stirred.

The connection here between poet and diviner—felt particularly in that final rhyme between "word" and "stirred"—embodies a thoroughly Romantic aesthetic. As Heaney once said in discussing this poem, the poet, like the diviner, makes "contact with what lies hidden" and makes "palpable what was sensed or raised." Moreover, the comparison argues for a Wordsworthian passivity on the part of the poet—he grips the wrists of others "nonchalantly," for example—and for the Romantic notion of the poet as a chosen vessel; only the diviner has the mysterious power to find the water.

Death of a Naturalist also introduces another, somewhat similar metaphor for the process of poetic creation, and this one informs much of Heaney's later work. In the first poem in the book, "Digging," Heaney defends his work as a poet by describing it as his version of the cutting of turf done by the men in his family before him:

The cold smell of potato mould, the squelch and slap
Of soggy peat, the curt cuts of an edge
Through living roots awaken in my head.
But I've no spade to follow men like them.

Between my finger and my thumb
The squat pen rests.
I'll dig with it.

At this point in Heaney's career, what the Romantic poet-as-archaeologist is likely to find is more individual than communal, more personal than public, as the final poem in the volume, "Personal Helicon," asserts: "I rhyme / To see myself, to set the darkness echoing."

Nonetheless, there are signs in *Death of a Naturalist* of more political concerns. The most ambitious poem in the volume, "At a Potato Digging," explores the relationship between present and past, specifically the past of the Great Famine of the 1840's, in which thousands of Irish died or emigrated when the potato crop failed for several consecutive years. This is a highly charged chapter in Ireland's long and troubled history—the English were (and, in some quarters, still are) blamed for much of the suffering—and Heaney uses the historical perspective to unearth certain cultural fears and attitudes, as well as to make the more general point about how current values, especially in Ireland, are inevitably shaped by the past. After a characteristically vivid description of harvested potatoes,

"Native
to the black hutch of clay
where the halved seed shot and clotted
these knobbed and slit-eyed tubers seem
the petrified hearts of drills"

the poem shifts to the past, relying on the phrase "live skulls, blind-eyed," used to describe the potatoes, as a fulcrum:

Live skulls, blind-eyed, balanced on
wild higgeldy skeletons
scoured the land in 'forty-five,
wolfed the blighted root and died.
. . .
Stinking potatoes fouled the land,
pits turned pus into filthy mounds:
and where potato diggers are
you still smell the running sore.

The ground here, like the landscape in a number of Heaney's later bog poems, is a cultural and political memory bank, a constant reminder of a history of injustice and suffering. And so, when the poem returns to the present, the relative prosperity of the contemporary potato farmer is made to seem precarious, shadowed by a disastrous past that is evoked in certain words and images associated with death and starvation, and so with the famine:

Under a gay flotilla of gulls
The rhythm deadens, the workers stop.
Brown bread and tea in bright canfuls
Are served for lunch. Dead-beat, they flop

Down in the ditch and take their fill,
Thankfully breaking timeless fasts;
Then, stretched on the faithless ground, spill
Libations of cold tea, scatter crusts.

SEAMUS HEANEY

DOOR INTO THE DARK

THERE are flaws in *Death of a Naturalist,* most of them the result of overwriting—of loading each rift with too much ore, of working too hard for the image that will shock (from "Waterfall": "water goes over / Like villains dropped screaming to justice"). Some of this is ironed out in Heaney's next book, *Door into the Dark.* The descriptions of rural life in Heaney's native County Derry tend to be somewhat sparer and more streamlined in this book, the lines less clogged with heavy stresses. In "Gone," for example, Heaney describes an absence rather than a presence, a place left uninhabited and therefore incomplete, all of which is reflected in the way that the poem resists the completeness of full rhyme and the stability of regular stanzas:

> Green froth that lathered each end
> Of the shining bit
> Is a cobweb of grass-dust.
> The sweaty twist of the bellyband
> Has stiffened, cold in the hand
> And pads of the blinkers
> Bulge through the ticking.
> Reins, chains and traces
> Droop in a tangle.
>
> His hot reek is lost.
> The place is old in his must.
>
> He cleared in a hurry
> Clad only in shods
> Leaving this stable unmade.

Similarly, the strain of violent sexuality that runs through a number of Heaney's nature poems in *Death of a Naturalist* is often tempered in *Door into the Dark*, usually by a gentle, wry sense of humor. In "Rite of Spring," Heaney playfully describes in sexual terms that are anything but threatening the process of thawing a frozen pump by wrapping it with straw and then setting the straw on fire:

> . . . then a·light
> That sent the pump up in flame.
> It cooled, we lifted her latch,
> Her entrance was wet, and she came.

And there is an erotic tenderness in "Undine" that is hard to find anywhere in *Death of a Natural-ist.* This poem retells a myth about a water spirit who has to marry a human and have a child by him before she can be human; and even though Heaney's version of the legend clearly suggests some kind of parallel between political and sexual conquest, it is finally a poem celebrating the union it describes:

> He slashed the briars, shovelled up grey silt
> To give me right of way in my own drains
> And I ran quick for him, cleaned out my rust.
>
> He halted, saw me finally disrobed,
> Running clear, with apparent unconcern.
> Then he walked by me. I rippled and I churned
>
> Where ditches intersected near the river
> Until he dug a spade deep in my flank
> And took me to him. I swallowed his trench
>
> Gratefully, dispersing myself for love
> Down in his roots, climbing his brassy grain—
> But once he knew my welcome, I alone
>
> Could give him subtle increase and reflection.
> He explored me so completely, each limb
> Lost its cold freedom. Human, warmed to him.

At the same time, a darkly introspective strain can be discerned in *Door into the Dark.* There is a poem, for example, entitled "Dream," in which Heaney describes himself driving a billhook into someone's skull; there is "The Forge," in which the image of the poet-as-diviner in *Death of a Naturalist* is replaced by that of poet-as-blacksmith, creating in darkness ("All I know is a door into the dark"); there is a poem entitled "Shoreline," in which Heaney sees the Irish consciousness as haunted by the nightmare of invasion:

> A tide
> Is rummaging in
> At the foot of all fields,
> All cliffs and shingles.
> Listen. Is it the Danes,
> A black hawk bent on the sail?
> Or the chinking Normans?

And, last but hardly least, there is the final poem in the collection, "Bogland"—Heaney's first bog poem—in which the landscape of the bog is presented as a memory bank holding all the past in its

271

watery embrace, and threatening to open a door into places unknown and terrifying:

> We have no prairies
> To slice a big sun at evening—
> Everywhere the eye concedes to
> Encroaching horizon,
>
> Is wooed into the cyclops' eye
> Of a tarn. Our unfenced country
> Is bog that keeps crusting
> Between the sights of the sun.
>   . . .
> They'll never dig coal here,
>
> Only the waterlogged trunks
> Of great firs, soft as pulp.
> Our pioneers keep striking
> Inwards and downwards,
>
> Every layer they strip
> Seems camped on before.
> The bogholes might be Atlantic seepage.
> The wet centre is bottomless.

In "Feeling into Words" Heaney described "Bogland" as a poem that laid down "an answering Irish myth" (*Preoccupations,* p. 55) to the legend of the American frontier—significantly, a vertical rather than a horizontal myth. But it was not until after the violence in Northern Ireland erupted that he was able to carry this idea an important step further, to use this notion of the bog as a means of unearthing in his poetry the cultural attitudes and values that lay beneath the terrible daily events that, as a poet born and brought up in Ulster, he could not ignore.

WINTERING OUT

THE difference between 1969, the year *Door into the Dark* was published, and 1972, when his next collection, *Wintering Out,* appeared, is registered forcefully in the dedicatory poem to *Wintering Out.* Here the pastoral landscape of Heaney's childhood, evoked so vividly in his first two books, gives way to one of war:

> *This morning from a dewy motorway*
> *I saw the new camp for the internees:*
> *a bomb had left a crater of fresh clay*
> *in the roadside, and over in the trees*

> *machine-gun posts defined a real stockade.*
> *There was that white mist you get on a low ground*
> *and it was déjà-vu, some film made*
> *of* Stalag 17, *a bad dream with no sound.*
>
> *Is there a life before death? That's chalked up*
> *on a wall downtown. Competence with pain,*
> *coherent miseries, a bite and sup,*
> *we hug our little destiny again.*

In *Wintering Out,* Heaney approaches this terrain of pain and misery along two principal routes—one linguistic, one metaphoric—each of which enables him to confront the violence while maintaining the integrity of his art.

Having grown up in an area both Protestant and Catholic, unionist and nationalist, Heaney understands full well the political depth charges buried in language—in the choice of one word over another, in the way the same word might be pronounced. In *Wintering Out,* Heaney re-views the places of his childhood through a linguistic lens, and thereby politicizes the landscape. As he said in an interview, "*Wintering Out* tries to insinuate itself into the roots of the political myths by feeling along the lines of language." And so the village of Toome, to the east of Mossbawn, emerges in this book more as a linguistic event than as a geographical one:

> My mouth holds round
> the soft blastings,
> *Toome, Toome,*
> as under the dislodged
>
> slab of the tongue
> I push into a souterrain
> prospecting what new
> in a hundred centuries'
>
> loam, flints, musket-balls,
> fragmented ware,
> torcs and fish-bones
> till I am sleeved in
>
> alluvial mud that shelves
> suddenly under
> bogwater and tributaries,
> and elvers tail my hair.
>   ("Toome")

Heaney is fully aware of the political implications of this kind of linguistic prospecting. The replacement of Irish by English as Ireland's principal language represents a crucial kind of conquest because it facilitates the erosion of Irish culture and traditions. Heaney does not, however, recommend turning back the clock of politics or of language. For better or worse, English is the modern Irish poet's language, and he must find ways to use the tongue of the conqueror to validate and maintain the heritage that it threatens. As he says in "A New Song":

> But now our river tongues must rise
> From licking deep in native haunts
> To flood, with vowelling embrace,
> Demesnes staked out in consonants.

If these lines argue for some kind of acceptance of English as Ireland's language—even some kind of "embrace" of those linguistic demesnes marked by consonants rather than vowels—they also, on a more strictly political level, insist that it is not realistic to assume that centuries of British presence in Ireland can be dismissed with the sweep of a hand, or of a hand grenade.

Wintering Out contains the first of Heaney's poems in which bogland is used metaphorically to interpret the conflict in Northern Ireland. In 1969, Heaney came across a photograph of a man from the Iron Age whose body was found preserved in the bogs of Jutland. The photograph appeared in a book entitled *The Bog People* (1969), and its author, P. V. Glob, argued that many of the bodies found strangled or with cut throats in the peat bogs of Jutland were victims of ritual sacrifices to an earth goddess, killed and buried each year to ensure the fertility of the land in the coming spring. For Heaney, as he later said in "Feeling into Words," the parallels with the political tradition of blood sacrifice in Ireland were striking:

Taken in relation to the tradition of Irish political martyrdom for that cause whose icon is Kathleen Ni Houlihan, this is more than an archaic barbarous rite: it is an archetypal pattern. And the unforgettable photographs of these victims blended in my mind with photographs of atrocities, past and present, in the long rites of Irish political and religious struggles.

(*Preoccupations*, pp. 57–58)

These correspondences came together in "The Tollund Man," a poem in which Heaney connects the Irish political tradition of blood sacrifice to a long history of fanaticism going back to the primitive Jutes, and suggests, chiefly through images of the victims, that this kind of ritualistic faith leads to sterility, not fertility:

> I could risk blasphemy,
> Consecrate the cauldron bog
> Our holy ground and pray
> Him to make germinate
>
> The scattered, ambushed
> Flesh of labourers,
> Stockinged corpses
> Laid out in the farmyards,
>
> Tell-tale skin and teeth
> Flecking the sleepers
> Of four young brothers, trailed
> For miles along the lines.

Like many of Heaney's poems about the North, "The Tollund Man" also turns a critical eye on its author, exploring with candor his own ambiguous position. At the end of the poem, Heaney concedes that as an Irishman he cannot help but identify to some extent with the violence and its motives, even though he is appalled by it. Imagining driving through Jutland, he sees himself as both alienated and implicated: "Out there in Jutland / In the old man-killing parishes / I will feel lost, / Unhappy and at home."

Heaney later said that when he wrote "The Tollund Man," he realized that it represented an important development in his work:

I had a sense of crossing a line really, that my whole being was involved in the sense of—the root sense—of religion. . . . And that was a moment of commitment not in the political sense but in the deeper sense of your life, committing yourself to something. I think that brought me a new possibility of seriousness in the poetic enterprise.

("An Interview with Seamus Heaney," *Ploughshares*, p. 20)

NORTH

THAT new possibility reached its full flowering in Heaney's fourth book of poems, *North*, which contains a series of poems in which the metaphor of the bog is used to delve into Ireland's rich, tumultuous past, and to exhume attitudes and values that explain, insofar as explanations are possible, the violence in contemporary Ulster. The bog poems in *North* see that violence as part of a long line of atrocity stretching back into the dimness of ancient history, and thus as a manifestation of a deep-seated human need to resort to bloodshed in the name of one cause or another.

In "The Grabaulle Man," for example, Heaney presents an arresting image of the body of a victim found in the bogs of Jutland—"The head lifts / the chin is a visor / raised above the vent / of his slashed throat / that has tanned and toughened"— and uses it to explore the human capacity for transforming such victims into political martyrs or heroes. Heaney also worries in this poem about how the artist can transform reality, sometimes in similarly disconcerting ways. For him, the Grabaulle Man, whom he first encountered in a photograph, has become "perfected in my memory," a product of his imagination. That abstracted image needs, Heaney says, to be weighed against the brutal reality of the victim's actual death and, more to the point, against "the actual weight / of each hooded victim, / slashed and dumped" in contemporary Northern Ireland.

This notion that the poet, like the political partisan, may be guilty of remaking reality for his own purpose is part of the self-reflexive doubt that runs through much of Heaney's writing about the North. Heaney's moral ambiguity about his responsibilities is perhaps nowhere more movingly expressed than in "Punishment," a poem in which the body of a Viking adulteress dug up from the bog, still bearing the marks of her public disgrace, is connected with the contemporary practice of tarring and feathering Ulster Catholic girls caught going out with British soldiers:

> Little adulteress,
> before they punished you
>
> you were flaxen-haired,
> undernourished, and your
> tar-black face was beautiful.
> My poor scapegoat,
>
> I almost love you
> but would have cast, I know,
> the stones of silence.
> I am the artful voyeur
>
> of your brain's exposed
> and darkened combs,

> your muscles' webbing
> and all your numbered bones:
>
> I who have stood dumb
> when your betraying sisters,
> cauled in tar,
> wept by the railings,
>
> who would connive
> in civilized outrage
> yet understand the exact
> and tribal, intimate revenge.

Part of Heaney's self-questioning here has to do with his commitment to writing poems about the North rather than taking some more obviously relevant action—with being, as he says, an "artful voyeur" of the catastrophe. But the poem is also concerned with the broader ambivalence explored in "The Tollund Man." On the one hand, from the perspective of "civilized outrage," Heaney abhors the violence and cruelty. On the other, he understands, in his bones, the feelings that lie behind it; as an Irishman—and as a human being—he cannot help but identify with that desire for "a tribal, intimate revenge."

North is divided into two sections, a division that proves significant in the development of Heaney's poetry. At the end of the first section of the book, in a poem titled "Hercules and Antaeus," Heaney retells the classical story of how Hercules defeated Antaeus by holding him up, keeping him from the ground that nourished him:

> Hercules lifts his arms
> in a remorseless V,
> his triumph unassailed
> by the powers he has shaken
>
> and lifts and banks Antaeus
> high as a profiled ridge,
> a sleeping giant,
> pap for the dispossessed.

This can be read as a version of the conquest of Ireland by England, of the destruction of the dark, vertical, earth-nourished culture of the Irish at the hands of the more rational, more "enlightened" culture of the English; robbed of its contact with the soil, the Irish tradition becomes "a sleeping giant" or, worse, "pap for the dispossessed." For Heaney, however, this myth had an additional significance; it represented an attempt on his part to put behind him the vertical, archaeological poetry of the first part of his career, and to try to establish for himself a more open, more socially conscious, more public voice. As he said in an interview, Hercules for him "represents the possibility of the play of intelligence," and he was at this time looking in his own work for "an intonation that could be called public," a voice that is "set *out . . .* a voice that could *talk out* as well as go into a trance" ("Seamus Heaney," *Viewpoints: Poets in Conversation,* p. 70).

That new Hercules voice sounds distinctly in the second part of *North.* "Whatever You Say Say Nothing," for example, is informed by the same self-criticism at work in "The Grabaulle Man" and "Punishment," but in this poem Heaney's questions about the efficacy of his art are expressed directly, even colloquially, and the richly suggestive metaphor of the bog is replaced by direct references to the seventeenth-century Battle of the Boyne:

Christ, it's near time that some small leak was sprung

In the great dykes the Dutchman made
To dam the dangerous tide that followed Seamus.
Yet for all this art and sedentary trade
I am incapable. The famous

Northern reticence, the tight gag of place
And times: yes, yes. Of the "wee six" I sing
Where to be saved you only must save face
And whatever you say, you say nothing.

The tone here is uncharacteristically acerbic, but that note of candid, critical self-examination informs much of Heaney's poetry in the late 1970's and 1980's. In the last poem of *North,* "Exposure," Heaney directs that inquiring gaze at his decision to move to Wicklow in 1972. To some extent, the poem can be read as a defense of that move—Heaney says that he is "neither internee nor informer"—but the poem ends in genuine doubt about the morality of his choosing to leave Ulster behind him, and about what he might have lost, as a poet, by doing so:

I am neither internee nor informer;
An inner émigré, grown long-haired
And thoughtful; a wood-kerne

Escaped from the massacre,
Taking protective colouring
From bole and bark, feeling
Every wind that blows;

Who, blowing up these sparks
For their meagre heat, have missed
The once-in-a-lifetime portent,
The comet's pulsing rose.

FIELD WORK

WHATEVER misgivings Heaney might have entertained when he was writing *North,* the move to Glanmore and the full commitment to writing proved to be, at least for his readers, good decisions. Heaney's next collection, *Field Work*—a book very much tied, as its title suggests, to Heaney's experience in Glanmore—was received by many critics as his most accomplished book by far. It also carried Heaney considerably forward in his attempt to develop a more Herculean poetics. In an interview conducted the year *Field Work* was published, Heaney said, "I remember writing a letter to Brian Friel [the Irish playwright] just after *North* was published, saying I no longer wanted a door into the dark—I want a door into the light" ("An Interview with Seamus Heaney," *Ploughshares,* p. 20). In the remarkably flexible and open voice that characterizes most of the poems in it, and in Heaney's willingness to speak directly and often autobiographically about events in the North, *Field Work* clearly opens that door.

Heaney's response to the Ulster violence in this book takes the form largely of elegies written about people he knew. Although this approach might be seen as a means of sidestepping unqualified political commitment—and Heaney does seem to be taking his cue in these poems from Yeats's observation in "Easter 1916" that the poet's role in such matters is chiefly "To murmur name upon name"—the form of the elegy provides Heaney with a way of writing about the pressing political and social realities of his native Ulster while maintaining the aesthetic distance from outright advocacy that he sees as necessary for the poet. This need for poetic independence is itself the theme of several of the elegies in *Field Work.* In perhaps the most moving of them, "Casualty," Heaney identifies his poetic self with a Catholic fisherman named Louis O'Neill, who was killed when he violated a curfew in Belfast. The curfew was imposed by Catholics in mourning for thirteen men shot to death by British paratroopers; O'Neill was killed, in other words, not

SEAMUS HEANEY

because of any political actions on his part but because he ignored restrictions placed on his individual freedom in the name of political necessity—placed there by his own "side" in the conflict.

Heaney's admiration for the fisherman rests on O'Neill's willingness to follow his own instincts, but characteristically, when he describes the scene of O'Neill's death, he asks a question that clearly interrogates his own instincts to steer clear of political advocacy in his art: "How culpable was he / That last night when he broke / Our tribe's complicity?" Nonetheless, Heaney insists that the poet must aim for some point beyond the day-to-day conflict. At the end of the poem, the scene of O'Neill's funeral dissolves into a memory of a fishing expedition that Heaney and O'Neill once took together, a memory in which Heaney both defines his essentially Romantic aesthetics (the poet, like the fisherman, hauls "off the bottom" and must surrender to rhythms and feelings that are "working you"), and affirms his faith in the need for the poet to follow his instincts "well out" and "beyond" the press of daily events:

> I missed his funeral,
> Those quiet walkers
> And sideways talkers
> Shoaling out of his lane
> To the respectable
> Purring of the hearse . . .
> They move in equal pace
> With the habitual
> Slow consolation
> Of a dawdling engine,
> The line lifted, hand
> Over fist, cold sunshine
> On the water, the land
> Banked under fog: that morning
> I was taken in his boat,
> The screw purling, turning
> Indolent fathoms white,
> I tasted freedom with him.
> To get out early, haul
> Steadily off the bottom,
> Dispraise the catch, and smile
> As you find a rhythm
> Working you, slow mile by mile,
> Into your proper haunt
> Somewhere, well out, beyond . . .

In the years before Robert Lowell's death in 1977, Lowell and Heaney became well acquainted, and when Lowell died, Heaney wrote an elegy for him in which Lowell becomes the vehicle for

Heaney's faith in the independence and integrity of art. From Heaney's point of view, he and Lowell had much in common; just as Heaney's writing had been inevitably shaped by the sectarian violence in Ulster, so Lowell had had to fashion his art in the context of the Vietnam War and a range of powerful political and social forces, some of which Heaney had observed during the year he spent at Berkeley at the beginning of the 1970's. "You drank America / like the heart's / iron vodka," Heaney says in "Elegy," but what he most admired about Lowell was his unwavering commitment, in the face of personal and public catastrophe, to "promulgating art's / deliberate, peremptory / love and arrogance."

If Kavanagh can be seen as an important influence in Heaney's early poems, Lowell strongly affected Heaney's work in the late 1970's and 1980's. That influence is most distinctly felt in the "Glanmore Sonnets," a sequence of ten poems in *Field Work* in which Heaney, taking Lowell's late sonnets as his model, defends his commitment to art, particularly to the new voice, something like Lowell's, that he is working to establish. The second sonnet, for example, drawing on the same kind of colloquial but compressed diction and rhythms observable in Lowell's sonnets, and written in the same autobiographical mode, describes this position:

> Then I landed in the hedge-school of Glanmore
> And from the backs of ditches hoped to raise
> A voice caught back off slug-horn and slow chanter
> That might continue, hold, dispel, appease:
> Vowels ploughed into other, opened ground,
> Each verse returning like the plough turned round.

By the time *Field Work* was published, the Wicklow experiment was over. Also, Heaney had lived through a decade in which his native Ulster was racked by sectarian violence—a situation that again and again had tested his commitment to being a poet. If the poems of *Field Work* may be taken as a reliable barometer, Heaney emerged from that test with a strengthened faith in his art; it is there in his elegy to Lowell, in the "Glanmore Sonnets," and, perhaps most movingly, in a poem titled "The Harvest Bow," set in the rural County Derry of his childhood. The poem opens with a description of Heaney's father tying a harvest bow from strands of straw, one of the local rituals that both defined a sense of place for Heaney and harkened back to a long tradition of lore and superstition, of magic and poetry:

> As you plaited the harvest bow
> You implicated the mellowed silence in you
> In wheat that does not rust
> But brightens as it tightens twist by twist
> Into a knowable corona,
> A throwaway love-knot of straw.

Like a poem or a story, the harvest bow opens a path for memory and imagination to travel. The middle of the poem recalls Heaney as a child out walking with his father, "You with a harvest bow in your lapel," a memory that leads to a final affirmation of a thoroughly Romantic faith in art's capacity to evoke the reality of the spirit, and thereby make something happen:

> *The end of art is peace*
> Could be the motto of this frail device
> That I have pinned up on our deal dresser—
> Like a drawn snare
> Slipped lately by the spirit of the corn
> Yet burnished by its passage, and still warm.

SWEENEY ASTRAY

THIS trust in art's authority, and the corresponding commitment to artistic independence, are major themes of Heaney's poetry in the 1980's. If the Tollund man or the Grabaulle man is the dominating figure in much of Heaney's work in the 1970's, in the following decade it is Mad Sweeney, the poet–hero of a Middle Irish romance and, for Heaney, a powerful symbol of poetic freedom. The story of Sweeney, which surfaced in Ireland in written form sometime between the thirteenth and sixteenth centuries, is one of rebellion against the establishment: Sweeney, a king, is put under a curse by a saint after preventing the construction of a church in his kingdom, and is transformed through the curse into a birdlike creature condemned to wander in exile and apparent madness. In his exile, Sweeney discovers that he has a gift for poetry, and much of the tale consists of the poems about Ireland that he writes in his wanderings.

This tale has been used by several modern Irish writers—most notably Flann O'Brien in his comic metafictional novel *At Swim-Two-Birds*—to explore the relationship between the artist and society. While he was living in Wicklow, Heaney worked on his translation of the story, publishing it in Ireland as *Sweeney Astray* in 1983. In his introduction he makes clear the ways in which, as a contemporary poet from Ulster living out of Ulster, he identifies with the figure of Mad Sweeney. "Insofar as Sweeney is also a figure of the artist," he says, "displaced, guilty, assuaging himself by his utterance, it is possible to read the work as an aspect of the quarrel between free creative imagination and the constraints of religious, political, and domestic obligation."

STATION ISLAND

THIS quarrel is at the center of Heaney's most important book of the 1980's, *Station Island*, arguably one of the most ambitious and accomplished collection of poems that he has published. The book is divided into three sections: a collection of various lyrics; a twelve-poem sequence entitled "Station Island" and based on a famous religious pilgrimage made by Irish Catholics; and a group of poems collected under the heading "Sweeney Redivivus" and spoken in the voice of a contemporary Sweeney. Several of the lyrics in the first section of the book explore the conflict between "free creative imagination" and the political obligations arising from the violence in Ulster, concluding with the same ambiguity and self-doubt that color much of Heaney's earlier work concerned with this question. In "Sandstone Keepsake," for example, Heaney depicts himself, in a clearly self-deprecating way, as inhabiting a world of illusion, alienated from social and political realities. The poem recalls an evening when he was out wading in an estuary across from a soldiers' camp:

> Anyhow, there I was with the wet red stone
> in my hand, staring across at the watch-towers
> from my free state of image and allusion,
> swooped on, then dropped by trained binoculars:
>
> a silhouette not worth bothering about,
> out for the evening in scarf and waders
> and not about to set times wrong or right,
> stooping along, one of the venerators.

An even less forgiving self-indictment occurs in the eighth section of "Station Island," describing an imagined encounter between Heaney, on his pilgrimage to Lough Derg, and the ghost of a cousin killed in the Ulster fighting and remembered earlier in a poem in *Field Work* titled "The Strand at Lough Beg." That poem opens with an epigraph taken from Dante's *Purgatorio,* and in "Station Island," Heaney turns this back on himself with a vengeance. The cousin tells him:

> You confused evasion and artistic tact.
> The Protestant who shot me through the head
> I accuse directly, but indirectly, you
> who now atone perhaps upon this bed
> for the way you whitewashed ugliness and drew
> the lovely blinds of the *Purgatorio*
> and saccharined my death with morning dew.

If Heaney seems in some ways to be atoning in "Station Island" for such poetic sins, on the whole this dream version of the actual pilgrimage that Irish Catholics have been making to Lough Derg for centuries to atone for their sins describes a renewed and strengthened faith in his art, and in his commitment to maintaining the aesthetic distance that he sees as necessary to it. On his imagined pilgrimage, Heaney meets a series of ghosts from his past and from the tradition of Irish literature— among others, a man named Simon Sweeney from his childhood (another version of Mad Sweeney), the Irish novelist William Carleton (whose "Lough Derg Pilgrim" is a centerpiece of nineteenth-century satire on Catholic superstition), Patrick Kavanagh, and James Joyce. Most of them advise him to steer clear of what Joyce's Stephen Dedalus describes as the nets of nationality, language, and religion. "Stay clear of all processions!" old Simon Sweeney tells Heaney just as he feels himself being swept up in the crowd of pilgrims heading for Lough Derg (section 1). Carleton, authorized by his own Sweeney-like rebellion against conventionality—both in his life and in his art—reminds Heaney that, for the artist, all experience must be seen as secondary; looking around at the pilgrims, he says, "All this is like a trout kept in a spring / or maggots sewn in wounds— / another life that cleans our element" (section 2).

Appropriately enough, it is Joyce—the exile who rebelled against nationality, language, and religion and then spent his life writing about them from a distance—who gets the last word in "Station Island." He begins by telling Heaney that "Your obligation / is not discharged by any common rite."

"That subject people stuff is," in Joyce's view, "a cod's game, / infantile, like your peasant pilgrimage." His final piece of advice—and the last voice that Heaney hears in "Station Island"—blends Joycean references to signatures and circles with Heaney's archaeological imagery of soundings, searches, and probes to make a powerful appeal for the kind of artistic authority and independence that, for Heaney and many other modern writers, Joyce is a model of:

> You lose more of yourself than you redeem
> doing the decent thing. Keep at a tangent.
> When they make the circle wide, it's time to swim
>
> out on your own and fill the element
> with signatures on your own frequency,
> echo soundings, searches, probes, allurements,
>
> elver-gleams in the dark of the whole sea.
>   (section 12)

That Heaney was listening to these voices, especially Joyce's, is evident in the "Sweeney Redivivus" section of *Station Island.* In a strikingly postmodern gesture, Heaney produces in these poems still another version of the Sweeney story that he translated and published as *Sweeney Astray,* this time written in the idiom of contemporary speech, and with Sweeney and Heaney more obviously, and sometimes quite overtly, merged into one figure of the contemporary poet. In "The First Flight," the reborn Sweeney unambiguously pictures himself as having escaped those Joycean nets that Heaney sees as threatening to the poet's independence and integrity, and he does so in terms that obviously invoke Heaney's situation as an Ulster-born poet confronted with the conflict in Northern Ireland:

> I was mired in attachment
> until they began to pronounce me
> a feeder off battlefields
>
> so I mastered new rungs of the air
> to survey out of reach
> their bonfires on hills, their hosting
>
> and fasting, the levies from Scotland
> as always, and the people of art
> diverting their rhythmical chants
>
> to fend off the onslaught of winds
> I would welcome and climb
> at the top of my bent.

"The Cleric" retells the story of Mad Sweeney's reaction to the saint's attempts to build a church in his kingdom but, again, its language and implications are distinctly contemporary:

> If he had stuck to his own
> cramp-jawed abbesses and intoners
> dibbling round the enclosure,
>
> his Latin and blather of love,
> his parchments and scheming
> in letters shipped over water—
>
> but no, he overbore
> with his unctions and orders,
> he had to get in on the ground.

Heaney's attitudes toward the Irish Catholicism of his upbringing are considerably more moderate than Sweeney's are here—he once said in an interview, "I've never felt any need to rebel or do a casting-off of God or anything like that"—but at the end of this poem, Sweeney and Heaney merge completely again, this time in an assertion of how the poet may achieve independence through confrontation with opposition, with those forces of "religious, political, and domestic obligation" that seem so powerfully ranged against his art. Sweeney here argues that even though it may seem that he has lost his battle with the saint, it was the struggle that enabled him to see the importance of his ultimate commitment to poetic freedom:

> History that planted its standards
> on his gables and spires
> ousted me to the marches
>
> of skulking and whingeing.
> Or did I desert?
> Give him his due, in the end
>
> he opened my path to a kingdom
> of such scope and neuter allegiance
> my emptiness reigns at its whim.

If this is Mad Sweeney recrowned as poet rather than political ruler, it is also Heaney crowned as a contemporary Irish poet, an artist of "neuter allegiance" who reigns by virtue of his "emptiness," his refusal to permit the political demands of the moment to control his art. And if there is a Yeatsian swell to the last line, it is one to which Heaney has, by this time in his career, earned every right.

Given Heaney's views on the precarious status and nature of art, that version of the poet as ruler, however high it may ride on the winds of Yeatsian self-confidence, cannot reign without qualification. *Station Island* does not end with it; the book instead concludes with the decidedly less ebullient image of the poet searching for inspiration, waiting for the spirit to "raise a dust / in the font of exhaustion" ("On the Road").

THE HAW LANTERN

AND it is that image which characterizes much of the atmosphere of *The Haw Lantern* (1987). Heaney was forty-eight when this book was published, and many of the poems in it are clearly the work of someone who has, in his life and art, been increasingly forced to confront loss. At the center of the book—in much the same way the "Glanmore Sonnets" are at the center of *Field Work*—is a sequence of sonnets titled "Clearances," written in response to the death of Heaney's mother in 1984. These poems offer moving testimony to Heaney's relationship with his mother and to his grief at her passing, but they are also, in the self-reflexive manner of much of his writing, concerned with the relationship between his mother's death and his writing about his mother's death. More specifically, they have to do with the question of how art is able to convert absence into presence, to create an artificial reality out of the loss of an actual one. In the final poem of the sequence, Heaney gets at this question by recalling a chestnut tree that he had planted when he was a child and that has since been cut down. The loss of the tree—like the loss of his mother—leaves a real vacuum, but in the hands of the artist that absence is made palpable, and the poem seeks to provide access to a spiritual reality made possible by a physical loss. What is empty is also, for the artist, "utterly a source":

> I thought of walking round and round a space
> Utterly empty, utterly a source
> Where the decked chestnut tree had lost its place
> In our front hedge above the wallflowers.
> . . .
> Deep planted and long gone, my coeval
> Chestnut from a jam jar in a hole,
> Its heft and hush become a bright nowhere,
> A soul ramifying and forever
> Silent, beyond silence listened for.

Poems like this clearly break new ground for Heaney, whose work tends to be deeply rooted in actual landscapes. In the essay "The Placeless Heaven: Another Look at Kavanagh," Heaney describes this new concern with the poetic evocation of the spiritual by comparing the early, realistic rural poems of Patrick Kavanagh with the spiritually inclined verse that Kavanagh, after recovering from what was thought to be a terminal illness, wrote late in his career. Heaney specifically talks about the image of the chestnut tree in the final sonnet of "Clearances":

> . . . all of a sudden, a couple of years ago, I began to think of the space where the tree had been or would have been. In my mind's eye I saw it as a kind of luminous emptiness, a warp and waver of light, and once again, in a way that I find hard to define, I began to identify with that space just as years before I had identified with the young tree.
>
> Except that this time it was not so much a matter of attaching oneself to a living symbol of being rooted in the native ground; it was more a matter of preparing to be unrooted, to be spirited away into some transparent, yet indigenous afterlife. The new place was all idea, if you like; it was generated out of my experience of the old place but it was not a topographical location. It was and remains an imagined realm, even if it can be located at an earthly spot, a placeless heaven rather than a heavenly place.
>
> (*Government*, pp. 3–4)

This is a richly Romantic passage, one showing that Wordsworth's importance for Heaney has become, if anything, even greater in his later work than it was in his earlier. In a poem titled "Hailstones," Heaney uses a distinctly Wordsworthian moment, or "spot of time," to evoke the idea of this placeless heaven that he sees as the rightful province of the poet. This poem, an important one for tracking recent changes in Heaney's poetics, opens with a striking metaphor for the notion of art as a process that is constantly consuming the experience on which it builds, constantly creating an absence by transforming the terms of experience into the terms of art:

> I made a small hard ball
> of burning water running from my hand
>
> just as I make this now
> out of the melt of the real thing
> smarting into its absence.

The poem concludes with a decidedly Romantic memory of a prophetic moment just after the end of a hail shower, a moment through which Heaney insists on art's capacity to create beauty and perfection out of the bleakly ordinary and transient:

> . . . there you had
> the truest foretaste of your aftermath—
> in that dilation
>
> when the light opened in silence
> and a car with wipers going still
> laid perfect tracks in the slush.

Much of *The Haw Lantern* is concerned with how art makes perfect tracks in the slush of experience, and an important part of that experience for Heaney is the political situation in contemporary Northern Ireland. In "From the Frontier of Writing," Heaney focuses on the process of artistic creation—in this case an experience connected to the Ulster violence—and he insists on the value of that process. In a postmodern gesture, the poem provides two versions of the same event: being stopped by soldiers at a roadblock. The first, supposedly the immediate, realistic account before the event is filtered through memory and imagination, underscores the feeling of emptiness or absence that the experience engendered:

> and everything is pure interrogation
> until a rifle motions and you move
> with guarded unconcerned acceleration—
>
> a little emptier, a little spent
> as always by that quiver in the self,
> subjugated, yes, and obedient.

In the second version of the incident, that loss is converted into gain through the power of the imagination to remake reality ("So you drive on to the frontier of writing / where it happens again"). The result is not subjugation but a kind of freedom:

> And suddenly you're through, arraigned yet freed,
> as if you'd passed from behind a waterfall
> on the black current of a tarmac road
>
> past armour-plated vehicles, out between
> the posted soldiers flowing and receding
> like tree shadows into the polished windscreen.

Art's ability to re-create experience is also investigated in *The Haw Lantern* through an exploration of allegory, fantasy, and parable. Even a listing of some of the titles in this volume indicates this interest in the wide variety of transforming forms that the artist has to hand: "Parable Island," "From the Republic of Conscience," "From the Land of the Unspoken," "The Song of the Bullets," "From the Canton of Expectation," "The Mud Vision," "The Riddle." In a number of these poems, Heaney specifically examines the political realities of contemporary Ireland through these deliberately distorting lenses (from "The Land of the Unspoken": "We are a dispersed people whose history / is a sensation of opaque fidelity"; from "Parable Island": "Although they are an occupied nation / and their only border is an inland one / they yield to nobody in their belief / that the country is an island"). "The Mud Vision," a characteristically self-doubting poem, questions whether the visionary power of poetry can have much effect on the real world. In this poem, Heaney imagines the routine of contemporary life in Ireland disrupted by the sudden appearance of a vision, "as if a rose window of mud / Had invented itself out of the glittery damp, / . . . sullied yet lucent." This symbol of spiritual possibility, or at least of radical societal reformation, is never understood, however; and when it fades, it leaves behind nothing but ignorance:

One day it was gone and the east gable
Where its trembling corolla had balanced
Was starkly a ruin again, with dandelions
Blowing high up on the ledges, and moss
That slumbered on through its increase. As cameras
    raked
The site from every angle, experts
Began their *post factum* jabber and all of us
Crowded in tight for the big explanations.
Just like that, we forgot that the vision was ours,
Our one chance to know the incomparable
And dive to a future. What might have been origin
We dissipated in news. The clarified place
Had retrieved neither us nor itself . . .

For Heaney, it seems, there must always be some nagging doubts about the worth of those clarified places that his art makes. At the very least, he is too much a postmodern poet not to be constantly scrutinizing himself and his work, constantly worrying about whether, in the end, poetry can make anything happen. In the title poem of *The Haw Lantern*, Heaney settles on a somewhat unlikely image to convey this postmodern need for the artist to monitor himself tirelessly; the poem describes the hawthorn berry as taking the form of Diogenes and his lantern, ever on the search for "one just man." It is a passage that says much about Heaney's own efforts to be both a poet and a just man:

But sometimes when your breath plumes in the frost
it takes the roaming shape of Diogenes
with his lantern, seeking one just man;
so you end up scrutinized from behind the haw
he holds up at eye-level on its twig,
and you flinch before its bonded pith and stone,
its blood-prick that you wish would test and clear
    you,
its pecked-at ripeness that scans you, then moves on.

Given who he is and the world in which he lives, it seems unlikely that Heaney can ever finally be tested and cleared. At the heart of his poetry is both a faith in the efficacy of his art and the need for constant reexamination of that faith. And if this is a process that seems to have no end, it is also one that perhaps identifies the position of the poet in contemporary society. Moreover, there is certainly much to admire in the candor and courage with which Heaney puts himself through the process, and in his unwavering if never wholly unqualified belief that poetry can make something happen, even if that something is not always immediately clear, not always even visible.

SELECTED BIBLIOGRAPHY

I. COLLECTED WORKS. *Selected Poems: 1965–1975* (London, 1980), reprinted as *Poems: 1965–1975* (New York, 1980); *Preoccupations: Selected Prose 1968–1978* (London and New York, 1980); *The Government of the Tongue: The 1986 T.S. Eliot Memorial Lectures and Other Critical Writings* (London, 1988; New York, 1989); *Selected Poems: 1966–1987* (London and New York, 1990).

II. SEPARATE WORKS. *Death of a Naturalist* (London and New York, 1966); *Door into the Dark* (London and New York, 1969); *Wintering Out* (London, 1972; New York, 1973); *Stations* (Belfast, 1975), a sequence of prose poems; *North* (London, 1975; New York, 1976); *Field Work* (London and New York, 1979); *Sweeney Astray* (London and

New York, 1984); *Station Island* (London, 1984; New York, 1985); *The Haw Lantern* (London and New York, 1987).

III. EDITED WORKS, INTRODUCTIONS, AND ANTHOLOGIES. *Soundings: An Annual Anthology of New Irish Poetry,* edited by Heaney (Belfast, 1972); *Soundings II,* edited by Heaney (Belfast, 1974); M. MacLaverty, *Collected Short Stories,* introduction by Heaney (Dublin, 1978); *The Rattle Bag: An Anthology of Poetry,* edited by Heaney and T. Hughes (London, 1982); *The Essential Wordsworth,* edited by Heaney (New York, 1988).

IV. UNCOLLECTED ESSAYS AND REVIEWS. "Out of London: Ulster's Troubles," in *New Statesman* (1 July 1966); "Old Derry's Walls," in *The Listener* (24 October 1968); "Celtic Fringe, Viking Fringe," in *The Listener* (21 August 1969); "Delirium of the Brave," in *The Listener* (27 November 1969).

"King of the Dark," in *The Listener* (5 February 1970); "King Conchobar and His Knights," in *The Listener* (26 March 1970); "Views," in *The Listener* (31 December 1970), essay on living in Berkeley; "Seamus Heaney Praises Lough Erne," in *The Listener* (4 February 1971); "A Poet's Childhood," in *The Listener* (11 November 1971); "The Trade of an Irish Poet," in *The Guardian* (25 May 1972); "Deep as England," in *Hibernia* (1 December 1972); "Mother Ireland," in *The Listener* (7 December 1972); "Lost Ulsterman," in *The Listener* (26 April 1973); "Land-Locked," in *Irish Press* (1 June 1974); "Summoning Lazarus," in *The Listener* (6 June 1974); "John Bull's Other Island," in *The Listener* (29 September 1977).

"Treely and Rurally," in *Quarto,* 9 (August 1980); "English and Irish," in *The Times Literary Supplement* (24 October 1980); "On Current Unstated Assumptions About Poetry," in *Critical Inquiry* (Summer 1981); "Envies and Identifications: Dante and the Modern Poet," in *Irish University Review,* 15 (Spring 1985); "'Place and Displacement': Recent Poetry from Northern Ireland," in *The Wordsworth Circle,* 16 (Spring 1985); "Place, Pastness, Poems: A Triptych," in *Salmagundi,* no. 68–69 (Fall–Winter 1985–1986); "The Glamour of Craig Raine," in *Ploughshares,* 13, no. 4 (1987); "The Pre-Natal Mountain: Vision and Irony in Recent Irish Poetry," in *The Georgia Review,* 42 (Fall 1988).

V. INTERVIEWS. "Poets on Poetry," in *The Listener* (8 November 1973); H. Cooke, "Interview," in *The Irish Times* (28 December 1973); C. Walsh, "The Saturday Interview," in *The Irish Times* (6 December 1975); "Interview," in M. Begley, *Rambles in Ireland* (Old Greenwich, Conn., 1977); S. Deane, "Unhappy and at Home," in *The Crane Bag,* 1, no. 1 (1977); J. Randall, "An Interview with Seamus Heaney," in *Ploughshares,* 5, no. 3 (1979); R. Druce, "Raindrops on a Thorn: Interview with Seamus Heaney," in *Dutch Quarterly Review of Anglo–American Letters,* 9, no. 1 (1979); J. Silverlight, "Brooding Images," in *The Observer* (11 November 1979); S. Deane, "Talk with Seamus Heaney," in *The New York Times Book Review* (2 December 1979).

J. Haffenden, "Seamus Heaney," in *Viewpoints: Poets in Conversation* (London, 1981); F. Kinahan, "An Interview with Seamus Heaney," in *Critical Inquiry,* 8 (Spring 1982); "An Interview with Seamus Heaney," in *An Gael,* 3, no. 1 (1985); J. Beisch, "An Interview with Seamus Heaney," in *The Literary Review: An International Journal of Contemporary Writing* (Fairleigh Dickinson University), 29, no. 2 (1986).

VI. CRITICAL STUDIES. R. Buttel, *Seamus Heaney* (Lewisburg, Pa., 1975); T. Curtis, ed., *The Art of Seamus Heaney* (Bridgend, Wales, 1982); B. Morrison, *Seamus Heaney* (London and New York, 1982); D. Annwn, *Inhabited Voices: Myth and History in the Poetry of Geoffrey Hill, Seamus Heaney and George Mackay Brown* (Frome, U.K., 1984); D. Johnston, *Irish Poetry After Joyce* (Notre Dame, Ind., and Mountrath, Ireland, 1985), contains chapter on Kavanagh and Heaney; H. Bloom, ed., *Modern Critical Views: Seamus Heaney* (New Haven, 1986); N. Corcoran, *Seamus Heaney* (London and Boston, 1986); R. F. Garratt, *Modern Irish Poetry: Tradition and Continuity from Yeats to Heaney* (Berkeley and Los Angeles, 1986); J. Genet, comp., *Studies on Seamus Heaney* (Caen, France, 1987); T. Foster, *Seamus Heaney* (Boston, 1989); R. Tamplin, *Seamus Heaney* (Milton Keynes, U.K., and Philadelphia, 1989); S. Burris, *The Poetry of Resistance: Seamus Heaney and the Pastoral Tradition* (Columbus, Ohio, 1990).

T. E. LAWRENCE

(1888–1935)

Stanley Weintraub

THOMAS EDWARD LAWRENCE, archaeologist and scholar turned war hero (as "Lawrence of Arabia"), became a legend even before the publication, in 1926, of his memoir *Seven Pillars of Wisdom,* one of the few modern epics in the English language.

Although it is Lawrence as myth and enigma who continues to provoke interest in the man and his work, his accomplishments alone inspire awe. More than a military leader, more than an inspirational force behind the Arab revolt against the Turks, he was a superb tactician and highly influential theoretician of guerrilla warfare. His *Seven Pillars of Wisdom* is stylistically self-conscious yet masterful, unique in its time. His sharply etched service chronicle, *The Mint* (1955), and his mannered prose translation of the *Odyssey* (1932) have added to a literary reputation further substantiated by the immense and fascinating correspondence that establishes him as one of the major letter writers of his day.

Lawrence was not his legitimate name. He once wryly told a friend that his *Odyssey* might well have been called "Chapman's Homer," for he was born in Wales (at Tremadoc, Caernarvonshire) on 15 August 1888, the illegitimate child of Sir Thomas Chapman and Sarah Junner, who was herself illegitimate. (According to some sources, he was actually born in the early hours of 16 August.) Junner had been the governess of Sir Thomas' daughters at Westmeath, and Chapman had fled with her from both marriage and Ireland. As "Mr. and Mrs. Lawrence," the couple had five sons (Thomas Edward was the second) during what was outwardly a marriage with all the benefits of clergy. In 1896 the family settled in Oxford, where T. E. (he preferred the initials to the names) attended the City of Oxford High School and later Jesus College. Medieval military architecture was his first interest, and he pursued the subject in its historical settings, studying crusader castles in France and, in 1909, in Syria and Palestine, submitting a thesis on the subject that won him first-class honors in history in 1910.

"The thesis was not for publication," Lawrence wrote Major Archibald Becke in 1929, "& I have no idea what happened to it; I lent it to Lord Curzon about 1919; and don't remember it since (except for a half-notion that he gave it me back & I burned it: but I don't remember this well enough to swear to it. It was only a thesis—a first study. Not worth printing): a typescript, it was, with plans & photos" (*T. E. Lawrence: The Selected Letters,* 1988, p. 435). *Crusader Castles* was published posthumously in 1936 by the Golden Cockerel Press in two volumes. The first volume contains the thesis submitted to Jesus College: "The Influence of the Crusades on European Military Architecture to the End of the 12th Century." The second includes selected letters written by Lawrence while on visits to crusader castles in France, England, Wales, and Syria in search of data.

Lawrence's first months after graduation were spent in desultory archaeological study in the British Museum and among the antiquities in Oxford's Ashmolean Museum. Toward the end of the year, he was awarded a postgraduate demyship (scholarship) from Magdalen College and joined an Oxford expedition to Jerablus (in today's northern Syria) to assist in the excavation of the great Hittite mounds at Carchemish, on the Euphrates. For most of the next three years the site of the dig was his headquarters. Between excavations he went off—dressed in the manner of the Arab workmen employed on the dig—on solitary walking tours, acquiring scant information and considerable fever and dysentery.

One of the sites to which he was directed in northern Syria led to what was—aside from a letter to the editor—his first publication, "The Kaer of Ibu Wardani," which appeared in the first volume of the *Jesus College Magazine,* in January 1913, under the initials "C. J. G." (From the very start Lawrence wrote under pseudonyms.) Although the Arabs believed the Kaer was built by an Eastern prince as a desert palace for his queen, Lawrence reported it was a ruin of the Roman period. Its gaping emptiness emphasized the harshness of the desert to Lawrence, who later adapted the piece to other uses in *Seven Pillars of Wisdom,* where the ruin emphasizes the forced simplicity of bedouin life (ch. 3).

Working from 1911 to 1914, first under Oxford archaeologist David G. Hogarth and then under Sir Leonard Woolley, Lawrence used his free time to travel on his own and get to know the language and the people. Early in 1914 he, Woolley, and Captain S. F. Newcombe explored northern Sinai, on the Turkish frontier east of Suez. Supposedly a scientific expedition, and in fact sponsored by the Palestine Exploration Fund, it was more a mapmaking reconnaissance from Gaza to Aqaba, destined to be of almost immediate strategic value. The cover study was nevertheless of authentic scholarly significance; written by Lawrence and Woolley together, it was published as *The Wilderness of Zin* in 1914.

Woolley was a prolific writer on archaeological subjects for years; the text does not separate the contributions of the collaborators, but parts of the book have the ring of the dramatic descriptive prose of Lawrence's letters home and of his *Crusader Castles* (the following is quoted in *The Essential T. E. Lawrence,* 1951):

The way down [the pass of Aqaba] is very splendid. In the hill-sides all sorts of rocks are mingled in confusion; grey-green limestone cliffs run down sheer for hundreds of feet, in tremendous ravines whose faces are a medley of colours wherever crags of black porphyry and diorite jut out, or where soft sandstone, washed down, has left long pink and red smudges on the lighter colours. The confusion of materials makes the road-laying curiously uneven. The surface is in very few cases made up; wherever possible the road was cut to rock, with little labour, since the stone is always brittle and in thin, flat layers. So the masons had at once ready to their hand masses of squared blocks for parapets or retaining walls. Yet this same facility of the stone has been disastrous to the abandoned road, since the rains of a few seasons chisel the softer parts into an irregular giant staircase; while in the limestone the torrent has taken the road-cutting as

a convenient course, and left it deep buried under a sliding mass of water-worn pebbles.

(p. 62)

Lawrence returned to England the month World War I began. His new role as a civilian employee of the War Office in London, charged with preparing a militarily useful map of the Sinai Peninsula, was brief. Soon he was in uniform.

SERVICE IN THE GREAT WAR

By December 1914, Lawrence was a lieutenant in Cairo. Experts on Arab affairs—especially those who had traveled in the Turkish-held Arab lands—were rare, and he was assigned to intelligence, where he spent more than a year, mostly interviewing prisoners, drawing maps, receiving and processing data from agents behind enemy lines, and producing a handbook on the Turkish Army. In mid 1915, however, his brothers Will and Frank were killed in action in France, and Lawrence was cruelly reminded of the "real" front in the west.

Egypt at the time was the staging area for Middle Eastern military operations of prodigious inefficiency—a sideshow of wasteful desert campaigns and a bloody, bungled frontal assault on the Dardanelles at Gallipoli. A trip to Arabia convinced Lawrence of an alternative method of undermining Germany's Turkish ally. In October 1916 he accompanied the diplomat Sir Ronald Storrs on a mission to Arabia, where Ḥusayn ibn 'Ali, emir of Mecca, had the previous June proclaimed a revolt against the Turks. Storrs and Lawrence consulted with Husayn's son Abdullah, and Lawrence received permission to go on to consult further with another son, Faisal, then commanding an Arab force southwest of Medina. Back in Cairo in November, Lawrence urged his superiors to abet the efforts at rebellion with arms and gold and to make use of the dissident sheikhs by meshing their aspirations for independence with Anglo-French military goals.

In their predicament, strategy planners were willing to listen to the young officer in Cairo then occupied in editing and writing a secret intelligence periodical, the *Arab Bulletin,* meant to keep British diplomats and military commands throughout the

Middle East informed about developments within Arab lands controlled by the Germans and Turks. Lawrence rejoined Faisal's army as political and liaison officer.

Lawrence was not the only officer to become involved in the incipient Arab rising, but from his own small corner of the Arabian Peninsula he quickly became—especially in his own accounts—its brains, its organizing force, its liaison with Cairo, and its military technician. His small but irritating second front behind the Turkish lines was a hit-and-run guerrilla operation, focusing upon the mining of bridges and supply trains and the appearance of Arab units first in one place and then another, pinning down enemy forces that otherwise would have been deployed elsewhere, and keeping the Damascus-to-Medina railway largely inoperable, with potential Turkish reinforcements thus helpless to crush the uprising. In such fashion Lawrence—"Emir Dynamite" to the admiring bedouins—committed the cynical, self-serving sheikhs for the moment to his kingmaker's vision of an Arab nation, goaded them with examples of his own self-punishing personal valor when their spirits flagged, and bribed them with promises of enemy booty and English gold sovereigns.

Aqaba, at the northernmost tip of the Red Sea, was the first major victory, seized after a two-month march on 6 July 1917. After that, Lawrence attempted to coordinate Arab movements with the campaign of General Edmund Allenby, who was advancing toward Jerusalem, a tactic only partly successful. In November, Lawrence was captured at Deraa by the Turks while reconnoitering the area in Arab dress and was homosexually brutalized before he was able to escape. The experience, variously reported or disguised by him afterward, left physical scars as well as wounds upon his psyche from which he never recovered. The next month, nevertheless, he took part in the victory parade in Jerusalem and then returned to increasingly successful actions in which Faisal's forces inched their way north, and Lawrence was promoted to the rank of lieutenant colonel and awarded the Distinguished Service Order (DSO).

By the time the motley Arab army reached Damascus in October 1918, Lawrence was physically and emotionally exhausted, having forced body and spirit to the breaking point too often. He had been wounded numerous times, captured, and tortured; had endured extremities of hunger, weather,

and disease; had been driven by military necessity to commit atrocities upon the enemy and even murder his own wounded to prevent the Turks from doing worse; and had witnessed in the chaos of Damascus the defeat of his aspirations for the Arabs in the very moment of their triumph, their seemingly incurable factionalism rendering them incapable of uniting as a nation. (Anglo-French duplicity, Lawrence discovered, had already officially betrayed them in a cynical wartime division of expected spoils: the Sykes–Picot Agreement of 1916 divided the Ottoman Empire between Britain and France.)

Disillusioned and distinguished, Lawrence left for home just before the Armistice and politely refused, at a royal audience on 30 October 1918, the Companion of the Bath and the DSO, leaving the shocked King George V (in his words) "holding the box in my hand."[1] He was demobilized as a lieutenant colonel on 31 July 1919, afterward calling his end-of-war status as a colonel (which expedited travel from Cairo to London) "temporary" and "acting."

EARLY POSTWAR WRITINGS

A colonel at thirty, Lawrence was a private at thirty-four. Before this voluntary demotion, he lobbied vainly for Arab independence at the Paris Peace Conference in 1919, even appearing in Arab robes; later in the same year he survived the crash of a Handley-Page bomber at Rome in which his shoulder blade was fractured. Meanwhile, he worked on *Seven Pillars of Wisdom,* his epic memoir of Arabia, acquiring for the purpose an All Souls College fellowship at Oxford; and all the while—beginning in London in August 1919—he was being transformed into a living legend by American journalist Lowell Thomas' long-running illustrated lecture, "With Allenby in Palestine and Lawrence in Arabia" (which Lawrence enjoyed going to see unobserved).

In March 1921, Lawrence was wooed back to the

---

[1]This quotation comes from a 1961 interview with Sir Basil Liddell Hart. Its substance is confirmed by Churchill in *Great Contemporaries,* 1937; Aldington in *Lawrence of Arabia: A Biographical Enquiry,* 1955; and Knightley and Simpson in *The Secret Lives of Lawrence of Arabia,* 1969. (See bibliography.)

Middle East as Colonial Minister Winston Churchill's adviser, redeeming where he could the idealistic wartime promises he had made. But the poetic ideal had splintered. Rather than an Arab nation, there were groupings of historically hostile tribes. And the Arabian lands had been divided into politically exigent states. One—the Palestine mandate—Lawrence helped split into Palestine and a Transjordanian Hashemite monarchy. The crazy lines that divided the postwar Middle East for the most part parceled out spheres of influence to various European powers and divided feuding Arab factions from one another. Reflecting upon either motive could not have made him happy with what he had helped bring about.

Lawrence had already written voluminous notes on his role and at least two versions of a war memoir based upon them, in which he expounded not only his dream for that troubled part of the world but his tribulations with the Arabs whom he had once loved as brothers. He had written not only of their loyalty, courage, and hardihood but, in disillusion, of their tribal feuds and treachery, which often destroyed his carefully laid plans. And he had described, in sorrow, the times when those on whom he had counted most would flee at the first sound of heavy artillery or desert their own cause when not bribed with British gold or enemy booty. Still, he had done what he could, and he bathed his accounts in a romantic nostalgia that sometimes turned the desert tribesmen into knights and princes of a near-medieval epic.

After the Cairo political settlements, Churchill asked Lawrence to remain in the Colonial Ministry, but Lawrence wanted no part of high government office and had already chosen a course opposite in the extreme. In August 1922, as "John Hume Ross," he enlisted in the Royal Air Force (RAF). By then he had completed the rough printing—on an Oxford newspaper press—of eight double-columned copies of his memoir—the first printed version of *Seven Pillars of Wisdom*. The biblical title came from the Book of Proverbs (9:1)—"Wisdom hath builded a house: she hath hewn out her seven pillars"—and had little relationship to the subject matter of Lawrence's book-in-progress other than a sentimental association with the same part of the world. He had intended using the title for an earlier work that he afterward curiously described as an "imaginary book on C P Cairo Smyrna Aleppo Jerusalem Urfa and Damascus, destroyed by T. E. S. in August 1914."[2]

The original *Seven Pillars* remains a mysterious work, but it was not an ex post facto invention of Lawrence's, meant to feed a myth about himself. "You will see, I think," he had written home in 1911 about a projected private press, "that printing is not a business but a craft. . . . And besides such a scheme would be almost sure to interrupt *The Seven Pillars of Wisdom* or my monumental book on the Crusades" (*The Selected Letters,* 1988, p. 29). A year later, clearly in response to a query from home about his writing, he explained (in a letter collected in *The Home Letters of T. E. Lawrence and His Brothers,* 1954):

I am not trying to rival Doughty. You remember that passage that he who has once seen palm-trees and the goat-hair tents is never the same as he had been: that I feel very strongly, and I feel also that Doughty's two years wandering in untainted places made him the man he is, more than all his careful preparations before & since. My books would be the better, if I had been for a time in open country: and the Arab life is the only one that still holds the early poetry which is the easiest to read.

(11 May 1912, p. 207)

Thus there *was* a book, "a youthful indiscretion book," he called it later. "It recounted adventures in seven type-cities of the East (Cairo, Bagdad, Damascus, etc.) and arranged their characters into a descending cadence: a moral symphony. It was a queer book, upon whose difficulties I look back with a not ungrateful wryness: and in memory of it I so named the new book" (*The Letters of T. E. Lawrence,* 1938, p. 451). He burned the manuscript, he said, the month the war began.

Even early in the war it was obvious that Lawrence had a compulsion to write, although his military channels necessarily had to be nonliterary ones. Aside from his *Arab Bulletin* papers he kept a scrappy journal and produced several lengthy political and military essays meant for official eyes (collected in *The Secret Lives of Lawrence of Arabia,* 1969). One, "The Politics of Mecca," written in January 1916, and meant for General Staff Intelli-

---

[2]"History of Seven Pillars," 1927, manuscript in the Harry Ransom Humanities Research Center, Austin, Tex.

gence in Cairo, stressed the instability of the Arabs as a potential nation and suggested shrewdly the value of such an insight to English power in the area. Yet even here he could not resist compelling literary touches. "If properly handled," he predicted of the Arabs, "they would remain in a state of political mosaic, a tissue of small jealous principalities incapable of cohesion" (pp. 58–59). Soon afterward he wrote a long memorandum entitled "The Conquest of Syria: If Complete," setting out the politics and tactics he proposed for the Arab revolt and which he carefully followed himself— and persuaded the Arabs to follow—as soon as he had the opportunity. Again it was a document with a wit and irony unusual in staff papers.

Equally dry and candid was his "Twenty-Seven Articles," a manual for political officers on how to manipulate Arabs that Lawrence wrote in August 1917, after nearly a year in the field with Faisal's army. "Handling Hejaz Arabs," he warned in a preface, "is an art, not a science" (p. 69). By the time Lawrence had worked over his successive manuscripts of the postwar *Seven Pillars* he was able to describe how his theories had worked in actual practice. He had followed them himself.

SEVEN PILLARS OF WISDOM

"Since eight copies were required, and the book was very large," Lawrence noted in the preface, "printing was preferred to typewriting." The Oxford substitute for a typewritten text with carbon copies was only an intermediate stage in a complicated development that would span a decade. Neither it nor the ultimate—and opulent—thirty-guinea subscription edition of 1926 was his first published chronicle of the Arab revolt, for as early as the month the war ended—his first weeks back in London—he had drawn on his service notes and his memories for a colorful and often wryly humorous account of the desert campaigns, published anonymously in the London *Times* in three parts on three days late in November of 1918 (reprinted in *Evolution of a Revolt, Early Postwar Writings of T. E. Lawrence*, 1968). He had just given testimony at a meeting of the Eastern Committee of the cabinet and clearly was using the influential *Times* to help mold opinion. The anonymity that was standard *Times*

practice was used to advantage by Lawrence who, still in uniform, was forbidden by army regulations to publish reports concerning his service without authorization. When he published two additional accounts in the *Times* in August 1920, it was again under the cloak of customary *Times* anonymity (also reprinted in *Evolution of a Revolt*).

By the time Lawrence's 1920 *Times* articles building up Faisal appeared, he had not only completed an elaborate version of *Seven Pillars* but had apparently written most of it twice. In a postscript to a letter to Charles Doughty written 25 November 1919, he confided, "I have lost the MSS of my own adventures in Arabia: it was stolen from me in the train" (*The Letters of T. E. Lawrence*, p. 296). The manuscript had been carried in a bag similar to those used by bank messengers and must have caused great disappointment to the purloiner at the railway station in Reading when he opened it. The nearly completed draft was never recovered, and Lawrence applied his already legendary energy and self-discipline to reconstruct (sometimes to invent) from his reports, notes, previously published articles—and memory—a new first draft.

There was no shortage of available personal documentary material. He had his two wartime diaries, although, as in most other modern conflicts before and since, there were futile service prohibitions against keeping a diary. From laconic entries he would later not only reconstruct the chronology of his movements but extrapolate vivid scenes. One such notation—"camel dead calf, suffering over skin"—referred to the death of the foal of Lawrence's Ghazala ("the old grandmother camel, now magnificently fit"). Frugally, his personal attendant, Abdullah, had skinned the carcass and carried the dry pelt behind his saddle, "like a crupper piece," until:

After an hour Ghazala lifted her head high, and began to pace uneasily, picking up her feet like a sword-dancer.

I tried to urge her: but Abdullah dashed alongside me, swept his cloak about him, and sprang from his saddle, calf's skin in hand. He lighted with a splash of gravel in front of Ghazala, who had come to a standstill, gently moaning. On the ground before her he spread the little hide, and drew her head down to it. She stopped crying, shuffled its dryness thrice with her lips; then again lifted her head and, with a whimper, strode forward. Several times in the day this happened; but afterwards she seemed to forget.

(p. 545)

Much of the new manuscript was written during weeks spent in an attic hermitage in Barton Street, Westminster, in space borrowed from his architect friend Sir Herbert Baker. Alone—and deliberately so—Lawrence forced himself into what might now be described as a "mind-expanding" state, exciting his imagination "with hunger and cold and sleeplessness," he thought, "more than did de Quincey with his opium." Explaining his method (but ignoring the considerable mass of preliminary material he had as foundation) he wrote, "I tie myself into knots trying to reenact everything, as I write it out. It's like writing in front of a looking-glass, and never looking at the paper, but always at the imaginary scene" (*Lawrence of Arabia: The Literary Impulse,* 1975, p. 20).

The 330,000 words—crowded into an accountant's ledger from Herbert Baker's office—were written in time taken from Lawrence's service with the Colonial Office in London and in the Middle East. The manuscript was begun (Lawrence noted in the ledger) on 1 September 1920 and completed on 9 May 1922. It was this rhetorically inflated text—slightly revised as it was set—which he had printed at the *Oxford Times* printing plant, beginning on 20 January 1922, even before he had completed the writing. On 24 June the last pages of his eight-copy edition came off the press. Three of the copies were afterward scissored up in the process of creating a final text.

The complex creative history of *Seven Pillars* was far from over when Lawrence lent his first copy to Rudyard Kipling and then to Bernard Shaw, for it was this Oxford text that Shaw and Lawrence pruned (about 13 percent of the text) and revised into the famous 127-copy Subscription Edition of 1926, and from which the 130,000-word abridgment *Revolt in the Desert* (1927) was taken.

Emotionally drained by the drafting of his memoir, he was willing to give up his £1,200 Colonial Office salary for the daily two shillings ninepence of a Royal Air Force aircraftman, not only to lose himself in the ranks but to acquire material for another book. He was successful only in the latter. The London press discovered him at the Farnborough base, the *Daily Express* breaking the story on 27 December. Embarrassed, the RAF released him early the next month.

Finding reinstatement impossible, Lawrence looked around for another service and through the intervention of a War Office friend who had served in the desert war, Sir Philip Chetwode, was able to enlist on 12 March 1923, as a private in the Royal Tank Corps, this time as T. E. Shaw, a name he claimed to have chosen at random, although one of the crucial events of his postwar life was his meeting in 1922, and subsequent close friendship with, Bernard and Charlotte Shaw. (In 1927 he assumed the new name legally.) Posted to Bovington Camp in Dorset, he acquired a cottage nearby, Clouds Hill, which remained his home thereafter.

From Dorset he set about arranging for publication of a definitive version of *Seven Pillars,* this one based upon editorial suggestions made by the friends among whom he circulated five copies of the Oxford text—notably Shaw, who suggested lowering the emotional pitch and blue-penciling the possibly libelous and politically questionable passages. (It may have been the puritan in Shaw that resulted, too, in excision of the most gamy passages about the homosexual behavior of the Arab troops when without women.) The famous Subscription Edition of 1926, sumptuously printed and bound and an instant rarity, was illustrated by notable artists such as William Rothenstein, Sir William Nicholson, and John Singer Sargent, commissioned by Lawrence.

Seven Pillars of Wisdom (a posthumous trade edition appeared in 1935, and several subsequent editions since) remains one of the few twentieth-century works in English to make epical figures out of contemporaries. Overpopulated by adjectives, often straining for effects and for "art," it is, nevertheless, an action-packed narrative, replete with incident and spectacle, filled with rich character portrayals and a tense introspection that bares the author's own complex mental and spiritual metamorphosis. Confessedly inexact and subjective, it combines the distance of heroic epic with the intimacy of autobiography.

However emotionally keyed up and graphically detailed, *Seven Pillars of Wisdom* has a mysterious ambiguity written into its most notorious event, continuously raising questions about Lawrence's sexual nature. It did not help that, elsewhere in the text, explicit—and largely sympathetic—analyses of rampant homosexuality in the Arab ranks, still included in earlier drafts that survive, were toned down or excised. But Lawrence's own essentially asexual nature emanates from his letters as it does from his other published writings.

"Unclean, unclean," he explained himself to E. M. Forster in a letter of 21 December 1927. Referring to a short story about a homosexual encounter that Forster had let Lawrence read in manuscript, T. E. responded, "I couldn't ever do it, I believe: the impulse strong enough to make me touch another creature has not yet been born in me" (*Selected Letters,* p. 360). But he *had* been touched. His only verifiable sexual experience came to him violently and perversely in the notorious episode he recounted dramatically but discreetly in chapter 80 of the Subscription Edition. Captured while on a spying mission, he was homosexually abused and beaten by Hajim, the bey of Deraa. Apparently unrecognized, he was then thrown into the street and painfully made his way back to friendly lines; but "the passing days confirmed . . . how in Deraa that night the citadel of my integrity had been irrevocably lost" (p. 447). That his self-deprivation of glory and self-punishment thereafter were reactions to feelings of humiliation and defilement would have been more clear to the few privileged readers of the Oxford narrative than to the still-few readers of the 1926 edition, for Lawrence dropped the most introspective passage about his own sexuality—the original last passage of the chapter, in which he had crept out of Deraa,

as though some part of me had gone dead that night . . . leaving me maimed, imperfect, only half myself. It could not have been the defilement, for no one ever held the body in less honour than I did myself. Probably it had been the breaking of the spirit by that frenzied, nerve-shattering pain which had degraded me to the beast level when it made me grovel to it, and which had journeyed with me since, a fascination and terror and morbid desire, lascivious and vicious perhaps, but like the striving of a moth toward its flame.

Carnality of any kind was repellent to Lawrence and had been so apparently since he had discovered as a boy that he had been illegitimately and sinfully conceived; after Deraa he could be sympathetic to the weakness in men that required some form of coupling, but he realized that such sympa-thies could be misplaced and misunderstood in public print. In *Some Notes on the Writing of the Seven Pillars of Wisdom,* [3] Lawrence referred to a homosexual encounter excised from chapter 84 as that "unpleasantly unnecessary incident." It concerned an Arab and an English soldier discovered committing sodomy. It was not possible for Lawrence to tolerate among Englishmen what he tolerated among Arabs. Arabs committed sodomy despite Muhammad's injunction, but they won Lawrence's sympathy by a "spiritual union" that was more than "the attraction of flesh to flesh," and he excused their conduct as encouraged by isolation and desert heat. In a letter from his barracks to Lionel Curtis on 27 March 1923, he explained that "surely the world would be more clean" if procreation were unnecessary, yet "you wouldn't exist, I wouldn't exist, without this carnality. . . . Isn't it true that the fault of birth rests somewhat on the child? I believe it's we who led our parents on to bear us, and it's our unborn children who made our flesh itch. A filthy business all of it" *(Selected Letters).* The heterosexual itch that brought Lawrence into sinful and illegitimate being and a world of pain revolted him more than the homosexual couplings he had described tolerantly in the earlier versions of *Seven Pillars.* But he understood the climate in which his book would be published. Sexual reticence was even more crucial than political reticence.

The 280,000-word production of the subscription edition had cost £13,000. Reproducing the plates alone had cost more than all the subscription income. To recover the costs, Lawrence agreed reluctantly to a trade edition of an abridgment, *Revolt in the Desert.* An agreement for the proposed "War in the Desert" was drawn up, calling for delivery of a 120,000-word manuscript by 31 March 1926 and an advance of three thousand pounds. Lawrence said half-seriously that he made the condensation by cutting out every other paragraph. Using a set of subscription edition sheets, a brush, india ink, and a wastebasket, he began by throwing away the first seven chapters. Other cuts involved removing consecutive pages, and whole chapters, elsewhere. It was a crude piece of work, made to keep the necessary readjustments to a minimum

[3]Some two hundred copies of this pamphlet, dated April 1927, were distributed to subscribers, and the notes were reprinted in the 1935 edition.

and to reduce the need for writing new material in those places where it was otherwise impossible to see the shortened version's "real shape across the gaps" (10 March 1926, *The Letters of T. E. Lawrence*).

Beginning with his arrival in Arabia (chapter 8 in the original), Lawrence concentrated on action rather than introspection—action, at that, of a variety likely to be approved by middle-class morality. Thus the introductory and magisterial passages on the origins of the Arab revolt were eliminated, as were the chapters on nationalism (chapter 14), on Lawrence's excruciating execution of an Arab (chapter 31), on his illness and his developing a theory of guerrilla warfare (chapters 32–33), on the arranging of the dead (chapter 52), on the origins of Christianity (chapter 63), on Lawrence's capture and torture at Deraa (chapter 80), on sex and discipline (chapter 92), on his guilty feelings about deception of the Arabs (chapters 100 and 103), and on the graphic horror of the Turkish hospital in Damascus (chapter 121). The symbolic concluding chapter (chapter 122) was also excised. Inevitably, it was a work inferior to *Seven Pillars,* although it captured much of the excitement of the original. In the process of cutting, the personal and subjective—the heart of the book—vanished, and was replaced, as Lawrence wrote to Forster, by "unity and speed and compactness" (*Selected Letters,* p. 347).

While plans went ahead for serializing part of the abridgment in the *Daily Telegraph* and for publication immediately thereafter, the private version made its very public appearance. November 1926 was the month for its distribution. The book was prefaced by an enigmatic dedicatory poem, "To S. A." Almost certainly the initial "A" represented Ahmed, a teenage Syrian boy who had worked for Lawrence at the Carchemish dig and who had died obscurely during the war. Ahmed, whom Lawrence called Dahoum, had helped save T. E.'s life in 1911, when Lawrence was seriously ill at the excavation site, and on recovering, he taught the boy to read and write, seeing in him the potential to rise beyond his circumstances. Evasively, Lawrence offered vague and contradictory explications of the poem—his "S. A.," the equivalent of Shakespeare's "W. H." But Ahmed seems a symbol for the Arab people, and Lawrence's perceived failure to gain the Arab lands for them becomes in the poem a "monument I shattered."

This edition of *Seven Pillars* came in two varieties: the subscription copies, complete in number (although variant in order) of plates; and the incomplete copies (missing some or most plates), which were given to comparatively impecunious friends who had served with Lawrence in Arabia or to others in acknowledgment of services rendered. "The *Seven Pillars,*" he reported in his notes to the book's subscribers,

was so printed and so assembled that nobody but myself knew how many copies were produced. I propose to keep this knowledge to myself. . . . I gave away, not perhaps as many copies as I owed, but as many as my bankers could afford, to those who had shared with me in the Arab effort, or in the actual production of the volume.
(pamphlet, April 1927)

A few diehards insisted that the Oxford version was superior to both the subscription edition and *Revolt in the Desert.* It was a conclusion that implied the special knowledge (and special favor) of having read the rare, semisecret Oxford text and was as much an announcement of having been "let in" as it was literary criticism. In the earlier version, however, no Procrustean games were played with the vocabulary and sentence structure to give a pleasing shape to each printed page. The basic question about *Seven Pillars of Wisdom* as a work of literature is whether it would still be read if the author were not the near-mythic Lawrence of Arabia. Yet the question is unanswerable, for the man cannot be separated from his work, and the best of the uneven parts of *Seven Pillars* rise from superior journalism to high art.

Most criticism of *Seven Pillars* has focused upon its synthesis of the man of action and the man of letters. It is difficult, also, to separate the artless from the artful in Lawrence's use of the confessional mode. That he lived much, if not most, of his introspective epic makes it seem almost coincidental, for example, that he was reading Joseph Conrad's *Lord Jim* (1900) at about the time he was writing his first draft of *Seven Pillars,* for the life of Conrad's Byronic, guilt-ridden, white-rajah hero bears an uncanny resemblance to that which Lawrence had already lived and largely recorded. (Lawrence also had a copy of *Lord Jim* with him in Paris in 1919 while he lobbied for the Arab cause at Versailles.)

The facts of the work's conception and development challenge a purely literary judgment. For R. A. Scott-James, writing in 1951, *Seven Pillars* is not merely the rare product of a man of action who was also by chance a man of letters: "The distinctive qualities which fitted him for literature were qualities without which he could not have succeeded in Arabia; and his literary ability needed, or appeared to need, important events shaped by himself for subject matter. He had an epic theme to handle; there would not have been this epic theme if he had not forced events to take that shape; and he produced the epic. His book is as full of heroes as the *Iliad,* and its Achilles is the author himself. What amazing egotism, one may be tempted to say, what colossal arrogance" (p. 190). Yet after some discussion of Lawrence's Doughty-inspired prose, Scott-James writes of the work's "muscular" language and the "drama and splendour in the portraits of the chiefs," concluding that the narrative "has the distances of heroic legend, yet the closeness of autobiography" (p. 192).

It is unclear to what extent a search for "distance" caused Lawrence to revise or romanticize his Arabian experience, but it is unquestionable that many events differ in details from the "facts" he reported in the *Arab Bulletin,* in his letters home or to friends, and in accounts by contemporaries on the scene. Discrepancies will continue to be alleged in reassessments of *Seven Pillars.*

Whether facts were falsified or magnified, invented or suppressed, belongs to history rather than to literature. Winston Churchill called the book "this treasure of English literature. As a narrative of war and adventure . . . it is unsurpassed. . . . If Lawrence had never done anything except write this book as a mere work of the imagination his fame would last." It gleamed, thought Churchill, "with immortal fire" (*Great Contemporaries,* pp. 133–134). Throughout his life his estimate never wavered. "Winston once told me," Lord Moran wrote, that "in his judgment [*Seven Pillars*] ranked with the greatest books ever written in the English language, with *The Pilgrim's Progress, Robinson Crusoe,* and *Gulliver's Travels.*"[4] Earlier Churchill himself had told Lawrence that.

The combination of profound introspection and naked confession in *Seven Pillars,* wrote Jean Béraud Villars in 1958, reminds one of Marcel Proust or André Gide. Villars found curious analogies between Lawrence and Gide, but a sentence like "I

punished my flesh cheerfully, finding greater sensuality in the punishment than in the sin, so much was I intoxicated with pride at not sinning simply," he thought, could in tone and in manner have been ascribed to any one of the three. Lawrence's "balance between romanticism and naturalism," Villars wrote, "was the essence of a new form of literature" to be seized upon by a generation of writers who were reacting to an upbringing pervaded by naturalism yet unable to withstand its attractions. By combining romanticism with naturalism, Lawrence gave new dignity to horror. It was a strangely mixed blessing, Villars implies, that plucked at fibers that were not accustomed to vibrating (*T. E. Lawrence; or, The Search for the Absolute,* 1958, pp. 296–297). Into *Seven Pillars* he infused the musty smells of homosexuality, of cruelty, and of death. And he expressed a certain sadism that had been carefully expurgated from the accounts of other war writers, who by tacit consent presented themselves as martyrs and paladins who were not supposed to have such troubled sensations.

Lawrence proved a forerunner. Before André Malraux, Arthur Koestler, Franz Kafka, and Jean-Paul Sartre, before the writers of the French Resistance and the postwar Europeans who described the Nazi and Soviet atrocities (and also before the authors of later commercial novels, those hybrids of brutality and pornography), he invented a style that was to be exploited by a whole generation of writers.

THE MINT

LATE in 1922, at the end of each long training day at the RAF camp at Uxbridge, Lawrence would sit in bed, blankets pulled over drawn-up knees, and write letters to friends or scribble notes for *The Mint.* His method was outlined not only in letters to Edward and David Garnett, to E. M. Forster, and to Charlotte Shaw, but in the work itself (the following is quoted in *Lawrence of Arabia: The Literary Impulse,* 1975):

Day by day I had been putting down these notes on our Depot life, often writing in bed from roll-call till lights out, using any scrap of paper. So I seemed only to be writing letters. They were now grown to an unmanageable crumpled bulk. Yet I could not send the earlier ones

[4]Lord Moran. *Churchill: Taken from the Diaries of Lord Moran* (Boston, 1966), p. 113.

away, for I often went back with fuller understanding to a past experience and implemented it; or ran the collected impressions of, say, three fire-pickets into one.

(p. 65)

The book began with a picture of the frightened would-be recruit; he was scruffy, hungry, and worried about being discovered or refused for enlistment—or both:

"Nerves like a rabbit." The Scotch-voiced doctor's hard fingers go hammer, hammer, hammer over the loud box of my ribs. I must be pretty hollow.

"Turn over: get up; stand under here: make yourself as tall as you can: he'll just do five foot six, Mac: chest—say 34. Expansion—by Jove, 38. That'll do. Now jump: higher: lift your right leg: hold it there: cough: all right: on your toes: arms straight in front of you: open your fingers wide: hold them so: turn round: bend over. Hullo, what the hell's those marks? Punishment?" "No Sir, more like persuasion Sir, I think." Face, neck, chest, getting hot.

"H...m...m..., that would account for the nerves." His voice sounds softer. "Don't put them down, Mac. Say *Two parallel scars on ribs*. What were they, boy?"

"Superficial wounds, Sir."

"Answer my question."

"A barbed-wire tear, over a fence."

"H...m...m..."

(pp. 13–14)

Lawrence's first enlistment—arranged through his friend at the air ministry, Chief of Air Staff General Sir Hugh Trenchard—came to an abrupt halt when his thin disguise as "John Hume Ross" was exposed.

"I had meant to go on to a Squadron, & write the real Air Force," he wrote E. M. Forster afterward, "and make it a book—a BOOK, I mean. It is the biggest subject I have ever seen, and I thought I could get it" (quoted in preface to 1955 edition). But his discharge broke the "rhythm" of composition. After the creatively uninspiring blank of his Tank Corps years (crowded by the preparation of *Seven Pillars,* and physical and emotional misery), his air force reinstatement in July 1925 provided him only, "for fairness' sake," with material to balance the bitterness and the savagery of the earlier experience. This renewal of the journal at the RAF base at Cranwell would become its third section, one built upon extracts from letters to his friends.

The organization of *The Mint* was worked out in India. Writing from the RAF base at Karachi (now Pakistan) while revising and augmenting his earlier material, Lawrence asked Charlotte Shaw to mail back to him the Cranwell notes of 1925 and 1926 which he had left with her, yellow slips of paper describing a hoisting of the colors ceremony, guard inspection, and his comments on a chaplain's sermon on the death of Queen Alexandra, the widow of Edward VII. The "final" version of the book he had begun in 1922 would be the assembling of his rewritten notes on his first RAF experience (the sections titled "Raw Material" and "In the Mill") with his happier life at Cranwell (the section titled "Service"). In a preface to the third section he stressed "how different, how humane" life could be under a benign regimen, an experience already suffused with nostalgia for him from the perspective of India. "There is no continuity in these last pages," he wrote, "—and a painful inadequacy: but perhaps some glint of our contentment may shine from between my phrases into your eyes" (1955 edition, p. 165). In a final sentence, given a paragraph to itself, he added, "How can any man describe his happiness?" It was an ironic bliss when, with a million and a half men unemployed in England, enlistment meant the open acknowledgment of defeat by life.

In its near-final form Lawrence's book followed the pattern of recruit training, but it amalgamated similar incidents taken from notes and letters into a single, more emphatic—and sometimes more hysterical—experience. He had reduced the fifty names in his notes to fifteen, both to avoid confusion and to protect himself in some places from too obvious identification. He tried to balance his scenes of contentment with air force life and his scenes of splenetic rage at the desecration of a recruit's essential inviolate humanity. He described dehumanization as an ironic good, but revealed the service's means toward that end—the metaphor of minting conveying the idea (as he wrote Air Marshal Trenchard early in 1928) of being shaped into the RAF's image of what the man in the ranks should be, "violently stamping an indelible mark on coarse material" (*Private Shaw and Public Shaw,* 1963, p. 145)—the molding "of a soldier's body and soul into a uniform pattern," as Villars describes it (*T. E. Lawrence; or, The Search for the Absolute,* p. 334). (But Villars does not mention the subtle reverberations of the title of the French translation, which Lawrence might have appreciated. *La Matrice* can mean "matrix," or "die mold"—or "womb.")

Lawrence also aimed at what he called the "feel" of a camp for recruit training, balanced by the "feel" of service at an RAF station. The complex of balances was worked out in short, journal-entry chapters: the lyrical ("landscape passages," he called them) opposed to the oppressive and the humdrum; the sentimental opposed to the stark and the obscene. As Shaw later told him, *The Mint,* in seeking that balance, wobbled between a document for the files and an artistic work.

Lawrence had already rejected one opportunity to write the RAF story literally from the files as well as for history. In 1924, while he longed for reinstatement in the air force, the RAF was searching for an author to write its young history. Trenchard suggested that the supplicant could re-enter the RAF as its official—and officer-rank—historian. "I thought for a night & then declined," Lawrence wrote to D. G. Hogarth. "The job is a hazardous one (T. wants a 'literary' history, the C.I.D. a 'technical'), attractive, very, to me by reason of its subject. The terms (three years) compare unfavourably with the six which the Army offers; and the responsibility is one which I'd regret as soon as I had shouldered it" (*Selected Letters,* p. 266). In a letter to Trenchard, Lawrence declined, and vowed to remain in the army until he could reenter the air force on the ground floor. It took him, even after high-level political intervention on the part of his friends, an additional two years to change his status from "Private Shaw" to "Aircraftman Shaw," but he had his way, as he did in writing his own air force book.

In July 1928, Trenchard wrote to Lawrence after having borrowed a typescript of *The Mint* (at Lawrence's suggestion) from Edward Garnett. "I read every word of it," he told Lawrence. "And I seemed to know what was coming each line, and I feel no soreness, no sadness, about your writing, and yet again I feel all of a tremble in case it gets out and into the hands of people who do not know life as it is" (*Letters to T. E. Lawrence,* p. 203). Lawrence assured Trenchard that it would not be published before 1950, if then; and their relationship remained as cordial as it could have been, given Lawrence's insistence upon remaining at the opposite pole in rank from that of his old friend. But

Trenchard also saw to it that there was an Air Force file, No. S44G8, marked "Precautions for Preventing Publication of *The Mint.*" No precautions ever had to be taken.

Without actual publication, *The Mint* enabled Lawrence again to luxuriate in close criticism of his work by those whom he thought his literary betters. The very fact of the criticism remaining private and personal appealed to his ego while it did not threaten his nagging sense of inferiority as a writer, which he may have feared that publication would expose. As a result the posthumous volume of *Letters to T. E. Lawrence* (1962) is packed with close critiques—mostly diplomatically favorable—of *The Mint* as well as of *Seven Pillars:* letters from John Buchan, Winston Churchill, Noel Coward, Edward Garnett, E. M. Forster, Augustus John, Rudyard Kipling, H. G. Wells, Bernard Shaw, and others. Lawrence was exhilarated not so much by praise as by the close attention creative people were willing to pay to his texts.

He never abandoned planning new touches for *The Mint,* toward its eventual publication, convinced it was his authentic claim to literary survival on its own merits and not on the accident of war. Perhaps for that reason he never felt satisfied that he had finished with the revising.

To E. M. Forster, Lawrence had written that he would not permit the book's publication while "the fellows with me in the force" would feel "horror . . . at my giving them away. . . . So *The Mint* shall not be circulated before 1950" (*Selected Letters,* p. 383). In 1936, however, shortly after Lawrence's death, the publisher of *Seven Pillars* in the United States, Doubleday, determined to protect the U.S. copyright via a limited edition of *The Mint.* Hoping to publish more of Lawrence in commercial editions, Doubleday, the American publisher of *Revolt in the Desert,* realized that since the U.S. was not a signatory to the International (Berne) Copyright Convention, what was needed was the technical reality of an American edition, which it printed with Lawrence's reluctant assent, in fifty copies. Because of the possibility of libel suits from persons identifiable in the text, and in response to Lawrence's own injunction, only ten of the fifty copies were placed on sale, at the prohibitive price of $500,000 per copy. But for three, the rest went into a vault. According to copyright law, two copies were deposited in the Library of

Congress—secretly, the publishers thought. One copy was technically "sold" to Lawrence's London agent, Raymond Savage, for one dollar, to secure British and international copyright, a gesture ruled invalid as "publication" or "release" of the book. But in Washington, Henry Seidel Canby, editor of the *Saturday Review of Literature,* turned up at the Library of Congress and demanded his rights as a reader. The review that resulted appeared in the 21 November 1936 issue.

Postwar arrangements for publication in London by Cape began in 1947, but in 1950 the martinet officer about whom Lawrence had written so viciously in chapter 20 was still alive. In 1955 *The Mint* was first released to the general public; and readers, expecting gross titillation after nearly three decades of rumor and secrecy had exaggerated the book's improprieties, were disappointed. Rather than appearing as a precursor of such "black" satires as Henry Miller's *Tropic of Cancer* (1934), Louis Ferdinand Céline's *Voyage au bout de la nuit* (1932), and Lawrence Durrell's *The Black Book* (1938), *The Mint,* because of its long delay in release and the intervening horror of another world war, became a contemporary, instead, of Norman Mailer's *The Naked and the Dead* (1948) and James Jones's *From Here to Eternity* (1951). Ironically, it thus became the embalmed document that Shaw had wanted unprinted but preserved. A generation late, its improprieties of language and its experiments in the surreal, the sadistic, and the grotesque had lost their force. Yet even in 1955 the trade edition timidly left white spaces where the limited edition had printed the four-letter words, apparently following the traditional but since discredited publishing philosophy that only the wealthy could be trusted to react appropriately to obscenity. (Current reprint editions print *all* the words.)

MINOR WRITINGS

APPREHENSIVE about attempting an original new work after *The Mint* yet hoping to fasten upon a new writing project, Lawrence had begun thinking about a translation of Homer. In the solitude of Miranshah—a remote RAF mountain base to which he had been transferred from Karachi—he began working on a version of the *Odyssey.* Homer effectively occupied a surplus of leisure time, and the first fifty lines came easily, but he worried over four drafts of the first book for a month. Bruce Rogers, an American book designer and illustrator, had agreed to commission a full translation if he liked a sample chapter, and Lawrence, eager to start another book, wanted the opportunity. As before, Lawrence ran both from and toward a literary career.

Continued at various RAF bases through Plymouth in 1931, it was published in 1932 under the name T. E. Shaw. Shaw's identity was by then an open secret; posthumous printings have used both Lawrence's real and adopted names. The work remains an effective prose translation of Homer, blending simplicity with archaic affectation, and using to advantage the know-how Lawrence had gained in primitive desert conditions as an aircraft mechanic and boat handler.

Lawrence's published critical output is small. The first critical piece under his own name was an introduction to the Medici Society's 1921 reprint of Charles Doughty's *Travels in Arabia Deserta* (first published in 1888), a travel classic that Lawrence revered. Doughty, old and in financial straits, needed the income, and only a "Lawrence of Arabia" introduction made the reprint possible. With kindness Lawrence wrote to Doughty, "I feel this as absurd as it would be to introduce Shakespeare. However they urged that I had an advertisement value . . . and so I said that I would do it, if you would allow it to be done. I'm afraid you will feel it rather an outrage on the book" (*The Letters of T. E. Lawrence,* p. 309).

What he produced was a personal essay, beginning, "It is not comfortable to have to write about 'Arabia Deserta.' I have studied it for ten years, and have grown to consider it a book not like other books, but something particular, a bible of its kind." Although the rest was praise, Lawrence privately had second thoughts about Doughty's style, especially after hearing the critical reaction to the obvious influence of *Arabia Deserta* on his own *Seven Pillars.* The antique manner was in one way self-defeating, he wrote David Garnett in 1927: "I regret Doughty's style, and find it unjustifiable; not that his skill in using it does not justify him, as a verbal artist, in using it, but because the difficulty of it had barred so many readers from what is, after

T. E. LAWRENCE

all, much more than a piece of verbal art. Philologically, too, he is all wrong; why should we borrow our syntax from the Sweden or Denmark of 80 years ago?"[5]

Later, Lawrence provided a preface to Richard Garnett's *The Twilight of the Gods* (1924) and a foreword to Bertram Thomas' *Arabia Felix: Across the Empty Quarter of Arabia* (1932). There could have been many more, as his name in a preface could have turned almost anyone's manuscript into selling copy, but he resisted all other blandishments. When Sir Ronald Storrs asked him to write a preface to a book by an acquaintance of his, he bristled, "No: I won't; forewords are septic things, and I hope never to do another. Bertram Thomas was like the importunate woman, but to strangers it is easy to say 'No.' "[6] As part of his intermittent literary hackwork he wrote flap-copy puffs for the Jonathan Cape firm, and even edited, anonymously, another traveler's journal of experiences in Syria, asking for payment in the form of books Cape would have sent him for the asking anyway.

Since he needed the money, Lawrence eventually agreed to do some criticism for publication. Francis Yeats-Brown, assistant editor of the *Spectator* in the mid 1920's, had asked him to review books on the Middle East. Lawrence agreed to occasional reviewing—but on any subject but Arabia, and only under a pseudonym. "The job comes very hard to me," he wrote, and added—strangely, considering his passion for criticism-laden correspondence—"I can't do it without trying my very best: and if I've ever in my past written decently it was under the dire command of some mastering need to put on paper a case, or a relation, or an explanation, of something I cared about. I don't see that happening with literature" (*Selected Letters,* p. 341).

Insisting upon anonymity, Lawrence suggested the identifying initials "C. D."—for "Colin Dale," he explained. To the uninitiated, it could have sounded like a name out of *Robin Hood,* or perhaps drawn from an early English pastoral. But Colindale—the pseudonym run together—was to Lawrence the station on the London underground

(actually above ground at that point) closest to Hendon Aerodrome. And Lawrence was "Aircraftman Shaw."

After a perceptive review of a collected edition of D. H. Lawrence's novels, there were others through the latter part of 1927 and into 1928. The best of them were "Hakluyt—First Naval Propagandist," and an overview of H. G. Wells's collected short stories. The Wells critique was as interesting for what it intimated about Lawrence, but it was nevertheless a substantial assessment of Wells as a writer of short fiction. As an author who felt "dry as a squeezed orange" (*Selected Letters,* p. 323), Lawrence was fascinated by Wells's ability to turn out so much writing of all kinds that the sixty-three stories in the volume represented only a fraction of the total. "His drafts," Lawrence mused, "would tell us if this huge production is due to industry or to a happy fluency. His writings let us into so many workshops and laboratories that we would like to see his own" (*Spectator,* 25 February 1928).

Colin Dale's enthusiasm for regular reviewing waned quickly; yet it was remarkable that he was able to do any of it at all, considering that his situation in the RAF ranks lay half a world away from the London literary scene he loved but ran from. Lawrence produced little other criticism after that; one effort, a piece intended for the *Spectator* early in 1928 but printed only posthumously, in David Garnett's *The Essential T. E. Lawrence* (1951), was an essay review of an edition of Walter Savage Landor.

No additional book by Lawrence was published in his lifetime other than a minor translation he had done, under his John Hume Ross pseudonym, of Adrien le Corbeau's *The Forest Giant* (1924). His wartime *Arab Bulletin* dispatches to Cairo (adapted into *Seven Pillars*) appeared posthumously in 1939 as *Secret Despatches from Arabia,* with a preface by his brother A. W. Lawrence, who published *Oriental Assembly* the same year. A literary-remains volume, it contains a brief diary from 1911, the suppressed opening chapter of *Seven Pillars,* two newspaper articles, and a preface to an exhibition catalog of drawings and paintings for the subscription edition. His earliest postwar writings, including a famous essay on guerrilla war and a magazine serial version of an early draft of *Seven Pillars,* have been edited by Stanley and Rodelle Weintraub as *Evolution of a Revolt* (1968). *Minorities: Good Poems by Small*

[5]Lawrence to D. Garnett, 30 November 1927. *Fifty Letters,* Humanities Research Center catalog (Austin, Tex., 1962), pp. 24–25.
[6]Lawrence to R. Storrs, 25 February 1935. R. Storrs, *Orientations* (London, 1937), p. 527.

Poets and Small Poems by Good Poets (1971) reproduced an anthology of more than one hundred poems Lawrence had collected in a notebook over many years, each associated with something, some moment, someone, in his life.

THE LETTER WRITER

LAWRENCE's literary impulses, never motivated by the desire for book income or for further public acclaim, were fed from within rather than from without. His largest body of writing—his correspondence—is thus integral to the rest. Many of his letters, in fact, have close textual affinities with both *Seven Pillars* and *The Mint,* and were not only the first working-out of material in the books but were actually retrieved to help in the writing. What remained for him to write in his later years were more letters, which he poured out without letup—perhaps the raw material of never-to-be-written books.

The thousand-plus Lawrentian letters published to date represent only a fraction of the total that survive in private hands and in library collections. As with all correspondences, even literary ones, many of the letters that have surfaced deal with the trivialities, the courtesies, the basic business of existence. Yet many of Lawrence's are rich in personal incident, yearning, and confession; metaphysical speculation; literary criticism and literary self-criticism; the history, politics, and geography of his world. They burn with self-doubt, gleam with arrogance and egotism, turn bleak with introspection, reach remarkable intensities of controlled hysteria, wearily achieve temporary inner peace. In sum, since he was as guilty of candor as he was of concealment, they are the autobiography that friends had vainly urged upon him, for they are more faithful to fact than are his own memoirs and closer to life in their arising out of emotional immediacy.

Having it both ways, Lawrence wrote to his friend K. W. Marshall on 6 September 1932: "My letters ceased being personal seven years ago, when an American magazine advertised a batch as 'characteristic products of a remarkable adventurer.' That cured me of writing sense" (*Selected Letters,* p. 464). But he had already written to Charlotte Shaw on 19 January 1930, "Perhaps I am not writing to you, but for my some-day 'Life and Letters' " (*Selected Letters,* p. 436). He was aware that recipients preserved his correspondence.

However crafted some letters seem, he wrote impulsively. He made few first drafts, and seldom used a typewriter. "Nobody ever wrote a good letter in a fair copy," he explained to Charlotte Shaw on 14 April 1927. "It's the first draft, or none" (*Selected Letters,* p. 324). He apologized to Eric Kennington, in a letter dated 6 August 1934,

It is very difficult to write a good letter. Mine don't pretend to be good . . . but they do actually try very hard to be good. I write them in great batches, on the days when at length (after months, often) the impulse . . . eventually comes. Each tries to direct itself . . . towards my picture of the person I am writing to: and if it does not seem to me (as I write it) that it makes contact—why then I write no more that night.

(*Selected Letters,* p. 495–496)

Candid and powerful, mordant and melancholy, lightened often by wry wit and encyclopedic erudition, Lawrence's letters are among the most compelling in English by a twentieth-century writer. Their prices as manuscripts on the auction block may reflect the fascinating qualities of the uneasy adventurer who wrote them and their rarity as objects for sale, more than their real literary merits, but they are likely to be read as long as people remember who Lawrence of Arabia was, or care to find out.

LAST YEARS

LAWRENCE's last years were spent among RAF seaplanes and seagoing tenders, although, because of his notoriety, officialdom refused him permission to fly. In the process, moving from bases on the English Channel to those on the North Sea and leading airmen and even officers charismatically from the lowest ranks as Aircraftman Shaw, he worked on improved designs for high-speed seaplane-tender watercraft, testing them in rigorous trials and developing a technical manual (*The 200 Class Royal Air Force Seaplane Tender,* 1932) for their use. A stenciled and duplicated production, it was as unpretentious as his first book had been opulent.

Recognizing his instinctive capacity to lead, Bernard Shaw had already used elements of Lawrence's personality in *Saint Joan* (1923). In Lawrence's last RAF years, Shaw gently parodied him as Private Napoleon Alexander Trotsky Meek in *Too True to Be Good* (1932). Lawrence eagerly read proofs of the play and suggested changes with, he wrote to Shaw, "inexpressible pleasure" (*Private Shaw and Public Shaw*, p. 219). The final text incorporated, in definitive detail, the colonel who had reduced himself to the ranks: his insignificant size; his pseudo-meek quick-wittedness, combined with a modest omniscience; his pleased abasement in rank; his knowledge of dialects and of tribal psychology; his genius for command, even from the bottom rung; his technical facility with mines, in blowing up bridges and trains; his shyness with women; his unseen but ear-shattering motorcycle. But for Lawrence the curious joy of the ranks was nearly over; at his age, he claimed to Bruce Rogers, he could not re-enlist at the lowest grade once his term of service concluded. Higher-ups, however, even the air minister, would have permitted it, but base officers uncomfortable with his leading from below were now reluctant to offer him anything but routine duty.

Discharged from the Royal Air Force on 26 February 1935, Lawrence returned to Clouds Hill to face a retirement, at forty-six, filled alternately with optimism about future publishing projects and a sense of emptiness. To Lady Astor, an old friend, he described himself as puttering about as if "there is something broken in the works . . . my will, I think" (*Selected Letters*, p. 537). A motorcycling crash on 13 May solved the problem of his future. He died six days later without regaining consciousness.

To the end, Lawrence had found despair as necessary as ambition. He lived on the masochistic side of asceticism, and the nonphysical part of his self-punishment involved creating within himself a sense of deep frustration that would immediately follow, and cancel out, high achievement, denying to himself the recognition he had earned. His behavior at its most extreme involved a symbolic killing of the self, a taking up of a new life and a new name. Under whatever guise, he was a haunted, many-sided genius who by his achievements denied himself the privacy he paradoxically sought and by the manufacture of his myth, however solidly based, created in his own person a characterization rivaling any in contemporary fiction.

SELECTED BIBLIOGRAPHY

I. BIBLIOGRAPHY. P. O'Brien, *T. E. Lawrence: A Bibliography* (Boston, 1988).

II. COLLECTED WORKS. *Oriental Assembly*, A. W. Lawrence, ed. (London, 1939; New York, 1940); *Secret Despatches from Arabia* (London, 1939), articles from the *Arab Bulletin; Men in Print*, A. W. Lawrence, ed. (London, 1940); *The Essential T. E. Lawrence*, D. Garnett, ed. (London and New York, 1951); *Evolution of a Revolt: Early Postwar Writings of T. E. Lawrence*, S. Weintraub and R. Weintraub, eds. (University Park, Pa., and London, 1968).

III. SEPARATE WORKS. *The Wilderness of Zin*, with C. L. Woolley (London, 1914; New York, 1936); *Seven Pillars of Wisdom: A Triumph* (London and New York, 1926; limited first trade edition, London, 1935); *Revolt in the Desert* (London and New York, 1927); *The Mint* (limited copyright ed., New York, 1936; New York and London, 1955); *Crusader Castles*, 2 vols. (London, 1936), 1 vol. (New York, 1937).

IV. TRANSLATIONS. A. Le Corbeau, *The Forest Giant* (London and New York, 1924); as T. E. Shaw, *The Odyssey of Homer* (London and New York, 1932).

V. ESSAYS, ARTICLES, INTRODUCTIONS, AND REVIEWS. Introduction to C. M. Doughty, *Travels in Arabia Deserta* (London, 1921; New York, 1923); introduction to R. Garnett, *The Twilight of the Gods* (London and New York, 1924); as C. D. (Colin Dale), "D. H. Lawrence," in *Spectator* (6 August 1927); as C. D., "Mixed Biscuits," in *Spectator* (20 August 1927); as C. D., "A Critic of Critics Criticised," in *Spectator* (27 August 1927); as C. D., "Hakluyt—First Naval Propagandist," in *Spectator* (10 September 1927); as C. D., "The Wells Short Stories," in *Spectator* (25 February 1928); foreword to B. Thomas, *Arabia Felix: Across the Empty Quarter of Arabia* (London and New York, 1932).

VI. ANTHOLOGIES. *Minorities: Good Poems by Small Poets and Small Poems by Good Poets* (London, 1971; New York, 1972).

VII. LETTERS. *The Letters of T. E. Lawrence*, D. Garnett, ed. (London, 1938; New York, 1939); *T. E. Lawrence to His Biographer, Robert Graves*, R. Graves, ed. (London and New York, 1938); *T. E. Lawrence to His Biographer, Liddell Hart*, B. H. L. Hart, ed.; *The Home Letters of T. E. Lawrence and His Brothers*, M. R. Lawrence, ed. (Oxford and New York, 1954); *T. E. Lawrence: The Selected Letters*, M. Brown, ed. (London, 1988; New York, 1989).

VIII. BIOGRAPHICAL AND CRITICAL STUDIES. L. Thomas, *With Lawrence in Arabia* (New York, 1924; London, 1925); R. Graves, *Lawrence and the Arabs* (London, 1927), published as *Lawrence and the Arabian Adventure* (New York, 1928); B. H. L. Hart, *"T. E. Lawrence" in Arabia and After* (London, 1934); V. Richards, *Portrait of T. E. Lawrence* (London, 1936); E. H. R. Altounyan, *Ornament of Honour* (Cambridge, 1937); W. Churchill, *Great Contemporaries* (New

York, 1937; London, 1941); A. W. Lawrence, ed., *Letters to T. E. Lawrence by His Friends* (London and New York, 1937).

C. S. Smith, *The Golden Reign: The Story of My Friendship with "Lawrence of Arabia"* (London, 1940); H. Williamson, *Genius of Friendship: "T. E. Lawrence"* (London, 1941); R. A. Scott-James, *Fifty Years of English Literature, 1900–1950* (London, 1951); R. Aldington, *Lawrence of Arabia: A Biographical Enquiry* (London and Chicago, 1955); F. Armitage, *The Desert and the Stars: A Biography of Lawrence of Arabia* (New York, 1955), published as *The Desert and the Stars: A Portrait of T. E. Lawrence* (London, 1956); E. Lönnroth, *Lawrence of Arabia: An Historical Appreciation* (London, 1956); J. Béraud-Villars, *T. E. Lawrence; or, the Search for the Absolute,* trans. by P. Dawnay (London, 1958; New York, 1959).

T. Rattigan, *Ross: A Dramatic Portrait* (London, 1960; New York, 1962); A. Nutting, *Lawrence of Arabia: The Man and the Motive* (New York and London, 1961); A. W. Lawrence, ed., *Letters to T. E. Lawrence* (London, 1962); J. R. Woolfenden, *Lawrence of Arabia* (New York, 1962), Columbia Pictures souvenir picturebook of the film scripted by Robert Bolt; V. Ocampo, *338171 T. E.* (London, 1963); S. Weintraub, *Private Shaw and Public Shaw: A Dual Portrait of Lawrence of Arabia and G. B. S.* (New York and London, 1963); S. Mousa, *T. E. Lawrence: An Arab View* (London and New York, 1966); P. Knightley and C. Simpson, *The Secret Lives of Lawrence of Arabia* (London, 1969; New York, 1970).

J. Meyers, *The Wounded Spirit: A Study of "Seven Pillars of Wisdom"* (London, 1973); R. Weintraub and S. Weintraub, *"Moby Dick* and *Seven Pillars of Wisdom,"* in *Studies in American Fiction* (Autumn 1974); C. Grosvenor, *The Portraits of T. E. Lawrence* (Pasadena, Calif., 1975); R. Weintraub and S. Weintraub, *Lawrence of Arabia: The Literary Impulse* (Baton Rouge, La., 1975); J. E. Mack, *A Prince of Our Disorder: The Life of T. E. Lawrence* (New York and London, 1976); H. M. Hyde, *Solitary in the Ranks: Lawrence of Arabia as Airman and Private Soldier* (London, 1977; New York, 1978); D. Stewart, *T. E. Lawrence* (New York and London, 1977); S. E. Tabachnick, *T. E. Lawrence* (Boston, 1978); T. J. O'Donnell, *The Confessions of Lawrence of Arabia: The Romantic Hero's Presentation of Self* (Athens, Ohio, 1979).

M. Larès, *T. E. Lawrence: La France et les Français* (Paris, 1980); National Trust, *Clouds Hill* (London, 1980); S. E. Tabachnick, *The T. E. Lawrence Puzzle* (Athens, Ga., 1984); R. Trevelyan, "T. E. Lawrence at Clouds Hill," in *Writers at Home,* S. Blow and J. Lees-Milne, eds. (London, 1985); M. Yardley, *Backing into the Limelight: A Biography of T. E. Lawrence* (London, 1985), published as *T. E. Lawrence: A Biography* (New York, 1987); V. M. Thompson, *"Not a Suitable Hobby for an Airman"—T. E. Lawrence as Publisher* (New York, 1986); C. Blackmore, *In the Footsteps of Lawrence of Arabia* (London, 1987); Bodleian Library, *T. E. Lawrence: The Legend and the Man* (Oxford, 1989), illustrated catalog of centenary exhibition; D. Fromkin, *A Peace to End all Peace: Creating the Modern Middle East, 1914–1922* (New York, 1989); S. Tabachnick and C. Matheson, *Images of Lawrence* (London, 1990); J. Wilson, *Lawrence of Arabia: The Authorized Biography of T. E. Lawrence* (New York, 1990); M. D. Allen, *The Medievalism of T. E. Lawrence* (University Park, Pa., 1991).

JOHN LE CARRÉ
(1931–   )

George J. Leonard

SINCE SMILEY AND the other spies in his novels use so many cover names, somehow it is satisfying to learn that "John le Carré" is itself only a cover name, adopted by the author, one reads, because people working in the Foreign Office were not allowed to publish under their real names. Another sound reason for the pseudonym would be le Carré's disinclination to have his bosses read, in *Call for the Dead* (1961), his first book, descriptions of themselves like these: "the professional civil servant from an orthodox department . . . , a man who could reduce any colour to grey . . . , the Head Eunuch" (ch. 1); and "a barmaid's dream of a real gentleman" (ch. 2). When *The Spy Who Came In from the Cold* (1963) was a hit, le Carré instructed his banker to notify him when his account reached a certain sum; when the call came, he gleefully resigned.

"There are few people more dishonest," le Carré has warned us, "than writers professing to recall how they came to do things." His pen name, he said, "came from nowhere that I can really remember," but he finally began telling "persistent" interviewers that he stole it from a shoe shop he used to pass en route to work. The shoe shop has never been located. He has stopped telling the story. Much of the information about him is of that quality, even when it comes directly from him.

So that is not his name. Later one discovers he never even worked "in the Foreign Office." Britian does not officially admit to having an FBI and a CIA for, respectively, domestic and international espionage—though everyone knows that such agencies exist. When a person is a domestic spy the British press writes, by long-standing gentlemanly agreement, that "he works in the Home Office"; if he spies on other nations, they write, "he works in the Foreign Office." (Everyone understands, just as they understand that "his constant companion" means "his mistress.")

We start then, fittingly, by removing his cover name and his cover job. We still have a long way to go. Like Peer Gynt peeling the onion to find its center, when we try to learn about le Carré we continually find cover stories within cover stories.

The cover name, in French, means "John the Square" and though the critics who long pondered it—John the Stolid? John the Straight Dealer?—have finally dismissed it as unsymbolic, it is not insignificant. He once remarked he wanted an upper-class-sounding name: that desire for upper-class status has been an obsession of his characters. He is also, almost in spite of his friendliest critics, exceptionally self-conscious of himself as the heir of the great spy novelists and loves to make filial allusions to them. One of the first stars of the genre was William LeQueux, whose *The Great War in England in 1897* appeared in 1894. John Buchan's famous *The Thirty-Nine Steps,* a pioneering 1913 spy novel, was first published under the pseudonym "H. de V." Too remote to have interested him? Le Carré has a scholar's love of allusion. One of Smiley's cover names, "Mr. Standfast," is the title of a 1919 Buchan novel.

The real-life David John Moore Cornwell was born on 19 October 1931. Before the stories about his father began to surface, Americans frequently assumed that Cornwell, an Oxford graduate and former Eton don, was a pillar of the Establishment, and they projected those politics onto his novels and his hero Smiley. Nothing could be further from the truth. He registers Labour party. Le Carré, although he has the old-boy manners and credentials, lived in that world, he has told us, virtually as a "spy." When he was three his mother left his father, Ronald Cornwell, a high-living professional swindler who, despite a prison sentence during David's youth, managed to accumulate two more wives and defraud enough people to achieve a spectacular bankruptcy, in debt about thirty million contemporary dollars. All the while David was in the exclusive Sherborne School he knew that "there was absolutely no money," and that "there was a lot to hide: women, the past, the present." His father sent him to school not to educate him but to turn him into "fake gentry," to plant him in the Establishment like a Russian "mole" in the secret services, to become useful later. To make a "gentleman" out of David, "my father always said he was prepared to steal; and I'm afraid he did."

It sounds like a novel and it eventually provided material for one: *A Perfect Spy* (1986). (In colloquial American English, the title means "a born spy" or "a natural spy.") If we were studying Dickens, it would make sense, at this point, to let the similarly autobiographical *David Copperfield* (1852) flesh out the sketchy notes on his childhood Dickens left his biographer, Forster. In le Carré's case, we have no less than four novels I consider autobiographical—indeed, nearly confessional, sometimes obsessive. The plots of *A Perfect Spy, A Murder of Quality* (1962), *A Small Town in Germany* (1968), and *The Naive and Sentimental Lover* (1971) are perfunctory. The writer seems intent on reliving an experience, understanding it, and exorcising it. "Factual" biographical data is, he himself warns us, hard to come by. For years his life involved matters still covered by Britain's Official Secrets Act. One thinks of the narrator/lawyer of *The Russia House* (1989), who carries the Act around, forcing people to sign. There are family considerations: he has been able to speak about his father only since Ronnie Cornwell died, and even so it caused strain in the family. Also, le Carré scholarship is in a primitive state: no autobiography, no standard biography, no collected letters or even collected essays, no bestselling exposé by an ex-wife. But we are not at a loss for evidence. What does a born spy, a habitually self-disguising person do when he has a need to "exorcise" experiences? This one writes novels.

Enough is now known about our man to help us glean from the novels what we need—not names and dates, but something we want even more and which novels supply even better than a witness could: what certain events meant to the young David Cornwell *emotionally;* how they colored his novels; and how they probably led him to his most famous creation, George Smiley. When we see le Carré, at thirty, sit down to create Smiley, we will know who he is. I will hold discussion of *The Naive and Sentimental Lover,* his novel of mid-life crisis, till its appropriate place in the middle of the story.

A PERFECT SPY

A PERFECT SPY is only superficially the story of Magnus Pym/Titch/Sir Magnus/Canterbury. (Le Carré's critics usually cope with his characters' many names by resorting to slashes.) Clearly, the author's purpose in writing the book was to depict his father, Ronnie (revealed in the book in the character of Rickie), and whenever this character is offstage the tension drops.

A Perfect Spy is an endless novel written in le Carré's lamented late lax style; its main interest is autobiographical. At the book's start Magnus has holed up in a room he keeps in Devon and is beginning a long memoir addressed to his son Tom. Meanwhile his wife, Mary, and his father-figure boss, Jack Brotherhood, ransack his home, because the CIA is claiming "the Firm" has been infiltrated by a Czech double agent, and Magnus has promptly disappeared. Inside Magnus' chimney they find a "small, clever-looking" Czech camera used for photographing documents (ch. 3). With this discovery all suspense ends, although the book will not for another four-hundred-odd pages. Unfortunately Jack and Mary, both in love with Magnus, need hundreds of pages to arrive at the same conclusion the reader has, and sitting with them while they come to their senses takes patience.

Crosscuts to Magnus' letter to Tom slowly reveal that Jack Brotherhood, when he recruited Magnus to the Firm in Berne, after the war, persuaded him to finger his best friend, the charismatic, war-wounded Axel, as a possible Russian agent. Magnus heard Axel taken away in the night. When he joyfully found Axel/Sgt. Pavel later in Austria, both of them were minor Army intelligence agents, but on opposite sides. They started trading secrets, advancing each other's careers. Some years later, a full-fledged agent, Magnus was arrested in Czechoslovakia and saved by Axel, who claimed him as a double agent, and since then he has been one, partly to take revenge on Jack Brotherhood—mostly, however, to sweep away, as Axel says, "the churches, the schools . . . , the class systems" and all the corrupt institutions and people who have produced "such sad little fellows as Sir Magnus" (ch. 15). Particularly people like Magnus' father, Rickie.

After his parents' separation, le Carré stayed with his father, whom he describes as a "colorful and curious personality" and, more significantly, as "a Micawber character." But Micawber was lovable. Ronald Cornwell, by contrast, was (his son has said) "perhaps a schizophrenic." Like Rickie in *A Perfect Spy*, Ronald was "the only son of religious lower-middle-class parents." And Ronald was "tremendously ambitious to get out, by any means."

Rickie gets out by knocking up the mousy daughter of Sir Makepeace Watermaster, pottery factory owner and chief minister in his workers' Tabernacle, a "dissenting" fundamentalist Protestant church. (The English Establishment belongs to the Church of England, headed by the monarch. The lower-middle and working classes belong to many small sects, often called simply "chapel.") Rickie had embezzled all the Tabernacle's funds and Magnus, it seems, is conceived as insurance because Rickie guesses—correctly—that Sir Makepeace will discover the theft. Magnus, like le Carré, grows up a "millionaire pauper," living in a succession of unpaid-for fine houses and hotels, his father surrounded by courtiers and "lovelies." For his mother, Dorothy (Dot), Magnus (Titch) has only pity, not love. All seven-year-old Magnus' love, even sexual interest, is wrapped up in the magical Annie Lippschitz called "Lippsie." "Life began with Lippsie, Tom," he writes to his son in chapter 4. Lippsie, a "German Four-by-Two . . . cockney rhyming slang for Jew," is a refugee Rickie acquires to be a maid of all work. A beauty, she eventually becomes the "trois" in a ménage à trois with Rickie and Dot. Rickie's man, Syd Lemon, says, "She was lonely, Titch. Adored the kids. Adored you." Magnus recalls this time as "Paradise" (ch. 4).

In jail and out, in trouble and out, Rickie bilks widows and old people of great sums of insurance and investment money. Le Carré has not sentimentalized his father here. Magnus prays Rickie will marry Lippsie. But Lippsie's "deepening melancholy" disturbs him. Her family is dead, she is sure—"Old Lippsie's on about her Jews," Syd Lemon says, "another lot's been done" (ch. 4).

At this time "Rick formed the determination to turn Pym into a gentleman" (ch. 4) and sends him to Grimble's school (based on St. Andrew's in Pangbourne). "And so we arrived," le Carré said later, "in educated, middle-class society feeling almost like spies," knowing there was "a great deal to conceal. . . . We learned to dissemble and be very watchful." The born spy. As a result, although institutions fascinate him, le Carré has "never felt at home in any social structure really." All through

his novels le Carré does not conceal his hatred for the smugness of the Establishment, represented in *A Perfect Spy* by insufferable little Sefton Boyd and his gang. He will always identify with Jews or anyone else who, like himself, does not fit in.

Rickie sends Lippsie with Titch to school, to labor as a kind of payment. He knows too that Lippsie is only "held to the world" through Titch. Lippsie teaches him his first German lessons, a language he loves throughout his life. But she tells Rickie "you made me to be a *teef*" (ch. 4)—a thief—and not long after, leaps from a school tower to her death. Syd leads us to think it is a case of survivor guilt: she has "the guilts she isn't dead" like her family (ch. 4). Sefton Boyd claims to have seen her vagina as she lay dead. Titch carves Boyd's initials in the beautiful wooden walls of the master's lavatory and Boyd is flogged. It is Pym's first important act of deceitful rebellion; later he betrays his father, and finally he betrays hated Establishment England. At the novel's end, he commits suicide.

Since Rickie is based on le Carré's real father—what of Lippsie? Could le Carré actually have had, in his youth, a Jewish surrogate mother who committed suicide because of his father? Amazingly, no one has ever asked him. Yet imagine the effect on his fiction. We have been searching through le Carré's books in emulation of his hero, Smiley, and here Smiley would pause, and mumble, "A Jewish heroine named Lippsie. . . ." He would think of *The Spy Who Came In from the Cold* and say, "Jewish heroine named Liz." Lippsie and Liz resemble each other physically; both die tragic deaths as a result of their Jewishness. He would reach for *The Honourable Schoolboy* whose heroine, Lizzie, is sometimes called Liza Worth (Liz Gold = Liza Worth?) and sometimes, most oddly, Liese, pronounced "Leesa" although it is a German name and she is not German. The wealthy man who keeps her, Drake Ko, makes her call herself that. Connie Sachs, with her "frightening" sixth sense, uncovers that Ko, orphaned young, was taken in by a German woman named Liese.

Lippsie, Liz, Lizzie, Liese—there is too much of this for it all to be coincidence. In a letter written 20 August 1990, le Carré confirms that there was a real-life original. After his mother left, he was for a while "entrusted" to a German Jewish girl named Annaliese. She was, he later decided, one of his father's conquests. Lippsie commits suicide. Annaliese, "most likely . . . as the consequence of a love affair" with his father, returned home to Germany just before the war—in retrospect, a kind of suicide, and his father's fault. Le Carré writes,

I was still in school in 1945, when the scale of the Holocaust became known. British newsreels at the cinema, and the British tabloid press, carried an almost unbearable diet of pictures of the atrocities, and they made an impact on all of us. I cannot tell you how much I was aware of the Holocaust before that, but I do remember that my fears for Annaliese grew as the war continued and the fate of the Jews in Central Europe became clearer.

Le Carré hunted for Annaliese after the war, when he was doing his national service as a lieutenant in the Intelligence Corps. "I spent most of my time interrogating and classifying refugees from all corners of Central and Eastern Europe. Some of these were survivors from the Holocaust, others claimed to be. All of them had tragic tales to tell." He visited the Dachau concentration camp, and Bergen Belsen, and "many" camps for refugees. Le Carré reports that he "used the military network in Austria and Germany to try to trace her, but I was unsuccessful."

Annaliese became Annie Lippshitz, "Lippsie." This is a figure of whom the novelist has written, "Life began with Lippsie. . . ." Knowing that the novelist, abandoned by his natural mother, acquired a beloved Jewish surrogate mother whom he believed died at the hands of the Nazis, a mother-figure he searched for among the concentration camp survivors, throws a whole new light on his novels. He has named three heroines after her, but that is almost superficial compared to the deep effects on his work. Finally we understand how le Carré, though not born Jewish, has written more about Jews than most Jewish novelists. He was a pioneer in what is now called Holocaust Studies. A large part of his work has been the empathetic study of what it means to be Jewish in the modern world.

His works contain, in particular, portraits of Jewish women strikingly at odds with current stereotypes. Lippsie and Liz Gold are almost supernaturally gentle, and nurturing, fantasy Jewish mothers. They are the most reverent portraits of Jewish women in contemporary literature and they stand shockingly alone. Le Carré writes counter to such tradition as exists—particularly within the Jewish community—a perplexing, scandalous situation. Woody Allen, Philip Roth, and Bruce Jay Friedman have popularized an image of the Jewish woman as "yenta" (nag or harridan) or "kvetch" (complainer).

Le Carré's beautiful portraits stand in lonely contrast. Though he never stereotypes, he is intensely conscious of both women as Jewish, and their Jewishness is central to their goodness, to the attractive parts of their personality. In *A Murder of Quality* one reads of masters telling British schoolboys that to show emotion is lowerclass. Le Carré's Jewish women are oases in an emotional desert: loving, emotionally expressive, volatile, nurturing, caring. In *A Perfect Spy*, Lippsie is warmer, more giving to a little English child starving for maternal love, than his own poor mother knows how to be. When he joins her in a bath, a beloved memory, it is more than a rebaptism, it is a rebirth.

A MURDER OF QUALITY

In *A Perfect Spy*, Magnus, at seventeen, like le Carré runs away from the Establishment idiocies of an English school to Bern, Switzerland, where he holds odd jobs and perfects his German at the university. Following military service (1950–1952) le Carré took a degree at Lincoln College, Oxford, studying German and French, graduating with first-class honors. His father's bankruptcy made the newspapers in 1954. That year le Carré married Alison Ann Veronica Sharp; together, they had three sons.

From 1956 to 1958 he taught German at Eton, most famous of the exclusive British private schools (called "public" schools). Eton is the heart of the Establishment, the old-boy network that has long run English life. "Let anyone who derides the notion of the Establishment," le Carré has warned—in his introduction to *The Philby Conspiracy* (1968), by Bruce Page, David Leitch, and Phillip Knightley—consider how it covered for the spy Kim Philby. During the Suez crisis, le Carré recalls most of the cabinet ministers were old boys from Eton. David Cornwell, the secret outsider, the born spy, loathed the place. Le Carré has been frank about it, but the best way to know the surprising intensity of his hatred is to read *A Murder of Quality*, which is otherwise of little interest.

Just as le Carré used the secret services as a "microcosm of the British condition," as he wrote in his introduction to *The Philby Conspiracy,* he tries to use Eton—or rather, Carne—as a microcosm of the British Establishment, a way to plunge quickly to its heart. On the first page we learn that the famous school Carne was "founded by obscure monks, endowed by a sickly boy king, and dragged from oblivion by a Victorian bully." In chapter 1, two boys in uniform discuss Stanley Rode—"You can tell he's not a gentleman"—and Terence Fielding, a senior don about to retire—"My Pater says he's a queer." Perkins, Fielding's head boy, quotes Fielding: "Emotionalism is only for the lower classes." Giving you the feel of this atavistic, oppressive little world, and making sure you hate it, is the novel's true goal. The plot is more of a tour—a short tour that other books have done better. In the end it turns out Fielding killed Rode's wife, to stop her from blackmailing him about a wartime incident with a boy. To solve the crime, Smiley must decipher the Hardyesque ramblings of Mad Janie, who lives in an abandoned church. A bad book.

A SMALL TOWN IN GERMANY

Far more deserving of our attention is *A Small Town in Germany*. This book, published in 1968, is set about two years ahead in the future. It deals with the rise of a neo-Nazi movement, led by Dr. Klaus Karfeld, while Britain, anxious not to offend Germany during certain trade negotiations, looks the other way. Le Carré shows us a British Establishment amoral and spineless as ever, once again desperate for peace at any price. At one point Karfeld's "mindless" crowds, "mediocre, ponderous and terrifying," shuffle pointedly toward "Chamberlain's hill" (ch. 17). Neville Chamberlain, British prime minister in 1938, had sold Europe out to Hitler. Chamberlain's speeches are some of le Carré's strong early memories.

During this crisis Leo Harting, a low-level diplomat, a "temporary" employee of the British Embassy in Bonn (the "small town" of the title) has disappeared with forty sensitive files, including an ultrasensitive Green File. Le Carré has written that although he left Harting's religion "ambiguous," he "never doubted" Harting was Jewish (unpublished letter, 20 August 1990). Harting had been a prewar child refugee in England with a certain member of the German parliament later known to be a Communist. The Foreign Office assumes that another Communist mole has decamped and sends in a Security man to investigate.

Foreign Office investigator Alan Turner, though an Oxford man, is defiantly working-class, Northern, and venomously anti-Establishment. He flies in from London and interrogates the embassy staff. The novel, little more than the record of Turner's inquest, offers the reader primarily a gallery of grotesques. *A Small Town in Germany* is a comparatively straightforward warm-up for the brilliantly intricate mole hunting in *Tinker, Tailor, Soldier, Spy* (1974).

Since le Carré had been, like Harting, a "second secretary" in the Bonn embassy, the novel is of considerable biographical interest. All le Carré's novels rest on his claim that "the British secret services" are "microcosms of the British condition, of our social attitudes and vanities" (introduction to *The Philby Conspiracy*). Turner and his creator reveal their disgust for the doglike complicity of all classes that keeps the effete Establishment secure. Le Carré describes, with a hatred bordering on relish, the diplomatic wives who manage to enter the English Church on Sunday, following, "quite by accident, the order of succession which protocol, had they cared about such things, would exactly have demanded" (ch. 2).

These institutional workaday fools are no match for the genius of Leo Harting, who, like a German Ronnie Cornwell, detaches their secret files from them simply by drinking with the men, flirting and sleeping with the women, listening to everyone's pathetic confidences, and—a brilliant touch—giving everyone hair dryers, then an expensive vanity item. There is something so tawdry about bribing people with hair dryers. *A Small Town in Germany* could have been titled after the Mann novel le Carré alludes to, *Confessons of Felix Krull, Confidence Man* (1954). Not even *A Perfect Spy* gives us a better feel for Ronnie Cornwell. There is rare knowledge behind le Carré's tour-de-force portrait of Harting's chameleon turns into each target's fantasy friend: with old Gaunt, the guard, Harting is the democratic aristocrat happy to sit like a regular chap and drink some tea and chew the fat; with dowdy Jenny Pargiter, he is a continental lover, a man of burning glances and barely bridled romantic passions; to bourgeois Cork, he becomes a sad and comic sidekick, flatteringly envious of Cork's wife and kids; with Mickie Crabbe the boozer, he is a drinking buddy to go whoring with; for Hazel Bradfield, his boss's wife, Harting becomes Lady Chatterley's lover, more sensitive and genuine than anyone from her class; to Rawley Bradfield, he is a present to appease his discontented wife. When Turner at last uncovers Harting's private lair deep inside the embassy, only we, looking at his mundane props, his thermos, his foot warmer, his hair dryers, finally envision him, like Laurence Olivier backstage: oddly colorless and normal, a small hard-working man.

Turner discovers, at book's end, that Leo Harting, no Communist mole, stole the files that proved Karfeld took part in the Chemical Research murder of thirty-one "hybrid" (half-Jewish) slave laborers. When Turner realizes the British decided to keep Karfeld's secret so that they could blackmail him if he came to power, his disgust and ours is complete. Turner only sees Harting at the instant Harting is murdered, while trying, critics claim, to assassinate Karfeld at a Nazi rally.

Le Carré's account of Leo Harting's lonely passion shines a great light backward on an experience we know le Carré to have had. One of le Carré's persistent themes is the presence of unpunished Nazi war criminals in Germany and the continued danger of naziism. A second is the Holocaust and its aftermath, including the state of Israel and contemporary Jewish unease. Obviously the two themes connect. Knowing more of le Carré's biography will help us understand why they fascinate him.

Drafted in 1949, le Carré was sent to Austria, where his good German was put to use interrogating DPs, "displaced persons," including former prisoners from concentration and slave labor camps. "Lippsies in the making," le Carré calls them in a scene from *A Perfect Spy* that depicts this time. Some "spoke of death and torture so casually that he became indignant at their unconcern. . . . If they described a night crossing over the hills, Pym crossed with them, lugging their Lippsie suitcases and feeling the icy mountain air" (ch. 13).

The interviews the twenty-year-old le Carré had with these survivors were some of the great formative experiences of his life. We know he was searching for Annaliese and probably picturing everything he heard happening to her. The marks of these interviews are all over his novels. *A Small Town in Germany* hangs on them: le Carré gave Leo Harting his own old job. Harting's youthful confrontation with the Holocaust so sears him that it produces the obsession still driving him two decades later. Le Carré wrote the 1968 *A Small Town in Germany* just before the deadline that motivates Leo: the twenty-year statute of limitations for Nazi war crimes was about to run out. "What's so damn holy about twenty years?" Praschko says Leo had shouted at him; Praschko's response was to say that we have gotten "old" and "tired" of remembering. Leo, Praschko relates, said he had "seen the living witness of evil," felt he was a "privileged" person who must bear witness (ch. 17); and so must le Carré. Leo dies in Turner's arms as Turner sees "his own life, his own face" in Leo's (epilogue).

The ghastly experiences available to most of us only through a movie like Claude Lanzmann's *Shoah* (1985), le Carré, at twenty, endured daily, and in the flesh. I helped an Auschwitz survivor write his memoirs fifteen years ago, and it is not an experience one can forget. ("Where were you standing when your mother fell off the train?") Le Carré was seeing Holocaust victims, while the wounds and memories were still fresh and emotions strong. In le Carré's first published novel, the very first thing Smiley does is visit a concentration camp survivor, Elsa Fennan, and interview her, "a slight, fierce woman" with hair "the colour of nicotine."

Although frail, she conveyed an impression of endurance and courage, and the brown eyes that shone from her crooked little face were of an astonishing intensity. It was a worn face, racked and ravaged long ago, the face of a child grown old on starving and exhaustion, the eternal refugee face, the prison-camp face. . . .

(*Call for the Dead*, ch. 3)

A face le Carré knows well. Interviewing her, Smiley feels "sick and cheap." She does not resent him. "He was an oppressor, but she accepted oppression." His quest for Annaliese led le Carré to write more about the Holocaust and its aftereffects than most Jewish novelists. The strongest pejorative in le Carré's characters' vocabularies to this day is "fascist." Indeed, the youthful le Carré probably, like Harting, acquired through his interviews information about Nazi war criminals, then watched the Western Occupation forces decide it was impolitic to prosecute them. "The war crimes investigation units themselves were near to disbandment," we learn in *A Small Town in Germany.* "There was pressure from London and Washington to bury the hatchet and hand over all responsibility to the German courts" (ch. 16). That is what motivates Elsa Fennan's spying in le Carré's first novel. At the end of the sequel, *The Spy Who Came In from the Cold,* we discover Elsa to have been correct. The entire British operation has been staged to protect a murderous former Nazi who is selling information to the British. A dedicated Jewish Communist is about to expose him, and the British discredit him, even accidentally unleash a new current of anti-Semitism. The Nazi even murders the hero's Jewish Communist girlfriend, Liz Gold. A few years later, as the Statute of Limitations approached, le Carré, who had been a "privileged" witness, wrote his only "message novel," challenging the Statute, telling what he had seen, arguing that Nazis still prominent in Germany could start all over again. When le Carré wrote of Israel later in *The Little Drummer Girl* (1983), he was only continuing his meditations on the Holocaust in another part of the world. It was hardly the ill-informed meddling in Jewish affairs that critics like Harold Bloom assumed it was at the time. When le Carré interviewed survivors in Israel twenty-five years after his original interviews, he was a person who—from the deepest personal interest—had spent much of his life work reflecting on what it meant to be a Jew after the Holocaust, a person who had written to warn against persistent Nazi strains operating in Germany.

CALL FOR THE DEAD

CALL FOR THE DEAD was published by a small house, Walker, in the United States, so many Americans who read *The Spy Who Came In from the Cold* did not realize that that novel was actually a sequel to the successful earlier book. *The Spy Who Came In from the Cold* reads differently, and its impact is even stronger, when it is read in the context of *Call for the Dead.* "In one of those old sixpenny note books" in which he wrote his first Smiley story, le Carré remembers, he made a sketch of that character as he "first imagined him. Tubby and perplexed, the weary pilgrim is struggling up a stony hill, carrying his exhausted horse on his shoulders."

Smiley is one of the great suggestive names in literature. Not only does the name make you instantly picture him, but even to pronounce it leaves your face in his polite, perpetually embarrassed smile. Although le Carré's concept of Smiley deepens, the center of the myth is present from *Call for the Dead's* first sentence: "When Lady Ann Sercombe married George Smiley," she described him to her amazed upper-class friends as "breathtakingly ordinary." In the second sentence she leaves him for a "Cuban motor racing driver." Smiley's appearance will not alter from this first page on: "Short, fat and of a quiet disposition, he appeared to spend a lot of money on really bad clothes, which hung about his squat frame like skin on a shrunken toad."

If the essence of popular literature is wish fulfillment, whose wish would be fulfilled by becoming George Smiley? One could understandably wish to be James Bond, but why would one identify with this unhappy little cuckold? Le Carré now admits, he did use a "model" for his depiction, at least for its "externals": the Reverend Vivian Green, his Oxford "tutor," who, like his student, knew Sherborne, having been chaplain there. Le Carré told the Book-of-the-Month Club Green was "tubby, bespectacled and in manner very quiet." Like Smiley, he dressed expensively but terribly, "white silk shirts that crumpled the moment he put them on." We recognize deeper Smiley traits: "When [Green] started a conversation he seemed to begin in the middle, as if he had read your thoughts thus far." He had the "ability to empathize, to affiliate himself with you without appearing to intrude."

In creating Smiley, le Carré was, I think, using an old father figure to create for himself the ideal father he never had. He acknowledged this when he told Joseph Lelyveld, in a 1986 interview for the *New York Times Magazine,* in reference to *A Perfect Spy,* that "it was only when I took leave of Smiley in my own mind" after *Smiley's People* (1980), "that I was able to address myself to my real father." He clearly implies that Smiley had long been his fictional one. Smiley may be the opposite of James Bond, but he is even more the opposite of Ronnie Cornwell: as faithful as Ronnie was fickle, as solid as Ronnie was shoddy. That gave Smiley his emotional fascination for his creator, who could write with all the power of a child's wish. Smiley is, unlike Ronnie, kind, gentle, sexually faithful (indeed, chivalric), respectable if not patrician—normal. He *belongs,* as Ronnie never did, and as Ronnie's children, by extension, never did. Ronnie's legacy of social ambiguity and the burden of all his lies are a theme throughout le Carré's novels. It intensifies le Carré's fury at the Establishment. We start to see how unreal, how dreamlike Smiley is when we realize he fits all of St. Paul's criteria for the perfect human being: Smiley suffereth long, and is kind; Smiley envieth not, doth not behave himself unseemly, is not puffed up; Smiley beareth all things, believeth all things, hopeth all things. And le Carré's fantasy father proved to be very close to the international reading public's.

Already, in this first book, Smiley works essentially alone, and wins. The individual still counts. Although he has been written of as an "organization man," whenever we actually see him he is as alone as a cowboy, as a samurai *ronin,* as a novelist. He returns from retirement, often, or works solo, only physically inside a corrupt organization. The spy in Western literature had been a sneak. During this century he became an affirmation of the individual's power against the megastate or megacorporation—the Circus (le Carré's term for the British secret service) or the Centre (his term for the Russian secret service)—which all others bow to as the sun. "It is sheer vanity," Smiley lectures himself in *Tinker, Tailor, Soldier, Spy,* "to believe that one fat middle-aged spy is the only person capable of holding the world together" (ch. 10). Le Carré dares to say it because he knows we will say "Not vanity at all!" We are readers and thinkers like Smiley, and his victories give us new faith in our own powers.

Call for the Dead begins when a Foreign Office employee, Samuel Fennan, whom Smiley had routinely questioned about Party membership in Oxford in the 1930's, kills himself, leaving a typed suicide note saying Smiley hounded him to death. Smiley is aghast. Fennan had known he was closing the file. "Half the Cabinet were in the Party in the '30s." The suicide seems unbelievable. "What was he like?" Peter Guillam asks, and readers who have not spent the time we have on le Carré's biography will flinch at Smiley's answer: "To look at, obviously a Jew" (ch. 2). The omniscient narrator sums up Smiley's thoughts later: "Samuel Fennan, the eternal Jew" (ch. 8). "I'm the wandering Jewess," his wife Elsa tells Smiley at the end of chapter 12.

Now that le Carré's reputation as a writer of serious literature has grown, and he is included in standard works like this one, people who never read *Call for the Dead* will become aware of it. Knowing nothing of le Carré, I fear they will misunderstand it, as many did *The Little Drummer Girl.* The important critic Harold Bloom—who is, alas, no le Carré expert—in a 1987 introduction he wrote to what is still the only collection of essays about le Carré, spent half the introduction blasting him for insensitivity to Jews. When le Carré writes that Israeli jets "bombed the crowded Palestinian quarter of Beirut," killing many children, Bloom retorts the passage "just won't do": "[it] makes me want to shout at le Carré" about the "rabbis and old men massacred by Palestinians last week in an Istanbul synagogue." Le Carré's sympathy, Bloom says, is "essentially . . . with the Palestinians in a very English tradition of choosing sides in that terrible and perpetual war."

I contend, on the contrary, that le Carré's extraordinary personal experience of the Holocaust, dramatized in Leo Harting's quest to bring Nazi murderers to justice, convinced him that the Holocaust was the most significant moral subject of his time. This conviction, and his deep personal identification with Jews—like himself, outsiders in Establishment England—have consistently drawn le Carré to where most gentile angels fear to tread. The narrator describes "the eternal Jew" in *Call for the Dead* this way: "cultured, cosmopolitan, self-determinate, industrious and perceptive: to Smiley, immensely attractive" (ch. 8).

Bloom is entirely right to hint at an English tradition of anti-Semitism. "We all knew who the Jews were in school," le Carré said with disgust later, "and made sure they knew it too." Anti-Semitism had been, le Carré well knew, particularly strong in the English thriller, which tended to play on spy mania and xenophobia. Sapper's (H. C. McNeile's) series character Bulldog Drummond led bands of black-shirted thugs to beat up Jews and foreigners. "The Jew is everywhere," a character tells Richard Hannay in chapter 1 of Buchan's seminal *The Thirty-Nine Steps* (1915) "but you have to go far down the backstairs to find him." Once you get past the gentile front men and "get to the real boss, ten to one you are brought up against a little white-faced Jew in a bathchair with an eye like a rattlesnake. Yes sir, he is the man who is ruling the world just now," and he wants a "return match for the *pogroms . . .* because his aunt was outraged and his father flogged" "Krauts. *Bloody* Krauts. God, I hate them!" Mendel says in *Call for the Dead.* "Forgive and forget.

Why bloody well forget? . . . Krupp and all that mob—oh no" (ch. 6). Superficially identical scenes. The difference is, le Carré's Mendel isn't "ruling the world," he is a retired police inspector. He is also Smiley's closest friend through all the novels. When Smiley is injured, Mendel even takes over as *Call for the Dead*'s protagonist for several chapters. And, the Jewish character here is not spoken about, described, but speaks *for himself.* Finally, Mendel's anger is, I will show, also le Carré's.

Call for the Dead treads on particularly dangerous ground for le Carré, since it is not a "Philby" novel (it does not deal with an Establishment mole) but a "Rosenberg" novel. The most famous American espionage case of the 1950's, still a bitterly sensitive subject in the Jewish community, was the prosecution of Julius and Ethel Rosenberg, American Communists, at the height of the McCarthy anti-Communist hysteria. They died in the electric chair as spies on 19 June 1953. Pablo Picasso painted them, scores of books and novels have been written about them. The American Jewish community has long considered them innocent martyrs to chauvinist hysteria. Smiley, investigating the case of Samuel and Elsa Fennan, will discover that Elsa is indeed guilty. What is more, her motive is her sense of herself as "the wandering Jewess," and she has even helped kill her husband because he endangered her mission.

That sounds as bad as Harold Bloom could fear. Pieced together with the widespread opinion that *The Little Drummer Girl* is anti-Semitic, it could suggest a very different le Carré than the one I see. But to read it as anti-Semitic one must know nothing of le Carré's biography or the "Never forget!" passions of *A Small Town in Germany.* Remembering that novel, we realize that Mendel's opinion about never forgiving Krupp is le Carré's. Le Carré wrote *A Small Town in Germany* to warn us that a policy of "forgive and forget" could lead straight to Klaus Karfeld's neo-Nazi crowds shuffling once more toward Chamberlain's hill, while the coward British Establishment seeks peace in our time. Le Carré plants a newspaper headline in *Call for the Dead* about the lynching of a Jewish shopkeeper in Dusseldorf to underline the reality behind Elsa's fears. What makes *Call for the Dead* so interesting is that le Carré thinks Elsa Fennan is *right,* but that nothing corrupts like being right, and being absolutely right has corrupted Elsa absolutely. Smiley, at the end, pictures Elsa and her Jewish controller, Dieter, tragically: "They dreamed of peace and freedom.

Now they're murderers and spies" (ch. 18). The double irony is that Smiley, too, is a spy; and he has just killed Dieter.

Dieter Frey, Elsa's controller from the Abteilung, the East German Intelligence Service, is not only a Jew—he was once Smiley's star pupil. "A tall, handsome, commanding cripple," Smiley says, "the idol of his generation; a Jew" (ch. 11). Change the last phrase to "a homosexual" and you have Bill Haydon, the mole of *Tinker, Tailor, Soldier, Spy.* During the war, Smiley, running a network of agents in Germany, recruits Dieter and trains him. Dieter somehow escapes the gas chambers and after the war follows his Socialist sympathies to East Germany.

Elsa survives a death camp, but is hospitalized for three years following. In the mid 1950's she watches the ascent of the "New Germany" and sees, like Mendel, that the "old names had come back, names that had frightened us as children. The dreadful, plump pride returned. . . . They marched with the old rhythm" (ch. 12). She becomes Dieter's agent, begins stealing her husband's Foreign Office papers and passing them to the Abteilung. When Dieter sees George Smiley interviewing Samuel Fennan, he fears the worst and has his "silent killer," Hans-Dieter Mundt, murder Fennan. Mundt is an ex-Nazi, and Dieter's association with him (symbolized by their shared name) is the mark of Frey's corruption. As for Elsa, her fear of a Nazi resurgence has led her to help a Nazi kill a Jew—her own husband.

In the end, Smiley tracks Dieter onto a bridge, Dieter pulls his gun, and they grapple. Dieter cannot bring himself to shoot his old mentor and Smiley, desperate, knocks him off the bridge. The crippled Dieter drowns while Smiley cries, "Oh dear God what have I done, Oh Christ, Dieter . . . why didn't you shoot?" Looking back on the way Dieter, not he, had honored their human connection with each other, Smiley muses, "Who was then the gentleman . . . ?" (ch. 16).

THE SPY WHO CAME IN FROM THE COLD

BUT what of Dieter Frey's "silent killer," Hans-Dieter Mundt? His escape from England at the end of *Call for the Dead* is hard to believe; and after he has killed Samuel Fennan and Adam Scarr and nearly killed Smiley, it is a strangely unsatisfying way for le Carré to leave the book. Unless, of course, he already had seen the book as part one of a two-part case.

Read as a sequel to *Call for the Dead,* we see that *The Spy Who Came In from the Cold* is, morally, a mirror reflection, a characteristic le Carré attempt to balance the moral scales. *Call for the Dead* describes an East German operation in which two idealistic East German Jews, Dieter and Elsa, descend to such savage means that they accept a Nazi as a cohort, who kills a Jew for their cause. *The Spy Who Came In from the Cold* is the story of the retaliatory English operation, in which the English descend to such savage means that they accept a Nazi as cohort, who kills a Jew for the cause. It is even the same Nazi, Hans-Dieter Mundt. In the first book he kills the German agent's love, Samuel Fennan; in the second, he kills the English agent's love, Liz Gold.

The Spy Who Came In from the Cold is le Carré's best written book, the one that made his reputation and rightly so. Only the transcendent Dickensian achievement of the Smiley character, in books much less beautifully designed, equals it. Everything came together for le Carré with awesome timing: the Berlin Wall went up and he was there; history prepared a spotlight for the material of which he had long been master.

In the famous opening, Alec Leamas, who has been running agents inside East Germany, watches the last one, Riemeck, shot as he tries to escape through the Wall. Hans-Dieter Mundt, now second man in the Abteilung, East German Intelligence, has rolled up the Berlin network. Leamas is tough, fiftyish, physical, unintellectual, a hardened fieldman used to "the cold"; "a man who was not quite a gentleman." The Circus is now run by Control, the symbolically nameless, inhumanly efficient professional. Control proposes a daring plan to Leamas, to "[take] care of Mundt." "If it's a question of killing Mundt, I'm game," Leamas says (ch. 2).

Le Carré, one notices, has been careful to put Smiley in retirement during the planning phase. Since killing Dieter, he has become so melancholy and thoughtful even Leamas thinks he is finished. Some revisionists have been overeager to claim Smiley as the villain of the piece. In le Carré's text, however, the plan is simply Control's, and matches his utilitarian strategy in *The Looking Glass War* (1965). In that book Control uses Smiley in several ways without letting him in on the secret until the

damage is done, whereupon Smiley recoils in horror. The Circus always works on a "need-to-know" basis. Control, moreover, gets sarcastic about Smiley's crises of conscience. There is every reason to believe that once Smiley is enticed back to the Service, he is given only a bit more knowledge than Leamas. His last line in the book shows that he had been misled about Control's plan for Liz Gold: "The girl, where's the girl?" (ch. 26).

The operation: Leamas seems to descend into drink, petty thievery, dismissal, disgrace, poverty, odd jobs, and a short jail term. Although Leamas does not know it, Control plants him in the Bayswater Library for Psychic Research so he will be near a shy, idealistic young British Communist, Liz Gold, in the hope that East Germany will later choose to question her about him. Evidence will be planted to indicate they had an affair. When Liz, the most convincing female lead in le Carré's fiction, falls for the apparently failing Leamas out of the natural charity of her heart, so much the better.

Leamas' old competition, the Abteilung, sizes up the seemingly embittered, impoverished spy, and after some tests, offers to buy information from him. They take him to East Germany. Meanwhile Control sends Smiley to Liz. Not even using a cover name, he pays all her expenses, as if accepting her as the dependent of an agent on a mission. He even leaves his card.

In Germany, Jens Fiedler, Mundt's Jewish second in command, "sweats" Leamas. Control had said, "Fiedler's a Jew . . . and Mundt is quite the other thing"—"He hates [Mundt's] guts" (ch. 12). The Circus knows Mundt's Nazi past. Leamas lets Fiedler work out of him information about a British agent Leamas only heard of, called Rolling Stone. Fiedler says, "Mundt escaped so easily from England; you told me yourself he did" (ch. 14). Fiedler, seemingly against Leamas' will, links the Rolling Stone dates to Mundt. He eventually reveals that he had suspected it, had been keeping a file on Mundt. Fiedler brings Mundt to trial.

Then Mundt produces a surprise witness, Liz. Fiedler, looking at her, "smiled very slightly, as if in recognition of her race" (ch. 23). She admits under questioning that one of Leamas' friends, George Smiley, has begun to protect her. Mundt realizes that Leamas had not fallen from grace; that he is an agent, there to discredit him. Leamas is exposed; Fiedler falls. "As for the Jew," a prison guard tells Liz, he will be shot. "Comrade Mundt knows what to do with Jews" (ch. 24). Mundt's rival is gone; he is stronger than ever.

And Leamas realizes that Mundt in fact *was* an English agent. He had not miraculously escaped after the Fennan affair. Captured, he had been "turned," given the choice of hanging or turning double agent and getting rich. To help Mundt rise to replace Dieter Frey, Control let him discover and kill Leamas' East German agents—to Control nothing more than a bunch of expendable Communist traitors, to be used any way that best advanced British interests. But—as we saw at the Wall—Mundt had to kill them on capture, before Fiedler could sweat them and learn anything valuable about the Circus or its methods. That aroused Fiedler's suspicions. So Leamas was duped. "We are witnessing," Leamas tells Liz, ". . . a filthy, lousy operation to save Mundt's skin. To save him from a clever little Jew. . . . They made us kill him, do you see, kill the Jew" (ch. 24). Control and Smiley only needed Liz and Leamas to be together "for a day" so that by bringing her money later they could make it look as if the Circus was paying for an agent's affair.

Mundt arranges a car for Leamas and Liz's escape. As they flee toward the Wall, Liz puts the book in so strange a light that le Carré's 1963 American readers probably took it as so much Communist nonsense. I know I did. The misleading Establishment image we had of le Carré also made it impossible to think he might in any way agree with Liz: "Fiedler was . . . doing his job," she tells Leamas, "and now you've killed him. Mundt is a spy and a traitor and you protect him. Mundt is a Nazi . . . he hates Jews. What side are you on?" (ch. 25). The one absolute in le Carré's world is anti-Semitism. Characters may act for communism or against it, but no character associated with anti-Semitic violence is ever excused.

Liz says it seems "odd" that Mundt let her go—"a Party member knowing all this." It isn't "logical" (ch. 25). They're given clear instructions on when to scale the Wall. They follow them, but the lights go on: only Liz is shot. Mundt—and Control—did not go through all this only to let this smart little English Communist endanger the entire operation. Smiley is shouting from the other side, "The girl, where's the girl?" so he obviously played his role thinking that she would be rescued with Leamas. Control will abuse Smiley's trust again in

the next book. The guards were instructed to kill only her, for when Leamas, coming "in from the cold" to side with his love, goes back down the Wall on the chance that she might still be alive, at first no one fires. She is dead. He stands, "glaring around him like a blinded bull in the arena" till they shoot.

The Spy Who Came In from the Cold is one of the best novels written in the second half of the twentieth century, a fusion of emotion and intellect that recalls the best work of Dickens. The style is more beautiful than Dickens, a unique compound of twentieth-century imagist descriptions and the elegant dialectical conversations of Jane Austen or Bernard Shaw.

THE LOOKING GLASS WAR

THE LOOKING GLASS WAR is one of le Carré's least read novels and the easiest to understand, so I will be brief—regretfully, for it is excellent. Le Carré is supposed to have said that the operation in *The Spy Who Came In from the Cold* was too brilliant, and he wanted to write of a normal operation in which everything goes wrong. That project is this book. The first scene, in which the silly ass Taylor accidentally gets drunk waiting for a film drop, parodies *The Spy*'s great tense opening. Accidents abound. People forget their orders or are too proud to say they never understood them.

Leclerc, a bureaucrat right down to his name, tries to find reasons for "the Department," a leftover arm of Military Intelligence, to exist. They do not even rate a staff car anymore. He decides he believes some hokey photographs suggest that the Russians are putting nuclear missiles in East Germany—another Cuban Missile Crisis? That threat pries loose some funding, not only for a car, but to reactivate one field agent. They train and send a trusting Pole, Fred Leiser, into East Germany. Leiser is caught and killed. Control, at the Circus, has been giving Leclerc enough rope to hang himself, as Smiley, who was liaison, realizes in horror at the end. Leiser was caught because Control gave Leiser outdated World War II radio equipment that Leclerc was too ignorant to refuse. (The way Control manipulates Smiley reinforces our sense of how things went in *The Spy Who Came In from the Cold*.) At book's end, Leclerc seems to have become senile from the shock, and the department will probably be disbanded.

The prose is beautiful but the book's real beauty lies in the delicacy of the characterizations, the portraits of average men trying to find some purpose in their lives. Le Carré quotes, ironically, from Rupert Brooke's early, innocent prowar poem, "1914," at the beginning of part 3: "To turn as swimmers into cleanness leaping / Glad from a world grown old and cold and weary." *The Russia House* is in some ways a heavy-handed replay of this theme. Organizations exist to perpetuate themselves, not to serve; Cold War organizations exist to perpetuate the Cold War, which they must feed on as if it were a host. Members of the Russian Writers' Union, in a 1989 interview with le Carré, expressed their fascination with *The Looking Glass War.* In the post–Cold War era, this fine book will be read intently, and we will all wonder how much of the Cold War was only Russian, American, and British Leclercs trying to save the departments they loved.

THE NAIVE AND SENTIMENTAL LOVER

THE year 1968 saw the publication of *A Small Town in Germany.* Two years later there was a "time out," in *Lover*'s own words. *The Naive and Sentimental Lover* was supposedly le Carré's attempt at a "straight novel" but is actually something less than that. *The Naive and Sentimental Lover,* both a critical and commercial failure, is a familiar male mid-life crisis novel, published in 1971, the year of le Carré's divorce from Ann, his wife of nineteen years.

The novel is the story of Aldo Cassidy, a youthful "tycoon" in his late thirties, a graduate, like le Carré, of Sherborne and Oxford. Nearing forty, Aldo runs away from wife and career to experience the joys of bohemian freedom. The novel is a period piece. There were countless like it in those years as the "silent generation" that had come of age in the sober 1950's and been good organization men for twenty years hit forty at the very minute that the hippie generation seemed to be having all the fun. One movie had the memorable title, *Middle-Aged Crazies,* and *The Naive and Sentimental Lover,* despite the pretentious title from Friedrich von Schiller, is about the same subject. "Cassidy," le Carré explained, "is the victim not of society, but of himself . . . a dreamer obliged to conform. But

with this difference: he could, he really could, be free. What defeats him is . . . the impossibility of middle-class love." Merely to read such sentiments, in all their dogged honesty, snaps one back to love beads and *Sgt. Pepper.*

It helps very little to know that the book was based on le Carré's actual ménage à trois with Susan and James Kennaway, the latter a fine Scottish novelist who died prematurely in 1968. (*The Looking Glass War* is dedicated to Kennaway.) If *The Naive and Sentimental Lover* had dealt with le Carré's feelings about Kennaway's death it might have been a deeper book, but le Carré confines it to domestic adventure. Parts are quite funny. Aldo's pride at having cleaned up by inventing a better baby-carriage brake is *very* funny. Le Carré worked hard on the novel, and in a somewhat pathetic letter to the bookstores before publication warned them that there would be, for once, no spies.

In *Rabbit Redux* (1971) John Updike, le Carré's contemporary, sends white-bread Rabbit off to learn about the free life from an African American named Skeeter. Aldo's mentor is the Irish artist Shamus, who addresses him as "lover." Shamus' beautiful wife, Helen, is first seen naked. Shamus says uncompromising things like, "Who wants the twilight when he can have the fucking sun?" (ch. 17). Le Carré's eye for English mores fails him for once: the artists use slang that sounds twenty years out of date, and Cassidy's naked fantasy girl, Helen, is first seen listening to Frank Sinatra! In a series of painfully familiar scenes, Cassidy gets his horoscope read, looks guiltily at his children as he reads them bedtime stories, sleeps with a hippie vegetarian with "broad, hard thighs" under a poster of Che Guevara: "She adored Castro but her greatest single regret was that she had not fucked Che Guevara before he died." The narrator is moved: "Time out; borrowed Time; a past unlived, too long imagined, belatedly made real . . . Cassidy stripped, stood in the fountain, and felt the edges of his existence" (ch. 29). This is the only time le Carré, that precise stylist, will write anything that sounds like Beatles lyrics.

After various mild *Walpurgisnacht* scenes, Shamus and Helen give him their last kisses. In chapter 38 Helen tells him to "put a value on *yourself.*" Shamus says, "Keep trying, lover. Never regret, never apologize"—which Henry Ford II once said was his father's motto. Critics who lamented the prose as self-indulgent did not understand that the whole novel is in praise of self-indulgence. In an epilogue Shamus becomes a successful serious artist and Cassidy goes back to his wife, although he allows himself some infidelities: "For in this world, whatever there was left of it to inhabit, Aldo Cassidy dared not remember love."

The Naive and Sentimental Lover was not for naught. Years later, when le Carré decided to draw the left-wing actress Charlie in the opening half of *The Little Drummer Girl,* he would satirize the hippie artist world with deadly, knowing accuracy.

TINKER, TAILOR, SOLDIER, SPY

SADDENED, perhaps chastened by the failure of *The Naive and Sentimental Lover,* le Carré returned to his forte, the secret world of spies, and created one of the most memorable characters in twentieth-century literature, his mature conception of George Smiley.

Dostoyevsky gives us a clue about Smiley in a letter appraising Smiley's precursor, Mr. Pickwick—a letter written when he was creating his "idiot," the gently charismatic Prince Myshkin. The most difficult thing in the world for the novelist to do, Dostoyevsky writes, is to "portray a *positively* good man." That was the challenge le Carré faced, too. The two successes Dostoyevsky says he knows of are Don Quixote and Pickwick, who succeed because they are "good only because at the same time . . . ridiculous." Pickwick, whom Dostoyevsky calls an "immense" conception, is "ridiculous and succeeds by virtue of this fact." So Smiley, in direct line of descent from that other British hero he so physically resembles, is good, ridiculous, and ultimately successful.

In recognizing that Smiley is an heir to Pickwick, we ascribe to him his legitimate fictional father: Dickens, not Graham Greene. Although they both use the same subgenre to write serious literature, in every important way le Carré is the opposite of Greene. Greene's most famous character, Pinkie, is a revelation of human evil; le Carré's George Smiley is a revelation of human virtue. Greene creates plausible evil characters; le Carré creates plausible good—almost saintly—characters. Greene has the imagination of sin and le Carré of human goodness: Even Smiley's antagonist Karla is a relative stick figure till *Smiley's People,* when le Carré can imagine

him as a distraught father transformed by "excessive love." Even Karla!

Since Greene accepts human evil he is friendly to coercive systems wherever he finds them: critics should not be bewildered by his friendliness to Catholicism *and* communism, even Stalinism. Greene understands anyone who wants to make us be good. Le Carré is an instinctive anarchist, so deeply does he believe in the goodness of the individual. He hates all organizations: his villains often seem to be not actively bad, merely mediocre wills an organization has soured or corrupted. *The Naive and Sentimental Lover* celebrated his own brief personal flouting of all social and sexual mores during the 1960's. Flower-child philosophy suited him well, brought out the most mawkish part of him. A central scene in all his novels concerns two people trying to make love while some bureaucrats refuse to leave them alone. Le Carré's version of glasnost in *The Russia House* sometimes seems to be little more.

At the beginning of *Tinker, Tailor, Soldier, Spy* Smiley is summoned from retirement for the third time straight to confer secretly with "Whitehall's head prefect" (p. 28), Oliver Lacon (ch. 3). The Circus has been betrayed. At Lacon's Ascot estate he shows Smiley a Far East gunrunner and Circus agent, "Tarr, sir. Ricki Tarr from Penang" (ch. 4), who has had a romance with Irina, a Russian agent. She has been executed, but not before passing Ricki her diary. One sentence introduces us to a new name and sets Smiley off on his great "quest": "Have you heard of Karla?" (ch. 8).

In the 1930's, Irina claims, Karla recruited a Communist university student, who became a deep-penetration agent, a mole in the Circus. (Le Carré has admitted to making up most Circus terms, although real spies have now adopted many of his inventions; the Circus itself never existed, though London tourists, thinking it as real as the Pentagon, try to find it.) As *Call for the Dead* used the Rosenberg case for a springboard, so *Tinker, Tailor, Soldier, Spy* uses the Philby case. Many novels did. In fact, the year before *Tinker, Tailor, Soldier, Spy* was published there was Brian Freemantle's *Goodbye to an Old Friend* (1973), the same year, Alan Williams' *Gentleman Traitor* (1974), and four years later Greene's pro-Philby pro-Communist reply, *The Human Factor* (1978).

Karla's origins may be traced to 1968, when le Carré wrote a lengthy, furious preface to *The Philby*

Conspiracy (1968, published in Great Britain as *Philby: The Spy Who Betrayed a Generation*). As he struggled to find the "apt phrases of outrage," he started to think that "none of us is yet equal to the dimensions of this scandal. Like a great novel, and an unfinished one at that, the story of Kim Philby lives on in us." *Tinker, Tailor, Soldier, Spy*, begun three years later, was his shot at finishing that great unfinished novel. In 1968 le Carré, reading, began to see Philby as the epitome of everything he had long hated about the British Establishment. "Let anyone who derides the notion of the Establishment read this book," he writes.

Guy Burgess, Donald Maclean, and Kim Philby were three leftist Cambridge students recruited in the 1930's to be Moscow's moles in SIS (British intelligence). Philby's father, St. John Philby, had been a man of the Empire, a more successful version of Lawrence of Arabia, a famous explorer and soldier who rose to become the Saud dynasty's general liaison with the West. Kim, born in India, nicknamed with amazing precognition after Rudyard Kipling's boy spy, had the British version of "the right stuff": he "was of our blood and hunted with our pack." He rose to become a master of the SIS and Britain's representative to the CIA. For ten years anything Britain (and maybe America) knew went to Moscow, and Moscow fed back disinformation. "In place of an all-seeing eye," SIS became "a credulous ear and a misleading voice."

When Burgess and Maclean's covers were blown in 1951 and the two fled to Moscow, all signs pointed to Philby as their protector. But the Establishment intervened, reasoning, le Carré fumed, " *'This Club does not elect traitors, therefore Kim is not a traitor.'* This Establishment is a self-proving proposition." One might as well have suggested a Roosevelt had been spying. Prime Minister Harold Macmillan publically exonerated Philby in 1956. When, in 1963, the British "turned" the chief of Polish Intelligence, Philby was identified. But the Establishment/SIS (le Carré argues that the two are "identical") became so embarrassed that Philby, even after a confession, was virtually put on his honor as a gentleman not to flee; he fled. So the Colonel Blimps had dithered away even his interrogation, the last chance at some repair.

In his preface le Carré goes beyond the book about Philby, claiming the "principal character" was still "missing": the Soviet controller who had "consciously seduced" the three boys. "We discern

his hand, his influence, his shadow: never once do we . . . hear his name." That will be le Carré's appointed task. The preface's suddenly dramatic prose, at this point, the rush of emotional energy, marks le Carré's first vision of a grand antagonist for George Smiley, the Hamletic English liberal, the man of agonizing conscience: Karla, equally brilliant but utterly convinced, as secure in his ideology as a twelfth-century heretic burner, Totalitarian Man.

"Have you heard of Karla?" Smiley has met him before, he tells Guillam after they have left Rickie Tarr. In a cell in Delhi, years before, he had tried to convince a Russian "calling himself Gerstmann" to defect (ch. 23). This Gerstmann was Karla. Smiley tried to reach him on an emotional level, even let him borrow his wife Ann's cigarette lighter, which Gerstmann kept: "I had convinced myself that Gerstmann ultimately was accessible to ordinary human arguments." Smiley had never faced a figure of such massive "philosophical repose," a priest without doubts, a monk beyond family or individual desire. Smiley, not yet aware, trying to make some "human" contact, exposes his own humanity, his doubts, his insecurity. "The political generality [is] meaningless," he tells Karla. "Don't you think . . . that there is as little worth on your side as there is on mine?" Smiley later understands that the supernaturally calm little figure only saw him as "the very archetype of a flabby Western liberal" (ch. 23). Smiley, notice, was in all ways temporarily mistaken: there *are* great differences between the two sides, he will insist in the end.

Now, to track Karla's mole, Smiley hides out in the Islay Hotel. With Guillam and Mendel as legmen, he conducts a sedentary paper chase, a scholar's exercise in reason. The mole he ultimately uncovers is Bill Haydon. Haydon's character is based upon Philby; he is also bisexual, like Guy Burgess. Smiley recognizes that Karla has had Bill sleep with his wife, Lady Ann, knowing that Smiley, the liberal endlessly attempting to be "fair," would, if he ever suspected Bill's treason, instantly doubt himself instead as a biased judge. Bill's Oxford schoolmate and lover, Jim Prideaux—whom he betrayed when Control, sensing there was a mole, sent Prideaux on a mission into Czechoslovakia—shadows Smiley and Guillam when they capture Bill, guesses the truth, gets into the prison, and breaks Bill's neck for him. Philby—who read that scene—commented wryly before his death that he suspected le Carré didn't like him, but was glad to have "contributed to his amazing affluence."

Bill, captured, is full of "half-baked political assertions" (ch. 38). Philby, le Carré had written, was not a political animal, but a vain, deceitful, self-important child frustrated by the diminished roles the diminishing Empire offered him to play. Kim (and Bill) loved "the great game," as Kipling termed spying in, fittingly, *Kim.* He loved deceit; above all, he loved the figure he cut as the grand betrayer. His half-baked politics were but an excuse to accept the starring role the Russian "seducer" had offered the boy. Le Carré will use this motive again in *The Little Drummer Girl,* when the born actress Charlie shifts her political loyalties 180 degrees to land a starring part in the "theatre of the real."

Smiley, at the end, is no more ideologically assured than when he first faced Karla. Le Carré hates Philby, but Smiley is someone else, and he does not hate Bill; he feels a "wasting grief" (ch. 38). Opposite Karla, "whatever intellectual or philosophical percepts he clung to broke down entirely now that he was faced with the human situation" (ch. 36).

THE HONOURABLE SCHOOLBOY

THE HONOURABLE SCHOOLBOY (1977) was le Carré's self-conscious attempt at "the Eastern novel," as one of the book's own characters styles it (ch. 5), giving learned references to Graham Greene *(The Quiet American),* André Malraux *(Man's Fate),* and Joseph Conrad *(Lord Jim* in particular). However much le Carré belongs in that company artistically, one telling difference immediately comes to mind: those men really knew something about "the East."

What would tempt le Carré to try this, when he had always been so careful to stay in his own backyard? He wrote of English spies operating in London, Germany, or "Czecho." They were almost always bookish, even academic, and the plots involved them with people connected in some way to the Holocaust. Although le Carré seemed a man of the world, it was a small world he was the man of. For him to decide to branch out by attempting a novel about the East (as in "Mysterious East"? how dated a concept, by 1977) was more radical a departure than his previous attempt at a romance.

He was driven to take such a chance because he

had been drawn back to the problem dramatized in *The Spy Who Came In from the Cold. The Honourable Schoolboy* is the second of what, since *The Russia House,* we see to be a pattern: I will call *The Spy Who Came In from the Cold, The Honourable Schoolboy,* and *The Russia House* his "star-crossed lovers" books. In all three, the characters, the theme, even the final plot twist show such deep structural similarities that if he had staged all three in Germany, the second two would be too familiar. In both later books, to reuse his Romeo and Juliet pattern le Carré has had to restage the action in another country, to give the pattern as much surface dissimilarity as possible.

The "star-crossed lovers" dramatize in the most moving and human way the central dilemma of his fiction: the conflict between personal and civic morality. Critics oversimplify when they say he writes of "ends and means." The wider civic morality, which Smiley has decided, with great reluctance, is worth upholding, frequently requires the individual to trespass against his or her personal morality. Le Carré has cited the English saying about a diplomat being an honest man "who lies for the good of his country." How much more dramatic a test case, then, is the spy, required to cheat and betray for his country. Le Carré never loses his sense that spying is sneaking. He is never interested in the genuine sneaks who do it, but only the "honest man" like Smiley who must descend even lower than the diplomat for the civic good. Smiley makes that moral descent in the first book, when he kills a former surrogate son, Dieter, and is forced to question himself thus: "Oh, God, who was then the gentleman?" Throughout the books le Carré's method will be to take his Pickwick and force him to act like a Fagin. "Smiley," le Carré told an audience at Johns Hopkins University in 1986, "sacrifice[s] his own morality on the altar of national necessity."

The star-crossed-lovers novels give the knife an extra twist. Here is their equation. Let Smiley, in his inevitable moral agony, take up the dirty sword to defend the civic good; then poise against him a surrogate son like Leamas or Westerby. Let the son, like Romeo, fall in love with a Juliet from the other side. He must then decide if Smiley's Way, the civic good, is worth betraying Juliet—must decide whether to betray his father or his wife, and whether to betray himself. Had the first novel, *Call for the Dead,* been written from Dieter's point of view, we might have seen how similar even *it* was to the later pattern.

Le Carré is *not* repeating himself. Rather, he debates his earlier self, and even repudiates himself. As he has come to different conclusions about this, his central moral conflict, he has been drawn back to this poignant knot. Each time he has returned to the star-crossed lovers, he has grown bolder in declaring for individual morality above the civic good.

Le Carré sought, in Hong Kong, a stage for his Romeo and Juliet at the maximum distance from the Berlin Wall. He needed new background shots, new clothes, new accents for his lovers, in short, new "nuts and bolts," as novelists contemptuously call all that. Most readers were charmed. Although many groaned at the glacial pace, *The Honourable Schoolboy* won a slew of prizes, and now forms the central book in le Carré's trilogy, retroactively dubbed *The Quest for Karla.* Really it is a reportorial tour de force: much of what seems cultural analysis is actually beautifully rendered surfaces, meticulous travelogues. The biggest card le Carré held was that his readers, like the aristocrats who bought Watteau's fantasies of the Chien Lung court, knew even less about the East than he did.

For his plot, le Carré has transplanted other familiar themes. Karla has had a high-ranking mole, Nelson Ko, inside the Chinese Communist hierarchy, just as he had Bill Haydon inside the Circus. Nelson's brother Drake is a filthy-rich, rags-to-riches, racehorse-owner, airline managing director, and opium smuggler working for Moscow Centre. The plot hangs on his stop-at-nothing Eastern determination to spring his brother from Communist China—which le Carré seems to picture surrounded by a Berlin Wall, manned by Chinese Mundts determined to shoot Chinese Liz Golds as they crawl to safety.

German efficiency was a poor paradigm with which to imagine China, 80 percent peasant, chaotic and corrupt, run by *ho-murr* ("back door" influence). Anyone with Drake Ko's money could have bought an exit visa for his brother. Enough complaining. Accept the book as a romantic fable, *orientalia,* or pass it by.

Smiley's patient tracking has uncovered a Russian "gold seam" (a flow of bribe money) leading to Drake Ko. Jerry Westerby becomes Smiley's Eastern agent and surrogate son, telling him, "You point me and I'll march" (ch. 5). Smiley and Jerry soon realize that Drake is holding Moscow's money in trust for his brother the mole.

Smiley plans to kidnap Karla's mole as he escapes from China to Drake's brotherly embrace. However, just as Leamas' conscience was awakened by his love for Liz Gold, Jerry's conscience is awakened by his love for Lizzie Worthington, Drake's mistress. Liz and Lizzie, Gold and Worthington, both women connected with the other side: the parallel seems deliberate. At the critical moment, Jerry's honor makes him side with the personal moral demands of his love against the moral demands of the state, even a state personified by Smiley.

Jerry betrays Smiley and tips off Drake, but, as the brothers are rejoined, the Americans shoulder Smiley's forces aside and snatch the mole for questioning. Le Carré, perhaps aware that the American readership might be less than outraged, considering the Circus' record, has Jerry rather pointlessly shot, either by Fawn, the Circus' most dangerous "silent killer," or by some faceless American in the departing black helicopters. We are supposed to expect a motive from neither.

Smiley drops into retirement, le Carré's favorite position for him. In the trilogy's last novel, the excellent *Smiley's People,* he can, yet again, be recalled to work from outside the system to save it.

SMILEY'S PEOPLE

LE CARRÉ came home to London, Paris, and Bern, the city of his student days, regaining his form to write the superb *Smiley's People.* This novel, the conclusion of *Quest for Karla,* is a central and satisfying book in the canon, but the reader is so familiar now with Smiley's world it can be sketched in very few words. As with *Tinker, Tailor, Soldier, Spy* we enter through a fun house of mysterious visits, multiple identities, false leads. When Smiley exposes the right path, we find that Karla has paid the price for his inhumanity. In the ultimate act of the Organization Man, that selfless, nonindividual assented to the purge of his lover. Communism, like all totalitarian systems since Plato's *Republic,* has resented the family. People are to identify with no cause but the state's. Karla purges his love, but his daughter, Tatiana, knows nothing of theory and she goes insane. His child's agony proves too much for whatever residual genetic cues in Karla still make him a human being. For the first time in his life he acts as an individual, breaks secretly with Party discipline, breaks rules, and even embezzles to find treatment for his daughter. Like the bloody Macbeth, he is left begging, "Cans't thou not minister to a mind diseased?"

First he makes a (for him) shockingly clumsy attempt to convince an old émigré, Maria Ostrakova, that Tatiana is Alexandra, the daughter she bore to "the Jew Glikman" and left in an orphanage twenty years ago when she fled Russia. Alexandra needs "the assistance of a mother," one of Karla's hoods, Kirov/Kursky, tells Ostrakova. Karla is willing to give Tatiana up to save her. Ostrakova looks at "several muddy photographs" and knows they do not depict her child (ch. 1). She alerts the old Estonian General Vladimir in London, who, after obtaining evidence, begs a meeting with the Circus. Vladimir is killed en route and power-broker Lacon brings Smiley back from retirement. When he uncovers the situation, he goes to Bern, blackmails the Russian diplomat, Grigoriev, who keeps Tatiana in a mental hospital there, and gets the evidence of Karla's corruption into the sin of paternal love.

There is the tremendously moving moment when Grigoriev, interrogated by Smiley, tells how the hard man he still does not realize is Karla had lapsed into emotion: "You must be a friend to this child. . . . Her father's twisted life has had a bad effect on her" (ch. 25). This had been the man Smiley once envied as utterly convinced, a rock of "philosophic repose." This only too plausible end reveals that Smiley's way, always to trust to one's individual conscience, "never acquiescing in a facile orthodoxy of [another], or of our own"—as Walter Pater put it (The Renaissance, 1868)—is a safer path than accepting the peace that dogma brings. It only remains to use Grigoriev's evidence to blackmail Karla: all is known, we are your only friends now, come to us and we will provide for you, care for Tatiana.

The last scene is at the Berlin Wall, the "icon of the cold war," where, two decades before, we and Leamas had waited for Reimeck, only to see him shot. After great suspense, Karla crosses safely to the West, a defection immeasurably greater than Bill Haydon's. He pauses and drops Ann's cigarette lighter—that reminder of their first meeting—at Smiley's feet. Smiley does not bother to pick it up. "George, you won," his disciple Guillam says. Smiley, with characteristic restraint, finally replies,

"Did I? Yes. Yes, well I suppose I did" (ch. 27).

Le Carré, writing in 1980, had no way of knowing that he had now written the last great Berlin Wall scene, as well as the first one. The Wall would not long outlast Karla, and it would crumble from within in a similar, inevitable, human way. All through the Cold War le Carré's novels argued that Karla's way, running against the human grain, could not endure.

THE LITTLE DRUMMER GIRL

IN 1983, when le Carré wrote The Little Drummer Girl, the problem with his prose that had been evident in The Honourable Schoolboy became a crisis. Buried beneath the flab of le Carré's late style is the muscle of a fine novel. He simply stopped editing. In The Spy Who Came In from the Cold, the crackpot Bayswater Library for Psychic Research, an important locale where Liz falls in love with Leamas, is captured in three perfect sentences:

The Library was like a church hall, and very cold. The black oil stoves at either end made it smell of paraffin. In the middle of the room was a cubicle like a witness box and inside it sat Miss Crail, the librarian.

(ch. 4)

Three and one-half lines of type, yet we have the look of it, chill of it, smell of it; plus the mental associations of churches, courtrooms, and prim older ladies who go by "Miss." In The Little Drummer Girl, by contrast, almost any location gets line after line of irrelevant, distracting detail, like this:

Their operations room in Freiburg city centre was a hastily rented ground-floor office in a busy main street, their cover the Walker & Frosch Investment Company, GmbH, one of dozens that Gavron's secretariat kept permanently registered. Their communications equipment had more or less the appearance of commercial software; in addition they had three ordinary telephones, courtesy of Alexis, and one of them, the least official, was the Doctor's own hot line to Kurtz.

(ch. 24)

That is only the start. The question is, why did le Carré omit the street name? Was it because it wouldn't mean a thing to the development of the story? That is a good reason. But by that logic, why include that this office was "ground-floor" or that the main street was "busy" or that its specific cover name was "Walker & Frosch"? From all this verbiage one does not learn as much as from the description in *The Spy Who Came In from the Cold,* not how it smells or how it feels on the back of your neck to stand there. "Walker & Frosch" or "busy main street" does not have the emotional resonance of "cubicle like a witness box." The description in *The Spy Who Came In from the Cold* tells us only what we need in order to feel how Liz feels, laboring in that hole with Miss Crail observing from her witness box. That mattered. When Liz jumps at the first live man to ever enter that chilly church hall we understand. Le Carré pruned away all else as potential distraction.

The Little Drummer Girl paragraph, a mere list, shows the unsuccessful replacement of inspiration by industry. One pictures le Carré, newly serious about his research, scribbling in his notebook about the exact color—"olive"—of the Dreisam, and noting the exceptional width of the window, and its Venetian blinds. It takes great self-discipline to throw out so much labor later, when you realize that readers want to know what will happen to Charlie and do not give a damn if it happens on the Dreisam or the Rhine. After *Tinker, Tailor, Soldier, Spy,* le Carré lacked that self-discipline. Writing *The Little Drummer Girl* he forgot that ten years earlier, even when he needed technical terms about spying, he had not done any research—he simply made them up, nearly two hundred of them. Not only did it not matter, but real spies, like the rest of the world, began to use them.

The Spy Who Came In from the Cold is a Rembrandt—one beam of light on St. Bartholomew's knife, another on his thoughtful forehead, the rest, darkness. *The Little Drummer Girl* is a pre-Raphaelite painting, every woodshaving on the carpenter's floor illuminated equally with Christ. The late novels, if they were stripped of unnecessary verbiage, would actually be the same length as the earlier ones. *The Little Drummer Girl* might have been *The Spy Who Came In from the Cold,* but it remains forever two months' work away from it.

No one has remarked how similar Magnus, "the perfect spy," is to Charlie. When le Carré used his left-leaning half sister Charlotte, an actress, as the model for the leftist actress Charlie in *The Little Drummer Girl,* he quite reasonably provided her with a father much like the one who made his sister

what she was. Not surprisingly, Magnus Pym, who shared that father, seems her brother. *The Little Drummer Girl* could have been called "A Perfect Actress." A confidence man like Ronald—an actor, essentially—would produce, as children, a pair of actors like Charlie and Magnus, both playing multiple roles under multiple names, Charlie on stage and Magnus in the "theatre of the real" as the novel terms it (ch. 12). Both are observers and mimics who use their skills to manipulate an audience (much as a novelist does, we note). Swindler, Actress, Novelist, Spy: Le Carré has now biopsied each profession, and shown them to be a family.

At the end of *The Little Drummer Girl,* Charlie can no longer act on stage, for she has "no stomach any more—and, worse, no understanding—for what passed for pain in Western middle-class society" (ch. 27). The book is meant to be her, and the middle-class audience's, education in the true depth of tragic suffering. The book begins with a suitcase bomb blowing apart an Israeli diplomat's home in West Germany. A child dies. Enter a team of experienced Israeli investigators, headed by a man we will later know as Kurtz. Critics rightly call him a Jewish version of Smiley. In the book he quests for the master terrorist Khalil, whose name is about as close as Arabic can get to Karla, particularly as le Carré pronounces it.

Khalil, the childkiller, is one villain; the next chapter brings out the other, Misha Gavron, Kurtz's chief, a Control-like figure. Gavron, like Smiley's feared American "Cousins," sees life in terms of good and bad groups, not individuals. Smiley wants to remove Karla, but the Cousins are endlessly ready to "bomb 'em all back to the Stone Age" (in the famous words of an American general about the North Vietnamese). Gavron too loves "American-style power-plays." Kurtz races to remove Khalil, before his terrorist provocations win Gavron the votes to bomb entire refugee camps back to the Stone Age. When the operation succeeds too late, "Kurtz's worst fears and Gavron's worst threats were fulfilled" (ch. 27) and the (historical) massive Israeli drive into Lebanon takes place.

American Jews were horrified when, after writing the book, le Carré met with PLO leader Yasir Arafat and decided he was "maligned," a "moderate." Le Carré is speaking in favor of moderation; if he mistakenly (I think) believed Arafat a moderate, that does not change what le Carré's values are.

Similarly, if readers think le Carré mistaken about the Lebanon expedition's strategic necessity, they should notice they are not arguing with le Carré about whether Jews or Israelis are "good" or "bad." Le Carré, emotionally involved with Jews all his life, is far beyond seeing Israel as a monolith. (People who argue that Jews or Israelis are "good" create, I submit, a historically dangerous precedent: the habit of picturing Jews as other than normal disagreeing individuals, as a kind of eerily cohesive mass.) *The Little Drummer Girl* is, in fact, specifically about a battle between factions and individuals—the same factions le Carré described battling in England, and almost the same individuals. Le Carré has even been criticized for doing a Middle Eastern Smiley and Karla Show, but he does it obviously, to bring out our feeling of eternal archetypes in battle everywhere. When Gavron's star ascends, Kurtz's body "seemed to shrink to half its size," his "Slav eyes lost all their sparkle" (ch. 27). Then, after a month of retirement, he "had vigorously resumed his strange running feud with Misha Gavron." Kurtz and Gavron are eternal enemies—how could anyone jell them into one political entity, "the Israelis"? Indeed, if le Carré's works have any single point, it is to express the need to see people as individuals, not as Jews, Germans, Russians, Palestinians.

Gavron's impending invasion is the deadline before which Marty Kurtz must remove the provocateur Khalil. Khalil is as much an enemy of the moderates as Gavron is, and for the rest of the book he will plan to kill the dovish Israeli professor Minkel. First Kurtz locates Khalil's skirt-chasing baby brother, Salim (also known as Michel), who, with a blonde groupie companion had delivered his brother's suitcase bomb. Khalil is kidnapped. Then the dashing Gabi Becker, an Israeli agent, beds a parlor Marxist and Palestinian sympathizer, the actress Charlie (short for Charmian).

The 1970's world le Carré took so seriously in *Naive and Sentimental Lover,* he now, in 1983, finds insufferable. Charlie's commitment to revolution has entailed reading some magazines, sleeping around, taking some drugs, and exchanging politically correct views with her theater friends. A type familiar to, sometimes prominent in, the theatrical and academic worlds, she is mercilessly anatomized. Kurtz and Becker know that she's been to some weekend introductions to "radical thinking" in which she was primarily introduced to "group

sex." She and her actor-lover Alastair attended a seminar on "bourgeois Fascism in Western capitalist societies" and signed a resolution against Zionism (ch. 7): "Charlie . . . knew the protest folk songs, and sang them in an angry mannish style." She's gung-ho, the little drummer girl herself. " 'You wait till my revolution dawns,' she'd warn them" (ch. 3). Le Carré means to give this middle-class radical, and the audience, an education in what the tough words Charlie uses so casually actually mean. Charlie will be forced to act in the "theatre of the real." "You've read Frantz Fanon," Kurtz baits her. "Violence is a cleansing force, remember?" (ch. 7).

Becker, torso covered with the scars of real violence and mideast battles, appears among Charlie's friends on a beach filled with middle-class "radicals" at play. " 'Isn't he *fabulous?*' said Lucy loudly. 'I'd have *him* with my salad any day.' 'Me too,' said Willy, louder still" (ch. 3). Becker, the first man of violent action Charlie has personally met, seduces her easily. It is no great achievement, nor is converting this perfect actress to the Israeli cause, once she is in love with him. Becker and Kurtz replace her surrogate family of actors with a new one of friendly young Israeli agents, then offer her what they make out to be the starring role in Kurtz's theatre of the real. Le Carré's concept, reminiscent of Hermann Hesse, is so surreally compelling one becomes furious with him for burying it under an endless drizzle of street locations, window widths, and river colors. The audience has to make out the action as if through a windshield spotted with rain. *The Spy Who Came In from the Cold* was complete by the time *The Little Drummer Girl* has reached the ninth of twenty-seven chapters.

Love letters between Salim/Michel and Charlie are forged—letters that show Michel has told Charlie compromising details about Khalil. Michel, when captured, had been traveling with two hundred pounds of Russian plastic explosives in his car. He is put back into the car, along with the blonde friend he bombed the diplomat's house with, and it is detonated. Terrorists Mesterbein and Helga use Michel's letters to find Charlie, to see what she knows. By stages she persuades them to accept her as Michel's replacement. She is trained in a Lebanese terrorist camp. Charlie, now acting in the theatre of the real, pretends to aid Khalil in blowing up the dovish Israeli Minkel; then, through a planted transmitter, brings Becker to where Khalil has been rewarding himself with her. "She saw Khalil's face burst" as the bullets hit. "She had gone deaf, so she could only vaguely hear her own screaming" (ch. 26). Covered with blood and vomit, she is taken to an ambulance. Reality is too much for this middle-class comedienne. Her mind breaks beneath the weight.

Charlie cannot continue to act in the theatre of the real but, literally and figuratively, she can no longer return to the romantic fluff of Western middle-class life: she cannot say her lines. Kurtz provides for her financially and Becker comes to be her lover at the end, but her last words in the book are "I'm dead, Jose. You shot me, don't you remember?" (ch. 27). *The Little Drummer Girl*'s great success is in making real the oceans of suffering the first world, like a ship, floats on. It makes the word "violence" real again. If the reader is in a university, leaving the book to go back to that world is, oddly, not like leaving a work of art for reality, but like leaving reality to watch people like the younger Charlie acting in a middle-class romantic play.

THE RUSSIA HOUSE

In the last few weeks of 1989 the Berlin Wall fell, the governments of Czechoslovakia, Poland, Hungary, and Bulgaria broke free of both communism and the Russians, and Romania captured and executed its tyrant of twenty-three years, Ceaucescu. All Europe was in upheaval. *Newsweek* said, "The cold war is over and we have won." The 1 January 1990 edition of *Time* magazine had Mikhail Gorbachev on its cover: "Man of the Decade"; inside, in a photo section titled "Icons of the Cold War," between a picture of Fidel Castro during the Cuban Missile Crisis and one of Senator Joe McCarthy conducting a Communist witch-hunt, appeared Richard Burton as the spy Leamas, from Martin Ritt's 1966 film version of le Carré's *The Spy Who Came In from the Cold.*

The photo shows the moment in which Leamas tries to pull his lover across the Berlin Wall, that icon of the Cold War and the centerpiece of so many le Carré novels. Burton pulls her up desperately by the wrists. The border guards are about to shoot them dead. A few weeks before the article

appeared, the Berlin Wall, to the world's astonishment, had been demolished; in the television news the dreaded "Vopo" Wall guards accepted flowers from girls and waved for the cameras.

In that moment all le Carré's novels changed. The Wall, falling, revised them all. They had been novels about a present, about a nuclear stalemate, a balance of terror that the world assumed would persist for hundreds of years, if not forever. When the Wall fell le Carré's novels became historical novels, available to *Time* for use as "icons of the Cold War," icons of the past. The novels were revealed to have been war novels, and the war he wrote about had ended. One might have wondered if le Carré, nearly sixty, his war finished, was finished as well.

But he had already embarked on a new phase. His prophetic *Russia House,* published four months before the Communist bloc collapsed, had the distinction of being the first novel of the post–Cold War era. *The Russia House* is the third of le Carré's star-crossed lovers novels, his ultimate declaration for individual morality above the civic good. Smiley, who had personified that good, has fittingly left the scene. Only the CIA Cousins have any power now, although they politely make use of a few British Establishment pawns like the narrator, a drone called Palfrey. Le Carré's distaste for everything American has become a phobia; all an apologist can say is that the Americans he has been forced to work with all his life have all been agents, either CIA, literary, or Hollywood. Someday he may discover the rest of the country.

Russia, however, he judged extremely well. Rupert, le Carré's half brother, was the London *Independent*'s man in Moscow during the 1980's. He undoubtedly helped. Le Carré also traveled there twice. When he stood by the book in a June 1989 interview predicting "the visible crumbling of power in the Soviet Union, the fragmentation of the Empire," the amazed interviewer wondered if "the cynical le Carré has simply gone soft."

The Leamas/Westerby role is now filled by Barley Blair, a saxophone-playing playboy, heir to a small-time publishing firm which sometimes sends him to Moscow for book fairs. The beautiful, committed Liz Gold role is played by the Russian Yekaterina Orlova ("Katya"), an editor and emissary of Professor Yakov Savelyev ("Bluebird" or "Goethe"), her Sakharov-like lover. Barley nicknames him "Goethe" because of his vision of European unity, beyond the claims of all nation states. Goethe's question is, do we dare to be traitors in order to be faithful to humankind? He sends Barley, via Katya and Niki Landau, a plucky Polish-English Jew, secrets he wants Barley to publish in the West—all on the strength of a drunken conversation they had had years before. Barley, a patriot, instead agrees to work for the "Russia House" wing of the British secret services, who want to acquire Goethe for themselves as a source.

But the Cousins turn out to have completed their acquisition of the British secret services. Barley is to be run not by London but by the people Bill Haydon once called "fascist puritans." When the arrangement leaves Katya in Liz Gold's unprotected position, and the Cousins do not care any more than Control did, Barley does something Leamas and Westerby never dared: he defects to Russia. He makes it seem Katya had been running him as a double agent, instead of vice versa, hands over the CIA's "shopping list" of questions (showing "the Sovs" exactly what the United States does not know) and saves Katya and her children. Like Goethe, he has left the "safe bastion of infinite distrust" and chosen the "dangerous path of love" (ch. 17).

In this, le Carré's third and probably final return to the star-crossed lovers, an ultimate point has been reached. In 1989 Barley acts out treason for his love, which Leamas, in 1963, must have thought of, but suppressed in horror; and his author did too. Love brought Leamas "in from the cold" yet he continues to function as agent until Liz's death. Then all he can do is attempt a suicidal gesture of rescue. Jerry betrays the Circus for the woman he loves, just as Barley betrays it for his Russian lover. Jerry will die. Barley will be allowed to survive. We see a clear progression from Leamas, who in 1963 doubts but obeys, to Jerry, who in 1974 disobeys but must die, to Barley, who in 1989 disobeys but is allowed to live happily ever after. At book's end he is living in Portugal, waiting confidently for Russia to complete its reforms and let Katya join him. The Berlin Wall fell a few months after the novel was published. He probably got his wish.

In *The Russia House,* then, le Carré, following his conscience, finally carries his lifelong individual-ism to virtually an anarchist position. If individuals follow their consciences, the civic good will take care of itself. The "state" does not exist; it is merely the sum total of its individuals, and if *they* act morally, it must in turn be moral.

In 1991's *The Secret Pilgrim,* le Carré reviewed, in linked stories, his own pilgrimage through the Cold War, and let George Smiley say good-bye. The book topped best-seller lists. Critics applauded his return to his old terse style. Chapter 10, Smiley's adventure with some cufflinks, is as sentimental as Dickens' "Christmas Carol" and as successful.

Like Barley Blair at the end of *The Russia House,* John le Carré looks forward to the future confidently. He is more than sixty now, the Cold War of which he was *the* master novelist is concluded, and one might have pictured him about to enter a decline. Instead, he seems rejuvenated, and has already begun writing about a new era.

SELECTED BIBLIOGRAPHY

I. COLLECTED WORKS. *The Incongruous Spy* (New York, 1963), includes *Call for the Dead* and *A Murder of Quality,* also published as *The le Carré Omnibus* (London, 1969); *The Quest for Karla* (London and New York, 1982), includes *Tinker, Tailor, Soldier, Spy, The Honourable Schoolboy,* and *Smiley's People.*

II. SEPARATE WORKS. *Call for the Dead* (London, 1961; New York, 1962), republished as *The Deadly Affair* (Harmondsworth, Eng., 1964); *A Murder of Quality* (London, 1962; New York, 1963); *The Spy Who Came In from the Cold* (London, 1963; New York, 1964); *The Looking Glass War* (London and New York, 1965); "Dare I Weep, Dare I Mourn?" in *Saturday Evening Post* (28 January 1967), short story; *A Small Town in Germany* (London and New York, 1968); "What Ritual Is Being Observed Tonight?" in *Saturday Evening Post* (2 November 1968), short story; *The Naive and Sentimental Lover* (London, 1971; New York, 1972); *Tinker, Tailor, Soldier, Spy* (London and New York, 1974); *The Honourable Schoolboy* (London and New York, 1977); *Smiley's People* (London and New York, 1980); *The Little Drummer Girl* (London and New York, 1983); *A Perfect Spy* (London and New York, 1986); *The Russia House* (London and New York, 1989); *The Secret Pilgrim* (London and New York, 1990).

III. SCREENPLAYS. *Smiley's People,* with J. Hopkin (BBC/Paramount Pictures, 1981).

IV. INTRODUCTIONS AND ARTICLES. "To Russia, with Greetings: An Open Letter to the Moscow *Literary Ga-*

zette," in *Encounter,* 26 (May 1966); "The Spy to End Spies: On Richard Sorge" in *Encounter,* 27 (November 1966); introduction to B. Page, D. Leitch, and P. Knightley, *Philby: The Spy Who Betrayed a Generation* (London, 1968; published in New York as *The Philby Conspiracy,* 1968); "At Last, It's Smiley," in the *London Sunday Telegraph Magazine* (21 October 1979); "Was There a Real George Smiley? Yes. No. Maybe," in *Book-of-the-Month Club Newsletter* (1979); introduction to D. McCullin, *Hearts of Darkness* (London, 1980; New York, 1981); "Memories of a Vanished Land," in *Observer Magazine* (13 June 1982); "The Betrayal," in *Observer Magazine* (3 July 1983); "Exiles in the White Hotel," in *Observer Magazine* (3 July 1983); "Hughes of Hong Kong," in the *London Sunday Times* (8 January 1984); "Le Carré: The Dishonourable Spy," in *Harper's Magazine* (December 1986), excerpt from "The Clandestine Muse," a speech given by D. Cornwell at Johns Hopkins University, Spring 1986; "The Unbearable Peace," in *Granta* 35 (Spring 1991).

V. INTERVIEWS. M. Dean, "John le Carré—The Writer Who Came In from the Cold," in *The Listener* (5 September 1974); J. Cameron, "The Case of the Hot Writer," in the *New York Times Magazine* (8 September 1974); M. Barber, "John le Carré: An Interrogation," in the *New York Times Book Review* (25 September 1977); S. Kanfer and D. Fischer, "The Spy Who Came In for the Gold," in *Time* (3 October 1977); G. Hodgson, "The Secret Life of John le Carré," in *Washington Post Book World* (9 October 1977); M. Gross, "The Secret World of John le Carré," in the *London Observer* (3 February 1980); H. McIlvanney, "The Secret Life of John le Carré," in *Observer Magazine* (6 March 1983); A. Gelber and E. Behr, "A Stellar Spymaster Returns," in *Newsweek* (7 March 1983); J. Lelyveld, "Le Carré's Toughest Case," in the *New York Times Magazine* (16 March 1986); P. Assouline, "Spying on a Spymaster," in *World Press Review* (August 1986); V. Orlik, "Spies Who Come In from the Cold War: A Session Between John le Carré and the Soviets," in *World Press Review* (October 1989); A. P. Sanoff, "The Thawing of the Old Spymaster," in *U.S. News and World Report* (19 June 1989), C. R. Whitney, "I Was Heartily Sick of It," in the *New York Times Book Review* (6 January 1991).

VI. CRITICAL STUDIES. R. J. Ambrosetti, "A Study of the Spy Genre in Recent Popular Literature," Ph.D. dissertation, Bowling Green State University, 1973; G. Grella, "John le Carré: Murder and Loyalty," in *New Republic* (31 July 1976); A. Burgess, "Peking Drugs, Moscow Gold: *The Honourable Schoolboy,*" in the *New York Times Book Review*

(25 September 1977); C. James, "Go Back to the Cold!: *The Honourable Schoolboy,*" in the *New York Review of Books* (27 October 1977); P. Vaughn, "Le Carré's Circus: Lamplighters, Moles, and Others of That Ilk," in the *Listener* (13 September 1979).

J. Halperin, "Between Two Worlds: The Novels of John le Carré," in the *South Atlantic Quarterly,* 79 (Winter 1980); R. W. Noland, "The Spy Fiction of John le Carré," in *Clues: A Journal of Detection,* 1 (Fall/Winter 1980); V. S. Pritchett, "A Spy Romance: *Smiley's People,*" in the *New York Review of Books* (7 February 1980); J. Kennaway, *The Kennaway Papers* (New York, 1981), a memoir largely concerning le Carré; A. Rothberg, "The Decline & Fall of George Smiley: John le Carré and English Decency," in *Southwest Review,* 66 (Autumn 1981); J. Wolcott, "The Secret Sharers: *The Little Drummer Girl,*" in the *New York Review of Books* (14 April 1983); J. Atkins, *The British Spy Novel: Styles in Treachery* (London and New York, 1984); L. O. Sauerberg, *Secret Agents in Fiction: Ian Fleming, John le Carré, and Len Deighton* (New York, 1984); P. E. Lewis, *John le Carré* (New York, 1985); D. Monaghan, *The Novels of John le Carré: The Art of Survival* (Oxford and New York, 1985).

T. Barley, *Taking Sides: The Fiction of John le Carré* (Philadelphia, 1986); F. Conroy, *"A Perfect Spy,"* in the *New York Times Book Review* (13 April 1986); S. Knight, "Re-Formations of the Thriller: Raymond Chandler and John le Carré," in *Sydney Studies in English,* 12 (1986–1987); D. Monaghan, *Smiley's Circus: A Guide to the Secret World of John le Carré* (London 1986); H. Bloom, ed., *John le Carré* (New York, 1987); M. Denning, *Cover Stories: Narrative and Ideology in the British Spy Thriller* (London and New York, 1987); K. M. Radell, "The Triumph of Realism over Glamour: Martin Ritt's Realization of le Carré's *The Spy Who Came In from the Cold,*" in D. Radcliff-Umstead, ed., *Transformations: From Literature to Film* (Kent, Ohio, 1987); P. Wolfe, *Corridors of Deceit: The World of John le Carré* (Bowling Green, Ohio, 1987); A. Bold, *The Quest for le Carré* (New York, 1988); J. R. Cohn, "The Watch on John le Carré," in *Studies in the Novel,* 20 (Fall 1988); J. Geoghegan, "The Spy Who Saved Me: A Thriller Starring John le Carré," in the *New York Times Book Review* (4 December 1988); W. Walling, "John le Carré: The Doubleness of Class," in *Columbia Library Columns,* 37 (February 1988); G. Hempstead, "George Smiley and Post-Imperial Nostalgia," in R. Samuel, ed., *Patriotism: The Making and Unmaking of British National Identity,* vol. 3 (London, 1989).

Critique: Studies in Contemporary Fiction, 31 (Winter 1990), issue dedicated to le Carré.

FLANN O'BRIEN

(1911–1966)

Joseph Devlin

ON AN EXTENDED visit to Germany in 1933, Flann O'Brien "managed to get himself beaten up and bounced out of a beer hall for uncomplimentary references to Adolph Hitler. . . . He also met and married 18-year-old Clara Ungerland, blonde, violin-playing daughter of a Cologne basket weaver. She died a month later."

The preceding statement is a bald-faced lie. Flann O'Brien told this lie to Stanford Lee Cooper, and the interview of which it is part appeared in the 23 August 1943 issue of *Time* magazine (pp. 88–92). The spoof is quoted here because it exemplifies much of O'Brien's artistic technique. It parodies journalistic writing with its agglomeration of fatuous adjectives—"blonde, violin-playing." The imaginative flippancy of O'Brien's writing surfaces in the assignment of the occupation "basket weaver" to Mr. Ungerland. Finally, the mock melodrama of Clara's early and convenient demise brings the episode neatly to a close. Evidently marriage did not agree with her.

The title of this essay is also somewhat of a lie. Flann O'Brien is actually the pseudonym of Brian O'Nolan, one of many pen names employed by O'Nolan during his career. Some of the others are Brother Barnabas, the O'Blather, and, most important to his Dublin compatriots, Myles na Gopaleen. I have used "Flann O'Brien" as the title because that is the name by which he is most generally known, though Myles na Gopaleen is in many ways as important. Myles is a persona, whereas Flann is merely a name attached to the novels. In the body of this essay, therefore, I will refer to the author as Brian O'Nolan except where the character of the pseudonymous entity is important.

O'Nolan began his writing career in the early 1930's and continued until the year of his death, 1966. He and the writers of his generation provide a link between the early-twentieth-century Irish literary renaissance and contemporary Irish writing. O'Nolan's comic sensibility exemplifies the most striking aspect of the Irish literary tradition: the tendency to treat serious subjects with laughter and to take that laughter seriously.

LIFE

O'NOLAN was born on 5 October 1911 in Strabane, a small town in County Tyrone, Ireland, the third of twelve children born to Agnes and Michael O'Nolan. Although he was a customs and excise officer working ultimately for the British government, O'Nolan's father held strongly nationalist opinions and made Irish the language of his household. Later in life O'Nolan published many articles and one remarkable novel in this language.

Like the Brontës, the O'Nolan children grew up in a semi-isolated world enlivened by their imaginations. The father's desire to have the children instructed only through the medium of Irish made finding a school difficult, so O'Nolan's formal education did not begin until he was almost twelve years old. Until then he spent his time playing with his brothers and sisters, especially his elder brothers Gearóid and Ciarán. In the spirit of the later Myles na Gopaleen Research Bureau, the brothers, using a kerosene lamp, projected drawings with captions onto the wall of a shed. Ciarán and Brian created heroic characters whose adventures and conflicts formed the basis of the "scripts."

Soon after his father was transferred to Dublin, O'Nolan began attending the Christian Brothers School at Synge Street. Writing about it later in his *Irish Times* newspaper column, "Cruiskeen Lawn," Brian remembered it as a place where "no matter how assiduous and even intelligent a student was he was bound to get a hiding every day of his school life" (Cronin, p. 25). Their fellow students treated the O'Nolan brothers as badly as did the teachers. The brothers' Strabane accents and ignorance of schoolyard politics made them targets. In 1927 the family moved within Dublin to Avoca Terrace, and O'Nolan entered Blackrock College, where his education was less Dickensian.

During his second year at Blackrock, Brian experimented with a particularly idiosyncratic and anonymous literary form known as the "letters controversy." He, Ciarán, and their friends the Kennys wrote letters to the *Catholic Standard,* a weekly newspaper, on that most pressing subject for all adolescents: homework. They did not sign their own names to these letters, however, but sent them in as the opinions of various parents and teachers. Not only did the *Catholic Standard* print the letters as genuine, but it advertised the controversy on a poster. During his university days and afterward, O'Nolan participated in other letters controversies, one of which led to his being hired as a columnist. He eventually gave up this epistolary practice, probably because the pay was not very good.

In the fall of 1929 O'Nolan entered University College, Dublin. During his first year he became active in the Literary and Historical Society, a debating club in front of which James Joyce had presented a paper on Ibsen many years before. By O'Nolan's time the conditions under which people spoke were very difficult. He describes these conditions in his contribution to a book of reminiscences about the society (collected in *Myles Before Myles, a Selection of the Earlier Writings of Brian O'Nolan,* 1988):

> It was large as such theatres go but its seating capacity could not exceed two hundred, whereas most meetings attracted not fewer than six hundred people.... A seething mass gathered and swayed in a large lobby outside the theatre.... This most heterogeneous congregation, reeling about, shouting and singing... came to be known as the mob, and I had the honour to be acknowledged its president.
>
> (pp. 16–17)

O'Nolan was able to hold the attention of both those seated in the theater and the mob outside with his wit and speaking ability. His attitude and actions in relation to the Literary and Historical Society point out an important aspect of his views on intellectual pursuits in general. He often took on

the role of willful philistine. His championing the mob was similar to his later ambivalence about censorship and his attacks on Albert Einstein and Frank Lloyd Wright. The difference was that his actions in regard to the society were reasonable, whereas in the other examples he began to sound like the mad philosopher–scientist de Selby of his novels *The Third Policeman* (1967) and *The Dalkey Archive* (1964).

Another important change in O'Nolan's life at this point was that he began to visit pubs with his friends. His problem with alcohol led to many accidents and probably contributed to his illnesses and early death. Particularly pertinent to this essay is that his addiction had a noticeable, adverse effect on his last novel, *The Dalkey Archive.* But this was far in the future.

O'Nolan's gift for satire, parody, and scathing personal abuse appears almost full-blown in his contributions to the student magazine *Comhthrom Féinne* (Fair Play). One of his favorite targets at this time, and for much of his writing life, was the group of writers associated with the Irish literary revival of the late nineteenth and early twentieth centuries. The romanticism and artificiality of William Butler Yeats, John Millington Synge, and their countless imitators made O'Nolan impatient with all forms of "Celtic twilightery." Writing under the pseudonym Brother Barnabas, he made this observation about the fictional poet Lionel Prune, who bears a striking resemblance to Yeats: "He is a journeyman-dilettante, an upstart, a parvenu, who must be persuaded, if civilisation is to be saved, to exploit to the full that one talent which he indubitably has, and steadily refuses to exercise or cultivate—the talent for being a silent corpse in a coffin" (*Myles Before Myles,* p. 34). Under the name Samuel Hall, O'Nolan wrote *The Bog of Allen,* the first of many parodies of Synge's work. This playlet contains the stage direction "Slowly the rich purple of the Celtic Twilight falls over the Bog" and stimulating dialogue such as

ALLEN (meditatively): Aye. (long pause) Surely.
MAGGIE: Musha.
ALLEN: Surely.
MAGGIE: Wisha.
ALLEN: Begorrah.
MAGGIE (her soul flooded with poetry): Anish, now, musha.

(*Myles Before Myles,* pp. 42–43)

The contributions to *Comhthrom Féinne* are very similar to the later "Cruiskeen Lawn" articles. "Are You Lonely in the Restaurant?" presents an extraordinarily elaborate scheme for providing companionship to solitary diners. Long descriptive lists enumerating "conditions of hire" and "classes of eaters" carry forth the original idea ad absurdum (*Myles Before Myles,* p. 50). This technique is similar to that employed in the book handling and ventriloquist schemes of Myles na Gopaleen, except that the later work is funnier. Another similarity between these early pieces and the *Irish Times* column is the nature of the pseudonymous persona Brother Barnabas. Like Myles na Gopaleen, Brother Barnabas has several mutually exclusive biographies and is likely to appear at any historic juncture. Brother Barnabas was a half-caste Russian Jew, led a carefree life in pre–World War I Vienna, thrashed Kaiser Wilhelm with a dog-whip, rented Trotsky's villa in Paris, and, perhaps his greatest contribution to civilization, invented mixed dancing.

From August 1934 to January 1935, O'Nolan, his brother Ciarán, and his friend Niall Sheridan produced a monthly satirical magazine called *Blather.* The opening issue introduced itself in this way:

Blather is a publication of the Gutter, the King Rat of the Irish Press, the paper that will achieve entirely new levels in everything that is contemptible, despicable and unspeakable in contemporary journalism. *Blather* has no principles, no honour, no shame. Our objects are the fostering of graft and corruption in public life, the furtherance of cant and hypocrisy, the encouragement of humbug and hysteria, the glorification of greed and gombeenism.

Blather doesn't care.

(*Myles Before Myles,* p. 97)

Obviously a publication with such lofty ideals needed an upstanding and talented man at the helm.

Should a man call at your door, probably attired in clerical garb and selling onions, send him away.

He is none other than the Editor of *Blather.*

Better still, invite him into the kitchen for a mug of tea and phone for the police.... When you try to telephone, you will find that the wires have been cruelly cut. That will bring home to you the desperate character of the man whom you have so foolishly invited into your kitchen for tea. It is no use telling us that you invited him in on our advice. Your reproaches, your hurt tones, will leave us unmoved. We are not called Ireland's Heartless

Hoaxer for nothing. In fact, we are not called Ireland's Heartless Hoaxer at all.

(*Myles Before Myles,* pp. 120–121)

This kind of guerrilla journalism involving brash, sarcastic attacks on the reader is typical of *Blather.* In addition to those who "so foolishly threw away" (*Myles Before Myles,* p. 104) threepence in order to subject themselves to this kind of abuse, O'Nolan sends up Éamonn de Valera, Yeats, Synge, the Abbey Theatre, retired British Army officers, and many others. The magazine did not catch on, however, and lasted only five months.

In July 1935, O'Nolan began work as a civil servant in the Department of Local Government in Dublin. His immediate superior, John Garvin, praised his work highly but added that "it took some time . . . to make him realise that official letters were not an appropriate medium for expressing his personality" (O'Keefe, p. 54). The position became extremely important in 1937 when O'Nolan's father died and Brian became almost the sole support of his large family. The civil service affected both the content and the tenor of O'Nolan's writings. His constant contact with politicians and bureaucrats kept these people and their foibles on his mind while he wrote his newspaper column. His position in the Department of Local Government entailed dealings with urban councils like the one in his play *Faustus Kelly* (1943). But perhaps the strongest influence on his writing came from the fact that his job often required attendance at the Dáil Éireann (Irish parliament). For a man of O'Nolan's intelligence and oratorical ability to sit quietly and watch men of less ability debate and decide national policy must have been difficult. The many references to the Dáil in "Cruiskeen Lawn" are not charitable. Though mute in the national forum, O'Nolan turned the *Irish Times* into his soapbox.

AT SWIM-TWO-BIRDS

O'NOLAN's first novel, *At Swim-Two-Birds,* was published on 13 March 1939. The work reveals a strikingly unorthodox attitude toward the novel, an attitude that was forecast five years earlier by O'Nolan's last contribution to *Comhthrom Féinne* under the name Brother Barnabas. "Scenes in a Novel" is, the author tells us, "probably posthumous," because the characters in the novel Barnabas is writing have a knife and plan to kill him. The trouble began with Carruthers McDaid, the main character of the book.

> Some writers . . . have started with a good and noble hero and traced his weakening, his degradation and his eventual downfall; others have introduced a degenerate villain to be ennobled and uplifted. . . . In my own case, McDaid, starting off as a rank waster and a rotter, was meant to sink slowly to absolutely the last extremities of human degradation. Nothing, absolutely nothing, was to be too low for him, the wheaten-headed hound. . . .
> (*Myles Before Myles,* p. 78)

But inexplicably, the hound balks at robbing a church poor box. In an earlier chapter Brother Barnabas had sent McDaid to a prayer meeting "for the purpose of scoffing and showing the reader the blackness of his soul. It appears that he remained to pray" (*Myles Before Myles,* p. 59). Meanwhile, Shaun Svoolish, the hero of the novel, has formed an unsuitable alliance with a servant girl and will have nothing to do with the "exquisite creature" the author has "produced for the sole purpose of loving him and becoming his wife" (*Myles Before Myles,* p. 79). Faced with a villain who has gotten religion and a hero who speaks of "the timeless passions of a man's heart" (*Myles Before Myles,* p. 80), Brother Barnabas decides to get tough. He threatens McDaid with anthrax and tells Svoolish that "railway accidents are fortunately rare . . . but when they happen they are horrible" (*Myles Before Myles,* p. 80). These actions stop the overt rebellion, but the conspiracy then turns ugly and the article ends with Brother Barnabas awaiting a grisly fate at the hands of his own creations. The idea of a book's characters having a private life independent of, and possibly inimical to, the authorized fiction of which they are part became an important component, but only one of many, in the new vision of the novel embodied in *At Swim-Two-Birds.*

O'Nolan began writing the book in 1935. His method of composition was very similar to James Joyce's in writing *Ulysses*—he devoured whatever scraps of writing he came across in his daily life and assimilated them into his work. His friend Niall Sheridan reports that a translation of a Catullus poem and a letter from a racing tipster both found their way into the novel. But O'Nolan went further than Joyce. The actual composition of the book became part of the plot. While writing, O'Nolan regularly gave Niall Sheridan excerpts to read; Sheridan was very surprised when a description of the narrator submitting an episode of a novel to Brinsley, a character in the book who is modeled on Sheridan, appeared in the piece he was given. The framing narrative, in which a college student writes a novel to which he refers as his "spare-time literary activities" (p. 9), is only partly autobiographical. The unnamed narrator lives with his uncle, whereas at this time O'Nolan lived in the well-populated family household. Sheridan stated that although a Catullus translation that appears in the book was really his, the bar scene in which the character Brinsley recites it is fictional.

The completed manuscript was edited by Sheridan, who cut the book by about one-fifth. Much of what was cut pertained to caricatures of the ancient Irish heroes, since Sheridan felt that "the weight of this material seriously unbalanced the latter half of the book" (O'Keeffe, p. 47). Graham Greene read manuscripts for the publisher Longmans at this time, and he was very enthusiastic about *At Swim-Two-Birds.* O'Nolan made minor changes at Longmans' request, including the deletion or watering down of "coarse words and references" (Cronin, p. 86).

The novel-writing narrator of the book explains his aesthetic theory to his friend Brinsley.

> The novel, in the hands of an unscrupulous writer, could be despotic. . . . a satisfactory novel should be a self-evident sham to which the reader could regulate at will the degree of his credulity. It was undemocratic to compel characters to be uniformly good or bad or poor or rich. Each should be allowed a private life, self-determination and a decent standard of living. . . . Characters should be interchangeable as between one book and another. The entire corpus of existing literature should be regarded as a limbo from which discerning authors could draw their characters as required, creating only when they failed to find a suitable existing puppet. The modern novel should be largely a work of reference.
> (p. 33)

The narrator's novel illustrates these ideas, but O'Nolan's novel does not. As the book opens, the narrator chews bread and reflects on his "spare-time literary activities," deciding that "a good book may have three openings entirely dissimilar" (p. 9). He then gives examples of the three possible openings. The first describes the Pooka MacPhellimey, "a member of the devil class" (p. 9); the second, John Furriskey, who had the distinction of being born at the age of twenty-five; the third, Finn Mac Cool, "a legendary hero of old Ireland" about whom it is said that "three fifties of fosterlings could engage with handball against the wideness of his backside" (p. 10).

But these three beginnings belong to the narrator's novel. O'Nolan's book has only one beginning, that of the student chewing bread. Throughout the work the fiction operates on these two planes: the framing narrative of the student, which is essentially realistic, and his novel-in-progress, which becomes increasingly outlandish and experimental. It is possible O'Nolan felt that so radical a departure from standard forms needed an anchor, a reference point from which the readers could get their bearings. The student and Brinsley afford the novel an extended discussion of technique, part of which appears above.

Inside this realistic narrative, however, lurk some unreal creatures. Chief among these is Dermot Trellis, "a member of the author class" (p. 138), who does not subscribe to the earlier stipulations regarding the rights of characters. He forces his characters to live with him in the Red Swan Hotel in order to keep an eye on them and make sure there is no boozing. Like Brother Barnabas, he requires that his minions perform shameful acts entirely alien to their natures. His hegemony is threatened, though, by his addiction to sleep. The characters learn that while Trellis sleeps, they may live as they choose. They therefore drug him and avoid his control.

The legendary Finn Mac Cool has fallen on hard times. Near the beginning of the book he trades stories with the Fianna, his heroic band, in parodies of Kuno Meyer translations such as "Finn that could carry an armed host from Almha to Slieve Luachra in the craw of his gut-hung knickers" (p. 24). The stories discussed at first have heroic titles but eventually descend to "the Little Brawl at Allen" and "the Churl in the Puce Great-coat" (p. 23). The ultimate humiliation occurs later in the work, when Finn takes up residence at the Red Swan Hotel and becomes a character in Trellis' sleazy melodrama. He is out of place in the modern world, and though the other characters refer to his tales as "the real old stuff of the native land" (p. 105), they tire of them quickly. They eventually refer to Finn as "Sir Storybook," O'Nolan's sardonic comment on modern Ireland's view of its ancient culture.

Another hero of ancient Ireland who stumbles into the book is mad Sweeny. Driven out of his wits by the curse of the cleric Ronan, Sweeny travels around the treetops of Ireland like a confused migratory bird. Originally the Sweeny narrative is a tale told by Finn, but later the birdman arrives in person and tells his own story. This material was translated by O'Nolan from an old Irish epic. The English is reasonably faithful to the original, with only occasional instances of parody, such as "the saint-bell of saints with sainty-saints" (p. 92), for a line that J. G. O'Keeffe translates as "the bell of saints before saints" (*Buile Shuibhne,* 1913, p. 13).

Although outside of *At Swim-Two-Birds* they are more than a thousand years apart, Sweeny and Jem Casey have much in common. They both enter the novel at about the same time through the narratives of other characters, then appear in the flesh later on. They are both poets. Sweeny composes mournful lays while resting between arboreal commutes, and Casey is described as "Poet of the Pick and Bard of Booterstown" (p. 168). Finn's description of Sweeny and his poetry reminds Shanahan of Casey. The most important parallel occurs after Casey has corporeally joined the band of characters and as Sweeny is about to. Shorty the cowboy is going to shoot Sweeny out of a tree when Casey stops him, saying, "I know a bloody poet when I hear one" (p. 178).

Shanahan describes Jem Casey as "a poor ignorant labouring man but head and shoulders above the whole bloody lot of them, not a man in the whole country to beat him when it comes to getting together a bloody pome" (p. 103). There follow heaps of praise regarding Casey's ability to use a pick and compose poetry at the same time. As proof of Casey's literary prowess Shanahan recites "Workman's Friend," a poem about a very inexpensive form of alcohol, plain porter.

> When money's tight and is hard to get
> And your horse has also ran,
> When all you have is a heap of debt—
> A PINT OF PLAIN IS YOUR ONLY MAN.
> (p. 108)

The poem continues this way for several stanzas, always with the same concluding line. After the recitation the group agrees that such a great poem will live forever.

The juxtaposition of Sweeny and Jem Casey highlights the differences and similarities of their poetic styles. The poetry of ancient Ireland is naive, yet natural and authentic. O'Nolan's touches of parody in Sweeny's "staves" are mild and playful and do not seem to question the validity of the poems as works of art. The attitude toward Casey is different. The ignorance with which the other characters insist on his literary immortality undercuts the reality of this claim. The paean to porter, though fun to read, probably will not "live as long as there's a hard root of an Irishman left by the Almighty on this planet" (p. 109), except perhaps because of its place in this novel. The satire of the modern proletarian poet cuts deeper than that of Sweeny, but both show O'Nolan's view of the inherent unreality and pretense of poetry as a genre.

Dermot Trellis' captive cast members eventually exact their revenge in a way appropriate to this book—they write a story about him. The narrator of this story is Orlick, Dermot's illegitimate semi-fictional son. Not finding "a suitable existing puppet" (p. 33) in other novels, the loathsome Trellis creates Sheila Lamont and becomes so obsessed with the beauty of his handiwork that he rapes her. The student narrator later discusses the difficulty of representing the half-human, half-fictional offspring resulting from this crime, stating that if he gave Orlick only half a body, a sedan chair would be needed to transport him. "For that reason I decided ultimately to make no outward distinction and thus avoided any charge that my work was somewhat far-fetched" (p. 207). Orlick, legs and all, becomes a writer like his father, and at the urging of the other characters uses his talent to avenge Trellis' treatment of his mother. In Orlick's story Trellis suffers the torments of the damned at the hands of the Pooka MacPhellimey. In the world of narrative reification that is *At Swim-Two-Birds*, Dermot is captured in his son's tale and actually undergoes these tortures.

O'Nolan's attitude toward his own stylistic innovations is highly irreverent. Brinsley puts into perspective the student's lengthy theoretical statement on the novel quoted above with the comment, "That is all my bum" (p. 33). The representation of these theories as belonging to a character in a book allows the author to explore and to disavow them at the same time. The levity toward the narrative sleight of hand resembles the tone of Cervantes' *Don Quixote*. The student expatiates on the problem of representing Orlick's paternal semihumanity, when in fact Trellis is also a fictional character. The entire episode seems a bubble created and inflated purely for amusement. O'Nolan's theories, like his novel, are a "self-evident sham to which the reader [can] regulate at will the degree of his credulity" (p. 33).

THE THIRD POLICEMAN

O'NOLAN's aesthetic playfulness continues in his second novel, *The Third Policeman*, but now the careless pursuit of theoretical constructs has a darker side. The plot of *The Third Policeman* is less complicated than that of *At Swim-Two-Birds*. It is not any less strange. The unnamed narrator begins by admitting to a murder, then recounts the story of his childhood. He becomes an orphan, and while away at a boarding school he discovers the writings of de Selby, an eccentric philosopher-scientist. De Selby's crackpot theories and the comical squabblings of his many commentators provide a farcical subplot to the novel.

While knocking around for a few months after graduating from school the narrator reports that:

I broke my left leg (or, if you like, it was broken for me) in six places and when I was well enough again to go my way I had one leg made of wood, the left one.

(p. 9)

He then hobbles home to his family's pub, which a man named John Divney has been running. Divney stays on and steals with impunity from both his employer and the customers. He eventually convinces the narrator to help him rob and murder an old man named Mathers.

Some time after the killing, the narrator goes into Mathers' house to retrieve the cash box Divney supposedly hid there. At this point strange things begin to happen. The dead Mathers appears and carries on a conversation with the narrator. The narrator begins to carry on a conversation with his own soul, to which he gives the unlikely name Joe. The murderer then leaves his animate victim and heads for the police barracks so he can inquire about the cash box. On the way he meets Martin Finnucane, who, like the narrator, has lost a leg and is also a robber and murderer. Finnucane plans to murder him, but relents when he finds out the narrator is one-legged.

Upon reaching the barracks the narrator meets Sergeant Pluck and Policeman MacCruiskeen, who introduce him to various miraculous inventions and theories. Eventually word arrives that Martin Finnucane has murdered Mathers, but since the police do not have him in custody, they decide to hang the narrator instead—this makes him the first man in history to be *framed* for a crime he *did* commit. The narrator then escapes in the confusion of a rescue attempt by Finnucane and bicycles back to Mathers' house. There he encounters Fox, the third policeman, who bears the face and voice of the murdered old man. After leaving Mathers' house, the narrator returns to his home and finds Divney, who is terrified at the sight of him and tells the narrator he has been dead for sixteen years. Divney then dies, and he and the narrator return to the barracks to start the cycle again. The reader learns that the narrator has been living in hell since he reached for the box in Mathers' house and set off a mine that Divney had planted. This plot device may seem as if it were taken from an old *Twilight Zone* episode, but at the time the book was written the idea was new and interesting. Certainly O'Nolan's idiosyncratic view of life in hell is like nothing before or since.

In the retreat sermon in Joyce's *A Portrait of the Artist as a Young Man,* the priest tries to make the eternity of hell comprehensible by using the image of a bird carrying away a mountain, one grain of sand at a time. But for O'Nolan it is the incomprehensibility of eternity that is hellish. The first intimation of this brand of torment occurs when the narrator is with the dead Mathers.

But the eyes were horrible. Looking at them I got the feeling that they were not genuine eyes at all but mechanical dummies animated by electricity or the like, with a tiny pinhole in the centre of the "pupil" through which the real eye gazed out secretively and with great coldness. Such a conception . . . disturbed me agonisingly and gave rise in my mind to interminable speculations as to the colour and quality of the real eye and as to whether, indeed, it was real at all or merely another dummy with its pinhole on the same plane as the first one so that the real eye, possibly behind thousands of these absurd disguises, gazed out through a barrel of serried peep-holes.

(pp. 24–25)

The unreality of the eye resembles the description of the landscape in hell, where trees do not seem to grow randomly but are carefully placed. The second part of the image shows the more common cause of fear and disgust in the novel. Even though the word "thousands" does not denote infinity, the series of holes is like two mirrors opposite each other, producing a continual repetition of the same image.

This being an Irishman's hell, it is naturally full of policemen. When the narrator reaches the barracks, Pluck and MacCruiskeen introduce him to various incomprehensible phenomena, the contemplation of which causes him great suffering. MacCruiskeen pricks the narrator's hand by holding a spear point half a foot away from it. The policeman explains that the real point is so thin it cannot be seen. "About an inch from the end it is so sharp that sometimes . . . you cannot think of it or try to make it the subject of a little idea because you will hurt your box with the excruciation of it" (p. 68). MacCruiskeen then shows the narrator a small, remarkably intricate and beautiful chest from which he removes a slightly smaller but identical chest. Chest after chest is methodically removed until they become extremely small. "At this point I became afraid. What he was doing was no longer wonderful but terrible. I shut my eyes and prayed that he would stop while still doing things that were at least possible for a man to do" (p. 73).

Sergeant Pluck later takes the narrator to a place that is actually called "eternity" and that resembles a complex of machine rooms. In addition to his confrontations with various conundrums, the narrator is shown things that *"lacked an essential property of all known objects. . . .* their appearance, if even that word is not inadmissible, was not understood by the eye and was in any event indescribable" (p. 135). In all these instances it is the contemplation of the incomprehensible, the eternal, the infinite, that torments the murderer.

De Selby, the philosopher-scientist, is one of the most original thinkers of all time. He denies the roundness of the earth but does not jump to the clichéd assumption that it is flat. He says it is shaped like a sausage. Believing that journeys are only hallucinations, he develops an ingenious method of traveling to Folkestone.

> Instead of going to the railway station . . . he shut himself up in a room . . . with a supply of picture postcards of the areas which would be traversed on such a journey, together with an elaborate arrangement of clocks and barometric instruments and a device for regulating the gaslight in conformity with the changing light of the outside day. . . . he emerged after a lapse of seven hours convinced that he was in Folkestone. . . .
>
> (p. 51)

Perhaps the strangest of de Selby's notions is that darkness is caused not by the absence of light but by an accretion of "black air," and that sleep is a succession of fainting fits caused by semi-asphyxiation due to this accretion. Although these ideas seem like harmless lunacy, they sometimes have unfortunate consequences. Defining a house as "a large coffin," de Selby designs his own "habitats" none of which give much protection from the elements—"more than one sick person lost his life in an ill-advised quest for health in these fantastic dwellings" (p. 21).

The only person crazier than someone who spends his life creating crackpot theories like those above is someone who spends his life studying the crackpot. The controversies and infighting between de Selby's commentators, recounted of course in footnotes, are an uproarious satire on scholarly criticism. Faced with de Selby's obvious incompetence in designing the "habitats" described above, the critic Le Fournier apologetically explains that the designs must have been merely doodles that were mistaken for plans. The best example of the silliness of de Selby's explicators is the controversy swirling around "the ill-starred Codex," a document written by de Selby. "The signal distinction of the manuscript is that not one word of the writing is legible" (p. 145). One passage deciphered by two critics is described as either a treatise on old age or "a not unbeautiful description of lambing operations on an unspecified farm" (p. 145). The German commentator Kraus, not understanding that the term "codex" merely refers to the unbound condition of the work, describes the code in which it is written. The critic Hatchjaw, as he does when facing any difficult crux in de Selby's works, declares the codex a forgery.

"The sardonic du Garbandier" (p. 93) is the only intelligent de Selby commentator. He states that "the beauty of reading a page of de Selby is that it leads one inescapably to the happy conviction that one is not, of all nincompoops, the greatest" (p. 92). He comments uncharitably on the fact that a man named Watkins is struck by lightning on the day he finishes the printing of a book by de Selby. In relation to Hatchjaw, who sees frauds and forgeries everywhere, du Garbandier implies that "Hatchjaw [is] not Hatchjaw at all but either another person of the same name or an impostor who [has] successfully maintained the pretence, in writing and otherwise, for forty years" (p. 172).

The narrator, who refers to du Garbandier as eccentric and unpleasant, is perfectly suited to the work of commenting on de Selby. He has a passive, overly intellectual personality and therefore, at the beginning of the novel, does not bother to curb Divney's depredations. When the subject of murder is broached, he allows Divney to persuade him to take part. He avoids acknowledging responsibility for the crime and blames his companion, even though he repeatedly struck Mathers in the head with a spade. De Selby is closely associated with the narrator's downfall. The eventual murderer's first crime is the theft of a book by de Selby from the school science master, and it is the contemplation of de Selby's works that distracts him from Divney's malfeasance. The argument that finally convinces him to help murder Mathers is that he can use the money to publish his "De Selby Index."

Forsaking his airy speculations for a moment, in his *Layman's Atlas* de Selby discusses "bereavement, old age, love, sin, death and the other saliencies of existence" (p. 93). He allows only six lines to these topics because he considers them "unnecessary." In the epigraph to the novel, de Selby states that since human existence is a hallucination, "it ill becomes any man of sense to be concerned at the illusory approach of the supreme hallucination known as death" (p. 5). The Roman Catholic religion, of which O'Nolan was a member all his life, takes a very different view of preparing for death. It is the narrator's unconcern, fostered by de Selby, for death and the other "unnecessaries" of human existence, that lands him in a hell where the same kind of fantastic theoretical insanity on which he wasted his life is made real in a terrifying and inescapable way.

But the view of imaginative speculation in the text is more problematic than that. Most of the theorizing, though patently false, is fascinating. For a book that champions common sense, it contains countless engagingly fantastic episodes. But, unlike John Milton, O'Nolan knows he is a member of the devil's party. It is the rejection of real life, not the exercise of imagination, that he satirizes.

O'Nolan was devastated by his publisher's rejection of *The Third Policeman* in 1940. To avoid explanations, he made up stories about having lost the manuscript. An unfortunate lack of self-confidence caused him eventually to agree, at least partly, with the publisher's appraisal. Later in life he could have published the book but did not, and the novel, one of his best, did not come out until after his death.

"CRUISKEEN LAWN"

In July 1940 Patrick Kavanagh published a book review and a poem in the *Irish Times.* These contributions provoked O'Nolan and friends of his to embark on a "letters controversy" that mercilessly scarified everything Kavanagh had to say and then veered off into uncharted realms of nonsense having nothing to do with the original topic. The controversy proved very popular, and R. M. Smyllie, the editor of the *Irish Times,* asked O'Nolan to write a regular column for the newspaper. Thus "Cruiskeen Lawn" (Irish for "the little brimful jug") was born. The pseudonym under which the articles appeared was Myles na gCopaleen (later Gopaleen), "Myles of the Ponies." O'Nolan wrote exclusively in Irish at first, but later alternated English and Irish pieces. Eventually the column was almost entirely in English.

One of the most entertaining of the innumerable schemes cooked up by Myles na Gopaleen is his escort service. This service is similar to the "eaters" scheme of O'Nolan's student days, in which the reader was offered conversation at meals for various prices. But Myles's escort speaks not only to you but for you—he is a ventriloquist. O'Nolan

here satirizes the middle- and upper-class woman who wants to be part of the nightlife of Dublin but is incapable of carrying on the bright and witty repartee she feels is required. The woman can rent a ventriloquist who will carry both halves of the conversation while she remains silent. The exchanges Myles transcribes as examples consist of trendy pseudo-intellectual nonsense, but a person who wants his service will not know that.

The escort business thrives but hits a snag when certain unscrupulous ventriloquists begin extorting money from theatergoers in return for not making embarrassing and insulting statements in their voices. Distributing threatening postcards signed "The Black Shadow" and "The Green Mikado," the escorts terrorize audiences and create pandemonium when their demands are not met. One unfortunate soul who refuses to pay finds himself accusing "a well-known and respected member of the justiciary" of having a "whiskey face," then adding, "I don't like you either, and I've a damn good mind to break your red neck" (p. 30).[1] The silent loudmouth is eventually punched, robbed, and arrested. In one theater, the ventriloquist scourge is particularly acute: "If you say something, no one will believe that you said it" (p. 33). Myles cannot resist the possibilities of the situation and says to a woman, "Hello, hag! How's yer ould one?" (p. 34).

"Cruiskeen Lawn" at times featured a strange pair of literary ne'er-do-wells: Keats and Chapman. Exactly how the Romantic poet and the Elizabethan translator of Homer came together in twentieth-century Europe to chase wealthy widows and generally make nuisances of themselves is unknown. Their first adventure involves a homing pigeon, owned by Chapman. The bird is ill and Keats pries open its beak, stares down its throat, and removes a piece of cork lodged there. Apparently unaware that he had done so a century before, Keats then writes the sonnet "On First Looking into Chapman's Homer." This tale set the pattern for Keats and Chapman episodes. They start with an elaborate buildup in which the heroes might be almost anywhere, pursuing almost any career or stratagem. All of the stories are constructed to set up a final excruciating pun

[1]Page citations for quotations from "Cruiskeen Lawn" are from *The Best of Myles,* (1968), unless otherwise noted.

FLANN O'BRIEN

delivered by Keats. Myles points out that the buildup should not lead directly to the outcome but should contain a certain amount of misdirection and even boredom. This is exemplified by the following:

Chapman was much given to dreaming and often related to Keats the strange things he saw when in bed asleep. On one occasion he dreamt that he had died and gone to heaven. He was surprised and rather disappointed at what he saw for although the surroundings were most pleasant, there seemed to be nobody about. The place seemed to be completely empty and Chapman saw himself wandering disconsolately about looking for somebody to talk to. He suddenly woke up without solving this curious puzzle.

"It was very strange," he told Keats. "I looked everywhere but there wasn't a soul to be seen."

Keats nodded understandingly.

"There wasn't a sinner in the place," he said.

(p. 190)

The urbane, unhurried tone of the story contrasts with the flippant abruptness of the ending. The three seemingly unnecessary repetitions regarding the emptiness of heaven prepare the reader for the final comic restatement. People with a low tolerance for puns should avoid Keats and Chapman. In one story the young Chapman is glued to the back of his school headmaster as a prank, and Keats remarks, "I like a man that sticks to his principals" (p. 181). When told of a gambler who sells a valuable painting to cover his losses, Keats comments, "F. Huehl and his Monet are soon parted" (*The Best of Myles,* p. 185). But, to quote Chaucer's innkeeper at the end of the Tale of Sir Thopas, "Namore of this, for Goddes dignitee!"

In addition to describing various characters from around Ireland, Myles is particularly interested in the Dublin Man. In one article this person is recounting some recent developments in his life. While visiting, his drunken brother-in-law sets fire to the Dublin Man's stairs, kills his wife by blowing up the kitchen, and kills his eldest son by knocking down part of the ceiling. The Dublin Man's response to all this is "and I wouldn't mind only on the way out he kicked the milk bottle to pieces and the young chisler Tomaus roaring his head off for his breakfast!" (*The Hair of the Dogma: A Further Selection from Cruiskeen Lawn,* p. 16).

The most extraordinary Dublin Man in "Cruis-keen Lawn" is a recurring character known as "the brother." He never appears in person, but *his* brother recounts his escapades to an unnamed auditor while the two wait for a bus. The brother is a great medical man who will not allow his sick landlady to call a doctor: "He still keeps working away at her and puts her on a special diet, milk and nuts and all this class of thing. . . . The brother is going to let her up for a while on Sunday" (*The Best of Myles,* p. 42). The brother is not above using his medical reputation for his own ends. In one episode the landlady is perfectly well, yet he insists she is deathly ill and sends her to Skerries for a rest. He then takes advantage of her absence by having a woman friend visit every night, something the landlady would never allow.

Usually, however, the brother's eccentricities do not point to his manipulativeness. He has some remarkable ideas about animals. When he is not busy listening to his dog talk, he is attempting to enroll the beast in the police force. A high-ranking police official wants the dog to be a sergeant, but the brother will not stand for any string-pulling and insists he start at the bottom like everyone else. The seal is another animal who behaves strangely in the brother's world. At night seals come out of the water to rob gardens, steal children, and sit on the upper decks of idle trams. "Begob the brother says it's a great sight of a moonlight night to see your men with the big moustaches on them sitting upstairs in the trams lookin out" (p. 53). But the most striking example of this man's love of animals is his refusal to use his talented dog to help round up an excess population of deer.

THE DEER, says the brother, IS MAN'S FRIEND. . . . And he's right. Because when did the deer harm you?
Never, I assure you.
And when did they take a puck at me?
Never.
When did they try to ate your men on the bicycles?

(p. 56)

This last exchange is an example of the idiomatic Dublinese that O'Nolan used in much of his writing. The phrases "take a puck" and "your men" are typical, as is the use of "ate" for "eat." Anthony Cronin, O'Nolan's friend and biographer, expresses uncertainty as to whether people spoke this way naturally or began to do so only after reading

Myles. Considering the popularity of "Cruiskeen Lawn," the latter suggestion is not as unlikely as it sounds. These idiosyncratic speech patterns, already in use by a segment of the population, probably became more widespread through their exposure in the column—life imitates art.

Another recurring feature in "Cruiskeen Lawn" is the Myles na gCopaleen Research Bureau. This inventive group bestows on mankind such boons as alcoholic ice cream and fake telephones for those who cannot afford real ones. In reference to Daniel Corkery's book *The Hidden Ireland,* which uncovered much that was unknown about Gaelic culture, the Bureau suggests "a scheme that should win the support of all right thinking citizens. *Hide Ireland again!"* (p. 133). The discussion of a gadget appearing in the column, in the same vein as the "Research Bureau" section that was introduced later, shows O'Nolan's impatience with literary pretension:

The article illustrated to-day . . . is a snow-gauge. . . . It . . . consists of a funnel or catch-pipe for the snow, which widens inwardly, then drops eighteen inches, allowing the snow to fall into a pan beneath. . . . By this arrangement the snow cannot escape; it melts and runs into the bucket beneath, where it is accurately gauged.

So what, you say. I will tell you what. . . . Supposing some moon-faced young man who reads Proust happens to be loitering about your house, blathering out of him about art, life, love, and so on. He is sure to have a few cant French phrases, which he will produce carefully at suitable intervals as one produces coins from a purse. Inevitably the day will come (even if you have to wait for it for many years) when he will sigh and murmur:

"[But where are the snows of yesteryear?]"

Here is your chance. This is where you go to town. Seize the nitwit by the scruff of the neck, march him out to the snow gauge and shout:

"Right in that bucket, you fool!"

I'll bet you'll feel pretty good after that.

(pp. 112–113)

The image of the homeowner is as ludicrous as that of the "moon-faced" young man. Imagine the homeowner waiting years, wringing his hands in anticipation, one eye on his guest and the other on the snow gauge. The author's method of direct address, referring to the homeowner as "you," is another example of the kind of comic abuse of the reader so common in *Blather.*

Pretentious intellectuals are one of Myles' favorite targets, but he also satirizes nonintellectuals, whom he lumps together in one officious mass known as "the plain people of Ireland." In regard to World War II, which was raging in Europe at the time, the P.P.O.I. voice the absurd concern that "the Swiss are thinking of having a go at the French" (p. 80). In response to their mistaken correction of his spelling, Myles defines the P.P.O.I. as "the ignorant self-opinionated sod-minded suet-brained ham-faced mealy-mouthed streptococcus-ridden gang of natural gobdaws!" (*The Best of Myles,* p. 81). But these gobdaws are capable of scoring off Myles. In the middle of a spiel of legal jargon such as "tenure by sochemaunce seisined by feodo copyholds . . ." they interrupt with the cogent comment, "This sounds like dirty water being squirted out of a hole in a burst rubber ball" (*The Best of Myles,* p. 85). Often the common man's naiveté is made fun of, but usually in a gentle way. The P.P.O.I. badger Myles for jokes and then pout when he does not produce them or when the jokes are too recherché for them to understand. When Myles starts writing an adventure serial in the column and the villain of the piece is knocked unconscious, the P.P.O.I. are completely caught up in the action and cannot help shouting, "Good enough for the dirty dog!" (p. 109).

There are a number of other recurring features in "Cruiskeen Lawn." One is the saga of "Sir" Myles na gCopaleen, who returns from the dead and squabbles with his heirs over his estate. For a price, the book-handling service offers to make the many books in your house appear as though you have actually read them. The "Myles na gCopaleen Cathechism of Cliché" provides such important questions and answers as

In what opulent manner does one deserve a thrashing? Richly.

(p. 216)

Particular types of bores are examined, such as "The Man Who Spoke Irish At A Time When It Was Neither Profitable Nor Popular" (p. 290). Comical transcriptions of court proceedings appear in the column, complete with impenetrable legal jargon. Some of the oddest pieces are detailed and extremely well-informed discussions of railway steam engines and the men who operate them.

Throughout the years Myles made innumerable references to literature. Two of his favorite topics are the literary giants of the generation preceding his own, W. B. Yeats and James Joyce. He wonders whether the name Yeats was ever misprinted as Yeast: "both, mind you, are noted for ebullience, for the capacity to transmute the base into the precious" (*The Hair of the Dogma,* p. 152). In the same article he discusses an excerpt from *The Celtic Twilight,* a book of essays published by Yeats in 1893, which he derides as an example of inauthentic or "stage" Irishness. This attitude goes back to O'Nolan's student days, when he satirized Yeats as the poet-dilettante Lionel Prune. But O'Nolan's aesthetic sense was too well developed for him not to appreciate Yeats's talent. While deploring the lack of talent among contemporary Irish writers, Myles states, "In the last century, Joyce and Yeats were the only two who were men of genius" (p. 256).

O'Nolan's attitude toward Joyce, expressed in "Cruiskeen Lawn" and elsewhere, is very complicated. Joyce received a copy of *At Swim-Two-Birds* shortly after it was published and enjoyed the book very much. Because of the mixture of realism and daring technical innovation in the novel, O'Nolan was continually compared with Joyce. He eventually began to resent these comparisons because he did not want to be thought of as a mere imitator, and because his aesthetic outlook differed more and more from Joyce's as his art developed. O'Nolan's unorthodox but strong Catholicism and customary apprehension toward things "artistic" prevented his wholehearted acceptance of Joyce. In an essay he contributed to an edition of the journal *Envoy* dedicated to Joyce (1951), O'Nolan states that the main difference between Joyce and Satan is that Satan never denied the existence of God.

This is a joke, but it illustrates O'Nolan's discomfort with Joyce's rebellion against religion and common morality. O'Nolan worked as a civil servant for years, supporting his brothers and sisters; at the same age Joyce went off to Europe to be an artist, leaving his family in squalor. This neglect of moral responsibility for intellectual pursuits is the kind of attitude O'Nolan attacks in his portrait of de Selby. About *Finnegans Wake,* which an unprofessional observer might easily mistake for a work by de Selby, O'Nolan writes in "Cruiskeen Lawn," "I say it with sorrow, but the reader can have my part of it and welcome" (*The Hair of the Dogma,* p. 155). "A Bash in the Tunnel," the *Envoy* article mentioned above, tells the story of a man who locks himself in the lavatory of an empty railway dining car and slowly drinks himself into oblivion with stolen whiskey.

But surely there you have the Irish artist?

Sitting fully dressed, innerly locked in the toilet of a locked coach where he has no right to be, resentfully drinking somebody else's whiskey . . . keeping fastidiously the while on the outer face of his door the simple word, ENGAGED?

I think the image fits Joyce: but particularly in his manifestation of a most Irish characteristic—the transgressor's resentment with the nongressor.

(*Stories and Plays,* p. 206)

And O'Nolan manifests the complementary characteristic—the nongressor's resentment of the transgressor.

Throughout the years Myles na Gopaleen made many comments, mostly unfavorable, on other Irish writers. The writers of the Irish literary revival associated with the Abbey Theatre believed "that poverty and savage existence on remote rocks was a most poetical way for people to be, provided they were other people" (*The Hair of the Dogma,* p. 102). Myles confesses to confusing Lady Gregory with Queen Victoria, and calls J. M. Synge a "moneyed dilettante" and "an affected interloper" (*The Hair of the Dogma,* p. 102). He takes Frank O'Connor and Sean O'Faoláin to task for "stage Irishness." Myles occasionally nettles Patrick Kavanagh and Brendan Behan, but their friendship with O'Nolan, and perhaps also their talent, protected them from the kind of abuse visited on others.

Considering his bias against arts that he felt were too self-consciously artistic, it is not surprising that Myles sides with Plato in deciding that "there is no excuse for poetry" (p. 239). The reasons he gives are that it does not pay well, it wastes space because of the way it is printed, and it promulgates illusion. "But a better case for the banning of all poetry is the simple fact that most of it is bad. . . . Moreover, poets are usually unpleasant people who are poor and who insist forever on discussing that incredibly boring subject, 'books' " (p. 239). Three of the chief offenders are Wordsworth, Shelley, and Tennyson. Myles derides Wordsworth for wearing elastic-sided boots and calls Shelley's "Ode to a Skylark" "base, effeminate, affected nonsense" (p. 261). He refers to all three poets as "Saxon windbags." A more lighthearted but no less devastating appraisal of a modern poet is given in verse:

> My grasp of what he wrote and meant
> Was only five or six %.
> The rest was only words and sound—
> My reference is to Ezra £.
>
> (p. 234)

As with the earlier depictions of Sweeny and Jem Casey, in "Cruiskeen Lawn" O'Nolan shows little patience with poetry, especially bad poetry.

One of the most common topics in "Cruiskeen Lawn," especially in the later years, is politics. O'Nolan's political stance is difficult to define because he is like an agile boxer, hitting and dodging. Anthony Cronin commented that O'Nolan had the unique ability of seeming to be on both sides of an issue at the same time. But throughout "Cruiskeen Lawn" and his other writings O'Nolan was basically conservative, though his independence of mind occasionally led him to say very unconservative things. Myles often poked fun at Sean O'Faoláin and his magazine *The Bell* for their stand against the censorship of books. Although it was ostensibly an attack on the trendiness and careerism of their arguments, it is clear that the censorship then practiced in Ireland did not greatly bother him. Another example of his conservatism is the assertion that only inferior people are concerned about their rights; successful people do not need to be.

O'Nolan heaped scorn on any politician unlucky enough to wander onto the pages of "Cruiskeen Lawn," but he unleashed an exceptionally virulent tirade against a spokesman for the British Labour Party who suggested a rapprochement with "the common man" of Ireland. He lampooned both the Britishness and the Labourness. O'Nolan's individuality prevented him from adhering dogmatically to one worldview, however. Myles ridiculed the British insurance companies' frantic attempts to avoid nationalization and the maudlin advertisements they used in this battle. In another newspaper column, "Bones

of Contention," which he wrote in the 1960's, O'Nolan presented a detailed and convincing argument against capital punishment. Perhaps the one constant in O'Nolan's political outlook was his deep disrespect for politicians of all persuasions. On the Dáil he commented, "The majority of the members of the Irish parliament are professional politicians, in the sense that otherwise they would not be given jobs minding mice at a crossroads" (*The Hair of the Dogma,* p. 171).

"Cruiskeen Lawn" appeared in the *Irish Times* until 1966, the year of O'Nolan's death. The first few years of the column produced the most inventive and funny pieces, but throughout its life "Cruiskeen Lawn" remained interesting and entertaining. For this essay it was useful to consider Myles's twenty-six-year span as one unit, but now it is necessary to move back in time.

THE POOR MOUTH

In 1941 O'Nolan published a satirical novel written in Irish, *An Béal Bocht (The Poor Mouth).* To "put on the poor mouth" means to "cry poverty" or claim to be as poor and miserable as possible, in order to gain sympathy or aid. The title refers to the first of two important targets of the satire in the novel, Gaelic literature. O'Nolan grew up speaking and reading Gaelic, and often visited places in the Gaeltacht (Irish-speaking regions) with his brothers. Because the Gaeltacht was so poor, the literature it produced spoke of this poverty—too frequently, in O'Nolan's opinion. The writers the book satirizes most are Séamas Ó Grianna (also known as Maire) and Tomás Ó Criomhthain. The other major satiric target in the work is the Gaeligores, English speakers who descended on the Gaeltacht to learn Irish and to observe the peasants and their way of life. In *The Poor Mouth* they are portrayed as ludicrous dilettantes with no real knowledge of the language and no real concern for the welfare of the peasants. The title of the novel, in addition to characterizing Gaelic literature, may be a swipe at the Gaeligore's linguistic inability.

The Poor Mouth was not attributed to Flann O'Brien, Brian O'Nolan, or Myles na Gopaleen. It is attested to be the autobiography of Bonaparte O'Coonassa, edited by Myles na Gopaleen. This is one of the few instances in literary history where an author uses not only a pen name but also a blue-pencil name. The autobiographical form mimics the Gaelic novels on which it is based. Another parallel between the parody and the originals is the use of certain characteristic phrases. The reason O'Coonassa chooses to write the story of his life in the mythical community of Corkadoragha is that "our likes will never be there again" (p. 11). This oft-repeated phrase is from Tomás Ó Criomhthain's novel *An t-Oileanach* (*The Islandman*). Although O'Nolan parodies Ó Criomhthain, he wrote elsewhere that he considered *The Islandman* to be a powerful and important work.

Bonaparte's grandfather, the Old-Grey-Fellow, says that when he was growing up, he was, like so many youngsters in Séamas Ó Grianna's books, "a child among the ashes" (p. 16). O'Nolan explodes this cliché by taking it literally. The Old-Grey-Fellow complains to Bonaparte's mother that she has cleaned all the ashes and soot from the floor "and not a bit left for the poor child. . . . It's an unnatural and unregulated training and rearing he'll have without any experience of the ashes" (p. 16). But traditional training and rearing are not as uplifting as the old man claims.

She took a bucket full of muck, mud and ashes and hen's droppings from the roadside and spread it around the hearth. . . . I moved over near the fire and for five hours I became a child in the ashes—a raw youngster rising up according to the old Gaelic tradition. Later at midnight I was taken and put into bed but the foul stench of the fireplace stayed with me for a week. . . .

(p. 16)

This literal-minded attack continues later in the novel when nineteen-year-old Bonaparte learns that life in the Rosses, where Ó Grianna's books take place, follows very definite patterns. In each home there are a character called the "Gambler," who plays cards and billiards when not off carousing in Scotland; an old man who tells stories by the fire with his "hooves" in the ashes; and a "comely lassie" for whom men come at night with "five noggin bottles" to press their suits of marriage. By reducing Ó Grianna's books to their skeletal plot and character elements, O'Nolan exposes their repetitive, formulaic nature.

Another stock situation in Gaelic literature is the protagonist's first contact with the English-lan-

guage educational system. When, on Bonaparte's first day of school, the venomous master Osborne O'Loonassa asks him, "Phwat is yer nam?" the youth is unable to answer because he does not understand the master's English (p. 30). But when a fellow student translates the question, Bonaparte recites his name and lineage in Gaelic. This response does not please O'Loonassa, who calls the child to the front of the room and splits his skull open with a wooden oar. Just before Bonaparte loses consciousness, he hears the master scream, "Yer nam . . . is Jams O'Donnell!" (p. 30). The other children do not learn from the boy's mistake; one by one they answer in Irish and are brutally christened Jams O'Donnell. When Bonaparte's mother later explains that all Gaels undergo this initiation and tells him that the Old-Grey-Fellow was once dubbed Jams O'Donnell, she voices the kind of lament heard throughout the book. "Alas! I don't think that there'll ever be any good settlement for the Gaels but only hardship for them always" (p. 34). When Bonaparte goes to prison at the end of the novel, he meets his father for the first time. He has never seen him before but knows this must be his father because the man's name is Jams O'Donnell.

The satire on the Gaeligores and the study of Gaelic begins with a pig wearing clothes. The Old-Grey-Fellow hatches a scheme to collect money from a government inspector by pretending that the family pigs are actually children. The scam works perfectly, but afterward one of the pigs disappears, still fully dressed. Meanwhile a Gaeligore from Dublin has been plying the locals with whiskey in an attempt to record Gaelic stories on his gramophone. When the clothed pig wanders into the darkened house where the recording is being done and starts grunting, the Dubliner is ecstatic because "he understood that good Gaelic is difficult but that the best Gaelic of all is well-nigh unintelligible" (p. 44). A group of eminent European scholars later declares the pig's comments to be some of the best Gaelic ever recorded.

Although the accuracy of Gaelic was said to increase with the poverty of the Gael, and Corkadoragha possessed the "choicest poverty," the Gaeligores, who by this time had become a mainstay of the local economy, decreased drastically in number. The Old-Grey-Fellow discovers that along with the constant downpours and the bad odors, the reason for the Gaeligores' desertion is

FLANN O'BRIEN

that "the poverty of the countryside [is] too poor" (p. 50). The Gaeligores choose to avoid Corkadoragha instead of helping, showing that their interest in the Gaeltacht is purely self-centered and mercenary.

The Old-Grey-Fellow decides that the only way to draw the Gaeligores back is to build a college for them to stay in so they can avoid the incessant rain and the stench of the people's cabins, and he organizes a feis (Gaelic festival) to raise money. The language enthusiasts descend like locusts on Corkadoragha the day of the feis and begin the revelry by taking honorary Irish titles. "There was a bulky, fat, slow-moving man whose face was grey and flabby and appeared suspended between deaths from two mortal diseases; he took unto himself the title of *The Gaelic Daisy*" (p. 52). The president of the feis delivers a speech that uses the words "Gael," "Gaelic," "Gaelicism," and "Gaelically" thirty-three times in one paragraph, for example—"We are all Gaelic Gaels of Gaelic lineage" (p. 54). In the midst of this Gaelic tirade the speaker asserts that the Gaelic language should be used only to discuss Gaelic subjects. In "Cruiskeen Lawn," Myles had already stated the opposite: that the Irish language would not survive unless it could be used to discuss things like nuclear fission. The inane repetition of the speech displays the solipsism of Gaelic studies at that time by reducing the self-referentiality to an absurdly literal level. When the speech is ended, Bonaparte reports that "this noble Gael sat down on his Gaelic backside" (p. 55).

Although the Gaelic world was ripe for satire in the early 1940's, it is important to remember that most of the complaints in the Gaelic novels were true. The countryside was gripped by numbing poverty, and English educational and legal institutions were unresponsive to the needs of non-English speakers. The language movement suffered from rampant careerism, chauvinism, and pretension, but it did help to stanch the loss of Irish culture and focus attention on the problems of the Gaeltacht.

Wandering alone at night, O'Coonassa is chased by a monstrous being called the "Sea-cat" and is lucky to escape with his life. When drawn on a piece of paper, the image of the Sea-cat resembles a map of Ireland. The editor Myles na Gopaleen makes this comment in a footnote: "It is not without importance that the Sea-cat and Ireland bear the same shape and that both have all

the same bad destiny, hard times and ill-luck attending on them which have come upon us" (p. 77). Stephen Dedalus describes his Irish nationality as a net, but for O'Nolan it is a hairy, vicious, foul-smelling beast. The truth in the Gaelic novels and the importance of the Gaelic revival only make the claims of the Sea-cat more suffocating and horrible. For a man of O'Nolan's temperament, that truth only makes the use of satire as a defense more necessary.

FAUSTUS KELLY

IN 1942 Myles na Gopaleen wrote a play called *Faustus Kelly*, which was first performed at the Abbey Theatre on 25 January 1943. Goethe's Faust sells his soul for the sublimity of forbidden knowledge, but in a typically O'Nolanesque reduction Kelly sells his for a seat in the Dáil and the affections of a wealthy widow. The play shows the inner workings of an urban council and the machinations of the council chairman, Kelly, in his attempt to be elected to parliament. The selling of Kelly's soul is quickly disposed of in a silent prologue, allowing the entire play to reveal the fallen world of Irish politics. In the council chamber Kelly's only impediment is a cantankerous council member named Reilly. Reilly, a bit of a crank, does not like automobiles or women in trousers, but he is the only member of the council who seems interested in honesty or good government. When Kelly and his minion, the town clerk, arrange a "ready-up" to have the devil illegally appointed as a tax collector, Reilly objects and threatens to expose the matter. In the meantime the devil engineers Kelly's successes with the widow Crockett and at the polls. After the election he insists that Kelly uphold his part of the bargain. In the end, however, the Prince of Darkness and Lord of the Underworld proves no match for an Irish politician.

The form and ideas of *Faustus Kelly* owe a large debt to the theater of Sean O'Casey. Both Shawn Kilshaughraun in *Kelly* and Seumas Shields in *Shadow of a Gunman* (1925) are obsessively concerned with "Irishness." The difference is that Shawn is an unthinking super-patriot, whereas Seumas is an unthinking denigrator of Ireland. But the O'Casey play O'Nolan had most in mind while writing *Kelly* was *The Plough and the Stars*

335

(1926). In a reply to a very positive letter from O'Casey about the recently published *An Béal Bocht,* O'Nolan discusses the success of a revival of *The Plough* at the Abbey Theatre and in the same breath states that he is about to start writing a play called *Faustus Kelly.* The main correspondence between the two plays is their concern with the nature and effects of oratory. At a political meeting in act 2 of *The Plough and the Stars,* a man on a platform is speaking in the phrases of Padraic Pearse about the need to achieve Irish independence, saying things like "bloodshed is a cleansing and sanctifying thing" and "the old heart of the earth needed to be warmed with the red wine of the battlefields." O'Casey's characters are agitated and enthused by this oratory. Fluther and Peter excitedly discuss their reactions, and Fluther says, "the blood was BOILIN' in me veins!" In the postindependence Ireland of *Faustus Kelly,* the function of oratory is different. Kelly is often carried away by the sound of his own voice and gives vent to such clichéd bombast as

Emigration, that is bidding fair to drain our land of its life blood and spelling ruin to the business life of the community. The flight from the land is another thing that must be arrested at no far distant day. Please God when I get as far as the Dail I will have a word in season to say on that subject to the powers that be.

(Stories and Plays, p. 153)

But Kelly is never so eloquent as when he is lying about his own honesty.

Will success crown their attempts to silence me? Will their gold once again carry the day and make me still another of their bought-and-paid-for minions? By God it won't! By God in Heaven it won't!

(Stories and Plays, p. 154)

When this tirade ends with Kelly shouting that he is not for sale, only the audience is aware of the irony of his making such a statement. In O'Casey's play oratory is an incitement, a call to arms, an invitation to bloodshed and catastrophe. In *Faustus Kelly,* however, it is not the violence of political speech that is satirized but the banality and hypocrisy. The gap between the backstairs politicking and the righteously indignant clichés spouted in public is, as Reilly would say, wide enough to drive a coach and four through.

THE HARD LIFE

ASIDE from his "Cruiskeen Lawn" articles, O'Nolan produced very little of note between *Faustus Kelly* and his next novel, *The Hard Life,* published in 1961. On 2 December 1948 he married Evelyn McDonnell, a typist in his section of the Department of Local Government. They were apparently happy in spite of his drinking, which grew steadily worse through the years. He would duck out during working hours to a nearby pub called the Scotch House, and seems to have proved a rather ineffectual employee. What got him into trouble, however, was the increasingly political nature of "Cruiskeen Lawn." The final straw was a devastating caricature, which appeared in the column, of the minister under whom O'Nolan worked, Patrick Smith. O'Nolan was allowed to retire in 1953 on a disability pension that paid him some money, but not enough. For about two years, under the pseudonym John James Doe, he wrote a newspaper column called "A Weekly Look Around." The problem with this column, as well as with the other hack journalism O'Nolan produced at the time, is that he was forced to "popularize" his writing in order to make it acceptable to newspaper editors. The creative freedom of "Cruiskeen Lawn" is rarely found in the newspapers of Ireland or anywhere else.

The 1960 reissue, to critical acclaim, of *At Swim-Two-Birds,* which had been out of print for many years, energized O'Nolan's creative faculties and led him to write *The Hard Life.* Although not as comically inventive as the earlier works, it is an interesting and entertaining novel.

Like *The Third Policeman, The Hard Life* is told as the autobiography of an orphan. Finbarr and his older brother, Manus, are sent to live with Mr. Collopy after the death of their mother. Collopy and a priest with the fragrant appellation Kurt Fahrt, S.J., engage in lengthy discussions on the role of the Jesuits in history and on public bathrooms for women. Finbarr's brother, as he grows older, becomes involved in various shady mail-order schemes. The first of these is Professor Latimer Dodd's high wire lessons; he soon branches out into the Excelsior Turf Bureau and the Zenith School of Journalism. When his business requires him to move to England, partly to avoid the police, he opens the London University Academy, which gives lessons by mail in everything from hypnotism to sausage manufacture in the home. When Mr. Collopy complains of rheumatism, Manus sends Finbarr a bottle of patent medicine called Gravid Water for him. The drug cures the rheumatism, but because Collopy accidentally takes too much, he mysteriously begins to grow heavier and heavier while his body stays the same size. A trip is made to Rome in the hope that an audience with the pope will result in a miracle cure. Unfortunately, during this audience Collopy's obsession with providing public rest rooms for women in Dublin arises and the pope decides he is crazy. No miracle occurs, and Collopy's enormous weight later causes him to fall through a stairway landing to his death.

The subtitle of the novel is *An Exegesis of Squalor,* and in many ways this is apt. Mr. Collopy is a likable but wretched man who is given to argument and obsession. He suffers from rheumatism, and his friend Fahrt constantly scratches because of psoriasis. Collopy lives "in sin" with Mrs. Crotty, who in the first half of the book slowly dies of an unpleasant disease. Manus' business dealings are certainly squalid, and the episode of his careless distribution of a dangerous substance, the Gravid Water, could easily occur in a sleazy melodrama. It is fitting that the book ends with Finnbar bringing up a "tidal surge" of vomit.

From 1960 until the year of his death from cancer (on the macabrely appropriate date of 1 April 1966), O'Nolan contributed a weekly column called "Bones of Contention" to the County Carlow *Nationalist and Leinster Times* under the pseudonym George Knowall. These are mostly good-natured, informative, and pedestrian pieces that lack the creativity and spleen of "Cruiskeen Lawn." But occasionally Myles peeks out from behind the genial Knowall mask, as in an article titled "Electors treated as half-wits." This piece begins with a tirade against the vulgarity and stupidity of the recent election campaign and goes on to discuss Fianna Fáil Party funding.

Not long ago an FG [Fine Gael Party] deputy asked the appropriate Minister to fix a minimum pork content for sausages. The Minister declined, saying that such an order "would not be in the public interest" or words to that effect. I have long eschewed, rather than chewed, the Irish sausage because I am convinced that certain brands *contain no pork at all!* The high spice content makes it impossible for the palate to distinguish pork from

horse. It must be taken that the firms benefiting from the Minister's astonishing attitude are heavy subscribers to the Party funds.

(*Myles Away from Dublin,* p. 111)

During the 1960's O'Nolan wrote a number of scripts for Irish television, most notably for a series starring the comedian Jimmy O'Dea.

THE DALKEY ARCHIVE

O'NOLAN's last completed novel, *The Dalkey Archive,* is a weaker effort than any of his previous books. His own battles with "cures" for his chronic alcoholism are pathetically mirrored in the protagonist Mick's continual resolutions to give up drinking. The plot of the work is often devoid of causation, so that new elements in the narrative seem tacked on rather than logically developed. The two main threads of the story, de Selby's plot and James Joyce's sudden reappearance, are never sufficiently tied together or resolved.

O'Nolan cannibalized the far superior, but at the time unpublished, *The Third Policeman* in writing *The Dalkey Archive.* The eccentric de Selby appears as a character rather than as a historical figure, and has a plan to destroy the world. Sergeant Fottrell speaks in a more pronounced version of the comically affected language of Pluck and MacCruiskeen. The section on the "Mollycule Theory" of Sergeant Fottrell is lifted almost verbatim from *The Third Policeman.* The germ of this theory is that by riding too much, people absorb the "mollycules" of a bicycle and eventually become mostly bicycle themselves. The bicycles also absorb human "mollycules" and mysteriously turn up by the kitchen fire on a rainy day with crumbs at their front wheels. O'Nolan plundered one of his best novels instead of trying again to publish it because he came to believe the earlier publisher's opinion. He unfortunately chose to rewrite *The Third Policeman* when his creative capabilities were far less acute than when he composed the original.

Despite its general mediocrity, *The Dalkey Archive* contains some clever ideas, particularly the appearances of Saint Augustine and James Joyce. Using a small amount of the substance with which he plans to end the world, de Selby calls Augustine down from heaven. Surprisingly, the early Christian speaks with a Dublin accent. Augustine comments on theology and the wily Jesuits, and settles the controversy stirred up by the scholar Binchy, who maintained that there were two Saint Patricks.

—Two Saint Patricks? We have four of the buggers in our place and they'd make you sick with their shamrocks and shenanigans and bullshit.

(p. 38)

The James Joyce of the novel is very different from the rebellious author of *Ulysses* and *Finnegans Wake.* In fact, he insists he never wrote those two books, that they are a hoax. He claims *Dubliners* is the only book he has written, along with, of all things, pamphlets for the Catholic Truth Society of Ireland. He attends mass every day, and his greatest wish is to become a Jesuit priest! Even though this playing with history is often inventive and funny, it does not save the book from the problems of bad construction and uninspired writing.

CONCLUSION

In May 1939 Niall Sheridan, in Paris on his honeymoon, delivered a copy of *At Swim-Two-Birds* to James Joyce. On the flyleaf O'Nolan had written that he was sending the book "with plenty of what's on page 305." The phrase "diffidence of the author" was underlined on that page. An examination of O'Nolan's career reveals many examples of this diffidence. The most obvious is his need to hide behind a dazzling number of pseudonyms. One could not be enough, because the identification with the real O'Nolan would become too strong. While shielding his own name with these masks, he leaves the narrators of *At Swim-Two-Birds* and *The Third Policeman* with the supreme anonymity of namelessness. In the early "letters controversies" and *Blather* the origin of particular pieces is vague, almost as if any claim of authorship would be an act of vanity.

The diffidence of O'Nolan caused him to accept too readily the opinions of others regarding his work. He allowed Sheridan to cut *At Swim-Two-Birds* for him and readily agreed to any publisher's request that he excise "obscenity" from his works. After the commercial failure of *At Swim-Two-Birds,* he wrote to William Saroyan that he guessed it was

a "bum book" anyway (Cronin, p. 99). When his publisher rejected *The Third Policeman,* O'Nolan was so mortified he could not admit to his friends what had happened and pretended to have lost the manuscript.

The reason for O'Nolan's tentative and ambivalent attitude toward his own talent and artistic integrity is that he, with his down-to-earth worldview, did not value such nebulous entities. What made his writing so worthwhile was this very devaluation, his ability to burst balloons of vanity and pretense. It is important to remember that Shakespeare did not bother to print his plays and that Swift, a more closely related artist, often created his best work for immediate political reasons rather than for perpetuity. Our expectation of how an artist should behave in respect to his art is one of the things O'Nolan so skillfully satirized.

SELECTED BIBLIOGRAPHY

I. Collected and Selected Works. *Cruiskeen Lawn* (Dublin, 1943), selections from the column; *The Best of Myles,* edited by K. O'Nolan (London and New York, 1968), selections from "Cruiskeen Lawn"; *Stories and Plays* (London, 1973; New York, 1976), includes *Faustus Kelly* and "A Bash in the Tunnel"; *The Various Lives of Keats and Chapman, and the Brother,* edited by B. Kiely (London, 1976), selections from "Cruiskeen Lawn" and a play adapted by E. Morrissey from O'Nolan's writings; *Further Cuttings from Cruiskeen Lawn,* edited by K. O'Nolan (London, 1976); *The Hair of the Dogma: A Further Selection from Cruiskeen Lawn,* edited by K. O'Nolan (London, 1977); *A Flann O'Brien Reader* (New York, 1978); *Myles Away from Dublin,* compiled by M. Green (London, 1985), selection of George Knowall columns; *Myles Before Myles, a Selection of the Earlier Writings of Brian O'Nolan* (London, 1988).

II. Separate Works. *At Swim-Two-Birds* (London, 1939 and 1960; New York, 1966); *An Béal Bocht* (Dublin, 1941), translated by P. P. Power as *The Poor Mouth* (London, 1973; New York, 1974)—all quotations in this essay are from Power's translation; *Faustus Kelly* (Dublin, 1943); *The Hard Life* (London, 1961; New York, 1962); *The Dalkey Archive* (London, 1964); *The Third Policeman* (London and New York, 1967).

III. Biographical and Critical Studies. I. del Janik, "Flann O'Brien: The Novelist as Critic," in *Éire-Ireland,* 4 (Winter, 1969); B. O'Conaire, "Flann O'Brien, *An Béal Bocht* and Other Irish Matter," in *Irish University Review,* 3, no. 2 (1973); T. O'Keeffe, ed., *Myles: Portraits of Brian O'Nolan* (London, 1973); C. Ó Nualláin (Ciarán O'Nolan),

"Myles na Gopaleen," in *Óige An Dearthár* (Dublin, 1973); R. Hogan and G. Henderson, eds., "A Sheaf of Letters," in *Journal of Irish Literature*, 3, no. 1 (1974); J. C. C. Mays, "Brian O'Nolan and Joyce on Art and on Life," in *James Joyce Quarterly*, 11, no. 3 (1974); M. Orvell, "Entirely Fictitious: The Fiction of Flann O'Brien," in *Journal of Irish Literature*, 3, no. 1 (1974); A. Clissmann, *Flann O'Brien: A Critical Introduction to His Writings* (Dublin and New York, 1975); S. Knight, "Forms of Gloom: The Novels of Flann O'Brien," in *Cunning Exiles: Studies of Modern Prose Writers* (London, 1975); M. Orvell and D. Powell, "Myles na Gopaleen: Mystic, Horse-doctor, Hackney Journalist and Ideological Catalyst," in *Éire-Ireland*, 10, no. 2 (1975); M. Orvell, "Brian O'Nolan: The Privacy of His Mind" in *ICarbS* (Carbondale, Ill.), 2 (1975); D. Jacquin, "Never Apply Your Front Brake First, or Flann O'Brien and the Theme of the Fall," in *Cahiers irlandais* 4–5 (1976); J. M. Silverthorne, "Time, Literature, and Failure: Flann O'Brien's *At Swim-Two-Birds* and *The Third Policeman*" in *Éire-Ireland*, 11, no. 4 (1976); B. Kennelly, *"An Béal Bocht:* Myles na gCopaleen (1911–1966)," in *The Pleasures of Gaelic Literature* (Cork, 1977); N. Mellamphy, "Aestho-Autogamy and the Anarchy of Imagination: Flann O'Brien's Theory of Fiction in *At Swim-Two-Birds*," in *Canadian Journal of Irish Studies*, 4, no. 1 (1978); M. Power, "Flann O'-Brien and Classical Satire: An Exegesis of *The Hard Life*," in *Éire-Ireland* 13, no. 1 (1978); R. Imhof, "Flann O'Brien: A Checklist," in *Études irlandaises*, 4 (1979).

B. Benstock, "A Flann for All Seasons," in *Irish Renaissance Annual*, 3 (1982); R. F. Peterson, "Flann O'Brien's Timefoolery," in *Irish Renaissance Annual*, 3 (1982); M. Gallagher, *The Poor Mouth:* Flann O'Brien and the Gaeltacht Studies," in *An Irish Quarterly Review*, 72 (Autumn 1983); J. Lanters, "Fiction Within Fiction: The Role of the Author in Flann O'Brien's *At Swim-Two-Birds* and *The Third Policeman*," in *Dutch Quarterly Review of Anglo-American Letters*, 13, no. 4 (1983); I. Mackenzie, "Who's Afraid of James Joyce? Or Flann O'Brien's Retreat from Modernism," in *Études de lettres*, 1 (1983); J. C. Voelker, " 'Doublends Jined': The Fiction of Flann O'Brien," in *Journal of Irish Literature*, 12, no. 1 (1983); J. Browne, "Flann O'Brien: *Post* Joyce or *Propter* Joyce?," in *Éire-Ireland*, 19, no. 4 (1984); J. Hassett, "Flann O'Brien and the Idea of the City," in M. Harmon, ed., *The Irish Writer and the City* (Gerrards Cross, U.K., and Totowa, N. J., 1984); E. Wäppling, *Four Irish Legendary Figures in "At-Swim-Two-Birds": A Study of Flann O'Brien's Use of Finn, Suibhne, the Pooka and the Good Fairy* (Uppsala, 1984); J. M. Conte, "Metaphor and Metonymy in Flann O'Brien's *At-Swim-Two-Birds,"* in *The Review of Contemporary Fiction*, 5 (Spring 1985); A. Horn, "The Half-Rusted Helmet: Julian Hawthorne's Poe and Flann O'Brien's Joyce," in *Essays in Literature*, 12 (Spring 1985); R. Imhof, ed., *Alive-Alive O!: Flann O'Brien's "At-Swim-Two-Birds"* (Dublin and Totowa, N. J., 1985); S. Pinsker, "Flann O'Brien's Uncles and Orphans," in *Éire-Ireland*, 20 (Summer 1985); P. Costello and P. van de Kamp, *Flann O'Brien, an Illustrated Biography* (London, 1987); B. P. O'Hehir, "Flann O'Brien and the Big World," in Wolfgang Zach and Heinz Kosok, eds., *Literary Interrelations: Ireland, England and the World*, Vol. 3 (Tübingen, 1987); J. Lanters, " 'Still Life' versus Real Life: The English Writings of Brian O'Nolan," in *DQR; Studies in Literature*, 3 (1987); W. Huber, "Flann O'Brien and the Language of the Grotesque," in B. Bramsback and M. Crughan, eds., *Anglo-Irish and Irish Literature: Aspects of Language and Culture*, Vol. 2 (Uppsala, 1988); A. Cronin, *No Laughing Matter: The Life and Times of Flann O'Brien* (London, 1989); R. L. Hunt, "Hell Goes Round and Round: Flann O'Brien," in *Canadian Journal of Irish Studies*, 14 (January 1989); T. B. O'Grady, "High Anxiety: Flann O'Brien's Portrait of the Artist" in *Studies in the Novel*, 21 (Summer, 1989); T. F. Shea, "The Craft of Seeming Pedestrian: Flann O'Brien's *The Hard Life*," in *Colby Library Quarterly*, 25 (December 1989); T. F. Shea, "Irony atop Peripeteia: Flann O'Brien's Indian Giving," in *Notes on Modern Irish Literature*, 1 (1989).

ALAN PATON

(1903–1988)

Randy Malamud

THE WORK OF South African writer Alan Paton is uniformly about the racial injustice of his country's society. From the time his first novel, *Cry, the Beloved Country,* was published in 1948 until his death in 1988, Paton was an unrelenting advocate of liberal reform. He was preeminently a moralist, secondarily a political activist. He considered writing to be his profession, but he gladly exploited his literary talent for his cause.

Paton is not essentially a *personal* moralist, though his fiction certainly is based on the personal, the individual character suffering in an oppressive society. His focus, always beyond the personal, is clearly on the larger social structure that must be changed. He is insistently pragmatic and proudly propagandistic in his writing. He is, stylistically, a better and more engaging writer of novels than of political essays, or newspaper broadsides, or South African biographies (and autobiography), but there is no change of focus as Paton moves from one of these genres to another; he uses whatever forum is available to advance a moral challenge to his country and to the world. "I should like to write books about South Africa which would really stab people in the conscience," he told an interviewer the year after his first novel was published; his mission, as he saw it, was "simply a question of stating an overwhelming truth that a man just cannot deny" (Breit, p. 92).

Paton's readers cannot help being drawn into the murky and anguished world of twentieth-century South Africa's ethical abyss. His fiction, however, does not present an exhaustive political overview of that country's condition; instead, it leads the readers to read more sophisticated and detailed political studies, historical sources, and even, at present, daily newspaper dispatches about the ongoing turmoil. As literal as Paton's scenarios are, they are at the same time a bit impressionistic: Paton is most successful when he distills into one consciousness (as he does with the Reverend Stephen Kumalo in *Cry, the Beloved Country* or Lieutenant Pieter van Vlaanderen in *Too Late the Phalarope*) varied sensibilities and impressions of the country's complex institutionalized racism. Certain political aspects may be highlighted or deemphasized to suit the narrative at hand. A political overview, however, is finally incomplete in his novels. It is more fully realized in his essays and biographies, but these, like his novels, tend to focus on isolated elements of politics and society. Paton's work, therefore, is not ultimately a self-sufficient entity. Rather, its success is marked by the extent to which it draws his audience into the turbulence of South African society. At that point of being drawn in, the difficult task of understanding (and, ideally, working to improve) South Africa's situation has only begun.

Virginia Woolf, in "Mr. Bennett and Mrs. Brown," complained about books that "leave one with so strange a feeling of incompleteness and dissatisfaction. In order to complete them it seems necessary to do something—to join a society, or, more desperately, to write a cheque. That done, the restlessness is laid, the book finished; it can be put on the shelf, and need never be read again." Woolf meant this criticism as derisive of her contemporary novelists; she felt the novelist should be interested "in things in themselves; in character in itself; in the book in itself" (*Collected Essays,* London, 1966, vol. 1, p. 326). That Woolf could write this way reflected a luxury Paton could not afford. Certainly, through her inspection of the enlightened and liberated consciousness, Woolf, too, advances a social vision, but Paton's work reflects an urgency that cannot brook her aesthetic subtlety. His writing is manifestly and intentionally the kind that, as Woolf writes, leaves the reader needing to do more, after finishing the book, to complete the experience.

It is perhaps also true, as Woolf asserts, that once such literature has raised one's consciousness, it

341

need never be read again. Woolf's aesthetic is still potent three-quarters of a century after she crafted it. Paton's writing may well date more quickly. Even forty years after he began writing, the specific scenarios on which he based his fiction were relatively obsolete—sadly, they are not yet rectified, but immeasurably more intricate as the discrimination caused by apartheid has increased vastly. Still, Paton's characterizations of oppressed humanity retain their poignancy, even if the nature and scale of oppression have changed. If and when a democratically representative government is instituted in South Africa, his writing may lose much of its fascination, except as a reminder of the past. Paton certainly would not have minded such a turn of events.

Harvey Breit, interviewing the newly acclaimed writer in 1949, found him "small and wiry and with a lean and hungry look. . . . His mind is lucid and tough, his speech is precise, unembellished and neutral, yet nevertheless touched as though with a bitter memory. The over-all sense of him is of iron—iron-minded, iron-willed and iron-muscled" (p. 90). This is exactly the kind of author that a reader would infer from the persona through which Paton narrates his novels. For several decades Paton was the most important and most publicized white South African voice for reform.

It is certainly a consequence of South Africa's racism that Paton cannot be said to be the transracial voice of reform: as morally forceful as he may be, he is constrained within the European viewpoint, which is—as all Africans know—the viewpoint of the oppressor, however mitigated it may be by Paton's personal goodwill. Paton writes essentially of whites, and for whites. Even his African characters are white people's Africans. The black South African writer Richard Rive categorizes two strains of writing about his country's troubled history: liberal writing by whites and protest writing by Africans. Liberal writing, of which *Cry, the Beloved Country* was the early international triumph, draws upon a tradition reaching as far back as Olive Schreiner's nineteenth-century stories that confronted the moral dilemma of racism; William Plomer and Laurens van der Post also predate Paton in this liberal South African literature, which is, Rive explains,

written by concerned, enfranchised white citizens for other white citizens in order to emphasize their moral, social and political responsibility toward blacks. The ap-

peal is directed at those who have the power to effect change or at least have the power to keep the controversy alive. The theme is the discrimination implicit in the black–white situation and the writing . . . is critical of white, racial domination. Concern, trusteeship and guardianship of the less privileged are amongst its primary concerns.

(p. 26)

Liberal writing reflects the indignation of those who are outraged by institutional injustices, though they are not directly affected by them—and certainly may, though unwillingly, benefit from white dominance. In the essay "Apartheid in Its Death Throes," Paton admits:

Do you want to know what it is like to live under apartheid? Then you should really ask a Black person. I am White and the laws of apartheid are made by White people to preserve the privileges of White people. . . .

The law also weighs heavily on White people—some White people—who hate apartheid, who try to reject it in their own lives, who are every day reminded of the cruelty of the laws that they cannot change.

Your cynical Black friend will say to you: "I am very sad about your suffering, but you continue to enjoy all the protection of the apartheid laws, all the days of your life." And he will be right too.

(*Save the Beloved Country*, p. 66)

Protest writing, such as that of Paton's contemporary Peter Abrahams, embodies the forthright political imperative of those who are actually being oppressed, and whose need to fight that oppression is not simply moral but pragmatic and immediate. Paton's "seeming emphasis of moral issues at the expense of political ones" in *Cry, the Beloved Country* is the basis of much African criticism of his writing. Rive argues: "They claim that Paton is preaching for a revolution of hearts rather than for a revolution in the social and political structure. They prefer the hard-line militant approach to that of the religious idealist" (p. 27).

As effective as Paton may be in capturing and publicizing the experience of the nonwhite South African, those who are themselves oppressed find a lack of substantial protest. "The liberal novel often has a strong moralistic streak and a didacticism which is superimposed on the work rather than emerging from it" (Rive, p. 28)—a self-righteous and possibly gratuitous morality. "There is little room in the protest novel for any form of didacticism. The anger flows directly out of the narrative sequence and often obscures it, so that in its rush of recrimination there is no time to ponder over the morality of what is happening." Liberal didacticism, Rive continues, often leads to a "built-in paternalism, an understanding at a level removed from those with whom it is concerned" (p. 29). Paton presents an example of such paternalism in his biography of Archbishop Clayton, published in 1973. He quotes the churchman in opposition to a policy of white supremacy, speaking of the need to allow Africans to transcend the oppressed position of inferiority in which the government had kept them: "It is a temptation to parents to prevent their children growing up and losing their endearing ways. But it is a temptation that has to be resisted. The children must grow up" (*Apartheid and the Archbishop: The Life and Times of Geoffrey Clayton, Archbishop of Cape Town,* p. 188). Paton shows at least some sensitivity to charges such as Rive's about paternalism; in a footnote to Clayton's quotation, he writes, "This was in 1949. One could not use such metaphors today" (p. 188). Still, when Paton began writing, in the late 1940's, he was certainly susceptible to the same paternalistic instincts as Clayton.

South Africa's institutionalized racism is so pervasive that even those whites who most strongly reject it cannot escape its taint; Paton, however well-meaning, cannot ultimately speak for those with whom his work is most concerned, because he is not one of them. Mitigating his charges of didactic paternalism, Rive admits that the commitment of liberalism "is a genuine one although not of the brand that more radical opinion, especially by blacks, would prefer. . . . It must be remembered that [Paton] grew up in an era before South African race politics had hardened into its present intransigence and that *Cry, the Beloved Country* appeared at a time when liberalism seemed to provide many answers to South Africa's problems" (p. 30).

The two primary groups of European settlers in South Africa were the Afrikaners (or Boers, Dutch for "farmers"), descended from Dutch, German, and French settlers who began coming to the continent in the seventeenth century, and the British, who bought parts of the country from the Dutch and seized others from the Boers in the nineteenth century. Paton's ancestry was British—his maternal grandparents settled in Natal in the 1850's, and his father came from Scotland in 1901, during the Boer War. Paton's parents called Britain home; he writes that he is proud never to have used that expression. Paton's heritage and culture were strongly British, but a brand of colonial British that was firmly rooted in Africa. As Afrikaners' nationalistic culture grew and came to dominate the country throughout the twentieth century, they regarded English-speaking South Africans as intrusively foreign; and they have resented, for generations, their humiliation and barbarism by the British during the Boer War. Paton was proud that he had a working knowledge of the Afrikaner language, Afrikaans, and recognized the value of the strong national sensibility that tied these people to the country they loved as fiercely as he did; yet throughout his career, he viewed Afrikaners as more susceptible to racial hatred, and as more responsible than English South Africans for the country's problems. Paton certainly did not wish to imitate the Afrikaners in their chauvinism; nevertheless, he promoted, gently but constantly, the contributions he felt British South Africans could offer: a presence that he saw as desirably reform-minded and beneficial for the future.

LIFE

ALAN STEWART PATON was born in Pietermaritzburg, Natal, on 11 January 1903. His parents were James Paton, a civil servant, and Eunice Warder James, a teacher. He attended high school at Maritzburg College and studied physics at Natal University College (now the University of Natal), where he became involved with religious and civic groups such as the Students' Christian Association and the Students' Representative Council. This involvement anticipated the mixture of religious and civic activism Paton was to embrace throughout his life, and his energetic leadership roles in these groups prefigured his later career.

On 2 July 1928, Paton married Doris Olive Lusted; their son David was born in 1930 and their son Jonathan in 1936. In *Kontakian for You Departed,* a tribute to Dorrie, who died of cancer in 1967, Paton makes clear how important his wife's life and death were as a source of inspiration for his work. Paton's secretary while he was writing that book, Anne Margaret Hopkins, became his second wife in 1969.

Paton's career can be divided into three phases: he was a teacher and schoolmaster from 1924 to 1935, a reformatory principal from 1935 to 1948, and a writer and political activist from the publication of his first novel in 1948 until his death on 12 April 1988, at Botha's Hill in Natal. During the public phase of his life, he was internationally acclaimed and honored—the institutions that awarded Paton honorary degrees include Harvard University (1971), Yale University (1954), Kenyon College (1962), and Edinburgh University (1971), along with such African institutions as Rhodes University (1972) and the University of the Witwatersrand (1975). His literary and humanitarian accolades included the American Ainsfield–Wolf Award and the London *Sunday Times* Special Book Award in 1949; the Benjamin Franklin Award in 1955; the American Freedom Award in 1960; and the Pringle Award in 1973.

TALES FROM A TROUBLED LAND

In the early years of his career, Paton was only vaguely concerned with social welfare. He was thrust much more forcefully into the arena of South Africa's social turmoil when he was named principal of Diepkloof reformatory at Potchefstroom, outside Johannesburg. Four hundred African boys, aged as young as seven, were incarcerated there for offenses ranging from trivial acts to murder. (When Paton applied for a principalship, he had expressed a preference *not* to work in an institution for Africans.) Paton spent thirteen years at Diepkloof, leaving shortly after the publication of *Cry, the Beloved Country*—the demands of life as a writer and political participant, he felt, necessitated that he give up his work in the reformatory. In many ways the novel grew out of his work at Diepkloof: he wrote it while on an extensive foreign trip in 1946 and 1947 to inspect prisons and reformatories in Europe and America, and to discover techniques he could implement in South Africa.

As principal, Paton learned to work with Africans. The reformatory's staff included Africans, to many of whom Paton grew quite close and to whom he credited the successes he was able to achieve there. For the first time, he developed a keen sensitivity to the African people at large through his extensive contacts with the boys. He learned the important lesson of making the best of an imperfect system in an imperfect society: juve-

nile African offenders and misfits certainly did not evoke great concern or sympathy on the part of white government officials and departments, yet Paton was able to improve reformatory conditions significantly. He worked hard and effectively to make the reformatory experience one that would prepare the inmates for a better life after they were released, instead of simply punishing and hardening them, as had been the case before his tenure.

Paton carried out urgently needed improvements in Diepkloof's physical plant: installing latrines to eliminate the putrid smell of the buckets for urination and defecation that had rested in the middle of each cell; getting rid of intimidating security fences and walls. He treated the boys with dignity and paternal affection. He implemented job-training programs and granted temporary furloughs. Morale increased greatly, and Paton gained a wide reputation as a pioneer in liberal reformatory administration. Paton's fiction, especially his collection of short stories called *Tales from a Troubled Land* (1961), is populated with numerous youthful offenders of whom the author offers sympathetic and understanding portraits. At Diepkloof, Paton learned to appreciate the touchingly delicate humanity of young Africans; he also learned how victimized the impoverished African homes and families were in a society dominated by white rulers whose policy was, at best, one of benign neglect.

The stories in *Tales from a Troubled Land* provide insights into harshly broken African families that evoke the cruelty described in nineteenth-century American slave narratives. Because the stories are often modeled closely on Paton's reformatory experiences, many of the characters are criminals. While they all dream of successful and meaningful lives, their opportunities constantly vanish in this "troubled land"—sometimes destroyed by others, sometimes sabotaged by themselves. In these stories, the reformatory principal—obviously an incarnation of Paton—narrates, looking on empathetically but impotently. The authority figure wrestles with the anguish of trying to "reform" people whose world is itself unreformable.

Paton certainly had some success with his charges, but these stories are more about the failures, who indicate the pervasively inhospitable world of South Africa. It is disquieting that so many of Paton's Africans are criminals, recidivists—constantly fighting, stealing, lying. This focus on Africans as criminals and misfits reflects one facet of his inability to escape whites' inherent limitations in viewing Africans. Still, the reformatory authority does not condemn them—he understands them, and somehow takes some of the guilt upon himself, as the representative of white society. Paton's Africans are imprisoned, yet, in a sense, freer of spirit than he is—one dreams of being a preacher, even though he is constantly in jail. Paton disturbs his readers, and means to, by creating a personal sympathy for these characters, then showing the pain in which their lives seem fated to end.

"Death of a Tsotsi" shows what Paton is constantly asserting in these stories: that omnipresent racism generates social corruption. Spike, a well-intentioned graduate of the reformatory, cannot escape involvement in the conflicts of local gangs. He has a good job and a concerned family, yet ends up pointlessly stabbed to death. At his funeral, the head of the reformatory reflects:

We were all of us, white and black, rich and poor, learned and untutored, bowed down by a knowledge that we lived in the shadow of a great danger, and were powerless against it. It was no place for a white person to pose in any mantle of power or authority; for this death gave the lie to both of them.

And this death would go on too, for nothing less than the reform of a society would bring it to an end. It was the menace of the socially frustrated, strangers to mercy, striking like adders for the dark reasons of ancient minds, at any who crossed their paths.

(pp. 105–106)

In "The Waste Land," Paton depicts the tenuous tightrope that any African continually walks in hoping to survive:

The moment that the bus moved on he knew he was in danger, for by the lights of it he saw the figures of the young men waiting under the tree. That was the thing feared by all, to be waited for by the young men. It was a thing he had talked about, now he was to see it for himself. . . .

His wages were in his purse, he could feel them weighing heavily against his thigh. That was what they wanted from him. Nothing counted against that. His wife could be made a widow, his children made fatherless, nothing counted against that. Mercy was the unknown word.

(p. 58)

Though the young men are African, that does not mitigate Paton's assertion that the story's "waste land" is created by white oppression. Whites have created a world in which Africans have to fear even themselves; a world reduced, through poverty and institutional inhumanity, to a vicious jungle in which a man can never attain security for himself and his family, no matter how hard he works or how good he is—a world corrupted, and beyond the control of its victims.

CRY, THE BELOVED COUNTRY

In "South Africa Today," a pamphlet Paton wrote in the 1950's to explain his country's plight to the rest of the world, he pinpoints the causes of the corruption and disintegration of African society, in what could be a précis of his first novel:

Many urban parents are at a total loss to understand the wayward behavior of their children, being too simple to recognize how they themselves were sustained. . . . The truth is that the impact of the cities on tribal life was shattering. Both fathers and mothers had to go out to work, the schools were full, and most children were educated in the streets. Prostitution began, and illicit liquor was obtainable. . . . law and custom began to wither away. . . . Theft and housebreaking became the occupations of the shiftless, often carried out with violence and murder. . . . It is then not to be wondered at that African tribal life has undergone a process of disintegration, and that crime, illegitimacy, and drunkenness disfigure African urban life. A whole nation has been rocked to its foundations.

(p. 18)

Cry, the Beloved Country brought Paton immediate international fame when it was published in 1948. It is a fusion of the eloquent rhythms of English, Zulu, Xhosa, and even Afrikaans speech and thought; of the African priest, the Anglican missionary, the prodigal son, the Sophiatown street urchin and prostitute, the European gentleman farmer—all are captured poetically and intertwined tenuously but insistently. Just as all these strands of social culture comprise South Africa's panorama, so they contribute to Paton's symphonic convergence of souls in *Cry*. Paton's vision of all these forces is incisively journalistic and sociological, but more prominently lyrical—with the lyricism, perhaps, of the Old Testament psalmist, cognizant of oppression and injustice, invoking hope for a soothing salvation. Maxwell Anderson and Kurt Weill confirmed Paton's lyrical force when they adapted the novel for their Broadway musical production, *Lost in the Stars:* the opening chorus is taken verbatim from the beginning of Paton's delicate prose narrative:

> There is a lovely road
> that runs from Ixopo into the hills.
> These hills
> are grass covered and rolling, and they are lovely
> beyond any singing of it.

Cry, the Beloved Country brought international attention to the violent and depressing plight of Africans living under white oppression; it is widely credited with bringing South Africa's shame to the world's attention—attention, of course, that was to increase drastically throughout the century, leading to the international isolation of the white South African government and a worldwide moralistic call for reform. Significantly, the novel was conceived and written abroad—in a burst of energy and inspiration Paton felt on his international tour of prisons and reformatories. He became inspired in a cathedral in Trondheim, Norway, as he describes in the autobiographical *Towards the Mountain:*

> It was now almost dark, and the cathedral itself was in darkness. . . . It has . . . one of the most beautiful rose windows in the world, and when we had finished our tour we sat down in two of the front pews and looked at it. There was still enough light in the sky to see its magnificent design and its colours. We did not speak, and I do not know how long we sat there. I was in the grip of a powerful emotion, not directly to do with the cathedral and the rose window, but certainly occasioned by them. I was filled with an intense homesickness, for home and wife and sons, and for my far-off country.
> (pp. 267–268).

Returning to his hotel room, Paton wrote the first chapter before dinner; later, he wrote, "I do not even remember if I knew what the story was to be" (p. 268). As he continued on his fact-finding tour, he completed the novel over the next four months, mostly while in America, and had it enthusiastically accepted by Scribners a month later—after a flurry of manuscripts rushed by mail back and forth across America. Newly made friends and enthusiastic supporters of this novel that he had dashed off hurried to help Paton complete all the arrangements before his return to Africa. The novel is significantly a product of the perspective Paton gained while abroad—his next novel, too, was written while he was on a trip to England—though he never acknowledged (or, perhaps, even recognized) this fact. While he described the novel as an expression of his homesickness, it is a homesickness in (temporary) exile. Other writers more consciously recognized the need to escape from the homeland in order to write about it without becoming mired down in it—James Joyce writing on Ireland from Paris, Doris Lessing writing about Rhodesia from London. Africa, as Paton has often written, is a land of mesmerizing beauty—and certainly of a grandeur that allows one to lose sight of human vanities. The predominant success of *Cry* is that, in it, Paton escapes from the limitations inherent in an uneasily inequitable society and presents for the world at large a picture of its suffering. The novel certainly could not have been written in South Africa.

Cry presents the wrenching moral consciousness of a liberal white man groping for answers, for reconciliation, for an antidote to the growing racism that is beginning to sunder a hapless African society. The novel is not about apartheid—apartheid did not begin, institutionally, until the victory of the white supremacist Nationalist Party almost four months after the release of the novel. Paton was not oblivious to the coincidental timing of these events—he wrote in *Towards the Mountain* that the publication of his novel "could justly be called one of the two decisive events in my life. The extraordinary thing is that the second decisive event happened soon after. . . . the event of May 26, 1948, brought my intention to nothing, and condemned me to a struggle between literature and politics" (pp. 303–304). Legislated apartheid proliferated in the early 1950's, a few years after *Cry* was published—yet it is not a mistake to associate the publication and reception of *Cry* with the origins of, and reaction against, apartheid.

Through fortuitous timing, and certainly with a kind of prescience on the author's part, *Cry* presents the anguishing challenge that South Africa would pose to the world as apartheid quickly crystallized into the brutal system of discrimination that has led the country to the crisis of the late twentieth century. As the situation became more complex over the next decades, he was increasingly criticized by some for maintaining a simplistic and unrealistic perspective on the country's problems. In defense of Paton, it can only be said that at the formative moment of his moral triumph, his country's later complexities had not yet burgeoned.

As in much African writing, the landscape is predominant in *Cry:* the vast veld, the rich soil, the dramatic valleys and rivers, the sights and sounds of birds and animals that seem to be more vitally conscious within the landscape than in any other national literature. In *Towards the Mountain,* Paton's boyhood memories of his country are lushly Edenic:

I cannot describe my early response to the beauty of hill and stream as anything less than an ecstasy. . . . As often as not a small stream ran down the kloof, and on its banks grew ferns and the wild begonia whose soft stems we would chew for their acid juice. . . . A glade of clivias in flower, in one of the larger stretches of bush that might be called a forest, is a sight not to be forgotten. . . . And one might, though perhaps only once in a lifetime, catch a glimpse of the small mpithi antelope, shy and delicate.

(pp. 4–5)

Paton begins *Cry* with a paean to this land: "Stand unshod upon it, for the ground is holy, being even as it came from the Creator. Keep it, guard it, care for it, for it keeps men, guards men, cares for men. Destroy it and man is destroyed" (p. 3). Yet the covenant between the Africans and their land had been abrogated by the intrusions of a society not their own, one that did not foster their symbiotic harmony with the ecosystem: "But the rich green hills break down. . . . Too many cattle feed upon the grass, and too many fires have burned it" (p. 3). The land "is not kept, or guarded, or cared for, it no longer keeps men, guards men, cares for men. . . . The great red hills stand desolate, and the earth has torn away like flesh. . . . The men are away, the young men and the girls are away. The soil cannot keep them any more" (pp. 3–4).

Reverend Stephen Kumalo, the respected *umfundisi* of the small Natal village of Ndotsheni, lives in one of the quickly disappearing places where Africans are still in touch with their land and able to control their own lives with relative stability. This control dissipates, though, as Kumalo is forced to forsake the peace of Ndotsheni for a journey to the urban chaos of Johannesburg, where his son, Absalom, and his sister, Gertrude, have gone in search of different lives: lives perhaps more immediately

stimulating but also inestimably more uncontrollable and ultimately destructive. Kumalo is entreated, in a letter from a fellow priest in the Johannesburg African slum of Sophiatown, to rescue his sick sister. Kumalo's quest represents his awakening to the sordid urban world that heralds the Africans' unpromising future. To pay for this trip, he must spend the small sum of money that had been scrupulously saved to send Absalom to St. Chad's, "to learn that knowledge without which no black man can live" (p. 9)—the knowledge for which Africans must fight so hard, against whites' intentions that they stay uneducated and unable to challenge white authority. But Kumalo's wife knows the implication of her son's having disappeared in Johannesburg without having sent any word home: "Absalom will never go now to St. Chad's" (p. 8).

The quest begins with a draining and dizzying train journey, on which Kumalo's countrypeople already start to lose their identities: in the train carriage he sees "some with strange assortments of European garments, some with blankets over their strange assortments, some with blankets over the semi-nudity of their primitive dress, though these were all women. Men travelled no longer in primitive dress" (p. 13). In his trip to the city, Kumalo learns of the other world that is increasingly attracting hordes of Africans—"All roads lead to Johannesburg" (p. 10). The train takes Kumalo away from the safe and the familiar, and toward the hostile and entropic world of the city:

One must catch buses too, but not as here, where the only bus that comes is the right bus. For there there is a multitude of buses, and only one bus in ten, one bus in twenty maybe, is the right bus. If you take the wrong bus, you may travel to quite some other place. And they say it is danger to cross the street, yet one must needs cross it. For there is the wife of Mpanza of Ndotsheni, who had gone there when Mpanza was dying, saw her son Michael killed in the street. Twelve years and moved by excitement, he stepped out into danger, but she was hesitant and stayed at the curb. And under her eyes the great lorry crushed the life out of her son.

(p. 12)

When Kumalo finally sees Johannesburg, it is as a terrifying dynamo:

Railway-lines, railway-lines, it is a wonder. To the left, to the right, so many that he cannot count. A train rushes past them, with a sudden roaring of sound that makes him jump in his seat. And on the other side of them, another races beside them, but drops slowly behind. Stations, stations, more than he has ever imagined. People are waiting there in hundreds, but the train rushes past, leaving them disappointed.

(pp. 16–17)

In Johannesburg, Kumalo finds a remnant of kindness in Msimangu, who had sent him the letter, and others who are not yet corrupted; but the city is predominantly a place where Kumalo learns firsthand "of the sickness of the land, of the broken tribe and the broken house, of young men and young girls that went away and forgot their customs and lived loose and idle lives" (p. 22). As Msimangu explains, "The white man has broken the tribe. . . . It suited the white man to break the tribe. . . . But it has not suited him to build something in the place of what is broken" (pp. 25–26). South Africa's hegemonic white power structure has divided and conquered the country's original inhabitants; Paton's scenario evokes the government's seizure of Africans' lands, dispersion of tribal and cultural strengths, and enforced economic dependence on the meager wages that African laborers receive from the country's vast natural wealth (the profits of which accumulate in white hands). Paton weaves such underlying causes of Africans' troubled lives into the background of his narrative when they do not directly fit the plot. In several interpolated choric passages, Paton shows Africans facing extreme housing shortages, discussing the politics of economic exploitation and oppressive antilabor tactics, planning strikes and boycotts, nurturing incipient stirrings for self-control and self-rule.

Kumalo, attempting to find and reunify his dissolving family, learns from Msimangu that Gertrude "has no husband now. . . . It would be truer to say, he said, that she has many husbands" (p. 23). She makes and sells "bad liquor . . . made strong with all manner of things that our people have never used. . . . These women sleep with any man for their price. A man has been killed at her place. They gamble and drink and stab. She has been in prison, more than once" (p. 23).

Paton learned of these neighborhoods, these worlds, from the inhabitants at Diepkloof. He knew how insidiously seductive they were, how dangerous, how inescapable. And as Paton reached out to the victims of these worlds at the reformatory, so Kumalo ventures deeper and deeper into Johannesburg's slums with only compassion for those it has overcome, and determination to bring his family out of it.

He is unsuccessful at extricating Gertrude and Absalom. Though he finds his sister, and convinces her to return home, she disappears just as they are about to leave Johannesburg; she is addicted to its depravity, unable to escape its lure. Kumalo does, though, bring home the son she has had in the city, representing the potential of a better life for the next generation and a hope that his people can learn from and surmount the oppressive lives of this generation. Similarly, Kumalo's son is no longer able to return to his home, having complicated and lost control of his life even more horribly than Gertrude. Absalom has been in the reformatory and, like the reformed Spike in *Tales from a Troubled Land,* has been unable to sustain his innocence in a world of violence. Following vague hints about where his wandering son has gone (unwillingly given by suspicious and fearful urban Africans), Kumalo spends wearying days trying to follow the faint trail Absalom left as he moved from shanty to shanty. As Kumalo traces each step in his son's odyssey, he learns more about Absalom's descent into the troubled, shady world of Johannesburg. Ironically, after Kumalo has spent a great deal of energy and money tracing his son, Paton shows the police retracing the same steps, quickly and easily. They intimidate all the people who know of Absalom's whereabouts, and extract from them the information they were so hesitant to give his father. The police are seeking Absalom because he is a suspect in the murder of a white engineer.

The murder of Arthur Jarvis, a fighter for justice, rocks Johannesburg. Jarvis, whose character is a composite of Paton himself and the contemporaries he admired, had been a popular speaker at liberal functions. In a paper on which he was working moments before he was killed, Jarvis explores the dynamics of South African society in the unmitigated terms of Paton's own moral sensibility:

It is not permissible to develop any resources if they can be developed only at the cost of the labour. It is not permissible to mine any gold, or manufacture any product, or cultivate any land, if such mining and manufacture and cultivation depend for their success on a policy of keeping labour poor. It is not permissible to add to one's possessions if these things can only be done at the cost of other men. Such development has only one true name, and that is exploitation. . . .

. . . Our natives today produce criminals and prostitutes and drunkards, not because it is their nature to do so, but because their simple system of order and tradition and convention has been destroyed.

(pp. 145–146)

Kumalo, as he reads of the killing in the newspaper, remembers that Jarvis' father is a farmer in the hills above Ndotsheni: "I know him well by sight and name, but we have never spoken"; he remembers Arthur, too, as "a small bright boy" (p. 72). Kumalo and his son are finally reunited in prison: brought together by the police rather than by a father's loving quest, and when it is too late to avert Absalom's tragedy. Absalom had carried a revolver, "For safety, he says. This Johannesburg is a dangerous place. A man never knows when he will be attacked" (p. 98). Kumalo poses many questions while trying to discover what happened— what Absalom was doing at Jarvis' house, why he has led the life he has. Presumably, Absalom was robbing the house, but all the precise questions his father poses "cannot be answered"—there are no neat answers, or reasons, in Absalom's profoundly unreasonable world. Absalom's only defense or explanation is "I was frightened when the white man came. So I shot him. I did not mean to kill him" (p. 98).

Kumalo and the elder Jarvis, who had never spoken, are now cruelly thrust together in this social morass. The novel's second book switches from Kumalo's perspective to Jarvis'. It begins identically to the first book: "There is a lovely road that runs from Ixopo into the hills. These hills are grass-covered and rolling, and they are lovely beyond any singing of it" (p. 129). It is, of course, the same country that Kumalo and Jarvis inhabit, and they are forced to acknowledge this bond through the sorrow their sons have brought them. For the rest of the novel, though the narrative extensively follows Absalom's trial, his contrition, his death sentence and ultimate execution, Paton concentrates more hopefully on the two fathers, and how they must confront their pain constructively and together. Paton is not a nostalgist—clearly, he would have preferred to explore the future of his country through the lives of the young men, Absalom

Kumalo and Arthur Jarvis, but both are dead. Paton leaves only the less satisfying recourse of considering, in the third and final book of the novel, how the fathers cope: how they try, in spite of their losses, to continue in a humanistic progression toward justice even in view of the pervasive injustice that afflicts both their lives; how they learn to communicate with each other, willingly and productively, instead of only through the necessity of the tragedy that brought them together.

Absalom, before his incarceration, had lived with a young woman in Pimville—an orphan, as badly off as everyone in the ramshackle satellite settlements outside Johannesburg—whom he planned to marry, and who is pregnant with his child. Kumalo reaches out to her with love, arranges for her to marry his son as he awaits execution, and brings her back to Ndotsheni; though he cannot bring his son, he brings the promise of a grandchild, rescuing mother and child from the misery of the city. When he returns to Ndotsheni, Kumalo is broken by what he has experienced in the city; nevertheless, he works to improve his people's lives, to uplift his village, to care for what is left of his family, in the hope that the sins of the parents will not be visited on the children rescued from Johannesburg.

Kumalo confronts drought and desolation in Ndotsheni, partly the result of the lack of agricultural education and partly of forced exploitation of land resources. The young son of the murdered Jarvis has returned to rural Natal, and reminds Kumalo of Arthur Jarvis as a boy. The murdered man's son wanders into the Africans' village and, with the innocence and kindness of youth, connects freely with them. Seeing their desolation, the boy acts as an intermediary to his grandfather, who delivers to the village much-needed milk, the gift of life, to help the Africans through the period of drought. The elder Jarvis, having learned the importance of his son's work to improve the lives of Africans, carries on this work by hiring an "agricultural demonstrator" to teach Africans how to farm more scientifically and productively. At the end of the novel, the continuation of Kumalo's and Jarvis' efforts to work for a better society heralds regeneration, the coming of dawn in this land of sublime beauty mixed with pervasive misery—not yet the time "of our emancipation, from the fear of bondage and the bondage of fear" (p. 277), for that hope is, Paton knows, still uncertain; but a dawn that may lead to that better dawn. The novel, as Edward Callan writes,

offers no blueprint for a utopian society. It offers instead recognition of personal responsibility. The crucial development in the characters of both Jarvis and Kumalo is that each comes to recognize how individual fear or indifference infects society with moral paralysis; and that the antidote for this paralysis is individual courage willing to go forward in faith.

(p. 41)

Horton Davies, in a 1959 study of the role of Christian ministry in the modern novel, finds that *Cry, the Beloved Country* asserts that "the ultimate reconciliation of racial tensions is to be found in Christian humility, forgiveness, and compassion" (*A Mirror of the Ministry in Modern Novels*, p. 129)— that is, in the spirit of religious transcendence embodied in the African Reverend Kumalo and the English Father Vincent (who assists Kumalo and Msimangu with their quest in the city, and whose character is based on a close friend of Paton's, an Anglican priest from Johannesburg). The novel, through its focus on the biblical motifs of the prodigal son, the redemptive value of suffering, the compassion shown by Reverend Kumalo, and the sublime forgiveness embodied in the elder Jarvis, finds its spirit of reassurance in Christian faith, Davies asserts; and Father Vincent stands out as the consummate spirit of understanding and Christian salvation. This interpretation illustrates grounds for criticism of Paton's vision based on this religious emphasis (which, for Marxist critics, will certainly appear as a kind of opiate in the strikingly unreligious world of the novel's victims and its immoral society) and on the depiction of benevolent whites. Though whites are marginal to the social morass that the novel describes, they are, as Davies and others have found, in some ways supremely omniscient and transcendent, paternalistic and possessed of a larger Christian humanity, compared with the noble but stumbling African protagonists. Edmund Fuller writes, "The primary story is pathetic, in that the suffering characters are more bewildered victims than prime movers in their difficulties" (*Books with Men Behind Them*, p. 95). As Richard Rive reminds us, the African tradition of protest literature finds this pathos belittling.

The novel's British edition bears the subtitle *A Story of Comfort in Desolation*. Paton finds this comfort in Absalom's repentance, Jarvis' forgiveness, and the promise of the children. Would a real-life Absalom have found comfort in this? Is it too tidy to look for comfort in the decadent and oppressive world in which Absalom falls? A. A. Monye rejects the sensibility of *Cry, the Beloved Country*, finding that its emotions

do not offer any positive solution to the problems of racism and colonial brutality in South Africa. We are merely invited to cry for a bruised and bleeding land and people. But the question is: Should we merely Cry? Is crying all we can do for these unfortunate victims of apartheid? . . . [Paton's sermon] is meaningless in a society where the basic requirements of life are denied a section of it. It is useless in a system where a negligible number of the population arrogate to themselves certain privileges and rights which they deny an integral part of that same just because of the pigmentation of the skin. To preach love to a people who are denied all their human rights, a people, who denied their ancestral heritage, are forced to the shanties and ghettoes by aliens who now occupy the richer part of the land, is quite unrealistic. Love in this society will only be realistic when what has been denied the Black South African is restored to him.

(pp. 74–75)

Monye, criticizing Paton from the tradition of protest writing, finds the characterizations of Africans naive and pointless:

I think this journalistic exercise—showing us a weeping people and expecting us to respect and pity them—is quite inadequate a solution to the reality of the Black man's predicament in racist South Africa. It could, at best, give us cue for action, but it is not positive action in itself. Today, the African writer is not content with only exposing the sufferings of his people for the world to see. He is now concerned with how to devise a positive solution to the problems of his people.

(p. 76)

Kumalo, Monye feels, is

like the absurd man in the proverb who leaves his burning house to pursue a rat fleeing from the flames. . . . [he] leaves reality and pursues shadows. He weeps when he should confront the enemy. He prays when he should use his position to lead his people in an organised revolt against the oppressive system of his country.

(p. 76)

ALAN PATON

TOO LATE THE PHALAROPE

PATON followed his first novel with *Too Late the Phalarope* in 1953. Here he focuses more intently on the portrait of an Afrikaner rather than an African. Pieter van Vlaanderen is the victim of social disintegration, and an emblem of the torturously confused personal morality that is a consequence of living in a society that is in moral turmoil. Taken as a companion to *Cry, the Beloved Country, Too Late the Phalarope* shows that great suffering (though not, of course, equal blame) lies on both sides of the color bar. Van Vlaanderen's tragedy is that "he was always two men" (p. 3) at the same time. One of his personalities is strictly in accord with the Afrikaner ideal: a police lieutenant, dispassionately enforcing law and order, oblivious to the social harm his people are inflicting. But the other person is a man with "strange unusual thoughts in his mind, and a passion for books and learning" (p. 2)—a person whose passion cannot be limited by the narrow-minded thinking of the Afrikaner Nationalists, and who knows that the law he enforces is wrong, that he cannot live by it. His aunt, narrating the story, records that it is "the story of our destruction" (p. 3); the outside world crashes down on van Vlaanderen's character just as it did on Kumalo's. Paton initially presents van Vlaanderen in his first role, as enforcer of apartheid: he stops a British boy who had been having some sort of possibly subversive (in the eyes of the police lieutenant) encounter with Stephanie, a young African woman. Van Vlaanderen stresses for the boy the importance of the Immorality Act:

The police have had instructions to enforce the Immorality Act without fear or favour. Whether you're old or young, rich or poor, respected or nobody, whether you're a Cabinet Minister or a *predikant* or a headmaster or a tramp, if you touch a black woman and you're discovered, nothing'll save you.

(p. 13)

The act, instituted in 1927 and strengthened by the Nationalists in 1950, was the cornerstone of apartheid, legislative "racial purity"; it reflected the fear and disgust its architects felt toward nonwhites. Afrikaners viewed the possibility of love between African and white people as extremely dangerous; their fear of such love seems to reveal their unease with their situation in Africa—a recognition of how fragile their condition is. In *Towards the Mountain*, Paton confirms that the terror of the Immorality Act had not lessened in the decades since he wrote of it in his novel:

If a white man of any substance, a minister of religion, a professor, a lawyer, a schoolmaster, is found guilty of breaking this law, his life is ruined, even if the court suspends his punishment. At the time I write this, three white men have committed suicide in the last few weeks rather than face trial.

(p. 16)

With the rise of the Nationalist government in Pretoria came the firmest commitment to legislated racial separation, and a conviction that such separateness was God's will. Paton writes in *Too Late the Phalarope*:

They set their conquered enemies apart, ruling them with unsmiling justice, declaring "no equality in Church or State," and making the iron law that no white man might touch a black woman, nor might any white woman be touched by a black man.

And to go against this law, of a people of rock and stone in a land of rock and stone, was to be broken and destroyed.

(p. 17)

Such is the incarnation of the "first person" that van Vlaanderen is—but the other person, a man of thought and passion, naturally cannot bridle his passion according to the cruelly irrational laws of a totalitarian government. When Pieter was a young boy, his father tried to raise him to be a stern, dispassionate, and unfeeling Afrikaner: he forbade the boy to pursue his hobby, his passion, of collecting stamps, which the father viewed as unmanly. Though Pieter was forced to repress this passion, he never abandoned it; and though the South African government tried to forbid interracial love, the older Pieter is similarly unable to forsake this passion when it comes his way.

He develops an infatuation for Stephanie in spite of his love for his wife and children, and in spite of his firsthand knowledge of the uncompromising way the police force and the government deal with such love. Stephanie has often been jailed, for the same kinds of offenses as Gertrude's in *Cry,* and she risks losing custody of her young child; she therefore allows the romance to develop, hoping to gain some power over Pieter that will enable her to keep her child. As Pieter gives Stephanie a little money, and tries to arrange a job for her, she lets him know where she will be at a certain time in the evening, in a deserted place. He is wrenchingly torn between the two people that he is, in a society that will not allow for such a range of personality; he cannot repress his "second person," but instead follows his impulse and passion: he goes to the place Stephanie had mentioned:

where it is dark, away from the three pools of light. And he came to the place where the blue-gums are, and the *kakiebos* weed in the vacant ground. And he stood there waiting in the dark, with the mad sickness and the fear.
And there, God forgive him, he possessed her.

(p. 153)

From that point, Pieter lives a nightmare of psychological terror and paranoia. When he returns home, a note pinned to his door states I SAW YOU, and he lives in constant fear of exposure. The note turns out to be a joke played by his friend Japie, a welfare worker, which referred to a trivial flirtation Pieter had had with a white woman. Nicholas H. Z. Watts observes that the phrase, in the present tense, is a traditional Zulu greeting "that acknowledges and respects the identity of the other. Pieter's reaction is a measure of how far apart he has drifted from those around him" (p. 253). He is tormented by the certainty that the society in which he has progressed so successfully according to its rules will turn on him. Yet in spite of his torment, he continues his relationship with Stephanie. Through this characterization, Paton asserts that Afrikaners—at least some—are not merely racist automatons, but have another aspect to their personalities, an individual pursuit of passion that defies legislated hatred.

J. B. Thompson asserts that Pieter's infatuation with Stephanie is not emotional: "Stephanie is no soul mate of Pieter's and not even a 'playmate,' but is joylessly used by him as a sexual object for sinister psychological purposes of his own" (p. 38): to undermine his people's blind faith in the force of racial purity. All Pieter feels for Stephanie, Thompson argues, "is the sort of benevolence he feels towards all members of 'the black nation' " (p. 38). Pieter's intent in the affair is to bring to the surface the second person that he is, and to destroy the first. "If his aim were to bring the maximum dis-

grace upon his family," Thompson writes, "he could not have made a better choice, and that, I feel, is precisely the point. It is a sort of blind irrational retaliation. . . . The consequence is an eruption of defiance" (pp. 40, 41). Myrtle Hooper, though noting, as Thompson does, the impersonal objectification of Stephanie, criticizes Paton for complicity in enforcing her silence, which represents the "elusion [of her character] of both author and reader" (p. 62). She asks, "As a prominent and respected member of his community, as a policeman, is [Pieter] not simply exploiting someone weaker than himself, disadvantaged, and voiceless?" (pp. 58–59). She argues that a character from J. M. Coetzee's novel *Foe* illustrates the same void that Stephanie represents in *Too Late the Phalarope*: "Many stories can be told of [Robinson Crusoe's "manservant"] Friday's tongue, but the true story is buried within Friday, who is mute. The true story will not be heard by art till we have found a means of giving voice to Friday" (p. 61).

The novel's enigmatic title comes from an episode in Pieter's relationship with his father, representing the dilemma of the Afrikaner who is in his prime trying to come to terms with the stoic and stubborn tradition of his people. For his father's birthday, Pieter has bought him a book—a dangerous gift, because the anti-intellectual old man scorns any literature except the Bible. This book, *The Birds of South Africa*, meets with some approval from the elder van Vlaanderen, who is, like all good Afrikaners, a lover of the land. It represents a potential connection between the "second" Pieter—the thinker, the member of a generation that is different from his father's—and the elder van Vlaanderen. But the book is by an Englishman, which offends the father's anti-British prejudices. The old man delights in finding mistakes in the book:

—Pieter, have you ever seen the phalarope?
—The what, father?
—The phalarope.
[His father] added impatiently, a bird.
Then his son, for politeness sake, took a step or two also until he stood by his father, but his father still did not turn to him, but stood as he was before.
—No, father.
—That Englishman of yours says they're birds of the coasts. Have you ever seen the *ruitertjie*, at the farm at Buitenverwagtig?

—Yes, father.

—And you've seen the phalarope there too, but you always thought it was the *ruitertjie.*

—It could be, said his son doubtfully.

His father turned to him.

—I didn't say it could be, he said, I said it was. Do you think I was blind when I was young?

—No, father, but . . .

But his father had turned round and faced us all. It gave him pleasure that we were all listening to him, but I write down here that it was not a vain pleasure, it was more a kind of mischief.

(pp. 115–116)

Much later, while on a family picnic, the father (whose incapacity for intimacy with his son mirrors Paton's relationship with his own father) spots a phalarope, and points it out to Pieter—confirming his own expertise and the Englishman's mistake—trying to share a moment of natural communion, the phalarope's flash of grace, with his son.

These are the novel's only references to the phalarope. From the title, the reader must infer that this is all too late—that is, the son tries to share the Afrikaner naturalist passion with his father through the son's medium, a book. The father also tries to share a part of his son's life by buying him a block of stamps for his birthday, decades after he had forbidden his son to collect them. But the essential connections have been lost; the time for possible understanding has passed, and Pieter has already taken the step that will earn his father's unrelenting hatred.

With an Afrikaner subordinate of van Vlaanderen's (who hates Pieter because he should have been his superior, but is of lower rank because he refused to fight with the English in World War II, as Pieter had), Stephanie conspires to reveal Pieter as her lover. When the father learns of Pieter's transgression with Stephanie, he crosses out his son's name in the family Bible, destroys every photograph and reminder of Pieter, and locks the front door, saying, "The door shall not be opened again" (p. 251). Pieter's wife and children leave him, and his father dies of shame eight days later. At the end of the story, Pieter receives a prison sentence, but the emphasis is not on society's punishment of him; rather, it is on the horrible crumbling of his family, their inability to survive the maelstrom of their country's irrational system, their unwillingness to face the human reality of uncontrollable passion. Pieter has lived his life unable to find com-

fort in the sober religion, the stern self-satisfaction, and the self-righteousness of his father.

Earlier, Pieter had heard a story told by a schoolmate of his who came to the aid of a woman in an auto accident: he rescued her from the car, holding her in his arms, until he saw that it was a Malay woman.

And he could not hold her any more; he let her go in horror, not even gently, he said, and even though a crowd was there. And without a word he pushed through the crowd and went on his way. For the touch of such a person was abhorrent to him, he said. . . .

(p. 126)

Pieter envies his friend's idiotic racism, his horror of nonwhites, "for to have such a horror is to be safe" (p. 126)—safe from confronting the unstable reality around him and the schizophrenic inclinations of his own character. But to be a thinking and feeling member of Afrikaner society, Paton asserts, is to be tormented. And, as in *Cry, the Beloved Country,* the beauty of the phalarope, and of the land, is no longer a sufficient force to overcome the turmoil that people have wrought in the land—it is too late.

AH, BUT YOUR LAND IS BEAUTIFUL

PATON's next novel, *Ah, But Your Land Is Beautiful* (1982), followed *Too Late the Phalarope* by nearly three decades—time Paton spent writing biographies and essays, and participating extensively in South African politics. In the novel (part of a planned trilogy, never completed), Paton returns to the 1950's, perhaps because that was a time he felt he understood better than the 1980's; a time when, in retrospect, the murky situation seemed clearer, and when it seems one could have done something, and found a clearer way out of the situation than was imaginable in the 1980's.

Paton's narrative becomes immensely more intricate in *Ah, But Your Land Is Beautiful* than in his earlier novels: numerous plots are intertwined and deal more explicitly with the political issues of the 1950's than in the earlier novels (which used these issues more as a backdrop against which an emotional human story was set). Among the issues discussed are civil disobedience, Indian resistance, the establishment of African homelands (and the usurping of more attractive African land by whites), the Group Areas Act (segregating living areas, and fragmenting African families and homes), "Bantu education" (the meager educational system for Africans), mixed worship laws, sanctions, segregation of sports associations, and, again, the Immorality Act and the idea of racial purity.

The various stories that encompass all these issues are, at first, difficult to follow and link together, but appreciating discrete individual stories is not the point of this novel: Paton succeeds at what he means to do, bombarding his readers with a pastiche made up of a vast range of anatomies of oppression and struggles to surmount this oppression. The reader gets not so much a feeling of empathy (as is evoked for Kumalo or van Vlaanderen) as a general sensitivity to the tenor of South African racism. Thematically, the novel indicates Paton's more mature view of apartheid. It depicts the years when the South African government constructed the harshest measures of apartheid with the most enthusiasm and dedication to isolating the different races and keeping nonwhites subordinate. No longer does Paton see the simple enduring spirit of a noble protagonist as a viable weapon against discrimination; instead, he points his readers toward the overwhelming panorama of oppression, all of which must be taken in and confronted by various members of the opposition, acting in some kind of unity. This novel is more aggressive and forthrightly activist than his first two, and more inspirational for direct political involvement in the specific issues Paton depicts in detail.

The voice of the oppressed is more authentic, more self-controlling, and more angry in this novel than in the earlier ones. Paton tells, for example, of a nurse–missionary who has devoted her life to the care of Africans in the slums, and who is killed during a riot provoked by the police:

Of course it is said, and how could it not be, that the Defiance Campaign is responsible for her death. And of course it is said, and how could it not be, that the real causes of her death are the laws of apartheid, and the poverty, and the frustrations, and the belief that the white rulers of South Africa know only one language, and that is the language of violence. It is the language they speak, and therefore it is the language in which they must be spoken to. It is not a campaign of protest, it is a war, and therefore everything white must be de-

stroyed, even the sisters and their hospitals and their clinics and their schools.

(p. 26)

While this confidently accusatory voice is not the only voice in the novel, it is for Paton newly radical, newly strong. Like *Cry, the Beloved Country,* the novel is a fusion of the various voices of South Africa; but in contrast with those in his first novel, the voices are more extreme, more directly combative, more isolated from each other in their own camps. African protesters proudly and fiercely chant, "Mayibuye! Afrika! Afrika! Afrika!" ("Come back, Africa," or, "Give Africa back to us.") At the other extreme, the voice of a woman who writes obscene letters signed "Proud White Christian Woman" to the liberal white reformer Robert Mansfield (who is, like Jarvis in *Cry, the Beloved Country* and the reformatory director in *Tales from a Troubled Land,* another incarnation of Paton), embodies a compulsive psychological sickness:

I have read about your speech in Cape Town. So you are against the Immorality Act. That's nothing to wonder about, because every time you poke your black dolly girls, you must be afraid of getting caught. What do they say? Caught in the act, ha! ha! I can see it, you and your dolly girl pawing at each other like two animals, breathing, panting, stinking of sex and sweat.

I bet you wake up at night and can imagine it all. How can you imagine such filth? You call yourself a Christian. How can you imagine such things? And that fuzzy hair, above and below.

Has your wife found any hair on the pillow yet? Or has she got her own black lover? You would both stoop to anything, I am sure.

(p. 99)

Another series of anonymous letters, from "The Preservation of White South Africa League," further explores the taint of such perverse hatred:

This is a letter of warning to you. It should be taken very seriously. We note that you have accepted the chairmanship of the Natal region of the Liberal Party. We regard your party as anti-Christian, and anti-White South African, and we have taken the decision that all the regional chairmen of the party, and all those who are foolish enough to become their successors, would be eliminated.

Do you know the meaning of the word *eliminated,* Mr. Mansfield? It has the same meaning as it had in Germany, under the great Führer Adolf Hitler.

(p. 77)

(In 1960, Paton had his passport suspended when he said, "We are not a Nazi country, but we are not a bad imitation of one" [*New York Times,* 12 April 1988]. It was not restored until 1970.) The novel presents pervasive conflict and tension: not just interracially but also whites against whites, Afrikaners against Afrikaners, party members in conflict with each other—Paton thus demonstrates the unavoidable turbulence and dissension that is ripping his society apart.

Paton's authorial voice is more aggressively critical of the government than in his earlier work, and totalitarian government leaders are more pointedly exposed as Orwellian villains. The obvious hypocrisy of this government is exposed, for example, through its opposition to the Freedom Charter (which demands basic rights for Africans—free education, abolition of apartheid, right to a fair trial, freedom of travel, abolition of pass laws and permits, and so forth—which the government views as treasonable, communistic). The government responds to this with language that evokes *Animal Farm:* Apartheid is "Dr. Hendrik's Great Plan for peaceful and harmonious separate coexistence" (p. 110); the government acts to protect "peaceful natives who appreciated that the apartheid laws were made for their advancement" (p. 168) from the supporters of the Freedom Charter. Paton's Orwellian sarcasm is evident in the attempts to prove that the Freedom Charter is a communist document, undertaken by three Afrikaner scholars who "are probably the greatest experts in the world on communism. Dr. Munnik's works in particular are said to be so profound that the number of people who understand them is small" (p. 143). And Nationalists fantasize about their own leadership: "Never in history have so few legislated so thoroughly and devotedly for so many divergent peoples, nor ever before in history have rulers shown such a high sense of purpose or idealism" (p. 67).

The novel is intentionally fragmented; while many of these fragments are even more propagandistic than Paton's earlier fiction, some are as incisively moving as anything Paton has written: a kindly white judge, for example, is asked to participate in the ceremony of washing feet at an African church's Maundy Thursday service. He agrees to be called to wash the feet of the elderly African woman who had nursed all of his children; when he begins to do this, he remembers how kind she has been to his family, and how she used to kiss

their feet after bathing them, and he does the same for her. A white newspaper reporter happens to witness this, and writes the story for his newspaper, causing a tremendous scandal and reactionary hostility among white society:

In the first place the judge's action at Bochabela ran counter to the racial policy of the Government.... Mixed worship is not compatible with racial separation, and racial separation is the mandate that was given to the Government in 1948, and renewed even more strongly in 1953....

[His action] is repugnant to most white Christian opinion, and certainly to most Afrikaner Christian opinion. The performance was melodramatic and tasteless.
(pp. 249–250)

Paton paints the scene as he depicted van Vlaanderen's transgression: as a simple act that rocks the false complacency of racist society; as a kind of personal tragedy for the transgressor but, more depressingly, as a ridiculously unnecessary trauma for society. Though these traumas fester unresolved in Paton's fiction, there seems to be a tentative hope that beyond the scope of the novel these traumas will awaken South Africans to the precarious state of their country and, after enough such traumas have taken place, will spur them to forsake and atone for their prejudices.

LIBERAL PARTY ACTIVITY

PATON did not exhort reform solely through his writing. For fifteen years, from 1953 until 1968, he was heavily involved in the formation and guidance of South Africa's strident, though often quixotic, Liberal Party. At the far left of the (white) political spectrum, the Liberals eventually called for universal adult suffrage, unqualified and regardless of race. The party attempted to be multiracial, thus drawing the condemnation of the vast majority of white South Africans, though in practice most politically active nonwhites found a more effective forum in such nonwhite groups as the African National Congress, the Pan-African Congress, and various Indian congresses. Some of these groups, Paton writes, "accused us of weakening the only true opposition in the country" (*Journey Continued,* p. 68). The party finally disbanded in 1968, when the government prohibited interracial organizations. Paton was vice president of the party at its formation, and became its national chairman in 1956 and its president in 1958. The Liberals suffered a battery of criticism, and Paton's descriptions of his party's work in his autobiographies illuminate the profoundly chaotic state of any South African political movement that challenges the status quo: In *Journey Continued,* he writes:

The critics of the right viewed our racial policies with abhorrence. What kind of people called for the repeal of the Mixed Marriages Act and the Immorality Act? We were obviously sex-obsessed, and we were particularly attracted by the thought of sex across the colour line.

Our critics on the left regarded us as useless. They accused us . . . of "blunting the edge of the revolution." They were angry with us for not joining the grand Congress movement. We were preventing black and coloured and Indian people from joining their own congresses, by offering them this pie-in-the-sky non-racialism.

We were accused . . . of making promises that we could never keep. I do not remember any of these promises. We promised blood and toil and tears and sweat, and that is what many of us got.

(p. 117)

The Liberal Party polled only one-third of one percent in the 1961 national elections, and did not run a candidate in the 1966 elections. Clearly, the party was based on an idealism that found only a negligible constituency in the real-life world of South African politics. Liberals were criticized for their political innocence and what seemed to opponents to be a willfully naive disregard for "the dynamics of history, the imperatives of economics, or the strategic devices of power. Liberals have tended to respond that the first are obscure, the second debatable, and the third are often morally dubious," writes Douglas Irvine (p. 120). African leaders, such as the African National Congress' president Chief Albert Luthuli, resented "white liberals' initial concern in the 1950s with 'civilization' as a criterion for voting rights, and impatience as well with what often seemed too great a regard for respectability and legality" (p. 118)—even the Liberals did not advocate full universal suffrage until 1960.

While the Liberals never found the groundswell of support they sought, they tenaciously forbore to engage in extensive government harassment, ban-

nings, police raids, and bombings, and used their platform as a soapbox from which to denounce the South Africans' increasing embrace of apartheid. At the party's final meeting in 1968, Paton admitted, "The party was small and not powerful. But it was formed to give expression to ideas that were not small, and were full of power": ideas such as freedom of the individual, of association, of employment, of residence. "The government was afraid of them. Therefore, it took merciless steps against those who held them" (quoted in Irvine, p. 133). Paton's energetic commitment to actual change through political involvements added to his writing the force of one who was not merely an idle or theoretical observer of events, but of one who had done everything within his power to affect them. Paton's historical overview in *Hope for South Africa* (1958), and his copious essays from the 1960's through the 1980's, collected in *Save the Beloved Country* (1989), embody a bitterly pessimistic assessment of South African society and government; but his bitterness reflects the experience of one who, though he has failed, has made a valiant effort to extend the moral vision of his literature into the world outside it.

BIOGRAPHIES

PATON wrote two full-length biographies: *Hofmeyr* (1964), abridged in an American edition as *South African Tragedy: The Life and Times of Jan Hofmeyr,* and *Apartheid and the Archbishop: The Life and Times of Geoffrey Clayton.* Paton knew both subjects personally and fairly intimately—he worked with both, and recorded in his autobiography that they were two of the most profound influences on his life and career. In his study of the politician Hofmeyr, whom Paton acclaims as a relatively positive moral force in the 1920's through the 1940's, Paton demonstrates the extremely dubious relativism that has always marked even the liberal end of the white South African political spectrum. (Certainly, his homage to Hofmeyr helps to explain Paton's own relativism and—in the eyes of Africans and the West—occasional deficiencies in his activism.) Hofmeyr was founding principal of the University of Witwatersrand; minister of finance, mines, education, interior, and public health; a leader of the United Party, a compelling statesman, and deputy prime minister during the Smuts era. Paton is adulatory of his boyhood schoolmate, and demonstrates in this work the biographer's stamina and dedication to factual precision; the work as a whole, though, concentrates on extreme technicalities and nuances of politics, often overdone. Paton shows Hofmeyr as a man possessing some degree of conscience in an unconscionable government. By tracing one man's (sometimes mild) opposition to racist legislation, he succeeds in intricately exploring the decades of development of what would become apartheid.

Hofmeyr, an Afrikaner, was rejected by more fiercely nationalist Afrikaners because he had been a Rhodes scholar at Oxford, where he learned to admire the British character, and because he was bilingual. He was, Paton writes, raised as a culturally committed Afrikaner, but "of a gentle kind"— not one of those xenophobes hardened by England's defeat and humiliation of South Africa in the Boer War. Especially in the earlier sections of the biography, Paton's role seems to be apologist. In a very tame rebuke of Afrikaner racism in the 1920's, he writes, "In those days, not only Hertzog, but also Smuts and Hofmeyr, entertained an idea of the white man's role in Africa which has proved erroneous" (pp. 95–96).

Paton believed that Hofmeyr always had the betterment of the nonwhite South African population in mind; at the same time, he is forced to admit that Hofmeyr largely accepted white dominance— he was perhaps critical of it, but never challenged it, because he was consummately a politician and represented a constituency committed to some kind of perpetuation of *baasskap*, white supremacy. Paton argues that when, for example, Hofmeyr fought for a small increase in the funds allotted to African education (which did not appreciably change the seven-to-one ratio in favor of education funds for whites), he was doing better than any other politician who hoped to keep his parliament seat and his ministry could do.

Hofmeyr was, seemingly, the least of many evils. Still, he frequently voted in support of bills that restricted the rights of non-Europeans and expressed a determination to keep them in an inferior position. Like many other South Africans, Hofmeyr envisioned extending European dominance in Africa as far north as Kenya. He unilaterally rejected claims for racial and social equality in his own country; his most liberal rapprochement to nonwhites was the institution of a kind of benevolent Christian trusteeship, in which a preeminent white race would do its best to uplift the rest of the population. And again, when Hofmeyr asserts, "We are revolted by the notion of social equality," Paton apologizes: "It seemed that he was talking of something felt by others . . . something that a politician could not ignore" (p. 192). Late in his career, Hofmeyr finally expressed his opposition to the color bar (and was blamed, as a result, for his party's loss of power in 1948, and the coming to power of the Afrikaner Nationalists, who immediately begain constructing apartheid). At the same time, however, Hofmeyr wrote to those (whites) who served as advocates for nonwhites in parliament, "saying he understood the reasons for their impatience and admitting that there were discriminatory laws. But to ask for their repeal forthwith was to ask for the impossible; while working for their repeal one had to live with the laws and, of course, obey them" (p. 338).

Hofmeyr never responded to calls from the Left to leave the compromising United Party and form his own; Paton, with his Liberal Party work in the 1950's and 1960's, seems personally to have picked up the mantle from Hofmeyr, and to have done what he imagined Hofmeyr would have done had he had another few decades to move forward at the slow pace palatable to his constituency. Paton's faith in Hofmeyr, and his respect for him, inspired his intense dedication to the biography over eleven years. In *Journey Continued* he writes, "I am often asked, 'Which do you regard as your best book?' To that I answer, 'I would not place *Hofmeyr* second to any of the others' " (p. 13). Current readers and critics would be unlikely to concur with that judgment, but it does point to Paton's belief that political efforts are of paramount importance in South Africa, and that Hofmeyr was, in Paton's estimation, a politician who had the unique attributes of being as enlightened and as successful (within the system as it stood) as was pragmatically possible.

Like *Hofmeyr, Apartheid and the Archbishop* (1973) provides, through a focus on one man, an intricate overview of a fundamental South African institution (the Anglican Church, but with considerable discussion of other religious institutions as well) over several decades. Also like the earlier biography, the study of Geoffrey Clayton is technically detailed, covering the church's personalities, political involvement, missionary activity, and social role as exhaustively as *Hofmeyr* explored the nuances of the United Party and Parliament.

Archbishop Clayton, whom Paton lauds for a commitment to the same kinds of values he admired in Hofmeyr—liberal tolerance and at least theoretical opposition to the color bar—seems to have had a greater degree of freedom in acting on his values. Though he, too, was to some extent co-opted by South Africa's racially oppressive society, a churchman's necessary compromises were less insidious than a politician's, and Clayton's platform in the church allowed him greater freedom of conscience than did Hofmeyr's in Parliament. Clayton solved his dilemmas about how to achieve moral results in a less-than-moral society by learning to compromise, or attain limited victories, just as Hofmeyr had often had to choose the lesser of two evils. Paton describes Clayton's philosophy: "When you could not see clearly how you would reach your objective, then *you must do the next right thing*" (p. 116). As Hofmeyr had had to make concessions to the status quo, voting for and upholding discriminatory laws that he knew were wrong, so under Clayton's rule, African Anglican priests were paid about one-third (or less) the stipends of white clergy. To put this in the context of "the lesser of evils," though, it must be remembered that in the Afrikaners' church, it was preached that racial segregation was divinely ordained.

Through Clayton, Paton further explores the dilemma of English-speaking South Africans' dual allegiances (and the consequent hostility on the part of Afrikaners). Clayton was a native of Leicester, England—like most officials in South Africa's Anglican Church, he was sent to serve for a few years in the "colonies," then expected to return to England. Clayton, however, spent his life serving in South Africa and, Paton notes to the archbishop's credit, never referred to England as "home," firmly adopting South Africa as his nation. South Africans of English ancestry were generally more liberal than the descendants of people from other European nations; consequently, Paton saw it as imperative that they be firmly rooted in South Africa and work there to proliferate their values.

With Hofmeyr's death in 1948 and the rapid passage of the most oppressive apartheid laws, Clayton was driven to carry on Hofmeyr's reformist work and became increasingly prominent as an activist opposed to apartheid. As Clayton became more outspoken, he became more alienated from the ruling Afrikaners and was charged with spreading, personally and through his church, anti–South African propaganda overseas. After earlier personal resistance to civil disobedience, he finally came to support it. Finally, at age seventy-three, after extensive deliberation, he wrote a letter to the prime minister announcing that he would urge his clergymen, from their pulpits, to entreat blatant disobedience of a proposed law: a clause in the Native Laws Amendment Act that explicitly extended the province of apartheid to the churches and mandated that church officials enforce segregation. Clayton saw this as a challenge to religious freedom, and took his strongest stand against apartheid; he died, however, before the letter was mailed. It was subsequently sent out and ignored by the prime minister. The law was passed, though in part through Clayton's publicized opposition to it, it was widely challenged and ignored.

In his decision to spend years researching and writing on Hofmeyr and Clayton, Paton showed his commitment to what he saw as the two most important callings in his career. *Hofmeyr* was a complement to Paton's own career in the Liberal Party and as a political reformer. *Apartheid and the Archbishop* confirmed Paton's strong religious faith and his commitment to bringing about, through that faith, the salvation of his country.

INSTRUMENT OF THY PEACE

PATON further demonstrated his faith in *Instrument of Thy Peace* (1968), a series of meditations on the prayer of St. Francis of Assisi: "Lord, make me an instrument of Thy Peace. Where there is hatred, let me sow love; where there is injury, pardon; where there is doubt, faith; . . ." The small book is an expansion on this theme. He writes:

I say to myself, this is the only way in which a Christian can encounter hatred, injury, despair, and sadness, and that is by throwing off his helplessness and allowing himself to be made the bearer of love, the pardoner, the bringer of hope, the comforter of those that grieve.

(p. 2)

The meditations make some reference to the troubles of Paton's society, and explain the Christian motivation behind his reformatory work: as St. Francis wrote, "It is in pardoning that we are pardoned," so Paton explains how his work at Diepkloof refuted "the extraordinary theological view that when a man commits an offence he rends the moral order of the universe, and that this damage is repaired only by his punishment" (p. 22). Instead of the sequence of "offence–punishment," Paton exhorts "offence–forgiveness–restoration." Primarily, though, Paton wrote these meditations not with reference to specific social problems but as a moral exhortation to persevere: "for those who are inclined to melancholy, for those who are inclined to withdraw rather than to participate, for those who are tempted to retreat into pietism because they are afraid of active engagement in the world" (p. v).

AUTOBIOGRAPHICAL WORKS

PATON's three explicitly autobiographical works—*Kontakion for You Departed* (1969), which focuses on his wife's death, *Towards the Mountain* (1980), and *Journey Continued* (1988)—are essentially a gloss on everything else he has written. The first of these is marked by a strong sense of loss and a tremendously vital and moving personal passion; the second embodies the energetic and idealistic optimism that Paton felt in his earlier years, as it follows his life up to the publication of *Cry, the Beloved Country;* and the third, finished just before his death, deals with the later period of political turmoil and frustration, and is thus more hardened. All three show not an advancement nor a development of his ideas but, rather, a commitment to saying the same thing over and over, never abandoning his moral onus. One senses, as in his novels and biographies, the writer's commitment to directing whatever topic is at hand—in this case, his own life—toward the enlightenment of those who believe in social inequity; and, at the same time, the ever-present implacable reality that Paton's voice is ultimately too small: the people who are causing the most harm in South Africa simply will not listen to him, and continue to live their lives in what often seems to be a universe that has no points of moral connection with his own.

"We Must Act Quickly" (1971) is the kind of essay that leaves Paton vulnerable to charges of tame activism, and perhaps even collaboration with the Nationalist government. Discussing the government's philosophy of "separate development" for whites and nonwhites (through which the South African government attempted to appease the nonwhite population with the same kind of paltry concessions that were given to American minorities until the "separate but equal" doctrine in *Plessy* v. *Ferguson* was declared unconstitutional in 1954), Paton equivocates on the potential of that maneuver. Tellingly, he structures the essay as a dialogue between "Alan" (representing idealism) and "Paton" (a pragmatic respondent), showing that he realizes he is espousing compromises that are arguably contradictory, hypocritical. "Alan" asks, "Do you honestly foresee the day when there will be eight or nine independent States, all economically strong, living in harmony together, in what we now call the Republic of South Africa?" "Paton" responds, "Of course not. Nobody does. But"—a word that recurs uncomfortably often throughout the essay—"I believe that the attempt to achieve such a goal may bring improvements in the conditions of Black men which they would never have achieved . . . in a supreme White Government" (*Save the Beloved Country,* p. 56).

The pragmatist "Paton" acknowledges that South Africa will not see racial harmony until the gap between white and nonwhite incomes is closed, but then sidesteps an activist attitude toward fulfilling this ideal; instead, he says, "All I can say is that [Africans'] moral case is extremely strong. And it is my belief that White South Africans are growing more vulnerable to moral demands" (*Save the Beloved Country,* p. 57). Any African activist could have told Paton that the oppressed majority had given up the hope that any change would come about through the moral conscience of a white South African government. Paton espouses a tentative stance, waiting and hoping that some positive results, even limited gains, can come from the Nationalists. By the 1970's, it was clear to most observers that the hope for liberation arising from limited tidbits thrown out by the ruling government was ephemeral. The Nationalists were in no essential way reform-minded throughout the 1970's and 1980's, but were merely stalling for time.

On other issues, too, Paton rejected stances of extreme confrontation with the government or full support of the country's increasingly radical elements. He seems jealous of, and unnecessarily confrontational with, Bishop Desmond Tutu in an essay entitled "Your Philosophies Trouble Me." (In response to Tutu's receiving the Nobel Peace Prize, Paton writes, "I have never won a prize like that. I am afraid that my skin is not the right colour" [*Save the Beloved Country,* p. 183]). Of Tutu's support for a political agenda that aggressively challenges the Nationalists, Paton writes, "I think your morality is confused just as was the morality of the Church in the inquisition, or the morality of Dr. Verwoerd [the architect of apartheid] in his utopian dreams" (*Save the Beloved Country,* p. 185). In "Indaba Without Fear" (1987), he is condescending toward Winnie Mandela; he calls her demand for the Nationalist government to abdicate and hand over power to the black majority "a forthright but quite useless suggestion" (*Save the Beloved Country,* p. 165). In "Where They Are Wrong" (1975), about student movements, he writes, "I am against the stupid kind of activism that demands everything NOW" (*Save the Beloved Country,* p. 221).

Paton had once occupied a position that seemed to the world to be the epitome of liberal reform-mindedness. As African movements caught up with and surpassed Paton's, other activists increasingly attacked him. Stephen Biko, the leading voice of the Black Consciousness movement that arose at African universities in the 1970's, specifically rejected Paton's involvement in his activism: while Biko felt Paton was generally committed to the same principles he himself espoused, he believed that the writer, like many white liberals, was insensitive to the proud and aggressive self-orientation of his group. While white leftists advocated improving Africans' lives, Biko asserted, they did not accept that this must adversely affect their own positions of privilege.

In the 1980's, in the face of a growing international movement to isolate and boycott South Africa economically by withdrawing investment in that country (support of which movement the government had made illegal), Paton demurred: "There is only one firm statement I can make on disinvestment—I will have nothing to do with it. I will not, by any written or spoken word, give it any support whatsoever" (*Save the Beloved Country,* p. 6).

Certainly, on this issue in Paton's camp there were other liberal politicians who feared, as Paton wrote, "that those who will pay most grievously for disinvestment will be the Black workers of South Africa" (*Save the Beloved Country,* p. 7). (In the event, as early 1990 saw major victories in the campaign for African liberation, the effects of international divestment were widely credited with having generated significantly important pressure on the white regime.)

Paton's stance on this issue, however, reflects his inclination in his later years to avoid the harshest possible criticism of the status quo and the hegemonic white power structure. He defends himself, somewhat simplistically, by analogy with his reformatory experience: he had learned in that phase of his life that "punishment was not the proper treatment for delinquent children. Punishment failed totally to treat the cause of delinquency. Punishment could change behaviour, but it was not a true reformatory instrument. . . . Punishment is no proper treatment for erring children, nor is it the proper treatment for erring countries" (*Save the Beloved Country,* p. 9). Again, he repeats the conviction, or at least the hope, that "the Afrikaner Nationalist is ready to behave better" (*Save the Beloved Country,* p. 9); presumably, Paton feels the rest of the world should simply wait for such improved behavior to be manifested. The fallacy in Paton's analogy is that racist totalitarian governments with extensively demonstrable records of harsh opposition to the human rights of tens of millions of their citizens are not like children. From his experience with children, Paton had learned to give a second chance, to forgive and hope for a better later effort. With the Nationalist government and its record, the stakes are different.

The older Paton, though, seemed oblivious to the differences in scale, and to the fact that the vast majority of South Africans had, over the decades of Nationalist rule, grown weary of waiting quietly on the sidelines for the white minority to improve the moral stance of their own accord. For these oversights, Paton lost some credibility and respect in the reform movement he once so influentially dominated. The force of his writing endures, however—if not as an effective contemporary manifesto, then as an acute psychological portrait of the human character torn by social hatred, and as a fiercely moral defiance of South African oppression.

ALAN PATON

SELECTED BIBLIOGRAPHY

I. BIBLIOGRAPHIES. E. Callan, "Selected Bibliography," in his *Alan Paton* (New York, 1968; rev. ed., 1982); and L. Bentel, comp., *Alan Paton: A Bibliography* (Johannesburg, 1969).

II. COLLECTED WORKS. *The Long View,* edited by E. Callan (New York, 1968); *Knocking on the Door,* edited by C. Gardner (New York and Cape Town, 1975); *Save the Beloved Country,* edited by H. Strydom and D. Jones (New York, 1989).

III. SEPARATE WORKS. *Cry, the Beloved Country* (New York, 1948); *South Africa Today,* Public Affairs Committee Pamphlet No. 175 (New York and London, 1951); *Too Late the Phalarope* (New York, 1953); *South Africa in Transition* (New York, 1956), with photographs by D. Weiner; *Hope for South Africa* (London, 1958); *Tales from a Troubled Land* (New York, 1961); *Hofmeyr* (Cape Town and Oxford, 1964), abridged as *South African Tragedy: The Life and Times of Jan Hofmeyr* (New York, 1965); *Instrument of Thy Peace* (New York, 1968); *Kontakion for You Departed* (New York, 1969); *Apartheid and the Archbishop: The Life and Times of Geoffrey Clayton, Archbishop of Cape Town* (New York, 1973); *Towards the Mountain* (New York, 1980); *Ah, But Your Land Is Beautiful* (New York, 1982); *Go Well, My Child* (Washington, D.C., 1985), with photographs by C. S. Larrabee; *Journey Continued* (New York and Oxford, 1988).

IV. DRAMATIC ADAPTATIONS. *Lost in the Stars* (1949), Broadway musical based on *Cry, the Beloved Country,* book by M. Anderson and music by K. Weill; *Cry, the Beloved Country* (1951), film directed by Z. Korda; *Sponono* (1964), Broadway play based on stories from *Tales from a Troubled Land,* adapted with K. Shah.

V. BIOGRAPHICAL AND CRITICAL STUDIES. H. Breit, *The Writer Observed* (Cleveland, 1956); H. Davies, *A Mirror of the Ministry in Modern Novels* (New York, 1959); E. Fuller, *Books with Men Behind Them* (New York, 1962); E. Callan, *Alan Paton* (New York, 1968; rev. ed., 1982); J. B. Thompson, "Poetic Truth in *Too Late the Phalarope,*" in *English Studies in Africa,* 24, no. 1 (1981); S. Watson, "*Cry, the Beloved Country* and the Failure of Liberal Vision," in *English in Africa,* 9 (May 1982); A. A. Monye, "*Cry, the Beloved Country:* Should We Merely Cry?" in *Nigeria Magazine,* 144 (1983); T. Morphet, "Alan Paton: The Honour of Meditation," in *English in Africa,* 10, no. 2 (1983); R. Moss, "Alan Paton: Bringing a Sense of the Sacred," in *World Literature Today,* 57, no. 2 (1983); R. Rive, "The Liberal Tradition in South African Literature," in *Contrast: South African Literary Journal,* 14 (July 1983); R. J. Linnemann, "Alan Paton: Anachronism or Visionary?" in *Commonwealth Novel in English,* 3 (Spring–Summer 1984); N. H. Z. Watts, "A Study of Alan Paton's *Too Late the Phalarope,*" in *Durham University Journal,* 76 (June 1984); D. Irvine, "The Liberal Party, 1953–1968," in J. Butler, et al., eds., *Democratic Liberalism in South Africa: Its History and Prospect* (Middletown, Conn., 1987); M. Hooper, "Paton and the Silence of Stephanie," in *English Studies in Africa: A Journal of the Humanities,* 32, no. 1 (1989).

BARBARA PYM

(1913–1980)

Mason Cooley

WHEN BARBARA PYM died early in 1980 at the age of sixty-six, she was becoming famous for the first time. Between 1950 and 1961 she published five novels that attracted favorable reviews and a small but loyal following. Between 1963 and 1977 she was unable to find a publisher for her work because her novels were felt to be out of tune with the taste of the period. In 1977, after Philip Larkin and Lord David Cecil named her one of the most neglected writers of the last seventy–five years in a survey conducted by the *Times Literary Supplement,* Pym again came into public view and published three more novels to increasing public recognition.

Since her death, her fame and her sales have continued to grow on both sides of the Atlantic. She has attracted sufficient attention among scholars and critics that a substantial number of books and articles about her, as well as *The Barbara Pym Newsletter,* are still in circulation. She has also attracted a good-sized segment of the reading public. To take advantage of the demand for her works, a number of writings were exhumed from the Pym archives at the Bodleian Library in Oxford and published posthumously. This combination of critical esteem and popularity among general readers is rare with modern writers. It probably rises from Pym's ability to write accessible, lucid, and entertaining prose without sacrificing a high standard of artistry and subtle comic intelligence.

LIFE

THE story of Pym's life is told in *A Very Private Eye: An Autobiography in Diaries and Letters* (1984) edited by her sister Hilary Pym and her literary executor Hazel Holt. Pym was born on 2 June 1913 in Shropshire, the daughter of a soliciter. As Hilary Pym has said, "It was a happy, unclouded childhood" (*A Very Private Eye,* p. 2). Anglican churchgoing was part of Barbara's and Hilary's lives from very early. Their mother was the assistant organist at the parish church of St. Oswald; their father sang bass in the church choir.

In 1931 Barbara went to St. Hilda's, Oxford, to study English. Three years later Hilary entered Lady Margaret Hall, Oxford, to study classics. The closeness of the two sisters lasted a lifetime. Barbara never married, and Hilary separated early from her husband. Hilary writes:

It was never our particular intention . . . to live together, but it somehow turned out that from about 1938 right up until the time of her death in 1980 we were never apart for more than a year or so at a time. In 1946, when I left my husband Sandy Walton, we started sharing a flat in London, then in 1961 we bought a house, and eventually, in 1972, a country cottage in Oxfordshire

(*A Very Private Eye,* p. 5).

Of their life together, Hilary concludes, it "started well and ran a good course."

During World War II Pym joined the Women's Royal Naval Service (Wrens) and served in Italy. In 1946 she went to work at the International African Institute as assistant editor of the institute's journal *Africa,* a post she retained until her retirement in 1974 after suffering a stroke. Thus Pym spent the chief part of her working life in the company of anthropologists. Though never much interested in the subject matter of anthropology, she was fascinated by the anthropologists themselves, their eccentricities, their folkways, and their intrigues. Shortly after Barbara's stroke, the sisters moved to the Oxfordshire village of Finstock, where Barbara Pym remained for the rest of her life.

Pym's inner life, seen only very partially through the reserve of her beautifully written letters and diaries, was dominated by literature and by a series of unhappy love affairs, beginning at Oxford and extending into middle age. She very early became convinced that she was not to marry and that her experience of love would be unrequited yearning for an unattainable beloved. That emotional experience is at the heart of her novels, but it is handled with cool detachment and an appreciation of its comic more than its tragic possibilities. As a writer, Pym is full of sentiment, but she is never overwhelmed by it. The love-yearnings of her heroines are treated with detachment and good-humored mockery, yet the yearnings are also given their due as legitimate sorrows.

Almost as important as the unrequited loves was Pym's powerfully literary turn of mind. Her thoughts were permeated by echoes from English literature; she worked full time as an editor for a quarter of a century; she wrote twelve published novels and hundreds of thousands of words of other matter; her writings are full of quotations from the English poets and allusions, both explicit and implicit, to classic novels. Almost invariably she framed her experience in literary terms, especially the terms of irony and comedy, which she used in her life as well as her work to deal with amorous and literary disappointments. She is a very complete instance of the English major as novelist.

Pym was more reserved about her religious life than either her romantic pursuits or her writing. She was a devoted lifelong communicant of the Church of England, and references to church matters are abundant in her work. But she says almost nothing directly about her faith. It is most in evidence during her final illness, when she felt sustained by it. Likewise in her novels, religious faith is kept under the surface, a hidden basis for the equilibrium that Pym's heroines manage, with some difficulty, to maintain.

CRAMPTON HODNET *AND* SOME TAME GAZELLE

PYM knew very early that she wanted to become a writer. She began her first novel after reading Aldous Huxley's *Chrome Yellow* when she was sixteen, but she did not actually publish her first book until she was in her mid thirties. Among the manuscript novels left unpublished at her death, *Crampton Hodnet* is by far the most successful.

Not published until 1985, *Crampton Hodnet* was begun just after the outbreak of World War II, in 1939. Pym completed a draft that she sent to her lifelong friend Robert Liddell in April of 1940. When she looked at the novel again after the war, it seemed to her to be dated, and she never sent it to a publisher. Whatever appeared dated to Pym in the 1940's contributes to what today's readers see as an attractive period aura. The novel is a playful and entertaining evocation of the lost world of pre–World War II England. It is also, as Hazel Holt has said, the most purely funny of Pym's novels.

In *Crampton Hodnet* Pym wrote a comic novel in which she both burlesques and glorifies British respectability. The novel is about genteel academic society in North Oxford at some indefinite moment in the first half of the twentieth century, probably the 1920's. Conflating two different epochs, the book combines representatives of stern Victorian moralism with characters who partake of Jazz Age playfulness and boldness. It presents a safe and stable community inhabited by a little band of gentlefolk who pursue their love affairs and gossip exempt from war, disease, aging, poverty, and the more imperious passions. Pym presents the quasi-Victorian world of North Oxford as a comic utopia, marred by pettiness and spite, but basically comfortable, reliable, and above all, impervious to change.

Both a romantic comedy and a satire on romantic comedy, *Crampton Hodnet* features three pairs of lovers who must make headway against the snoops and gossips and nosy relatives of North Oxford.

The youngest, most conventional, and least interesting pair are Anthea Cleveland, the pretty daughter of an Oxford don, and Simon Beddoes, an Oxford undergraduate with political ambitions. They have a light romance in which both of them, experienced players, attend to the rules of courtship observed by their generation, kissing more frequently than their elders would approve of, but not *much* more. Their story offers Pym little opportunity for the surprising twists and turns of erotic attachment that are her signature, and she never again gave more than cursory attention to the love of an ingenue for a juvenile lead. The other two couples are more characteristically Pymean.

One is composed of a handsome curate, Mr. Latimer, and Jessie Morrow, thirty-five and already drab and spinsterish. Ironic, detached, and observant, Jessie makes the best of her often uncomfortable position as a paid companion to Miss Maude Doggett, a neo-Victorian spinster devoted to rooting out every unsuitable manifestation of Eros. Her definition of unsuitability is comprehensive—Miss Morrow must listen to dance music on Radio Luxembourg like someone listening to a forbidden newscast in a totalitarian country, with her hand on the switch in case she should hear Miss Doggett approach.

After Mr. Latimer takes a room in Miss Doggett's house, he and Miss Morrow strike up a friendship. Out for a walk, they are caught in a heavy rainfall. They are so late getting back that Mr. Latimer misses his evening service and makes up a story about having been called to the fictitious parish of Crampton Hodnet to assist a fellow clergyman who was ill. Having done so, he feels he is in Miss Morrow's power, since she can expose him at any time. That, and his fear of the amorous attentions of his female parishioners, turn his thoughts toward marriage, and he proposes to Miss Morrow.

The third couple are Francis Cleveland, Anthea's father, and Barbara Bird, a beautiful undergraduate with an intense love of literature. Every meeting between these two is eagerly observed and reported by one or another of the snoops and gossips of Oxford. Things come to a head when Miss Doggett visits her relatives, the Clevelands, to denounce Francis to his wife. Despite the distractions offered by everyone involved in snapping off the ends of gooseberries, Miss Doggett manages to force a crisis. Francis is made so angry that he announces he is indeed in love with Miss Bird, and stamps out. The lovers make a plan to run away to Paris.

In a reversal of the usual procedure of romantic comedy, the three pairs of lovers end by separating from one another, not because of any external obstacles in the way of their union but because they do not care enough for one another to continue. Simon meets someone else and drops Anthea, who in due course recovers (chiefly from wounded vanity) and finds a new young man, a friend of Simon's. Jessie Morrow refuses Mr. Latimer's offer of marriage because he has nothing more romantic than "respect and esteem" to offer her. She does not marry Mr. Latimer, handsome

and well-off though he is, because she is too romantic to do so.

Francis Cleveland and Barbara Bird miss the boat train to France and are going to have to spend a night in a Dover hotel. When Barbara sets eyes on the room's enormous double bed, she realizes the whole arrangement is impossible. She likes romance, but not the prospect of actually having sex with Francis. She leaves after deciding to take refuge with her nearby friend Sarah Penrose:

I'm, free, she thought; there won't be any going to Paris. There won't be any more love, or at least not *that* kind of love. I've run away from Francis. Not *run* away, I've left him, I've given him up. I've *renounced* him. There was nothing shameful about renunciation; on the contrary, it was noble. "I must not think of thee. . . ." There was that poem in the *Oxford Book of Victorian Verse* about it. Barbara had often read it, but never before had she really understood what it *meant*.

(p. 190)

When Francis finds out that Barbara has left him, he at first feels stricken but soon is relieved not to have to keep up the altogether too-strenuous comedy of adulterous love. He returns, with a bad cold, to his wife. She puts him to bed and fusses over him, paying no attention to his amorous adventure, which she buries under an avalanche of domesticity.

The only fulfilled romance is Mr. Latimer's. He returns from his vacation in an ecstatic state to announce his engagement to a very young and pretty woman. Otherwise, everything returns to the way it was at the opening of the novel, which ends as it began, at a beginning-of-term tea party at Miss Doggett's. The final lines are given to Miss Doggett, and to Michael and Gabriel, a gay couple:

"Oh, Miss Doggett, isn't it *frightful*, we're in our third year," said Michael and Gabriel, rushing to greet her. "Change and decay in all around we see, but not *here*."

"No, I do not think you will find any change and decay in Leamington Lodge," said Miss Doggett, smiling.

And Miss Morrow was inclined to agree with her.

(p. 216)

The conservative impulse could scarcely go further. The novel began by presenting the oppressiveness of Leamington Lodge, the scene of Miss Doggett's tyrannical reign. At the end, Leamington Lodge has become virtually the Great Good Place. The seductions of the familiar have prevailed over the forces of change. Even Miss Morrow, who has the least to gain from the existing state of affairs, takes comfort in the durability of North Oxford. The comedies of amorous love are transitory entertainments riding along on the steady, satisfying course of daily life. With German bombers about to appear overhead, the security of Miss Doggett's drawing room comes to seem the very picture of happiness.

The first novel to appear in print in Pym's lifetime was *Some Tame Gazelle.* It was begun in 1934 but not finally published by Jonathan Cape until 1950, after it had been revised three times. Perhaps as a result of this long period of forced gestation, Barbara Pym's literary personality was fully formed by the time she began to publish. The work combines youthful hilarity with the assurance and control of a skilled artist—a reflection perhaps of the novel's beginnings in the author's youth and its completion in her maturity.

The beginning of *Some Tame Gazelle* foreshadows to a remarkable degree the entire body of Pym's subsequent work:

The new curate seemed quite a nice young man, but what a pity it was that his combinations showed, tucked carelessly into his socks, when he sat down. Belinda had noticed it when they had met him for the first time at the vicarage last week and had felt quite embarrassed. Perhaps Harriet could say something to him about it. Her blunt jolly manner could carry off these little awkwardnesses much better than Belinda's timidity. Of course he might think it none of their business, as indeed it was not, but Belinda rather doubted whether he thought at all, if one were to judge by the quality of his first sermon.
(p. 7)

The tone is discreetly comic. The characters are realistically individualized creations based on the comic stereotypes of the foolish clergyman and the curious old maid. The setting is an idyllic, unhistorical English village untouched by war, death, or poverty. It is the village of pastoral and romantic comedy.

The dramatic situation is so genteel as to be almost a parody of itself. A young clergyman is paying a call on two middle-aged sisters, Belinda and Harriet, who live happily together on a private income (never specified as to source or amount) sufficient to keep them in the style of prosperous country gentlefolk. The talk is well bred, the demeanor polite. Propriety appears to reign. But one detail in the decorous picture is awry, and as a result so are the thoughts of the heroine.

The young clergyman's long underwear shows above his socks. His hostess, noticing, is in a state of agitation and embarrassment, a state of mind typical of Pym's excessively conscientious heroines. Spinster and clergyman are voyeur and unwitting exhibitionist, the nervous female experiencing the naughty infantile pleasures of peeping, the clergyman oblivious to his breach of proper appearance. Ages and gender roles are scrambled. The lady is peering at the gentleman's underwear, not the gentleman at the lady's. The woman is older and more judicious, the man young and somewhat dizzy. The woman suffers from agonizing quixotic preoccupations with etiquette and propriety; the man is well pleased with himself and at ease. In Pym's world the woman worries while the man talks on contentedly. The man is the self-absorbed child, the woman the all-too-attentive parent, afraid to interfere but unable to turn her attention elsewhere.

The dramatic situation is one of apparent impasse. Belinda's mind scampers busily around the problem. But the rules of etiquette hem her in at every point; she can neither speak up about nor ignore the underwear, only remark waspishly to herself on the curate's general thoughtlessness as reflected both in his sermons and the arrangement of his dress. The solution is that the visit ends in due course, as visits always do, and Belinda's mind can move on to the next problem. In Pym's world issues are not so much resolved as simply left behind by the progress of daily life from meal to meal and day to day.

The two middle-aged sisters are Pym's way of imagining herself and her sister Hilary thirty years later (prophesying their real-life living situation with uncanny accuracy). Belinda and Harriet are excellent women, devoted church workers, each with a hopeless love. Belinda has loved the vain and affected Archdeacon Hoccleve for thirty years; he lives next door and has been married all this time to her college rival, the dry and stingy Agatha. Harriet's hopeless love (which is quite cheerful) is for whatever curate happens to be in residence, invariably a wispy young man much younger than herself. Both Belinda and Harriet are courted by suitors appropriate in age and social class, but the

BARBARA PYM

sisters drive the suitors away and return contentedly to their lives with each other and their unattainable beloveds.

The novel ends with wedding bells, but they are not ringing for the protagonists. The curate marries Miss Olive Berridge, an expert on the medieval poem *The Owl and the Nightingale.* The colonial bishop rejected by Belinda marries a faint local lady who plays the harp. In the final episode of the novel, Belinda reflects with satisfaction that nothing has changed. The suitors are gone. There is a new curate for Harriet; Belinda can return to her love for the Archdeacon.

Some Tame Gazelle both celebrates and mocks romantic comedy. Much of the book is constructed out of traditional comic materials. The two sisters have their origins in the first great comic novel, Cervantes' *Don Quixote.* Belinda—tall, thin, excessively bookish, and idealistic—is a female Quixote. Harriet—plump, earthy, and sometimes altogether too realistic—is a literary descendant of Sancho Panza. The symmetries of classic comedy are evident in the profusion of matched pairs: two sisters, two suitors, two unattainable beloveds, two rejected proposals, two marriages of minor characters at the conclusion. The village is constructed along literary rather than sociological lines, endowed with an Edenic existence outside history.

Pym plays havoc with romantic convention as much as she exploits it. Two of the leading conventions of romantic comedy are that the lovers, after a struggle, are happily paired off at the end. In addition, the lovers themselves are young and beautiful. The two sisters are unromantic in appearance: both in their fifties, one too plump, the other too thin, and, in addition, both are bespectacled. The suitors fare no better. Mr. Mold is a heavyset man with a flushed face, probably the result of excessive drinking; he suggests what Harriet might become if she completely lost control of her too-hearty appetite. The bishop of Mbawawa reminds Belinda "of a sheep" (p. 162), and his oleaginous moralizing suggests what Belinda might fall into if she completely lost control of her acute conscientiousness. Belinda and Harriet wind up at the end of the novel happily united to one another, which is the way they want it. Their determined resistance to change and their preference for imaginary loves over real ones creates a pleasant disturbance among the structural rules of romantic comedy.

Some Tame Gazelle establishes Pym as an accomplished writer of comedy, with an assured range from farce to the rarefied mental acrobatics of high comedy. It also establishes her as a writer who delights both in embodying and reversing or parodying literary convention. Her interest in playing with convention springs in part from the comedian's desire to create a happy (and usually temporary) disorder, the upsetting of rules being one of the prime motifs of comedy. Pym is also interested in showing, here and throughout her work, that amorous love manifests itself in an amazing variety of forms, involving people who may be young lovers or old women with parrots; it pays little heed to the rules.

EXCELLENT WOMEN *AND* JANE AND PRUDENCE

PYM's next novel, *Excellent Women* (1952), remains her most popular and is also one of her best. Shortly after it was published, the novel was dramatized by BBC radio and selected by a book club. If one were going to read only a single Pym novel, *Excellent Women* would be a good choice.

Excellent Women introduces us to the first fully developed instance of Pym's prototypical heroine—the "excellent woman." The book achieves the balance of comedy and realism that characterizes most of the author's subsequent novels. It gives a masterful picture of the London of Anglican parishes and gentlefolk in reduced circumstances. All the elements in the Pym mixture, including moments of real farce, are in evidence.

Yet the comic mode is subdued in relation to the high spirits and frequent hilarity of *Some Tame Gazelle.* A meticulous and highly selective realism chastens the comedy, as does the sometimes melancholy coloring of the narrative. In writing this work, Pym mastered the difficult art of achieving comic effects without disrupting the realistic surface. Indeed, so discreet are some of her comic touches that they are easy to mistake for matterof-fact detail. The novel demonstrates convincingly Pym's premise that the comic is inherent in life itself, not merely a matter of literary perspective.

The setting is the shabby district of Pimlico in London during the period of austerity immediately following World War II. The hard times in Britain following the war were even more psychologically devastating for many than the war itself, when people were sustained by a sense of heroic struggle. The housing shortage is acute, so that even the elegant Rocky and Helena Napier must content themselves with a humble flat in Pimlico. Rationing is still in effect, with milk, eggs, and meat in particularly short supply. The reader sees nothing of the bombed-out working-class East End of London, but is told of the peeling paint on parish-house walls, the inadequate heating, the neglect and decay in the West End.

Britain has won the war but has become an impoverished country faced with the immense task of rebuilding after wartime devastation. With the empire lost and the industrial plant antiquated, Britain no longer holds a prominent position in world affairs. The country is saddled with an enormous war debt; a Labour government has imposed ferocious taxes on income; there has been a general decline in the middle-class standard of living. It is a hard, gray, austere time in the London of *Excellent Women,* and some of this grayness is shared by the heroine.

The novel is narrated by Mildred Lathbury, the daughter of a country clergyman, now living on her own in London. Mildred establishes the character type of the "excellent woman," who is at the center of most of Pym's fiction. She is educated and in her early thirties; she considers herself "spinsterish." Plain and retiring, she thinks of herself as an uninteresting person with little claim on the attention of others, though she has a very active curiosity about those around her. She has a small private income and works part-time for a society for distressed gentlefolk. To her chagrin, she lives in a flat with a shared bathroom. A devout Christian and a devoted church worker, she is a particular friend of the clergyman of her parish and his unmarried sister. Her parents are dead; she has no lover, no network of friends outside the church, and no career. In every possible sense, she is a lone woman. She lives by a philosophy of stoic making-do—albeit a little reluctantly—with what life has offered her.

Mildred can be read as a sad case, a representative of a vanished order. She has an old-fashioned regard for the details of propriety that seems more Edwardian than post–World War II. For instance, after hearing a lecture at an anthropological society, she is much agitated when the discussion afterward is slow to get under way, and she is unnerved when a woman sitting near her gets up

and leaves before the meeting is over. Like her immediate predecessor Belinda Bede, she is often obsessed with worries about minor issues of "suitability." When she buys a new lipstick, she worries about whether it may be of too vivid a shade. She is much put out when she encounters Everard Bone outside the office of the charity for which she works part time; she is casually dressed for warm weather, without the hat, gloves, and stockings that would be proper attire for a meeting with a male acquaintance.

Mildred is part of a semidispossessed class, the lesser gentry made up of the squires and parsons of England, once prosperous and powerful, but now far less so. Trying to keep up a code of behavior that few even remember, she is a genteel spinster, a defenseless and (in her own eyes) "superfluous" creature. The austerity of her life and the austerity of the London in which she lives mirror one another. Her philosophy of trying to be satisfied with little, both emotionally and materially, is appropriate to the hard historical time in which she lives. If Mildred had appeared in a novel about the swinging London of the 1960's, she would have been a forbidding figure representing puritanical asceticism. In a novel about London immediately after the war, she represents the cheerful acceptance of inevitable privations.

But there is more both to London and to Mildred than grayness and austerity. Despite appearances, London is a lively, busy place, a great aggregation of semi-autonomous villages—with their gossiping, working, joking, planning, shopping, and courting. In a quieter way, it partakes of some of the vitality and humorous exaggeration of Dickens' London, and its inhabitants have no awareness whatever of being the exhausted inhabitants of a nation in decline. They are far too busy pursuing their own affairs and commenting on those of their neighbors.

There is also more to Mildred than dun-colored and defeated respectability. She is witty, brave, independent, observant, and kindhearted. Her keen curiosity keeps drawing her into the lives of the people around her, though her dislike of emotional complications occasionally sends her scurrying back to the shelter of her privacy. To her glamorous neighbors the Napiers, the husband a just-returned naval officer, the wife an anthropologist, she makes herself useful as confidante, messenger, negotiator, comforter, and even supplier of more than her share of toilet paper for the bath-room they share. But she is never quite taken in by either the wife's brassy self-confidence or the husband's flirtatiousness. She is also skeptical about the self-consciously "sweet" manner of the husband-hunting clerical widow, Allegra Gray. Though full of self-doubt, Mildred never quite yields to the seductiveness of her worldly friends or to the cant of her religious friends. She has an ironic and detached clarity that sometimes takes a while to come into focus, but ultimately saves her from being taken in. The mixture of worry, sharp-wittedness, and irony directed both toward herself and others is evident in Mildred's reflections after she has seen the vicar Julian Malory holding hands with Allegra Gray in the park:

I worried over the problem in bed that night and wondered if I ought to do anything. I suddenly remembered some of the "Answers to Correspondents" in the *Church Times,* which were so obscure that they might very well have dealt with a problem like this. "I saw our vicar holding the hand of a widow in the park—what should I do?" The question sounded almost frivolous put like that; what kind of an answer could I expect? "Consult your Bishop immediately"? Or, "We feel this is none of your business"?

(p. 108)

The conception of the excellent woman is rooted in the comic stereotype of the old maid, to whom is imputed an excessive concern with propriety, a passion for prying and gossip, a censorious tongue, an obsessive interest in good housekeeping, and a hopeless hunger for a man. Pym takes these stock attributes and transforms them into a complex, many-sided character suitable to be a protagonist rather than a two-dimensional minor figure. In particular, the old-maid characteristic of curiosity is enriched and elevated, though without losing its comic dimensions.

It is curiosity that keeps Mildred attached to life; she does not expect to find love or riches or adventures, but she very much wants to know what is going to happen next. Her good housekeeping and family background of clerical hospitality make her a provider of sympathy and "endless cups of tea" for those who seek her out. Mildred certainly wants to find a man but has little expectation that she will, and her fastidiousness and ironic spirit limit the field of choice. Not a search for a man but

a spirit of curious investigation is what leads her from one involvement to another, if the word "involvement" is not too strong to describe her somewhat tentative connections with those around her.

Excellent Women lays down the zigzag pattern of approach and retreat that all of Pym's subsequent plots follow. Like Chekhov's short stories, Pym's novels seem scarcely to have plots at all, so naturally, even aimlessly, do the incidents appear to unfold. The heroine is not struggling toward a goal, and the conflicts, such as they are, tend to be muffled and inconclusive. The sequence of episodes is loose and seemingly casual rather than tightly interlocked. But Pym is not an aimless writer of local color, and she reveals a larger pattern of meaning through the meandering course of daily life.

The novel begins with the heroine standing in front of her building. Though she does not admit it to the churchwarden, Mr. Mallett, who is teasing her on the subject, she is observing the unloading of a furniture van, which has brought the belongings of the tenants moving into the flat directly beneath her own.

"Ah, you ladies! Always on the spot when there's something happening!" The voice belonged to Mr. Mallett, one of our churchwardens, and its roguish tone made me start guiltily, almost as if I had no right to be discovered outside my own front door.

"New people moving in? The presence of a furniture van would seem to suggest it," he went on pompously. "I expect *you* know about it."

"Well, yes, one usually does," I said, feeling rather annoyed at his presumption. "It is rather difficult not to know such things."

I suppose an unmarried woman just over thirty, who lives alone and has no apparent ties, must expect to find herself involved or interested in other people's business, and if she is also a clergyman's daughter then one might really say that there is no hope for her.

(p. 5)

This first incident establishes curiosity as one of Mildred's chief motives, the one that will keep leading her on in her slightly disapproving friendship with her new neighbors. It initiates the story of the arrival of strangers in an enclosed world, the excitement and disturbance they cause, and the subsiding wake left after their departure. It also establishes the initial milieu of "churchiness" and small domestic concerns.

To this parish world the Napiers add glamor and,

in the person of Rockingham Napier, an almost all-inclusive flirtatiousness. He is an ex-naval officer whose function in Italy was to entertain women officers at his admiral's parties and give them someone to dream of and gossip about. He continues to practice on Mildred, who is wise enough to realize that there is nothing very personal in his pseudo-amorous but genuinely friendly attentions.

Helena Napier, an anthropologist, brings with her into Mildred's life the brash, modern, contentious world of professional anthropologists. Noisy, mobile, full of the unexpected, this milieu is the opposite of the respectable, predictable world of the parish. Mildred's potential suitor, Everard Bone, is both a churchman and an anthropologist.

Mildred navigates successfully but uneasily between these two worlds for a time. She is courted by Everard in a manner so equivocal as to be almost unrecognizable. At the end of the novel, the Napiers have moved away, and two retired governesses have moved in, older versions of the "excellent woman." Mildred is going to do some editorial work for Everard, and Julian has been rescued from the husband-hunting widow. The new people have come and gone. There are no wedding bells, no deep insights, no transformations of character. Everything is much as it was at the beginning.

But now Mildred's spirits have improved. She has found that she is less superfluous than she had imagined, and the ceaseless flow of her self-criticism has moderated. She has met a man who might become a suitor. (In a subsequent novel we discover that Mildred and Everard have married.) Her life is fuller than it was, and she feels more confident that she will find her existence sustaining.

The eros of amorous love has not appeared, but the agape that informs daily life is comfortingly in evidence. Barbara Pym has little to say directly about Christian faith, but at the end of *Excellent Women* she shows that Mildred has achieved the blessing of a cheerful and accepting mind, one of the most Christian of goals. Her attitude toward the world has changed from a sad to an equable stoicism, and her austerity from a melancholy asceticism to a good-humored acceptance of shortages both of goods and loves.

The melancholy of *Excellent Women* dissipates in the course of the novel; it is replaced by a mild cheerfulness that feels genuine because it is based on an acceptance of things as they are. The auster-

ity of the story is not a matter of puritanical harshness but of matter-of-fact circumstance. The mildness and conciliatory spirit that prevail are the story's essence.

With the publication of *Excellent Women,* Pym achieved a small but faithful following and seemed assured of a friendly critical reception for subsequent books. From both inclination and necessity, she continued to work for the International African Institute, and settled into a pattern of writing that enabled her to finish four books in the next ten years.

Jane and Prudence followed *Excellent Women* in 1953. A less ambitious and more playful novel than *Excellent Women,* it is more obviously "literary" in its inspiration and more explicitly comic. The slight plot derives from romantic comedy. It is based on a love triangle involving a vain widower, a beautiful young woman with a taste for unhappy love affairs, and a plain but resourceful lady's companion, Jessie Morrow, resurrected from *Crampton Hodnet* and in this incarnation determined to marry and free herself from thralldom to Miss Doggett. The story is told mostly from the point of view of Jane Cleveland, the clever but addled wife of the local vicar, who has a taste for matchmaking and compares herself alternately to Chaucer's Pandarus and Jane Austen's Emma Woodhouse, the most famous (though finally unsuccessful) matchmakers of English literature.

The setting is a nameless village in the south of England, not far from London, a few years after World War II. The village is neither timeless and idyllic like the one in *Some Tame Gazelle* nor grimly modernized like the village in Pym's last novel, *A Few Green Leaves.* Pym does not make any particular historical point about the setting; it is simply a village as it would have been in the early 1950's. It has a too-large, rather desolate vicarage, inadequately heated, a tea shop that serves light meals and has to struggle with food shortages, and a pub where the slightly disreputable are likely to appear at lunchtime. Unlike a Jane Austen village, this one is not at all a self-enclosed world. The social horizon of the village is widened by the characters' frequent trips to and from London. It partakes both of the fluid movement of people in the metropolis and the intimacy of a small community.

The Jane and Prudence of the title are Jane Cleveland and Prudence Bates, a pair of women friends who, like the sisters Belinda and Harriet

Bede, have their roots in *Don Quixote.* They do not embody the contrast between don Quixote and Sancho Panza, as Belinda and Harriet do. Rather, Jane and Prudence are both like don Quixote: together they attempt a literary reconstruction of the world around them into one filled with adventure.

Prudence looks for amorous adventures. Beautiful, imaginative, and sentimental, she is at twenty-nine still occupied with reconstituting the busy romantic life she enjoyed as a university student. She is always ready to idealize some quite ordinary man and turn her relations with him into a high-flown romance, as don Quixote did with the dirty, flirtatious servant-maid Dulcinea del Toboso. For Prudence, romance is by definition star-crossed and destined to end unhappily; consequently, she is often looking for someone new. This trait makes her an ideal subject for Jane the matchmaker, who, in order to practice her trade, needs someone whose affections are mobile.

Prudence has constructed an artificial world out of romantic narrative. Like don Quixote and Emma Bovary, she is a great reader of love stories. Here she is in bed with a book that

described a love affair in the fullest sense of the word and sparing no detail, but all in a very intellectual sort of way and there were a good many quotations from Donne. It was difficult to imagine that her love for Arthur Grampian could ever come to anything like this, and indeed she was hardly conscious of him as she read on into the small hours of the morning to the book's inevitable but satisfying unhappy ending.

(p. 47)

Jane, in addition to encouraging the amorous imaginings of Prudence, turns every commonplace event into an adventure out of a book. Having studied English at Oxford and written a short book of essays, she is still a great reader. She reads life by the light of the book, trying to force literary conceptions on an often recalcitrant reality. When she first began her life as a clergyman's wife, Jane had "taken great pleasure in imagining herself" in this role, "starting with Trollope and working through the Victorian novelists to the present-day gallant, cheerful wives who ran large houses and families on far too little money and sometimes wrote articles about it in the *Church Times* [a key publication in Pym's works]" (p. 8).

But Jane is too fantastical, impractical, and ab-

sent-minded to be successful as a clergyman's wife. She scarcely knows the location of the kitchen in her own house, turning the preparation of meals over to her daughter and the daily cleaner. Her conversation with her husband's parishioners often follows the course of literary association rather than the actual social situation, leaving those who do not know her well feeling puzzled and obscurely offended:

. . . she began to ask Mr. Oliver about his work. It must be so interesting working in a bank, she thought.

"Interesting?" he echoed. "Well, yes, it is in a way, I suppose."

"I always think of the medieval banking houses in Florence; great times those must have been," went on Jane rather wildly.

"I should think there have been a good many changes since then," observed Nicholas dryly. "What department do you work in?"

"I'm in the Executor and Trustee Department at the moment," said Mr. Oliver.

"How that must put you in mind of your own mortality!" said Jane, clasping her hands under her chin in rather an affected way. "You must see the worst and best sides of people too—I believe it always comes out over money."

(pp. 63–64)

Out of literary language, Jane has constructed an artificial world that only incidentally parallels the real one. Jane often tries to sacrifice the event to the phrase.

Given two female characters who want to make life follow literature, it is inevitable that when they meet in chapter 1 at a college reunion, courtship and matchmaking should become the theme of their revived friendship. The target is to be the handsome, vain widower Fabian Driver. Jane muses to herself as she conceives her plan:

Really, she was almost like Pandarus, she told herself, only it was to be a courtship and marriage according to the most decorous conventions. Fabian was a widower and Prudence was a spinster; there wasn't even the embarrassment of divorce. No, when she thought it over, Jane decided she was really much more like Emma Woodhouse.

(p. 96)

Prudence and Fabian get off to a promising start, but events do not unfold accordingly. For one thing, the lovers do not like each other very much.

Prudence is all too aware that Fabian is vain and boring. Fabian is discomfited by Prudence's cleverness and her graceful "literary" letters. Both are good-looking enough not to be particularly grateful for the attentions of a good-looking person. Plain Jessie Morrow, who lives next door to Fabian, is taken by his looks and loves him enough not to mind his affectations and selfishness. She rather easily wins him away from Prudence, to the consternation of her tyrannical employer, Miss Doggett, and to the temporary disappointment of Jane Cleveland, who has assumed, mistakenly, that handsome people naturally couple with one another.

The novel ends with Jane planning to bring together Prudence and the local Member of Parliament, who now seems to her much more "suitable" than Fabian Driver. For both Jane and Prudence, the game is more important than the goal. Through matchmaking and courtship, they keep transmuting the dullness of ordinary life into drama and excitement. If one of Prudence's romances ended in a match, the game would be over. Better to keep losing so as to be able to keep playing.

Jane and Prudence is one of Pym's most purely funny novels. It handles the theme of appearance and reality, convention and fact, in a light and playful way. It develops with delightful invention and variety Pym's perennial thesis that, though there is a love story in everyone's life, eros never plays by the book.

LESS THAN ANGELS *AND* NO FOND RETURN OF LOVE

IN *Less than Angels* (1955), Pym returns to London and to a circle of professional anthropologists. Unlike the genteel London of *Excellent Women,* the London of *Less than Angels* is the scruffy bohemia of research students and their sexual partners. There are no parish churches to provide a center, no network of neighborhood friends, no clergymen or pious spinsters. The concrete community of Pimlico has been replaced by the abstract "community" of a learned profession.

We are in an entirely modern world, postreligious and fragmented, in which human relations are noncommittal and in flux. Lovers and friends come and go, in pursuit of new people or new career opportunities. A kind of busy, crowded isolation is the usual condition of life. Typically, characters adopt a stance of detachment, either ironic or matter-of-fact, to protect themselves from the shocks of frequent engagements and disengagements. London is represented as a crowd of people constantly crisscrossing the city on foot and by bus, by underground, and by taxi. They notice one another only in a hurried and oblique way, all intent on following their own paths.

The theme of isolation is embodied in all three milieus represented in the novel as well as in the central characters. It is seen not as a special condition but as a common fate. Isolation is most intense in inner London, in the pubs and libraries where the anthropologists gather. The research students in anthropology are preoccupied with their own individual misery, and comparatively indifferent to that of their colleagues, who are all potential competitors for grants and jobs.

. . . the room, as well as being a general dumping-ground for unwanted anthropological specimens, was also regarded as a kind of no-man's land, where former students of the department, who had nowhere else to go, might find a corner in which to write up their field-notes. There were one or two tables spread with papers and these were spasmodically occupied by these shabby hangers-on. They lived in the meaner districts of London or in impossibly remote suburbs on grants which were always miserably inadequate, their creative powers stifled by poverty and family troubles.

(pp. 48–49)

The senior anthropologists live in comfort, but at their gatherings, they talk furiously without listening, observe with malice, and keep themselves constantly on the lookout to settle old scores and form new alliances.

In the suburbs where the young anthropology student Deirdre Swan lives with her mother and aunt, the isolation is not so naked but is equally pervasive. The mother and aunt spy on Alaric Lydgate, who lives next door, from their upstairs window, a mode of one-way contact that they prefer to actually talking to him. Alaric himself makes a particularly poignant statement of the attractions of solitude by putting on an African mask in the evening:

He often sat like this in the evenings, withdrawing himself from the world, feeling in the stuffy darkness of the mask that he was back again in his native-built house, listening to the rain falling outside. He often thought what a good thing it would be if the wearing of masks or animals' heads could become customary for persons over a certain age. How restful social intercourse would be if the face did not have to assume any expression—the strained look of interest, the simulated delight or surprise, the anxious concern one didn't really feel. Alaric often avoided looking into people's eyes when he spoke to them, fearful of what he might see there, for life was very terrible whatever sort of front we might put on it.

(p. 57)

Even in the traditional English farming village where Tom Mallow goes to visit his family, people maintain a distance, either suspicious or indifferent, from one another. When Tom arrives, his uncle barely looks up from the television, and his brother gives him only a cursory greeting.

The description of Alaric in his mask is as close as Pym comes to making an explicit statement about isolation. In her work, isolation is not merely a lack or defect. It is a strategy for living in peace and safety, especially suitable for those who are too fragile to withstand the shocks and jars of direct human contact. Isolation exacts a terrible price in emptiness and sadness, but is no more condemned by Pym than are the odd loves that often engage her characters. Any love is to be preferred to isolation, but for some, isolation is what life has brought them to, and Pym writes about it with the acceptance she brought to every condition she felt to be true to human life.

The isolation of the heroine in *Less than Angels* springs more from her situation than her temperament. Catherine Oliphant is the only one of Pym's protagonists who is a writer. A free-lancer who composes fiction for women's magazines, she works at home alone. She has no family visible in the novel, no religious faith or church affiliation, no network of professional friends. She knows many people and is generous and hospitable, but she has no close friends, no confidante. She leads a brave, self-reliant, lonely life. She has a considerable capacity for sentiment, but is used to drawing back from it with an ironic shrug. Her characteristic manner is one of friendly, good-humored mockery.

Catherine's lover, Tom Mallow, recently returned from Africa, lives with her, but on an uncommitted, permanently "temporary" basis. He has detached himself from his family of country gentry in order to become an anthropologist; he

detaches himself from Catherine by getting involved with the very youthful Deirdre. He detaches himself from Deirdre by returning to Africa, where he can live the life of neutral observation thought to be suitable to his profession. As he prepares to leave, Catherine says,

"Your people wait for you. . . . How soothing it will be to get away from all this complexity of personal relationships to the simplicity of a primitive tribe, whose only complications are in their kinship structure and rules of land tenure, which you can observe with the anthropologist's calm detachment."

(p. 186)

Catherine herself lives the life of an outside observer, but her mode of observation is lively and inventive, warm and playful. In the opening scene of the novel, she is alone, sitting in a cafeteria in central London and observing the cafeteria line moving past the stained glass windows and the mosaic peacocks on the walls of the elaborately decorated establishment. She entertains herself by imagining her fellow diners to be tourists moving in a line through a Byzantine church in Ravenna, embroidering the theme with humor and speculation. By reinventing what she observes she invests it with something of herself. Like a reader absorbed in a book, she has no awareness of being alone.

By the use of her imagination, Catherine animates her world and overcomes the distance between herself and others. She has the magical privilege of the writer—that of being simultaneously inside and outside of events. Pym does not present Catherine as "the artist," since Catherine writes potboilers for women's magazines. The way her imagination works is seen as a general human characteristic present to a greater or lesser degree in everyone, not a special prerogative of the writer.

The changing fortunes of Tom Mallow are the basis for the rather slim story that runs through the novel. He returns from Africa to finish his thesis, moves back in with Catherine, meets Deirdre, moves out of Catherine's (at her insistence), finishes his thesis, and returns to Africa. There he is killed by accident in the course of a local election riot that his curiosity led him to mingle in.

The news of his death is handled with Pym's characteristic comic displacement of accent. To report his death, Pym as author interrupts a conversation between Catherine and Deirdre about the problems of sending and receiving Christmas cards to Tom in Africa. Pym's narratorial report ends with an account of a young official's worry about what to do with Tom's Christmas cards, which he has found already addressed.

As is characteristic in Pym's work, the death has a rather tonic effect on the survivors, and they bestir themselves to make good their loss. Deirdre takes up with another young anthropologist, who will inherit Tom's grant; Catherine gets together with Alaric Lydgate. The characters have the wit and energy to stay a little ahead of the sadness that pursues them. Tom disappears from the world, but his loss is soon covered over by the busy network of connections and disconnections the characters weave for themselves. Pym has enough ironic detachment to do justice both to the fact of death and to the scramble to get away from it and move life along. At the end, the characters are left dancing as hard as ever, in tenuous couples or alone.

No Fond Return of Love (1961) opens with the heroine, Dulcie Mainwaring, attending a conference of indexers and bibliographers in a girls' boarding school in the depths of the country. Her fiancé has just broken off their engagement, giving the unconvincing reason that she is too good for him. The first sentence of the novel is, "There are various ways of mending a broken heart, but perhaps going to a learned conference is one of the more unusual." The learned conference and the yearning heart are two of the major components of the novel. The third, which drives the plot along, is amorous curiosity.

The novel is set largely in comfortable middle-class suburban London. The characters are mostly academic, or semi-academic—editing journals, running libraries, doing indexes and bibliographies. The milieu is one of apparent respectability and dowdiness, but eccentricity crops up everywhere, and eros is at work creating odd and fantastical longings and alliances. The novel is full of caricatures, slightly modified comic stereotypes, and odd couples.

This profusion of caricatures may be accounted for by the traditional oddities attributed to the learned professions, their abstractedness and inconsequence having long been objects of satire. The stereotypes are derived from the familiar *dramatis personae* of romantic comedy: the handsome brothers, the pair of ladies in pursuit of a beloved, the affected and amorous widow, the ingenue and

the juvenile romantic interest, the servant-confidante, the courtly gnome, and so on. The couples are a characteristic Pym gallery, in which there is almost everything except a regular married couple: women friends living together, mother and daughter, brother and sister, widow and lodger, even, in a minor way, ingenue and juvenile lead. Eros is busy matching and mismatching, coupling and uncoupling in this seemingly subdued world in which everyone has a love interest of one kind or another.

Dulcie Mainwaring's love finds expression largely through her voracious curiosity about her beloved, the handsome Aylwin Forbes. Aylwin edits a learned journal and seventeenth-century poetic texts, and has come to the conference to give a paper on "Some Problems of an Editor." Comically, he faints while delivering the paper and is revived by Dulcie's smelling salts. As a result of this episode in which the traditional genders of fainter and rescuer are reversed, Dulcie falls in love and virtually turns into a private detective investigating the life of her beloved.

In this respect, the character is similar to the author. In *A Very Private Eye*, Hazel Holt says of Barbara Pym:

She had always had a passion for "finding out" about people who interested or attracted her. Tracking people down and looking them up were part of her absorbing interest (that continued all her life) in "research into the lives of ordinary people." Her researches ranged from looking people up in *Who's Who, Crockford* or street directories to the actual "tailing" of the object of her investigation. She was very resourceful at this and often said that she would have made a good detective.

(p. 10)

Pym's heroines are generally characterized by their lively curiosity, but with Dulcie curiosity becomes a mania that overrides her otherwise highly developed sense of propriety and makes her forget all about "suitability." She looks up Aylwin's name in reference books. She smuggles herself under an assumed name into a jumble sale being given in the house of Aylwin's mother-in-law and makes a purchase from Aylwin's estranged wife. She visits the church of Aylwin's clerical brother, also very handsome and much pursued by amorous women, and draws his housekeeper into conversation. She visits the country hotel owned by Aylwin's eccentric mother, finds out *her* story, and eavesdrops on conversations between Aylwin and his wife and mother-in-law. She visits the grave of his father.

As Sherlock Holmes must have Dr. Watson to assist in his curious investigations, so must Dulcie have a partner in prying. Viola Dace, already in love with Aylwin, supplies the need. The two contrasting women, Dulcie and Viola, blond and brunette, quiet and theatrical, neat and messy, subdued and extravagant, become a pair of damsels errant in search of their beloved. They share strategies and speculations and support one another in their enterprise, which seems more suitable to schoolgirls in pursuit of a rock star than to two presumably staid women in their thirties in pursuit of the editor of a learned journal. Their goal is not to capture the beloved, or even catch up with him, but to have him always in view and know all about him. In true voyeur fashion, they are terrified of being discovered, of being seen rather than seeing.

Though Viola makes a great point of being unusual and "literary," she abandons her presumably romantic quest the moment she attracts the attention of Bill Sedge, who deals in women's knitwear. Bill likes her and wants to marry her, and that is good enough for Viola. Dulcie is disappointed in Viola, feeling that despite all her theatrical sensibility, Viola is a commonplace woman incapable of following the high romantic road of love-yearning for an unattainable beloved. Bizarre-looking Viola, it turns out, merely looks strange. Normal-looking Dulcie really *is* strange, and continues her quixotic enterprise.

The object of this pursuit is a typical Pym beloved—handsome, vain, nervous, self-absorbed, all too willing to exploit his women admirers, but absentmindedly rather than systematically. He is the romantic beloved as fuddy-duddy. Aylwin has the looks to be a hero, but he is forty-seven and seems pathetically old to eighteen-year-old Laurel, whom he courts unsuccessfully. He is also unable to hang onto his wife, Marjorie. They have been separated, and after an attempted reconciliation, Marjorie runs off with a man she meets on a train. At the end of the novel, Aylwin has gone through the available supply of women, except for Dulcie, and so decides to turn to her.

The novel ends as his taxi pulls up in front of her suburban house, and he gets out with a bouquet in his arms. The lodger next door looks on from the upstairs window, wondering what is going on. Dulcie's last thought recorded in the novel is puzzlement as to why he is bringing flowers when she already has so many in the garden. Typically, the tale ends with a voyeur, an offbeat thought, and a romance not yet defined or legitimized.

Curiosity has had its wild run, and perhaps Dulcie will now, somewhere beyond the end of the novel, settle down to all the tedium of knowing more than she wants to about Aylwin.

AN UNSUITABLE ATTACHMENT *AND* A GLASS OF BLESSINGS

COMPLETED in 1963, *An Unsuitable Attachment* did not find a publisher until 1982, two years after Barbara Pym's death. After it was refused by her usual publisher, Jonathan Cape, Pym unsuccessfully offered it to almost every major English publisher. She entered a "time in the wilderness" when for seventeen years she could find no publisher for her work. *An Unsuitable Attachment* is not one of Pym's best books, but it is full of attractive characters and scenes, certainly worthy of publication. Pym's characteristic mildness, which is especially in evidence in this novel, was unacceptable to the 1960's taste for spice and flash and revolt. Pym suffered a loss of confidence in her talent, but kept writing nevertheless, encouraged by her friends and her own hopeful sense that perhaps her work was only out of fashion, not intrinsically inferior to what it had been.

By 1982 the revival of interest in Pym reached a point where readers seemed eager for everything she had written. The novel was issued with a foreword by Philip Larkin, in which he mixes praise for the characteristic Pymean touches with criticism of the weakness of the central story. One can only agree with his judgment.

The main narrative thread is the courtship of Ianthe Broome and John Challow. The daughter of a Church of England clergyman, Ianthe is a thirty-five-year-old librarian. She is unmistakably a lady of the old school, quiet, correct, gentle, and shy. John Challow is five years younger and of a lower social class. The two meet when he comes to work in the library after a rather mixed work history, including a stint as a movie extra. When Ianthe first meets John, she thinks, ". . . his shoes seemed to be a little too pointed—not quite what men one knew would wear" (p. 49). That is about the extent of

John Challow's unsuitability. His shoes testify that he is slightly less of a gentleman than a suitor of Ianthe should be; Ianthe is slightly more of a prim lady than she should be in the libertarian times in which she lives. But after some slight misunderstandings the two get together and the novel ends with their marriage.

Ianthe Broome is the only one of Pym's heroines to be awarded a marriage at the end of her novel. The other heroines either do not marry at all or do so somewhere beyond the end of their book, as we find out incidentally in a subsequent novel. Ianthe is neither silly nor ironic, but just sweetly conventional. She has more affinities with romance than with comedy and learns the Pymean lesson, in a very gentle form, that love is where you find it. The unsuitability of the unsuitable attachment is too insubstantial to create much dramatic interest. Pym's narrative lines are usually rather slight, but this one is the slightest of all, and does not quite fulfill its function of generating enough dramatic energy to carry the novel forward.

The supporting couples supply the comedy and dramatic interest lacking in Ianthe Broome and John Challow. Mark and Sophia Ainger, the vicar and his wife, are notably "good," though unobtrusively eccentric, and have about them a slight flavor of pathos. Sophia's cat, Faustina, is an independent spirit amid all the conventionalities and timidities of the human characters. Sophia's sister, Penelope ("the Pre-Raphaelite beatnik" as she is called on page 39), is desperate to find a man; she is courted in a lackadaisical and ambiguous way by the anthropologist Rupert Stonebird. Penelope's ever-alert search for a man and her clumsy efforts at being glamorous provide the comedy that is missing in the ever-correct Ianthe. Around these couples is a group of curious parishioners, a gently caricatured chorus that comments on the activities of the main couples.

The major success of the book is its picture of the Italian trip; it is the only time Barbara Pym ventured onto foreign soil in her published novels. (Among her draft novels, she has one with a Finnish setting and another with a brief trip to Hungary.) Mark Ainger organizes an Easter trip to Rome for a group of his parishioners. From the moment of their arrival, they behave like parodies of the English abroad. One traveler looks out the window of the plane to see if she can catch an Italian kicking a dog or beating a horse, since for-

eigners are known to be cruel to animals. Another regrets her failure to use the bathroom on the plane, since she fears she will not find another clean one in Italy. As soon as they have checked into their pensione, the whole party goes to Babbington's, the famous outpost of Victorian Englishness, to have tea and play with the resident cat, after which they feel much better.

Aside from the satire on the English abroad, who are more English even than when at home, there is a more ambitious satire on the literary tradition of the Italian Journey. In Goethe, Stendhal, Forster, Mann, and Gide, among others, the journey of North Europeans or the English to the sunny South, to Italy, signifies a casting off of puritanical restraints, an awakening of passion and love of art, an encounter with "real" sex, and possibly with disease or danger.

Pym satirizes all these conventions of the Italian Journey. To begin with, she makes a point of telling us (accurately) that Italy is not all that sunny. Much of the time the weather is cloudy or drizzly. Pym's visitors enact their own homely, down-to-earth version of the journey of aesthetic discovery. They do not develop a passion for art, but dutifully busy themselves with the chores of the tourist, making the rounds of museums, churches, and historic sites. Like her less robust literary ancestor, Henry James's ingenue Daisy Miller, middle-aged Sister Dew visits an ancient amphitheater by moonlight. Daisy Miller falls ill and dies; Sister Dew sprains her ankle and is carried off to a nearby emergency ward. Ianthe does not meet a passionate Italian, but comes to realize while she is away from him that she is in love with John Challow.

The high point of the satire comes when Sophia and Ianthe go to Salerno to visit Sophia's aunt, who has lived in Italy for many years with her lover. We are to meet the romantic English lady and her Italian demon lover. The aunt, now sixty or so, seems a little raffish and almost sinister, with hair dyed a startling black. The demon lover is a Dottore/Professore wearing a striped suit that suggests the skin of an animal. But he is formidably articulate and correct, and the uneasy party of four sit through their meeting scrambling (successfully, on the whole) for conversational common ground. The Dottore finds out that the ladies live in North London and directs the conversation to Kensal Green Cemetery, a theme on which they all dutifully enlarge. So much for the romance of *that* encounter with the exotic South and its imperious passions.

But deflation is not the final point. Shortly after the visit, Sophia with delight unwraps a little bundle of lemon leaves to reach the delicious raisins nested in them. In this small object there is surprise and a modest joy. The magic of Italy is not on a stagey terrace above Salerno, but in an inconspicuous nest of lemon leaves. Again, Pym has the food of daily life offer the fulfillments that are missing from the more seemingly important experiences of life.

An Unsuitable Attachment has enough of Pym's invention and characteristic turns of incident to please her devoted readership, but it is not strong enough to be a satisfactory introduction to her work.

A Glass of Blessings (1958) is set in a different London from that of *Less Than Angels;* it is the London of the privileged upper middle class—people who have servants, automobiles, and well-appointed houses in the West End. In *Less Than Angels,* Catherine Oliphant earns an uncertain living as a freelance writer and is sponged on by anthropology research students who show up suspiciously close to mealtimes. In *A Glass of Blessings,* Wilmet Forsyth is married to an upper-level civil servant and lives like a permanent guest or a pampered adolescent in the luxurious home of her mother-in-law, Sybil. Her only domestic duties are to help occasionally with the flower arranging; she is childless and has no outside job. Her husband and her mother-in-law are concerned only that Wilmet should keep herself amused.

Wilmet's social life at home is urbane, witty, and decorous, with no awkward intrusions of ignorance, bad manners, or ill temper. Her social life in her parish has a lively mixture of ages, manners, and classes; the parishioners are sometimes a little vulgar and quarrelsome. Wilmet enjoys her parish life as long as she can retreat easily to the uniform elegance of her mother-in-law's home. Wilmet is attractive, well-dressed, charming, and lively, but also snobbish and more than a little vain. She regards love and admiration as the natural right of attractive women like herself, and cannot imagine how less attractive women ever manage to attract lovers or husbands. She is mystified by the "burden-bearing" women she knows through her church. Though she enjoys her freedom, Wilmet is sometimes restless. Since she has no desire to get a

job, is not interested in drink, and has an aversion to doing charity work, Wilmet naturally turns to extramarital romance for entertainment.

Like Emma Bovary, she is the bored young wife of a stolid, reliable husband, and she wants some excitement. Wilmet, however, is prudent and cool-headed, with no plans to do anything that would endanger her comfortable place in life. When Harry, the husband of her best friend, Rowena Talbot, makes a pass at her, she has lunch with him but at no point considers a sexual affair. When she runs into Rowena's "unsatisfactory" but very handsome brother, Piers Longridge, she is much attracted, and takes an evening extension language course from him. Here is the way she thinks of "doing good" for her two admirers.

> Still, there could be no harm in having lunch with Harry or walking with Piers in the park. I could show Harry what a good wife Rowena was; and as for Piers, drifting and rootless, perhaps often drunk, it might be that my friendship could be beneficial to him. It seemed an excellent winter programme.
>
> (p. 47)

The idea is to have adventures that combine the romantic and the edifying. But of course Harry is not interested in getting together with Wilmet to discuss his wife's virtues. Piers has already been rescued, it turns out, by a working-class lover, Keith, who fusses and nags and cleans up and generally forces Piers to pull himself together. After the initial shock of these discoveries, Wilmet accepts them equably enough, and proceeds to make friends with Piers and Keith. This slender narrative is the main story line of the book, but the chief interest lies not in the story, but in Wilmet's changing way of looking at the world.

In the course of the novel, almost every one of her beliefs is overturned by the course of events. She believes that unimaginative men like her husband Rodney never look at other women. But he confesses near the end of the book that while she was seeing Harry, *he* was keeping dinner engagements with Prudence Bates (of *Jane and Prudence*). She believes that handsome men are the rightful property of attractive women like herself. But the gloriously good-looking Father Ransome marries plain Mary Beamish, Wilmet's best friend in the parish.

Wilmet also believes that erring men are rescued,

if at all, by respectable women like herself. But Piers is rescued by a vulgar, bossy young man who makes his living as a model for a knitwear magazine. Finally, she believes that romance is the privilege of the young, or at least youngish. But her sixty-nine-year-old mother-in-law marries Professor Root, and Rodney and Wilmet have to move out of her house to make room for him. Life, it seems, obeys none of the rules laid down by the conventions Wilmet has learned.

Wilmet is intelligent, adaptable, and good-humored, so that she gets the point quickly when it is made in an unmistakable way, and accepts things as they are without undue discomfort. Love in *A Glass of Blessings* breaks all the rules, as it usually does in Pym's novels. Taking people and their loves on their own terms is, in essence, a kind of informal Christian charity. Acceptance without judgment always clears the air and opens a way to further developments.

Acceptance is carried far enough to become Christian charity proper in the incident of Wilf Bason, Father Thames, and the jeweled Fabergé egg. Wilmet has found a male cook, Wilf Bason, for the clergy house. She discovers to her horror that he is a kleptomaniac and has taken possession of Father Thames's valuable Fabergé egg. After she has persuaded Wilf to put it back, Wilmet has tea with Father Thames:

> Father Thames had picked up the Fabergé egg and was saying in an indulgent tone, "So my egg is back again. I wondered how long it would be away this time."
> "You mean . . . ?" I faltered.
> "Oh yes, Bason borrows it every now and then. He doesn't realize that I know, of course. He thinks I don't notice." Father Thames smiled. "He is very fond of beautiful things, you know."
> "Yes, I did know," was all I could think of to say.
> "It seems selfish to keep one's possessions too much to oneself, doesn't it, when they can give so much pleasure to others."
> I could hardly fail to agree with him, and after that there seemed to be nothing more to say.
>
> (p. 183)

By the end of the novel, Wilmet Forsyth has not turned into a Sister of Charity. But she has shed her more conventional expectations and her self-absorption. She finds that taking people on their own terms gives her more than it takes away. She has opened her heart not to a new romance but to a charitable love that includes Keith, Mary Beamish—and even her own husband.

A Glass of Blessings is the most elegant and gossamer of Barbara Pym's comedies, and it is the one that most consistently embodies the theme of the moral education of the heroine, an education conducted with a light and playful hand. Wilmet does not have to confront the darker facts of existence. She merely has to learn that other people are likely to act to suit themselves rather than her, and that they are likely to play by their own rules, not hers. For a vibrant young woman with a good deal of self-confidence, such knowledge is merely surprising, not upsetting. Wilmet is Pym's smiling tribute to the blessing of a lively temperament and a fortunate life.

THE SWEET DOVE DIED
AND QUARTET IN AUTUMN

BARBARA PYM worked on *The Sweet Dove Died* (1978) from 1963 to 1969, cutting and recasting until she achieved a level of polish and brilliance unequalled by her other works. Apparently her inability to find a publisher made her adopt an almost Flaubertian standard of perfection. The rather relaxed fun and geniality of her earlier novels are replaced by tense economy and a cutting irony. The mood is one of carefully restrained bitterness. The novel is built on a series of love triangles, and has at its center Leonora Eyre, the least appealing of Pym's heroines, but one of the most compelling.

The exploration of Leonora's character is the chief concern of the novel. She is another of Pym's educated, unmarried women living in London. But in Leonora, Pym explores the darker possibilities of the type—self-absorption, contempt for others, emotional and sexual coldness, ruthless manipulation. Leonora is an aging beauty of exquisite taste and refinement. With a private income and a beautiful flat, she does not work. She has no ties to a parish or any other institution. Her chief activity seems to be shopping for beautiful clothes and perfect antiques. She has reached middle age without ever having a real love affair—only decorous flirtations in the great gardens of Europe.

Earlier Pym heroines may be prim and nervous, but they are also generous and warmhearted. Their humanity is not impaired by their aloneness.

Leonora's aloneness is the product of her disdain for other people and her distaste for lovemaking. She worships perfection in things and in people—not moral perfection but perfection of style and appearance, the unflawed vase, the unlined face. She lives to be admired, but even her admirers scarcely arouse her liking.

Leonora embodies the central theme of the novel, which is the sexual politics of narcissism, the diplomacy and warfare not so much of love as of self-love. The theme is also realized in James, the young man she comes to idolize, and in his subsequent lover, Ned. All three are strikingly attractive, self-involved, and unfeeling toward others.

There is a circle of minor female characters around Leonora who serve to put her into sharper relief. Each of the other female characters loves something or somebody in a way that is not just a reflex of vanity. Leonora's dowdy middle-aged friend Meg is attached to a gay young man who disappears when he has a lover and returns when he does not. She patiently keeps his favorite Riesling in the fridge, and forgives him when he returns. Leonora, on the other hand, coolly turns James away when he returns after such an escapade, regretting that she has permitted him to ruffle her life so disagreeably.

James's girlfriend before he takes up with Ned is a vague, badly dressed young woman named Phoebe, who lives in a messy cottage in the country and does literary research. She is timid and unfocused, but she feels a quick sexual passion for James and acts on it at once. In contrast, for Leonora, one of James's chief merits is that the question of sexual relations does not arise as they play at their artificial comedy of beautiful mother and adoring surrogate son.

Leonora's neighbor Liz, embittered by divorce, spends all her time and love in breeding Siamese cats for competition. Her love has only that one outlet, but the cats have the merit over Leonora's furniture of being alive. Leonora's friend Joan, who lives in the country, is attached to her noisy children and pipe-smoking husband and finds the stiff, overdressed Leonora something of a problem when she comes for the weekend.

The first triangle is formed at a rare-book auction, where Leonora meets Humphrey Boyce, a sixty-year-old antiques dealer, and his very handsome, sexually ambiguous nephew James. Humphrey likes Leonora, who likes James. She cultivates Humphrey in order to get to James. This pattern of crisscrossed attractions brings the first triangle of Leonora, Humphrey, and James into play.

Each of the three is more interested in possession and display than in genital love. Leonora does not want James as a sexual partner, but as a young and beautiful trophy. Humphrey is willing to play along because he likes being seen with Leonora in elegant restaurants and at the opera. James likes Leonora's flattering attentions, but he will also sneak off to his sexual lovers, first a woman, then a man. The erotic merry-go-round of Viennese bedroom farce is adapted to the conditions of British high comedy. The comedy of opening and closing bedroom and closet doors is replaced by the maneuvering of lovers who spend much of their time in verbal sparring and discreet spying on one another.

Past forty, Leonora is enchanted by James's youthful good looks. James receives her love offerings with detachment and slight surprise. Leonora is delighted by his humdrum conversation, and this makes James feel, a little uncertainly, that he may be more interesting than he had imagined. Leonora manages to break up the affair between James and Phoebe and thus end the second triangle: that of Leonora, James, and Phoebe. Leonora then fixes up a flat in her house for James. While he is living there, they play the roles of adoring, glamorous older woman and perfect son-lover-friend.

The flimsy nature of this ostentatiously "perfect" arrangement becomes evident when James is seduced by Ned, a sexually accomplished young American academic on sabbatical leave. With this move, the third triangle of Leonora, James, and Ned comes to the foreground. Leonora is a sentimental narcissist, James a passive one. Ned, however, is interested in power, and he successfully undertakes to separate James from Leonora just to show that he can do it. He has little difficulty in persuading James to move out. Leonora is stricken:

The days seemed long and hopeless and Leonora began to wish she had not given up working, for a routine job would at least have filled the greater part of the day. Yet she lacked the energy and initiative to find herself an occupation; she remembered the dreadful woman . . . she had met at the Murrays' party and the impertinent suggestions she had made about the useful voluntary work one could do. But when Leonora came to consider them each had something wrong with it: how could she do church work when she never went near a church, or work for old people when she found them boring and physically repellent, or with handicapped children when the very thought of them was too upsetting?

(p. 181)

Her chief solace in her loneliness is her possessions.

She had always cared as much for inanimate objects as for people and now spent hours looking after her possessions, washing the china and cleaning the silver obsessively and rearranging them in her rooms. The shock of finding that James had taken the fruitwood mirror had upset her quite disproportionately. . . .

(p. 182)

The episode of Leonora-James-Ned has a cold brilliance and wit that suggest Restoration comedy with its rakes and coquettes and their intrigues and their dance of ever-changing partners. *The Sweet Dove Died* presents this triangle as filled with a fascinating, often amusing perversity, but it also does justice to Leonora's aching sense of loss. She turns out to be more adept at suffering than at love.

After Ned leaves for America, the original triangle of Leonora-James-Humphrey is reestablished. This time Humphrey wins Leonora, whatever that may mean, and James is sent away. Leonora decides to give up being the admirer and go back to her old position of the one admired. This is the last paragraph of the novel:

The sight of Humphrey with the peonies reminded her that he was taking her to the Chelsea Flower Show tomorrow. It was the kind of thing one liked to go to, and the sight of such large and faultless blooms, so exquisite in colour, so absolutely correct in all their finer points, was a comfort and satisfaction to one who loved perfection as she did. Yet, when one came to think of it, the only flowers that were really perfect were those, like the peonies that went so well with one's charming room, that possessed the added grace of having been presented to oneself.

(p. 208)

The Sweet Dove Died has no truly likable characters, and thus the reader is denied easy access to the story through identification. As readers, we are forced into a somewhat detached position where we experience the book more through our intelligence than our feelings. From that vantage, reading and rereading reveal the beauty and fierce but restrained imaginative energy of the book. It is compact, intense with life, and complete, one of Pym's major successes.

Written in 1973–1976, when Pym was in her sixties and had little hope of finding a publisher, *Quartet in Autumn* (1977) is often considered her best book. It is a masterpiece of concentration and dark irony. In her diary in March of 1972, Pym wrote down the germinal idea for the novel: "Have thought of an idea for a novel based on our office move—all old, crabby characters, petty and obsessive, bad tempered" (*A Very Private Eye,* p. 267). The novel is often thought to be the one work in which Pym turned away from comedy to write tragedy, or at least a very dark and sad realism.

However, in a BBC talk entitled "Finding a Voice," Pym defined her intention in *Quartet in Autumn* as fundamentally comic (*Civil to Strangers and Other Writings,* pp. 385–386):

It's about four people in their early sixties—two men and two women—working in a London office. During the course of the story, the women retire and one of them dies. I wanted to write about the problems and difficulties of this stage in one's life and also to show its comedy and irony—in fact I'd rather put it the other way round; my main concern was with the comedy and irony, the problems and difficulties having been dealt with almost excessively, one might say, elsewhere

Comic the novel may be in its emphasis on incongruity and straying logic, but the comedy is very stark. It is a bleak and minimalist version of her characteristic themes; such laughter as there is has a bitter flavor. The domestic realism goes beyond drabness. The protagonists are not merely inconspicuous and lonely, but old, almost poor, and of no interest to others.

Pym's characteristic narrative of failed human contact is doubled and enacted in an extreme form. A typical Pym novel has two characters who might become a couple, but do not. *Quartet in Autumn* has a quartet of two men and two women of symmetrically contrasting characters who take active measures to maintain their distance from one another. Although the four work together in the same small office, they avoid making friends with each other, each vigilantly guarding an empty privacy. The characters all live alone and only one, Edwin, has ever been married. He is mild-mannered and loves to tour different churches; Norman is angry and sarcastic. Letty is polite, friendly, and kind; Marcia is silent and disturbingly odd.

The women retire and continue to see the men at lunch from time to time. Marcia dies of anorexia and leaves the house she inherited from her mother to Norman, for whom she has never shown any particular regard. The book ends with the three survivors having lunch together in Marcia's house. Marcia's death has brought them together, at least temporarily.

The emptiness and sadness of these lives are transformed by Pym's humorous perspective and by the intensity of the quartet's absorption in the routines of their daily life. Their work is dull and superfluous, and their department is to be abolished when they retire; their personal relations are slight. Yet each character lives busy and absorbed inside a small world of tenaciously retained habits and preoccupations. They pursue their grudges and suspicions energetically. Only Letty is directly aware from time to time of the fuller life that is missing.

After her retirement, Marcia becomes increasingly isolated. She seldom leaves her dusty house in North London, spending her days sitting in the kitchen or rearranging her collection of tinned food and plastic bags. Her only nourishment is tea and biscuits, and often she forgets even those. Her mind drifts in semi-vacancy, yet her life is controlled by a submerged love-longing that she is scarcely aware of. She once followed Norman into the British Museum at lunchtime, but left without speaking to him. One day she drags a shovel through the weeds in her back garden, looking for the grave of her long-dead cat, Snowy, without being quite aware of what she is looking for.

Her great love-longing, however, is for Mr. Strong, the surgeon who performed her mastectomy a few years earlier. On her last vacation before retirement, she takes a long bus ride to the suburban neighborhood in which Mr. Strong lives and stands for a long time in the road, looking at his empty house. The detective impulse that sent Dulcie Mainwaring in *No Fond Return of Love* actively sleuthing after her beloved has here turned into a love-pilgrimage to the shrine of the beloved: a starving old woman looks at the house of her surgeon, imagining with a sense of fulfillment the complete and privileged life he lives there.

After Marcia's final collapse, her chief concern is to be sure that her new nightgowns accompany her in the ambulance to the hospital, where she will be reunited with Mr. Strong. In the high tradition of tragic romance, her nightgown is soon to become her shroud, and her beloved is the harbinger of death. Marcia expresses her amorousness only in these submerged ways, yet it is the governing spirit of her existence. Her anorexia is an expression of her indifference to mere ordinary living, and her bizarre oddities are an expression of her blank but powerful love-hunger.

Marcia is the ultimate romantic who grandly refuses the bread of daily existence. All of Pym's other characters are content to take refuge in the daily round and find comfort in its small pleasures. Marcia is Pym's limit case of the stubborn and willful one who eludes social workers, friends, and the apparatus of the welfare state. For Marcia, avoiding food is no sacrifice but rather a victory over those who try to make her buy fresh vegetables, go for a walk, or take a vacation. Her eventual death is a triumph of the will over the forces of reason and appetite.

The surviving three of the quartet are carried along on the current of daily life, enlivened by efforts to catch one another in small misdemeanors or errors of logic. Their conversation expresses both familiarity and distance. They deal with subjects connected to their loneliness and fears of the future, but their manner is contentious and matter-of-fact. Norman is reading aloud from a newspaper:

"Hypothermia," he read the word slowly. "Another old person found dead. We want to be careful we don't get hypothermia."

"It isn't a thing you *get*," said Marcia bossily. "Not like catching an infectious disease."

"Well, if you were found dead of it, like this old woman here, you could say you'd *got* it, couldn't you?" said Norman, defending his usage.

Letty's hand moved over to the radiator and lingered there. "It's a state or condition, isn't it," she said, "when the body gets cold, loses heat or something like that."

"That's one thing we've got in common then," said Norman, his snappy little voice matching his small spare body. "The chance of being found dead of hypothermia."

Marcia smiled and fingered a leaflet in her handbag, one she had picked up at the library that morning—something about extra heating allowances for the elderly—but she kept the information to herself.

"Cheerful, aren't you," said Edwin, "but perhaps

BARBARA PYM

there's something in it. Four people on the verge of retirement, each one of us living alone, and without any
close relative near—that's us."

(pp. 6–7)

Their common plight does not lead to a common
bond. Letty and Marcia both put their hands out to
extra sources of warmth, literal and symbolic, but
covertly. Letty silently warms her hand at the radiator; Marcia silently fingers the leaflet about heating supplements. Each one keeps separate and
secret inside an envelope of solitariness. However
much desolation may go along with solitude, it
offers security from the complications of personal
relations and from difficult-to-manage emotions.

Barbara Pym's quartet is scarcely an edifying
group. They are cranky and petty, stingy, suspicious, and narrow-minded. They do not care
much for one another or even for themselves. Yet
Marcia, in destroying herself, has some of the
stubborn, unconsciously brave persistence of a
tragic hero. Letty and Norman and Edwin are
timid and conventional, but they are making (for
the moment) a successful stand against oblitera-
tion. With the approach of old age, they remain
completely, incorrigibly, and powerfully themselves. *Quartet in Autumn* is a tribute to the human
ability to make life, to make interest, in characters
in the narrowest of circumstances, with the most
circumscribed of imaginations. Realism has always had the validation of the commonplace as
one of its major goals; *Quartet in Autumn* presses
that project to a new limit.

A FEW GREEN LEAVES

A FEW GREEN LEAVES (1980), Pym's last novel, was
the only one written after her "return from the
wilderness" in 1977. Completed two months
before her death from cancer early in 1980, it is
both a summation and a farewell. As Robert
Emmet Long says, "Remarkably, the novel shows
no sign of haste, and reveals an absolute composure
of mind" (*Barbara Pym,* p. 188).

The setting is a fictional West Oxfordshire village loosely modeled on the village of Finstock,
where Barbara Pym and her sister Hilary had
moved in 1974 after a stroke had led to Barbara's

retirement from the African Institute. Not merely
a convenient setting, the collective life of the village is itself the chief subject.

This village has little in common with the idealized pastoral community in *Some Tame Gazelle.* It
belongs to the England of the 1970's, the world of
the welfare state, television, plastics, synthetic fabrics, junkyards, dying religion, and triumphant
medical science. The traditional inhabitants have
moved out to the modern bungalows that ring the
village. Middle-class people from London and the
universities occupy the village center; they go in
for local customs and, from time to time, church
attendance. The old inhabitants prefer television,
transistor radios, and modern conveniences. The
center of influence has shifted from the church to
the doctor's surgery, and the family of the local
squire have long since moved away. The old order
no longer prevails, but still has a somewhat ghostly
existence in the antiquarian interests of the new
inhabitants and in the old cottages, now renovated
for their urban inhabitants.

The chief representative of the old order is the
local clergyman, Tom Dagnall, his influence now
much diminished. He lives with his sentimental,
discontented sister Daphne in a huge Victorian rectory that he can scarcely afford to heat. His chief
occupation, aside from wandering vaguely around
the village, is doing research on the location of the
deserted medieval village reputed to be somewhere
nearby. He also meditates on death and burial customs while the two doctors preach the doctrine of
healthy living.

Dr. Gellibrand, the older doctor, is gradually
being supplanted by his younger colleague, Dr.
Shrubsole, who also wants to purchase the rectory
from Tom in order to house his growing family and
to signify his growing social predominance. The
old doctor likes expectant mothers; the young one
is interested in geriatrics—a shrewd choice in a
time when old people are multiplying more rapidly
than babies. This crisscrossing of interest and generations brings typical Pymean ironies to bear on
the theme of old and new, past and present.

Into this ancient village with its diminishing but
still visible past comes Emma Howick, an anthropologist in her early thirties, who is staying in
her mother's cottage while she writes up her field
notes. She had planned on her first weekend to
"observe the inhabitants in the time-honoured

manner from behind the shadow of her curtains" (p. 1). But Emma surprises herself by abandoning her post of observation and going out to join the walking party that is forming in front of her house. For the first time in Pym's novels, a protagonist in the first scene acts on her impulse to join in.

Still, Emma's ironic distancing of herself and her distinctly modern taste in landscape set her apart from the rest of the walking party:

Emma glanced at the flowers in the distance. She was becoming rather tired of daffodils. Their Wordsworthian exuberance had been overdone, she felt, crammed into cottage gardens and now such poetic drifts of them in the park and woods. She would have liked to have seen the woods bare in winter, the stark outlines of noble trees. . . .

(p. 4)

This modern preference for bare trees over daffodils is compatible with her disdain for her mother's studies of the Victorian novel and her interest in maintaining her anthropologist's post of disinterested observation.

Emma, however, becomes more old-fashioned as the novel proceeds. At the end, she comes to prefer the absentminded clergyman to the dull and selfish anthropologist with whom she has been having a half-hearted affair. She also decides to write a novel rather than anthropology field notes. She has joined, in a surprisingly thoroughgoing way, the community she thought she would be interested only in observing.

There are intimations of death and dying throughout the novel. The church graveyard is much in Tom Dagnall's thoughts because he has so much trouble finding someone to mow it; Tom and the old doctor often meet in the de Tankerville mausoleum. Tom ruminates at length on Anthony á Wood's discourse on burying in woolens. There are a number of elderly women in uncertain health, who have intimations of their mortality in their faces. Nevertheless, there is only one death, and that one is rendered in a gentle, offbeat way.

The old governess who was at the manor in the old days comes unexpectedly from London for a visit. Taken ill, she is found unconscious in the woods. The buildup is for a death scene in which an old gentlewoman looking for her past returns to the scene of her youth and dies in a poetically apt fashion. But in fact the governess recovers and goes on to enjoy her visit. The even older lady who lives nearby dies instead, during a power outage.

In the next-door cottage Miss Lickerish had not bothered to put on the light at the normal time. She boiled a kettle on the fire and then sat in her chair with a cup of tea at her side and a cat on her knees. But some time during those dark hours the cat left her and sought the warmth of his basket, Miss Lickerish's lap having become strangely chilled.

(p. 227)

When Death comes, it comes gently—to the oldest inhabitant of the village when the lights are off. The cat is the first to know. The young elderly are still intact, even flourishing. Death's dominion is coming, but very gradually.

Religious faith has waned in the village to the point that the church is often almost empty during services. A sign of the times is the loss of faith of Terry Skate, the young gay florist who looks after the de Tankerville mausoleum. Terry has been upset by a trendy clergyman on television, wearing a turtleneck rather than a clerical collar. His faith is not destroyed by intellectual doubt but by the manners of the age. A clergyman in sporty clothes overturns the iconography in Terry's mind. He believes in clerical collars, and when those go, so does his faith.

But in a few others, faith is still intact. After Tom has a disconcerting conversation with Terry Skate about his loss of faith, he speculates about the faith of Miss Lee, who polishes the brasses and wood in the church. He sets out to ask her about her faith but in embarrassment he deflects his question to something simpler and more direct:

"Do you ever wish we had a brass lectern?" he asked. "As they have in some other churches?"

"Oh no, rector," she answered. "I *love* that old wooden bird, and I *love* polishing it. A brass one may look more brilliant, but wood can be very rewarding, you know, and I think I can flatter myself that nobody can get a better polish on it than I do."

Tom turned aside, humbled by her words. It was almost an idea for a sermon, what she had said about brass looking more brilliant but wood being very rewarding. Of course Miss Lee never had doubts! And if she had, she was much too well-bred ever to dream of troubling the rector with such a thing.

(pp. 201–202)

Religious faith may be in decline, but in some, like Miss Lee, it is still strong. Even though her faith is bound up in polishing the wooden bird, as Terry's has been bound up in clerical collars, the much-polished wooden eagle is an emblem of a steady devotion expressed in a domestic task faithfully performed. Religious faith is not a matter of deep thought or transcendent emotion, but of a settled and active piety in daily life. This oblique statement made in the incident of Miss Lee and the wooden eagle is as close as Pym ever came to stating a religious credo. Otherwise she treats church-going and parish life as social rather than religious phenomena, in the manner of Anthony Trollope.

In her valedictory, Pym ends with the few green leaves of love and faith that appear even in an autumnal time. Emma Howick falls in love with a good man, and Miss Lee goes on polishing the eagle.

CONCLUSION

PYM's fiction continues and enlarges on a number of notable traditions of literature. Perhaps the most pervasive of these are realism and comedy. She presents scrupulously accurate pictures of middle-class domestic life in all its ordinariness and repetition, painting her scene in subdued colors that suggest a scrupulous faithfulness to the actual. Yet she constantly shows this milieu as shot through with the antic spirit of comedy. Rules and proprieties raise neat hedges on every side, yet underwear shows where it should not, lovelorn dons peer out of the shrubbery, dignified spinsters behave like schoolgirls in pursuit of a rock star, and clergymen appear in flowered aprons, festooned with drying tobacco leaves. Something of the wildness of farce manages to surface from Pym's quiet world of shabby gentility. This blending of realism and comedy is as old as Aristophanes writing in fifth-century Athens, and it continues as a central tradition in both drama and prose narrative to the present.

Only slightly less central to Pym's work is the tradition of romantic comedy, of which we have the first surviving instances in the Roman dramatists Plautus and Terence. Romantic comedy descends through medieval romance and Shakespearean comedy and the eighteenth-century novel to one of its supreme flowerings in the work of Jane Austen. The apparatus of romantic comedy has survived in recognizable form from ancient times. The list of constituents is this: one or more pairs of lovers; blocking figures, usually elders; desired suitors, and usually, matching these, undesired suitors; confidantes and helpers; messenger/servants and comic foils; clowns and braggarts. At the end, there are weddings and a feast.

Pym makes free use of this tradition thoughout her work, sometimes employing it in a straightforward fashion, sometimes parodying it or turning it upside down. Her endings are the clearest examples of inverting the tradition. They almost never include marriage and feasting, marking only a modest improvement in the protagonist's situation or simply a happy return to the state of affairs that existed at the beginning of the narrative. Such endings, of course, gain their significance from their contrast with the standard feasts and marriages a reader expects at the end of romantic comedies.

Pym has closer affinities with Jane Austen than with any other classic writer, though Pym modestly disclaimed Austen as an ancestor on the grounds that no modern novelist should *dare* to claim such august lineage. Nevertheless, her world of quiet gentlefolk resembles Austen's, and the authors share central themes of courtship and marriage, though in Pym these may decline into unrequited love (a kind of one-way courtship) and devoted spinsterhood (a kind of one-way marriage). Equally they share a quiet but pervasive irony, and a sharp eye for the illogic and incongruity of everyday interchanges. Pym also shares with Austen the cool and detached gaze of the writer of high comedy, delighted by the follies she depicts, but keeping a careful emotional distance. Both mix politeness and playfulness, disillusionment and gaiety.

There is no way of knowing what Pym's position will be in the annals of literature, but it is clear already that even in her most casual utterances she is never less than an artist—complete in style, imagination, and wit.

SELECTED BIBLIOGRAPHY

I. SEPARATE WORKS. *Some Tame Gazelle* (London, 1950; New York, 1983); *Excellent Women* (London, 1952; New

York, 1978); *Jane and Prudence* (London, 1953; New York, 1981); *Less than Angels* (London, 1955; New York, 1957); *A Glass of Blessings* (London, 1958; New York, 1980); *No Fond Return of Love* (London, 1961; New York, 1982); *Quartet in Autumn* (London, 1977; New York, 1978); *The Sweet Dove Died* (London, 1978; New York, 1979); *A Few Green Leaves* (London and New York, 1980); *An Unsuitable Attachment* (London and New York, 1982); *A Very Private Eye: An Autobiography in Diaries and Letters,* ed. by H. Holt and H. Pym (London and New York, 1984); *Crampton Hodnet* (London and New York, 1985); *An Academic Question* (London and New York, 1986); *Civil to Strangers and Other Writings,* ed. by H. Holt. (London and New York, 1987); *The Barbara Pym Cookbook,* arranged by H. Pym and H. Wyatt. (London and New York, 1988).

II. CRITICAL STUDIES. P. Larkin, "The World of Barbara Pym," in *The Times Literary Supplement* (11 March 1977); K. Miller, "Ladies in Distress," in *The New York Review of Books* (9 November 1978); J. Updike, "Lem and Pym," in *The New Yorker* (26 February 1979).

I. Finlayson, "An Interview with Barbara Pym," in *Literary Review* (23 February 1980); L. Snow, "The Trivial Round, the Common Task: Barbara Pym's Novels," in *Research Studies,* 48 (June 1980); B. Brothers, "Women Victimized by Fiction: Living and Loving in the Novels of Barbara Pym," in T. F. Staley, ed., *Twentieth Century Women Novelists* (Totowa, N. J. and London, 1982); H. Calisher, "Enclosures: Barbara Pym," in *The New Criterion* (September 1982); P. Binding, "Barbara Pym," in J. L. Halio, ed., *British Novelists Since 1960: Dictionary of Literary Biography* (Detroit, Mich., 1983); C. Burkhart, "Barbara Pym and the Africans," in *Twentieth Century Literature: A Scholarly and Critical Journal,* 29 (Spring 1983); I. Kapp, "Out of the Swim with Barbara Pym," in *The American Scholar,* 52 (Spring 1983); E. B. Wymard, "Secular Faith of Barbara Pym," in *Commonweal* (13 January 1984); P. Howe, "The 'Cruelly Perceptive Eye' of a Born Novelist," in *Listener* (5 July 1984); R. Liddell, "Two Friends: Barbara Pym and Ivy Compton-Burnett," in *London Magazine,* 24 (August–September 1984); F. M. Keener, "Barbara Pym Herself and Jane Austen," in *Twentieth Century Literature: A Scholarly and Critical Journal,* 31 (Spring 1985); M. A. Schofield, "Well-Fed or Well-Loved? Patterns of Cooking and Eating in the Novels of Barbara Pym," in *University of Windsor Review,* 18 (Spring–Summer 1985); J. Nardin, *Barbara Pym* (Boston, 1985); L. V. Sadler, "Spinsters, Non-Spinsters, and Men in the World of Barbara Pym," in *Critique: Studies in Modern Fiction,* 26 (1985); D. Benet, *Something to Love: Barbara Pym's Novels* (Columbia, Mo., 1986); R. E. Long, *Barbara Pym* (New York, 1986); C. Burkhart, *The Pleasure of Miss Pym* (Austin, Tex., 1987); J. Rossen, *The World of Barbara Pym* (New York, 1987); D. Salwak, ed., *The Life and Work of Barbara Pym* (Iowa City, Iowa, 1987); H. Hazel, *A Lot to Ask: A Life of Barbara Pym* (New York, 1991).

JEAN RHYS

(1890–1979)

Judith Kegan Gardiner

FORGOTTEN FOR DECADES and thought dead during her lifetime, Jean Rhys has ultimately achieved an international reputation, a reputation that came only late in her lifetime and has since continued to grow. Writing a week after her death in 1979, Alfred Alvarez judged her "one of the finest British writers of this century," and her short stories and novels, especially *Wide Sargasso Sea* (1966) have earned, appreciation as women's fiction, as West Indian fiction, and, despite their sometimes depressing subject matter, simply as great writing.

LIFE

THE author who signed her books "Jean Rhys" was born Ella Gwendolen Rees Williams in Roseau, Dominica, the West Indies, on 24 August 1890. (She lied about her age, and many sources still list her birth year as 1894. She also used a variety of names.) Her father, William Rhys Williams, was a Welsh doctor who had immigrated to the West Indies. Her mother, Minna Lockhart, was a Creole native of the West Indies and a descendent of plantation owners. Rhys had two older brothers and also two sisters, one older, one younger, but in her unfinished autobiography, *Smile Please* (published posthumously in 1979), she describes her childhood as relatively solitary and her favorite playmates as black children and books. Although her family was Anglican, she attended a Catholic convent school. In 1907 she went to England with her father's sister, her aunt Clarice. There she attended the Perse School for Girls in Cambridge, but she soon dropped out; she had decided to study acting, and during 1909 she was enrolled at the Academy of Dramatic Art, later to become the Royal Academy. After her father died, leaving the family impoverished, she remained in England—despite her

mother's objections—and joined the touring company of a musical comedy as a chorus girl. During 1910 she was involved in a love affair with Lancelot Hugh Smith, a wealthy, middle-aged bachelor; the liaison lasted nearly a year and a half. An "illegal operation" followed the end of the affair, and Rhys continued to receive financial help from her first lover until her marriage years later.

Rhys and her critics trace her personality and her sad, autobiographical characters to the influences of her early life. In the vignettes of *Smile Please,* she presents her first sexual affair as a watershed. Before it, she was young and hopeful; after it, despondent. Some later affairs recapitulated this cycle of attraction to and dependence on an older man, followed by abandonment and despair. But earlier phases of her life also seem to have defined her personality. She describes her father as kind, financially reckless, rarely available to his family, and sometimes frightening. She speaks about her mother with considerable regret as a woman fond only of babies, who indulged little Ella until her younger sister was born seven years later. Perhaps the most traumatic incident of Rhys's childhood does not appear in these and other passages from *Smile Please* but in her unpublished notebooks (held at the University of Tulsa). She said that when she was in early puberty an elderly gentleman took a flattering interest in her. When alone with her, he took her for walks and told her about love: "A lover smiles at you. And beats you . . . cruelty submission that was the story." Rhys wrote about the incident decades later, still so emotionally involved that she crossed out the climactic part of the description. Whatever the abuse she experienced, it made her doubt Freud. In Paris she read Freud's judgment that "women of this type will invariably say they were seduced when very young by an elderly man. In *every* case this story is fictitious." Rhys angrily records her reply: "No honey I thought, it is *not* fictitious in every case. Anyhow how do you know" (Tulsa manuscripts).

When her first love affair ended in England, she purchased a number of notebooks and wrote down everything she remembered. The writing alleviated her loneliness by bearing witness to her grief and disappointment, but she carried these notebooks around with her for years before writing anything else. After several drifting years involving men, drink, and some odd jobs, including canteen work during World War I, in 1919 she married Jean Lenglet, a half-French, half-Dutch songwriter and journalist who had served in the French Foreign Legion. They moved to Paris; in a vignette from *Smile Please* that is titled after the city, Rhys describes herself as happy there "because both sides of me were satisfied—the side which wanted to be protected . . . and the side which wanted adventure, strangeness, even risk." In 1920 their son, William, was born; he died when he was three weeks old. That same year, Rhys followed Lenglet to live in Vienna and later in Budapest, during the course of his employment as secretary and interpreter with the Interallied Disarmament Commission. His position was short-lived. The two then returned to Paris, but circuitously: in 1922 Rhys gave birth to their daughter, Maryvonne, while they were temporarily living in Brussels, and they placed the child in foster care.

Rhys and Lenglet, once in Paris, existed precariously on odd jobs and with virtually no permanent address. Then, in 1923 or perhaps 1924, Lenglet was arrested for activities that seem to have included illegal entry into France and currency offenses. Rhys, meanwhile, had made the acquaintance of a woman who took an interest in her writing and provided her with an introduction to Ford Madox Ford, first arranging for Ford to read the notebooks. In 1924 Lenglet was imprisoned and extradited to Holland; Rhys moved in with her new mentor—Ford—and his companion Stella Bowen and began an affair with Ford.

In 1924 Rhys's short story "Vienne" appeared in the *Transatlantic Review,* an influential literary journal edited by Ford. She published under the pen name "Jean Rhys," borrowing names from her husband and her father. Her first book, a collection of short fiction titled *The Left Bank and Other Stories,* appeared in 1927 with an introduction by Ford. Ford helped her obtain the job of translating from French to English the novel *Perversité,* by Francis Carco; when the English edition appeared in 1928, it erroneously listed Ford as its translator. In 1927 she met and began living with Leslie Tilden-Smith, who became her literary agent. Her novel *Quartet,* based loosely on the circumstances of her affair with Ford, appeared in 1928 under the title *Postures,* a change demanded by the publishers, who feared that its content was libelous. Her second novel, *After Leaving Mr. Mackenzie,* was published in 1931. In 1932 she received a divorce from Lenglet and married Tilden-Smith, who inherited some money not long thereafter. The 1930's was a period of relative prosperity for Rhys. Maryvonne Moreman describes visits with her mother in those years as "marvellous, with everything a child could wish for: books, ballet, music, pantomimes, circus, in summer camping and caravaning and summer places on the Thames" (*Smile Please,* p. 150). Rhys visited the West Indies in 1936 for four months, her only trip back to her childhood home. In 1939 she published *Good Morning, Midnight.* All of these books were modest critical successes, but they seem not to have brought her much money.

Rhys remained in London during World War II. She lost touch with Maryvonne, who was active in the Dutch Underground and was briefly imprisoned by the Gestapo during the Nazi invasion of Holland, but both Maryvonne and Jean Lenglet survived the war. Tilden-Smith died in 1945, and two years later Rhys married his cousin George V. Max Hamer. In 1950 Hamer was charged with having fraudulently appropriated funds from the legal firm at which he worked; he was convicted and served the next two years in prison. In 1949, Rhys herself had spent five days in Holloway Prison after a brawl with a neighbor, and friends describe her life in the 1940's and 1950's as difficult: she suffered from poor health, as did her husbands; she drank; she sometimes flew into rages; she was isolated from her London friends; and she had very little money. Hamer and Rhys left London to live in Cornwall in the mid 1950's and then in 1960 moved to a rather dilapidated little cottage in Cheriton Fitzpaine in Devon, where Rhys remained for the rest of her life.

Rhys's comeback began in 1957, when BBC radio dramatized *Good Morning, Midnight.* Selma Vas Dias—who was to play the lead role—and others involved in the production were not even sure that the author was still alive. Rhys answered an ad asking for information about her, and her "reappearance" led to encouraging correspondence with Vas Dias and also with the writers Francis Wyndham and Diana Athill, all of whom urged her to continue her writing and to publish. She returned to a novel about the West Indies upon which she had long been meditating, and she published some short fiction in magazines. In July 1964 Rhys was hospitalized after a heart attack. Hamer died in 1966, and that same year Rhys at last published *Wide Sargasso Sea*, the novel set in the West Indies that had been nearly finished but stalled in its completion for years. It won the W. H. Smith literary award and an award from the Royal Society of Literature. Thus, although four of her five novels appeared in little more than a decade—between the wars, when she was in middle age—fame and success came only when she was seventy-six years old. "When I was young and lovely I had only one dress," she commented, "and now Dior and Chanel offer me their masterpieces" (Campbell, 1979). Her earlier novels were reprinted, and *Tigers Are Better-Looking*, an anthology of short stories including a selection reprinted from *The Left Bank*, appeared in 1968. Rhys continued to publish short stories, some drafted decades earlier, which were collected in *Sleep It Off, Lady* in 1976. In all, Rhys wrote about fifty stories during more than fifty years, from the 1920's through the 1970's. In 1978 she was made a Commander of the Order of the British Empire for services to literature. She died on 14 May 1979, having lived almost to the age of ninety despite alcoholism, poverty, and heart disease. Her unfinished autobiography, *Smile Please*, was published posthumously in 1979; a collection of her letters appeared in 1984; and her novels were collected into one edition in 1985.

THE LEFT BANK

SHORT, intense, catching a slice of life, absorbing us in its mood, the twentieth-century short story is a form that many women have written with grace and precision. Rhys joins writers like Katherine Mansfield, Katherine Anne Porter, Doris Lessing, and Tillie Olsen as masters of this exacting form. Like James Joyce, Mansfield, and Lessing, she was an exile as well, and her first collection of short stories gives a vivid sense of the settings as well as the times in which Rhys lived. Ford's preface to *The Left Bank* praises Rhys's "very remarkable technical gifts," her "singular instinct for form"—an instinct he found shared "by almost no English women writers"—and her "terrific—almost lurid!—passion for stating the case of the underdog." Ford claims that the book is "so very good, so vivid, so extremely distinguished by the rendering of passion, and so true" that he wanted his name associated with hers in its production.

When her first story appeared, Rhys was already thirty-four and had spent half her years to that point drifting through Europe, often seeing the underside of life there. Her stories reflect these experiences. "Vienne" draws vignettes of a predatory world in which men circulate women in a market as volatile as the stock market. In the story's opening vignette, Rhys describes a "little dancer" who "was so exquisite . . . that it clutched at one, gave one a pain, that anything so lovely could ever grow old, or die, or do ugly things." Buying and selling these vulnerable women are restless men like Fischel, the former German fighter pilot, who cruises the city each night to find a new woman. Rhys connects sexual and global politics from the very beginning: a Japanese colonel calls European women "war material," and he approves "the German Army and the German way of keeping women in their place" (p. 220).

The final part of "Vienne," labeled "The Spending Phase," introduces us to the first-person autobiographical heroine central to Rhys's fiction: a passive, pleasure-loving, acutely observing woman who falls prey to men, circumstances, and her own lazy ways. When she has money, she feels happy: "the great god money—makes possible all that's nice in life—youth and beauty, the envy of women, and the love of men—even the luxury of a soul." It is the summer of 1921, and her euphoria suddenly deflates. Her husband's money and luck run out, and the couple make a desperate run for the border. The earliest version of the story ends in an angry manifesto against the "haves" on behalf of the "have-nots." Rhys underscores her meanings here in a way that seems crude in comparison with her later prose: "If there's one hypocrisy I loathe more than another, it's the fiction of the 'good' woman and the 'bad' one" (p. 224), she says, and " 'eat or be eaten' is the inexorable law of life" in this "detestable world" (p. 230).

The narrator of the sketches in "Vienne" is both angry and defensive. She knows women are getting

JEAN RHYS

a raw deal, yet she believes the usual stereotypes
about women and so seethes with self-hatred:

It's not my fault. Men have spoilt me—always disdain-
ing my mind and concentrating on my body. Women
have spoilt me with their senseless cruelties and stupidi-
ties. . . . Lord, how I hate most women here. . . . They
are animals, probably. . . . Even Jesus Christ was kind but
cold and advised having as little as possible to do with
them. . . . How lonely I am"
(*Tigers Are Better-Looking,* pp. 236–237).

Hating herself and others, inevitably this character
is lonely. She sees all action as so likely to produce
evil that she prefers the role of the passive victim,
but this victimization also produces rage; the narrator sometimes lashes out at the reader as just another respectable hypocrite like those the sketches
satirize.

A similar tone pervades many of the stories of
The Left Bank. "Discourse of a Lady Standing a Dinner to a Down-and-Out Friend" experiments with
a Brownian satirical monologue in prose. The entire story gushes from the self-satisfied mouth of a
philanthropist annoyed at what she interprets as
the lazy, improvident ways of the woman for
whom she has purchased supper and whom she
silences with her volubility. "It is dreadful to try to
help poor people. They will not help themselves,"
the rich woman laments. "One comfort. It is always people's own fault" (p. 106). The obverse of
this story is "Hunger," a monologue by a woman
describing her "semi-starvation" on bread and
coffee until all efforts seems futile: "Women are
always ridiculous when they struggle."

Rhys shows her sympathy for underdogs simply
and sometimes sentimentally. One story she chose
for inclusion in *The Left Bank* was her translation of
Jean Lenglet's story, "The Sidi," about an Arab
prisoner in a French jail who cannot understand the
other prisoners' tapping code. Her sketch in "Mixing Cocktails" about a little girl growing up in the
Antilles is also a portrait in alienation, here of the
"well-behaved little girl" who longs, unsuccessfully, to be like other people (*Tigers,* p. 189). Several early stories romanticize self-pity, early death,
and suicide, although the narrators sometimes
catch themselves in these poses and reject them,
like the woman in "A Night," who dreams of a
perfect love and then splutters, "What rot!" (p.
111). At other times, the narrator falls prey to these

poses. In "Tea with an Artist," she admires a former prostitute with the "poisonous charm of the
life beyond the pale" (Tigers, p. 185), and the narrator of "In the Rue de L'Arrivée" defends a pure
victim who is "a harmless creature pathetically incapable of lies or intrigue or even of self-defense"
(p. 114). From this position, she believes that "only
the unhappy can either give or take sympathy"
(pp. 120–121).

Her own sympathy is mixed for the bohemian
artists she portrays. In "Tea with an Artist," she
admires a painter who will not sell or exhibit his
pictures, but she is wary about the sensible English
portrait painter, "Miss Bruce," whose secrets include a closet of beautiful dresses she is ashamed
to wear in public and her lesbian attraction to other
women. Rhys's narrators here, like "Miss Bruce,"
are caught in the contradictions of believing that
artists and women are opposite and irreconcilable
types of people.

The best of the these early stories, "La Grosse
Fifi," satirizes bourgeois standards of morality and
aesthetics while indicating that its own sentimentality is passé and sadly laughable. A respectable
English couple at a resort despise Fifi, a fat, middle-
aged French tart with a heart of gold who befriends
a sad, young West Indian woman recovering from
a bad love affair. Fifi excuses her gigolo's infidelities and recites soupy lines of French poetry that
say "I have laid my life in the hands of my lover."
Unfortunately, she has. The gigolo murders her,
and instead of poetry for an epitaph, she receives
only the crass headlines of the local tabloid. The
young woman cries over Fifi's death—until she
imagines "her friend's gay and childlike soul, freed
from its gross body, mocking her gently for her
sentimental tears" (*Tigers,* p. 216).

QUARTET

In his introduction to *The Left Bank,* Ford claims he
wants to share Rhys's reputation. The wish was
ironically fulfilled when her first published novel
appeared in 1927, based loosely on her affair with
Ford and sufficiently obvious that one publisher
feared a libel suit and another insisted that its title
be changed to *Postures.* Reprints have returned to
Rhys's original title, *Quartet.* Rhys's epigraph for the
novel, ". . . Beware / Of good Samaritans . . ." refers

390

somewhat caustically to Ford as well as to the novel's character Heidler. As with other first novels, *Quartet* invites inquiry into its sources, chiefly Ford's literary influence and the influence of personal autobiography, especially Rhys's affair with Ford. The temptation toward gossipy pleasures offered by a roman à clef led to much attention focused on the novel's autobiographical element. That approach seems particularly justifiable since Ford was a self-aggrandizing mythographer who put versions of himself and other people, including Rhys and Henry James, into his own novels.

Not only Ford, but in fact each of the "quartet" of characters involved in the affair wrote a version of it: Ford in *When the Wicked Man* (1932); Stella Bowen, Ford's companion, in her memoir, *Drawn from Life* (1941); and Rhys's husband Jean Lenglet, under the pen name Edouard de Nève, in the novel *Sous les verrous,* which Rhys herself translated as *Barred* (1932), because she thought it was only "fair"—after deleting a few sentences she thought "too unfair" to herself, as her editor Diana Athill recounts in the foreword to *Smile Please* (p. 9).

All Rhys's writing had its source in events that had happened to her, and her first concern was to get the experience down as accurately as possible, but that first draft was never the novel; it was followed by "a great deal of slow, meticulous and entirely conscious work." Rhys "could rely on her infallible instinct to tell her what her people would say and do" within each novel, Athill claims. Rhys herself, writing to Francis Wyndham in September 1959, judged *Quartet* "angry and uneven . . . but it has some life and it wasn't an autobiography, as everyone here seemed to imagine though some of it was lived of course."

The novel centers on Marya Zelli, a young woman married to Stephan, a Polish art smuggler who sells the treasures of Europeans ruined by World War I to the rising nouveaux riches—in chapter 2, for example, he intends a Mrs. Butcher of Pennsylvania to buy an amethyst necklace with a pendant "the size of a pigeon's egg," and he also trades in "twelfth-century Madonnas" and "Napoleon's sabre." When Zelli is arrested, Marya moves in with a respectable art dealer, the middle-aged Hugh Heidler. In order to remain in control over her husband, Lois Heidler encourages him to have manageable affairs under her nose. At first, Heidler pursues Marya passionately. Eager for love and protection, she submits, and her love soon becomes "this perpetual aching longing, this wound that bled persistently and very slowly" (p. 122). Meanwhile, he loses interest, as his wife had known he would. When Stephan is released from jail and finds out about the affair, he is furious. Neither man can countenance the idea of "sharing" their woman. Heidler leaves Marya. Her husband refuses to take her back. Instead, he strikes her, and she crumples lifeless to the floor. He flees across the border, picking up another woman on the way.

Clearly, much of this plot parallels events in Rhys's life, but much does not. Rhys shapes the novel away from the raw facts of autobiography to make certain literary points. Stella Bowen wrote that "Ford had fallen in love with a very pretty and gifted young woman. . . . a really tragic person" whose "gift for prose" and "personal attractiveness" were offset by "bad health, destitution, shattered nerves, an undesirable husband, lack of nationality, and a complete absence of any desire for independence. . . . Ford gave her invaluable help with her writing, and I tried to help her with her clothes" (p. 167). That is, Bowen saw Rhys primarily as a writer and as a rival, and she saw herself as a victim both of the Ford–Rhys affair and of Rhys's version of it. "Life with Ford had always felt to me pretty insecure. Yet here I was cast for the role of the fortunate wife who held all the cards" (p. 167). Thus Bowen objects that Rhys is *not* writing biography but has recast the situation in creating the fictional "wife" of her novel. Moreover, unlike Rhys, Marya is not an author, and, obviously, Rhys was not murdered as a result of the affair.

Rhys was not merely disguising the facts with these changes but shaping the novel aesthetically—much in line with Ford's own aesthetic views. Ford prided himself on his talent for tight, elliptical plot construction, cumulatively building plots, freedom from unnecessary details, and evocative metaphorical language, and he praised Rhys for her similar technique. Rhys's own imagery, with its caged animals and ironic musicality, sometimes recalls Ford's, especially that in *The Good Soldier* (1915), which had been reissued in 1927, the same year *Quartet* appeared. Ford's novel also concerns an adulterous quartet, "a minuet . . . a prison full of screaming hysterics" (part 1), although Ford's treatment of the situation is both more elegant and more melodramatic than Rhys's. Ford's adulterous woman is a shallow, vicious conniver, whereas Marya of *Quartet* makes a case for herself as a victim, not as a predator, in a social system that is stacked against her. Her indictments of this system, especially of its division of women into virtuous wives and vicious strumpets, recur throughout the novel.

In addition to Ford, Rhys also satirized Ernest Hemingway. Cairn, the Hemingway character, is introduced in chapter 10 as an "ugly, broad-shouldered, long-legged, slim-hipped" American writer. Marya's conversation with him quietly parodies Hemingway's famous simple style: "They talked about Cairn's new hat—whether it was or was not too small for him, and about a short story that he wished to write and about money. 'Haven't any,' said Cairn gloomily. Then they talked about Life." As Bowen suggests, however, the main target of satire in the novel is not other writers but the bourgeoisie. Bowen thought Rhys was "a rather feeble and egotistical" kind of anarchist: she "took the lid off the world that she knew, and showed us an underworld of darkness and disorder, where officialdom, the bourgeoisie and the police were the eternal enemies and the fugitive the only hero. . . . She regarded the law as the instrument of the 'haves' against the 'have nots.' " (pp. 166–167).

Rhys's satire in the novel can be playful. For example, as she describes slyly, among expatriates in Paris in the 1920's parties were "full of That Important Feeling and everything—even sin—was an affair of principle and uplift if you were an American, and of proving conclusively that you belonged to the upper classes, but were nevertheless an anarchist, if you were English" (ch. 8). Sometimes the satire is more pointed, as when Marya complains of the "essential craziness of existence . . . prisons and drains and things, tucked away where nobody can see" (ch. 7). The climactic satirical vision of the novel is Marya's bitter picture of Heidler in church, peacefully praying as he ruins her life; she imagines Heidler thinking, "God's a pal of mine. . . . I prayed to him to get you and I got you. . . . nobody owes a fair deal to a prostitute. . . . Intact or not intact, that's the first question. An income or not an income, that's the second" (ch. 21).

AFTER LEAVING MR. MACKENZIE

After Leaving Mr. Mackenzie, the quietest of Rhys's novels, followed closely upon *Quartet.* It parallels the period of Rhys's life in which she had finished the affair with Ford, who becomes the self-satisfied title character, and began to see Leslie Tilden-Smith, who provides a model for Mr. Horsfield. Julia Martin is an English woman from a poor middle-class family, from which she had fled to a youthful affair, to a marriage that failed, and then to the affair with Mr. Mackenzie, which is already over as this novel begins. Alone in a Paris hotel room, Julia receives a final check from Mr. Mackenzie via his lawyer. In a fit of impractical pique, she makes a scene at a restaurant and flings it back at him. At loose ends and broke, she meets other men, including the kind, vague Mr. Horsfield. Notified that her mother is dying, she returns to England and finds her mother in a coma, unable to recognize her. After her mother dies, Julia and her sister, Norah, bitterly quarrel, filled with mutual envy and recrimination, even though both seek only emotional warmth and respite from their money troubles. Norah and her apparently lesbian roommate send Julia away without her share of the inheritance. Julia consoles herself by seducing Mr. Horsfield. Back in Paris, she is reduced to borrowing a small sum from Mr. Mackenzie, who concludes in the last scene of the novel that "women go phut quite suddenly."

Although Mackenzie and others are shown as cold hypocrites, Rhys does not tell the story exclusively from her heroine's point of view. She reads other people's minds as well, and we learn that all the characters have moments of compassion, though it is baffled by mutual misunderstanding. Julia, for example, wears makeup to hide her feelings, as a "substitute for the mask she would have liked to wear" (part 1, ch. 1) and as a sign that she's still making an effort to keep up appearances, although her family interprets her painted face as proof of her fallen and hardened condition.

The plot seems to hinge on the passive, masochistic, and narcissistic relations women have with men. Men like Mackenzie, at first passionate and kind to women, throw them over. "He had lied; he had made her promises which he never intended to keep; and so on, and so on. All part of the insanity, for which he was not responsible" (part 1, ch. 2). His victim Julia becomes a predator herself, though a wounded and inefficient one, asking everyone she knows for small handouts and seducing the mild Mr. Horsfield. After his second night with her, Mr. Horsfield suddenly sees Julia "not as a representative of the insulted and injured, but as a solid human being" who needs food, shelter, companionship, and understanding (part 2, ch. 13). But this access to empathy frightens him with its implied responsibility, and he backs off from the relationship.

Julia's relations with men, and by implication, all women's, are those of dependency and sexual use, not companionship. Julia visits her first lover twenty years after their affair and realizes for the first time that he is a connoisseur of fine art: "I didn't know anything about him, really," she marvels. "I was for sleeping with—not for talking to" (part 2, ch. 14). The only way she could imagine equality with a man is if he too were poor. She used to pray that her rich lover would lose all his money. She realizes these fantasies are foolish, excessive, like those of the "girl I knew, who used to pray that the man she loved might go blind . . . so that he might be entirely dependent on her." The image recalls Charlotte Brontë's Rochester in *Jane Eyre,* a figure to which Rhys will return in her own novel *Wide Sargasso Sea.*

After Leaving Mr. Mackenzie directly criticizes the sexual double standard and other restrictions against women. When Mr. Horsfield gives Julia money, he feels "powerful and dominant. Happy" (part 1, ch. 3). For poor women, the alternative to dependence on men is no better. Respectable Norah sacrifices her life to caring for her sick mother and becomes a bitter and envious old maid.

This is the only one of Rhys's novels that ends without implying that the heroine may be about to die, though like all the others, the reader leaves her poorer and worse off than she began. Perhaps the heroine does not have to die to give a shape to this narrative, because Julia's mother dies instead, halfway through the novel, indicating the core of the heroine's psychology. Her dying mother is both the cause of Julia's own damaged personality, in Freudian terms, and also a metaphor for the devalued condition of women, a condition Julia and her mother share. The novel thus illustrates what has been called "matrophobia," the fear of becoming one's mother. Contemporary psychology maintains that women often experience ambivalent feelings about their mothers that take shape in childish rages, a blurring of boundaries between themselves and other people, confusions about gender roles, and difficulties in forming adult erotic attachments. Julia's reaction to her mother's deathbed demonstrates these difficulties at the same time

that it shows her enormous unfulfilled longing for maternal recognition and nurture.

The dying mother epitomizes the female condition. Unconscious, she is all body and no mind, passive, immobile, dependent, and isolated. She must be fed and changed like a baby—a frightening reversal for the daughters, who still want to be cared for themselves—and, like a baby, the mother cries in inarticulate pain. Julia approaches the deathbed hoping for some soothing and restorative communication, for reconciliation: "Oh darling," she pleads, "there's something I want to explain to you" (part 2, ch. 5). Although her mother is unconscious, she yearns for her acceptance and fears her disapproval, which she thinks "would finish her; it would be an ultimate and final judgment." The only thing that the dying mother says is "orange trees"—a reminder of the mother's own childhood and unfulfilled longings. Julia remembers "that when she was a very young child she had loved her mother. Her mother had been the warm centre of the world. You loved to watch her brushing her long hair; and when you missed the caresses and the warmth you groped for them." This period of idyllic closeness had been short. Her baby sister appeared, and her mother, "entirely wrapped up in the new baby . . . had gradually become a dark, austere, rather plump woman, who, because she was worried, slapped you for no reason."

At the center of the novel, then, is the death of the mother—who is like the heroine, who has failed the heroine, and who represents the sad lot of women, colonials, and the poor. Her mother, her sister, and sex with men all promise Julia an intimacy and sense of connection that fail—a failure, the novel makes clear, that is not just the result of her idiosyncratic family history but of society's treatment of women. Julia cries at her mother's funeral while thinking about her mother's life and her own "long succession of humiliations and mistakes and pains and ridiculous efforts. . . . She was a defiant flame shooting upwards not to plead but to threaten. Then the flame sank down again, useless" (part 2, ch. 9). Following the funeral and the quarrel with her sister, she feels "peaceful and purified, as though she were a child. Because she could not imagine a future, time stood still" (part 2, ch. 10). Without a mother any longer, a lover, or a child, she is freed from time, outside the cycle of generations, immersed in a kind of down and out Zen. "It's childish to imagine that anybody cares," Julia tells her Uncle Griffiths (part 2, ch. 3).

After her mother's death, she seeks comfort in sex. She wakes up the morning after she has seduced Mr. Horsfield "well and rested, not unhappy," thinking "every day is a new day. Every day you are a new person " (part 2, ch. 12). This moment of peace gives her romantic, Wordsworthian ideas about innocence and childhood: "When you are a child you are yourself and you know and see everything prophetically. And then . . . you become what others force you to be. You lose your wisdom and your soul."

Julia ends the novel still longing for maternal nurture. She sees "a slim woman with full, soft breasts" at a coffee counter and thinks, "If I could talk to her, if only I could go up and tell her all about myself and why I am unhappy, everything would be different afterwards" (part 3, ch. 1). But, of course, she cannot tell the café woman all about herself, though the novel can appeal to its readers for just such consoling understanding. Perhaps this is why the novel, like the wallpaper in Julia's hotel room, creates a somewhat equivocal response in the reader: "The effect of all this was, oddly enough, not sinister but cheerful and rather stimulating" (part 1, ch. 1).

VOYAGE IN THE DARK

JEAN Rhys's *Voyage in the Dark* (1934) is often discussed as though it is her first novel, because she wrote the notebooks on which it is based after her first affair and because its heroine is a young woman. In *Smile Please,* Rhys describes writing those notebooks compulsively, for days and nights on end, as though in a trance: "My fingers tingled, and the palms of my hands. I pulled a chair up to the table, opened an exercise book, and wrote *This is my Diary.* But it wasn't a diary. I remembered everything that had happened to me in the last year and a half. I remembered what he'd said, what I'd felt" ("World's End and a Beginning"). She kept the notebooks with her for years. Stella Bowen said, "When we met her she possessed nothing but a cardboard-suitcase and the astonishing manuscript"—"an unpublishably sordid novel of great sensitiveness and persuasiveness" (p. 167). Rhys must have agreed at the time, since she did not try to revise the notebooks for publication until 1933, when she was married, in tolerable financial circumstances, and regularly seeing her daughter. It was, in fact, during one of the more stable periods in her life in which, as a woman in her mid forties, she began to give artistic shape to those notebook reminiscences about her youth.

The novel is quite sophisticated, her first absolute triumph in the form. An adolescent coming-of-age novel, it reflects ironically on the optimistic pattern of books like Joyce's *A Portrait of the Artist as a Young Man* (1916), or perhaps D. H. Lawrence's *Sons and Lovers* (1913), in which a young man moves from the country to the city, loses his innocence, and gains a vocation with the love and help of women. Career choices are different for women, however. For Anna Morgan, love is a vocation, and a dangerous and degraded one at that.

Abandoning the third-person narration of Rhys's first two novels for a fluid, first-person account, *Voyage in the Dark* records its heroine's steady decline. Anna Morgan is a pretty young chorus girl from the West Indies who is touring England in the years before World War I with a shabby acting troupe. The company is cold, hungry, and poor, and Anna's girlfriends urge her to make money from men. After an illness, she accepts help from the rich bachelor Walter Jeffries and is soon his devoted mistress. This first love affair fills part 1 of the novel. After her lover discards her, she suffers a long breakdown and illness, described in the second part of the novel. Part 3 shows her repeating this cycle in a more dissolute and desperate way. She becomes a housemate and manicurist for a forty-year-old masseuse, but men seem more comforting and profitable, and she drifts into casual prostitution. Once again, sex leads to breakdown and disease. The female rake's progress slides joylessly downward to the brief, final section, Anna's abortion.

Throughout the novel this grim decline contrasts with Anna's memories of a happier childhood. Compared to England, the island Dominica was a fragrant, Technicolor paradise filled with warm if sometimes frightening black people. Rhys said the novel's "big idea" was "something to do with time being an illusion." Its original title was "Two Tunes," meaning "Past and Present" (*Letters,* 18 February 1934 and 6 November 1957).

The opening of the novel shows the disjunction between Anna's past life and her life in the present, a disjunction that is unbridgeable and absolute. Everything about Anna seems split, divided. She even describes her two worlds in two different styles of narration, using many adjectives and rich imagery for her sensuous island past, while speaking of the cold English present in fragments and simple phrases. Similarly, there is a split between Anna's real self—her private memories, fantasies, and feelings—and her compliant and submissive adapted self. The first lines of the novel establish the heroine's experience as divided in a way that may disorient its readers: "It was as if a curtain had fallen, hiding everything I had ever known. It was almost like being born again. The colours were different, the smells different, the feeling things gave you right down inside yourself was different." The feeling "right down inside yourself" sounds intimately female but vague, and indeed the key events of the novel—Anna's loss of virginity and her botched abortion—take place "right down inside" herself. The novel's success or failure depends on its ability to create empathy with Anna's responses to these intimately internal, yet socially defined events. Thus a reader, especially a female reader, begins to join the narrator in her "voyage in the dark," back through the falling curtain to peek at the lost home from which Anna feels so cut off.

"I didn't like England at first," Anna reminisces as the novel begins. "I couldn't get used to the cold. Sometimes I would shut my eyes and pretend . . . I was standing outside the house at home, looking down Market Street to the Bay." Much of the novel details Anna's futile efforts to find a home: in boarding houses on tour as a chorus girl; in the rich, disapproving house of her lover; and in the flat she later shares with a man-hating manicurist. Instead, she is outside in a "market": in her memories, black women sell fishcakes "all sweet an' charmin' " in the market where, in slavery days, they were themselves bought and sold; in the flesh markets of England, Anna too becomes a "sweet an' charmin' " young thing for sale. "It seems to me now that the whole business of money and sex is mixed up with something very primitive and deep," Rhys wrote in *Smile Please*. "I am sure the woman's deep-down feeling is 'I belong to this man. I want to belong to him completely.' It is at once humiliating and exciting" ("Christmas Day").

"Sometimes it was as if I were back there and as if England were a dream. At other times England was the real thing and out there was the dream, but I could never fit them together," Anna goes on to say, and from this opening the novel plunges its

readers into a similar sense of confusion and dislocation. The imagery is dreamlike, and the dream is one from which it is difficult to awaken, in part because the sensations described are so visceral, so much a matter of feelings "right down inside."

When Anna first meets her lover Walter, her response is cool: "In my heart I was always sad, with the same sort of hurt that the cold gave me in my chest" (part 1, ch. 1). This passage illustrates Rhys's deliberately simple style, with its apparent childishness linking physical and emotional sensations while separating Anna's inner truth from her false and conforming outer actions. Rhys later made fun of this style, telling a friend that she wrote the novel "almost entirely in words of one syllable. Like a kitten mewing" (*Letters,* 18 February 1934).

In one pivotal scene, Anna's stepmother, Hester, rejects her because she has become Jeffries' mistress and therefore no longer respectable; at the same time, she accepts the situation because she does not wish to continue to support the girl financially. Anna responds to this rejection by counterattacking Hester: "You're trying to make out that my mother was coloured" (part 1, ch. 6). Anna thus shifts the discussion away from the dangerous category of moral virtue in order to make the issue one of race and class, and Hester eagerly translates her grievances into these terms: "I tried to teach you to talk like a lady and behave like a lady and not like a nigger." Hester identifies Anna with the black West Indian servant Francine: "When you were jabbering away together in the pantry I never could tell which of you was speaking."

Anna's life in England contrasts coldly with her memories of the warm, black culture on the island, with its easy acceptance of the female body, the reproductive cycle, and nurturing nature: "The thing about Francine was that when I was with her I was happy. . . . While she sucked [mangoes] you saw that she was perfectly happy. . . . when I was unwell for the first time it was she who explained to me, so that it seemed quite all right" (part 1, ch. 6). Yet Anna's identification with Francine is illusory: "She disliked me too because I was white," she realizes, responding to this rupture with self-hatred: "I hated being white. . . . I felt I was more alone than anybody had ever been in the world before." Throughout the novel, Anna identifies with oppressed black people but is not one of them. Cut off from black people, from her lover, from her potential baby, and from her female friends, who leave her when she finds herself in trouble, she can only break out of solitude by addressing her story's readers, the equivalent of the witnessing "diary" of her first notebooks.

The published novel ends with Anna thinking "about being new and fresh. And about mornings, and misty days, when anything might happen. And about starting all over again, all over again. . . ." The ellipses, a common device with Rhys, are in this context the author's way of hedging the future and also of complying with her editors: presumably Anna has learned the rules by which her world runs, and even if she cannot profit by her knowledge, perhaps the reader can. Anything might happen, but the author leaves us with slim expectations. Rhys objected to letting Anna live at the end; in *Smile Please* she complains that her editor wanted Anna to recover and meet a rich man. "But how horrible," I said. "How *all wrong.* . . . can't you see that a girl like that would be utterly bewildered from start to finish? She's dying and there's no more time for her as we think of time" ("The Dividing Line"). Rhys's manuscript for the novel implies that Anna dies from her butchered abortion. Bleeding and feverish, she hallucinates the carnivals of her childhood. Instead of the blacks being comforting, however, they are now rejecting, showing white culture what they think of it by wearing white masks: "*A pretty useful mask that white one watch it and the slobbering tongue of an idiot will stick out.*"

As in all of Rhys's fiction, a strong society overpowers a weak woman, and, as in her other novels, Rhys corrects men's views about women. Early in the novel, Anna is reading Émile Zola's *Nana* (1880), and her friend Maudie says, "I bet you a man writing a book about a tart tells a lot of lies" (part 1, ch. 1). Ironically, as a novel by a woman about female initiation, *Voyage in the Dark* is also "a book about a tart." Without sentimentality, it shows Anna as the victim of poverty caused by the limited economic opportunities open to women before World War I, and also as the victim of female biology, the double standard, and the puritanical attitudes of the time. Alienated and isolated, she imagines but is not part of a rich, non-European culture with more accepting attitudes toward women and sexuality.

The Rhys hero is always marginal with respect to love and work, which intersect differently for men and for women. Since Rhys sees sex and money as connected for all women, she admits no moral divide, only a division of security and status, between wives and prostitutes. Rhys's heroines demonstrate this by inhabiting both and neither sides of female roles: they are unprofessional prostitutes or abandoned wives, mothers whose children are aborted or have died, and inefficient workers about to be fired. In all these respects, the Rhys hero is a sadly representative figure, standing for the disabilities that women so often face in their lives, more than she stands for Rhys herself.

GOOD MORNING, MIDNIGHT

WRITTEN shortly after *Voyage in the Dark, Good Morning, Midnight* (1939) repeats the use of a first-person perspective and a fluid shifting between the heroine's present and her past. *Good Morning, Midnight* also shares the dark title imagery and the four-part structure of the preceding novel, but instead of being a retrospective look at England before World War I, it peers closely at a troubled Europe heading toward World War II. Rhys's representative heroine, here named Sasha Jansen, is, as always, in difficulty; but this latest character is a mature woman, and her novel fits the genre of the midlife identity crisis rather than that of the youthful bildungsroman. Reversing the relationship in *Voyage in the Dark* between an innocent young woman and an older man, *Good Morning, Midnight* shows an older woman becoming involved with a younger man. However, the later novel is more subtle and more complex than the earlier one. Whereas *Voyage in the Dark* was structured in terms of irreconcilable polarities, in *Good Morning, Midnight* all such divisions break down, and it is hard to tell the exploiters from the victims.

Sasha Jansen is a woman of independent, though limited, means visiting Paris. Moody and depressed, she bursts into tears in cafés when she thinks about her past. An acquaintance arranges for her to visit the studio of a left-wing Russian artist. He tells her about a mistreated mulatto woman who came to him crying and drunk and whom he comforted; Anna, too, drinks and cries. But his pictures bring her a moment of happiness, and she buys a painting of a Jew with a banjo.

Earlier in the narrative, a young gigolo attracted

by her prosperous-looking clothing has made overtures to her; wanting to take vengeance on him for the evils men have done to her, she finds herself, to her surprise, instead beginning to desire him. "I was a fool, wasn't I?" she muses, "to think all that was finished for me." Embracing him, she is happy: "Now everything is in my arms on this dark landing—love, youth, spring, happiness, everything I thought I had lost" (part 4, ch. 3). He comes up to her hotel room, and she longs to come alive, but freezes and rebuffs him. He calls her stupid and threatens rape. After he leaves, she unlocks the hotel room door and hopes for his return—as she waits, a sinister commercial traveler enters the room and approaches her bed.

Throughout this slight plot, Sasha's memories interweave the emotions of her past with her anesthetized present existence. The atmosphere is dreamlike, as in a surrealist film. Like other Rhys heroines, Sasha lives in a world where other people are not independent beings but extensions of her desires and fears, and objects often are more animated than people. Rooms, cafés, and mirrors speak to her, and the streets she walks on seem to disappear on either side of her.

At the same time that *Good Morning, Midnight* seems dreamy and cut off from external reality, it is precise about its setting: Paris, October 1937. Rhys believed in accurate details, and she saw all writing as inevitably tied to its place in history: "After all books and plays are written some time, some place, by some person affected by that time, that place, the clothes he sees and wears, other books, the air and the room and every damned thing" (*Letters*, 3 March 1953).

The title of the novel, from a poem by Emily Dickinson, looks forward to all the other oppositions within the narrative that collapse into one another: among others, memory and history, light and dark, past and present, despair and hope, inside and outside, nature and art, life and death, male and female. Rhys's narrative voice in the novel builds our identification with Sasha's viewpoint; at the same time literary devices like allusion and humor create a world that we and Rhys share which is considerably more spacious, less bitter, and less claustrophobic, than that of the aging Sasha.

Portraying herself as timid and often confused as things happen to her, Sasha grows bolder and wiser in hindsight. In one passage, for example, she remembers her employer at a fancy dress shop, who fired her for getting rattled after he mispronounced his instructions. "Well, let's argue this out, Mr. Blank," she thinks:

You, who represent Society, have the right to pay me four hundred francs a month. That's my market value, for I am an inefficient member of Society. . . . We can't all be happy, we can't all be rich, we can't all be lucky. . . . Let's say that you have this mystical right to cut my legs off. But the right to ridicule me afterwards because I am a cripple—no, that I think you haven't got."

(part 1, ch. 2)

Talking to herself, or the reader, Sasha ruminates: "Close-up of human nature—isn't it worth something? . . . If you're determined to get people on the cheap, you shouldn't be so surprised when they pitch you their own little story of misery sometimes" (part 2, ch. 1). Presumably we readers are "determined to get people on the cheap" with our vicarious interest in the sorrows of others, and we shouldn't be surprised when she pitches us her "own little story of misery," a story that both solicits our empathy and defends itself against our criticisms and conventional clichés.

Sasha's memories are mainly harrowing, like the one about the maternity clinic where her son was born and promptly died. Yet Rhys's wit, her mastery of language, and her satire of cliché, inform the traumatic scene. Each woman at the clinic cries out her need in deft, ironic orchestration: " 'Jesus, Jesus,' says one woman. 'Mother, Mother,' says another" (part 1, ch. 6). After these conventional appeals to a male god and to female nurture, Sasha's own cry for "chloroform, chloroform" is both funny and chilling. In a moment of birth and transformation, her own childlike self seeks consolation from pain, quiet, even death. In such a setting, when all words run the risk of turning into lies and clichés, the most consoling contact is nonverbal. The midwife comforts Sasha with "her old, old language of words that are not words."

Sasha too sometimes thinks in clichés, in stereotypes, but she knows how false and harmful they are. She fantasizes herself as a masochistic moll and the gigolo René as her matinee idol and master: "Now he ill-treats me, now he betrays me. . . . If he were to die I should kill myself" (part 4, ch. 3). Such clichés are used not to think but to keep people in their places, and since her place is nowhere, a well-off relative calmly asks her, "Why didn't you drown yourself in the Seine?" (part 1, ch. 4). "Everything in their whole bloody world is a cliché," Sasha fumes. In contrast, she wants to know and tell the truth, but that is not what people want to hear. "You imagine the carefully-pruned, shaped thing that is presented to you is truth," she tells us, but "the truth is improbable, the truth is fantastic; it's in what you think is a distorting mirror that you see the truth" (part 1, ch. 9).

From the epigraph by Emily Dickinson to a conclusion that comments upon James Joyce, Rhys situates her novel as a commentary on the literary currents preceding and surrounding her. Allusions throughout the book to Anatole France, the Romantic poets, Virginia Woolf, and others make sure we know we are reading one life among many novelistic versions of women's lives, implying a range of freedom and potentiality that elude Sasha herself, even as Sasha's story implicitly criticizes some other fictions. For example, Rhys admired Colette, whose popular *Chéri* novels of the 1920's romanticized love between a middle-aged courtesan and a handsome young man, giving the woman resources and control over her situation that Sasha cannot muster.

More overtly, Rhys comments on James Joyce's Molly Bloom, who ends *Ulysses* (1922) saying, "yes I said yes I will Yes." Apparently Rhys thought this version of female sexuality was one of those attractive lies that people wanted to hear, a point she makes in the last line of her own novel with a woman in bed saying "yes" to a man. But Sasha is not a woman in whom nature and her own sexuality are at one. She is split into two voices and contrary desires. Although the man she takes to bed with her is a traveler like Ulysses, he is a sinister stranger, possibly a killer, rather than a hero. "I look straight into his eyes and despise another poor devil of a human being for the last time. . . . Then I put my arms round him and pull him down on to the bed, saying: 'Yes—yes—yes. . . .'" Sasha's sad, repeated "yes" stands entirely at odds with the "yes" of Molly Bloom and with Joyce's views of women.

WIDE SARGASSO SEA

As we have seen, Rhys's short stories and novels written between 1924 and 1939 draw not only on her West Indian background and bohemian life in Europe but also on the modernist literary tradition of writers including Joyce, Woolf, Ford, Hemingway, and Joseph Conrad. Her wonderful last novel, *Wide Sargasso Sea* (1966), appeared an entire generation—twenty-seven years—after *Good Morning, Midnight,* and it makes sense to look at the novel in the context in which it actually appeared as well as to see it as the successful culmination of Rhys's earlier characters, techniques, and themes.

Wide Sargasso Sea shares the culture of nostalgia, pastiche, and global sophistication found in many of the so-called postmodernist novels written after World War II. Like Doris Lessing's *The Golden Notebook* (1962), *Wide Sargasso Sea* focuses intently on women's psychology and shows female identity being shaped by larger social forces. Like Gabriel García Márquez' *One Hundred Years of Solitude* (1967), Rhys's novel is a historical yet magical fiction that disputes the superiority of Western reason and civilization over other cultures. And, like the novels of Joseph Heller or Thomas Pynchon, *Wide Sargasso Sea* engrosses us is in its logic of paranoia. Thus *Wide Sargasso Sea* is at once a novel of its time and unmistakably Rhys's in every passage. It is also a tribute to and a revision of Charlotte Brontë's *Jane Eyre* (1847), the most influential nineteenth-century novel of female development.

The title of the novel does not allude to *Jane Eyre.* The Sargasso Sea is neither sea nor land but a huge mass of seaweed in the mid-Atlantic that tricks and traps ocean travelers with the appearance of solid land. In his poem "Portrait d'une femme," Ezra Pound calls a woman's confused mind "our Sargasso Sea." Rhys also thought of the novel as a "wild sea of wrecks" (*Letters,* 8 April 1964). Moreover, the novel itself traverses the Atlantic, moving from the colonial Caribbean islands to nineteenth-century Britain.

Wide Sargasso Sea tells the story of Antoinette Cosway, starting with her childhood as the daughter of a white, West Indian plantation owner. At the opening of the novel, he has just died, leaving his young wife and two children poor and stranded on an isolated estate. Slavery has been abolished, and the former slaves do not wish to work for their former masters. The beautiful garden runs wild, and the family feels marooned, especially after the former slaves poison the only horse. The mother devotes herself to her feeble little son, while Antoinette plays with a black friend, Tia, whose warmth and assurance attract her. Yet Tia too absorbs the islanders' attitudes: "Real white people, they got gold money," Tia taunts her after winning some pennies, and then she steals Antoinette's dress and calls her a "white nigger" (part 1). In order to save her family, the mother remarries a wealthy Englishman, Mr. Mason. He tries to revive the plantation by importing coolie labor rather than hiring the local blacks, who angrily burn down the house. A parrot flying from the flames stops the superstitious rioters, but the feeble son dies from the fire nonetheless. Maddened by her losses, Antoinette's mother turns against her husband, who consigns her to degraded black caretakers, by whom she is sexually abused.

Antoinette goes to a local convent school and becomes friends with a colored relative, Sandi Cosway. Her stepfather and her mother die. When she is sixteen, her stepfather's son, Richard Mason, arranges a marriage for her with a fortune-hunting Englishman, a younger son estranged from his own father. By English law, the bridegroom acquires all of Antoinette's property. The novel switches to the young man's viewpoint. He finds the island seductive but alien and frightening. Similarly, he finds his passionate young wife attractive only briefly; he projects his own unease with sexuality back on her and distrusts her desire for him. She goes to her old black nurse, Christophine, for a potion to regain her husband's love and succeeds in seducing him at the expense of his further alienation. He punishes her by having sex with a black servant so that his wife overhears them, and he entertains rumors that she is hereditarily insane, "intemperate and unchaste." Although Christophine and Sandi urge her to run away from her hostile husband, he has all her money and the law on his side. He takes her to England.

Time passes, and the scene shifts. A woman identifies herself as Grace Poole, attendant to a madwoman. This is the first clear indication that the narrative has joined the story of Brontë's *Jane Eyre*, if we have missed the significance of Mason's otherwise rather common name. (Antoinette's husband is unnamed, though his circumstances and sometimes his language are those of Brontë's character Edward Rochester.) Grace admires her charge, Antoinette, for her continued fierceness and desire to escape. Part 3, the final section of the novel, returns to Antoinette's mind. Imprisoned in her attic, angry and confused, Antoinette rages against the man who hates her, and she derives comfort from a red dress that reminds her of her island

home. Dreams persuade her that her destiny is to set the house aflame and jump to freedom. Like other Rhys novels, the book ends at the point where we think the heroine is about to die.

Rhys said she was fascinated with Rochester's mad first wife in *Jane Eyre* because of her West Indian origin, and she thought Brontë treated the character unfairly. By rewriting *Jane Eyre*, Rhys places her novel in a women's tradition—unlike her earlier books, which looked primarily to male novels like Zola's *Nana* as their points of comparison. In their study *The Madwoman in the Attic* (1979), feminist critics Sandra Gilbert and Susan Gubar suggest that nineteenth-century women writers like Brontë create plots in which such a madwoman is the angry, rebellious double for the virtuous heroine and her author. Rhys explicitly makes this mad rebel into her heroine.

Wide Sargasso Sea rereads *Jane Eyre* in a fashion that points up the earlier novel's British chauvinism and middle-class bias and its ambiguous attitudes about sexuality and male dominance. The novel is a tribute as well as a criticism of its predecessor, and Rhys makes her character Antoinette a double for Jane Eyre as well as her opposite. Like Jane, Antoinette is an orphan, neglected and rejected at home and treated cruelly by other children. Both girls find refuge and tender maternal care at boarding school and, as young women, both passionately desire love. Both are sensitive to the natural world and appeal to it when hurt, and both have prophetic dreams. Similarly, in *Wide Sargasso Sea*, Rhys repeats some of *Jane Eyre*'s key images—horses on a bad road, solitary trees, a garden, an isolated house. However, where Jane finds support in kind relatives, a protective husband, the voice of her dead mother, and a convenient legacy, Antoinette can turn only to a few black people—themselves poor and devalued. Brontë describes her madwoman as a large, frightening woman, a hyena and a demon. She is a rageful overgrown baby, and at the same time she expresses the sexuality that Victorian women were not supposed to exhibit. Rhys corrects these aspersions by redramatizing the story so that the madwoman's bestiality makes human sense: for example, she bites her stepbrother only after he insists that he cannot tamper with Rochester's legal control over his wife.

Wide Sargasso Sea can be classified as a women's novel of development; as a Gothic novel, complete with haunted house, men who mean evil, witchcraft, and exotic historical settings; or even as an upscale "bodice ripper," sexually obsessed and socially disturbing, though without the conventional happy ending. As with such formulaic popular fiction, we know the basic plot of *Wide Sargasso Sea* before we begin reading it, and the novel is in some sense a repetition of its Victorian precursor. This repetition, however, is an intentional means of commenting upon and revising the popular model and not of merely following its pattern. Despite some formulaic components, the novel is also genuinely tragic. It invokes our pity and terror, and it invites us to feel that choosing one's own death may be the only heroism available to women and the oppressed. Thus the novel questions the nineteenth-century notions of character, choice, freedom, and individual success implied by novels of development like *Jane Eyre,* from the perspective of more elevated and also more popular genres.

Yet, despite its conventional elements, much of the novel's intensity comes from its having personal, biographical relevance to Rhys, who began subscribing to nationalist West Indian journals after the 1936 visit to her homeland. Many details from Rhys's life make their way into the novel. Her maternal grandmother had a pet parrot and faced a riot by freed slaves. Rhys's childhood nurse told her stories about zombies and the local practice of witchcraft, or obeah. Moreover, her father was, like Rochester, a younger son on poor terms with his own father. He too fell ill with fever upon arriving in the islands and married when he recovered. "I probably romanticised my father," Rhys says in *Smile Please,* "perhaps because I saw very little of him" ("My Father"). Such fantasies may have informed her sympathetic, sometimes furious portrait of the powerful Rochester. Rochester is thus a psychologically convincing character as well as a representative of patriarchal power, although the most complex and affecting character in the novel is Antoinette.

Antoinette's personality, like that of other Rhys heroines, dominates the novel. Rejected, misunderstood, and persecuted, Antoinette is the damaged, narcissistic daughter of a damaged, narcissistic mother, a syndrome also evident in *After Leaving Mr. Mackenzie.* Dreams and symbols throughout the novel expand Antoinette's personality to archetypal status. In a frightening dream of being pursued, she wears a dirty white dress. In contrast, she feels most herself, most at home, in a dress "the colour of fire and sunset" (part 3). The white dress stands for her passive, subordinate self; the red one for her rage, her "spunks." Before the fire at her childhood home, she lives in an Edenic world: "Our garden was large and beautiful as that garden in the Bible—the tree of life grew there," she says early in the novel. Rochester fears the lush nature of the island, and Antoinette says, "It is as indifferent as this God you call on" (part 2). Where Jane had Christianity as a reliable guide, Antoinette lives in an animistic, superstitious world. Although the black religion seems more true to her than any other belief, it does not always work for her: nature is simply indifferent.

Christophine is a powerful figure in the novel, who illustrates a version of womanhood that stands as an alternative to the harmful "civilised" expectations that Antoinette as a white woman is required to meet. An unmarried mother, she keeps her money and lets no man own her. Rhys feared she had made Christophine too articulate for a realistic portrayal, but the characterization succeeds as myth. At the center of the novel, we hear her "judge's voice," disrupting our identification with Rochester. The novel does not enter the minds of its black characters, but it awards Christophine correct perceptions: "Everybody know that you marry her for her money and you take it all," Christophine accuses Rochester. "And then you want to break her up, because you jealous of her. She is more better than you" (part 2).

Christophine understands Rochester's own witchcraft of treating Antoinette like a doll, not a person, and of calling her Bertha rather than her actual name.

But Rochester's magic works on Antoinette. In her attic she realizes that "names matter, like when he wouldn't call me Antoinette, and I saw Antoinette drifting out of the window with her scents, her pretty clothes and her looking-glass" (part 3). Her former identity gone, Antoinette wonders, "What am I doing in this place and who am I?" In her childhood, when Coulibri was burned down, Antoinette looked to her black friend Tia for help: "I will live with Tia and I will be like her," she thought, but "when I was close I saw the jagged stone in her hand but I did not see her throw it. I did not feel it either, only something wet, running down my face. I looked at her and I saw her face crumple up as she began to cry. We stared at each other, blood on my face, tears on hers. It was as if I saw myself. Like in a looking-glass" (part 1).

Antoinette's final dream picks up and weaves together all the former scenes and symbols in the novel. In it she calls on Christophine and is answered with a wall of fire. She hears the parrot croaking *"Qui est là?"*—the request for identity so difficult for her—and sees Tia beckoning to her at the pool at Coulibri. "I called 'Tia!' and jumped and woke. . . . Now at last I know why I was brought here and what I have to do," Antoinette concludes upon awakening. She steals Grace Poole's candle, "and it burned up again to light me along the dark passage," she says, of her own and other women's lives and also of all the literary passages from Brontë to Rhys.

Thus while its end is foreknown, the novel makes the causes that lead to that end both inevitable, in terms of character and circumstance, and also mysterious. This ending has occasioned considerable debate. Like the similarly ambiguous drowning at the end of Kate Chopin's *The Awakening* (1899), Antoinette's suicide can be read either as a defeat, in which she succumbs to her repressive society, or as a victory, bringing her freedom and vengeance.

LATE STORIES

WIDE SARGASSO SEA is so good, so clearly a culmination of themes and skills developed in Jean Rhys's first four novels, that it tends to overshadow her late short stories, some of which she had worked on for decades; she devoted attention to writing short stories until she was well into her eighties. Yet the late stories show a remarkable range and a perfection in their form that should not be overlooked.

Viewed as a whole, Rhys's stories take women through the life cycle. First there is the innocent but violated child, then the seductive working girl, followed by the happy, pregnant madonna. Less cheery is the abandoned mistress, who may become the attempted suicide, the solitary old drunk, or the unwanted ghost. Because these characters have rather similar viewpoints, their changing relationships to their contexts tend to be overlooked. Especially in her later fiction, Rhys is far more responsive to history than critics and readers perhaps have noticed. Her characters are embattled before World War I, adrift in the 1920's,

depressed in the 1930's, struggling on the home front during World War II, and later alienated from postwar conformity.

Late stories written about girlhood reflect on the repressions of Victorian culture. In "Goodbye Marcus, Goodbye Rose," collected in her 1976 volume *Sleep It Off, Lady,* handsome old Captain Cardew treats twelve-year-old Phoebe like a grown-up. She appreciates his attentions until he takes her on a walk: "His hand . . . darted towards her, dived inside her blouse and clamped itself around one very small breast" (p. 25). The child feels confused, shocked, and wicked, sure she will never be able to become a proper wife and mother. In "The Day They Burned the Books" (from *Tigers Are Better-Looking,* 1968), a twelve-year-old girl observes the conflicts of her young friend Eddie Sawyer, the son of a bigoted Englishman and a colored mother. Eddie rejects the local admiration for English things like strawberries and daffodils, but rages at his mother when she burns his father's library of European classics. "Fishy Waters," included in *Sleep It Off, Lady*—a late, complex story told through newspaper exchanges about a court case and through the views of a woman new to the island—has at its center a violated child, a poor black girl beaten in an apparently unmotivated attack. Mystery and controversy surround the case. A drunken white socialist carpenter is accused of the crime, but rumor points instead toward a respectable middle-class Englishman whose wife, telling the story, suddenly finds her husband alien and frightening to her.

Set in July 1914, "Till September Petronella," a story Rhys shortened from a novel (collected in *Tigers*), shows a social world that is complacent yet full of conflict, seething with sexual and class antagonisms, which prefigure the conflicts of World War I. Two well-off young men patronize Petronella, an artist's model who does not want to be seduced, at a nasty summer party in the country. A model and therefore an object for men to look at and transform into their fantasies, Petronella herself fantasizes about escaping her hard life through a Cinderella myth—she will appear as a triumphant beauty in an opera box, though she has never been to an opera—and her handsome prince will come. Literature also helps Petronella fantasize. Reading long novels is for her almost like having a baby, almost like creating her own artwork: "What is not there you put in afterwards, for it is alive, this book, and it grows in your head" (p.

10). The young men are so bored with themselves they want to "blow everything up" just for a little excitement, and of course, the guns of August soon will answer their wish, intervening before their date with Petronella in September.

Rhys describes the unleashed decadence of the cosmopolitan 1920's in stories like "Night Out 1925" (in *Sleep It Off, Lady*), in which a man takes a respectable girl on a date to a brothel just to "stare and jeer" at the unfortunate women (p. 109), while "Tigers Are Better-Looking" features a journalist in the 1930's who is depressed about the times, his circumstances, and human nature. He cannot get into the swing of celebrating the jubilee of King George V in 1934, and getting into the swing is what is important about writing and about fitting into society. In "Let Them Call It Jazz" (from *Tigers*), another poor artist has trouble getting into the English swing of things. A black West Indian woman, persecuted in England, goes to the Holloway women's prison for making too much noise in a white neighborhood when she is drunk. She hears and remembers another woman's song in jail and later sells the song to a commercial musician. The anthem of women's solidarity then enters the heartless commercial market—as Rhys may have felt her stories of the oppressed were to do.

If Rhys remembers World War I for destroying a generation of young men and their pretensions, she remembers the home front in World War II as destroying women's hopes. For instance, Audrey, an overworked government typist in "The Insect World" (in *Sleep It Off*) hates the war for making her an old maid in a world without men. Audrey has a painfully divided consciousness and thinks of herself as "twins." Her nonconforming side feels she is "a wanderer in a very dark wood. The other told her that all she accepted so meekly was quite mad, potty" (p. 131). Yet things are amuck, of course, during the Blitz, and Audrey superstitiously walks through London, thinking, "If the siren goes when I'm in this street it'll mean it's all U.P. with me."

"A Solid House" (in *Tigers*) extends the destruction of World War II into allegorical dimensions. Teresa is a middle-aged woman recovering from drugs, alcohol, and attempted suicide in an odd but restful London boardinghouse during the bombings. Her landlady, Mrs. Spearman, holds séances and always gets "good results" after an air raid. Then she warns Teresa that "many people simply won't believe they are dead" (p. 146). Perhaps Teresa's suicide attempt was successful after all, and she joins dead England in an embalmed eternity Rhys sees as a Victorian parlor filled with stuffed birds.

In these last stories, as in the early ones, rejection and abandonment face the heroines, now often older women rejected by younger ones. In "The Sound of the River," a story from *Tigers* that recalls Rhys's second marriage, an old couple cheerily goes on vacation—but then the wife wakes up to find her husband dead in bed. In the title story of *Sleep It Off, Lady,* we sympathize with another solitary old woman when her horribly rejecting neighbors leave her to die of shock after she faints near her trash bin, afraid of a giant rat. Yet we can also see the situation as they do: that the evidence points to her being a fanciful and fearful old drunk.

Whereas one of the romantic figures of the twentieth century is the macho alcoholic, reckless and daring in his escapades, the female version of this figure has never been so honored. Rhys, like Hemingway or Malcolm Lowry a great writer, an exile, and an alcoholic, writes a bitter self-parody of the drinking woman author in her story "The Lotus" (in *Tigers*). The Lotus is an annoying drunk who is writing a novel about a "girl who gets seduced" (p. 115)—that is, a novel like Rhys's *Voyage in the Dark.* Humiliated by a snobbish young couple, the pathetic old woman runs out into the street naked. Even more than her story about a seduced young woman, the Lotus exposes herself as the text that is the hardest for her society to take—a naked, aging, no longer desirable female body, a nude no one wants to paint, whose story no one wants to hear.

CONCLUSION

In the chapter of her memoirs titled "From a Diary" Rhys wrote, "I must write. If I stop writing my life will have been an abject failure. . . . I will not have earned death." Dedicated to her craft, she has in fact earned immortality for her works, which she held as far more valuable than her life: "for all of a writer that matters is in the book or books. It is idiotic to be curious about the person," she continues in "From a Diary," and she requested that no biography of her be written. Her memoirs, letters, and reissued novels have appeared posthumously; *Quartet* has been made into a movie; and novels and poems by contemporary women writers allude to her work and so embrace this solitary and alienated writer into a living tradition that honors her.

SELECTED BIBLIOGRAPHY

I. BIBLIOGRAPHIES. R. C. Reynolds and B. J. Murray, "A Bibliography of Jean Rhys," in *Bulletin of Bibliography*, 36 (October–December 1979); R. A. Roberts, "Jean Rhys: A Bibliographical Checklist," in *American Book Collector*, 3 (November–December 1982); E. W. Mellown, *Jean Rhys: A Descriptive and Annotated Bibliography of Works and Criticism* (New York and London, 1984).

II. NOVELS. *Quartet* (originally published as *Postures*, London, 1928; as *Quartet*, New York, 1929); *After Leaving Mr. Mackenzie* (London, 1931); *Voyage in the Dark* (London, 1934); *Good Morning, Midnight* (London, 1939); *Wide Sargasso Sea* (London, 1966); *The Complete Novels of Jean Rhys* (New York, 1985), with an intro. by D. Athill.

III. SHORT STORIES AND OTHER WORKS. "Vienne," in *Transatlantic Review* (January 1925), short story; *The Left Bank and Other Stories* (London, 1927), short stories, with a preface by F. M. Ford; *Perversity* (Chicago, 1928), trans. of novel by F. Carco; *Barred* (London, 1932), trans. of novel by E. de Nève (pseudonym of J. Lenglet); *Tigers Are Better-Looking* (London, 1968), short stories, including a selection from *The Left Bank*; "I Spy a Stranger" and "Temps Perdi," in J. Burnley, ed., *Penguin Modern Short Stories* 1, (Harmondsworth, 1969), short stories; *My Day: Three Pieces by Jean Rhys* (New York, 1975), essays; "Whatever Became of Old Mrs. Pearce?" in London *Times* (21 May 1975), essay; *Sleep It Off, Lady* (London, 1976), short stories; "Four Poems," in London *Observer* (20 February 1977), poems; "The Joey Blagstock Smile. 7 September 1974," in *New Statesman*, 94 (23–30 December 1977), sketch; "Making Bricks Without Straw," in *Harper's* (July 1978), essay; "The Whistling Bird," in *The New Yorker* (11 September 1978), story; *Smile Please: An Unfinished Autobiography* (London, 1979), with a foreword by D. Athill; *The Letters of Jean Rhys*, F. Wyndham and D. Melly, eds. (New York, 1984; published as *Jean Rhys Letters 1931–1966*, London, 1984).

Manuscripts of Jean Rhys are in the McFarlin Library, University of Tulsa; Evelyn Scott Collection, Humanities Research Center, University of Texas at Austin; the British Museum; and the possession of Francis Wyndham, her literary executor.

IV. INTERVIEWS AND BIOGRAPHICAL AND CRITICAL STUDIES. S. Bowen, *Drawn From Life: Reminiscences* (London, 1941); M. Bernstein, "The Inscrutable Miss Jean Rhys," in *Observer Magazine* (1 June 1969), interview; K. Ramchand, "Terrified Consciousness," in his *The West Indian Novel and Its Background* (London, 1970); J. Hall, "Jean Rhys," in *Guardian* (10 January 1972), interview; E. Mellown, "Character and Themes in the Novels of Jean Rhys," in *Contemporary Literature*, 13 (Autumn 1972); N. Casey, "Study in the Alienation of a Creole Woman—Jean Rhys's *Voyage in the Dark*," in *Caribbean Quarterly*, 19 (September 1973); A. Alvarez, "The Best Living English Novelist," in *New York Times Book Review* (17 March 1974); M. Cantwell, "A Conversation with Jean Rhys," in *Mademoiselle* (October 1974), interview; A. Luengo, "*Wide Sargasso Sea* and the Gothic Mode," in *World Literature Written in English*, 15 (April 1976); D. Porter, "Of Heroines and Victims: Jean Rhys and Jane Eyre," in *Massachusetts Review*, 17 (Autumn 1976); J. Thurman, "The Mistress and the Mask," in *Ms.* (January 1976); L. James, *Jean Rhys* (London, 1978); N. Robertson, "Jean Rhys: Voyage of a Writer," in *New York Times* (25 January 1978), interview; H. Tiffin, "Mirror and Mask: Colonial Motifs in the Novels of Jean Rhys," in *World Literature Written in English*, 17 (April 1978); E. Abel, "Women and Schizophrenia: The Fiction of Jean Rhys," in *Contemporary Literature*, 20 (Spring 1979); A. Alvarez, "Against the Odds," in *Observer* (20 May 1979); E. Campbell, "From Dominica to Devonshire: A Momento of Jean Rhys," in *Kunapipi*, no. 2 (1979); C. M. L. Dash, "Jean Rhys," in B. King, ed., *West Indian Literature* (London, 1979); T. F. Staley, *Jean Rhys: A Critical Study* (Austin, Texas, 1979); E. Vreeland, "Jean Rhys: The Art of Fiction LXIV," in *Paris Review*, no. 76 (1979), interview; P. Wolfe, *Jean Rhys* (Boston, 1980); H. Nebeker, *Jean Rhys: Woman in Passage* (Montreal, 1981); R. Scharfman, "Mirroring and Mothering in Simone Schwarz-Bart's *Pluie et vent sur Télumée Miracle* and Jean Rhys's *Wide Sargasso Sea*," in *Yale French Studies*, no. 62 (1981); J. K. Gardiner, "Rhys Recalls Ford: *Quartet* and *The Good Soldier*," in *Tulsa Studies in Women's Literature*, 1 (Spring 1982); J. K. Gardiner, "Good Morning, Midnight: Good Night, Modernism," in *Boundary 2*, 11 (Fall–Winter 1982–1983); E. R. Baer, "The Sisterhood of Jane Eyre and Antoinette Cosway," in E. Abel, M. Hirsch, and E. Langland, eds., *The Voyage In: Fictions of Female Development* (Hanover, N. H., and London, 1983); P. Delany, "Jean Rhys and Ford Madox Ford: What 'Really' Happened?" in *Mosaic*, no. 4 (1983); S. James, *The Ladies and the Mammies: Jane Austen and Jean Rhys* (Bristol, 1983); D. Plante, *Difficult Women: A Memoir of Three* (New York, 1983); M. Kappers-den Hollander, "Jean Rhys and the Dutch Connection," in *Journal of Modern Literature*, 11 (March 1984); C. Angier, *Jean Rhys* (Harmondsworth, England, 1985); N. H. Brown, "Jean Rhys and *Voyage in the Dark*," in *London Magazine*, 25 (April–May 1985); A. Davidson, *Jean Rhys* (New York, 1985); N. J. Leigh, "Mirror, Mirror: The Development of Female Identity in Jean Rhys's Fiction," in *World Literature Written in English,* 25 (1985); J. C. Oates, "Romance and Anti-Romance: From Brontë's *Jane Eyre* to Rhys's *Wide Sargasso Sea,"* in *Virginia Quarterly Review,* 61 (Winter 1985); *Review of Contemporary Fiction,* 5 (1985), special issue on Rhys; T. F. O'Connor, *Jean Rhys: The West Indian Novels* (New York and London, 1986); N. Harrison, *Jean Rhys and the Novel as Woman's Text* (Chapel Hill, N.C., 1988); L. Tracy, *"Catching the Drift":*

Authority, Gender, and Narrative Strategy in Fiction (London, 1988); R. Webb, "Swimming the Wide Sargasso Sea: The Manuscripts of Jean Rhys's Novel," in *British Library Journal,* 14 (Autumn 1988); J. K. Gardiner, *Rhys, Stead, Lessing, and the Politics of Empathy* (Bloomington, Ind., 1989); D. K. Kloepfer, *The Unspeakable Mother: Forbidden Discourse in Jean Rhys and H. D.* (Ithaca, N.Y., and London, 1989); M. L. Emery, *Jean Rhys at "World's End": Novels of Colonial and Sexual Exile* (Austin, Tex., 1990).

I. A. RICHARDS

(1893–1979)

John Paul Russo

> Poetry is the supreme use of language, man's chief co-ordinating instrument, in the service of the most integral purposes of life.
>
> —*Coleridge on Imagination*

A FOUNDER OF modern literary criticism, Ivor Armstrong Richards began his teaching career at Cambridge University after World War I. *The Meaning of Meaning: A Study of the Influence of Language upon Thought and of the Science of Symbolism* (1923), coauthored by C. K. Ogden, pioneered the study of semantics. *Principles of Literary Criticism* (1924) and *Science and Poetry* (1926) offered a cultural critique, psychological theories of value and communication, and poetic analysis. In *Practical Criticism: A Study of Literary Judgment* (1929), his most influential book and his masterpiece, he examined hundreds of undergraduate comments on poems of varying quality, classified them by type of misreading, and proposed a corrective method. With its strategies for determining authorial tone and attitude, belief or "doctrine" in poetry, and irony, ambiguity, and sincerity, Richards' method of "close reading" proved capable of interpreting high modernist texts, some of the most difficult literature ever written. Richards hastened the overwhelming acceptance of what we now call high modernism (represented in the poetry of T. S. Eliot, Ezra Pound, and Wallace Stevens) in university study. In Great Britain he taught two of the principal critics of their generation, William Empson and F. R. Leavis, and his influence expanded across the commonwealth. In America he is the acknowledged father of New Criticism, which occupied the theoretical high ground in the academic study and teaching of literature from the 1940's through the 1960's. His method remains standard in the Anglo-American classroom to the present day. Beyond specific achievements, Richards raised the theory of criticism to the status of a field in the Anglo-American university.

EARLY LIFE

RICHARDS was born in Sandbach, Cheshire, on 26 February 1893, the youngest of three sons. His father, a chemical engineer, came from a prominent Welsh family of architects and builders in Swansea (Richards' great-uncle was a Liberal M.P.) and was head manager of a chemical factory. His mother was from Yorkshire; her family dealt in textile imports. When Richards was nine, his father died of cancer. Shortly afterward his mother moved the family to Clifton, a suburb of Bristol, where she could send her three sons to Clifton College as day boys to spare expenses. Richards' studies were interrupted for over a year by the first of three bouts of tuberculosis in ten years. He was originally enrolled in what at Clifton was called the Classical side, but on his return he entered the Military and Engineering side, and finally settled on the Modern side. Because of his illness he was allowed to pace himself: "They let me live in the library, where I entertained myself. They were sensible enough to realize that though I wasn't sitting listening to things being said in class, I was getting an education—which was very unusual for a school in those days" ("Fundamentally, I'm an Inventor," 1973). In 1909–1910, Richards became acquainted with E. H. C. Wethered, one of the organizers of the Extension (Adult) School in Bristol, who invited him to teach his first classes. Richards chose as his subject the Book of Job, to which he would come back often in his career. To his surprise, the adult students greeted his angry denunciations of unjust godhead with amiable British toleration.

In 1911 Richards entered Magdalene College, Cambridge, having won a small scholarship in history. As he recalled, however, he "couldn't bear history";[1] he said that he "hated the past" for its suffering and tragedy and that he always looked ahead, "even now" (it was 1972). Upon the prompting of a fellow undergraduate, C. K. Ogden, he switched after one or two terms to philosophy, or moral science, as the field was then known at Cambridge. Richards suffered a second attack of tuberculosis and left school for a year (1912–1913). He eventually graduated with first-class honors in part one of the tripos examination in 1915.

Four individuals played a shaping role in Richards' undergraduate years. A. C. Benson, the popular Edwardian literary figure and later master of Magdalene, tutored Richards in essay writing and argued points of taste. Benson's diary gives an amusing portrait of Richards as "the votary of liberty," "a mixture of [Percy Bysshe] Shelley and [Edward] Carpenter [the turn-of-the-century socialist and writer on sexuality]," a "very able, well-read, thoughtful and a delightful creature too, full of modesty." Benson's remark that his young student was well-read is something to note, because occasionally Richards is wrongly thought to have wandered into literature from linguistics, philosophy, or psychology. Benson played a part in Richards' having to be disciplined once while at Magdalene. Richards had taken up mountaineering in North Wales and the Valais Alps and practiced at night on Magdalene's roofs and chimneys. When a dummy was found suspended from a weathercock, an irate Benson and the local constable put their heads together and solved the mystery. But Benson appreciated this one of his "two ablest" students and alerted him when Thomas Hardy (who was an honorary fellow) dined at Magdalene, so that Richards could sit forward and "see Hardy close up." Many of Richards' weekly essays for Benson have survived and are among the earliest manuscripts in the extensive Richards collection at Magdalene College.

The neo-Hegelian idealist J. M. E. McTaggart was Richards' first supervisor in moral science, and while he reacted sharply against McTaggart, he felt his influence "very deeply." McTaggart reinforced the Romantic-idealist strain in his thinking, originally drawn from the English Romantic poets and their Victorian successors. "I knew Swinburne by heart—and Shelley much better," said Richards. McTaggart's notion of the dialectical relatedness of things came to have increasing importance in Richards' later career, although he would return to its source in Plato and give it a highly linguistic orientation. Richards rejected McTaggart's neo-Hegelianism, his concept of the absolute, and his denial of the existence of time. "More judicious, more balanced, more interested in trying to say and restate what others thought" than McTaggart was W. E. Johnson, Richards' supervisor for his final two years. Johnson was a logician who had also lectured on philosophical psychology. Richards praised his "lessons in intellectual integrity." Under him Richards wrote a report on William James's *A Pluralistic Universe* (1909). At some point in these years he also studied James's *Principles of Psychology* (1890), a book he never tired of recommending.

By far the most important influence on Richards at Cambridge was the commonsense philosopher G. E. Moore. "I spent seven years studying under him and have ever since been reacting to his influence," he recalled of his "master" in 1968. "Where there is a hole in him there's a bulge in me" ("An Interview with I. A. Richards," 1969). Moore's philosophical stance and problems absorbed him: the repudiation of idealist metaphysics, the appeal to direct intuition and common sense, realism, the test of "absolute isolation," theories of definition, the relations between language and the "proposition" contained therein, the setting of works of art among the highest goods. Richards admired Moore's Socratic character and was fascinated by the way Moore in lecture teased and prodded language, turning phrases over dozens of times to make them yield up their meanings or propositions. Although Richards' preference for micrological textual study cannot be traced to Moore alone, Moore intensified his involvement in linguistic analysis and offered strategies to develop it. "He could hardly ever believe that people could mean what they said," Richards observed. "I've come to think they hardly ever can say what they mean" ("An Interview with I. A. Richards"). "Meaning" henceforth became a key word in his criticism. At the same time, Richards believed that Moore resorted too hastily to intuition which should be saved as a last resort; he felt Moore's commonsense

---

[1]Quotations that appear without citations refer to the author's private conversations or correspondence with Richards.

conclusions might have been formulated before considering what other thinkers had written on a subject or before exhausting other options. Nor did he care for Moore's aesthetic theory, believing it to be entirely too abstract. Another student in Moore's lecture hall before the war, equally puzzled by the master, was Ludwig Wittgenstein.

The revolution in philosophy associated with Moore and Bertrand Russell resulted in a return to native British empiricism, albeit on new foundations, after a generation or two of idealism (as represented by T. H. Green, F. H. Bradley, and McTaggart). Russell went so far as to include the new psychology of behaviorism in one version of his philosophy. Moreover, the language of philosophy was increasingly at issue. Language could no longer serve as a mere windowpane through which one looked at the world, but was an object of study in its own right, a primary constituent in framing our view of the world. Richards was one of the immediate beneficiaries of, and participants in, this revolution and worked on the borders of adjoining fields: linguistics, neurophysiology, and psychology. Eliot had also been trained in philosophy and was determined to bequeath to criticism a more precise language of comparison and analysis. After Eliot and Richards the general tone of criticism changed dramatically from rhapsodic appreciation and dry historicism to the technical critique of specific works of art. From the perspective of history, Richards ushered the age of analysis into literary criticism.

In a yet broader way Richards' university education shaped his thought. At the turn of the century there existed a liberal body of beliefs that may be termed Cambridge humanism. Thinkers and artists associated at some point with Cambridge were, according to J. M. Keynes, completing a revolution in ethics and feeling that had begun with a focus on the intellect in the mid-Victorian generation. As espoused by Goldsworthy Lowes Dickinson, E. M. Forster, F. M. Cornford, Leonard Woolf, Moore, Russell, McTaggart, and Keynes, Cambridge humanism meant directness in speech and writing; rationalism; antiauthoritarianism; agnosticism; personalism; a strain of idealism that envisages the ultimate harmony of the good, the true, and the beautiful; and a meliorist faith in human endeavor. These values permeate Richards' theories and method and, much later, his poetry and plays. Richards claimed that Lowes Dickinson's *A Modern*

Symposium (1905), which preached personal idealism, the perfectibility of man, internationalism, and toleration, "*had* a tremendous influence on me politically" ("Beginnings and Transitions: I. A. Richards Interviewed by Reuben Brower," 1973). Richards joined the Cambridge Heretics, a radical society whose moving spirit was Ogden. The Heretics championed such causes as academic reform, coeducation, adult education, civil liberty, opposition to compulsory college chapel, women's suffrage, syndicalism, internationalism, psychoanalysis, and birth control. Although Richards rarely made a political statement, he was a leftward-leaning liberal, with a strong current of individualism and utopianism. In 1960 he said in the preface to *The Screens and Other Poems* that his political ideal was a "good police" in a society "as nearly anarchic as possible" (p. 7).

THE FOUNDATIONS OF AESTHETICS

SOON after he graduated, Richards succumbed to his third, most severe, tubercular lesion (1915–1916), which kept him out of the war. Among the mountains of North Wales he lived alone for a year, recuperating and exercising his skills in rock climbing and high mountaineering, which became a lifelong passion. It was in 1917, on a mountaineering trek in Wales, that he met his future wife, Dorothy Eleanor Pilley (1894–1986). She was the daughter of a wealthy food manufacturer, a budding journalist and at the outset of a career as one of the great figures in British mountaineering. She was already keeping her remarkable diary (1910–1986). Their sometimes stormy courtship was to last nine years. Before the end of the war, Richards returned to Cambridge and took up premedical subjects with the intention of going into medicine and eventually "psychological medicine"—as late as June 1918 he declared this plan to Ogden. He also made a point of attending Moore's lectures, which were delivered across the street from the Cavendish Laboratory.

On the night of the armistice, 11 November 1918, Richards and Ogden met after a melee in which students had rioted and broken into Ogden's bookshops—for this Cambridge polymath had edited and published the *Cambridge Magazine* during the war and was reputed to be a pacifist.

They began discussing "meaning" and found they could agree on a theory of definition. "It's a most extraordinary experience," Richards recalled in 1969, "finding you can agree with someone. Decades later it wasn't the case that we could understand one another *at all*" ("An Interview with I. A. Richards"). This was the immediate origin of their collaborative efforts over the next five years, which resulted in *The Foundations of Aesthetics* (1922) and *The Meaning of Meaning*. The meeting with Ogden influenced Richards' entire career, for in the 1930's he shifted his primary focus of interest from the theory of criticism to Ogden's Basic English movement and language training. The theme of conciliation and agreement is among the strongest in his work.

Meanwhile Richards, a recent tubercular patient and impoverished student, was living a precarious life, rapidly losing interest in medical subjects and growing tired of waiting for a teaching post in moral sciences in one of the colleges. To his good fortune, Cambridge had ratified a degree in English studies in 1917 and teachers were being recruited to prepare for large numbers of returning soldiers in 1919. In an interview with Mansfield Forbes, to whom Richards went for recommendations as a mountaineering guide, the conversation quickly turned to literature. Two hours later Richards emerged with the position of freelance lecturer with a stipend directly proportional to the number of undergraduates enrolled in his courses. The year 1919, Richards reminisced while in his seventies, was "quite beyond anything you could imagine. It was World War I survivors come back to college. . . . There was an atmosphere, such a dream, such a hope. . . . Those who got back to Cambridge from all that slaughter were back *for reasons*" ("An Interview with I. A. Richards"). After serious illness and vocational uncertainty, Richards had regained his original path. Now, what should he teach? His answer typically combined high seriousness, spontaneity, pleasure, and modesty: "What would be fun? What could we talk about *without disgracing ourselves?*" In the autumn of 1919 Richards gave his first lectures in two courses, theory of criticism and the contemporary novel.

Within a few years, still in his twenties, Richards had become a spellbinding lecturer, one of the greatest teachers of his generation. So many students thronged to his lectures that at times they had to be held in the streets—something, Empson said, that had not happened since the Middle Ages. What was his subject? Not a crowd-pleasing theme, nor a political speech on the economy, nor a moral diatribe. He was reading poetry and explaining how to analyze it. His voice was pitched high and relatively neutral, though superb in modulation and timing. (He always disliked the way actors typically read poetry in a histrionic manner.) Richards' antirhetorical mode consorted with the times—one thinks of Ernest Hemingway's attack on patriotic oratory in *A Farewell to Arms* (1929) or Pound's "liars in public places" in *Hugh Selwyn Mauberly* (1920). Christopher Isherwood, one of Richards' early students, summed up the appeal in his autobiography, *Lions and Shadows:* "He was infinitely more than a brilliant new literary critic; he was our guide, our evangelist, who revealed to us, in a succession of astounding lightning flashes, the entire expanse of the Modern World" (Norfolk, 1947, pp. 121–122). He combined Cambridge analysis and modern science with a Romantic sense of the mysterious, the magical, and the oracular.

As with Moore, the lecture format suited Richards' approach to the analysis of meaning. For him, theory was for books, practical criticism for the lecture hall. There he could try out different rhythms, introduce some of the numberless shadings of a word or phrase, advance sudden qualifications and expansions, and draw the irradiated strands together, not always in smooth organic union, but in deliberate, disturbing disunion. In these exercises in practical criticism Richards had a microscopic eye, for the literary critic a gift perhaps even greater than theoretical brilliance. No detail—of sound, rhythm, word order, tone, line break, allusion—seemed at first glance too insignificant to be ignored; it might be the axis of the poem's world. He had the ability to contemplate a poem long and steadily, until its separable meanings each came into sharp focus, while retaining their vital connections to one another and to the whole. Since he believed that the voice was better able than the printed page to convey the "meanings" of a poem, he published fewer close readings than his pupils would have wished. For those who heard him lecture, Richards left the unforgettable impression of having gazed upon the ultimate particles of poetry.

Although Richards had conceived most of his major ideas before his thirtieth year, he constructed his theory and method slowly, from his first published essay, "Art and Science," in 1919 to *Interpreta-*

tion in Teaching in 1938. Arguing against the aesthetic formalism of Clive Bell and Roger Fry, "Art and Science" contends that the concept of truth is as "decisive" in building an art theory as it is in science: "Any aesthetic worth considering must use truth as a main instrument" (in *Complementarities*, 1976, p. 4). The real difference between science and art is not that one claims truth and the other does not but that the propositions of art do not necessarily form a logical system; in science, they do. Art "is interested in propositions for their own sake, not as interconnected" (p. 5). The test of truth in art lies within individual interiority, a matter of intuition, which is "self-evident" and "inevitable." Richards never abandoned his belief in truth as the "decisive notion" in art, though he would add to intuition a pragmatic test.

The Foundations of Aesthetics was a summer's project with Ogden and the artist James Wood in 1920. The authors present sixteen theories of beauty, not with the intention of bringing them into conflict but, as is stated in the preface to the first edition, "by distinguishing them to allow to each its separate sphere of validity": theories of intrinsic beauty (like Moore's in *Principia Ethica* [1903]), imitation, form, the medium, emotion, genius, pleasure, social effectiveness, empathy, and the authors' preferred theory of synaesthesis. This is essentially a psychological theory that includes notions of equilibrium, harmony, and freedom. In equilibrium, we have "no tendency to action"; "any concert-goer must have realised the impropriety of the view that action is the proper outcome of aesthetic appreciation." In harmony, the various impulses "work together": "such disciplined co-ordination in action is much to be desired in other places" (ch. 14). As the latter phrase indicates, Richards does not want to break the hidden relations between art and moral action, although he is yet to explain how they may be connected. (The power that *bad* or commercialized art *does* have over individuals—through best-sellers, the cinema, the media, advertising—was for Richards always the best reason to believe in the power that good or great art, if properly understood, *might* have.) Harmony is the process by which the conflicting impulses and attitudes, aroused by the work of art, strive together toward an end-state of consciousness. Yet it is easier to define lack of harmony or false harmony. Thus in "oscillation" or "deadlock," two or more conflicting states of mind fail to resolve;

phases alternate either too rapidly or too weakly for either side to make its appropriate claim in the end result; or phases keep their independence and do not mutually inform one another. False balance shares the feeling of completeness with synaesthesis and so may be mistaken for it. Such balance wins its way by the suppression of rival emotional groups, which nonetheless keep up a menacing pressure and threaten the balance.

The experience of beauty as synaesthesis strengthens inwardness, freedom, and possibility: "As we realise beauty we become more fully ourselves the more our impulses are engaged. . . . Our interest is not canalised in one direction rather than another. It becomes ready instead to take any direction we choose. This is the explanation of that detachment so often mentioned in artistic experience" (ch. 14). Richards employs "impulse" to mean the force behind a mental event, or the deeper drives and interests; it is not merely a neural event, the nerve impulse. His statement accords with the humanism of Matthew Arnold. Not a "loss of self," but a larger, more inclusive, and fully integrated self emerges from the experience of great art. Richards would later refer to poetry as the "completest mode of utterance" (*Coleridge on Imagination*, p. 163) for its power to create such states of mind. Synaesthesis foreshadows the psychological side of Richards' writings in the 1920's. It contains the synthetic-dynamic principle of the "equilibrium of opposed impulses" (*Principles of Literary Criticism*, p. 251), and takes into account his notions of clarity, alertness, readiness to act (without a specific, overt action), impersonality, freedom, and "completed being" (p. 252).

At the same time, without entirely abandoning psychology, Richards would trace psychological effects to their proximate causes in the objective work of art and emphasize linguistic analysis. A quick, subtle thinker, Richards moves from one to another phase of communication—artist, poem, reader—without losing sight of the whole, and this should be a warning against pigeonholing his aesthetic theory with either objectivist (or formalist) or subjectivist (or psychologistic) labels. His practical experience ensured that he would examine both the reader's "responses" and the aesthetic object, along with the vital interplay between them. One of his weaknesses, however, is already present in his first book: the failure to examine the social and historical origins of the various theories of art. Like so many others of his generation, he reacted against nineteenth-century historicism and biographical criticism. On this point, to the detriment of his criticism, Richards never yielded.

In 1923 Richards and Ogden published *The Meaning of Meaning.* It has been called the most famous book ever published in the field of semantics. Born of the antiwar consciousness following World War I, it is a search conducted over five hundred pages for a new "meaning of meaning" and directive for civilization. In the spirit of Arnold, the authors address persons "of learning and sincerity" and observe that "new millions of participants in the control of general affairs must now attempt to form personal opinions upon matters which were once left to a few." "At the same time," the authors continue, "the complexity of these matters has immensely increased" (preface to the first edition). How will the new voting masses be properly educated in the arts of language? How can they learn to break the spell of words—as propaganda, publicity, yellow journalism, language coming over the air waves, through the loudspeakers, in the cinema halls—if they do not possess a practical understanding of the use and abuse of words?

THE MEANING OF MEANING

MANY books in one, *The Meaning of Meaning* contains a historical compendium of attitudes to language; a partly mentalist, partly behaviorist approach to meaning; a critique of philosophic definitions of beauty; a functional theory of language; and a practical guide to improvement in speech, writing, and translation. What unifies the work is an inner theme: words are not a part of and do not correspond to things but to thought and emotion. Words " 'mean' nothing by themselves"; "it is only when a thinker makes use of them that they stand for anything" (ch. 1). Only contexts have meaning. Instead of regarding the meaning of a sentence, for example, to be the result of the meaning of individual words, Richards and Ogden begin the other way around, with the meaning of the sentence or larger discourse in context, and work backward. The readers' applications of this principle increases their interpretive skills and enhances the freedom that language can afford for intellectual and moral growth. Conversely, the failure to benefit from the principle leaves one bound to language or by those ever present manipulators of language. The authors subject the word "meaning" to one of their critical strategies, multiple definition: twenty-two current definitions of "meaning" are examined. Clearly, the authors conclude, philosophy had run aground on language. Not only philosophy—all intellectual disciplines were suffering from not taking language sufficiently into account. Many contemporary thinkers such as John Dewey, Henri-Louis Bergson, and Ludwig Wittgenstein, were roughly handled, but this was quite calculated. Richards said *The Meaning of Meaning* was all "written in the spirit of 'here's a nice half-brick, whom shall we throw it at?' " (*Complimentarities,* p. 256).

The most serious abuse of language, the authors find, is treating words as things. They illustrate this "disease" of "Word Magic" from primitive times to recent philosophy in which the error is linked to entrapment by hypotheses, universals, linguistic fictions (Bentham's theory of Fictions was relevant), and even hypostatized grammar. Words have habitually led us to think in terms of the categories, beliefs, values—the "meanings"—for which they have stood at some point in their history. Long after the meanings have shifted, the words continue to give them life, piloting us along similar lines and leading us to repeat the errors of the past. Words assume the place of active thinking and "think" for us; we succumb to the "devastating disease" of "word-dependence." Other linguistic traps include the "proper meaning superstition," by which a word has a single meaning belonging to itself, and the "doctrine of usage" whereby grammarians insist on fixed denotation based on (usually one) "correct" use. The aim is to be "word-free" or "word-independent" (ch. 10).

The authors hope to reduce confusion with their "Thought or Reference" triangle in chapter 1:

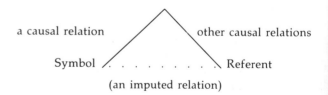

a causal relation   other causal relations

Symbol   Referent

(an imputed relation)

This is now a standard device in semantics textbooks. A *symbol* is a word that stands for some object, depending on an empirical test; *thought* or *reference* is the psychological context to which the word belongs in the individual history of the speaker or reader; *referent* is the spatio-temporal particular. If no external referent exists, there is no "symbol" but rather an emotive "sign" for something in the psychological context.

In their elaboration of "context" the authors borrowed from John B. Watson's theory of behaviorism, which was new, radically different, and therefore suspect, thus adding to the book's notoriety. Richards drew again on Watson, as well as the neurophysiologist C. S. Sherrington, in *Principles of Literary Criticism,* and despite his protestations, he was ever afterward dubbed a behaviorist. A careful scrutiny, however, shows that Richards and Ogden, faithful to the Cambridge philosophical tradition, remained mentalists, with strong leanings toward the sciences. They realized the virtues and limitations of behaviorism, and preferred the employment of multiple models, which they termed the "double language hypothesis": reality is the unknowable x but it may be described in one or another languages or systems. Richards was practicing Niels Bohr's principle of complementarity, announced in 1927, even before he preached it in his later criticism as expressing his position on the nature of models: the inevitable mixing of the model with reality in experimental results, and the safeguard of using multiple models. Richards' most explicit critique of behaviorism appeared in a review of Watson's *Behaviorism* in 1926.

To determine the meaning of a given utterance, Richards and Ogden propose a functional theory of language, which was supported in a supplement to *The Meaning of Meaning* by the anthropologist Bronislaw Malinowski. According to the theory, language fulfills a "plurality of functions," jobs, purposes: it can convey emotion, it can depict objects, it can adjust a tonal relation to an audience. Five functions are analyzed in *The Meaning of Meaning.* With the "referential" or "scientific" function, the uppermost purpose of the language is neutral description and analysis. The value-laden "emotive" function of language is exemplified by political speeches, advertising—and poetry. In most cases all the functions are more or less present in the given utterance. Analysis untangles the various functions and assesses the manner in which they help or hinder one another. One must assess the individual intentions behind the various functions as well as the intention of the whole utterance within its situation or context. By examining the surrounding context, physical and psychological, one determines the total meaning of the utterance.

By 1955 Richards had raised the number of language's functions to eight (indicating, characterizing, realizing, valuing, influencing, controlling, purposing, venting). He said that one could have as many functions as one preferred so long as each was given its specific duty within an utterance. This is a late statement; in *The Meaning of Meaning* the authors had put the accent on the rigid twofold division of referential and emotive language instead of on the multiple functions, placing language within a limited view of reality split between the objective and the subjective, between facts and values—a position with which they became identified. But what is more interesting in light of their later work is their presentation of multiple functions (and models). Richards' and Ogden's discussion of the referential versus emotive use of language anticipates aspects of the logical positivism of the Vienna Circle, while their more flexible approach to multiple linguistic functions and the significance of context adumbrate elements in the later Wittgenstein and J. L. Austin.

PRINCIPLES OF LITERARY CRITICISM

Having focused on referential or "scientific" language in *The Meaning of Meaning,* Richards turned to the poetic uses of language in *Principles of Literary Criticism.* With scientific language, references must be correct (match up to referents) and the "connections and relations of references to one another must be of the kind which we call logical." In the poetic use, the "series of attitudes due to the references should have their own proper organisation, their own emotional interconnection" (ch. 34). As in "Art and Science," Richards claims that poetry need not convey a "logical" picture of reality to claim truth. His psychological model served a triple purpose: to account for value, thereby showing why the arts are among the highest goods; to specify the nature of communication; and to supply concepts and terms for analyzing the objective work of art. Besides the specific model, psychology furnished Richards with an abundance of ideas. Nor was he inclined to a "mechanical" view of mental action, as is sometimes thought, for he borrows equally from associationists (Alexander Bain, John B. Watson, Margaret Washburn) and antias-sociationists (James Ward, G. F. Stout, the Wurz-burg School), as well as from William James. Freudian theory is noteworthy for its relative absence, but this is because the psychological component of Richards' criticism largely predated the diffusion of Freud's ideas in England. In any case, the originality of Richards' model lies not so much in its parts as in its assembly and the use to which it was put.

The central feature in the model is taken from C. S. Sherrington's description of the "final common path" in *Integrative Action of the Nervous System* (1906). Reading "upward" from a physical to a psychological model, Richards portrays the mind as a vast system of impulses and interests, either allied with or antagonistic to one another as they compete for action pathways. When a large number of impulses converge upon one of these paths, the group that wins through the "final common path" brings about the particular action. However, when opposing groups are more or less evenly balanced, they are halted and resolve into "attitudes," which are "imaginal and incipient activities" or "tendencies to action" (ch. 15) but not action itself. Lack of immediate physical action, which in Sherrington is "attention," allows for the opportunity to try out the experience imaginatively and receive "backwash" emotional effects, to learn from the potential experience and test its worthiness. If action does ensue, the poetic experience will have rendered it more subtle and appropriate than might have been the case.

Since an individual benefits from the most varied attitudes, Richards postulates a theory of value by which ideal mental states "involve the widest and most comprehensive co-ordination of activities and the least curtailment, conflict, starvation and restriction" (ch. 8). Breadth of mental experience, equipoise, and readiness of response (what Richards calls in *Science and Poetry* "command of life"), and not immediate satisfaction, are his higher values which may be termed a critical eudaemonism. He admires "those fortunate people who have achieved an ordered life, whose systems have developed clearing-houses by which the varying claims of different impulses are adjusted. Their free, untrammelled activity gains for them a maximum of varied satisfactions and involves a minimum of suppression and sacrifice." At the other

extreme are persons "hag-ridden by their vices, or their virtues, to a point at which the law of diminishing returns has deprived even these of their appropriate satisfactions" (ch. 7); these are subject to what Freud deemed excessive repression. Eliot, in a 1927 *Dial* article, mocked Richards' moral ideal as "Efficiency—a perfectly working mental Roneo Steel Cabinet System," although he admitted that his psychology "is probably quite true." (In fact, Richards' attempt to bridge the gaps between physical and mental action in his model is not as successful as Eliot appears to have assumed.)

Underlying Richards' psychology is the pragmatic principle of continuity by which aesthetic experiences are "only a further development, a finer organisation of ordinary experiences," and not a "new and different kind of thing" (ch. 2). This was his rebuke to aestheticism or any kind of formalism that separated the arts from other human activities, including moral action. The greatest theories in the history of criticism, he believed, were the moral theories. On the other hand, unlike Tolstoy, Richards did not advance a specific moral doctrine. As Richard Foster summarizes in "The Romanticism of I. A. Richards" (1959), "through intelligent experiencing of the arts our minds pass from relative chaos to relative order, from a condition relatively wasteful of their inherent resources to one relatively complete in its realization of them" (p. 93).

How can one produce ideal states of mind? Who has the best ones? For Richards, the "artist's organization," both in the "creative moment" and "in its aspect as a vehicle of communication" (the poem), presents "conciliations of impulses which in most minds are still confused, intertrammelled and conflicting" (ch. 8). The poet "makes unconsciously a selection which outwits the force of habit; the impulses he awakens are freed, through the very means by which they are aroused, from the inhibitions that ordinary circumstances encourage . . . and upon the resulting simplified but widened field of impulses he imposes an order which their greater plasticity allows them to accept" (ch. 32). Linking poetry to whatever human progress there is, Richards remarks that the poet's mind in the creative moment is "the point at which the growth of the mind shows itself" (ch. 8). In Richards' theory of communication, while the reader's response cannot be identical to the artist's original experience (even in the most ideal circumstances), nonetheless they should be closely similar. When reading well, the reader reenacts the poet's imaginative progress in the work itself or in what Richards terms the "poetic process." In one definition, a poem is a class of experiences that do not differ within certain limits from the artist's experience. Conceding that we cannot know the artist's exact psychological experience, Richards argues that the properly interpreted poem supplies abundant evidence for that experience. "Qualified readers," who can avoid the pitfalls of misreading and observe the poet's numerous linguistic controls, can achieve either agreement or mutual understanding through one or another permissible "variant readings." The way was now open for Richards to analyze how a poem works and where readers go wrong, the two fields of his most original research.

As with empirical philosophy and psychological textbooks, Richards starts with imagery. Some readers indulge in irrelevant personal imagery, like daydreaming, and lose the poem. Instead of reading the poet's poem, they read a "private poem." Other readers who do not have a strong visualizing capacity undergo no loss of meaning. They may be less distracted. (The discussion of overvisualization contains an implicit critique of the rising "image" culture and its hegemonic claims over "word" culture.) Richards distinguishes "free" from "tied" imagery (ch. 16). Free images—visual, aural, taste, etc.—are mental signs of sensory qualities and vary somewhat from person to person because life-histories inevitably are different. To Richards, the sensory qualities of the images, however different, are less important than the ways in which these images stand for a verbal sign, the more generalized item, within the poetic structure. This sign structure ensures against totally subjective interpretations. Tied images are either auditory ("the sound of the word in the mind's ear") or articulatory (the feel of the words on the lips and tongue and in the throat). The performance of the language—not necessarily spoken aloud, but in the imagination—ought to play a significant role in both the poetic experience and the analysis.

With regard to the sense of a poem—prose paraphrase, theme, allusion, reference, "local" as opposed to the "total meaning" of a poem—Richards takes a novel approach. Sense is only one of the components of a poem, and often not the most important. In *Science and Poetry* he introduces the

term "pseudo-statement" (ch. 6) to indicate the kind of sense or reference in poetry that was justified primarily through its power to bring about attitudes that are "true" to the feelings, though not necessarily "true" to external reality. The pseudo-statement may be true to external reality and pass a scientific or historical test, but that is not its main purpose. If the question "Is this true in the strict, scientific sense?" has to be asked, we are not in the presence of emotive language. Some critics wrongly interpreted "pseudo-statement" to mean simply a false statement. Richards wanted to account for poetic organicity, the manner in which the functions of language and poetic qualities work together in the poetic process. This meant not imposing a priori preferences. "Many arrangements of words," he writes, "evoke attitudes without any reference being required *en route.* They operate like musical phrases. But usually references are involved *as conditions* for, or *stages in,* the ensuring development of attitudes, yet it is still the attitudes not the references which are important" (ch. 34). In different poetries, the various components of a poem will be weighed differently.

In Swinburne's poetry, he comments in "The Analysis of a Poem" (ch. 16), we may encounter "vague thoughts" that are not closely linked to one another; feeling or mood is predominant over sense:

There glowing ghosts of flowers
Draw down, draw nigh;
And wings of swift spent hours
    Take flight and fly;
She sees by formless gleams
She hears across cold streams
    Dead mouths of many dreams that sing and sigh.

At the other extreme, Hardy's poetic argument requires far more attention to the logical sense of the words:

    "Who's in the next room?—who?
        I seemed to see
    Somebody in the dawning passing through
        Unknown to me."
    "Nay: you saw nought. He passed invisibly."

Richards, whose taste in poetry was very broad, admired both writers deeply. Indeed, while his method gained fame from its treatment of complex metaphysical and modernist poetry, it is open to the widest variety of "poetries" (he himself liked to stress the plural). If in his early books he emphasized the emotive functions, it was because he hoped to check the excessively "message"-oriented reading then current, with its sharp division between form and content. In *The Meaning of Meaning,* he writes that "a poem—or a religion . . .—has no concern with limited and directed reference. It tells us, or should tell us, nothing" (ch. 7). Here he uses "tell" in the special sense of the scientific or referential function. In *Science and Poetry* he argues that "it is never what a poem *says* which matters, but what it *is*" (ch. 2). Such statements were wrongly interpreted as an attack on sense itself in poetry, though as Gerald Graff notes, Richards is "severe with readers who fail to construe the 'Sense' of a poem accurately."[2] With the success of his method, Richards dropped these warnings against overvaluing sense. His practical criticism devotes more space to sense than to any other aspect of a poem.

With regard to rhythm and meter Richards, like Benedetto Croce, spurns the traditional vocabulary—feet, meters, stanzaic patterns—as the imposition of a rigid, inorganic order upon the fluid individuality of the poem. At best, classical prosody can describe only the *"general* movement" of the rhythm. Reading aloud, the indispensable aid in determining the exact rhythm, is a reminder that the power of rhythm does not derive from "perceiving a pattern in something outside us, but to our becoming patterned ourselves" (ch. 17). Rhythm and its more specialized form of meter contribute to distancing and the sense of impersonality. Most important, a rhythmic pattern establishes expectations of a certain order, but vetoes nothing outright, and leaves open the unexpected possibility, a violence of order. Thus rhythm is "much more a negative thing than a positive," that is, it sets limits, but does not prescribe. "Much more a negative thing," a characteristic phrase, implies more than the fact that the rhythmic pattern may result in the unexpected. It is a warning against the easy satisfaction, against the premature imposition of an accepted form and for the possibility of something unexpected and possibly better. No one valued more than Richards the significance of surprise in aesthetic experience. He

developed a phrase for this leitmotiv in his work: *Neti, neti,* the Vedantist injunction against trying to characterize what as yet lies beyond one's grasp— *"Not that, not that;* the positive utterance being beyond our means" (*So Much Nearer: Essays Toward a World English,* 1968, p. 120).

For Richards, sound imagery is more primordial than rhythm, but its effects are usually either "too subtle" or "too mingled" with other elements in the context to be assessed critically. The sound pattern of a good poem on a recording drum might be "indistinguishable" from "rubbish." In *Practical Criticism* he concocts a stanza of nonsense verse whose sounds exactly parallel a stanza from Milton's Nativity Ode, proving that sound is only "valuable" in context with all other elements of meaning. The rhythm "which we seem to detect actually *in* the sounds, and which we seem to respond to, is something which we only *ascribe* to them, is, actually, a rhythm of the mental activity through which we apprehend not only the sound of the words but their sense and feeling" (ch. 4). Only very occasionally does he comment on sound by itself, usually in the act of correcting a student comment. He notes the difference between "tingling" and "tinkling" in D. H. Lawrence's "Piano," in which the proximity of the child's ear to the piano provides the acoustic clue: "tingling" when he sat beneath the piano and felt physical vibrations, "tinkling" when he stood farther off. Here Richards has onomatopoeia for a guide.

Tone, a major poetic component, is treated most extensively in *Practical Criticism.* In fact tone is multiple, being the attitude of the artist toward the audience, the subject matter, or himself; or of the speaker within the poem toward the audience, subject matter, or himself. In this way Richards distinguishes the poem's intentions from the poet's, further adding to distancing and impersonality. Eighteenth-century poets often pay readers "too much deference"; poets like Shelley and Swinburne, on the other hand, sometimes "please themselves" and "neglect the reader" (ch. 3). Even lyric poems have a dramatic element, and so establish relationships between themselves and their readers. Richards' "speaker" is the origin of the New Critical concern with "voice," "narrator," "persona," and "mask." His concepts of tone and the speaker proved among the most useful of all his contributions.

With regard to the "total meaning" of the poem

[2]G. Graff, *Poetic Statement and Critical Dogma,* 2nd ed. (Chicago, 1980), p. 26.

or "wholeness," Richards treats the question from the viewpoint of both the reader's response and the work of art. It is a psychological experience that has its roots in the stimulating object. Yet the "balance" experienced by a reader is not mirrored in the object (many works of art do not exhibit external symmetries or balance) or we would have a "formula for beauty." Other aestheticians with less practical experience of reading poetry had erred in this regard. Richards' definition of wholeness in *Principles of Literary Criticism* subsumes his discussion of synaesthesis in *The Foundations of Aesthetics.* It begins with the reader: "The equilibrium of opposed impulses, which we suspect to be the ground-plan of the most valuable aesthetic responses, brings into play far more of our personality than is possible in experiences of more defined emotion" (ch. 32). The greater poetries overcome the "more defined" emotion not with "less defined," but with a wider interplay of emotions themselves. Irony is one by which a poet creates the interplay and tension in the work of art, so creating the conditions for wholeness or equilibrium. Classical irony is stating one thing and meaning the opposite; for Richards, following Romantic concepts, irony "consists in the bringing in of the opposite, the complementary impulses" (ch. 32) without eliminating or suppressing the original impulses. It gives amplitude to the poem's world and makes certain that the poem has earned its strength and stability through conflict with other views, to the point of including them in the final response.

In a "poetry of inclusion" the sets of impulses or interests do not have the same direction. Instead, the poem has an "extraordinary heterogeneity" of interests and impulses; "more than heterogeneous, they are opposed." Richards has no quarrel with poems of "more defined" emotion that win their success through eliminating or suppressing these other points of view: Housman, Bridges, Burns, and Fitzgerald practice a "poetry of exclusion." But he preferred the poetry of inclusion or "synthesis," which contains its own counterpositions, often in dialectical relation to its main themes, such as "Sir Patrick Spens," Donne's "Nocturnall upon S. Lucie's Day," or Keats's "Ode to a Nightingale." The poetry of inclusion can bear "ironical contemplation"; with the poetry of exclusion, however, readers may undermine the poem's stability by supplying, consciously or otherwise, the other position (through questions, nagging doubts). This is

why poetry which is "exposed" to a reader's irony "is not of the highest order, and why irony itself is so constantly a characteristic of poetry which is" (ch. 32). Hopkins and E. M. Forster strive for inclusion and fail; Dostoyevsky, Eliot, and Joyce are among the premier modern artists of inclusion.

Ambiguity is another literary device that expands the intellectual and emotional perimeters of a poem. In *Principles of Literary Criticism* Richards writes that, while the thoughts occasioned by the words happen first, "more important are the further thoughts caused by the sense, the network of interpretation and conjecture which arises therefrom" (ch. 32). In 1926 he argued that "very much of the best poetry" is "necessarily ambiguous in its immediate effect." Then he defended Gerard Manley Hopkins against a charge of mere "obscurity" and applauded writers who "can compel slow reading," remarking that the "peculiar intellectual thrill which celebrates the step-by-step conquest of understanding may irradiate and awaken other mental activities more essential to poetry." In *Practical Criticism* he declared that ambiguity "in fact is systematic" and can be plotted within poems. (His student William Empson came out with *Seven Types of Ambiguity* the following year.) One of Richards' examples is a poem by G. H. Luce, on which he performs a close reading. In the line "O frail steel tissue of the sun," "frail" is the opposite of steel-like, hard steel is the opposite of soft tissue, and tissue is midway between opacity and transparency. "We have to gather millions of fleeting semi-independent impulses into the momentary structure of fabulous complexity, whose core or germ is given us in the words." By *Coleridge on Imagination* (1934) he would speak of doctrinal oppositions coming together in "ambiguity (or rather completeness)," where ambiguity is a means of securing inclusion, and completeness an ideal state of mind. In view of subsequent critical trends—Empson's ambiguity, William Wimsatt's and Cleanth Brooks's irony and paradox, Allen Tate's tension, Philip Wheelwright's "plurisignifications," Paul De Man's "free presence" of the word, and Jacques Derrida's floating signifiers—Richards' promotion of ambiguity to a major literary device marks a historic moment in criticism.

Since the advent of historicism, the concept of aesthetic universality has been infrequently raised. The critical tendency has been to assess how a work expresses its sociohistorical circumstances,

415

not how it escapes them. By revealing the hidden ambiguities of language, Richards helped to show how works once considered strictly doctrinal were far more hedged by doubt than hitherto suspected; or how authors left traces of a struggle against counterpositions, proving they did not arrive at their conclusions without entertaining alternatives. The ambiguity of poetic language ensured that the emphasis might fall as much upon the poets' questions, not answers, so leaving their works ever open to study. As Richards writes in *Principles of Literary Criticism:*

The arts are our storehouse of recorded values. They spring from and perpetuate hours in the lives of exceptional people, when their control and command of experience is at its highest, hours when the varying possibilities of existence are most clearly seen and the different activities which may arise are most exquisitely reconciled, hours when habitual narrowness of interests or confused bewilderment are replaced by an intricately wrought composure.

(ch. 4)

Paul Ricoeur writes that Richards' "pioneering" work on metaphor in *The Philosophy of Rhetoric* (1936) "cannot be overestimated" (*The Rule of Metaphor,* p. 76). In neoclassic theory, the two parts of a metaphor—sometimes called the idea and the image—were placed in a strict hierarchy, the prejudice favoring the idea over the image. Some theorists refused to concede how much of the "idea" was actually embedded in, and drawn from the image. To refer to one side as the "idea" or "meaning" is to assume that the other side is ornamental and that the logic of the discourse might survive without it. Richards' originality consisted in granting parity to the two parts to prevent prejudice in judgment prior to analysis. He coined terms for these parts to reinforce objectivity and neutrality: "tenor" (or "principal subject") and "vehicle" (what the principal subject is compared to). What is shared by the two parts is the "ground" of the metaphor. In "Achilles is a lion," the tenor is Achilles, the vehicle is lion; the ground is "strength"; but the "whole double unit" is the metaphor, not the vehicle alone. And neither tenor nor vehicle go through the metaphorical process unchanged. The tenor is affected by the context of the vehicle, and vice versa, each exchanging elements from the other's context. In this exchange,

what the tenor excludes from the vehicle's context, and vice versa, is probably more important to the production of the metaphor than what is specified. *Neti, neti.* Richards' definition of a metaphor is a "transaction between contexts." If ever so slightly, the life histories of the words are changed permanently. Even more important, unlike neoclassic theory, Richards' theory can no longer take the doctrinal security of the tenor for granted. His theory is one for an age of relativity and pluralism.

Through the 1920's Richards suggested different textual features as forwarding or controlling the process of poetic "wholeness": rhythm, sense, "movement and sound" together, "passional structure," tonal control. Richards' difficulty in deciding reflects his close experience in reading, for he came to appreciate the variety of means by which poems structure themselves. Later essays stress the poem's "autonomous being": "How Does a Poem Know When It Is Finished?" (1963) or "How a Poem Protects Itself" (unpublished lecture, ca. 1967). The poem's strongest means of protection—against political movements, literary fads, bad readers—is "contextual check," the interplay of literary devices and linguistic functions. Contextual check provides the grounds for distinguishing legitimate "variant readings" from outright "misreading" and thus shifts (part of) the burden of judgment from subjective taste to argument and analysis. While the "equilibrium of opposed impulses" serves as Richards' best description of a poem at the beginning of his career, "oppositions and collaborations among words" does so in his final years. For this reason, his general theory of criticism has, with justice, been termed "contextualism."

Proceeding from literary devices to larger forms in *Principles of Literary Criticism,* Richards prefers tragedy before all other genres because it is the "most general, all-accepting, all-ordering experience." Its essence is conflict and reconciliation, such as the opposition between pity ("the impulse to approach") and terror ("the impulse to retreat"), along with other groups of discordant impulses. The unified response issues in catharsis as we undergo a "sense of release," of "repose in the midst of stress," of "intricately wrought composure." He claims, "This balanced poise, stable through its power of inclusion, not through the force of its exclusions, is not peculiar to tragedy. It is a general characteristic of all the most valuable experiences of the arts" (ch. 32). Next to tragedy, Richards thought that "universal satire" embraced heterogeneity, as in the juxtaposition of the sublime and tawdry slang. In this category he placed Shakespeare's *Troilus and Cressida* and his treatment of Falstaff, *Don Quixote, Candide,* Flaubert's *Bouvard et Pécuchet,* and Wyndham Lewis' *Childermass.*

Through irony, ambiguity, tension, tragic conflict, and heterogeneity, Richards emphasized disturbances rather than harmonies in works of art. His main specimens for the "equilibrium of opposed impulses" were writers whose thematic materials are immensely varied, whose societies are in states of transformation or disintegration, or whose ideologies drive them in contrary directions. At the same time, he believed that wholeness in a work of art could lead to wholeness of character. Ideally he preferred that state of "vigilance" and "openness" to experience that contained equilibrium, but was ready to be broken apart and transformed by something more valuable, that is, a more capacious self with a greater "command of life." In the 1926 edition of *Science and Poetry* Richards spoke of "complete equilibrium" as an end-state of poetry; when he republished it in 1935 he changed "complete" to "wider," the comparative of degree indicating his awareness of a person's need for stability and an equal awareness of the dangers of habit and entrapment, with the thrust toward ever-widening perspective. So that they would not lose out on this crucial experience, Richards warned his students not to forget the distinction between "what a poem does" to us in imaginative reading and "how it works" in discursive analysis. As he said, even where the boundaries between reading and analysis are not fixed and are likely to change when analysis incorporates itself into a subsequent reading, nonetheless "there is a risk that we may lose the poetry in the poetics." It is "easier to measure time lengths than sprinklings of grace" (ch. 3).

SCIENCE AND POETRY
AND PRACTICAL CRITICISM

SCIENCE AND POETRY (1926), a short popularization of Richards' ideas, has a manifesto air. It appeared in the Psyche Miniatures series as a pocket-sized edition. As with many of his books, he begins by painting the contemporary situation in the bleakest terms. The war has brought human progress to a halt. He says in chapter 5 that science has "neutralized" nature and has destroyed the "Magical View of the world" (Richards probably took this concept from Max Weber, who speaks of the "de-magification" of the world in modernity). Myths that supported humankind for thousands of years have collapsed in a century. Voices of ideology and propaganda—what Jakob Burckhardt prophesied as the "terrifying simplifiers"—assail us on all sides. Language has become debased by the media. Within this *Waste Land* scenario Richards mingles pessimism with optimism. The very suddenness with which all these circumstances have converged can shock us into awareness. Yet science, which has been responsible for so much of the transformation of modernity, can neither replace religion, nor fulfill emotional needs once answered by religion, nor redirect the search for new values. Invoking Matthew Arnold, Richards sees a way through the crisis: "We shall be thrown back up . . . upon poetry. It is capable of saving us; it is a perfectly possible means of overcoming chaos" (ch. 7). Richards did not mean that world literature in its major statements held the key to the future, but that great literature must be restudied, not by the few, but by the many, and at a much deeper level of linguistic comprehension, for its insight and debate over central human themes. Only then would individuals be in a better position to confront the "contemporary situation" and freely choose their future. Richards was fond of citing Francis Bacon's equation of knowledge and power, and thought that the new sciences (e.g., linguistics, psychology, anthropology) would enhance our understanding of poetry. If we could learn more about how a poem works, we would know more about how a mind works—and this was the point—how to assess and rank its possibilities in terms of growth, power, control, and moral action. Poetry was capable of saving us—with the help of science.

The psychology that Richards employed to examine literature in the 1920's represents the first phase of his interest in science. He later found means of applying the media and technology to develop his language learning programs and combat illiteracy. His criticism as a whole illustrates what many thinkers have seen as the twentieth-century search for a comprehensive theory of mind: introspective psychology, neurophysiology, behaviorism, linguistics, cybernetics. Adding the other scientific concepts that absorbed him—from evolutionary theory, relativity, Niels Bohr's complementarity, the engineer's communication model, embryological growth—his writings present a tableau vivant of contemporary science.

To be sure, Richards' views on science were never popular. Part of his audience withdrew in aesthetic horror or fastidious disdain. To confirmed religious believers, science was useful, but beside the point on the most important questions, and they accused Richards of making poetry a substitute religion. To say poetry is capable of saving us, wrote Eliot in *Selected Essays,* is "like saying that the wall-paper will save us when the walls have crumbled." To nonbelievers like Wells or Shaw, Richards' attitude toward science must have had a period flavor. Writing in the journal *Scrutiny,* Denys Harding said that Richards was attempting "to meet the friendly and intelligent Philistine on his own grounds" ("Evolutions I: Richards," 1933).

Speculating in *Science and Poetry* on what happens to a mind when it reads a poem, Richards quotes Wordsworth's sonnet "Composed upon Westminster Bridge" (1807). In one of his arcane metaphors he likens the mind to a system of magnetic balances; the poem moving through the mind restores equilibrium. In a chapter entitled "What Is Valuable," he asks us to consider what we would wish for a friend given one final hour of life, blocking out any considerations of an afterlife and assuming that the person is otherwise well. This test resembles G. E. Moore's introspective concept of "absolute isolation." Would we not want for our friend the "fullest, keenest, most active and completest kind of life"? "What does such life feel like, how is it to live through? the answer is that it feels like and is the experience of poetry" (ch. 3).

Practical Criticism is the most empirical and experimental—and scientific—of all Richards' studies, the most evenly balanced between theory and practice. His rhetoric is thoroughly under control, as he was not attempting to change human nature, only reading habits. The origin of this famous study in the pathology of interpretation traces to a dinner-hall conversation with A. C. Benson in 1923. Benson's diary records Richards' suggestion that a good test of reading would be to ask students for their comments on a small group of poems without any clue as to author or date and "containing one really *worthless* piece." Richards began the experiment in 1925 and resumed it upon his return from the Far East in 1927. The book consists of 176 pages of student comments or "protocols" on thirteen poems interspersed by Richards' analysis; this is followed by an equally lengthy section on the method of "close reading" and a summary of recommendations. The poems range in quality from John Donne's "At the Round Earth's Imagined Corners Blow," Gerard Manley Hopkins' "Spring and Fall, To a Young Child," and Thomas Hardy's George Meredith elegy, to lyrics by G. A. Studdert Kennedy and J. D. C. Pellew. Often the students blamed their own faulty readings on the poet and condemned the poem. These were honors students at Cambridge. (Richards tried his experiment elsewhere with similar results.) Sometimes the poet *was* in error, captured by his own stock response or sentimentality; in these cases the poem had been foisted upon the student by tradition or bad teaching. However, the results of the experiment documented serious deficiencies in education, and Richards concluded that a "decline in speech" was well under way. Would it end in a new barbarism?

Among the causes of decline in the arts of language Richards noted the hidden connections between mass education and mass media. He saw that the "economics" of the media industry did not permit transmission of "new, delicate, and subtle ideas," which "cost too much labour" in production and distribution. The media function at their best with "stereotyped ideas" that can be " 'put across' quickly" (*Principles of Literary Criticism,* ch. 31), a prescient remark on the importance of time in mass media. Readers who lack sufficient roundedness and inwardness may succumb to the "*attractiveness* of the idea (in light of some particular desire)" rather than its "*relevance.*" "Widespread diffusion" leads to a "standardisation" and thence a "levelling down" (*Practical Criticism,* part 3, ch. 5). Violence in the media, for example, does not mean simple mimetic response in the audience; rather, such experiences are turned inward to reemerge in "sinister" mass forms: in 1924 Richards had already warned of the "sinister potentialities of the cinema" (*Principles of Literary Criticism,* ch. 5) "The extent," he writes, "to which second-hand experience of a crass and inchoate type is replacing ordinary life offers a threat which has not yet been realised" (ch. 31). The situation will only worsen "as world communications, through the wireless and otherwise, improve" (*Practical Criticism,* part 4, "Suggestions Towards a Remedy").

I. A. RICHARDS

Typical among student errors were "stock responses" and "irrelevant associations," hobby horses, sentimentality, inhibitions, and confusions over the poet's "sense," feeling, or tone. One understood Alfred Noyes's metaphor "king / Of all our hearts" to be about a real king (part 2, "Poem 9"), an error of sense. Others failed to construe the delicate, wistful tone of Hopkins' speaker, calling him "reproachful," "sermonising," "patronising": "The *parent or whoever it is* who is advising Margaret *is a bitter, hard individual* who seems to be trying to take away all the hope and happiness of the child" (part 2, "Poem 6"). Still others jumped to conclusions on the basis of a misread rhythm or image and rode a hobby horse such as a preference for rhyme. Richards defined their behavior in terms of a "stock response" which is something already-made, implying convenience, speed, and standardization; a stock response costs the reader less than a response "made out of raw or partially prepared materials." Many readers tended to substitute stock responses instead of fashioning a response appropriate to the experience of the poem. "Nearly all good poetry," he notes, is "disconcerting, for a moment at least" (part 3, ch. 5).

One of the most serious errors was a student's espousal or rejection of a poem because of its particular "doctrine"—which was why Richards, in the Introduction, could describe his book as "field-work in comparative ideology." The climax of *Practical Criticism* is a chapter on "Doctrine in Poetry" that concludes with a discussion of sincerity. No theme in Richards is more symbolic of its age: skepticism, relativity, the mixing of traditions, unbelief, personalism. His interest in belief went back to his undergraduate years when, on 5 March 1915, as a member of the Moral Science Club, he delivered his very first paper on J. H. Newman's psychology of belief (Bertrand Russell signed the minutes, which said the paper was "short but highly interesting"). According to Richards, the personal context that one brings to a poem should be as open as possible to the experience of all kinds of beliefs. That meant holding personal beliefs in temporary abeyance lest they interfere with the poetic process. "We need no such beliefs," he said in *Science and Poetry,* "and indeed we must have none, if we are to read *King Lear*" (ch. 6). To entertain the poet's belief as a kind of make-believe, then drop it, or to devote all one's attention to formalistic or historical matters was in either case to avoid the central problem. The reader must make an effort to translate the import of the great writers of the past: "There is something a little ridiculous, at least, in admiring only the rhythms and 'word harmonies' of an author who is writing about the salvation of his soul" ("Belief," 1930). For Richards, the behaviorist reading Dante is the acid test: "*Qua* psychologist he denies the existence of the soul or the self, and stands prepared to translate all statements about the 'spiritual' into terms of visceral reaction systems and yet *qua* imaginative individual he fully undergoes all transformations of feeling and attitude that the poet compels."[3] Clearly the higher claims of belief in major artists should influence conduct and effect "permanent modifications in the structure of the mind" (*Principles of Literary Criticism,* ch. 16).

The tradition of Anglo-American philosophical psychology stands behind Richards' theory of belief, notably the theories of Alexander Bain, J. H. Newman, James Ward, and especially William James in "The Will to Believe" (1897). For Richards, belief is either intellectual ("verifiable," "scientific") or emotional. Intellectual belief ranges from commonsense habits to scientific reasoning where the logical connections among the beliefs are crucial; such belief makes few claims upon our emotions. In fact, it has so little emotional import that Mill called it "knowledge." An emotional belief can be any other kind of belief, from belief in the gods to belief in ideals and values. The philosophical tradition had two tests of belief: the first was a pragmatic test of action and the second the far more elusive test of feeling. In the first, one asks how much belief must one place before committing oneself to action. But with emotional belief, are we ready to perform a practical action? Richards saw clearly that emotional belief is both weaker and stronger than intellectual belief. It is weaker in that it cannot be proven true or false by physical evidence, stronger in that it is the faith that can move mountains. In the pragmatic test of action, there is a "backwash effect" on the feelings. Both intellectual and emotional beliefs prompt initial feelings of "acceptance" or "satisfaction." But emotional beliefs have longer-range effects: the sense of "ease,"

[3]From a review of Wyndham Lewis' *Time and Western Man,* in *Cambridge Review* (9 March 1928), pp. 325–326.

419

of "free, unimpeded activity." In reading poetry, one should suspend intellectual belief—how else could one read of Homer's gods?—and retain emotional belief, and let it be tested by experience and the backwash effect of feeling (after the James-Lange theory of emotion: feeling follows action). Its "success will be in ordering the growth of the personality or in aiding the good life" (part 3, ch. 7).

Emotional belief places a heavy burden on individual taste, judgment, and character, on an intuitional event that concerns a moment of choice leading to action—in a word, on sincerity. Aware that sincerity could be invoked by anyone to justify anything, Richards attempts to define his ideal rigorously and to safeguard it as far as possible from unbridled relativism or self-deceit. Whatever sincerity is, he said, expressing his difficulty in finding a usable formula, it is "the quality we most insistently require in poetry" and "most need as critics." His concept is indebted to a variety of sources, from English Romanticism to Tolstoy. But his most important source was the *Chung Yung,* the "Doctrine of the Mean, or Equilibrium and Harmony" of ancient Confucian books. He cites ten passages that may be grouped under the headings intuition, self-completion, and the union of internal and external. Intuition, Richards warns, must only follow a period of "unremitting research and reflection" (ch. 7). Self-completion means "obedience to that tendency which 'seeks' a more perfect order within the mind," an interpretation in which Richards' radical Protestant inwardness prevails. This is especially true for the last part, union of the internal and external. Whereas in Confucian philosophy conflict is suppressed through imitation of the sage, the highest social and moral repesentative, thus reinforcing the conservative social order, in Richards the emphasis falls on the individual him/herself becoming the ideal of imitation in a democratic pluralism: "freedom calls out freedom"; "those who are 'most themselves' [that is, artists in their creative moments, readers in theirs] cause others about them to become also 'more themselves.' " Sincerity is action according to "one's true nature," obedience to *a tendency towards increased order"* (ch. 7).

If one's judgment about the value of the poem still remains unresolved, Richards suggests a "technique" or "ritual" of sincerity—the words carry scientific and religious associations, and Richards hoped for a meeting point beyond them. He drew on Moore's "absolute isolation" as well as on oriental meditation:

When our response to a poem after our best efforts remains uncertain, when we are unsure whether the feelings it excites come from a deep source in our experience, whether our liking or disliking is genuine, is *ours,* or an accident of fashion, a response to surface detail or to essentials, we may perhaps help ourselves by considering it in a frame of feelings whose sincerity is beyond our questioning. . . . Consider with as full "realisation" as possible—
i. Man's loneliness (the isolation of the human situation).
ii. The facts of birth and death in their inexplicable oddity.
iii. The inconceivable immensity of the Universe.
iv. Man's place in the perspective of time.
v. The enormity of his ignorance.

(ch. 7)

In historical terms, there are close links between Richards' method of close reading and modernist literary texts. This literature was ambiguous, allusive, ironic, conceptually obscure, and in Eliot's prescriptive term, "difficult." The method could deal with ambiguity, irony, allusion, and arcane metaphor.

He championed Eliot's poetry and wrote the most influential review-essay of *The Waste Land,* which he called "equivalent in content to an epic." Eliot held his poem by a "music of ideas," a structural technique by which "heterogeneous ideas" are arranged "not that they may tell us something," but that their effect may "combine into a coherent whole of feeling and attitude." His theme of pathological sex was "the problem of our generation." Moreover, Eliot "had effected a complete severance between his poetry and all beliefs." Eliot accepted Richards' theory of belief with reservations but chose Richards' as a main example of the "modern mind" and satirized his ritual of "sincerity" in *The Use of Poetry and the Use of Criticism* (1933). On Joyce's *Ulysses* (1922) Richards said that "shock, perhaps severe shock" may be the effect of its "titanlike convulsions." Richards values Joyce's "inclusion," the "robust acceptance of everything" "however painful, repellant, or abhorrent." Controlling his varied materials, Joyce creates a resolution that has an "enheartening calming effect." Richards also wrote one of the first serious studies of Gerard

Manley Hopkins and considered Hardy a major poet. Yeats, however, eluded him for a time. While Richards appreciated the early poetry as well as the criticism in *Ideas of Good and Evil* (1903), he disliked Yeats's use of the "supernatural." When Yeats's *The Tower* appeared in 1928, however, he sharply reversed himself.

Explicating modernist texts was not the main justification of Richards' method, only its immediate historical context. His intention was to clear blocks in the channel of literary communication, ancient and modern. Often enough, earlier literature was found to be far more ambiguous than at first suspected.

THE ORIENTAL SOJOURN AND BASIC ENGLISH

RICHARDS first visited the Far East on a voyage around the world in 1926–1927, during which he was married to Dorothy Pilley in Honolulu on 31 December 1926. After completing *Practical Criticism,* he took a leave from Cambridge to teach at Tsing Hua National University in Peking (1929–1930) and Harvard University (January–June 1931). In Peking, a potent warning of the gulf separating East and West occurred during his lectures on Thomas Hardy's *Tess of the D'Urbervilles.* When Richards read the passage in which Tess is executed for child murder, his Chinese students broke out into a loud and spontaneous applause: they had been waiting to see her punished for disobeying her father early in the novel. Richards was astonished. Could he have failed to comprehend how vastly different was their cultural system? What did this mutual miscomprehension mean for the future? Richards' sojourn was to have long-range effects on his career, but above all it deepened his enormous respect for the Chinese people. At a time when China was on the brink of violent political disorder, Richards recalled, here were "the sons of Han, that stable, humane, nonviolent, mutually respectful, custom-ruled, law-abiding, frugal society. . . . It was a deep lesson in *what matters*" ("The Future of Reading," 1971).

One immediate outcome of his Chinese journey was *Mencius on the Mind: Experiments in Multiple Definition* (1932). Richards shared with the Chinese philosopher Mencius (372–289 B.C.) a focus on inwardness and the self, an interest in language, a

belief in the inherent goodness of humanity, and an optimistic outlook. A passage from Mencius is paraphrased interpretatively, with multiple definitions of the key psychological terms such as *hsing* ("complex of impulses," "incipient activity" [ch. 2]), *ch'i* (source of the will power, libidinal energies), and *ming* ("decree of heaven" [ch. 1]). Mencius' goal is the unity of the self: "The knowledge of heaven that results is no mystical vision, but simply the development of the possibilities of human nature" (ch. 1). No less than the Confucian Sage in Lowes Dickinson's *Letters from a Chinese Official* (1903), Mencius resembles the ideal Cambridge Humanist. Richards also comments on Mencius' language. Reading him is like reading Shakespeare and "much modern writing"; that is, his is a language of highly condensed thought, bold analogy, and sometimes indefinite syntax—a language not merely of "senses" but of "gestures" (another casually used word that became an important term later, particularly in the criticism of R. P. Blackmur). Unlike Ezra Pound or Ernest Fenollosa, however, Richards did not view the Chinese nondualism of mind and matter as culturally superior to Western ideas. But neither was it inferior, and Richards saw in modern pragmatism and instrumentalism a certain parallel with ancient Chinese philosophy.

Experiments in Multiple Definition, the subtitle of his Mencius study, calls attention to a common feature in Richards' criticism, which in sum contains about two hundred fifty such analytical definitions, ranging from a sentence to several pages. Multiple definition symbolizes his lasting concern for the dictionary, for lexical range, subtlety, and precision as the foundation of the critic's task. In the "Prologue" to *Beyond* (1974), Richards hailed the "Dictionary" as the "inestimable successor to Holy Writ" and reveled in its "endless paranomastic play." It was rumored in the 1960's that he took only one book on vacation to the Caribbean: a dictionary.

At Harvard, Richards taught two spring semester courses on "Practical Criticism" and "Contemporary English Literature (1890 to the Present Time)." The latter included Joseph Conrad's *The Secret Agent,* Joyce's *Ulysses* (he risked prosecution because a ban against the book was in effect), and Fyodor Dostoyevsky's *The Possessed.* Back in Cambridge, England, he gave his first series of lectures on Coleridge and "The Philosophy of Rhetoric"

(1931–1932). He returned to North America in 1933 to attend two conferences concerning Ogden's Basic English. Although he had kept up with Ogden, they had not collaborated for ten years, with the sole exception of Richards' contribution to Ogden's *The Meaning of Psychology* (1926). Ogden had followed the "referential path" from *The Meaning of Meaning,* published on Bentham's theory of Fictions, and whittled down the wordlist of his original invention, "Basic English." Richards had chosen the "emotive path," pursuing literary theory and methodology. Now their paths were again to converge.

Basic English is an idiomatic version of the language based on 850 words and simplified grammatical patterns. The 850 words are not the most frequently used words in English, but the most efficient (many of course are among the most frequently used). Although Ogden expected that non-English speakers would acquire words *off* the list immediately and thought of Basic only as a first, capacious landing stage, he needed Basic to be as complete as possible for marketing and teaching purposes. Five hundred words might have sufficed, but he would have had to sacrifice every trace of ease and naturalness. Within a few years the enterprising Ogden had groups interested in Basic from Peking and Moscow to New York and Australia. At the same time many people, wrongly thinking that 850 was an absolute limit, accused Ogden of a crime against English literature. Others raised the charge of British linguistic imperialism, especially as the movement gathered momentum and spread to many countries. In 1943 a speech by Winston Churchill praising the efforts of Ogden and Richards on behalf of Basic gave wings to this charge. According to a subtler critique, Basic seemed to offer an ideal of technological efficiency that reduces language from a complex instrument of intellectual analysis to a collection of purely functional phrases. For Ogden and Richards, Basic was only the simplest form of referential language.

For almost forty years, beginning in the mid 1930's, Richards worked to improve the design and further the goals of Basic English in China and the United States. Initially he was attracted by Basic's experimental potential for teaching processes of reasoning. His *Basic Rules of Reason* (1933), written in Basic, argues for a rationalistic empiricism and performs multiple definitions on twenty-six Basic words such as "fact," "knowledge," "true," and

"belief." Richards also saw Basic's educational usefulness in promoting world literacy. It was clear by the 1890's that English would be the international language. By the 1930's it dominated communications, film, science, aviation, and world business. With so many people wanting to learn English, Richards saw an opportunity to yoke the teaching of English to studies in the art of interpretation as well as a liberal approach to world culture. Richards was not alone in recognizing the merits of Basic. Ezra Pound recommended it for "training and exercise," for examining the intellectual content of a work of art, and for the "diffusion of ideas"; he indicated he might even write a "Basic Canto" (he did not). G. B. Shaw supported it; William Empson learned to write in it and promoted it over the radio; Lawrence Durrell used it to teach foreign students. Eliot thought Richards' case in *Basic English and Its Uses* (1943) was "unassailable."

In the midst of his growing interest in Basic, Richards completed *Coleridge on Imagination* (1934), which has been called the foundation of twentieth-century studies in Coleridge. In Richards' view, Coleridge did not leave a huge, incomplete jigsaw puzzle of criticism, as some have thought, but created a huge interlocking system, though it might show deep fissures here and there as if earthquake struck. He accepted Coleridge's insistence on the difference between "fancy," a less potent faculty that retrieves images from memory and merely rearranges them, and imagination, which brings the "whole soul of man into activity" in the creative act. A complex argument in sometimes elliptical prose, the book does not pretend to be a historical reconstruction of Coleridgean theory. Rather, Richards extracts the principle of imagination from all its surrounding materials and "translates" Coleridge's metaphysical, theological, and psychological systems and language into modern terms through which, he hoped, their value and relevance would be readily apparent. One by one, Richards takes up Coleridge's "facts of mind" (central intuitive experiences) and faculties of mind (Inner Sense, Realizing Intuition, Primary and Secondary Imagination, Fancy, Transcendent Will and Empirical Will, Understanding and Reason). Through the "translation" of reason Richards sustains Coleridge's moral claims for imagination. The last chapters were written with a view toward the contemporary political crisis in Europe. Foreseeing a "wrecked universe" as a consequence of the warlike "myths" raging across the globe, Richards made a bold plea for the "myth-making" power of the Coleridgean imagination, now reassembled for use, as the "necessary channel for the reconstitution of order" (ch. 9).

The challenge to play a role in the constitution of that new order propelled Richards from working on the upper levels of education to research in elementary language training, second-language learning, and literacy. Although others saw only the division of his career in this anxious decade, he aimed toward a higher level of unity that is breathtaking in scope and intention. As he said in a 1973 *Harvard Magazine* interview: "Little by little, I decided that work towards unifying the planet was worth so much more than any sort of work I'd dreamt of before." In 1936 he decided to return to China and assist the newly founded Basic organization, first stopping in the United States to deliver the Mary Flexner Lectures at the University of Virginia. These lectures, which contained the most sophisticated version of his theory of metaphor, appeared as *The Philosophy of Rhetoric* in 1936. While preparing them, between January and March, he wrote *Interpretation in Teaching* (1938), a kind of *Practical Criticism* for prose, an attack on modern theories of grammar, and a contribution to the history of rhetoric and education. Richards was a fast writer, but nothing he did ever surpassed in speed the writing of what would become 558 printed pages in seven weeks, his tenth and eleventh books in sixteen years. In *Interpretation in Teaching,* Richards collected about two hundred student responses to prose passages for analysis; by comparison, in *Practical Criticism* he collected a thousand responses to poems, though just under four hundred were cited. In *Interpretation in Teaching* he spread the protocols throughout the book, making for a choppy, sprawling effect; in *Practical Criticism* the protocols are treated conveniently together in an opening section. Moreover, the prose passages were not "literary" (e.g., novelistic) but "expository" (e.g., from philosophical and critical sources) and less immediately compelling in interest. Although Richards considered it his best book, it was not successful—his first real failure to win an audience and a sign of things to come, even if it contains the blueprint for many of his tracts and projects in language training for the next thirty years.

The sojourn in China was spent largely in combining his creative efforts with those of the Ortho-logical Institute, the name of Ogden's Basic organization, and in bringing Basic to the attention of university and government organs through his personal prestige. He was obliged to return to Magdalene in early 1937, but realized that he had to get back quickly if he were to take advantage of the Chinese government's interest in a nationwide "Basic" experiment. This was needed to test Basic's potential and perhaps score a victory over its competitors in English language training. Magdalene granted another leave, and Richards returned to Peking to lobby the government and lay plans for the teaching program. On 26 June 1937 a high-level government committee of the Ministry of Education, meeting in Nanking, adopted a three-year pilot program of Basic for middle schools. Richards was overjoyed and cabled his wife in Peking: HAVE EVERYTHING I WANT. SOMETHING MUST BE WRONG.

Two weeks later the Japanese invaded northern China. Richards was in Peking at the time and witnessed the attack. With typical pluck and imperturbability, he began his summer school teacher-training program just outside the city walls. The war swept by the city; by mid August it was impossible to carry on the work of the Orthological Institute, and the decision was made to explore the feasibility of moving south of the fighting line. Richards would also attempt to keep interest in Basic alive by meeting with the ministry's subcommittee on vocabulary. Joined by William Empson, who had arrived to teach in Peking and who was also drawn into the Basic movement, Richards and his wife made a three-thousand mile journey across China and Indochina by train, boat, plane, bus, and finally donkey, from Peking to Tientsin, Hong Kong, Changsha, Kueilin, Hanoi, and finally Yunnan fu in extreme southwestern China. Nevertheless, it was clear that any nationwide experiment was out of the question.

At this point (October to December 1937), near some of the world's sublimest mountains, Richards and his wife journeyed into the Li-chiang snow range (Jade Dragon Mountain), which stretches for hundreds of miles across the immense loop of the Yangtze River. In Yunnan fu they had consulted the anthropologist Joseph Rock, who was studying the Na-Khi tribes of this region. (Pound's reading of Rock would later lead to his setting the paradisal section of the *Cantos* among these mountain tribes.) Rock probably gave them good maps because they often traveled the length and breadth of the range without a guide. The Richardses climbed Gyi-nà nv-lv (Black Water snow peak), approximately 19,300 feet high, the highest peak in their long career in mountaineering, and Ha-pa Shan (18,700 ft.), of which Dorothy wrote nonchalantly, "If it hadn't been for 100 m.p.h. gale it would have been an easy snow peak." Eventually Richards and his wife recrossed China and settled in Tientsin where he completed his *First Book of English for Chinese Learners* (427 pages) and a teacher's handbook in the spring of 1938. He sailed for Vancouver in May.

Looking back on the collapse of his projects in 1975, he said: "*All* went down the drain! . . . For *ALL* here was something very big and wide and successful." In his Chinese period Richards appears as a curious mixture of the adventurous, the committed, the ingenious, and the naive. What could he have thought as he trekked across the entire nation, with its strange mountains and rivers, under siege as it was at the time, only a few days ahead of bombing raids, and always further and further from his goal? It is an arresting picture of one of the great critical minds of the twentieth century.

LANGUAGE RESEARCH IN AMERICA

On his journey homeward in 1938 Richards pondered the advantages of integrating the modern media with elementary- and second-language training. Properly designed programs could free teachers from potentially tedious repetitions to concentrate on individual problems. Film, audio, and tape were already available, and some of the programs could even be self-teaching, either partly or wholly. Moreover, technology could be the answer to mass illiteracy. But where to try a broadscale experiment? In 1939 Richards accepted a five-year grant from the Rockefeller Foundation and a university lectureship at the Harvard School of Education to pursue research in language training. As the lectureship came to an end and his work was still in progress, he was offered one of five distinguished university professorships at Harvard, to begin in 1944. He held this position until 1963, teaching a highly popular course on Homer, the Old Testament, and Plato in the undergraduate general education program as well as graduate courses in the School of Education and in English. In 1941 he created the Commission on English Language Studies, which in 1950 became Language Research, Inc., a nonprofit institution that produced his teaching designs. From 1945 his work was most frequently coauthored by Christine M. Gibson, an Englishwoman who had come to the Harvard School of Education in 1939 to study foreign-language learning under Richards. For nearly forty years they worked together on books and projects, making theirs one of the most fruitful collaborations in twentieth-century education.

Richards had three objectives in his American career: to conduct experiments in literacy and second-language learning; to prepare textbooks in beginning and advanced reading, including classics, gradually expanding the Basic vocabulary; and to adapt Basic English so that it could be taught by the media. The preparation of texts and adaptation of Basic to the media raised trouble with Ogden, who did not relish changes in his design or what he considered a premature use of the media. They were separated during the war, Ogden remaining in England, and their differences were not easily ironed out. In 1947 they broke off relations and Richards renamed his program Every Man's English.

Employing analogies taken from George W. Corner's *Ourselves Unborn: An Embryologist's Essay on Man* (1944), Richards believed that the clue to language learning lay in proper sequencing. His principle is one of "preparation": "*We learn through what we have learned,*" his corollary being "*and how we have learned it.*" The principle is indebted to Coleridge's concept of "progressive transition" in the *Treatise on Method* (1818), one of the works in the Coleridgean canon that Richards had restored to prominence. Emphasis in Richards' programs falls on the earlier stages, in which the pupils are at their most helpless, having to make all sorts of intellectual and imaginative leaps in quick succession to find a way in; here they are most in need of exact guidance. But they are also at their most interested in these stages. Meanwhile, as a subject is being taught, so too are intellectual processes such as comparison, analogy, opposition, and ordering. Richards was himself always at his best in the early stages of his programs, "when all the possibilities are open," as in the new English School at Cambridge after World War I or the new general education program at Harvard after World War II.

The principle of preparation is supported by five practical rules. "Economy" means clarifying procedures and reducing the number of items to be remembered. In *First Steps in Reading English* (1957) ten letters of the alphabet take the pupil through forty pages, then letters are added slowly. "Intelligibility" ensures that the pupils are made aware of how the design is teaching them while they are learning a subject. The art of comparison can be introduced by the letters themselves: *p, b, q,* and *d* appear similar. Space and time may be presented by simple contrast or experiments in typography. Richards and Gibson believed that a language has an optimal order in which sentence-in-situation pictures could be presented. "Sequencing" facilitates progress, as the learner knows that an answer lies in the neighborhood of what has already been learned. Richards felt this was the heart of the program. There are two kinds of programming. In "contiguity programming," the pupil attempts to solve the problem by filling in a missing piece of information in a series: *a, b, c ? e f.* The mind performs its act more or less mechanically—this is "stock response" learning which encourages "blind automatic rote." "Similarity programming" relies on proportion, analogy, opposition, and sameness in difference; it requires that a pupil give an analogous part of an incomplete whole. Most simply, *a:c::d:?.* Richards summarizes in *So Much Nearer,* "Contiguity conforms; Similarity explores. Both are exercises of structure but Contiguity reproduces while Similarity extends and develops" (ch. 1).

Lastly, "Depiction, Machines, and Channel Interplay" played an increasingly larger role in Richards' designs. He kept up with the swiftly developing media in the 1940's through the 1970's, from film and tape to long-playing records, television, video, and home computers. He believed that computer-handled, television or satellite-distributed, "sentence-situation" depiction games could be the answer to world literacy problems, film's "second chance" to redeem itself from its dismal failure to serve education. He devised machines in which three perceptual channels work in concert: the eye seeing marks on paper or on a screen, the ear sensing the sounds, the vocal organs repeating them. Each acted as a stimulus and control of the other. Such "feedback" and what Richards called "feedforward"—success in the form of a correct response that enables a pupil to regenerate and reinforce the process—are vital because many of Richards' designs are "graded direct," that is, progressive and self-teaching.

One literacy project made use of a hand-wind phonograph, which could be used even where there was no electricity and thus could be taken to the farthest corners of the globe. It symbolized Richards' belief that the teacher and student must ultimately be found in the same person. In all his programs the vehicle and goal are one: self-corrigibility. Explaining the organization of his *English Through Pictures, Book II* (1958), which carried the theme of the "mutual dependence" of parts from language learning to global politics, he said that the two key themes of his career were "internal unity and self-control."

Richards' programs also included "translation" or controlled paraphrase of English into simpler English or into Basic English, in which the pupil makes the "translation" an interpretation and analysis of the original text. Richards himself experimented with translations because he wanted newcomers to English to have major works of the Western tradition available in simplified form. He relearned Greek in middle age in order to translate Plato's *Republic* (1942) and Homer's *Iliad* (1950) into slightly expanded versions of Basic (under 2,000 words). During World War II the U.S. government arranged for the distribution of two million copies of a pocket edition of his Plato to armed forces overseas. He also made a play out of Plato's four dialogues on the death of Socrates, *Euthyphro, Apology, Crito,* and *Phaedo* in simplified English. Entitled *Why So, Socrates?* (1964), Richards himself took the role of Socrates when it was performed on local educational television.

Critics excoriated Richards' translations, particularly the Homer, because he had reduced the texts by about half and flattened the poetry. Arnold had said that an ideal translation of Homer must be rapid, plain in words and style, simple in ideas, and noble. Richards succeeds in the second and third, and sometimes the fourth, but loses Homer's sublimity; and because of the drastic cuts he is too rapid, costing Homer his massiveness. Richards may have kept the skeleton entire but there was some question at least whether he did not cut out the heart. He made two unpublished plays out of the *Iliad,* "The Wrath of Achilles" and "Homage to Hector" (1970–1971), and in the latter he took the role of the Trojan rhapsode in a local production.

Although Language Research, Inc., operated with a small staff, in one or two rooms on a shoestring budget, its accomplishments over the years are impressive: to name only a few, the Language Through Pictures series in seven languages, the

Learning the English Language series, radio courses for Spanish and Portuguese speakers in South America, local literacy programs, the training of a thousand Chinese seamen in six weeks, thirty-six half-hour programs of *English Through Television.* A glance at the bibliography will confirm Richards and Gibson's success, which should be contrasted with today's educational programs funded by vast sums, involving large teams of researchers and secretaries, making use of extensive technology—and with often pathetic results.

In sometimes vatic pronouncements Richards expressed his belief that technology was the answer to the problem of mass education. "The Technological Crisis" (1962) argued that teachers were not keeping up with the needs resulting from the accelerated pace of technological society. A severe critic of the media since the 1920's, he nonetheless believed that its failures were human ones, for example, overprofessionalization in educational television. He never quite understood that there might be something in the relentlessly simplifying nature of mass media and technology that might be inimical to individual autonomy or complex uses of language. Nor did he attempt to confront serious critiques of the media and technology as in the work of Jacques Ellul. At some point, Richards hoped, wise individuals would take control of technology and direct it toward good ends. He was his own best example: in 1957–1958 he had his own weekly television program, "The Sense of Poetry," which aired on WGBH-TV, Boston. Curiously, Richards never owned a television himself (or learned to drive a car or even to typewrite).

In 1942 Richards published *How to Read a Page: A Course in Effective Reading, with an Introduction to a Hundred Great Words,* which was his ironic response to Mortimer Adler's *How to Read a Book* (1940), with its list of great books. Richards advocated the micrological method of reading; a page ought to be read as *slowly* as its textual density required. *How to Read a Page* is not, however, about literary "close reading." Instead, Richards analyzes passages of philosophy and examines 103 key words from the Basic list, words such as "make, "get," give," "reason," "purpose," and "work." As usual, Richards' multiple definitions are not disconnected from a larger argument leading to dialectical reasoning and the apprehension of the Platonic good. He wants to show that even small errors in reading and interpretation are symptomatic of much larger ones in the person-

ality and in the state. Some of these themes carry over to *Speculative Instruments* (1955), a collection of essays on education, linguistics, and close reading. Notable in the latter category is an essay on Shakespeare's *Troilus and Cressida.* The book itself presents a Richards divided between careers. And he was about to take on another.

POETRY AND DRAMA

At the age of fifty-nine, Richards began writing poetry. Someone compared him to the aging Socrates who learned to play the lyre. In the next twenty-seven years Richards published four volumes of poetry and three verse plays. What he said of his poem "Whose Endless Jar" in *Beyond* applies to all his verse: it "amounts to an experiment intended to support the view that more intricate and more highly organized meanings can be conveyed more adequately in verse than in prose" (ch. 6). He wanted his own verse to assume an "impersonality, a detachment, and an authority no prose of mine would ever pretend to" (ch. 6). Richards' poetic themes are few: old age; resignation; courage before death; high mountaineering, his lifelong "passion"; scientific and metaphysical topics such as opposition, complementarity, Faustian striving, choice, creativity, and the Good; and the nature of language itself. But his vocabulary is extremely varied and he experimented with stanzaic form, rhyme scheme, capitalization, indentation plans, line break, and orthography. In the main his poems have a rough texture and high surface tension, which together with his themes suggest life's puzzling challenge, resistances, but also variousness and play. The burden of assimilation placed on the poems is often great, so intent is he to activate as many resources of language as possible. When a Richards poem fails, it is not from lack of conviction, so much as lack of fusion.

In verse and prose, and mixing satire and comedy with moments of tragic pathos, *A Leak in the Universe* (written in 1954 but not published until 1956) consists of five scenes set in an Institute for Advancing Studies. Its action centers around the investigation of a familiar magic trick, the box into which everything disappears—the "leak in the universe." The conjuror has lost his pen, watch, and magic wand, and cannot retrieve them. A Nobel Prize–winning physicist fails to answer the riddle: science is helpless. The conjuror repairs to a medium, Mrs. Nemo, and a Japanese Buddhist, Professor Omori, who pronounces that the box is designed by the "Rebel" Lucifer and serves as a symbol of the power of mind, a nothingness out of which all is created. For Richards, the Jamesean pragmatist, the universe is imperfect and unfinished; it "leaks," though much to its own advantage.

Goodbye Earth and Other Poems (1958) appeared in the midst of the space craze. In the title poem, "Goodbye Earth: Farewell to the Planet," an elderly poet contemplates death and examines the "raw materials" and the choices through which his life was made, and the "symbiotic tensions that impel us." We build our personal spaceships with our lives and then "take off." Mindful of the failures of Basic English in China and elsewhere—failures only measured against the high goal of "unifying the planet"—the poet describes the arc of his career as he saw it at this time: "SUCCESS, ADVENTURE, FAILURE, COMPREHENDING." Richards has written some of the finest poems in English on being over sixty-five: "Future Intimative," "And So to Bed," and "Annual Club Dinner." In "To Dumb Forgetfulness" he confronts the impairment of memory in old age. "Forget, forget . . . Forget what you forget," he advises the frustrated elderly person who cannot recollect the "lost quote" or "choice statistic," or more importantly, the sighs, glances, and profiles of persons, whatever might disclose the keys to one's "formula of fate." The strict form of the villanelle with its many mnemonic repetitions symbolizes a kind of victory, not over forgetfulness (which is progressive), nor death (which is inevitable), but for the final harmony of the person. In "Hope" (in *The Screens and Other Poems,* 1960), Richards tries to comfort his wife, who had been hospitalized after an automobile accident, by recounting one of their narrow escapes in the mountains:

> "Leaping crevasses in the dark,
> That's how to live!" you said.
> No room in that to hedge:
> A razor's edge of a remark.

Richards often repaired to his experiences of high mountaineering in his poems and plays to express enduring age, death, the fate of self-knowledge and meaning in a Heraclitean flux, and the search for ultimacy. Mountains are not mere backdrops, but proving grounds for extreme tests of mental and physical strength. In *Internal Colloquies* (1971), thoughts are "edges" or "ledges" of rock; time is the strung rope. The sky beckons like a "cragsman's paradise" ("Conditional") or "Hell's own throat" ("Model Yourself"). "Eye-perpendicular," the cliffs are the cracking "Tissue of *buts* and *ifs,* / Of let and bar" ("Gravitation and Delinquency"). In his essay "The Lure of High Mountaineering" (1927) Richards called the momentary exaltation that ensues the successful overcoming of tensions "serenity amid stress": climbing high mountains gave him an experience analogous to reading sublime poetry. In *History* (1973) Robert Lowell's two sonnets on Richards have high mountaineering for their theme, the key to his character, the mountaineer's courage to "move on" and upward.

Tomorrow Morning, Faustus! (1962) is an "infernal comedy" with tragic undertones. Mammon, Belial, Moloch, and Beelzebub, members of the Futurity Foundation, are summoned by the chairman Satan for a General Epochal Meeting in preparation for a new age. The scene switches to Faustus, who reveals the pact made long ago: if the fiends can be tricked into teaching him what he most needs to know about himself, he must deliver himself to them forever. Meanwhile, they spy on him to discover what they are. Man, the "bare chameleon" (p. 13), reflects the fiends' uncertainty, multifacetedness, and lack of unity: man is what the fiends are becoming. The fiends are projections of rebellious man through the ages. (As Richards writes in "The Proper Study": "The desolate aims / Through which the soul is wrought / Are mirror imaged / In the selves they've wrought.") Old and near death, Faustus travels to his final meeting. After various machinations, Faustus and Satan offer each other the "Psy-ray," which would enable them to enter each other's consciousness. Satan accepts and perceives through Faustus the human lot. But Faustus will not be tricked into accepting what would spell the abrogation of his pact and refuses the Psy-ray, preferring the active striving after truth to perfect knowledge. Critical of one's intellectual possessions, and creative through and beyond them, understanding that "gods" and "fiends" are but self-images, humanity must continually "remake" itself. Sometimes Faustus (and Richards) makes it look easy: "The answer to thinking's another way to think" (p. 51). At other times it proves an undertaking as dangerous as climbers on a "wintry cliff" that is "biscuit thin and brittle" (p. 55):

with one twist of the mind
I can shoulder out exits for the lot of you.
Once through, you are that. That cold void gulf
Is you; not in it, IT. You're back; you've gone
Back to the matrix . . .

The play ends with Faustus' death and triumph as he vanishes with Satan, each having absorbed the other's knowledge.

Richards, in his review of *The Waste Land,* remarked of Eliot: "When a writer has found a theme or image which fixes a point of relative stability in the drift of experience, it is not to be expected that he will avoid it." Two images are recurrent in Richards' poetry, the one natural, the other technological: the eddy and the circuit. Perhaps they resolve to one image, the vortex: energy and rotation about a center. He writes of circuits with which one constructs the spaceship about to spin into the heavens in "Goodbye Earth"; the "coils" that bind Faustus and Satan in their "eddying" into the afterlife; the "whirl of being" ("Ars Poetica) a residual form amid the flux; the Earth itself, "Stable because a-spin and swinging round" ("Tomorrow Morning, Faustus!"); "eddying Depths" that open between extremes, like valleys into which one peers dizzyingly from mountain peaks ("A:B::B:C"); thought itself, a form of turning things around— fast: "To spin a clue you do not stand your ground," even as the stars move with their "cyclic wobbles," "Distinctive vortices worked out within" ("Sunrise"). Richards sees the eddy as a circular countermovement within a larger one, the smaller receiving energy from the larger but separate from it. A mental eddy is a kind of equipoise amid a chaos or a cosmos only partially knowable. In "The Daughter Thought" (in *Goodbye Earth*) he envisions the boundless and the unimaginable "order" within it:

> But, but within all let or lour
> There rules an order without bound:
> Cyclic, unsearchable, but found
> When the unthinkable junctures flower.

But "wobbles" may depict poor human creatures better that swirling graceful eddies. "My wobble now salutes your wobble, you." We are all wobbles, saluting each other across a void.

BEYOND

In his eighty-second year, Richards published his first book of close readings, *Beyond.* With the meditative power and range of last things, the book explores the dialectical relation between Homer and the Olympians, Job and Javeh/Shaddai, Dante and the Christian godhead, and Shelley and Demogorgon—all texts with which Richards had lived for a lifetime. In the poetic dialogues the human characters strive "beyond" themselves to question power and its limits, justice, loss and undeserved suffering, immortality, and the nature of the soul. Images of godhead and the self-images of the questioners stand in a mirrored or dialectical relation; oblique answers and cruel silences may derive from the nature of the questions. For Richards, the human characters emerge from these encounters as the ethically superior beings. Thus in the *Iliad* (1:188–222) Achilles is tempted to kill Agamemnon for seizing Briseis when Athena appears and urges him to hold down his wrath, telling him that great gifts come to him. For Richards, she is not wise counsel but merely policy and covetousness. She "misconceives" Achilles for whom heaps of booty will not matter; she is *"a foil"* for him and proves him the "greater and deeper being" that the goddess of wisdom can only attempt to fathom (ch. 1).

The finest sections of *Beyond* concern the Book of Job and Plato. Richards wonders who in Job is really being tested: Jaweh, Job, or Satan? Job seeks to penetrate the mystery of injustice in a world ruled by God; and God in response speaks past him to the mystery of power and creation. Separating the prose folktale (1:1–2:13 and 42:10–17) from the poem (3:1–42:9), Richards reveals the dynamic oppositions between two formal structures, two Jobs, two godheads, and two forces of evil. Despite attempts by early editors and by tradition to iron out differences, the poem's "indeterminateness" provokes and enacts the very questionings that occur in the narrative. Plato's Socrates is equally a paragon of virtue who is put "on trial" and pressed to an extreme. The Job poet's quest and Plato's quest, Richards finds, are "radically the same," that is, to comprehend what is "central to the human endeavor," the quest for self-knowledge and the power that enables us to reach it: "Beyond even the concept of the Good—the Universal which orders all universals, beyond any other machinery it may contrive as a help to itself in its conceivings, its bodying forth of itself and its world—the mind ... finds *Itself*" (pp. 80, 82–83). Richards also treats the Job poet and Plato on immortality. In the *Apology* Socrates posits either an endless sleep or a philosopher's immortality whereby souls that have "remained, or become, sufficiently like the divine source they come from, return to it"; "by doing right" souls are able "to become nearly like a God as it is possible for a man to be."

Instead of analyzing Dante's poetry extensively, Richards comments on Dantescan themes in the three cantos of "Whose Endless Jar," corresponding to Hell, Purgatory, and Heaven. Were they Richards' best poems (as he thought them—but they are not), their presence among the august masterpieces of the Job poet, Plato, and Dante might constitute an act of hubris. Yet there is characteristic daring in Richards' decision to turn to poetry, the "completest mode of utterance," to express himself on these themes. In harmony with earlier chapters is the sense of greater risk, pushing oneself "beyond." In his career, too, he had turned finally to poetry. In the paradisal section of "Whose Endless Jar" Richards envisions human beings in control of their fates, seeking their own highest perfection in mutual dependence on one another, making a paradise of the natural rhythms of the earth, and bequeathing a better world to the next generation. These are Romantic concepts and a reminder of Richards' original feelings for poetry. *Beyond* concludes with a brilliant reprise of its major themes through close readings of Shelley's 1820 *Prometheus Unbound* (the only English work treated): the colloquy between Asia (whom Richards, after E. H. Gombrich, interprets as *Humanitas*) and Demogorgon; Asia's transfiguration; and Prometheus on the role of the arts in a redeemed world. After the tragic tone of the previous chapters, Richards ends on a note of Shelleyan hope.

CONCLUSION

IN summer 1974, after thirty-five years of residence in Cambridge, Massachusetts, Richards returned to Cambridge, England, and lived in a house adjoining the Magdalene Fellows' garden. In the autumn he delivered the Clark Lectures, "Some Futures for Criticism." Two of the four lectures criticized modern scholarship and biography for losing the poem in its various sources, e.g., the author, social history, politics. The third concerned retributive justice, with examples from Milton; the fourth treated Justus Buchler's theory of assertive, active, and exhibitive judgment, with an analysis of Shakespeare's sonnet 60, "my favorite among the sonnets." In the same year he published his last book on language training, *Techniques in Language Control,* coauthored by Gibson.

In these final years at Cambridge the pace of travel barely slackened: the Alps in the summer and New England in the fall. Although he was increasingly prone to illness, at eighty-six he decided upon an ambitious lecture tour of China in the spring of 1979, hoping to rekindle interest in his English language training programs. After a month of strenuous travel and lecturing, he collapsed in Peking in June and never recovered. He died in Cambridge, England, on 7 September 1979.

Richards' current reputation rests almost entirely on the work of his career in the theory and method of criticism through the 1930's. Although many early reviewers did not object to his psychological importations or his links to science, Eliot, Conrad Aiken, and Mark Van Doren criticized the pragmatic theory of value. In *Scrutiny* in 1933 D. W. Harding blasted Richards' belief in art as the most "organized" activity as a crude "Darwinian" notion of progress, while two years later in the same journal F. R. Leavis launched a severe attack on *Coleridge on Imagination* for its straining of Coleridge's ideas through Benthamism and science. At the same time Leavis' studies in mass civilization and language as "continuity" are deeply indebted to Richards (in *Scrutiny*, 1935), and Leavis also counseled that Richards' treatment of metaphor is "probably better than any to be found anywhere" (*Scrutiny*, 1937).

In his *Seven Types of Ambiguity* (1930) and *The Structure of Complex Words* (1951), without rejecting the reader's psychological response, Empson emphasized the objectivist side of Richards' poetics and brought the style of close reading to near perfection. The American New Critics—John Crowe Ransom, Robert Penn Warren, Cleanth Brooks, William Wimsatt, Reuben Brower—abandoned the psychology entirely and concentrated on "the poem itself." Initially, the sheer brilliance of their close readings exerted a liberating effect on criticism and brought textual analysis to the forefront of academic study after World War II. They borrowed heavily from Richards' terms and concepts of contextualism, antihistoricism, polysemousness, tension, equilibrium, attitude, response, belief, tenor and vehicle of metaphor, tone, the speaker, gesture, poetries of inclusion and exclusion, gesture, irony, and ambiguity. At the same time the New Critics narrowed Richards' scope. They dispensed with his interest in "science," which they thought inimical to poetry, and ignored his studies in "scientific" or expository prose, as in *Interpretation in Teaching.* By the "intentional fallacy" William Wimsatt and Monroe C. Beardsley cut the poem's intentions from those of the poet. By the "affective fallacy" they exposed the "error" of treating a poem in terms of its psychological effects, upon either belief or action. Actually Richards thought it entirely possible for a poem to exert emotive effects without resulting in vague impressionism or moral relativism, and he had predecessors such as Aristotle on catharsis and Longinus on the sublime. Oddly enough, in the 1950's when Richards considered his own career at its nadir on account of the failure of his language-training programs, the influence of his early books on criticism was reaching its zenith.

With the decline of the New Criticism in the 1960's, Richards' writings on theory and method fell under a historical shadow. To be sure, myth-and-symbol critics such as Northrop Frye perpetuated his influence, and many of the new generation of poststructuralist or deconstructionist critics—J. Hillis Miller, Paul De Man—in the 1970's and 1980's had begun their careers under the impact of New Criticism. And one must not forget that "close reading" remained the method of choice in teaching, and remains so to this day. Still, Richards' books were neglected. Even *Practical Criticism* was more often acknowledged through its offspring, the numberless introductory textbooks and reader's guides to literature. Despite the revival of interest in expository writing, Richards' studies in referential language are infrequently mentioned.

The situation is similar regarding Richards' second career in elementary and second-language training. No comprehensive test has ever been conducted to ascertain his program's efficacy over that of its competitors. It is noteworthy, however, that Richards and Gibson's Language Through Pictures

series in book and cassette form continues to sell across the globe since its introduction in the 1950's, which cannot be said for most of its rivals.

Students in criticism and intellectual history now examine Richards' writings in relation to their social and critical background and extensive influence. His indebtedness to, and impact upon literary modernism remains to be further clarified. His second career is still seen as detached from his first and has yet to earn the attention it deserves, particularly regarding his studies in the media and technology. Beyond the divisions of his career into criticism, education, translation, applied science, and poetry, there is a need to understand Richards' thought and humanistic project as a whole. The opening of the Richards Collection at Magdalene College, Cambridge, and the deposit of the Language Research, Inc., collection at Harvard University are likely to encourage these studies.

In many ways, Richards is the most representative critic of the English-speaking world in the twentieth century. One can point to his primary focus on language (so common today we almost forget the critical practice of 1914); his concern for the systematic nature of criticism; his interests in science, psychology, and technology; his application and critique of modern media; his interdisciplinary approach; his adoption of complementarity; his work in translation; his internationalism. His contributions to education extend from the most elementary to the most sophisticated levels. His criticism covers most phases of the communication process, from the artist to the work of art to the reader's response and moral duty. In one way he can never be representative: in his comprehensiveness.

Richards' unique achievement, what sets him in the company of the greatest critics, grew out of his insight into the situation of a reader in the process of reading a text. No critic has come closer to uncovering so many sides of that infinitely complex process, or to analyzing what helps and hinders that fundamental act. One of his invaluable messages as a critic is that good theory (and method) can save readers from bad theory, but should not get in the way of something potentially better—and no theory can decide a case, at any rate, a case that matters. That decision is ultimately ethical because it means stepping into a larger context of circumstance and choice. The great strength of

Richards' criticism is that it forces attention back toward the work of art. He makes the interaction between the mind and the work of art the center from which criticism departs on its theoretical investigations, and to which criticism returns to gain its bearings. Contrary to those who have found his work formalistic, "scientific," or mechanical, his formalism is an expression of humanism, a celebration of what reason and the imagination can accomplish.

SELECTED BIBLIOGRAPHY

I. BIBLIOGRAPHY, MANUSCRIPTS, AND COLLECTIONS. J. P. Russo, "A Bibliography of the Books, Articles, and Reviews of I. A. Richards," 1919–1973, annotated, in *I. A. Richards: Essays in His Honor*, R. Brower, H. Vendler, and J. Hollander, eds. (New York, 1973); supplement for 1973–1979 in J. P. Russo, *I. A. Richards: His Life and Work* (Baltimore and London, 1989).

The Richards Collection, Magdalene College, Cambridge University (letters to and from Richards, private papers, manuscripts, personal library, Dorothy Pilley Richards' diary); Houghton Library, Widener Library, and School of Education Library, Harvard University (books, pamphlets, manuscripts, audiovisual and other materials regarding the teaching of Basic English, Every Man's English, and foreign languages; letters and private papers from his American period [1939–1974]; Christine M. Gibson papers) [see B. Reutlinger, "Listing of Materials Transferred from Language Research, Inc., to the Harvard Graduate School of Education, June 1984, together with Tables of Contents of Master File of Supporting Materials and Projects File" (Cambridge, Mass., 1984), 4 vols.]; Rockefeller Foundation Archives, N. Tarrytown, New York (Basic English and Language Research enterprises from the 1930's to 1950's); Otto G. Richter Library, University of Miami, Florida (Language Research productions, English and foreign-language training materials).

II. SEPARATE WORKS. *The Foundations of Aesthetics*, with C. K. Ogden and J. Wood (London, 1922), published originally as "The Sense of Beauty," in *Cambridge Magazine*, 10:2 (1921); *The Meaning of Meaning: A Study of the Influence of Language upon Thought and of the Science of Symbolism*, with C. K. Ogden (London, 1923); *Principles of Literary Criticism* (London, 1924); *Science and Poetry* (London, 1926; rev. ed., 1935), rev. ed. repr. as *Poetries and Sciences* (New York, 1970); *Practical Criticism: A Study of Literary Judgment* (London, 1929).

Mencius on the Mind: Experiments in Multiple Definition (London, 1932); *Basic Rules of Reason* (London, 1933); *Coleridge on Imagination* (London, 1934); *Basic in Teaching: East and West* (London, 1935); *The Philosophy of Rhetoric* (New York, 1936); *Interpretation in Teaching* (New York, 1938); *A First Book of English for Chinese Learners* (Peking, 1938).

How To Read a Page: A Course in Effective Reading, with an Introduction to a Hundred Great Words (New York, 1942); *The Republic of Plato: A Version in Simplified English* (New York, 1942); *Basic English and Its Uses* (London, 1943); *Words on Paper: First Steps in Reading*, with C. M. Gibson (Cambridge, Mass., 1943); *Learning Basic English: A Practical Handbook for English-Speaking People*, with C. M. Gibson (New York, 1945); *The Pocket Book of Basic English: A Self-Teaching Way into English*, with C. M. Gibson (New York, 1945), repr. as *English Through Pictures* (1952); *Learning the English Language, Books I–III*, with C. M. Gibson (Boston, 1945); *Nations and Peace* (New York, 1947).

The Wrath of Achilles: The Iliad of Homer, Shortened and in a New Translation (New York, 1950); *French Self-Taught Through Pictures*, with M. H. Ilsley and C. M. Gibson (New York, 1950); *Spanish Self-Taught Through Pictures*, with R. Metcalf Romero and C. M. Gibson (New York, 1950); *German Through Pictures*, with I. Schmidt Mackey, W. F. Mackey, and C. M. Gibson (New York, 1953); *Hebrew Through Pictures*, with D. Weinstein and C. M. Gibson (New York, 1954); *Speculative Instruments* (Chicago, 1955); *Italian Through Pictures*, with I. Evangelista and C. M. Gibson (New York, 1955); *A Leak in the Universe*, a verse play in five scenes, in *Playbook* (New York, 1956); *Goodbye Earth and Other Poems* (New York, 1958); *English Through Pictures, Book II*, with C. M. Gibson (New York, 1958); *A First Workbook of English*, with C. M. Gibson (New York, 1959).

The Screens and Other Poems (New York, 1960); *Tomorrow Morning, Faustus! An Infernal Comedy* (New York, 1962); *Why So, Socrates? A Dramatic Version of Plato's Dialogues: Euthyphro, Apology, Crito, Phaedo* (Cambridge, Eng., 1964); *So Much Nearer: Essays Toward a World English* (New York, 1968): *Design for Escape: World Education through Modern Media* (New York, 1968).

Internal Colloquies: Poems and Plays (New York, 1971); *Beyond* (New York, 1974); *Techniques in Language Control*, with C. M. Gibson (Rowley, Mass., 1974); *Poetries: Their Media and Ends*, T. Eaton, ed. (The Hague, 1974); *Complementarities: Uncollected Essays*, J. P. Russo, ed. (Cambridge, Mass., 1976; Manchester, Eng., 1977); *New and Selected Poems* (Manchester, Eng., 1978); *Verse v. Prose* (London, 1978).

III. ARTICLES, TALKS, AND REVIEWS. "Art and Science—I," in *Athenaeum* (27 June 1919), repr. in *Complementarities: Uncollected Essays* (1976); "Mr. Eliot's Poems," review of T. S. Eliot, *Poems 1909–1925*, in *New Statesman* (20 February 1926), repr. in Appendix B, *Principles of Literary Criticism;* "The Teaching of English," in *New Statesman* (23 July

1927); "The Lure of High Mountaineering," in *Atlantic,* 139 (1927), repr. in *Complementarities;* "Belief," in *Symposium,* 1 (1930), repr. in *Complementarities;* "Between Truth and Truth," in *Symposium* 2 (1931), repr. in *Complementarities;* "Multiple Definition," in *Proceedings of the Aristotelian Society,* 34 (1933), repr. in *Complementarities;* "What is Belief?" in *Nation* (18 July 1934), repr. in *Poetries: Their Media and Ends* (1974); "Empson's Poems," review of W. Empson, *Poems,* in *Cambridge Review,* 57 (1936).

Times of India Guide to Basic English, part 4, with C. K. Ogden, A. Myers, ed. (Bombay, India, 1938); "William Empson," in *Furioso,* 1:3 (1940); "What is Involved in the Interpretation of Meaning?" in *Reading and Pupil Development: Proceedings of the Conference on Reading Held at the University of Chicago,* vol. 2 of Supplementary Educational Monographs, no. 51 (Chicago, 1940); "The Interactions of Words," in *The Language of Poetry,* Allen Tate, ed. (Princeton, 1942), repr. as "The Interinanimations of Words," in *Poetries and Sciences* (1970); "Psychopolitics," *Fortune,* 26 (1942); "A World Language," speech delivered on 16 November 1943 (New York, 1943), repr. as "Common Language," in *Vital Speeches* 10 (1943); "Responsibilities in the Teaching of English," in *Essays and Studies by Members of the English Association,* 32 (1947); "Literature, Oral-Aural and Optical," a talk delivered on BBC radio, 5 October 1947, repr. as "The Spoken and Written Word," in *Listener* (16 October 1947) and in *Complementarities.*

"The Eye and the Ear," in *The English Leaflet,* 47 (1948); "Emotive Meaning Again," in *Philosophical Review,* 57 (1948); "Emotive Language Still," in *Yale Review,* 39 (1949); "Religion and the Intellectuals," in *Partisan Review,* 17 (1950); "Communication Between Men: Meaning of Language," in *Cybernetics: Circular Causal and Feedback Mechanisms in Biological and Social Systems: Transactions of the Eighth Conference, March 15–16, 1951,* H. von Foerster, ed. (New York, 1952), repr. in *Speculative Instruments* (1955); " 'A Cooking Egg': Final Scramble," in *Essays in Criticism,* 4 (1954); "Percy Bysshe Shelley," in *Major British Writers, II,* G. B. Harrison, ed. (New York, 1954); "The Sense of Poetry: Shakespeare's 'The Phoenix and the Turtle,' " television broadcast, WGBH-TV, Boston (ca. 1957–1958), printed in *Daedalus,* 87:3 (1958), repr. in *Poetries;* "Beauty and Truth," on Keats's "Ode on a Grecian Urn," television broadcast, WBGH-TV, Boston, 1958.

"Poetic Process and Literary Analysis" and "Variant Readings and Misreading," in *Style in Language,* T. A. Sebeok, ed. (Cambridge, Mass., 1960); "The Future of Poetry," in *The Screens and Other Poems* (1960); "How Does a Poem Know When It Is Finished?" in *Parts and Wholes: The Hayden Colloquium on Scientific Method and Concept,* D. Lerner, ed. (New York and London, 1963); " 'A Valediction: Forbidding Mourning' by John Donne" and " 'The Extasie' by John Donne," in *Master Poems of the English Language,*

O. Williams, ed. (New York, 1966); Introduction to C. K. Ogden, *Opposition: A Linguistic and Psychological Analysis* (Bloomington, Ind., 1967); "A Talk on 'The Childermass,' " in *Agenda,* 7:3 (1969).

"Jakobson's Shakespeare: The Subliminal Structures of a Sonnet," review of Roman Jakobson, *Shakespeare's Verbal Art in "Th'expence of Spirit,"* in *Times Literary Supplement* (28 May 1970), repr. in *Poetries;* "The Future of Reading" and "Instructional Engineering," in *The Written Word,* (Rowley, Mass., 1971); "Sources of Our Common Thought: Homer and Plato," *The Great Ideas Today 1971* (Chicago, 1971), repr. in *Poetries;* "John Milton," in L. Kronenberger, ed., *Atlantic Brief Lives: A Biographical Companion to the Arts* (Boston, 1971); "Functions of and Factors in Language," in *Journal of Literary Semantics,* 1 (1972), repr. in *Poetries;* "Powers and Limits of Signs," *73rd Yearbook of the National Society for the Study of Education* (Chicago, 1973), repr. in *Poetries;* "Literature for the Unlettered," *Uses of Literature,* M. Engel, ed. (Cambridge, Mass., 1973), repr. in *Poetries;* "Walter De la Mare," in *New Republic* (31 Jan. 1976); "Some Notes on Hardy's Verse Forms," in *Victorian Poetry,* 17 (Spring–Summer 1979).

IV. INTERVIEWS. "An Interview with I. A. Richards," by B. A. Boucher and J. P. Russo, in *Harvard Advocate,* 103 (1969); "Beginnings and Transitions," by R. Brower, in *I. A. Richards: Essays in His Honor,* R. Brower, H. Vendler, and J. Hollander, eds. (New York, 1973); "Fundamentally, I'm an Inventor," by J. Watkins, *Harvard Magazine,* 76 (September 1973).

V. BIOGRAPHICAL AND CRITICAL STUDIES. T. S. Eliot, "Literature, Science and Dogma," *Dial* 82 (1927); J. C. Ransom, *The New Criticism* (Norfolk, Conn, 1941); T. C. Pollock et al., *A Theory of Meaning Analyzed* (Chicago, 1942); S. E. Hyman, *The Armed Vision: A Study in the Methods of Modern Literary Criticism* (New York, 1948); M. Black, *Language and Philosophy: Studies in Method* (Ithaca, N.Y., 1949); R. Wellek, *A History of Modern Criticism 1750–1950,* vol. 5 (New Haven, 1955); W. Wimsatt and C. Brooks, *Literary Criticism: A Short History* (New York, 1957); E. M. W. Tillyard, *The Muse Unchained: An Intimate Account of the Revolution in English Studies at Cambridge* (London, 1958); R. Foster, "The Romanticism of I. A. Richards," in *ELH,* 26 (1959).

R. Lowell, "I. A. Richards as Poet," in *Encounter* (February 1960); W. H. N. Hotopf, *Language, Thought and Comprehension: A Case Study of the Writings of I.A. Richards* (Bloomington, Ind., 1965); R. P. Blackmur, *A Primer of Ignorance,* J. Frank, ed. (New York, 1967); J. P. Schiller, *I. A. Richards' Theory of Literature* (New Haven, 1969); G. Cianci, *La Scuola di Cambridge: La critica letteraria di I. A. Richards, W. Empson, F. R. Leavis* (Bari, Italy, 1970); G. Graff, *Poetic Statement and Critical Dogma* (Evanston, Ill., 1970; 2nd ed. 1980); R. Brower, H. Vendler, J. Hollander, eds., *I.A. Richards: Essays in His Honor* (New York, 1973); C. Karnani,

Criticism, Aesthetics and Psychology: A Study of the Writings of I. A. Richards (New Delhi, India, 1977); P. Ricoeur, *The Rule of Metaphor,* R. Czerny, trans. (Toronto, 1977).

H. Vendler on Richards as a teacher, in *Masters: Portraits of Great Teachers,* J. Epstein, ed. (New York, 1981); J. Needham, *"The Completest Mode": I. A. Richards and the Continuity of English Literary Criticism* (Edinburgh, Scotland, 1982); P. McCallum, *Literature and Method: Towards a Critique of I. A. Richards, T. S. Eliot and F. R. Leavis* (Dublin, 1983); S. Dev Jaggi, *I. A. Richards on Poetic Truth* (Delhi, India, 1985); R. Shusterman, *Critique et Poesie selon I. A. Richards: De la confiance positiviste au relativism naissant* (Talence, France, 1988); J. P. Russo, *I. A. Richards: His Life and Work* (Baltimore and London, 1989).

OLIVE SCHREINER

(1855–1920)

Anne McClintock

OLIVE SCHREINER'S LIFE was distinguished by paradox. Born in 1855 to missionary parents in an obscure corner of colonial South Africa, she consecrated herself to an impassioned refusal of empire and God. At the age of eight, she shook her fist at the heavens and reneged on the church. Although a daughter of empire, she devoted her life and writings to championing the dispossessed, abetting the Boers against the British during the Anglo-Boer War (1899–1902), and then later the Africans against both. Schooled in discipline and decorum, and destined from childhood for domesticity, she flouted Victorian and parental decree by becoming a feminist, a best-selling writer and intellectual, and one of the most sought after celebrities of her time.

Schreiner's life spanned the heyday of South African mining colonialism, the rise and demise of the late Victorian industrial empire, and the outbreak of World War I. Migrating restlessly between colonial South Africa and fin-de-siècle Britain, she was unusually well positioned to testify, as she did in her novels, essays, political writings, and activism, to the major tumults of her time: the discovery of precious minerals in South Africa, the crises of late Victorian industrialism and the Great Depression, the socialist and feminist upheavals of the turn of the century, the Anglo-Boer War and the great European conflagration of World War I. Her diverse literary output—including three novels *(Undine, The Story of an African Farm, From Man to Man),* two exceptional prose books *(Thoughts on South Africa* and *Woman and Labour),* an allegorical novella *(Trooper Peter Halket of Mashonaland),* political essays, and three volumes of short stories—was written, she said, "in blood" *(Letters).* Her work amounts to an impassioned and lifelong denunciation of social injustice in the colonies and Britain, and a fierce defense of the disempowered: Africans and Boers, prostitutes and Jews, working-class women and men. In this respect, Schreiner was an exception in her time.

A few years after the 1867 discovery of diamonds in South Africa, when she was fifteen, Schreiner joined the pell-mell rush to the Fields, where among the tents, the brothels, and tin shanties of New Rush she witnessed at firsthand the convulsions of colonial capitalism. Sailing to Britain in 1881, she saw in the fetid slums and rookeries of the East End the calamities of late Victorian industrialism. The 1883 publication in Britain of her novel, *The Story of an African Farm,* when she was twenty-eight, won her overnight fame, the admiration of some of the great luminaries of her time, and the distinction of being the first South African writer to be widely acclaimed in Britain.

In 1889 she returned as a celebrity to South Africa, yet immediately pitched her solitary voice against the swelling crescendo of British jingoism, publicly condemning the notorious Jameson Raid of 1895 and Rhodes's bloody mauling of Mashonaland. From newspaper and podium, she decried the British ravaging of the Afrikaners during the Anglo-Boer War and then the clandestine blood brotherhood of mining capitalism and Afrikaner nationalism that was spawned soon after. The British interned her during the war for her Boer sympathies, and the Afrikaners in turn vilified her for supporting the Africans.

Schreiner's life and writings were crisscrossed by contradiction. Solitary by temperament, she hobnobbed with celebrities. Hungering for recognition, she shrank from publicity when it came to her. Insisting on women's right to sexual pleasure, she suffered torments in confronting her own urgent sexuality. At odds with her imperial world, she was at times the most colonial of writers. Startlingly advanced in her antiracism and in her political analysis, she could fall on occasion into the most familiar racial stereotypes. Revering monogamy, she waited until she was in her forties to marry. When she found "the perfect man," she chose to spend most of her married life apart from her husband. Haunted by longing for a home, she wandered from country to coast, farm to city, continent to continent, unable to settle. She was a political radical, yet she aligned herself with no party. A belligerent pacifist, she supported the Boers in their armed struggle against the British, and was a supporter of the African National Congress when it emerged in 1912.

Yet it is precisely by exploring with the utmost passion and integrity what it meant to be both colonized and colonizer, in a Victorian and African world, that Schreiner pushed the contradictions of empire to their limits, and she allows us thereby to explore some of the abiding conflicts of race and gender, of power and resistance, that haunt our time.

EARLY LIFE

OLIVE SCHREINER was born on 24 March 1855 to an English Dissenting mother and a German Lutheran father in a mud-floored house on a mission called Wittebergen, which lay in a remote African reserve on the borders of Basutoland. The tiny cluster of buildings stood solitary in the veld, scourged by lightning, the red wind of the karoo, and a sun that struck like a damnation. The Schreiners' closest neighbors were the Fingo and Sotho, and some few surviving Khoisan. The nearest post office was a hundred miles away.

In 1837, the same year that Queen Victoria ascended the throne, Rebecca Lyndall had married Gottlob Schreiner. Born into the plush sobriety of a Dissenting Yorkshire parsonage, Rebecca, Olive Schreiner's mother, was carefully groomed for her destiny as adornment to a middle-class man's career. As befitted a daughter of the cloth, she was bequeathed the demure accomplishments proper to her class: French and Italian, singing, drawing, and a generous exposure to books. Cultivated and brilliant, she wanted to be a doctor, but, as a girl, her education was intended to be decorative and not practical; the portals of university and hospital were closed to her. Olive Schreiner later described in a letter her mother's own account of her parent's house, as a sad place of cold meats

and catechism, sinners and psalms. Destined for the listless slumber of bourgois marriage and maternity, she glimpsed in empire the radiant promise of escape. At one of her father's services, she met a young German missionary, Gottlob Schreiner, and agreed almost at once to marry him. Within three weeks of marrying, they had sailed for South Africa.

At once the Schreiners took their place in an imperial narrative already two centuries in the making. Their mission work was inseparable from the politics of empire, and since Schreiner's own background cannot be understood outside this context, something must be said about the colonial situation into which she was born.

Europe first saw the southern African coastline in the fourteenth century, when the Portuguese rounded the Cape and sailed triumphantly into the Indian Ocean on their way to the spoils of the East. In the fifteenth century, the Dutch East India Company founded a tiny refreshment station at the Cape to provide fresh provender for ships plying their unseemly trades up and down the two great coasts of Africa. The Dutch saw little reason for establishing a colony at this unpromising spot, and in 1642, when Jan Van Riebeeck's ships scraped their keels on the bright beaches, the Dutch sailors built a hedge of sour almonds to segregate themselves from the continent of Africa. Nevertheless, over the centuries, small bands of Europeans arrived in sporadic waves and, lured into the interior by the promise of barter and hunting, became the unglamorous vanguard of white expansion.

Contrary to the colonial "myth of the empty lands," the vast grasslands into which these white intruders pushed had been widely populated for centuries. A diversity of sophisticated chiefdoms, some strong, some weak, with different settlement patterns, skills, and military systems, had migrated south in long, slow sweeps through the grasslands, the Nguni along the eastern seaboard, the Tswana and Sotho on the high savannas. Along the southern coast, the gentle Khoikhoi and Khoisan greeted the white visitors with curiosity and a frank enthusiasm for barter. But the sailors and settlers, piqued by the Khoi reluctance to part entirely with their herds, were not fussy about preserving good relations. Grisly colonial records tell of sportive killing raids of hair-raising cruelty, when white men rode out at dawn to massacre at random the sleeping Khoi. Those who did not succumb to smallpox or massacre were dragooned into slavery on the white farms.

Inequities certainly existed between African royals and commoners, seniors and juniors, men and women. Nevertheless, military conflicts were ritualistic and not very bloody affairs, and sophisticated social systems of communal and familial responsibility made southern Africa in some respects a more democratic place than much of medieval and Renaissance Europe (Allister Sparks, *The Mind of South Africa,* 1990). There seemed to be plenty of room for everyone. Only as the white nomads pushed steadfastly east and north, borne rapidly on their extraordinarily wasteful system of farming, did land become scarce, tensions flare over cattle and water, and chafing wars break out along the tattered frontiers. When the British took over the Cape in 1806, most of the settlers were Dutch, so in the 1820's the British Government sponsored the arrival of thousands more settlers to stimulate farming and swell the British presence on the frontiers. It was along these same frontiers that missionaries were settled to serve as a buffer between the colonials and the Africans, and it was among a settlement of Khoikhoi in the eastern Cape that Olive Schreiner's parents had their first mission station.

Rebecca's life there refuted in almost every detail the prototype of the faded, crushed petal of idle Victorian womanhood: the same bourgeois prototype her daughter later passionately denounced in her writings. At the same time, her life bore witness to the subtle betrayals of empire. During the wedding, the minister brusquely tore the garland from Rebecca's bonnet. The frivolity of flowers was improper for a missionary wife, and the clergyman's rebuke foretold a life plucked bare of frippery and frills. On the Schreiners' arrival in South Africa, the illusions of empire were as rudely snatched away. From the moment of beaching at the wind-tossed Cape, until she died a rancorous and destitute invalid in a convent, Rebecca's life was an inclement round of woe.

By all accounts, Gottlob Schreiner, Olive's father, sinned only in his lack of greed and guile. The son of a German village shoemaker, he had given up cobbling at the age of eighteen and set out to join the missionary throng. After an unpromising beginning, he was ordained into the London Missionary Society, then the largest evangelical institution peddling its spiritual wares in the arena of empire. Gottlob arrived in South Africa in 1837 and took his place among "the superfluous men" as H. Rider Haggard called them, the imperial ragbag of unemployed poor, the younger or ill-gotten sons of the clergy and fallen gentry, for whom an industrializing Europe had no place.

Nothing in Rebecca's background could have prepared her for the appalling trial that awaited her. For decades she and Gottlob trekked from mission to mission, lumbering in ox wagons across the scorching wastes of the frontier with their large family. Dogged by disappointment and poverty, natural hazards and the anger of Africans, Rebecca's only revenge was fanatacism, and her only comfort the perpetually deferred promise of heaven.

Rebecca ruled her mission household with unswerving ferocity. Pregnant for the better part of two decades, she had delivered eleven children by the time Olive arrived. Two boys died in infancy, and just before Olive's birth a third son died. Rebecca found solace only in pacing frantically back and forth in the churchyard until Olive was born. In a macabre requiem, Schreiner was named after her three dead brothers: Olive Emilie Albertina Schreiner. Her identity thus took its first shape around a female grief and the mourning of a lost male identity.

For Rebecca, the fanaticism of the civilizing mission cloaked a severe crisis in social identity, and her own fall from class somewhat represents in microcosm the more general crisis in the legitimacy of colonial power. Lacking the accoutrements of the croquet, the cricket, the brass bands, and the sundowners of the colonial gentry, Rebecca could distinguish herself from the Africans and the Boers only by a frank racism, an unswerving sexual puritanism, a diet of self-denial, and a regimen of guilt.

From her mother, Schreiner inherited her precocious intellect, her ethical fervor and her longing for the infinite, her tendency toward self-scrutiny and sexual guilt, her gifts as a raconteur, and her passion for medicine. Her mother also bequeathed to her the secret, ambiguous knowledge of the power of women.

Rebecca appears clearly to have abused her children, whipping them furiously for the smallest sin. More than Gottlob, Rebecca saw herself as the avenging angel of a punitive God. The children were forbidden to speak Dutch, for English was the language of the racially elect. Schreiner wrote that her earliest memory was of receiving fifty vicious lashes from her mother at the age of five, for swinging on a door handle and using a taboo Dutch word, exclaiming: "*Ach,* it is so nice outside." At a stroke, she recalls, she inherited the "unutterable bitter rebellion" against "God and man" that would wreak havoc with her childhood *(Letters)* and last the rest of her life. The unfathomable injustice of the thrashings was the major reason she became a freethinker and why, at the age of eight, without precedent or example, she summarily swept the heavens clear of her parents' creed and refused any longer to go to church. Henceforth, she would always be an outcast and a pariah.

Identity comes into being only through community, and from the outset Schreiner's earliest relations with her family were shaped by an obscure economy of identity through denial. She learned very young that she would be rewarded with her mother's love only if she denied herself. As a result she fell into the quandary of winning affirmation of self only through a ritualistic self-negation, a sad logic of Christian masochism that left its mark on her life long after she rejected Christian dogma.

Schreiner might have learned to negotiate these childhood dilemmas more successfully had an obscure calamity not befallen her. Shortly after renouncing her parents' creed, at the age of nine in 1865, she was punished by the death of her beloved baby sister, Ellie. Inconsolable with grief, she insisted on cradling the tiny corpse in her arms for an entire day and into the night. After the burial, she haunted the grave for weeks, crouching next to the small mound and talking fervently into the earth. Schreiner would later insist that the death of her sister was the most important event of her childhood: it was to Ellie that she owed her lifelong love for women, her mystic faith in the unity of the cosmos, her pacifism, and her desire to be a doctor *(Letters,* 29 October 1892). The death of a female child was an enigma that haunted her, and the premature mutilation of female life returns as a theme in much of her writing.

In the trauma of the early thrashings, her renunciation of Christianity, and her sister's death, Schreiner's identity became fashioned around a tortuous logic of rebellion and guilt, autonomy and punishment. Pleasure in the body, she learned, could be answered inexplicably by an annihilating pain. Transgressing the threshold of domesticity brought violent retribution, and an unholy alliance reigned between forbidden words and power. Transgression offered the shimmering promise of autonomy and the potency of self-creation, but it also threatened her with the catastrophe of negation, of herself or another. Negotiating the boundaries between identity and difference, desire and punishment, love of the other and loss of self became a lifelong activity fraught with peril. In all of Schreiner's writing boundary images preside: doorsteps and windows, seashores and deathbeds, noon and midnight. Characteristically, her imagination was pitched at the dangerous borders between domesticity and wilderness, love and autonomy, obedience and scandal.

At about this same time in her childhood, Schreiner became afflicted by phobias. She would awake at night crying and shouting, then clamber under her bed to lie face down on the cold floor for hours in a paralysis of dread. She found relief from "the agony of there being no Hereafter" *(Letters,* 4 December 1884) only in biting and mauling her hands and beating her head against the wall until she was insensible. Schooled in sacrifice, she went into the veld one day to solicit a final answer from God, an event she recreates in *The Story of an African Farm.* On an altar of twelve flat stones, she offered up a fat lamb chop and waited in the sacrificial heat for the torch of God. But the conflagration never came, and in a paroxysm of disbelief, she smeared her body with dung. In this way, at the very moment of abandoning Christianity, she was rehearsing the masochistic logic of Christianity, mortifying the body in a bid for salvation from mortification of the soul. Inflicting punishment on herself preempted the power of the mother to punish her and at the same time licensed her own willful mutinies.

Clearly, these "desperate romps" of anger and bewilderment were a hysterical protest against her situation *(Letters).* From an astonishingly early age, Schreiner saw her suffering as gendered: "When I was a young girl—a child, I felt this awful bitterness in my soul because I was a woman" *(Letters,* 27 June 1908). The main force of her refusal of her colonial world came from a deeply felt sense of exile, and much of her motivation to write stemmed from her urgent yearning for an alternative community. Yet, at the same time, colonial life bequeathed to her as a white child a greater measure of physical freedom than that enjoyed by most British girls of her class and time. Easily dodging the overworked Africans and her distracted mother, Schreiner found in the vast veld the promise of redemption from the limits of her situation.

Beyond the sepulchral mission lay an immense, hot country of cactus and red sand, of flat rocks and aromatic thorn trees, where the only sounds were the cries of the sheep and the cough of baboons from the crags. In this beloved place, Schreiner wandered the streambeds and stood alone with her small bewilderments under a blue cathedral of sky. There she developed her precocious talent for introspection: "In such a silence," she later wrote, "one could only think and think" (Letters). Pondering the crystal drops of the ice plant and the spoor of leopard in the sand, tracing the enigma of origins in fossils, and examining the scarlet veins of an ostrich heart, she came to read in nature a hidden hieroglyphics of divinity.

Born of colonial stock, Schreiner inherited a Bible and a European culture out of place with the African history of her beloved karoo. With her renunciation of the Bible, she lost forever the dialogue of prayer and inherited instead a haunting sense of exile and solitude. Yet she was incapable of abandoning all solace, and she projected onto the steadfast immensity of sky and veld the metaphysical silhouette of her lost religion. The tendrils of the palm fern, the tracery of ants in the sand, the mierkat's small footfall all offered an alternative allegory of God. If the thunderous God of the Bible had lost his voice, that voice was now ventriloquized through nature. Nature drew her close "with that subtle sympathy which binds together all things, and to stones and rocks gives a speech which even we can understand" (The Story of an African Farm). In almost all of Schreiner's writings there is a ritualistic moment when a child frantic with despair is spoken to and calmed by nature. Moreover, Schreiner's god of nature is not a male god, but is consistently feminized. In her allegories and novels, nature is a projection of a female principle, speaking with a female voice, and figured as a long-robed mother bending over and smoothing her child's dishevelled hair.

In this way, the weird, compelling beauty of the karoo gave Schreiner the lifelong respite of a metaphysical solace: "The Universe is One, and It lives!" (Letters, 29 October 1892). A monist vision of the cosmos animates all her writing with a mystical faith in the unity of all things. In her favorite allegory, "The Ruined Chapel," an angel of God ex-

poses a human soul to an unbelieving man. In this soul the man discovers "in its tiny drop" the whole universe, the inner nature of stars, lichen, crystals, the outstretched fingers of infants. Gazing at the fully naked soul, he shudders and whispers: "It is God" (Stories, Dreams, and Allegories, 1923). In The Story of an African Farm, Waldo moves his hands "as though he were washing them in the sunshine." So too Schreiner found absolution for unbelief in the sacrament of sun.

Yet there is a paradox. The vast veld gave Schreiner material grounds for her longing for the infinite, but it also concealed the very real history of colonial plunder that gave her privileged access to this immensity. There was nothing "infinite" about the karoo; it was fenced by land laws, the history of dispossession, and colonial rout. Schreiner's theological skepticism would always be tempered by a mystical faith in the divinity of the cosmos. Yet this faith was won at the cost of ignoring, for a long time, the history of colonialism that guaranteed her privileged access to the land. In later life, Schreiner wandered naked among the hot rocks and bush, calm in the knowledge that there was no one to disturb her. In her rhapsodies to the infinite, it was easy to forget she was walking on stolen land.

Her pantheism, for all its emotional integrity, was very much a metaphysical abstraction. As an abstraction, it served to conceal, and thereby to ratify, the very real imbalances in social power around her. Schreiner's early reluctance to look squarely at the politics of race is rendered most vividly and problematically in the figure of the hostile, ominous, and unsympathetic "Hottentot" that stalks many of her stories. Schreiner swore she never had a mother, yet in fact a number of mother figures attended her childhood. Essentially, it was to the shadowy presence of the African women in the household that Schreiner owed her sense of racial privilege, yet this presence was paradoxical.

Some of Schreiner's first experiences of the limits to her power and pleasure, and hence to her identity, were forged about the figure of an angry and punitive black woman. The Story of an African Farm, "The Child's Day" (published as the prelude to From Man to Man, 1926), and many of her early stories are haunted by the figure of the angry "old Ayah," a reflection, however oblique and denied, of the resistance of African women. The African woman has no name; she bears only a labor category and the identity of servitude, and yet she possesses a secret and appalling power to judge and punish. In later life, Schreiner confessed to Havelock Ellis her phobic loathing of eating in front of strangers. In "The Prelude," Rebekah is similarly tormented by the African women who look from their corners with strong, steady disapproval while she eats *(From Man to Man)*.

Schreiner was caught in a paradox she never resolved. Her mystical monism assuaged her loneliness and sense of exile, but was at odds with the social history of racial and gender difference that shaped her experience. She swung between an agnostic vision of the "awful universe" as capricious and blind and a contrary belief in a universal "Truth" driving the destiny of planets *(The Story of an African Farm)*. For years she was tormented by an impossible choice between fidelity to an abstract, universal "Truth" and fidelity to the historical value of human community. The conflict between these values is a theme around which much of her writing revolves, and she came to feel her inability to resolve the paradox with the force of a lifelong and inconsolable grief.

Schreiner's childhood was marked by a sense of exile that was twofold. As Lyndall cries in *The Story of an African Farm:* "To be born a woman is to be born branded." To the man the world cries "Work! To woman it says: Seem" (part 2, ch. 4). Lyndall's image of the girl sitting beside the window, her pale cheek pressed wistfully against the pane, symbolizes the invisible glass barriers that stand between women and the world. Her furious, failed attempt to smash the window pane and prize open the stubborn shutters bears witness to Schreiner's own bleak sense of the barriers facing women's power. At the same time, Schreiner's sense of exile was very much the outcome of the social alienation of the colonial intruder in a foreign land. Unable to find clues to the social history of her loneliness, she took refuge in the solitary vocation of language, in flights of fantasy and the autonomy of self-creation.

Schreiner was by all accounts an extravagantly intelligent child, a beautiful and ardent girl whom people remembered for her "flashing eyes" and brilliant conversation. Three of the Schreiner sons were sent to Cambridge; the youngest, Will, later succeeded Cecil Rhodes as prime minister of the Cape Colony. As a girl, Schreiner was deprived the formal education of her brothers, but her mother,

"all intellect and genius" (*Letters,* January 1893), educated her at home, teaching her political philosophy, economics, theology, and history, indulging her passion for poetry, and imbuing in her a lasting love of medicine.

From the outset, books held an inordinate value for her. By the age of seven, Schreiner had fallen in love with John Milton, and could recite large sweeps of Samuel Taylor Coleridge and Alfred Lord Tennyson. In books she glimpsed the delirious possibility that her solitude was not the affliction of an accursed infidel, but rather the mark of a persecuted community of truth-seekers and seers. When the family lived near Cradock, one of the garrison towns strung along the northern frontier, Schreiner was allowed to rifle at will through the local, privately endowed library, a freedom not available to many white girls of her time and certainly not to African women or men. She read voraciously, doggedly pushing her way through Plato, Percy Bysshe Shelley, Edward Gibbon, Baruch Spinoza, Henry David Thoreau, John Ruskin, Thomas Carlyle, William Lecky, Johann Wolfgang von Goethe and Heinrich Heine, Charles Dickens, the Brontë sisters, George Sand, Robert Browning, and Charles Darwin. By the age of twelve, she was spending six hours a day reading and writing. Discovering Ralph Waldo Emerson (after whom she named Waldo and Em in *The Story of an African Farm,* and from whom she took her own pseudonym, Ralph Iron) rescued her from a suicidal crisis, and "gave her more strength than anything else has ever done," her husband later recorded in *The Life of Olive Schreiner* (1924).

On one momentous evening, moreover, when Schreiner was sixteen, a traveler arrived wet and disheveled at the door. (He in fact became the model for the German "stranger" in *The Story of an African Farm.*) After conversing intensely with Olive, the traveler, Willie Bertram, lent her a copy of Herbert Spencer's *Principles.* She devoured it in three days, and she credited Spencer's rationalist arguments for cosmic unity as having reset the "broken leg" of her "blank atheism." "He helped me believe in a unity underlying all nature; that was a great thing" (*Letters,* 28 March 1884).

At about this time, at the age of sixteen, Schreiner summarily changed her name. She had been called Emily since birth, and now she insisted that she was to be called Olive. As Antoinette in Jean Rhys's *Wide Sargasso Sea* (1966), says: "Names matter."

Names reflect the obscure relations of power between self and society, and women's names mirror the degree to which women's status in society is relational, mediated by a social relation to men: first father, then husband. Schreiner associated the name Olive with her mother's family, and her stubborn change of name expressed a newfound, willful determination to fashion her own identity. At the same time, the choice of the mother's name expressed an identification with her mother's history and power. Much of the inspiration for Schreiner's writings sprang from a desire to redeem the deformed narrative of her mother's life, and both Rebekah in *From Man to Man* and Lyndall in *The Story of an African Farm* are named after her mother. Later, when she married, Schreiner refused the symbolic surrender of women's autonomy in names, and insisted that her husband, Samuel Cron Cronwright, take her name, while she kept her own.

Schreiner created stories from earliest childhood. Servants and visitors alike were struck by the eerie spectacle of the child pacing feverishly back and forth on the veranda, hair disheveled, hands clenched behind her back, mumbling stories to herself. There on the veranda, between domesticity and veld, scandal and decorum, autonomy and dependence, Schreiner began the radical project of identity and the vocation of selfhood. Throughout her life, she paced in this way, driving neighbors and landladies to distraction with the restless tread of her feet. Indeed, pacing to and fro between extremes can be seen to be the quintessential activity of Schreiner's life.

From the outset Schreiner's attitude to language was marked by paradox. She discovered in language a magician's power to conjure from nowhere the miracle of her mother's approval. The sorcery of writing promised self-justification and autonomy. Yet language was also the realm of peril, for words were always linked to transgression. In language the boundaries of selfhood were permanently ambiguous, and words could occasion, she had learned, the swift annihilation of rejection and retribution, a sense that deeply shaped her future relations with her public. Moreover, her brother Will, eavesdropping on her, retold her stories to the family at dinner and claimed them for his own. This male appropriation of language drove Schreiner into convulsions of rage and imbued in her a precocious sense of storytelling as a gendered contest over authorship and authority.

The bewilderments of Schreiner's childhood might have been less decisive had they not been overdetermined by the crises and contradictions of her colonial situation. Her father's life was in every sense marginal. As a German, Gottlob was an outsider to the British and the Dutch. As a colonial, he was an outsider to the Africans. The white farmers bitterly resented him for training the Africans in industrial skills, since Africans, they thought, were predestined to be no more than hewers of wood and drawers of water. If he was an honorary member of the white elite, the fiction of racial superiority was belied by his sheer lack of talent for any occupation and the consequent poverty and chronic distress of his family. From her docile and visionary father, Schreiner inherited her hatred of injustice, her generosity, her compassion for the dispossesed, and a lifelong sense of exile.

In the mid 1860's, the family narrative took shape around the disgrace of the colonial father. Meandering from mission to mission, Gottlob Schreiner was beset by failure and financial distress. In 1865, the same year that baby Ellie died, after a number of dismissals and censures, he was finally expelled from the ministry for his infringment of laws banning trading. After twenty-seven years of mission work, the aging and inept preacher tried his hand at commerce. Ambling about the country on horseback, he peddled eggs, hides, coffee, and pepper to the Africans, but one after the other his stores failed. Hounded by debt and disgrace, he surrendered to his creditors and plunged into destitution.

The family scattered. Rebecca went to live in a outbuilding, and Schreiner's parents spent the rest of their lives leaning on the charity of their children. Olive was farmed out to her older brother Theo, a headmaster at Cradock, under whose tyrannical tutelage her life became a "hell on earth." Theo embued in her a lasting sense of her intellect as a deformation and a crime: "He turned away so utterly when I began to think" (*Letters,* 10 July 1884).

All the elements that shaped Schreiner's attitude to writing and the vocation of selfhood were now in place. Her childhood and adolescence were rife with contradiction. Contrary to colonial dogma, her family lived scarcely better than the fairly prosperous African farmers around them. Contrary to patriarchal dogma, her mother was the dominant power in the household. Contrary to Christian dogma, her parents' faith had been rewarded only by "disaster and disaster and trouble" (*Life*). The Victorian ideology of the family was a mockery and failure. All things considered, the evidence of her life could admit no easy evangelism, and the failure of empire to keep its promise bred in Schreiner a precocious pessimism.

Nonethless, her mystical experiences in the immensity of the veld and her timely contact with Spencerian ideas of progress and cosmic unity rescued her from the sense of being everywhere in exile and from the blank atheism toward which she tended. Her love for her sister, too, released her from the lonely soliloquy of selfhood, from the terrors of solipsism. She recalled, "I had no self, she was myself. . . . I sometimes think my great love for women and girls, not because they are myself, but because they are not myself comes from her" (*Letters,* 29 July 1893).

In writing, as in love, the boundaries of identity were blurred and there she could glimpse a longed-for community of identity. Feminists have commented on this characteristic feature of women's social identity: it is figured not as autonomous or inherent, but rather as coming into being *in relation* to an other, through community. Indeed, Schreiner frequently revealed the degree to which her writing was not only an expression of her identity, but an *extension* of her identity: "My work and my people seem more real to me than I myself" (*Letters,* 29 March 1885). She had great difficulty distinguishing between her characters and herself: "Sometimes I really don't know whether I am I or one of the others. Bertie is me, and Drummond is me, and all is me" *(Letters).*

In the semiautobiographical prelude to *From Man to Man,* which Schreiner first conceived in a flash of intuition in 1887, we find almost all the obsessive themes that characterize her writing. A "little mother" groans in the agony of childbirth. Abandoned in the spellbinding heat of a mission garden, a child uncovers her head to the forbidden sun and makes her way to a secret place in the veld, where in a small allegory of the mother's labor of creation, she builds a tiny house of stone. There she waits for a visitation that never comes. This is an almost ritualistic moment in the colonial narrative: a solitary self sits alone in the wilderness waiting for communion. Bereft of response, she cups her fingers into the shape of a mouse and projects herself into an other-self, confusing the boundary of flesh and symbol, self and other, and in this commerce

with creativity redeems the lost moment. Returning to the house, the child crosses a forbidden boundary, climbs through a closed window, and finds in the cool, dim room a sleeping child. Careful not to wake her, she bequeathes the child her gifts: an alphabet book, a Bushman stone, a silver needle and thread, a Queen Victoria's head, and a chocolate. Thereby she symbolically restores to her sister the sacred elements stolen from women: writing, history, creative labor, political power, and sensual pleasure. Yet the gift giving is aborted, for her sleep next to her sister is interrupted by the wrathful "old Ayah," the unforgiving midwife of death and difference, who berates her for her trespass and furiously points out that the baby is dead. Returning to the veld, the girl lies under a tree, cradling in her arms a book instead of a baby, and enters a series of dreams within dreams in which the eternal symmetry of the cosmos and her unity with nature is revealed to her. From the house, there comes the cry of a newborn child.

In this small parable of female creativity one finds many of the themes that preoccupied Schreiner throughout her career: her sense of exile from social community redeemed by a revelation of cosmic unity, the interdependence of women, the fluid sliding between the roles of mother and child, the allegorical association between writing and childbirth, her projection of the principle of difference onto the anger of African women, and her sense of writing as a radical project of self-creation and self-justification.

Just at the time when Schreiner was beginning the lifelong task of fashioning her own identity, a new economy began to be forged in South Africa. So it is not surprising that the contradictions of her society entered her life and writings with overwhelming force.

FIRST WRITINGS

UNTIL THE 1860's, South Africa held scant allure for the imperial powers. But in 1867 a small child happened to pick up the first diamond discovered in South Africa, and with it drew this unpromising outpost of empire into the turbulence of modern imperial capitalism. Overnight, South Africa was transformed from an isolated, pastoral land into a modern industrial economy. Overnight, a motley scramble of thousands of adventurers, fortune seekers, and entrepreneurs tumbled ashore and rushed up-country for the mines. In 1871, a surveyor's wife, while on a picnic, chanced upon another diamond, revealing at a stroke the world's richest deposit of blue diamond-bearing kimberlite. The discovery sparked the New Rush; within a few months thousands of frantic diggers were gouging a huge hole in the bare hillside where the diamond had been found.

Next to the hole a town called Kimberley was born. From the town emerged a small syndicate of ambitious white capitalists jockeying for control of the riches. From the syndicate was formed the De Beers Consolidated Mines, a monolithic corporation destined to control two-thirds of the world's entire stock of diamonds. One of the most flamboyant and ambitious of these ambitious men was Cecil John Rhodes, a vicar's son from England and the future prime minister of the Cape, who summed up the spirit of the age when he said, "I would annex the stars, if I could."

In 1872 Olive Schreiner, destined to become one of Rhodes's most famous and vexing antagonists, joined her brothers at New Rush in the pell-mell dash for the diamonds. There, standing on the tip of the gaping, noisy hole, among the black diggers and their frenzied white overseers, Schreiner witnessed the beginning of a new and cataclysmic economic dispensation for South Africa.

Those who were called the "diggers" at New Rush were nothing of the kind. The "diggers" were white, and did no digging: the men who dug were black. At the same time, Africans were entirely denied possession of the diamonds they dug from the earth. A law was quickly rushed into force by the white invaders: no African would be allowed to own, buy, or sell a single diamond.

Britain, until then indifferent to the region, quickly threw its paramountcy over the territory, and the lieutenant governor of Natal, supposedly adjudicating between the rival claims of the Boers and the Africans for the land, awarded the fields to a tractable man of Khoi descent called Witbooi. Without any ado, Witbooi requested and received British citizenship, whereupon the diamond fields passed immediately and conveniently into British hands. It was there in the diamond fields in 1872, amid the hubbub and tumult of the new history, that Schreiner began to write in earnest. She was seventeen.

The same year, at Dortrecht while visiting relatives, Schreiner met a man named Julius Gau, the brother of an intimate friend of hers. She traveled the long, slow journey of a hundred miles home with Gau, alone and unchaperoned, an unusual and decidedly improper event at the time. In a letter dated 18 August 1872, after an inexplicable silence in her letters about the journey, she summarily announced to her sister Kate that she was engaged to marry Gau, adding enigmatically: "It may be very soon, that is in four or five months, or it may not be for at least a year to come. I will be able to tell you more definitely next week." Yet nothing was ever again said of the matter, and Gau vanished from the scene.

The incident might have been inconsequential, were it not soon apparent that Schreiner was suffering a severe breakdown, unable to sleep or eat. While any conjecture about the incident remains hypothetical, the semiautobiographical recreations in her novels suggest that she had sexual intercourse with Gau, and that she had been swiftly abandoned. Whatever the event, Schreiner seems to have inherited from it an intense terror of sexual involvment, an abiding fear of rejection, and a lifelong fury at the social hypocrisy of sexual relations. In her unforgiving mission community, the squandering of virginity outside the sanctity of marriage was as great a sin as a woman could commit, tantamount to losing all celestial and earthly credit in the eyes of God and the world. Sexual desire could be answered only by guilt and punishment, and Schreiner marked in her journal: "To be carnally minded is death" (Life).

From this time on, Schreiner was tormented by incessant bouts of asthma, and the restless migrations of her life were to a large degree shaped around this malady. Beaten as a child for speaking out of turn, unable as an adolescent to discuss religion, politics, or philosophy with her family, and now unable to speak to anyone about this latest calamity, her life's breath, cheated and strangled like her words, turned inwards. For Schreiner, asthma represented a way of voicing her voicelessness; it served as a form of symbolic protest or a kind of convulsive bellowing for help. Indeed, Schreiner often expressed frustration at the inability of other people to interpret the malady allegorically: "It's as much my mind as my body" (Letters). Illness features prominently in her novels and yet medical reasons for the ill health of her characters are never given: illnesses are emotional affairs, physical protests at insoluble conflicts. By heaving and gasping for breath, by physically exhibiting her suffocation and voicelessness, in a voice like a "rusty bellows," she maintained that she was attempting to give voice to her inability to speak. A woman deprived of love, she wrote in the preface to *Woman and Labour* (1911), could only draw a "half-asphyxiated" life.

Asthma was thus a portmanteau malady, rich in paradoxical meaning. It gave Schreiner a motive for mobility, as well as an excuse for failure. It gave her power over people, when she appeared at her most vulnerable. As soon as a relationship became stifling, asthma allowed her to pack up and leave. Asthma absolved her of the sin of self-sufficiency and autonomy: it was not her fault she had to leave her family, live in boarding rooms, live apart from her family and husband. Asthma muted her power, and thus made her appear more "feminine." At the same time, when she was well, she could be free to enjoy the robust strength and physical prowess of which she was alternately proud and ashamed. Asthma allowed her to punish herself and thus preempt the punishment of others.

UNDINE

LIVING among the tents and shacks of New Rush, in 1872 Schreiner began to write *Undine,* and this semiautobiographical tale, written over a period of two years, marks her first willful assumption of the vocation of selfhood. Drawing on her experiences at the diamond fields, and motivated by a haunting sense of exile, *Undine*—although not published until 1929—was Schreiner's first, halting effort to find clues to the history of her solitude. The words that open the novel, "I was tired of being called queer and strange and odd," belong as much to Schreiner, as her motive for writing the book, as they do to the heroine Undine. Writing in itself became for Schreiner a plea for self-justification, and creating *Undine* amounted to a fierce rebuttal of male, colonial decree and an effort to reinvent the scope of women's identity in a world mismanaged by men.

Undine, the daughter of a devout Boer family, is beset, like Schreiner, by precocious disbelief, and she suffers, like Schreiner, the scourge of social stigma for her temerity and tomboy ways. Militantly "unwomanly," she refuses to genuflect to convention or creed and flouts at every turn her family's dogmas and decorum. She forgets to wear her bonnet in the flaming sun, risking a dark complexion—the ungodly sign of racial and gender transgression. She scandalizes propriety by rescuing her monkey, Socrates, from a tree, enacting a small, allegorical rehearsal of Schreiner's lifelong effort to rescue for women the right to natural intelligence and freedom of the body. Yet if *Undine* is a vehement defense of female mutiny, the narrative also bears testimony to the tragic limits of women's revolt, and it initiates Schreiner's abiding theme of the intolerable impasse between love and autonomy.

When Undine sees Albert Blair, the uncaring object of her adoration, she lets fall the book she is reading, symbolically abandoning the world of the mind for the traitorous allure of love. Blair schools Undine in submission, adjusting her gloves, forcing her to betray her convictions in the hypocrisy of church-going, and proclaiming that the essence of femininity is the mediocre and the mundane: "A woman to be womanly should have nothing striking or peculiar about her; she should shun all extremes in manners and modes of expression; she should have no strong views on any question" (ch. 8).

At the diamond fields, Undine discovers that she is the victim of a far more perilous exclusion. As a woman, she is historically barred from the male contest over the diamonds and the economy of mining capitalism. Denied the right to labor, land, and profit, peering into the forbidden depths of the mine, she mourns: "If she had been a man, she might have thrown off her jacket and set to work instantly, carrying the endless iron buckets and coils of rope" (ch. 15). Henceforth money, public autonomy, and sexual power will be reserved for white men, while her alloted fare is dependency and servitude, ill health and grief, and her only profession the vocation of matrimony.

Here arises one of Schreiner's obsessive themes: "All women have their value in coins." Throughout her life, Schreiner responded to the matrimonial trade in women—the barter of female bodies to guarantee male privilege and power, and the rites of domestic dependence—with loathing and fear. For Schreiner, "the unenviable fate of both women and pictures" is to be bought and sold by men (*Undine*). Undine's only access to capital is vicarious: bartering her body to Albert Blair's unsavory father, on the condition that he offer a tidy sum of money, she is seduced and betrayed by the false promise of matrimony, and she ends her life betrothed only to grief. At its heart, *Undine* is a fraught attempt to answer the question that the French feminist Luce Irigiray posed a century later in *This Sex Which Is Not One* (1985): "Can the commodity refuse to go to market?" If Schreiner seems to answer here in the negative, the novel *Undine* prefigures the necessity of a far more incendiary, if at that moment unimaginable, revolt.

In *Undine,* Schreiner was indifferent to the racial implications of the plundered profits of the diamonds. Undine's gendered rebellion is not matched by any more-radical racial or class rebellion, and her understanding of her social situation remains stillborn. Frustrated by her inability to express the truth of her situation, Schreiner denounced the book as unformed and incomplete, and she later begged Havelock Ellis to have it burned.

THE STORY OF AN AFRICAN FARM

DENIED the pulpit of her father and the political podium of her brothers, Schreiner's only destiny was domesticity. Since no husband seemed imminent, it was inevitable that she enter paid domestic work, and from the ages of fifteen to twenty-two Schreiner worked as a governess in colonial homes.

The colonial governess was in every sense a threshold creature. Graced with an education but not with the opportunity to use it, racially a member of the white elite but in reality a member of the serving class, protected by racial privilege but not by economic security, lodging among black servants but not with them, paid for work that the housewife did for free, the white governess embodied some of the abiding contradictions of the colonial economy of female labor. Schreiner's early experience in domestic service gave significant shape to her later feminism, and an acute understanding of the contradiction between paid and unpaid work animates *Woman and Labour.*

In March 1875, when she was twenty, Schreiner took a position as governess with the Fouché family, on a remote farm in the karoo called Klein Ganna Hoek. There she lived in a single, mud-floored room under the roof of the kitchen, washing in the cold water of a nearby stream. The roof of her room leaked, so she sat under an umbrella,

scribbling and jotting, and it was there at Ganna Hoek, in the stolen, exhausted hours after work, that she wrote most of the novel that secured her fame, *The Story of an African Farm.*

The Story of an African Farm is a towering denunciation of the unholy trinity of empire, family, and God—the three grandiose illusions that had graced Schreiner's infancy with their radiance, only to become the traitorous figures of her despair. The animating vision of the book is the failure of both empire and patriarchy to keep their promises, and the radical significance of the book lies in Schreiner's conviction that a critique of the violence of colonialism also entails a critique of the patriarchal family and the institution of marriage.

From the outset, the "African farm" is figured as pathological. The colonial family is in disarray. The white father has vanished, lingering only as an obsolete afterimage in the figure of Otto, the quixotic, dreaming, German overseer, modeled on Schreiner's own father. There is no mother. The household is presided over by a grossly animalistic and monstrous aunt, Tant' Sannie, a deformation of maternal power. Lyndall is an orphan, Waldo a disinherited son. Although Schreiner offers no explicit critique of the white ownership of the farm, it is clear that there will be no legitimate colonial heir to the future. The movement of the plot is flight: flight from the patriarchal house and the economy of colonial agriculture. Waldo flees to the coast, Lyndall flees to the mines, but the ultimate destination is death. Neither marriage, nor empire, nor God can redeem the colonial narrative.

The Story of an African Farm begins, like many of Schreiner's allegories, pitched under a midnight moon, a complex symbol of the uncertain half-light of transcendence. The moon, promising but not ensuring redemption, casts its eerie radiance over the ostrich farm, which lies still under the rule of sleep. Waldo, son of the hapless German overseer, Otto, lies awake in the wagon house, swathed in solitude, listening with dread to the clicking clock. The clock is a repeated motif in Schreiner's tales: almost all Schreiner's children lie in the dark, spellbound by fear of the clock's metronome, measuring time with death: "Dying, dying, dying . . . Eternity, eternity, eternity!" (part 1, ch. 1). For Schreiner the clock symbolizes the grotesque parody of the Victorian concept of industrial progress: mechanical, mundane, deadly. The clock, like the multiplication table, like ancient arithmetic, like the Latin grammar, offers only the cold algebra of reason. The soul, however, "has seasons of its own; periods not found in any calendar" (part 2, ch. 1). The singular struggle of the novel, indeed the struggle of much of Schreiner's life, is to discover, and to render in words, an alternative, redemptive calendar of the soul.

It is not surprising, therefore, that Schreiner preferred the literary form of the allegory. All of her writings are allegories: "except in my own language of parables I cannot express myself" (*Letters,* 29 October 1892). All of her plots are interrupted by allegories, parables, and dreams that flash their crystalline uncertainties like prisms, refracting themes and images in myriad directions and dispersing their irregular radiance slantingly across the linear progress of plot. From the outset Schreiner wanted her writing to imitate the unpredictable disorder and imprecision of life, "the method of the life we all lead. Here nothing can be prophesied. There is a strange coming and going of feet. Men appear, act and re-act upon each other, and pass away" she says in the preface to *The Story of an African Farm.*

Waldo, like Schreiner, is afflicted with insomnia of the soul. For Waldo, as for all allegorists, the world is the word made flesh: "has it never seemed to you that the stones were *talking* with you?" (part 1, ch. 2). In the beginning was the Word, and nature is the book of God, a divine script destined to be read by visionaries and poets. Nature is the "open secret." The fossil footprints of great birds, the skeletons of fish, the filaments of a spider's web are miniature allegories of an unchanging reality that animates all things: "All true facts of nature of the world are related" (part 2, ch. 2). Under the allegorist's gaze, the varied and multitudinous forms of life dissolve into a many-colored, many-shaped singular form of existence: the thorn tree sketched against a midwinter sky has the same form as the tracery of crystals in a rock, which has the same form as the beetle's tiny horns. The human body, too, is a hieroglyph, offering hints and intimations of divine meaning. The underlying unity of all things is revealed in this beautiful similitude of form: "How are these things related that such deep union should exist between them all?" Schreiner questions in *The Story of an African Farm* (part 2, ch. 1).

For Waldo, books, like nature, reveal "the presence of God." Books offer the delirious, imperial promise of knowing the final secrets of the world: "Why the crystals grow in such beautiful shapes, why lightning runs to the iron, why black people are black." Books offer Waldo, as they did Schreiner, a refuge from cosmic abandon and the scourge of loneliness: books reveal men and women to whom not only kopjes and stones were calling out imperatively, "What are we, and how came we here? Understand us, and know us," but to whom "the old, old relations between man and man . . . could not be made still and forgotten. . . . So he was not alone, not alone."

In *The Origin of German Tragic Drama,* Walter Benjamin asserts that allegory is always shadowed by its dark side. The allegorical vision is guaranteed by an occult faith that the relation between words and things is cosmically ordained, yet the allegorical project is inherently ambiguous. Allegory has its etymological origins in the Greek words *allos* and *agoreuei:* to speak in public of other, or secret, things. Allegory's power is precisely this doubleness, speaking to the chosen few of secret truths, concealing them from the profane. All allegories involve a doubling, or even multiplying, of a text by another. "Art," as Schreiner put it, "says more than it says." Yet, allegory, as a result, is paradoxical and perilous, its ambiguity always threatening to undermine its intelligibility. When Tant' Sannie finds Waldo's book on political economy, his precious "pollity-gollity-gominy" is unintelligible to her, and she feeds it to the bonfire.

Hence the tragic quality of allegory: "Words are very poor things" *(Letters).* Oblique and strangely incomplete, with its origin in exegesis, allegory both solicits and frustrates desire for original meaning. Words are the sacred emissaries of truth, but they are never fully adequate to their burden, and thus they both illuminate and obscure meaning: "If I say that in a stone, in the wood, in the thoughts of my brain, in the corpuscles of a drop of blood under my microscope, in a railway engine rushing past me in the veld, I see God, shall I not be darkening counsel with words?" (*Letters,* 29 October 1892).

Allegory, moreover, lies on the cusp of memory and forgetting: it points beyond itself to an originary history that at every moment threatens to vanish. In Benjamin's words: "An appreciation of the transience of things, and a concern to rescue them for eternity, is one of the strongest impulses in allegories" (*The Origin of German Tragic Drama.*)

Here we come directly upon one of Schreiner's central motivations to write: the desire to rescue history, the flesh, and language from oblivion—her cry "not to let the thing die!" Language was a passionate rebuttal of the intolerable enigma of death and the inevitable process of dissolution and decay. Allegory offered Schreiner the promise that language could redeem matter—as she believed as a child, talking for days down into her dead sister's grave. Hence Schreiner's entirely modernist fascination with ruins, with the breathing dead, the interred living. As Lyndall remarks darkly in *The Story of an African Farm:* "Not all that is buried is dead" (part 2, ch. 4).

Yet, for Waldo, "writhing before the inscrutable mystery," such intimations of immortality are repeatedly imperiled by the catastrophic possibility that all is illusion: "If there should be no God" (part 2, ch. 1). Wandering clumsy and ragged in the veld, he scans the stubborn sky and sand for signs of God, yearning "for a token from the inexorably Silent One." Here Waldo rehearses a recurrent, almost ritualistic moment in colonial narratives, whereby the solitary self, standing dumbfounded before an inexpressible landscape, cries out "This *I*, what is it?": "For an instant our imagination seizes it; we are twisting, twirling, trying to make an allegory. . . . Then suddenly a loathing comes to us; we are liars and hypocrites" (part 2, ch. 1). That man in the pulpit lies! The brass-clasped hymn book lies! The leaves of the Bible drop blood; the stones do not give voice to God.

Waldo's crisis, however, which Schreiner here figures strictly as the existential crisis of the universal soul, is more properly speaking a crisis of colonial legitimacy. The sorrow of finitude that haunted Schreiner is a peculiarly colonial predicament. The colonial intruder who cannot find words to fit the landscape stands in a world gone suddenly quiet. The effort to give voice to a landscape that is felt to be unspeakable because it inhabits a different history creates a deep confusion, a kind of panic, which can be warded off only by adopting the most extreme of defensive measures. A colonial culture, Dan Jacobson says in the introduction to *The Story of an African Farm,* "is one which has no memory."

Cut off from the metropolis and arrogantly ignorant of indigenous culture, estranged from all tradition, the colonial is marooned in a time and place bereft of history. At the same time that Schreiner expressed the hope of redeeming history through allegory, her imperial faith that a singular universal meaning animates the world, that the radiance of a "naked simplicity" imbues the colonial landscape with intelligible form, also confirmed the degree to which, despite herself, she was still a colonial writer *(Letters).*

BRITAIN AND FEMINISM

FOR seven years Schreiner worked as a governess in colonial homes. Then in 1881, she left South Africa for Britain, to fulfill her long desire to become a doctor. From childhood, Schreiner had shared her mother's thwarted ambition to enter medicine: "I could not remember a time when I was so small that it was not there in my heart" *(Letters,* 2 May 1884) As a child in the veld, she dissected the hearts of ostriches and sheep, unfolding their sacred centers "with a startled feeling near akin to ecstasy" *(The Story of an African Farm,* part 2, ch. 1) The scarlet, lacy filaments and mysterious chambers of blood yielded intimations of infinity, and the allegorical promise that "in the center of all things is a Mighty Heart" (part 2, ch. 1).

If part of Schreiner's ambition to be a doctor flowed from her imperial desire to penetrate to the heart of the universe, it also flowed from a stubborn determination to redeem her mother's disappointed life. Thus Schreiner took her place in women's historic attempt to reclaim the traditionally female skill of healing, so violently wrenched from them in the centuries before. In this way, medicine offered Schreiner the hope of reconciling the conflict between her imperial, and conventionally male, "impulse to span the infinite," and the conventionally female activities of duty, service, and compassion *(The Story of an African Farm).* Becoming a doctor, she hoped, could satisfy her "hunger for exact knowledge of things as they are" *(From Man to Man, ch. 7),* while at the same time rescue her from the guilt of her intelligence. "A doctor's is the most perfect of all lives; it satisfies the craving to know, and also the craving to serve" *(Letters,* 2 May 1884).

In South Africa, however, the medical profession was jealously closed to women and black men. In Britain a medical college had recently opened its doors, so in 1881, at the age of twenty-six,

Schreiner reversed the trajectory of her mother's life and traveled back to the metropolis, carrying with her two completed manuscripts, *Undine* and *The Story of an African Farm,* and an unfinished work titled "Saints and Sinners."

The years Schreiner spent in Britain, from 1881 to 1889, were momentous ones. Social crises were reverberating through the country and its colonies. The land crisis loomed, as economic power passed from the ancient gentry to the desks of manufacturers and mining magnates. Vast industrial fortunes were made in the great shipyards and the belching mills, while mass unemployment and strikes, the diseases of poverty, and the hardships of economic depression signaled a profound crisis in class relations. The first socialist party, the Democratic Federation, was formed in 1881, the same year Schreiner arrived in Britain.

The class crisis was matched by an acute crisis in gender relations. Mutinous women were crowding and buckling the doors of male privilege. Since midcentury, working-class women had become militant in an effort toward fairer working rights and conditions. Now middle-class women were clamoring for better education, the right to paid work, the right to the franchise. The Married Women's Property Act was passed in 1882, the Guardianship of Infants Act in 1886, and women won the right to divorce in France in 1884. The "new woman" became a figure deeply feared and derided by many men, emblematic of social chaos and misrule. Masculinity itself was under contest, in the discovery of the Cleveland male brothel in 1889, the trial of Oscar Wilde in 1895, and the pathologizing of homosexuality. Ruling class men lashed back, rioting at Cambridge to oppose women's admission to the brotherhood and voting overwhelmingly at the Oxford Union in 1896 against allowing women to receive the B.A. degree. The police drove their horses against the suffragettes, who were arrested, beaten, and violently force-fed in the prisons. William Gladstone opposed the amendment to England's Reform Bill that might have granted women suffrage, and the franchise became a dead issue until 1905.

The metropolitan calamities were compounded by crises in the colonies: sporadic rebellion and chronic agrarian unrest in Ireland, the upheavals in the Caribbean, the aftershocks of the 1857 Rebellion in India, and the ignominious defeat of General Charles Gordon by an Islamic fundamentalist at Khartoum in 1885. England's Great Depression coincided, not accidentally, with the rise of the new imperialism. In 1886 gold was discovered in South Africa. That same year, the European powers sat down at a table in Berlin and carved up Africa among them; not one African leader was present.

In the second half of the nineteenth century, the social crises of Victorian industry and empire were figured increasingly within an intricate discourse on evolutionary theory. Beginning about midcentury, scientists, medical men, and biologists became enthralled by the magic of measurement, tirelessly calibrating skulls and skeletons from around the world and pondering the evidence of racial and gender degeneration. From geometric allegories of the body's skeleton, they improvised multifarious legends of racial and sexual difference, baroque in their inventive intricacy and flourish of fictive detail. Scientific racism attempted to grace social inequity with the sanction of science and nature.

At the same time, the Woman Question was fiercely debated at every level of society, and the "riddle" of female identity was answered in a way that placed gender at the center of an imperialist politics. Female sexuality was figured, in Freud's words, as "a dark continent," and a host of expert geographers and explorers set out to chart the terra incognita of the female body. An intricate analogy between race and gender, women and the colonized, figured women who insisted on working for wages—mining and factory women, domestic workers, prostitutes—as a race apart, as barbaric survivals of a degenerate prehistory, and as an imminent threat to the moral and economic rectitude of the imperial body politic. The analogy between race and gender reached into almost every nook and cranny of British social life, influencing at least two generations of writers and scientists, politicians and lawmakers, theologians and doctors. Indeed, it is Schreiner's immense distinction to have been the only intellectual in Britain to offer a sustained public challenge to these racial and gender stereotypes.

From the outset, however, Schreiner's ambition to become a doctor was doomed by asthma. After a few days at the Edinburgh Royal Infirmary, ill health forced her to abandon her training. In despair over the ruination of her dream, she began peddling her manuscripts to publishers, concealing her female identity under the pseudonym Ralph

Iron. *The Story of An African Farm* was quickly accepted and published in 1883. The book won instant acclaim, and almost overnight this obscure colonial governess became one of the most sought after intellectuals of her time. Gladstone sent his congratulations; George Moore and Oscar Wilde were eager to meet her; Edward Avering reviewed the book favorably in *Progress;* Rider Haggard praised it as among the most meaningful of the age; the politician Sir Charles Dilke compared it with *Pilgrim's Progress;* and a Lancashire working woman voiced its importance for women: "I think there is hundreds of women what feels like that but can't speak it, but *she* could speak what we feel." Hugh Walpole declared that it marked an epoch "as scarcely any other book can do" (First and Scott, *Olive Schreiner,* p. 347).

Schreiner was courted as a celebrity, invited to hobnob with the intellectual elite of the time. She developed intimate friendships with such luminaries as Eleanor Marx (Karl Marx's daughter) and Havelock Ellis; these two attachments in particular lasted for the rest of her life. Temperamentally averse to the glare of podium politics, she was reluctant to join organizations, and, despite her acclaim and august acquaintances, she led a solitary, fitful life, wandering from boarding house to boarding house, driven by asthma and the "hidden agony of her life" to the continent and then back to London (*Letters,* 18 March 1889). As a single woman living alone, she cut an improper figure, and outraged landladies would burst into her room, insinuating scandal, when she was visited by male friends. She swung between elation and despondency, taking large doses of potassium bromide and reaching out to the people she loved in voluminous epistolary outpourings.

Schreiner was soon invited to join the elite coterie of the Men and Women's Club. Karl Pearson, the renowned eugenicist and enthusiast of empire, founded the club in 1885, inspired, it seems, by both matrimonial and scientific ambitions to gather about him an assemblage of socialist and feminist intellectuals to discuss, without emotion or prurience, the great sexual issues of the time: prostitution and pornography, marriage and monogamy, and, above all, the vexing and inevitable Woman Question. The women of the club were mostly middle-class philanthropists and reformers, single, demure, and a trifle intimidated by the membership's overbearing men. The men were tweedy Oxbridge types, who moved easily between the old-boy enclaves of the aristocratic clubs and the radical bohemia of London's avant-garde. By and large, the club was elitist in its atmosphere. The odors of cigar and port and the faded perfume of philanthropy hung about its discussions, despite its revolutionary agenda and scandalous topics. In this decorous Victorian setting, with its pretensions to rational sobriety, Schreiner's loud gestures and extravagant voice, flashing eyes and passionate tirades disquieted some of the more primped and coiffured members, who privately patronized her as a colonial upstart who had lived too long among "coarse and brutal natures." Schreiner viewed them in return as "a lot of old maids and manhaters" (*Letters,* 11 October 1885).

The privileged language of the club was Darwinism. The object was to discover the precise and scientific nature of women's role in the evolutionary advancement of the race and to bring the alarming feminist upheavals under male scrutiny and guidance. Feminism was seen as the maidservant of evolution, necessary but dangerously fickle. Women's proper vocation was service to the species, their rights secondary to their duties: "We must first . . . settle . . . what would be the effect of her emancipation on her function of race reproduction before we can talk of her rights," Pearson proclaimed grandly (Walkowitz, p. 45).

Schreiner, unused to Victorian restraint, was quick to criticize Pearson's condescension and inconsistencies. Women, as Schreiner rightly noted, were seen by the male club members as the objects, not subjects, of study, while male sexuality was a natural given. The male insistence on the language and "revealed truth" of science shrouded the men's own imprecisions, their vested interests, and unconscious desires. Charlotte Wilson, likewise, scolded Pearson roundly for his assumption that women's lusts were less than men's. Women's chastity, she argued, was "a hard battle," enforced by male society and won only at the cost of extreme toil. Nevertheless, Schreiner's frank independence of mind did not prevent her from developing an equally frank but calamitous passion for Pearson. A cold fish by all accounts, Pearson was bent on keeping his fixation with female sexuality under the wraps of scientific pretensions. Obsessed with race survival and scathingly scornful of the female "shopping dolls" of the middle class, he publicly advocated female sexual power, but was clearly unmanned in reality by passionately sexual and intellectual women. Schreiner's relationship with Pearson became increasingly unsteady; he rebuffed her advances with characteristic iciness, and she left the club in emotional disarray.

FROM MAN TO MAN

NONETHELESS, the club offered Schreiner an unprecedented arena for enriching and expanding her ideas on women's sexuality and labor. During these years she wrote many of the dreams and allegories that would be bound in *Stories, Dreams, and Allegories* (1923). During this time, she also worked almost continuously on *From Man to Man,* the novel in which she gave fictional form to her twin obsessions, the issues of marriage and prostitution. This was the book of her heart: "I love it more than I love anything in the world, More than any place or person" (*Letters,* 11 April 1889). Dedicated to her dead baby sister, and later to her own dead daughter, *From Man to Man* is an impassioned homage to women. "The most womanly book that ever was written," as Schreiner wryly put it, the novel is "the story of a prostitute and of a married woman who loves another man, and whose husband is sensual and unfaithful" (*Letters,* 2 February 1889).

Set in colonial South Africa and London, *From Man to Man* is a radical rebuttal of the presiding tenets of late Victorian and colonial society: evolutionary Darwinism, the imperial ideology of racial and gender degeneration, and the bourgeois Victorian institution of the sexual double standard. The thematic center of the book is the dialectical relation between monogamy ("for women only," as Friederich Engels pointed out in his *Origin of the Family, Private Property, and the State*) and prostitution for men. In this fictional account of two sisters, one wretchedly bound in marriage to a careless philanderer, the other a prostitute, Schreiner adamantly refuses the Victorian dichotomy of housewife-madonna and whore. For Schreiner, like Engels, the matrimonial trade in women's bodies was the "crassest prostitution," and marriage without love "the uncleanest traffic that defiles the world" (*The Story of an African Farm,* part 2, ch. 4). At the same time, prostitution was a source of unceasing grief and anger for her: her singular outrage was

that the professions of marriage and prostitution were well-nigh the only vocations open to the majority of women.

Born into the luxuriant beauty and torpor of a Cape colonial farm, and hungering restlessly for knowledge of the world, Schreiner's character Rebekah can attempt to escape the inertia of her parents' colonial life only through marriage. In Cape Town her husband indulges in a careless round of inamoratas—their African maidservant, actresses, pimply schoolgirls, and respectable matrons—yet Rebekah is forbidden the balls and parties, lest she discover her husband's infidelity and lest she attempt to do the same. The novel is a scorching, griefstricken indictment of the lethal tradition of the sexual double standard. Baby-Bertie, Rebekah's sister, is seduced by her beloved tutor, who immediately bolts for Europe, and when she confesses this indiscretion to her fiancé, she is again summarily abandoned. As in *The Story of an African Farm,* the movement of plot is flight from the family and social constraint. Bertie escapes to join her sister in Cape Town, where she becomes the pretty darling of society, until a jealous socialite discloses her shame to the world. Ostracized and vilified, she takes up with a wealthy man, who sets her up in his boudoir before throwing her to the streets and a life in prostitution.

From Man to Man bitterly condemns the suffocation of the female intellect in matrimony. Immured in the matrimonial house, Rebekah's longing for truth is encaged in her tiny closet of a study; her writings dwindle to a trickle of fragments and outlines. Muffled in the torpor of maternity, she is condemned to soliloquy. Neglected and alone, pacing feverishly in her airless study, she expounds her creed of cosmic monism, the same creed that sustained Schreiner through the blank atheism of despair: "Rebekah is me; I don't know which is which anymore" (*Letters*). In the central, allegorical chapter, Rebekah ventriloquizes Schreiner's challenge to the "old Christian conception" of the universe as the creation of a single, male "individual Will," capricious and violent, capable on a whim of reducing the "shreds and patches and unconnected parts" of existence to nothingness (ch. 7). Refusing to be the figment of a single, male mind, Rebekah offers an alternative vision of cosmic unity: the sheen on a bird's feather, the tilt of the planets, the rainbow lights in a crystal all partake of the great universal life. The prism flings light on the sun, the fossil illuminates the structure of the hand that holds it. Every fragment is a tiny allegory of the whole truth, enigmatic yet redolent with meaning.

Yet here we come upon the familiar paradox in Schreiner's vision. Rebekah finds phantasmagoric solace for her very real social alienation by projecting onto the "great, pulsating, always interacting whole" (ch. 7) of the universe the hope of metaphysical communion. The problem of social community is thus deferred and postponed, and her historical, gendered travail is rendered as a universal condition of the human soul. The book initially poses marriage as a social problem, then displaces the dilemma of female community onto the metaphysical realm. As a consequence, no social solution to the problem of marriage can be found.

To Schreiner, marriage in its present form was a "barbaric relic of the past" (*Letters,* 4 December 1893), but she was always baffled when people reviled her as an advocate of free love or promiscuity. On the contrary, she protested, from the age of thirteen she had held the view that the only ideal was "the perfect mental and physical lifelong union of one man with one woman" (1889). True marriage, a sacred and deathless thing, was a mutually contracted monogamy. "No kind of sex relationship can be good and pure but marriage" (4 December 1893). The legal and ceremonial aspects of marriage, however, were "a mere bagatelle" (1895). True marriage was a question of mutual mental, spiritual, and erotic fulfilment. But the Victorian institution of marriage was no more than the symbolic and contractual surrender of a woman's sexual, property, and labor rights to a man. As a result, it was deeply inconsistent with women's freedom, and Schreiner herself feared she could never marry under such a system: "If I am to live I must be free" (5 January 1886).

Schreiner's critique of Victorian matrimony was fundamentally economic. A true marriage, "the most holy, the most organic, the most important sacrament of life," should be entirely "independent of monetary considerations." "The woman should be absolutely and entirely monetarily INDEPENDENT OF THE MAN" (*Letters,* 1895). Without economic independence, women had no power and no redress. Here Schreiner went beyond the emergent feminist critique of marriage, which tended to focus on sexual and emotional exploitation. Unlike most Victorian feminists who came from comfortable middle-class homes, Schreiner's own class background was so contradictory, and her economic situation so precarious, that she was more aware than most that the real issue was "the sex purchasing power of the male" *(Woman and Labour)*.

Schreiner was most vehement in her denunciation of the paucity of professional options available to women outside of marriage. To those who argued that women were free to choose not to marry, she retorted, as Lyndall does in *The Story of an African Farm:* "Yes—and a cat set afloat on a pond is free to sit in the tub till it dies there" (part 2, ch. 4). Lyndall, who refuses to marry without true love, is forced to iron and wash men's shirts for a pittance until she starves to death. To those who argued that women did not want independence, Schreiner retorted: "If the bird does like its cage, and does like its sugar, and will not leave it, why keep the door so very carefully shut?" (part 2, ch. 4).

At the same time, Schreiner was almost alone among her contemporaries in insisting that women's sexual needs are as urgent and compelling as men's. Women's desires are laced and corsetted, crimped and curtailed, she maintained, while men were given privileged access to prostitution, the marriage market, and the double standard. For a woman, unlike a man, premarital or adulterous sex was fraught with punitive dangers. In a world without dependable contraception or legal, safe abortion, "a woman's character is like gossamer" *(From Man to Man,* ch. 7). If a woman bartered her virginity outside the matrimonial contract, she was seen by God and the world as having squandered forever her moral and social credit. Bertie, for one, having spent her virginity, has no recourse but to become a "kept women," languishing in opulent ease among the scarlet cushions and chandeliers, the ornamental kittens and ribbons of the wealthy man's apartment, prone to ennui and weeping fits.

The radical thrust of the book, in fact, is that Bertie's luxurious confinement and Rebekah's martyred solitude in marriage are merely different kinds of prostitution. "All other matters seem to me small compared to matters of sex, and prostitution is its most agonising central point," Schreiner once asserted *(Letters).* Prostitution always held a fascination and horror for Schreiner, and she seems to have identified deeply with prostitutes themselves: perhaps, in a way, as the mirror projection of her own sexual guilt. Her fictional portrayal of Bertie's social ostracism and frantic flight from social shame might be read as a semiautobiographical attempt to exorcise the trauma of Schreiner's own feelings of ostracism following the Gau fiasco. The novel would thereby offer some insight into Schreiner's own incessant patterns of flight.

Yet it is Schreiner's distinction that, almost alone of her contemporaries, she gives prostitution a *social* history. *From Man to Man* is a massive refusal of the often "documented" Victorian stereotype that prostitution was a genetic flaw, an atavistic regression and racial pathology of the body politic. Instead, Schreiner, like Engels, locates prostitution historically alongside the cultural structures of traditional matrimony and the fetish of virginity. "The man with the long purse" has the buying power (*Woman and Labour,* ch. 6); women are driven by economic duress into bartering their sexual services for profit.

In her obsession with prostitution, Schreiner was very much Victorian. Until the 1850's, the widespread tolerance of prostitution in England was reflected in the absence of any serious legislation. But from the 1850's onwards, a discourse on sexuality and venereal disease entered parliamentary debate with great heat and ferocity and became ever more deeply informed by constructions of race, gender, and imperialism. In the 1860's the notorious Contagious Diseases Acts were passed and only repealed after a national avalanche of protest. The acts were clearly designed less to abolish prostitution than to place control of "sexwork" in the hands of the male state. The initial impetus for the legislation had come from the recent blows to male, national self-esteem in the arena of empire. The public argument ran that the real threat to the prowess and potency of the national army lay in the syphilitic threat that prostitutes supposedly posed to the genital hygiene of the army. If women who served the garrison towns could be forcibly examined and cordoned off, the purity of the army and of respectable middle-class patrons could be assured. The acts therefore gave police the right forcibly to impose physical examinations, registration, and incarceration on working-class women thought to be working as prostitutes in designated garrison and naval towns. At the same time, the regulation of sexual behavior served as a means of policing the unruly working-class population at large.

In 1885, a few years after Schreiner arrived in Britain, W. T. Stead had set London aflame with his lurid revelations about child prostitution, published in *The Pall Mall Gazette* as "The Maiden Tribute of Modern Babylon." Stead's tales of hapless virgins entrapped by lascivious aristocratic roués gave middle-class women a language in which to express for the first time the sexual distress, frustration, and secret terrors of Victorian marriage. The prostitute became the projection of middle-class anxieties and hypocrisies, while prostitutes' own voices, lives, motives, and powers were swept away in the ensuing storm of middle-class outrage and voyeurism.

Schreiner was thoroughly Victorian in the way that prostitutes figured in her writings as objects of grief and rage. Like many Victorian women, she had virtually no knowledge of prostitutes' real lives, and her identification with them, intense and heartfelt as it was, served more as a projection of her own very real sense of sexual exploitation and vulnerability. Like most Victorians, she saw prostitution as a reflex of male sexual needs, and it never occurred to her that sexwork could also be a form of resistance to patriarchal control in the family and marriage, as well as to economic distress and social immobility. For many women prostitution was preferable to marriage and expressed a stubborn refusal of precisely the "sex parasitism" that Schreiner condemned in the marriage of convenience.

Certainly, Schreiner was never able to resolve satisfactorily the tension between her feminist and socialist understanding, on the one hand, with her Spencerian faith in a cosmic unity and design governing the universe, on the other. For the remainder of her life, Schreiner carried the manuscript of *From Man to Man* about with her, working and reworking the remarkable book, able neither to finish nor abandon it. In the same way that she carried the small white coffin of her dead baby with her, unable to entrust it to the earth, she could not entrust "this greatly loved offspring of her mature mind" to the public *(Life).* Closure eluded her, and she died with the novel still unfinished. As was only fitting, the scandalous, incomplete book was published posthumously. As Lyndall says in *The Story of An African Farm,* "We can say things to the dead that we cannot say to the living" (part 2, ch. 4).

While in Britain, Schreiner was besieged by social invitations and a sprinkling of marriage proposals, and she fled for a while to London's East End to evade callers. Although she was averse to meetings and public gatherings, in the next few years she met Gladstone and Spencer; the Sheffield socialist Edward Carpenter; the novelist George Moore; and also W. T. Stead and Arthur Symons. An unsystematic commitment to socialism drew her to the large socialist crowds that were swelling in the East End, and to the river during the great Dock Strike of 1889, when casual labor finally won the right to unionize. But by the middle of 1889, she had made up her mind to return to South Africa.

In 1886 gold had been discovered in the Transvaal. A year before, Rhodes had formed the De Beers Consolidated Mines Company, and in 1889 he received a charter from the imperial government to operate in Rhodesia. In October of 1889, Schreiner set sail for South Africa, with the "nervous feeling" that she would marry Rhodes *(Letters)*.

SOUTH AFRICA AND WAR

RHODES became prime minister of the Cape Colony in 1890, and far from marrying him, Schreiner's attraction paled almost immediately. While she continued to admire the man personally, and while he never withdrew his great admiration for her and her writing, she became his most vocal opponent, devoting herself to public denunciation of his imperial policies. The country was brewing for war, though few observers besides Schreiner could see it.

Schreiner settled in the lonely town of Matjesfontein. There she formed the habit of meeting traveling politicians on the station platform to engage in conversation before their trains departed. There, too, she began a series of brilliant and prophetic articles on South African political life, collected in 1923 as *Thoughts on South Africa*.

In 1892, Schreiner met Samuel C. Cronwright, a farmer and former member of the Cape Parliament. She married him two years later. He was priggish and pedantic, yet every inch the colonial male. A surviving photo of the couple is revealing: Cronwright-Schreiner stands fully erect, head back, legs apart, his hands thrust manfully in his pockets, the image of the proprietory husband. Olive sits on a log at his knee, self-consciously coy and a trifle smug. Their dog is resting its dutiful head on her knees. This traditional family tableau notwithstanding, Schreiner was clearly the dominant

party, obliging Cronwright to leave his beloved farm and move to Kimberley on account of her asthma.

In 1895, at the age of forty, Schreiner gave birth to a longed-for baby girl. The child seemed sturdy, but it lived only until the next morning, and Schreiner's grief was unstaunchable. The baby's death coincided with national crisis. Afrikaner agitation against British maneuvers in the Transvaal began to swell. Schreiner and Cronwright publicly denounced the incipient capitalist and Bond brotherhood, and they condemned Rhodes's African policy of dispossession, a brutal policy neatly summed up in his frank admission: "I prefer land to natives." Schreiner vehemently opposed the Flogging Bill for which Rhodes voted: "Edward," she wrote to Edward Carpenter, "you don't know how bad things are in this land; we flog our niggers to death and wealth is the only possible end and aim in life" *(Letters,* 23 November 1892).

In 1899 Schreiner published her antiwar pamphlet, *An English South African's View of the Situation,* and delivered speeches as part of the women's protest movement in the Cape. In 1896 she and her husband had published *The Political Situation*—a document that cried out presciently, if fruitlessly, against the "small and keen body of men amalgamating into rings and trusts" who were quickly settling "their hands round the mineral wealth of the country." Indeed, the deep-level gold mining of South Africa needed huge inputs of capital, advanced technology, and very cheap, ample labor. But the labor requirements of the mines came into swift competition with the labor needs of the farmers. Moreover, the miners' need for a centralized transport system and a unified economy and state began to strain against the rustic economy and political structure of the Transvaal. Out of these contradictions exploded the bloody Boer War.

In 1896 Rhodes had been briefly disgraced by the failure of the notorious Jameson Raid, the botched outcome of a plot by two of the largest mining companies, among others, to take over the Afrikaner Transvaal for the British. Schreiner publicly deplored the raid, an extremely unpopular position and one that earned her the enmity of the British settlers and her family's outraged contempt. Rhodes was indeed obliged to resign as prime minister of the Cape, but in the uncertain aftermath of the raid he busied himself further north in Matabeleland, where the infamous Rudd Concession of

1889 had given him a monopoly over all the minerals in Lobengula's kingdom in return for some guns and ammunition, a paltry annual grant, and a steamboat. In 1893 Rhodes had marched on Lobengula's seat, Bulawayo, with a column of white mercenaries, and in the next three years Matabeleland was subjected to an unrelentingly brutal mauling, during which almost all the Africans' land and all their cattle passed into white hands. The country was christened Rhodesia: the name summing up that inimitable colonial presumption that the entire history of a land and people can be subsumed under the personal identity of a single white male. Rhodes returned to the Cape a hero.

One morning, during the time that Rhodes was "pacifying" Rhodesia, Schreiner awoke with her allegorical novella *Trooper Peter Halket of Mashonaland* (1897) "full fledged" in her mind (*Letters,* August 1896). The allegory is a visionary diatribe against the Mashonaland massacres, centering on the lynching of three Africans, and it is structured as a dialogue between Christ and Trooper Peter Halket. Schreiner wrote the piece in anguish, terrified of the risks she was taking in condemning Rhodes, dreading her family's response, but unable to keep silent. That year she suffered three miscarriages, two of them probably due to the trauma of the isolation and rejection that followed the book: "The attacks from my family . . . kill me," she wrote (*Letters,* October 1896). But despite the great personal cost to Schreiner herself, and despite the book's immense circulation, *Trooper Peter Halket* could do nothing to prevent the eruption of the Anglo-Boer War in 1899.

Schreiner did everything she could to alert the public in Britain and South Africa to the impending calamity. She sent cables, held interviews, attended congresses against annexation, and suffered a heart attack under the pressure. During the war, at women's congresses, she vehemently protested the British burning of the Boer farms; she cried out against the infamous concentration camps into which the British herded Afrikaner women and children. Twenty-five thousand women and children died of starvation and ill-treatment in these frightful places. Schreiner was renowned as an incendiary public speaker—when she spoke, according to one source, "she was transfigured into flame."

The thrust of her great prose collection, *Thoughts on South Africa,* is a fiercely protective defense of the Boers. Having lived among the Afrikaners as a governess, she had "learnt to love" them, particularly the Boer woman, who was "the true citadel of her people" *(Thoughts on South Africa).* She voiced her admiration of Boer women in the language of the international women's movement, praising their rugged strength and labor and urging them never to give up their wagon whips and white caps for hats with paper flowers and croquet mallets: "The measure of its women is ultimately the measure of any people's strength and resistile power" *(Thoughts On South Africa).* Although the Boers had admittedly been cut off from the Enlightenment, she wrote, they were also untouched by the "god of commerce." In her paeans to the Boers, Schreiner refused the dominant British stereotype of Afrikaners as a racially fallen, idle, and degenerate race, but her arguments were riven by a fundamental flaw. In her sentimental fidelity to the besieged Boers, she represented the war as an agon between two white cultures, and the fundamental issue of the preeminent African claim to the land and minerals went for the moment ignored. The Afrikaners were ferocious racists, and their labor practices were by and large appalling. Yet Schreiner was uncritical of the Boer republics until after the war, when she saw them coming to power and no longer felt they needed her protection: "It is the Boers who are top dog now" *(Letters).*

WOMAN AND LABOUR

WHILE the Boer War was shaking the country, Schreiner wrote her great prose work *Woman and Labour.* She had begun a book on the Woman Question in her youth, despite her isolation from any feminist inspiration. Motivated only by her own precocious sense of gendered travail, she had set herself the task of uncovering the historical clues to the "hidden agony" of her life. In the decades that followed she worked continuously at this monumental "sex book," until 1888, when she had only the last section to complete.

In its original form, the most notable feature of Schreiner's "sex book" was the sheer immodesty of its scope. Like Engels' *The Origin of the Family, Private Property and the State,* the book was frankly audacious in its attempt to embrace the whole of human history in a grand global schema. Borrowing its form from the bildungsroman and the narrative of evolution, the book attempted to chronicle the epic unfolding of the world historical condition of women. Beginning in prehistory, the narrative traced the shambling climb of humanity through the tumultuous centuries into the rattle and glare of industrialism.

Almost none of this vast and ambitious undertaking survives. The introduction to *Woman and Labour* is a truncated requiem to the lost labor and the lost years. In 1899 Schreiner left Johannesburg because of ill health. Two months later, the Anglo-Boer War broke out, and martial law confined her to the Colony. In her absence, British soldiers broke into her study, forced open her desk, and lit a bonfire in the center of the room with all her papers. When she returned, the great intellectual labor of her life was a bundle of charred and blackened scraps that fell to ash as she touched them. She had no copy.

Some months later, interned by the British for her pro-Boer sentiments in a house on the outskirts of a village, surrounded by armed guards and a high barbed-wire fence, forbidden reading material or news, Schreiner resolutely forced her thought "from the horror of the world . . . to dwell on some abstract question" and rewrote from memory one chapter of the larger book of twelve. The chapter was published as *Woman and Labour* in 1911, a broken shard of the original monument, yet hailed by many prominent feminists of her generation as the Bible of the women's movement.

The circumstances of *Woman and Labour* bear tragic testimony to the gist of its argument. Incomplete and mutilated, radical and incendiary, and, above all, stubbornly and triumphantly rebellious, the book amounts to a miniature allegory of Schreiner's life. Condemned to labor in the shuttered dark, forbidden consort with the public world of news and history, surrounded by the male technology of violence, her life and labor were subject to the disfiguring violence of male imperatives.

The fundamental point of the book is its attempt to give to women's labor and women's subjection a social history. Schreiner dismantles women's subjection as universal, natural, and inevitable. The stories of women's disempowerment and revolt are historical and political stories: the lessons of gender are not written immemorially in the blood. Morover, women have power, and women resist; they are not the mute and passive sufferers

of victimization. But the effects and potential for resistance take different forms in different social moments and are shaped by the enabling conditions of the time.

For Schreiner, rifling through the ancient and modern tomes of biology and science, medicine and botany, the lesson of evolution was that "sex relations may assume almost any form on earth." In the majority of species, she argued, the female form exceeds the male in size, and often in predatory nature. Nor are parenting tasks inherent in nature. Contrary to the dominant Victorian notion that saw the male hunter as the herald of history, Schreiner placed historical agency into the hands of women, offering the life-giving mother, who, carrying both child and fodder, stood erect to take history forward. Nonetheless, Schreiner never fully throws off the evolutionist mantle. As she saw it, the custodian of progress is "ancient Mother nature sitting as umpire" (ch. 4). Here the familiar contradiction emerges: she debunks the ancestral opposition between a male culture and female nature, but then reinvents history as presided over by a benificent—and natural—female force.

Woman and Labour has been best remembered for Schreiner's analysis of women's labor, and the condition of "sex-parasitism" to which many women were then condemned. The fundamental tense of *Woman and Labour* is the imperative: *"Give us labour and the training which fits us for labour!"* (ch. 1). Schreiner's was a cry to open up all labor for women and to reclaim for women their ancient economic power. Henceforth, there was no fruit in the garden of knowledge that women were not determined to eat:

From the judge's seat to the legislator's chair; from the statesman's closet to the merchant's office; from the chemist's laboratory to the astronomer's tower, there is no post or form of toil for which we do not intend to fit ourselves.   (ch. 4)

Moreover, contrary to Victorian dogma, women had always worked: "We hoed the earth, we reaped the grain, we shaped the dwellings, we wove the clothing, we modelled the earthen vessels." In the now-famous slogan of the feminist movement: "Women have always worked, we have not always worked for wages." As herbalists and botanists, women were the "first physicians of the race." As childbearers, they bore the race on their shoulders. But as society progressed in technical skills, she wrote, men no longer spent their lives in fighting, and they returned from the hunt to invade the women's realm. The spinning wheels were broken, the hoes and grindstones were taken from women's hands, the rosy milkmaids vanished. Women's "ancient field of labor" shrank (ch. 1), and they were condemned to a passive and incessant "sex-parasitism" upon the male (ch. 2).

Yet there are points where Schreiner's sense of historical agency is uncertain. She does not question the gendered division of labor between hunting and agriculture, nor does she offer a systematic theory of historical change. No reason is given why men should want to wrest economic control from women, nor why they were able to. Beyond a vaguely Spencerian notion of inevitable progress, Schreiner lacks a theory of gender conflict and a theory of historical change.

Nonetheless, Schreiner's radical challenge was to address the doctrine of "separate spheres" and the emergent Victorian image of the "idle woman." She denounces Victorian middle-class hypocrites who oppose women's waged work because they see it as contrary to an idealized female role as "divine childbearer"; she points out that this same oppression does not carry over into anguish for the "woman who, on hands and knees at tenpence a day, scrubs the floors of the public buildings." For the Victorian male, she notes, "that somewhat quadrupal position is for him truly feminine" (*Woman and Labour,* ch. 6). Such men were not disturbed by the old tea drudge bringing them tea in bed, but rather by the woman doctor with an income who spent the evening smoking and reading. Schreiner's insight here is into the class hypocrisy of the objection to women's work: men only wanted women out of the prestigious, powerful, and profitable realms of labor. As Lyndall cries in *The Story of an African Farm,* "When we ask to be doctors, lawyers, lawmakers, anything but ill-paid drudges, they say, No" (part 2, ch. 4).

An equal amount of Schreiner's fierce indignation is directed at the systematic inequities of women's recompense for "equal work equally well performed." She was unusual among feminists for her recognition, born from the contradictions in her own class background, that the "idleness" of middle-class women depended on the vast, invisible labor of working-class women, both black and white: "Domestic labor, often the most wearisome and unending known to any section of the human race, is not adequately recognised or recompensed" (introduction to *Woman and Labour*).

She was also exceptional in her insistence that women's sexual needs are as powerful as men's. Yet here, too, Schreiner's arguments are ambiguous, for she deplores the ravages of celibacy, yet she also sees sex as a sacred sacrament, properly taken within the context of a monogamous love. Yet, in a world lacking anything close to reliable contraception, where abortion was a grisly, agonizing, and often fatal last resort, where loss of virginity outside of marriage carried, as she well knew, catastrophic social stigma, Schreiner knew that women were condemned to a social situation where sex could not be "taken" otherwise. The material conditions were not yet present for a fundamental transformation of sexual relations. Schreiner, in fact, never condemns the monogamous, heterosexual family. Furthermore, her views on male homosexuality were no more enlightened than the prevailing depictions of perversion and pathology, and there seems to be no evidence that she had any interest in lesbianism.

Schreiner's special distinction, however, lies in the extraordinary foresight of the views on African politics that she developed at this time. Yet despite the brilliance of her political essays, they remain by far the most neglected aspect of all her writing—a neglect stemming no doubt from the very ethnocentricism and racism she attempted to challenge.

During the decades surrounding the turn of the century, Schreiner formulated a view unique to herself alone: that the Labor Question and the Native Question in South Africa were inseparable. Her analysis of race was founded on an analysis of class, and she saw the African and land questions as an extension of the Labor Question of Europe, only deeply complicated by race. Almost alone, she recognized that the fundamental issue was territory: in order to understand South Africa's political problems, "the first requisite is a clear comprehension of their land."

Certainly, Schreiner's views on Africans are at times blemished by condescension and a patronizing pity, but in her political analyses, she was breathtakingly ahead of her time. As early as 1891 she had foreseen some form of union between the various states, and she even predicted the date: 1910, off by exactly five months. She foresaw that the country was "bound ultimately to become free, self-governing, independent and republican," decades before South Africa did indeed become a republic, albeit a racially exclusive one. More profoundly, she argued that solutions such as separate territories for the different South African peoples were unthinkable, despite the fact that the Bantustan, or black state, solution was not systematically implemented until after 1948. She recognized the Africans "as the makers of our wealth," and deplored the shunting of the Africans into locations and slums. She stressed the political indivisibility of all South African peoples, anticipating by decades the nonracial position of the African National Congress. Indeed, she argued in *Thoughts on South Africa* that the distinctive bond uniting all South Africans "is our mixture of race itself." She recognized the problem of a racially divided working class, which even the South African Communist party did not see in the 1920's, at a time when white workers mobilized under the banner Workers Unite for a White South Africa.

Schreiner forecast, moreover, that a time would come when the future of the world would be in the hands of the American and Russian nations. She was, at the same time, vehemently opposed to the virulent anti-Semitism that contaminates much white South African culture, and she insisted on the need for recognizing the invaluable contribution of the Jewish people to the world. She was also prescient in deploring the senseless slaughter of the African wildlife and in calling for conservation and wildlife reserves.

It is to Schreiner's lasting credit and distinction that she was a political activist as well as a political writer. In the last years of her life, she struggled to implement her vision of racial and gender equality within the political activism of the international suffrage movement. The Cape Women's Enfranchisement League hailed her as the genius of the suffrage movement of South Africa. She was in close contact with the British suffrage movement through radical friends like Constance Lytton and Emmeline Lawrence. It is also to Schreiner's credit that she, alone of all the others, insisted that the franchise could not be seen as a gender issue alone. She was fully, if uniquely, aware that the issue was as much an issue of class and race, and when the Women's Enfranchisement League, a white, middle-class group, refused to demand a nonracial franchise, she resigned in protest in 1913—the year of the notorious Native Land Act by which black

South Africans were allocated a meagre 13 percent of the most broken, arid, and devastated land in the country.

Indeed, in all her writings and political work, Schreiner took the contradictions of colonialism, and women's situation under colonialism, to the very edge of historical transformation. Yet, as she herself well knew, social transformation is a collective issue, and no single visionary is capable of inaugurating a new epoch. Perhaps a fitting epigraph to her situation is found in the lines from Antonio Gramsci's prison notebooks: "The old is dying and the new cannot be born; in this interregnum there arises a great diversity of morbid symptoms."

Schreiner left South Africa for the Continent in 1913, a year after the African National Congress was formed, and she was traveling in Germany when the darkening cataclysm of World War I engulfed the globe. In 1920 she sailed back to South Africa, a year after the peace treaty of Versailles. She died—at Wynberg, on 11 December 1920—as she had lived, in a boarding-house room between homes, alone, a book against her heart, her pen still held firmly in her hands, her eyes steadfastly open to the darkness around her.

SELECTED BIBLIOGRAPHY

I. BIBLIOGRAPHIES. E. Verster, *Olive Emilie Albertina Schreiner, 1855–1920* (Cape Town, 1946); R. Davis, *Olive Schreiner, 1920–1971* (Johannesburg, 1972).

II. SELECTED WORKS. A. Purcell, ed., *Olive Schreiner's Thoughts About Women,* (Cape Town, 1909); S. C. Cronwright-Schreiner, ed., *The Letters of Olive Schreiner, 1876–1920* (London, 1924); N. Nuttal, ed., *The Silver Plume* (Johannesburg, 1956); U. Krige, ed., *Olive Schreiner: A Selection,* (Cape Town, 1968); H. Thurman, ed., *A Track to the Water's Edge: The Olive Schreiner Reader* (New York, 1973); C. Clayton, ed., *The Woman's Rose* (Cape Town, 1986); C. Barash, ed., *An Olive Schreiner Reader* (London, 1987).

III. SEPARATE WORKS. *The Story of an African Farm* (London, 1883), novel, pub. under the pseudonym Ralph Iron, repr. (London, 1910); *Dreams* (London, 1890), short stories; *Dream Life and Real Life* (London, 1893), short stories, pub. under the pseudonym Ralph Iron; *The Political Situation* (London, 1896), treatise, written with S. C. Cronwright-Schreiner; *Trooper Peter Halket of Mashonaland* (London, 1897), novella; *An English South African's View of the Situation* (London, 1899), antiwar pamphlet; *A Letter on the Jew* (Cape Town, 1906); *Closer Union* (London, 1909), on federalism; *Woman and Labour,* (London, 1911), prose; *Thoughts on South Africa* (London, 1923), prose; *Stories, Dreams, and Allegories* (London, 1923), short stories; *From Man to Man; or, Perhaps Only . . .* (London, 1926), novel; *Undine* (London, 1929), novel; *Diamond Fields: Only a Story of Course* (Grahamstown, South Africa 1974).

IV. Biographies. S. C. Cronwright-Schreiner, *The Life of Olive Schreiner* (London, 1924); V. Buchanan-Gould, *Not Without Honour: The Life and Writings of Olive Schreiner* (London, 1948); J. Meintjes, *Olive Schreiner. Portrait of a South African Woman* (Johannesburg, 1965); Z. Friedlander, ed., *Until the Heart Changes: A Garland For Olive Schreiner* (Cape Town, 1967); R. First and A. Scott; *Olive Schreiner: A Biography* (London. 1980).

V. Critical Studies. C. P. Gilman, "Woman and Labor," in *Forerunner,* 2 (July, 1911); V. Woolf, "Olive Schreiner," in *New Republic,* 42 (March 1925); M. Fairley, "The Novels of Olive Schreiner," in *The Dalhousie Review* (July 1929); M. Friedmann, *Olive Schreiner: A Study in Latent Meanings* (Johannesburg, 1955); M. Harmel, *Olive Schreiner, 1855–1955* (Cape Town, 1955); D. L. Hobman, *Olive Schreiner: Her Friends and Times* (London, 1955); L. Gregg, *Memories of Olive Schreiner* (London, 1957); R. Heard, "Olive Schreiner and Death," in *English Studies in Africa,* 2 (March 1959); J. Van Zyl, "Rhodes and Olive Schreiner," in *Contrast,* 21 (August 1969); M. Dyer, "Olive Schreiner's Liberalism," in *Reality,* 2 (November 1970); R. Rive, "An Infinite Compassion: A Critical Comparison of Olive Schreiner's Novels," in *Contrast,* 29 (October 1972); R. Rive, "Olive Schreiner: A Critical Study and Checklist," in *Studies in the Novel,* 4 (1972); A. R. Cunningham, "The New Woman Fiction of the 1890's" in *Victorian Studies,* 17, no. 4 (1973); R. Rive, "New Light on Olive Schreiner," in *Contrast,* 8 (November 1973); R. Beeton, *Olive Schreiner: A Short Guide to Her Writings* (Cape Town, 1974); J. A. Berkman, "The Nurturant Fantasies of Olive Schreiner," in *Frontiers,* 2, no. 3 (1977); *Quarterly Bulletin of the South African Library,* 31 (June 1977); A. Davin, "Imperialism and Motherhood," in *History Workshop Journal,* 5 (1978); B. Fradkin, "Havelock Ellis and Olive Schreiner's 'Gregory Rose'," in *Texas Quarterly,* 21 (Fall 1978); J. Liddington and J. Norris, *One Hand Tied Behind Us: The Rise of the Women's Suffrage Movement* (London, 1978); K. Parker, ed., *The South African Novel in English: Essays in Criticism and Society* (London, 1978); J. A. Berkman, *Olive Schreiner: Feminism on the Frontier* (Montreal, 1979); L. Dowling, "The Decadent and the New Woman in the 1890's," in *Nineteenth Century Fiction,* 33 (March 1979); J. Marcus, "Olive Schreiner: Cartographer of the Spirit/ A Review Article," in *Minnesota Review* (Spring 1979); J. Marquard, "Olive Schreiner's 'Prelude': The Child as Artist," in *English Studies in Africa,* 22 (March 1979); C. Wilhelm, "Olive Schreiner: Child of Queen Victoria, Stories, Dreams, and Allegories," *English in Africa,* 6 (1979); E. Wilson, "Pervasive Symbolism in *The Story of An African Farm,*" in *English Studies in Africa,* 6 (1979).

S. Christie, G. Hutchings, and D. Maclennan, *Perspectives on South African Fiction* (Johannesburg, 1980); M. Friedmann, "Trooper Peter and Zimbabwe," in *London Magazine,* 19 (March 1980); N. Gordimer, " 'The Prison-House of Colonialism': Review of Ruth First and Ann Scott's *Olive Schreiner,*" in *London Times Literary Supplement* (15 August 1980); S. Gardner, " 'No "Story," No Script, Only The Struggle': First and Scott's *Olive Schreiner,*" in *Hecate,* 7, no. 1 (1981); L. Stanley, "Olive Schreiner," in D. Spender, ed., *Feminist Theorists* (London, 1982); R. Beeton, *Portraits of Olive Schreiner: A Manuscript Sourcebook* (Johannesburg, 1983); M. van Wyk Smith and D. Maclennan, eds., *Olive Schreiner and After: Essays in Honour of Guy Butler* (Cape Town, 1983); C. P. Sarvan, "Olive Schreiner's *Trooper Peter*—An Altered Awareness," in *International Fiction Review,* no. 1 (1984); C. Clayton, "Olive Schreiner: Life Into Fiction," in *English in Africa,* 12 (May 1985); L. Stanley, "Feminism and Friendship: Two Essays on Olive Schreiner," in *Studies in Sexual Politics,* 8 (1985); C. Barash, "Virile Womanhood: Olive Schreiner's Narratives of a Master Race," in *Women's Studies International Forum,* 9, no. 4 (1986); J. Walkowitz, "Science, Feminism, and Romance: The Men's and Women's Club, 1885–1889," in *History Workshop,* 21 (Spring 1986); J. A. Berkman, *The Healing Imagination of Olive Schreiner* (Amherst, Mass., 1989); U. Laredo, "Olive Schreiner," in *Journal of Commonwealth Literature,* 8 (December 1989).

STEVIE SMITH

(1902–1971)

Suzanne Fox

TWENTY YEARS AFTER her death, Stevie Smith remains as puzzling as a writer as she is endearing as a personality. As "Stevie," the literary spinster of Palmers Green, she is domestic, cozy, and classifiable; as "Stevie Smith," the poet, she is charming but elusive, as difficult to analyze as she is to categorize. Her life has been the subject of two full-length biographies as well as a play (Hugh Whitemore's *Stevie: A Play,* 1977) which was adapted into a popular film (*Stevie,* starring Glenda Jackson, 1978) while her work has been left relatively unexplored by the critical establishment. Many well-known contemporary writers have commented on her work, but all have done so briefly; both of the longer studies now in print are overviews, too general in scope to address her poetics in detail.

Stevie Smith herself created the skittish, companionable persona that has fed her posthumous popularity. For any writer, but for women writers particularly, the cultivation of such an eccentric mask both brings privilege and exacts a price. The roles that Smith played so enthusiastically—the dotty spinster, the childlike naïf, the impish witch—effectively released her from many of the personal and creative constrictions facing women writers of her generation. Yet they also have helped to abet what can only be called her poetic marginalization; Smith herself helped to manufacture the pickets that would be used to fence her out of the garden of serious poetry. Although the two women are dissimilar in personality, purpose, and magnitude of achievement, it is instructive to think in this regard of Emily Dickinson: another woman writer whose withdrawal from accepted sexual and maternal roles, deliberate eccentricity, and apparent childishness helped delay serious critical consideration of her work.

Even without the confusion engendered by the persona—one is almost tempted to say the product—that became "Stevie," Smith's poetic oeuvre would confound the critical expectations traditionally brought to bear upon and define serious poetry. Her output was bewilderingly large—more than a thousand poems as well as extensive work in prose. Many of the poems are brief—a couplet or one or two quatrains in length; many are undeniably slight in ambition and effect; many bear obvious relation to casual, "easy" genres such as nursery rhyme, song, or nonsense verse; many are humorous or offhand in tone. Smith insisted on singing, rather than respectably intoning, her poems at readings and on publishing them accompanied by her own drawings. This practice would seem to deny the self-sufficiency and seriousness of her poetic enterprise even if the drawings had, say, William Blake's visionary intensity rather than her own doodling, almost self-deprecating delicacy. Finally, her work displays little in the way of progression, either technically or thematically. The same strategies and subjects seen in her first book are found in her last, making it unhelpful to study her work through the familiar method of chronological development or improvement. In short, her individual poems and her oeuvre alike challenge Romantic and traditional assumptions that great poetry must be serious, pure, intense, painstakingly wrought, and difficult.

The issue here is neither to deny that such qualities can characterize great poetry nor to digress into the tempting but complex realm of critical parameters and expectations. Instead, it is simply to point out that the unconsidered application of these criteria has not served the study of Smith's particular gifts well. As Mark Storey writes, the critical establishment seems to have acknowledged her existence without accommodating her into the terms of its discourse (p. 42). Smith is widely praised, but too often the admiration seems bestowed despite her method rather than because of it. Her longer, most carefully composed, or most "serious" poems are singled out for note while her brief, humorous, or apparently offhand works are dismissed. Such an assessment finds her on her weakest ground and reinforces the very values she habitually rejected. In fact, serious consideration of Smith's oeuvre discloses a consistent resistance to this type of hierarchical ranking—a resistance she maintained even when that apostasy brought her decades of unwelcome critical obscurity.

The foundation of Smith's aesthetic is her deliberate persistence in scrambling the signals of poetic seriousness. Thematically as well as formally, her impulse is one of inclusion; she juxtaposes contradictory orders—silliness and despair, grandiosity and deflation, childishness and wisdom, enchantment and irony, irregularity and order, brevity and expansion, freedom and constraint, plain speech and mystery—until the falsity of such distinctions is revealed. Her work is so companionable, so unpretentious, so unfailingly lucid, that the profound anarchism inherent in this strategy goes unnoticed, leaving only an impression of originality and freshness along with a suspicion that the tidy boundaries of language have been gleefully transgressed. Smith's value in twentieth-century poetry is not her intermittent willingness to meet the aesthetic demands of the good or competent poem, but her boldness in stepping beyond them.

LIFE

WRITERS on Stevie Smith have often wondered how this dull, suburban spinster could create such a provocative, vividly unique body of work. In fact, though few readers would wish to live Smith's life, recent biographies suggest that it was not only sufficient but also bountiful in nurturing her particular gift. It fed her richly on the great hymns, ballads, and children's rhymes that informed her innately receptive ear; taught her the literary canon without exposing her to the academy's factionalism or self-consciousness; brought her into the heart of London literary life while offering her an escape from it; and provided what was, for her, the wholly necessary security of a fixed home, a familiar routine, and a trustworthy, undemanding, unvarying companion. Some of these advantages came to her by chance; others, by choice—Smith

understood perfectly what supported her work and stuck to it even when it ran directly contrary to prevailing notions of creative imperatives. They are not by themselves enough to "explain" her originality, the fact that she wrote like no one else either then or since. But what artist's life, however dramatic or sophisticated, is like another's? The originality of her work is ultimately a function of the originality of her mind. Smith's mind, with its peculiar combination of rueful wit, moral and intellectual probity, verbal ingenuity, and sheer intelligence, would have been just as astonishingly sparkling in a salon in literary bohemia as it was immured in Palmers Green.

Stevie Smith was born Florence Margaret Smith on 20 September 1902, in the port of Hull. Called Peggy until her middle twenties, when a friend likened her to the popular jockey Steve Donoghue, she was the second daughter of Charles Ward Smith and Ethel Spear Smith. The Smith and the Spear families were solidly middle class, but by the time of Stevie's birth the family stability and fortunes had both begun to slip. The blame can be laid chiefly on Charles Ward Smith, whose lifelong desire to go to sea had been thwarted by a domineering mother. He took over his father's forwarding agency instead, but had little interest in the work. Slackly run, the firm began to founder; Smith's marriage seems to have been unsatisfactory as well, and in 1906 he left his wife and two children to work for the White Star Shipping Line. There was no legal separation, but Charles Smith never lived permanently with his wife and children again. Neither did he contribute to his family's tenuous livelihood, a failing that exacerbated Smith's later distaste for her father. He visited intermittently and sent brief, noncommittal postcards. Pompey, the autobiographical protagonist of Smith's *Novel on Yellow Paper,* remembers the words "Off to Valparaiso love Daddy" as the entire text of one of his cards and adds, "And a very profound impression of transiency they left upon me" (p. 76).[1] This experience of abandonment was the first of a series of childhood losses that affected Smith deeply.

In 1906, Mrs. Smith, her two daughters, and her sister Madge Spear moved to 1 Avondale Road, Palmers Green, the house in which Smith was to live for the rest of her life. Palmers Green, a suburb

[1]Page references for the *Novel on Yellow Paper* are from the Virago Press edition first published in London in 1980.

of London, was still primarily rural at the time the Smiths arrived. It offered Smith and her sister Molly fields, woods, and parkland to play in, an idyllic landscape given added spice by such suburban touches as a small railway station complete with poster advertisements. Smith loved Palmers Green even fifty years later, when it had grown crowded and shabby; she described it as an ideal setting for children and frequently memorialized it, only thinly disguised as Syler's or Bottle Green, in her essays and poems. The continuity, space, and unpretentious briskness the town offered were tremendously important to Smith, and she extolled her particular suburb's virtues even as she scathingly satirized the inanities of what she called the "suburban classes."

Smith's acclimatization to the new world of Palmers Green was interrupted almost immediately when she contracted a form of tuberculosis, at that time still impossible to treat quickly. With the exception of summer visits to the seaside with her family, she spent the next three years at the Yarrow Convalescent Home in Broadstairs, Kent. Her early days there were not unpleasant, but she became progressively lonelier and more homesick as her stay went on. She later attributed her first thoughts of suicide to this period, writing in *Novel on Yellow Paper* that her recognition at the age of eight that one could choose not to live was what made life bearable; in the same book she recommended, not entirely jokingly, that children be educated about the availability of suicide in order to "brace and fortify" them. Smith recovered and was able to leave the children's home at the age of nine, but chronic fatigue and a tendency to nervous strain were to remain constants throughout her life.

Smith returned from Broadstairs to Palmers Green to begin her formal education. The Palmers Green High School taught English literature and the classics intensively, with an emphasis on memorization that helped Smith further develop her storehouse of literary models and hone her acute poetic ear, a process that her family's attendance at Anglican worship, with its great hymns and liturgy, supported as well. Smith enjoyed this first school but was less happy at North London Collegiate, which succeeded it. During this period the Smith family held a stable if financially rather precarious place in the community of Palmers Green. Gradually, however, Ethel Smith's health began to decline. In 1919 she died of an extended and pain-

ful respiratory illness. The exhaustion and depression engendered by her mother's death, her relatively poor academic showing, and the family's lack of funds combined to steer Smith away from university training. Instead, she enrolled in a secretarial academy. Her first position after graduation was with an engineering firm. Within a year, however, she had found the job with the Pearson (later Newnes) publishing organization that she was to hold for thirty years.

By 1922, the basic patterns that Smith was to follow for most of her life were established. The house in Palmers Green; a quiet routine with Madge Spear, her "Lion Aunt," who became her lifetime companion until the aunt's death in 1968; her undemanding job at Newnes; intensive reading and writing; a cycle of lunches, dinners, and weekend visits with friends: these fixed points characterized most of Smith's life. Her routine was far from idyllic. Palmers Green was inconvenient and at times confining. Her job at Newnes was emotionally deadening and would prove financially inadequate. Even life with the Lion Aunt, who was stalwart, loving, protective, and, to Smith's mind, happily unliterary, had its strains. Yet clearly the fixity of her life satisfied a deep need, for Smith made few serious attempts to change it. She had romantic relationships of varying degrees of seriousness with one woman (whose name is not revealed) and several men, including Karl Eckinger and Eric Armitage (the "Karl" and "Freddy" of her novels and poems) and, reportedly, George Orwell. But by the time she was thirty, she seems to have acknowledged that marriage, children, and even serious romantic relationships were not for her. She preferred the more intermittent rhythms of friendship and was, according to contemporary accounts, a witty, scathing, entertaining, and at times demanding companion. She was gregarious and had a wide circle of friends, but the bond with her aunt formed the single long-term emotional commitment of her adult life.

Spurred in part by her embarrassment at not having attended university, Smith read voraciously during the 1920's. She kept a series of notebooks that list, comment on, and quote from her reading of the period, reading that broadened her knowledge through the addition of more modern and more varied works. These notebooks attest to the tremendous range of her reading, which included history, biography, theology, fiction, and literary criticism; they note works by authors including Euripides, Jean Racine, William Blake, Joseph Conrad, Edgar Allan Poe, D. H. Lawrence, Virginia Woolf, Franz Kafka, James Joyce, and lesser known writers of her period. The notebooks conclusively prove Smith's familiarity not just with classic literature but also with the literary trends of her own time, contradicting entirely the idea that she was either a naïf or a miraculous original without antecedents or influences. Many of the works she read during this period turn up later, their subjects adapted and their texts echoed, quoted, or parodied, in her poems and novels. The single area she appears to have avoided in her reading was contemporary poetry, which she seems to have feared imitating too closely.

Smith had begun writing verse while still at school but did not make her first sustained attempts at poetry until the mid-1920's. Her early poems display many of the hallmarks of her later style set within somewhat more timid and more derivative forms. She concealed her writing from most of her intimates for over a decade. In 1934 she sent a large group of poems—she was always a prolific writer—to the Curtis Brown literary agency, whose reader they bewildered and dismayed. A second group, sent to Chatto & Windus in 1935, received a more positive response. Ian Parsons, Smith's contact there, was unable to publish them but encouraged her to write a novel first in order to help establish her name.

Hesitant at first, Smith composed *Novel on Yellow Paper* during an intensely productive ten-week period in the fall of 1935. Despite revisions intended to make it more conventional in structure and punctuation, Chatto & Windus refused to publish the book. It was brought out by Jonathan Cape in September 1936. Its reviewers, who included some of the most prominent critics of the day, were not without their complaints, but virtually all recognized a new and original literary voice. This favorable response and the book's engaging, energetic, intimate tone—which seemed to suit its times perfectly—helped to make it a notable success. During this same period six of Smith's poems, including the strikingly insouciant "Freddy," were published by *The New Statesman.* By the beginning of 1937, Smith had decisively arrived, with force and fanfare, on the English literary scene. Perhaps the only negative voice was that of her employer, Newnes,

which disliked her new notoriety and distrusted the increasingly idiosyncratic, childlike dress and persona she slowly began to adopt.

Smith's success created an immediate interest in her work—her reviews and essays as well as her poems. At the same time it dramatically expanded her circle of literary friends, contacts, and correspondents. She enjoyed and took advantage of the wider opportunities both changes afforded her. A highly social being, Smith welcomed the excitement and exposure to new ideas her friendships with prominent writers, editors, and critics brought to her life. The reassurance of success and the vein of creativity tapped by the composition of *Novel on Yellow Paper* yielded a steady stream of new work to meet the growing demand. Her poems appeared widely in periodicals, and her first collection of poetry, *A Good Time Was Had by All,* was published in 1937. A second book of poems, *Tender Only to One,* and a novel, *Over the Frontier,* both appeared in 1938. The response to the poetry was excellent, fueled by the recognition of the quirky uniqueness of her voice. *Over the Frontier,* a far less effervescent production than *Novel on Yellow Paper,* was reviewed widely but to mixed notices by critics uncomfortable with its midstream switch from the familiar chatty narrative voice to an ominous, mysterious lyricism. Smith wrote a third novel, "Married to Death," in 1937 but abandoned the manuscript when a friend, the editor David Garnett, reluctantly declared it to be virtually unreadable.

By the early 1940's the war had helped to change the English national climate from gaiety to sobriety. Smith did volunteer work in London but, as always, refused both to ally herself with any political movement and to exaggerate the gloom of the times, since she found what she called "world-worrying" to be both prideful and self-aggrandizing. She began having difficulty publishing her work at this time—as several commentators have pointed out, its apparent lightness may have been considered unsuited to the somber wartime years. Smith's third volume of poetry, *Mother, What Is Man?,* did not appear until 1942, and *Harold's Leap* not until 1950. *The Holiday,* her final novel, was composed during the war but not published until 1949. She continued to write reviews, but her work was to stay out of fashion through the 1940's and much of the 1950's, an extended obscurity that affected her income, her confidence, and her sense of connection to a literary circle. In response to this frustration, as well as to those of chronic depression, a dreary job, and a tiring home life with her aging aunt, Smith attempted suicide in 1953. She was retired as a result and used her free time to write additional reviews and poetry. She received a pension from Newnes but her finances remained tenuous, as they had been for some time.

The André Deutsch organization rather reluctantly published *Not Waving But Drowning,* Smith's fifth collection of poems, in 1957. It received wider and more positive attention than her books of the 1940's and early 1950's, and marked the turn of the tide of both public taste and Smith's popularity. The 1960's were as generous with recognition as the previous years had been sparing. The decade saw the publication of her *Selected Poems* in England in 1962 and in America two years later; frequent appearances on BBC Radio; the acceptance of her work by leading periodicals in both England and America; widespread and favorable reviews of the *Selected Poems* (1962) and the subsequent *Frog Prince and Other Poems* (1966); recognition by peers including Robert Lowell, Philip Larkin, and Sylvia Plath; and the honor of the Cholmondeley Award for Poetry in 1966. Smith reveled in these honors, which were especially welcome after the drought of so many years. Though they were physically draining, she also enjoyed her many opportunities to appear at the poetry readings and festivals that became hugely popular during this period. Her poetry, so often influenced by sung or spoken models, was ideal for performance. By all accounts she was a frail, eccentric, and captivating stage presence, a star who sang her poetry boldly in a high, oddly tuneless voice, outshone fellow readers who included some of the century's best-known poets, and was surprisingly popular with the young people in her audiences.

By 1969, when she was awarded the Queen's Gold Medal for Poetry (she believed she disconcerted the queen with her odd dress and chat about poetry and murder), Smith was a lively but increasingly fragile sixty-seven. Her beloved aunt had died in 1968 at the age of ninety-six, after a long period of invalidism, leaving Smith lonely and grief-stricken. Her sister, Molly, suffered a stroke in January 1969, requiring Smith to make frequent visits to Devon. Smith was at her sister's when, in the fall of 1970, she began experiencing dizziness

and difficulties with speech. Her symptoms worsened quickly, and a biopsy revealed an inoperable brain tumor. She died on 7 March 1971. *Scorpion and Other Poems,* a posthumous collection, was published in 1972. It had as its final poem her second work titled "Come, Death," a work she had recited for visitors to her hospital room during her final illness.

I feel ill. What can the matter be?
I'd ask God to have pity on me,
But I turn to the one I know, and say:
Come, Death, and carry me away.

Ah me, sweet Death, you are the only god
Who comes as a servant when he is called, you know,
Listen then to this sound I make, it is sharp,
Come Death. Do not be slow.

POETIC THEMES

STEVIE SMITH wrote a poetry of isolation in a determinedly social voice. Her poems are typically engaging in tone, direct in manner, and unpretentious in approach. Their slightness and eccentricity often mask the darkness of their vision, just as their diversity of subject and persona tend to obscure the relentless persistence with which she examined her few, central concerns. Smith's simple, apparently naïve surfaces echo off of, collide with, underscore, mock, or are mocked by her stark themes of desolation, loneliness, and despair. This disjunction between content and manner explains, though it does not support, the frequent classification of this most "deathwards" of poets among the practitioners of light and children's verse.

In a recorded conversation with a friend, the writer and editor Kay Dick, Smith commented that "being alive is like being in enemy territory" (Dick, p. 45). Though uncharacteristically portentous in tone, this remark provides a useful key to her thematics. The sense of inhabiting an unfamiliar, even hostile domain; the necessity of remaining always wary; the feeling of being odd, incongruous, mysteriously misplaced: all are constants in her poetry. Her eye—and, even more intensely, her ear—has the wicked acuity of the eternal observer rather than the complacence of one at home; whether they misunderstand or are misunderstood, for

Smith's characters all language seems a foreign language at times. Her comment prepares one, too, for the movement in her poetry, the frequency with which her characters find themselves traveling, seeking, wandering, departing or, even when at rest, restless. .

In itself, this recognition of the human's innate alienation is not new. What distinguishes Smith from the many other modern writers who share it is her particularly rueful response. She is acutely aware of the essential comicality of incongruity, and she exploits it in both the form and the content of her poetry. She venerates a kind of sardonic stoicism that finds moral virtue in the simultaneous acknowledgment of and resistance to the yearning for consolation. She abhors sentimentality, exaggeration, and self-aggrandizement, whether born of love or of despair. Smith satirizes, teases, and debates the man-made tidinesses—Christianity, marriage, class and political groupings—that try to mask the essential isolation and confusion of life with a spurious order. Above all she welcomes Death as god, servant, friend, father, prince, and deliverer: the primal force, at once all-controlling and controllable, who ends life's exile and thus, paradoxically, makes it possible to live joyfully in that exile.

Smith's large oeuvre is as remarkable for the important genres it excludes as it is for those it encompasses. She wrote virtually no conventional love lyrics, little visually descriptive nature poetry. Instead she found her most natural voice in two modes: the poem of philosophical or moral speculation and the narrative. Her poems in the former category muse on religion, human and animal relationships, and the many passing subjects that caught Smith's attention: illegitimacy, river pollution, the validity of cheap editions of Walt Whitman. Some are brief and aphoristic, such as "From the Greek":

> To many men strange fates are given
> Beyond remission or recall
> But the worst fate of all (tra la)
> 's to have no fate at all (tra la).

Others, such as "This Is Disgraceful and Abominable," "Oh Christianity, Christianity," or "Pretty," are extended and conversational arguments. At their best their sustained attention to a topic yields rewards, but they always flirt with and often surrender to the dangers of polemicism. They become overly essayistic and declamatory: intelligent and sharply sarcastic, but without the necessary edge of irony.

Instead, Smith's most comfortable mode is that of monologue and narrative, genres she knew well from her extensive early reading. At the heart of her brief poetic stories are people; her *Collected Poems* (1975) has the air of a cocktail party given by an individual of large and diverse acquaintance: The crowds are lively, the personalities heterogeneous, and the chatter immensely varied. She lifts characters from her own life; adapts historical figures from Hadrian to Cranmer; reworks mythical, legendary, or biblical beings such as Eve, Rapunzel, King Arthur, and Persephone. She invents a gallery of her own improbable characters, some handed simple, suburban names like Pauline, Elinor, and Amelia, others the fruit of a gleeful wordplay: the Romans Tenuous, Precarious, Hazardous, and Spurious, among others; the child killer, Malady Festing and her daughter Angel Boley; Lord Barrenstock and Lord Say-and-Seal; the commercial villains Profit and Batten; widowed Mrs. Courtly; and renegade Lady 'Rogue' Singleton. She writes often about children and almost as often about animals, from the Hound of Ulster to the lions that ate the Christian martyrs (whose contribution to the church she feels has been overlooked).

Smith presents all of her characters sparingly, without physical description, detailed characterization, or narrative resolution. Her monologues offer a chatty surface, but the stories themselves are truncated, mysterious, and oblique.

> I shall be glad to be silent, Mother, and hear you
>   speak,
> You encourage me to tell too much, and my thoughts
>   are weak,
> I shall keep them to myself for a time, and when I am
>   older
> They will shine as a white worm shines under a green
>   boulder.
>
> ("The White Thought")

> Standing alone on a fence in a spasm,
> I behold all life in a microcosm.
> Behind me unknown with a beckoning finger
> Is the house and well timbered park. I linger
> Uncertain yet whether I should enter, take possession,
>   still the nuisance

Of a huge ambition; and below me is the protesting
    face of my cousin.

                             ("The Cousin")

Smith includes only what captures her imagination, that is, the alienation of her characters from themselves, others, their language, and their world. Their relationship to those around them is typically one of failed communion and missed connections; they are excessive or eccentric, wistfully or defiantly out of step, time, and tune. Virtually all share, in one way or another, the misfit, misunderstood loneliness, at once excruciating and comical, of "The Songster":

Miss Pauncefort sang at the top of her voice
(Sing tirry-lirry-lirry down the lane)
And nobody knew what she sang about
(Sing tirry-lirry-lirry all the same).

The poems' apparently offhand quality is deliberate. Casual, brief, or light-verse forms—nursery rhymes, nonsense stanzas, clerihew quatrains, songs—echo her characters' marginality. The childlike rhythms refract their painful subjects, functioning like prisms whose simple transparency makes visible a rainbow of distinct and complex colorations. Smith's songster (perhaps not incidentally, she performed her own poems by singing them) is savored by her creator, in the poem and in the drawing of a buxom, wide-mouthed, platter-hatted woman that accompanies it, as an undeniably comical figure. Yet her painful isolation and patent absurdity are heroic: She resists assimilation or, in this case, silence. The poem, like many of Smith's best, leaves the reader "on the fence in a spasm," hovering between pity and laughter, admiration and ridicule. The subtle indeterminacy of the parenthetical lines adds a characteristic element of ambiguity to Smith's habitually lucid literal surface.

Smith models many of her poems on children's literature, especially nursery rhymes and fairy tales. She writes often and unsentimentally about children, whom she finds powerful and anarchic rather than sweet. Her children are uncannily canny beings; the key to lack of innocence is perhaps their parents, who emerge again and again in Smith's oeuvre as misguided or malevolent figures—"But Murderous," "Mother," "Advice to Young Children," "A Mother's Hearse," "Little

Boy Lost," and "Parents" are only a few examples. Whether scheming or indifferent, they fail to provide the nurturing necessary for helpless infants. Virtually all of her children are "cynical babes," as she says in "Infant," and, as she adds, not without cause. They have a premature prescience that both protects and isolates them.

My mother was a romantic girl
So she had to marry a man with his hair in curl
Who subsequently became my unrespected papa,
But that was a long time ago now.

        . . .

I sat upright in my baby carriage
And wished mama hadn't made such a foolish
    marriage.
I tried to hide it, but it showed in my eyes
    unfortunately
And a fortnight later papa ran away to sea.

He used to come home on leave
It was always the same
I could not grieve
But I think I was somewhat to blame.

                      ("Papa Love Baby")

Here Smith juxtaposes the sentimentally simplistic family history with the sophisticated, even jaded voice of the child. In this world it is adulthood that is naïve and foolish, overly susceptible to dreams of romance, and childhood that is ironic and detached. This deliberate self-distancing becomes the child's salvation from the uncertainty of the adult's insincere, arbitrary love. "The Orphan Reformed" is not "right" until she ceases "looking for parents and cover," until she realizes that "really she is better alone," until "when she cries, Father, Mother, it is only to please" rather than with the expectation of true love. "The Wanderer" uses echoes of the supernatural ballad to explore the same theme, though in a manner that allows the underlying longing to surface even as it is denied.

Twas the voice of the Wanderer, I heard her exclaim,
You have weaned me too soon, you must nurse me
    again,
She taps as she passes at each window pane,
Pray, does she not know that she taps in vain?

Her voice flies away on the midnight wind,
But would she be happier if she were within?
She is happier far where the night winds fall,
And there are no doors and no windows at all.

465

Many of Smith's characters share this sense of premature weaning, this "Dream of Nourishment," to use the title of one of her poems. "I had a dream of nourishment / Against a breast," it begins, then continues, "But in my dream the breast withdrew." For Smith, surrender to the longing for nurture inevitably courts rejection, just as surrender to the yearning for home risks alienation. As the speaker of "Fairy Story" says, "I sang a song, he let me go, / But now I am home again there is nobody I know." It is safer to remain unloved and unrooted like the Wanderer or the narrator of "Lightly Bound," who says, "Do you suppose I shall stay when I can go so easily?" Smith habitually uses images of wind and air to describe the refuge chosen by these characters: the windy flight of the Wanderer, the elopement with the north wind of "Lightly Bound," the journeying and "rushing air" of "In My Dreams." Such flights are cold and isolating, but they are safe because they permit no false hopes, ask only for the freedom they can give themselves.

In my dreams I am always saying goodbye and riding
    away,
Whither and why I know not nor do I care.
And the parting is sweet and the parting over is
    sweeter,
And sweetest of all is the night and the rushing air.

In my dreams they are always waving their hands and
    saying goodbye,
And they give me the stirrup cup and I smile as I
    drink,
I am glad the journey is set, I am glad I am going,
I am glad, I am glad, that my friends don't know
    what I think.

                  ("In My Dreams")

Unlike so many other writers concerned with blighted love, Smith never overvalues the intimacy her characters fail to achieve. Alienation, for her, is in the nature of things, engendered both by love— ". . . if she were not so loving / She would not be so miserable," she writes in "Unpopular, Lonely and Loving"—and by the avoidance of love. The choice is not between intimacy and isolation but between an isolation masked by apparent closeness (and thus terrifying) and the less dangerous isolation of actual aloneness.

Isolation, in this sense, becomes a function of language. Like the narrator of "The After

Thought," Smith's characters often find they cannot be heard: "What is that darling? You cannot hear me? / That's odd. I can hear you quite distinctly." Even when heard, they are frequently misunderstood. Language, the medium of intimacy, is almost always the medium of misperception as well.

I love little Heber
His coat is so warm
And if I don't speak to him
He'll do me no harm
But sit by my window
And stare in the street
And pull up a hassock for the comfort of his feet.

I love little Heber
His eyes are so wide
And if I don't speak to him
He'll stay by my side.
But oh in this silence
I find but suspense:
I must speak have spoken have driven him hence.
                        ("Heber")

This variation on both nursery rhyme and Blake's "The Chimney Sweeper" is far more troubling and unsettled than its models. Heber appears as both human and animal, raising doubts about the potential for either response or understanding. The poem's indeterminate conclusion, straddling the future and the past, denies closure. Most important, perhaps, speech itself—more typically regarded as a bridge to intimacy—becomes a dangerous and alienating force, an action tabooed by a mysterious interdict. The text itself announces this: Afraid to speak, its persona takes refuge in the comforting patterning of regular stanzas and apparent lightness of nursery rhyme repetitions— they create a form of discourse that is childish enough to seem safe. Inevitably the freight of emotion is too heavy for this slight vehicle; the rigid self-control of the stanzas literally breaks down, spilling over into two desperately unwieldy final lines.

"Lady 'Rogue' Singleton," another poem about human relationships, pits two forms of language, rather than speech and silence, against one another:

Come, wed me, Lady Singleton,
And we will have a baby soon
And we will live in Edmonton
Where all the friendly people run.

I could never make you happy, darling,
Or give you the baby you want,
I would always very much rather, dear,
Live in a tent.

I am not a cold woman, Henry,
But I do not feel for you,
What I feel for the elephants and the miasmas
And the general view.

The pedestrian regularity, stilted repetitions, and flat-footed rhymes of Henry's first-stanza proposal mimic the conventionality of his mind. Its invitation to marriage, baby, and suburban bliss debase the erotic passion of the love lyrics on which it is based in the same way its choices of diction—the specificity of "Edmonton," the banal "friendly"—do. In contrast, Lady Singleton is delicate, dangerous, and unpredictable. Her rhythmic boldness and its range of diction—from the flat, conversational "I am not a cold woman" to the vagueness of "miasmas"—make her words simple, memorable, and irreducible: It is as impossible to explain the symbolism of Lady Singleton's three "true loves" as it is to forget them. Yet underneath the humor Smith's typical seriousness can be glimpsed. Lady Singleton has forsaken the security of marriage without gaining any significant compensation except freedom from its stifling conventionality: the elephants, the miasmas, and the general view are at best indifferent, at worst threatening—in any case, they provide neither solace nor company.

Smith's most famous poem, "Not Waving But Drowning," plays with similar concerns. The lilting chime of "waving," "drowning," and "larking" is exactly its point: Not only do friends not understand, but language itself has gone awry—there is not enough linguistic difference between the terror of "drowning" and the childish play of "larking" to allow the narrator's peril to *be* understood. The betrayal is as much that of language as that of love.

Nobody heard him, the dead man,
But still he lay moaning:
I was much further out than you thought
And not waving but drowning.

Poor chap, he always loved larking
And now he's dead
It must have been too cold for him his heart gave
    way,
They said.

Oh, no no no, it was too cold always
(Still the dead one lay moaning)
I was much too far out all my life
And not waving but drowning.

So inadequate is the man's communication during his lifetime that he continues to "moan" after his supposed death, like a spirit doomed to search forever for the human connections that eluded him in life. Language itself is, for Smith, something that appears to be waving even as it is drowning; her speakers are seduced by its charms even as they are victimized by it.

Smith conducted a lifelong argument with Christianity, and many of her debates with it are voiced through her poems. In significant ways, Christianity was for Smith both a parent promising a spurious safety and a deeply unreliable construct of language. She and her personae long for the comfort, the fatherhood, the companionship of a God. Yet she distrusts the form in which this comfort is offered, the neat package of beliefs, rules, and dogmas. They offer a solace that denies what Smith believed to be the harsher, more random nature of reality; they are ultimately too tidy, too human, too convenient, and thus too dangerous to accept. Her conscience and her temperament lead her to insist on the "emptiness of an indifferent universe" (Barbera and McBrien, pp. 218–219) and to reject the wishful thinking that prefers spurious coziness. "Write that word right, say 'hope,' don't say 'belief,' " she wrote in her essay "The Necessity of Not Believing" (Barbera and McBrien, p. 218). We must learn to "be good without enchantment," she says in the conclusion of the long poem "How Do You See":

I do not think we shall be able to bear it much longer
    the dishonesty
Of clinging for comfort to beliefs we do not believe
    in,
For comfort, and to be comfortably free of the fear
Of diminishing good, as if truth were a convenience.
I think if we do not learn quickly, and learn to teach
    children,
To be good without enchantment, without the help
Of beautiful painted fairy stories pretending to be
    true,
Then I think it will be too much for us, the
    dishonesty,
And, armed as we are now, we shall kill everybody,
It will be too much for us, we shall kill everybody.

Again and again Smith's poems attack organized religion, particularly the Christian church. She found the concepts of sin and damnation cruel, even monstrous, and wondered how a God of love could condemn his own creatures, exiling man from the same grace he simultaneously created. She disliked the dominating, hectoring element so prominent in Christian doctrine. Above all, perhaps, Smith distrusted what she called its tidiness, the neatness of rules and hierarchies that she felt bore the "mark of our humanity" (Spalding, p. 235) far more than the mark of a god. "A god is Man's doll, you ass, / He makes him up like this on purpose. / He could have made him up worse. / He often has, in the past," she wrote in "Was He Married?" Yet Smith admitted that her feelings on God and religion fluctuated widely over time; she could never entirely discard the plentiful attractions of belief. In the end, as she said of Blake, though she herself "rows and grumbles at God and nags him . . . he cannot forget Him" (Spalding, p. 241). The intimacy and personalization of her verbs are both poignant and telling.

Paradoxically, the intensity of her feelings about Christianity weakens most of Smith's poems about it. They are among her most aggressively prosy and argumentative works, imbued with an insistent rationalism that precludes mystery. It is as though the lure of belief is so strong that she cannot afford to give in to its enchantment—in contrast with the works discussed earlier that embody enchantment even as they expose it. Far more successful are the poems that meditate on or invent Smith's own gods rather than allowing Christianity to constrain them. Among these "God the Eater" is notable and worth quoting in full.

There is a god in whom I do not believe
Yet to this god my love stretches,
This god whom I do not believe in is
My whole life, my life and I am his.

Everything that I have of pleasure and pain
(Of pain, of bitter pain and men's contempt)
I give this god for him to feed upon
As he is my whole life and I am his.

When I am dead I hope that he will eat
Everything I have been and have not been
And crunch and feed upon it and grow fat
Eating my life all up as it is his.

All of Smith's strengths are here. The voice of the poem is complex, at once seductive and disturbing. It is disenchanted, in the sense that it offers no easy escape, no placid, sentimental vision of godhead: This god feeds with relish on his flock rather than nurturing them. Yet the power, the attraction, of merging with a god (however ominous) is palpable within it. It is a poem that is at once highly controlled—note the regular stanzas—and thoroughly abandoned; the speaker submits herself entirely to her god, leaving the dangerous overtones of this submission unverbalized, to resonate within the reader. Unlike so many of the poems on Christianity, its "meaning" can neither be paraphrased nor reduced. It is unresolved, unresolvable, and thus haunting.

Ultimately, for Smith, death was the one truly satisfactory god. His very bleakness is his attraction: He makes no false promises, offers no neat orders. Smith again uses the imagery of air to denote the freedom from false shelter and confining structure that forms death's paradoxical appeal:

Why do I think of Death as a friend?
It is because he is a scatterer
He scatters the human frame
The nerviness and the great pain
Throws it on the fresh fresh air
And now it is nowhere
Only sweet Death does this
Sweet Death, kind Death,
Of all the gods you are best.
("Why Do I . . .")

Or, as she writes in "The Donkey," ". . . at last, in Death's odder anarchy / Our pattern will be all broken up." "I aspire to be broken up," she concludes.

Unlike parents, lovers, spouses, friends, or even other gods, death is entirely reliable. "Your friends will not come tomorrow / As they did not come today / You must rely on yourself, they said," the poem "Company" states. Its speaker responds by invoking death: "Sweet Death it is only you I can / Constrain for company." Confident in him as in no other, Smith and her personae engage in dialogue with death, sometimes wistfully, as in Scorpion's poignant "Scorpion so wishes to be gone," and at other times peremptorily. She believes that an awareness of the availability of suicide affords control over the potentially unbearable despair, exhaustion, or isolation her characters so often face. Yet, as she writes in *Novel on Yellow Paper*, "It is just as possible to be ignoble in self-slaying as in every other department of human activity" (p. 160). Death should not be chosen out of fear or self-pity, but earned by attempting to live life; awareness of the presence of death should be used to make life possible and to enrich the possibilities and awareness of the moment. Hers is, essentially, a Stoic's philosophy.

> Yet a time may come when a poet or any person
> Having a long life behind him, pleasure and sorrow,
> But feeble now and expensive to his country
> And on the point of no longer being able to make a
>   decision
> May fancy Life comes to him with love and says:
> We are friends enough now for me to give you
>   death,
> Then he may commit suicide, then
> He may go.
>
>   ("Exeat")

Ironically, perhaps, the only poems in which Smith abandons her insistent focus on disjunction and isolation are those about death. In this single relationship she found no strain, no abandonment, no conflicting or inadequate languages, no need to mask pain or longing in bravado or irony. In the end, though still as oblique and scrupulous as ever, Smith comes the closest to a love poetry of tenderness and reciprocation not to parents, children, lovers, or friends, but to death.

> I have a friend
> At the end
> Of the world.
> His name is a breath
>
> Of fresh air.
> He is dressed in
> Grey chiffon. At least
> I think it is chiffon.
> It has a
> Peculiar look, like smoke.
>
> It wraps him round
> It blows out of place
> It conceals him
> I have not seen his face.

> But I have seen his eyes, they are
> As pretty and bright
> As raindrops on black twigs
> In March, and heard him say:
>
> I am a breath
> Of fresh air for you, a change
> By and by.
>   . . .
> But this friend
> Whatever new names I give him
> Is an old friend. He says:
>
> Whatever names you give me
> I am
> A breath of fresh air,
> A change for you.
>   ("Black March")

POETIC FORM

A quick reading of Stevie Smith's best-known poems may suggest that she was unpracticed at conventional stanza and metrical structures, like a fledgling tennis player who knows the rules but cannot control her swing. Closer scrutiny proves Smith to be capable of, in fact skilled at, orthodox poetic practice. What begins to strike the reader instead are the arbitrary limitations the sport imposes. To continue the analogy, Smith's strategy is to flout those restrictions, acknowledging but breaking the rules and even mixing different games together. To read her work carefully is to become aware of the rigidity not just of traditional or metrical poetic structures but of most free verse as well.

Smith's is a highly referential poetry, rife with parodies, variations, and adaptations of other literature. She learned and loved the work of Tennyson, Browning, Milton, the seventeenth-century religious writers, Blake, Wordsworth, Coleridge, and many other poets. Borrowings from them, as well as from Shakespeare, Racine, fairy tales, the Bible, and the classics, abound in her poems. Sometimes these are accurate renderings, but more often they are fragmentary or twisted. The rhythms as well as the words of other literature are insistently heard. Smith writes capably and at times conventionally in a range of meters and uses traditional stanzaic patterns including heroic couplets, tercets,

469

and a variety of quatrain forms. Her work is always reminding the reader of its highly traditional roots—in fact, it does so far more obviously than the work of many more overtly conventional poets.

Yet—and this is certainly the key to its popularity if also to its critical difficulty—it does not look, does not *sound,* like the canon on which it is modeled. One reason is suggested by the fact that Smith performed her work by singing rather than by reading it. She did not just read but memorized virtually all of the poets just mentioned—that is, she apprehended them by ear, not just by eye—and, equally important, was deeply familiar with Anglican hymns, old English and popular ballads, folk songs, nonsense and children's verse, and nursery rhymes. She was intensely aware of the rhythms of everyday speech, the music of ordinary language. The influence of these sung or spoken models is of tremendous importance to her work. Its heritage intersects—one might even say collides—with her borrowings from a more purely literary tradition. This deliberate conjunction of disparate modes, with its inclusion of the rhythms and formats of marginal or "low" discourses along with those of higher and more academic ones, helps to locate Smith's originality even as it helps explain her exclusion from the canon of "great" poetry. It also allows her to be simultaneously one of the most and one of the least literary of modern writers.

Informed by a broad knowledge of verse structures but ultimately holding herself accountable to none, gifted with a perceptive, mimetic, and musical ear, Stevie Smith is a master of the poetic line. She works it with the virtuosity of a fisherman, flinging it out in a single extended cast, then reeling it in with uninterrupted fluidity. Read silently or spoken aloud, her lines declare themselves endlessly malleable, infinitely plastic. Her oeuvre encompasses everything from regular lines fit into formal stanzas—

> Forgive me forgive me for here where I stand
> There is no friend beside me no lover at hand
> No footstep but mine in my desert of sand.
> ("Forgive Me, Forgive Me")

> I shall be glad when there's an end
> Of all the noise that doth offend
> My soul. Still Night, don cloak, descend.
> ("Up and Down")

—to longer, almost prosy ones, apparently formless but underlain by the casual rhythms of colloquial speech.

> And would people be so sympathetic if they knew
>   how the story went?
> Best not put it to the test. Silence and tears are
>   convenient.
> ("Silence and Tears")

> "It's the truth," Mrs Simpkins affirmed, "there is no
>   separation
> There's a great reunion coming for which this life's
>   but a preparation."
> ("Mrs Simpkins")

Yet Smith's distinctiveness stems not so much from her ability to play in a variety of line lengths and meters as from her willingness to combine different modes—long lines with short, regular lines with irregular ones, fixed patterns with shifting structures—within the confines of a single work. She simultaneously establishes and rejects the contract of form; first embraces, then discards, a predictable pattern. Both strategies work by creating a norm, then interjecting one or more lines that are obviously too long, too awkward, or too unwieldy within its context. The dislocation of expectations is refreshing—and unsettling. It forces the reader to question the original patterning and to adapt to a new, more pluralistic text. Consistent with Smith's distaste for false orders and deceptive tidinesses—whether personal, religious, economic, or political—it accommodates a world of disjunctive realities even as it teases conventional assumptions about poetic unity. "Lady 'Rogue' Singleton" is typical of this strategy. So is "Pad, Pad," which shares its concern with failed love and its distinctive mix of popular, Latinate, and archaic diction:

> I always remember your beautiful flowers
> And the beautiful kimono you wore
> When you sat on the couch
> With that tigerish crouch
> And told me you loved me no more.

> What I cannot remember is how I felt when you were
>   unkind
> All I know is, if you were unkind now I should not
>   mind.
> Ah me, the power to feel exaggerated, angry and sad
> The years have taken from me. Softly I go now, pad
>   pad.

STEVIE SMITH

The poem's abandonment of the limerick form of its first stanza, with its inherent comicality and bravado, for the messier line and less controlled mode of the second verse is not just witty but entirely to the point, as is the break between voices. "Do Take Muriel Out" is radically different in effect but similar in strategy. Smith uses the simple, spare quatrains of the ballad—one of her favorite forms—as a foundation for its ominous narrative.

> Do take Muriel out
> She is looking so glum
> Do take Muriel out
> All her friends have gone.

The regularity begins to falter in the third stanza, though the rhyme and parallel structure are retained:

> All her friends have gone
> And she is alone
> And she looks for them where they have never been
> And her peace is flown.

The intrusion of the long, loping line into the grimly neat stanzas prefigures the poem's startling end, which intensifies the impact of another irregular line with a deliberately blighted rhyme. The point of the variation, its chilling relevance, becomes clear with the recognition that the release from the etiquette of Muriel's stark, overly ordered existence can come only with the great anarchy of death:

> Do take Muriel out
> Although your name is Death
> She will not complain
> When you dance her over your blasted heath.

Stevie Smith used rhyme extensively. End rhymes were, as Hermione Lee points out in her introduction to *Stevie Smith: A Selection*, "her most pronounced device for controlling the line" (p. 21), a fact that helps to explain the weakness of some of the unrhymed works scattered throughout her books. Not surprisingly, her use of rhyme flouts conventional expectations. Smith is not afraid of full, thumping rhymes, the kind that would be laughed out of a contemporary poetry workshop: "Your sins are red about your head / And

many people wish you dead," for example, from "Lord Barrenstock"; but she also uses polysyllabic rhymes frequently: "introspective/reflective," "protocreation/imagination," "calculating/revolting," "ecstasy/artery." She rhymes English with Latin or French—for example, "Where speaking sub specie humanitatis / Freddy and me can kiss" ("Freddy"). Even more frequently, and contrary to standard poetic practice, she rhymes on the unaccented last syllable of a polysyllabic word: "nightfall/radical," "estuary/Mary," "frequently/distinctly," "instant/confidante." Such rhymes fracture the normal spoken rhythm of her lines—one stumbles over them, trying to force both rhyme and stress to work naturally at the same time. The effect is to hammer home the artificiality, the "createdness," of the poetic construct.

Smith's frequent and masterful use of impure and slant rhymes gives her work a subtle, offbeat quality. Like the couples in her poetic narratives, the rhymes form pairs that are never quite compatible. The mismatching of her half rhymes reflects the misfitting within the poems. For example, from "Magna Est Veritas":

> With my looks I am bound to look simple or fast I
>   would rather look simple
> So I wear a tall hat on the back of my head that is
>   rather a temple
> And I walk rather queerly and comb my long hair
> And people say, don't bother about her.

Similarly, in "The Orphan Reformed" the felicity of the rhyming stems from the fact that within the poem "for ever" and "Mother" rhyme as badly in concept as they do in sound; the same is true of "tedious" and "generous" in "Child Rolandine":

> But still she cries, Father, Mother
> Must I be alone for ever?
> Yes you must. Oh wicked orphan, oh rebellion,
> Must an orphan not be alone is that your opinion?
>   ("The Orphan Reformed")

> Likely also, sang the Childe, my soul will fry in hell
> Because of this hatred, while in heaven my employer
>   does well
> And why should he not, exacerbating though he be
>   but generous
> Is it his fault I must work at a work that is tedious?
> Oh heaven sweet heaven keep my thoughts in their
>   night den
> Do not let them by day be spoken.

471

But then she sang, Ah why not? tell all, speak,
 speak,
Silence is vanity, speak for the whole truth's sake.
                                        "Childe Rolandine"

As in the "gone/alone" and "death/heath" from "Do Take Muriel Out," Smith's unusual rhymes are not always comical; often they work to unsettlingly beautiful—or beautifully unsettling—effect. Like that of her lines, Smith's manipulation of rhyme is tremendously versatile, capable of engendering a delicate, chilling, brittle, fragile, admonitory, haunting, or poignant effect. Whichever emotional resonance Smith chooses, her slant rhymes always subtly prevent resolution, keeping the poem, and the reader, gently off balance.

Thieves honor him. In the underworld he rides
  carelessly.
Sometimes he rises into the air and flies silently.
                                        ("The Ambassador")

Oh Man, Man, of all my animals dearest,
Do not come till I call, thou thou weariest first.
                                        ("God and Man")

As with her line lengths, Smith's success with rhyme lies not only in the virtuosity of individual pairings but also in her willingness to establish regular schemes, only to abandon or transmute them. "So to Fatness Come" takes advantage of this freedom, moving from an unrhymed stanza to a series of rhymed couplets and then back, to intensify its deliberate, somber persistence.

Poor human race that must
Feed on pain, or choose another dish
And hunger worse.
              . . .
I am thy friend. I wish
You to sup full of the dish
I give you and the drink,
And so to fatness come more than you think
In health of opened heart, and know peace.

Grief spake these words to me in a dream. I thought
He spoke no more than grace allowed
And no less than truth.

As many of the excerpts suggest, Smith's diction is tremendously rich and astonishingly varied. She mined the potential of varied vocabularies to the full, welcoming the anarchic energy released by allowing clashing idioms to meet. She savored the almost tangible textures of archaism, slang, cliché, the grand formulations of literature, the jargons of religion, science, and scholarship. Her characteristic strategy is to confront the highest of idioms—Latinate, archaic, biblical, or purely poetic language—with the lowest. The combination creates poetry that is very much the product of its own time, place, and class, yet finds a paradoxical freedom within its specificity of manner. Both "The River God" and "Magna Est Veritas," for example, mix the chatty, offhand locutions of suburban England—"plenty of go," "dear," "in a bit"—with direct and indirect echoes from the literary canon.

Hi yih, yippety-yap, merrily I flow,
O I may be an old foul river but I have plenty of go.
Once there was a lady who was too bold
She bathed in me by the tall black cliff where the
       water runs cold,
So I brought her down here
To be my beautiful dear.
Oh will she stay with me will she stay
This beautiful lady, or will she go away?
She lies in my beautiful deep river bed with many a
     weed
To hold her, and many a waving reed.
                                        ("The River God")

I regard them as a contribution to almighty Truth,
     magna est
veritas et praevalebit,
Agreeing with that Latin writer, Great is Truth and
     will
prevail in a bit.
                                        ("Magna Est Veritas")

Where many modern poets have sought to reduce the elitism, artificiality, and distance of poetry by eliminating purely "poetic" diction entirely, Smith takes a different tack: By accommodating the most popular, the least pretentious of idioms, she is able to accommodate the grandest as well without sacrificing the colloquial, apparently spontaneous transparency of her surfaces. Her use of nonsense syllables like "tra la" or "yippety-yap"; her inclusion of contemporary slang and clichés; her love for simple, almost childlike words; her dismissal of all but essential punctuation; her use of companionable, engaging questions, appositions, invocations; and her heavy emphasis on the exclamations and qualifiers—"rather," "dear," "oh," "really," "well," "a bit," "quite"—that are usually excised from all discourse but everyday speech, help mask the sophistication of her subjects and models. When used without careful relation to content, these techniques can seem gimmicky or disingenuous. At her best, however, Smith is adept at using them simultaneously to deflate, intensify, and enliven the themes and models of her poems.

Technically, Smith remains distinctive for the confidence with which she discards conventional assumptions about poetic consistency, unity, and purity and for the boldness with which she brings together what has been kept apart. Her deliberate combinations of tight with loose forms, metrical with irregular lines, full with off rhymes, and high with low diction expand the sheer possibility within her work exponentially—the potential permutations are endless. Moreover, her aesthetic of combination keeps each poem open to change or adjustment at every moment in its progression: The establishment of one pattern never precludes another. The risk of Smith's strategy is dilution of effect, and there are poems in which she succumbs to this danger. More often, however, she reaps its rewards, obtaining for herself a poetic method that is uniquely adaptable, responsive, and *alive*.

NOVELS

IN addition to a thousand or more poems, Stevie Smith wrote four novels, several short stories, a smattering of essays, and scores of reviews. Among her prose pieces the stories are charming but slight, without either great intensity of feeling or strength of technique. Smith's essays are by turns provocative and lyrical; her reviews—on works of technology, history, biography, and anthropology as well as fiction—intelligent, lucid, at once companionable and imbued with an authority essentially moral rather than literary. All of these brief prose works remain enjoyable to readers today, though few are of real literary importance. Instead, it is Smith's three published novels (a fourth was abandoned and the manuscript destroyed), written between 1936 and 1949, that stand out as her most significant prose achievement.

Smith's biographer Francis Spalding calls her *Novel on Yellow Paper* "a poet's book." This descrip-

tion fits all of Smith's novels well. They are books, written by a poet and studded with the author's poems, that are as much "about" their own extravagant, overweening language as any poem. They are also books that adopt the privilege, familiar from collections of poetry but rarer in extended fictions, of presenting truth as a series of disjunctive possibilities rather than as a single consistent reality. They offer a plethora of opinions on subjects from the philosophy of Boethius to the paintings of George Grosz at the same time they withhold a unified tonal, structural, or imagistic resolution. Their unfixed quality alternately enchants and unsettles, enlivens and baffles. The writer and editor David Garnett, commenting on the manuscript of Smith's abandoned novel "Married to Death," commented to her that "A book must have shape, bones, foundations. It ought to be built like a house. This is liquid, a flowing stream of words" (Spalding, p. 141). Smith's three published novels all share the fluidity Garnett identified, partaking of the speed, adaptability, and liveliness of liquid as well as of its often frustrating formlessness.

Smith's novels, which have often been likened to the equally eccentric, talkative *Tristram Shandy*, are almost entirely plotless. Their events occur in succession but not in response to one another; their narratives are propelled by the quicksilver dartings of a curious consciousness rather than by external causality. Smith makes little attempt to convey a sense of place or sustain a chronologically accurate narrative. Nor, though her characters are based so recognizably on her friends and acquaintances that libel was always a risk, did she attempt to create rounded or realistic characterizations. In her experimentalism Smith reflects the interest of the 1920's and 1930's in new and disjunctive fictional structures. She had certainly read Joyce's *Ulysses* and had commented on Virginia Woolf's *The Common Reader*, whose essays "Modern Fiction" and "The Russian Point of View" espouse the same fluidity she was to exploit, in her reading notebook. She was influenced by American fiction as well. She must have been familiar with Gertrude Stein, whose playful inversions and repetitions heavily influenced her novelistic rhythms. She admired Sinclair Lewis's novels *Arrowsmith* and *The Man Who Knew Coolidge;* the latter, like her novels, takes the form of a single extended monologue. She enjoyed the jazzy energy of Anita Loos and Dorothy Parker, from whom she picked up what she called "this sort of pseudo (for me) American accent" (Dick, p. 47), a brassiness of tone and a wisecracking approach, most evident in *Novel on Yellow Paper,* that she came to dislike quite heartily.

Smith's extended interior monologues attain neither Woolf's lyrical intensity nor Joyce's opulence of detail. Instead, as the critics of the time immediately recognized, the originality and freshness of her achievement lies in her voice: in her own words, the "talking voice that is so sweet, how hold you alive in captivity, how point you with commas, semi-colons, dashes, pauses and paragraphs?" (p. 39). The rhythm of this voice shifts slightly over time, from the skittish teasing of *Novel on Yellow Paper* to the dreamlike narrative of *Over the Frontier* and again to the melancholy introspection of *The Holiday.* Yet in all three novels it remains essentially similar and intensely distinctive. It is a swift, engaging voice, at once vigorous and sensitive, ruthlessly attentive and quickly distractible, pliable and brittle, honest and arch. It takes full advantage of the discontinuities of spoken conversation, yet at the same time is far more exaggerated and mannered. As does her poetry, it blends a potpourri of idioms that are rarely mixed, jumbling foreign words, archaisms, slang, and literary quotations and echoes together. Spoken through the ventriloquistic mouths of her protagonist/narrators Pompey Casmilus, in *Novel on Yellow Paper* and *Over the Frontier,* and Celia Phoze in *The Holiday,* this complex voice is both the novels' most memorable achievement and one of their greatest limitations.

Nowhere is this more true than in Smith's first book, *Novel on Yellow Paper.* This soliloquy, which loosely traces the progress of Pompey Casmilus' love affairs with Karl and Freddy in between interludes in her office, at her home, and among her friends, is the most entertaining of Smith's novels. Pompey is highly conscious of her audience, whom she flirts with, teases, provokes, admonishes, informs, questions, and, sometimes, rejects; her tone is by turns humorous, plaintive, cruel, and lyrical. Her address to the reader on the subject of her book is characteristic in its wit, its liveliness, its velocity, its slangy colloquiality, and its bravado:

But first, Reader, I will give you a word of warning. This is a foot-off-the-ground novel that came by the left hand. And the thoughts come and go and sometimes they do not quite come and I do not pursue them to embarrass them with formality to pursue them into a harsh captivity. And if you are a foot-off-the-ground person I make no bones to say that is how you will write and only how you will write. And if you are a foot-on-the-ground person, this book will be for you a desert of weariness and exasperation. So put it down. Leave it alone. It was a mistake you made to get this book. You could not know. . . .

Foot-on-the-ground person will have his grave grave doubts, and if he is also a smug-pug he will not keep his doubts to himself; he will say: It is not, and it cannot come to good. And I shall say, Yes it is and shall. And he will say: So you think you can do this, so you do, do you?

Yes I do, I do.

That is my final word to smug-pug. You all now have been warned.

(pp. 38–40)

When, immediately after, Pompey says, "So now I will go back again to play with and pet for a moment this delicious idea . . ." (p. 40), her verbs are entirely apt. She toys with and discards an astonishingly wide range of emphemera: ruthless portraits of people; disquisitions on books; childhood memories; previously unpublished poems (Pompey assures her readers that they "get the first look in"); folk and popular songs; discussions of the Christian church, marriage, death, and the education of children; a compendium of favorite quotations whose sources include Gibbon, overheard conversations, Henry Adams, and the *East African Courier;* retellings of the stories of *Phèdre* and *The Bacchae*—and more. The book's ability to accommodate the weight of this diversity, like a fairy-tale sack capacious enough to encompass an endless (and endlessly motley) assortment of objects, is due to the deftness of the narrator's conversational voice. The language of Pompey's soliloquy, if at times irritating, is also astonishingly tensile and elastic. Its velocity blurs the disparate elements of its own discourse into unity. It overtly rejects consistency and refuses to be responsible for the reader's need for resolution or explanations—a rejection made explicit in both the content and the style of the first words of the book:

Beginning this book (not as they say "book" in our trade—they mean magazine), beginning this book, I should like if I may, I should like, if I may (that is the way Sir Phoebus writes), I should like then to say: Goodbye to all my friends, my beautiful and lovely friends.

STEVIE SMITH

And for why?
Read on, Reader, read on and work it out for yourself.

(p. 9)

Despite the sassiness and effervescence that both charmed and exhausted contemporary readers, *Novel on Yellow Paper* is essentially a somber book, its gaiety born of desperation. In a 1957 letter to a friend, the critic Hans Häusermann, Smith wrote:

How right you are about the nervousness of the writing, there is some dreadful fear that pursues always, and that has no form or substance . . . It *is* like the sea, sunny and bright (sometimes) on the surface and black and so cold seven miles down, and with such pressure the water lies. . . . So now you know why I don't want to write another novel.

(Spalding, p. 180)

This pressure is evident in the book's insistent motion—Pompey seems unable to still her mind, yet even an incessant mental liveliness cannot protect her from the fear. In the midst of the bright chatter she relates her recognition of the falsity of adult love and her discovery of suicide at the age of eight, describes her pain at the agonizing death of her mother, shares a moment of anguish over her breakup with Freddy, and discovers a demon of horrific emptiness in a sea of ice cream wrappers.

So round about Hythe and all through the streets of this little town, and up on the hills by the canal, there were pieces of paper, and there were cartons that had held ice cream and there were those little cardboard spoons that go with it. And there were newspapers and wrapping papers.

There was every sort of paper there, only the devil was there too, and he was not wrapped up in paper. And I had this vision of the fiend, and he was looking like—well he was certainly not looking like that great angel Lucifer that was so fallen, so changed, but was still that great angel that raised impious war in heaven and battle proud. . . .

No this was the fiend that is so. That is so. That is.

Oh I went too far for my walk that evening and I was wishing my dear Freddy, my sweet boy Freddy, was there to bring me home, and hold my arm, and be so loving and giving, as he is so sweet. . . .

(pp. 70–71)

It is characteristic that even in the midst of relating this uncanny and frightening vision, Pompey's tone shifts with great speed. From the flat, stark repetitions of fear she moves to grandiose literary echoes, wordplay (the clichéd "Oh I went too far . . ."), and sentimental posturings. She distracts herself from the peculiarly modern devil of meaninglessness with the less frightening, because more human, presence of Milton's Lucifer and the insipid charms of Freddy. And yet the shift is also Smith's backhanded way of acknowledging the exaggeration inherent in such visions—and thus their innate comicality. In her preface to the Virago edition of the novel (1980), Mary Gordon writes that Smith's work is always "balanced between terror and hilarity" (p. vii). In *Novel on Yellow Paper* the balance is not that of the scales, which settle into stasis, but that of the seesaw, liable at any moment to lurch from an unfixed airiness, with a thudding crunch, onto solid ground, from elation at the joyous plenitude of life to an intolerable despair.

Pompey's only immediate response to her terrific vision of the fiend, the painful "tearing inside" (p. 236) that she feels after breaking off with Freddy, her helplessness during her mother's death, or her inexplicable despair is to shift the subject. Yet she is not entirely without defenses against her own desolation. As it is in Smith's poetry, in *Novel on Yellow Paper* death is the presence that saves Pompey from unbearable despair. She meditates on it at length. One of the novel's most crucial passages is inspired by Pompey's childhood memory of a maid she knew at the convalescent home. The maid's affectionate actions were like those of Pompey's mother, yet the child Pompey perceived that underneath them lay not a steady love but an absence of feeling, a void "without depth or significance" (p. 156). This perception gives Pompey her first taste of real terror and her first intuition of the benevolence of death.

It was a little early perhaps you see, to encounter the deceitfulness of outward similarity, and that perhaps is why this maid, who was so thoughtlessly and you would think harmlessly affectionate, terrified me first in such a way that I had never before been terrified, and touching my pride, sent my thoughts again toward death.

And the thought of death, and I understood it so far that it is possible to die by falling off a high cliff, or out of a high window, the thought of this death was very consoling and very comforting to me. It was also a great source of strength, so that I came out of that experience very strong and very proud.

(p. 156)

"Always the buoyant, ethereal and noble thought is in my mind: Death is my servant," Smith writes (p. 159). Later, she lectures with a parodic heartiness on the value of educating children about their power to avail themselves of death. The deliberately mocking tone and unsophisticated diction do not hide the urgency with which she insists on the relief afforded by death's accessibility.

To brace and fortify the child who already is turning with fear and repugnance from the life he is born into, it is necessary to say: Things may easily become more than I choose to bear. . . . But that "choose" is a grand old burn-your-boats phrase that will put beef into the little one, and you see if it doesn't bring him to a ripe old age. If he doesn't in the end go off natural I shall be surprised. Well look here, I am not paid anything for this statement, but look here, here am I. See what it's done for me. I'm twice the girl I was that lay crying and waiting for death to come at that convalescent home. No, when I sat up and said: Death has got to come if I call him, I never called him and never have.

(pp. 160–161)

Pompey's surname, Casmilus, underscores the centrality of death to the novel. Smith found the name in Lemprière's *Classical Dictionary*, where it was listed as one of the appellations used for the Greek god Hermes. (Actually, her edition misprinted Camilus, the correct name.) Hermes' character as trickster–messenger, a capricious and sometimes untrustworthy figure, is closely related to the quickly changing, often cruel Pompey. Even more important, his role as the conductor of souls to the underworld allowed Hermes to fly freely from life to death and back again. Like Hermes Camilus, Pompey holds dual citizenship in these realms. She is able to travel back and forth between them; in doing so, she makes the two realities one.

Not surprisingly, the novel ends with an image that brings together heroism and burlesque, veers from poignancy to absurdity, and bridges life and death. The tigress Flo, whose slapstick story concludes the book, completes its circle by balancing the image of the horse Kismet from the first page of the novel. Kismet, a "great eater," suggests the death hidden within the life force, the mingling of destructiveness with its motion, power, and appetite. Flo might be looked on as Kismet's mirror image, an exemplar of the vitality and courage necessary to embrace death.

There was pity and incongruity in the death of the tigress Flo. Falling backwards into her pool at Whipsnade she lay there in a fit. The pool was drained and Flo, that mighty and unhappy creature, captured in what jungle darkness for what dishonourable destiny, was subjected to the indignity of artificial respiration. Yes, chaps, they worked Flo's legs backwards and forwards and sat on Flo's chest, and sooner them than me, you'll say, and sooner me than Flo, that couldn't understand and wasn't raised for these high jinks. Back came Flo's fled spirit and set her on uncertain pads. She looked, she lurched, and sensing some last, unnameable, not wholly apprehended, final outrage, she fell, she whimpered, clawed in vain, and died.

(pp. 251–252)

The Holiday was Smith's favorite among her novels. In it she replaces Pompey Casmilus with Celia Phoze, who works in a government ministry. Like Pompey, Celia simultaneously savors and satirizes her London friends; labors at a dull job; writes, reads, and quotes poems; muses on a bewildering variety of subjects; and lives with a stalwart and affectionate aunt. Yet the voices of the two narrators differ, less because of an adjustment to Smith's characterization than because her own voice had changed over time. *The Holiday* finds her less energetic but also less self-conscious. A tone of melancholy passivity supersedes the air of arch skittishness. The novel accommodates more reflection and stronger physical descriptions; the schoolchildren in South Kensington, the park in Celia's suburb, the flat shore landscape of the holiday are effectively evoked. Like its predecessors, *The Holiday* is a structure built around emptiness and pain, but its surfaces are plainer, its design less baroque.

Though its first half is thickly populated with Celia's London colleagues, employers, and acquaintances, the key characters in *The Holiday* are few. Smith seems to have developed them in a series of complementary pairs, which include Celia's friend and colleague Tiny and his repugnant brother Clem; her aunt and her Uncle Heber, a vicar, in whose house she spends the holiday of the title; her mad cousin Tom, whom she fears yet considers marrying, and her cousin Casmilus or Caz, whom she loves and yet who is denied her by the suspicion that they share the same father.

This possibility can neither be proved nor disproved, leaving the cousins in a state of limbo Celia calls "eternally ridiculous and eternally unbearable" (p. 181).[2] The theme of incest is underscored by Smith's bestowal of Pompey's surname on Caz, a tactic that suggests a splitting of the previously single protagonist into a male and a female persona. Whatever her intentions, Smith has invested the unfulfillable yearning of the relationship of Celia and Caz with some of the power of the Platonic myth of creation, in which an androgynous whole is divided into halves that eternally long for reunification. Caz is, as he tells Celia, "the most flesh and blood" of any of her dreams (p. 149), and perhaps the most flesh and blood of Smith's novelistic males. Like all of her characters, he is roughly and rather vaguely sketched. Yet the interludes between the cousins have a tremendous power, particularly compared, say, with her distanced, satiric depictions of the relationship of Pompey and Freddy. Smith is never explicit, but the intensity of the thwarted physical passion between the cousins is undeniable—the language used to describe their meetings attains at times a stark simplicity rare among Smith's lively chatter.

Caz now led me away and we went off together, treading the dark forest rides until we came to a patch of bracken and trod it down and lay down together, close together against the chilly night; where we lay for an hour.

(p. 185).

The mingled poignancy and desperation of this central relationship helps suffuse *The Holiday* with its predominant sad, restless tone.

Smith wrote *The Holiday* during the early 1940's but was unable to find a publisher for it until 1949. To update it's setting to the postwar period, she revised it extensively before publication. There are oversights in her emendations—the most notable occurs in Chapter Nine, when an escaped German prisoner parachutes from a burning Hurricane. Yet Smith succeeds brilliantly in evoking "the trivial, the boring, the necessary, the inescapable" postwar period (p. 184), that era of "the war won, and the peace so far away" (p. 155), of which "it cannot be said that it is war, it cannot be said that it is peace, it can be said that it is post-war; this will probably go on for ten years" (p. 13).

The characters of *The Holiday,* though the panic and violence of war have passed, have taken with

them its intensity, urgency, and energy. Celia admits that "there is something devilish about war, devilish exciting I mean" (p. 184). What is left in its wake is deprivation without the redemptive possibility of heroism. The novel depicts a peace that has left food still scarce, London in ruins, the staff of Celia's ministry still deciphering codes, and the British Empire beginning to dismantle itself. There is none of the ease or comfort of victory. "The peace goes badly, it goes very badly for us" (p. 7), Celia remarks, proceeding on her mundane daily rounds of "this work that is so bustling and so cosy" (p. 32) while wondering what, if anything, this work adds up to.

Early in the novel, Celia exclaims rebelliously, "Yes, certainly, it is the Devil of the Meridian, it is the devil of a middle situation that has us by the throat. . . . So that is how it is and we are rightly wretched. Courage, we should rather cry: Work in silence for the time to pass" (p. 53). The postwar period is a time of what can only be called middleness, against which no action but waiting is possible. Celia's inner life also reflects the difficulties of the "middle situation." She sees herself as dark and corrupt, yet longs for innocence. She cannot believe in Christianity, which "too much bears the human wish for something finished off and tidy" (p. 43), yet she is unable to relinquish it entirely; her ambivalence makes her life a painful exile—"If we are to be taken back, oh why were we sent out, why were we sent away from God?" she cries (p. 116). Celia finds herself, as well, in middle age, a phase of the life cycle dominated by an uncongenial "intellectuality." In contrast, she feels,

. . . . *instinctuality,* that brings with it so much glee, so much pleasure that cannot be told, so much of a vaunting mischievous humility, so much of a truly imperial meekness, runs with childhood and old age; and as I am by nature of this type of person, it is perhaps because I now run in these *middle* years that I am not enjoying it but must cast ever backwards to my childhood and forwards to my old age . . .

The feeling of full enjoyment will flood in again, we must get through these middle years.

(p. 124)

Perhaps most important, like her predecessor Pompey, Celia is poised irresolute between life and death. When asked by her cousin why, if she wants to die, she does not, she answers, "One part of us

---

[2]Page references for *The Holiday* are from the edition published by Virago Press in London in 1979.

477

wants to die, I suppose, and the other part does not, and the two are always crying out against each other . . ." (p. 159). Humorously, Caz offers a metaphor that at once captures and deflates the sense of passive waiting, at once anticipatory and apprehensive, which characterizes the book.

Life is like a railway station, said Caz, the train of birth brings us in, the train of death will carry us away, and meanwhile we are cooling our heels upon the platform and waiting for the connection, and stamping up and down the platform, and passing the time of day with the other people who are also waiting.
. . . you are romantic about death. Yes, he said, the train of death that you are waiting for is an excursion train, yes, that is what it is: All aboard for a day in the country.

(p. 155)

This lighthearted, ironic view is balanced by the death wish engendered by true despair. The first morning of Celia's holiday, she makes a serious suicide attempt and is saved only by her cousin's arrival.

But now the earth's moisture, drawn in spirals round my knees, struck upward to my heart, and I was oppressed by such a sense of melancholy sweet sadness, of a tragedy of huge dimension but uncertain outline, of wrongs forgotten whose pain alone remains, that I cried out in fear and threw myself upon the ground. There is not one thing in life, I cried, to make it bearable.
I decided to go for a swim . . . I swam straight out and turned on my back to let the current carry me down into the lake. Oh, God, I thought, we are not innocent, yet innocence is what one would wish for. The water was as cold as ice. I had a sleepy feeling that I was floating away from the Ministry, and the London parties, and Lopez, and the Indian problems, and going to have a fine long sleep and no dreams.

(pp. 102–103)

The novel's postwar accidie and irresolvable relationships provide a dual focus for this despairing sadness, an emotion felt not just by the sensitive Celia but also by characters such as Tiny. All agree that it is a time of sadness, coldness, the time of a "black split heart." Yet though what Smith called a "loamish" sadness is dominant, the reader cannot ignore the joy, strain, volatility, euphoria, and terror the novel also evokes. The shifting play of emotion can become exaggerated in degree, yet entirely accurate to the swift fluidity of a sensitive—perhaps oversensitive consciousness. Celia, like Pompey, seems at times too vulnerable, too permeable, as though she lacks the protective membrane necessary to protect the psyche.

This sadness cuts down again upon me, it is like death. And the bright appearance of the friends at the parties, makes it a terrible cut, like a deep sharp knife, that has cut deep, but not yet quite away.

My teacup fell from my hand and I began to cry and scream, for there was such a pain in my heart as twisted my heart and muscles, so that I was bent backwards as though it was an overdose of strychnine.

(p. 171)

The pain in such passages becomes almost excruciating, particularly when surrounded, as it so often is, by bright chatter or intellectual play.

Late in the book, Celia's Uncle Heber is quoted: "There is no answer, he says: You would not expect an answer? No, no, I say, feeling at once immensely lightened, I should not wish for an answer, and I smile at my Uncle and I say that I suppose an answer suffocates" (p. 145). *The Holiday* risks no such suffocation. Celia's affair with Caz neither ends nor is fulfilled; the volatility of her consciousness continues, fixing on neither life nor death, joy nor despair, as a point of stasis; the postwar middleness drags on. Celia searches for the source of her sadness, wondering, "Shall I ever be rid of this misery, is it papa's legacy, or my mama's, or is it the war, or is it the guilt of our social situation that is so base bottom bad?" (p. 42), yet she can find no answer. Significantly, the novel ends on a note of indeterminacy, with the ominous but unconfirmed suggestion that Celia's holiday may not end: that she may never go, or perhaps will not be welcomed, back to the ministry at which she worked before this respite. As in so many of Smith's poems, it has been made apparent that the only resolution, the only relief, the only true holiday is death.

SELECTED BIBLIOGRAPHY

I. BIBLIOGRAPHY. J. Barbera, W. McBrien, and H. Bajan, *Stevie Smith: A Bibliography* (London and Westport, Conn., 1987).

II. SELECTED AND COLLECTED WORKS. *Selected Poems* (London, 1962; New York, 1964); *The Collected Poems of Stevie Smith* (London, 1975; New York, 1976); *Me Again: The Uncollected Writings of Stevie Smith,* ed. by J. Barbera and W. McBrien (London, 1981; New York, 1982); *Stevie Smith: A Selection,* ed. by H. Lee (London, 1983); *New Selected Poems* (New York, 1988).

III. SEPARATE WORKS. *Novel on Yellow Paper* (London, 1936, 1980; New York, 1937, 1982); *A Good Time Was Had by All* (London, 1937); *Over the Frontier* (London, 1938; New York, 1982); *Tender Only to One* (London, 1938); *Mother, What Is Man?* (London, 1942); *The Holiday* (London, 1949; New York, 1982); *Harold's Leap* (London, 1950); *Not Waving But Drowning* (London, 1957); *Some Are More Human Than Others* (London, 1958); *The Frog Prince and Other Poems* (London, 1966); *The Best Beast* (New York, 1969); *Scorpion and Other Poems* (London, 1972).

IV. INTRODUCTIONS. *Cats in Colour,* ed. and with intro. by Smith (London, 1959; New York, 1960); *The Batsford Book of Children's Verse,* ed. and with preface by Smith (London, 1970), repr. as *The Poet's Garden* (New York, 1970).

V. BIOGRAPHIES. H. Whitemore, *Stevie: A Play* (London and New York, 1977); J. Barbera and W. McBrien, *Stevie: A Biography of Stevie Smith* (London, 1985; New York, 1987); F. Spalding, *Stevie Smith: A Critical Biography* (London, 1988; New York, 1989).

VI. CRITICAL STUDIES. K. Dick, *Ivy & Stevie: Ivy Compton-Burnett and Stevie Smith* (London, 1971, 1983); D. J. Enright, "Did Nobody Teach You? On Stevie Smith," in *Encounter,* 36 (June 1971), repr. in his *Man Is an Onion: Reviews and Essays* (London, 1972); M. Tatham, "That One Must Speak Lightly . . . A Study of Stevie Smith," in *New Blackfriars,* 53 (July 1972); C. Bedient, "Stevie Smith," in his *Eight Contemporary Poets* (London, 1974); J. Williams, "Much Further out Than You Thought," in *Parnassus: Poetry in Review,* 2 (Spring/Summer 1974); S. Heaney, "A Memorable Voice," in *Irish Times* (3 April 1976), repr. in *Preoccupations: Selected Prose 1968–1978* (London, 1980); S. Wade, "Stevie Smith and the Untruth of Myth," in *Agenda,* 15 (Summer/Autumn 1977); J. Thaddeus, "Stevie Smith and the Gleeful Macabre," in *Contemporary Poetry,* 3, no. 4 (1978); M. Storey, "Why Stevie Smith Matters," in *Critical Quarterly,* 21, no. 2 (1979).

C. Ricks, "Stevie Smith," in *Grand Street,* 1 (Autumn 1981), rev. and repr. as "Stevie Smith: The Art of Sinking in Poetry," in his *The Force of Poetry* (Oxford, 1984); J. C. Oates, "A Child with a Cold, Cold Eye," in *New York Times Book Review* (3 October 1982); A. C. Rankin, *The Poetry of Stevie Smith: Little Girl Lost* (Gerrards Cross, U.K., and Totowa, N.J., 1985); M. Pumphrey, "Play, Fantasy and Strange Laughter: Stevie Smith's Uncomfortable Poetry," in *Critical Quarterly,* 28, no. 3 (1986); S. Sternlicht, *Stevie Smith* (Boston, 1990).

STEPHEN SPENDER

(1909–   )

David Adams Leeming

STEPHEN SPENDER is an enduring but neglected presence in the literary world of the twentieth century. Sometimes praised for great lyrical moments and original critical insights, he has just as often been scorned or simply passed over as the poet who wrote "I think continually of those who were truly great," but who never became great himself. Much of the treatment of Spender derives from the association of his career with that of his friend W. H. Auden.

The linking of Auden and Spender in the "Auden Group" or "Oxford School" was the inevitable result of several factors. As undergraduates at Oxford, they read their poems to each other, discussed literature and personal philosophies, and generally shared a variety of aesthetic, sexual, and political interests. The fact that Spender in 1928 printed small books of poems by himself *(Nine Experiments: Being Poems Written at the Age of Eighteen)* and by Auden on his own handpress added a Wordsworth-Coleridge note to their relationship. Later their common opposition to fascism in the context of the Spanish Civil War would draw them even closer together in the public mind. But most important, as "new poets" of the 1930's generation, publishing against a background of the socio-political upheavals of their time, Auden and Spender, with Cecil Day Lewis and sometimes Louis MacNeice, were collectively drafted by the critics to fill the enormous gap left by the slaughter of the previous generation of young poets in World War I.

If the influence of Auden was dominant in the group it was because he was a more intellectual poet, more of a theoretician than the others. As Spender noted in a 1980 interview with *The Paris Review,* because Auden was "very conscious of his own mental superiority" he was perfectly willing to insist on his point of view. His influence is perhaps most evident in the group's tendency to make poetry out of the modern industrial landscape. In the early years Auden, following T. S. Eliot, insisted on this. What Auden added to Eliot's view was an attitude toward the social decline between the wars that was less gloomy, a younger generation's sense that the decline was not altogether a bad thing, that, in fact, it provided exciting material for poetry.

As far as Spender's career is concerned, Auden's dominance was to have both a beneficial and a detrimental effect. It seems clear that Auden, always eccentric, vocal, and somewhat imperative, imposed his views on his rather reticent and shy friend. To the very end of Auden's life Spender craved his approval and reserved for his somewhat older colleague the kind of slightly resentful adulation usually reserved for demanding mentors. In his *Journals 1939–1983* (1985), Spender is perfectly candid about his feelings: "To measure my attitude to Auden, it is that of a somewhat battered observer. Moreover when a friend forms an idea of one when both he and you are very young and retains the same attitude throughout one's life, one feels a bit resentful" (p. 356).

It is true that during the Oxford years Auden rightly prevailed upon Spender to curb his Romantic tendencies as a poet, but it is also true that the attachment to Auden placed Spender in the position of having to be constantly compared to a poet of entirely different sensibilities and talents. Thus it is commonplace that Spender is overshadowed by Auden. Compared to Auden, his detractors say, Spender is a minor writer, one whose personal vagueness and old-fashioned English awkwardness are mirrored by clumsy lines and imprecise thoughts. Spender himself, always self-effacing and shy, seems to join happily in the criticism: "My mind is not clear, my will is weak, I suffer from an excess of ideas and a weak sense of form," he wrote in *The Making of a Poem* in 1955 (1973 reprint, Westport, Conn., p. 49).

But to see him in Auden's light is to miss the point about Stephen Spender. While it can be useful to compare his poetry to Auden's as a means of differentiating the two poets and illustrating Spender's unique voice, it is just as important to avoid the commonplace by not evaluating Spender according to how well he lives up to Auden's understanding of the techniques and functions of poetry. As Spender stated in a 1970 interview in *The Review,* "For better or worse—probably for *my* worse—we are absolutely different kinds of writer. We really have very little in common" (p. 27). It seems fair to say that Auden was an intellectual poet influenced by the discoveries of psychoanalytical practice, while Spender, as he describes himself in his autobiography, *World Within World* (1951), was "an autobiographer restlessly searching for forms in which to express the stages of my development" (pp. 125–126).

The first thing that must be said of Spender is that the many facets of his career stand together as a coherent whole. He has been a poet in the broad sense of that word, a public presence following a vocation that has transcended his role as a writer of verse, a critic, a playwright, a novelist, a teacher, a journalist, and a recorder of significant moments with the great people of his day. By applying his considerable talents in each of these areas Spender has been faithful to a credo he articulated in 1937 when he wrote in *Fact* magazine, "the poet is essentially sensitive to the life of his time" (p. 18). Samuel Hynes in *The Auden Generation* suggests that Spender's attitude towards poetry is based on "a romantic notion of the artist, as a man with a superior morality and a higher responsibility" to reveal "the truth about historic public issues" (p. 105).

As a man not given, like Auden, to sharp wit, satire, or hard, self-contained images, Spender analyzes the public world by way of an often disarmingly honest and almost old-fashioned lyrical use of events in his own life. If that life is marked by ambiguity, by the scars resulting from a peculiarly English upper-middle-class, duty-bound background, by a naive innocence that cohabits with a tendency toward hedonism, and by a humility that borders at times on masochism, it serves well as a source for metaphors, and it provides the poetic voice that is Stephen Spender with a large capacity for spiritual and moral exploration that reminds us more of William Wordsworth, Wilfred Owen, and T. S. Eliot than it does of W. H. Auden. Spender is

an artist of conscience, in the best sense a moralist, at once a confessional poet and a socio-political one translating and probing for significance in the events of his time.

As all aspects of Spender's literary and personal life are so closely intertwined, it seems best to consider his career in a biographical context, studying the verse, the criticism, the fiction, and the journalism as pieces in a larger "poem" that Spender has been composing since the 1920's.

EARLY LIFE AND WORK

STEPHEN HAROLD SPENDER was born in London on 28 February 1909. In his parents and his relationship with them we find seemingly clear sources for much of what was to become the struggle in Spender between the public life and the confessional mode. His father, Edward Harold Spender, was a well-known journalist and sometimes politician committed to the values of the Liberal Party as articulated by Lloyd George in what can now be seen as its dying days. An author of books on Byron, on mountaineering, on home rule, on Herbert Asquith, and on Lloyd George, he was the son of the Victorian novelist Mrs. J. K. Spender. Harold Spender's ideals were those of the upper-middle-class reformers who before World War I had optimistically believed in the possibility of preserving respectability and dignity and even the class system by applying the new scientific and unsuperstitious principles to old social wrongs. Desperately clinging to those ideals after the war, Harold Spender and men like him were fervent supporters of the League of Nations and free trade. But as Stephen Spender was to realize later, looking back at his childhood in his autobiography, *World Within World,* "the war had knocked the ballroom floor from under the middle-class English life. People resembled dancers suspended in mid-air yet miraculously able to pretend that they were still dancing" (p. 2). The result for the Spender children, Christine, Humphrey, Michael, and Stephen, and others of their class, was a childhood characterized by virtuous isolation in a world drifting into chaos and immorality: "My brothers and sisters and I were brought up in an atmosphere which I would describe as 'Puritan decadence'" (*World Within World,* p. 285). The mood was tragic; calamity loomed everywhere, as evident in "My Parents," first published in 1933 as "Parents," in the collection titled *Poems.*

My parents kept me from children who were rough
Who threw words like stones and wore torn clothes.
. . .
They were lithe, they sprang out behind hedges
Like dogs to bark at my world. They threw mud
While I looked the other way, pretending to smile.
I longed to forgive them, but they never smiled.
("My Parents")[1]

Spender seems to have felt from an early age a mild aversion to his father, his ardently journalistic outlook, his commitment to public rather than personal needs. Harold Spender inhabited "a world of rhetorical situations" in which his son's having to play football was meant "to harden the tissues of my character."

Old man, with hair made of newspaper cutting
A public platform voice,
Tail coat and top hat strutting
Before your constituents' applause—
("The Public Son of a Public Man")

Yet Spender learned his father's lesson well to the extent that throughout his life he has found it necessary to turn to journalism, to public issues, even against the advice of men and women as important to him as T. S. Eliot and Virginia Woolf. He has done so out of a real moral commitment to a later version of his father's liberalism, but he has always done so with a tinge of regret for a quieter, more withdrawn life better suited to his Romantic sensibilities:

O father, to a grave of fame I faithfully follow
Yet I love the glance of failure, tilted up,
Like a gipsy's amber eyes that seem to swallow
Sunset from the evening like a cup.
("The Public Son of a Public Man")

The dark mood of the Spender childhood was compounded by the semi-invalid state of Spender's mother, Violet Hilda (Schuster) Spender. One of the poet's earliest memories was of his mother's reaction to the childrens' playing trains in the nursery above her bedroom by appearing "with a white face of Greek tragedy" and exclaiming "like Medea: 'I now know the sorrow of having borne children'" (*World Within World,* p. 3).

Still, Spender remembers his mother as being also "intelligent and sensitive," a delicate woman whose "painting, embroidery, and poetry had a sacred, unchallenged reputation among us" (p. 4). That reputation was justified when a book of her poetry was published posthumously in 1923. If she was understandably a moody woman, Violet Spender nevertheless provided her son with a set of aesthetic and personal values that could to some extent temper the public ones he inherited from his father.

Much of Spender's early childhood was distinctly colored by World War I. The family moved to Sheringham on the east coast during the war years, and some of Spender's earliest memories are of nearby military camps and Zeppelin raids and of the news that his mother's favorite brother, Alfred Schuster, had been killed on the front. War was to remain an important theme in the background that provided the setting for his life's work. Some of his best poetry was inspired by the Spanish Civil War and by World War II. War provided a dynamic context for the meeting of Spender's public and private sides and the result was an often subtle combination of deep compassion and bitter anti-war sentiments:

The killed, filled with lead,
On the helpless field
May dream pious reasons
Of Mercy, but alas
They did what they did
In their own high season.
("The War God")

Spender traces the beginning of his interest in verse and his prediliction for romanticism to a summer spent in Wordsworth country near Derwentwater in the Lake District of England. Stephen was nine years old. The extraordinarily beautiful countryside and his father's reading aloud of Wordsworth "fused" in his mind and "the seed of poetry was planted in me." The poems of Wordsworth conveyed "a sense of the sacred cloaked vocation of the poet" (*World Within World,* p. 79). Wordsworth remained a primary influence for Spender, a reminder that even public issues could be approached by way of nature and the inner self.

[1]Unless otherwise noted, all poems quoted in this essay are from *Collected Poems 1928–1985* (London, 1985).

The Derwentwater summer was the happy prelude to several years of misery. In the fall he entered the Old School House Preparatory School of Gresham's School, Holt, and was immediately overcome by homesickness of such intensity as to preclude any kind of social or academic success. Spender wrote movingly of his school experience in *World Within World*, and he used it as the basis for his first novel, *The Backward Son* (1940), a rather terrifying representation of the kind of educational and class hypocrisy against which Spender would always stand. The principled, if somewhat naive and romantic child isolated in the world of the Old School House was, as Spender later recognized, a mask for the man he would become:

The fact remains that I am and was the same person: when I was a child there were moments when I stood up within my whole life, as though it were a burning room, or as though I were rowing alone on a sea whose waves were filled with many small tongues of fire . . .

(*World Within World*, p. 304)

The Old School House experience confirmed the young Stephen Spender in his sense of his own difference. By the time he moved on to a London day school, University College School in Hampstead, he had other immediate problems to confront and was better able to cope with that difference.

Violet Spender died when Stephen was twelve; Harold Spender died when he was seventeen. After their mother's death, the day-to-day care of the Spender children was left to a pair of old family servants, later joined by a companion for Christine, and at about the age of fifteen Stephen came under the important influence of his maternal grandmother, Hilda (Weber) Schuster. Mrs. Schuster was above all a loving woman and one whose "view of life was entirely personal" (*World Within World*, p. 10). She provided her grandson with much-needed counterbalance to the public and rhetorical views of his father and the emotional distance of his mother. Like Stephen, Mrs. Schuster was an innocent; she encouraged her grandson in his appreciation of modern art and "advanced" ideas without any thought as to the "proper" interests of an upper-class English school boy. She also encouraged him in his writing of poetry. In short, she provided legitimacy to what his peers perhaps considered his oddities.

Spender had always known that his grandparents' origins were German, but it was not until he was about sixteen that he discovered that his grandfather, Ernest Joseph Schuster, had been a Jew. For Spender, always anxious to understand the sources of and the nature of his difference from others, this was an important and welcome discovery; it helped solidify his sense of virtuous isolation from the ordinary upper-class English ways epitomized by school life. He began to realize that he "had more in common with the sensitive, rather soft, inquisitive, interior Jewish boys, than with the aloof, hard, external English" (*World Within World* p. 12).

Before going off to the University College, Oxford, Spender was sent by his grandmother on a trip to the Continent. This was the beginning of what was to become a pattern. For most of his life Spender has lived almost as long a time abroad as in England. During and after his Oxford years he lived for extended periods in Germany. Later he taught and lectured regularly in the United States at the University of Cincinnati, the University of California at Berkeley, the University of Connecticut at Storrs, Northwestern University, the University of Florida at Gainsville, Wesleyan University, Cornell University, Loyola University, Emory University, and elsewhere. And he still spends a great deal of every year at a home in the south of France. The effect of Spender's living abroad has been to make his writing singularly un-insular and cosmopolitan. His concerns have been international rather than national; his poetry has been composed in the context of a wide knowledge of European and American as well as English literature. If Wordsworth has been important to Spender, so have Rainer Maria Rilke and Robert Lowell. If British public policy has been a concern, so, for instance, has censorship in the third world or the status of indigenous Palestinian Jews in Israeli kibbutzim. Spender has traveled widely in most parts of the world, not as a tourist but as a poet driven by a need and a duty to concern himself with "the life of his time."

When, after his first European tour, he entered Oxford, Spender was appalled by what he considered to be the dominance of English public school attitudes there. He resisted and masked his own extreme shyness and insecurity by affecting pacifist and socialist points of view and by associating with other outsiders. Eventually he met and became friendly with Louis MacNeice, Christopher Isherwood, Isaiah Berlin, and Auden. These connections and his reading of modernists such as James Joyce, Virginia Woolf, Ernest Hemingway, Ezra Pound, Eliot, and D. H. Lawrence, changed his idea of what art was. He began to see that "unpoetic-seeming things were material for poetry," that anything created by humans must be seen to be symbolic of "an inner state of consciousness within them" (*World Within World*, p. 86). He took in Auden's remark that the most beautiful walk in Oxford was the one along the canal near the power plant. Joyce's *Ulysses* and Eliot's *The Waste Land*, especially, were proof that "modern life could be material for art."

What excited me about the modern movement was the inclusion within new forms, of material which seemed ugly, anti-poetic and inhuman. . . . [Joyce and Eliot] showed me that modern life could be material for art, and that the poet, instead of having to set himself apart from his time, could create out of an acceptance of it.
(*World Within World*, p. 86)

Furthermore, Joyce, Eliot, and Woolf opened up new sensibilities and demonstrated that the creative process itself could be the writer's subject. And D. H. Lawrence appealed to Spender's Romantic nature, pointing the way to a modernist approach to the depiction of deep emotion and nature. What Spender learned in his Oxford reading has remained with him throughout his career. His own writing has always been based on the understanding, learned from the great modernists, that "poetry was a use of language which revealed external actuality" of all sorts "as symbolic inner consciousness" (*World Within World*, pp. 86–87). Although he later turned away from such self-conscious use of the industrial landscape, in his early poem "The Pylons," for instance, Spender makes use of singularly unpoetic objects to symbolize, as the *The Waste Land* had done, the inner consciousness of a civilization that is in danger of losing its interconnected and personal center:

The secret of these hills was stone, and cottages
Of that stone made,
And crumbling roads
That turned on sudden hidden villages.

Now over these small hills, they have built the concrete

That trails black wire;
Pylons, those pillars
Bare like nude, giant girls that have no secret.

In the summer of 1929, at the invitation of a German Jew he had met at Oxford, Spender made the first of his many trips to Germany. In Hamburg, where his host lived, he was suddenly confronted with the "fusion of naked liberation with a kind of bitter pathos" that was characteristic of Weimar Germany. "Intoxicated" by the sense of abandonment so foreign to his English experience, he eagerly embraced, physically if not spiritually, the free love, the atonal music, the homosexuality, the nudism, the bare modernist art: "It was easy to be advanced. You had only to take off your clothes" (*World Within World*, p. 96ff).

The Hamburg summer and aspects of other trips to Germany are recorded in *The Temple*, an unveiled autobiographical novel begun in 1929 and finally revised and published in 1988. *The Temple* is most successful as a semi-historical document—a resource for those interested in the mores and attitudes of young Germans between the wars. And it conveys something of the attitudes of Spender and his friends—Auden and Isherwood appear in the book as the characters Simon Wilmot and William Bradshaw—towards English repressiveness during the same period. As Spender suggests in his introduction, in writing the novel he "had the sense of sending home to friends and colleagues dispatches from a front line in our joint war against censorship" (p. xi). But there was a sense, too, of something ominous in the new life of Weimar as depicted in *The Temple*, something Spender described also in a prophetic poem about his friendship with two Germans in the summer of 1929:

Our fathers' misery, their spirits' mystery,
The cynic's cruelty, weave this philosophy:
That the history of man, traced purely from dust,
Is lipping skulls on the revolving rim
Or war, us three each other's murderers–
("In 1929")

The voice that tells the German story in *World Within World*, in the poems of the period, and in *The Temple*, revels in the freedom of this very un-English experience, but it never loses its sense of poetic distance from the events being described. Here, too, in this seemingly liberated paradise

Stephen Spender was somehow out of place, driven by his poetic vocation to see in the events he was describing the externalization of a national consciousness and, in this case, a national despair. The young men with whom the British poet frolicked were part of a generation "which had been born into war, starved in the blockade, stripped in the inflation—and which now, with no money and no beliefs and an extraordinary anonymous beauty, sprang like a breed of dragon's teeth waiting for its leader, into the center of Europe" (*World Within World,* p. 105).

POLITICS AND WAR

SPENDER never completed his Oxford studies. Determined to pursue a career as a writer, he followed Christopher Isherwood to Germany in 1930 and for the next three years lived at least half of the year there writing poetry and observing the rise of fascism in Berlin and Vienna. These years are described by Spender in *World Within World.* Somewhat older, more established in his commitment to writing, Isherwood was an important presence in Spender's life at the time. Most of all, he gave his friend confidence in his abilities as a poet. In spite of disagreements, Spender and Isherwood remained close friends until Isherwood's death in 1988.

It was in 1932, with the publication of an anthology of poetry called *New Signatures* (1932), edited by Michael Roberts, that Spender had his first taste of fame. Among the London literary circle Spender was already considered a poet as a result of his *Nine Experiments* and the 1930 publication by Basil Blackwell of *Twenty Poems,* a collection of his better undergraduate writing; but it was the *New Signatures* collection that solidified his association with Auden and Day Lewis in the minds of critics. It should be pointed out that Spender, Day Lewis, and Auden never met under the same roof until 1949, but in his introduction to the book, Roberts finds a means of creating a "school": "The writers in this book have learned to accept the fact that progress is illusory, and yet to believe that the game is worth playing; to believe that the alleviation of suffering is good even though it merely makes possible new sensitiveness and therefore new suffering" (p. 12).

It seems unlikely that Spender thought of progress as illusory. He was already interested in communism as a means of combatting fascism and soon he joined the Communist Party for a short time. The poets of *New Signatures* did have in common with each other and their older mentors, William Butler Yeats and Eliot, a sense of a society's death agony, and they shared a belief in the need for revolutionary change. They were torn between a distrust of polemical writing and a sense that in those days they had no choice but to go public against fascism. "Why should poetry be concerned with public affairs rather than with the private interests of the individual?" Spender asked in 1937. "The answer is that it is precisely within the consciousness of many separate individuals that the political struggle is taking place. . . . the central drama of our time . . . is the historic struggle as it effects the mind of the individual . . ." ("Poetry," *Fact,* pp. 18–19).

The German years culminated for Spender with the 1933 publication of his *Poems* and with an enlarged version of the same book a year later. With this little volume Spender came into his own as a poet, and over the next twenty years produced some eleven books of verse, most notably *Vienna* (1934), *The Still Centre* (1939), *Ruins and Visions* (1942), and *The Edge of Being* (1949), before Faber printed his *Collected Poems 1928–1953* (1955). New poems came less frequently after the early 1950's, but there were a few volumes, including *Inscriptions* (1958) and *The Generous Days* (1969; enlg. ed. 1971), before a new large collection, *Selected Poems* (1964), and the comprehensive *Collected Poems 1928–1985* (1985).

It is especially in *Poems* that Spender takes up the Eliot-Auden challenge to bring the powers of verse to bear on the technology, the agony, the fragmentation, and the material tyranny of his time. His subjects are "The Pylons", "The Express", "Unemployed", "The Prisoners", "In Railway Halls":

After the first powerful plain manifesto
The black statement of pistons, without more fuss
But gliding like a queen, she leaves the station.
("The Express")

In railway halls, on pavements near the traffic,
They beg, their eyes made big by empty staring
And only measuring Time, like the blank clock.
("In Railway Halls")

However imprecise the imagery in these poems, the effect of a loss of values on the inner consciousness of a civilization and of immanent disaster is clearly if subtly expressed.

Vienna, the volume that followed *Poems,* was a continuation of Spender's commentary on the decline of the civilization of his time. This commentary depicted the brutal suppression in Austria of a socialist insurrection.

> The Reichstag that the Nazis set on fire–
> And then our party forbidden–
>
> ("Perhaps")

In *Vienna* Spender attempted, unsuccessfully, to relate this political and historical event to a love experience of his own: ". . . in a world where humanity was trampled on publicly, private affection was also undermined" (*World Within World,* p. 174.) The problem with the poetry of *Vienna* is, as Spender recognized, its failure to maintain the proper tension and, therefore, the proper relationship between the public and the personal. The tragic events of the rise of fascism are treated in self-conscious images rather than in poetry grounded in the poet's person: the poem fails to "attain a unity where the inner passion becomes inseparable from the outer one" (p. 174). Most readers, however, recognized the validity of Spender's attempt.

Poems and the publications that followed established Spender more fully in London literary society. The process of his acceptance had begun in 1929 when he met Eliot, who had read some of Spender's early Oxford verse and been impressed by it. Eliot remained Spender's friend and supporter and, as a director at Faber and Faber, he became his principle publisher. The meeting with Eliot may have been the beginning of what became one of Spender's major occupations in life, the cultivation of his relations with the famous. This never became a name-dropping activity as some have suggested. Given Spender's sense of the poet's role in society as an articulator of his time, it was natural that he should seek out others bent on the same goal.

> I think continually of those who were truly great.
> Who, from the womb, remembered the soul's
>   history.
>
> ("The Truly Great")

Spender became close to the Bloomsbury group—particularly to the Woolfs—although his politics were considerably more radical than theirs. He knew E. M. Forster, Harold Nicolson, and Vita Sackville-West. He was introduced to Yeats in Lady Ottoline Morrell's living room, a meeting he describes amusingly in *World Within World,* remembering how badly the meeting went until Virginia Woolf was summoned by phone to save the day. He remembers Yeats explaining to Virginia Woolf that her novel, *The Waves,* could be understood in light of modern theories in physics and new discoveries in psychic research (*World Within World,* p. 149).

Spender's *World Within World* and *Journals 1939–1983* sparkle with such anecdotes. Few people can be said to have known and so acutely observed nearly all of the major figures in the arts from W. B. Yeats and Virginia Woolf to Allen Ginsberg and Margaret Drabble. He writes with characteristic humility in *World Within World,* "What can I feel but gratitude that I was taken into this great wave of the talent of my time? When I had bathed in it, I was imperceptibly changed" (p. 151).

CULTURAL STUDIES

SPENDER'S interest in the literary overview, in the relationship between the artist and his or her time, became evident in his first major critical work, *The Destructive Element: A Study of Modern Writers and Beliefs,* published in 1935. The central figures here are particular Spender favorites—Henry James, Yeats, Eliot, and Lawrence—each of whom is evaluated in the context of the Conradian "destructive element," the loss of values and order in the fragmented modern wasteland. Does James's world foreshadow that wasteland? How is the poetry and prose of Eliot, Yeats, and Lawrence related to it? *The Destructive Element* is Spender's most Marxist work, focusing as it does on literature in the context of the collapse of capitalist-bourgeois civilization. Later he would reject its philosophical premise, but nevertheless it is a brilliant work, the first segment in a literary commentary that continues into the 1990's.

The Destructive Element began as a book on Henry James, a writer to whose revival Spender may be said to have contributed, and whether or not Marxist in origin, it contains serious insights into James's work in the context of his era. Spender suggests that James, faced with the destructive element, "retired more and more into the inventions of his own mind" (p. 47); it was history itself that was responsible for the Jamesian late style. The same history is seen to be the source of Yeats's "magical system," Eliot's religion, and Lawrence's sexual preoccupations. But if James and the others took refuge in the subjective world of their own individuality, in James's late works, at least, Spender saw "a profound indictment of our civilization." He wondered whether it was time now for a more social and objective form of art, for a Marxist confrontation with the destructive element.

In the mid 1930's Spender continued to search in a variety of formats for an understanding of his world. His first attempt at fiction, five short stories, was published in 1936 as *The Burning Cactus.* These stories are autobiographical in that their heroes are suffused with Spender's sensitivity and his sense of isolation in a fragmented world. In the long essay *Forward from Liberalism* (1937) Spender urged liberals to accept the methods of communism in the interest of defeating fascism. The Communist versus Fascist theme from a much less Marxist perspective is pursued in Spender's first attempt at drama, a verse tragedy titled *Trial of a Judge,* produced in London in 1938 at the Group Theatre. Here Spender, having been disillusioned by his experience in the Spanish Civil War, has his judge condemn both sides for their betrayal of essential human values of justice.

In *The Still Centre* Spender's sense of the disintegration of civilization achieves its highest articulation.

> At night I'm flooded by the future
> Incoming tide of the unharnessed war.
> ("The Uncreating Chaos")

The Still Centre contains some of Spender's most memorable poetry, particularly that which grew out of his experience in the Spanish Civil War in 1937. Spender had been sent to Spain by the Communist Party as a propagandist but soon found that the stretching of truth involved in that work was incompatible with his nature. He wrote an article for the *New Statesman* in April 1937 in which he denounced the tendency of propaganda to turn the war dead into heroes in order to justify abstract political ideologies. The civil war poetry, as Samuel Hynes suggests in *The Auden Generation,* is in the spirit of Wilfred Owen, a young poet of World War I. Spender's war poetry does not take sides. Like Owen's, it focuses on human suffering and conveys the poet's moral indignation. Perhaps most important, it takes its emotional power from a deep compassion conveyed by the poet's personal relation to his subject. In these poems Spender succeeds where in *Vienna* he had failed. The public and the personal serve each other. The dead boy in "Ultima Ratio Regum," for example, is strikingly real because we feel in the poet's treatment of him a consuming passion, a sense of loss that is based not only on the poet's moral concerns but on his physical longing:

> The guns spell money's ultimate reason
> In letters of lead on the Spring hillside.
> But the boy lying dead under the olive trees
> Was too young and too silly
> To have been notable to their important eye.
> He was a better target for a kiss.

In *The Still Centre,* as the title of the volume indicates and as A. K. Weatherhead suggests in *Stephen Spender and the Thirties,* Spender seems to be seeking "unity of being or an image of the integrated self" (p. 177).

He was frantically seeking unity of being in his personal life as well. In 1936, after several difficult relationships with both men and women, Spender married Inez Pearn, an Oxford student involved with the Spanish Aid Committee. The decision to marry was impulsive on both sides: "we both saw marriage as a solution of temporary problems," a means "to fill the emptiness of living alone" (*World Within World,* p. 187). The end of the marriage in 1939 coincided with the fall of Republican Spain, further disillusionment with communism, the Munich settlement, the German invasion of Czechoslovakia, and the terminal illness of Margaret Spender, his sister-in-law and confidante. For Spender this was a difficult period. It was in all likelihood the more serious nature of his sister-in-law's predicament that saved him from despair, that and necessarily distracting events involved in the beginning of World War II.

> . . . to accept the worst
> Is finally to revive
> ("Elegy for Margaret")

It was at this point, during the "phony war" of 1939, that Spender planned the literary cultural review *Horizon* with Cyril Connolly and Peter Watson. He was already on the board of John Lehmann's *New Writing,* but *Horizon* provided his first concentrated editorial experience. Although *Horizon* became in many ways Connolly's magazine, it remained an important social and cultural place in Spender's life until the death of Connolly in 1973. Spender's most significant piece for *Horizon* was "Rhineland Journal," an account of meetings with German intellectuals during his postwar service in Germany as a civilian member of the occupying forces with a commission to report on the attitudes of the intelligentsia. A 1946 book, *European Witness,* was an outgrowth of the *Horizon* article.

Horizon was evacuated to the Devon coast during the German Blitz of 1940. Spender felt frustrated at being away from London. He could watch air raids as they occurred in Plymouth, not far away:

> A buzz, felt as ragged but unseen
> Is chased by two Excaliburs of light
> A thud. An instant gleams
> Gold sequins shaken from a black-silk screen.
>   ("Air Raid Across the Bay at Plymouth")

After an unsuccessful term as a school teacher in Devon, Spender joined the National Fire Service in London. In 1940 France fell. The potential for despair was great.

> Yet under wild seas
> Of chafing despair
> Love's need does not cease.
>   ("The War God")

And in April 1941, Spender married Natasha Litvin, a concert pianist. The Spenders produced two children, Matthew and Elizabeth (Lizzie), both of whom have made careers in the arts.

The marriage and the continued association with *Horizon* colleagues, with new Hampstead friends such as Anna Freud and her brother, Ernst Freud, as well as with older friends—Eliot, E. M. Forster, Elizabeth Bowen, and others—made the war years more than bearable. There was not a great deal of time for writing, what with the constant tension of the bombing and his duties as a firefighter, but Spender still managed to produce several important works.

The autobiographical novel *The Backward Son,* about his boarding school years, appeared in 1940, and the first of several collections of earlier and some new poems, *Selected Poems,* was also published in 1940 by Faber and Faber and Random House. It immediately became the sourcebook for those who saw Spender as primarily a poet of the thirties. *Ruins and Visions* is a revision of *The Still Centre* with a few new poems. *Life and the Poet* (1942) is, in a sense, a formal rebuttal of Spender's more Marxist position in *The Destructive Element.* In this long essay he emphasizes, much as Henry James had done in "The Art of Fiction" (1884), the necessity of allowing the artist his freedom of subject and approach. A propagandist cannot be expected to represent reality faithfully. In 1943 Spender published, with William Sansom and James Gordon, *Jim Braidy: The Story of Britain's Firemen,* an outgrowth of his wartime job. Another work related to the war is *Citizens in War—and After* (1945). And in 1945 he began a subsidiary career as an art critic with his introduction and notes to a collection of ten Sandro Botticelli reproductions.

During the middle of the war Spender privately printed a small book of sonnets, *Spiritual Exercises (To Cecil Day Lewis)* (1943), a meditation on death in the context of war. *Spiritual Exercises* (revised as "Spiritual Explorations" in *Poems of Dedication*) is part of Spender's continuing search for personal identity in a world dominated by public realities. In their spirituality the poems of this collection rank among Spender's most Romantic poetry, but the imagery is modernistic, almost surrealistic, reminding us more of Eliot in the *Four Quartets* than of Wordsworth, as seen in this untitled first poem of the series:

> Revolving with the earth's rim through the night
> We conscious fragments, pulsing blood and breath,
> Each separate in the self, yet reunite
> For that dark journey to no place or date
> Where, naked beneath nakedness, beneath
> Our human generation, we await
> The multitudinous loneliness of death.

Immediately after the war Spender returned to Germany and soon after published *European Witness* (1946), a work based on that trip and one that reflects a renewed idealism, a hope for a new Europe based on the free interplay of ideas. If this is a naive work it is nevertheless reflective of the valid hope of an artist who is true to his mission as a sounding board for his era. But perhaps the most significant work of the early postwar period is the little volume called *Poems of Dedication* (1947), containing the sonnet series "Spiritual Explorations" and "Elegy for Margaret," a long poem in reaction to the death of Spender's sister-in-law on Christmas Day, 1945. This is arguably Spender's most ambitious poem. The emotions are profound, based as they are on Spender's spiritual intimacy with Margaret and his preoccupation with death. Yet the emotional content of the poem is communicated with a clarity that owes much to the sure use of the elegiac form, with its dependency on a nature imagery compatible with the poet's Romantic inclinations. Margaret's death is universalized, like that of Milton's elegiac hero Lycidas, in the imagery of death by drowning:

> Darling of our hearts, drowning
> In the thick night of ultimate sea

Her struggle with death is crystalized in the image of

> . . . a tree choked by ivy, rotted
> By yellow spreading fungus on the bark
> Out of a topmost branch
> A spray of leaves is seen

But images of nature veil the agony as well and make the emotion bearable:

> Poor child, you wear your summer dress
> And your shoes striped with gold
> As the earth wears a variegated cover
> Of grass and flowers
> Covering caverns of destruction over
> Where hollow deaths are told.

And in keeping with the pastoral tradition, this modern Adonis is celebrated by the forces of nature, who absorb her and by so doing give death a larger meaning that transcends individual sorrow:

> Already you are beginning to become
> Fallen tree-trunk with sun-burnished limbs
> In an infinite landscape among tribal bones
> Encircled by encoraching ritualistic stones.

Even the death agony finds concrete expression in terms of "a final act of love" in nature:

> . . . the world-storm fruit
> Sperm of tangling distress,
> Mouth roaring in the wilderness,
> Fingernail tearing at dry root.

And finally, the heroine of the elegy achieves her Adonis-like resurrection, not in terms of the classical or Christian year-spirit myths, but in terms—borrowed again from nature—expressive of the poet's own idealism in the face of a world he does not pretend to understand. To accept Margaret's death is to celebrate her life and in so doing to overcome death:

> As she will live who, candle-lit,
> Floats upon her final breath,
> The ceiling of the frosty night
> And her high room beneath,
> Wearing not like destruction, but
> Like a white dress, her death.

When Spender made his first trip to America, in 1947, he went as an established man of letters to join a faculty at Sarah Lawrence College that included such notables as Mary McCarthy, Robert Fitzgerald, Horace Gregory, Joseph Campbell, and Randall Jarrell. In the summer following the 1947–1948 academic year, the Spenders visited Christopher Isherwood in Los Angeles and Frieda Lawrence and the remnants of the D. H. Lawrence circle in Taos, New Mexico. Spender, driven by Leonard Bernstein, returned to the Lawrence ranch later in the summer and stayed there for six weeks writing his autobiography, *World Within World*. In deciding to write an autobiography, Spender seemed to be signaling, perhaps mostly to himself, that he had finally achieved a tangible identity, a fusing of his personal and public life.

World Within World is a classic among modern autobiographies, an extraordinarily honest and moving portrait of an ambivalent and introverted individual whose background, historical circumstances, and apparent vocation demanded that he seek a meaningful public identity. *World Within World* is the major source for information about Spender's life and thought to the 1950's. Later, with the publication of *Journals 1939–1983,* more is revealed about Spender's private thoughts from the early period on through into the mid 1980's.

After his stay in Taos, Spender continued to cultivate his American connections. Much of 1948 was spent on lecture tours and developing further acquaintance with American intellectuals. It was also the year in which he wrote an essay for *The God That Failed: Six Studies in Communism* (1950), a work in which Spender and other intellectuals renounced communism in a series of essays.

In 1949 Spender published *The Edge of Being*, for the most part a collection of World War II poems that are much less Romantic than his Spanish Civil War poems, much more grounded in the real and not necessarily heroic concerns of survivors of the London bombings:

> Against an acrid cloud of dust, I saw
> The houses kneel, revealed each in its abject
> Prayer, my prayer as well: 'Oh God,
> Spare me the lot that is my neighbour's.'
> ("Rejoice in the Abyss")

Spender in 1949 was not, as some have suggested, a poet whose technical ability was not equal to wider experience and new depth of thought. If there is no longer the old naïveté or the sweeping lyrical lines of the early poetry, there is a new hardness more in keeping with the postwar, McCarthy era through which Spender, then in his forties, was moving. Spender held to his view that the poet's role was to be "sensitive to the life of his time."

In keeping with that role, in 1953 Spender accepted a position as coeditor of a new journal called *Encounter*. He remained with the magazine until 1967, when he discovered that some of its funding came from the Central Intelligence Agency. In spite of this questionable and covert connection, *Encounter* remained during Spender's tenure a moderately anti communist journal that published views from all sides of the political spectrum and served as a literary review as well.

Spender's position with *Encounter* tended to encourage him to address public issues. In 1952, for instance, he published *Learning Laughter*, a book on the plight of indigenous Palestinian Jewish children in the Israeli kibbutzim. He became active in movements in support of political and cultural freedom in general, most especially PEN and later the *Index on Censorship* of which he was a founder. He

attended conferences on the major postwar issues. But Spender never lost the poet's need to internalize his public life, to bring it into conjunction with more personal feelings. In 1956 he attended a meeting in Venice of Soviet and Western intellectuals where ideological debates were dominated by Jean-Paul Sartre and Maurice Merleau-Ponty, a friend who many years later would be "translated" by Spender into verse:

> I walked with Merleau-Ponty by the lake.
> Upon his face, I saw his intellect.
> Energy of the sun-interweaving
> Waves, electric, danced on him. His eyes
> Smiled with their gay logic through
> Black coins flung down from leaves.
> ("One More New Botched Beginning")

Another creative result of the Venice conference for Spender was a satiric novella called *Engaged in Writing* (1958).

In the 1950's Spender continued to search for a public and personal significance that could replace the disintegration of values he had described in *The Destructive Element* during his Marxist years. In 1953 he published a sequel to that book, called *The Creative Element: A Study of Vision, Despair and Orthodoxy Among Some Modern Writers*. Spender writes in the introduction:

The creative element is the individual vision of the writer who realizes in his work the decline of modern values while isolating his own individual values from the context of society. He never forgets the modern context, in fact he is always stating it, but he does so only to create the more forcibly the visions of his own isolation.

The Creative Element is a continuation of Spender's study of modernism. The Marxist idealism of *The Destructive Element* gives way in this study to a developing belief, already inherent in the early poetry, that the poet "must restore the lost connection between man-made objects and inner life" (p. 39), that there is a heroism in the visionary isolation of the great modernist writers—Yeats, Eliot, Rimbaud, Rilke, Lawrence—who have had to struggle against the destructive element that "was simply society itself" (p. 12). For these "visionaries" and for Stephen Spender at this stage, values, significance, and belief, are grounded in the act of creation, itself the only source of meaning.

STEPHEN SPENDER

In *The Making of a Poem* (1955) Spender collects his essays on Goethe, Auden, Dylan Thomas, and others, emphasizing the confessional tendency of English poetry, including his own, rooted, as he suggests it is, in repression and guilt. The title essay is a highly sensitive analysis of the connection between poetry and experience. It can be said to be itself a metaphor for what has been Spender's lifelong pilgrimage to establish the connections between the public and the private, between life and art.

Spender continued during the 1950's to write poetry, drama, and fiction, if somewhat sporadically, given his career in teaching and journalism. His *Collected Poems 1928–1953* appeared in 1955 with a few new poems added to ones already published. Several small volumes of verse, *Sirmione Peninsula* (1954), *I Sit at the Window* (1955), and *Inscriptions* (1958) also appeared. And Spender found time to adapt two plays for New York and London productions, Friedrich von Schiller's *Mary Stuart* (1959) and Frank Wedekind's *Lulu.*

The 1960's found Spender still wrestling in his critical writing with the question of modernism. *The Imagination in the Modern World* (1962) and *The Struggle of the Modern* (1963) grew out of lectures delivered at Northwestern University, the University of California, and the Library of Congress in Washington, D.C. In these books Spender continues to point to the characteristically modern splits between art and life and between the inner and outer life. He sees in modernism an attempt to heal the wounds by way of a creative juxtaposition of the past with the present. Joyce, Eliot, and Yeats, for instance, all use the mythic past to bring significance to the materialist present.

By the 1960's Stephen Spender had attained the stature of a major literary figure. He received the CBE (Commander of the British Empire) in 1962, and in 1965 he was named Poetry Consultant at the Library of Congress for the academic year. In 1966 he was invited to give the Clark Lectures at Cambridge University. These lectures, published as *Love-Hate Relations: A Study of Anglo-American Sensibilities* (1974), outline the general cultural and specifically literary relationship between Britain and America. His early focus is Henry James, always in his mind one of the "truly great," whose work was grounded in that relationship and who maintained European cultural and literary values while remaining sensitive to the realities that informed the

new American independence from those values. Spender traces the American literary pilgrimage through an early dependence on Europe to a new sense of *patria* based on "the severance of the American future from the European past" (p. xviii). He discusses the contemporary American threat to the European past itself. If Americans were at first overwhelmed by their European past, they have now developed a chaotic culture that defies tradition and threatens in turn to Americanize Western culture. For Europeans, America itself has now become the destructive element that, because of its commitment to instant profit or gratification, to "self-involvement," threatens the effective operation of past traditions in the present reality. "Americans fear the European past; Europeans fear the American future" (p. 62). There are various reactions to Americanization. Some in England have retreated into a Georgian past as a means of maintaining "distance and sanity." In spite of his sympathy for the "studied provincialism" of the sort practiced in England by poet Philip Larkin, however, Spender seems unwilling to dismiss the more "orgiastic" approach of America altogether. He prefers the attitude of D. H. Lawrence, another of his heroes who recognized that he had much in common with writers like Walt Whitman and Herman Melville, but maintained "a hierarchy of values within the chaotic and vague concept of 'life'" (p. 318) that marks the works of these and other Americans.

America has always interested Spender, but unlike Isherwood and Auden he seems never to have been tempted by expatriation. In fact, in spite of his international outlook Spender is much more at ease in Philip Larkin's England than he is in Allen Ginsberg's America. It seems likely that it is his commitment to the idea of the artist as social chronicler that has led to his fascination with a nation that has in so many ways dominated his era.

Spender's preoccupation with America reached a high point in the 1960's. America during the time of the student revolution fascinated him in much the way that Germany had fascinated him thirty years earlier. The ideological struggles on the American campuses where he spent so much of his time "reminded me of ideological debates in my own youth" (*Journals,* p. 258), and he decided to write about them. But first he visited Paris, Berlin, and Prague to study the revolts there. The result of his study of young students in America and Europe was *The Year of the Young Rebels* (1969), a book generally acclaimed by critics as a sensitive and perceptive view of the subject. In *The Young Rebels* Spender wonders whether the students of the 1960's will be able to avoid the pitfalls of the students of the 1930's, who succumbed to such destructive ideologies as fascism and communism.

At the age of sixty, Spender was appointed Professor of English Literature at University College London, a position he held until his retirement in 1975. In 1971 he received the Queen's Gold Medal for Poetry for *The Generous Days,* an expanded version of a book of poems published under the same title in 1969. The poet of the Spanish Civil War poems who is at once confessional and sensitive to his time is still present in these poems, but, as Doris Eder has suggested, the poems in *The Generous Days* show "a new leanness . . . compressing more meaning into smaller compass" (p. 362). If the poet still seeks a means of closing the gaps between the public and the private, between poetry and life, between bodily needs and spiritual ones, he does so with a new efficiency that Auden himself, whom Spender visited whenever he was in New York in the 1960's and 1970's, could admire. In the title poem of *The Generous Days* Spender writes:

> His are the generous days that balance
> Spirit and body. Should he hear the trumpet
> Echoing through skies of ice–
> And lightning through his marrow—
> At once one with that cause, he'd throw
> Himself across some far, sad parapet,
> Spirit fly upwards from the sacrifice,
> Body immolated in the summons.

The 1970's were a productive decade. Aside from *Love-Hate Relations* and *The Generous Days,* Spender wrote *T. S. Eliot* (1975), a major critical overview, and an anecdotal collection of essays and journal entries titled *The Thirties and After: Poetry, Politics, and People (1933–1975)* (1978) in which the author shares his unique experience of at least two generations of culture.

This same period was also marked by the deaths of old associates and friends. Auden died in 1973 and Cyril Connolly in 1974. Spender published *Cyril Connolly: A Memoir* in 1978 and edited *W. H. Auden: A Tribute* in 1975. And he worked on a formal five part elegy to Auden in the spirit of Auden's "In Memory of W. B. Yeats." As his *Jour-*

nals make clear, Spender agonized for several years over what was to be one of his finest poems. He wanted it to be a poem that would satisfy Auden's technical standards. It was almost as if he feared Auden's disapproval:

> One among friends who stood above your grave
> I cast a clod of earth from those heaped there
> Down on the great brass-handled coffin lid.
> It rattled on the oak like a door knocker
> And at that second I saw your face beneath
> Wedged in an oblong shadow under ground.
> Flesh creased, eyes shut, jaw jutting
> And on the mouth a grin . . .

Spender was in his seventies when in 1981 he traveled for three weeks with his friend David Hockney, in China. *China Diary* (1982) contains paintings and photographs by Hockney and a text by Spender. He continued to teach in the United States, as recently as the fall of 1987 at the University of Connecticut in Storrs. In 1983 he completed for an Oxford production a reworking of the Theban plays by Sophocles. These were produced again for a tour of India in 1989.

In 1983 Stephen Spender was knighted by Queen Elizabeth II. As if to round off his career, he published *Journals 1939–1983* in 1983 and *Collected Poems 1928–1985* in 1985. And then in 1989 his novel *The Temple,* which he had begun in 1929, was published. In the early 1990's he was at work on another novel and several new poems. He continued, as well, to write for literary journals and to accept interviews.

Of the later works, the *Journals,* in addition to the *Collected Poems,* deserve special attention. They are an extraordinary record of a dialogue between art and life, of a poet's conscientious attempt to listen to the messages and to comprehend the patterns of his time. They are the story of the poet at work, absorbing the world around him, recording the words and actions of the "great." Spender's *Journals,* his many works of literary and cultural criticism, and his works of drama and fiction are themselves ample evidence of his importance, and they must be included in any overall evaluation of his place in literary history, but when all is said, it is verse that has been the dominant medium in the long autobiographical poem that has been Stephen Spender's career, and it is on his verse that his reputation will most depend.

CONCLUSION

REPRESENTING fifty-six years of work, *Collected Poems 1928–1985* contains the best of Spender's poetry. The artist who emerges from this collection is not a passé 1930's poet but a major poet whose verse deserves serious reconsideration. To some extent such reconsideration has begun. Geoffrey Thurley in *The Ironic Harvest,* while still concentrating, as most critics have, on the early poems, makes the somewhat revolutionary claim that Spender was "Auden's superior as a poet . . . the most powerful English poet of his time" (p. 79). Others have reached similar conclusions. A. K. Weatherhead calls Spender "one of the purest lyrical talents of the century" (*A Library of Literary Criticism,* 1975, p. 496). For Thurley, Spender's verse is of a superior quality because it "strives more continuously than [Auden's] for a unifying context both transcending and undercutting the immediate perception" (p. 80). Spender's consciousness of his role as a poet involves a personal commitment that makes possible a moral depth that compensates for his lack of Auden's technical skill: "Both in rhythm and body of verse, Spender's poetry is more powerful and more deeply organized than Auden's" (Thurley, p. 80).

Whether or not one agrees entirely with Thurley, it can be said that he provides a starting point for an understanding of a Stephen Spender released from Auden's shadow. He isolates Spender's difference, suggesting that it is precisely to Spender's naïveté and his "clumsiness" that the particular power of his early poetry can be attributed. The naïveté is a mask for a "genuine innocence of eye" (Thurley, p. 81) that gives his verse a peculiar freshness and the clumsiness is an effect of genuine searching resulting in a sense of moral depth. If Auden's precision and dexterity and his irony are missing, there is, instead, what an anonymous critic reviewing *Collected Poems* in the *Times Literary Supplement* called "a stumbling eloquence or a sweeping gesture suddenly arrested" (1955). The images may not fully succeed visually or be used in the early poetry as efficiently as they might be, but the thought is so felt as to be deeply moving. What we see is not so much the external world as the world of the inner consciousness reflected in the external. In this connection, Doris Eder points to the surrealistic aspect of Spender's imagery and

reminds us of his interest in painting, pointing to an early poem, like "Not Palaces":

> Eye, gazelle, delicate wanderer,
> Drinker of horizon's fluid line;
> Ear that suspends on a chord
> The spirit drinking timelessness;

In lines like these, Eder sees Spender's "sensitive eye" as "a dilated pupil looking inward quite as much as it gazes on the outward scene" (p. 356). This quality and power to move is found throughout Spender's poetry, in such lines as these from the early poem "The Room Above the Square":

> The light in the window seemed perpetual
> When you stayed in the high room for me;
> It glowed above the trees through leaves
> Like my certainty.

And from "Grandparents," a later poem:

> We looked at Matthew's child, our granddaughter,
> Through the glass screen where eight babies
> Blazed like red candles on a table.
> Her crumpled face and hands were like
> Chrysalis and ferns unrolling.
> "Is our baby a genius?" he asked a nun.
> We went to the Uffizi and he looked at
> Italian primitives, and found
> All their *bambini* ugly.
> He started drawing Maro and her daughter
> Nine hours after Saskia had been born.

It is important to note here, as has been suggested earlier, that some of the early naïveté and lyricism gives way in the later poetry to more concreteness. But in both stages, the poetry reveals the deep emotional reaction of the poet to what he sees so clearly in the physical world. In the early poem light serves as the symbol of a feeling that is "explained" by the abstraction, "my certainty." In the later poem the images themselves—babies that "blazed like red candles" and "her crumpled face and hands" like "Chrysalis and ferns unrolling"— reveal the emotion directly. The poet has become more efficient, but he is very much the same poet, the poet who understands his experience by making it objectively public in art. Whether the subject matter is war or the birth of a grandchild, we are always reading the autobiography of the man whose primary and consistent goal is to be "sensitive to the life of his time."

Spender was asked in the late 1980's to write an article on his beliefs. In "What I Believe" (*The London Review of Books*, 26 October 1989, pp. 24–25) he articulates the belief system that has been the basis for a long and distinguished career as a poetic voice for his era, a career that extends from the 1920's into the 1990's. It is a belief system based on intellect and the "hero worship" of true intellectuals: "The friends of my life-time whom I have most admired and loved, the books and paintings I love—people and masterpieces I compare myself with, much to my own disadvantage—exemplify for me what I most profoundly believe. I believe in intellect. . . ." Spender defines intellect not in the sense of the mental activity of "public figures who can be induced to sign manifestos," but in a Proustian sense, the work of the intellect being the idea, the act, or the object of art that reminds us of a significance beyond our comprehension that is the source of our being. The creators of such works are heroes, the "truly great."

Who, from the womb, remembered the soul's history
Through corridors of light, where the hours are suns,
Endless and singing. Whose lovely ambition
Was that their lips, still touched with fire,
Should tell of the Spirit, clothed from head to foot in
    song.
And who hoarded from the Spring branches
The desires falling across their bodies like blossoms.
                              ("The Truly Great")

SELECTED BIBLIOGRAPHY

I. BIBLIOGRAPHY. H. B. Kulkarni, *Stephen Spender, Works and Criticism: An Annotated Bibliography* (New York, 1976).

II. COLLECTED WORKS. *Selected Poems* (London, 1940); *Collected Poems 1928–1953* (London, 1955); *Selected Poems* (New York, 1964); *Collected Poems 1928–1985* (London, 1985).

III. SEPARATE WORKS. *Nine Experiments: Being Poems Written at the Age of Eighteen* (privately printed, London, 1928).

Twenty Poems (Oxford, 1930); *Perhaps* (privately printed, 1933), poems; *Poems* (London, 1933; rev. ed. 1934); *Poem* (privately printed, 1934); *Vienna* (London, 1934), poem; *At Night* (privately printed, Cambridge, Eng., 1935), poem; *The Destructive Element: A Study of Modern Writers and Beliefs* (London, 1935; pprbk. ed., Philadelphia, 1953); *The Burning Cactus* (London, 1936, repr. 1955), short stories; "Poetry," in *Fact,* 4 (July 1937), essay; *Forward from Liberalism* (London, 1937), political essays; *Trial of a Judge* (London, 1938), five-act play; *Danton's Death* (London, 1939), adaptation of play by Georg Büchner, trans. with G. Rees; *The New Realism: A Discussion* (London, 1939), essay; *The Still Centre* (London, 1939), poems.

The Backward Son (London, 1940), novel; *Life and the Poet* (London, 1942), essays; *Ruins and Visions* (London, 1942), poems; *Jim Braidy: The Story of Britain's Firemen* (London, 1943), with W. Sansom and J. Gordon; *Spiritual Exercises (To Cecil Day Lewis)* (privately printed; London, 1943), sonnets; *Botticelli* (London, 1945), introduction and notes on ten reproductions; *Citizens in War—and After* (London, 1945), essays; *European Witness* (London, 1946), essays; *Poetry Since 1939* (London, 1946), literary criticism; *Poems of Dedication* (London, 1947); *Returning to Vienna 1947: Nine Sketches By Stephen Spender* (Paulet, Vt., 1947), poems; *The Edge of Being* (London, 1949), poems

World Within World: The Autobiography of Stephen Spender (London, 1951); *Europe in Photographs* (London, 1952), photographs with commentary; *Learning Laughter* (London, 1952), travel essays; *Shelley* (London, 1952), essay; *The Creative Element: A Study of Vision, Despair and Orthodoxy Among Some Modern Writers* (London, 1953); *Sirmione Peninsula* (London, 1954), poems; *I Sit at the Window* (Baltimore, 1955), poem; *The Making of a Poem* (London, 1955), essays on writing; *Engaged in Writing and The Fool and the Princess* (London, 1958), satire; *Inscriptions* (London, 1958), poems; *Mary Stuart* (London, 1959), adaptation of play by Friedrich von Schiller.

The Imagination in the Modern World (Washington, D. C., 1962), three lectures; *Rasputin's End* (Milan, 1963), play, with N. Nabokov; *The Struggle of the Modern* (London, 1963), essays on modern life, art, and literature; *Ghika: Paintings, Drawings, Sculptures* (London, 1964), essays, with P. L. Fermor; *Chaos and Control in Poetry* (Washington, D. C., 1966), lecture; *The Magic Flute, Retold by Stephen Spender* (New York, 1966), children's story; *The Generous Days* (Boston, 1969; enlg. ed., London, 1971), poems; *The Year of the Young Rebels* (London, 1969), essays on student rebellion.

Art Student, (London, 1970), poem; *Descartes* (London, 1970), poem; *W. H. Auden: A Memorial Address* (privately printed, 1973); *Love-Hate Relations: A Study of Anglo-American Sensibilities* (London, 1974), essays on the relationship between English and American literature; *Eliot* (London, 1975) repr. as *T. S. Eliot* (New York, 1976); *Cyril Connolly: A Memoir* (Edinburgh, 1978); *Henry Moore: Sculptures in Landscape* (London, 1978), with G. Shakerley; *Recent Poems* (London, 1978); *The Thirties and After: Poetry, Politics, and People (1933–1975)* (London, 1978), reminiscences and literary criticism; *America Observed* (New York, 1979), with P. Hogarth; *Venice* (London, 1979), with F. Roiter.

Letters to Christopher, ed. L. Bartlett (Santa Barbara, Calif., 1980), Spender's letters to Christopher Isherwood 1929–1939 and two 1930's journals; *China Diary* (London, 1982), contains paintings and photographs by David Hockney and text by Spender; *Oedipus Trilogy* (London, 1984), drama; *Journals 1939–1983,* J. Goldsmith, ed., (London, 1985); *Henry Moore: A Memorial Address* (London, 1987); *The Temple* (London, 1988), novel "What I Believe," *The London Review of Books* (26 October 1989), pp. 24–25, article.

IV. Works Edited, Translated, or Containing Contributions by Spender. M. Roberts, ed., *New Signatures* (London, 1932), an anthology of young poets; R. Crossman, ed., *The God That Failed: Six Studies in Communism* (London, 1950), contains an essay by Spender; *Penguin Modern Poets 20* (London, 1971), an anthology with J. Heath-Stubbs and F. T. Prince; *The Lulu Plays and Other Sex Tragedies,* by Frank Wedekind, translated by Spender (London, 1972); *W. H. Auden: A Tribute* (New York, 1975), edited by Spender.

IV. Interviews. P. Orr, ed., *The Poet Speaks: Interviews with Contemporary Poets* (New York, 1966), pp. 239–244; "A Conversation with Stephen Spender: The Creative Process," in *English Record,* 18 (April 1968).

"A Conversation with Stephen Spender," in *The Review,* 23 (London, 1970), pp. 21–27; "A Conversation with Stephen Spender," in *American Poetry Review,* 6, no. 6 (1977); "The Art of Poetry XXV," in *The Paris Review,* 77 (Winter/Spring 1980); G. Plimpton, ed., *Writers at Work: The Paris Review Interviews,* sixth series (New York, 1984), pp. 39–78.

V. Biographical and Critical Studies. L. MacNiece, *Modern Poetry* (Oxford, 1938; rev. ed. 1968); M. L. Rosenthal, *The Modern Poets* (Oxford, 1965); J. J. Connors, *Poets and Politics: A Study of the Careers of C. Day Lewis, Stephen Spender and W. H. Auden in the 1930's* (New Haven, Ct., 1967); A. T. Tolley, *The Early Published Poems of Stephen Spender: A Chronology* (Ottawa, 1967); Derek Stanford, *Stephen Spender, Louis MacNeice, Cecil Day Lewis: A Critical Essay* (Grand Rapids, Mich., 1969); H. B. Kulkarni, *Stephen Spender: Poet in Crisis* (Glasgow, 1970); G. Thurley, "A Kind of Scapegoat: A Retrospect on Stephen Spender," in *The Ironic Harvest: English Poetry in the Twentieth Century* (New York, 1974), pp. 79–97; A. Kingsley Weatherhead, *Stephen Spender and the Thirties* (Lewisburg, Pa., 1975); S. Hynes, *The Auden Generation: Literature and Politics in England in the 1930s* (London, 1976); D. L. Eder, "Stephen Spender," in *The Dictionary of Literary Biography,* vol. 20 (New York, 1983), pp. 351–365; R. Carter, ed., *Thirties Poets: "The Auden Group"* (London, 1984).

LYTTON STRACHEY

(1880–1932)

Michael Rosenthal

LYTTON STRACHEY'S ASSESSMENT of Jonathan Swift, in his *Spectatorial Essays,* that "the interest attaching to his name has always depended as much upon his character as upon his works" (p. 141), can aptly be applied to Strachey himself. For certainly Strachey's reputation as a critic and biographer rests as much on his unique character and the public image he created as on his literary production. A larger-than-life figure, all angles and beard and mannerisms, Strachey was an indispensable member of the Bloomsbury group, that legendary coterie of writers, artists, and intellectuals who flourished during the first three decades of the twentieth century. However formidable a person in his own right, it is nevertheless difficult to think of him outside of the Bloomsbury context. Strachey cannot be thoroughly appreciated without having some sense of the Stephen sisters, Virginia (Woolf) and Vanessa (Bell), the writers Leonard Woolf and E. M. Forster, and the art critics Clive Bell and Roger Fry, the economist John Maynard Keynes, the painter Duncan Grant, and the host of other talented, eccentric people—Lady Ottoline Morrell, Dora Carrington, and Ralph Partridge, to name a few—to whom Strachey was attached. Requiring the sustenance of the Bloomsbury friendships, he provided a powerful social presence around which the group's varied relationships cohered. More than anyone else, Strachey embodied what came to be thought of as the Bloomsbury way of life.

CHILDHOOD AND CAMBRIDGE YEARS

STRACHEY'S early years gave no indication that he would ever embody anything other than the loneliness and unhappiness frequently conferred upon shy, frail, physically awkward little boys. Giles Lytton Strachey was born at Stowey House, Clap-

ham Common, London, on 1 March 1880, the eleventh of thirteen children (three of whom died in infancy). His father, Sir Richard Strachey, aged sixty-three at Lytton's birth, was a talented man with a host of varied interests. Having served with distinction in the British army in India, he went on to make significant contributions to the running of that country. During his thirty years' service there he helped develop its canals and railways, encouraged the decentralization of financial and administrative authority, and restructured its vital Public Works Department. In his spare time he explored the Himalayas, became a decent painter, and wrote papers on a number of scientific subjects. Science, indeed, was his real passion. Twice he served as president of the Royal Geographical Society; for his groundbreaking work in Indian meteorology he received the prestigious Symons medal from the Royal Meteorological Society.

As befitted a proper Victorian gentleman, Sir Richard's interests did not include extensive relationships with his children, particularly his eleventh. Those responsibilities, along with all other matters pertaining to family management, were left to Lady Strachey, twenty-three years her husband's junior. A vivacious woman, and a lover of literature, Jane Maria Grant Strachey was superficially far more involved with her children than her husband. She read to them from the Elizabethan dramatists, entertained them by playing the piano, and shared with them her love of parlor games, puzzles, and even billiards, at which she was extraordinarily talented. But despite her energy and accessibility, she had a personal vagueness about her that prevented her from making any substantial emotional contact with her children. Looked after and even at times suffocated by his mother, Strachey was never entirely understood by her.

When Lytton was four, the family moved to 69 Lancaster Gate, which was to be his home for the next twenty-three years. Thinking back on his past in 1922, Strachey wrote in his diary that Lancaster Gate marked the beginning of his conscious life. His recollection of the house's immensity reveals more about his own sense of impotence and vulnerability than about the actual dimensions of his home. The architectural reality was clearly distorted by the feelings of a little boy oppressed and frightened by a home environment in which he could not comfortably locate himself: "Its physical size was no doubt the most obviously remarkable thing about it; but it was not mere size, it was size gone wrong, size pathological; it was a house afflicted with elephantiasis" (in *Lytton Strachey by Himself,* 1971, p. 18). The vast spaces Strachey claims to remember reveal his bewilderment in a house that he defines as "the crowning symbol of the large family system" (p. 20). His description of the drawing room—"When one entered that vast chamber, when, peering through its foggy distances, ill-lit by gas-jets, or casting one's eyes wildly towards the infinitely distant ceiling overhead, one struggled to traverse its dreadful length, to reach a tiny chair or a far-distant fireplace, conscious as one did so that some kind of queer life was clustered thick about one" (p. 20)—suggests the extent to which the young Lytton felt overwhelmed by the experience of Lancaster Gate.

With its murkiness, its genteel decomposition, and even its quirky individuality, the drawing room came to represent for Strachey the "concentrated product of an epoch" (p. 20). To peer into it was to read "the riddle of the Victorian Age" (p. 20), a complicated task in which he was more or less engaged for the rest of his life. Although as an adult he dissected some of its pathologies in *Eminent Victorians* (1918), Strachey was at the same time an authentic product of that age. If he came to abhor what he called the "restriction and oppression— the subtle unperceived weight of the circumambient air" (p. 27) of the household, he also absorbed a great deal of it. Lancaster Gate shaped his values and attitudes, fashioning in Strachey's soul a past of that same Victorian sensibility he would one day come to criticize. He concludes of the house, "To reconstruct, however dimly, that grim machine, would be to realize with some real distinctness the essential substance of my biography" (p. 27).

While life in that grim and gloomy machine was not without its pleasures, Lytton was fundamen-

tally thwarted by lack of real emotional contact with anybody in the family. The "incubus" that, he later wrote, "sat upon my spirit" (p. 27) catered to an intellectual precocity (which he could develop in isolation) at the expense of other capacities. Endlessly ill (a condition that remained with him throughout his life, no doubt as much a product of the incubus as of any somatic cause), beset by an increasing sense of his own unworthiness and unattractiveness, and without any sustaining human relationships, Lytton had no more life outside Lancaster Gate than he had within. His early schooling consisted of tutoring at home and essentially private tutoring at a small school in Dorset. When Lytton was thirteen, Lady Strachey evinced her characteristic lack of understanding by deciding that what he needed was a bracing masculine environment in which he could make friends and flourish physically. She picked Abbotsholme, a purportedly "advanced" school founded four years earlier by Dr. Cecil Reddie, to provide this. It would have been difficult to have made a worse choice.

Intent on building masculine character and rescuing England's national life from decline, Reddie claimed that Abbotsholme was based on "natural methods" and significant educational innovations. In fact, although Reddie's "natural methods" required the boys to defecate in the fields rather than in lavatories, and physical training included manual labor along with the traditional rugby and cricket, the school could not genuinely be called progressive in any serious way. Obligatory and high-minded chapel, a spartan physical regimen that included cold baths, anti-intellectualism, the ritualized bullying system in which the older boys (prefects) were entitled to tyrannize the younger (fags), and therapeutic public floggings—all these features of the conventional public school existed here as well.

Lytton, needless to say, was miserable at Abbotsholme. Although he wanted to be part of the school's life, he failed: he was not strong enough to endure the physical rigors of the place; his literary gifts were neither recognized nor rewarded; and he was treated as an outcast by the other boys, who were hardier and more adept at games. He left before the year was out, with both his health and his self-esteem in more perilous condition than when he began. Perhaps the one major benefit of the experience was his exposure to the self-righteousness and self-importance of Dr. Reddie, who clearly contributed to the scathing portrait of Dr. Thomas Arnold of Rugby in *Eminent Victorians.*

The next educational choice was only slightly better. Leamington College was a decidedly minor public school with all of the limitations of such institutions. Foremost among them was the cruelty meted out to those who did not conform. Lytton's ungainliness and lack of stamina made him an inevitable target. Immediately called "Scraggs," which seemed the proper sound to fit his peculiar frame, he was relentlessly bullied at the outset. But gradually his tormentors lost interest, and Strachey even began to ingratiate himself into various school groups. He participated in theatrical events, and, by the end of his time there, was performing quite creditably in his academic work. While real friendships continued to elude him, at least he began to explore the possibilities of such relationships. Twice Lytton fell in love—the sort of schoolboy crushes common in public schools where older, accomplished boys are frequently idolized by the more timid and less renowned. Neither passed the stage of unrequited romantic fantasy, but they did represent his first stumbling efforts to break out of his loneliness and into communion with others. His infatuation with these schoolboy heros was a benign expression of Lytton's desperate need, which remained constant throughout his life, to invest each new lover with all the burdens of his unfulfilled longings for personal completion and acceptance. Strachey's yearning to escape the confines of his awkward self for the perfection he imputed to others never wavered, thereby guaranteeing eventual disappointment.

Upon leaving Leamington in 1897, Strachey was judged by his mother to be too young—he was seventeen—for Oxford or Cambridge, and so the third unfortunate choice was made for him: Liverpool University College, where he would spend the next two years. His time at Liverpool was unutterably boring. Although he read widely and began writing poetry, he was even lonelier here than he had been at Leamington; indeed, Leamington looked good by comparison to the depressing solitude of Liverpool. "My life is a turmoil of dullness," he wrote in his diary during this period (in *Lytton Strachey by Himself,* p. 88). The major happy consequence of his time at Liverpool was the friendship he formed with Professor Walter Raleigh, with whom he studied English literature and whose interest in him helped Lytton survive the bleakness of those two years.

Lytton's liberation from both the stultifying influence of Lancaster Gate and the boredom of inappropriate schools occurred when he went up to Cambridge in 1899. For Strachey, like so many other sensitive, intellectually gifted young men of his generation who had been bullied and mocked at the public schools where they were misfits, Cambridge was an unimaginable paradise. Suddenly they were immersed in a world where talents other than skill at games were affirmed, where idiosyncrasy openly abounded, where men of like mind could come together to share their interests in art, literature, and philosophy. The crippling conformity of the public schools gave way to a marvelous new freedom in which people felt no obligation to be other than themselves.

In addition to giving Strachey license to develop (rather than obscure) his odd individuality, Cambridge supplied him with a set of friends who were to remain lifelong companions. Through the Midnight Society, a reading club he helped to form at Trinity College, he became closely tied to Clive Bell, Leonard Woolf, Saxon Sydney-Turner, A. J. Robertson, and Thoby Stephen (brother of Virginia and Vanessa). More important, in 1902 Strachey was elected to the Cambridge Conversazione Society, generally known as the Apostles. Founded in 1820, the Apostles was probably the most distinguished and select society in the entire university. It met on Saturday evenings to hear a brief paper given by one member, to which all Apostles present would reply in turn. Each session ended with a vote taken on some proposition or problem connected with the paper. Election to the society was an enormous honor, and Strachey was thrilled to be asked to join the company of Forster, Bertrand Russell, Keynes, G. E. Moore, and Fry, among others. He relished the friendships and intellectual excitement he found there, as well as the considerable boost to his self-esteem conferred by membership in such an august group. Apostleship, in a sense, officially recognized the completion of his journey from bumbling schoolboy outcast to significant Cambridge figure.

Strachey spent six years at Cambridge: three as an undergraduate, three in an unsuccessful effort to gain a fellowship. He left having achieved substantial notoriety as a formidable intellectual and an imposing, at times terrifying, personal presence, outspoken in his intolerance of religion and in his defense of homosexuality. His highly evolved personal style contributed to his reputation: there was a cruel Strachey wit, cutting through pretense and pomposity; a Strachey way of walking, of sitting, of standing; even a Strachey voice—high-pitched and supercilious—that many undergraduates sought to emulate. Although the torments of self-doubt never subsided, Strachey succeeded in fashioning an image that exuded authority and confidence. Whatever else he managed to do at Cambridge, his creation of himself stands as his greatest achievement.

By the time he left Cambridge in 1905, Strachey had already started, rather tentatively, to embark on a career as journalist and writer. His first published essay, a scathing review of Elizabeth Lee's translation of selections from La Bruyère and the marquis de Vauvenargues, appeared in the *Independent Review* in 1903, when Lytton was twenty-three. "Two Frenchmen" is an astonishingly sophisticated performance, full of the wit and sparkle characteristic of his mature essays. Strachey's prose was elegantly crafted from the very start of his career. Its polish and balance match that of the men he is reviewing. He writes of La Rochefoucauld: "Too proud not to be a master of his art, too magnificent to care whether he was or no, he shows, in every line he wrote, that supreme detachment which gives him a place either above or below humanity. When he speaks of love, he is as icy as when he speaks of death; when he speaks of death, it is as if he were already dead" (in *Literary Essays,* p. 101). Here too we find his splendid contempt for the sloppy and second-rate: while Elizabeth Lee claims that Vauvenargues never understood the art of writing,

he understood it better than Miss Lee, whose English is never good. . . . And if Miss Lee has failed with Vauvenargues it was not to be expected that she would succeed with La Bruyère. This would have required a special talent, a fine instinct, and a reverent mind; without these qualities it were better to leave untouched one of the great writers of the world.

(p. 103)

"Two Frenchmen" was the first of a half-dozen essays Strachey contributed to the *Spectator* and the *Independent Review* while at Cambridge. Along with the formal papers delivered at the Apostles meetings, they constituted the bulk of the evidence on which Strachey could test the credibility of his fervent yearnings for public success. Accomplished as some of this work was, however, it could do little to protect Strachey from the utter despair generated by his inability to win a fellowship. The rejection of his lengthy dissertation on Warren Hastings, a well-known English colonial administrator in India, shattered Lytton's arduously constructed and always precarious self-confidence. Seeing two-and-a-half years' work result in nothing exacerbated the sense of worthlessness that he was always fighting to subdue. Exiled from the Cambridge he loved and forced to return to the gloom of Lancaster Gate, he felt old and depressed, a total failure. At twenty-five, his life seemed over.

EARLY BLOOMSBURY

ALTHOUGH his nontriumphant reentry into the confines of Lancaster Gate was painful, Strachey refused to succumb to the defeat he thought he had unjustly suffered at the hands of the Trinity College examiners. His ambitions were too great for that. Since writing was not only what he did best, but also what appeared to be the only way to earn money, he began churning out reviews regularly for the *Independent Review, New Quarterly,* and, most frequently, the *Spectator,* edited by his cousin St. Loe Strachey. Equally important, he remained actively engaged in the gradually expanding network of friendships, initially formed at Cambridge but now reestablishing itself in London, that came to be known as the Bloomsbury group. Originally used by Molly MacCarthy as a lighthearted descriptive label for the loosely connected set of friends (she actually called them the "Bloomsberries") who used to meet at several apartments at Gordon Square in the Bloomsbury section of London, the term rapidly took on large cultural meanings. Such critics as Wyndham Lewis, F. R. Leavis, and D. H. Lawrence saw Bloomsbury as representing all that was effete, snobbish, and morally trivial, in art and in life. For them, Bloomsbury consisted of a pack of sterile, socially useless aesthetes who were committed to pursuing their own interests at the expense of anyone who opposed them. Stopping at nothing to destroy those who did not share their dubious values, Bloomsbury was taken as vivid evidence of the decline of modern culture. Furthermore, to appreciate the evil of Bloomsbury, one had only to know Strachey, the embodiment of reprehensible behavior and attitudes.

Time has been kind to the Bloomsbury group, however. Far from being reviled, its members are now celebrated as socially progressive and artistically important, praised for their openness in sexual matters, their freedom from gender stereotyping, their refreshing skepticism about received moral and institutional truths. No longer cautionary, Bloomsbury has become exemplary, and Strachey a figure for whom no one need apologize.

Despite the conflicting metaphoric meanings attached to the name, the fact is that Bloomsbury was never a club or movement, nor did it have a coherent (or even incoherent) social policy. It had no membership list, no oath of initiation, no dogma. Instead, it consisted of a fluid, constantly expanding group of friends (most of whom lived elsewhere) who shared, as friends usually do, a number of assumptions about life. They believed in the importance of art and friendship (both of which had been espoused as prime values by Moore, a Cambridge philosopher whom Bloomsbury revered); they tended not to believe in religion, placing their faith instead in the power of the human intellect. They were irreverent toward authority and tradition, largely upper middle class, at times condescending, and above all enormously talented and productive, leaving behind them a wealth of serious work in fiction, painting, sculpture, economics, biography, and art and literary criticism. One of the assumptions not shared concerned the relative merits of each other's work, as all tended to be quite critical about what everybody else was doing.

Among friends who were equal, it is perhaps fair to say that Lytton was more equal, less by virtue of accomplishment than by strength of personality and character. His withering honesty, his pleasure at shocking in the service of doing away with stale and restricting conventions, and his willingness to fight for his beliefs generated a moral force that tended to sweep all before him. He single-handedly changed the behavior patterns of his friends. Clive Bell notes in *Old Friends* that a letter he received from Strachey on 25 November 1906, beginning "Dear Clive," marked the first time that

Bloomsbury friends, who had formerly addressed each other by last name, used Christian names in their correspondence with each other. "It was entirely Lytton's doing," Bell writes. "Henceforth between friends manners were to depend on feelings rather than conventions." Similarly, Strachey's pointing to a stain on a friend's dress and asking if it were semen initiated an entirely new frankness in speech regarding sexual matters among the Bloomsberries. David Garnett attributes his own conversion to a life of libertinism to his having attended a public reading of *Ermyntrude and Esmeralda,* Strachey's mildly pornographic and rather silly story poking fun at traditional sexual pruderies. Those critics, such as F. R. Leavis, who object to Bloomsbury largely because of a personal abhorrence of Strachey were at least right in understanding the privileged position Strachey held among his friends.

Lytton's social growth following his return from Cambridge was not without its emotional complexities. Unabashedly homosexual, he fell passionately in love with two fledgling painters: first Duncan Grant, then Henry Lamb. Both were handsome younger men, radiating that physical beauty to which Lytton, consumed with a sense of his own unattractiveness, was especially vulnerable. Strachey's extreme possessiveness and ready sexual jealousy made long-term relationships impossible, and the frustration and final collapse of these two liaisons—most painfully with Grant, who also was sexually entangled with Strachey's good friend Maynard Keynes—anticipated the course of love affairs during the rest of his life. The turmoil surrounding his difficulties with Grant also helped precipitate one of Strachey's oddest acts: his marriage proposal to Virginia Stephen on 17 February 1909. No plausible explanation exists for such behavior other than its being a rather bizarre attempt to escape from the tribulations of his homosexuality and his general unhappiness into the socially respectable state of marriage. To his horror, Virginia accepted. The ludicrous notion of such a union fortunately occurred to both of them at about the same time. Strachey wrote to his brother James a month later, "It was an awkward moment, as you may imagine, especially as I realized the very minute it was happening, that the whole thing was repulsive to me. Her sense was amazing, and luckily it turned out that she's not in love. The result was that I was able to manage a fairly honourable retreat" (*Virginia Woolf and Lytton Strachey: Letters,* p. 32). Virginia and Lytton remained good friends, and he never again resorted to such an extreme solution to his problems.

During this period of sorting out his identity, Strachey decided on two measures that helped bolster his self-image: he grew a beard, which provided him with both a distinctive and distinguished feature and a means of obscuring, to some degree, the exaggerated angularity of his face; and he dropped the Giles from his name, opting for the more theatrical Lytton. With beard and name in place, Strachey continued to fashion himself into the formidable presence he wanted to be.

The centrality Lytton achieved among his Bloomsbury acquaintances was not immediately matched by comparable public recognition. Although an industrious reviewer and essayist (between 1905 and 1910 he contributed nearly ninety reviews to the *Spectator* alone), he nevertheless was writing essentially journalistic pieces that necessarily partook of the ephemeral nature of the genre. Although Strachey's essays are always sensible, they are not the stuff of which reputations are built. The satisfaction in reading them comes less from an encounter with penetrating new insights than from the exposure to a cultivated sensibility capable of expressing ideas in an original—and often arresting—way. Small pleasures, perhaps, but real, as when, in comparing the genius of *King Lear* with the pedestrian version of the same material that preceded Shakespeare, Strachey comments in his *Spectatorial Essays,* "Ingredients which in a common vessel will give you tolerable broth will raise immortal apparitions if you put them in a wizard's cauldron" (p. 66). Even taken together, the individual merits of Strachey's critical essays still do not add up to a significant body of work. His criticism is of a purely belletristic sort in which a civilized intelligence roams freely over a range of literature, lingering, without lengthy analysis, over things that interest it, whether Blake's punctuation or Pope's couplets or Thomas Browne's prose style. By its nature this intelligence speaks in a minor voice, avoiding large claims and extreme positions. If such literate reviewing has a distinguished lineage and undoubtedly will always have some role to play in our culture, it was nevertheless not the kind of writing designed to satisfy Strachey's de-

sire for wider acclaim. For that he would need a book.

LANDMARKS IN FRENCH LITERATURE

BUT the book would have to be his second, *Eminent Victorians,* not his first, for *Landmarks in French Literature* (1912) was hardly the work to appeal to a large audience. Commissioned by H. A. L. Fisher for the Home University Library series, it was intended as a one-volume survey of French literature from its origins to the nineteenth century. In a sense Strachey was an odd choice for the assignment, for he was by no means an authority on French literature. Fisher, however, had been impressed by some of Strachey's occasional pieces on French subjects, particularly "Two Frenchmen," and admired his prose style. He convinced the editors of the series that Strachey was right for the job; and in 1910, armed with the model of John W. Mackail's *Latin Literature* (1895), Strachey began his reading for it. Covering the development of French literature in an impossibly small space (roughly fifty thousand words), the book immediately reveals the constraints of its form: it is necessarily superficial, marked as much by those authors it mentions only in passing—Alain Le Sage, Madame de Sévigné, Choderlos de Laclos, and Abbé Prevost, for example—as by those it excludes entirely: Emile Zola, Arthur Rimbaud, Gérard de Nerval, and Stéphane Mallarmé, among others.

Indeed, there is little room in *Landmarks* for more than a general narrative of how one age follows or resists the last, interspersed with capsule descriptions of writers' achievements and some of their significant works. What obviously cannot be included is any complex sense of how artists emerge from or are shaped by their age, detailed examination of specific texts, or sustained discussion about the value of individual authors. Since Strachey was not in any case particularly interested in working out complicated critical judgments, the absence of these in the book is not surprising, and owes as much to his predilections as to space constraints. Metaphoric effusions about beauty and genius generally tend to substitute for the rigors of fine-grained analysis.

Minimally useful as a convenient outline for students of French literature, *Landmarks* is not without interest for students of Strachey. In addition to seeing how he is able to elaborate what is essentially the methodology of his essays and reviews into a book-length study, as well as experiencing his passion for French, we can trace, through some of his enthusiasms, ideas central to his moral and intellectual development. His celebration of François Rabelais, for instance, who rejected the "superstitious gloom and the narrow asceticism of the Middle Ages" (p. 35) in favor of the energy and light of the Renaissance, points clearly to the path Lytton trod away from what he perceived as the stultifying taboos of Victorianism. Rabelais's "hatred of stupidity" and the "pedantic education of the monasteries," his "jovial acceptance of the physical facts of life" (pp. 35–36) are Strachey's as well and define exactly some of the major issues with which he was obsessed throughout his life. Similarly, his enormous admiration for Voltaire's "abhorrence of fanaticism" and his commitment to rooting out the "superstitious bigotry" (p. 178) that has always made possible hideous acts of violence, almost seems to announce the central focus of *Eminent Victorians.*

Although *Landmarks* was generally well received, it is difficult to make much of a case for it today. Its strengths are the strengths found in the essays: Strachey's intelligence, his wit, his capacity for such happy formulations as Bossuet "saw all round his age, but he did not see beyond it" (pp. 119–120). Its weaknesses, in addition to the superficiality imposed by the format, stem largely from the fact that serious literary criticism was not altogether congenial to Strachey. He was infinitely more comfortable with civilized discourse about the glories of literature than he was grappling with the circumstances that produced those glories or dealing with the richness of complicated texts. The final paragraph of the book, combining the vague rhetoric to which he was prone with his genuine feeling for French literature, neatly summarizes the mixed nature of his achievement:

Finally, if we would seek for the essential spirit of French literature, where shall we discover it? In its devotion to truth? In its love of rhetoric? In its clarity? . . . The one high principle which, through so many generations, has guided like a star the writers of France is the principle of

deliberation, of intention, of a conscious search for ordered beauty; an unwavering, an indomitable pursuit of the endless glories of art.

(p. 247)

EMINENT VICTORIANS

REGARDLESS of its merits, the writing of *Landmarks* was an important event for Strachey, heralding what he called his "Spiritual Revolution." The responsibility placed upon him by the commission, and his capacity to put together a serious book within a year, provided him with a vital infusion of self-confidence. No longer simply a reviewer and occasional essayist, he was now very much an author. Having finished one book, he was prepared to start another; and in the fall of 1912, as he was awaiting the publication of *Landmarks,* he was beginning to mull over some inchoate ideas about Victorian biographies that gradually evolved into the conception for *Eminent Victorians.*

Strachey's early notions about the book were quite different from what emerged six years later. He originally planned a volume of about a dozen brief biographies, tentatively titled "Victorian Silhouettes," treating both scientists, who were largely to be admired, and nonscientists, who were mainly to be criticized. In addition to the four—Cardinal Manning, Florence Nightingale, Thomas Arnold, and General Gordon—who made their way into the completed book, the original list of possibilities included Charles Darwin, John Stuart Mill, Benjamin Jowett, Thomas Carlyle, G. F. Watts, the duke of Devonshire, Professor Henry Sidgwick, and Lord Dalhousie. As Strachey's thinking about his project deepened, his disparate candidates for portraits began to sort themselves into a more coherent book than he had first anticipated, and one with a rather different tone. The outbreak of World War I contributed significantly to the sharpening of the book's focus, for Strachey came rapidly to feel that the mindless slaughter was both futile and avoidable, a product of the worship of power, the self-delusion, the hypocrisy of the previous generation. From a pleasant retelling of assorted Victorian lives that "might be entertaining if it was properly pulled off," as Strachey wrote to Ottoline Morrell in 1915 (in Holroyd's *Lytton Strachey*), the book turned into a fiercely sustained (if no less entertaining) criticism of corrupted Victorian ideals and mythmaking.

The moral energy flowing through *Eminent Victorians* was not limited to the book. Strachey's abhorrence of the war led him, in 1916, to file for conscientious objector status, a courageous action to take in a country that did not look kindly upon such behavior. Although Strachey's physical frailty was in any case guaranteed to render him unfit for military service (as indeed it did), he chose instead to state his principled opposition to the war, prepared, if necessary, to go to prison for his conviction that "the whole system by which it is sought to settle international disputes by force is profoundly evil; and that, so far as I am concerned, I should be doing wrong to take any active part in it" (in *Lytton Strachey by Himself,* p. 136). In rejecting his petition, the Hampstead Advisory Committee gave Strachey an opportunity for one of his deftest mockeries of fatuous respectability. When asked the outrageous question invariably asked of all those opposed to the war—what he would do if he saw a German raping his sister—Strachey, whose homosexuality was well known, immediately replied that he would try to interpose his body between the two. There was no response.

Not even Strachey could have predicted the brilliant success of *Eminent Victorians.* Reprinted in Britain six times in the first year alone, it also sold extremely well in America and was soon translated into French, German, Italian, Spanish, and Swedish. If it is difficult now to appreciate fully how reinterpreting four Victorian lives could produce such an enormously popular book, it is important to recognize the disillusion and exhaustion throughout England and Europe spawned by the war. Strachey's artful irreverence, his insistence on seeing beneath facades to underlying—and not altogether pleasing—truths of human nature, delighted those weary of the lies and nationalistic nonsense they had been fed for four years. His impertinence toward a hallowed Victorian past was a liberating gift to them. British critic Cyril Connolly perhaps best assessed its importance when he suggested, "It might be described as the first book of the 'twenties. . . . It appeared to the post-war young people like the light at the end of a tunnel" (quoted in Holroyd, rev. ed., pp. 731–732).

The book's originality consists not just in its fresh view of established figures but in its methodology as well. The truth of an individual or an era, Strachey argues in the preface, cannot be found by the accretion of all known facts; rather, it is discovered by the delicate intuition of the biographer (or historian) extracting the illuminating insight from the "great ocean of material" (p. v) surrounding each subject. Compressing four lives into one volume, the very form of *Eminent Victorians* is intended to make the point that one arrives at biographical truth not through compiling turgid masses of information but through the careful sifting and shaping of that information. Skillful brevity, not implacable industriousness, becomes the hallmark of the true biographer. In providing the postwar generation with a refreshing view of its past, Strachey also sought to free biography from its dependence on "those two fat volumes, with which it is our custom to commemorate the dead" (p. vi).

Not that Strachey refused to avail himself of those volumes. On the contrary, he was content to extract his lives from the existing secondary and biographical material about them. Unlike the modern biographer, who relishes the search for useful primary sources, Strachey had no difficulty accepting the scholarship of others as the basis of his own work. His achievement was as an interpreter rather than as an original investigator.

In his preface, which is a marvelous mixture of irony, disingenuousness, and confusion, Strachey argues that he is not interpreting so much as simply laying "bare the facts of some cases, as I understand them, dispassionately, impartially, and without ulterior intentions" (p. vii). His choice of subjects, he claims, is haphazard, "determined by no desire to construct a system or to prove a theory, but by simple motives of convenience and of art" (p. vi). Needless to say, Strachey's stance as objective biographer is nothing more than a deliciously wrought pose. The coherence of the book, with its unified moral focus, makes it clear that the four lives were not selected arbitrarily, but instead constituted for Strachey part of the truth of the Victorian age he was intent on exposing. In this regard, his comment that "human beings are too important to be treated as mere symptoms of the past" (p. vi), while admirable in itself, is completely misleading. For it is precisely as symptoms of the past or, more specifically, as symptoms of Victorian pathologies that Strachey is drawn to his subjects. Manning, Florence Nightingale, Arnold, and General Gordon together form the case studies on which he documents his diagnosis of the age.

It is important to remember that Strachey's anti-Victorianism emerged from a moral sensibility formed in the Victorian hothouse of Lancaster Gate. All of Bloomsbury's denizens, no matter how advanced their views on certain subjects, particularly sexual ones, brought with them much Victorian baggage from their pasts, and none more so than Strachey. The perspectives from which he criticized Victorian abuses and excesses were as much Victorian perspectives as anything else. *Eminent Victorians* is not the wholesale rejection of Victorian values it is sometimes taken to be but, rather, a focused criticism of particular forms of exploitation and dishonesty that did not come to an end with the death of Queen Victoria. In addition to its marvelous wit and elegance, *Eminent Victorians* retains a moral relevance that keeps it very much alive today.

"CARDINAL MANNING"

THE first—and most unrelenting—of the four essays, which Strachey came to see as the separate movements of a string quartet, deals with Henry Edward Manning, who left the Church of England and ended up a powerful cardinal in the Church of Rome. In Manning's career Strachey establishes the central themes that resonate throughout the book: his hatred of religion, of intellectual dishonesty, of the myriad ways people serve their own interests while pretending to serve those of others. For Strachey, Manning is the paradigm of the individual whose lust for worldly power, albeit in the spiritual realm, becomes his sole consuming obsession, compromising his humanity in the process. Strachey contrasts the flawless calculation behind Manning's conversion and rise through the church hierarchy with the similar path taken, for altogether different reasons and in an altogether different way, by Cardinal Newman. The Newman-Manning opposition, insisted upon throughout the essay, provides an effective structural principle. Newman: artistic, humble, impeccably honest. Manning: political, ambitious, completely expedient. Strachey uses Newman's spiritual purity as a scourge to flay Manning's worldly aspirations.

But even more devastating to Manning's charac-

ter than the counterpoint posed by Newman is the fierce and at times outrageous irony and innuendo of Strachey's prose. The movement from the general literary survey of *Landmarks* to the moral intensity of *Eminent Victorians* required a significant change in Strachey's style. The pleasant, sensible style with which Strachey takes the reader through eight or so centuries of French literature would not do for the scathing assault on the varieties of mendacity he was pursuing here. For the task of exposure he would need a far more acerbic, incisive language than he chose to employ in the earlier book.

From the very first page it is clear that the transformation from affable tour guide to implacable moral assessor has been complete. Sentences fairly crackle with irony as Strachey punctures all of Manning's pretensions at sanctity, undercutting all explanations of his behavior other than the basest self-interest. Every detail is carefully crafted to further the impression of a man endlessly scheming for self-advancement, for whom life in the relatively parochial Church of England would never suffice. Relating a trivial incident in which the young Manning outwitted a schoolmaster, for example, Strachey elaborates it into a significant pattern of adult behavior by portentously commenting that on this occasion "he gave proof of a certain dexterity of conduct which deserved to be remembered" (p. 7). Innuendo casts suspicions on even the blandest of actions. When his father's bankruptcy dashed his political ambitions, Manning was encouraged to think instead of heavenly goals by a sister of one of his Oxford friends, Strachey tells us, "as they walked together in the shrubbery" (p. 8). His youthful marriage is made to seem but another calculated decision toward furthering a brilliant career. Forgetting about Miss Deffell, the woman, according to Strachey, whom he originally loved, Manning "married his rector's daughter. Within a few months the rector died, and Manning stepped into his shoes: and at least it could be said that the shoes were not uncomfortable" (p. 9).

If marriage was the first step in the right direction, his wife's premature death was even more important, a loss the future cardinal would one day include "among 'God's special mercies' " (p. 17). Strachey concludes his discussion of Manning's marriage by noting that in later years, when obviously it was not convenient to acknowledge that he had ever been married, "the memory of his wife seemed to be blotted from his mind; he never spoke of her; every letter, every record, of his married life he destroyed" (p. 10).

By the end of the brief first chapter (from which all these quotations are taken), Strachey has effectively demolished Manning's claim to any credibility. Using these same techniques for the rest of the essay, Strachey presents every part of Manning's life as a consciously contrived effort to achieve through the church the honors and glory he had originally hoped to find in politics. Perhaps the most notorious example of Strachey's skill at insinuation concerns the interview Manning had with the pope before his conversion. Noting that during his time in Rome, Manning kept a detailed diary of conversations with nuns and priests, Strachey observes as a remarkable omission that there is no substantive description of his meeting with Pius IX. Speculating in the next chapter on the reasons for Manning's conversion, and pointing out that Manning was not a man who "was likely to forget to look before he leaped" (p. 60), Strachey returns to the interview three years earlier, curious to know what had taken place. With a marvelous indifference to acceptable biographical method, he rhetorically supplies the damning evidence he could not possibly know: "What did Pio Nono say? It is easy to imagine the persuasive innocence of his Italian voice. 'Ah, dear Signor Manning, why don't you come over to us? Do you suppose that we should not look after you?' " (p. 60).

As unforgiving as he is of Manning, Strachey is that accepting of Newman. The ironies with which he depicts the meanly ambitious Manning turn to loving effusions when describing Newman: "a creature of emotion and memory, a dreamer whose secret spirit dwelt apart in delectable mountains, an artist whose subtle senses caught, like a shower in the sunshine, the impalpable rainbow of the immaterial world" (pp. 16–17). A man of ideas rather than of action, Newman was led to Rome by the logic of his own theological beliefs rather than, as Strachey suggests is true for Manning, some sense of personal gain. Once the two men arrived at Catholicism, Manning came to see Newman's purity and reputation as a threat to his own status. It was, of course, no contest; Newman was defenseless in the face of Manning's rapacity. On the issue of whether Newman could return to Oxford to establish an oratory Strachey writes, "It was the meeting of the eagle and the dove; there was a hovering, a swoop, and then the quick beak and the relentless talons did their work" (p. 87). Denied permission as a result of Manning's efforts, Newman was successfully crushed.

Although the Manning-Newman contrast proves an effective way to focus on Manning's obsession with power, it is unlikely that either man was precisely as Strachey depicted him. Certainly Newman was not the passive, helpless, dreamy soul he is made out to be. He had far more resilience, with much more intellectual bite than he is permitted here. And Manning, while without doubt colder and harder than Newman, was hardly the monster he appears to be. His spiritual concerns, which Strachey touches upon almost as an afterthought, were no doubt as genuine as his calculating self. The finely tuned biographical truths, in this case, are subordinated to a moral vision that Strachey is intent on pursuing, regardless of what all the dull facts say.

The distinction Strachey maintains between Newman and Manning should not obscure the reality that both were men of religion, and that it is religion itself, as much as those who use it for their own advancement, which is the target of Strachey's attack. Throughout the essay Strachey delights in savaging religious dogma and mocking what he considers the preposterous nature of religious debate. He quotes with pleasure John Keble's assertion that England would be far better " 'were it vastly more superstitious, more bigoted, more gloomy, more fierce in its religion than at present it shows itself to be,' " (p. 20), and he relishes Newman's attention to the "dialectical splitting of dogmatical hairs" (p. 24). The issuance of the Catholic *Syllabus errorum*, "in which all the favourite beliefs of the modern world—the rights of democracies, the claims of science, the sanctity of free speech, the principles of toleration—were categorically denounced" (p. 94), particularly pleases him, as does the doctrine of papal infallibility. In the figures of his two ecclesiastics, one humble, one not, Strachey expresses his hatred of religion, a hatred that colors all four of the lives of his *Eminent Victorians*.

"FLORENCE NIGHTINGALE"

"Florence Nightingale," the second of the lives, represents an important change of focus for Strachey, a change that many readers have failed to appreciate. For it was less Nightingale herself than the myths about her that Strachey is determined to debunk. Although the Nightingale whom Strachey depicts is certainly a woman out of touch with her feelings, driven by impulses she cannot comprehend, she is by no means as calculatedly self-absorbed as Manning. However complicated or pathological their origins, her ambitions, unlike Manning's, are directed outward in the service of others, rather than inward for the aggrandizement of self. With all of her failings and lack of understanding, Nightingale remains essentially admirable, a woman who in the face of enormous obstacles managed to achieve monumental changes in military health care.

That she did so by being the "saintly, self-sacrificing" woman of popular mythology, "the delicate maiden of high degree who threw aside the pleasures of a life of ease to succour the afflicted" (p. 135), is the nonsense that Strachey is out to remedy. No woman in the middle of the nineteenth century could take on the rigidities and prejudices of the army establishment and triumph over them through the simple goodness of her soul; and if Strachey's Nightingale is excessively fierce, that ferocity is surely closer to the truth than the image of the gentle "Lady with the Lamp," "consecrating with the radiance of her goodness the dying soldier's couch" (p. 135).

While Strachey endorses both her extraordinary accomplishments and the strength of resolve with which she pursued them, it is in his analysis of Nightingale's motivation that he engages in his characteristic mockery. Unlike his systematic undercutting of Manning's aura of selflessness, Strachey's exposure of the force behind Nightingale's behavior seems both fuzzy and not altogether deserved. For Strachey, the truth of Nightingale "was not as facile fancy painted her. She worked in another fashion, and towards another end; she moved under the stress of an impetus which finds no place in the popular imagination. A Demon possessed her. Now demons, whatever else they may be, are full of interest" (p. 135).

But however interesting demons are, they are hardly plausible constructs to enable us to understand complex human beings. And while Strachey has great fun at Nightingale's expense, her demon is finally a slightly silly feature in an otherwise substantial portrait of a determined woman who fought against the gender restrictions and adminis-

trative inefficiencies of her age. Strachey insists upon her oddness from the very beginning. While every other well-to-do young woman of her acquaintance happily accepted it as her destiny to marry and live happily ever after, Florence had other dreams: "Why, as a child in the nursery, when her sister had shown a healthy pleasure in tearing her dolls to pieces, had *she* shown an almost morbid one in sewing them up again? Why was she driven now to minister to the poor in their cottages. . . . Why was her head filled with queer imaginations of the country house at Embley turned . . . into a hospital, with herself as matron moving about among the beds?" (p. 136).

Although the emergence of an individual unwilling to accept the constraints imposed on women by her age and class is no doubt a mysterious process, there is no reason to make it seem vaguely pathological, as Strachey does here. To present Nightingale's craving for a significant life as something associated with demons and peculiar desires runs counter to the very real admiration Strachey expresses for her courage. Indeed, part of the moral impact of "Florence Nightingale" is precisely the clarity with which Strachey delineates the plight of the talented woman in the nineteenth century. A strong supporter of the early women's rights movement, Strachey celebrates Nightingale's refusal to bow to the conventional expectations of how women should lead their lives. While the gentle mockery of the impulses that animate her provide good reading, the humor it generates finally does not serve Strachey's purposes.

The outbreak of the Crimean War, exposing the complete administrative collapse of British military health care, gave Nightingale the opportunity for which she had unwittingly been preparing. The horrors of the British military hospital at Scutari gave Strachey the opportunity for some of his most powerful descriptive writing:

Want, neglect, confusion, misery—in every shape and in every degree of intensity—filled the endless corridors and the vast apartments of the gigantic barrack-house, which . . . had been hurriedly set aside as the chief shelter for the victims of the war. . . . The structural defects were equalled by the deficiencies in the commonest objects of hospital use. There were not enough bedsteads; the sheets were of canvas, and so coarse that the wounded men recoiled from them. . . . There were no basins, no towels, no soap, no brooms, no mops, no trays, no plates;

there were neither slippers nor scissors, neither shoe-brushes nor blacking; there were no knives or forks or spoons.

(pp. 146–147)

Into this mess stepped not the shy, retiring angel of mercy but a competent, implacable administrator who attended to details, understood the uses of power, and was unsparing in her denunciation of the mediocrity around her. The passages describing her achievements at Scutari are among Strachey's finest. But, as Strachey emphasizes, Nightingale's work in the Crimean War was only a small part of her career. After the war it was not simply the military hospitals that needed reforming, but the whole Army Medical Department, and finally nothing less than the War Office itself.

In the battle against the rigid bureaucrats and the fatuous policies of the Medical Department and the War Office, Nightingale enlisted the gentle Sidney Herbert on her side. Strachey is fascinated by their relationship and the reversal of traditional gender roles they seemed to enact: the passive, responsive Herbert and the commanding, willful Nightingale. Strachey, in a sense, makes Sidney play Newman to Florence's Manning. In fact, the eagle-dove contrast in the first essay reappears here in altered form as Strachey describes the power Nightingale exercises over Herbert. Herbert is depicted as a comely, gallant stag "springing through the forest." "But," the analogy continues, "the forest is a dangerous place. One has the image of those wide eyes fascinated by something feline, something strong; there is a pause; and then the tigress has her claws in the quivering haunches; and then—!" (p. 173).

With her own unrelenting labor, and that of Herbert, Nightingale succeeded in establishing critical reforms throughout every aspect of army health care. The two years during which Herbert served as secretary of state for war constitute for Strachey "an important epoch in the history of the British Army" (p. 181). Hospitals were remodeled, an army medical school was established, and the entire Army Medical Department was reorganized. In addition, Nightingale applied what she had learned about health practices in the army to the country at large, writing an essential text on hospital construction and management and, by opening a training school for nurses, effectively becoming the founder of modern nursing in Britain. For all of these immense achievements Strachey has the highest regard. But her mania for work never slackened—nor did her demands on Herbert. Strachey returns to the notion of Nightingale's demon by suggesting that it was her refusal to let Herbert rest from the task of reforming the War Office that actually killed him: "If Miss Nightingale had been less ruthless, Sidney Herbert would not have perished; but then, she would not have been Miss Nightingale. The force that created was the force that destroyed. It was the Demon that was responsible" (p. 186).

The death of Herbert marked the end of Nightingale's campaign against the War Office, and Strachey devotes the last pages of the life to charting her slow decline into muddled religious contemplation. The woman whose practical skills had changed the organization and delivery of army medical care would now set right the "religious convictions of mankind" (p. 191). Strachey renders the ineffectual Nightingale a figure of fun with a conception of God that appears at times to be that of "a glorified sanitary engineer " (p. 193); in her speculations she "seems hardly to distinguish between the Deity and the Drains" (p. 193). Growing fat and senile, she finally receives the Order of Merit three years before she dies, long after she accomplished the remarkable work that has almost been obscured by the persistent myth of the Lady with the Lamp.

"DR. ARNOLD"

"Dr. Arnold" is the funniest, the cruelest—and perhaps the most indefensible—of the four lives. Whereas both Manning and Nightingale are formidable people who despite, or even because of, their manias are taken seriously by Strachey, Thomas Arnold is treated essentially as a buffoon. Strachey denies him any particular human complexity; the "slightly puzzled look" he wears on his face, and his legs, "shorter than they should have been" (p. 210), suggest the extent to which Strachey's portrait of him is more a caricature than anything else.

Strachey's wickedly comic savaging of Arnold should not be read, however, as playful indifference toward his subject. Strachey, as we have seen, loathed his own public school experience with its sterile curriculum, its anti-intellectualism, its cloying religiosity. Insofar as Arnold, when he became headmaster of Rugby in 1828, failed to implement any salutary reforms, Strachey quite properly saw him as contributing to the very public school conditions he detested. Failing to provide any solution, Arnold thus became for Strachey part of the public school problem. It was a problem about which he had very strong feelings.

The Rugby that Arnold took over was, in Strachey's words, "a system of anarchy tempered by despotism" (p. 211). Morally it was a disaster, a reflection of the system the legendary Keate had instituted at Eton in which order and discipline were achieved through floggings. Intellectually it was no better: learning was largely confined to the forced ingestion of Greek and Latin. Arnold was appointed headmaster with the expectation that he would change all of this. Unfortunately, he was up to none of it. Strachey is unforgiving of Arnold's utter inability to exploit the opportunity given him to improve not just Rugby but the entire system of public schools throughout England:

Was he to improve the character of his pupils by gradually spreading round them an atmosphere of cultivation and intelligence? By bringing them into close and friendly contact with civilised men, and even, perhaps, with civilised women? By introducing into the life of his school all that he could of the humane, enlightened, and progressive elements in the life of the community? On the whole, he thought not.

(p. 213)

Instead, Arnold chose to convert the system, prevalent in most public schools of the day, in which the oldest students—the sixth-form boys—were responsible for helping keep discipline in the classrooms, into one in which the sixth formers were actually charged to help govern the entire school, reporting only to the headmaster. Strachey's judgment of this innovation, like everything else about Arnold, is merciless:

This was the means by which Dr. Arnold hoped to turn Rugby into "a place of really Christian education." The boys were to work out their own salvation, like the human race. He himself, involved in awful grandeur, ruled remotely, through his chosen instruments, from an inaccessible heaven.

(p. 214)

The assault on moral evil that Arnold fought with his sixth formers and his dramatic chapel sermons was aided by the fact that "he had no theoretical objection to corporal punishment" (p. 216). Not only did he believe in the value of flogging, but he extended the authority to flog to his sixth-form prefects.

Strachey's contempt for Arnold's moral improvements is matched by his criticism of Arnold's failures to establish a curriculum that had any relevance to the lives of the students. There was no physical science, and though he introduced modern history, modern languages, and mathematics into the school, too little time was devoted to them to make much difference. Greek and Latin remained the major study at Rugby, but less the pleasures of the literature than the deadening rigors of syntax and prosody: "Boys," Arnold remarked, "do not like poetry" (p. 219).

Strachey's irony is insistent. Noting that Thomas Carlyle praised Arnold's diligence, as shown in his seventeen volumes of published work, Strachey begins his next paragraph with the diabolical "Mrs. Arnold, too, no doubt agreed with Carlyle. During the first eight years of their married life, she bore him six children; and four more were to follow" (p. 230). Undercutting Arnold's claim to be a liberal by citing his own words to the effect that he was opposed to the spirit of 1789, the French Economistes and the American Revolution, Strachey concludes his description of Arnold's political beliefs with the following thrust: "He believed in toleration, too, within limits; that is to say, in the toleration of those with whom he agreed" (p. 223).

It is fair to argue, as some have done, that Strachey's portrait of Arnold is excessively biased and that he clearly could not have been as ludicrous as Strachey makes him appear. But to argue this is to miss the point. Strachey's target here is less Arnold than the British public school system that he played such an essential role in shaping. Strachey's ridicule of Arnold is in the service of a larger moral mission—to criticize the means by which a country has chosen to educate its elite—and to hold Strachey to some strict criterion of biographical truth may be legitimate but is ultimately futile. Arnold's failure to take advantage of the opportunity the culture presented him to effect significant change in an important institution—"Under him, the public school remained, in essentials, a conventional establishment, devoted to the teaching of Greek and Latin grammar" (p. 240)—constituted for Strachey a failure of the gravest sort. The greatest irony of Arnold's reign at Rugby was that the respectable behavior which he substituted for the chaos of Keate's time, and the prefect model of school governance he established, turned irresistibly into the "worship of athletics and the worship of good form" (p. 241), both of which would have distressed the "earnest enthusiast who strove to make his pupils Christian gentlemen" (p. 241). Arnold's final legacy is an attitude that makes it seem "that an English public schoolboy who wears the wrong clothes and takes no interest in football is a contradiction in terms" (p. 241). For Strachey, it is an attitude symptomatic of the moral and intellectual bankruptcy that helped lead to the meaningless devastation of World War I.

"THE END OF GENERAL GORDON"

AFTER the narrow focus and almost exclusively comic treatment of Dr. Arnold, Strachey turns, in his concluding life of General Charles George Gordon, to a far broader canvas and a much more complicated character—indeed set of characters. Moving among China, Egypt, and the equally exotic labyrinth of the English government, Strachey charts the drama of Gordon's progress to his unnecessary and marvelously self-indulgent end in Khartoum. In the life and especially the death of Gordon (the title of this last essay is "The End of General Gordon"), Strachey orchestrates to the fullest the pernicious consequences of religious fanaticism and unfettered ambition—themes he has been pursuing throughout each separate life. But, perhaps most important, Strachey presents Gordon's fate not simply as a product of his own compulsions but of the malign workings of British imperialism as well. For despite all of his strength and majestic obsessions, Gordon would never have been transfixed by dervishes' spears and then hacked to death if he had not also been a willing dupe of the imperialist wing of the British government. Gordon's life provides Strachey with his opportunity to inveigh eloquently against the evils of imperialism.

In contrast with the monochromatic Arnold, for whom he has no sympathy, Strachey is both repelled and attracted by the elusive, complicated Gordon. Appalled by his religious fatalism, by the "intoxicated heart" (p. 247) that drives him to pursue glamour and power and leaves him vulnerable to the political manipulations of others, Strachey at the same time cannot help but admire his extraordinary strength of character, his practical abilities, his energy, and his courage. His absurd religious concerns are countered for Strachey by his capacities as a decisive man of action; in addition, we do not have to look too deeply into the biographer's psyche to understand the appeal to him of a subject who was always uneasy in the company of women and who "was particularly fond of boys" (p. 257), invariably happy in the company of street urchins and young sailors. Strachey portrays him as a creature of "intertwining contradictions—intricate recesses where egoism and renunciation melted into one another" (p. 260). It is a tribute to Strachey's biographical skill that he is able to handle Gordon's complexities and his own ambivalences toward them with confidence and clarity. His treatment of a genuinely complicated man is never itself confused.

Structurally, Strachey brackets Gordon's fanaticism between his confrontations with two similar fanatics: Hong-siu-tsuen, who in a sense launched Gordon on his career, and the Mahdi, who very definitely terminated it. With all three he plays variations on the central theme of the God-intoxicated heart: Hong declaring himself "the prophet of God; he was more—he was the Son of God; he was *Tien Wang*, the Celestial king; he was the younger brother of Jesus" (p. 249); Mahommed Ahmed proclaiming himself the Mahdi, the forerunner of the Messiah whose task it was to purge the world of corruption and sin; and Gordon himself, making no claim for his own divinity but nevertheless firmly believing that the "Will of God was inscrutable and absolute; that it was man's duty to follow where God's hand led" (p. 259), thereby investing "the wildest incoherences of conduct or of circumstances with the sanctity of eternal law" (p. 260).

If Gordon's military prowess was sufficient to defeat Hong and his fervent Wang followers, it could not prevent his head from being cut off by the Mahdi after the fall of Khartoum. But it was not the Mahdi alone who is responsible for Gordon's death. The players in Gordon's demise in-

LYTTON STRACHEY

cluded William Gladstone, the Liberal prime minister, who preferred to interfere as little as possible in Egypt's affairs; Sir Evelyn Baring, consul general at Cairo, who wanted to see the British withdrawn from the Sudan altogether; Lord Granville, the foreign secretary, who was reluctant to relinquish British authority in the area; Lord Hartington and Lord Wolseley, who, as leaders of the imperialist faction of the government, opposed the policy of British withdrawal from the Sudan; the newspaper editor W. L. Stead; and assorted pashas.

The issue was whether to send Gordon to Khartoum to carry out the evacuation of the British from the city menaced by the Mahdi's forces. Strachey focuses on the maneuverings and negotiations that concluded with Gordon, a man who never retreated in his life, going to Khartoum, over the explicit objections of Baring, to oversee the British withdrawal. As Strachey notes, "The whole history of his life, the whole bent of his character, seemed to disqualify him for the task for which he had been chosen. He was before all things a fighter, an enthusiast, a bold adventurer; and he was now to be entrusted with the conduct of an inglorious retreat" (p. 289).

Strachey relishes the political intrigue that resulted in Gordon's ostensibly being asked to perform a mission for which he was temperamentally unqualified. To document the government's duplicitous motives in sending him, Strachey employs a characteristic series of charged questions whose interrogative form obscures their firmly declarative intent:

Was it not at least possible that, once there, with his views and his character, he would, for some reason or other, refrain from carrying out a policy of pacific retreat? Was it not possible that in that case he might so involve the English Government that it would find itself obliged, almost imperceptibly perhaps, to substitute for its policy of withdrawal a policy of advance? . . . In short, would not the dispatch of General Gordon to Khartoum involve, almost inevitably, the conquest of the Sudan by British troops, followed by a British occupation?

(p. 293)

While he claims to have insufficient evidence to answer all these questions in the affirmative, their rhetorical weight is such that they clearly constitute Strachey's firm conviction regarding the politi-

cal reality behind the decision to send Gordon to Khartoum. Once there, of course, Gordon acted precisely as Strachey suggests the British imperialists knew he would act: he eschewed all thought of leaving, and prepared his defense of the city. Radiant in his self-importance—"He was already famous; he would soon be glorious" (p. 298)—Gordon waited for the government to send troops to rescue him. But Gordon did not count on Gladstone's principled opposition to interfering in the Sudan, or Evelyn Baring's judicious minimizing of his risks and maximizing of his opportunities "to become an institution," or even the ponderous slowness of Lord Hartington.

As the politics worked themselves out, the Mahdi's threat grew ever graver. By the time Lord Hartington announced to Gladstone that he would resign his cabinet position unless relief forces were sent, there was no time left to act. When Sir Charles Wilson at last arrived in Khartoum, the Egyptian flag was no longer flying: "The relief expedition was two days late" (p. 343). Strachey clearly enjoys the delicious irony that with all the complications surrounding the issue of Gordon—British and Egyptian policies, the Mahdi's fanaticism, internal power struggles—his fate "was finally determined by the fact that Lord Hartington was slow" (p. 295).

Gordon's death and the massacre of those with him was but the beginning of the devastation unleashed by the potent combination of imperial ambitions and bureaucratic incompetence. The British public needed its revenge, and thirteen years later Major Kitchener achieved it at Omdurman with his Maxim-Nordenfeldt guns. The essay's final sentence—hence the concluding sentence of *Eminent Victorians*—distills perfectly the irony and moral outrage for which the book is justly known: "At any rate, it had all ended very happily—in a glorious slaughter of twenty thousand Arabs, a vast addition to the British Empire, and a step in the Peerage for Sir Evelyn Baring" (p. 350).

DORA CARRINGTON

THE publication of *Eminent Victorians* brought Strachey both the acclaim and the financial security he had long been seeking. He was now an internationally known writer with sufficient resources to make needed improvements in the Mill House at Tidmarsh, the country cottage into which he had moved in 1917. As important to Strachey as the fame, the money, and the house was his discovery during the summer of 1915 of Dora Carrington, the fey, exuberant painter with whom he was to share the rest of his life. The circumstances of their meeting indicate the unique nature of the relationship they maintained for the next sixteen years. Walking with her in the woods near Asheham, a house rented for several summers by the Woolfs, Strachey suddenly embraced her. Carrington broke away in anger, and later complained to her friend Barbara Hiles about what he had done. Hiles assured her that since Strachey was homosexual, she had no reason to worry, an explanation that failed to comfort Carrington very much—she seemingly did not know what a homosexual was. Intent on revenge, she crept into his bedroom the next morning with a pair of scissors to remove the marvelous full beard that had become such an essential ingredient of his selfhood. As she leaned over him, prepared to cut, Strachey opened his eyes and stared into hers. A bonding as mysterious as it was instantaneous took place, and from then on, Carrington was absolutely devoted to Strachey. Neither the affairs each conducted nor even Carrington's eventual marriage to Ralph Partridge could separate them or diminish the love that existed between them. Loyal companions regardless of whom they were sleeping with, they nourished and supported each other to the end of Strachey's life.

Confident in the reputation generated by the success of his *Eminent Victorians* and living happily at Tidmarsh, Strachey began to cast about for a new project. An early notion, soon rejected, was another volume of brief biographies, this time of the scientists who had been on the initial list of possibilities for *Eminent Victorians*. It was Walter Raleigh, his old friend from the Liverpool days, who first suggested in May 1918 that he bring his new biographical method to bear on Queen Victoria herself. Lytton liked the idea and immediately began some serious exploratory reading. By January 1919 he was sufficiently convinced that he had found his subject to inform Chatto and Windus that his next book would be on the queen. The thought that her son might do to Victoria what (she felt) he had done to his previous four figures caused Lady Strachey to try to change his mind, but Strachey disregarded these maternal reservations and in 1921 published *Queen Victoria*.

QUEEN VICTORIA

LADY STRACHEY need not have worried. The book was not only an instant popular triumph (all five thousand copies of the first English printing sold out within twenty-four hours) but a critical one as well. Reviews from even the most august and conservative quarters were enthusiastic, and in 1922 *Queen Victoria* received the prestigious James Tait Black Memorial Prize. Most important for Lady Strachey's sense of propriety, the book was particularly praised for Lytton's delicate, judicious, even loving portrait of the queen. For those who came to the book expecting to find the same excoriation of Victorian folly that structured the lives of Lytton's four eminences, its gentleness of tone must have constituted an enormous shock. In place of the acerbic irony there is an accepting and even good-natured humor; and tolerant understanding of human imperfection replaces his attack on the follies of his *Eminent Victorians*.

If Strachey's new voice surprised people, it really should not have. As was suggested earlier, Strachey was very much a Victorian himself, and *Eminent Victorians* represented less a repudiation of an entire culture than an attack on the abuses of the culture's ideals. Having criticized them once, Strachey had no need to do it again. In addition, with his anger at the war now behind him, and, after the success of *Eminent Victorians*, imbued with new confidence in his own powers, he was mellow and relaxed in a way he had not previously been. Strachey wrote *Queen Victoria* not as a fiercely engaged moralist but as a genuine biographer, interested in recounting the lives of diverse and complex characters.

This is not to suggest by any means that Strachey had been defanged or that his portrait of Victoria is uncritically bland. Few absurdities escape him, and Victoria's limitations—her rigidity, her indifference to some of the pressing social and intellectual issues of the day, her lack of imagination, and even her rather peculiar grasp of English grammar, among others—are as clearly revealed here as elsewhere. But her weaknesses, like those of Albert and the other characters, are simply human weaknesses, offset by a host of human virtues; and Strachey embraces both as he tells the story of a distinctly human queen and the era over which she presided.

Strachey's greatest challenge clearly lay in the immensity of his task: how to capture in one relatively slim volume the life of a queen who ruled for nearly two-thirds of the nineteenth century. His response—the only one really available to him, given his talents—was to channel as much historical material as possible into the depiction of character, and then to organize Victoria's life (and times) around the interplay of successive relationships. Thus we see her as a teenage monarch listening adoringly to Melbourne as he explains more or less everything to her, and fighting with Sir Robert Peel about the political loyalties of her ladies of the bedchamber. We find her, as a mature queen, opposing Lord John Russell on the Schleswig-Holstein affair, resenting Gladstone's treating her like an institution instead of a woman, and expanding "to the rays of Disraeli's devotion like a flower in the sun" (p. 350). Throughout all of these relationships, Strachey traces the development of her imperiousness, her sense of duty, the sincerity "which gave her at once her impressiveness, her charm, and her absurdity" (p. 250), and her commitment to the respectable middle-class virtues of home and family that together helped define her.

The central relationship of Victoria's life, of course, was not with her ministers but with Prince Francis Charles Augustus Albert Emmanuel of Saxe-Coburg-Gotha, known familiarly as Prince Albert, her husband. She made clear the importance of the marriage to her when, at Albert's premature death in 1861, at age forty-two, she indicated that her own real life had also come to an end. The very form of Strachey's biography mirrors this fact: almost three-quarters of it are devoted to Victoria's first forty-two years; the second half of her life, as long as the first but endured in bereavement, occupies the remaining quarter of the book.

The relationship between the two distant cousins is complicated from the start. Entranced by a physical beauty that only she seemed to appreciate, Victoria fell passionately in love with Albert at the outset; he married less out of feelings of love than a sense of obligation, and even the faint stirrings of

ambition at what he might achieve in his position. She was the queen, adored by a nation, while he was a foreigner, looked upon with great suspicion. And both were willful people, used to having their ways. Strachey includes the no doubt mythical story of Victoria's inability to get Albert to open a locked door until she ceased to identify herself as the queen of England and instead claimed only to desire admission as his wife as an apt summary of the problems the marriage imposed upon each of them.

It is hard not to feel that in the portrait of Albert as the outsider seeking recognition, Strachey had poured a good deal of himself. Albert's loneliness and his sense that his talents were not truly appreciated clearly speak to the frustrations that Strachey himself experienced as a younger man. And although it is only delicately hinted at in the text, the fact that he had no physical passion for Victoria and never flirted, even with the prettiest ladies in the court, supports Strachey's suggestion that Albert was homosexual—an interpretation he confirmed in conversation with fellow biographer Hesketh Pearson as retold by Holroyd in *Lytton Strachey: A Critical Biography*. Unsatisfied to the end, trying to find through his maniacal devotion to work the acceptance fated always to elude him, Albert emerges from the pages of the biography as a vulnerable and richly conceived character. The garish monument Victoria commissioned to honor his memory—at which Strachey pokes great fun—serves only to emphasize how little the queen's adoration of her husband had to do with her truly understanding him.

While his *Queen Victoria* is necessarily a book about those who exercise public power and make the decisions that determine the destinies of countries—the queen, prince consort, and various ministers, for example—Strachey is also interested in another species of characters who exhibit another form of power: those who stand behind the great presences and derive their fulfillment by influencing them privately. Strachey treats three such figures here: Baroness Lehzen, Victoria's governess, who scrutinized and was responsible for every aspect of her early development; Baron Stockmar, the faithful adviser of Victoria's Uncle Leopold who in large part also became the creator of Alfred, and whose satisfaction "lay in obscurity, in invisibility—in passing, unobserved, through a hidden entrance, into the very central chamber of power, and in sitting there, quietly, pulling the subtle strings" (p. 80); and to a lesser extent, John Brown, the Highland gillie who, after Albert's death (and always with her consent), took to bullying and ordering Victoria about. In the various ways they wielded power and derive satisfactions, the three illustrate aspects of "the curious diversity of human ambitions" (p. 47) that absorbs so much of Strachey's interest as a biographer.

Unlike some of the questionable assertions and allegations in *Eminent Victorians,* Strachey took pride in the extensive secondary research that went into *Queen Victoria.* He announces with pleasure before the opening of chapter 1, "Authority for every important statement of fact in the following pages will be found in the footnotes," a claim he could not have made earlier. Given his relatively scrupulous attention to plausible psychological analysis and documentary sources, his extraordinary final sentence, evoking through a series of almost stream-of-consciousness images Victoria's recapitulation of her past as she lay blind and dying, is a particularly powerful and imaginative conclusion. Depicting her moving from her silent state, where she seems "to be divested of all thinking" (p. 423), Strachey returns us gradually to the beginning of her life, from the spring woods at Osborne, where she and Albert used to summer, to memories of "Albert's face under the green lamp, and Albert's first stag at Balmoral, and Albert in his blue and silver uniform," concluding with specific images of "Lehzen with the globes, and her mother's feathers sweeping down towards her, and a great old repeater-watch of her father's in its tortoise-shell case, and a yellow rug, and some friendly flounces of sprigged muslin, and the trees and the grass at Kensington" (p. 424).

Bringing us back, through the mind of the dying woman, to the start of it all, causes us to reflect in a special way on the meaning of the spectacle that has been unfolding before us. Strachey's adaptation of the deathbed staple of Victorian literature to his own purposes here provides an effective note on which to end. It reveals something as well about the development of his artistic imagination that the last paragraph of *Queen Victoria* was in fact the first Strachey wrote. Arriving at his resonant conclusion before he starts, and shaping the rest of the narrative to guarantee that the conclusion makes sense, Strachey demonstrates a mastery of his material not found even in the neatly orchestrated movements of *Eminent Victorians.*

ELIZABETH AND ESSEX

IN the years following the publication of *Queen Victoria,* Strachey enjoyed his fully certified eminence: traveling, writing, preparing a number of earlier essays for publication in a single volume, *Books and Characters* (1922), and conducting his endlessly complicated love life. In the winter of 1924 he moved from the Mill House, finding it too damp for his health, to Ham Spray House, between Newbury and Hungerford. He was to remain there, with Carrington and their assorted lovers, for the rest of his life.

Not until the fall of 1925 did Strachey begin to consider some serious possibilities for his next full-length undertaking. Having earlier rejected a half-serious idea about attempting a life of Christ, he began thinking about a book of famous love affairs: Robert and Elizabeth Barrett Browning, Byron and his half sister, and Queen Elizabeth and the earl of Essex, among others. But within two months the fascination of the young earl and the old queen had seized his imagination, and he decided to devote a whole book to them. On the morning of 17 December 1925, he wrote the first sentences of *Elizabeth and Essex.*

Although it is ostensibly a biography, the book's technique, prose, and overall purpose bear little resemblance to Strachey's previous biographical work, particularly *Queen Victoria.* Whereas the impulse behind *Queen Victoria* was genuinely biographical, *Elizabeth and Essex* is more an uninhibitedly imaginative re-creation of Elizabethan passions and intrigues than an attempt at a faithful and factual rendering of late-sixteenth-century England. Cut loose from the self-imposed constraints that shaped the writing of *Queen Victoria,* Strachey's prose here is effusive, poetic, often outrageously self-indulgent. Strachey feels free to play with language as he has not done before; its exuberance and excess make the style of *Elizabeth and Essex* as different from its predecessor as *Queen Victoria* is from the harshness of *Eminent Victorians.*

The liberties Strachey takes with his prose mirror the license he gives himself as teller of the tale he subtitles *A Tragic History.* Strachey has no reluctance to enter the minds of the various characters in his story, not only to explore motivation and explain behavior but also to reveal actual thought processes and depict emotional responses to events. Claiming access on various occasions to what his protagonists think and feel, Strachey in a sense functions as the omniscient narrator of a novel, going in and out of his characters' thoughts at will. While scrupulous biographers are well aware that the private thoughts of those living in the sixteenth century (or any century, for that matter) cannot be captured, novelists, moving freely in worlds of their own making, can know everything about the characters they have invented. Although a number of critics have suggested the influence of Elizabethan dramatic soliloquies as a means of understanding the ways in which Strachey exposes the minds of his characters to scrutiny, I believe it is preferable to think of him as exercising the traditional prerogative of novelists to do whatever they can to bring their creations to life. To ascribe this fictional quality to *Elizabeth and Essex* is not to deny its historical usefulness or the insights it offers about real people in a real historical context, but simply to try to define its special quality as a biography.

As befits its novelistic nature, the book's strengths lie in Strachey's absorption with his characters and his capacity to bring them before us. From the beginning, both Essex and his doting queen, thirty-three years his senior, are fully conceived with a rich verbal energy and endowed with characteristically Stracheyan dual natures. Strachey is at his best when dissecting their complications, their ambitions, their pathologies. His fascination with them never flags, nor does his success in making us share that fascination. However idiosyncratic some of his conclusions about motivation or character may be, the portraits of Elizabeth and the earl she put to death are absolutely compelling.

The book falters when Strachey's lush prose tips over into the ponderous and the turgid, as, for example, in the following clotted meditation on the meaning of human relationships:

Human relationships must either move or perish. When two consciousnesses come to a certain nearness the impetus of their interactions, growing ever intenser and intenser, leads on to an unescapable climax. The crescendo must rise to its topmost note; and only then is the preordained solution of the theme made manifest.

(p. 6)

It also falters when Strachey strains to make the queen, her earl, and their relationship emblematic of various social and intellectual currents flowing through the sixteenth century. This is particularly true of his insistence that Essex somehow embodied "the spirit of the ancient feudalism," which, almost extinguished, "flamed up" once more in his person, so that "the spectral agony of an abolished world is discernible through the tragic lineaments of a personal disaster" (p. 2). But Essex was no more the old than Elizabeth was the new, and the creaky prose of these metaphoric assignments suggests how forced they are. Both Essex and Elizabeth flourish in the book when Strachey delights in them for themselves, not as representing larger meanings.

Essex moved implacably toward his doom, impelled essentially by his own pride, stubbornness, and blindness, but also helped along by the politics and intrigue of Elizabeth's court. The supporting players in his downfall included Sir Walter Raleigh, deeply envious of the queen's fondness for Essex; the crippled and brilliant Robert Cecil, working to rise in Elizabeth's graces until he finally became, under the queen, the most powerful person in England; and the Bacon brothers, particularly Francis, whose "multiplicity was not merely that of mental accomplishment, but of life itself" (p. 44). All play their roles, and all are splendidly realized characters, but of these Strachey clearly finds Francis Bacon the most interesting.

Just as Essex is identified throughout the book with imagery of fire, so is Bacon associated with a specific image, the serpent:

The detachment of speculation, the intensity of personal pride, the uneasiness of nervous sensibility, the urgency of ambition, the opulence of superb taste—these qualities, blending, twisting, flashing together, gave to his secret spirit the subtle and glittering superficies of a serpent. A serpent, indeed, might well have been his chosen emblem—the wise, sinuous, dangerous creature, offspring of mystery and the beautiful earth.

(p. 44)

Strachey admires Bacon's superb intellect but sees him as terribly flawed by his inability to understand anything—including himself—outside of the realm of that intellect. Attaching himself initially to Essex, Bacon did his best to warn him of the perils of confronting the queen, unable to appreciate that Essex totally lacked a capacity for dissimulation and could not feign the subservience that Bacon counseled.

Led by his cold calculus of self-interest, Bacon turned against Essex, when the latter was facing trial, in order to do the bidding of the queen. He played a significant role in Essex's condemnation, earning £1,200 from Elizabeth for his efforts. The human cost of living a solely intellectual life, however, was greater than any compensation Bacon received from the queen. He ended his life alone and miserable, a victim of his own emotional impoverishment. It is difficult to imagine another writer capable of rendering Strachey's judgment of Bacon's failure: "The same cause which made Bacon write perfect prose brought about his worldly and his spiritual ruin. It is probably always disastrous not to be a poet" (p. 46).

The book is dedicated to James and Alix Strachey, Lytton's brother and sister-in-law. Although dedications normally have little to do with the focus or meaning of what follows, in this case the choice of the Stracheys is significant. Psychoanalysts as well as students and translators of Freud, James and Alix provided Lytton with his basic exposure to those Freudian ideas which play such a major role in his interpretation of the Elizabeth–Essex relationship. Strachey's use of Freudian theorizing was sufficiently arresting to earn the admiration of Freud himself, who, in a 1928 letter, praised Strachey for being "steeped in the spirit of psycho-analysis," for his talent in exposing Elizabeth's "most hidden motives," and his skill in tracing "back her character to the impressions of her childhood" (pp. 615–616). In the case of a child whose father has chopped off her mother's head, of course, it is not difficult to assume that some sort of trauma has occurred, but the specific diagnoses Strachey makes of some of the Virgin Queen's peculiarities—that her physical "ailments were of an hysterical origin," that she had a "neurotic condition," and that "her sexual organisation was seriously warped" (p. 20)—suggest the specific influence of the Freudian ideas that Lytton absorbed from James and Alix.

A rather more daring use of psychoanalytic insight occurs near the end of the book, during Strachey's evocation of Elizabeth's thinking as she determined to execute Essex after he had been found guilty of high treason. Imagining the satisfaction Elizabeth takes in teaching Essex that she indeed is made of the same stern stuff as her father, and that she, too, can punish the perfidy of those she most loves, Strachey then moves to a deeper and subtler understanding of her motives:

But in a still remoter depth there were still stranger stirrings. There was a difference as well as a likeness; after all, she was no man but a woman; and was this, perhaps, not a repetition but a revenge? After all the long years of her life-time, and in this appalling consummation, was it her murdered mother who had finally emerged? . . . Manhood—the fascinating, detestable entity, which had first come upon her concealed in yellow magnificence in her father's lap—manhood was overthrown at last, and in the person of that traitor it should be rooted out. Literally, perhaps . . . she knew well enough the punishment for high treason.

(pp. 263–264)

The punishment for treason to which Elizabeth refers includes castration, which is meted out to several people in the course of the narration, complete with gory attendant detail. Strachey's interpretation of the execution of Essex as Elizabeth's method of getting back at her father not only for killing her mother but even for possible sexual transgressions against her as a girl (the "detestable entity" concealed in her father's lap that she considers literally rooting out) is precisely the sort of exploration of hidden motives that earned Freud's approbation. (In fact, despite Strachey's speculations, Elizabeth was content simply to remove Essex's head.) There is more explicit treatment of sexual material in *Elizabeth and Essex* than in any other of Strachey's serious works.

Enormously popular and certainly highly entertaining, *Elizabeth and Essex* had a deservedly mixed critical reception. It is full of brilliance and originality, and when the prose works Strachey achieves extraordinary heights. But there is also much about it that is self-conscious, strained, and downright awkward. It is perhaps fair to say that it is both more ambitious and more flawed than *Queen Victoria*.

Exhausted by his efforts to finish the book,

which came out in 1928, Strachey never again attempted another. His last years were spent without substantial writing of any sort. Mostly he read and enjoyed his many friends. By 1931 he became ill with a condition that was variously diagnosed as typhoid fever, colitis, some form of paratyphoid or enteric fever. Several experts later, it was determined that he was suffering from ulcerative colitis. This remained the diagnosis of choice, although no treatment seemed to help. He died of cancer on 21 January 1932. On 11 March, Carrington committed suicide, unable to bear the idea of living without Strachey.

SELECTED BIBLIOGRAPHY

I. BIBLIOGRAPHY. M. Edmonds, *Lytton Strachey: A Bibliography* (New York and London, 1981).

II. COLLECTED WORKS. *Portraits in Miniature and Other Essays* (London, 1931); *Characters and Commentaries* (London, 1933); *Collected Works*, 6 vols. (London, 1949), consists of *Landmarks in French Literature, Eminent Victorians, Queen Victoria, Elizabeth and Essex, Biographical Essays,* and *Literary Essays; Spectatorial Essays* (London, 1964); *Ermyntrude and Esmeralda: An Entertainment* (London, 1969); *Lytton Strachey by Himself: A Self-Portrait,* M. Holroyd, ed. (London, 1971); *The Really Interesting Question and Other Papers,* P. Levy, ed. (London, 1972); *The Shorter Strachey,* M. Holroyd and P. Levy, eds. (Oxford and New York, 1980).

III. SEPARATE WORKS. *Landmarks in French Literature* (London, 1912); *Eminent Victorians* (London, 1918); *Queen Victoria* (London, 1921); *Pope* (Cambridge, 1925), the Leslie Stephen Lecture; *Elizabeth and Essex: A Tragic History* (London, 1928).

IV. EDITED WORK. *The Greville Memoirs,* ed. with R. Fulford, 8 vols. (London, 1938).

V. CONTRIBUTIONS TO COLLECTIONS. "Ely: An Ode," in *Proclusiones academicae* (Cambridge, 1902); "The Cat," "Ningamus Serta Rosarum," and "When We Are Dead a Thousand Years," in *Euphrosyne: A Collection of Verse* (Cambridge, 1905).

VI. CORRESPONDENCE. *Virginia Woolf and Lytton Strachey: Letters,* ed. by L. Woolf and J. Strachey (London, 1956).

VII. BIOGRAPHICAL AND CRITICAL STUDIES. A. Huxley, *On the Margin* (London, 1923); H. Nicolson, *The Development of English Biography* (London, 1927); C. Bower-Shore, *Lytton Strachey: An Essay* (London, 1933); B. Dobrée, "Lytton Strachey," in *The Post-Victorians,* W. R. Inge, ed. (London, 1933); F. Swinnerton, *The Georgian Literary Scene* (New York, 1934); G. Boas, *Lytton Strachey* (London, 1935);

K. R. S. Iyengar, *Lytton Strachey: A Critical Study* (London, 1939); C. Clemens, *Lytton Strachey* (Webster Groves, Mo., 1942); M. Beerbohm, *Lytton Strachey* (Cambridge, 1943); J. M. Keynes, *Two Memoirs* (London, 1949).

C. R. Sanders, *The Strachey Family, 1588–1932: Their Writing and Literary Associations* (Durham, N.C., 1953); J. K. Johnstone, *The Bloomsbury Group* (London, 1954); R. A. Scott-James, *Lytton Strachey* (London, 1955); C. Bell, *Old Friends: Personal Recollections* (London, 1956); C. R. Sanders, *Lytton Strachey: His Mind and Art* (New Haven, 1957); M. M. S. Yu, *Two Masters of Irony: Wilde and Lytton Strachey* (Hong Kong, 1957); J. Clive, "More or Less Eminent Victorians," in *Victorian Studies,* 2 (September 1958).

M. Kallich, *The Psychological Milieu of Lytton Strachey* (New York, 1961); G. K. Simson, "Lytton Strachey's Use of His Sources in *Eminent Victorians,*" Ph.D. dissertation (University of Minnesota, 1963); R. Altick, *Lives and Letters: A History of Literary Biography in England and America* (New York, 1965); M. Holroyd, *Lytton Strachey: A Critical Biography,* 2 vols. (London, 1967–1968), rev. ed., 1 vol. (London, 1973).

D. Garnett, ed., *Carrington: Letters and Extracts from Her Diaries* (London, 1970); S. P. Rosenbaum, ed., *The Bloomsbury Group: A Collection of Memoirs, Commentary and Criticism* (London, 1970); D. Gadd, *The Loving Friends: A Portrait of Bloomsbury* (New York, 1974); S. J. Darroch, *Ottoline: The Life of Lady Ottoline Morrell* (New York and London, 1975); L. Garber, "Techniques of Characterization in Strachey's *Elizabeth and Essex,*" in *Dalhousie Review,* 56 (Autumn 1976); L. Edel, *Bloomsbury: A House of Lions* (London, 1979); D. Garnett, *Great Friends: Portraits of Seventeen Writers* (London, 1979).

J. Halperin, "*Eminent Victorians* and History," in *Virginia Quarterly Review,* 56 (Summer 1980); M. Holroyd, "A Survey of Lytton Strachey's Centenary," in *Études anglaises,* 33, no. 4 (1980); G. Merle, *Lytton Strachey (1880–1932): Biographie et critique d'un critique et biographe,* 2 vols. (Paris, 1980), and "Lytton Strachey ou la stratégie du style," in *Études anglaises,* 33, no. 4 (1980); G. Simson, "Eminent Chinese: Lytton Strachey as Dramatic Herald from the Court of Pekin," in *Études anglaises,* 33, no. 4 (1980); R. Strachey, *A Strachey Boy,* S. Strachey, ed. (London, 1980); I. Nadel, "Strachey's 'Subtler Strategy': Metaphor in *Eminent Victorians,*" in *Prose Studies,* 4 (September 1981); F. Partridge, *Love in Bloomsbury: Memories* (London, 1981); B. Redford, "The Shaping of the Biographer: Lytton Strachey's 'Warren Hastings, Cheyt Sing and the Begums of Oude,'" in *Princeton University Library Chronicle,* 43, no. 1 (Autumn 1981); D. H. Johnson, "The Death of Gordon: A Victorian Myth," in *Journal of Imperial and Commonwealth History,* 10 (May 1982); S. G. Putt, "A Packet of Bloomsbury Letters: The Forgotten H. O. Meredith," in *Encounter,* 59 (November 1982); L. Edel, "Biographer and Subject: Lytton Strachey and Van Wyck Brooks," in *Prose Studies,* 5 (December 1982); N. Kiell, ed., *Blood Brothers:*

Siblings as Writers (New York, 1983); I. B. Nadel, "The Smallest Genius and the 'Wittiest Mind': Max Beerbohm and Lytton Strachey," in *English Literature in Transition*, 27, no. 4 (1984); E. Overend, "Attitude, Drama, and Role in Strachey's *Elizabeth and Essex*," in *Biography: An Interdisciplinary Quarterly*, 7 (Spring 1984); B. Strachey, *The Strachey Line* (London, 1985); W. Epstein, *Recognizing Biography* (Philadelphia, 1987); J. Marcus, ed., *Virginia Woolf and Bloomsbury: A Centenary Celebration* (Bloomington, Ind., 1987); P. Meisel, *The Myth of the Modern: A Study in British Literature and Criticism After 1850* (New Haven, 1987); J. Ferns, *Lytton Strachey* (Boston, 1988).

J. R. R. TOLKIEN
(1892–1973)

Karl Kroeber

In 1954 the British publishers Allen and Unwin, in association with Houghton Mifflin in the United States, issued an edition of 3500 copies of *The Fellowship of the Ring,* the first volume of a lengthy fantasy by J. R. R. Tolkien, a professor at Oxford known only to a handful of philologists and medievalists. But the book was so popular that the publishers quickly brought out the second and third volumes, *The Two Towers* (1954) and *The Return of the King* (1955). The trilogy, known as *The Lord of the Rings,* was so immediately successful that a new, larger printing was required, and soon another, still larger printing became necessary. In 1965 when the first paperback edition of *The Lord of the Rings* was issued, its 50,000 copies were instantly sold out. Since then millions more have been printed and the trilogy has been translated into a dozen languages. So popular had Tolkien become that over a million hardback copies of his posthumously published *The Silmarillion* (1977) were purchased in the first year of its publication. Tolkien's work, in fact, initiated the success of the mass marketing of literary fantasy, now a major part of the publishing industry.

How did so reclusive, even pedantic, a scholar produce such an innovative and commercially successful book? What qualities of *The Lord of the Rings* have made it so esteemed by so many for more than a generation, especially by students and young adults? Do those qualities suggest that Tolkien's book, like analogous literary sensations of earlier times, is likely to fade into obscurity, or will it endure as a classic? Answers to such questions probably are to be found in the nature and social function of literary fantasy in the second half of the twentieth century.

LIFE AND WORK

JOHN RONALD REUEL TOLKIEN (always called Ronald by his family) was born on 3 January 1892, at Bloemfontein, South Africa, where his father Arthur had taken a position with the Bank of Africa. The Tolkien family had been prosperous piano manufacturers, but the business had failed. Mabel Suffield, Arthur's wife, was the daughter of a once successful drapery manufacturer in Birmingham, England, who had gone bankrupt and survived by selling disinfectant to shopkeepers around the city.

In the spring of 1895 Mabel sailed back to England because the African climate was damaging Ronald's health. Arthur hoped to return to England soon, but he contracted rheumatic fever the following autumn and died early in 1896. After a few months of living with her parents, Mabel rented a cottage on the edge of Birmingham, and from then until her death in 1904, she and her two sons lived in rented houses on the edges of the city. In 1900 Mabel Tolkien had converted to Roman Catholicism, and after her death her parish priest, Father Francis Morgan, took responsibility for the upbringing and education of her sons.

Ronald's only means of escape from a lower-middle-class commercial life was by winning an academic scholarship, which, with some difficulty, he did in 1910, gaining entrance to Exeter College, Oxford. In 1908 Tolkien fell in love with Edith Bratt, like him an orphan, three years his senior, but in 1910 Father Francis forbade him to communicate with her until he was of age. Tolkien obeyed. At Oxford he began studying classics but soon concentrated on English language and literature, being awarded first-class honors in his final examination in 1915. He revisited Edith five days after his twenty-first birthday, and they were formally betrothed in 1914 when, at Tolkien's insistence, she converted to Roman Catholicism.

With the rise of patriotism at the outbreak of the First World War, Tolkien's decision to stay at the university to earn his bachelor's degree was an act of moral courage—he was condemned by both family and friends for not at once enlisting. But since he was engaged and had no money he felt he had to obtain his degree before volunteering. As soon as he received it he entered the army, receiving a commission as a second lieutenant and being given training as a signal officer. When his battalion was notified it was being sent to France in March 1916, he used his last leave to marry Edith. In France he was caught up in the bloody horror of the Somme offensive that gained no ground and cost the British 600,000 casualties in four months. Tolkien was not wounded, but in November he was evacuated back to England suffering from a severe case of trench fever. His recovery was slow, and he never returned to the battlefields of France. While convalescing in early 1917 he began to develop "The Book of Lost Tales," imaginative writings he had begun in 1914, work that would become *The Silmarillion,* published more than sixty years later.

The first of Tolkien's four children was born in November 1917. After the Armistice Tolkien joined the staff of the *Oxford English Dictionary,* and in 1920 he was appointed Reader in English Language at Leeds University, where, with E. V. Gordon, he shaped an edition of *Sir Gawain and the Green Knight,* a work that helped lead to his election as Professor of Anglo-Saxon at Oxford University in 1925. For the next thirty-four years Tolkien taught at Oxford, where he became known as an eccentric and often incomprehensible lecturer but one dedicated to helping advanced students. Not a highly published scholar, Tolkien's most significant academic accomplishment was the Gollancz Memorial Lecture at the British Academy in November 1936, "Beowulf: The Monsters and the Critics," which was influential in establishing the Anglo-Saxon poem as a masterpiece of world literature.

At Oxford Tolkien enjoyed informal meetings with small groups of academics who shared his interest in translating medieval literature, such as Norse sagas, or in reading to each other their own unpublished writings—stories, poems, sections of novels—which would then be discussed and criticized. The best known of these groups in which Tolkien participated was the Inklings, a shifting collection of Oxford scholars and writers, of whom the most talented was Tolkien's best friend, C. S. Lewis, who from their earliest meetings until the end of his life admired Tolkien's stories and encouraged him both to write and to publish.

Except for a few poems, however, Tolkien published none of his creative work until, in 1936, he was persuaded by friends to let the firm of Allen and Unwin consider his typescript of *The Hobbit; or, There and Back Again* (1937), a story that had delighted all those to whom he had read it, including his own children. Since it was a children's book, Sir Stanley Unwin, the chairman of the company, employed his ten-year-old son Rayner as reader of the manuscript for the fee of a shilling. Rayner's one-paragraph critique of the book is as good as any brief review that has ever appeared, concluding that the book "should appeal to all children between the ages of 5 and 9" (quoted in Carpenter, p. 181). *The Hobbit* was published to excellent reviews, a couple written anonymously by C. S. Lewis, and it sold so well that Unwin asked Tolkien to write a sequel.

Tolkien wished to oblige, but it took him fifteen years to complete that sequel, which we know as the trilogy *The Lord of the Rings. The Hobbit,* in fact, had been an aberration in Tolkien's creative career. In the summer of 1928, earning a little extra money to support his growing family by reading examinations of secondary school students seeking university admissions, he happened on an examination with a blank page, and in a moment of relief he wrote on the page, "In a hole in the ground there lived a hobbit." Where that sentence came from he never understood, and it was some time before he began developing, slowly, that now famous opening sentence of his first book into a narrative—began, indeed, to imagine what hobbits might be and do.

Tolkien had written his first story, about a dragon, when he was seven. But it was not until he was recuperating from his experiences in the First World War that he began composing in earnest, although only for his private satisfaction or, later, to entertain his children. What he wrote after the war and throughout the entire decade of the 1920's and into the 1930's was published posthumously as *The Silmarillion,* followed by a series of "Lost Tales" volumes—*The Book of Lost Tales Part I* (1983), *The Book of Lost Tales Part II* (1984), *The Lays of Beleriand* (1985), and *The Shaping of Middle-Earth* (1986). These writings shall be referred to in this essay as "Silmarillion materials." None of this writing contained anything to do with hobbits. *The Hobbit,* however, includes some references to the history and mythology of the Silmarillion material that throughout his life was the primary focus of Tolkien's imaginative activity.

To write what became the 600,000-word sequel to *The Hobbit,* between 1937 and 1952, Tolkien had to imagine the relationship of his relatively recently imagined creatures to the vast, complicated world of Silmarillion materials that he had created over the previous two decades. Following the enormous success of *The Lord of the Rings,* when his publishers were clamoring for anything Tolkien cared to write, he spent nearly twenty years procrastinating and not perfecting the intricate Silmarillion material. *The Silmarillion,* which was finally published four years after Tolkien's death on 2 September 1973, was edited by his son Christopher.

The Hobbit, under wartime pressure of paper shortages, went out of print in 1942, and its subsequent popularity largely derives from the success of *The Lord of the Rings.* Tolkien's fame, and whatever critical repute is awarded him, depends principally on the trilogy. "On Fairy-Stories" (1947) is the most intellectually original and provocative modern discussion of fantasy, and seems sure to gain in esteem of historians of criticism. "Beowulf: The Monsters and the Critics" (1936) will hold a distinctive place in Anglo-Saxon studies, having confirmed beyond question *Beowulf's* artistic merit, and having used the poem to establish fundamental differences between the heroic literatures of northern and southern Europe. The former, Tolkien argued persuasively, centers on martial heroism as its own end in full recognition that the wages of heroism is death. Furthermore, Tolkien's essay proved that Grendel, his mother, and the dragon are brilliant successes of artistic imagination.

Tolkien's few short stories all have charm, though none is a masterpiece. "Leaf by Niggle" (1945; collected in *Tree and Leaf,* 1964) dramatizes the difficulties of being an artist such as Tolkien was, obsessed with details even while worriedly striving to attain a large, dominating form. And he was unsure of his own artistic ability, evidenced in his own self-criticism and self-parody. In *Farmer Giles of Ham* (1949) Tolkien parodies medieval literary forms and conventions, making special fun of *Sir Gawain and the Green Knight* and Chaucer's *Canterbury Tales,* but also entertainingly spoofs academic scholarship and his own fantasies. *Smith of Wootton Major* (1967) is a late story evocative of the bereavements of old age. *The Silmarillion,* and to a much lesser extent the subsequent books retrieved from his father's manuscripts by Christopher Tolkien (who makes use of his father's original, won-

derfully apt title for *The Silmarillion, The Book of Lost Tales*), will always be a joyous resource to enthusiasts. But the material in these volumes remains the matrix for Tolkien's most perfected artistry, of which *The Hobbit* and *The Lord of the Rings* are the dominant expressions.

A way of explaining Tolkien's curious talent of writing enormous numbers of stories but then being slow, even reluctant, to publish is to examine his reaction to the success of *The Lord of the Rings.* Although he was grateful for the wealth it brought him, and sometimes flattered by his fame, he was, unlike most bestselling authors, embarrassed and troubled by the popularity of his books, and did virtually nothing to exploit it. He never, for example, visited the United States, where he would have been lionized and could have earned a fair sum of money through a few lectures. Why not? One reason was that Tolkien was more than anything else a professor.

Many hours of a professor's life are spent in preparing classes, lecturing, and reading and writing on students' work. In addition, university professors find themselves engaged in an array of departmental and university meetings that often leave little time for what initially lured them to the university—research, the analysis and the reevaluation of a narrow field of knowledge. But Tolkien loved the professorial life, despite its time-consuming responsibilities, as a life motivated by passionate commitment to an intellectual discipline that goes on forever. His specialty was philology, the study of the history of words, and he observed that we do not know with certainty the origin of *any* ancient word. The imaginative reconstructions of verbal origins devised by each philologist are gradually absorbed, and lost, within the ever-developing history of the discipline: one finds oneself by losing oneself within an imaginative tradition.

There is a further source of pleasure for a scholar like Tolkien principally concerned with literary texts: the delight of the great art that is his constant study. There is a difference, however, between studying literary art and making literary art, being an artist. Indeed, the occupations are almost adversarial, as Tolkien demonstrates in his two finest critical essays, "Beowulf: The Monsters and the Critics" and "On Fairy-Stories," since the artist primarily pursues beauty, as does the painter Niggle in Tolkien's story *Leaf by Niggle.* It is rare that a genuine professor, such as Tolkien was, achieves success as a creative artist. But the peculiar accomplishment of Tolkien's imaginative creations can only be understood as having emerged from and having been shaped by the special focus of a professorial life that Tolkien himself recognized as, nevertheless, hostile to artistic activities.

nu karne vaiya   under red skies,
úri nienaite híse   a bleared sun blinking
píke assari silde   on bones gleaming
óresse oilima?   in the last morning?

Hui oilima man kiluva   Who shall see the last eve-
hui oilimaite?   ning?

(*The Monsters and the Critics and Other Essays,* pp. 214–215)

ORIGINS OF THE SILMARILLION MATERIAL

THE Silmarillion material that Tolkien began to compose in 1914, and that he added to and emended for the rest of his life, consists of invented legends about the creation of the world and its early history. These stories are like the myths and wonder-laden tales of the northern European peoples—Finnish, Anglo-Saxon, Norse, Germanic and Celtic—whose literatures were the center of Tolkien's professional studies. Some of his invented legends were written in prose, some in various verse forms, as was true of the myths and stories he studied. Moreover, he regarded his invented legends as having been "originally" composed in invented languages. Tolkien devised several of these languages, the most important being Quenya (which was influenced by Finnish in the complexity of its declensions) and Sindarin (whose closest analogue is Welsh), which possess large vocabularies, complete systems of tense and declension, a complex syntax, as well as coherent phonological structures. Tolkien even composed a few works in these languages.

The conclusion of a poem, "The Last Ark," which Tolkien recited to an Esperanto Congress to illustrate his "secret vice" of the pleasure in linguistic invention (which for him lay in the new relations thus created between sounds and notions), exemplifies his practice:

Man kiluva lómi sangane,   Who shall see the clouds gather,
telume lungane   the heavens bending
tollalinta ruste   upon crumbling hills,
vea qualume   the sea heaving
mandu yáme,   the abyss yawning,
aira móre ala tinwi   the old darkness
lante no lanta-mindon?   beyond the stars falling upon fallen towers?

Man tiruva rusta kirya   Who shall heed a broken ship
laiqa ondolissen   on the green rocks

Mostly, however, in composing stories he fantasized that he was translating and reconstructing, as he did in his scholarly work with Norse sagas, the Anglo-Saxon *Beowulf,* or the Finnish *Kalevala.* He thus fused his creative imagining and his professional scholarship.

Tolkien is the only major fantasy writer to have created his fantasy world from a beginning in the systematic invention of languages. And he did this on the basis of a profound scholarly study of medieval northern European philology and literature. Critics without his knowledge tend to misjudge the form of his art. The difficulty in describing the Silmarillion material points to its essential nature of not being entirely coherent. It is deliberately inchoate. That is to say, Tolkien makes the Quenya and Sindarin legends exist as do the medieval legends and myths of northern European peoples in Germany, Scandinavia, Ireland, and Britain for twentieth-century scholars. *The Kalevala,* which fascinated Tolkien and was an important inspiration for him, has often been called the Finnish national epic. But in fact it is a collection of diverse traditional songs, some narrative, some lyric, some magical incantations, which was painstakingly gathered together and edited in the middle of the nineteenth century by a Finnish doctor, Elias Lonnröt, to serve as a poetical museum of vanishing Finnish rural life. Tolkien created the Silmarillion material as an analogous collection of remnants of the various songs and stories of what he called Elvish people. From both Elves and medieval Finnish peasants only fragments of historical and cultural coherence could be reconstructed by even the most diligent present-day philologist-collector.

Quenya and Sindarin are Elvish languages, and the Silmarillion material consists of Elvish myths, legends (on the edge between history and fairy tales), and songs. Elves, as Tolkien presents them, are the "first-born," like men (the "followers") but a little taller and handsomer, more sensitive to the beauty of the world, and doomed to be immortal. Elves who bring the world to high achievements of beauty and courage gradually fade away as the followers grow and absorb the life the Elves have shaped, the special gift (or doom) of men, the followers, being mortality.

Tolkien's conception of an immortal, humanlike race that precedes mankind as we know it, fading as our world comes into being, becoming like carved "figures barely visible in weathered stone in unpeopled lands" (Lord of the Rings, vol. 3, bk. 6, ch. 6), imaginatively repeats an idea very widespread in human mythologies—although so far as one can tell, Tolkien was unaware of this universality, since his knowledge of mythology was limited to Europe, where the conception has been somewhat concealed by the superimposition of later philosophical/religious systems. Many Native American cultures, for example, conceive of a world inhabited by firstborn and then followers in a fashion similar to that described by Tolkien. The difference lies in angle of imagination. Whereas Tolkien conceives of a different kind of person, Elves, inhabiting our familiar world, some Native Americans thought of their firstborn as inhabiting a world different from ours, one in which, for example, animals could speak. Native Americans did not, therefore, make modern man's distinction between myth and history, between what we call fictional and factual stories. All the Native American stories are realistic—it is just that the conditions of reality were different when their firstborn were living here. The distinction is worth noticing because it illuminates what Tolkien wished to accomplish, what he means by the "secondary world" produced by the "subcreation" of a writer of fantasy. To write a fantasy, or to tell a story about the firstborn, is to imagine a different kind of reality from that currently prevailing for the imaginer and his audience. Such imagining can be a way of escaping from the actual conditions in which the imagining takes place. But it also can be a way of assessing those conditions, and even of finding ways to improve them. Preliterate cultures, such as those of medieval northern Europeans, recognized the practical advantages of creating such perspectives on their own culture, and modern fantasy, Tolkien believed, could function in an analogous fashion.

The origins of contemporary fantasy may be found in a reaction to Enlightenment rationalism in the eighteenth century. In the middle of the century James Macpherson became famous through his popular European work, Fragments of Ancient Poetry Collected in the Highlands of Scotland. These fragments purported to be translations of ancient Gaelic legends unearthed by scholarship. Attractive to eighteenth-century readers because of its pseudo-biblical poetic prose that appealed more to sentiment than to logic, its many romantically exotic names of peoples and places, and its themes of failed grandeur, unhappy love, and heroic enterprise amidst the storms of a bleak northern landscape, Macpherson's work claimed to be "authentic," not an imaginative invention, and it was in fact very loosely based on Gaelic historical materials.

A few years later William Blake in a series of books combining brilliantly colored etchings and startling poetry created a bewildering "death-filled hellish" world through parody of the Bible and traditionally religious literary works such as Paradise Lost. Blake, a devout Protestant who lived during a time of enthusiastic utopianism, utilized his personal re-imaginings of myths central to Western civilization to challenge both orthodox religious and scientific thought of his day, hoping to reconstitute Western culture by reestablishing imagination as the primary human capacity.

Like other writers who survived the First World War, Tolkien was more pessimistic, willing to settle for the recovery of a little imaginativeness to lighten the hyperrationalizing of modern, industrial culture. So the tone of his works is closer to the nostalgic melancholy of Macpherson, just as his medium is a somewhat archaic prose, not bewilderingly innovative poetry. Yet the analogy to Blake ought not to be entirely dismissed, for both Tolkien and Blake understood that the imagination does not operate freely unless its possessors have the energy and courage to try reinventing the world around them—and its history.

This view helps to distinguish Tolkien from other writers of fantasy of the later nineteenth and early twentieth century, such as George Macdonald, Lord Dunsany, or William Morris. The latter's Earthly Paradise makes use of both Greek and Norse myths in a decorative poem that evades confronting the real difficulties of imaginatively reconstituting earlier mythological or legendary practices. The anthropological comparative analyses of James Frazer in The Golden Bough at the turn of the century in fact are closer to Tolkienian imaginings. But Tolkien never developed a deep interest in the Eastern or classical myths that were among Frazer's chief concerns. And Tolkien's way of inventing stories was by inventing languages which the stories embodied. He had no interest in simply retelling old stories, which is one reason he found the tales of King Arthur unadaptable to his purposes.

This point suggests how Tolkien's training as a comparative philologist, one who analyzes texts in terms of the history of the forms of its words and grammatical structures, paradoxically associates him with contemporaneous literary artists and literary trends he consciously ignored or disdained. It is less important that T. S. Eliot drew on Frazerian anthropology for *The Waste Land,* or that William Butler Yeats's poetry was founded on the basis of an original mythopoetic vision, than that while Tolkien was writing *The Silmarillion,* James Joyce was writing *Finnegans Wake.* This is no mere coincidence. The intellectual life of the first years of the twentieth century was dominated by a fascination with language, as is demonstrated by the psychology of Sigmund Freud and the philosophy of Ludwig Wittgenstein. This salient characteristic of modern intellectualism is highlighted by the work of Ferdinand de Saussure, who revolutionized the study of linguistics by turning it from philology to structuralism, a turn Tolkien's work seeks to counteract.

Comparative philology was the first historical science, having its origins in a monograph by Sir William Jones in 1786 which argued that Germanic and Celtic languages, as well as Greek, Latin, and Sanskrit, so closely resembled each other formally that they must have arisen from a common source—what soon came to be called Indo-European. This study of linguistic phenomena, therefore, depends on comparisons between languages and the reconstruction of processes of historical change, extrapolated backward behind any existent language to sources that can only be imagined. Tolkien pointed out that this approach permits an appreciation of a dead language, such as Homeric Greek, unavailable to those who used it when it was alive. Of course the later scholar cannot recover the nuances and meaning and connotations of the original speakers, nor the subtleties of pronunciation, but the scholar does have a perspective from which to see, with a special clarity that was formerly unavailable, the complexities of word

forms, the interrelationship of those forms, and their connection to word meanings.

Tolkien recognized that a keen source of pleasure for a philologist is perceiving relationships of word sounds and word forms to the ideas they express. This pleasure is intensified in the invention of languages, because, as all linguists agree, the meaning of words is arbitrary. "Arbitrary" here means that it is perfectly reasonable for the Romans, for example, to have called what we refer to as a tree by the name of arbor. It is reasonable because "arbor" is part of a complete, intricately organized linguistic system, a language, a human construct. But it is characteristic of languages that their intricate systems contain subtle complexities of meaning that change in time, taking on a history. To imagine a language as Tolkien did is to practice imagining complexities in words' meanings, how these change in time, and how particular words relate to or differ from words with similar meanings in other languages. This practice accounts for Tolkien's peculiar skill, for example, in deploying commonplace words so as to exploit their complicated metaphoric connotations. A simple but striking instance in *The Lord of the Rings* is "shadow," a word (like the phenomenon to which it refers) that we encounter casually every day, but which carries a rich freight of connotations, of fear, of doubt, of moral darkness, dangerous supernatural forces, and so on. It is these connotations of the ordinariness of "shadow" that Tolkien uses to evoke our imagination of Sauron's evil which, we realize when the Ring is destroyed, is also "shadowy" in being insubstantial.

Comparative philology requires imaginative contemplation of words, leading as it does inevitably to reconstruction, the speculative creation of a source word in a vanished language, such as Indo-European. This imagining is the reverse of irrational. It adheres to severely logical systems of morphology and phonology. Tolkien's fiction is an extension of that combination of rigorous logic and fantasy. He understood when he once overheard a man murmur thoughtfully to himself, "Yes, I think I shall express the accusative case by a prefix," that the speaker shared what Tolkien called his "secret vice" of inventing languages. He understood because he and the other man shared a knowledge of the strict discipline of linguistic science.

Most of the best poets and novelists of the early twentieth century experimented—"radically"—with language. Tolkien, too, was intrigued by what language could be made to do, for in good measure increased interest in what language is and how it works had been stimulated by the scholarship of philologists, culminating in works such as Milman Parry's discovery of the formulaic system of Homeric poetry and the production of the *Oxford English Dictionary*. But whereas Gertrude Stein or James Joyce manipulated language of the present day, Tolkien clung to the philological tradition of exploring the developmental, historical nature of words—even when he worked as an artist. Joyce, for example, seems to have been ignorant of scientific linguistics. He plays with words, principally by punning, as verbal counters that may have a symbolic, that is, unhistorical, significance, but he almost never draws upon their morphological history. Joyce's inventiveness with language is purely semantic, as in the sentence from *Finnegans Wake*, "There's many's the ice-polled globetopper is haunted by the hottest spot under his equator like Ramrod, the meaty hunter, always jaeger for a thrust." Tolkien's experimenting with language, contrarily, seeks to develop the *historical* (not symbolic) implications within the forms of ordinary words used in ordinary ways, even when he is describing imaginary places with invented names:

They entered the circle of white trees. As they did so the South Wind blew upon Cerin Amroth and sighed among the branches. Frodo stood still, hearing far off great seas upon beaches that had long ago been washed away, and sea-birds crying whose race had perished from the earth.
(*The Lord of the Rings*, vol. 1, bk. 2, ch. 6)

Here it is worth noting the strange analogy in Tolkien's art with Wittgensteinian language philosophy, of which he appears to have been ignorant. One of Wittgenstein's simplest but most resonant insights was that a private language is an impossibility. Tolkien had his "secret vice" of making up private languages. But in fact Tolkien recognized (in accord with Wittgenstein's perception) that to invent anything truly resembling actual language one must imagine it as used by a specific society and expressive of a distinctive historical culture. Tolkien's stories of unusual peoples are necessary validations of his philological imaginings.

This is why names are so important in his fanta-

sies. A name, of course, is a word that refers to a specific thing, place, or person, but specific persons are part of a society with a particular occupation, a set of relationships to family and others, living in a determinate way in a particular place, all of which characteristics have historical-cultural dimensions that can be suggested by the name and its relation to other names—as is most obvious in names such as John-son, or simply Smith. The implication of social dimensions intrinsic to names is more subtly illustrated by Tolkien's fondness for emphasizing that a particular person or place is named differently by different peoples. Thus "Rohan" is the Gondorian name given to the country inhabited by famous horsemen, who themselves call their homeland "the Riddermark." The place called "Rivendell" in our language, is called "Imladris" in the invented language Sindarin.

Even more revealing is the name Gollum, the hobbit Frodo's principal antagonist in *The Lord of the Rings*. "Gollum" is, in fact, an onomatopoeic nickname derived from a sound he began to make in his throat after acquiring the Ring by murdering his brother, who had found it. His real name was Trahald, meaning "worming in," of which the Anglicized version is Sméagol. These different names for the same character, which are extended by Sam Gamgee's calling him Slinker and Stinker, help to dramatize the changes in Gollum after he obtains the Ring, is driven out by his family after his brother's murder, loses the ring to Bilbo, and so on. For Gollum, like Bilbo and Frodo, is a hobbit, but both his physical form and his moral character are transformed by his history; his name-history represents his character-history.

Significant, too, is the first legendary figure Tolkien invented, one who appears in Shelleyan verses he wrote in 1914, "The Voyage of Eärendil the Evening Star," inspired by his reading of Cynewulf's Old English poem, *Crist*. Tolkien's poem portrays Eärendil's journey across the darkened firmament until he disappears in the light of dawn, and it puzzled Tolkien's friend G. B. Smith, who asked him what it was about. "I don't know," replied Tolkien. "I'll try to find out." *The Silmarillion* can be understood as his attempt to discover the fullest meaning of the name that had aroused his imagination, as the several hundred pages of *The Hobbit* are his attempt to discover what he meant when he wrote on a blank examination page, "In a hole in the ground there lived a hobbit."

J. R. R. TOLKIEN

THE earliest events treated by the Silmarillion material are parts of a cosmogonic myth, of which the most important elements are the Valar, powers deriving from divinity, like angels in Christian theology, existing before the making of the world. That world inhabited primarily by humankind Tolkien came to call Middle-earth. But first it was the scene of Elves' activity, the principal concern of *The Silmarillion* proper. The history of the Elves, who confront the griefs and burdens of deathlessness in a world of time and change, originates in a series of falls, like that initiated by the Christian angels. The first falling away from Eru or Iluvatar, "Father of All," is of Vala Melchar, or Morgoth, who creates his own music in discord with the cosmic music deriving from Eru. This "creative discord" is continued by those deriving from Morgoth. Of these the most significant is Fëanor, finest of Elven craftsmen and leader of the greatest of the Elven peoples, the Noldor. He succeeds in capturing the wondrous light of the Two Trees of the Valar in three jewels, the Silmarils. The story of these events and the subsequent self-exile of the most gifted of the Elves and their followers from Valinor, the home of the gods in the far west, and their reentry into Middle-earth, the place of their origin but now dominated by Melchar/Morgoth's evil creations against which they strive, constitute the history of the beginning of Middle-earth's First Age.

The struggles of this era are focused on the Silmarilli jewels, crafted by Fëanor and imprisoning within them the "radiance of pure light" (the meaning of Silmaril) of Valinor. The downfall of the Elves comes from the possessiveness of the creator of the Silmarilli, Fëanor, and his seven sons. When the jewels are captured by the Morgothian Enemy and set in his Iron Crown and Fëanor is slain, the sons of Fëanor take a disastrous oath of vengeance against any, even gods, who shall claim any part of the Silmarilli. They pervert most of their kindred, who rebel against the gods, leave Valinor, and wage desperate war against the Enemy in the northwest portion of Middle-earth. The evil of the oath of vengeance dogs all the Elves' efforts, and, despite many victories and much heroism, their efforts lead to the catastrophe of Elves slaying Elves.

The next stories concern men resisting the evil ruler of Middle-earth who retreat to the West, where they have heard they may find allies. There they encounter the self-exiled Elves in the midst of their war against the great Enemy. The central story of this part of the First Age (and keystone narrative of *The Silmarillion*) tells of Beren, an orphaned, outlawed mortal, who with the help of his lover Lúthien, an Elf maiden, penetrates the stronghold of the Enemy and wrests one of the Silmarilli from the Iron Crown. The marriage of Beren and Lúthien is the first between mortal and immortal. But—and this is an aspect of the tale that focuses a recurrent motif in Tolkien's cycles—the supreme triumph of the recapturing of the Silmaril leads to disaster, for the oath of the sons of Fëanor comes into play, and lust for the Silmaril brings the kingdoms of the Elves to ruin, as we learn from stories such as the *Children of Húrin* and *The Fall of Gondolin,* which are found in the *Lost Tales* series (a version of the latter story appears in *The Silmarillion*).

The Second Age is a dark one, much of west Middle-earth being desolated. The exiled Elves return to the island of Eressëa, within sight of Valinor, but from which they have excluded themselves. For their valor and good faith men of the Three Houses were permitted to inhabit the great western island of Númenor. Meanwhile, in Middle-earth Sauron, originally a noble being of Valinor perverted to evil, repents but, instead of returning to Valinor, lingers, disregarded by the Valar, and slowly he rebuilds Middle-earth. In the process Sauron becomes the reincarnation of evil lusting for complete power. During the Second Age his shadow grows and extends over Middle-earth. Meanwhile the Elves who remain become obsessed with fading, and as they grow sadder they become friendly with Dwarfs, to whom they had traditionally been hostile, and with them develop smithcraft (the art of forging in smithies) to its apogee. Some (though not all) allow themselves to be persuaded by Sauron that they could make Middle-earth as beautiful as Valinor, and these Elves fall into ways of magic and machinery. Their supreme product are the Rings of Power, whose chief potency is to arrest change, preserving what is loved as beautiful.

But secretly Sauron himself manufactures one Ruling Ring that contains and controls the power of the others and makes its wearer invisible while rendering things of the invisible world visible to him. Aware of what Sauron had done, the Elves hide their chief three Rings of Power and try to destroy the others. Sauron wars on the Elves and seizes many of the Rings of Power thus becoming almost supreme in Middle-earth, the last Elf Kingdom being that ruled by Gil-galad on the extreme west shores near the Havens of ships, while Elrond, son of Eärendil, maintains an enchanted sanctuary of Imladris (Rivendell, in English). But Sauron, through the power of the One Ring rules a growing empire from his great, black tower of Barad-dûr in Mordor, next to fire-riven Orodruin, Mount Doom, within which the greatest Ring was secretly forged.

This One Ring, unbreakable by any smithcraft and indissoluble in any fire, except that in which it was forged, determines the plot of *The Lord of the Rings,* which is the story of how, in fact, the One Ring was brought back to Barad-dûr in Sauron's Mordor (black land) and annihilated when thrown back into the fires in the Crack of Doom out of which it was created. Sauron's own being is thereby made to disintegrate, his power dematerializing as he becomes truly a shadow, an ominous, insubstantial memory of possessive will.

In the latter part of the Second Age the focus is on the glory and fall of Númenor, where dwell the only men who speak in an Elvish tongue. The Númenoreans rise to great wealth and wisdom, but eventually become overbearingly proud and try to gain dominion over the world. Outraged by this perversion of the gifts they have bestowed on the Númenoreans, the Valar consent to the island-continent's destruction by a great flood. From this only Elendil and a few faithful followers escape on their ships to Middle-earth, where he establishes and rules the kingdoms of Arnor and Gondor. The Second Age ends with the Last Alliance of Elves, led by Gil-galad, and Men, led by Elendil, resulting in a siege of Mordor, the seat of evil, and the destruction of Sauron in a great battle. Gil-galad and Elendil, however, are also slain in defeating Sauron, and Isildur, Elendil's son, cuts the One Ring from Sauron's hand. But Isildur, worked on by the temptation embodied in the Ring, refuses to cast it into the fires that will dissolve it. He marches away with it, but is soon drowned, and the Ring is lost to all knowledge.

The Third Age begins with Mordor and its Dark Tower empty, but not obliterated, while the Enemy's monstrous servants, including counterfeit creatures of illusion such as trolls, balrogs, and orcs, persist. Gradually the world becomes literally shadowed as Sauron regains existence and power. In this age the hobbits appear, chiefly in what is called the Shire. Through an odd chance an undistinguished hobbit, Bilbo Baggins, becomes possessed of the One Ring, and eventually his nephew and heir, Frodo Baggins, carries the Ring back to the Dark Tower just as the revived Sauron appears to have attained mastery over all of Middle-earth. As the Ring disintegrates in its founding fires Sauron and all his powers of evil crumble and disappear—at least for a time.

COMPOSITION OF THE LEGENDS

EVEN so schematic a sketch suggests what Tolkien himself recognized, that the hobbits for which he is most celebrated not only had no part in his original imaginings, but remained always secondary and peripheral features of his mythology. *The Hobbit* was written as a children's story, whereas the Silmarillion material was never directed to children. *The Hobbit,* moreover, contains relatively few references to either the details or general structure of *The Silmarillion.* But it is the hobbit books on which Tolkien's fame is based, and it seems unlikely that *The Silmarillion* would even have been published, let alone strengthened Tolkien's celebrity, without the success of the two hobbit books.

Understanding the order in which Tolkien's legends were invented illuminates an interesting feature of Tolkien's art. All that has been said about the One Ring appears nowhere in the Silmarillion material composed roughly between 1914 and 1937. The whole concept of the One Ring and how it was made and the effects of its unmaking was only imagined by Tolkien in the process of writing *The Lord of the Rings* between 1937 and 1952. Bilbo Baggins, the protagonist of *The Hobbit,* which was written between 1930 and 1936, happens upon a ring that makes him invisible and plays some part in his adventures, but which is not tremendously important. It was only when trying to devise a sequel to *The Hobbit* that Tolkien thought to make Bilbo's ring the One Ring with all its powers and significance. This new idea in fact required Tolkien for later editions to rewrite part of *The Hobbit* to make the role of the Ring congruent with its enhanced importance in *The Lord of the Rings.* Even so, careful readers notice that the role of this Ring in the first book is inconsistent with what is made of it in the trilogy.

What makes this peculiarity of composition so interesting is that it is a private, as it were miniaturized, version of what happens all the time in actual legends of preliterate peoples, illuminating the mode of what might be called inchoate composition that distinguishes genuine mythological literatures. These are formed by a variety of storytellers over a considerable span of time. Such living myths are not repeated verbatim; they are constantly being made anew by retellings, retellings that can vary enormously. The living myths of preliterate peoples, the original form of even the Greek and Norse myths, which we know only in their written, systematized, belated forms, were only to a degree systematic. Living myths are hospitable to innovation and radical change because human societies have to contend with changing conditions and new situations, climatological and geographical and social, in relations to other societies and cultures, as well as to interior economic and political self-transformations. The study of any large mythological system reveals, therefore, countless instances of the kind of rethinking and revaluation Tolkien's imagining of the One Ring epitomizes. Suddenly an unimportant object, character, or motif is given prominence in a new version of an old story to meet the exigencies of some change in the circumstances of the teller and his audience. Sometimes an important figure, even a divinity, abruptly vanishes from a traditional narrative. Or a central story of the mythology begins to be told in a new way radically incongruent with its original form.

The existence of the analogy between Tolkien's composition of his fantasies and this inchoateness of living oral mythologies is not merely coincidental. Tolkien was a profound, lifelong student of works such as the *Kalevala* and the Norse sagas that function thus inchoately. These works are fascinating, and indeed aesthetically attractive, precisely because they are so open, able to accommodate radical differences and shifts in perspective, structure, and meaning while remaining expressive of the ways and beliefs of specific peoples. Tolkien was aware that myths are genuinely alive only so long as they retain this power of self-reconstituting creativeness and do not attain the self-sufficient, self-contained perfectedness of form modern criticism tends to identify as the highest achievement of art. The chief reason why Tolkien never "completed" *The Silmarillion* was his commitment to this quality. The book published posthumously under that title, for example, includes material on Sauron and the One Ring supporting the description given above, because after the publication of *The Lord of the Rings* in the mid 1950's Tolkien added to and revised the Silmarillion material to make it congruent with *The Lord of the Rings,* which is supposed to deal with a later period.

Tolkien's fantasy is the only modern fantasy that is composed according to principles equatable with the way in which myths and legends are created by oral cultures. This uniqueness is especially impressive because a large number of modern works of fantasy and science fiction—*Islandia,* Isaac Asimov's *Foundation* series, Frank Herbert's *Dune* novels, for instance—present carefully developed whole cultures and complete geographies. Indeed, many fantastic romances attempt to recreate complete societies, many with far more scrupulosity of concrete detail than Tolkien. He is, in fact, sparse and vague on many practical details of ordinary life and the processes by which things are done or made; one senses that he does not have the faintest idea of how in practice a ring might be forged. But no other fantasy writer has reproduced, as Tolkien has, the *method* of imagining characteristic of oral cultures.

No other writer of modern fantasy has had the knowledge to do what Tolkien thus did. No other writer of modern fantasy has spent a lifetime studying in an intensely scholarly way the "fantasies" of sophisticated preliterate peoples, the northern medieval peoples for whom what we call "fantasy"—the use of imagination to conceive of what one was unlikely to experience in everyday existence—was an important part of their life, perhaps the most important part. Tolkien's profession of philologist is decisively significant for Tolkien's art. For it is through the historical analysis of words in texts representing, with varying degrees of accuracy, accounts and stories originally told orally, that philologists are able imaginatively to reconstruct how particular tales and accounts came into being and their probable relation to other tales and accounts.

Both *The Hobbit* and *The Lord of the Rings,* especially the latter, gain from the Silmarillion-material references a peculiar resonance, or a beauty like that of a glimpse of distant towers in a sunlit mist. Almost all other works of fantasy are in themselves exhaustive—the full extent of the fantasist's imagination is realized in the book we read. One feels that there is no more that is significant for *this* invented world than what is depicted. The hobbit books appear as amidst both a nimbus and penumbra of history, genealogy, and other, untold, stories—facts and imaginings far more extensive and of a different kind from what we read. And the inchoateness is helpful to this resonating effect, because many of the implications and references in the hobbit books are vague, uncertain, inconsistent, seldom exactly fitting any determinate structure.

MODERN INFLUENCES

YET the inspiration (no other word seems appropriate) of hobbits also enabled Tolkien to realize his Silmarillion fantasies with a vividness and cogency that would otherwise have been impossible. The imaginary hobbits, paradoxically, enable Tolkien to link a twentieth-century readership to the ancient Silmarillion world. In Tolkien's stories hobbits are frequently referred to as halflings, that is half-humans—and they are at least that. Except that they are usually only three or three and half feet tall, and that because of their rather large and hirsute feet they prefer not to wear shoes, hobbits are anatomically, in their dress, social life, and habits—notably their fondness for smoking tobacco and drinking beer—identical to humans—very English bourgeois humans. More exactly, perhaps, hobbits are, except for height and feet, like lower middle-class Tolkiens and Suffields holed up in and around Birmingham in the first half of the twentieth century.

Tolkien once remarked that the name "hobbit" owed something to Sinclair Lewis' character George F. Babbitt. If we turn to the opening two pages of *Babbitt* (1922) we will see what Tolkien meant:

The towers of Zenith aspired above the morning mist; austere towers of steel and cement and limestone, sturdy as cliffs and delicate as silver rods. They were neither citadels nor churches, but frankly and beautifully office-buildings. . . . pouring out the honest wares that would be sold up the Euphrates and across the veldt. The whistles rolled out in greeting a chorus cheerful as the April dawn; the song of labor in a city built—it seemed—for giants. . . .

Plainly enough, prosperous, well-fed Bilbo Baggins, the original hobbit, owes something to the creation of Sinclair Lewis. Tolkien set himself the problem of constructing a connected body of legendary tales, ranging from the cosmogonic to the fairy story, "cool and clear" and possessing a "fair elusive beauty" as he confessed to one correspondent, that would form a majestic whole, yet leave scope for imaginative work by "other minds and other hands"—and this in a world in which the dominant literary form was realistic fiction! Tolkien himself observed the absurdity. Yet he tried to make this gift to England, his native land he loved so deeply that he almost never voluntarily left it, by combining his knowledge of its medieval past with his experience of the contemporary bourgeois world in a fashion that would allow the former historically to enoble the latter. This ambition also explains the vein of comedy that runs through the hobbit books, and the remarkably unobtrusive fact that in them two different styles of speech coexist. Bilbo, for instance, speaks in the modern idiom: "Don't wait to knock! Tea is at four." But characters like Gandalf, Thorin Oakenshield, and Aragorn speak archaically. And their speech reflects patterns of thought and behavior such as one encounters in *Beowulf, The Niebelungenlied,* and the Norse Sagas. Thus Gandalf tells Aragorn:

It is not our part to master all the tides of world, but to do what is in us for the succour of those years wherein we are set, uprooting the evil in the fields that we know, so that those who live after may have clean earth to till. What weather they shall have is not ours to rule.

Then Gandalf asks the king, "For do I not guess rightly, Aragorn, that you have shown yourself to him in the Stone of Orthanc?" and receives a "kingly" answer: "I did so ere I rode from the Hornburg. . . . I deemed that the time was ripe . . ." (*The Lord of the Rings,* vol. 3, bk. 5, ch. 9,).

Against the heroic codes emphasizing rank, courage, and sheer will expressing itself in joy at violence and personal combat, Bilbo and Frodo are modern middle-class figures concerned about respectability; they are self-distrustful, and capable, like protagonists of that modern form the bildungsroman, of radical personality change, whereas their more archaic peers define themselves by unyielding adherence to traditional patterns of behavior. Aragorn can be himself only by behaving royally, Gandalf by behaving as a wizard.

Absurd as it may have been to try to link these two historically distinct ways of life, the ideal of a continuity of English civilization fired Tolkien's imagination, as can be seen in his 1929 essay *"Ancrene Wisse* and *Hali Meiðhad"* (published just after Tolkien had written "In a hole in the ground there lived a hobbit"), which remained his most elegant piece of scholarly writing. In that article, on the basis of a rigorously logical analysis of carefully marshalled linguistic details, Tolkien arrives at a vision of the survival, somewhere in the west of England, of a small group of isolated people adhering to the oldest English language traditions, undisturbed by the Danish and Norman invasions that distorted the pure lines of development from Old English to our present speech. It is that recognizedly visionary ideal on which the hobbit's Shire is founded, but because it is an ideal, Tolkien's "escape" to it is more than a mere evasion of modern life.

There are, of course, as with any work of art, many sources for *The Hobbit* and *The Lord of the Rings,* some ancient, some contemporary. "Mirkwood" and the "Misty Mountains" are lifted directly from Norse sagas—Dwarf names and Gandalf's come from the *Voluspa.* Yet it seems a fair guess, both because rats, moles, and badgers live in holes, and because we know Tolkien's Inkling associates, especially C. S. Lewis and Charles Williams, were deeply influenced by the book, that some inspiration for hobbits came from Kenneth Grahame's *The Wind in the Willows.* That book combines in a peculiarly English way fantasizing with amusing (because the characters are, after all, rather unattractive animals) representations of the most egregiously ordinary aspects of middle-class life—with the women left out. The accessibility of the hobbit books owes much to this kind of sub-fantasy, one might call it, of gently satiric representation of the most conventional of English conventionalities—to which Sam Gamgee, Frodo's chief supporter in his adventures, also contributes.

That Sam's quietly selfless loyalty, good-humored tenacity under difficulties, and thick-headed unimaginativeness about what does not immediately impinge on him, his master, and their families, are traits of an enduring British type was dramatized by the letter to Tolkien written by a real Sam Gamgee, inquiring how he had become a character in the professor's book. The real Sam, of course, had not read the book—he had picked up his name from a dramatization his daughter heard on the radio. He was not offended, or especially interested, that Tolkien's Sam was heroic, only mildly curious—as Tolkien's Sam would have been.

The difficulty with Tolkien's Sam is the overtness of his literary heritage; he is a later example of English forelock-tugging retainers who defend to the death the class system at its most rigid. Worse, as his girl Rosie and old Gaffer back in the Shire remind us, he is modeled directly on Charles Dickens' Sam Weller. It is unwise to imitate an incomparable performance, and what makes this imitation especially painful is Sam's incapacity for Dickensian humor. The independence implicit in Weller's shrewd humorousness, moreover, is missing from Gamgee—and from Tolkien's world. Gamgee's loyalty to Frodo is blind (as are all Tolkienian loyalties), whereas Weller's to Mr. Pickwick is not. Sam Weller freely chooses to serve Mr. Pickwick, thereby teaching us much about the dignity of service to others and the human rewards that may accrue to good people even if they behave ridiculously. That kind of wisdom is beyond Tolkien, and this failure has encouraged condemnations of his work as both psychologically and ethically simpleminded.

THE SIGNIFICANCE OF ADULT FANTASY

THE charge seems to carry weight because Tolkien's moral system appears crude and superficial. For example, he has no taste for the contradictoriness of trickster figures—in Norse mythology superbly embodied in the figure of Loki. Because Tolkien was incapable of challenging his own system of belief, he imagines "goodness" and "badness" in terms of the simplest popular stereotypes; they are not arranged to compel his readers to reassess their firmest presuppositions about what constitutes goodness and badness.

Yet the student revolutionaries of the 1960's invoked Tolkien the pious Catholic as often as Blake the radical Protestant—who became a popular poet only in that decade, two centuries after his birth. I remember at the University of Wisconsin in Madison in the late 1960s perceiving through a tear-gas haze the conjunction of a sign hoisted by the occupiers of the Education Building quoting Blake's Proverb of Hell, "The Tygers of Wrath are Wiser than the Horses of Instruction" with a giant graffiti scrawled on an unfinished building looking like a ruined tower at the foot of the hill, FRODO LIVES. The vast majority of student protestors were by neither temperament nor background very radical: what they principally desired was the revival of some moral commitments in a world increasingly demoralized because entirely rationalized and pragmatized. Tolkien's moralism, less energetic and demanding than Blake's calls to active self-examination, was in important respects more congenial exactly *because* it was so conventionalized.

The young people of the 1960's were attracted to Blake and Tolkien by these writers' unashamed imaginativeness. The young people were imaginatively starved to emaciation, and the avidity with which they, and their successors, seized on *The Lord of the Rings* is a symptom of the imaginative under-nourishment to which modern society subjects its youth.

The bravest and the brightest were drawn to daring innovators such as Blake, but for the majority, to whose suburbanized sensibilities Blake's authentic radicalism and uncompromising passionateness could only be troubling, Tolkien's quieter, far more conventionalized stories, encouraging escape rather than confrontation, were more congenial. Perhaps the least attractive aspect of Tolkienian conventionality is its sexism. Females play very minor parts in both *The Hobbit* and *The Lord of the Rings*, and most of their appearances are somewhat embarrassing, the most painful being that of Shelob. Sam and Frodo's encounter with this spider monster reads like an elementary Freudian text describing male fear-fantasies of female sexual power.

Tolkien's biography is not in these matters attractive. He was one of those good, responsible husbands whose unwitting selfishness damaged a long-suffering wife. One must not forget, however, that in these matters Tolkien adhered to long-established attitudes and patterns of behavior dependent on male-bondings fostered by the English public-school system and universities. The pipe-smoking, beer-drinking, all-male groups, such as the Inklings, served to protect and sustain male imaginativeness. In the modern world, which began earliest in England, the social systems sustaining masculine public fairy-tale telling had been increasingly destroyed. And many men, too. When the Armistice came in 1918 only one of Tolkien's friends from school and university was still alive. Tolkien's conventional attitudes toward women were a price he (and his wife) paid for being free to imagine dragons in the company of other men. And a degree of conventionality in a writer of fantasy is not necessarily a bad thing.

Take dragons for example. No story with a dragon in it can be a total failure. Because dragons are not real, an author who includes one has exercised *some* imagination. But precisely because dragons are human artifacts, not natural creatures, they take shape through conventions of art. And Tolkien's great dragon, Smaug, the best part of *The Hobbit,* is wonderful because carefully crafted to the conventions of dragon depiction. We perceive the care because Smaug is so unlike the terrific dragon in *Beowulf* that Tolkien publicly admired. Beowulf's dragon, after all, came from a time when the imaginariness of dragons was not firmly established. He is truly frightening. When he blasts out of his burrow a fury of claws, scales, and searing flame, one does not approve of Beowulf's companions' pell-mell desertion of their leader, but one understands it. Bravely, Tolkien sacrificed most of what distinguishes the dragon he loved in *Beowulf* (retaining principally his deep malice and stupid exactness as to the contents of his hoard) to produce a more conventional, and therefore for our age, a more convincing and interesting, dragon. For example, Smaug is a clever wordsmith, like many subsequent dragons in twentieth-century literature. Tolkien deserves the credit for having restored dragons to a respectable place in literature: every dragon that has appeared after *The Hobbit* is a direct descendant of Smaug.

That *The Hobbit* is a book for children is no longer ground for denigrating its aesthetic accomplishment, since children's literature has become the object of increased scholarly attention. But *The Hobbit* is not quite in the top rank of children's stories, though as young Rayner Unwin predicted, it satisfies the five-to-nine-year-old crowd. Its weakness lies not in occasional condescensions of style, which Tolkien later deplored more strongly than anyone else. Nor is it the poetry, which is as undistinguished as most—though not all—of Tolkien's verse. (It seems oddly characteristic of comparative philologists to lack the ear needed for the music of genuine poetic form.) *The Hobbit* does not triumph as a children's book because Tolkien was so polemically committed to the recreation of *adult* fantasy. His conservatism and conventionality were enlivened by his conviction that there was inherent value in imaginary stories for everyone living in the modern world. Twentieth-century existence was not so unmitigatedly splendid, Tolkien suggested in his essay on fairy tales, that imaginative escapes from it should be programmatically condemned. And he was consistently explicit that his purpose in *The Lord of the Rings* was to create a long story that would simply amuse, delight, and quicken the emotions of his readers. Tolkien hated the allegorization of imaginative narrative (even resisting W. H. Auden's praise of his work as a splendid realization of the quest archetype). For Tolkien allegory degraded storytelling by imposing some extrinsic meaningfulness upon narrative that could be entirely satisfying intrinsically.

Exactly contrary to Bruno Bettelheim, the psychologist who wrote that fairy tales were composed primarily for the benefit of children, Tolkien wished to reclaim fairyland as an abandoned province of adulthood. This being his heroic quest, he could never hope to address children with that sincere innocence distinguishing the finest of children's writers, such as Beatrix Potter and Jean de Brunhoff.

Tolkien's purposes are revealed by the intriguing fact that the plot structure of *The Hobbit* and *The Lord of the Rings* is identical. The earlier work begins with an "Unexpected Party," which results in Bilbo Baggins learning of the treasure it will become his task to steal from Smaug. The later story begins with a "Long-Expected Party" that leads to Frodo Baggins learning of the Ring it will be his doom to carry back to Sauron's tower. In the first part of the journey from the Shire each hobbit picks up a valuable sword and reaches Rivendell, where there is a conference with the Elf Elrond and the wizard Gandalf. Both hobbits leave Rivendell with a party led by Gandalf that is prevented by storms from passing over the Misty Mountains, so that they must pass through the mountains by means of caverns in which they fend off an attack by Orcs,

encounter Gollum for the first time, and lose Gandalf. The latter portion of both quests involves journeying down a river to a desolated land dominated by powerful evil, climbing a mountain, and penetrating through another tunnel to their goal. The climax of both quests is marked by huge battles engaging a variety of peoples and creatures, in which a king atones for previous errors by a heroic death after leading a decisive charge, and the arrival of a flight of eagles assuring victory for the good. Celebrated for their heroism by Elfs, Dwarfs, and Men, both Bilbo and Frodo return to the Shire to find that in their absence those hostile to them have gained power, so they must struggle to regain their home and restore the tranquility of earlier hobbit life.

Few readers notice this structural identity because the *Lord of the Rings* is so much longer and richer in incidents and diverse characters; it is, in fact, the fulfillment of the hobbit history that Tolkien did not yet know he was trying to write when he undertook his children's story. And the parallelism dramatizes an extraordinary inversion. Bilbo's quest fits the traditional pattern: he seeks out and wins something precious to himself and those with whom he is associated. Frodo's quest is unusual in being an attempt to return and get rid of a dangerous burden. Bound up in that twist is Tolkien's most important contribution to modern fantasy.

It is Gollum, the marvelously slimy-sympathetic, vicious but victimized last possessor of the Ring before Bilbo, who calls the Ring "My Precious," and it is Gollum's relentless quest to recover the Ring that has debased him which finally destroys him and allows Frodo to succeed. In a climactic struggle Gollum bites off the hobbit's finger on which he wears the ring, leaps back, and falls into Sauron's fiery Crack of Doom. The true "power" of the Ring is not that it bestows longevity and invisibility, or even that it controls other powers, but that it becomes overwhelmingly precious to its wearer—and therefore deadly. Modern commentators are reminded of Lord Acton's aphorism on how political power corrupts, but Tolkien is reviving an ancient truth known to many peoples but overlooked in the modern consumerist world— that every gift is a curse, like Helen's beauty that left so many Greeks and Trojans dead. Many cultures have recognized more perceptively than ours the dangers inherent in powers to cure: often the healing doctor through exercise of restorative forces is transformed into a destructive demon. For change and chance, despite the delusions of stability fostered by modern industrialized society, is the rule of life, and it is a function of fantasy to remind us of that rule.

To do this, fantasy writers must resist the lures of psychology and symbolism. Frodo and Bilbo (like most of Tolkien's characters) are little more individualized than Cinderella, or the disregarded youngest son who finally slays the monsters and wins the princess. Bilbo and Frodo are, simply, hobbits, halflings, representatives of small, unnoticed people, upon whom, all unrecognized, the destiny of great events frequently depends. Characters in fantasy are not individuals as are the characters in realistic novels, but the representatives of social subgroups, such as outcasts, or embodiments of social types, such as stuffy stay-at-homes who do not want adventures, or dramatic illustrations of how patterns of force, such as the accidents of life, can suddenly distort normal existence. The portrayal of fantasy characters tells us little or nothing about personal psychology because their function is to enable us to imagine how unimportant individuals, like ourselves, may affect and be affected by the interplay of vast natural or cultural forces—an interplay more difficult to conceive, and to explain, than personal motives or idiosyncrasies of behavior.

In the modern world, where nature is supposedly conquered and life is supposedly entirely rationally ordered, only the realm of personal psychology seems free and untrammeled, and with what imaginativeness it has left, modern literature concentrates on personal psychology. It is this focus from which the fantasist must escape, in part because it leads to an overvaluation of symbolism. One's private hangups, for example, have no significance for anyone else except so far as they embody universal principles. So Freudian psychology isolates individuals in secret rooms to bring to light the specific case of a meta-historical pathology needing to be exorcised. The modern psychologist is in this sense like the modern structural linguist (not philologist), a definer of universal principles that reduce the particular incident, usage or person, to relative unimportance, no more than a case. As Tolkien reactionarily clung to comparative philology, imagining reconstructions from minute particulars of language usage, so his stories reac-

tionarily return to premodern forms and styles in which what a story means, what it may symbolize, is less important than simply what it is.

The weakness of most contemporary fantasy is a determination to be meaningful, to symbolize beyond itself. Here Tolkien's center of scholarly interest, northern European sagas, legends, myths, and folktales, saved him, for this literature has been little contaminated by a quest for symbolic significance. We are still able to read *Beowulf* and many of the Norse sagas simply as gripping stories. And a major function of storytelling is to renew our appreciation of events as events, the potency of living in a world where things happen all the time, where everything always changes. Narrative art, Tolkien thought, degenerates into magic or machinery, when it strives to overcome, not simply confront, that endlessly transformative activity.

Let us return for a moment to the climactic moment in *The Lord of the Rings* to clarify fantasy's resistance to symbolism. Gollum inadvertently saves Frodo from the evil potency of the Ring by inadvertently destroying himself and the Ring. This emphasis upon chance at the story's climax is consistent with the prominence of contingency throughout the book. Neither aesthetic nor ethical patterning is allowed to outweigh happenstance. There is, of course, much order and logic in the trilogy, and even the possibility of a spiritual system, a "logic" of forgiveness and retribution, is raised, but never, as the climax demonstrates, is sheer chance eliminated. It is this characteristic above all else that makes Tolkien's work bothersome to many readers, for whom imagining is justified only if the fantasizing possesses significance. Tolkien's willingness to accept contingency as contingency in his stories derives from his profound knowledge of medieval literature, in which this characteristic often prevails, and from his commitment to philology, which is a severely logical discipline that finally compels the scholar to make an imaginative leap.

For example, in *"Sigelwara land,"* a scholarly essay published before Tolkien had begun *The Lord of the Rings,* he deployed an intricate array of philogical evidence to prove that the first part of an Anglo-Saxon word, "Sigelhearwan," *sigel,* had originally meant both "jewel" and "sun." But in combination with *hearwan* it came to refer to creatures "with red-hot eyes that emitted sparks, with faces black as soot." Such monsters, produced by Tolkien's imaginative word-history, suggest the terrible balrog who almost destroys the magician Gandalf in *The Lord of the Rings,* while the *silmarils,* the jewels filled with light from which *The Silmarillion* derives its name, find a source in Tolkien's speculation about *sigel.*

Philology encourages this kind of imagined history because a philologist must deal simultaneously with two separate variables, meanings of words and the forms of words. The developments of forms and meanings remain independent even when affecting one another. Tolkien cites the example of "yelp," which for a long time meant "to speak proudly" and was most often linked to major promises, as when a knight vowed to undertake a dangerous deed. Quite suddenly, without any change in form, for no discernible reason, "yelp" began to mean the noise made by foxes or dogs. Because the philologist can find no reason for this change, he must learn to live with the sheer fact, the contingency. In the study of *any* word, moreover, the philologist must keep in mind that there may always be homophones, phonetically indistinguishable elements that possess different meanings and therefore are simultaneously the same word and different words—Tolkien's example is the Indo-European stem (or stems) *men,* meaning "stick out" and "think." And he must remember that semantic change, as in the case of "yelp," is often radical, but may have left no evidence of its violence (if, for instance, the earlier usage of "yelp" as "proud speaking" had not chanced to survive in what texts remain). Seldom can a philologist know whether to weight form or meaning more heavily in tracing linguistic developments, and more often than not the very rigor of his systematic methods compels him to recognize that no fully coherent explanation is possible, that he must use his imagination to deal with inescapable contingencies if he is to be true to his scientific procedure.

This is why Tolkien insists in "On Fairy-Stories" that "fantasy does not destroy or even insult Reason . . . nor obscure the perception of Scientific verity" (*The Tolkien Reader,* p. 54). He argues that "the clearer is the reason the better fantasy it will make," because fantasy is founded on "recognition of fact, but not slavery to it" (p. 55). The strengths and weaknesses of Tolkien's fantasy stories, and the admiration and distaste they have aroused, derive from his carrying into his art his pleasure in imagining provoked by philological uncertainties.

Upon that transfer depends, finally, Tolkien's understanding of the function of fantasy fiction, most forcefully stated in his preface to the first paperback edition of *The Lord of the Rings.* The book, he asserts, has no symbolic meaning or message, no purpose other than to "hold the attention of readers, amuse them, delight them, and at times maybe excite them or deeply move them" (p. ix). Admitting his "book is too short" (p. x)—a splendidly medieval view of a 200,000-word story—Tolkien goes on to observe that he prefers history "true or feigned" (p. xi) to allegory; the latter implies domination by the author, whereas history bestows freedom on the reader, since it represents accidents, real or imagined, as accidents, things that just happen to happen.

Tolkien's preference for history over symbolism explains why in *The Lord of the Rings* magic appears, at best, as a dubious skill, even though Tolkien had argued in "On Fairy-Stories"—composed just as he was beginning *The Lord of the Rings*—that fantasy depends upon enchantment. The art of fantasy for Tolkien is subcreation that aspires to "the elvish craft, Enchantment" which, however much it may resemble magic, is "wholly different from the greed for self-centered power which is the mark of the mere Magician" ("On Fairy-Stories," p. 53). Magic in Tolkien's view is not true art but technique, craft, and its purpose is power, not the delight of joint enchantment. Unlike enchantment, magic produces, or claims to produce, an alteration in the primary world. Tolkien defines enchantment in terms of joining and sharing of creator and audience "in making and delight," whereas magic can only establish separateness and power relations. So he associates magic with technology and manufacturing and their evil consequences.

Among these the worst for Tolkien is possessiveness and materialism, Babbitt's disease, with which Bilbo was dangerously infected, and which, theoretically at least, the youthful protestors of the 1960's rejected. Resistance to possessiveness is the ground for Tolkien's readiness to defend fantasy as "escape," which he identified with recovery, his version of what literary critics call defamiliarization. The "drab blur of triteness or familiarity" ("Of Fairy-Stories," p. 57) of the modern world Tolkien thought originated in our possessiveness: what is familiar is what we have appropriated mentally or legally. What we "know" in some way we "own," whether it be our car or our spouse. In no sense, then, does fantasy deny the facts of the primary world, especially its accidents. To the contrary, fantasy arises from a recognition of the intractability of chance that our familiarity with the rationalized organizations of modern life has obscured, and which we prefer obscured so as to feel secure of our possessions.

For Tolkien, therefore, "escape" in the contemporary world is not, as most literary critics assert, the flight of a deserter. The "realism" these critics applaud, he felt, means behaving like a collaborator, accommodating oneself to a reality recognized to be, if not detestable, needing radical improvement. The escape of the fantasist is a resistance to accepting what the currently dominant (but of course evanescent) fashion of defining reality treats as inexorable. In such arguments Tolkien's cordial dislike for many features of the modern world surfaces, particularly his scorn of improved means to deteriorated ends, and his grumpy professorial opinion that much of today's "serious" literature is only play under a glass roof beside a swimming pool.

CONCLUSION

Tolkien's strengths and weaknesses depend upon his conservatism, even his reactionariness. He is an erratic writer, sometimes awkward, often prolix, occasionally portentously unprogressive in telling his tale, at other moments brilliant, as in the riddling match between Bilbo and Gollum, or in his conception of the Ents, great tree-creatures whose language is composed of enormously long words used to tell very slowly long, long, long stories. But Tolkien's primary virtue is his steady resistance to any temptation to be led away from the satisfaction of the imaginative story. Sauron's evil has no more significance as evil than shadows have significance—other than marking the absence of light we need and love, although we can scarcely conceive of human love in a shadowless land.

How Tolkien's reputation will thrive or dwindle, then, depends largely on whether his conception of the function of storytelling—embodied in his endeavors to recover something of northern medieval narrative art—gains or loses support. Nothing defines more clearly his sense of historical fantasy's opposition to what is dominant in contemporary

literature than his insistence on a happy ending, what he called, coining a new critical term, the "eucatastrophe" essential to fairy stories. The eucatastrophe does not deny the existence, even the probability, of sorrow and failure, but it lifts the heart with a glimpse of possible joy.

Tolkien ends his essay "On Fairy-Stories" with a characteristic reference to an ancient, little-known poem, "The Black Bull of Norroway"; it represents exactly the ultimate effect he thought art could attain and toward which all his fiction aimed.

"Seven long years I served for thee,
The glassy hill I clamb for thee,
The bluidy shirt I wrang for thee,
And wilt thou not wauken and turn to me?"
He heard and turned to her.

Happy endings are not assured; they depend on luck, on chance, and for just that reason they bring a catch in the breath at finding in this harsh world a momentary deliverance or beauty's grace or the heart's desire.

SELECTED BIBLIOGRAPHY

I. BIBLIOGRAPHY. J. A. Johnson, *J. R. R. Tolkien: Six Decades of Criticism.* Bibliographies and Indexes in World Literature, 6 (Westport, Ct, 1986), comprehensive, with succint, accurate annotations for the hundreds of entries, and excellent indexes.

II. SEPARATE WORKS. *The Hobbit; or, There and Back Again* (London, 1937), literary fantasy, illustrated by the author; *Farmer Giles of Ham* (London, 1949), literary fantasy, illustrated by P. Baynes; *The Fellowship of the Ring: Being the First Part of The Lord of the Rings* (London, 1954; Boston, 1955), literary fantasy; *The Two Towers: Being the Second Part of The Lord of the Rings* (London, 1954; Boston, 1965), literary fantasy; *The Return of the King: Being the Third Part of The Lord of the Rings* (London, 1955; Boston, 1956), literary fantasy; *The Adventures of Tom Bombadil and Other Verses from the Red Book* (London, 1962; Boston, 1963), poems, illustrated by P. Baynes; *Tree and Leaf* (London, 1964; Boston, 1965), essays and short fiction, reprints "Leaf by Niggle," an expanded version of "On Fairy-Stories," "The Homecoming of Beorhnoth Beorhthelm's Son," and "Smith of Wooton Major." *The Tolkien Reader* (New York, 1966), illustrated by P. Baynes, includes "The Homecoming of Beorhtnoth," "On Fairy-Stories," "Leaf by Niggle,"

"Farmer Giles of Ham," and "The Adventures of Tom Bombadil;" *Smith of Wootton Major* (London, Boston, 1967), short fantasy, illustrated by P. Baynes.

Posthumous Works: *The Silmarillion* (London, Boston, 1977), a collection of epic poems and fantasies; *Unfinished Tales of Númenor and Middle-Earth* (London, Boston, 1980), short fiction, ed. by C. Tolkien; *The Book of Lost Tales Part I* (London, 1983; Boston, 1984), ed. by C. Tolkien; *The Book of Lost Tales Part II* (London and Boston, 1984), ed. by C. Tolkien; *The Lays of Beleriand* (London and Boston, 1985), ed. by C. Tolkien; *The Shaping of Middle-Earth: the Quenta, the Ambarkanta, and the Annals, together with the two earliest "Silmarillion" and the First Map* (London and Boston, 1986), ed. by C. Tolkien. The last four entries contain previously unpublished stories, poems, plans, and notes primarily relevant to *The Silmarillion* and *The Lord of the Rings*.

III. ESSAYS. "Ancrene Wisse and Hali Meiðhad," *Essays and Studies by Members of the English Association*, 14 (1929); "Beowulf: The Monsters and the Critics," *Proceedings of the British Academy*, 22 (1936), reprinted in *The Tolkien Reader;* "On Fairy-Stories," in C. S. Lewis, ed., *Essays Presented to Charles Williams* (Oxford, 1947; Grand Rapids, Mich., 1966), revised and reprinted in *Tree and Leaf* and *The Tolkien Reader; The Monsters and the Critics, and Other Essays* (London, Boston, 1984), critical and biographical essays, ed. by C. Tolkien.

IV. LETTERS. *The Letters of J. R. R. Tolkien* (London, Boston, 1981), ed. by H. Carpenter with C. Tolkien.

V. BIOGRAPHICAL AND CRITICAL STUDIES. N. D. Issacs and R. A. Zimbardo, eds., *Tolkien and the Critics* (Notre Dame, Ind., 1968), among the best of critical essays, including essays by W. H. Auden and C. S. Lewis; C. R. Stimson, *J. R. R. Tolkien*, Columbia Essays on Modern Writers series (New York, 1969), a cogent but hostile critique.

P. H. Kocher, *Master of Middle-earth: The Fiction of J. R. R. Tolkien* (Boston, 1972), detailed and thoughtful study; R. Sale, *Modern Heroism: Essays on D. H. Lawrence, William Empson, and J. R. R. Tolkien* (Berkeley, Calif., 1973), interesting comparisons, somewhat critical of Tolkien; R. Foster, *A Guide to Middle-earth* (New York, 1971), annotated glossary with page references; H. Carpenter, *Tolkien: A Biography* (London and Boston, 1977), judicious, perceptive, factually accurate account.

P. H. Kocher, *A Reader's Guide to the Silmarillion* (Boston, 1980); R. Noel, *The Languages of Tolkien's Middle-Earth* (Baltimore, Boston, 1980), includes glossaries, guides to grammars and pronunciation; R. Helms, *Tolkien and the Silmarils: Imagination and Myth in "The Silmarillion"* (Boston, 1981), a thorough guide; N. D. Issacs and R. A. Zimbardo, eds., *Tolkien: New Critical Perspectives* (Lexington, Ky., 1981); T. A. Shippey, *The Road to Middle-Earth* (London, 1982), highly opinionated, but informed analysis of the philological basis of Tolkien's art; R. L. Purtill, *J. R. R. Tolkien: Myth, Morality, and Religion* (San Francisco, 1984), analysis of the religious dimension of Tolkien's art; L. D. Rossi, *The Politics of Fantasy: C. S. Lewis and J. R. R. Tolkien* (Ann Arbor, Mich., 1984), useful comparison of the two friends and very different writers of fantasy.

NOTE: There are Tolkien societies in both Great Britain and the United States. Each publishes its own journal:

Mallorn, published by the Tolkien Society of Great Britain, 9 Kingston Road, Ilford, Essex, England.

Mythlore, published by the Mythopoeic Society, Box 24560, Los Angeles, Calif. 90024. In 1973 *The Tolkien Journal*, a publication of the Tolkien Society of America, P. O. Box 373, Highland, Mich. 48031, merged with *Mythlore*.

Index

All references include volume numbers in bold-face Roman numerals and page numbers either in Arabic, to indicate the text of an essay, or in lowercase Roman, to refer to the introduction in a volume. Extended treatment of a subject is indicated by bold-face page numbers.

"Haunter, The" (Hardy), **VI**: 18
Haunter of the Dark, The . . . (Lovecraft), **III**: 345
Haw Lantern, The (Heaney), **Supp. II**: 268, **279–281**
Hawes, Stephen, **I**: 49, 81
Hawk in the Rain, The (Hughes), **Supp. I**: 343, 345, 363
"Hawk in the Rain, The" (Hughes), **Supp. I**: 345
Hawkins, Lewis Weldon, **VI**: 85
Hawkins, Sir John, **II**: 143
Hawthorne, Nathaniel, **III**: 339, 345; **VI**: 27, 33–34
Hawthorne (James), **VI**: 33–34, 67
Haxton, Gerald, **VI**: 369
Hay Fever (Coward), **Supp. II**: 139, 141, **143–145**, 148, 156
Haydon, Benjamin, **IV**: 214, 227, 312
"Haystack in the Floods, The" (Morris), **V**: 293
Hayter, Alethea, **III**: 338, 346; **IV**: xxiv–xxv, 57, 322
Hazard, Paul, **III**: 72
Hazlitt, William, **I**: 121, 164; **II**: 153, 332, 333, 337, 343, 346, 349, 354, 361, 363, 364; **III**: 68, 70, 76, 78, 165, 276–277; **IV**: ix, xi, xiv, xvii–xix, 38, 39, 41, 50, **125–140**, 217
"He" (Lessing), **Supp. I**: 244
He Knew He Was Right (Trollope), **V**: 98, 99, 102
"He Revisits His First School" (Hardy), **VI**: 17
"He saw my heart's woe" (Brontë), **V**: 132
"He Thinks of His Past Greatness . . . When a Part of the Constellations of Heaven" (Yeats), **VI**: 211
"He thought he saw a Banker's Clerk" (Carroll), **V**: 270
Headlong Hall (Peacock), **IV**: xvii, **160–163**, 164, 165, 168, 169
Health and Holiness (Thompson), **V**: 450, 451
Heaney, Seamus, **Supp. II**: **267–281**
Hearing Secret Harmonies (Powell), **VII**: 352, 353
"Hears not my Phillis, how the Birds" (Sedley), **II**: 264
"Heart, II, The" (Thompson), **V**: 443
"Heart Knoweth Its Own Bitterness, The" (Rossetti), **V**: 253–254
Heart of Darkness (Conrad), **VI**: 135, **136–139**, 172
"Heart of John Middleton, The" (Gaskell), **V**: 15
Heart of Mid-Lothian, The (Scott), **IV**: xvii, 30, 31, 33–34, 35, 36, 39; **V**: 5
Heart of the Matter, The (Greene), **Supp. I**: 2, 8, 11–12, 13
Heartbreak House (Shaw), **V**: 423; **VI**: viii, xv, 118, **120–121**, 127, 129
"Heart's Chill Between" (Rossetti), **V**: 249, 252

Heat of the Day, The (Bowen), **Supp. II**: 77, 78, 79, 93, 95
"Heather Ale" (Stevenson), **V**: 396
Heather Field, The (Martyn), **VI**: 87, 95
Heaven and Earth (Byron), **IV**: 178, 193
Heavenly Foot-man, The (Bunyan), **II**: 246, 253
"Heber" (Smith), **Supp. II**: 466
Hebrew Melodies, Ancient and Modern . . . (Byron), **IV**: 192
Hecatommitthi (Cinthio), **I**: 316
Heel of Achilles, The (Koestler), **Supp. I**: 36
Hegel, Georg Wilhelm Friedrich, **Supp. II**: 22
Heine, Heinrich, **IV**: xviii, 296
Heinemann, William, **VII**: 91
"Hélas" (Wilde), **V**: 401
Helena (Waugh), **VII**: 292, 293–294, 301
Hellas (Shelley), **IV**: xviii, 206, 208
Hellenics, The (Landor), **IV**: 96, 100
Héloïse and Abélard (Moore), **VI**: xii, 88, 89, **94–95**, 99
Hemans, Felicia, **IV**: 311
Hemlock and After (Wilson), **Supp. I**: 155–156, 157, 158–159, 160, 161, 164
"Hendecasyllabics" (Swinburne), **V**: 321
"Hendecasyllabics" (Tennyson), **IV**: 327–328
Henderson, Hamish, **VII**: 422, 425–426
Henderson, Hubert, **VII**: 35
Henderson, Philip, **V**: xii, xviii, 335
Henderson, T. F., **IV**: 290n
Hengist, King of Kent (or *The Mayor of Quinborough*) (Middleton), **II**: 3, 21
Henley, William Ernest, **V**: 386, 389, 391–392; **VI**: 159
Henn, T. R., **VI**: 220
"Henrietta Marr" (Moore), **VI**: 87
Henrietta Temple (Disraeli), **IV**: xix, 293, 298–299, 307, 308
"Henrik Ibsen" (James), **VI**: 49
Henry Esmond (Thackeray), *see History of Henry Esmond, Esq.* . . . , *The*
Henry for Hugh (Ford), **VI**: 331
Henry James (ed. Tanner), **VI**: 68
"Henry James: The Religious Aspect" (Greene), **Supp. I**: 8
"Henry Purcell" (Hopkins), **V**: 370–371
Henry II (Bancroft), **II**: 305
Henry IV (Shakespeare), **I**: 308–309, 320
Henry V (Shakespeare), **I**: 309; **V**: 383
Henry VI trilogy (Shakespeare) **I**: 286, 299–300, 309
Henry VI's Triumphal Entry into London (Lydgate), **I**: 58
Henry VIII (Shakespeare), **I**: 324; **II**: 43, 66, 87; **V**: 328
"Henry VIII and Ann Boleyn" (Landor), **IV**: 92
Henry Vaughan: Experience and the Tradition (Garner), **II**: 186n
Henslowe, Philip, **I**: 228, 235, 284; **II**: 3, 25, 68
Her Triumph (Jonson), **I**: 347
Herakles (Euripides), **IV**: 358

Herbert, Edward, pseud. of John Hamilton Reynolds
Herbert, Edward, *see* Herbert of Cherbury, Lord
Herbert, George, **II**: 113, **117–130**, 133, 134, 137, 138, 140–142, 184, 187, 216, 221
Herbert of Cherbury, Lord, **II**: 117–118, 222, 237, 238
Hercule Poirot's Last Case (Christie), **Supp. II**: 125
"Hercules and Antaeus" (Heaney), **Supp. II**: 274–275
Hercules Oetaeus (Seneca), **I**: 248
"Here" (Larkin), **Supp. I**: 279, 285
Here Comes Everybody: An Introduction to James Joyce for the Ordinary Reader (Burgess), **Supp. I**: 194, 196–197
Heretics (Chesterton), **VI**: 204, 336–337
Hering, Carl Ewald, **Supp. II**: 107–108
Heritage and Its History, A (Compton-Burnett), **VII**: 60, 61, 65
"Hermaphroditus" (Swinburne), **V**: 320
Hermetical Physick . . . *Englished* (tr. Vaughan), **II**: 185, 201
Hermit of Marlow, the, pseud. of Percy Bysshe Shelley
"Hero" (Rossetti), **V**: 260
"Hero and Leander" (Hood), **IV**: 255–256, 267
Hero and Leander (Marlowe), **I**: 234, 237–240, 276, 278, 280, 288, **290–291**, 292
Hero and Leander, in Burlesque (Wycherley), **II**: 321
"Hero as King, The" (Carlyle), **IV**: 245, 246
Hero Rises Up, The (Arden and D'Arcy), **Supp. II**: 31
Heroes and Hero-Worship (Carlyle), **IV**: xx, 240, 244–246, 249, 250, 341
Heroic Idylls, with Additional Poems (Landor), **IV**: 100
"Heroic Stanzas" (Dryden), **II**: 292
Heroine, The: Or The Adventures of Cherubina (Barrett), **III**: 335
Herrick, Robert, **II**: **102–116**, 121
Herself Surprised (Cary), **VII**: 186, 188, 191–192
"Hertha" (Swinburne), **V**: 325
"Hervé Riel" (Browning), **IV**: 367
Herzog, Werner, **IV**: 180
"Hesperia" (Swinburne), **V**: 320, 321
Hesperides, The (Herrick), **II**: 102, 103, 104, 106, 110, 112, 115, 116
Heylyn, Peter, **I**: 169
Heywood, Jasper, **I**: 215
Heywood, Thomas, **II**: 19, 47, 48, 68, 83
Hibberd, Dominic, **VI**: xvi, xxxiii
Hide and Seek (Swinburne), **V**: 334
Higden, Ranulf, **I**: 22
"High Life in Verdopolis" (Brontë), **V**: 135
"High wavering heather . . ." (Brontë), **V**: 113
High Windows (Larkin), **Supp. I**: 277, 280, **281–284**, 285, 286

Pater, Walter Horatio, **V:** xiii, xix, xxiv–xxvi, 286–287, 314, 323, 324, 329, **337–360**, 362, 400–401, 403, 408, 410, 411; **VI:** ix, 365
"Pater on Style" (Chandler), **V:** 359
"Path of Duty, The" (James), **VI:** 69
"Patience, hard thing!" (Hopkins), **V:** 375
Patmore, Coventry, **V:** 372, 379, 441
"Patmos" (Durrell), **Supp. I:** 125
Paton, Alan, **Supp. II: 341–359**
"Patricia, Edith, and Arnold" (Thomas), **Supp. I:** 181
Patrician, The (Galsworthy), **VI:** 273, 278
Patriot (Johnson), **III:** 121
Patriot for Me, A (Osborne), **Supp. I:** 335, 337
"Patrol: Buonomary" (Gutteridge), **VII:** 432–433
Pattern of Maugham, The (Curtis), **VI:** 379
Pattern of Painful Adventures, The (Twine), **I:** 321
Pauli, Charles Paine, **Supp. II:** 98, 116
Pauline: A Fragment of a Confession (Browning), **IV:** xix, 354, 355, 373
Paul's Departure and Crown (Bunyan), **II:** 253
Paul's Letters to His Kinsfolk (Scott), **IV:** 38
"Pavilion on the Links, The" (Stevenson), **V:** 395
"Pawnbroker's Shop, The" (Dickens), **V:** 45, 47, 48
Paying Guest, The (Gissing), **V:** 437
Payne, W. L., **III:** 41n
"Peace" (Brooke), **VI:** 420
"Peace" (Collins), **III:** 166, 168
"Peace" (Hopkins), **V:** 370
"Peace" (Vaughan), **II:** 186, 187
Peace and the Protestant Succession, The (Trevelyan), **VI:** 392–393
Peace Conference Hints (Shaw), **VI:** 119, 129
Peace in Our Time (Coward), **Supp. II:** 151, 154
Peace of the World, The (Wells), **VI:** 244
Peaceable Principles and True (Bunyan), **II:** 253
"Peaches, The" (Thomas), **Supp. I:** 181
Peacock, Thomas Love, **III:** 336, 345; **IV:** xv, xvii–xix, xxii, **157–170**, 177, 198, 204, 306; **V:** 220; **VII:** 200, 211
Pearl (Arden), **Supp. II:** 39–40
Pearsall Smith, Logan, **VI:** 76
"Peasants, The" (Lewis), **VII:** 447
Peckham, Morse, **V:** 316, 335
Pedlar, The (Wordsworth), **IV:** 24
Peele, George, **I: 191–211**, 278, 286, 305
"Peele Castle" (Wordsworth), *see* "Elegiac Stanzas, Suggested by a Picture of Peele Castle . . ."
"Peep into a Picture Book, A" (Brontë), **V:** 109
Pelican History of English Literature, The, **II:** 102
Pell, J. P., **V:** 161

Pelles, George, **VI:** 23
"Pen, Pencil and Poison" (Wilde), **V:** 405, 407
Pen Portraits and Reviews (Shaw), **VI:** 129
Pendennis (Thackeray), *see History of Pendennis, The*
Penelope (Maugham), **VI:** 369
Penitential Psalms (Wyatt), **I:** 101–102, 108, 111
"Pennines in April" (Hughes), **Supp. I:** 344
"Penny Plain and Twopence Coloured, A" (Stevenson), **V:** 385
Penny Whistles (Stevenson), *see Child's Garden of Verses, A*
"Penshurst, To" (Jonson), **II:** 223
"Pension Beaurepas, The" (James), **VI:** 69
Pentameron and Pentalogia, The (Landor), **IV:** 89, 90–91, 93, 100
Pentland Rising, The (Stevenson), **V:** 395
Pepys, Samuel, **II:** 145, 195, **273**, 274, 275, 278, **280–288**, 310
Per Amica Silentia Lunae (Yeats), **VI:** 209
Percy, Thomas, **III:** 336; **IV:** 28–29
Percy Bysshe Shelley (Swinburne), **V:** 333
Peregrine Pickle (Smollett), **III:** 149, 150, 152–153, 158
Perelandra (Lewis), **Supp. I:** 74
Perennial Philosophy, The (Huxley), **VII:** xviii, 206
"Perfect Critic, The" (Eliot), **VII:** 163
Perfect Spy, A (le Carré), **Supp. II: 300–302**, 304, 305
Perfect Wagnerite, The (Shaw) **VI:** 129
Pericles (Shakespeare), **I:** 321–322; **II:** 48
Pericles and Aspasia (Landor), **IV:** xix, 89, 92, 94–95, 100
Pericles and Other Studies (Swinburne), **V:** 333
Peripatetic, The (Thelwall), **IV:** 103
Perkin Warbeck (Ford), **II:** 89, 92, 96, 97, 100
Perkins, Richard, **II:** 68
Pernicious Consequences of the New Heresie of the Jesuites . . . , The (tr. Evelyn), **II:** 287
Peronnik the Fool (Moore), **VI:** 99
Perry, Thomas Sergeant, **VI:** 24
"Persian Eclogues" (Collins), **III:** 160, 164–165, 175
"Persian Passion Play, A" (Arnold), **V:** 216
Personal History, Adventures, Experience, and Observation of David Copperfield, The (Dickens), *see David Copperfield*
Personal Landscape (periodical), **VII:** 425, 443
Personal Record, A (Conrad), **VI:** 134, 148
Persons from Porlock (MacNeice), **VII:** 408
Persse, Jocelyn, **VI:** 55
Persuasion (Austen), **IV:** xvii, 106–109, 111, 113, 115–120, 122
"Pervasion of Rouge, The" (Beerbohm), **Supp. II:** 45
"Pessimism in Literature" (Forster), **VI:** 410

Peter Bell (Wordsworth), **IV:** xviii, 2
Peter Bell the Third (Shelley), **IV:** 203, 207
"Peter Grimes" (Crabbe), **III:** 283, 284–285
Petrarch's Seven Penitential Psalms (Chapman), **I:** 241–242
Peveril of the Peak (Scott), **IV:** xviii, 36, 37, 39
Phaedra (Seneca), **II:** 97
"Phaèthôn" (Meredith), **V:** 224
Phantasmagoria (Carroll), **V:** 270, 273
Pharos, pseud. of E. M. Forster
Pharos and Pharillon (Forster), **VI:** 408
Pharsalia (tr. Marlowe), **I:** 276, 291
Phases of Faith (Newman), **V:** 208n
"Phebus and Cornide" (Gower), **I:** 55
Philanderer, The (Shaw), **VI:** 107, 109
Philaster (Beaumont and Fletcher), **II:** 45, 46, **52–54**, 55, 65
Philby Conspiracy, The (Page, Leitch and Knightley), **Supp. II:** 302, 303, 311–312
Philip (Thackeray), *see Adventures of Philip on His Way Through the World, The*
Philip Sparrow (Skelton), **I:** 84, 86–88
Philip Webb and His Work (Lethaby), **V:** 291, 292, 296, 306
Philips, Ambrose, **III:** 56
Philips, Katherine, **II:** 185
Phillipps, Sir Thomas, **II:** 103
Phillips, Edward, **II:** 347
"Phillis is my only Joy" (Sedley), **II:** 265
"Phillis, let's shun the common Fate" (Sedley), **II:** 263
Phillpotts, Eden, **VI:** 266
"Philosopher, The" (Brontë), **V:** 134
Philosopher's Pupil, The (Murdoch), **Supp. I:** 231, 232–233
Philosophical Discourse of Earth, An, Relating to . . . Plants, &c. (Evelyn), **II:** 287
Philosophical Enquiry into the Origin of Our Ideas of the Sublime and Beautiful, A (Burke), *see On the Sublime and Beautiful*
Philosophical Lectures of S. T. Coleridge, The (ed. Coburn), **IV:** 52, 56
"Philosophical View of Reform, A" (Shelley), **IV:** 199, 209
"Philosophy of Herodotus" (De Quincey), **IV:** 147–148
Philosophy of Melancholy, The (Peacock), **IV:** 158, 169
Philosophy of Necessity, The (Bray), **V:** 188
Philosophy of Rhetoric (Richards), **Supp. II:** 416, 423
Philosophy of the Unconscious (Hartmann), **Supp. II:** 108
Phineas Finn (Trollope), **V:** 96, 98, 101, 102
Phineas Redux (Trollope), **V:** 96, 98, 101, 102
Phoenix (Storey), **Supp. I:** 408, 420
Phoenix, The (Middleton), **II:** 21, 30
Phoenix and the Turtle, The (Shakespeare), **I:** 34, 313